DATE DUE

			PRINTED IN U.S.A.

Literature Criticism from 1400 to 1800

Guide to Gale Literary Criticism Series

For criticism on	Consult these Gale series
Authors now living or who died after December 31, 1959	*CONTEMPORARY LITERARY CRITICISM (CLC)*
Authors who died between 1900 and 1959	*TWENTIETH-CENTURY LITERARY CRITICISM (TCLC)*
Authors who died between 1800 and 1899	*NINETEENTH-CENTURY LITERATURE CRITICISM (NCLC)*
Authors who died between 1400 and 1799	*LITERATURE CRITICISM FROM 1400 TO 1800 (LC)* *SHAKESPEAREAN CRITICISM (SC)*
Authors who died before 1400	*CLASSICAL AND MEDIEVAL LITERATURE CRITICISM (CMLC)*
Authors of books for children and young adults	*CHILDREN'S LITERATURE REVIEW (CLR)*
Dramatists	*DRAMA CRITICISM (DC)*
Poets	*POETRY CRITICISM (PC)*
Short story writers	*SHORT STORY CRITICISM (SSC)*
Black writers of the past two hundred years	*BLACK LITERATURE CRITICISM (BLC)*
Hispanic writers of the late nineteenth and twentieth centuries	*HISPANIC LITERATURE CRITICISM (HLC)*
Native North American writers and orators of the eighteenth, nineteenth, and twentieth centuries	*NATIVE NORTH AMERICAN LITERATURE (NNAL)*
Major authors from the Renaissance to the present	*WORLD LITERATURE CRITICISM, 1500 TO THE PRESENT (WLC)*

ISSN 0740-2880

Volume 51

Literature Criticism from 1400 to 1800

Critical Discussion of the Works of Fifteenth-, Sixteenth-, Seventeenth-, and Eighteenth-Century Novelists, Poets, Playwrights, Philosophers, and Other Creative Writers

Marie Lazzari
Editor

GALE GROUP

Detroit
San Francisco
London
Boston
Woodbridge, CT

STAFF

Marie Lazzari, *Editor*

Jelena O. Krstović, *Contributing Editor*
Pam Revitzer, *Associate Editor*
Janet Witalec, *Managing Editor*

Maria Franklin, *Permissions Manager*
Kimberly F. Smilay, *Permissions Specialist*
Kelly A. Quin, *Permissions Associate*
Sandra K. Gore, *Permissions Assistant*

Victoria B. Cariappa, *Research Manager*
Patricia T. Ballard, Tamara C. Nott, Tracie A. Richardson,
Corrine Stocker, Cheryl L. Warnock, *Research Associates*

Gary Leach, *Graphic Artist*
Randy Bassett, *Image Database Supervisor*
Mike Logusz, Robert Duncan, *Imaging Specialists*
Pamela A. Reed, *Imaging Coordinator*

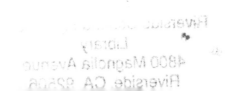

Contents

Preface vii

Acknowledgments xi

The Aesopic Fable
Introduction 1
Representative Works 1
The British Aesopic Fable 1
The Aesopic Tradition in Non-English-Speaking Cultures 55
Political Uses of the Aesopic Fable 67
The Evolution of the Aesopic Fable 89
Further Reading 100

The English Realist Novel, 1740-1771
Introduction 102
Representative Works 102
Overviews 103
From Romanticism to Realism 123
Women and the Novel 159
The Novel and Other Literary Forms 176
Further Reading 198

The Levellers
Introduction 200
Representative Works 201
Overviews 201
Principal Figures 230
Religion, Political Philosophy, and Pamphleteering 287
Further Reading 312

The Revolutionary Astronomers
Introduction 314
Representative Works 315
Overviews 316
Principal Figures 325
Revolutionary Astronomical Models 352
Further Reading 365

Literary Criticism Series Cumulative Author Index 369

Literary Criticism Series Cumulative Topic Index 441

LC Cumulative Nationality Index 449

LC Cumulative Title Index 451

Preface

*L*iterature Criticism from 1400 to 1800 (LC) presents critical discussion of world literature from the fifteenth through the eighteenth centuries. The literature of this period is especially vital: the years 1400 to 1800 saw the rise of modern European drama, the birth of the novel and personal essay forms, the emergence of newspapers and periodicals, and major achievements in poetry and philosophy. *LC* provides valuable insight into the art, life, thought, and cultural transformations that took place during these centuries.

Scope of the Series

LC provides an introduction to the great poets, dramatists, novelists, essayists, and philosophers of the fifteenth through eighteenth centuries, and to the most significant interpretations of these authors' works. Because criticism of this literature spans nearly six hundred years, an overwhelming amount of scholarship confronts the student. *LC* organizes this material concisely and logically. Every attempt is made to reprint the most noteworthy, relevant, and educationally valuable essays available.

A separate Gale reference series, *Shakespearean Criticism,* is devoted exclusively to Shakespearean studies. Although properly belonging to the period covered in *LC,* William Shakespeare has inspired such a tremendous and ever-growing body of secondary material that a separate series was deemed essential.

Each entry in *LC* presents a representative selection of critical response to an author, a literary topic, or to a single important work of literature. Early commentary is offered to indicate initial responses, later selections document changes in literary reputations, and retrospective analyses provide the reader with modern views. The size of each author entry is a relative reflection of the scope of criticism available in English. Every attempt has been made to identify and include the seminal essays on each author's work and to include recent commentary providing modern perspectives.

Volumes 1 through 12 of the series feature author entries arranged alphabetically by author. Volumes 13 through 47 of the series feature a thematic arrangement. Each volume includes an entry devoted to the general study of a specific literary or philosophical movement, writings surrounding important political and historical events, the philosophy and art associated with eras of cultural transformation, or the literature of specific social or ethnic groups. Each of these volumes also includes several author entries devoted to major representatives of the featured period, genre, or national literature. With Volume 48, the series returns to a standard author approach, with occasional entries devoted to a single important work of world literature. One volume annually is devoted wholly to literary topics.

Organization of the Book

Each entry consists of a heading, an introduction, a list of principal works, annotated works of criticism, each preceded by a bibliographical citation, and a bibliography of recommended further reading. Many of the entries include illustrations.

> The **Author Heading** consists of the most commonly used form of the author's name, followed by birth and death dates. Also located here are any name variations under which an author wrote, including transliterated forms for authors whose native languages use nonroman alphabets. Uncertain birth or death dates are indicated by question marks. Topic entries are preceded by a **Thematic Heading,** which simply states the subject of the entry. Single-work entries are preceded by the title of the work and its date of publication.

- The **Introduction** contains background information that concisely introduces the reader to the author, work, or topic that is the subject of the entry.

- The list of **Principal Works** is ordered chronologically by date of first publication. The genre and publication date of each work is given. In the case of foreign authors whose works have been translated into English, the title and date (if available) of the first English-language edition is given in brackets following the original title. Unless otherwise indicated, dramas are dated by first performance, not first publication. Lists of **Representative Works** by different authors appear with topic entries.

- Reprinted **Criticism** is arranged chronologically in each entry to provide a useful perspective on changes in critical evaluation over time. The critic's name and the date of composition or publication of the critical work are given at the beginning of each piece of criticism. Unsigned criticism is preceded by the title of the source in which it appeared. All titles by the author featured in the text are printed in boldface type. Footnotes are reprinted at the end of each essay or excerpt. In the case of excerpted criticism, only those footnotes that pertain to the excerpted text are included. Criticism in topic entries is arranged chronologically under a variety of subheadings to facilitate the study of different aspects of the topic.

- Critical essays are prefaced by brief **Annotations** explicating each piece.

- A complete **Bibliographical Citation** of the original essay or book precedes each piece of criticism.

- An annotated bibliography of **Further Reading** appears at the end of each entry and suggests resources for additional study. In some cases, significant essays for which the editors could not obtain reprint rights are included here.

Cumulative Indexes

Each volume of *LC* includes a series-specific cumulative **Nationality Index** in which author names are arranged alphabetically by nationality. The volume or volumes of *LC* in which each author appears are also listed.

Each volume of *LC* includes a cumulative **Author Index** listing all of the authors that appear in a wide variety of reference sources published by The Gale Group, including *LC*. A complete list of these sources is found facing the first page of the Author Index. The index also includes birth and death dates and cross references between pseudonyms and actual names.

LC includes a cumulative **Topic Index** that lists the literary themes and topics treated in the series as well as in *Nineteenth-Century Literature Criticism*, *Twentieth-Century Literary Criticism*, and the *Contemporary Literature Criticism* Yearbook.

Each volume of *LC* also includes a cumulative **Title Index,** an alphabetical listing of all the literary works discussed in the series. Each title listing includes the corresponding volume and page numbers where criticism may be located. Foreign-language titles that have been translated into English followed by the tiles of the translation—for example, *El ingenioso hidalgo Don Quixote de la Mancha (Don Quixote)*. Page numbers following these translated titles refer to all pages on which any form of the titles, either foreign-language or translated, appear. Titles of novels, dramas, nonfiction books, and poetry, short story, or essay collections are printed in italics, while individual poems, short stories, and essays are printed in roman type within quotation marks.

A Note to the Reader

When writing papers, students who quote directly from any volume in the Literary Criticism Series may use the following general format to footnote reprinted criticism. The first example pertains to material drawn from periodicals, the second to material reprinted from books.

Eileen Reeves, "Daniel 5 and the *Assayer*: Galileo Reads the Handwriting on the Wall," *The Journal of Medieval and Renaissance Studies,* Vol. 21, No. 1, Spring, 1991, pp. 1-27; reprinted in *Literature Criticism from 1400 to 1800,* Vol. 45, ed. Jelena O. Krstović and Marie Lazzari, Farmington Hills, Mich.: The Gale Group, 1999, pp. 297-310.

Margaret Anne Doody, *A Natural Passion: A Study of the Novels of Samuel Richardson*, Oxford University Press, 1974, pp. 17-22, 132-35, excerpted and reprinted in *Literature Criticism from 1400 to 1800,* Vol. 46, ed. Jelena O. Krstović and Marie Lazzari. Farmington Hills, Mich.: The Gale Group, 1999, pp. 20-2.

Suggestions Are Welcome

Readers who wish to suggest new features, topics, or authors to appear in future volumes, or who have other suggestions or comments are cordially invited to call, write, or fax the editor:

Editor, *Literature Criticism from 1400 to 1800*
The Gale Group
27500 Drake Road
Farmington Hills, MI 48133-3535
1-800-347-4253
fax: 248-699-8049

Acknowledgments

The editors wish to thank the copyright holders of the excerpted criticism included in this volume and the permissions managers of many book and magazine publishing companies for assisting us in securing reproduction rights. We are also grateful to the staffs of the Detroit Public Library, the Library of Congress, the University of Detroit Mercy Library, Wayne State University Purdy/Kresge Library Complex, and the University of Michigan Libraries for making their resources available to us. Following is a list of the copyright holders who have granted us permission to reproduce material in this volume of *LC*. Every effort has been made to trace copyright, but if omissions have been made, please let us know.

COPYRIGHTED MATERIAL IN *LC*, VOLUME 51, WAS REPRODUCED FROM THE FOLLOWING PERIODICALS:

—*Cultural Critique,* v. 1, Fall, 1985. © 1985. Used by permission of Oxford University Press, Inc., and the author. —*The Critical Review,* n. 29, 1989. Reproduced by permission. —*The Journal of British Studies,* v. XX, Fall, 1980. Reproduced by permission. —*The Western Political Quarterly,* v. 36, March, 1983. Reproduced by permission. —*Eighteenth Century Studies,* v. 25, Winter, 1991/92; v. 27, Winter, 1993-94. © 1991, 1993-94 by The American Society for Eighteenth-Century Studies. Both reproduced by permission. —*Eighteenth-Century Fiction*, v. 6, January, 1994. © Macmaster University 1994. Reproduced by permission. —*Manuscripta*, v. XXII, November, 1978. Reproduced by permission. — *Papers on French Seventeenth Century Literature,* n. 11, Summer, 1979. Reproduced by permission. — *PMLA,* v. 97, January, 1982. Copyright © 1982 by the Modern Language Association of America. Reproduced by permission of the Modern Language Association of America. —*Prose Studies,* v. 9, September, 1986. Reproduced by permission of Frank Cass & Co. Ltd. —*Studies in Philology,* v. XCI, Winter, 1994. Copyright © 1994 by the University of North Carolina Press. Reproduced by permission of the publisher.

COPYRIGHTED MATERIAL IN *LC*, VOLUME 51, WAS REPRODUCED FROM THE FOLLOWING BOOKS:

—Alliston, April. From "Female Sexuality and the Referent of Enlightenment Realisms" in *Spectacles of Realism: Body, Gender, Genre.* Edited by Margaret Cohen and Christopher Prendergast. University of Minnesota Press, 1995. Copyright © 1995 by the Regents of the University of Minnesota. All rights reserved. Reproduced by permission. —Castle, Terry. From *The Carnivalesque in Eighteenth-Century English Culture and Fiction.* Stanford University Press, 1986. © 1986 by the Board of Trustees of the Leland Stanford Junior University. —Daly, Lloyd W. From *Aesop without Morals.* Thomas Yoseloff, 1961. Copyright © 1961 by A. S. Barnes and company, Inc. Reproduced by permission. —Dow, F. D. From *Radicalism in the English Revolution.* Basil Blackwell Ltd., 1985. © F. D. Dow. Reproduced by permission of the publisher. —Ferris, Timothy. From *Coming of Age in the Milky Way.* William Morrow and Company, 1988. Copyright © 1988 by Timothy Ferris. All rights reserved. Reproduced by permission of William Morrow and Company, Inc. In the British Commonwealth with permission Owen Lester for the author.—Fitzgerald, Laurie. From *Shifting Genres, Changing Realities: Reading the Late Eighteenth-Century Novel.* Peter Lang, 1995. © 1995 Peter Lang. Reproduced by permission. — Goldsmith, Maurice. From "Levellers by Sword, Spade and Word: Radical Egalitarianism in the English Revolution," in *Politics and People in Revolutionary England: Essays in Honor of Ivan Roots.* Colin Jones, Malin Newitt, and Stephen Roberts, eds. Basil Blackwell, Ltd. 1986. © Basil Blackwell Ltd. 1986. Reproduced by permission of the publisher. —Green, Katherine Sobba. From *The Courtship Novel, 1740-1820: A Feminized Genre.* The University Press of Kentucky, 1991. © 1991 by The University Press of Kentucky. Reproduced by permission. —Heinemann, Margot. From "Popular Drama and Leveller Style–Richard Overton and John Harris," in *Rebels and Their Causes: Essays in Honour of A. L. Morton.* Edited by Maurice Cornfield. Lawrence and Wishart, 1978. Copyright © Lawrence and Wishart, 1978. reproduced by permission. —Hemmings, F. W. J. From *The Age of Realism.* Penguin Books, 1974. Copyright © Penguin Books, 1974. Reproduced by permission of the Peters, Fraser & Dunlop Group Ltd.

—Heninger, Jr., S. K. From *The Cosmographical Glass: Renaissance Diagrams of the Universe.* The Huntington Library, 1977. Copyright 1977 The Henry E. Huntington Library and Art Gallery. Reproduced by permission of the Henry E. Huntington Library. —Hill, Christopher. From *The Experience of Defeat: Milton and Some Contemporaries.* Bookmarks, 1994. First published in 1984 by Faber & Faber. Copyright Christopher Hill. Reproduced by permission. —Keller, John E. and Clark Keating. From *Aesop's Fables with a Life of Aesop.* The University Press of Kentucky, 1993. Copyright © 1993 by The University Press of Kentucky. Reproduced by permission. —Kettle, Arnold. From *An Introduction to the English Novel, Vol. 1.* Hutchinson University Library, 1967. Reproduced by permission. —Lenaghan, R. T. From *Caxton's Aesop.* Harvard University Press, 1967. © Copyright 1967 by the President and Fellows of Harvard College. All rights reserved. Reproduced by permission of Harvard University Press. —Lewis, Jayne Elizabeth. From "Aesopian Examples: The English Fable Collection and its Authors, 1651-1740," in *The English Fable: Aesop and Literary Culture, 1651-1740.* Cambridge University Press, 1996. © Cambridge University Press 1996. Reproduced by permission of the publisher and the author. —Morton, A. L. From *The Matter of Britain: Essays in a Living Culture.* Lawrence & Wishart, 1966. Copyright © A. L. Worton. Reproduced by permission. —Patterson, Annabel. From *Fables of Power: Aesopian Writing and Political History.* Duke University Press, 1991. © 1991 Duke University Press, Durham., N.C. All rights reserved. Reproduced by permission. —Reichenbach, Hans. From *Copernicus to Einstein.* Translated by Ralph B. Winn. Philosophical Library, Inc., 1942. Copyright MCMXLII by Philosophical Library, Inc. Renewed 1970 by Philosophical Library, Inc. Reproduced by permission of Philosophical Library, N.Y. —Robertson, D. B. From *The Religious Foundations of Leveller Democracy.* King's Crown Press, 1951. Copyright 1951 by D. B. Robertson. Reproduced by permission. —Ross, Deborah. From *The Excellence of Falsehood: Romance, Realism and Women's Contribution to the Novel.* The University Press of Kentucky, 1991. © 1991 by The University Press of Kentucky. Reproduced by permission of The University Press of Kentucky. —Rousseau, Pierre. From *Man's Conquest of the Stars.* Translated by Michael Bullock. W. W. Norton & Company, Inc., 1959. English translation copyright © 1959 by Jarrolds Publishers (London) Ltd. —Warner, William. From "Licensing Pleasure: Literary History and the Novel in Early Modern Britain" in *The Columbia History of the British Novel.* Edited by John Richetti. Copyright © 1994 Columbia University Press, New York. All rights reserved. Reproduced with the permission of the publisher. —Watt, Ian. From *The Rise of the Novel: Studies in Defoe, Richardson and Fielding.* University of California Press, 1962. Copyright © 1957, renewed 1985 by Ian Watt. Reproduced by permission of the publisher. In North America by the author. —Zagorin, Perez. From *A History Of Political Thought in the English Revolution.* Humanities Press, 1966. First published in Great Britain 1954 by Routledge & Kegan Paul Ltd. Reproduced by permission of the publisher and the author.

PHOTOGRAPHS AND ILLUSTRATIONS APPEARING IN *LC 1400-1800,* VOLUME 51, WERE RECEIVED FROM THE FOLLOWING SOURCES:

The New York Public Library Picture Collection for the Johannes Hevelius engraving of astronomers and astronomical instruments, p. 314; The Library of Congress for the picture of Ptolemy, p. 316.

The Aesopic Fable

INTRODUCTION

Stories and verses based on fables believed to have originated with a Greek slave named Aesop (circa 620 B.C. to circa 564 B.C.) have been popular for centuries. The Aesopic fable—a short allegorical tale usually featuring personified animal characters displaying the foibles of human nature—is so well-known that it is regarded as the standard example of the fable genre.

Aesopic fables have been collected and translated into a variety of languages. Prose versions in Latin were used to teach this language in the Middle Ages and Renaissance. Heinrich Steinhöwel published a Latin-German edition in 1476-77, and William Caxton brought out an English version in 1484. A Spanish edition became available in 1489. According to John E. Keller and L. Clark Keating, Aesopic fables were extremely popular in Spain, where they had originally been circulated by Greek colonists and Roman conquerors. In the seventeenth century, the French writer Jean de La Fontaine drew on Aesop's works to produce his own collection of fables in verse, which are among the most renowned and popular in world literature.

During Aesop's time fables were often used as an indirect method of conveying subversive messages. Tomoko Hanazaki asserts that "the use of fictitious beasts to attack political powers or persons is the very essence of the Aesopic tradition." Annabel Patterson has shown that in seventeenth-century England, when Aesopic fables were used to teach ethics and morals, a strong tradition also existed of employing fables politically as a form of satirical commentary on abuses of power and even philosophically to question the morality of the actions of the state.

Throughout their long history, however, Aesopic fables have served primarily to instruct and entertain. With the advent of didactic children's literature in the nineteenth century, editions of Aesop generally included a brief summation of the moral that the reader or listener should learn from the tale. In a reaction against this trend, Lloyd W. Daly produced *Aesop without Morals* in 1961. Throughout the twentieth century, the fables have been most commonly regarded as entertainment for children, and numerous illustrated editions have been produced. In additional, audio tapes, compact disks, animated television shows and films, and online sources make the ancient fables newly accessible.

REPRESENTATIVE WORKS

Aesop's Fables [translated by Samuel Croxall] 1722

The Fables of Aesop [translated by Joseph Jacobs] 1894

Aesop without Morals [translated by Lloyd W. Daly] 1961

Caxton's Aesop [translated by William Caxton] 1484

Aesop's Fables [edited by Samuel Richardson] 1740

Fables from Aesop and Others [translated by Charles H. Bennett] 1857

The Morall Fabillis of Esope the Phrygian by Robert Henryson, 1570; [translated by George D. Gopen, 1987]

La vida del Ysopet con sus fabulas hystoriadas, 1489; [translated as *Aesop's Fables with a Life of Aesop* by John E. Keller and L. Clark Keating 1993]

THE BRITISH AESOPIC FABLE

R. T. Lenaghan (essay date 1967)

SOURCE: "Introduction," in *Caxton's Aesop,* pp. 3-21. Cambridge, Mass.: Harvard University Press, 1967.

[*In the following essay, Lenaghan traces the textual history of William Caxton's 1484 English translation of Aesop's fables, discusses the popularity of the fable format during the Middle Ages. Lenaghan suggests that Caxton's treatment of the fable anticipates aspects of Renaissance humanism.*]

Aesop's fables have been popular from papyrus to television. While our children read them in school, we read Marianne Moore's translations of La Fontaine or Thurber's fables in *The New Yorker* and thus repeat once more an old pattern, for Roman and medieval schoolboys did their primer fables while their parents read about the Horatian mice or Chauntecleer and Pertelote. The practice of attributing such fables to Aesop is centuries-old, but since for almost as many centuries there has been no firm knowledge about him, the identification has been more legendary than biographical.

Under the impulse of their unquestionable vitality fables proliferated, particularly during the Middle Ages, in a variety of collections which were usually credited to Aesop as the ultimate source but which were quite different from one another in significant ways. Since no fables can be surely identified as Aesop's, his name is best taken as a generic label, and it is more accurate to speak of the Aesopic fables in a given collection than of Aesop's fables. The chief ancient collections are those of Babrius, a hellenized Roman whose Greek fables were probably composed in the latter half of the first century A.D., and of Phaedrus, a Roman writer whose Latin verse fables were composed toward the middle of the same century. Although both these collections were unknown in the West during the Middle Ages, the fables of Phaedrus did circulate in a prose reworking that went under the name Romulus. The fables of the Romulus collection were accepted as Aesop's by a German physician and man of letters, Heinrich Steinhöwel, when he attempted to assemble Aesop's fables in the fifteenth century.

The fifteenth century was an age of transition in northern Europe, and in England William Caxton conveniently embodied some of this transitional division. He was a printer, hence modern, of traditional books, hence medieval. He was born about 1432 and spent most of his adult life as a mercer in Bruges when that city was the seat of the Dukes of Burgundy and an important cultural center. There Caxton developed the literary interests which animated his work as a printer when he returned to England and set up his press at Westminister in 1476, Since Aesopic fables were both popular and traditional, they were a natural choice for early printers, and Caxton was no exception. Steinhöwel's collection was the largest available in the fifteenth century, and it had been translated into French by an Augustinian monk in Lyons and printed there in 1480.[1]

Caxton's Aesop

In 1483 William Caxton began to print his translation of the French translation of Steinhöwel's fables:

> *Here begynneth the book of the subtyl historyes and Fables of Esope whiche were translated out of Frensshe in to Englysshe by wylliam Caxton at westmynstre In the yere of oure Lorde M.CCCC.lxxxiij.*

Inasmuch as the colophon dates the completion of the book on March 26, 1484, the second day of Caxton's new year, he must have done most of the printing in 1483.

> And here with I fynysshe this book/ translated & emprynted by me William Caxton at westmynstre in thabbey/ And fynysshed thexxvj daye of Marche the yere of oure lord M CCCC lxxxiiij. And the fyrst yere of the regne of kyng Rychard the thyrdde

Three complete or nearly complete copies of this edition are known to survive: a perfect copy in the Royal Library at Windsor; a copy in the British Museum, which lacks the first leaf but has the complete text; and a copy at the Bodleian, which lacks eight leaves. Caxton printed only this one edition, but the London printer, Richard Pynson, printed two more editions, one about 1497 and one about 1500. All these editions are profusely illustrated with woodcuts modeled on those in the French *Esope,* which were traced copies of the original German woodcuts.

Caxton's *Aesop* contains 167 fables and tales and a *Life* of Aesop which is itself a composite of various types of folktales. Although Caxton's collection is basically an English version of the one assembled by Steinhöwel,[2] its contents do differ slightly from those of its basic source. It does not include two tales which Steinhöwel took from Petrus Alphonsus and one which he took from Poggio; the same tales were omitted by the intermediate French translator and editor, Julien Macho. On the other hand, at the end of the selection from Poggio it does include six tales neither in Steinhöwel nor in the French.

Caxton's edition is divided into seven main parts: (1) the *Life of Aesop* translated into Latin from the Greek by the Italian humanist, Rinuccio da Castiglione of Arezzo; (2) the four books of the Romulus collection of Aesop's fables; (3) a fifth book of seventeen fables of Aesop which had not been included in the registers of the Romulus collection; (4) seventeen fables of Aesop newly translated by Rinuccio and so also not included in the Romulus collection; (5) a selection of twenty-seven fables of Avianus, a Roman fabulist of about A.D. 400; (6) a selection of thirteen tales from the *Disciplina Clericalis* of Petrus Alphonsus, a Spanish Jew converted to Christianity in the twelfth century; and (7) a group of thirteen tales, attributed by Caxton to the Italian humanist, Poggio Bracciolini (of these, seven came from Poggio's *Facetiae* through Steinhöwel and the French text; to them Caxton added four other tales from the *Facetiae* and two more which are apparently original with him). These components range in date from the late fourth century to the mid-fifteenth; the older ones, having been popular for centuries, were no doubt easily accessible to Steinhöwel, and both Poggio's *Facetiae* and Rinuccio's fables were in print in the 1470's.

(1) *The Life of Aesop.*[3] The *Life,* as taken from Rinuccio, is a crude, episodic 'biography,' presenting in a series of tales Aesop's rise from slave to royal adviser and concluding with his death at the hands of the jealous Delphians. The earliest version comes from Egypt and dates from the first century A.D.,[4] but most of the versions known in modern times have been associated

with the name of Maximus Planudes, a thirteenth-century Byzantine monk who was an emissary to Italy. Steinhöwel's version of the *Life* was formerly thought to derive from the Greek of Planudes, but Professor Perry has shown that the versions of Rinuccio and Planudes descend from different branches of a complex of manuscripts stemming ultimately from an eleventh-century Byzantine reworking of an ancient version of the *Life*.[5]

(2) *The Romulus Collection.*[6] These fables make up the largest unit in the collection, accounting for almost half of its total number of fables and tales. The Romulus collection is dated between A.D. 350 and 600 by its editor. The name, Romulus, comes from a prefatory letter in which a writer of that name recommends to his son the collection of Aesop's fables he has translated from Greek into Latin, though in fact the fables are a prose reworking of the verse fables of Phaedrus. Since the fables of Phaedrus survived as the Romulus collection, that collection became Aesop's fables in the Latin West, and medieval references to Aesop's fables usually meant the Romulus fables. The Steinhöwel-Caxton version of these fables, like most other versions of the collection, is divided into four books, but it is the only version that is evenly divided into four books of twenty fables each. This unique symmetry produces some peculiarities of omission (the boy and the scorpion, *Aesopica*, 199; and the thirsty crow, later included as the twentieth fable in the selection from Avianus) and addition (the pine tree and the reed, Romulus IV, 20).

(3) *The Fifth Book.*[7] This book is made up of seventeen fables ascribed to Aesop. Caxton, following the French translator, says they are Aesop's despite the fact that they were not included in any of the registers for the books of the Romulus collection. Steinhöwel calls them *extravagantes antique* because they were old (*antique*) and because they were not fixed in the books of the standard Romulus collection of Aesop's fables (*extravagantes*). Eleven of the seventeen do, however, appear in a collection contained in a fifteenth-century manuscript in Munich along with twenty-eight fables from the standard Romulus collection. Inclusion of these fables in another Romulus collection would presumably have been a satisfactory warrant for Steinhöwel to attribute them to Aesop as *extravagantes antique*. No doubt these eleven fables had been 'extravagant' for some time: five of them appear, wholly or in part, in the twelfth-century collection of Marie de France, and, of course, separate episodes and motifs can be found in versions antedating those of the Munich manuscript (e.g., no. 16 and no. 86 of the *Dialogus Creaturarum*). Although Steinhöwel designated all seventeen fables as *extravagantes,* six of them appear for the first time in his collection and therefore present rather more of a problem than the other eleven. There seems no way of deciding whether Steinhöwel was following a collection now lost, which contained all seventeen *extravagantes,* or whether he simply added to those of the Munich manuscript six more fables and tales which he thought were also *extravagantes*. He does say at the end of the book that he is not certain whether these fables are Aesop's, but because the French translator omits this passage, no such doubt appears in Caxton's text, and he attaches the *extravagantes* as an additional fifth book to the traditional four of the Romulus collection.

(4) *The Selection from Rinuccio's Fables.*[8] This grouping of seventeen fables comes from the collection which Rinuccio translated from the Greek in 1448 and which was accompanied by his *Life of Aesop*. Rinuccio asserts that he has translated only those fables he chanced to find and that he makes no claims to completeness; nevertheless, his collection is large, numbering one hundred fables. Some of them are also in the Romulus collection, and since Steinhöwel had already included these fables of Aesop in his collection, there was no need to duplicate them from Rinuccio. However, there are also fables in Rinuccio's collection which do not appear elsewhere in Steinhöwel and which he did not include in his selection from Rinuccio. This is the first suggestion that Steinhöwel would be satisfied with something less than completeness. Of course, aside from reasons of practicality and convenience, it is quite possible that Steinhöwel may have rated Rinuccio's authority less than that of tradition (he speaks of the *new* translation) and so have felt freer to exercise a choice about what was to go into his collection. In this case the French translator and Caxton repeat Steinhöwel's editorial remarks and inform their readers that these fables are Aesop's, but from a new translation instead of the old one made by Romulus; therefore, the selection is not given a book number like the fables of Romulus or designated by the name of the author like the non-Aesopic sections of the collection.

(5) *The Selection from the Fables of Avianus.*[9] This selection of twenty-seven fables is taken from the collection of Avianus, which is a reworking in distichs of forty-two fables from the Greek of Babrius and dates from about 400. Of the fifteen fables which do not appear in this section of the Steinhöwel-Caxton collection, only one appears elsewhere.

(6) *The Selection from the Disciplina Clericalis of Petrus Alphonsus.*[10] Caxton's selection numbers thirteen fables (really, twelve tales and one fable, Al. 9), twelve of which are taken from the thirty-four tales of the *Disciplina Clericalis*. Steinhöwel may have added the additional tale (Al. 12) to his selection, or he may have used a variant text which included this tale. The *Disciplina Clericalis* is the oldest medieval collection of 'Eastern' tales and was written in the early twelfth century by Petrus Alphonsus.

(7) *The Selection from the* Facetiae *of Poggio Bracci-olini*.[11] The *Facetiae* are a collection of frivolous stories assembled sometime after 1450 for the amusement of Poggio's colleagues of the papal Curia. The selection which Caxton prints as 'fables of Poge theFlorentyn' is made up of thirteen fables and tales. Seven of these tales come straight from the intermediate French edition where Julien Macho reduced Steinhöwel's selection of eight by one. Four additional tales come from the *Facetiae* independently of Steinhöwel and Macho, and the last two tales are apparently Caxton's own. These last six tales form a textual unit in that they follow one another without separate numbering, the only pieces in the entire collection which are so presented. Following the pattern set for the first seven tales of the selection, Caxton credits Poggio with the first four tales of the additional unit, the ones taken independently from the *Facetiae*. He then introduces his own tale of the widow's reply (Poggio no. 12) impersonally and he introduces himself at the beginning of his last tale—of the good, simple priest (Poggio no. 13), 'Now thenne I wylle fynysshe alle these fables wyth this tale that foloweth whiche a worshipful preest and a parsone told me late.'

It is something of a question how Caxton, who followed the French translation of Steinhöwel's collection so faithfully, obtained his four additional tales from the *Facetiae* independently of the French translator and of Steinhöwel. Robert H. Wilson, on the strength of the appearance of one of the four in a French *Esope* of 1532, suggests a common source for the French collection and Caxton.[12] Brunet does mention an early French translation of some of the *Facetiae* and cites an attribution to Julien Macho,[13] but I have been unable to learn anything more about the book. If this book existed in the 1480's, it could have been Mr. Wilson's hypothesized source. It is also quite possible, however, that Caxton (or someone else) could have taken the tales directly from the *Facetiae* and appended them just as Steinhöwel might have appended his *extravagantes* to the fifth book of fables. While the tale of the widow's reply (Poggio no. 12) could have been associated with Poggio's collection before Caxton made his additions to the selection from it, it could also have been his own rather more sober variation of the usually frivolous 'reply' as represented elsewhere in the *Facetiae*. As for the last tale, I see no reason to doubt Caxton's attribution to a 'worshipful preest.' Whatever the source of these last two tales or the details of their transmission, their overt morality has the effect of returning the reader to a serious atmosphere of instruction, and by virtue of their strategic final position they do much to shape an impression of the book.

Caxton's *Aesop* is shaped, then, in the pattern Steinhöwel gave his original collection. At the center is the Romulus collection—Aesop's fables—to which the *Life* is an obviously suitable preface. The *extravagantes*

antique and the fables from the new translation of Rinuccio, though not perhaps of equal authority, supplement the basic collection. The selection from the fables of Avianus, though they were never supposed to be Aesop's, was an appropriate addition to the collection because these fables had long been paired with the fables of Romulus as school texts and thetraditional link between them must have been very strong. The selections from the *Disciplina Clericalis* of Petrus Alphonsus and Poggio's *Facetiae* are less clearly appropriate, and some of Steinhöwel's editorial remarks show that he felt this diminished suitability. Though Caxton does not make explicit any such editorial doubts, his reshaping of the last part of the final selection implies that though he wanted to entertain his reader, the traditional literary function of instruction was still an active principle in his work. It is the special quality of the fable that it is the most elementary combination of the two functions.

The Aesopic Fable in the Middle Ages

Perhaps just because the fable is so rudimentary a combination of the basic literary functions, it was an extremely popular literary form during the Middle Ages, and perhaps for the same reason fables were freely altered and recast throughout the period. Consequently the history of the medieval fable is a complicated one and any survey must be either very short, a general designation of the main sources, or very long, an analysis of the intricacies of relationship among the various collections. A brief sketch should be sufficient to locate Caxton's *Aesop* against the general medieval background.

There are two main source collections for the medieval fable, both of late Latin origin: the prose fables of Romulus and the verse fables of Avianus. Those of Avianus were selected and translated from the Greek fables of Babrius. Those of Romulus are prose reworkings of the 'standard' ancient Latin collection, the fables of Phaedrus, which were unknown in their original form through most of the Middle Ages. The Romulus fables became the most important Aesopic collection during the Middle Ages, in part perhaps because they were derived from the 'standard' antique collection, in part because they were more numerous than the fables of Avianus, but chiefly because of the prefatory letter which claimed that they were Aesop's fables translated directly from the Greek. Whatever the cause, the Romulus fables were taken as Aesop's fables during the Middle Ages. They were translated, versified, recast with new or additional morals, and selected for smaller collections. The fables of Avianus underwent the same process. The resulting tangle of versions and collections can be most easily appreciated by scanning the lists and tables of Leopold Hervieux's *Les Fabulistes latins*. Accretion to so varying a corpus was almost inevitable. The process of this accretion and, indeed, the whole tangle of the medieval fable are conveniently ordered in Ben Edwin Perry's *Aesopica* where the development of the Aesopic corpus is clearly laid out.

Caxton's *Aesop* can be seen as a historical anthology of the medieval Aesopic fable. The *Life* establishes an identity for the legendary author of the fables. Then come Aesop's fablesthemselves, in the Romulus collection, some medieval additions to that corpus, and the variant, parallel collection of Avianus. The tales of the *Disciplina Clericalis* serve as a reminder that the fable was often combined with other sorts of didactic literature and was often thought of more as one kind of moral narrative than as an independent literary genre. The *Aesop* also implies a rounding off of this medieval history by inclusion of the work of the fifteenth-century Italian humanists, Rinuccio and Poggio Bracciolini. Rinuccio's translation is newly made from Greek sources and is an early sign of the re-established contact with the Greek world. Although Poggio's tales are usually unlike the typical Romulus fable in several ways, the novel difference is implicit in his title, and explicit in his preface where he says that entertainment and style are his only concerns; the tales are not concerned with morality. That the new mixes so easily with the old testifies both to the vitality and the elasticity of the fable as a genre.

The vitality of the genre is an obvious incentive to the collector but its elasticity is just as obviously a problem for him. He has to decide what a fable is before he can assemble a collection. Ancient and medieval authorities defined the fable as a fiction made up to represent some aspect of human activity.[14] This amounts to saying that the fable is a fundamental form of literature. The definition sets out the combination of the traditional literary elements—story and moral—and the concomitant aims—amusement and instruction. Caxton's *Aesop* is true to this tradition; it is an unsophisticated collection of literary elements unabashedly confident in the worth of those elements. Because, however, their combination in the fable is so rudimentary, it is difficult to say which of the elements is more important, and so the genre carries about it an ambiguity of intention that makes it difficult to declare the actual primacy of one or the other of the two aims. Caxton is not especially sensitive to this ambiguity, but the original collector, Heinrich Steinhöwel, was much more conscious of the problem. He apologizes for the unseemly tales of Poggio, and his preface insists that fables are valuable for their morals. There can be no misunderstanding Steinhöwel's conception of the fable's purpose: it is didactic. He provides an index to help to realize that aim by arranging appropriate fables under topical headings like *Aigensinnig, Ayd, Alter*.[15]

When Steinhöwel turns from the fable's function to its nature, or make-up, his discussion becomes more con-fusing. He borrows a definition from the medieval encyclopedist, Isidore of Seville, which is really a combination of definitions. He starts with etymology: 'The poets have taken the name fable from the Latin word *fando,* that is to say in German that fables are not about things which actually happened but are only verbal inventions, and they have been composed so that through the invented words of unreasoning animals lower than himself a man may recognize an image of the ways and habits of human virtue.'[16] He then defines by description and division of fables according to their characters.He finally defines by function: some fables are composed to give pleasure, some to represent human nature for didactic ends, and some to give allegorical explanations of natural phenomena (*Steinhöwels Äsop,* p. 5). Steinhöwel, Isidore, and most twentieth-century readers would agree that a fable is a moralized animal tale. But in picking up Isidore's etymology, Steinhöwel emphasizes what medieval authorities considered the essential feature of the fable: it is 'made up'; it narrates events that did not happen. Steinhöwel's borrowed definition is really a combination of at least four different, though not mutually exclusive, definitions: (1) it is fiction in the sense that it did not really happen; (2) it is literary entertainment; (3) it is poetic fiction with double or allegorical significance; and (4) it is a moral tale, usually with animal characters. The first seems to be the essential definition but it is very general. The fourth is most familiar to modern readers, and if Isidore's examples are indicative, it seems to have been uppermost in his mind. Since the fourth is easily contained in the first, it is possible that *fable* may often refer specifically to a moralized animal tale even when the context stresses its more general definition as fiction. These two principal definitions are ancient and medieval commonplaces, one from rhetoric and one from grammar. The rhetorician defined *fabula* as fiction, that type of narration which describes events that could not have happened. The grammar teacher stressed the utility of the fable as a simple, instructive tale. Although Steinhöwel's definition of the fable only confuses his discussion, tacitly admitting the ambiguity of the genre, he does come down squarely on the side of the grammar teacher in his insistence on the morality of the fable.

The grammar teacher, probably more than anyone else, was responsible for the medieval currency of the Aesopic fable. He was actively aware of the reasons for the durability of the genre. The suitability of the fable as primer material is obvious. The lists of school authors are seldom without an Aesopic collection and the same is true of certain earlier manuscripts which seem to have served as primer texts in the ninth and tenth centuries. The fable was also the vehicle of the first of a series of paraphrase exercises in composition which are described in Priscian's *Praeexercitamina*.[17] Though the series probably did not survive intact through the Middle Ages, there is ample evidence that fables did serve as paraphrase vehicles for teaching composition. This pedagogical utility is due to the simplicity that so strongly characterizes the genre; yet that very simplicity, enforced by association with the schoolroom, makes the fable especially suitable for a special kind of sophisticated irony that subordinates instruction to amusement. By virtue of the naïveté associated with the genre, a sophisticated fabulist can take the ironic stance of Socratic mock innocence. Chaucer's *Nun's Priest's Tale* is a fine single example of this sort of fable, and the Reynard tales are often expanded developments of the same kind of irony.

The conclusion to be drawn, then, is that in the fifteenth century, as for many centuries before, the fable was a literary genre, most obviously a simple one, but also possessed of a basic ambiguity sufficient to invite sophisticated, ironic manipulation.

Because of its generic ambiguity, then, the fable was many things in the fifteenth century: folktale, pedagogical device, sermon exemplum, literary genre; it could reach a wide range of intelligences; it could be bluntly assertive or cleverly ironic; didactic or skeptical. It is no wonder that the definition Steinhöwel appropriated from Isidore turns out to be a rather confusing combination of definitions. A man may emphasize any feature or function he chooses. Steinhöwel chose with the grammarians to emphasize the didactic function, but by quoting Isidore, he noticed almost all the others. Texts of such various appeal, sanctioned by so long a tradition, would naturally suggest themselves for printing. Practical financial questions aside, the problem would have been to make a selection from the welter of texts circulating in the fifteenth century. Heinrich Steinhöwel, Italian-educated and prominent both because of his social position and his literary activities, had the authority to make that choice. His decision was quite simple: he made a collection of collections, and Johann Zainer printed the lavish German and Latin edition of 1476/77.

The *Esopus* was widely reprinted; it was translated into French by Julien Macho of Lyons and printed there in 1480. Caxton translated the French text, and so within six years of its first printing Steinhöwel's collection passed through an intermediate French edition into Caxton's English.

The Editions of Steinhöwel and Julien Macho

In one sense, description and discussion of Caxton's collection make superfluous any discussion of its originals, Steinhöwel's collection and its French translation, because much of what should be said of them has already been said. Still, Caxton's collection does differ

in certain respects from its originals, and a full view of his work is impossible without a look at them and the process of their transference into his collection.

Steinhöwel's *Esopus* was an unmistakably lavish production, offering a profusion of woodcuts, more fables than any earlier edition, a bilingual text, and, for the first three books of fables, still another Latin version in distichs. The pattern of the collection indicates that Steinhöwel was a self-conscious, and, to a degree, a discriminating collector ('completed are the *extravagantes antique,* ascribed to Aesop, I do not know whether truly or falsely'[18]). Steinhöwel included, either complete or in part, almost all the major collections of fables popular in the Middle Ages. His printer undertook to produce a book worthy of such a collection, and perhaps the best measure of this is the presentation of the first three books of Romulus in three parallel versions: the Latinprose of the Romulus collection itself, the German translation of it, and a set of Latin verse fables.

Of these three versions, the Latin prose of the Romulus collection is basic, and Steinhöwel's German version tends to follow it closely with some expansion.

> Verum ut vitam hominum et mores ostenderet, inducit aves, arbores, bestias et pecora loquentes, pro vana cuiuslibet fabula, ut noverint homines, fabularum cur sit inventum genus, aperte et breviter narravit. Apposuitque vera malis. Composuit integra bonis. Scripsit calumnias malorum, argumenta improborum.

> Aber darumb daz er das leben der menschen und iere sitten erzögen möchte, hat er in syn fabeln redend fogel, böm, wilde und zäme tier, hirs, wolf, füchs, löwen, rinder, schauff, gaiss und andre gezogen, nach gebürlikait ainer ieden fabel, daruss man lycht und verstentlich kennen mag, warunb die gewonhait in fabeln ze schryben sye erfunden. Er hat die warhait zuo den bösen geseczet, das guot zuo guoten. Er beschrybt die böslist der untrüwen ankläger der gericht, und erdichte fürzüg der unfrummen.[19]

The translation is close, 'translated from Latin into German by Doctor Heinrich Steinhöwel not well but clearly, taken not word for word, but meaning for meaning, to the greater clarification of the text often with a few added or deleted words.'[20] The most obvious change is the expansion of the *dramatis bestiae,* but also noteworthy are the change of *vana fabula* to *syn fabel* and the reminder in *nach gebürlikait ainer ieden fabel* that there are traditional expectations for certain animals (the lion is a king; the fox is clever; the wolf is violent).

The third of the parallel versions—the Latin verse fables—derives from the basic Romulus collection as a poetic version of it, but it has more the status of an independent collection. These distichs date from the twelfth century and are attributed to an unknown Walterius. They were already extremely popular; Hervieux lists 129 Latin and vernacular manuscripts of it. The fifteenth-century Italian translations by Zuccho and Tuppo seem to have been more popular than the Latin translations made from the Greek by Lorenzo Valla and Rinuccio. To judge from the number of editions, however, the most popular fifteenth-century verse collection was the *Esopus Moralisatus,* which was nothing more than Walter's collection with the superaddition (by the thirteenth century) of a set of moralizations appended to the epimythia of the fables. Thus, by including the fables of Walter, Steinhöwel in effect appropriated the major rival collection of the fifteenth century.

Though Steinhöwel's sources are all identified, the specific texts he used have not been established. In any event, Steinhöwel would have felt free to exercise his own judgment in preparing his texts. For example, though Rinuccio says that fables are important for their wisdom and although his *Argumentum fabularum* describes an explicitly moral wisdom, in his prologue it is a rather worldly wisdom. Steinhöwel resisted the lead suggested by Rinuccio and poured the 'new' translation into the old moral bottles so that it became formally indistinguishable from the old. He added Latin and German promythia, the initial, generalized statements of the morals, to all except three of his selections from Rinuccio's fables (and he managed a German promythium for one of the three). The effect, though he may have intended nothing more than to produce a formal similarity, is certainly to underscore the morals. Similar literary and didactic standards can also be seen in his treatment of his selection from Poggio. After a tale of unquestionable impropriety (Poggio no. 4), he writes a lengthy apology: he included such stories not because he liked them but because of his respect for the famous Poggio, and when he thinks of how he has fallen from his high purposes to such stories, he sees that he must have done with them. To prove his sincerity he devotes a page to describing, occasionally in detail, the stories he will not tell. He does, however, conclude the book with four harmless tales, the last being a fable of a fox and a cock (Poggio no. 7). Needless to say, Steinhöwel is hard put to find edifying morals for improper material, but it is testimony to his determination that he supplies promythia for three of the eight pieces. These promythia are more interesting for what they reveal about Steinhöwel's sense of genre than for any applicability of moral to tale. The concluding fable he introduces, 'Concerning this, hear a fable,' but each of the two tales (Poggio no. 6 and one which does not appear in Caxton) he introduces, 'Concerning this, hear an amusing tale.' This kind of apology and this kind of discrimination are editorial manifestations of Steinhöwel's interest in

the questions of the nature and function of the fable, and they are precisely what, for lack of interest or for lack of space, are omitted from Julien Macho's translation and therefore from Caxton's.

Steinhöwel's collection was reprinted several times immediately after the first edition. The German text alone was reprinted by Gunther Zainer in Augsburg in 1478 and twice more in Augsburg (1479 and 1480) by Anton Sorg, who also reprinted the Latin text alone in 1480. The French translation was made by an Augustinian monk of Lyons, Julien Macho, an obscure figure about whom little is known aside from the fact that he translated and edited a number of books for Lyonnais printers.[21] The more or less automatic expectation, particularly in view of his other translations, is that he would have made the French translation from a Latin text. This would seem to be borne out by a comparison of some sample passages.

> Quidam ex scolaribus percipiens Xanthum vino paulisper gravatum ait: Dic mihi, preceptor, homo unus mare totum bibere posset? Quid ni, Xanthus ait, nam egoipse totum ebiberem. Et scolaris inquit: Et si non biberis, quid deponis? Domum, Xanthus air (*Steinhöwels Äsop,* p. 23).

> Et adoncques vng des escolliers voyant que xantus estoyt bien devin charge. Mon maistre ie te demade si vng homme pourroit boire tout la mer. Et pourquoy non dist xantus moy mesme le la boyray toute.

> Et lescollier luy dist. et si tu ne la boys que veulx tu perdre.

> Et xantus dist ma maison.[22]

Furthermore, there are occasional mistakes which would suggest that the translator had his eye on the Latin text: 'vng prestre qui auoit nom Isidis,' 'ecce Ysidis sacerdos,' 'ain prester der gottin Ysidis'; or 'lesquelz seruiteurs auoient nom Grammaticus Saltes & esope,' 'hi fuerunt grammaticus, psaltes atque Esopus,' 'die warent ain grammaticus, ein harpfer und Esopus.'[23]

On the other hand, there are passages which suggest that the translator had his eye on the German text:

> de grece au pres de troye la grande dune ville appelle amonneo, is . . . natione Phrygius, ex Ammonio Phrygie pago fuit, der gegent Phrigia, dar inn Troya gelegen ist, von Ammonio dem wyler geboren.[24]

Steinhöwel offers a full Latin version of the fable of Venus and the hen (Rom. III, 8) but stops his German version short, saying he will not put what the hen said into German. The French translator follows the German version, 'We shall leave it in Latin,' even though the Latin he leaves it in is not in his book (see note 239; p.110). The promythia of the fables of Avianus also indicate that the translator sometimes followed the German text. There are no promythia for some of the fables in this collection, but Steinhöwel, perhaps because of an understandable reluctance to imitate the poetry of Avianus, did not supply the missing Latin promythia, as he did for the fables of Rinuccio. Instead he contented himself with supplying German promythia, which some of the French promythia very much resemble. Although Steinhöwel no doubt modeled some of his German promythia on the corresponding Latin epimythia, the final, generalized statement of a fable's moral, and the French translator could easily have done the same (e.g. Avianus no. 9), there are other cases where it is unlikely that the French translator followed Steinhöwel's Latin (Avianus no. 3), or impossible (Avianus no. 8). It therefore seems clear that Julien Macho made some use of the German text.

If a comparison of the texts suggests that the French translation follows both the German and Latin texts, the obvious original for the translation would seem to be Steinhöwel's first bilingual edition printed at Ulm. Unfortunately for this conclusion, there are woodcuts in the French edition of 1480 which are not in Steinhöwel's first edition but do appear in the subsequent editions printed at Augsburg.[25] Since none of these editions was bilingual, Julien Macho probably worked from the bilingual first edition, and the designer of the woodcuts had one of the Augsburg editions.

The French translation is a much reduced version of the lavish Steinhöwel first edition. It is not bilingual, and gone with the Latin texts are three of Steinhöwel's tales (Alphonsus nos. 13, 14 and Poggio no. 1). Also dropped is Steinhöwel's editorial apparatus: his introduction about the nature and function of the fable, his topical index of morals, and his apology for Poggio's tales. Apparently, Julien Macho was less concerned than Steinhöwel to define the fable as a literary genre and saw less need to stress the didactic function of that genre. He does, however, make his position clear by adding to the preface to the second book of Romulus some remarks on the function and value of fables (which reappear in Caxton's edition, p. 89):

> Every fable is invented to show men what they ought to follow and what they ought to flee. For fables mean as much in poetry as words in theology. And so I shall write fables to show the ways of good men.[26]

Still, the omission, for whatever reason, of so much of Steinhöwel's express emphasis on the morality of the fable does have the effect of leaving the reader free to read with as little attention to morality as the fables themselves permit. The result is that the French translation concentrates somewhat less on instruction than does Steinhöwel's collection, and so permits relatively more attention to entertainment.

Caxton's Prose

Caxton's dependence on Steinhöwel is counterbalanced less by his own independence of judgment than by his dependence on the French translator. This is not to minimize the independence implicit in his additions to the collection but simply to state the obvious—Caxton could only see Steinhöwel's collection as the French translator chose to show it to him. The pattern of Caxton's *Aesop* reveals the larger shape of this dependence, but the actual processes of translation best reveal its particulars, as can be seen by comparing passages from Caxton's edition with passages from the French edition of 1480.

> Des mocqueurs esope a fait vne telle fable dung asne qui recontra vng lyon. Et lasne luy dist. Mon frere dieu te gart. Et le lyon commence a [c 8] branler la teste par grant ayr et a grant paine peust il refraindre son yre que de ses dens ne le deuourast. Et Adoncques dist en soy mesmes il nappertient pas que vne dens si noble touche a vne beste si ville. Car celluy qui est saige ne doit blesser le fol auoir cure de ses parolles mais le fault laisser aller pour tel quil est.

> Of them whiche mocken other esope reherceth such a fable Ther was an asse which met with a lyon to whom he said my broder god saue the & the lyon shaked his hede [e 4ᵛ] and with grete payne he myght hold his courage/ to haue forth with deuoured hym/ But the lyon sayd to hym self/ It behoueth not that teethe soo noble and sofayre as myn be touchen not/ ne byten suche a fowle beest/ For he that is wyse must not hurte the foole ne take hede to his wordes/ but lete hym go for suche as he is (Rom. I, II)

The most important point is again the obvious one: Caxton follows the French closely, word for word at times. His changes are usually minor: for example, the addition of 'ne byten,' the omission of *par grant ayr,* the alteration of *dung asne* to 'Ther was an asse,' the expansion of *Des Mocqueurs* to 'Of them whiche mocken other.' There are occasional difficulties: his infinitive is an awkward rendering of *que de ses dens ne le deuourast.* As might be expected in so faithful a translation, Caxton anglicizes and directly adopts many of the original French words. But Caxton's syntax is clearly English. Occasionally difficulties arise from a lapse into French patterns (e.g. 'took of the most best metes,' 39:24), from the reproduction of difficulties in the French original, and from requirements made by our English but not by Caxton's (e.g. pronouns, 102:21-24; omitted subject, 172:1, and levels of discourse, 91:12-14). In short, Caxton wanted to render the fables directly into English and on the whole he did his work efficiently.

He made some changes, and the most important of these—the additions to the selection of tales from Poggio—have already been discussed. There are also two fairly long omissions: a passage in the *Life* about urinating (see note 43; p. 35), and another of heavy-handed quibbling (see note 50; p. 39). Caxton might seem to be acting from a moral or aesthetic sensitivity, especially since there is a comparable graphic omission in the deletion from his frontispiece of the striking French example of hindsight (see Caxton's frontispiece in appendix); but there are too many indelicate episodes which are not slighted to admit of generalizations about Caxton's delicacy. Similarly, in a tale of cuckoldry (Poggio no. 1) he changed French *dieu* to the Holy Ghost, but whether this tempers or refines the irreligion is hard to say. It is probably safest to regard these changes as fortuitous.

It is possible, however, to make some general inferences about Caxton's handling of his text. To start negatively, Caxton is often neglectful of narrative precision or nicety. He sometimes abridges the French narrative and drops out words or phrases on which a later statement depends. For example, the country mouse gave his urbane cousin 'of such mete as he had,' instead of 'some grains of wheat and some water to drink' which better anticipates the conclusion, 'I had leuer ete some corne in the feldes' (see note 160; p. 81). There are other such places (e.g. note 78; p. 53), places where his narrative is less tidy (e.g. note 349; p. 152), and places where he changes the identity of an animal in spite of a clearly corrective woodcut (e.g. Aesop before Croesus in the *Life,* or Romulus IV, 14). That such blemishes are more matters of carelessness than ineptitude is clear from the direct and effective narration of Caxton's own concluding tale (Poggio no. 13).

If such careless omission and alteration show that narrative precision was not a major interest, a positive interest in style may be inferred from one kind of addition Caxton made to his text. A casual reading shows that he is not always as direct as he is in his final tale; indeed he often swells up his prose to a remarkable prolixity (e.g. 91:6-8). This tendency suggests an interest in elevation of style, but the focused augmentation of doubled phrases is a safer basis for inference than the more general notion of prolixity. Caxton obviously wants to use two words where one would suffice. This doubling was common enough in his day and, on the sample of the first half of his book, I found that thirty per cent of Caxton's doublets are simply translations of doublets in the French text. Of the remainder, slightly more than half are formed by adding an English word to the French ('doubte ne drede' from 'doubter,' 'tryst and sorowful' from 'tryste'). A glance at almost any page will provide further examples of these counterpoised doublets. They are best understood in the light of the dilemma Caxton describes in the prologue to his *Eneydos;* he was attracted to the book by 'the fayr and honest termes and wordes in frenshe' and he had been urged by great clerks 'to wryte the moste curyous termes,' but others wanted him to stick to 'olde and homely termes.'[27] Caxton's response is often to do both, or at least to link an English word with a French one. As a result, some doublets did have the effect of 'augmenting' the language, and in some cases this effect seems to have been intentional (see notes 239; p. 109 and 190; p. 93). In other doublets, however, there are no French words, or else the French word had long been naturalized and could not be considered 'curyous.' Caxton's enrichment of his native language was occasional and unsystematic; it came naturally in the effort to elevate his style. Professor N. F. Blake has remarked that doublets in Caxton's *Reynard the Fox* come most frequently in didactic or descriptive passages and in beginnings and endings rather than in the course of the narrative.[28] This is less clearly true of the fables, where there are a good many doublets added in the narrative sections; but in some fables the frequency of doublets goes up quite markedly in the promythia and epimythia. These are statements of *sentence,* and the doublets are the straightforward means of lending them dignity.

Caxton's prose, especially the doublet, is a guide to the nature of his book. His method of elevating his style was consistent with contemporary Burgundian literary values and was thus old-fashioned or medieval. His famous prologue to his *Eneydos* was similarly old-fashioned, but its deference showed a receptivity, a willingness to be taught, and further suggested that this willingness was proper for gentlemen concerned with humane studies. In other words Caxton's general concern with style, though it was old-fashioned and Burgundian in its particulars, put him in the humanistic channel through which the new instruction was eventually to come. In his *Aesop* Caxton actually had harbingers of the new age, the humanists, Rinuccio and Poggio, but there is no sign that he had any practical recognition of this fact. Steinhöwel, of course, did have some idea of the values of the Italian humanistsand his *Esopus,* with its pedagogical associations, is a partial and elementary reflection of those values. By eliminating the Latin texts of the *Esopus,* Julien Macho eliminated the explicit signs of that reflection and so Caxton stands almost as far from Steinhöwel as his woodcuts are from their German originals. Yet Caxton's treatment of his text betrays some apprehension of the general values which animated Steinhöwel's collection and which, because of the traditional link between the Aesopic fable and elementary grammatical study, were still implicit even in the reduced version that Caxton translated and printed.

Notes

[1] Ben Edwin Perry's *Aesopica* (Urbana, 1952) is the authoritative text but his volume in the Loeb Classical Library, *Babrius and Phaedrus* (Cambridge, Mass., 1964), is a more convenient introduction to the Aesopic fable. For Caxton, Nellie Slayton Aurner's *Caxton: Mirror of Fifteenth Century Letters* (London, 1926) is a good general introduction, as is, more briefly, the relevant part of the *Oxford History of English Literature:* H. S. Bennett, *Chaucer and the Fifteenth Century* (Oxford, 1947), pp. 203-213.

[2] *Steinhöwels Äsop,* ed. Hermann Österley (Tübingen, 1873).

[3] There is no modern edition of Rinuccio's *Life and Fables.* The incunabula are listed in *Der Gesamtkatalog der Wiegendrucke,* nos. 335-344.

[4] Ben Edwin Perry, *Aesopica,* p. 5; *Babrius and Phaedrus,* p. xlvi.

[5] *Aesopica,* pp. 22, 28.

[6] *Der Lateinische Äsop des Romulus und die Prosafassungen des Phädrus,* ed. Georg Thiele (Heidelberg, 1910).

[7] The closest thing to a source text for these fables is *Monachii Romulleae et Extravagantes Fabulae,* ed. Leopold Hervieux, *Les Fabulistes Latins,* 2nd ed. (Paris, 1894), II, 262-290, and *Aesopica,* pp. 696-704.

[8] *Der Gesamtkatalog der Wiegendrucke,* nos. 335-344.

[9] Avianus, *Fables,* ed. Robinson Ellis (Oxford, 1887); the fables of Avianus are also included in a volume of the Loeb Classical Library, *Minor Latin Poets,* ed. J. Wright Duff and Arnold M. Duff (Cambridge, Mass., 1935).

[10] Petrus Alfonsus, *Disciplina Clericalis,* ed. Alfons Hilka and Werner Soderhjelm (Helsinki, 1911).

[11] Poggio Bracciolini, *Facetiae,* ed. anon. (Paris, 1879).

[12] 'The Poggiana in Caxton's *Esope,' The Philological Quarterly,* 30:350 (1951).

[13] Gustave Brunet, *La France Litteraire au XVe Siecle* (Paris, 1865), p. 165.

[14] Ben Edwin Perry's 'Fable,' *Studium Generale,* 12:19-23 (1959), is an authoritative modern definition.

[15] 'Obstinate, Oath, Old Age.'

[16] 'Die poeten den namen fabel von dem latinischen wort fando habent genommen, daz ist ze tütsch reden, wann fabel synt nit geschechene ding, sonder allain mit worten erdichte ding, und sint darumb erdacht worden, daz man durch erdichte wort der unvernünftigen tier under in selber ain ynbildung des wesens und sitten der menschlichen würde erkennet' (*Steinhöwels Äsop,* p. 5).

[17] Priscianus, *Praeexercitamina,* ed. Heinrich Keil in *Grammatici Latini* (Leipzig, 1858), II, 430.

[18] 'Finite sunt extravagantes antique, ascripte Esope, nescio si vere vel ficte' (*Steinhöwels Äsop,* p. 241).

[19] 'But because he wanted to instruct the life of men and their customs he has drawn into his fables speaking birds, trees, wild and tame beasts, stags, wolves, foxes, lions, oxen, sheep, goats and others, according to the requirements of each fable, from this one may easily and clearly recognize why the custom of writing fables was invented. He has told the truth to the wicked, good to the good. He describes the wickedness of the false accusers of the just and sets down the progress of the ungodly' (*Steinhöwels Äsop,* p. 78).

[20] 'uss latin von doctore Hainrico Stainhöwel schlecht und verstentlich getütschet, nit wort uss wort, sunder sin uss sin, um merer lütrung wegen des textes oft mit wenig zugelegten oder abgebrochnen worten gezogen' (*Steinhöwels Äsop,* p. 4).

[21] J. B. Wadsworth, *Lyons, 1473-1503* (Cambridge, Mass., 1962), pp. 22-25.

[22] And then one of the scholars, seeing that Xantus was full of wine, said, 'Master, I ask you if a man can drink all the sea?' 'And why not?' said Xantus, 'I shall drink it all myself.' And the scholar said to him, 'And if you do not drink it all, what will you forfeit?' And Xantus said, 'My house.'

[23] 'a priest who was named Isidis'; the French translator apparently missed the genitive, *Ysidis,* and read it in apposition with *sacerdos,* a reading impossible from the German; 'the which servants were named Grammaticus, Saltes and Aesop'; the translator read *grammaticus* and *psaltes* as proper names like *Esopus,* again a reading impossible from the German.

[24] 'from Greece in the country of Troy the great of a town called Amonneo.' The Latin locates Ammonio in Phrygia; the German joins it with Troy and the French drops Phrygia.

[25] Claude Dalbanne and E. Droz, 'Etude sur l'Illustration des Fables,' *Les Subtiles Fables d'Esope* (Lyons, 1926), p. 160.

[26] Toute fable est trouuer pour demonstrer aux hommes quelle chose ilz doyuent ensuyure et quelle chose ilz

doyuent fouyr. Car autant veult dire fable en poesie comme parolles en theologie. Et pource iescripray fables pour monstrer les meurs des bons hommes.

[27] *Caxton's Eneydos,* ed. W. T. Culley and F. J. Furnivall, *Early English Text Society, Extra Series 57* (London, 1890), pp. 1-3.

[28] 'William Caxton's *Reynard the Fox* and his Dutch Original,' *Bulletin of the John Rylands Library,* 46:320-321 (1964).

Annabel Patterson (essay date 1991)

SOURCE: "Fables of Power: The Sixteenth Century," in *Fables of Power: Aesopian Writing and Political History,* pp. 45-80. Durham: Duke University Press, 1991.

[*In the following essay, Patterson refutes the contention that fables were meant exclusively as moral or educational tools, arguing instead that the English fables of the Middles Ages and Renaissance were intended as political commentary.*]

> O wretch that thy fortunes should moralize
> Esops fables, and make tales, prophesies.
> Thou'art the swimming dog whom shadows
>   cosened,
> And div'st, neare drowning, for what's
>
>   vanished.
>
> —*John Donne:* Satire 5

The history of the fable in the sixteenth century is, from one perspective, continuous with that of the late middle ages. John Lydgate's *The Horse, the Goose, and the Sheep,* which included comments on the fable's function as a medium of communication, "under covert," of social protest by the poor and their advocates, was printed by Caxton in 1477, and by Wynkyn de Worde in 1499 and again in 1500. Lydgate's *The Churl and the Bird* was, likewise, printed by Caxton in 1478 and by De Worde in 1520. The latter poem, claiming to be a translation from a French "pamphlet" and indeed an expansion of a clerical fable by Petrus Alfonsi,[1] becomes in Lydgate's treatment an extended meditation on the fable tradition in the world of political power structures, especially in its relation to freedom of expression.

For *The Churl and the Bird,* whose center is a Chauntecleer-like tale of how a captured bird out-witted her captor, is, quite unlike the *Nun's Priest's Tale,* a moving account of the problems of poets who are forced to operate under any kind of social constraint, from clientage to more extreme forms of repression. (Lydgate himself wrote to order for Henry V, Henry VI, and

Humphrey, duke of Gloucester, and *The Churl and the Bird* ends by recommending itself "unto my maister.") Having trapped the bird, the churl (peasant) "cast for to make, / Withyn his hous a praty litel cage, / And with hir song to rejoissh his corage." But here is the bird's response:

> I am now take & stond undir daungeer,
> Holde streite, & I may not flee;
> Adieu my song & al my notis cleer
> Now that I have lost my liberte,
> Now am I thral, and sometyme I was fre,
> And trust weel now I stonde in distresse,
> I can-nat syng, nor make no gladnesse.
>
> And thouh my cage forged were of gold,
> And the pynaclis of beral & cristall,
> I remembre a proverbe seid of old,
> "Who lesith his fredam, in soth, he leseth
>   all;
> For I have lever upon a braunche small,
> Meryly to syng among the woodis grene,
> Than in a cage of silver briht and shene.
> Song and prisoun have noon accordaunce,
> Trowistow I wole syngen in prisoun?
>
>   . . . . .
>
> Ryngyng of ffeteris makith no mery soun,
> Or how shold he be glad or jocounde
> Ageyn his wil that lith in cheynes bounde?[2]

In addition, Lydgate opened his fable with several metacritical stanzas that implicitly relate this central issue to the "liknessis & ffigures" with which, from time immemorial, fables have been constructed. Beginning with Jotham's fable, in Judges 9, of how the trees of the forest went about to choose themselves a king, Lydgate proceeded to the secular tradition in which monarchy involves consideration of parliamentary government:

> And semblably poetes laureate,
> Bi dirk parables ful convenyent,
> Feyne that briddis & bestis of estat—
> As roial eglis & leones—bi assent
> Sent out writtis to hold a parlement,
> And maade decrees breffly for to sey,
> Some to have lordship, & som to obey.
>
>   (2:469)

These poems today exist on the fringes of "literature," as supposedly minor productions of a poet whose reputation has faded into insignificance beside Chaucer. Yet their history of publication in the fifteenth century and early sixteenth century implies that their message was noticed and valued, that it carried an application to early Tudor England. It seems inarguable to me that Lydgate established an English tradition of political fabling as a form of resistance to unjust power relations, which ran continuously alongside (or beneath) the more conventional and conservative notion that the content of fables was merely ethical, and that they could, therefore, serve as benign texts in the elementary education of children. Lydgate's reminder in *The Churl and the Bird* that "Poetes write wondirful liknessis, / And under covert kept hem silf ful cloos" (2:469), was, as we shall see, a cardinal principle of sixteenth- and seventeenth-century fabulists.

Yet the established critical position has been that the fable does not or should not do what Lydgate believed it had always done. Rather, we have been told, it should eschew topicality (or political allegory) and speak to the most general (and hence socially neutral) moral concerns. As Lessing remarked in his *Abhändlungen über die Fabel,* published in 1759, "the fable only becomes an allegory when to the invented individual case which it contains [the animal plot] a similar and real one [of human, historical circumstance] is added; and the word allegory must be regarded as not at all connected with the strict definition of the fable, which in its essence ought to convey a general moral precept."[3] This eighteenth-century opinion remains as an uninspected premise in modern criticism of the fable, reinforced by other prejudices—against allegory as a mode of figuration and against historical circumstances as a subject of representation or an object of interpretation—inherited respectively from Romanticism and New Criticism. Denton Fox's desire to ignore the evident topicality of Henryson's fables[4] is related to Derek Pearsall's critique of Lydgate's. For Pearsall, Lydgate's fables are only of interest insofar as they can be compared, unfavorably, to Henryson's, as in their common interest in *The Wolf and the Lamb.* Henryson is praised for his development of narrative as distinct from its moralization and for "realism, the sense of a significance attaching to life in its literary imitation." Lydgate's handling of the fable is described as "bookish, moralistic, typically medieval," and although the further charge of "quietism" is leveled, you would never elsewhere guess from Pearsall's description that Lydgate's fables were driven by politicalactuality, were everywhere concerned with what Lydgate calls "tyranny," especially in the legal system.

More telling still is the comparison, again unfavorable, with Chaucer. Chaucer is praised for "his gradual sloughing-off of the externally imposed moralisation" endemic to fable tradition:

> The *Nun's Priest's Tale* explodes the fable in a cascade of literary fireworks, so that the mock-serious injunction at the end, "Taketh the moralite, goode men," can evoke the bewildered response,

"Which one?" The moral is mortified into absurdity and irrelevance, and our attention directed back to the body of the tale. . . . In the *Manciple's Tale* Chaucer provides as the moral a string of unctuous platitudes which reflect back not upon the tale but upon the narrator, and upon the whole concept of the fable as a vehicle of moral wisdom. These very platitudes, parodied by Chaucer, are presented by Lydgate with a perfectly straight face.[5]

If one starts, however, with a bias *in favor* of political consciousness, it greatly enhances one's capacity to recognize its presence. And in fact Chaucer's fables clearly contain their own brand of politics. The *Nun's Priest's Tale* of Chauntecleer's escape from the fox may avoid explicit social commentary (which in Pearsall's vocabulary is not distinguished from moral platitude), but it gratuitously expresses contempt for "Jakke Straw and his meynee" (l. 3394), Chaucer's only reference to the Peasants' Revolt of 1381. The early *Parliament of Fowls* completely suppresses from the idea of a "parliament" any political implications; it is merely the forum for aristocratic dynastic-marital disputes; and the *Manciple's Tale* anticipates Lydgate's use of the caged bird motif, in language that Lydgate evidently remembered:

> Taak any bryd, and put it in a cage,
> And do al thyn entente and thy corage
> To fostre it tendrely with mete and drynke
> Of alle deyntees that thou kanst bithynke,
> And keep it al so clenly as thou may,
> Although his cage of gold be never so gay,
> Yet hath this brid, by twenty thousand foold,
> Levere in a forest, that is rude and coold,
> Goon ete wormes and swich wrecchednesse.
> For evere this brid wol doon his bisynesse
> To escape out of his cage, yif he may.
> His libertee this brid desireth ay.
>
> (Ll. 163-74)

Yet having admitted the problem of constrained speech, Chaucer's tale decides against the bird and against freedom of expression. The manciple's fable of the crow, once white but transformed to black by Apollo for betraying the adultery of its mistress, concludes with a moral precisely the opposite of Lydgate's theory of the fable. In fifty lines Chaucer's manciple repeats over and over the injunction to silence:

> My sone, be war, and be noon auctour newe
> Of tidynges, wheither they been false or trewe.
> Whereso thou come, amonges hye or lowe,
> Kepe wel thy tonge, and thenk upon the
> crowe.
>
> (Ll. 359-62)[6]

It might be possible to argue that the manciple is mocked for Polonius-like sententiousness; but there is nothing in the *Manciple's Tale* to suggest that its *message* is to be held suspect. It appears that Chaucer did what he could to neutralize the fable's potential for protest or resistance and that Lydgate did what he could to reverse the process.

Early Tudor writers had reason continually to assess these rival models. In the 1520s John Skelton developed the model of the bird in the cage with unsurpassed brilliance, but not without a certain equivocation between the extremes of outspokenness and silence. *Speke, Parott* is a tour de force of vituperation directed against Cardinal Wolsey, in which the conceit of a truly talkative bird who is nevertheless a court pet and learns by rote permitted Skelton to encode some of his most violent accusations in a seemingly random medley of foreign tongues:

> For trowthe in parabyll ye wantonlye
>   pronounce
> Langagys divers; yet undyr that dothe reste
> Maters more precious than the ryche
>   jacounce.

> (Ll. 363-66)[7]

Yet, as Arthur Kinney has shown, the complexity of Skelton's biblical sources renders the fabulist plot almost invisible in a far more learned project. His Parrot, in fact, "pretendith to be a bybyll clarke" (l. 119).[8]

At about the same time Wynkyn de Worde had printed, as well as Lydgate's *The Churl and the Bird,* an anonymous *Parliament of Birds,* which may also have been intended as anti-Wolsey persuasion. In sharp distinction to Chaucer's poem with a similar title, this *Parliament* makes no bones about the institution's political function:

> This is the parlyament of byrdes,
> For hye and lowe and them amyddes,
> To ordayne a meane: how it is best
> To keepe among them peace and rest,
> For muche noyse is on every side
> Agaynst the hauke so full of pride.
> Therfore they shall in bylles bryng
> Theyr complaint to the egle, theyr kyng;
> And by the kynge in parlyament
> Shall be sette in lawful judgement.[9]

In fact, the poem divides into two complaints, one against the hawk, represented as a gray-headed chief minister of the realm, and the crow, an upstart who has received, with the eagle's initial encouragement, borrowed feathers from each of the birds to permit him to come to attend the parliament in proper array.

Eventually this arrangement causes more outrage than the crow's initial absence, and is consequently reversed:

> Then was plucked fro the crowe anone
> All his feders by one and by one,
> And lefte in blacke instede of reed.

> (P.66)

It is possible that this episode refers, by way of allusion to the red of the cardinal's robe, to Wolsey's fall in 1529, which was also the year of the Reformation Parliament; but a more interesting form of political commentary is represented by the hawk, whose role in the poem is less to defend himself than the system as it stands, and especially to articulate the position of Chaucer's *Manciple's Tale,* against freedom of speech:

> The hauke answered the prating pye:
> "Where is many wordes the truth goeth by;
> And better it were to seace of language sone,
> Than speake and repent when thou hast done."

> Than sayd the sterlynge: "Verament,
> Who sayth soth shal be shent;
> No man maye now speke of trouthe
> But his heed be broke, and that is routhe."

> The hawke swore by his heed of graye:
> "All sothes be not for to saye:
> It is better some be left by reason,
> Than trouthe to be spoken out of season."

> Than spake the popyngeiay of paradyse:
> "Who saythe lytell, he is wyse,
> For lytell money is sone spende,
> And few wordes are sone amende."

> The hawke bade: "For drede of payne
> Speke not to moche of thy soverayne,
> For who that wyll forge tales newe
> Whan he weneth leest his tale may rewe."

> (P.60)

Echoes of this debate would be heard in the *The Mirror for Magistrates* in the years following Elizabeth's accession,[10] in Spenser's *Shepheardes Calender,* and Sidney's *Arcadia,* and, from the perspective of the hawk, in Lyly's *Euphues his England.* But by the end of the century this thematic continuity would have seemed less obvious, perhaps, than a newly ratiocinative and *applied* approach to the fable. John Donne took it for granted that a fabulist mode of reference was a necessary part of the thinking man's intellectual machinery. The fifth of his satires, quoted as this chapter's epigraph, concluded with an appeal to the typical late Elizabethan, trapped in a world of entrepreneurial greed and humbug, and seeing himself in Aesop's *Dog and the Shadow.* One of the most famous of his verse letters, *The Calme,* begins with a metaphor that equally depends on familiarity with the Aesopian fable, in this instance the famous *Frogs Desiring a King.* "The fable is inverted," wrote Donne of his voyage to the Azores in 1597, "and farre more / A blocke afflicts, now, then a storke before." The first poem printed in the 1633 edition of Donne's poems was *Metempsychosis,* an amalgam of the ancient animal fable with its related concept of metamorphosis, the whole underwritten by Pythagorean notions of the transmigration of souls, but the purpose political satire.[11] And in one of his epigrams Donne identified himself as "Esops selfe," the man of wisdom who recommends himself for sale in the slave market by admitting he knows nothing, whereas his fellow slaves profess omnicompetence.[12] The metaphor derives from one of the earliest episodes in the *Life* of Aesop, and speaks to that text's continual contrast between conventional values and alien insights, wisdom from below.

I take this *congeries* of allusions to indicate that the second half of the sixteenth century in England was the time (and place) where the Aesopian fable entered early modern culture decisively. In Donne's practice the details of fable plots were not merely an educational residue, a reminder that boys in the grammar schools would probably read Aesop as their first classical author. In Donne's glancing allusions the fable was evidently a reflex of the political imagination; and in other hands (Sidney and Spenser) it had already become the medium in which opposing political theories were debated with considerable precision and even, perhaps, constructed. It is also evident that throughout the early modern period writers who reused the Aesopian materials frequently consulted their English predecessors, and conducted their debates with their support or against their opposition; which is not to say that the literary system operated solely by the mechanism of internal reflexes. On the contrary, it appears that the relation between old forms and their new application to events in the real world was taken so seriously that later fabulists consulted earlier ones as carefully as if they were historians or political philosophers.

In the last decades of the sixteenth century there were created in England the conditions that promote Aesopian writing in the looser modern sense; that is to say, a flexible and constantly renewable system of metaphorical substitutions for actual events, persons, or political concepts that can, but need not, be recognized as such. Among those conditions were a great increase in formal education (including, of course, access to the ancient fabulists); a large group of dissatisfied intellectuals, like Donne himself; and, perhaps most importantly, a determination by the authorities (the queen and her privy council) to exert political control over all the public media of expression at a time when the spread of print technology made such control more difficult, and therefore more obvious in its legal manifestations and public justifications.

The result was a steadily increasing tendency to recuperate not only the fable as a genre, but the genre's own political history, as implied in the *Life* of Aesop and by Phaedrus. Thus certain ancient fables, *The Dog and the Wolf,* which Phaedrus had identified as a liberty-text, or *The Frogs Desiring a King,* which Phaedrus attributed to Aesop on the occasion of a coup by Pisistratus in Athens, inevitably carried with them their original historico-political context, which allowed them to become both exemplars of how to construct a topical fable and permanent tropes in the public discourse of early modern Europe. Others, particularly those that featured the lion, quickly became metaphors for the strengths and limitations of monarchical government in emergent nation states. And still others, like the famous fable of *The Belly and the Members* attributed to Menenius Agrippa and reported both by Livy and Plutarch became, as in Shakespeare's *Coriolanus,* an extremely complex text in which event the tiniest verbal variations could become the bearers of an individual political posture.

Also, a great deal of formal innovation took place within the fable as a genre. It could be massively expanded into a longer narrative, as, for example, by Edmund Spenser in *Mother Hubberds Tale,* one of the chief models for John Dryden's *Hind and the Panther* a century later. Expansion could also be dramatic rather than narrative. In the first decade of James's reign Ben Jonson refashioned the many fables that featured a quick-thinking fox into the plot of *Volpone,* producing an astringent but morally ambiguous analysis of Jacobean legacy hunters, parasites and catamites, professional politicians, and ultimately the entire legal system.[13] No one did more, in the mid-seventeenth century, to expand the fable's possibilities as local political commentary than John Ogilby, in whose hands Aesopian originals became at once definitively lyrical (as distinct from merely being versified) and definitive markers of both civil war and Restoration thinking; yet Ogilby too looked back to Spenser for technical innovation, while enlisting the fable as far as was possible to the support, rather than the critique, of the monarchy then in defeat or exile.

It is one of the fable's habits (and this book's objectives) to oscillate between "literary" exempla and others not normally thought of as literature. If a by-product of this chapter is a clearer sense of what that distinction means and whether it can be maintained, so much the better; but the chief objective is to show the habit itself, the deep penetration of the fable into the culture. I begin with a striking example that itself straddles the divide. In July 1586 there was discovered a Roman Catholic plot against Elizabeth by young aristocrats

led by Anthony Babington; the leaders were all executed in September in a public spectacle, complete with
the full horrors of disembowelment; and early in 1587
there was rushed into print a new edition of "Holinshed's" *Chronicles*. Though Raphael Holinshed himself was dead, a committee of antiquaries including
John Stow continued the history of England through
Elizabeth's reign and literally up to the moment. Its
conclusion was devoted to an account of the Babington plotters, their discovery and trial, and the public
satisfaction at the rigors of the punishment. The chronicle described how, in the Tower, the conspirators
"occupied their wits in dolorous devises . . . savouring
more of prophane poetrie than christianitie, of fansie
than religion"; and Babington, in an appeal for clemency on the basis of his rank, managed to distribute certain poems, which were promptly illegally printed: "the
copies are common (yet never authorised for the print)."

The chronicler continued:

> Furthermore, . . . to procure the speedier com-
> miseration (in his fansie) he falleth into a familiar
> tale of a certaine man, that having a great flocke of
> sheepe, mooved either with a sheepish unruliness,
> or for his better commoditie, threatened everie daie
> by one and one to dispatch them all: which he dailie
> performed according to his promise, untill such time
> as the terror of his accustomed butcherie strake the
> whole flocke into such a fear, as whensoever he
> came and held up his knife, advising at that instant
> but the slaughter of one, the whole number of them
> would quake, fearing each one his particular chance.
> Which tale he applieth to himself, being one of the
> brutish herde (as he confesseth) that for their dis-
> ordinat behaviour the law justlie condemneth, and
> threatneth to dispatch one after another.[14]

This extraordinary insert, marked out for readerly interest, indeed, *literary* attention, by the marginal gloss
"A fable or tale which Babington applieth to his present
case of wretchednesse," demonstrates with a fearful
economy all but one of my opening postulates about
how the fable functions in the world. Clearly, it speaks
to unequal power relations, and to the need for those
without power in those relations to encode their commentary upon them, not to preclude understanding, but
in order to claim for their protest the sanction of an
ancient form; and equally clearly, Babington hoped that
wit or literary ingenuity (which the chronicler degraded as "fansie") would emancipate him, save him from
the Tower and the scaffold.

The chronicler assumed this to be "a familiar tale." In
fact, it was a remarkable adaptation of the Aesopian
fable of *The Sheep and the Butcher* which appeared in
Steinhöwel's edition (and hence also in Caxton's) with
a woodcut showing the butcher cutting the throat of
one sheep while the rest of the flock look on . . . . The
moral of the original fable was that personal safety

depends on group solidarity. In Caxton's translation
the fable reads as follows:

> Whenne a lygnage or kyndred is indyfferent or in
> dyvysyon not lyghtly they shalle doo ony thynge
> to theyr salute as reherceth to us this fable Of a
> bocher whiche entryd within a stable full of
> whethers. And after as the whethers sawe hym none
> of them sayd one word. And the bocher toke the
> fyrst that he fonde. Thenne the whethers spake al to
> gyder and sayd lete hym doo what he wylle. And
> thus the bocher tooke hem all one after another
> sauf one onely. And as he wold have taken the last
> the poure whether sayd to hym Justly I am worthy
> to be take by cause I have not holpen my felawes.
> For he that wylle not helpe ne comforte other
> ought not to demaunde or aske helpe ne comforte.
> For vertue which is uny[t]ed is better than vertue
> separate.[15]

Caxton's translation had been telling in its own time,
in its substitution of "lygnage or kyndred" for the Latin
"Parentes vel amici," thus appealing to precisely that
standard of loyalty based on lineage in an honor culture that was already being eroded, as much by the
internecine Wars of the Roses as by the long international development of centralized monarchies.[16] And
in 1484 this fable would have had a specific, horrific
charge, published as it was the year after Richard III
took over the throne, an event accomplished by the
summary executions of Earl Rivers and Lord Hastings,
not to mention the probable murder of the young king
Edward V and his brother.

But whereas Caxton was content to let the fable do its
work in 1484 with only minimal adjustment to the
circumstances, Babington, through the voice of the
chronicler, had apparently rewritten the fable so as to
add to its "familiar" message an unmistakable indictment of the psychology of repression. Caxton's sympathy for the "poure whether" and the brutal implications
of "bocher" are retained, which already ran counter to
the sheep's confession that he suffered justly for his
earlier passivity, for nonintervention in the deaths of
his colleagues; but he nowhere anticipated the brilliance of Babington's conception whereby the shepherd terrifies his flock into submission by a daily, ritual execution of one of their number. This was a genuine insight into the Elizabethan theory of public executions as, literally, exemplary ritual; a theory to
which, of course, the 1587 *Chronicles* subscribed or
claimed to subscribe.[17]

Yet however much the law-and-order mentality of the
narrator attempts to control the fable's power by editorial comment, the story transmits its own message. A
"sheepish unrulinesse" (which is only hypothetical, and
may actually be an excuse for the shepherd's "better
commoditie") scarcely justifies such "accustomed
butcherie" as indeed, common sense asserts, must surely work *against* the economy of sheep farming; while

the metaphor itself has disturbing implications for the idyllic versions of pastoral, with the queen as shepherdess, which were already fashionable in Elizabethan courtly poetry and drama.

Today's reader can therefore speculate on the complexities of a cultural process that produces such a document; not least because, as we now know, this fable fell victim to censorship. The new "Holinshed" was called in by the Privy Council almost as soon as it appeared in January 1587, and large sections of it dealing with the most up-to-the moment events, especially the Babington Plot, were deleted and replaced with a briefer and more neutral account.[18] In this unusually careful revision, largely carried out by Abraham Fleming, a second, different fable significantly survived.

A few pages later, the chronicler had paused to moralize on the Babington plot and its consequences, and, marking the spot with another marginal gloss ("A prettie apolog allusorie to the present case of malcontents") proceeded to rewrite for the occasion the ancient Aesopian fable of *The Frogs Desiring a King:*

> God make prince and people of one mind, and plant in all subjects a reverend regard of obedience and contentment of present estate, supported with justice and religion: least longing after novelties, it fare with them as with the frogs, who living at libertie in lakes and ponds, would needs (as misliking their present intercommunitie of life) with one consent sue to Jupiter for a king, and so did. Whereat he woondering, granted their desires, and cast them an huge trunk of a tree, which besides that it made a great noise in the water as it fell, to their terrifieng; so it was cumbersome by taking up their accustomed passage: insomuch that discontented therewithall, they assaulted Jupiter with a fresh petition, complaining that (besides diverse mislikes otherwise) the king whom he gave was but a senselesse stocke, and unworthie of obedience: wherefore it would please him to appoint them another indued with life. Whereupon Jupiter sent the herne among them, who entring into the water, devoured up the frogs one after another: insomuch that the residue, seeing their new king so ravenouslie gobling up their fellowes, lamentablie weeping besought Jupiter to deliver them from the throte of that dragon and tyrant. But he (of purpose unchangeable) made them a flat answer, that (will they nill they) the herne should rule over them.

> (4:922)

"Whereby we are taught," the chronicler concluded, "to be content when we are well and to make much of good queene Elizabeth, by whom we enjoie life and libertie" (2:1576). Again, the applied topical moral asserts that passive obedience to the queen is the best policy. In the uncensored text these two fables would have reverberated with each other in a most uncomfortable fashion, since the second replicates the narrative premise—sequential execution of the powerless—of *The Sheep and the Butcher.* In the censored version, where *The Frogs Desiring a King* appears in splendid literary isolation, it is more easily controlled by the concluding official platitudes.

Yet, as we shall see, both the original and the subsequent political history of this fable admitted that its own structure was too complicated for certain application. On the one hand it appears to argue for a divinely sanctioned monarchy and the required obedience of subjects, no matter how harsh the rule; on the other it implies a contractual relationship, whereby the frogs freely brought monarchy upon themselves; and although the gods may argue that they now have no more choice in the matter, once the contractual basis of sovereignty has raised its logical head it is hard to lay it down. In fact, the chronicler has made matters worse than they were in simpler versions of the fable by emphasizing the earlier, republican state of the frogs, "living at libertie in lakes and ponds" or "intercommunitie" (a word here recorded for the first time in English), and moving to petition "with one consent," an important political term implying a general will. All of this jars unnecessarily with the "libertie" that is finally said to derive from Elizabeth's rule; and even more puzzling, if one puts any pressure on the metaphor, is whether she was to be identified with King Log or King Herne.

The 1587 *Chronicles,* then, establish the terms of reference for this chapter, which will broadly survey political fabling in England during Elizabeth's reign and a little beyond. One of the first major contributions was made in Edmund Spenser's *Shepheardes Calender,* published in 1579 in the context of court factionalism—the competition for influence between Burghley, on one side, and the circle of Leicester, Walsingham, and Sir Philip Sidney on the other, who were associated with a more militant Protestantism than Elizabeth herself was prepared to countenance. In 1579 those tensions were exacerbated by the queen's proposed marriage to the French duke of Alençon, a member of the same family that the English held responsible for the St. Bartholomew's Day massacre of the Huguenots. Dedicated to Sidney, and written (though anonymously) by Leicester's secretary, the *Calender* was unlikely to be neutral on these issues; though discreet it certainly had to be, given Elizabeth's extreme antipathy to any public discussion of the match. Spenser was certainly aware of the fate of a too-outspoken critic of the queen's plans, John Stubbs, whose authorship of a pamphlet attacking the marriage had been grounds for his trial for seditious libel in October of that same year. In a notorious case of political censorship, Stubbs's pamphlet, *The Goping Gulf,* was burned, and its author, printer, and publisher were sentenced to lose their right hands. Mysteriously, the printer, Hugh Singleton, appears to have been reprieved; only to reappear as the printer of *The Shepheardes Calender.*

Although the dominant genre of the *Calender* is, obviously, theeclogue-book on the model of Virgil's, Spenser, through E. K., apparently intended a close and interesting relationship between pastoral and Aesopian discourse. There is a frontal emphasis on fables and fabulist thought, beginning with E. K.'s "Epistle" to the reader, where we are warned that those who do not cherish the vernacular are "like to the Mole in Aesopes fable, that being blynd her selfe, would in no wise be perswaded, that any beast could see," and also "Like to the dogge in the maunger, that him selfe can eate no hay, and yet barketh at the hungry bullock, that so faine would feede."[19] The "February" eclogue contains a fable of *The Oake and the Briar,* which, as E. K. remarks, "he telleth as learned of Chaucer, but it is cleane in another kind, and rather like to Aesopes fables" (p. 426); and the "May" eclogue, in case the reader had failed to notice its relation to *The Wolf and the Kid,* is also carefully glossed as "much like to that in Aesops fables, but the Catastrophe and end is farre different" (p. 440). For good measure, E. K. inserts into the notes to "February" the remark that old men who have lost their fear of God are "lyke unto the Ape, of which is sayd in Aesops fables, that oftentimes meeting the Lyon, he was at first sore aghast and dismayed," but later lost both fear and respect (p. 427). I take this fabulist insistence to be one of Spenser's strategies for making the *Calender* speak to "the meaner sorte" as well as to a courtly audience, balancing his lyric praise of Elizabeth with a strong strain of popular protest. And indeed, in the "September" eclogue he anticipated Donne's reference to *The Dog and the Shadow,* placing it, with a self-ironizing bitterness resembling Donne's, in the mouth of a spokesman for anticlerical and social reform. "To leave the good, that I had in honde, / In hope of better, that was uncouth:" says Diggon Davy, "So lost the Dogge the fleshe in his mouth" (p. 453).

But the full-fledged fables he produced are, to put it mildly, extremely difficult to read, or at least to "apply" in the manner to which an Elizabethan schoolboy was likely to have been accustomed. In "Feb-ruary," Spenser probably started with Aesop's fable of *The Bush and the Aubyer,* where a woodcutter is induced by one tree to cut down its rival. In this tale of "The Oak and the Briar," however, we follow the fate of an ancient oak who is finally cut down by a "husbandman" at the urging of an upstart briar, who will ultimately suffer from the loss of shelter that the great oak had provided. Spenser's fable has therefore absorbed the tradition represented by *The Hospitable Oake* in Edward's reign, whereby great patrons or political protectors were envisaged as powerful yet vulnerable shade trees.[20] But while one of "February's" referents

was plausibly Leicester's fall from influence over Elizabeth, its length and complexity of detail invoke a larger scenario. The Oak is represented in terms that would better apply to a venerable religious institution:

> The Axes edge did oft turne againe,
> As halfe unwilling to cutte the graine:
> Seemed, the sencelesse yron dyd fear,
> Or to wrong holy eld did forbeare.
> For it had bene an auncient tree,
> Sacred with many a mysteree,
> And often crost with priestes crewe,
> And often halowed with holy water dewe.
> But sike fancies weren foolerie,
> And broughten this Oake to this miserye.

(Ll. 203-11)

Such ambivalence—half awe and half critique—is consistent with Spenser's view of the pre-Reformation church; and when the Briar finds himself without shelter, he suffers from the same weather that oppresses the poet in "January" and "December" ("The biting frost nipt his stalke dead / . . . And heaped snowe burdned him so sore / that nowe upright he can stand no more"). The reader's allegiances are, therefore, subtly shifted from one side to the other as the fable proceeds, although even the notion of a "side" seems too precise for the experience; and the result is no simple recognition of hero and villain, still less the assignment of blame to a single error (rivalry, ambition, inexperience, superstition) but a tragic fable of mixed allegiances and the misunderstanding of roles and values.

In "May," Spenser produced a version of the ancient fable of *The Wolf and the Kid,* and by substituting a fox for the adversary achieved a greater emphasis on cunning. This was appropriate to the fable's most evident goal, which was anti-Catholic satire. In one of his glosses, Spenser's mysterious commentator E. K. identifies the trinkets in the fox's basket as "the reliques and ragges of popishe superstition": and he directly asserts that the "morall of the whole tale" is "to warne the protestaunt beware, howe he geveth credit to the unfaythfyll Catholique," and cites as an example the massacre of the Huguenots, "practised of Late yeares in Fraunce by Charles the nynth." In so doing, Spenser through E. K. was also identifying the topical value of Protestant alertness at the time of the *Calender*'s publication, since at this very moment Elizabeth was considering a marriage with Charles IX's brother.

But, as with "February," today's alert reader (and probably many of Spenser's original audience) might well experience a credibility gap between this explicit moral and the complex text they face. Neither court factionalism nor Protestant fervor seem sufficiently to motivate Spenser's innovations in this fable's plot and texture. Its power resides in the remarkable development of the domestic setting and—unusual in early modern poetry—of the mother-child dyad:

Thilke same Kidde (as I can well devise)
Was too very foolish and unwise,
For on a tyme in Sommer season,
The Gate her dame, that had good reason,
Yode forth abroade unto the greene wood,
To brouze, or play, or what shee thought
     good.
But for she had a motherly care
Of her young sonne, and wit to beware,
Shee set her youngling before her knee,
That was both fresh and lovely to see,
And full of favour, as kidde mought be:
His Vellet head began to shoote out,
And his wrethed hornes gan newly sprout:
The blossomes of lust to bud did beginne,
And spring forth ranckly under his chinne.
My sonne (quoth she) (and with that gan
     weepe:
For carefull thoughts in her heart did creepe)
God blesse thee poore Orphane, as he mought
     me,
And send thee joy of thy jollitee.
Thy father (that word she spake with payne):
For a sigh had nigh rent her heart in twayne)
Thy father, had he lived this day.
To see the braunche of his body displaie,
How would he have joyed at this sweete
     sight?
But ah False Fortune such joy did him
     spight,
And cutte of hys dayes with untimely woe,
Betraying him into the traines of hys foe.
Now I a waylfull widdowe behight,
Of my old age have this one delight,
To see thee succeede in thy fathers steade.

(Ll. 173-203)

This news, that the father of the family has already fallen prey to the Fox, creates a genuine dramatic irony, and also connects with that other classic tale of fatal heredity—*The Wolf and the Lamb*—at least as Caxton told it.

Yet here Spenser evidently recognized, and exploited to the full, that ambiguity resident in Aesopian tra-dition with respect to the relationship between speech and power, wit and innocence, one's sense of justice and one's sympathy for the oppressed. All the widow's warnings against opening the door to strangers are rendered useless by the histrionic skills of the Fox, who comes to the door disguised as a "poore pedler." It is not his trinkets that gain him entrance,

but his apparent physical distress:

A Biggen (handkerchief) he had got about his
     braine,
For in his headpeace he felt a sore payne.
His hinder heele was wrapt in a clout,
For with great cold he had gotte the gout,
There at the dore he cast me downe hys pack,
And layd him downe, and grones, Alack,
     Alack.
Ah deare Lord, and sweete Sainte Charitee,
That some good body woulde once pitie mee.

(Ll. 242-48)

He employs, in effect, the very pathos that the fable's opening claimed in its address to the reader; and when the Kid takes pity upon him, and opens the door to his own undoing, he is only showing the sympathy that the fable assumes and encourages in its audience. A false victim claims a true one; and the reader is therefore required to rethink the role of suffering as a claim to authenticity—certainly a more serious approach to Protestant polemic than the usual focus on trinkets, and possibly an insight of more than ecclesiastical pertinence.

We are looking here at a remarkable achievement, though one remarkably underacknowledged. In his first independent publication, Spenser had apparently established an original position on the Aesopian fable, one that was both unimaginable from what had preceded him and unprecedented in terms of the freedoms he took with his models. Nor did Spenser's reputation as a fabulist rest only on the *Calender*. More important as precedent, at least for John Dryden, was *Prosopopeia. Or Mother Hubberds Tale,* which appeared under similar protocols ("Base is the style, and matter meane withal") that had indicated the *Calender*'s populist thematics. This story of how the Fox and Ape conspire to take over the kingdom of beasts while the true ruler, the Lion, "sleeping lay in secret shade, / His Crowne and Scepter lying him beside, / And having doft for heate his dreadfull hide" (ll. 951-53) was loosely based on two Aesopian originals, *The Lion and the Mouse* (already developed by Henryson in terms of Scottish politics) and *The Ass in the Lion's Skin.* Together they produced and emblem of royal negligence, which permits knaves to take over the government.

Unlike the majority of Aesop's fables, this one ends well, with the Lion recalled to duty by Mercury, and the Fox and the Ape (who has been wearing the Lion's skin) captured and punished. But there is an earlier phase of the narrative which does not offer the same optimism. The Fox and the Ape have been begging, the Ape got up like a wounded veteran of the wars. They encounter a "simple husbandman" who offers the Ape the job of shepherd on his farm, with the Fox as his sheepdog. Not surprisingly, the rogues ravage the flock, eating the lambs as fast as they are born; and when the time comes that they should "render up a reckning of their travels / Unto their master" they simply flee the area. "So was the husbandman left," concludes Spenser of this episode, "to his losse" (l. 341). The effect is of two parallel fables of governance by false deputy, the first a tragedy whose tone matches those of the fables within *The Shepheardes Calender*, the second a satirical comedy; and also of two contrasting models of the lawful monarch, the good but naive husbandman, and the supreme but slothful beast of prey.[21] It was not an encouraging pair of alternatives, nor, for all the summary justice of its conclusion, a respectful representation of the Elizabethan state.[22]

But precisely because it is so expanded, at the level of detail *Mother Hubberds Tale* resists any single explanation. There areelements of the Fox's behavior when in power that would certainly have suggested the fiscally-prudent Burghley (whom Elizabeth herself called her Fox)[23] especially the charge (which we now know to have been unjust) that under "the cloke of thrift, and husbandry, / For to encrease the common treasures store" he had made himself wealthy, and the concomitant complaint that during his ministry the power of the great noble families had diminished:

> For he no count made of Nobilitie,
> Nor the wilde beasts whom armes did glorifie,
> The Realmes chiefe strength and girlond of
>   the crowne,
> All these through fained crimes he thrust
>   adowne,
> Or made them dwell in darknes of disgrace:

> (Ll. 1183-87)

But in the earlier phase of the fable, when the tricksters first embark on their partnership, the Fox advises practices that belonged to the bottom strata of society, and justifies them by appealing to precisely that concept of liberty that Aesopian tradition, especially when governed by the *Life* of Aesop, could itself be seen to stand for. "Thus therefore I advise," says the Fox to the Ape:

> That not to anie certaine trade or place,
> Nor anie man we should our selves applie:
> For why should he that is at libertie
> Make himselfe bond? sith then we are free
>   borne,
> Let us all servile base subjection scorne:

Just as the appeal to pathos was transferred from the Kid to his destroyer, so here the appeal to liberty is transferred to *this* rapacious entrepreneur, and heard as

a rationalization for further rapacity. Further, and even more skittishly, Spenser develops this specious claim in the language of sixteenth-century egalitarianism, of protest from below:

> And as we bee sonnes of the world so wide,
> Let us our fathers heritage divide,
> And chalenge to our selves our portions dew
> Of all the patrimonie, which a few
> Now hold in hugger mugger in their hand,
> And all the rest doo rob of good and land.
> For now a few have all and all have nought,
> Yet all be brethren ylike dearly bought:
> There is no right in this partition,
> Ne was it so by institution
> Ordained first, ne by the law of Nature,
> But that she gave like blessing to each creture
> As well of wordly livelode as of life,
> That there might be no difference nor strife,
> Ne ought cald mine or thine.

> (Ll. 129-49)

As all of Spenser's readers would have realized, this was the language by which the Puritan protest of the 1580s and 1590s was linked, at least in official propaganda, with radical social protest from the Peasants' Revolt onward. In Richard Bancroft's *Survey of the Pretended Holy Discipline,* published in 1593 as anti-Puritan propaganda, the dissenters are compared to the insurrectionists of 1381:

> We live in a worlde (you know) that crieth out: *the first institution, the first institution:* everything must be brought to the *first institution.* The wordes be good, if they be well applied. But something was amisse in the Priestes application of his text, being such a like saying amongst a multitude of rebels, viz: *When Adam digged and Eve spanne, who was then the Gentleman.*[24]

It is impossible to determine whether the Fox's appeal to the "institution / Ordained first" was intended really to discredit this tradition of protest and so to distance Spenser from his own earlier populism, or whether it merely warns that the ancient Edenic tropes of equality were capable of being abused by racketeers. *Mother Hubberds Tale* as a whole was scarcely a prudent document. Containing hints of previous censorship, it was finally published in 1591; and unsold copies of the *Complaints,* the volume in which it appeared, were apparently called in by the authorities.[25]

Spenser's fables, then, are marked by contradictions: an insistence on the Aesopian base, but considerable independence from the model; a theoretical grasp of the Aesopian ideology, but as great an interest in how those beliefs may mislead; a strong indication (through what L'Estrange referred to as "Hints and Glances") that topical meaning is present, but an equally strong resistance to having that meaning easily decoded. The story that Spenser's fabulist practice tells has itself the structure of a fable: If you find yourself in the position of the Lamb or the Kid, you had better learn how to write, at least, like a Fox.

Working in precisely the same political context—the French marriage crisis and the struggles of the Leicester-Walsingham axis to retain any influence over Elizabeth's policy—Sir Philip Sidney also turned to Aesopian tradition, but with very different effect. His position was both more exposed and more protected than Spenser's, not only because he was Leicester's nephew, but also because he had taken it upon himself to write the queen a personal letter strongly advising against the marriage. It is generally assumed that Sidney's retreat to his country estate during 1580-81, there to write most of his pastoral romance, the *Arcadia,* was a form of political prudence, if not of actual protest; and into the center of his romance Sidney inserted a long and extremely complex neo-Aesopian fable.

The fable is presented as a song within a song within the pastoral romantic narrative frame. Its singer is Philisides, manifestly Philip Sidney's own persona, and its source, he reports, is another non-fictional person, Hubert Languet, Sidney's Huguenot friend and mentor. Some of his readers, therefore, would have expected the fable to bear some relation to the political theories of the Huguenots, who argued for a monarchy limited by a contractual relation to those (the people) who bestow on any individual the sovereign power; and also for the right of reformers or "subaltern magistrates" to depose a monarch if he breaks his contract and becomes tyrannical. Sidney's fable was, indeed, loosely based both on *The Frogs Desiring a King* and its biblical analogue, Jotham's fable of the trees; but it explores in a more complex way than either, at the level of political philosophy as regenerated by Machiavelli, the origins, sanctions, and disadvantages of monarchy as an institution.

Here, because we are dealing with political *argument,* we shall need to quote most of this long poem. Before the existence of Man, the poem claims ("Such manner time there was"), the animals all lived "freely" together:

> The beasts had sure some beastly policy;
> For nothing can endure where order nis.
> For once the lion by the lamb did lie;
> The fearful hind the leopard did kiss;
> Hurtless was tiger's paw and serpent's hiss.
>   This think I well: the beasts with courage clad
>   Like senators a harmless empire had.

At which, whether the others did repine
(For envy harb'reth most in feeblest hearts),
Or that they all to changing did incline
(As e'en in beasts their dams leave changing parts),
The multitude to Jove a suit imparts,
   With neighing, bleating, braying, and barking,
   Roaring, and howling, for to have a king.

. . . . .

Jove wisely said (for wisdom wisely says):
"O beasts, take heed what you of me desire.
Rulers will think all things made them to please,
And soon forget the swink due to their hire.
But since you will, part of my heav'nly fire
   I will you lend; the rest yourselves must give,
   That it both seen and felt with you may live."

Full glad they were, and took the naked sprite,
Which straight the earth yclothed in his clay.
The lion, heart; the ounce gave active might;
The horse, good shape; the sparrow, lust to play;
Nightingale, voice, enticing songs to say.
   Elephant gave a perfect memory;
   And parrot, ready tongue, that to apply.

The fox gave craft; the dog gave flattery;
Ass, patience; the mole, a working thought;
Eagle, high look; wolf, secret cruelty;
Monkey, sweet breath; the cow, her fair eyes brought;
The ermine, whitest skin spotted with naught;
   The sheep, mild-seeming face; climbing, the bear;
   The stag did give the harm-eschewing fear.

The hare her sleights; the cat his melancholy;
Ant, industry; and cony, skill to build;
Cranes, order; storks, appearing holy;
Chameleon, ease to change; duck, ease to yield;
Crocodile, tears which might be falsely spilled.
   Ape great thing gave, though he did mowing stand:
   The instrument of instruments, the hand.
Each beast likewise his present brings;
And (but they drad their prince they oft should want)
They all consented were to give him wings.
And ay more awe towards him for to plant,

To their own work this privilege they grant:
  That from thenceforth to all eternity
  No beast should freely speak, but only he.

Thus man was made; thus man their lord
  became;
Who at the first, wanting or hiding pride,
He did to beasts' best use his cunning frame,
With water drink, herbs meat, and naked hide,
And fellow-like let his dominion slide,
  Not in his sayings saying "I," but "we";
  As if he meant his lordship common be.

But when his seat so rooted he had found
That they now skilled not how from him to
  wend,
Then gan in guiltless earth full many a
  wound,
Iron to seek, which gainst itself should bend
To tear the bowels that good corn should
  send.
  But yet the common dam none did bemoan,
  Because (though hurt) they never heard her
  moan.

Then gan he factions in the beasts to breed;
Where helping weaker sort, the nobler beasts
(As tigers, leopards, bears and lion's seed)
Disdained with this, in deserts sought their
  rests;
Where famine ravin taught their hungry chests,
  That craftily he forced them to do ill;
  Which being done, he afterwards would kill

For murder done, which never erst was seen,
By those great beasts. As for the weakers'
  good,
He chose themselves his guarders for to been
Gainst those of might of whom in fear they
  stood,
As horse and dog; not great, but gentle blood.
  Blithe were the commons, cattle of the field,
  Tho when they saw their foen of greatness
  killed.

But they, or spent or made of slender might,
Then quickly did the meaner cattle find,
The great beams gone, the house on shoulders
  light;
For by and by the horse fair bits did bind;
The dog was in a collar taught his kind.
  As for the gentle birds, like case might rue
  When falcon they, and goshawk, saw in
  mew.

Worst fell to smaller birds, and meanest herd,
Who now his own, full like his own he used.
Yet first but wool, or feathers, off he teared;
And when they were well used to be abused,

For hungry throat their flesh with teeth he
  bruised;
  At length for glutton taste he did them kill;
  At last for sport their silly lives did spill.

But yet, O man, rage not beyond thy need;
Deeme it no gloire to swell in tyranny.
Thou art of blood; joy not to make things
  bleed.
Thou fearest death; think they are loath to die.
A plaint of guiltless hurt doth pierce the sky.
  And you, poor beasts, in patience bide your
  hell,
  Or know your strengths, and then you shall
  do well.[26]

Like the 1587 chronicler's version of *The Frogs Desiring a King,* Sidney's fable tells how all the creatures had once enjoyed a well-balanced "policy," which combined aspects of the biblical peaceable kingdom with those of the Roman republic ("Like senators a harmless empire [they] had") until it occurred to them to ask Jove for a king. Jove first warns them, as Jotham did the Israelites, that monarchy will only lead to tyranny, and then accedes to their request, on the condition that if he provides the life principle, the creatures will all contribute their own characteristics to the new creation. The result is Man, a mixture of good and sinister qualities, which in combination give him absolute power. A part of the fable's effectiveness derives, I submit, from its subtle contest between conventions, the traditional attributes of the different species being reallocated so as to cross the normal boundaries between strong and weak, the benign and the untrustworthy. Traditionally monarchical symbols, the lion and the eagle (and, in the special case of Elizabeth, the ermine, symbol of purity) are combined with animals more often associated with courtiers (parrot, wolf, fox, and dog) or with the common people (industrious ant, perpetually victimized sheep). The ape provided the "Instrument of Instruments," the hand; and for the ultimate gift the creatures, who have previously all enjoyed "perfect speech," agree on a great sacrifice: "That from thenceforth to all eternity / No beast should freely speak, but only he."

It is hardly a surprise, then, when Jove's prediction is fulfilled and Man becomes a tyrant, driving away (like the Fox in Spenser's fable) the great wild beasts, forcing them, in desperation, to become predators and so susceptible to punishment; and turning those who are weaker into either his servants or his prey. This section of the poem is clearly represented as an allegory of class relations, and of the extent to which class warfare can be conceived as neither necessary nor perennial, but rather produced by stress emanating from the top of the political system. It is also clearly specific to the Elizabethan system. The distinction between those of "great" lineage who have been exiled and criminalized, and those of "gentle blood" who are employed to serve the state and to police their superiors is directly pertinent to Elizabeth's reliance on Burghley, and prophetic of her later struggle with the second earl of Essex. Indeed, Sidney's use of the term "factions" as the *consequence* of monarchical manipulation is a sardonic comment on what has been claimed as Elizabeth's greatest contribution to the pragmatics of rule, her ability to manage rival interest groups. This poem suggests that she actually fostered faction in order to maintain her own supremacy.

Instead, then, of the crude antithesis between the passivity of King Log and the cruelty of King Stork, Sidney provided a subtle analysis of current and competing theories of monarchy, in which divinely sanctioned power (Jove's "heavenly fire") is incorporated into an anatomy of the role such as Machiavelli might have produced, had he chosen to extend his analogy of how the prince is composed of both the lion and the fox.

Sidney resolutely extended the original fable's capacity to suggest how the theory of monarchy's acceptance is dependent on two conflicting premises, divine origin and that particular version of contract theory that supposes a people, initially capable of self-government, consenting to transfer the common sovereignty to a single figure.[27] While his attitude toward the "multitude" acting as such contains a measure of aristocratic disdain,[28] his theory of commonwealth is carried not only by the utopian "beastly policy" and "harmless empire," but also by the triple appearance of "common." So long as the monarch is uncertain of his power he "fellow-like" adopts a corporate rhetoric, "Not in his sayings saying 'I,' but 'we'; / As if he meant his lordship common be" (a sardonic gloss on the so-called "royal we"). When he turns to violence, however, his first step is to violate "the common dam," the maternal earth that he shares with the animals, who in fact preceded his late arrival on or from it; and one of his primary strategies is to persuade the "commons, cattle of the field" that it is in their interest that the great wild beasts (whom he has forced into a posture of hostility to the commons) be destroyed. Behind this satire lies an intuitive and perhaps nostalgically feudal notion in which diversity of rank would not be incompatible with peaceful cooperation, and in which the weak would be protectedrather than preyed on by the strong.

When the fable ends, Sidney remarks that its shepherd audience was bemused by "the strangeness of the tale . . . scanning what he should mean by it" (p. 259). Subsequent criticism has experienced the same difficulties;[29] but one obvious key to its interpretation was the textual reference back, at the close, to *The Frogs Desiring a King.* When recording that fable, Phaedrus had explained its original historical context—a coup d'état by Pisistratus in the mid-sixth century B.C., by

which Athenian democracy, already under internal strain, was temporarily ended. At the end of his version of the fable, Phaedrus had also explained that as Jove told the frogs to endure the misery of the crane, so Aesop instructed the Athenians to accept their present misfortune, lest worse befall:

> . . ."Vos quoque, o cives," ait
> "hoc sustinete, maius ne veniat, malum."

Here, clearly, is the source of Sidney's final moral also: but with a certain difference. His fable ends with a double message, addressed to a double audience:

> But yet, O man, rage not beyond thy need;
> Deem it no gloire to swell in tyranny.
>
> . . . . .
>
> And you, poor beasts, in patience bide your
>   hell,
> Or know your strengths, and then you shall do
>   well.

The traditional advice to the frogs to observe a stoical patience is now qualified: first by the warning directed to the monarch; second, by that adjectival "poor," as in Caxton's version of *The Sheep and the Butcher,* a candid direction of sympathy; and especially by that barely explicit threat of an alternative ("Or know your strengths") to passive obedience.

Here, then, is another kind of metafable—an overview of the system by which human failings are emblematically recognized in the animal kingdom and then, at a second level of translation, perceived to be somehow intensified, mimetically actualized, in the sphere of political action. Given the unsettled state of political theory in Europe at the end of the sixteenth century, given Sidney's own uneasy situation as one of Elizabeth's courtiers, it would have been surprising to find anywhere, let alone in a courtly poem, an unequivocal definition of an acceptable polity; but, nevertheless, the choices are distinguished with remarkable clarity, and the political issues unmistakable. Compared to Spenser's fables, Sidney's is direct. The difference is partly required by his subject, which is not the temporary shifts in the factional balance at Elizabeth's court, but political theory in the abstract; but while Spenser's response to political censorship was to create a smokescreen, Sidney's was to render articulate even the conditionsof the fable's telling. His choice of genre for this central poem in the *Old Arcadia* is surely to be found in his insistence on the last and greatest gift that the creatures gave their king—the renunciation of their freedom of speech. Unnecessary to the fable's plot, this gesture explains why the fable itself became a necessary ingredient of Elizabethan discourse. It is deeply connected to the theory of language built into the ancient *Life* of the Father of the fable, which contains three premises: the first, that the fabulist mysteriously recovers the Adamic prerogative of differentiating (naming) the creatures; the second, that he thereby recalls a still more innocent age when beasts themselves could speak;[30] and the third, that by making them speak again as metaphors for a brutal society he emancipates his own speech, which would otherwise remain forbidden and unfree.

That actual censorship was on Sidney's mind as the *Old Arcadia* took shape seems indisputable; for another poem prior to Philisides' fable seems to address it directly (as well as recalling the late medieval bird poems, especially the anonymous *Parliament of Birds* that De Worde had printed in the 1520s, and that Kitson had reprinted in 1565).[31] In a debate as to how shepherds (poets) can educate their society, Geron ("old man") warns a younger colleague against imprudent critique of the powerful:

> Fie, man; fie, man; what words hath thy
>   tongue lent?
>
>   . . . . .
>
> We oft are angrier with the feeble fly
> For business where it pertains him not
> Than with the pois'nous toads that quiet lie.
> I pray thee what hath e'er the parrot got,
> And yet they say he talks in great men's
>   bow'rs?
>
>   . . . . .
>
> Let swan's example siker serve for thee,
> Who once all birds in sweetly singing passed,
> But now to silence turned his minstrelsy.
> For he would sing, but others were defaced:
> The peacock's pride, the pie's pilled flattery,
> Cormorant's glut, kite's spoil, kingfisher's
>   waste,
> The falcon's fierceness, sparrow's lechery,
> The cuckoo's shame, the goose's good intent,
> E'en turtle touched he with hypocrisy.
> And worse of other more; till by assent
> Of all the birds, but namely those were
>   grieved,
> Of fowls there called was a parliament.
> There was the swan of dignity deprived,
> And statute made he never should have voice,
> Since when, I think, he hath in silence lived.[32]

In January 1581, while Sidney was probably at work on his romance, the House of Lords introduced an "Act against seditious words and rumours" (23 Eliz. Cap. II), sometimes referred to as the "statute of silence." The measure was clearly in response to the French marriage negotiations and Elizabeth's insistence that they not be discussed in press or pulpit; and between this real parliament and Arcadia's fabulous one there is a more than coincidental resemblance.

Sidney, then, looked to the Aesopian fable as a medium of comment on the *concept* of monarchy, Spenser as a medium of criticism of its *practice*. Given that shift in political relations which, all over early modern Europe, centralized power in single figures controlling larger geographical units than before, both were predictable responses to what some have called the age of absolutism. Although in England monarchy was never so absolute—not subject to constitutional limitation—as was claimed at the time and has been subsequently argued by both its supporters and opponents, there were obviously phases in the reigns of all the Tudors, with the exception of Edward VI, when the relationship between sovereign and subject seemed unduly weighted in favor of the former. The period of the French marriage negotiations (1579-81) was one such juncture, the time of the Babington plot in 1586 was evidently another. And the fable's usefulness as an increasingly complex medium of political analysis (and hence of political resistance) is demonstrated in part (though the argument must here remain entirely circular) by its appearance and reappearance at moments of crisis, or at least of visible strain on the ligaments of the social body.

But sometimes, and also at moments of strain, we can witness the turn to fable for what seems a contrary purpose—by writers convinced that contemporary power relations were the best they could be. In the same year that Spenser produced *The Shepheardes Calender,* John Lyly, notorious for his efforts to ingratiate himself with Elizabeth, produced the second instalment of his mannered novella whose protagonist Euphues gave his name to a certain kind of stylistic excess. Licensed for the press in July 1579. *Euphues and His England* offered its readers an intensely nationalistic reading experience, whereby Euphues, as a visitor to England from Greece, is treated, mostly through conversation, to an idealized survey of English life and customs. And whereas in the first installment Lyly had peppered his text with what Sidney was later to call "unnatural natural history," similes derived from the plant and animal kingdom, in *Euphues and His England* this habit revealed its affinity with a certain kind of fabulist practice.

Euphues and His England in fact offers its readers three extended tales of the birds, the beasts, and the bees; and although only the central one is (almost) identified as a fable, all three are generically related and share the same political philosophy. And while Euphues himself introduces the first, the second and third are produced by good old Fidus of Canterbury, whose name, location, and vocation (gardener and husbandman) ostentatiously proclaim his function as a reliable narrator, the same claim that Sidney made for "old Languet" and his "old true tales." The fabulist mode is established when Fidus, offering Euphues hospitality, begins apologizing for his house; to which Euphues replies with a version of the parliament of fowls:

> When all the birds were appointed to meet, to talk of the Eagle, there was great contention at whose nest they should assemble, every one willing to have it at his owne home, one preferring the nobility of his birth, another the statelinesse of his building: . . . at last the swallow said they should come to his nest, beeing commonly of filth, which all the Birds disdaining, said: Why, thy house is nothing else but dirt. And therefore (answered the Swallow) would I have talke there of the Eagle: for being the basest, the name of an Eagle will make it the bravest.[33]

Partially hidden in this deferential statement is a reference to yet another parliament of birds ("all the birds were *appointed* to meet, to talk of the Eagle"); but "talk of the Eagle" in a parliamentary context is the last thing that Lyly intends to recommend. For Fidus embarks on the second, much longer and more complex fable by remarking that "as Kings pastimes are no playes for every one, so their secrets, their counsels, their dealings, are not to be either scanned or enquired of any way, unlesse of those that are in the like place, or serve the like person." The tale he proceeds to tell is of uncertain status. "I cannot tell," he says, "whether it bee a Canterburie tale, or a Fable in Aesope, but prettie it is, and true":

> The Foxe and the wolfe going both a filching for food, thought it best to see whether the Lion were asleepe or awake, lest beeing too bold, they should speed to badde. The Foxe entring into the Kings denne (a King I call the Lion) brought word to the Wolfe that hee was asleepe, and went himselfe to his owne kennell: the Wolfe desirous to search in the Lions denne, that hee might espie some fault, or steale some pray, entred boldly, whom the Lion caught in his pawes, and asked what he would? The sillie wolfe (an unapt terme for a Wolfe, yet fit, being in a Lions hands) anwered, that understanding by the Foxe, hee was a sleepe, he thought he might be at liberty to survay his lodging: unto whom the princely Lyon, with great disdaine, though little despight (for that there can be no envy in a King) said thus: Doest thou thinke that a Lion thy prince and governour can sleepe, though hee winke, or darest thou enquire whether hee winke or wake? . . . you shall both well know, and to your griefes feele, that neither the wilines of the Foxe, nor the wildnesse of the Woolfe, ought either to see or aske, whether the Lion either sleepe or wake, bee at home or abroad, dead or alive. For this is sufficient for you to know, that there is a Lion; not, where he is, or what he doth.

(Pp. 43-44)

Lyly's fable was evidently a clever variant on the Aesopian *The Lion and the Mouse,* where the moral was the lion's high-minded generosity in freeing the mouse who has dared to play on his body while he sleeps; that royal magnanimity receives its reward when the mouse later frees him from the hunter's net. But it is also clear that Lyly was alert to the satirical potential of the notorious laziness of lions between hunting periods—precisely that characteristic that Spenser turned to political critique in *Mother Hubberds Tale.* Rather than denying its zoological credit, he bypassed the question of moral respon-sibility and translated the problem into one of political theory. All of the monarch's doings are transferred by Lyly (in a move that James I would later insist on for himself) to the territory of *arcana imperii,* the mysterious realm of government which is beyond criticism because it is beyond secular limitation. As old Faithful moralizes his text for Euphues, it is the subject's only duty to "understand there is a king, but what he doth, is for the gods to examine, whose ordinance he is; not for men, whose overseer he is."

And then, using as a transition a condensed version of the fable of the Body (which had so vast a tradition of political use that it will require a chapter of its own), Fidus moves on to a fully structural account of the English form of government as he understands it, by way of analogy with the commonwealth of bees drawn, or so his says, from his own experience as apiarist. The classical source here was of course not Aesop, but rather Virgil, who had devoted the fourth book of his *Georgics* to beekeeping, and in an extended account of the internal regulation of the hive had provided a metaphorical compliment to Augustus, which entered the Renaissance as a paradigm of effective monarchical or imperial government.[34]

"Then how vain is it," Fidus continues, " . . . that the foot should neglect his office, to correct the face; or that subjects should seeke more to know what their Princes doe, then what they are? wherein they shew themselves as bad as beasts, and much worse then my Bees. . . . " He then proceeds to claim that the bees choose their king and direct all their endeavors to his protection:

> whom if they finde to fall, they establish again in his Throne, with no less dutie than devotion, garding him continually, as it were for fear he should miscarry, for love he should not: whom they tender with such faith and favour, that whithersoever he flieth they follow him, . . . If their Prince die, they know not how to live, they languish, weepe, sigh, neither intending their worke, nor keeping their old society. And that which is moost marvellous, and almost incredible: if there be any that hath disobeied his commandments, either of purpose or unwittingly, hee killeth himselfe with his own sting, as executioner of his owne stubbornnesse. The King

himselfe hath his sting which hee useth rather for honour then punishment.

(Pp. 44-45)

However implausible this may be as an empirical account of apian behavior, its message is unmistakable. Lyly seeks to produce in his readers the same internalization of loyalty, of subjection to the monarch, as that which is found (he claims) in the best of the insect communities. And if this honor community is entomologically implausible, what are we supposed to think of what follows? For here the bee-king himself supervises the means of production, and thereby provides an alternative answer to the charge of monarchical indolence:

> The King himselfe not idle, goeth up and downe intreating, threatning, commanding, using the counsell of a sequell, but not losing the dignitie of a prince, preferring those that labor [to] greater authoritie, & punishing those that loiter with due severity. Al which things being much admirable, yet this is most, that they are so profitable, bring unto man both honey & waxe, each so wholesome, that we all desire it, both so necessarie that we cannot misse them.

(P. 46)

In these last lines the language of natural community is particularly potent, blending as it does the novella's middle-class readership into that alluring "we all," bringing together into one "wholesome" construct authority, profit, rewards, punishments, honey, wax, needs, desires, and their gratification.

Seldom does one find so instructive an example of how, it is now often claimed, literature serves hegemony. Yet we can be reasonably sure that Lyly produced this powerful rhetorical magic as a defensive strategy, defensive against the troublesome spirits of 1579, like Spenser and Stubbs, who had taken it upon themselves to question royal policy (or perhaps, in the context of the French marriage proposal, royal desires and needs). And it is possible to detect the point at which Lyly *felt* defensive, to discern a slight crack in the idealizing armature where political critique might be recognized. It occurs at the point where the concept of choosing a king (the premise of Aesop's fable of the frogs) has to be given some rational, instrumental extension.

Notes

[1] For the different versions of the story, originating in the Latin *Disciplina clerica* of Petrus Alfonsi, see J. O. Halliwell, ed., *Lydgate's Minor Poems,* in *Early En-*glish *Poetry, Ballads, and Popular Literature,* 2 vols. (London: Percy Society, 1940), 2:179.

[2] John Lydgate, *The Minor Poems,* ed. H. N. Mac-Cracken, 2 vols. (London: EETS, 1934), 2:472. It appears that Sir Thomas Wyatt remembered these lines when imprisoned by Henry VIII in 1541, subsequent to Thomas Cromwell's fall from power and influence. Wyatt wrote to his friend Sir Francis Brian: "Syghes ar my foode, drynke are my teares; / Clynkinge of fetters such musycke wolde crave"; and in another related poem, he ironically contrasted his incarcerated self to that of his own hunting birds: "Luckes, my faire falcon, and your fellowes all, / How well plesaunt yt were your libertiee!" See Sir Thomas Wyatt, *Collected Poems,* ed. Kenneth Muir (London, 1949), pp. 159, 160.

[3] Gotthold Lessing, *Abhandlungen über die Fabel,* in *Gesammelte Werke,* vol. 1 (Berlin and Weimar, 1981), pp. 359-60. The fable in question here was *The Horse, the Hunter, and the Hart* (Romulus, 4:9), in which the horse "allowed itself to be bridled by the man . . . in order to revenge himself on the deer." As Lessing complained, this fable became allegorical by its occasion, as related by Stesichorus, "at a time when the Himerenses had made Phalaris the commander of their forces, and were about to furnish him with a body guard" (Aristotle, *Rhetoric,* 2:20). "All is here allegorical," Lessing complained, "but only because . . . the bridle [is not made applicable] to every first encroachment upon liberty, but simply to the unrestricted commandership of Phalaris."

[4] See chapter 1, pp. 33-34.

[5] Derek Pearsall, *John Lydgate* (London, 1970), pp. 197, 196, 194-95. These views are largely repeated by Lois Eben, *John Lydgate* (Boston, 1985), pp. 105-11.

[6] Geoffrey Chaucer, *Works,* ed. F. N. Robinson (Cambridge, Mass., 1957), pp. 225-27.

[7] Quotation from *John Skelton: The Complete English Poems* (London, 1983). For an argument that Skelton wrote *Speke, Parott* as a bid for renewed royal favor, and that he badly miscalculated Wolsey's capacity to survive, see Greg Walker, *John Skelton and the Politics of the 1520s* (Cambridge, 1988), pp. 88-100.

[8] Arthur Kinney, *John Skelton: Priest as Poet* (Chapel Hill, N.C., 1987), pp. 15-30.

[9] Malcolm Andrew, ed., *Two Early Renaissance Bird Poems: The Harmony of Birds, The Parliament of Birds* (London and Toronto, 1984), p. 59.

[10] See "Howe Collingbourne was cruelly executed for making a foolishe rime," in Richard III's reign, specifically for not remembering to "Touche covertly in ter-

mes," but for writing a poem in which "The Cat, the Rat, and Lovel our Dog, / Do rule al England, under a Hog," whereof, Collingbourne complains, "the meanyng was so playne and true, / That every foole perceyved it." *The Mirror for Magistrates,* ed. Lily B. Campbell (New York, 1960), pp. 347, 349.

[11] For an account of the poem as an extended satire on the ministry of Burghley's son, Robert Cecil, from Donne's perspective as a supporter of Ralegh and ambivalent toward Essex, both of whom could be seen as Cecil's victims, see M. van Wyk Smith, "John Donne's *Metempsychosis,*" *Review of English Studies* n.s. 24 (1973): 17-25, 141-52.

[12] For the texts, in order cited, see John Donne, *Poetical Works,* ed. H. J. Grierson, 2 vols. (Oxford, 1912), 1:171, 178, 78. The epigram was directed against the newssheet, *Mercurius Bello-Gallicus,* which Donne regarded as a source of misinformation.

[13] For Jonson's return to the beast epic of *Reynard the Fox* (one branch of which was also translated by Caxton in 1481), see R. B. Parker, "*Volpone* and *Reynard the Fox,*" *Review of English Studies* n.s. 1 (1950): 242-44. Parker provides an invaluable summary of the evolution and dispersal of the Reynard legends, and shows how Jonson's play shares the confusion of tone endemic to medieval tales "which all commentators see as a tug-of-war between an anarchic identification with the fox and a satiric condemnation of the evils and institutions he represents" (p. 35).

[14] Raphael Holinshed, *Chronicles of England, Scotland and Ireland* 6 vols. (London, 1808; repr. New York, 1965), 4:912.

[15] Lenaghan, ed., *Caxton's Aesop,* p. 126.

[16] On this transition, and the collapse of aristocratic dissidence into passive obedience to the monarchy, see K. B. McFarlane, "The Wars of the Roses," in *England in the Fifteenth Century: Collected Essays,* intro. G. L. Harriss (London, 1981), pp. 87-119, 260; and Mervyn James, *Society, Politics and Culture: Studies in Early Modern England* (Cambridge, 1986).

[17] Compare Holinshed, *Chronicles,* 4:916, on the meaning of the crowds at the execution: "although the assemblie were woonderfull great, and the traitors all goodlie personages, clothed in silkes, &c: and everie waie furnished to moove pitie . . . yet . . . there appeared no sadnesse or alteration among the people, at the mangling and quartering of their bodies."

[18] See Elizabeth Story Donno, "Some Aspects of Shakespeare's Holinshed," *Huntington Library Quarterly 50* (1987): 229-47.

[19] Edmund Spenser, *Poetical Works,* ed. J. C. Smith and E. de Selincourt (London, 1912), p. 417.

[20] See Annabel Patterson, *Pastoral and Ideology* (Berkeley, Calif., 1987), pp. 49-57.

[21] While Spenser usually refers to the Lion as male, there is one line (629) in which her female sex slips through the convention.

[22] In fact, these two fables are only the frame for an extended critique on Elizabethan society, including more than 100 lines of anticlerical satire, and an even longer diatribe on how knaves succeed at court and the miseries of clientage. "What hell it is," wrote Spenser, "in suing long to bide . . . To have thy Princes grace, yet want her Peeres" (ll. 895, 900).

[23] For this long-standing interpretation, as well as a theory that the *Tale* was composed in two parts, one in 1579-80, the other in 1591, see Edwin Greenlaw, *Studies in Spenser's Historical Allegory* (Baltimore, 1932), pp. 112-24.

[24] Richard Bancroft, *A Survey of the Pretended Holy Discipline* (London, 1593), pp. 8-9.

[25] See H. S. V. Jones, *A Spenser Handbook* (New York, 1930), pp. 74-75, who lists references to the "calling-in" by Gabriel Harvey (1592), Thomas Nashe (1593), John Weever (1599), and Thomas Middleton (1604). Jones adds that the *Tale* was omitted from the Folio of 1611, presumably to avoid offending Burghley's son, Sir Robert Cecil, but that it reappeared in editions following Cecil's death in 1611.

[26] For the text see Jean Robertson, ed., *The Countess of Pembroke's Arcadia* (Oxford, 1973), pp. 254-59.

[27] For a clear account of this theory and its chief exponents, see J. P. Sommerville, *Politics and Ideology in England,* 1603-1640 (London and New York, 1986), pp. 64-85.

[28] There is disagreement as to Sidney's attitude toward the "commons," and especially toward popular protest, as articulated in the *Arcadia.* Compare Stephen Greenblatt, "Murdering Peasants," *Representations* 1 (1983): 1-29; and Richard M. Berrong, "Changing Depictions of Popular Revolt in Sixteenth-Century England: The Case of Sidney's Two *Arcadias,*" *Journal of Medieval and Renaissance Studies* 19 (1989): 15-33.

[29] This fable has occasioned much scholarly dispute as to its meaning. For a recent summary of previous arguments (as well as a proposal, with which I disagree, that the fable rejects the antimonarchism of Hubert Languet), see Martin N. Raitiere, *Sir Philip Sidney and Renaissance Political Theory* (Pittsburgh, 1984), pp. 57-101.

[30] This concept Aesop himself articulates in his first fable as delivered to the Samians: in the words of the *Life,* the fabulist reconstructs what it was like "In elder Times when Beasts had speech."

[31] See Andrew, ed., *Two Early Renaissance Bird Poems,* p. 26.

[32] Sidney, *Old Arcadia,* pp. 78-79.

[33] John Lyly, *Euphues and His England* (London, 1609), p. 39. There were previous editions in 1579, 1580, 1582, 1586, 1597, 1606, and several more in the reigns of both James I and Charles I. Whether one understands such a publication history as proof of a works' popularity or of its political usefulness, it is worth noting that *Euphues and His England* continued to be republished long after the fashion for Euphuism had become a subject for mockery.

[34] Sincy Lyly shared with antiquity the belief that bees were ruled by a king, not a queen, he missed an opportunity to "apply" his natural history to Elizabeth in a gender-specific way. This opportunity was first used in the 1630s in relation to Henrietta Maria. But in Lyly's case the resulting masculinization merely matches his strategy in the fable of the lion, the wolf, and the fox (as was also the case in *Mother Hubberds Tale*). There seems to have been no attempt in Elizabethan fables to adapt their protagonists' sex to the special circumstances of a female monarch.

Edward Wheatley (essay date 1994)

SOURCE: "Scholastic Commentary and Robert Henryson's *Morall Fabillis:* The Aesopic Fables," in *Studies in Philology,* Vol. XCI, No. 1, Winter, 1994, pp. 70-99.

[*In the following essay, Wheatley asserts that Henryson's edition of Aesopian fables depends on paraphrases and interpretations, intended to educate medieval readers about social or spiritual issues.*]

I

Modern critics have examined Robert Henryson's *Morall Fabillis* in relation to the sermons, popular literature, and political events of Henryson's day, but the fables have never been systematically compared to common educational texts, even though Henryson, a school-master, acknowledges the source for some of his fables as the classroom Aesop of his era. The Middle Scots poet took seven tales from one of the so-called "Romulus" collections, a group of sixty Latin verse fables probably written in the late twelfth century and generally attributed to Gualterus Anglicus (Walter of

England).[1] This collection became popular enough to displace Avianus's fables as the curricular representative of the genre in European grammar schools, earning "Aesop" a place among the *Auctores octo,* the group of eight authors including Cato, Theodulus, and Alain de Lille.

Like most widely studied "pagan" texts during the Middle Ages, these Aesopic fables acquired scholastic commentaries. The 160 extant manuscripts of the fables and/or their commentaries[2] indicate that anyone in the medieval educational hierarchy, from schoolboys to highly learned adults, could attempt to pen a commentary: the surviving body of work extends from the charmingly childish to the highly learned. The more expert commentators typically wrote a paraphrase of each fable and then offered interpretations of the fable's meaning, sometimes leaving the interpretation on a social, earthly level, sometimes providing a Christian allegory, and sometimes doing both.

The most perceptive modern critic of Latin commentaries, Rita Copeland, has described the motivation for this kind of text as follows:

> Latin exegetical practice in the Middle Ages carries the rhetorical force of *hermeneia,* or primary or productive discourse: it works to displace the original text, materially by paraphrase, and conceptually by reconstituting the argu-mentative structure of the text. . . . Latin com-mentary substitutes itself for the text in question, inserting itself into the *auctoritas* of that text, hence appropriating that authority, and to varying degrees performing in lieu of the text. The dynamic effect of exegesis is to achieve a certain difference with the source.[3]

Although Copeland focuses upon elevated philosophical texts (and highly educated commentators, for a schoolboy writing a commentary would hardly think of himself as appropriating the authority of "Aesop"), her remarks hold true at least for the most scholarly fable commentaries.

Indeed, fables were probably even more available for appropriation than any other texts in the Middle Ages, since one of the standard classroom practices from antiquity demanded paraphrase. Priscian's influential *Praeexercitamina,* a standard guide for medieval educational theory, suggested that students learn Aesopic fable plots and then retell them in abbreviated form (*"modo breviter"*) and/or lengthened form (*"modo latius"*); he reproduces one fable in each form.[4] Thus educated medieval readers would have learned early in their schooling that fables existed in order to be rewritten. As a schoolmaster, Henryson must have presided over such student activity repeatedly, and, as we shall see, he certainly knew the commentaries that grew out of this activity.

The most popular commentaries associated with the Aesopic fables came to be held in almost as much esteem as the tales themselves. By Henryson's day, two branches of commentary on the fables had achieved such popularity that one or the other was nearly always printed with the fables. Probably written in the thirteenth century, the older branch, with the incipit *"Grecia disciplinarum mater,"* was generally published with the fables alone under the title *Esopus moralizatus.* A commentary written roughly a century later and beginning with the words *"In principio huius libri"* was most often published with the fables as part of the *Auctores octo* collection.[5] These two commentaries were printed with the fables at least twenty-five times in several countries before 1500.[6]

In spite of the broad dissemination of not only these published commentaries but also many others in manuscripts, they have received practically no modern scholarly attention on their own, and very little in relation to vernacular fables derived from Walter's collection. Only Douglas Gray, in his book simply entitled *Robert Henryson,* has suggested connections between some of the author's fables and the allegories in the *Esopus moralizatus* and *Auctores octo,* but Gray devotes a mere three pages of his book to discussing similarities in subject matter (125-28). In this article I will examine the Prologue, *moralitates,* and some structural principles of the Aesopic fables in Henryson's *Morall Fabillis* in relation to the scholastic language, educational theory, and allegories in fable manuscripts and books available in the late fifteenth century. Many of the comparisons here are based on the *Esopus moralizatus* and *Auctores octo* commentaries, but I will also cite similarities between the Middle Scots fables and commentaries found only in manuscripts, especially BL MS Add. 11897, the commentary which is strikingly similar to much of Henryson's work.

Henryson's project, which uses both beast-epic and Aesopic fable as primary sources along with numerous works of Christian and pagan *auctoritas* as secondary sources, is the most scholarly vernacular fable collection to emerge during the Middle Ages. The *Morall Fabillis* includes the entire spectrum of figuration and allegory, from homiletic morals which leave the relation between a character and its moral role undefined to full allegorization in which, to pervert a metaphor, no stone is left unturned into something else. In a sense, this collection is a compendium of approaches and attitudes toward fable, here expanded to include the sister genre of beast-epic. (Although the *moralitates* of Henryson's beast-epic fables [Fables III, IV, V, and IX, X, and XI] are structurally indebted to scholastic fable commentaries, they will not be discussed here.)

However, the variety of subject matter and interpretative technique has proved disconcerting to critics unfamiliar with the diversity which typifies the scholastic fable tradition. A substantial number of critics in the 1950s, 1960s, and even the 1970s found Henryson's changes of interpretative mode so opaque that they chose not to read the narratives and *moralitates* as integrated,[7] a baby-and-bathwater rejection which neither elucidates Henryson's work nor shows an understanding of fable as a genre. Wisely, most Henryson critics in the past three decades have followed Denton Fox's advice in his 1962 article "Henryson's *Fables*,"[8] that the two parts of each fable should be considered together, and that the collection should be viewed as a unified work of literature rather than a random compilation.

Nevertheless, curiosity and confusion about Henryson's moral messages remain, even in the work of the sensitive critic Douglas Gray, who calls the *moralitates* "selective and arbitrary" (124). On one level, this judgment is irrefutable: why Henryson chose to apply one *moralitas* and not another to a certain fable was entirely his own decision. By comparing his work to scholastic fable commentaries, however, we can see clearly that Henryson viewed his own work as part of a tradition (even though the very tradition had long been based on selectivity and arbitrariness).

In the following discussion I will differentiate between social and allegorical readings of the fables. A social reading entails generalized social roles, with animals representing good or bad people, powerful or weak people, etc.; these demand little rethinking of the narrative. Allegorical readings call upon the reader to think the fable into a different spiritual plane, and on the whole such interpretations are much more detailed than social readings.

II

In the prologue to the *Morall Fabillis* Henryson draws upon two parts of the standard Latin fable curriculum: Walter of England's verse prologue and several of the *accessus,* or scholastic introductions, which accompanied the Latin collection in manuscripts and books. These sources are combined with common fable theory in such a way that Henryson prepares his audience for a vernacular collection of broader concern than any of its sources.

The tone of Henryson's prologue is instructive, seeking to justify the project in terms of scholastic endeavor:

> Thocht feiyeit fabils of ald poetre
> Be not al grunded vpon truth, yit than,
> Thair polite termes of sweit rhetore
> Richt plesand ar vnto the eir of man;
> And als the caus quhy thay first began
> Wes to repreif the of thi misleuing,

O man, be figure of ane vther thing.

(1-7)[9]

Here Henryson criticizes the genre because of its basic falsity, a criticism which could have reached him through patristic writings,[10] but he immediately negates that criticism by emphasizing the importance of figuration. The word "caus" in line 5 would havereminded Henryson's contemporaries of the Aristotelian form of scholastic introduction;[11] indeed, this stanza may represent an adaptation of the *"causa materialis"* which the *accessus* to the *Esopus moralizatus* gives for Walter's collection, *"Causa materialis vel subiectum huius libri est sermo fabulosus in respectu ad vertutes morales."*

While the horticultural imagery in the prologue's second stanza is taken directly from Walter's prologue,[12] it is noteworthy that although Walter speaks metaphorically of himself as a gardener tending the growth of his rhetorical flowers, Henryson's narrator distances himself from verbal horticulture through a simile; poetry, "in lyke maner" (8) to a garden bringing forth flowers and grain, has "ane morall sweit sentence" (12). The shift from first-person metaphor to depersonalized simile serves two purposes. First, it separates Henryson's own poetic activity from that of the original cultivator, Aesop/Walter. Our narrator can compare himself to the *auctor* but cannot presume to play the same part as the master of the genre. Second, this distancing simile frees our narrator for another role, as we shall see.

The next stanza, a justification for mixing pleasure and instruction which is as indebted to Walter as it is to Horace, closes with Henryson's quotation of the second line of Walter's prologue, *"Dulcius arrident seria picta iocis"* (line 28). To medieval readers, this verse was doubtless familiar enough to serve as a clear identifier of the collection which Henryson was "translating." The line presents one of Walter's justifications for the genre in which he writes, but Henryson apparently places it here in order to prepare his audience for what is to follow: a citation of the "serious thing" inherent in a traditional modesty *topos,* but adorned with the pleasantries of some unexpected role-playing on the part of the narrator. This passage initially appears to be a light-hearted, satirical depiction of the traditional scholastic use of fables, but comparison with scholastic texts brings out its darker aspects. The poet writes of Aesop:

> Of this poete, my maisteris, with your leif,
> Submitting me to your correctioun,
> In mother toung, of Latyng, I wald preif
> To mak ane maner of translatioun—
> Nocht of my self, for vane presumptioun,
> Bot be requeist and precept of ane lord,

Of quhome the name it neidis not record.

Superficially Henryson's modesty *topos* seems quite traditional, but a closer examination of the stanza reveals unique aspects of the author's narratorial self-creation. One change is signaled by the word "maisteris," a term appropriate to the classroom.[13] In asking leave of his masters to begin his translation, the narrator places himself in the role of a studentspeaking to his teachers.

While the translation of fables was an age-old classroom exercise, the satirical edge of this passage becomes clearer in light of the fact that translation myths were also part of the standard scholastic introductions to Walter of England's fables. The *Esopus moralizatus* tells us that the emperor Romulus ordered the fables translated into Latin because he wanted his sons to be instructed by them, though no translator is named. The *Auctores octo* commentary first credits Socrates with a translation ordered by Emperor Theodosius, but later states that *"magister Romulus"* undertook the work at the behest of the emperor Tiberius. In these prologues, great care is taken to mention the name of the patron who has requested the translation, so that his commission will redound eternally to his greater glory. Henryson, on the other hand, leaves his readers doubting whether his narrator really has been commissioned, for surely someone submitting his work for the consideration of "maisteris" would not be qualified to undertake a translation for a lord.

But we should examine the passage yet again. Henryson's narrator brings into play a sin, "vane presumptioun," which will not taint his translation, and then tells us that he need not name the lord by whose precept he is working. Henryson here could be hinting at the ways in which his Christian fable collection will differ from earlier texts: his work need not glorify and earthly lord, because it is written to glorify the spiritual one. Through this calculated ambiguity, Henryson prepares his readers for the fact that his collection will examine both the relationship between earthly nobles and their subjects, and that between the heavenly lord and his creatures.

The narrator further denigrates his own abilities in lines 36-42, which on their own seem a wholly traditional disclaimer of verbal skills:

> In hamelic language and in termes rude
> Me neidis wryte, for quhy of eloquence
> Nor rethorike, I never vnderstude.
> Thairfoir meiklie I pray your reuerence,
> Gif ye find ocht that throw my negligence
> Be deminute, or yit superfluous,
> Correct it at your willis gratious.

(29-42)

Here Henryson satirizes both the dictates of Priscian's *Praeexercitamina* and his own narrator. The narrator's self-declared lack of rhetorical talent directly contradicts the generic requirement of fable cited in the prologue's first stanza, providing further evidence that he is ill-qualified for the task. Rhetorical sweetness, the genre's primary *raison d'être,* must pave the way if instruction in proper living is to follow. Furthermore, to adhere to Priscian's pedagogical model, a student was required to make a fable either "deminute" or "superfluous"; the narrator's request for correction expresses fears based upon scholastic practice, though even at the outset of his project, Henryson must have known that the "superfluities" added to the original fables would be his stamp upon them.

Of course Henryson gives his narrator the lie not only by means of his elegant rhyme royal stanzaic form but also in the very terms expressing inarticulateness: this stanza includes no fewer than seven latinisms, betokening an elevated rhetorical style.[14] Indeed, Bengt Ellenberger has pointed out that the prologue contains 2.6 times the average number of latinisms per line of the *Morall Fabillis* as a whole. Thus Henryson paints the narrator as a man who is classically educated, as any fabulist should be, but who wears his learning lightly.

In the next two stanzas, Henryson clarifies the balance that he is attempting to strike between the fables' classroom role and their value as *exempla.* The narrator attributes to Aesop/Walter a far more ambitious agenda for fables than the source itself posits:

> My author in his fabillis tellis how
> That brutal beistis spak and vnderstude,
> And to gude purpois dispute and argow,
> Ane sillogisme propone, and eik conclude;
> Putting exempill and similitude
> How mony men in operatioun
> Ar like to beistis in conditioun.
>
>   (43-49)

Here Henryson plays brilliantly upon Priscian's dictates that fables be rhetorical models for school children, the curricular role for which Walter probably wrote his Latin fables. Henryson has raised the curricular stakes by writing forms of academic discourse into the fables rather than simply allowing those forms to be the subject of that discourse. But if this idea begins as a witty satire of scholarly *disputatio,* it is balanced by a dead-serious indictment of sinfulness in lines 47-49 and the following stanza:

> Ne merveill is, ane man be lyke ane beist,
> Quhilk lufis ay carnall and foull delyte,

> That schame can not him renye nor arreist,
> Bot takis all the lust and appetyte,
> Quhilk throw custum and the daylie ryte
> Syne in the mynd sa fast is radicate
> That he in brutal beist is transformate.
>
>   (50-56)

In his edition's notes to these lines, Fox cites the standardscriptural passages in which sinful men are compared to irrational beasts, 2 Peter 2:9 ff., and Jude 10, but while these verses are certainly part of the broader background of Henryson's stanza, the idea of the incongruity of humans acting in beastly fashion could also have been borrowed from this passage of the *Auctores octo* introduction:

> Magister Aesopus de civitate Atheniensi, auctor huius libri, volens omnes homines communiter informare quid agere et quid vitare debeant, hoc opus composuit in quo fingit bruta irrationalia animalia et inanimata loqui nobis; per hoc in-conveniens docet nos cavere cavenda et sectari sectanda: nam fingit gallum loqui et lupum, ut patet in littera; hoc est totum figurative: ut id quod minus videtur inesse inest et id quod magis.

This passage also shares with the final stanza of Henryson's prologue the emphasis on the figurative nature of the poet's project ("Esope . . . be figure wrait his buke," 57, 59).

By the end of his introduction, then, Henryson has begun to sketch the role of his narrator in the collection: that of a learned but modest man playing the student before his superiors, while addressing spiritual concerns superior to his listeners. He has touched upon his familiarity with the classroom use of fables, but he will be taking them beyond those traditional confines.

Like Walter's first fable, Henryson's "The Cock and the Jasp" tells of an ignorant creature who cannot see beyond extrinsic beauty to intrinsic value. Having found a jasper while scraping for food in the dunghill, the cock uses rather high rhetorical style to tell the stone that it is useless to him. He concludes:

> "Quhar suld thow mak thy habitatioun?
> Quhar suld thow duell, bot in ane royall tour?
> Quhar suld thow sit, bot on ane kingis croun
> Exalt in worschip and in grit honour?
> Rise, gentill Iasp, of all stanis the flour,
> Out of this fen, and pas quhar thow suld be;
> Thow ganis not for me, nor I for the."
>
>   (106-12)

Then the narrator interjects a self-conscious first-person sentence to point out that he intends to explain the tale's moral:

> Bot of the inward sentence and intent
> Of this fabill, as myne author dois write,
> I sall reheirs in rude and hamelie dite.

> (117-19)

Here the narrator's change of tone and person is reminiscent of Walter's original *moralitas,* in which he uncharacteristically addresses the cock and the jasper, telling them what they represent (*"Tu Gallo stolidum, tu iaspide pulchra sophye / Dona notes; stolido nil sapit ista seges"*). In each case, the narrator apparently wants to guide his readers through the first interpretation. Henryson's transition from fable to *moralitas* offers an implicit warning, however, in that the narrator intends to write in the low style—"rude and hamelie dite"—unlike the cock, whose high-flown rhetoric masks his foolishness. Here Henryson points out that rhetorical eloquence does not have a monopoly on wisdom, and by extension, that lesser genres such as the fable need not be in-eloquent.

The *moralitas* begins with a stanza about the seven properties of jasper, information obviously borrowed from a lapidary. This stanza confuses Henryson's modern editor, Denton Fox, who writes,

> It seems very possible that [this] is a fragment which Henryson intended to cancel or rewrite. This stanza treats the jasp as a magical stone and deals exclusively with earthly things, while in the following stanzas Henryson makes the jasp into a figure of wisdom and contrasts it to 'ony eirthly thing' (n., line 130).

Even though he finds no aesthetic justification for the passage, Fox goes on to cite several English lapidaries (198).

Actually, one of the best-known lapidaries in the Middle Ages had been associated with Walter's fables at least half a century before Henryson rewrote them. In BL MS Add. 11897, a late fourteenth- or early fifteenth-century German manuscript of Walter's fables with a highly learned commentary, the scribe has written the following lines in the margin alongside the fable of the cock and the jasp: "In lapidaris dicitur, 'jaspidis esse decem species septemque feruntur. Caste portatus fugat et febres et iidropes. Optimus in viridi translucentique colore'" (2r). These lines are taken from the verse lapidary *De Gemmis,* romantically attributed to Evax, King of Arabia, who describes the jewel under the fourth heading in his work.[15]

BL MS Add. 11897 was copied during the lifetime of John Lydgate, who rewrote seven of Walter's fables in English as *Isopes Fabules*. Although his acquaintance with this specific manuscript seems highly unlikely, he, too, associated Evax's lapidary with Walter's first fable. Lydgate has the cock address the jewel as follows:

> "Evax to the yeveþ praysyng manyfolde,
> Whos lapydary bereþ opynly wytnesse,
> Geyn sorow & woe þou bryngest in gladnesse.
> The best iacyncte in Ethiope ys founde
> And ys of colour lyke the saphyre ynde,
> Comforteþ man þat ly in prison bounde,
> Makeþ men strong & hardy of hys kynde,
> Contract synewes þe iacyncte doþ unbynde.

> (152-59)[16]

Since Lydgate's fables survive in only two manuscripts, both of which are miscellanies of his poetry, we cannot assume that the tales reached a large audience; therefore, Henryson's knowledge of them seems only slightly more plausible than his knowledge of the German manuscript. Regardless of whether he was acquainted with either of these texts, their very existence suggests that Henryson probably knew of some precedent for the use of lapidaries in relation to this particular fable. Furthermore, Henryson may have been echoing Evax's verse, *"Et tutamentum portanti creditur esse,"* in the following verses about the jasp:

> It makis ane man stark and victorious
> Preseruis als fra cacis perrillous;
> Quha hes this stane sall haue gud hap to speid,
> Of fyre not fallis him neidis not to dreid.

> (123-26)

Henryson's next stanza contrasts the properties which God has given the jasper and those which the fabulist gives it:

> This gentill iasp, richt different of hew,
> Betakinnis perfite prudence and cunning,
> Ornate with mony deidis of vertew,
> Mair excellent than ony eirthly thing,
> Quhilk makis men in honour ay to ring,
> Happie, and stark to haif the victorie
> Of all vicis and spirituall enemie.

> (127-33)

Whether the comparison with "only eirthly thing" describes the jasper, as Fox believes, or virtue, as I think more likely, must be left open to debate, but the fact that the subject leads to victory over vices is a mark in favor of the latter interpretation. We should note, too, that a jasper representing virtue would help people to triumph over their "spirituall enemie"; Henryson's jewel leads to a spiritual fortitude absent from Walter's jasper, which is symbolic of moral wisdom.

At this point the jasper is subsumed in the allegorical interpretation until the author has described the cock:

> This cok, desyrand mair the sempill corne
> Than ony iasp, may till ane fule be peir,
> Quhilk at science makis bot ane moik and
>   scorne,
> And na gude can; als lytill will he leir—
> His hart wammillis wyse argumentis to heir,
> As dois ane sow to quhome men for the nanis
> In hir draf troich wald saw the precious stanis.

(141-47)

The closing lines of this stanza, which Fox identifies as an obvious reference to Matthew 7:6, "Neither cast ye your pearls before swine . . . ," also reflect the *Auctores octo* commentary. In the plot summary of the fable, that commentator initially refers to the stone not as *"iaspis,"* but only as *"margarita."* In his moralization he writes, *"Per margaritam (intellige) sapientem."* Just as Henryson alludes to the pearl of great price but returns to the jasper at the end of his *moralitas* (155 ff.), the *Auctores octo* commentator changes his pearl back to a jasper at the end of his moralization, where he gives the etymology for the word *"iaspis."*[17]

In general, fable commentaries call several forms of interpretation into play early in Walter's collection, thus familiarizing readers with several avenues of interpretative pursuit, any of which might be followed in subsequent fables. In the *moralitas* of "The Cock and the Jasp," Henryson appears to follow the example of scholastic commentators by giving several kinds of interpretation to the first fable in his collection: he uses more than one type of allegory, in this case the natural (the lapidary), the social (the earthly fool), and the biblical (the allusion to the pearl before swine). What to modern readers appears a confusing variety of allegorical forms created by Henryson may have suggested to medieval readers the multiplicity of interpretative forms available for this genre.

Henryson's fable of the city mouse and the country mouse, a lengthy adaptation of Walter's twelfth fable, is not as clearly indebted to scholastic commentaries as most of Henryson's other fables, perhaps because the commentaries generally offer only social interpretations similar to that provided in the verse fable itself. The *Auctores octo* commentary reads the country mouse as *"bonos homines spirituales, de securitate semper letos,"* and the city mouse as *"pravos homines et seculares semper gaudentes tam de illecebris quam de utilitate."* The BL MS Add. 11897 commentator repeats this interpretation.

Henryson includes only a vague echo of this reading when writing the country mouse's farewell, after the cat has interrupted dinner; this speech contains the only mention of God by either of the characters: "Almichtie God keip me fra sic ane feist" (350).

In the *moralitas,* Henryson's passing mention of "sickernes (with small possessioun)" (380) reflects the commentary's use of *securitate* quoted above, but this is the only word implying a debt to the commentary.

Henryson concludes his *moralitas* by citing a biblical authority:

> And Solomon sayis, gif that thow will reid,
> 'Vnder the heuin I can not better se
> Than ay be blyith and leif in honestie.'
> Quhairfoir I may conclude be this ressoun:
> Of eirthly ioy it beiris maist degre,
> Blyithnes in hart, with small possessioun.

(391-96)

Although this scriptural citation itself has not been identified with any certainty, Henryson's use of Solomon as *auctor* in his moral is clearly traceable to the commentary tradition, where he is quoted repeatedly in relation to *moralitates.* In the *Auctores octo,* Solomon is quoted four times, one instance of which appears in the comment on the fable following that of the two mice.[18]

After the first triad of beast-epic fables, Henryson returns to Walter's collection for "The Sheep and the Dog," which tells of a canine who falsely accuses a sheep of being in debt to him and who bribes false witnesses to support his claim in court. Perhaps to mark the change from one kind of source to another, this fable begins with an approximate translation of the standard introduction to comments in the *Esopus moralizatus, "Hic autor ponit aliam fabulam";* Henryson writes "Esope ane taill puttis in memorie . . ." (1146), a phrase which must have reminded many of his contemporaries of scholastic commentary.

Less a generalized scholastic fable than a pointed satire on legal corruption, Henryson's version of the narrative devotes as much attention to the victimized sheep as to the corrupt court proceedings. In rewriting the fable slightly as a satire of legal injustice, Henryson rejects the spiritual allegory available to him in scholastic commentaries, where the trial is allegorically recast as divine judgment of a human soul. Instead, Henryson opts for detailed social figuration: the sheep represents "the figure / Of pure commounis" (1258-59), the wolf is likened to "ane schiref stout" (1265), and the raven represents "ane fals crownair" (1272).

Here Henryson is obviously not writing a fable general enough for all times and places: these are medieval characters in a contemporary situation.

Among the three roles, figurative specificity shifts strangely. The role of a poor common person comes up quite often in fable commentaries as *"paupes"* or *"impotens,"* but a definite role for a powerful person almost never appears; these remain at the general level of *"potentes"* or *"tyranni."*[19] Evidently willing to sacrifice generality at the altar of satire, Henryson goes against the precedent set by scholastic commentary when he assigns the wolf and the crow specific roles within the legal system. Perhaps because of this alteration, Henryson introduces the figurative roles differently. The sheep "may present the figure / Of pure commounis" (1258-59); the use of "may" is standard for the author as he introduces figurative roles. However, turning to the other two animals, he writes, "This volf I likkin to ane schiref stout" (1265), and "This rauin I likkin to ane fals crownair" (1272). The narrator's personal intervention here might betray Henryson's discomfort with the substantial change which he makes to his source and to standard figurative treatments of the genre as a whole.

Once the figurative identities have been established, the sheep speaks up again in the middle of the *moralitas,* an interruption which strikes the modern reader as bizarre. In spite of our expectations, this kind of direct address in the *moralitas* had been established in scholastic commentaries before Henryson's day. For example, in the *"Allegoria"* section of the *Auctores octo* comment on Fable XXXV, *"De lupo et capite,"* this sentence concludes the comment: *"Lupus, id est deus, ait, O vos decores depicti huius mundi hominis, sed heu, sine voce, id est gratia mea et regno patris mei."* This kind of direct address must be based on the fact that the statement is general enough to fit the wolf as well as God (or in this case, Christ); in fact, only the first half of the wolf/deity's statement strikes the appropriate level of generality.[20] In Henryson's fable of the sheep and the dog, the animal's plaint is as appropriate to poor people as to himself, to the degree that he becomes confused about his own identity: the group on whose behalf he complains is "we pure pepill" (1317).

But Henryson's changes to the scholastic model are aesthetically significant, for the sheep's plaint is not a mere repetition of what he has said in the fable. There, he has presented his case formally, using legal terminology. In the *moralitas* he bemoans his unjust sentence as symptomatic of the evil in the upper strata of society:

"Se how this cursit syn of couetice
Exylit hes baith lufe, lawtie, and law.
Now few or nane will execute iustice,
In falt of quhome, the pure man is ouerthraw.

The veritie, suppois the iugis knaw,
Thay ar so blindit with affectioun,
But dried, for meid, thay thoill the richt go
     doun.

"Seis thow not, lord, this warld ouerturnit is,
As quha wald change gude gold in leid or
     tyn?
The pure is peillit, the lord may do na mis,
And simonie is haldin for na syn.
Now is he blyith with okker maist may wyn;
Gentrice is slane, and pietie is ago.
Allace, gude lord, quhy tholis thow it so?

                                        (1300-13)

In effect, this declamation, which continues to the end of the *moralitas,* is as truthful and relevant to the sheep's case as the speech which he makes before the court (1187-1201), and it could certainly have found a place in the fable narrative itself. Alternatively, the lines in the *moralitas* could have been left in the voice of the narrator, and the moral lesson which they teach would have been much the same. However, Henryson has marginalized the plaint, making the sheep the commentator on the fable in which he appears. This structure suggests that the universe defined by the fable is too corrupt to encompass certain truths: they must be marginalized in a world which is "ouerturnit," i.e., upsidedown. By the same token, the structure gives the sheep's voice greater authority, since it inhabits the *moralitas,* where the greatest wisdom of a fable must lie.

The exclusion of truth from its proper realm remains an important theme in the framing narrative of Fable VII, "The Lion and the Mouse," in which the narrator dreams that Aesop visits him and grudgingly tells a fable. This frame is another element in Henryson's fables that has bothered modern critics, notably Dieter Mehl, whose article "Robert Henryson's *Moral Fables* as Experiments in Didactic Narrative" includes perceptive readings of the lessons Henryson teaches.[21] However, because Mehl is unfamiliar with the variety of didactic experiments in scholastic fables and commentaries, he believes that the frame undermines the possibility of unity among Henryson's fables as a collection. Mehl writes,

The originality of the frame makes it very unlikely that the poet wrote the fable as part of a collection; to justify its place in the Bassandyne-order by pointing out that it stands exactly in the centre of the thirteen tales is tempting, but does not explain the individual character of the tale. The arrangement is more likely to be the afterthought of some ingenious compiler, but it should not be made the basis for elaborate theorizing about the structure of the whole collection.

                                        (87)

Pace Mehl, the fables of Walter of England, undeniably a collection, include two framing narratives, in Fable VII, *"De femina et fure,"* and Fable L, *"De patre et filio."* In both of these, a wise man faced with a social problem (a neighborhood potentially overrun by thieves, and a wayward son, respectively) attempts to change his listeners' behavior by telling a relevant fable. We cannot deny the possibility, then, that Henryson could have conceived of his framed fable as one in a collection.

Furthermore, extant scholastic commentaries include at least one example of a commentator sketching a framing narrative in which Aesop himself tells a fable, as he does in Henryson's work. Walter's twenty-first fable, *"De Terra Atheniensium Petente Regem,"* was apparently written to incorporate two fables, though some manuscripts divide them. The first narrative accords with the title above, and the second tells an analogous story of frogs begging Jupiter for a ruler, only to be given first an inert log and then a hungry hydra. The fable as a whole begins with a sort of promythion, two lines describing why fables were first created(*"Fabula nata sequi mores et pingere vitam, / Tangit quod fugias, quodque sequaris iter"* [Hervieux 325]), and the lines that serve as a transition between the two sections mention Aesop himself (*"Vrbem triste iugum querula cervige gerentem / Esopus tetigit, consona verba movens"* [Hervieux 326]). In MS II. 216 of the Biblioteca Comunale Ariostea in Ferrara, the commentator believed the two stories were one fable, the first describing the historical situation in which Aesop himself came forward to tell the exemplum of the unfortunate frogs (84v). That Aesop should tell both that commentator's version of the tale and Henryson's fable of the lion and the mouse is coincidental in subject matter as well, for both narratives are concerned with the need for just government.

As is the case with MS Add. 11897, the Ferrara text predates Henryson's *Fabillis* by about a century, but no clear link can be drawn between it and his fables; even so, the inspiration for having Aesop tell a fable may have been available to him through another commentary.

While these fables or a commentary may have provided structural models for Henryson, he carried the idea of a framing narrative much further, not least in complicating the identity of Aesop by making him a Christian born in Rome and therefore deserving an authority different from that belonging to pagans. His first words to the dreamer are "God speid, my sone" (1363), and he says that he dwells in heaven (1374). But Aesop's Christianity is tinged with despair, as he betrays when replying to the dreamer's request for a fable:

Schaikand his heid, he said, "My sone, lat be,
For quhat is it worth to tell ane fenceit taill,
Quhen haly preiching may na thing auaill?

"Now in this warld me think richt few or nane
To Goddis word that hes deuotioun;
The eir is deif, the hart is hard as stane;
Now oppin sin without correctioun,
The e inclynand to the eirth ay doun.
Sa roustit is the warld with canker blak
That now my taillis may lytill succour mak."

(1388-97)

Why would Henryson have decided to make Aesop Christian? Pagan authors, too, deserved respect, especially when their work was given the Christian meaning that not only Henryson but also scholastic commentators gave to Walter's fables. One explanation for the change of religion is that Henryson extrapolated it from a scholastic commentary. The *accessus* of neither the *Esopus moralizatus* nor the *Auctores octo* states that Aesop was a pagan, and in the latter work, the fables appear alongside several clearly Christian works including the *Facetus, De Contemptu Mundi, Tobias,* and the *Floretus.*

Aesop's Christianity lends credence to his assertion that "haly preiching" is no longer efficacious. While the narrator does not go so far as to disagree with Aesop's appraisal, he persists in requesting a fable, asking, "Quha wait nor I may leir and beir away / Sum thing thairby heirefter may auaill?" (1402-3). Vague as it is, this rebuttal persuades Aesop to begin recounting the fable of the lion and the mouse.

The *moralitas* which Aesop gives the fable is purely social, tacitly acknowledging that the fable is no sermon. The lion represents royalty, and the mouse the common people. In his closest brush with allegory, Aesop makes the forest stand for "the warld and his prosperitie, / As fals plesance, myngit with cair repleit" (1582-83). In one sense this role represents only an allegorical synecdoche based on place: the part represents the whole. However, the religious connotations of "the warld and his prosperitie" give the moralization a different twist, one which is anticipated in MS Ambrosiana I. 85 supra, copied by Johannes Brixianus (i.e., of Brescia) in 1415. Like Henryson's Aesop, he states that the lion and the mouse represent earthly figures (*"homo pius"* and *"homo paupertas"*), but the forest represents "this world" (*"per silvam habemus istam mundum"*); the commentator has chosen the demonstrative adjective with slightly pejorative overtones, instead of the more neutral *"hic."* He and Henryson's narrator share the medieval Christian contempt for that which is purely worldly, a widely available sentiment which presumably teachers would want to inculcate in their pupils at an early stage.

The final stanza of the fable returns us to the dream vision, in which Aesop bids farewell to the dreamer:

> Quhen this wes said, quod Esope, "My fair
>   child,
> Perswaid the kirkmen ythandly to pray
> That tressoun of this cuntrie be exyld,
> And iustice regne, and lordis keip thair
>   fay
> Vnto thair souerane lord baith nycht and day."
> And with that word he vanist and I woke;
> Syne throw the schaw my iourney hamewart
>   tuke.

(1615-21)

Aesop basically urges the narrator to give a sermon to churchmen, inasmuch as a sermon should partly be a persuasion to prayer, but again Henryson colors Aesop's message with despair; instead of exhorting the narrator to preach to the lords who are apparently close to losing faith in their leader, Aesop tells him to preach to the clergy, as if preaching to the nobility were doomed to failure.

A. C. Spearing is correct to point out that this fable and its framing narrative are both structurally and inspirationally central to the *Morall Fabillis*.[22] I would add to his theory of centrality that the fable also delineates the central problem which Henryson as a poet confronts both in the Prologue and here: how to take a pagan fable based on social figuration and give it religious meaning. Even as a Christian, Aesop seems unable to bridge this gap, leaving the narrator with a challenge not to tell a fable but to preach. Of course scholastic fable allegory links these kinds of discourse, and significantly, both of the direct borrowings from commentaries occur after this point in Henryson's collection, as we shall see below.

If the fable of the lion and the mouse questions the efficacy of preaching, that question is given a bleak answer in the following fable, "The Preaching of the Swallow." In fact, the fable opens with a kind of sermon on God's omnipotence as evidenced by nature and the seasons. This encomium serves as a transition to the fable narrative, but at fifteen stanzas, it is much longer than necessary if Henryson, a poet capable of impressive verbal economy, were not emphasizing its homiletic aims. Thus, by the time we reach the preaching swallow himself, we see similarities between the bird and the narrator.

Both the narrator and the swallow embellish their sermons with quotations from curricular *auctores*: the narrator cites Aristotle's *Metaphysics* in line 1636, and

the swallow has recourse to half of one of the distichs of Cato in line 1754. Modern readers might associate the use of such *auctoritates* with Chaucer and *The Nun's Priest's Tale,* where the presence of a plethora of authoritative aphorisms is clearly satirical, in keeping with the rest of the tale; therefore we might infer that Henryson simply did not understand Chaucer's intention and consequently thought that such elevated *auctores* could be linked to lowly fables even when the tone of the work is serious. In fact, the idea of associating auctoritates and fables belonged to neither Chaucer nor Henryson, but scholastic commentary. Biblioteca Marciana MS 4658 quotes no fewer than 22 *auctoritates* in its fable commentary, and BL MS Add. 11897 no fewer than 37. Aristotle and Cato are cited in both manuscripts (and in the latter, complete or partial distichs are reproduced twelve times). Thus while the modern reader might be conditioned to feel a certain disjuncture of tone between Aesop and Aristotle, educated medieval readers would not have responded in the same way.

In commentaries written or printed in several countries during the century before Henryson wrote, the scholastic allegories for this fable are remarkably similar to each other and to Henryson's *moralitas:* the fabulist's debt to scholastic fable commentary is far clearer than has been acknowledged.

The *Esopus moralizatus* commentary as published by Heinrich Quentell in Cologne in 1489 gives the following allegorization after thesummary of the fable's plot:

> Allegorice per aves intelligere possumus peccatores, per hyrundinem vero spirituales, qui sepe ammonent peccatores ut desistant et abstineant a peccatis. Sed peccatores, spirituales ammonitiones spernentes, tandem per rethia capiuntur et eterno igni traduntur.

(Fable XX)

This is one of only nine spiritual allegories among the sixty fable interpretations in this commentary.

The *Auctores octo* commentary printed by Jehan de Vingle in Lyon in 1495 summarizes the plot and then turns to this allegory:

> Allegoria: tu debes insudare bonis operibus, ne dyabolus te seducat ab eis. Per aves intelligimus peccatores, per irundinem spirituales qui semper monent eos ut se abstineant; illi vero respuentes monitionem, venit dyabolus et rapit per rhetia, id est per opera mala et deducit eos ad infernum.

(Fable 20, *Fabularum Esopi*)

Because BL MS Add. 11897 differs from the printed commentaries in lacking plot summaries, its allegorical interpretation includes more details of setting and plot than do the other comments. The allegorizer offers spiritual meanings for nearly every aspect of the story:

> Allegoria: per yrundinem intellige spiritualem praedicatorem qui a(d)monet certas aves, id est homines, ut evellant linum, id est peccatum maximum cordis seu cogitationis que habent se, et seminaria aliorum peccatorum de agro cordis sui, ne agricola, id est dyabolus, ex eisdem diversa rethia, id est diversas temptationes quibus solet decipere homines, faciat. Sed ipsi homines consilium predicatorum spernentes sinunt crescat linum, id est peccata ex quibus dyabolus texit rethe. Quando illa capiant illos ducendo eos in consuetudinem peccandi et tandem reddens obstinatos in peccatis et finaliter impenitentes, ducit ipsos ad penas inferni eternales.

(8v)

Although this keenly detailed allegorization may exist in only one manuscript, we shall see that it has more in common with Henryson's *moralitas* than does either of the comments from incunables, earlier editions of which Henryson was far more likely to have known.

Allegories which interpret the swallow as a religious person or preacher, the other birds as sinners, and usually the man as the devil also appear in a large number of late fourteenth- and early fifteenth-century manuscripts in libraries throughout Europe.[23]

Following the first stanza of the *moralitas* of "The Preaching of the Swallow," in which the poet eulogizes Aesop for the "morall edificatioun" inherent in his fables, the narrator states that the tale has "ane sentence according to ressoun" (1893-94). This gratuitous statement, unique among his fables, could be the poet's acknowledgment that the scholastic allegories associated with the fable are unusually uniform. The reason for this uniformity may not be far to seek: the figure of the bird-catcher was conventionally read as symbolic of the devil,[24] the interpretation which Henryson reproduces:

> This carll and bond, of gentrice spoliate,
> Sawand this calf, thir small birdis to sla,
> It is the feind, quhilk fra the angelike state,
> Exylit is, as fals apostata,
> Quhilk day and nycht weryis not for to ga,
> Sawand poysoun and mony wickit thocht
> In mannis saull, quhilk Christ full deir hes
>   bocht.

(1895-1901)

The seed sown "in mannis saul" is substantially similar to that sown in the heart of sinners, mentioned in BL MS Add. 11897. That manuscript also emphasizes

"consuetudinem peccandi," vocabulary duplicated in Henryson's next stanza:

> Ressoun is blindit with affectioun,
> And carnall lust grouis full grene and gay,
> Throw consuetude hantit from day to day.

(1905-7)

The narrator goes on to tell us that wicked thoughts sown by the devil grow in the minds of sinners until "the feynd plettis his nettis scharp and rude" (1911), an action which also appears in the manuscript's allegorization quoted above (*"linum . . . ex quibus dyabolus texit rethe"*).

Henryson then gives ornamented descriptions of the birds' allegorical roles as mentioned in the commentaries:

> Thir hungrie birdis, wretchis we may call,
> Ay scraipand in this warldis vane plesance,
> Greddie to gadder gudis temporall,
> Quhilk as the calf ar tume without substance.

(1916-19)

As in the scholastic comments, the swallow as preacher is mentioned only in passing; Henryson devotes most of his attention to the pains which sinners will suffer at the hands of the devil:

> This swallow, quhilk eschaipit is the snair,
> The halie preichour weill may signifie,
> Exhortand folk to walk, and ay be wair
> Fra nettis of our wickit enemie
> Quha sleipis not, bot euer is reddie,
> Quhen wretchis in this warldis calf dois scraip,
> To draw his net, that thay may not eschaip.

(1923-29)

The narrator gives us three more stanzas of exhortation to avoid sin, the last of which begins in the first-person plural but shifts to third-person singular at the end:

> Pray we theirfoir quhill we ar in this lyfe
> For four thingis: the first, fra sin remufe;
> The secund is to seis all weir and stryfe;
> The thrid is perfite cheritie and lufe;
> The feird thing is, and maist for our behufe,
> That is in blis with angellis to be fallow.
> And thus endis the preiching of the swallow.

(1944-50)

The abrupt change of person and focus from the allegorical mode to a homiletic tone shares formal similarities with the *Auctores octo* commentary, in which we are given no transition between the second-person command and the third-person allegorization.

The stanza shows the narrator following the instructions of Aesop in the final stanza of the previous fable: he is persuading people to pray. In doing so, he is transformed. His voice merges with that of the swallow, a transformation emphasized by the last line, in which the bird's preaching is said to end simultaneously with the narrator's. The reader has been partially prepared for the reappearance of an animal voice in the *moralitas* by the strange renaissance of the sheep in the final verses of the fable of the sheep and the dog, where the animal supplies the moral. In addition, the conjunction of human and animal voices recalls the human-into-beast translation described in Henryson's prologue. It is therefore appropriate that he use first-person plural in addressing his audience, for he, like us, has debased his human nature through beastly sinfulness. Also implied in this audience are the "maisteris" to whom the narrator appeals in the prologue. We must all pray together for guidance.

The penultimate fable in the *Morall Fabillis,* "The Wolf and the Lamb," evidently owes little to the scholastic commentary tradition. Rather, it seems to have been placed here in order to summarize the moral interests of the three previous fables from the beast-epic tradition. The figurative roles of the lamb as "pure pepill" (2707) and the wolf as "false extortioneris / And oppressouris of pure men" (2711-12) reflect Walter's *moralitas* as much as any scholastic commentary. Indeed, the lengthy, formally structured description of the kinds of wolves which rule in the world (2714 ff.) clearly grew from the final clause of Walter's moral, *"Hii regnant qualibet urbe lupi"* (317).

Henryson's version of Walter's third tale, *"De mure et rana,"* rewritten as the final Middle Scots fable, "The Paddock and the Mouse," evidently has nearly as unified an allegorical tradition as the fable of the swallow and the linen. In both of the incunables the commentators include both social and allegorical readings. The *Esopus moralizatus,* after an elaborately embellished plot summary, gives this allegorical reading:

> Allegorice per ranam potest intelligi caro humana; per murem autem intelligitur anima que adversus carnem semper militat. Caro concupiscit adversus spiritum et spiritus adversus carnem. Caro enim nititur trahere animam ad terrena, et carnales delectationes. Anima vero resilit ad bona opera. Et istis sic ligantibus venit milvus, id est diabolus, quasi bolus in morsus duorum, scilicet corporis et anima. Virtus aliter sicut tangitur in fine littere: per ranam intelligant [*sic*] deceptores bonum dicentes deceptationemque intendentes; conantur enim alios decipere. Et sic quandoque cadunt in insidias quos aliis paraverunt. Sic dicitur in psalmo, "Incidit in foveam," etc.[25]

Here the commentator has interpreted not only the fable but also his own interpretation, by writing a situational etymology for the "diabolus," which the kite is said to represent. This is an interesting example of the displacement of the authoritative source, cited by Copeland: the commentator finds his own text rather than the authoritative fable worthy of interpretation on the verbal level.

The *Auctores octo* commentator remains more faithful to the fable plot in his summary, and he gives much the same allegory as above:

> Allegoria: per ranam intellige corpus cuiuslibet hominis, per murem animam qui nititur ad bona opera vel ad regnum dei; sed corpus retrahit eam, et sic milvus, id est diabolus, venit utrunque rumpens, scilicet corpus et animam. Fructus talis est quod non promittamus prodesse cum possimus nosmetipsos iuvare et volumus obesse.

As for other fables, BL MS. Add. 11897 gives a reading similar to that in the *Auctores octo* text, but the commentator allegorizes more of the elements of the plot, thus more closely approaching Henryson's *moralitas:*

> Allegoria: per mure intelligere possumus anima que ad bonum et ad celestia regna nititur et tendit, per rana corpus hominis quod vivit in deliciis presentis seculi, per lacum vero presensseculum aut mundum, deliciis et occupacionibus variis fluctuans. Unde sic rana promiserat mure velle transducere ipsum per lacum, licet pretendebat dolum quia nitebatur, per hoc murem submergere. Sic corpus humanum educatum in deliciis promittit animae servitutem in istis temporalibus, in quibus non est salus nec servitas. Anima non nititur in hereditatem celestibus. Iuxta illud ratio semper deprecatur ad optima. Et ita ipsis contra se reluctantibus, secundum quod dicit apostolus, "Caro concupiscit adversus spiritum et spiritus adversus carnem." Tandem supervenit milvus rapax, id est diabolus, qui rapit utrunque et pena cruciat eternaliter. Fructus apologi est: Ne dum promittimus prodesse intendemus ut conemur obesse, ut dum nitimur decipere alios redundat pena in nosmetipsos.(3r)

Again, we see the double *moralitas,* which includes both social figuration and spiritual allegory.[26]

Henryson reproduces the structure of this two-fold interpretation, placing the social reading first. This *moralitas* is structurally similar to that for the fable of the two mice: each of its first three stanzas, written in the eight-line ballade form, concludes with an identical message, in this case a warning about the evils of finding oneself with a wicked companion (Middle Scots "marrow"). The second of these stanzas reads as follows:

Ane fals intent vnder ane fair pretence
Hes causit mony innocent for to de;
Grit folie is to gif ouer sone credence
To all that speiks fairlie vnto the;
Ane silkin toung, ane hart of crueltie,
Smytis more sore than ony schot of
   arrow;
Brother, gif thow be wyse, I reid the fle
To matche the with ane thrawart fen yeit
   marrow.

(2918-25)

It is possible that the image of the painful arrow of de-ceit has as its source an *auctoritas* from the commentary tradition; in BL MS Add. 11897, the same image, drawn from Geoffrey of Vinsauf's *Poetria Nova,* appears in marginalia adjacent to the *moralitas* of Walter's fable. The line reads *"Gaufredus in Poetria: Sepe sagittantem didicit referire sagitta,"* a reference to line 201 of Geoffrey's work.[27] If Henryson had this mar-ginal gloss in mind, his warning against false friends tacitly includes its own warning to the liars them-selves.

After the three ballade stanzas the poet returns to the rhyme royal form and simultaneously signals the change from social figuration to spiritual allegory. The narra-tor's opening words here, referring to the diatribe against false friends, tell us a good deal about how fables were read in Henryson's day:

This hald in mynd; rycht more I sall the tell
Quhair by thir beistis may be figurate.

(2934-35)

Readers are meant to keep in mind both the social interpretation which the narrator has just conclud-ed, and the religious allegory which immediately fol-lows. Henryson expects us to balance these two forms of interpretation as we read, retaining both lessons as we should when studying the *Auctores octo* and MS Add. 11897 comments above. Henryson also could have borrowed from these commentators the idea that the narrator should make a self-conscious dec-laration that the type of figuration is about to change; as *"Fructus talis est"* prepares us for a different kind of allegorical exploration, so does Henryson's couplet.

Henryson translates the first of the comments' allego-rized animal roles as follows:

The paddok, vsand in the flude to duell,
Is mannis bodie, swymand air and late
In to this warld, with cairis implicate:
Now hie, now law, quhylis plungit vp,

quhylis doun,
Ay in perrell, and reddie for to droun.

(2936-40)

"Mannis body" is more directly indebted to the *Auc-tores octo* and MS Add. 11897 commentaries, which use the phrase *"corpus (cuiuslibet) hominis,"* than to *"caro humana"* in the *Esopus moralizatus.*

On the other hand, while the basic mouse/*anima* alle-gorization could have been taken from any of these sources, the concluding portion of this description seems to reflect the *Esopus:*

This lytill mous, heir knit thus be the schyn,
The saull of man betakin may in deid—
Bundin, and fra the bodie may not twyn,
Quhill cruell deth cum brek of lyfe the
   threid—
The quhilk to droun suld ever stand in
   dreid
Of carnall lust be the suggestioun,
Quhilk drawis ay the saull and druggis doun.

(2948-54)

The final verses of this stanza are quite close to the sentence in the *Esopus moralizatus* which warns that the flesh strives to drag (*"trahere"*) the soul toward earthly things and carnal delights (*"carnales delecta-tiones"*).

While Henryson's allegorization of the water as the world is a logical extension of the roles for the mouse and the frog, it also bears a striking resemblance to the description in BL MS Add. 11897:

The watter is the warld, ay welterand
With mony wall of tribulatioun,
In quhilk the saull and bodye wer steirrand,
Standand distinyt in thair opinioun:
The spreit vpwart, the body precis doun;
The saull rycht fane wald be brocht ouer, I
   wis,
Out of this warld into the heuinnis blis.

(2954-60)

In both the poem and the manuscript comment the water is described with a present participle denoting motion (*"fluctuans"* and "welterand") associated with the trou-bles which the soul will find therein (*"deliciis et occupacionibus variis"* and "tribulations"), and both morals mention that the mouse/soul wants to cross the water in order to reach the heavenly king-dom (*"hereditatem celestibus"* and "heuinnis blis"), an idea which in both texts exists independently of any directly stated allegorical correlation between the opposite bank and heaven.

Henryson's allegorization of the kite as death seems to be his own:

> The gled is deith, that cummis suddandlie
> As dois ane theif, and cuttis sone the battall:
> Be vigilant thairfoir and ay reddie,
> For mannis lyfe is brukill and ay mortall.

(2962-65)

Because of the change of roles for the kite, Henryson's fable is more hopeful than is his source; the body and soul are taken by death rather than chewed to pieces by the devil, and the poet leaves the destiny of the soul to the imagination of the reader.[28]

Fidus, "albeit they live under a Prince, they have their privilege, and as great liberties as strait lawes":

> They call a Parliament, wherein they consult for lawes, statutes, penalties, chusing offices, and creating their King, not by affection, but reason: not by the greatest part, but by the better. And if such a one by chance bee chosen (for among men sometimes the worst speed best) as is bad, then is there such civil warre and dissension, that untill he be pluckt down, there can be no friendship.

(p. 45)

And as Fidus's first fable had developed the theory of *arcanaimperii* in a way that seems less pertinent to Elizabeth than to James I's style of government, or at least his pronouncements upon it, so the apologue of the beehive introduces into fabulous discourse the central terms of dispute between James and his parliaments—parliamentary privilege and the "great liberties" of consultation which were constantly invoked to balance royal prerogative. More surprising still, Lyly's fable actually invokes the threat of "civill warre and dissension" that James's son experienced. Lyly's example shows that even the most determined apologist might have difficulty in appropriating Aesopian tradition to the support of society's most powerful agents; but others would certainly try. In the next chapter we shall see just how prophetic *Euphues and His England* was, both of the real political developments, and of how fabulist traditions expanded to meet them.

Henryson works with the scholastic fable tradition in much the same way that modern scholars work with critical material: sometimes adopting it wholeheartedly with very few changes, at other times rejecting it entirely, but most often simply showing that the tradi-

tion has been understood and absorbed. Furthermore, the poet/schoolmaster must have felt comfortable enough with the structure and function of fable allegory (which he had probably taught many times) to detach it completely from fable and transfer it to beast-epic, as the same variety of approach characterizes the *moralitates* of the six fables excluded from this discussion.

As a collection, the *Morall Fabillis* contains textbook examples of what Rita Copeland has helpfully categorized as "primary translations" and "secondary translations":

> Primary translations . . . operate according to the terms of exegesis: they give prominence to an exegetical motive by claiming to serve and supplement a textual authority, but they actually work to challenge and appropriate that textual authority. Secondary translations, on the other hand, give precedence to rhetorical motives, defining themselves as independent productive acts: characteristically they supress any sign of exegetical service to a specific source, even though they produce themselves through such exegetical techniques.[29]

The primary translations in the collection are the four fables most clearly allied with scholastic exegesis: Henryson has cited the authoritative source for the fables but not the commentary, which he then covertly uses to appropriate much of the authority of the fables themselves. Of course Henryson cannot hide his source for "The Two Mice," "The Sheep and the Dog," and "The Wolf and the Lamb," but he treats them differently from the other Aesopic fables. This trio shows relations to scholastic commentary while allowing the poet to make full use of the topics and common places of fifteenth-century Scottish political and legal dialectic. Henryson employs some of the tools of exegesis in the fables' *moralitates,* but they are serving his vision of society rather than the source text.

III

In sum, it appears that Henryson's choices for the roles assigned to the characters of the Aesopic fables were largely but not entirely determined by what he had learned from the scholastic commentaries on Walter's fables. While his debt to this source extends to basic content in at least two fables, he owes even more to fable commentary for the form which some of his *moralitates* take, a form which he applies successfully to beast epic. That form is most clearly scholastic when it is most deeply allegorical, but like the scholastic commentators, Henryson employed a broad range of figurative and allegorical interpretations, some apparently his own, to make his collection richly multi-dimensional.

By explaining the elements of the *Morall Fabillis* which educated fifteenth- and sixteenth-century readers would have viewed as traditional but which we as modern readers find unsettling, we can begin to dispense with modern scholars' prejudices that Henryson was to some degree delighting in being perverse. Simultaneously we can begin to appreciate him both for preserving the variety inherent in the scholastic fable tradition and for embellishing it with a few new flourishes.

Notes

[1] This identification was made by nineteenth-century editor Léopold Hervieux in *Les Fabulistes Latins depuis le siècle d'Auguste jusqu'à la fin du moyen âge,* vol. 1 (Paris: Firmin Didot, 1893-99), 475-95; who cites a group of medieval manuscripts and incunables attributing the fables to Gualterus Anglicus. Hervieux goes on to identify this Gualterus as chaplain of Henry II of England. I am using this name not because I believe that Hervieux's identification is reliable enough to invite biographical speculation about the fables' author, but simply for the sake of convenience. The collection's other common name, the *Anonymus Neveleti,* is not based upon any medieval aspect of it, but rather, upon its appearance in the anthology *Mythologia Aesopica,* published in Frankfurt in 1610 by Isaac Nevelet.

[2] For lists of manuscripts, see Hervieux, I. 503-602; Klaus Grubmüller, *Meister Esopus* (Munich: Artemis, 1977), 82, n. 180; and Paul Oskar Kristeller, *Iter Italicum,* vols. 1-6 (Leiden: E. J. Brill, 1963-1991). Kristeller places this fable collection under the index heading "Aesop," where it can be identified by its incipit, *"Ut iuvet."*

[3] *Rhetoric, Hermeneutics, and Translation in the Middle Ages: Academic Traditions and Vernacular Texts* (Cambridge: Cambridge University Press, 1991), 103.

[4] Prisciani Caesariensis, *Opuscula,* vol. 1, ed. Marina Passalacqua(Rome: Edizioni di Storia e Letteratura, 1987), 33-34.

[5] In this article I will refer to the *Esopus moralizatus cum bono commento* printed in Cologne by Heinrich Quentell in 1492, and to the *Auctores octo* published by Jehan de Vingle in Lyon in 1495. Since neither book is paginated, I will cite passages according to the number of the fable in which they appear.

[6] Hervieux, I. 602-35. Deriding the fable commentaries as "puerile," Hervieux does not consistently indicate which commentaries appear in the editions that he lists.

[7] See, for example, James Kinsley, *Scottish Poetry* (London: Cassell, 1955); David Murtaugh, "Henryson's Animals," *TSLL* 14 (1972): 408-9; and H. Harvey Wood, *Two Scots Chaucerians* (London: Longman, 1967), 17.

[8] *ELH* 29 (1962): 337-56.

[9] All quotations of Henryson's work, cited by line number, are taken from *The Poems of Robert Henryson,* ed. Denton Fox (Oxford: Clarendon Press, 1981).

[10] See, for example, Augustine's *Contra Mendacium* (469-528 in *Corpus Scriptorum Ecclesiasticorum Latinorum,* vol. 41; Leipzig: Freytag, 1900), 508-9; Macrobius, *Commentary on the Dream of Scipio,* trans. William Harris Stahl (Columbia: Columbia University Press, 1952), I.ii.9.

[11] For a description of the categories used in this type of prologue, see A. J. Minnis, *Medieval Theory of Authorship,* 2nd ed. (Philadelphia: University of Pennsylvania Press, 1988), 28-29.

[12] Hervieux, II.316.

[13] See Fox's discussion of the term's scholastic usage in his edition of Henryson's poems (xv).

[14] *The Latin Element in the Vocabulary of the Earlier Makars Henryson and Dunbar,* Lund Studies in English 51 (Lund: Gleerup, 1977), 57.

[15]

> Iaspidis esse decem species septemque
>   feruntur
> Hic et multorum cognoscitur esse colorem
> Et multi nasci perhibetur partibus orbis.
> Optimus et viridi translucentique colore,
> Et qui plus soleat virtutus habere probatur.
> Caste portatus fugat et febres et hydropem
> Appositque iuvat mulierem parturientem,
> Et tutamen portanti creditur esse.
> Nam consecratus gratum facit, atque potentem.
> Et sicut perhibent, phantasmata noxia pellit
> Cuius in argento vis fortior esse putatur.
>   (n.p.)(*De Gemmis Scriptum Evacis Regis
>   Arabum* [Lubeck: H. Rantzovius, 1575]).

[16] *The Minor Poems of John Lydgate,* ed. Henry Noble McCracken, *EETS* o.s. 192 (London: 1934), 571-72.

[17] "Nota quod jaspis dicitur quasi 'iacens inter aspides vel in fronte aspidis,' vel dicitur ab 'yos' grece, quod est viride latine, quia est viridi coloris."

[18] In his article, "Chaucer's Influence on Henryson's Fables: The Use of Proverbs and Sententiae" (*MÆ* 39: 20-27), Donald McDonald cites Chaucer as the source for Henryson's repeated use of proverbial *auctoritates* such as this reference to Solomon, but it seems equally possible that Henryson, at least in this work, picked up the technique from scholastic commentary.

[19] In the *Esopus moralizatus,* these roles appear in Fables II, V, VIII, XIII, and XIV.

20 For other examples of direct address used by characters in *moralitates,* see Fables XVIII, XXII, XXXII, XXXIV, XXXVIII, XLI, and LXI in the *Auctores octo.* In these examples, it is not the fable character but rather the figurative or allegorical representative who speaks, generally paraphrasing something which the fable character has said. While these examples do not represent exactly the technique employed by Henryson, they show the manner in which commentators made the division between fable character and its figurative or allegorical cognate less distinct.

21 In Ulrich Broich, ed. *Functions of Literature: Essays Presented to Erwin Wolff on his Sixtieth Birthday* (Munich: Niemeyer, 1984), 81-99.

22 *Medieval to Renaissance in English Poetry* (Cambridge: Cambridge University Press, 1985), 195-99.

23 Some of these manuscripts are as follows: Augsburg, Universitätsbibliothek MS II.1.4°.27; Basel, Universitätsbibliothek MS F.IV.50; Berlin, Staatsbibliothek Preussischer Kulturbesitz MSS Lat. Qu. 18 and Lat. Qu. 382; Freiburg, Universitätsbibliothek MS 21; Halle, Universitäts- und Landesbibliothek Sachsen-Anhalt MS Stolb.-Wern. Za 64; Leipzig, Universitätsbibliothek MS 1084; Mainz, Stadtbibliothek 540; Milan, Biblioteca Ambrosiana MS Trotti 161;Munich, Bayerische Staatsbibliothek Clm 609, 7680, 14529, 14703, 16213, 19667, 22404; Stuttgart, Würtembergische Landesbibliothek MSS HB XII.4 and HB I.127; Treviso, Biblioteca Comunale MS 156; Trier, Stadtbibliothek MSS 132, 756, and 1109; Wolfenbüttel, Herzog August Bibliothek MS 185 Helmst.; Wroçlaw, Biblioteka Uniwersytecka MSS II.Q.33, IV.Q.4, IV.Q.81, IV.Q.88.

Having seen only about 100 of the 160 extant manuscripts of the Latin fables, I assume that this allegory for the fable appears in other manuscripts as well.

24 See B. G. Koonce, "Satan the Fowler," *MS* 21 (1959): 176-84.

25 This phrase appears in Psalm 7:16, part of a passage referring to God's punishment of a wicked man:

15. Behold, he hath been in labour with injustice; he hath conceived sorrow, and brought forth iniquity.

16. He hath opened a pit and dug it: and he is fallen into the hole [*incidit in foveam*] he made.

17. His sorrow shall be turned on his own head: and his iniquity shall come down upon his crown. (Douay-Rheims)

26 In his brief exploration of the similarities between scholastic commentaries and Henryson's fables, Douglas Gray also makes this point (127).

The same allegory, though not always the same two-fold interpretation, is reproduced in all but three of the manuscripts listed in note 23; those lacking the allegory are Augsburg Universitätsbibliothek MS II.1.4°.27, Munich Bayerische Staatsbibliothek Clm 22404, and Stuttgart Würtembergische Landesbibliothek MS HB XII.4.

27 Of course the similarity of this imagery may be entirely coincidental, since each of these stanzas features a rhyme-word at the conclusion of the sixth line which anticipates "marrow"; Henryson also uses "barrow" and "tarrow." Even though he could certainly have arrived at the use of this word without external influence, the numerous similarities of the *Morall Fabillis* to BL MS Add. 11897 make this coincidence worth a passing mention.

28 Ian W. A. Jamieson, in his dissertation, "The Poetry of Robert Henryson: A Study of the Use of Source Material" (University of Edinburgh, 1964), notes the similarity between Henryson's *moralitas* and that given for the same fable in the MS 141, No. 328 of the Municipal Library of Bern (qtd. in Henryson 325, n.1). The fabulist responsible for this collection, which Hervieux called the "Bern Romulus," wrote after his very brief version of the fable, *"Sic maiores et minores inter se disceptantes. Sic etiam dyabolus animamet corpus dissipat"* (Hervieux, II.738). Jamieson could not explain the relationship between this fifteenth-century manuscript, of which only one copy is extant, and Henryson's *Morall Fabillis,* but a similar branch of fable commentary doubtless explains the resemblance.

29 *Rhetoric, Hermeneutics, and Translation in the Middle Ages,* 177.

Jayne Elizabeth Lewis (essay date 1996)

SOURCE: "Aesopian Examples: The English Fable Collection and its Authors, 1651-1740," in *The English Fable: Aesop and Literary Culture, 1651-1740,* pp. 14-47. Cambridge: Cambridge University Press, 1996.

[*In the following excerpt, Lewis examines the ways in which British writers such as John Ogilby and Samuel Richardson either modified Aesop's fables or alluded to them in their own writing in order to reflect the political instability that occurred in the country during the late-seventeenth to mid-eighteenth centuries.*]

Prevailing Tales: The Major Collections

More than one European country adopted fables into a native literary tradition during the late seventeenth and eighteenth centuries, and the major fable collections produced in England between 1651 and 1740 are no exception. Despite their differences from one another, they are very uniquely and deliberately English, and together they consitute a figural response, often self-consciously organized within the English language, to England's notoriously unstable political history and the crisis of signification that that history wrought.[23] Ogilby's own *Fables* "englished" the fable collection partly by incorporating political slang left over from the wars. Often posing as translators or teachers of written English, later fabulists consistently situated themselves amid the different competitions that characterized not only England's political experience between the Civil Wars and the death of Walpole but also its emerging literary marketplace and commercial culture generally.[24] In their very diversity, the fable collections reflected the demands and desires that vied in the world around them. They ranged in price from a penny to several pounds, and in size from a "Pocket Manual" to that of "a Folio more than double that Bulk."[25] Their authors could be as obscure as an anonymous Grub Street hack or as eminent as John Locke. Likewise, their illustrators could be unknowns or celebrated artists like Francis Barlow, their readers barely literate children or aged and illustrious poets. The object of a fable collection could be to teach schoolboys how to read English, French, or Latin. But it could also be to preach proper conduct to young ladies or to arguefor a complex political perspective that might, in turn, be Whig or Tory, Williamite or Stuart.

It is fitting that Aesop's fables themselves tell tales of competition among individuals of radically different stripe. Set in a world where power is never balanced and self-interest decides value, their themes mirror the instability of the England in which they were put to use. After beginning with the story of the cock who digs up a precious gem, only to announce that he would have preferred a barleycorn, a typical collection went on to tell of a wolf with a craving for mutton who accuses a lamb of sullying his drinking water and then devours him. A jay strutting in peacock's feathers is plucked apart for her pretensions. A frog explodes when she tries to puff herself up to the size of an ox. A wolf hires a stork to fish the lamb bones out of his throat and, when she demands remuneration, reminds her that his sparing her head should be compensation enough. A fox trapped in a well persuades the goat stuck with him to offer his head for a step ladder; gaining freedom, the fox leaves the goat to perish, jeering over his shoulder that his ex-partner has not "half so much Brains as you have Beard."[26] Since Aesop's plots uncover craft and machination in the service of brutal desire, the morals attached to them were usually cynical and pragmatic: "A Wise Man [. . .] leaves Nothing to Chance more than he needs must." "In a Wallowing Qualm, a Man's Heart and Resolution fail him, for want of Fit Matter to Work upon." "Perfidious people are naturally to be suspected in reports that favour their own interest."[27]

Skeptical and combative though their themes and morals might be, however, Augustan fable collections also practiced a strikingly conciliatory figural method. Structurally they employed a "Method of recommending [. . .] Principles by pleasing Images."[28] Practically, fables provided primary reading material to most English grammar schools, thereby supplying a reservoir of shared figures to several otherwise divided generations of readers and writers. In other words, Augustan fable collections struck a delicate balance between a mode of representation so simple and sensible as to seem unmediated—almost non-linguistic—and the admission that all authoritative signs can be appropriated, manipulated, and inverted. A less than flattering view of the human reader prompted Ogilby's own commitment to this delicate equipoise. His famous epigraph maintains that fables' primary task is to "make Men lesser Beasts," to offer precepts "Men" can agree upon and that can forestall reversion to what we may fairly call a state of nature. Ironically, it is only by commissioning the sensible, familiar, but also belligerent elements of that state that fabulists may forestall such reversions, for only these elements are deemed genuinely and universally impressive.

It is not surprising then that Ogilby's first Aesopian quarto should have appeared in the same year as Thomas Hobbes's *Leviathan* (1651). Hobbes found the germ of cultural stability in a *rapprochement* between human signifying practice and the state of nature. He argued that "Man"'s native penchant for conflict can be averted only when "Men" craft a consensual sign system. Thus a brutal and divisive "Nature" composes itself into the "Artificial Animal" of social order. What holds this prodigious beast together are symbolic tokens which its members have agreed to exchange. Hobbes allowed these tokens to be words themselves, as long as they remain grounded in the shared sensible world, and as long as those who use them consent to do so in the same way.[29] As Ogilby's epigraph makes clear, fables (particularly when "adorn'd" with impressive "Sculptures") are perfect candidates to become such tokens. And the persuasive image of Hobbes's own Leviathan predictably bears more than a passing resemblance to the beasts in Aesop's menagerie.

But Hobbesian theory also promises that clashing appetites will continue to drive, and divert, the traffic of signs. Especially when viewed in light of its metamorphoses over the 1650s and 1660s, Ogilby's fable collection acts out this promise and the paradox that attends it. In the first edition of *Fables,* the former dancing master, theater manager, and Royalist soldier offered Cromwellian London eighty-one "Tale[s] adorn'd with Sculpture." Alluding to the recent wars, he guaranteed that any one of these "Tale[s]" could "make Men lesser Beasts." Laudatory poems by James Shirley and William Davenant praised Ogilby's "humble Moralls" for their ability both to "convince the subtile, and the Simple gaine." In Davenant's far from un-shared view, Ogilby's fables "invade[d]" their reader's "will" not with "force" but rather with homely imagery to which all and sundry are naturally amenable.[30]

Despite the high aroma of conciliation emanating from *Fables,* however, Davenant sent his verses "from the Tower," and Ogilby pointedly dedicated the volume to the royalist Heneage Finch. As both Annabel Patterson and Mary Pritchard have shown, individual fables were fraught with royalist dogma. The Aesopian canon al-ready housed simple stories about amphibian monar-chies, ingenuous trees that lend woodsman wood for their axe handles, and foxes that grow so accustomed to the sight of "the Scepter'd *Lion*" that the latter loses all power to awe, hence rule. In Ogilby's hands, such narratives became intricate political allegories, some critically sympathetic to the royalist cause, others hos-tile to the government that had supplanted it.[31] To com-plete the picture, ominous images of decapitation haunt Francis Cleyn's "Sculptures." Such gestures undercut the fables' superficial pursuit of the peaceable author-ity of the naturalized and textualized example by con-spicuously, even violently, twisting the implications of individual signs.

Just so, in 1660, the fabulist himself was to be found designing "Ænigmaticall Emblems" for the triumphal arches at Charles II's coronation. He went on to be-come Master of the Royal Imprimerie and, at the end of the decade, Cosmographer Royal, in which capacity he devised elaborate atlases of the world's continents as well as road maps of England that instituted the statute mile. Ogilby took easily to a position of cultur-al authority, and his Aesop just as effortlessly traveled with him from the margins to the mainstream of sev-enteenth-century literary culture. The contemporary value of Ogilby's fables, in other words, was not re-stricted to the political critique they mounted. Rather, equally viable in two very different Englands, they offered literary figures that acknowledged the faction-al, and fictional, nature of all meaningful signs even as they continued to identify themselves with a natural world whose preceptive authority few wished to deny. Ogilby's fables thus confirmed the vision of effica-cious symbolic order set forth in *Leviathan.* Unlike Hobbes's treatise, however, Ogilby's fables and others like them proved structurally equipped to comment on the ironic juxtaposition of two axes of signification, one combative and motivated, the other busy minting a new symbolic currency that could create cultural coherence.

For example, when Bernard Mandeville applied Hobbes's argument to a modern commercial society, he naturally did so in the form of a fable. It is even a lion who, in one of the footnotes to *The Fable of the Bees* (first complete edition, 1729), remarks that, in suc-cessful human societies, "Millions [. . .] well-join'd

together [. . .] compose the strong *Leviathan.*"[32] Mandeville's fable earmarks "private Vices" as the predicates of "publick Benefits," injustice and dis-proportionate lack as prerequisites of cultural order. Fabulists like Ogilby had already made this paradox a feature of signification itself. Ogilby's headstrong, truculent animals often comment ironically on their own absorption into a stable and transmissible symbol-ic system: "Here I the Emblem of fond Mortals sit, / That lose the Substance for an empty Bit," one dog mourns, after he has dropped a shoulder of mutton by snapping at its reflection. The dog's own words reveal what made him a significant object. He is thus a con-vincing reminder not only of the follies of unbridled desire ("an Emblem of fond Mortals") but also of the greed and guile that turn meaningless "Substance" into meaningful sign.[33]

Throughout all of Ogilby's collections, fables like "The Dog and the Shadow" meld sensible images ("Sculp-tures") with linguistic structures ("Tales") that docu-ment those images' progress toward the status of mem-orable and authoritative signs. A similar desire to de-mystify the act of attaching moral and political signif-icance to phenomenal signs apparently motivated the other major collection of the Restoration period, the celebrated artist Francis Barlow's *Æsop's Fables with his Life.* While English readers identified Ogilby's Aesop with its writer, they associated Barlow's equally sumptuous and oft-reprinted volume with its illustra-tor.[34] For a first edition of 1666, however, Barlow com-missioned the text of the fables (in English, French, and Latin) from one Thomas Philipott. Then for a new edition of 1687 he invited the "ingenious" playwright, poet, and romance writer Aphra Behn to "perform the English Poetry."[35] Behn obliged and the resulting col-lection flourished well into the eighteenth century.

In his dedication to the Earl of Devonshire, Barlow claimed aspecial symbolic status for "his" fables—"a thing," he declared, "much practis'd by the Ancient *Greeks* and the *Orientals*" who used them as "Portrai-tures in their Temples, design'd as Memorial Charac-ters of Philosophic Notions to be the Subject of Ado-ration." In place of these antique idols, Barlow osten-tatiously offers his own modern English readers a "Book, ascrib'd to Esop in a Plain and Simple Form." As the "Plain and Simple" book supplants the arcane icons of the past, it openly confesses its own political and historical contingency; equally transparent are its fictive strategies for recommending "the conduct of Life." After all, Barlow points out, "'tis the Misfortune of Mankind, that the present Times as little dare to relate Truths, as the Future can know them." Obvious-ly fictional and factional, Barlow's carefully fused "Ornaments of Sculptures and Poetry" further Ogil-by's quest for a symbolic form that might wed a pic-ture's immediate impact to language's power of skep-tical exposition.

Each a quatrain with a moralizing couplet tacked onto it, Behn's fables deftly "perform[ed]" the Aesopian premises that Barlow's dedication had sketched. Behn feminized a number of Aesop's fables, somewhat improbably turning the "kingly Eagle" who steals a young fox into a female, along with the kid whom a wolf woos away from its mother. A female ape begs in vain for an inch of a fox's tail to "vaile" her "bum" and the fable of the dog in the manger is moralized as a story about how "aged Lovers" who court "young Beautys [. . .] / Keepe off those joys they want the power to give" (p. 59). Behn's verses not only bent fables with the crowbar of witty feminism she had perfected in the Restoration theater; writing in the last days of the Stuart monarchy, which she supported, Behn also included barely oblique references to the Stuart predicament. To the brief chronicle of a family of adders whom "the Porcupines deceiv'd / Of their warme Nest which cou'd not be retriev'd," for example, she appended the observation that "Crownes got by force are often times made good, / By the more rough designes of warr, and blood" (p. 81). Other fables, like that of the mouse who saves a lion from a snare by gnawing through the ropes, caution their readers not to "despise the service of a Slave" since "an Oak did once our glorious Monarch save" (p. 47). More than veiled political commentary, Behn's fables fulfilled Barlow's dedicatory promise that the "Plain and Simple Form" of the Aesopian example ought to convey the impossibility of "relat[ing] Truths." Because each fable also appeared in French and Latin versions that were unmolested by tendentious reference, Behn's "Plain and Simple" English verses all the more plainly displayed their own distortions. And since these same verses were printed as captions to Barlow's illustrations, throughout the collection visual images were virtually soldered to tendentious English words. The resulting figures effectively ironized—even parodied—the very notion of an indisputable emblem.

The revised edition of Barlow's collection appeared just before James II's abdication and the accession of William and Mary. The next fifteen years saw a fresh flurry of Aesopian activity, particularly by writers who, like Behn, sympathized with the lost Stuart cause. The simplest explanation for the rash of fable collections during the Williamite period is that fables' seemingly innocent preoccupation with animal affairs made them safe, while yet exceptionally convincing, ways to resist the prevailing political tide. While many fables were written from the ruling side, this explanation can begin to account for the most copious, notorious, and widely read fable collection of the 1690s, Roger L'Estrange's immense *Fables of Æsop and Other Eminent Mythologists* (1692 and 1699).

By his own confession, L'Estrange was already "on the wrong Side of Fourscore" when he published the first edition of his *Eminent Mythologists*.[36] A Cavalier who had prudently spent the middle of the seventeenth century abroad, he became a prolific propagandist for the Stuarts after the Restoration, publishing a blizzard of pamphlets and two newspapers that, along with his watchdog post as Surveyor of the Press and Chief Licenser, presciently earned him the Aesopian nickname "Towzer."[37] Throughout the reigns of the last Stuart kings, L'Estrange's jobs as censor and propandist put him in exactly the spot where old (centripetal) images of sovereign right met the new (centrifugal) cultural authority of the printing press. Predictably, his Stuart and Roman Catholic sympathies ousted him from this influential position in 1688. No less enterprising than Ogilby, L'Estrange thereupon launched a remarkably successful career translating Seneca, Tacitus, and Terence, as well as select modern texts in French and Spanish. *Eminent Mythologists* belongs to this paradoxical period of political dis-enfranchisement and swelling belletristic prestige. Officially L'Estrange's collection is also a translation, of Aesop and a number of "Other Eminent Mythologists," ancient and modern.[38] The identities of these other mythologists merge into that of Aesop, whose portrait and biography, as in Barlow's *Fables,* are an integral part of the collection. L'Estrange's own likeness—flowing Cavalier ringlets, canine bone structure and all—appears at the beginning of the volume, so that readers so inclined could also identify the motley and gargantuan collection with a single English author.

Rendered in a pithy and colloquial prose with morals and long "Reflexions" that offered a clandestine protest against the constitutional structure of the new political order,[39] L'Estrange's versions of Aesop's fables looked and sounded quite unlike Ogilby's intricate verses, or even Behn's quipping quatrains. Nor were L'Estrange's fables illustrated, though his preface described them as "Precepts in Emblem," as "Emblem[s] and Figure[s]," even as "Images of Things."[40] However, it is this very assumption that graphic signs—the words that communicate the fable, in conjunction with the words that moralized and reflected on it—can persuade as powerfully as images do that placed *Eminent Mythologists* in line with its recent English predecessors. As was the case with earlier Aesops, L'Estrange's collection was more than Jacobite propaganda tucked under "the Vaile of *Emblem,* and *Figure.*"[41] Like them, it mixes political reaction with an almost obsessive attention to the sensible and potentially mediatory properties of the printed page.

Whereas Ogilby and Barlow had dedicated their work to notable aristocrats, L'Estrange officially intended his collection to be used in English classrooms, where it might instill a proper sense of the English language. His long and lively preface scorns the "Book" of Aesop's fables as he maintained it had been "universally

Read, and Taught in All our Schools" (sig. B4r). For too long, L'Estrange claimed, Aesop's fables had languished in the form of empty "Rhapsody," foaming with "Insipid *Twittle-Twattles,* Frothy *Jests,* and Jingling *Witticisms.*" The English language had languished right along with them, for, rife with nonsensical word games, the old Aesops had taught children to read "as we teach *Pyes* and *Parrots,* that pronounce the Words without so much as Guessing at the Meaning of them; Or to take it Another Way, the Boys Break their Teeth upon the Shells, without ever coming near the Kernel" (sig. B2r).[42]

Although his pedagogical approach makes L'Estrange a different breed of author from Ogilby or Barlow, or Behn, he shared their conviction that modern fables could coax signs away from obscurity and excessive figurality into a more durable and trustworthy symbolic register. As his contempt for "pronounc[ing]" suggests, that register is implicitly textual. L'Estrange even maintained that fables affect their readers as sense experience does, impressing reading minds as writing might a page: "Children are but *Blank Paper,* ready Indifferently for any Impression, Good or Bad, and it is much in the Power of the first Comer, to Write Saint, or Devil upon't, which of the two he pleases" (sig. A2v). As primary reading material, fables openly wielded "the Power of the first Comer." Like Ogilby's preceptive examples and Barlow's "Ornaments of Sculptures and Poetry," L'Estrange's fables capitalize on the materiality of the text, transferring to self-revealing graphic signs more and more of the powerful immediacy that iconic signs had once possessed. It seems unlikely that L'Estrange really expected his fables to be used in "the Schools." Instead, his speculations about how printed fables viscerally impress young readers build a trope for Aesopian authority. This trope in turn openly acknowledges the pages of the fable collection to be a proper arena of political activity. Once that activity is conceded to be a matter of making meaning, the physical body of the fable collection can be seen to participate in its moral, political, and thematic mission.

Though eighteenth-century readers complained about its raunchy and colloquial style, its Jacobite morals, even L'Estrange's fondness for the contractions and abbreviations that made it speak almost *too* current an English, *Eminent Mythologists* remained the most popular collection in the nation for the next thirty years.[43] Other Aesops came and went without attracting half the notice that it did. None was more often abridged, revised, and discussed. But in 1722 the Whig clergyman Samuel Croxall decided that the time was ripe for a new collection of Aesop's fables. He proceeded to devise one whose political sensibilities aggressively countered and ultimately deposed L'Estrange's "eminent mythologists," with new editions proliferating well into the twentieth century.

Writing in the self-congratulatory pseudo-stability of early Georgian England, Croxall touted his *Fables of Æsop and Others* as a patriotic antidote to L'Estrange's *Eminent Mythologists.* His dedicatee was the five-year-old Baron Halifax, whom Croxall depicted as an English political hero in the making, already precociously adept in the "English Tongue" and "by Birth intitled to a Share in the Administration of the Government."[44] Croxall filched L'Estrange's trope of the Aesopically influenced English reader in order to promote his own *Fables* as a book with consequences for the nation: In theory, if Halifax ingested its contents early, then later the "Country [would] feel the Benefit of these Lectures of Morality" (sig. A5r). Thus would Croxall's Aesop personally advance "the Peace and Prosperity of my Country" (sig. A6v). Superficially, this approving image of a peaceful and prosperous Britain set Croxall against the confirmed malcontent L'Estrange, whom Croxall claimed had twisted the fables so as to exaggerate "Party Animosities" and "factious Division." It was in order to endorse and replicate the "liberal" politics of Hanoverian Britain that Croxall resolved to detoxify L'Estrange's "pernicious . . . Principles, coin'd and suited to promote the Growth, and serve the Ends of Popery and Arbitrary Power" (sig. B5v). His acrid preface parrots L'Estrange's diatribe against earlier collections to express contempt for the "Insufficiency of *L'Estrange'*s own Performance." In Croxall's book, this frightful "Insufficiency" went beyond objectionable political views to encompass the "insipid and flat" morals and "course and uncouth [. . .] Style and Diction" that, like those views, had diverted Aesop's fables from the "Purpose for which they were principally intended" (sigs. B4v-r). Insisting that this "Purpose" was to argue against political absolutism, Croxall revised L'Estrange's fables so that they would better suit the "Children of *Britain,*" who are "born with free Blood in their Veins; and suck in Liberty with their very Milk" (sig. B5r).

It is not hard to catch the ironic resemblance between Croxall's conception of what a fable collection should be and that of his loathed predecessor. Like L'Estrange, Croxall implied that the future of England's linguistic and political integrity depended on the proper transmission of Aesop's fables to a new generation of English readers. To this end, he too stressed the material ties that bind the Aesopian text to the phenomenal world that it depicts. Thus one of Croxall's most strident criticisms of L'Estrange's stupendous folio was that it was physically inadequate to the task of impressing the appropriate "Morality" on the "blank Paper" of its reader's mind. L'Estrange, Croxall charged, had "swell'd [the collection] to so voluminous a Bulk, . . . I don't see how it can suit the Hand or Pocket, of the Generality of Children" (sig. B8v). L'Estrange's "noxious Principles" were inseparable from his "Prolixity." As cumbersome textual matter, his fables embodied their author's unpalatable political designs. Nonetheless, this very materiality became the condition of Croxall's own opposition to L'Estrange. It permitted him to point the fables plausibly in new directions and thus it demonstrated not simply the reassuring substantiality of written signs but also how easily they can be stolen and deformed. For example, Croxall took L'Estrange's version of "A Lyon and a Man," literally inverted its title to "The Forrester and the Lion," and applied its moral directly to writing, noting tersely that "contending Parties are very likely to appeal the Truth to Records written by their own Side."[45]

As Richardson would observe, the "depreciating of *Lestrange's* Work seems to be the Corner-Stone of [Croxall's] own Building."[46] From an Aesopian perspective, this "depreciating" is both a natural action and a textual strategy; it is equally constructive and destructive. To show L'Estrange's unjust "Manner of drawing his Reflections," for instance, Croxall cited Old Towzer's version of the fable of a dog who describes his life of leisure to a wolf. In the fable, the wolf is nearly persuaded to join the dog on the other side of the fence—until he notices the marks that the dog's collar has worn into his fur. The wolf interprets these marks as badges of servitude and flees. In L'Estrange's view, the moral of the fable was that freedom of mind is preferable to mental bondage. Croxall disagreed, seeing such a conclusion as a debased apology for political oppression. Rather than simply shift the moral, however, Croxall turned the fable itself into a vivid example of L'Estrange's willingness to "perver[t . . .] Sense and Meaning" (sig. B6r). Croxall himself becomes the wolfish reader who easily sees through the dog L'Estrange's "long, tedious, amusing Reflection, without one Word to the Purpose." The "Reflection" is, in Croxall's eyes, a flagitious attempt to "justify Slavery":

> He tells us at last *that the Freedom which Æesop is so tender of here, is to be understood as the Freedom of the Mind.* Nobody ever understood it so . . . If the Wolf was sensible how sweet the Freedom of the Mind was, and had concern for the liberty of his person, he might have ventur'd to have gone with the Dog well enough: But then he would have sav'd *L'Estrange* the spoiling of one of the best Fables of the whole Collection. However, this may serve for a Pattern of that Gentleman's Candour and Ingenuity in the Manner of drawing his Reflections.

(sig. B7v)

For Croxall—as ironically for the Stuart-sympathizing fabulists of the last century—fables embody not only morals but also "Manner[s] of drawing [. . .] Reflections." They translate often contentious literary relations into a sensible "Pattern." That pattern accommodates the new author himself, and it in turn becomes an integral part of the story a fable tells. Indeed, it makes possible the fable's replication across parties and generations, creating a coherence within conflict—authorial integrity within a dispute about authority—that neither Croxall nor L'Estrange acknowledge directly.

In 1739, however, Samuel Richardson did acknowledge it. As Margaret Anne Doody suggests, the London printer's interest in Aesop, resulting in his popular *Æsop's Fables,* may betray a nascent sympathy to the Jacobite cause.[47] Certainly, it was L'Estrange, not Croxall, whose text Richardson finally decided to abridge and illustrate. In any event, Richardson was no mean entrepreneur, and he quite unapologetically aimed to mold his readers' morals. He thus naturally wanted to make the fables in this new collection as physically impressive as possible. Just as Ogilby had found Aesop's fables the kind of graphic "Examples" that may best "prevaile" over their readers, just as L'Estrange deemed them the most persistent of the primary characters that one could hope to engrave on children's brains, and just as Croxall pronounced them as digestible as the "Milk of Liberty," so Richardson, "sensible of the alluring Force which Cuts or Pictures, suited to the respective Subjects, have on the Minds of Children," took care to include "in a quite new Manner, engraved on Copper-Plates, at no small Expence, the Subject of every Fable." Illustrations would further "excite [readers'] Curiosity, and stimulate their Attention, [. . .] especially as [they] are distinctly referred both to Page and Fable in every Representation" (p. xi).

But if the physical properties of the page promised to forge a happy coherence among author, reader, signifier, and signified, the fabulist still had to account for the split political personality of the English fable collection, as exemplified in the glaring discrepancies between Croxall's *Fables* and those of L'Estrange. Richardson's preface scrupulously weighs the relative merits of "the Knight" (L'Estrange) and the "Worthy Gentleman" (Croxall), and finds that the latter "has strained the natural Import of some of the Fables near as much one way, as Sir Roger has done the other" (p. viii). For Richardson, however, such "strain[ing]" may be explained as a consequence of historical accident, and he specifically defended L'Estrange by reasoning that, "were the Time in which he wrote considered, the Civil Wars so lately concluded in his View, and the Anarchy introduced by them, it is the less wonder that one Extreme produced another in the opposite Party, in its Turn" (p. vi).

As he conceded authorial vulnerability to historical and political circumstance, Richardson *de facto* admitted those same circumstances as key features of every figure. His own collection could yield "better-adapted and more forcible Morals' precisely because in both preface and in practice it recognized that signs acquire meaning in a contentious and reversible world. Richardson thus had no trouble imagining Croxall and L'Estrange in reversed positions: "Had [the former] lived when Sir *Roger* did, he might have been the *Lestrange* of the one *Court;* as *Lestrange,* had he been in his place, mighthave taken Orders and become *Chaplain* in the other" (p. ix). The two authors could have cancelled each other out; instead, they demonstrate the same provisional model of symbolic authority.

What made the fables in the English collection contestable was also what made them durable, reproducible, and effective—their "natural Import," their tendency to reduce complex symbolic systems into discrete, concrete, historically responsive terms whose maneuvers could be monitored and whose origins could be investigated. As he strove to reconcile Croxall and L'Estrange in the "natural" space of his own text, Richardson perforce conceded that an individual figure's "natural Import" is never entirely separable from its use, and therefore that symbolic authority survives only through its conscious alienation. This is in many ways the moral of the two epistolary novels that Richardson published in the 1740s, and it is no accident that the letter writers in both *Pamela* (1740) and *Clarissa* (1747-1748) make liberal use of Aesop's fables. In the fifth edition of *Pamela,* an advertisement for Richardson's *Fables* even slyly footnoted Pamela's allusion to "the grasshopper in the fable, which I have read of in my lady's books."[48] The links between Richardson's novels (which looked toward the future of English fiction) and his fables (which mark the end of the Aesopian period as I have described it) are not only literal ones. First, Richardson's work has never been known for its tropological richness. On the contrary, he disavowed all sympathy with his most metaphorically accomplished character, Lovelace, whose narcissistic but self-immolating enthusiasm for convoluted imagery brands him a libertine. Aesop's fables, on the other hand, supply Richardson's correspondents with images so natural, so shareable, and so carefully and conspicuously invested with meaning that they seem to avoid the predatory centerlessness of Lovelacean figuration.

Furthermore, in both *Pamela* and *Clarissa* the most meaningful signs are the words that make up individual letters—minute textual particulars burdened with the task of representing their authors to a world of jealous and acquisitive readers. Both of Richardson's besieged heroines are anxious because they recognize that these graphic signs are continuous with their own bodies and minds—with "Virtue" in Pamela's case, and with moral and spiritual integrity in Clarissa's. For the same reason, both heroines understand, and experience, interpretation (readers' assignment of morals and meanings) as violence. As Terry Castle and other feminist readers of Richardson have shown, this is what makes the symbolic texture of *Clarissa* in particular so very agonized and agonizing.[49] English fabulists from Ogilby forward, though, had sculpted Aesop's fables into concrete textual figures that demonstrated these very trepidations and thereby stood a chance of weathering them.[50] In Richardson's novels, these same fables thus naturally supply a symbolic currency common even to characters as antagonistic as Lovelace and Clarissa. More important, they work almost as forcibly as sensible impressions to control and limit a letter writer's meaning, without denying the fragility of all claims to symbolic mastery.

Pamela offers an especially clear case in point. Because Richardson's laboring-class heroine cribs her fables from her dead mistress's library, Aesop demonstrably mediates between the aristocratic Lady B—and her nominal servant Pamela. And as Pamela claims to have consulted "a *book* of Fables" (p. 109)—not, for instance, the gossip of other household menials—fables' textual status supersedes even their conventional appeal to the natural world. Early in her one-sided correspondence with her parents, Pamela uses Aesop to figure her own deracinating upbringing by Lady B, an upbringing that, she claims, has made her "like the grasshopper in the fable." Pamela goes on to reproduce, *verbatim,* the tale of "a hungry grass-hopper (*as suppose it was poor me*)" who, "having sung out the whole season" of summer, come wintertime "beg[s] charity" of a colony of industrious ants (Pamela's reader-parents), only to be told to "dance in winter to the tunes you sung in summer" (p. 108).

Pamela applies the fable directly to herself: "So I shall make a fine figure with my singing and dancing, when I come home to you" (p. 108). The fable participates in Aesopian tradition not just because the author so ostentatiously adopts it as her own ("suppose [the grasshopper] was poor me") but also because in so doing she uses a piece of text, lifted from a different book, to foreground the process through which meaningful figures themselves are constructed. This in turn lets Pamela rearrange a conventional relationship between the figural and the literal. Pamela is literally as like Aesop's grasshopper as she can be, for she was taught exactly the arts—"singing and dancing"—that he perfected. But she uses the image of the grasshopper to project a personal future in which, returning to her parents' humble household, she wryly expects to "make a fine figure" as useless as the one the grasshopper cuts at the end of the story. The Aesopian example regulates a delicate exchange between the literal and the figural. It witnesses the transformation of the one into the other. This is why Pamela intuitively uses it to guide her parents' reading of her: It gives her authority over the self-portrait her letters compulsively paint. Significantly, in the long run Pamela manages to keep the most undesirable of future selves—the "figure" of the feckless servant girl ignominiously returned to her roots—from materializing. Seen from this perspective, Aesop's fable manages the ratio between the material and symbolic aspects of the author's own character.

In *Clarissa,* the stakes are higher, and Aesop's fables are accordingly much in evidence, in Lovelace's letters as well as in Clarissa's. Whereas Lovelace applies most of his fables to others, Clarissa shares Pamela's inclination to shield herself (or at least her social image) with Aesopian imagery.[51] For instance, when Lovelace pretends to propose to dress her in his sister's clothes and take her to meet his family, Clarissa declines by comparing herself to "the jay in the fable" (p. 456) who masqueraded inpeacock feathers only to be stripped of her borrowed finery by its rightful owners. Like Pamela, Clarissa uses the Aesopian figure to control the figural destiny of her own body in the social and symbolic space where her letters too acquire their meanings.

Aside from Clarissa's body, those letters are the most imperiled and material signs in Richardson's novel. It is thus appropriate that Clarissa's most memorable fable appears in the "odd letter," written after Lovelace rapes her, that she "throw[s . . .] in fragments under the table" (p. 889). The "fragments" offer their own graphic testimony to the state of their author's mind and body; the scribbled fable condenses this terrible equation of mind, body, and letter into a single figure. In the story, "a lady [who] took a great fancy to a young lion, or a bear, I forget which—but a bear, or a tiger" is "tor[n . . .] in pieces" when the animal "resume[s] its nature" and seeks to "satisfy its hungry maw" (p. 891). Clarissa moralizes this chilling tale by asking "who was most to blame, [. . . t]he brute, or the lady?" She concludes that it was "the lady, surely.—For what *she* did, was *out* of nature, *out* of character at least: what *it* did, was *in* its own nature" (p. 891). Although Clarissa casts herself as the lady in the fable in order to maintain a sense of agency—and supplies a moral for the same reason—the fable itself serves less to protect its teller's physical body than to confirm the yoked fragmentations of body, letter, and meaning in a way that later will protect her symbolic body—her reputation.

Clarissa's fable of the lady broken to bits by the beast she befriended has itself begun to break down: Was "the brute" a lion or a tiger or a bear? Was the lady's "great fancy" for the creature as unnatural as she wishes to believe? Because it refuses to answer these questions, yet remains an impressive image, the fable takes us to the apocalyptic edge of the history of Aesopian figuration in England, at least as it had been theorized and practiced in the major fable collections from Ogilby to Richardson. As Ogilby's exemplifications of Hobbesian sign theory had made apparent, fables themselves reveal brutal nature masquerading in social and even typographical character. Via his epistolary heroines—the authors in his own texts—Richardson smuggled fables' power of revelation out of the fable collection and into the English novel. But unlike the other fabulists we have seen, including Richardson himself, his female fabulists are utterly powerless. In their hands,

the talent for reactive mediation that had given the Aesopian example its cultural cachet was finally swallowed up by its capacity to demonstrate the violence that makes things mean.

Significant Miniatures: The Minor Collections

The fabulists we have met so far were only the most eminent Aesopians of their day. Along with their high visibility as "AUTHOR[S]" and the extraordinary longevity of their work, their self-consciousness as the sculptors of a new form of symbolic authority sets them apart from the droves of other fabulists whose collections inundated both the popular press and English classrooms between 1651 and 1740. Like their more illustrious counterparts, however, the "minor" collections made it clear that "things" do not "hold discourse" without some authorial hugger-mugger behind the scenes. At the same time, in order to impress their readers, these same collections relied on fables' well-publicized close kinship with natural signs to impress their readers. Particularly since many of them were designed for schools or for quick and easy consumption, the relatively obscure Aesops to which we now turn trained English readers to tolerate the resulting paradox, even to expect it. Both in their manner of ordering and moralizing their fables, and in their prefatory catalogues of fables' distinguishing traits, they thus paved the way for the more self-reflexive and complex collections we have been examining.

Among their distinguishing features, one of the most conspicuous was fables' urgent address to the eye. Despite their alleged origins in oral culture, fables were identified with "pleasing Images," not sounds. Edmund Arwaker's collection of 1708 described them in typically pictorial terms:

> A Man that would describe another Man's Person to me, must need a great many Words, & yet after all perhaps give me but a very imperfect Idea of him; but he that shows me his Picture well-painted, though it be in Miniature, does all this much better at one View and in a Moment. It is the same thing in Writing: a Man may drag up the Artillery of twenty Heavy Ornaments to attack a Vice, one of which may strike by the Way, the rest be either not understood, or not remembered. But a Fable shall describe the sordidness of this Vice at once, and convince us pleasantly and quickly.[52]

The preface to Robert Samber's popular 1721 translation of Antoine Houdart de la Motte's *Fables nouvelles* (1719) also described the fabulist as a writer who "by Discourse paints to the Ears."[53] In 1689 Philip Ayres found that writing fables is "like the Placing of Pictures before [readers'] Eyes, whereby more firm and lasting Impressions of Virtue may be fix'd in them, than by plain parallel Rules and Maxims." John Jackson compared a "Fable" to "a Picture or Image of

Truth," and characterized every fable in his collection as a "painted Scene."[54]

Ut pictura poesis is of course one of the oldest literary principles in the book, and it is not surprising to find so many fabulists staking claims to it. As they became more and more like images, fables were expected to make ever "more firm and lasting Impressions" on their readers. But, as La Motte hints, they were never expected absolutely to abandon the verbal register that lent them a skeptical reflexivity. Indeed, many of the collections whose prefaces treat fables as images actually lack illustrations. Instead their visible activity takes place typographically, in the form of demonstratively yoked typefaces.

Another reason that editors of fable collections likened their contents to "miniature" pictures was because they reckoned diminutive size a virtue: English fabulists readily adopted La Fontaine's maxim that "Brevity is the Soul of Fable." Addison described fables as "Pieces." Richardson and Croxall deliberately scaled their collections down to "such a *Size,* as should be fit for the *Hands* and *Pockets* for which it was principally designed."[55] Meanwhile, an extremely anglicized La Motte grumbled that fables' "laconick Original," Aesop could even be "too concise, and I have often wonder'd at it, for he was a Greek, and they are great Talkers in that Country, as witness our divine Homer." *Æsop Naturaliz'd* (1711) noted flat out that "One reason why Stories and Fables seem most suitably contrived to Inform the Understanding is . . . because they are unusually short; and the shortest way to Instruction is the Best; they only aim to teach us one Point at a Time, and are Quick in doing it."[56]

Like their affinity with images, fables' brevity claimed them for a symbology which assumes that the perceptible world is itself organized in particles, and that therefore the most penetrating signs will also be the most irreducible and concrete. As they had been in the sixteenth century, fables were tirelessly likened to compact, palatable substances that, in L'Estrange's words, "go kindly down." They were touted as "Chymical drops," as nuts, as "Chinks" and "Crannies" of light, as "Gilt and Sweeten'd . . . Pills and Potions," as honey-rimmed cups. Traditionally such analogies suggested sweet deception, and could be applied, as in Sidney's *Defence of Poetry* (1595), to figurative language generally. Augustan fabulists used these metaphors more precisely to stress fables' likeness to particular small things. Their lilliputian size physically "adapted [fables] to the Palate and Capacity" of those who took them in.

But fables' compactness equipped them for cultural action as well as for natural impact: it made them easy to transport from text to text, and indeed from language to language. And it aligned them with a symbolic system in which items acquire authority, significance, and value according to their capacity for transportation and exchange.[57] The fact that fables were most often preserved in collections not only invokes a cultural system that identifies knowledge with accumulation. It also displays the instability of resulting systems of meaning, insofar as these consist of many discrete restless particles. Augustan enthusiasm for fable collections—as opposed to fables printed individually, or fables interspersed with other kinds of writing—suggests that skeptical display mattered at least as much as fables' materiality relative to other literary forms.

Such displays seemed to keep authors honest. Aesop himself was promoted as a "hireless Priest of Nature" who exposed "that which was by Art for Profit hid, / And to the Laities as to Spies forbid."[58] The eye-oriented and atomistic structure of the fable collections showed just how symbolic authority got cobbled together. By contrast, the long, sinuous moral tales of the Brahmin fabulist Pilpay were considered too esoteric and mystical for liberated English readers: Pilpay "lock'd up all his politicks; it was a Book of the State and Discipline of Inclosing," one preface noted with disapproval. And "besides his Fables are not distinct and separate enough; he crouds up one within another, [. . .] an extravagant Romance of Brutes, Men, and Genii."[59] *Aesop's* fables were always arranged in distinct sequence, as if to confirm Aesop's reputation for having "set the Truth in so clear a Light, as to make it stand in no need on any further Proof." For he "knew very well that Fable did not consist absolutely in Fiction but in a Collection of Circumstances which concurred to make a Truth understood." While on one level fables' brevity and resulting collectibility seemed to unite them with the physical world, on another level it also spotlit the canny contrivances that "concu[r]" to produce meaning.[60]

Unless we remember that by 1688 the open negotiation of political authority had come to define the character of the English nation, it's hard to see how anyone could have deemed Aesop's talking animals more probable than Pilpay's "extravagant Romance of Brutes, Men, and Genii." Yet while, as one fabulist observed, "the only Word, Fable, awakens [. . .] the Idea of Animals endowed with Speech," this "Idea" offended remarkably few sensibilities. Certainly, loquacious beasts could simply indicate a fabulist's willingness to employ a familiar and accessible style. La Motte, as liberally translated by Samber, interrupted one of his own fables to declare that "I who write of Brutes, a simple Fabulist, must write most plain and easy, and follow Nature in her Tracts" (p. 183). For "elevated Expressions impose upon and seduce us, tho" they are the best chosen, whereas the Familiar cannot gain any Respect but through Justice and a happy Application" (p. 44). But the "Familiar" style could also make rhetorical design explicit. As La Motte put it, fables "make

Plants and Animals speak . . . so that if there is a Necessity for it, the Spring may complain against its Stream; the File laugh at the Serpent, the Earthen and the Iron Pot discourse with each other and swim in one another's Company" (p. 38). Such voluble bodies fail to "impose upon and seduce us" because they point out what human designs "necessit[ate]" linguistic invention. Hence John Dennis (a fabulist himself) with reason doubted that anyone could "be so simple as to believe, that Reynard, Bruin, Isgrim, and Grimalkin say really of themselves the things that Æsop puts into their Mouths."[61] La Motte too assumed that the speaking animal pretense exposes its own cultural origins. One of the most important "Species of the Merry Stile of Fable," he decided, "transfer[s] to Animals, those extrinsical Denominations we make use of to one another" (p. 45).

Because it works at the sociable level of "extrinsical Denomination," the body of the Aesopian brute shares an important affinity with the manifestly invented, printed body of the fable itself. The frontispiece to John Jackson's 1708 collection depicts a potbellied Aesop surrounded by an admiring entourage of beasts. It announces that "in this Figure, the Fables are represented addressing themselves to Æsop, as their Prime Patron." Jackson's preface even more vigorously mixes textual and animal estates: "With great Judgement [Æsop] dresses up Brutes with humane Forms and Qualities. [. . .] The Lyon, the Fox, the Horse, and other Animals, even the Mute-Fish, are his Speakers, and read Lessons of Morality for the Instruction of Youth in the Concerns of Life."[62]

Despite their plea to be read like the pages that cage them, Aesop's creatures are most conspicuously distinguished by the power of speech. In turn, fable collections great and small naturally figured speech as a matter of power. The wolf upstream locks in verbal combat with the lamb below, whom he accuses of sullying the water that actually flows from his mouth to hers; the lion tries to convince the fox to step into his cave, the fox persuades the crow to drop her breakfast into his waiting mouth, and so on. As Joan Hildreth Owen has observed, the differences between Aesop's interlocutors often extend to ethical systems and ways of life; these, like discrepancies of power, are made visible by positional and morphological distinctions.[63] Aesopian animals of the late seventeenth and early eighteenth centuries were especially aware that spatial arrangement decides signifying potential: When one of Ayres's lambs stands at a window and berates a wolf as a "cruel and murderous Beast," the wolf "refuse[s] to be offended by his Abuses" and observes himself that "'tis not thou, but that secure Place wherein thou art, that injures me."[64]

While places might be "secure" in a given fable, an animal's tenure there is less so. In fables, animals sig-

nify only in opposition to each other, and in the context of the visible discursive field that they inhabit at a particular moment. They are not, that is, enslaved to traditions of static correspondence in which serpents always represent wisdom, lions power, diamonds knowledge, and so forth. While their bodies remain the same from fable to fable (and this could be literally true, since most Aesopian motifs were transmitted from illustrator to illustrator with little change), the meaning of those bodies is defined in a discursive field whose constituent terms can always be rearranged. Indeed, many fable collections openly rebelled against fixed correspondence: in the story of the farmer who warms a snake on his bosom and is stung for his pains, John Toland noted that "the Serpent is not always the Emblem of Wisdom, as that Passage of our Saviour seems to imply, when he charges his Disciples to be as Wise as Serpents and as Harmless as Doves." Even within a fable collection, a creature's significance can change from fable to fable, in response to his or her competition at a given moment. When an eagle outwits a fox, Toland concludes that "this Fable represents the Eagle in quite a different Character from what the former [where a crow imposes on him] did. There he plaid the part of a generous but overcredulous Prince. . . But here we see him put the Cheat upon the Fox."[65]

In Augustan fables character is emphatically situational, not essential, and hence it is always open to dispute. A moral, thus, might hoard the possibility of contradiction until the last possible moment: "'Tis a Kind of *School Question* that we find started in the Fable, upon the Subject of Reason and Intellect," L'Estrange had noted at the end of the fable of the crow who drops stones into a pitcher until she manages to raise its contents to her beak.[66] Likewise, musing over another story, Toland wondered:

> Does Æsop intend hereby to inform us of the great Family of Manking? Or is it to let us know [the eagle was] insensibly debauch'd by the Air of the Court? Or does Aesop by this Fable undertake to show that we are not obliged to keep our word with wicked Men? If the last be Aesop's intention, we entirely dissent from him; for, on the contrary, we are of Opinion, that if one must break one's word, 'tis more proper doing it to a good than to a Bad Man.

Even the less self-examining (and proportionally more conservative) collections of fables of the Augustan period throve "on the contrary" and on "dissent." As the anonymous preface to *Fables, Moral and Political* (1703) observed, "We may say of all human things, that they have two Handles, a right and a left: So we may with equal reason say of all the old Fables that they have an infinite number."[67] Readers caught on quickly. In the front of a collection of 1651, one of them scribbled that "Time brings opposites to pass/ And various maxims teaches."[68]

But while Augustan fable collections reflected a precarious world, they often did so for conservative reasons—to teach English readers a single habit of interpretation, to reflect to them a single image of themselves as interpreters and potential producers of signs. The preface to *Fables, Moral and Political* tells us that "that all Men might be sufficiently convinc'd of the above-mention'd Truths in one and the same Manner, the Wise Ancients invented many fictitious Stories, Comparisons, Apologues, Parables and Fables, to make them well comprehend and retain those Truths."[69] The possibility of inversion did not ultimately threaten a fable's authority, so long as that fable maintained a single, reliable "Manner" of representation, guaranteed to instill a single, reliable "Manner" of approaching written signs.[70]

Even the editors of classroom Aesops reinforced this symbolic practice by introducing fables' caprices alongside their stalwart simplicity. At Dryden's Westminster School "Esops Fables" came first in Headmaster Busby's syllabus of texts by which "Schollers learne the rudim*ts* of Grammer & Syntaxis in English."[71] In 1736 the *Gentleman's Magazine* described how "Aesop's tales at once instruct and please" students in the "first and least" class. But fables' rudimentary virtues grew less important as students grew more accomplished: at Westminster, the mornings were devoted to "conster[ing]" and "transcrib[ing]" a "Fable in Esope"; but in the afternoons, schoolboys were to "peirce the lesson they construed out of Esope." Likewise, the *Gentleman's Magazine* reported that the very fables that "instruct and please" in the first form laterteach more subtle lessons about how business is actually conducted in a contentious symbolic field. In the second form

> *Aesop* in a clearer light is seen,
> Here they perceive to what his fables lean,
> Can smoke the *Fox* comending from below
> The voice, the shape, the beauty of the *Crow;*
> Who perch'd on high, far from his reach was
>   sat,
> Bless'd (what he wanted) with a piece of
>   meat.[72]

Even in the classroom, Aesopian instruction was two-tiered, stacking interpretive skepticism (seeing "in a clearer light," "perceiv[ing] to what [. . .] fables lean") on top of a rudimentary reassurance that written words can cohere with the physical world. Such a pedagogical strategy naturalized the myth of the discerning eye that keeps the viewer an ostensibly free subject of literary experience.

Aesopian instruction increasingly imbued the act of reading with the dominant political principles of an emerging England. This was true even when the language to be learned was not English. In a typical collection like Charles Hoole's *Æsop's Fables. In English and Latin* (1687), "every [fable was] divided into its distinct period and marked with Figures, so that little Children may [. . .] learn to imitate the right Composition, and the proper Forms of Speech, belonging to both Languages."[73] Hoole brooke Aesop's fables into small syntactic units whose counterparts in different languages were easy to pick out in matching typefaces. Superficially, this reinforces a fairly even exchange between the two languages: the fable of the fox and stork, for instance, typographically varies parts of the story so that they may be compared with corresponding Latin phrases. In the English version

1 A Fox invited a Stork to Supper.

2 He poured the meat upon a Table, which, because it was thin, the Fox licked up, the Stork striving in vain to do so with her bill.

3 The Bird being abused, went her way; she was ashamed and grieved at the injury.

4 After a few days, she comes again and invites the Fox.
5 A glass was set full of meat; which vessel, because it was narrow-mouthed, the Fox might see the meat, and be hungry, but he could not taste of it.

6 The Stork easily drew it out with her bill.

7 Mor. Laughter deserves laughter, Jesting, jesting, Knavery, knavery, and Deceit, deceit.[74]

Across the page we find "De Vulpecula et Ciconia," a Latinversion of the story that corresponds to the English point for point, down to the moral: "Risus risum, jocus jocum, dolus dolum, fraus meritur fraudem." The fable's plot performs the acts of matching and exchange that occur linguistically. Symbolic elements become body parts (bills and mouths) and visible objects (the glass, the table, the meat). All of these signs move in three directions at once. They are tokens in a series of transactions between the stork and the fox. They signify a moral that presents reciprocity as a fact of life. And they are linguistic counters that can be exchanged for their Latin equivalents across the page. At the same time, however, exchange is presented thematically as cruel and aggressive deceit. Hence, like Aesop's pedagogical productions, the fable ironizes its own assertions about language. It is not self-conscious about the irony; this is what distinguishes Hoole from fabulists like Ogilby and Barlow. But collections like Hoole's inculcated the reading habits that make it possible to recognize the predatory subtext of modern English signifying conventions.

For this reason, fables like that of the fox and stork enjoyed a high life in the cheap political fables that flourished on Grub Street at the turn of the century. Contrived by hack writers no doubt raised on classroom collections, these penny pamphlets all responded to the "late Change of Government" in 1688. Their titles moved Aesop from place to place in order to protest against or to welcome the prevailing political wind "They were as likely to be written from the Whig as from the Tory side: *Æsop at Tunbridge, Æsop at Whitehall, Æsop at Bathe, Æsop Return'd from Tunbridge* were all Tory; *Old Æsop at Whitehall, Æsop at Epsom, Æsop at Amsterdam, Æsop from Islington* and *Æsop at Westminster* all were Whig, Some others—*Æsop the Wanderer, Æsop in Portugal, Æsop at Oxford, Æsop at the Bell-Tavern, Æsop at Paris*—exploited Aesop's itineracy to address more global political situations: when Aesop went to Paris, for example, he became a French undersecretary. Others, like *Æsop at Richmond,* stole the "Aesop at . . ." formula for their titles but dished up social satire instead.

The bulk of the Grub Street Aesops, though, used the political climate of the day to justify their authors' choice to write in fables: "Who the De——l but a Modern Man would venture to write Truth this Time of Day?" one queried. Fables themselves were up for grabs in the recently renegotiated world of Williamite England. "I write Fables too," one Aesop noted, "only with this difference, mine are for the Government and his against it."[75] Fables' flagrant promiscuity went hand in hand with their materiality. One Aesop describes a rival's attempt to "squeeze itself into the press" and Aesop at Tunbridge reports the discovery of a "Parcel of Papers" dropped along Tunbridge Road: "Picking 'em up, I found they were the following fables."[76] Even the most ephemeral of all Augustan fable collections showed figures at the beck and call of a skeptical nation and a materialist age.

When Aesop at Epsom told the story "Of the Fox and the Stork," he captured exactly this preoccupation: writing against Aesop at Tunbridge, this Whig Aesop casts himself as the stork and his opponent as the fox, thereby demonstrating that it is now his turn to "make the Tallies even." He means that it is now his turn to eat, to speak, to laugh at the expense of the other. The fable turns the superficially egalitarian space of the dining table into an example of how power is organized in modern English culture. That culture's dominant political instrument is a press willing to spin its web of equally factitious and substantial signs for anyone who asks it to. In such a world, meaning waits on an imbalance that masquerades as parity: the fable would lose its own significance if the stork had the "narrow long neck'd glass" before her at the same time that the fox is supplied with his "liquid feast." Aesopian figuration repeats a national history that unfolds as a series of inversions and temporary subordinations.

Because all of the Grub Street Aesops speak the same language, only one of them can occupy Aesop's skin at a time. The conventional prefatory banter that always challenges an Aesopian predecessor of the opposing party invariably gives way to fables about unequal exchange, nervous compromise, contest over bodies which, like what one pamphlet describes as the "fine, empty" body of Aesop himself, are finally not worth the quarrel. As "Æsop Return'd from Tunbridge" put it:

> When the small ones give their Voice,
> Who shall be most Empower'd,
> They have but liberty of Choice
> By whom they'll be devour'd.[77]

Such jingles capture the tension between stability and subversion that organized both major and minor English fable collections between 1651 and 1740. Without denying the manifold differences among those collections, we can say that they shared at least one cultural aim—to create a common figural system. To the extent that reactive mediation between opposing sides was one perceived virtue of that system, these very differences may even be interpreted as marks of success.

Notes

[23] Gerard Reedy gives an excellent summary of this crisis in "Mystical Politics," in *Studies in Revolution and Change,* ed. Korshin, 20-46. Not overlooking Ogilby's own role in crafting the iconography of Charles II's Restoration, Reedy points out that the "symbolic texture of the day" (p. 20), thanks to the "demythologiz[ing]" mania of the Interregnum, was characterized by a deep skepticism about the "mystical nature of noumenal essence" and by a conviction that kingly authority was little more than "a concept to be manipulated" (p. 45) as a "political tool" (p. 21). We can generalize this insight to suggest that all previously unchallengeable correspondences between "phenomenal" signifiers and "noumenal" signifieds found themselves under fire by 1660.

[24] In *Stability and Strife,* W.A. Speck offers an overview of the conflictual structure of eighteenth-century English politics. Compelling essays on various conflicts of the period may be found in *Culture, Politics, and Society in Britain, 1660-1800,* ed. Jeremy Black and Jeremy Gregory (Manchester, 1991). Jean-Christophe Agnew's *Worlds Apart: The Market and the Theater in Anglo-American Thought, 1550-1750* (New York, 1985) traces and theorizes the way an emerging market shaped symbolic forms in early modern England.

[25] This is how Roger L'Estrange described his own prodigious fable collection's metamorphosis from the diminutive to the mammoth, so that it might better "answe[r] all the *Parts* and *Pretences* of the

Undertaking, as well *Publique* as *Private.*" L'Estrange, Address to the Reader, in *Fables and Storyes Moralized, Being a Second Part of the Fables of Æsop* (London, 1692 and 1699), sig. A3v. Future references to this preface will be designated "Address."

[26] L'Estrange, "A Fox and a Goat," in *Eminent Mythologists,* 80.

[27] *Ibid.;* Samuel Richardson, "A Cock and a Fox" in *Æsop's Fables, with Instructive Morals and Re-flections* (London, 1739), 20.

[28] Arwaker, Preface to *Truth in Fiction,* vi.

[29] Thomas Hobbes, "The Introduction" to *Leviathan,* ed. C.B. Macpherson ((1651) Harmondsworth, 1968), 81. For Hobbes's elaboration of the "generall use of Speech," "*Markes,* or *Notes,*" and "*Signes,*" see *Leviathan,* I.iv, "Of Speech." Hobbes's discussion of language's culturally constructive uses actually begins with a discussion of writing—"a profitable Invention for continuing the memory of time past" (p. 100), and his discussion of words very often seems to assume that at their most efficacious they would be graphic. On Hobbes's use of the exemplary potential of the page, and on its centrality to his notion of obedience to certain forms of cultural authority, see Richard Kroll, "*Mise-en-page:* Biblical Criticism and Inference during the Restoration," in *Studies in Eighteenth-Century Culture,* ed. O.M. Brack, Jr. (Madison, 1986), 3-40.

[30] William Davenant, "To My Friend Mr. Ogilby, Upon the Fables of Æsop Paraphras'd in Verse," in Ogilby, *Fables* (1651), n.p.

[31] Ogilby, "Of the Fox and the Lion," in *Fables,* 194-195. Patterson analyzes several of Ogilby's fables as instances of his having "appropriated fabulist tradition," rendering individual fables "vehicle[s] of protest and solidarity for the Royalist nobility and gentry" and thereby eventually "alter[ing] the *status* of the fable"(*Fables of Power,* 86-87). Her close readings of several of Ogilby's most tendentious fables enhances Pritchard's interpretation of *Fables* as a sustained plea for cultural integration reflected in the "narrative unity" of the collection itself (p. 17).

[32] Bernard Mandeville, "Remark P," in *The Fable of the Bees* (1705-1729), ed. F.B. Kaye. 2 vols. (Oxford, 1924), II: 178.

[33] John Ogilby, "Of the Dog and Shadow," in *Fables of Æsop.* 4.

[34] On Barlow's contributions to Aesopian represen-

tation in England, see Edward Hodnett, *Francis Barlow: First Master of English Book Illustrations* (London, 1978). Philip Hofer analyzes Barlow's fable collection as a "private venture" that was "in direct competition" with Ogilby's Aesop, even though Barlow apparently supplied illustrations for one of Ogilby's collections. Hofer sees Barlow as wishing to "produce a finer book" than Ogilby (pp. 281-282). See Hofer, "Francis Barlow's Aesop." *Harvard Library Bulletin* 2 (1948), 279-295.

[35] Francis Barlow, Dedication to *Aesop's Fables with his Life, in English, French and Latin* (London, 1687), n.p. Future references to Barlow's Dedication and to Behn's fables will be to this edition (in Bibliography see *s.v.* Behn).

[36] L'Estrange, "Address," sig. A3v.

[37] Contemporary lampoons depicted L'Estrange as a dog with "a thousand dog tricks, viz. to catch for the Papists, carry for the Protestants, whine to the King . . . and cring [*sic*] to the Crucifix," none of which could compare with his "damn'd old trick of slipping the halter." See the anonymous "Hue and Cry" appended to "Strange's Case Strangely Altered" (London, 1680), n.p.

[38] L'Estrange's biographer, George Kitchin, points out that, though L'Estrange was knighted much earlier, he only became "the celebrated L'Estrange" after he turned to polite letters. *Sir Roger L'Estrange: A Contribution to the History of the Press in the Seventeenth Century* (London, 1913), 390-407.

[39] Patterson, *Fables of Power* (139-143), treats L'Estrange's *Fables* as political satire responding to England's return to constitutional government after 1688.

[40] Roger L'Estrange, Preface to *Eminent Mythologists* (London, 1692), sig. A2v. L'Estrange berates the "Morose and Untractable Spirits in the World, that look upon Precepts in Emblem" as trivial, the strict province of "Women and Children" and uses the terms "Figure" and "Fable" interchangeably. Future references to this preface will be to this edition and will appear in the text.

[41] L'Estrange, "Address," sig. A3v.

[42] L'Estrange's choice of words here is not original. In the preface to *The Midwives Book* (London, 1671), Jane Sharpe remarks on her own choice to communicate anatomical, gynecological, and obstetrical precepts in lay words: "It is not hard words that perform the work, as if more understood the Art that cannot understand Greek. Words are but the Shell, that we oft times

break our Teeth with them to come at the Kernel. I mean our Brains to know what is the Meaning of them" (pp. 3-4).

[43] Mr. Spectator was voluble on the rampant "Humour of Shortning our Language" that, exemplified by L'Estrange, threatened to "have confounded all our Etymologies, and have quite destroy'd our Tongue." Joseph Addison, *Spectator* 135 (August 4, 1711), in *The Spectator,* ed. Bond, II: 35. For the most minute of many contemporary engagements with L'Estrange's fables, see *Some Observations on the Fables of Æsop, as Commented upon by Roger L'Estrange* (Edinburgh, 1700). The "Divine of the Church of Scotland" responsible for the *Observations* added morals to L'Estrange's fables, examined their sometimes contradictory relations to each other, and furnished details that he felt L'Estrange might have mentioned. The depth and detail of the *Obser-vations* show how deeply L'Estrange's fable collection engrossed contemporary readers and writers.

[44] Samuel Croxall, Preface to *Fables of Æsop and Others* (London, 1722), sig. B5v. Future references to Croxall's preface are to this edition and will appear parenthetically in the text.

[45] Croxall, "The Forrester and the Lion," in *Fables of Æsop and Others,* 96.

[46] Richardson, Preface to *Æsop's Fables,* iv. Future references will appear parenthetically in the text.

[47] As would his choice of names like "Charles" and "Charlotte" for protagonists in his last novel *Sir Charles Grandison* (1753-1754). For Richardson's uncommonly sympathetic response to L'Estrange, see Margaret Anne Doody, *A Natural Passion: A Study in the Novels of Samuel Richardson* (Oxford, 1974), 25-28. And on Richardson's possible Jacobitism, Doody's "Richardson's Politics," *Eighteenth-Century Fiction* 2 (1990), 113-126.

[48] Samuel Richardson, *Pamela; or, Virtue Rewarded* ((1740) Harmondsworth, 1980), 108. Future references to *Pamela* will be to this edition and will appear parenthetically in the text.

[49] Terry Castle, *Clarissa's Ciphers: Meaning and Disruption in Richardson's "Clarissa'* (Ithaca, N.Y., 1982).

[50] Richardson's footnotes to his novels notoriously multiplied over successive editions as he sought to protect the authority he had conceded by writing in the epistolary form. As they simultaneously assert and surrender the authority to control interpretation, we are thus encouraged to read the novels as we would fables.

[51] For example, Lovelace cites a fable in which Mercury, disguised, asks a statuary "what price that same statue of *Mercury* bore," only to be told it is worth nothing. Lovelace applies this fable to his correspondent Belford, who like Mercury "prizes" Clarissa's "good Opinion" and whom Lovelace rewards with the bruising information that "she dislikes thee." Samuel Richardson, *Clarissa; or The History of a Young Lady* ((1747-1748) Harmondsworth, 1985), 355. Future references to *Clarissa* will be to this edition and will appear in the text.

[52] Arwaker, Preface to *Truth in Fiction,* vi.

[53] Antoine Houdart de la Motte, *One Hundred New Court Fables,* trans. Robert Samber (London, 1721), 331. La Motte, whose *Fables nowelles* appeared in an ornate and theoretically eloquent edition in Paris in 1719, was extremely important for English fab-ulists (particularly Whiggish ones); Samber ventured that this was because he "seem[ed] to have the utmost Allusion to Arbitrary Government, and dares say so; Through all his Fables may be discovered a spirit of liberty" (ix). (Of course, La Motte's fables were also dedicated to the king.) All fables being trans-lations at some level, English fabulists habitually made few, if any, qualitative distinctions between an original fable and a translation. I thus treat Samber's important collection as a full participant in English Aesopian conventions.

[54] Philip Ayres, "Epistle Dedicatory to Lewis Maydwell, in *Mythologia Ethica, or Three Centuries of Æsopean Fables in English Prose* (London, 1689), sigs. A3r-A4v; John Jackson, Preface to *A New Translation of Æsop's Fables, Adorn'd with Cutts* (London, 1708), lxvii.

[55] Richardson, *Æsop's Fables,* x. Like Richardson, Croxall likewise wanted his book to "suit [. . .] the Hands of the Generality of Children." See Croxall, *Fables of Æsop,* B8v.

[56] La Motte (trans. Samber), "The Sheep and the Bush, in *Court Fables,* 248. *Æsop Naturaliz'd: In a Collection of Fables and Stories from Æsop, Lockman, Pilpay and Others* (3rd ed., London, 1711), sigs. A3v-A4r.

[57] Susan Stewart's *On Longing: Narratives of the Miniature, the Gigantic, the Souvenir, and the Collection* (Baltimore, 1984) touches on some of the ideological underpinnings of the culture of miniaturism in which Aesop's fables so openly participated. James H. Bunn gives a brilliant and persuasive account of how mercantilism informed eighteenth-century linguistic activity in "The Aesthetics of British Mercantilism," *New Literary History* 11 (1980), 303-321.

[58] William Davenant, "To My Dear Friend Mr. Ogilby," in Ogilby, *Fables of Æsop* (1651), n.p.

[59] La Motte (trans. Samber), *Court Fables,* 31.

[60] *Free-Thinker* 47 (September 17, 1718), in *The Free-Thinker* 1 (London, 1722), 34; La Motte (trans. Samber), *Court Fables,* 61.

[61] John Dennis, *The Stage Defended* (1726), in *Critical Works of John Dennis,* ed. Hooker, II: 308.

[62] Jackson, "Preface," xvii-xviii.

[63] Joan Hildreth Owen, "The Choice of Hercules and the English Fable," 57.

[64] Ayres, *Mythologia Ethica,* 74.

[65] Toland, "Of the Eagle and the Fox," in *Fables,* 427.

[66] L'Estrange, "A Crow and a Pitcher," in *Eminent Mythologists,* 208.

[67] Anon., *Fables, Moral & Political* (London, 1703), sig. A11r.

[68] *Æsop's Fables with their Morals in Prose and Verse* (1651); facing page: British Library copy.

[69] *Fables Moral and Political,* sigs. A4v-A4r.

[70] On the "oppositional seam" that structures standard discursive formations of the period, such as the maxim, see Roland Barthes, "Reflections on the Maxims of La Rochefoucauld," *New Critical Essays,* trans. Richard Howard (New York, 1980), 3-19.

[71] Shaftesbury document, reproduced in James Winn, *John Dryden and his World* (New Haven and London, 1987), 523.

[72] "Westminster-School," in *The Gentleman's Magazine* 6 (October, 1736), 611.

[73] Hoole, *Æsop's Fables.*

[74] Hoole, "Of the Fox and the Stork," in *Æsop's Fables,* 22.

[75] *Æsop Return'd from Tunbridge* (London, 1698), sigs. A2r-A3v; *Æsop at Epsom* (London, 1689), sig. A2v.

[76] "To the Reader," *Æsop at Tunbridge* (London, 1698), 1.

[77] "Sharpers and Cullies," in *Æsop Return'd from Tunbridge,* 13.

THE AESOPIC TRADITION IN NON-ENGLISH-SPEAKING CULTURES

Joseph R. Berrigan (essay date 1978)

SOURCE: "The Latin Aesop of Ermolao Barbaro," in *Manuscripta,* Vol. XXII, No. 3, November 1978, pp. 141-48.

[*In the following essay, Berrigan looks at the Italian Renaissance tradition of teaching languages as well as morals via translations of Aesop's works.*]

The Latin translators of Aesop in the first half of the Quattrocento comprise a small group of Italians, whose contributions to the field of fable literature have been the subject of study for the past century by both classical and Renaissance scholars. A particularly significant cluster of articles has been authored by Professor Chauncey E. Finch.[1] Before taking up Ermolao Barbaro and his apologues, I would like to provide the context of the Renaissance fable and the several men who busied themselves with Aesop in the early Quattrocento.

Our starting point has to be that the fable played a significant role in early Byzantine education as well as in the initial stages of a child's instruction in the medieval West.[2] Anyone familiar with the character, the inherent charm of apologues would acknowledge the wisdom of coating the painful first steps of acquiring Greek with the sugary delights of the Fox and the Grapes, let us say. How much more sensible this approach is than the familiar introduction of a student to Greek through Xenophon or Latin through Caesar! The schoolmasters of the early Quattrocento were intimately acquainted with the nature, goals, and methods of Byzantine education. Adapting them to the exigencies of the Italian classroom was especially the work of Guarino da Verona, who had followed Chrysoloras to Constantinople and lived in his home for several years.[3] We have the firmest of evidence that Guarino employed Aesop in his introductory Greek lessons. Of this evidence more in a little while.[4] Aesop must have had a very powerful impact upon Guarino, for he named his second son, apparently born in September of 1422, Aesop or Esopo.[5] Filosa is surely right in pointing to the schools of Guarino and Vittorino as the centers of Aesopic diffusion.[6] For of the six early translators or composers of apologues four are associated with these two schools: Barbaro and Valla with Guarino, Ognibene and Correr with Vittorino. The other two are apparently independent: Leonardo Dati of Florence and Rinuccio Aretino. I suppose of them all the most important is the last, for his translation of Aesop was printed in 1474 in Milan by Buono Accursio along with the Greek text of the fables that formed the basis of the vulgate

Aesop until the early nineteenth century.[7] Rinuccio apparently translated these fables in 1488.[8] Unlike all the other fables we are dealing with, Dati's are written in verse. They remained unpublished until 1912 when they were presented on the basis of a single, quite faulty German manuscript.[9] They are dedicated to Gregorio Correr; this helps us date Dati's translation to the very late 1420's or early 1430's.[10] Correr was working on his own fables in 1429 and was in Rome, where he could have encountered Dati, and writing his satires in 1433.[11] What I find particularly intriguing about this connection is Dati's subsequent composition of the fourth tragedy of the Renaissance, the *Hiensal,* and its possible inspiration by Correr's earlier tragedy, the *Progne.*[12] The ring then is closed. Dati translated and versified forty fables. They turn out to correspond to the first forty-four fables of Vat. Pal. gr. 195 with the interchange of two fables and the omission of four.[13]

As Professor Finch pointed out in his article on the fables of Gregorio Correr, the two sets of apologues translated in the school of Vittorino are related to each other.[14] Ognibene da Lonigo composed his set first and dedicated them to Gian Francesco Gonzaga, the lord of Mantua.[15] Shortly thereafter Ognibene's fellow student, Gregorio Correr, fresh from his labors over the *Progne,* composed his set of fifty-nine fables.[16] He claims, in his own preface, that he has composed a full sixty, but there are only fifty-nine. Subsequently, he would revise both the preface, by shortening it and excising all reference to Ognibene and his fables, and his apologues, by reducing them to fifty-three.[17]

Like the fables of Correr those of Barbaro still remain unpublished. As far as I have been able to discover, they exist in only a single manuscript, British Museum, Additional MS 33782.[18] This manuscript came to London in the very late nineteenth century from Verona. From every indication it is a holograph and therefore similar to the Marciana MS of Correr.[19] Unlike Correr's fables those of Barbaro are translated directly from the Greek and therefore resemble the other collections of apologues. Before turning to the contents of the manuscript, I would like to say a few words on Ermolao Barbaro himself.[20] He is another of those young Venetians who left their city to study under Guarino or Vittorino. There is some disagreement over when he was born: Sabbadini suggests that he was born in 1407 or 1408.[21] The most recent research indicates a somewhat later date, 1410.[22] If we take that as the correct year, then he would have been a year older than Vittorino and only twelve when he translated his fables, for we are sure from the colophon of the manuscript that he finished this work in 1422.[23] His family, too, was quite distinguished. His uncle Francesco had studied under Guarino, too, had gone to Florence, and then written one of the important tracts of the early Quattrocento, the *De re uxoria*[24] Like Correr, Ermolao Barbaro would enter the clergy; he became a very active

prelate in the service of a series of Renaissance popes. Interestingly enough, when he was not on diplomatic missions or in Rome, he lived in his episcopal city, Verona, the same city that Correr called home for most of his later life. Barbaro, too, was opposed to a world dominated by classicism and wrote a book against some of the classic poets.[25]

The British Museum MS consists of a preface and thirty-three fables. That number should ring bells in the minds of Renaissance Aesop scholars, since it is the same number of fables that ·Valla would turn into Latin in 1438. The fables are dedicated to the famed scholar-monk, Ambrogio Traversari, whom Barbaro had met on a trip to Florence. Consequently, the preface has already been published in the Epistolario of Traversari, edited by Mehus in 1759.[26] In it Barbaro explains that Traversari had encouraged him to pursue the study of Greek and so he was dedicating these first fruits of his youthful efforts as a monument and pledge of their mutual love to Traversari. He alludes to the several other scholars who had inspired him by their example as much as their words to embark upon the pursuit of Greek. He mentions Carlo Marsuppini but particularly emphasizes the role of Niccolo Niccoli, who had played the role of a Varro to him in his generous nurturing of youthful talent. Once he had been convinced that he should study Greek, Barbaro did not have to look around for some new teacher; he had only to return to the man who had been educating him in Latin for several years, Guarino da Verona, his father, as he says, and his teacher. "Now in the same way I hoped to acquire the knowledge of Greek letters, zealously to make this knowledge part of myself, then to fix it as the basis of a good and happy life."[27]

Barbaro then explains that he had recently translated some of Aesop's fables with Guarino and dedicated them to Traversari, not because Traversari would need a Latin translation to help him decipher the Greek but because, by sending them to Traversari, he was sure to win praise for himself. "Just as fruit placed in precious bowls or golden vessels acquire the finest embellishment from these receptacles, so if these fables are deposited and lodged with you, the most excellent of vessels, aglow with a great variety of jewels, they will be adorned, by your judgment and witness, with the choicest honor and glory."[28] Barbaro then appends a brief encomium of Aesop and his fables, the use that Plato and Plutarch had made of them, and their sturdy contributions to the moral character of their readers. After the thirty-three fables Barbaro concludes the work with the colophon I have already alluded to: "Here end the fables of Aesop translated by me, the young Ermolao Barbaro, a patrician of Venice, on October 1, 1422, under the supervision of Guarino da Verona, my father and teacher."[29] From preface, fables, and colophon we can surely make the conclusion that Guarino employed Aesop in the very early stages of teaching a boy Greek.

Barbaro had only recently decided to pursue that language, these fables were the first fruits of that study, they were written as exercises under the direction of Guarino. The place of Aesop in Renaissance Greek and subsequently Latin education was clearly established by Guarino and would have a long and happy life. In passing, I would like to mention an incident from the mid-nineteenth century, when young Milton Humphreys, subsequently to become one of America's greatest classicists, left his Appalachian home and went to Charleston, Va., as it was then before the Civil War. There he was introduced to Aesop in Latin and was so delighted that he rolled off the bed laughing.[30]

As I have intimated, even before reading the British Museum MS my suspicions had been aroused by the number of fables translated in 1422 by Barbaro: thirty-three. I wondered if it were only a coincidence that Valla too had translated thirty-three. I am a devoted believer in serendipity but not when it comes to Renaissance Latin translations of Aesop. My suspicions this time turned out to be entirely justified, for the fables translated by Barbaro are precisely the same as the fables translated some sixteen years later by Valla. They are the same in number, in order, and in subject matter. A note on the fly-leaf of the British Museum manuscript does indeed note the relationship of the two translations and provide the equivalent references for the Hudson edition of Aesop. The note, written in a nineteenth-century hand, makes a crucial mistake, however, for it says that Valla had translated these same fables *antea*. Surely it was *postea*, around 1438.[31]

Because of their identity with the Valla fables, these efforts by Barbaro should be familiar to Aesopic scholars. There is a generous bibliography on Valla and Aesop, with the names of Achelis and Finch being the most prominent.[32] Its conclusions on the Greek manuscripts of Aesop, those which are closest to Valla's translation, would also apply to Barbaro's, given the identity of the fables presented.

An obvious conclusion from what I take the facts to be is that Valla got the Greek text he translated from Guarino or else accidentally came across a text that was the same as the one employed by Guarino in his teaching. I find the latter supposition untenable, particularly when we remember that Valla says that he obtained his copy of Aesop from a shipwreck.[33] Surely, from what we know, the borrowing of a codex from Guarino makes more sense than the unlikely, really unbelievable linkage of a shipwreck and the identity of manuscripts being translated. Even serendipity has its credible limits. There is nothing inherently absurd in suggesting that Valla obtained a text of Aesop from Guarino. They were very good friends. Guarino thought very highly of Valla. He wrote to the younger man upon receiving his diatribe on Bartolus, "Laurenti, laurea, et Valla, vallari corona ornandus es."[34] We know

of this cordial relationship and can point to at least one occasion, in 1433, when Valla visited Guarino in Ferrara for two days.[35] To summarize, we know from Barbaro and his fables that Guarino had a Greek Aesop with 33 fables; we know that Valla subsequently translated a Greek Aesop with the same 33 fables; we know that Valla and Guarino were friends and the former could very well have received the Aesop from the latter.

I do not wish to leave the impression that Valla published Barbaro's version or even used it. As you might expect, there is a great difference between the Latinity of the two translations. Barbaro was after all still a young school-boy when he did his translation, Valla was in his early thirties when he did his and he was already a master-stylist. Barbaro's fables have remained unpublished and to a great extent unread until now; Valla's enjoyed enthusiastic success throughout Renaissance Europe. There is apparently only one manuscript of Barbaro's Aesop; there are scores of copies of Valla's, both handwritten and printed.

The very uniqueness of Barbaro's translation is an argument for its being a holograph. The whole character of the manuscript supports that view. The handwriting is that of a child, perhaps a precocious child and one writing in the new humanistic style, but still a child. There are a number of misspellings, especially in the doubling or nondoubling of consonants, that bespeak its north Italian origin. There are several instances of mistranslation of particular Greek words but these are, after all, quite few in number. The remarkable thing is how close Barbaro remains to the Greek text, how clearly the Greek shines through.

Some thirty-six years later, Guarino's younger son, Battista, dedicated his own translation of Xenophon's *Agesilaus* to this same Ermolao Barbaro, by then bishop of Verona. In his preface he addresses Ermolao and asks, "What shall I say of your learning? Everyone knows that from your earliest years you were educated admirably, first under my father's direction and then under your uncle Francesco, in both Latin and Greek letters. From among all men I have chosen you to dedicate the first-fruits of my studies of the Greek language."[36] From Aesop to Xenophon, from dedicator to dedicatee, from honoring the father to being honored by the son—such is the circle of Renaissance education that appropriately begins with a fable like that of the fox and the goat.

Notes

[1] See his "The Alphabetical Notes in Rinuccio's Translation of Aesop," *Mediaevalia et Humanistica*, 11 (1957), 90-93; "The Greek Source of Lorenzo Valla's Translation of Aesop's Fables," *Classical Philology*, 55 (1960), 118-120; "The Fables of Aesop in Urb.

Gr. 135," *TAPA,* 103 (1972), 127-132; "The Renaissance Adaptation of Aesop's Fables by Gregorius Corrarius," *Classical Bulletin* 49 (1973), 44-48.

[2] Norman H. Baynes, *The Byzantine Empire* (London: Oxford University Press, 1925), p. 153; Carlo Filosa, *La Favola* (Milano: Vallardi, 1952), p. 75.

[3] W. H. Woodward, *Vittorino da Feltre and Other Humanist Educators* (Cambridge: Cambridge University Press, 1897), p. 17.

[4] See below, note 29.

[5] Remigio Sabbadini, ed., *Epistolario di Guarino Veronese,* III (Venice: R. Deputazione di storia patria, 1919), p. 148.

[6] Filosa, pp. 75-76.

[7] Ben E. Perry, *Babrius and Phaedrus* (Cambridge: Harvard University Press; and London: Heinemann, 1965), p. xvii.

[8] T. O. Achelis, "Die Hundert äsopischen Fabeln des Rinucci da Castiglione," *Philologus,* 83 (1928), 60.

[9] *Rheinisches Museum,* 67 (1912), 285-299.

[10] T. O. Achelis, "Zu den äsopischen Fabeln des Dati und Corraro," *Rheinisches Museum,* 70 (1915), 387; Otto Tacke, "Eine bisher unbekannte Aesopübersetzung aus dem 15. Jahrhundert," *Rheinisches Museum,* 67 (1912), 280.

[11] J. R. Berrigan, "Gregorii Gorrarii Veneti Liber Satyrarum," *Humanistica Lovaniensia,* 22(1973), 10.

[12] J. R. Berrigan, "Latin Tragedy of the Quattrocento," *Humanistica Lovaniensia,* 22 (1973), 1-9.

[13] Paul Marc, rev. of "Eine bisher unbekannte Aesopübersetzung aus dem 15. Jahrhundert," by Otto Tacke, *Byzantinische Zeitschrift,* 21 (1912), 566.

[14] Finch, "Corrarius," 45.

[15] In his presidential address to the Classical Association of the Middle West and South in 1963 Professor Finch stated that it would not be difficult to establish the classification of the manuscript upon which Ognibene da Lonigo's version rests. Thanks to a grant from the Mellon Foundation and the kind assistance of the Knights of Columbus Vatican Film Library at Saint Louis University, I have been able to do so relatively simply. Vat. Ottobon. lat. 1223 contains the fables by Ognibene from f. 73^r through f. 87^r; his preface to Gian Francesco Gonzaga, the lord of Mantua, occupies f. 72^r to f. 73^r. Ognibene provides forty fables, and my

examination of their sequence shows that they follow the order of Hausrath's Class IIIa manuscripts. Even more specifically, they occur in the pattern of Vat. Barb. gr. 105. I hereby append the sequence in which these forty fables appear in the Barb. gr. MS: 1-1, 2-3, 3-4, 4-5, 5-6, 6-7, 7-8, 8-9, 9-10, 10-12, 11-13, 12-19, 13-21, 14-24, 15-26, 16-27, 17-29, 18-30, 19-31, 20-32, 21-33, 22-35, 23-36, 24-38, 25-41, 26-42, 27-43, 28-45, 29-47, 30-53, 31-57, 32-65, 33-71, 34-73, 35-78, 36-79, 37-87, 38-98, 39-99, 40-113. Both the Ottob. lat. and the Barb. gr. MSS were placed at my disposal in microfilm copies and are available in the Knights of Columbus Film Library at Saint Louis University.

[16] Ottob. lat. 1223, ff. 92^r 93^v.

[17] J. R. Berrigan, "The 'Libellus Fabellarum' of Gregorio Correr," *Manuscripta,* 19(1975), 131-138.

[18] Sabbadini, p. 142.

[19] Berrigan, "Liber Satyrarum," 12.

[20] Other than Sabbadini, p. 142, there is the recent brief biography of Barbaro by E. Bigi in *Dizionario biografico degli italiani,* 6(Rome: Enciclopedia italiana, 1964), pp. 95-96.

[21] Sabbadini, p. 142.

[22] Bigi, p. 95.

[23] See below, note 29.

[24] Most conveniently accessible in Eugenio Garin, ed., *Prosatori latini del Quattrocento* (Milano: Ricciardi, 1952), pp. 103-137.

[25] Bigi, p. 96.

[26] Sabbadini, p. 142.

[27] B.M., MS Add 33782, f. 4^r.

[28] *Ibid.,* f. 5^r.

[29] *Ibid.,* f. 39^v.

[30] Typescript autobiography, Alderman Library, University of Virginia, p. 124.

[31] T. O. Achelis, "Die Aesopubersetzung des Lorenzo Valla," *Munchener Museum, 2(1913), 242.*

[32] Finch, "Valla," 118-120; Achelis, "Die Aesopübersetzung," 239-278; Achelis, "Aesopus Graecus per Laurentium Vallensem traductus Erffurdiae 1500," *Münchener Museum,* 2(1913), 222-229; Achelis, "Die

lateinischen Aesophandschriften der Vaticana und Laurentiana," *Münchener Museum,* 3(1914), 217-225.

[33] Achelis, "Dati und Corraro," 387.

[34] Sabbadini, p. 299.

[35] *Ibid., p. 300.*

[36] *Ibid., p. 504.*

Roseann Runte (essay date 1979)

SOURCE: "Reconstruction and Deconstruction: La Fontaine, Aesop and the Eighteenth-Century French Fabulist," in *Papers on French Seventeenth Century Literature,* No. 11, Summer 1979, pp. 29-46.

[*In the following essay, Runte compares the Aesopic fable with the work of French writer Jean de la Fontaine, identifying this distinction: while Aesopic fables treat the reader as a student to be instructed, La Fontaine's fables in verse treat the reader as a co-participant in interpreting the fable's meaning.*]

"Une ample comédie à cent actes divers," La Fontaine thus characterized his collection of fables.[1] Critics have not been remiss in exploring the dramatic qualities of these "scènes parfaites pour les caractères et le dialogue."[2] Dialogue has been explored primarily on the level of the plot line and in terms of the characters created by the fabulist: "Le Fabuliste fait de ses animaux ce qu'un Dramatique habile fait de ses Acteurs."[3] However, a second level of exchange exists in the fables. This is the dialogue which the author maintains with his reader. The presence of an authorial persona has been noted since the eighteenth century. La Harpe, for example, stated that La Fontaine, "a tellement imprimé son caractère à ses écrits, et ce caractère est si aimable, qu'il s'est fait des amis de tous ses lecteurs."[4] Marmontel suggested that the fabulist had designed a role for himself: that of a simple and credulous man to create an illusion by which to seduce the reader. La Fontaine was not a *conteur,* declared Marmontel, but "un témoin présent à l'action et qui veut vous y rendre présent vous-même."[5] Chamfort went a step further and exclaimed, "Que dirai-je de cet art charmant de s'entretenir avec son lecteur . . . ?"[6] It is this art which we shall attempt to define.

La Fontaine has created three authorial personae: the translator, the commentator, and the author. As translator he denies authorship of the fables and sets the stage for the second persona who is thus free to comment on and react to both fable and moral discourse. As non-author, he may disagree with either the allegorical pretense or the moral conclusion. This persona often makes personal application of the moral and it is thus that "La Fontaine nous fait rire, mais à ses dépens, et c'est sur lui-même qu'il fait tomber le ridicule."[7] The author as persona admits timidly to the creation of some fables such as "La Mort et le bûcheron." He is self-conscious of his art and extends his discussion of choice of character, form and style beyond the prologues and epilogues. A self-commentary extends through the entire collection. For example, he is concerned about length, "Je pourrais tout gâter par de plus longs récits," (289) and correction of language, "J'ai regret que ce mot soit tropvieux aujourd'hui," (101). Finally, the author's presence in the text is indicated through the choice of stylistic devices including rhetorical figures and parenthetical expressions which imply an overall system of values and establish a personality. In the first two manifestations of the authorial persona, the first person singular is the referential axis of discourse. The last instance is impersonal but nonetheless indicative of an opinion either through an overt statement: "[Un lion] Manda des médecins; / Il en est de tous arts" (184) or through the juxtaposition of opposites, the shortening of a line, the use of unexpected expressions, exaggeration and contrast, etc.

The translator's presence is evidenced through numerous statements of this nature: "Voici comme à peu près Esope le raconte" (133), "Pilpay conte qu'ainsi la chose s'est passée" (306). The translator assumes a guise of humility before his illustrious predecessors as well as his reader.

The commentator is present on both an impersonal and on a personal level, maintaining in each instance a rapport with the reader. He introduces his plot with expressions such as, "J'ai lu" (88) and "le conte m'en a plu toujours infiniment" (232). He reflects on character, situation and moral: "je le crois" (232, 377), "j'entends" (259), "je ne vois point" (228). The personal contact paints a human portrait of the fabulist which corresponds to some extent to the legendary interpretation of the artist who was seen as a *fablier,* a *bonhomme.* "On adore en lui cette *bonhommie,* devenue dans la postérité un de ses attributs distinctifs, mot vulgaire anobli en faveur de deux hommes rares, Henri IV et La Fontaine."[8] Just as the translator denies authorship, the commentator denies omniscience. He constantly underlines his human frailty and the limits of his prescience: "Je ne sais s'il avait raison" (86), "Concluons que la Providence / Sait ce qu'il nous faut mieux que nous" (135). He is naïve and appears to believe that which the reader is too sophisticated to admit: "Quand pour expliquer comment un cerf ignorait une maxime de Salomon, il nous avertit que ce cerf n'était pas accoutumé de lire . . . nous rions, mais de la nouvéte du poète, et c'est à ce piège si délicat que se prend notre vanité."[9] This character is forgetful (not always able to recall his source); insouciant: "ce ne sont pas là mes affaires" (100); misogynous as in "Le Mal Marié"; indolent: "Une souris tomba . . . / Je ne l'eusse pas ramassée" (223); nostalgic: "ai-je passé le temps d'aimer?" (219); impractical and prone to reverie: "Solitude où je trouve une douceur secrète" (268); slightly anti-social lacking paternal instincts: "O père de famille / (Et je ne t'ai jamais envié cet honneur)" (267). In short, he admits imperfection and reveals his personal flaws to establish intimacy with the reader. By the same token he authenticates his persona on whose reality depends the illusion of veracity, which in turn lends interest to the tale and credibility to the moral.

The three personae address themselves to two readers. One is the critic against whom the second reader is asked to join forces with La Fontaine. The presence of the critic demonstrates the merits of the second reader with whom we are asked to identify and with whom La Fontaine dialogues. We are invited to be the friend of the author (213) and to scorn the critic: "Maudit censeur, te tairas-tu?" (52). We want La Fontaine to conclude his *conte* and are obviously separate from "les délicats" who are "malheureux! / Rien ne saurait les satisfaire" (52). An example of the exchange between the reader-commentator and the second reader is in the fable, "Le Lion et le Moucheron": "Quelle chose par là nous peut être enseignée? [Author asks reader] J'en vois deux . . . . [Author confides and perhaps replies to reader]" (59).

La Fontaine's extended system of dialogue between authorial personae and readers is unique. "Aesop's" fables present a narration in the third person punctuated by occasional recourse to limited dialogue between animal characters.[10] If morals are presented, as in Nevelet, they are voiced by an impersonal, omniscient narrator. La Motte aptly summed up the effect: "En un mot je vois dans Esope un Philosophe qui s'abaisse pour être à la portée des plus simples."[11] The case is clear and may be easily illustrated by comparing the conclusion of the fable, "Le Corbeau et le renard," with La Fontaine's familiar verse. Esope in Nevelet reads: "Alors le corbeau dupe gémit de sa stupidité. Ceci montre combien l'intelligence a de valeur. Toujours, même sur le courage, prévaut la sagesse."[12] There is no complicity between author and reader. The author is present through omniscience, absent through intratextual signs. The author condescends to elucidate the reader. In La Fontaine's fables, the contrary is the rule. The reader condescends to join the poet in evaluating the allegorical relation and the moral as implied or stated. The Aesopian fable is straightforward while La Fontaine's is devious. The seventeenth-century poet plays with illusion and warns us: "Les fables ne sont pas ce qu'elles semblent être" (132). With La Fontaine the artistic veil of allegory extends beyond the simple *récit* to envelop its framework and moral.

The case of the eighteenth-century fable is necessarily more complex and difficult to analyze because of the extensive number of authors. Cognizant of the risks of generalities it may be advanced that these fabulists returned to the Aesopian norm of impersonal and omniscient narrator. The reader does not conspire with the narrator. The reader is the subject of the tale and the object of the moral. The author is ever aware of his weighty task of correcting the faults of the reader.[13] Unlike the Aesopian narrator who addresses a general public guilty of a myriad of imperfections, the eighteenth-century fabulist often singles out one social group: *belles, libertins* or an individual (often thinly masked by a plural): *rois, ambassadeurs,* etc. Rather than personalize the fable, this device reduces the scope of the moral application and the fable becomes exclusive instead of inclusive. When Aubert names his readers "Incrédules mortels, ceci s'adresse à vous. / Race ingrate, parlez: sera-ce quand la foudre / Aura réduit ce globe en poudre, / Que d'un être vengeur vous craindrez le courroux?" the effect is alienation.[14] The reader instinctively denies any relationship with these "incrédules mortels" and rejects personal application of the moral. Similarly, Benninger's vehement outcry, "O que ne pouvez-vous en accrocher autant, / Maudits flatteurs, que l'imbécile honore, / Mais que le sage abhorre," inspires neither identification nor participation.[15] The psychological effect contradicts the author's intention and the charm of the tale is lost in the thunder of the sermon.[16] Chamfort, in comparing La Fontaine to Molière, said that the former makes us aware of ourselves and our shortcomings, while the latter illustrates the vices of others. The impact of the first is necessarily greater than that of the second which the reader/spectator refuses to acknowledge.[17] The parallel may be aptly extended to the case under consideration. La Fontaine's fifteen-line fable, "Le Corbeau et le renard" may be compared to Le Noble's seventy-two-line fable of the same title. Eighteen lines are separate from the allegorical tale and are moralistic: "Oh la dangereuse fumée, / Que celle d'un Encens flatteur, / Malheur, malheur à ceux dont l'âme est si affamée / D'un mets si doux, si séducteur. . . . "[18] The subtitle of Richer's inversion of the same fable, "Leçon allégorique à ceux qui se croyent plus fins que les autres" is in itself indicative of the tone of omniscience. The narrative is imbued with serious moral purpose.[19] It is furthermore an invitation to telescope rather than to magnify the moral thrust. The eighteenth-century fabulist's method is deductive and both the premises of the argument and the conclusion of the syllogism are clearly indicated to the reader whose only action is to accept or reject the lesson. La Fontaine presents the evidence or observations and invites the reader to actively participate in induction.

These distinctions are at first view incompatible with history. La Fontaine's enormous popularity and the hommage paid to his genius during the eighteenth century have been established.[20] He was openly regarded by his successors in the genre as a model. This fact is the key to the seeming paradox. The eighteenth-century fabulists analyzed La Fontaine's works to discover the elements of his success. It is ironic that this very research should have been responsible for their failure. On the most obvious level, they became self-conscious authors following an established set of rules. Grozelier said: " . . .[La Motte and D'Ardenne] ont établi des règles . . . ainsi j'ai dû me conformer à ces règles, au lieu d'en proposer de nouvelles."[21] In complying with an abstract formula, the author's individual characteristics tended to be obscured, and the fable became less personal. Among the precepts for perfection were polished language and style. La Fontaine was considered inelegant and negligent.[22] The attempt to regularize and correct also contributed to the sterility of the form. Creation was preceded and dominated by critical theory. The stilted result again removed the fable from the realm of author-reader correspondence. It is a question of temporal and stylistic distance. The creative process continues as the reader participates with La Fontaine. In the eighteenth-century fable, a finished production is presented. The creative process begins and ends with the author.

Nivernais echoed the sentiment of most eighteenth-century fabulists when he prefaced his fables: "Ce ne sont pas contes pour rire / Que j'offre ici; / Je veux instruire. . . . "[23] La Fontaine's successors maintained that the master had neglected his moral purpose. La Motte even hypothesized that he had written the fable and then sought a moral to justify its existence. In reversing the situation, the eighteenth-century poet became didactic. He concentrated on idea rather than format and conscious of his moral mission, emphasized the moral to the detriment of the allegorical tale.[24] Fearing that the reader would fall victim to the artifice and neglect to read beneath the surface features of the text, the narrator constantly raised the level of comprehension to a conscious level. In La Fontaine it was subconscious and followed the act of reading. That is, where La Fontaine is implicit, the eighteenth-century fabulist is explicit. For example, in addition to his moral he often explains the allegory: "Le Malheur de ce rejetton / Opprimé par ce Chêne antique, / Est celui de Boston sous la loi Tyrannique / De l'orgueilleuse Albion: / Et la France est le Bûcheron / Qui, par sa valeur héroïque, / Le tire de l'oppression."[25]

In their quest for success, the eighteenth-century fabulists considered the question of authorship. With D'Ardenne, most admitted that previously invented situations or truths (morals) might be employed if counterbalanced by originality in other aspects of the narration. La Motte proposed the creation of new characters: "Les acteurs les moins usités et les plus bizarres deviennent naturels et méritent même la préférence sur d'autres."[26] This resulted in a reduction of simplicity and an increase in the distance between the reader and the text. Metaphysical and symbolic beings: "La Lune et la jarretière," "Le Crime et le châtiment," the bizarre: "La Vessie," "Le Gras de la jambe et le téton," "La Jonquille et le grate-cul," "Le Pot de chambre et la trophée," "L'Oeil et le pantoufle," the obscure: "La Métamorphose d'un professeur de philosophie en cigale," "Les Femelles des oiseaux en ambassade devant Jupiter," remove the fable from the terrain of the familiar. Abstractions such as pregnant ignorance giving birth to Miss Opinion who is named Truth by Pride and indolence, lack the warmth and spontaneity of Jean Lapin.[27] The reader is further separated from the text by the tone inspired by these characters. Moreover, since the authors insisted on originality (novelty), they necessarily rejected the role of translator and removed their own personal presence from the text.

While the eighteenth-century fabulists recognized in La Fontaine a quality they termed variously, *le génie, le plaisant, le sublime du naturel, le riant, le je ne sais quoi,* they had difficulty in defining it.[28] Rules were nonetheless established for reproducing the effect. However, its role was limited to that of stylistic ornamentation and the conscious presence of figures such as the use of familiar nomenclature (Maître Corbeau, Jean Lapin) is not consonant with the overall tenor of the fable. Mile Opinion and Dame Pleine Lune, as well as carefully chosen plays on words, are anachronistic. The effect is neither continuous nor extensive. They do not appear casual. They are formal literary devices, obvious to the reader as they stand out from the text. Instead of revealing a confidant, a reader with a human character present in the tale, they unveil an author who is unsuccessfully attempting to create an illusion.
The overriding desires of the eighteenth-century fabulists are to be moral, to justify their productions through their claim to originality and uniqueness, and to regularize the genre while capturing the charms of naïveté. The author as persona was replaced by the author as moral artist. The authorial personae in La Fontaine dialogue; the moral artist or omniscient narrator sermonizes. The first posit their imperfection and surprise the reader who discovers unsuspected merit. The second claims expertise and invites criticism. La Fontaine reduced his commentator to a level beneath that of the reader. The eighteenth-century fabulist attempted to raise the reader to his own level of literary and moral perfection. La Fontaine conspires with his reader and inspires confidence. His successors conspired against the reader and alienated him.

The structure and tone of La Fontaine's fables meet the conditions described by many critics as characteristic of irony. Socrates was a midwife to his disciples' intelligence. He would dissimulate urbanely and ask his followers for plain answers suited to his own professed ignorance.[29] La Fontaine's authorial personae claim to be something less than they are in reality. They play the role of an *eiron*.[30] They operate a brachylogy, renouncing exhaustiveness and placing confidence in the reader to interpret and understand, to complete the textual implications. It is an elliptical rather than an encyclopaedic manner.[31] "The reader is not exposed to attack but admitted to an alliance upon which the whole force of the rhetoric depends."[32] " . . . We have come to apply the term irony to the fusion in a spectator's mind of superior knowledge and detached sympathy."[33] The preceding discussion of the exchange between authorial personae and reader in La Fontaine illustrates the manner in which his form suits the description of Socratic Irony.

Irony requires an unconscious art.[34] It may be found in simplicity. "Irony by its very nature instructs by *pleasing*. To ignore the pleasure, and its civilized implications, is inevitably to simplify and falsify the total effect."[35] It has been demonstrated that the eighteenth-century fabulist was conscious of his art and tended to make pleasure secondary to instruction. In so doing, he ignored some of the implications of irony.

Verbal and situational irony create tension. Alternatives of perspective, the clash between appearance and reality, the trembling equipoise between jest and earnest create a sense of irony.[36] Irony is false modesty, false naïveté, and false negligence, according to Jankélévitch (or artistry in Thompson).[37] The eighteenth-century fabulist failed to recognize the illusion which was deliberately created by La Fontaine. When he spokeseriously of insignificant matters it was ironic. The fabulists of the next century did not interpret correctly the ironist's mask. They saw it as a true face. They mistook the appearance for reality. The result is the difference between La Fontaine and his successors. The first has "l'apparence du sérieux," the second, "le sérieux de l'apparence."[38] That is, La Fontaine's pleasantries seem serious, while during the enlightenment, what was serious was made to seem amusing. La Fontaine, the ironist, stood halfway between the illusion of his allegory and the truth of his moral, fluctuating between hypocrisy and good faith. The eighteenth-century fabulist never deviated from his moral intention. He refused to allow either himself or his reader to be confidently unaware that appearance is only appearance.[39] Both are eternally witness to reality. Text and context are unified.

In dramatic irony there are three roles: the victim, the audience and the author,[40] In La Fontaine the author and reader collaborate to unmask the victim, while in the fables of the later period, the victim is the audience. One role has been omitted and the effect is not ironic. It is closer to satire.[41]

Irony, in general terms, is the clash between connotative and denotative signs. The superficial text makes a statement which is counter to the implied meaning. To interpret such a text the reader must engage in a process of reconstruction. He must peer into the text and unmask the *eiron*. He executes a *pas de deux,* tearing down the surface features and reconstructing meaning. The author invites the reader to form a new conclusion. La Fontaine, through his authorial personae, commences the process within the text itself. He dramatically engages with the reader in discovering the implications of the allegory.[42] The eighteenth-century fabulist, in placing the reader in a role of passive detachment, has deconstructed the possibilities for surface tension and a search for hidden meaning.

La Fontaine's fables are vertical in structure while those of the eighteenth century are horizontal. La Fontaine's dialogue gives the fables a double layer. They are, like irony, a two-storied phenomenon.[43] The reader is encouraged to sound the depths and move to a new level. The eighteenth-century fable's surface is flat; the significance is apparent. The thesis is explained in the lecture, the moral in the sermon. There are no further levels of application for the reader to explore.

La Fermière, an eighteenth-century fabulist, saw the mask in the fable: "Ce genre antique, inventé par un sage, / Offre toujours un voile officieux / Que l'amour-propre emploie à son usage. / La Fable plait quand la Satire outrage, / Et par-là même elle instruit beaucoup mieux."[44] However, he did not completely understand its function. He interpreted it as a shield for the reader who would otherwise be wounded by the author's satiric barbs. It was more than this. It was a delicate cornerstone of the ironic structure of the fable. La Fontaine offered the veil not only as protection, butalso as enticement to the reader to enter into the process of reconstruction. The eighteenth-century fabulist denied the veil, or rather misapplied it and purposefully filled it with holes. He feared it would effectively hide his moral and did not trust the reader to infer the meaning. For example, La Fermière himself concludes a fable: "Expliquons l'allégorie; / Dans ce combat le Lecteur / Verra la Philosophie aux prises avec l'Erreur."[45]

In effect, the eighteenth-century fabulist assumed the role of philosopher fighting error. Like Aesop, he used the fable as an illustration for his moral. Fable and moral were one. Connotative and denotative meaning were congruous. La Fontaine socratically asked his reader to become a philosopher and discover both his own and the author's errors. The invitation is indicated by the tension between overt and covert significance and is delivered in the dialogue between authorial personae and reader which frames the allegorical narration. The double-tiered literary structure parallels the intellectual construction the reader will build by the juxtaposition of antipodal meanings. The reader of Aesop and the eighteenth-century fabulist is a witness, while La Fontaine's reader is co-author, continuing the creative function in reconstructing in his own terms the significance of the fable: "La véritable auteur du récit n'est pas seulement celui qui le raconte, mais aussi, et parfois bien davantage, celui qui l'écoute."[46]

Notes

[1] Jean de La Fontaine, *Oeuvres complètes* (Paris: Gallimard, 1954), p. 115. Further references to this work appear in the text. When appropriate, spelling has been modernized. See also Pierre-Augustin Caron de Beaumarchais, *Oeuvres complètes* (Paris: Léopold Collin, 1809), II, 5-6: "La Fable est une comédie légère, et toute comédie n'est qu'un long apologue: leur différence est, que dans notre comédie les hommes sont souvent des bêtes, et qui pis est, des bêtes méchantes."

[2] Jean-François de La Harpe, "Eloge de La Fontaine," *Recueil de l'Académie des Belles-Lettres, Sciences et Arts* (Marseilles, 1774), p. 16.

[3] La Harpe, p. 17.

[4] La Harpe, *Lycée ou cours de littérature* (Paris: H. Agasse, 1798), VI, 325.

[5] Jean-François Marmontel, "Fable," *Encyclopédie ou dictionnaire raisonné des sciences, des arts et des métiers* (Stuttgart: Friedrich Frommann, 1966), VI [1756], 346.

[6] Sébastien-Roch-Nicolas Chamfort, "Eloge de La Fontaine," *Les Trois Fabulistes: Esope, Phèdre et La Fontaine* (Paris, 1976), III, 186.

[7] Marmontel, p. 348.

[8] La Harpe, *Lycée,* p. 325.

[9] Marmontel, p. 348.

[10] "Aesopian fables" here refers to fables collected and transmitted in such works as *Mythologia Aesopica Isaaci Nicolai Neveleti* (Frankfort, 1610).

[11] Antoine Houdar de La Motte, *Fables nouvelles* (Paris: Grégoire Dupuis, 1719), p. xiv.

[12] La Fontaine, *Fables,* ed. R. Radouant (Paris: Hachette, 1929), p. 16.

[13] See Roseann Runte, "The Paradox of the Fable in Eighteenth-Century France," *Neophilologus* (to appear) and "A Study of Thematic Artifice: The Eighteenth-Century French Fable," paper delivered at the 1976 conference of the American Society for Eighteenth-Century Studies, University of Virginia.

[14] Abbé Jean-Louis Aubert, "Les Mites," in Lottin [Hérissant], *Le Fablier français ou élite des meilleures fables depuis La Fontaine* (Paris: Lottin le jeune, 1771), pp. 70-71.

[15] Benninger, "Le Corbeau et le renard," *Choix des plus belles fables qui ont paru en Allemagne imitées en vers français* (Kehl, 1782).

[16] Saint-Marc Girardin, *La Fontaine et les fabulistes* (Paris: Michel Lévy frères, 1867), II, 466, 243 ff.

[17] Chamfort, p. 176.

[18] Eustache Le Noble, *Contes et fables* (Lyon: Claude Rey, 1697), II, 85-86.

[19] Henri Richer, "Le Corbeau et le renard," in Gaigne, *Encyclopédie poétique ou recueil complet de chef-d'oeuvres de poésie sur tous les sujets possibles* (Paris: Gaigne et Moutard, 1778), IV, 330-32.

[20] See for example G. Saillard, *Essal sur la fable en France au dix-huitième siècle* (Toulouse: Privat, 1912), pp. 12-57.

[21] Pere Nicolas Grozelier, *Fables nouvelles* (Paris: De Saint et Saillant, 1790), p. v.

[22] See Runte, "Paradox."

[23] Louis-Jules Barbon Mancini-Mazarini duc de Nivernais, *Fables* (Paris: Nivernais, 1796), I, 3.

[24] Saillard, p. 156: "Ils ont sacrifié la forme au fond."

[25] Demarie, "Le Chêne, l'arbrisseau, et le bûcheron," *Journal de littérature, des sciences et des arts,* 5 (Paris: Au bureau du journal, 1781), 5.

[26] La Motte, p. xxviii.

[27] Marmontel, p. 347.

[28] Pierre Clarac, *La Fontaine: l'homme et l'oeuvre* (Paris: Boivin, 1947), p. 154.

[29] S.C. Muecke, *The Compass of Irony,* (London: Methuen, 1969), p. 57 and G.C. Sedgewick, *Of Irony Especially in Drama* (Toronto: University of Toronto Press, 1948), p. 13.

[30] J.A.K. Thompson, *Irony, An Historical Introduction* (London: George Allen and Unwin Ltd., 1926), pp. 10-18.

[31] Vladimir Jankélévitch, *L'Ironie* (Paris: Félix Alcan, 1936), p. 89.

[32] A.E. Dyson, *The Crazy Fabric. Essays in Irony* (London: Macmillan and Co., 1965), p. 152.

[33] Sedgewick, p. 33.

[34] Thompson, p. 109.

[35] Dyson, p. 13.

[36] Sedgewick, p. 26, Thompson, p. 166, Cleanth Brooks, *The Well-Wrought Urn: Studies in the Structure of Poetry* (New York: Harcourt Brace and World, 1947), p. 195.

[37] Jankélévitch, p. 90 and Thompson, p. 131.

[38] Jankélévitch, p. 111. See also Marmontel, p. 346: "c'est le sérieux avec lequel il mêle les plus grandes choses avec les plus petites. . . . "

[39] See for example Normal Knox, "On the Classification of Ironies," *Modern Philology,* 70 (1972), p. 53.

[40] Jankélévitch, p. 111; Muecke, *Irony* (Norfolk, Great Britain: Methuen, 1970), p. 35.

[41] Dyson, p. 1.

[42] Cleanth Brooks, "Irony and 'Ironic' Poetry," *College English* 9 (1948), 237; Muecke, *Compass,* 21, 29; Wayne C. Booth, *A Rhetoric of Irony* (Chicago: University of Chicago Press, 1975), passim, especially Ch. 11; Dyson, p. 5.

[43] Muecke, *Compass,* p. 19.

[44] [La Fermière], *Fables et contes* (Paris: Lacombe, 1775), title page.
[45] [La Fermiere], p. 175.

[46] Gérard Genette, *Figures III* (Paris: Seuil, 1972), p. 267.

John E. Keller and L. Clark Keating (essay date 1993)

SOURCE: "Introduction," in *Aesop's Fables with a Life of Aesop,* translated and edited by John E. Keller and L. Clark Keating, pp. 1-6. Lexington: University Press of Kentucky, 1993.

[*In the following essay, Keller and Keating trace the history of Aesopic fables in Spain until the fifteenth-century publication of the Spanish* Ysopet.]

Aesop's Fables, with a Life of Aesop—in Spanish *La vida del Ysopet con sus fabulas hystoriadas*—along with versions with similar titles in many western languages, represents the apogee of that body of stories we know as Aesop's Fables. This may seem an unusual statement to make, since the *Ysopet,* as we shall term it in this introduction, was not translated into Castilian until the late fifteenth century and not printed in its entirety in Spain until 1489. An incomplete version was printed in Saragossa in 1482 with woodcuts colored by hand. According to Victoria Burrus, who pointed out to me the existence of this incomplete incunable, the 1489 edition we have used as the basis of our translation is a corrected and augmented version of the 1482 text. While the 1482 edition should be the basis of a critical edition, since it is incomplete it cannot be the text from which a translation should be made. The edition of 1488, printed in Toulouse and edited by Victoria Burrus and Harriet Goldberg, would not have influenced the many Spanish versions listed by Cotarelo y Mori in his introduction to the facsimile edition of *Ysopete hystoriado* of 1489. The edition of 1482 would quite probably have been the one used by the printed in Toulouse. Be that as it may, since the text of 1482 is incomplete, and since the text of Toulouse of 1488 contains woodcuts not asexcellent as those in the printing of 1489 in Saragossa, we are confident that our choice of edition is best for the present translation, which is the first into the English language.

To begin with, we do not know if indeed in the sixth century B.C. there actually lived an author named Aesop any more than we can be certain that about three thousand years ago a man named Homer flourished. But we believe in an Aesop because ancient writers of consequence—Herodotus, Plato, and Aristotle, to name but three—mention him as a fabulist and because various ancient writers—Babrius, Phaedrus, Avianus, and others—gathered and set down fables they attributed to him. No manuscripts of Aesop have survived from that early period and, what is worse, nothing like a complete collection of those fables has survived the ages. We do not know, therefore, how many fables go back to the original collections. But fables attributed to Aesop were gathered and set down in writing across the centuries, some collections copious and some limited as to number, in both Greek and Latin. Wherever Greek colonists went in ancient times, they surely took some of the fables with them, and in Spain this would have scattered Aesop along the eastern seaboard. Roman conquerors and settlers surely brought Aesop with them to Rome's favorite colony.

Closer to us, because Aesop began to appear in the vernacular literatures of the West, is the impact of Aesop in the Middle Ages. In Spain, Odo of Cheriton's *Fabulae,* containing a great deal of Aesopic material, was probably translated from the Latin in the thirteenth century, when Odo flourished, even though the only extant manuscript of it in Spanish translation, *El libro de los gatos,* is of fifteenth-century vintage. The collection of eastern fables and stories *Kalila wa Dimna,* translated from the Arabic in 1251 at the behest of Prince Alfonso (to be crowned in 1252 as Alfonso X) and entitled *Calila e Digna,* contained some

Aesopic fables, attesting to the fact that Aesop had penetrated the literatures of the Islamic world. In the fourteenth century Juan Ruiz, Archpriest of Hita, inserted more than twenty-five Aesopic fables into his *Libro de buen amor,* and his contemporary Don Juan Manuel adapted several in his *Conde Lucanor.* In the first quarter of the fifteenth century the Archdeacon Clemente Sánchez used a considerable number in his *Libro de los exenplos por a.b.c.,* the most copious book of brief narratives in the medieval Spanish language. Aesop, then, was well known in Spain long before the printing of the *Ysopet.*

We must trace the ancestry of Spain's great corpus of Aesopic fables as they appeared in the West to the Middle Ages' most comprehensive anthology collected and written down in one volume in medieval Greek by Maximus Planudius, ambassador to Venice from Constantinople in 1327. From what sources this ecclesiastic garnered the many fables he set down is not known, nor do we know the authorship of the fictitious thirteenth-century *Life of Aesop* which Planudius included as an important preface to his anthologyof fables. It is certain that he did not stop with fables considered as belonging to an Aesopic tradition, for he included a good many brief narratives definitely not fables at all. These stemmed from eastern tales, many of which originated in the *Panchatantra,* written in Sanskrit, and passed through Pahlevi into Arabic and thence into Planudius's native Greek. It is even possible that a few included by him were taken from folklore.

Had Planudius's anthology remained in Greek, the fate of Aesopic fables in the West would have been far less happy than it is. Though we owe much to Planudius, since he saved many fables from virtual oblivion, we owe almost as much to his translator into Latin, one Rinuccio Thesalo or d'Arezzo, who toward the middle of the fifteenth century brought into Western Europe the first nearly complete anthology of Aesopic material. Some debt is owed, too, to Cardinal Antonio Cerdá of Mallorca, to whom d'Arezzo dedicated his book, for it is likely that this important ecclesiastic did much to publicize Aesop and to aid in the dissemination of d'Arezzo's translation. It may be more than coincidence that Saragossa in the Kingdom of Aragon became a center of Aesopic fables in Spanish so that eventually the *Ysopet* was published there. Lending support to this statement is the fact that d'Arezzo's Latin work was translated into Castilian probably in the 1460s at the behest of Enrique, viceroy of Cataluña under his cousin Ferdinand of Aragon, who married Isabella of Castile. Enrique, to whom the manuscript of the *Ysopet* had been submitted for approval in the 1460s, could not see it printed, since printing did not reach Spain until 1480.

It should be noted that d'Arezzo's translation from the Greek was also translated into other European tongues, but the way in which this affected the course of Aesopic fables in Spain will be treated below. Suffice to say that one important center of translation was Germany.

The work of d'Arezzo in Latin had great success in most of Europe, at least among the erudite, but much less among vernacular speakers whose Latin was weak or nonexistent. Almost as soon as the printing press was invented in Germany vernacular versions of Aesop began to appear. Doctor Heinrich Steinhöwel's translation from d'Arezzo was published by Johannes Zeiner in Ulm and Augsburg at some time between 1474, when printing reached Ulm, and 1483, when it came to Augsburg. The Steinhöwel translation followed the order of fables in d'Arezzo, as might have been expected, and included the lengthy "Life of Aesop," which should be regarded as an important contribution to the rise and development of the European novel. This fictitious biography runs to just over twenty-five pages. It contains a frontispiece illustrating Aesop himself and twenty-eight woodcuts, each depicting an event in his life.

The corpus of fables is divided into eight separate sections variously called "books" or "parts." In the Editio Princeps' table of contents each fable or other form of brief narrative is listed by title. Books I, II, III, and IV contain twenty fables each andare composed of many fables we recognize as belonging to the Aesopic tradition. Book V contains seventeen fables and bears the title *Fabulas extravagantes,* possibly because these stories belong to less familiar collections, such as the *Roman de Renart,* the French *fabliaux,* and folkloric sources. We have labeled this book *The Fanciful Fables of Aesop,* since this is one meaning of *extravagantes.* Book VI also contains seventeen fables and bears the title *Las fabulas de Remicio,* that is, fables of Rinuccio d'Arezzo, a significant fabulist.

Book VII, *Las fabulas de Aviano,* comes from fables written by one Avianus, who flourished sometime between the second and fifth centuries. It contains twenty-seven stories. Book VIII, *Las fabulas collectas de Alfonso e de Poggio y de otros en la forma e orden seguiente,* contains twenty-two. The Alfonso of the title is Petrus Alfonsus, the Aragonese Jew whose twelfth-century *Disciplina Clericalis* was perhaps the most oft quoted of collections. Poggio is Poggio Bracciolini (1380-1459), whose humorous and often scatological *Facetiae* were among the most popular of fable anthologies. We have not been able to identify "los otros" as to source.

In 1489, just six years after the printing in Augsburg, a German printer named Jan Hurus, transplanted to Saragossa, published the Editio Princeps of *La vida del Ysopet con sus fabulas hystoriadas.* Hurus must have known the German version. He had brought the science of printing to Aragon, and he embellished his printing of *Ysopet* with the same woodcuts, or virtually identical copies, printed in the editions of Zeiner in Ulm and Augsburg. One can state, therefore, that the relationship between the German translation of d'Arezzo and the Spanish is remarkably close. The only noticeable difference between the two, insofar as content is concerned, lies in the section entitled "Collectas," in which there are four fables not found in the German text. In a Spanish version of 1496 four more were added. The similarity of the woodcuts and ignorance of the origin of the Spanish translation have led some to believe that the Spanish *Ysopet* was a translation of the German—an obvious error, since both the German and the Castilian were translated from the Latin of d'Arezzo.

Such, in the very briefest terms, is the history of the definitive collections of Aesopic fables in Spain.

The famous woodcuts deserve more attention, for they served not only to enliven the fables and other brief narratives but to fix them in the memories of readers. Narrative art in book illustration had, in medieval times, developed to a remarkable extent. It is not strange, then, that this art continued in the Renaissance in a form not well known in earlier times, that is, in woodcuts, which could be printed as easily as letters. It was primarily in Germany and the Netherlands that this art reached its height. These were the times of Dürer and the "little masters," Aldorfer, Behams, and Pencz, who first began to forsake religious topics in woodcuts to produce, with a touch of the decorative quality learned from Italian masters, the humor and studied debauchery of everyday life.

And so it was that the Editio Princeps of the *Ysopet,* printed in 1489 and made available to thousands, began the centuries-long influence of the greatest fables of the ancient world. From this first volume all the later Spanish editions came, and from this tradition all Spanish writers who mentioned Aesop or used his fables in their works drew their references. It can be stated without fear of contradiction that the romantic life of Aesop and the collection of fables made available to Spaniards in 1489 was the most widely read body of literature across at least two centuries in Spain. Nor should we wonder at this. After all, the same fables from their inception in distant Antiquity until the present, have attracted and held human attention. It is fortunate that the Royal Spanish Academy in 1929 published a complete facsimile of the single extant copy of the Editio Princeps, thereby preserving it for posterity. With the scholarly intro-\duction by Emilio Cotareli y Mori, it contributes vastly to our understanding of a great work of the past.

Today Aesop is read for the pleasure his fables afford rather than for the utilitarian value of their lessons, although these lessons are present, as they were in the fifteenth century and, for that matter, in all the previous centuries. These lessons are universal and are at home in any age and any culture, for they are based upon life itself and the practical wisdom one needs to survive. One can, of course, dispense with the lesson and simply enjoy the stories *per se,* as children do. And yet it may be impossible to divorce *dulce* (story) from *utile* (lesson), because the moralization found in each fable is actually a component of narrative technique perhaps as much as are plot, conflict, characterization, and the other elements of narrative. People expected the moralization, even if they did not always realize they were imbibing it. Moreover, the fables led to the creation of proverbs, which are always a delight and a convenience—even a necessity in daily parlance. In Spain, where proverbs are still a way of life, the *Ysopet* must have generated more of such witty or sententious sayings than anywhere else. In our own daily parlance we seldom pass a day without uttering an "Aesopic proverb," even in abbreviated form, as in "like a dog in the manager," "sour grapes," "cat's paw," and many more.

In the Middle Ages and the Renaissance the Roman Catholic Church allowed Aesopic fables to creep into its sermons and homilies, despite the fact that Aesopic "morality" in its utter utilitarianism was a far cry from the tenets of Christianity. Not even the weak excuse that examples of duplicity and selfishness could be used to teach the avoidance of such qualities actually justified the telling of such fables in the pulpit. The influence of Aesop was everywhere. People heard the fables recited and read them in books, they were depicted in sculpture, in tapestries, in carvings of wood and ivory and stone, they were seen on the capitals of columns and in frescoes and other paintings, and most of all they were familiar in book illustrations.

And today where does one find Aesop? His fables appear in story books for children; some can be found in school books; reciters of folktales include Aesopic fables; in some parts of the world professional tellers or readers offer such fables in their repertories; anthologies like ours in translation contain them; and fables concerned with adultery and cuckoldry, which are not found in true Aesopic fables but are often found accompanying them, have appeared in as popular a magazine as *Playboy* in its "Ribald Classics." Stories in this last category have reached perhaps the largest possible audience, upwards of more than two million subscribers, not counting the many others who read each copy. Aesop's fables are not dead.

The language of *La vida del Ysopet con sus fabulas hystoriadas* is good fifteenth-century Castilian colored somewhat by Aragonese, since it is quite likely that the translator was a native of Aragon. But since translations are often shaped to some degree by the original tongue, specialists may see something not quite typical. They should consider, even so, that a work accepted by a humanist of such consequence as the Viceroy of Cataluña could not have been regarded by him as faulty or dialectal. To the reader of the modern English version none of this is significant, of course. In short, the Spanish from which the present translation was made must have been well received in the Peninsula, to judge by the number of subsequent editions.

The present translation of the *Ysopet* follows to a rather remarkable degree the philosophy of the translator from the Latin, and one may read that interesting concept of the translator's art in the first few lines of the *Ysopet*. The approach to translation taken by the author five hundred years ago and the present-day translators are surprisingly parallel. Modern scholars can improve upon the original, however, and can achieve better success in rendering the imagery, speech, concepts, and thought of the Spanish text. Our parlance is of the most modern American vintage. We have broken up the inordinately lengthy sentences of the original into more manageable form, have created paragraphs, have punctuated where the original did not, and have avoided many of the archaisms and strictures that Hurus's book contained. We believe we have succeeded in offering to modern readers one of the most complete anthologies of Aesopic fables, together with a number of those non-Aesopic tales that by the fifteenth century tended to be included with the true fables. Readers of our translation of *La vida del Ysopet con sus fabulas hystoriadas* are in essence reading what d'Arezzo gave his readers in Latin and therefore what Maximus Planudius offered his readers in Greek.

POLITICAL USES OF THE AESOPIC FABLE

Annabel Patterson (essay date 1991)

SOURCE: "The Fable Is Inverted: 1628-1700," in *Fables of Power: Aesopian Writing and Political History*, pp. 81-109. Durham: Duke University Press, 1991.

[*In the following essay, Patterson maintains that in seventeenth-century England the Aesopic fable was refined into a verbal weapon. No longer limited in range to local or temporal political issues, the genre was used to dealt with larger, more universal issues such as the conflict between absolute and parliamentary power.*]

The world is chang'd and we have Choyces,
Not by most Reasons, but most Voyces,

The Lion's trod on by the Mouse,
The lower is the upper House:

. . . . .

The feet, and lower parts, 'tis sed,
Would trample on, and off the head,
What ere they say, this is the thing,
They love the Charles, but hate the King;
To make an even Grove, one stroke
Should lift the Shrubb unto the Oake.

Anon: "A Madrigall on Justice"

If Elizabeth's reign was, for all its strategic successes and overall stability, occasionally vulnerable to the subversive critical analysis that fables made possible, we would expect the same to be even more true of the earlier seventeenth century, when the first two Stuarts were less accomplished in maintaining the stance defined by Lyly's Lion, of being above question. Indeed, to begin with, the fable under James continued on the track pioneered by Spenser; as Hoyt Hudson has demonstrated, *Mother Hubberds Tale* spawned a whole series of animal satires, with the cast of characters extended as necessary. The earliest was Michael Drayton's *The Owle* (1604), an extended bird polity marking the accession of James as the Eagle. Richard Niccols produced two such satires, the first, *The Cuckow* (1607), in obvious imitation of Drayton's bird kingdom, the second, *The Beggers Ape,* written before 1610 but unpublished until 1617, virtually a sequel to *Mother Hubberds Tale. The Cuckow* was a generalized attack on sexual looseness that unfavorably contrasted Jacobean mores with Elizabeth's ethos of chastity, and *The Beggers Ape,* which retained Spenser's Fox and Ape as the villains, was primarily directed against the sale of titles as a means of raising revenues. William Goddard's *The Owles Araygnement* (c. 1616), pointed "with some plainness" to the murder of Sir Thomas Overbury by the agents of Carr and Frances Howard; and, finally, John Hepwith's *The Calidonian Forrest,* another fable of misgovernment by false deputy (Buckingham as the Hart) extended the genre into Charles's reign. Although written at the time of Buckingham's death in 1628, Hepwith's poem was not published until 1641 when, Hudson speculates, it may have appeared in order to counter the effect of James Howell's Royalist tree-fable, *Dodona's Grove: or the Vocall Forrest,* the first instalment of which appeared in 1640.[1]

While the very existence of these neo-Spenserian texts is proof of the fable's functionality, their procedures—to attack either generalized corruption or egregious local instances of it—render them relatively inaccessible today. It was the more theoretical model provided by Sidney that would gradually emerge on the cutting edge of seventeenth-century politics. In that model, central elements of classical fables, or of the fable's history as a genre, are used as ideological principles, and against them are measured the new historical circumstances that motivated the writer to return to Aesop. For the fable to do its work in the world, a contemporary vocabulary and issues cannot merely be grafted upon a traditional matrix, but past and present must be seen to be *structurally* related. And the more people wrestled to accommodate received systems to vast social and cultural changes, the more it became evident that the fable was no rudimentary signifying system, but capable of doing advanced work in the arena of political definition.

The major issue in need of definition from Elizabeth's death to the outbreak of civil war was, in fact, peculiarly adapted to Aesopian tradition: the sanctions of royal power and its limitations, if any. In James's reign the theoretical relationship between the sovereignty vested in the king and responsibilities vested in parliament, became, of course, widely debated and contested, not least because James himself had published his views on the subject; the stock phrases that registered the contest were royal prerogative and the liberties of the subject. Parliamentary history shows a series of confrontations between king and parliament in which attempts to deal with other issues (the proposed union between England and Scotland, monopolies, impositions, the Great Contract of 1610) foundered in the impasse created by those terms; and of those confrontations, the most disruptive was the 1628-29 struggle over the Petition of Right and the resulting decision by Charles I to rule without parliament indefinitely.

In the records of the House of Commons for May 22, 1628, there appears an instance of fabulist discourse that is almost too good to be true, in its making explicit the procedure by which an old metaphor was reappropriated and reinterpreted in terms of the current crisis, and in showing how a literary training and imagination could function in political debate; not, as one might too easily assume, merely to add rhetorical force or emotive content, but to clarify and demystify an otherwise ill-defined constitutional abstraction.

The context of the discussion was whether the Petition of Right should be circumscribed by a proviso proposed by the Lords excluding the king's "sovereign power" from the terms proposed. In opposing the Lords' amendment, Sir Henry Marten (father of the regicide) spoke with unusual forcefulness and color:

> Horace dislikes the painter that *humano capiti* would join a horse's neck. Yet if he made a horse's neck alone it was good. The King may not require money but in parliament. It is a man's head; but add this clause, "unless it be by sovereign power," then it is a lion's neck, and it mars all. . . . It implies the King is trusted with a power for the destruction

and also for the safety of the people. It admits also he may use "sovereign power," and if he do we may not refuse it, for it is for our protection. So it bounds up my mouth that I cannot but say that it is for the good of the people. "Sovereign power" is transcending and a high word. There is a tale in *Aesop's Fables,* the moral whereof shall be that when actions are regulated by law you may guess at the proportion, but if it be regulated by the prerogative, there is no end. The ass, the lion and the fox agreed to go on hunting, and they found good prey, and the ass was willing to make a division, and so he did laying all into three heaps, and said to the lion, "It is your prerogative to choose." The lion took it ill and said, "It is my prerogative to choose," and he tore the ass and did eat him up. He said to the fox, "Divide you," so he took a little part of the skin, and left all the rest. The lion asked him what he meant. He answered him, "All is yours." The lion replied, "This is my prerogative," and he asked the fox who taught him that. Said he, "The calamity of the ass."[2]

The fact that this episode was recounted in four of the parliamentary journals, and in one of them with such precision, suggests a paradox: that Marten's speech was so remarkable that its textual nuances were seen as essential to the record; and that the fable he chose was so familiar that Marten could count on his audience to recognize and appreciate his divergences from it. The preexistent fabulist plot on which he depended was simple: in *The Lion, the Cow, the Goat, and the Sheep,* which usually appeared early in the Aesopian corpus, the lion and three non-predators agree, unnaturally, to go hunting together and to divide the spoils; but when the time comes for division, the lion claims all the shares one by one, by a series of rationalizations, and none dare gainsay him. In Caxton's version, already quoted in my introduction, the lion offers a four-point claim to all four shares, culminating in naked threat: "who so ever toucheth the fourthe part he shalle be myn mortal enemy." And therefore, Caxton moralizes, "this fable techeth to al folk that the poure ought notto hold felawship with the myghty. For the myghty man is never feythfull to the poure."[3] The disparity in power relations was more emphatic in Caxton than in some other versions, where the strees fell on the fragility of the original agreement. So, for example, the reader might be admonished that reads: "Faithfulness hath been ever rate; it is more rare now-a-days: but it is and hath always been most rare among potent Men. Wherefore it is better that you live with your equals. For he that liveth with a potent man, must necessarily part ofttimes with his own right: you shall have equal dealings with your equals."[4]

The moral of Marten's version, however, is not predetermined by cultural precedent but "shall be" arrived at. The lion is bound by convention to be recognized as the king; but by retelling an ancient tale of "might makes right" in terms currently hot, especially the central and ironically repeated "prerogative," the immediately topical application is secured. The sub-theme of censorship ("it bounds up my mouth that I cannot but say that it is for the good of the people") connects this fable to Sidney's in the *Arcadia,* while at the same time permitting the parliamentarian to open his mouth after all. The fox learns by the calamity of the ass to let the prerogative alone, but the fabulist learns by the example of Aesop to let the animals speak for him. And by setting his intervention in the frame of Horace's *Ars Poetica,* where the rules are established for a probable, rather than a fantastic mimesis, Marten implied that not only parliamentary debate, but the constitution itself, should be governed by the rules of a natural decorum. Men should keep their own heads on their own necks; a king who roars like a lion has become a monster.

Marten's warning, as we know, was inefficacious. In 1629 Charles's second parliament dissolved in undignified confusion, to be followed by eleven years of prerogative rule, and then by the ultimate confrontations of 1640 to 1649. The broadside ballad verses cited at the opening of this chapter show both how pervasive fabulist thinking had become, in the sense that they literally circulated on the street, and how clearly the *inversion* of the old fables were connected to the inversion of conventional power structures in England, in which process parliament itself is seen as the primary agent. But for a truly intelligent attempt to rethink Aesopian concepts in relation to the civil war and the republican experiment, we need to turn to John Ogilby and his *Fables of Aesop Paraphras'd in Verse,* first published in 1651 with illustrations by Francis Cleyn. Ogilby's interpretations of Aesop stand at the midpoint of both the century and the revolution, and they significantly altered the status of the fable in the second half of the century.

In Mary Pritchard's pioneering study of the political fable, Ogilby is given credit for converting the fable into a medium of historical representation. His system was signaled to the seventeenth-century reader by "politically charged" language, unmistakably referring to persons and events:

> There are, for example, several references to covenants and covenanters (Fables 3, 8, 42) and one to the "Solemn League and Cov'nant" (32). Civil war is likewise mentioned in four fables (6, 21, 40, 72) along with a multitude of references to various kinds of rebellion. Cromwell's cavalry regiment, Ironsides, is alluded to in Fables 8 and 27, while the term "malignants," a common epithet used by the Parliamentarians to describe the Royalists, occurs in Fables 13, 17, 22, 39, 40 and 71 as both adjective and noun. Two fables, 29 and 72, mention sequestration, and four, commonweal or commonwealth (32, 47, 75 and 77). Reference is made to two issues with which Cromwell was particularly concerned during his Parliamentary career: the draining of the fens (15) and the Root and Branch bill (40, 42 and 67).[5]

This careful analysis is useful confirmation that Ogilby's *Aesop* is indeed as topical as it feels. Nor would one wish to quarrel with Pritchard's larger conclusion, that the theme of the volume as a whole is a principle of order and hierarchy, which war and rebellion subvert. But in order to substantiate my claim that Ogilby significantly altered the *status* of the fable, we need to go deeper; and one can hardly do better than begin where the seventeenth-century reader began, with the commendatory poem by William Davenant that preceded the 1651 edition.

It was certainly part of the effect intended that Davenant addressed himself to the reader "From the Tower Sep. 30. 1651," underlining the condition of many Royalists after the battle of Worcester that very month. His poem on Ogilby's paraphrases is an elegant play on ideas of imprisonment, appropriating for both politics and aesthetics the tradition of the fable as the political language of slaves, and connecting both ancient and recent styles of bondage to the freedom with which Ogilby had treated his material. Davenant begins by praising Aesop for having rescued from Egyptian priests the ancient system of hieroglyphs, by which animal symbolism conveyed knowledge of the divine, and for having restored it to "the Laitie," a challenging application of Reformation imagery to one who clearly opposed the current "reformers." He then proceeded to praise Ogilby for having performed a comparable act of rescue for Aesop:

> Blest be our Poet too! whose fire hath
>   made
> Grave Aesop warme in Death's detested
>   shade.
> Though Verses are but Fetters deem'd by
>   those
> Who endlesse journeys make in wandring
>   Prose,
> Yet in thy Verse, methinks, I Aesop see
> Less bound than when his Master made him
>   free:
> So well thou fit'st the measure of his
>   mind,
> Which, though the Slave, his body, were
>   confind,
> Seem'd, as thy wit, still unconstrained
>   and young.
>
>   (A5v)

And he concludes with a classic defense of poetry as a form of passive resistance:

Laws doe in vain with force our wils invade;
   Since you can Conquer when you but
      Perswade.

(A6r)

What Davenant's poem suggested, everything that we know about Ogilby's career confirms, from his early service in Wentworth's household in Ireland, through his lost Royalist epic, the *Carolies,* to his remarkable prestige and privileges at the Restoration.[6] This was to be a Royalist collection of fables, speaking to a social and cultural elite of sudden reversals in the power relations; and to that end the classical fable was to be not only "paraphrased" but converted to a use hitherto alien to it. Instead of representing the voice of the slave or laboring class, of the disenfranchised, the powerless, the uncouth, negroid, or base, the fable is now, by the vagaries of political fortune, discovered as a vehicle of protest and solidarity for the Royalist nobility and gentry who seemed to have lost the war and had certainly, with the execution of Charles I in 1649, lost their leader. Since it was now widely understood that the only hope for the restoration of the monarchy lay in strategic acceptance of the Engagement, consolidating their position under Cromwell and waiting for the revolution to burn itself out, Ogilby's fables as a group adopted a position that was somewhere on the fine line between active and passive resistance.[7]

In accordance with this program, which required Ogilby to seem to have rightfully appropriated fabulist tradition, his fables were constructed as elegant and complex lyric structures, which nevertheless incorporated, wherever possible, the more basic strengths of earlier English fabulists. Ogilby had obviously read his Spenser. His Fable 36, *Of the Husbandman and the Wood,* combines the original Aesopian tale—a wood foolishly provides the woodcutter with a handle for his axe—with "February's" fable of the Oak and the Briar. But taking seriously the Spenserian implications of age and rootedness, and the hints that the Oak was both person and institution, Ogilby abandoned the theme of rivalry between two trees for a far more complex narrative of political interests. For the tree with a long history he substituted an ancient forest system, "Neer a vast Comons," in which the oak is only one element:

> This wealthy grove, the Royall Cedar grac'd,
>   Whose head was fix'd among the wandring
>   stars,
>   Above loud Meteors and the elements Wars,
> His root in th'Adamantine Center fast;
>   This all surpast
> Crown'd Libanus; about him Elmie Peers,
> Ash, Fir, and Pine, had flourish'd many years,
> By him protected both from heat and cold.

> Eternall plants, at least ten ages old,
>   All of one mind
>   Theyr strength conjoyn'd,
>   And scorn'd the wind;
> Here highly honour'd stood the sacred Oke,
>   Whom Swains invoke,
> Which oracles, like that of Dodon, spoke.

The ancient forest, then, is clearly the English political system, in which all the trees are distinguished by their height, that is to say, their rank, from the "Comons," and in which the "Royal Cedar" (the king) is distinguished from the "sacred Oke" (the national church or its greatest representative, Archbishop William Laud). Even to name them, however, as Ogilby had no need to, detracts from the dignity that inheres naturally in the very idea of a great forest, and culturally in the concept of solidarity ("All of one mind") with which Ogilby has endowed the English aristocracy.

But the fable's point is that this defensive unity does, after all, give place to the rivalry between different types of tree that Aesop and Spenser had recognized. There is an equally clear historical referent for "the under cops (that did complain / Their Soveraign / A Tyrant was)," as well as for the "rotten-hearted Elms, and Wooden Peers," who support the husbandman's plans for chopping down some of their colleagues in order to give themselves more room. Central to the tragedy, also, is the shortsightedness of the royal cedar, who is persuaded to give the husbandman the wood he needs for a handle to his axe, thus enabling his own destruction and that of his entire kingdom—a none-too-inscrutable allusion to the Nineteen Propositions in which Charles I, many of his own supporters thought, had given away the constitutional grounds of his sovereignty; while the husbandman himself is both villain and victim, who weeps to behold "the havock his own hands had made." And if, as in Spenser's fable, the husbandman stands as he must for the monarch who mistakenly destroys something or someone of value to the land, Ogilby's husbandman must logically be the English nation itself. But the fable as a whole is, if not impersonal, honestly judicious. It offers not a narrowly partisan but a polytropic explanation of the causes of the civil war, in which there can be no simple apportionment of blame, and, because it is a tragic fable, a final moral (that kings should not put weapons into their subjects' hands) whose very inadequacy is part of the somber effect.

The tone established here is continued in another Spenserian recall, Ogilby's version of *The Wolf and the Kid,* which Spenser had adapted to the purposes of anti-Catholic propaganda. Ogilby returned in his version (*Of the She-Goat and Kid,* Fable 72) to the wolf of the Aesopian original, but the psychological details of his account, in which much is made of the goat's widowhood and her devotion to her only child, "her comfort and her care," are unmistakably derived from Spenser's "May" eclogue. They are equally unmistakably adapted to the new historical circumstances of 1651:

> A She-Goat Widowed by Civill War,
> (As many other wofull Matrons are)
> Although her sequestration a small fine
>   Had taken off,
>   Had little cause to laugh,
> For when she rose, she knew not where to
>   dine.

"Sequestration" was a technical term employed by the Long Parliament to describe the temporary confiscation of Royalist estates, which could subsequently be released by taking the Engagement and (usually) paying a fine. Like Spenser's fable, Ogilby's dwells on the death of the kid's father at the hands of the wolf and the mother's fears for her son, whom she must leave alone to go foraging for food. But what the wolf brings to the door in 1651 is not the grab bag of religious superstition or a deceptive martyr complex, but the allure of a political loyalty that is bound to destroy its adherent. Disguising himself as "the King and Father of the Heard," the wolf addresses the kid in the language of those who had attempted to drum up military support for Charles II for the abortive campaign that ended on the field at Worcester; or, perhaps, of those who might, disguising themselves as the king's adherents, attempt to betray a trusting young man to engage in a destructive and doomed conspiracy:

> I live, whom Fame reported dead, and
>   bring
> Good tydings, never better was the King.
> The Lyon now is fourty thousand strong,
>   Enumerous swarms,
>   Both old and young, take arms,
> And he will thunder at their Gates ere
>   long,
> Changing their tryumph to a dolefull
>   Song.
>   And now the Conquering Boar,
>   Of those subdu'd before,
>   Doth speedie aid implore,
> But the dissenting Brethren in one Fate,
>   Too late,
> Shall rue they turn'd this Forrest to a
>   State.

The result, for this kid, is a situation in which all of the most sacred values of his culture are invoked to lure him to disaster: "Whom Pan, his Parents, and his King obey'd, / Duty, Belief, and Piety betraid." It is fair to ask whether Ogilby would have conceived of rendering this problem—of the psychology of loyalty in defeat—in these touching familial and adolescent

terms if he had not been able to appropriate Spenser's insights, and particularly the dangers to themselves of idealism in the young; but where Spenser's message is obscure, and his effects achieved by expansive, even self-indulgent description, Ogilby's psychology is as deft as his political meaning is unavoidable.

Given the strategic compromises required by Engagement politics, Ogilby's fables also explore the psychological territory between unwise resistance and total capitulation. His version of *The Oke and the Reed* (67) somehow merges the traditional values of massivestrength and ductility by suggesting the merits of postponement:

> Though strong, resist not a too potent foe;
> Madmen against a violent torrent row.
> Thou maist *hereafter* serve the Common-
>   weale,
> Then yield till time shall better days repeale.
>   (Italics added)

But while his own later career amply confirmed the wisdom of Ogilby's position, it was not merely a rationalization of timeserving. The ancient fable of the war between the birds and beasts, in which the bat, biologically a compromise between the warring species, decides on neutrality, now becomes in Ogilby's version (29) a traitor to *both* sides:

> The treacherous Bat was in the battell took:
> All hate the traitors look,
>   He never must display,
>   Again his wings by day,
> But hated live in some foul dustie nook,
> Cause he his Country in distresse forsook.

And the Moral points specifically to those who compounded with the new government in order to save their estates: "Or King or State their ruin they'l endure, / May they from Sequestration be secure."

Given this careful definition of the indefinable, a condition of loyal and unselfserving temporizing, we can see why Ogilby attempted to adapt to current circumstances *The Frogs Desiring a King* (12), a fable whose precedent history in the theory of political obedience had assumed a transition from a frog republic to different styles of monarchy. But because English history had, in effect, released into practice the contradictions inherent in the fable from its origins, those contradictions admitted by Holinshed's *Chron-icles* and exploited by Sidney, Ogilby's version of the fable (figure 6) needed radical adjustment. It opens with the voices of the frogs, speaking from the position of whose who have once enjoyed a king but are now experiencing—and negatively—a republic:

> Since good Frogpadock Jove thou didst
>   translate,

How have we suffer'd turn'd into a State?
In severall interests we divided are;
Small hope is left well grounded peace
    t'obtain,
        Unlesse again
        Thou hear our prayer
Great King of Kings, and we for Kings
    declare.

It continues with considerable wit to describe the two sovereigns, neither of whom would have suggested, in 1651, an exact political correlative.[8] First comes the log, with a huge splash:

At last all calm and silent, in great State
On silver billows he enthroned sate,
Admir'd and reverenc'd by every Frog:
His brow like fate without or frown or smile
    Struck fear a while;

        . . . . .

But when they saw he floated up and down,
Unactive to establish his new Crown;
Some of the greatest of them without dread
Draw neerer to him; now both old and young
    About him throng,
    On's Crown they tread,
And last, they play at Leap-Frog ore his head.

Straight they proclame a fast, and all repair
To vex Heavens King again with tedious
    prayer,
This stock, this wooden Idoll to remove;
Send them an active Prince, a Monarch stout
    To lead them out,
    One that did love,
New realms to conquer, and his old improve.

The effect of this readjusted series of choices, from monarchy to republic and back again, must have been unsettling at least in 1651, where the frogs' request for the Restoration is so cynically undermined by its predetermined consequences. The Moral is emphatically not a translation of Aesop's advice to the Athenians to endure the current tyranny without complaint or resistance, but a general observation of the fickleness of the nation that assumes an objective distance from both Royalist and republican sentiment:

No government can th'unsetled vulgar please,
Whom change delights think quiet a disease.
Now Anarchie and Armies they maintain,
And wearied, are for Kings and Lords again.

But in 1665, when Ogilby reissued his *Fables,* he also added Aesop's final address to the Athenians, "To you, O Citizens, bear this, he said, / Lest you a greater mischief do invade." The referential system had in the

interim become both clearer and more complicated. On the one hand, the repeated requests made to Cromwell during his Protectorate that he should assume the crown would have made it possible to identify that extremely "active Prince" as the stork; on the other, five years of experience of Charles II had already produced such considerable disillusionment with the ideal of Restoration that the frog fable took on a new lease of life. Even before the Restoration, John Milton had responded in a fury to a sermon delivered in 1656 by the Royalist divine, Matthew Griffith, which had featured *The Frogs Desiring a King* in an antipopulist argument. Milton claimed that Griffith had distorted the true meaning of the fable:

The frogs (being once a free Nation saith the fable) petitioned Jupiter for a King: he tumbl'd among them a log. They found it insensible: they petitioned then for a King that should be active: he sent them a Crane (a Stork saith the fable) which straight fell to pecking them up. This you apply to the reproof of them who desire change: wheras indeed the true moral shews rather the folly of those, who being free seek a King; which for the most part either as a log lies heavy on his Subjects, without doing ought worthie of his dignitie and the charge to maintaine him, or as a Stork, is ever pecking them up and devouring them.[9]

When the Stuarts were reinstalled, this republican version of the fable was likely to appear in opposition poetry. Two of Marvell's verse satires assume its immediate intelligibility. One of the predictions of *Nostradamus's Prophecy* remarks of Charles II that "The Frogs shall then grow weary of their Crane / And pray to Jove to take him back againe"; and in *The Dialogue between the Two Horses,* itself formally related to the animal fable, one of the horses asks the other, "What is thy opinion of James Duke of York?" "The same that the Froggs had of Jupiters Stork," is the by now predictable answer.[10] In 1674 John Freke's ballad, *The History of Insipids,* was more outspoken still, completely abandoning the fable's classical statement of its purpose:

Then, farewell, sacred Majesty,
Let's pull all brutish tyrants down!
Where men are born and still live free,
There ev'ry head doth wear a crown.
Mankind, like miserable frogs,
Is wretched, kinged by storks or logs.[11]

Perhaps because *The Frogs Desiring a King* was no longer controllable, it did not appear to John Dryden a useful medium for debating the political and religious issues of 1687; at least not centrally. Yet because *The Hind and the Panther* anticipates and attempted to avert the revolution of 1688, as Milton had anticipated and attempted to avert the Restoration, Dryden does in fact allude in a single line to *The Frogs Desiring a King,* as also to the episode in 1 Samuel 8 with which, in constitutional theory, it was aligned. When the doves, in their rivalry with the chickens, summon the buzzard from abroad to be their "Potentate," and one who, Dryden's fable warns, will ultimately make them his prey, the allusion to the stork (or crane) of the classical fable is not only plausible, it is authorially encouraged; for the buzzard is, among many other alarming and reprehensible characteristics, described as "A King, whom in his wrath, th'Almighty gave."[12] Yet the warning against those who would once more disrupt the political system by displacing James II and bringing over William and Mary to restore a Protestant dynasty is, of course, only the last item in Dryden's ambitious polemical program.

In part because the poem is so argumentative, it is easy to underestimate how powerful and consistently it engages with fabulist tradition. Dryden's framing fable can be too easily forgotten as he struggles with his defense of Catholic dogma from the awkward posture of a new convert to that religion; but the fact remains that the Hind, as a nonpredatory representative of a faith now claimed as the only true one, has been chosen by Dryden to stand in for the innocent and yet highly intelligent hero of the *The Wolf and the Lamb*. Indeed, Dryden explains his move by remarking that "the Sheep and harmless Hind / Were never of the persecuting kind" (1:286-87). Against the "milk-white" Hind stands the Anglican panther, spotted by her Reformation antecedents and like them a beast of prey, yet unlike the Baptist boar, the Arian fox, or the Presbyterian wolf, potentially redeemable, "least deform'd, because reform'd the least" (1:409). Dryden thereby suggested that the fable might turn on its own history, and by means of a talking cure allow the powerless (his own tendentious image of Roman Catholicism) not merely to survive but to change the world for the better.

It is the Hind who alludes, in her debate with the Panther, both to *The Dog and the Shadow* and *The Wolf and the Lamb,* and adjusts them each to new circumstances.[13] In the first instance, the Hind complains that the Anglican compromise over the Real Presence in the Eucharist is mere wordsmanship:

> Then said the Hind, as you the matter state
> Not only Jesuits can equivocate;
> For *real,* as you now the word expound,
> From solid substance dwindles to a sound.
> Methinks an Aesop's fable you repeat,
> You know who took the shadow for the meat.

(2:44-49)

This witty play on the relationship between physical and spiritual eating also connects fabling with equivocation, a relation which, as we shall see, Dryden himself exploited at the level of metapoetics. But

sustenance connects the theological issue to the ecclesiastical, in the sense that the poem debates the respective rights of Anglicans and Roman Catholics to royal protection and preferment. With the Catholic James now on the throne, the newly Catholic poet takes the position that the Established Church is always on the verge of returning to the wolf, the Romans in England of becoming the lamb:

> If *Caesar* to his own his hand extends,
> Say which of yours his charity offends:
>
> . . . . .
>
> When at the fountains head, as merit ought
> To claim the place, you take a swilling
>   draught,
> How easie 'tis an envious eye to throw,
> And tax the sheep for troubling streams
>   below,
> Or call her, (when no farther cause you find,)
> An enemy profess'd of all your kind.
> But then, perhaps, the wicked World wou'd
>   think,
> The *Wolf* design'd to eat as well as drink.

(3:109-10, 123-30)

There is also evidence that Dryden saturated himself in earlier English developments of the fable. In his invaluable edition of *The Hind and the Panther* and in his monograph on Dryden's poetry, Earl Miner demonstrated that the two long fables-within-a-fable that constitute most of the third part of the poem are derived from Ogilby's *Fables*. That told by the panther, the story of the martin's prophecy of disaster to the swallows, their failure to heed it, and their fatal refusal to fly south before winter, is a rewriting of Ogilby's Fable 40, *The Parliament of Birds*. That told by the hind, the story of the rivalry between the pigeons ("a sort of Doves") and the "Domestick Poultry" on an estate, echoes Ogilby's Fable 20, *Of the Doves and Hawks,* in which the doves, engaged against their will in a defensive war with the kites, call in the hawks to assist them but then become the victims of their own mercenaries. Miner showed how the essentially political premises of Ogilby's fables were adapted, by fusion with the biblical typology of dove, swallow, and cock, to Dryden's more complex subject, more complex because the politics of both church and state were involved;[14] and that in the second fable, Ogilby as model is fused with Chaucer, whose *Nun's Priest's Tale* of Chauntecleer and the Fox is used as an allegory of the dissolution of the monasteries by Henry VIII. So the Protestant pigeons berate the cock for waking them up in the morning, warning that contemporary Roman Catholics may share the fate of their imprudent forebears:

Such feats in former times had wrought the
  falls
Of crowing *Chanticleers* in Cloyster'd Walls.
Expell'd for this, and for their Lands they
  fled,
And Sister *Partlet* with her hooded head
Was hooted hence, because she would not
  pray a-bed.

(3:1020-25)

But Miner did not, I think, realize that a crucial passage in the first part of the poem, which raises the problem of man's relation to the beasts, is also a rebuttal of Sidney's fable of the origins of monarchy; crucial because, in Dryden's argument, the survival of Catholicism in England is tied to the survival of a monarchy without constitutional limitation.

When Dryden stands, in the first part of his poem, "like *Adam,* naming ev'ry beast" (1:309) who will participate in his fable, he appropriates to himself the role assigned to Aesop, who in 1687, the same year as *The Hind and the Panther,* had appeared on the frontispiece of Francis Barlow's new and more elaborate polyglot edition (see figure 3) as a mild and plebeian Adam surrounded by the animals, the spokesman for a peaceable kingdom. But Dryden's animal world is considerably more threatening; and he is careful to observe that the various beasts of the Reformed churches are politically dangerous also. The Wolf brings with him no mark of his kinship with "*Wickliff's* brood," "But his innate antipathy to kings" (1:177); together with the Fox, he engages in political sabotage abroad (the Protestant version, Dryden suggests, of Jesuit missions, which in their own terms had been antimonarchical). Significantly, Dryden links "Holland" (the Dutch republic) and Scotland as hotbeds of this heresy, both "Drawn to the dreggs of a Democracy," (1:211).

The question thus raised, about what sort of Adamic kingship was required for this more savage kingdom, was answered in terms readily transferable to James II. In the address "To the Reader" that accompanied the poem in the spring of 1687, Dryden complimented James on his famous or notorious "Declaration for Liberty of Conscience," issued April 4, 1687, and part of his campaign both to extend the royal prerogative, to surround himself with Roman Catholic appointees, and to seek the support of those to the religious left of the established church, the Dissenters or Nonconformists. As Dryden very well knew, this "Declaration" by James had precisely the same unconstitutionality that had forced his brother to withdraw a similar proclamation, similarly motivated, in 1672. Calmly finessing this issue in his preface, Dryden asserted that "some of the Dissenters in their Addresses to His Majesty have said that *He has restor'd God to his Empire over Conscience:* I Confess I dare not stretch the Figure to

so great a boldness: but I may safely say, that Conscience is the Royalty and Prerogative of every Private man. He is absolute in his own Breast, and accountable to no Earthly Power, for that which passes only betwixt God and Him" (p. 120). This plan, to conceal the teeth of the prerogative by metaphorical transubstantiation, is then subtly developed in the first part of the poem, where Dryden, following Sidney, creates *his* image of a natural monarchy by describing Adam's creation.

Beasts are the subjects of tyrannick sway,
Where still the stronger on the weaker prey.
Man onely of a softer mold is made;
Not for his fellows ruine, but their aid:
The noble image of the Deity.

One portion of informing fire was giv'n
To Brutes, th'inferiour family of heav'n:

. . . . .

But, when arriv'd at last to humane race,
The god-head took a deep consid'ring space:
And, to distinguish man from all the rest,
Unlock'd the sacred treasures of his breast:
And mercy mix'd with reason did impart;
One to his head, the other to his heart:
Reason to rule, but mercy to forgive:
The first is law, the last prerogative.
And like his mind his outward form appear'd;
When issuing naked, to the wondring herd,
He charm'd their eyes, & for they lov'd, they
  fear'd.
Not arm'd with horns of arbitrary might,
Or claws to seize their furry spoils in fight,
Or with increase of feet t'o'ertake 'em in their
  flight.
Of easie shape, and pliant ev'ry way;
Confessing still the softness of his clay,
And kind as kings upon their coronation day.

(Ll. 245-71; italics added)

Here too, evidently, the royal prerogative is disarmed by being defined, not as individual freedom of conscience, but as the choice of an absolute monarch to set aside law when he feels compassion—a genial if somewhat disingenuous metaphor for a royal but illegal declaration of toleration. But, in addition, and in ways not apparent unless one were familiar with Sidney's fable of the origins of monarchy, Dryden here offered his own substitute for the fable of *The Frogs Desiring a King.* Unlike Sidney's first man, created as an amalgam of the divine and the bestial, this Adam matches the figure appropriated by Robert Filmer for the central arguments of the *Patriarcha,* that peculiar defense of absolute monarchy as established in Eden, published in 1680 and promoted as a tool to be used against the Whigs throughout the

Exclusionist crisis. Dryden's original ruler is created solely by God, and receives no characteristics from the animals, who, in turn, make no request for a sovereign. Whereas Sidney's Jove reluctantly consented to the new creation by giving the animals "part of [his] heav'nly fire" and allowing them to finish the job, Dryden's God gave "One portion of informing fire" to the inferior creation, but created Man in "the noble image of the Deity." Nakedness and pliability are now essential characteristics, not, as in Sidney's fable, a temporary pose of vegetarian restraint. And though Dryden's fable of the origins of monarchy chooses to acknowledge the ending required by his scriptural plot (his Adam loses his innocence; "pride of Empire sour'd his balmy bloud," "the murtherer *Cain* was latent in his loins"), this transition from meekness to savagery in the ruler naturally avoids Sidney's double advice to his participants: "O man, rage not beyond thy need. . . . And you, poor beasts, in patience bide your hell, *Or know your strengths.*"

But there remains the half-acknowledged problem of monarchical violence. The passage ends by casually switching fables, with a bland allusion to James as the "British Lyon" who is merciful even to his foes. The prototype of the merciful lion is, of course, the ancient fable of *The Lion and the Mouse.* In Ogilby's version of this fable the politics of monarch and subject are fully developed. The mouse, when caught, explains: "think not, great Sir, / I came to pick a hole in Royal Fur, / Nor with the Wolf and Fox did I contrive / 'Gainst you, nor question'd your Prerogative." The moral of the fable is ambiguous:

> Mercy makes Princes Gods; but mildest
> Thrones
> Are often shook with huge Rebellions;
> Small Help may bring great Aid, and better
> far
> Is Policy than Strength in Peace or War.[15]

This advice was not only descriptive of James's strategy in declaring toleration for nonconformity, but also of Dryden's strategy in *The Hind and the Panther,* designed, as the preface indicates, to persuade more of the "Sects" to withdraw themselves "from the Communion of the Panther" and join the king.

By thus representing monarchy *both* by Adamic kingship, as Robert Filmer had done, and by the fabulist tradition which made the lion the king of the beasts, Dryden was in fact admitting to a chasm in his own argument. As John Locke was to argue in 1689 (or indeed, if we accept Peter Laslett's argument, had *already* argued in his not yet published refutation of Filmer and support for Shaftesbury's position), the Stuart position on monarchy's origins as based on Genesis was fundamentally illogical:

> [Adam] was Created, or began to exist, by God's immediate Power, without the intervention of Parents or the preexistence of any of the same species to beget him, when it pleased God he should; and so did the Lion, the King of Beasts before him, by the same Creating Power of God: and if bare existence by that Power, and in that way, will give Dominion, without any more ado, our Author, by this Argument, will make the Lion have as good a Title to it as he, and certainly the Ancienter.[16]

And if conceived as a lion, James or any other sovereign was immediately resituated on the other side of the ethical line Dryden is attempting to draw, along with the Panther and the other beasts of prey.

It was for this reason, I suggest, that at the opening of part 3 of his poem Dryden identified yet another important model in the adaptation of Aesopian tradition:

> Much malice mingl'd with a little wit
> Perhaps may censure this mysterious writ,
>
>   . . . . .
>
> Let Aesop answer, who has set to view,
> Such beasts as Greece and Phrygia never
>   knew;
> And mother Hubbard in her homely dress,
> Has sharply blam'd a British Lioness,
> That Queen, whose feast the factious rabble
>   keep,
> Expos'd obscenely naked and a-sleep.
> Led by those great examples, may not I
> The wanted organs of their words supply?[17]

Why was Spenser's *Mother Hubberds Tale* so chosen for special mention? Because, I suggest, the earlier poem offered a *structural* solution to the "king of the beasts" dilemma, with its ethical ambiguities.

First, Dryden seems to have used Spenser's authority as permission to admit that the dilemma existed. By mentioning Spenser's "blaming" of the British lioness Dryden indicated that he read it as criticism of Elizabeth (and adjusted the lion's sex accordingly). And he seems to have connected Spenser's impertinence in showing the queen "Expos'd obscenely naked and a-sleep," with the famous trick played by Aesop on his master's wife, whose nakedness was thereby displayed to the philosophical community. This genealogy connects Spenser's delinquent lioness to the various lions in the English royal dynasty, and especially to Henry VIII, "A Lyon old, obscene, and furious made by lust" (1:351), linked by the word "obscene" to Spenser's critique of Elizabeth, literally her father, and whose role in bringing about the English Reformation was a primal cause of the current religious divergences.

By having admitted the liabilities of the lion myth, Dryden was freed to maneuver, and to suggest that Spenser's satirical view was not the only possibility. Indeed, in *Absalom and Achitophel* he had already introduced James as a noble lion, though that image was discolored by being put in the mouth of Shaftesbury, as part of his temptation of Monmouth, the king's illegitimate son, to lead a popular rebellion. There, Absalom advises violence to prevent violence:

> Then the next Heir, a Prince, Severe and
>   Wise,
> Already looks on you with Jealous Eyes;
> Sees through the thin Disguises of your Arts,
> And markes your Progress in the Peoples
>   Hearts.
> Though now his mighty Soul its Grief
>   contains;
> He meditates Revenge who least Complains,
> And like a Lyon, Slumbring in the way,
> Or Sleep dissembling, while he waits his
>   Prey,
> His fearless Foes within his Distance draws;
> Constrains his Roaring, and Contracts his
>   Paws;
> Till at the last, his time for Fury found,
> He shoots with suddain Vengeance from the
>   Ground:
> The Prostrate Vulgar, passes o'r, and Spares;
> But with a Lordly Rage, his Hunters teares.

> (Ll. 441-54)[18]

In 1681 James had not yet properly succeeded to leonine status. In 1687, as the "British Lyon" who reappears in Dryden's bestiary, he is not only awake and alert but also merciful, pacific, a creature of courage and integrity, and legitimately king. But because of his species it is impossible to separate him absolutely from earlier members of the dynasty. Just at the moment when Dryden makes explicit his identification of the Lion with James II he carefully represents him as a figure of power under rational control, thereby admitting (by denying) the savage potential of the fabulist metaphor:

> So when the gen'rous Lyon has in sight
> His equal match, he rouses for the fight;
> But when his foe lyes prostrate on the plain,
> He sheaths his paws, uncurls his angry mane;
>
> . . . . .
>
> So James, if great with less we may compare,
> Arrests his rowling thunder-bolts in air.

> (3:267-74)

But Spenser had *also*, in *Mother Hubberds Tale*, provided the model for an alternative metaphor for monarchy: The caring, if too incautious husbandman, owner of the sheep farm. Turning this too to the purposes of support rather than critique, Dryden makes his final representation of James the "Plain good Man" of the hind's own fable, a figure whose social status, as a landowner with three "lineal" estates, is carefully balanced by signs of humility and statements of personal attentiveness:

> Another Farm he had behind his House,
> Not overstock't, but barely for his use;
> Wherein his poor Domestick Poultry fed,
> And from his Pious Hands receiv'd their
>   Bread.

> (3:993-96)

This characterization was, of course, also modeled on that of the poor widow in Chaucer's *Nun's Priest's Tale*, the modest owner of Chauntecleer. As in Chaucer, the story and its teller gets its authority from the world of Aesopian materialism, or, as Leonardo put it in his fable of the razor, of "rustici villani." But in Dryden's adjustment, it elegantly supported his implied plea for toleration between the rival religions ("He therefore makes all Birds of ev'ry Sect / Free of his Farm, with promise to respect / Their sev'ral Kinds alike, and equally protect" (3:1244-46).

By once again inverting the fables he inherited, Dryden hoped to purge the image of monarchy of the negative inferences (tragic irresponsibility in the husbandman, reprehensible sloth in the lion) that had previously seemed so "natural." Yet precisely by reacting to Spenser and following his binary model, Dryden offered a view of the king's conduct in 1687 that was, while transparent in its sympathies, ambiguous at least in its rhetorical effect. Was the king a lion or a careful farmer, the Declaration of Indulgence an act of beneficence or an unconstitutional exertion of the prerogative? In the line of the best political fables, *The Hind and the Panther* remained, if not argumentatively, *structurally* evasive on this, the central political point.

As with the case of La Fontaine, I do not think we need to give this discovery a deconstructive edge. To do so is, I believe, to misunderstand Dryden's assertion that his poem is a "mysterious writ." In Steven Zwicker's account of Dryden's career, it is claimed that Dryden in *The Hind and the Panther* collated three kinds of "mysterious writ": his newly adopted theology, with its insistence that true religion consists of mysteries and hence requires one central and infallible interpreter; the indeterminacy of reference with which all language is infected; and the fable genre itself. Zwicker suggested that ambiguity was part of Dryden's subject and his special contribution; and that, therefore, the resistance of the interpolated bird fables to interpretation, and in particular the apparent confusion between William III and Gilbert Burnet as alternative prototypes for the buzzard, was fully intentional, part of Dryden's chosen disguise, a way of speaking his mind without being fully held to account.[19] It is not clear to me why being thought to refer *both* to William and Burnet was a form of personal insurance against career damage; and although it is certain that Dryden in this poem was fascinated by problems of interpretation in Scripture, and in the technical meaning of "equivocation" as saying something, under pressure, other than what one truly believes, the poststructuralist notion of the indeterminacy of language in general is not a useful interpretive tool here. As in Bellosta's account of La Fontaine and his interest in the *Life* of Aesop, a belief in the indeterminacy of language in general works against, rather than strengthening, the fable's claim to indeterminacy. A text that with-holds its full meaning because of the sociopolitical constraints against open discussion is a text committed to referentiality; this does not prevent it from advertising its writerly mystery. As Hegel put the paradox, *because* the fabulist "dare not speak his teaching openly," he can "only make it intelligible in a kind of riddle which is at the same time always being solved."

But we cannot leave Dryden and the fable in 1687. For in 1700 he marked the turn of the century by producing a volume of *Fables Ancient and Modern* that contained, as its only fable in the strict sense, a new version of Chaucer's *Nun's Priest's Tale,* already, I have argued, a bulwark against the political implications of the fable as Lydgate would recover them. In his *Preface* to *Fables,* Dryden, who had read his Chaucer in editions that included the *Plowman's Tale,* noted, in order to dispose of it, the mistaken tradition of Chaucer's political radicalism: "In *Richard's* Time, I doubt, he was a little dipt in the Rebellion of the Commons; and being Brother-in-Law to *John of Ghant,* it is no wonder if he follow'd the Fortunes of that Family; and was well with Henry the Fourth when he had depos'd his Predecessor. Neither is it to be admir'd . . . if that great Politician should be pleas'd to have the greatest Wit of those Times in his Interests, and to be the Trumpet of his Praises." The effect is to make any supposed democratic sympathies disappear into the territory of patronage and political self-interest.

As Steven Zwicker defined the tone of *Fables,* its method is "not primarily figural or historical," and its context is "not political crisis" as it had been for *The Hind and the Panther,* "but poetry and eternity," "literary self-consciousness," "the sense of place and tradition in literary terms."[20] Just so. The *Preface* establishes Chaucer as "the Father of *English* Poetry" (replacing, we might add, Aesop as the Father of the fable), and conceives of poetry in terms of lineage and property inheritance, significantly by primogeniture: "for we have our Lineal Descents and Clans, as well as other Families: *Spencer* more than once insinuates, that the Soul of *Chaucer* was transfus'd into his Body; and that he was begotten by him Two hundred years after his Decease." And by translating the *Nun's Priest's Tale* into early modern idiom, therefore, as he claimed, preserving it for posterity, Dryden located himself in the same lineage.

Nevertheless, Dryden took this solemn occasion as an opportunity to *rewrite* Chaucer in more than linguistic terms. Consider, for instance, his description of Chauntecleer's sexual prowess. Where Chaucer had merely written that:

> This gentil cok hadde in his governaunce
> Sevene hennes for to doon al his plesaunce,
> Whiche were his sustres and his paramours,

> (Ll. 2863-65)

Dryden expatiates on the very problem of lineage that his *Preface* renders literary but his era had seen as the center of political controversy:

> This gentle Cock for solace of his Life,
> Six Misses had beside his lawful Wife;
> Scandal that spares no King, tho' ne'er so
>   good,
> Says, they were all of his own Flesh and
>   Blood:
> His Sisters both by Sire, and Mother's side,
> And sure their likeness show'd them near
>   ally'd.
> But make the worst, the Monarch did no
>   more,
> Than all the *Ptolomeys* had done before:
> When Incest is for Int'rest of a Nation,
> 'Tis made no Sin by Holy Dispensation.
> Some Lines have been maintain'd by this
>   alone,
> Which by their common Ugliness are known.

> (Ll. 55-66)

If this passage recalls the witty opening of *Absalom and Achitophel,* in which Charles II's sexual pro-miscuity is given an ironic dispensation from disapproval by scriptural precedent, it also glances nastily at the fact that William III's father married his first cousin Mary, daughter of Charles I. And the rest of the poem gradually reveals that, for Dryden, it has become an allegory not of ecclesiastical but of political history. In Chauntecleer's tale of how a man dreamed his own murder, where Chaucer wrote, "the peple out sterte" (l. 3043), Dryden substituted, "The Mob came roaring out" (l. 276); and into a second tale, of how an equally prophetic dream of shipwreck was disregarded, Dryden inserted the following passage of mockery:

> Dreams are but Interludes, which Fancy
>   makes,
> When Monarch-Reason sleeps, this Mimick
>   wakes:
> Compounds a Medley of disjointed Things,
> A Mob of Coblers, and a Court of Kings:

> (Ll. 325-29)

These seemingly petty alterations collate with Dryden's treatment of the brief Chaucerian allusion to the Peasants' Revolt, which is carefully brought up to date. Where Chaucer wrote, in describing the barnyard clamor that follows Chauntecleer's seizure, "The dokes cryden as men wolde hem quelle" (l. 4580) Dryden substituted: "The Ducks that heard the Proclamation cry'd, / And fear'd a Persecution might betide" (ll. 736-37). And where Chaucer made a negative comparison between this uproar and "Jakke Straw and his meynee," whose uprising he had designated mere occupational rivalry ("Whan thay they wolden any Flemyng kille"), Dryden ventured his own opinion that popular protest is itself a form of persecution:

> *Jack Straw* at *London*-stone with all his
>   Rout
> Struck not the City with so loud a Shout;
> Not when with *English* Hate they did
>   pursue
> A *French* Man, or an unbelieving *Jew*.

> (Ll. 742-45)

Finally, Dryden's Fox is presented, as Chaucer's certainly was not, as the protagonist in an act of sedition. Having made the same mistake as his victim, and opened his mouth incautiously, thereby losing his prey, this Reynard reveals himself as a would-be king-napper:

> Th'appearance is against me, I confess,
> Who seemingly have put you in Distress:
> You, if your Goodness does not plead my Cause,
> May think I broke all hospitable Laws,
> To bear you from your Palace-Yard by
>   Might,
> And put your noble Person in a Fright:
>
>   . . . . .
>
> I practis'd it, to make you taste your Cheer,
> With double Pleasure first prepar'd by fear.
> So loyal Subjects often seize their Prince,
> Forc'd (for his Good) to seeming Violence,
> Yet mean his sacred Person not the least
>   Offence.

A vision of the late 1640s, when Charles I was a prisoner of the army, here blends, in poetic retrospective, with the arguments of Shaftesbury as Dryden had represented them in *Absalom and Achitophel,* advising Monmouth to lead a popular rebellion:

> Commit a pleasing rape upon the crown.
> Secure his person to secure your cause:
> They who possess the prince, possess the
>   laws.

> (Ll. 474-77)

It is fair to say that when Dryden entered the field, the need or fashion for fables was at its height. Ogilby's first collection was reissued in 1665, 1668, and 1675, and supplemented in 1668 with a new collection of *Aesopics,* written to take into account the changed political circumstances of the Restoration. Following Ogilby's lead, if not his partial independence from the fabulist canon, Francis Barlow had introduced in 1666 the first version of his polyglot edition, which combined the attraction of an illustrated Aesop, accompanied by a *Life,* with an encouragement to read the fables in a broader European context. This version and its main competitor, the translation of the fables and the *Life* by W. D., were constantly reprinted throughout the last three decades of the century. In both W. D.'s and Barlow's edition, as also in the anonymous *Aesop Explained . . . accommodated to the Lives and Manners of Men in this present Age* (1682), or *Aesop Naturaliz'd and Expos'd To the Publick View* (1697), the political implications of the text were either implicit or dormant, the translators apparently being content to draw on the market that had been created for them by Ogilby. Not so, however, with the two major translations that would follow and shape the eighteenth-century perception of fabulist discourse, the rival contributions of Sir Roger L'Estrange and Samuel Croxall, who took up positions diametrically opposite on the fable's social function, and chose those positions in relation to actual political parties.

Because L'Estrange and Croxall cannot be separated, I choose to postpone discussion of them until my last chapter, where the story of the fable's political afterlife is briefly and selectively told. The publication of Dryden's *Fables* conveniently serves to mark a real turning point, not least in its retrospective quality, reminding Dryden's readers of what had motivated fabulist activity throughout the century, but especially from its turbulent center onward. In its own turn towards *literary* history, even when, as in the prefatory discussion of lineage, the literary serves as a metaphor for the political, rather than the converse, *Fables Ancient and Modern* indeed looks forward to the demise of the Aesopian fable proper, or rather to the gradual disappearance of its strong relation to the real history of its early modern discoverers and rediscoverers.

Notes

[1] See Hoyt Hudson, "John Hepwith's Spenserian Satire upon Buckingham: With Some Jacobean Analogues," *Huntington Library Bulletin* 6 (1934): 39-71.

[2] Robert Johnson et al., eds., *Commons Debates* 1628, 5 vols. (New Haven, Conn., and London, 1977), 3:532.

[3] Lenaghan, ed., *Caxton's Aesop,* p. 77.

[4] *Aesop's Fables, with Their Morals in Prose and Verse, Grammatically Translated,* 14th ed. (London, 1698), p. 7.

[5] Mary H. Pritchard, "Fables Moral and Political: The adaptation of the Aesopian Fable Collection to English Social and Political Life, 1651-1722" (unpublished Ph.D. dissertation, University of Western Ontario, Canada, 1976), pp. 36-37.

[6] For Ogilby's biography, see Katherine Van Eerde, *John Ogilby and the Taste of His Times* (Folkestone, England, 1976); and see also Marion Eames, "John Ogilby and His Aesop," *Bulletin of the New York Public Library* 65 (1961): 73-78; Earl Miner's facsimile edition of the 1668 *Fables* (Los Angeles: Augustan Reprint Society, 1965), pp. i-xiv; Margret Schuchard, *John Ogilby,* 1660-1676; *Lebenbild eines Gentelman mit vielen Karieren* (Hamburg, 1973).

[7] For Engagement politics see David Underdown, *Royalist Conspiracy in England,* 1649-1660 (New Haven, Conn., 1960), pp. 30-51, 73-96.

[8] Compare, however, Philip Massinger's play, *The Emperor of the East,* which appeared in 1631-32, at the beginning of Charles I's period of prerogative rule, and whose fictional protagonist complains:

> . . . O the miserable
> Condition of a Prince! who though hee varie
> More shapes than Proteus in his minde, and manners,
> Hee cannot winne an universall suffrage,
> From the many-headed Monster, Multitude.
> Like Aesops foolish Frogges they trample on him
> As a senselesse blocke, if his government bee easie.
> And if he prove a Stroke, they croke, and rayle
> Against him as a tyranne.

See *The Plays and Poems of Philip Massinger,* ed. Philip Edwards and Colin Gibson, 5 vols. (Oxford, 1976), p. 428.

[9] John Milton, *Complete Prose Works,* ed. D. M. Wolfe et al., 8 vols. (New Haven, Conn., 1953-80), 7:748.

[10] Andrew Marvell, *The Poems and Letters,* ed. H. M. Margoliouth, rev. Pierre Legouis, 2 vols. (Oxford, 1971), 1:179, 212.

[11] John Freke, *The History of Insipids, in Anthology of Poems on Affairs of State,* ed. George de F. Lord (New Haven, Conn., and London, 1975), p. 143.

[12] John Dryden, "The Hind and the Panther," pt. 3, l. 1198, in *Poems 1685-1692,* ed. Earl Miner and Vincent Dearing, in *Works,* 20 vols. (Berkeley and Los Angeles, 1956-87), vol. 3 (1969).

[13] In *Dryden's Poetry* (Bloomington, Ind., and London, 1967), pp. 157, 339, Earl Miner points out that the text is sprinkled with other, less obvious allusions to fables, and that in one passage (1:438-47) there are three allusions within ten lines, to *The Husbandman and the Wood, The Gourd and the Pine,* and *The Sun, the Wind, and the Traveller.*

[14] Miner's commentary is available both in his notes to the edition, cited above, and in *Dryden's Poetry,* pp. 144-205.

[15] John Ogilby, *The Fables of Aesop Paraphras'd in Verse,* Fable 9.

[16] John Locke, *Two Treatises of Government,* ed. Peter Laslett (Cambridge, 1967), p. 169. For Laslett's argument about dating see pp. 45-66.

[17] Dryden, *Works,* 3:161.

[18] Dryden, *Absalom and Achitophel,* cited from *Poems 1681-1684,* ed. H. T. Swedenberg, Jr., in *Works,* vol. 2 (1972).

[19] Steven Zwicker, *Politics and Language in Dryden's Poetry: The Arts of Disguise* (Princeton, 1984), pp. 123-58.

[20] Ibid., p. 164.

Tomoko Hanazaki (essay date 1993-94)

SOURCE: "A New Parliament of Birds: Aesop, Fiction, and Jacobite Rhetoric," in *Eighteenth-Century Studies,* Vol. 27, No. 2, Winter 1993-94, pp. 235-54.

[In the following essay, Hanazaki examines the function of animals, and particuarly bird characters, in eighteenth-century British Aesopic fables employed for purposes of political satire.]

I

The fable, one of the most popular traditional generes in English literature, assumes a newly distinctive character in the decades around the turn of the seventeenth century. This, when seen in perspective, has implications for post-Revolutionary political rhetoric and the subsequent history of imaginative literature. Its marked trajectory between 1630 and 1680 has been perceived and illustrated,[1] but from a rather misleading angle. Certainly, the political history of the fable had been generally understood by the 1720s, but Samuel Croxall's "new" collection (1722), with which Annable Patterson begins her essay, testifies to a change: the genre became, ostensibly, depoliticized in the mid-century in the hands of hired, mostly second-rate, writers. Rebelling against L'Estrange's Jacobite reading, but anxious for promotion, the Hanoverian chaplain rewrote Aesop with morals more general in their application. John Gay's 1727 collection of fables, the urbane irony of which made it deservedly celebrated at the time, was aimed primarily at amusement for a court audience, and Edward Moore's imitations of Gay, first published in 1744 both in London and Dublin, were intended to inculcate domestic virtues in a female audience. By contrast, fables published singly in broadsheet and collectively in pamphlet form during Queen Anne's reign had reflected ministerial feuds and party strife; they were clearly intended for a political audience and often for an audience familiar with Dryden's *The Hind and the Panther.* Some of them adopted his animal-types representing religious sects in order to satirize the factious and rebellious as well as to allude to the subject of toleration, which remained controversial long after the 1688 Revolution.[2] *The Hind and the Panther,* published in 1687, was felt at that time to go far beyond the acceptable bounds of imagination both in content and form, for in a highly complex debate between the two animals on religious policies since Henry VIII it expressed a heartfelt wish that the nation be united under the Catholic king James II. The poem's scope and depth of imagination continued to have a strong hold on the reader, and the vituperative fervor that Dryden's "intelligent animals" aroused in political readers at the time of publication may well have been remembered and have had its impact on the succeeding political fables.[3]

The process of change in the early decades of the century was complicated, as is recognized, by two fundamentally opposing and equally long traditions in Aesopic writing; its combination of allusion with instructiveness had rendered it a proper form of advice to a prince, hence the educational purport, but the fable's political nature also resided there. Fables published after the 1688 Revolution demonstrate varied effects of the two impulses, though their major preoccupation is no doubt political. Concerns over the Revolution Settlement and the increasing economic power of the Nonconformists are duly expressed in fables mostly by "minor" writers now almost forgotten. Looking at those published toward the last years of Queen Anne's reign, we see that familiar birds emerged as a new convention of the English fable addressing a wider political audience, before the genre became a mere device for pedagogues. In what follows I shall document this burst of bird typology in the context of its literary as well as its sociopolitical genesis. While in agreement with Thomas Noel's main thesis that the Aesopic fable was widely popular in the eighteenth century, this factual focus will, it is hoped, give a much clearer view of the genre than his survey of fable theories in Europe: a clearer view showing that the path which the English fable took to advance its popular appeal was distinct from that of its continental counterparts.[4]

II

Fable publication surged ahead conspicuously in 1698 when a host of fable pamphlets assailed the Town, featuring a narrator, an ugly, hunch-backed sage, "Æsop," masquerading at various social and political centres, observing people's follies and quibbles. Some allude to current political and literary topics, such as the where-abouts of the former *Surveyor of the Imprimerie,* L'Estrange, recently released from his imprisonment.[5] But the political intent of these fables is rather minimal; mostly they are quick to respond to "humors," fashionable topics, changes of manners, and the social structure in town. Some of them clearly voice the discontent of a hack who tries to sell his work by making the best of the gossip current in town. A confidential note and a personal interest in "Æsop" are characteristic of the 1698 Aesopic pamphlets satirizing the *beau monde* and intelligentsia. The anonymous author of *Æsop Return'd from Tunbridge,* for instance, intimates a wish *"to write Truth"* by saying:

> But let me whisper one thing in thy Ear, upon condition of secrecy, if thou wilt give me thy Word and Honour not to disclose it to any Body.

("The Preface")

This is a little device for winning the reader's attention, since in full confidence the author at once reveals that:

> Æsop, it seems, has been a little disturb'd of late, and it has been argu'd Pro & Con, amongst the Virtuosi, whether his Indisposition was the effect of Tunbridge Waters, or Company. He himself has absolv'd the Waters, and condemn'd the Company, which has oblig'd 'em in their own Justification to send him to Bedlam to have his own Brains set right, for endeavouring to rectifie theirs.

(ibid., "The Preface")

"Æsop" is certainly inherited in the titles of many pamphlets published in the following decades reporting parliamentary debates and ministerial feuds over the succession.[6] A distinctive tone, either surreptitious or provocative, is also echoed there. However, what is exploited in later works is not only the Aesop persona but also his fictitious and "innocent" beasts. They are a rhetorical means, for instance, by which to bait those in the "present administration":

> *He has too great an Opinion of our present Administration . . . to think that they'll take Offence at what a Parcel of irrational Animals, and volatile Creatures act, and talk among them-selves; or be angry at a few* Innocent Fables.

> ("The Publisher's Preface" to *Æsopat the Bell-Tavern in Westminster, or, A Present from the October-Club, in a few select Fables. From Sir Roger L'Estrange* [1711.])

The lapse of the Licensing Act in the House of Commons in 1695 has been considered to relate directly to the sudden growth in the production of political literature in the succeeding decades,[7] but the increase of Aesopic publication suggests inherent contradictions in the "tradition of the fable as the political language of slaves" (Patterson, 283): it must be inferred either that in the post-Revolutionary era, fable was published following Elizabethan precedents for "subversive critical analysis" (ibid., 278) of affairs of state and for advocacy of free speech (ibid., 296),[8] or that fable's political purport and its very limited effect on the course of politics became so familiar that writers operated the vehicle in an increasing spirit of amusement. The extent of any legal impact on literary publication is hard to measure, and it is likely that the 1695 expiry of the Act was one of the factors contributing to the rash of fable publications in the period. Political events aside, there are at least three other factors which appear to have been influential in the revival of Aesopic fables during 1698 to 1720: the first is a recent topic in town,[9] now known as the controversy between the Ancients and the Moderns; the second is a species of classical literature called "Vita Esopi"; the third is, in a sense, its modernized version, a contemporary drama, *Æsop,* by Sir John Vanbrugh, enacted at Drury Lane in January 1697 (or possibly "as early as December 1696").[10]

The controversy between Sir William Temple and the Hon. Charles Boyle on one side, and Richard Bentley and William Wotton on the other, was certainly a "battle of the books," since Temple's claims for the superiority of ancient literature had been based upon Phalaris and Aesop,[11] and Bentley's counterargument was demonstrated through his detailed professional dissertation.[12] However, merits of literature and scholarship aside, the battle aroused strong interest in society because of its class implications; Temple was a dilettante aristocrat and regarded Bentley, the grandson of a stonemason, as an insolent invader of territory naturally his own. The changing social structure in which the hacks emerged was reflected in contemporary Aesops. "The Mouse and the Lion" in *Æsop Naturaliz'd* (Cambridge,

1697), for instance, tells of the marriage of a poor tradesman (a mouse) with a lady of quality. All ten fables in *Æsop Return'd from Tunbridge* describe those who do not—and indeed cannot—earn their own living. The fable of "The Grasshopper and the Ant" (vi) recasts the old story in a modern scene where an idle beau (or man of quality) asks "the frugal grave *Cit*" for bread. The *Cit* advises him to go to "the *Fleet,* or *King's-Bench*" (18). The persona Æsop in these pamphlets represents a hack, and his fables occasionally in hudibrastics express frustrated ambition, sometimes tinged with self-pity. The "Ass," the declared author of *The Life of Æsop of Tunbridge . . . Part II* (1698), for instance, describes himself as "a poor moneyless Pretender to Poetry, which some people call an honest, others a foolish, and every body, a drunken fellow."[13]

On a political level, however, the question of Aesop's authenticity is understood to be alluding more specifically to the metamorphosis of L'Estrange.[14] Though strongly Tory in the long "Reflection" added to each fable, his prose translation first published in 1692 proved widely popular, largely on account of his elegant, yet vigorously familiar style.[15] His work might well have been encouraging to a pack of minor scribes awaiting a chance to rise. A "Jacob Dash" boldly justifies his new attempt at fable by satirically quoting his predecessor, an "Æsop," or a modern hack whom L'Estrange was seen to represent:

> SINCE nothing now but Dogrel [*sic*] Rhimes
> Will please the Readers of our Times,
> And every Scribler of the Town,
> Of Little, Great, or No Renown,
> Pesters the World with Frippery Stuff,
> And thinks his Verses well enough.
> Since Æsop strols from Place to Place,
> Like banish'd Tory in Disgrace,
> And checks the Frenzy of the Age,
> In Deathless and Immortal Page.

> He took up Quarters in *Whitehall,*
> And there, like *Rochester* of old,
> Spoke Truth undauntedly and bold:

> (*Æsop at Richmond . . . A Poem
> in Burlesque,* ll. 1-18)[16]

In "The Preface" to *Æsop Return'd from Tunbridge,* a text probably published earlier that year, the author puns on the word "title" by referring to the recent Aesopic issues by L'Estrange and competing hacks; there might well be a suppressed allusion to the Pretender's (il)legitimate claim to the throne:

> *Upon these comes yet another; whether with better Title than the former, is a question,* Reader, *we leave thee to decide. Only I shall take the liberty to give thee some Hints, for the better Information of*

thy Judgment. First then as to his Person, it has re-
semblance enough to old Æsop's (or the Picture
of him, at least, as Planudes, and others, have
drawn it) that had he left any Legitimate Issue
behind him, Ours might very well plead his Figure
in evidence of his Descent from the old Beau
of Samos; *and the Posture and Condition of their*
Intellects, make out the Relation be-twixt him
and the Bully *of* Tunbridge. *For this confesses*
himself out of his Wits when he writ, and t'other, by
universal Consent, mad to Write what he writ.

Aesop's genealogy herein questioned, whether politically or not, recalls another tradition contributing to
the fashion of resuscitating "Æsop." The "Planude"
above-mentioned is one of the alleged authors of
"Vita Esopi,"[17] first printed in 1505 and conventionally adapted through the seventeenth century, for instance
in Francis Barlow's *Fables* published in 1666 and
in L'Estrange's *Fables.* Vanbrugh's comedy, the third
factor concerned, also adapts the topic. The story,
now seldom appreciated,[18] is one typical of Molière
and Restoration comedy.[19] An old, rather silly father,
Learchus, plans to marry his pretty daughter, Euphronia, to the famous sage, Æsop. His am-bition for fame
through his daughter's marriage fails when Euphronia
finally marries her handsome young lover, Oronces.
Act III starts with a dialogue between Æsop and Jacob Quaint, "a Genealogist." Quaint boasts of his
knowledge of all the pedigrees in the town, including
that of "the Noble *Æsop.*"

> ÆSOP: Dost thou then know my Father Friend? for
> I protest to thee, I am a Stranger to him.

> QUAINT: Your Father, Sir, ha, ha; I know every
> Man's Father, Sir, and every Man's Grand-father,
> and every Man's Great Grand-father.

> (Act III)[20]

Vanbrugh also characterizes Æsop by making him frequently resort to his fables whether requested or not[21]
and emphasizing his physical appearance, to much
theatrical advantage. Informed of the marriage planned
by Learchus between Æsop and Euphronia, Oronces
blurts out:

> ORONCES: Condemn'd? to what? Speak! Quick.

> DORIS: To be married.

> ORONCES: Married? When, how, where, to what,
> to whom?

> DORIS: *Æsop, Æsop, Æsop, Æsop, Æsop.*

> ORONCES: Fiends and Spectres: What, that piece
> of Deformity, that Monster; that Crump?

> (Act II)[22]

At the sight of Æsop, a Country Gentleman laughs:

> Haux, haux, haux, haux, haux: Joular, there
> Boy, Joular, Joular, Tinker, Pedlar, Miss,
>   Miss,
> Miss, Miss, Miss—Blood—Blood and
> Oons—O there he is; that must be he, I
> have seen his Picture.

> (Act IV)[23]

This picture, well-known at the time from the impressive frontispieces in John Ogilby's *Fables of
Æsop* (first illustrated by Francis Cleyn in the 1651
edition) and Francis Barlow's own *Fables,* is described
in more detail in "To the Reader" to *Æsop at Richmond:*

> He [*Æsop*] added, that he was beholden, not only
> to the Poets and Painters for representing him to
> the World with such Charms, as a Scythe-Leg,
> Beetle-Brow, Goggle-Eye, Blobber-Lip, swarthy
> Phiz, &c.[24]

III

Conventional as it was in 1698 to emphasize the sage-
cum-writer Aesop both in his appearance and parent-
age, the early decades of the next century saw a more
prominent role played by his creatures, in representing
major scenes of political life both domestic and European. Fables in the period are mostly occasioned by
the (impending) deaths of the monarchs William III
and Anne, and recall previous parliamentary debates
regarding the Revolution Settlement. This alone might
seem to suggest that fable was a form of writing strongly
favoured by Jacobites,[25] but when we look at a larger
number of the fables then published, such a statement
needs modification. The sixteen fables in *Æsop in
Masquerade* (1718), for instance, contemplate on the
one hand, the royal succession in England and Europe,
and on the other, the increasing numbers and influence
of the Nonconformists, to whom satirists were soon
conventionally to ascribe an inordinate love of money
and attendant moral decay in the nation at large.[26] The
first of the twelve tales in *Canterbury Tales, rendred
[sic] into familiar verse* (1701) alludes to the new
allegations made by William Fuller early in 1701 against
the Popish Lords.[27] In December 1691 Fuller had "confessed" his Jacobite intrigue with the Lords then in the
Tower, was examined in Parliament in 1691-92,[28] and
convicted of libel on failing to provide evidence he
originally claimed to have. The culprit, however, repeated his trick ten years later; his accusations, this
time supported by four letters, were carefully examined and proved yet again that he gave the House of
Commons "amusement."[29] The fable's intention is to
deride anti-Jacobites as well as potential Jacobites. The
Lion is here James II, the Tyger (now "the Sov'raign

Beast"), William III. The Ape (Fuller) asserts that

> The *Lion* has no Living Son.
> I'le prove his Birth is Spurious.
> Hold—said the Sov'raign Beast, thou Sot,
> And strait withdraw thy Phiz,
> Should such a Rascal say, he's not
> Legitimate, and true Begot,
> The World will think he is.
> Moral
> *Thus for the* Teller's *sake*
> *the* Tale *we slight, And* F-ll-rs *only* Read
> *what* F-ll-rs *write.*

("The Plain Proof," 29-37)

Mockery of all the participants in the anti-Jacobite paranoia pervades the text; it is in fact anticipated in "The Preface," which explains how these "Tales" fell into the publisher's hands, and why they are now entitled "Canterbury Tales" "when they seem Calculated for the Meridian of London": because they "were found in . . . that City" which "is the Metropolis of the County [Kent]." The twelve tales have beasts, birds, humans, and, unusually, fish as characters, and the political sentiments expressed are various. Likewise, *The Chaucer's Whims* (1701) have no relation to the poet, and his name in the title suggests some provocation on the part of the anonymous author, presumably William Pittis. Satirical pamphlets alluding to Chaucer and his works had been published since the civil wars,[30] and the provocative use of traditional narrators, Chaucer or Aesop, was common in the early eighteenth century: *Brown Bread and Honour, A Tale. Moderniz'd from an ancient Manuscript of Chaucer* (1716) is another instance.

The reign of Queen Anne, and her last five years in particular, however, contains more promising examples of Jacobite fables. A technique frequently encountered in contemporary political literature was to exploit Aesopic creatures to voice the authors' satiric reviews of domestic events such as the Sacheverell trials (e.g., *The Bull-Baiting: or, Sach—ll Dress'd up in Fire-Works* [1709]), the aggravating split between the Lord Treasurer and Secretary of State (*'Tis Pity They Shou'd Be Parted; Or the Fable of the Bear and the Fox* [1712]), and partisan comments on graver issues such as the peace negotiation to end the War of the Spanish Succession (*Æsop at Utrecht* [1712], which is also and more notably allegorized in John Arbuthnot's prose *History of John Bull*). Alongside conventional Aesopic beast types such as lion, eagle, wolf, fox, cat, dog, and frog, however, there appeared commonly between 1708 and 1716 a relatively consistent use of bird typology: the Eagle represents Queen Anne; the Cock commander in chief, Marlborough; Jays and Pyes party factions and perjurers; the Owls supporters of the Hanovers; the Swan an eloquent and noble high Tory St John;

and more familiar birds like the Robin and the Blackbird epitomize, if fictiously, those faithful to the Queen, respectively Robert Harley and a bard (i.e., a hack), whose fables are published often with significant allusions printed in black letters. Edmund Stacy, "the Author of the Black-Bird's Tale (or Song)," has been identified as a Tory propagandist.[31] Considering his other pamphlets, such as a fable on Guiscard's attempted assassination of Harley (1711), a partisan defence in verse of the Church of England (*The Picture of a Church Militant* [1711]), and a verse translation of L'Estrange's *Fables* (1717, second edition, 1720), it may be that he was one of the hacks hired by Harley, but he himself was undoubtedly a high Tory. Stacy's High Church position is consistently evident. His *Black-Bird's Tale. A Poem, The Black-Bird's Second Tale. A Poem,* and *The Tale of the Robin-red-breast,* all published in 1710, are in the "advice-to-princes" tradition; the bird, the author's persona, warns Queen Anne against the "parrots, jays, chattering pies" (2), and "all sorts of vicious fowls" (6). The Royalist birds in the *Black-Bird's Tale* are swans, as in convention,[32] and the Blackbird warns the Queen that they

> took their Flight,
> And all good *Birds* will leave you quite.

(*The Black-Bird's Tale,* 7)

Further, the Robin warns secretively:

> Of the Cuckows take heed,
> They're a *villanous Breed;*
> But chiefly, *Madam,* be arm'd,
> 'Gainst the *Fowls* that of late
> Would have seiz'd your *Estate,*
> And so boldly the *Village* alarm'd.

(*The Tale of the Robin-red-breast,* 11-12)

"Cuckows" represent Dissenters,[33] and "Fowls," a reminder of the discontented and rebellious fowls in Part III of Dryden's *Hind and the Panther,* refer to Williamites. Stacy's fear that factious Whigs and Nonconformists may lead the country to another revolution is even more strongly expressed in *The Tale of the Raven and the Blackbird* (1715). Unlike the preceding tales, this mostly consists of a dialogue between the two birds on their "new Landlord" (George I) and repeatedly emphasizes the Blackbird's honest and faithful design to continue warning the monarch.

Stacy's fables with vivid images of "highflyers" apparently had considerable circulation among political readers. "The Mag-pie and Black-bird" in *The Welchman's Tales* (1710), for instance, defends the Black-bird whom "a certain Pye" persecuted because he advised, out of genuine concern, that she should make her nest higher. *The Tale of My Lord the Owl, told by the Blackbird* (1718), a mock imitation of the Blackbird series, enacts a dialogue between the two birds, and wryly illustrates that the Blackbird's high Tory patriotism and moral argument are no longer to prosper. The Owl, a newly elected Whig Lord (l. 8), is scornful of the Blackbird:

> 'Twas you the *Party War* began,
> Which blindly still you carry on,
> Without considering that by this
> You only do us *Services.*(21)

The Blackbird signifies Harley's tools, Bolingbroke (a high Tory) and a high Tory hack (like Stacy), in *Robin-Red-Breast's Answer to the Black-Bird's Song* (1715). The poem satirizes the late minister now facing impeachment, in his mock answer to Stacy's work published in March that year; it accuses Harley of embezzlement, high treason, and treachery with regard to the Jacobites. Bolingbroke's flight to the court of the Pretender at St. Germain, mentioned early in this text, is told in a more notable adaptation of Stacy: *A Tale concerning a Swan. How that Swan did swim; and several other matters fit for Babes to hear, and know, and be instructed in* (1715). This prose fable, occasioned by Anne's death and George I's accession to the throne, shows intriguing rhetorical features. "The Translator's Preface" explains how he found the manuscripts, reminding us of the Scriblerian fiction in *The Memoirs of Martinus Scriblerus*. The tale tells us of the court of the Phoenix (Queen Anne), of her minister Robin-red-breast (Robert Harley), his relation with other birds, and her trust in a beauteous bird, the Swan (Bolingbroke), that finally came to her, "laden with golden Feathers from distant Shores" (7). The fifth chapter, on the Phoenix's death, alludes to an expected Jacobite rising and is printed in a deliberately obscure manner (for example, "*** call the Owls ** dark Birds *** Mysterious Things ***great Expectation from *Paradise*** Ashes scatter'd in Foreign Kingdoms *** will rise ***" [14]), a mode we associate with Swift. The tale closes with the Owl's speech to the Eagle on behalf of the Swan, the bird impeached for treason. One is left with a temptation to read a Jacobite plot into the *Tale,* but this the anonymous author mocks by adding a note:

> *N.B. There is a famous Chymist preparing a Spirit, by which 'tis hop'd, in time, more of this Manuscript will be recover'd, to be the unspeakable Benefit of Mankind.*(20)

IV

The bird typology thus commonly exploited by Tory hacks and their opponents features in early eighteenth-century fables on the succession. Contemporary fables satirizing Nonconformists use beasts as well as birds. The Geese are a satirical image of the Papists, who hold the doctrine of passive obedience.[34] "Volpone," the cunning and treacherous fox in Jonson's city comedy as well as French medieval lore, lends its satirical catch-name to Godolphin in his moderate church policies and in promoting the union with Scotland.[35] Though different in ministerial allegiance, those more or less sympathetic to the ancient theory of the divine right of kings were major exponents of bird typology. *The Eagle and the Robin* (1709), so popular as to be pirated as well as reprinted in the same year, for instance, uniquely attacks Robert Harley as "quarrelsome" Robin, but is complimentary to the queen in depicting her favour for Marlborough. The story begins thus:

> A LADY liv'd in former Days,
> That well deserv'd the utmost Praise;
> For Greatness, Birth, and Justice fam'd,
> And every Virtue cou'd be nam'd.
> Which made her Course of Life so even,
> That she's a Saint (if dead) in Heaven.
>
> (ll. 1-6)[36]

The fable's strong hold on the Stuart supporters is a combined force of icons with extraordinary fiction in which birds and beasts "talk like you and I." A penchant for tales is certainly characteristic of the age, but unlike the Jacobite Tories, at whom Steele sneered,

> 'Tis incredible! with what ridiculous Joy the *Tories* invent and receive Stories of this Sort; Stories! so wild, so inconclusive, that they are too low for the silliest Nurse that ever fondled a Changling to entertain. Amongst a vast Number of these, the FAITHFUL (for so I shall call the *Jacobites* hereafter, who are arriv'd to believe every Thing that pleases) with great Delight give out, That Sir Richard Steele is gone over to their Party.[37]

Walpolean writers liked stories that were not necessarily of the Aesopic stock. Joseph Mitchell, for instance, adopted only two well-known Aesopic fables, "Reasonable Fear: or, The Frogs and Fighting Bulls. A Fable from Phædrus Applied to All People of Inferior Condition" and "Ways and Means: or, The Belly and the Members. A Fable from Menenius Agrippa. Applied to the Subjects of Great Britain" in *A Tale and Two Fables in Verse* (1727); these warn the public to obey the government. Amorous tales and romances, which Mitchell and Croxall wrote in profusion, were apparently the form of story favored by Walpolean writers.

Fiction such as fable was subject to misreading, since you could easily amplify its allusion by way of allegory. When it was written by Tories, it was in particular liable to be (mis)taken, if half-mockingly, as relating

Jacobite intrigues. Such a suspicion is certainly justifiable in an elegantly abbreviated version of *Mother Hubbards Tale* (1715) and William Meston's *A Tale of a Man and his Mare, found in an old Manuscript, never before printed* (second edition, 1721). The latter is very entertaining, its octosyllabics satirizing George I as a man ideally suited to digging turnips. The Renaissance Protestant tradition of condemning any poetry as no more than the devil's work was exploited to attack those Tory sympathizers sufficiently competent to write fiction.[38] *The British Blood-Hounds; or a Chase after the State Run-a-ways, A Fable, with a true Copy of the Pretender's Last Will* (1715?), an allegorical dialogue in prose between a "Citizen" and a "Forrester" on Anne's death, the Jacobites' intrigue, and the "happy" prospect of the Hanoverian succession is deliberately given the misnomer "fable," to deride those who might believe in such a thing as "The Pretender's Last Will," herein revealed by the Citizen (12-16). The political implications of bird icons cannot be neglected in this context. The use of fictitious beasts to attack political powers or persons is the very essence of the Aesopic tradition (from which Swift's later invention of the Yahoo, the most repugnant animal on earth, may be considered to descend), but bird typology, a new convention, conjures up ideas of flight and freedom. It suggests the flight of the Jacobites after the 1715 rising on the one hand,[39] and on the other, the idea of "free speech," which in retrospect has been attributed to Aesopic fables in general. Gay's achievement aside, the decline of fable protesting against the fast-ascending Whig oligarchy in the 1720s involves interpretations of "power" and "free speech." The concepts can be deployed by both the revolutionary and the reactionary to implement their respective ideologies, but as interpretations of "liberty" in the eighteenth century necessarily involved those of "property,"[40] so they were likely to be claimed more dominantly by those already in power to buttress their established authority: hence the growing return of the fable collection in the mid-century as an instrument of indoctrination, for enforcing the existing political order and codes of behaviour (as Croxall's *Fables* represented it), rather than for the subversion of them. The civilwar period, when the Aesopic machinery was exploited by Royalists to reassert the divine right of the king, and when familiar biblical icons served parliamentarians to report satirically on the cavaliers' conduct in battle, was far distant;[41] traditional Aesopic icons such as beasts and trees (in particular oaks) returned but as an appropriate reminder of the great chain of being.[42]

The short period during which bird icons flourished in England was a transitional time in which party politics were being established, and here the Tory hacks' role in promulgating bird typology cannot be ignored. Their presumed loyalty to the monarchy (and to individual ministers such as Harley and Bolingbroke) is, on a secular and poetic level, to be seen in their preference for the "ancient" English tradition of poetry; Chaucer's title is echoed in Stacy's *Parliament of Birds, with an account of the Late and Present Ministry,* published by John Morphew in London and reprinted in Dublin by C. Carter, both in 1713. This parliament is a daydream about the Stuart succession. The fiction, however, is delicately made, since it artfully collates the wishful ideology with actual parliamentary proceedings (June 1712-July 1713) on the peace treaty and the removal of the Pretender from Lorraine.[43] Stacy rewrites history by making "a wealthy *Gander*" (15) propose a motion to impeach all factious fowls that had joined the "Foreign Leagues" (16). In indicating his intention to publish a sequel, Stacy is certainly not optimistic. But he seems to have hoped that his fable might move a larger part of the political audience towards Jacobitism. The underlined parallel between the aftermaths of 1641 and 1688, which both worked to reduce the "*old* Hereditary *Right*" (4), becomes evident and evaluated when the first vote is disclosed for the constitutional monarchy over Republicanism:

> The Question's put, and they divided,
> And when it came to be decided,
> Upon a Scrutiny the Sum,
> Was *Eighty Eight* to *Forty One.*

(11)

The second vote, "Three Hundred against Forty five" (12), wins an overwhelming support for the Stuarts. Stacy's *Parliament* won popularity, indeed; a pirated as well as a third edition appeared in the same year as the first, 1713.

If the debate in the fable recalls the repeated tension during the pre-Revolutionary years, then the style in which it is couched also carries a note of familiarity. Speakers are depicted partly as birds, partly as individual ministers, to ensure that no contemporary readers will mistake their identities and implied satire:

> A *Jay,* the Scandal of the Age;
> A turbulent mischievous Bird.
> That had been Pander to a Lord.
> Who got him to the *Oak* preferr'd
> This Antick by his Tricks and Sport.
> Had gain'd a Favourite at Court;
> And, as 'tis said, had sometimes been
> The *Junto*'s Spie upon the *QUEEN.*

(9)

Other rhetorical features are variations on the double structure (praising virtues and blaming vices) of formal verse satire, familiar sayings, proverbial expressions,[44] and stock ideas of birds:

> a Cock, that lost his Battle
> Stands up, and thus began to rattle.

(8)

The partisan content aside, the style in the following address to the Queen made by "a Linnet, hatch'd in Hertfordshire" (6) is simple and accommodated to a larger political audience:

> *We likewise [sic] our own Constitution*
> *Has been impair'd by Revolution;*
> *Our antient Rights, and Forrest Laws*
> *Mangled to serve a Modern Cause:*
> *And many treach'rous Matters done*
> *To lessen or subvert the Crown;*
> *Madam, to these we will apply*
> *A sure and lasting Remedy.*

(7)

The familiar tone thus created recalls an oral tradition (in which fable probably originates) and helps to enforce the political message arguing for the ancient constitution: both point to an esteem for the ancient.

The modern element, however, is also present in bird fables. In retelling public events they are original in plot and fundamentally self-referential. The "Brethren of the Quill"[45] who fought for the peace treaty are listed here with contempt by the belligerent Cock:

> *The* Robin-redbreasts *and the* Larks,
> *The* Blackbirds, Linnets, *and such Sparks*
> *May, with their artful Notes a while*
> *Some thoughtless Fowls and Birds beguile,*
> *But we, with all their Cunning. [sic] know*
> *They're labouring their own Overthrow,*
> *And this a little time will show.*

(*The Parliament of Birds,* 8)

More than beasts, birds readily lend themselves to verbal plays and puns (such as birds and bards), and these feature in later bird fables, which were occasioned by less public events, but which nonetheless show the writer's allegiance to an old set of morals—good sense and loyalty. As is well-known among fable readers, Swift's *An Answer to Delany's Fable of the Pheasant and the Lark,* published in 1730 in Dublin, was occasioned by charges against his friend, Delany, for writing an epistle to Carteret insinuating that the Lord should increase his salary. Swift's fable expresses his respect and admiration for Delany on the one hand,

and on the other, his contemptuous irritation at those who had no wit to appreciate good poetry; it is conducted in a characteristically Swiftean mode, self-mockery hinged on a series of puns and verbal games upon which fable finally rests. After punning on the word "Nightingal," with ostentatious elan, the author-bird flies off leaving the intended reader, Sheridan, in the silent darkness of the owl:

> One Clincher more, and I have done,
> I end my Labours with a Pun.
> *Jove* send, this Nightingal may fall,
> Who spends his Day and *Night in gall.*
> So Nightingal and Lark adieu,
> I see the greatest Owls in you,
> That ever screecht or ever *flew.*

(ll. 101-7)[46]

The frequent appearance of birds in English political fables only tantalizes the modern reader with glimpses of the ideal of fable as a democratic mode of speech. "Aesopian writing" might be an increasingly common form of political resistance in Eastern Europe recently (Patterson, 273),[47] but insofar as early eighteenth-century England is concerned, fable looms large as a medium for traditional moralists who fought to restore the Stuart sovereignty and vigorously ridiculed Whigs by pinning them down as a variety of impious, squalid, noisy fowls. A spirited variation on the stock-opening common in tales ("In ancient time")—such as

> IN Ancient Days when *Birds* cou'd speak
> As plain as *Men* do now,
> And learned Sayings us'd to break
> From ev'ry Hedge and Bough.

(*A Tale of the Finches* [1716], ll. 1-4)[48]

—marks a brief but memorable period in which "birds" (talented writers) and "bards" (hacks) both participated inpolitical discourse and represented the Jacobite cause, before they disappeared and the fable, an ancient form of fiction, became a largely dogmatic kind of writing intended for women and children.

Notes

[1] Annabel Patterson, "Fables of Power," *Politics of Discourse: The Literature and History of Seventeenth-Century England,* ed. Kevin Sharpe and Steven N. Zwicker (Berkeley: Univ. of California Press, 1987), 271-96. Subsequent references to this article cited more than once will appear in parenthesis in the text. Patterson's recent book, *Fables of Power: Aesopian Writing and Political History* (Durham, N.C.: Duke Univ. Press, 1991) seems, one may add, an extension of this article, and is rather weak on eighteenth-century fables.

[2] See pp. 12 and 13 below. Among other numerous examples are "The Panther and his Son" in *Æsop the Wanderer* (1704); "The Revolution" in [William Pittis] *Canterbury Tales* (1701) and *A Tale. Robin's Tame Pidgeons [sic.] Turn'd Wild* (1713), both of which draw on Dryden's inlaid fable of the pidgeons; "Æsop's Thanks" in *Bickerstaff's Æsop* (1720), where the two universities are alluded to as "Two Milkwhite Hinds" (l. 1). Cf. *A Poem in Defence of the Church of England, In Opposition to the Hind and Panther. Written By Mr. John Dryden* (1709).

[3] For a short catalogue of abusive pamphlets published during the year 1687, see Hugh MacDonald in *Essential Articles for the Study of John Dryden,* ed. H. T. Swedenberg, Jr. (London: Frank Cass & Co., 1966), 22-53. The present essay does not concern itself with a detailed discussion of *The Hind and the Panther,* for reasons indicated below.

[4] Thomas Noel, *Theories of the Fable in the Eighteenth Century* (New York: Columbia Univ. Press, 1975), in particular chapter 3.

[5] See "To the Reader" in *Æsop at Richmond, recovered of his late illness. A poem in burlesque,* and also George Kitchin, *Sir Roger L'Estrange: A Contribution to the History of the Press in the Seventeenth Century* (London: Kegan Paul, Trench, Trübner & Co., Ltd, 1913), 372. Other Aesopic pamphlets published in the year include: *Æsop at Tunbridge; or, a few select fables in verse. By no person of quality;. Æsop Return'd from Tunbridge: or, Æsop out of his wits. In a few select fables in verse; Æsop at Epsom, by a cit; Æsop at Bath; or a few select fables in verse by a person of quality; Æsop at Whitehall, giving advice to the young Æsops at Tunbridge and Bath; or, some fables [in verse] relating to Government. By a person of what quality you please.*

[6] See, for example, *Æsop in Paris* (1701), *Æsop in Spain* (1701, 1703), *Æsop at Portugal* (1704), *Æsop in Scotland* (1704) and *Æsop in Europe. Or a general survey, of the present posture of affairs in England, Scotland, France* (1706).

[7] J. A. Downie, *Robert Harley and the Press* (Cambridge: Cambridge Univ. Press, 1979), 1.

[8] See also Joseph Jacobs, *The Fables of Aesop. As first printed by William Caxton in 1484 with those of Avian, Alfonso and Poggio, now again edited etc.,* 2 vols. (1889). Vol. 1, *History of the Aesopic Fable,* 38-40.

[9] Swift, *A Full and True Account of the Battel Fought last Friday, Between the Antient and the Modern Books in St. James's Library* (written 1697, printed 1710), in *The Prose Writings of Jonathan Swift,* ed. Herbert Davis, 14 vols. (Oxford: Basil Blackwell, 1939-68). Vol. 1, 1939, p. 145; G. V. Bennett, *The Tory Crisis in Church and State 1688-1730: The Career of Francis Atterbury Bishop of Rochester* (Oxford: Clarendon Press, 1975), 41.

[10] *The Complete Works of Sir John Vanbrugh,* the Plays edited by Bonamy Dobrée, the Letters edited by Geoffrey Webb, 4 vols. (New York: AMS Press, Inc., 1967), 2:7.

[11] "Ancient and Modern Learning" in *Five Miscellaneous Essays by Sir William Temple,* edited, with an Introduction, by Samuel Holt Monk (Ann Arbor: The Univ. of Michigan Press, 1963), see p. 64 in particular.

[12] Bentley, *A Dissertation upon the Epistles of Phalaris . . . and the Fables of Æsop* (1697, to-gether with Wotton's *Reflections upon Ancient and Modern Learning,* 2d ed.), 146; see also Boyle *Dr. Bentley's Dissertations,* (1698), 236. For a detailed and comprehensive account of the battle see Joseph M. Levine, *The Battle of the Books: History and Literature in the Augustan Age* (Ithaca: Cornell Univ. Press, 1991).

[13] The "Epistle Dedicatory." See also *Æsop at Richmond* (ll. 15-16).

[14] Kitchin, *L'Estrange,* 392, and further, 393-400; H. J. Blackham, *The Fable as Literature* (London and Dover, New Hampshire: The Athlone Press, 1985), 84-87; Patterson, "Fables of Power," 271-74.

[15] Reviews by Motteux in *The Gentleman's Journal* (1691-92) and De la Crose in *Works of the Learned* (1692) (mentioned in Kitchin, *L'Estrange,* 400). L'Estrange's *Fables* were reissued repeatedly(1694, 1699, 1704, 1708, and 1714), commentated on in detail, possibly by James Gordon (1701), and adapted by other Tory writers, probably William Pittis in *Æsop at the Bell-Tavern in Westminster* (1711) (D.F. Foxon, *English Verse 1701-1750. A Catalogue of Separately Printed Poems with Notes on Contemporary Collected Editions,* 2 vols. [Cambridge: Cambridge Univ. Press, 1975), 1:425]) and Edmund Stacy (1717), whom I shall discuss later.

[16] This poem, not an Aesopic beast fable in the conventional sense, starts by referring to "Æsop" as an honest outspoken Tory (1-2), but in the main it portrays social types (such as the "modern Beaux"—"a cully'd Man o'th' Law," "a sneaking sniv'ling Cit," "the Country-Lass," "a Man of Wit" or just "Dick"; "most" of these are, the narrator says, courting "in Prose" or "in Chime") gathering at Richmond Wells, merely "to show" "their Foppery" (6-7), and unconcerned with the current moral or political state of affairs.

[17] There is one other version, which was translated into Latin by Rinuccio de Castiglione in 1474, and then,

through French and German texts, into English by Caxton (published in 1484).

[18] Madeleine Bingham, *Masks and Facades: Sir John Vanbrugh The Man in his Setting* (London: George Allen & Unwin, 1974), 58-60; Robert D. Hume, *The Development of English Drama in the Late Seventeenth Century* (Oxford: Clarendon Press, 1976), 419-20; and Leo Hughes, *A Century of English Farce* (Princeton N.J.: Princeton Univ. Press, 1956), 126. For a brief but good introductory account, see Kerry Downes, *Sir John Vanbrugh: A Biography* (London: Sidgwick & Jackson, 1987), 133-38.

[19] It is largely an adaptation of a French play written by Boursault, enacted as *Ésope à la Ville* on 10 January 1690, but printed at Paris in 1693 under the title of *Les Fables d'Ésope* (see Vanbrugh's Prologue).
[20] Dobrée, *Works,* 2:33

[21] For instance, see Act III in Dobrée, *Works,* 2:29. For the frequent digression in the work, see Bingham, *Masks,* 59; Hume, *Development,* 419-20; and also Mahlon Ellwood Smith in *PMLA* 46 (1931): 225-36.

[22] Dobrée, *Works,* 2:22.

[23] Ibid., 45.

[24] See also the "Preface" to *Æsop Naturaliz'd & Expos'd to the Publick View in His Own Hape and Dress.*

[25] For thematic traits in Jacobite writing, see Paul Kléber Monod,*Jacobitism and the English People 1688-1788* (Cambridge: Cambridge Univ. Press, 1989), 49-54.

[26] See, for example, "The Consequences of a Standing Army" (ii), "Trade and Empire Inconsistent" (vi), "The Effect of Naturalizing Acts" (xi).

[27] *The Parliamentary History of England, from the Earliest Period to the Year 1803,* 36 vols. (London, 1806-1820), 5 (1809), 1336-37.

[28] Ibid., 671-75, 689-90.

[29] Ibid., 672, 1337.

[30] See, for example, *A Canterbury Tale translated out of Chaucer's old English into Our Now Usuall Language . . . by A.B.* (1641), *Catalogue of the Pamphlets, Books, Newspapers, and Manuscripts Relating to the Civil War, etc.,* collected by George Thomason, 1640-1661, 2 vols. (London: William Clowes & Sons, 1908), 1:29.

[31] Foxon, vol. 1, S702.

[32] Ogilby's Royalist swans (Fable V) in *Æsopics* (1668).

[33] *The Fable of the Cuckoo* (1701), 96-99 wherein the Cuckoo represents the malicious, stubborn and barbarous element among the Dissenters.

[34] "The Passive Goose" in *Three Belgic Fables; or, Hieroglyphic Ridles* [sic] (1729).

[35] See, for example, Joseph Browne's *The Fox Set to Watch the Geese* (1705; reissued under the title *Volpone, or, the Fox* [1706]), and an anonymous prose *Vulpone [sic]: or The Scotch Riddle* (1707).

[36] The text is taken from the one published by J. Bradford.
[37] *Chit-Chat* (1716), no. 3, *Richard Steele's Periodical Journalism 1714-16,* ed. Rae Blanchard (Oxford: Oxford Univ. Press, 1959), 266.

[38] "Time was, when it was question'd much in Story,/ Which was the Worst, the *Devil,* or a *Tory?*" (*The Tripe Club. A Satyr* [1706]).

[39] As one might expect, imagery of rape, suggested by H. Erskine-Hill as a "defining characteristic" of Jacobite writing ("Literature and the Jacobite Cause: Was There a Rhetoric of Jacobitism?", *Ideology and Conspiracy: Aspects of Jacobitism, 1689-1759,* ed. Eveline Cruickshanks [Edinburgh: John Donald Publishers Ltd, 1982], 49-69), is not found in Aesopic writing.

[40] H. T. Dickinson, *Liberty and Property: Political Ideology in Eighteenth-Century Britain* (London: Methuen, 1977).

[41] See, for example, *Be Wise as Serpents, innocent as Doves* (20-26 July, 1644), *A Dog's Elegy; or, Rupert's Tears for the Defeat at Marstonmoore* (2 July 1644), *England's Wolfe [sic]* with Eagles Clawes (1646).

[42] For a wider acceptance of the idea in the eighteenth century, see Arthur O. Lovejoy, *The Great Chain of Being: A Study of the History of an Idea* (Cambridge, Mass.: Harvard Univ. Press, 1970; first 1936), 183-207.

[43] *The Parliamentary History of England,* 6 (1810), 1141-44, 1165, 1207-14, 1224-26, 1232-37.

[44] See, for example, *The Eagle and the Robin,* ll. 120-23; *The Emulation of the Insects* (1754), the penultimate couplet. Some fables are also quoted like familiar proverbs. For instance, "'Tell him he may e'en gan his get, I'll have nothing to do with him I'll stay like the poor Country Mouse, in my own Habitation.' So Peg talkt," John Arbuthnot, *The History of John Bull,* ed.

Alan W. Bower and Robert A. Erickson (Oxford: Oxford Univ. Press, 1976), part 1, chapter 4, p. 55, ll. 23-25; see also chapter 6, p. 58, ll. 25-27.

45 "The Dedication" in *Bickerstaff's Æsop: or, The Humours of the Times, Digested into Fables* [1720].

46 *The Poems of Jonathan Swift,* ed. Harold Williams, 3 vols. (Oxford: Oxford Univ. Press, 1958), 2:515.

47 See also Lev Loseff, On the Beneficence of Censorship: Aesopian Language in Modern Russian Literature (München: Verlag Otto Sagner in Kommission, 1984)

48 See also "The Succession" in *Chaucer's Whims* (1701), ll. 1-6; *Volpone, or, the Fox* (1706), ll. 1-10; *The Eagle and the Robin* (1709), ll. 1-6; "The Mag-Pye and Black-Birds" in *The Welchman's Tales* (1710), ll. 1-4; the opening of Delany's fable; and Pope's *Dunciad,* Book I, ll. 9-12.

THE EVOLUTION OF THE AESOPIC FABLE

Lloyd W. Daly (essay date 1961)

SOURCE: "Introduction," in *Aesop without Morals,* translated and edited by Lloyd W. Daly, pp. 11-26. New York: Thomas Yoseloff, 1961.

[*In the following excerpt, Daly asserts that the morals that appear at the end of Aesopic fables are additions made by later generations which do nothing to clarify the meaning of the original tale.*]

The Fables. "Know thyself," commanded one of the legends inscribed on the temple of Apollo at Delphi, and Socrates echoed to the Athenian court that condemned him, "the unexamined life is not worth a man's living." This introspective bent, this disposition toward self-criticism, was part of the Greek genius for "seeing life steadily and seeing it whole." It might express itself in tragedy, or it might express itself in comedy; Nietzsche labeled its more austere and measured expression Apollonian, its more enthusiastic and irrational side Dionysian.

When the Greek looked at himself, he was not always happy with what he saw. The extreme reaction is represented in the story of King Midas' capture of the sage Silenus, the boon companion of Bacchus and an embodiment of the proverb *in vino veritas*. When forced to answer the foolish king's question, Silenus said that the best thing for man was never to be born and the second best to die as soon as possible. The outlook

finds its standard portrayal in the legend about the philosopher Diogenes who went about with a lantern and, when asked what he was looking for, replied simply, "An honest man." Though ancient Cynicism did not deny human sincerity and goodness, it found these qualities rare.

The Aesopic fables are one of these reflections from the mirror of self-examination. The Greek looks into his glass and sees a horrible picture of himself. It is always difficult to be honest with oneself, and it is as though the fables were saying, "It is not I but the animal in me that is like this." Then comes the moralist and says, "No, you fool; this is yourself even more truly than any ideal you may have." The Aesopic fables have been pap for children in schools for so many hundreds of years that it is perhaps difficult to think of them in any other light, but the cynical vein of the stories themselves runs so strong that it must be obvious they were not intended for the edification of youth, and it is in such a light that I would present them in this new translation, freed from the encumbrance of the added morals, which are at best supererogatory.

If we dispense with the morals, which are little more than an insult to our intelligence, how are we to understand the existence of such a collection of tales? If these fables were not intended to serve a moral and instructional purpose, were they brought together to serve any other purpose? The answer to this question is not, perhaps, too difficult to divine, for we know something of the place the fables occupy in our own consciousness. Pointed stories capable of a wide variety of application have always been in demand. We have only to recall *fishing in muddy waters, out of the frying pan into the fire, the goose that laid the golden eggs, the dog in the manger, the boy who cried wolf, the ant and the grasshopper, the hare and the tortoise,* and *the wolf in sheep's clothing* to realize the proverbial and paradigmatic function the stories serve with us. We depend on the very mention of a fable to say, "Oh yes, everyone recognizes that kind of behavior; it's just like that of the animal in the fable." Still, the analogy of modern understanding is not always a reliable index to the attitudes of other times or other places, and a proper insight into a literary product of any age other than our own can be gained only by looking at it in the light of what we know of its genesis and development.

The first appearance in the Hellenic world of anything that can be identified as an Aesopic fable is in the *Works and Days* (lines 201 ff.) of the poet Hesiod, whom the ancients regarded as a contemporary of Homer and who may have lived as early as the eighth century before Christ. Hesiod says:

And now I will tell a fable for kings even though they are wise: Thus spoke the hawk to the speckled-necked nightingale as he seized her in his claws and carried her up among the clouds—and pitifully did she whimper as the crooked claws pierced her through—masterfully did he bespeak her: "Simple creature, why do you cry aloud? One far mightier than yourself now holds you in his grip, and you will go wherever I take you for all your singing, and I will make a meal of you if I choose, or I will let you go. Foolish is he who would match himself against those who are stronger; he is robbed of victory and suffers pain as well as shame."

The fable is told as something that is already familiar, for it begins in the middle; to judge from the lesson that is drawn, it should have begun by saying that the nightingale was inordinately proud of her song, so proud that she boasted she was the better of any winged creature.

Other early Greek poets make use of similar talking-beast tales, but it is not until the fifth and fourth centuries before Christ that we find such writers as Aristophanes, Plato, and Aristotle ascribing the stories they tell to Aesop. These stories obviously had currency by word of mouth for a long time, even, to use a close parallel, as shaggy-dog stories have in recent times.

A story told by Plato of Socrates sheds an interesting light on the status of the fables in his day. In the *Phaedo* (60 D ff.) one of the friends of Socrates, who is in prison awaiting execution of his sentence, asks him about some poems he is said to have been composing there. Socrates says that he has been doing this in response to a command that he had often received in a dream. He says that he has composed a hymn but "realizing that the poet, if he is really to be a poet, must write stories rather than addresses, and since I was no storyteller, I took the fables of Aesop, which I knew and came readily to hand, and turned the first ones that occurred to me into verse." It is reasonably certain that Socrates is not supposed in this anecdote to have had a copy of *Aesop's Fables* at hand in the prison. Indeed there is no reason to suppose that there was in existence among the Greeks any such collection of what would have been looked upon as trivialities in this day when books were still a relatively scarce commodity. Socrates would merely have drawn on his familiarity with such fables for simple plots. It will also bear noticing that this is the first instance in which there is any suggestion of the idea of versifying Aesop, an idea that has since borne generous fruit.

These instances in which fables were used by ancient poets and other writers of Greece also give us an opportunity to see in what way the fables were used in this period before there is any evidence of their having been brought together into a collection. The example chosen from Hesiod above is perhaps somewhat misleading, for it is only he and a moralist such as the Socrates of Xenophon's *Memorabilia* (II 7, 13) who

make use of a fable to point a generalized moral lesson. In most of the other instances in which there is sufficient context preserved to allow us to make any observation, the fables are used to make a point or support an argument. The Greeks are known for their love of disputation, and this use of the fable is only one of their many devices for forceful expression aimed at making a point or carrying conviction. And there was more than one way of using a fable for such a purpose. Herodotus in his *History* (I 141) tells how Ionian Greeks, who had resisted the Persian king, Cyrus, once they heard that Croesus and the Lydians had already been subjugated, sent an ambassador with offers of submission. Cyrus' only reply was to tell a fable. "A flute player saw some fish and started to play, with the idea that the fish would come out on the land. When they disappointed him, he took a net, cast it, and hauled out a great quantity of fish. When he saw them jumping around, he said to them: 'You don't need to dance for me now, since you wouldn't come out and dance when I played my flute.'" Herodotus assures us the Ionians did not miss the point of Cyrus' fable.

The romanticized biography of Aesop gives a perfect illustration of this allegorical use of a fable. Aesop, a slave recently freed for his good advice to the people of Samos, was called upon for further advice. Croesus had demanded tribute of the Samians, and their public officials had advised sending it. But the assembly of the people asked Aesop's advice. The master of the fable replied, "If I say 'don't give it,' I'll mark myself as an enemy of Croesus." The assembly still called loudly for him to speak, and reluctantly he responded, "I will not give you advice but I will speak to you in a fable. Once, at the command of Zeus, Prometheus described to men two ways, one the way of freedom and the other that of slavery. The way of freedom he pictured as rough at the beginning, narrow, steep, and waterless, full of brambles and beset with perils everywhere, but finally a level plain amid parks, groves of fruit trees, and water courses where the struggle reaches its end in rest. The way of slavery he pictured as a level plain at the beginning, flowery and pleasant to look upon with much to delight, but at its end narrow, hard, and like a cliff." In his *Rhetoric* (II20) Aristotle comments on this use of the fable. "Fables," says he, "are suited to popular oratory and have this advantage that, while historical parallels are hard to find, it is comparatively easy to find fables. For fables have to be invented, like illustrations, if one has a faculty of seeing analogies, and invention is facilitated by cultivation."

The first indication that any Greek took the fables seriously enough to make a written collection of them does not come until the fourth century B.C. Diogenes Laertius in his biography of Demetrius of Phalerum (V 5, 80) reports that this scholar left, among many other works, "collections of Aesopic Fables." These collections have not survived, but fragments of a papyrus scroll of the first century after Christ have been found containing fables in Greek prose, and this scroll may well be a copy of them.

The earliest extant collection is a versified Latin version of some of the fables done by the freedman Phaedrus in the first century of our era. The five short books of Phaedrus contain not only Aesopic fables but also anecdotes and topical material of contemporary interest, which indicates how little feeling there was that the fables had a fixed form and independent existence in their own right rather than being floating, common property. Phaedrus retold the fables he chose in iambic verse, which had always been felt to be appropriate for satire or invective. The fables do not in themselves point a satirical finger at anyone, at least not explicitly. In a collection who can say that any one fable is aimed at an individual? Some of them may be so aimed, and those who are sensitive or vulnerable may feel wounded. Some, at least, of Phaedrus' fables were taken as personal satire, for we are told that under the emperor Tiberius he was punished for offence he gave through his fables to the emperor's powerful favorite, Sejanus. This satirical bent eventually found its fullest expression in the French *Fables* of La Fontaine, many of which are based directly upon Phaedrus.

In France the *Fables* of La Fontaine have been familiar to generations of school children through exercises in memorization, recitation, and paraphrasing. This is precisely the pedagogical practice advocated for Roman school children by Quintilian in the first century in his *Education of the Orator* (I 9, 1). The pupils of the elementary teacher "should," he says, "learn to paraphrase Aesop's fables, the natural successors of the fairy stories of the nursery, in simple language, and subsequently to set down this paraphrase in writing with the same simplicity of style: They should begin by analyzing each verse, then give its meaning in different language, and finally proceed to a freer paraphrase in which they will be permitted now to abridge and now to embellish the original so far as this may be done without losing the poet's meaning." The poet in this case we can only presume to have been Phaedrus.

Phaedrus did not find an emulator in Latin until about 400 A.D., when Avianus turned forty-two fables into elegiac verse, which enjoyed the greatest popularity throughout the Middle Ages and served as a mediator of the fable to modern times. But Avianus' model was not Phaedrus. His stories are all taken from Babrius, who, at an uncertain date not later than the second century, did the work Socrates had conceived and left iambic renderings in Greek of the fables in ten books, of which we now have two.

But it is the prose versions of the fables with which we are here concerned. Aside from the one small papyrus fragment already referred to, the Greek prose versions are preserved by manuscripts written at various times ranging from the tenth to the sixteenth century. Yet the formation of the collection upon which these late copies are based may be assigned with confidence to some time within the first three centuries after the birth of Christ. This is not to say that every fable in the collections has been preserved in precisely the form in which it would have appeared in the original collection; it is, in fact, clear that the precise literal form of the fables was not regarded as anything like sacrosanct and that variations on the nature of the collections were produced from time to time by the addition, omission, and rearrangement of fables.

It is these prose versions of the *Fables* which may be considered as the true Aesop, the basis in one sense or another for all others. While it is clear from allusions in the poet Archilochus that some of these fables are as old as the seventh century before Christ, at least one (262) was pretty clearly added in Christian times, since it is the fable told by Jotham to the men of Shechem in the book of Judges (IX 8).

The fables are, as everyone knows, beast stories in which the beasts not only talk but also behave in other ways very much like humans. Isidore, the seventh century Bishop of Seville, says that fables are told in order to produce a recognizable picture of human life through the conversations of imaginary dumb animals. He goes on to say that fables are either Aesopic or Libystic. "They are Aesopic when dumb animals or inanimate things such as cities, trees, mountains, rocks, rivers are supposed to have talked to one another, but they are Libystic when there is supposed to be some oral communication of men with beasts or beasts with men." There are fables of both kinds represented in our collections, but there are also other kinds, and the distinction is of no significance. Some fables, such as that of *The Thieving Boy and His Mother* (200), have only human characters.

Far from being highly moral stories, the fables are not always even conducive to moralizing. The fable of *The Boys and the Butcher* (66) presents two juvenile delinquents of antiquity stealing from a butcher. The point of the story lies in the boy who stole the meat saying that he didn't have it and the one who had it saying he hadn't stolen it. The butcher's remark that even if they deceive him with their lies, they will not deceive the gods, is very lameindeed. Again in the story of *The Bat and the Weasels* (172), in which the bat escaped death at the hands of weasels once by claiming to be a mouse instead of a bird and again by claiming to be a bird instead of a mouse, there is no moral content, and even the moralist can only say, "Obviously, we too must not always stand on the same ground but remember that people who adapt themselves to circumstances often manage to escape the most serious perils." On occasion they may serve very special purposes. For example, the fable of *The Bat, the Bramble, and the Coot* (171) is aetiological, that is it serves to explain the origin of the peculiar habits of each of the members of this trio. That of *Zeus and the Turtle* (106) is a *Just So Story* explaining how the turtle got his shell. Still the vast majority of the fables are paradigmatic, which is to say that, whatever their content, they serve as examples, usually horrible, of human behavior. You may take them as you like, but they must usually have been told in antiquity with the expectation that someone specific would find that the shoe fit and would have to put it on. That is why they so readily turn into satire in the hands of Phaedrus or La Fontaine.

In our collections nearly all the fables are equipped with morals at the end. *This fable teaches* is one of the familiar introductory formulae. Upon such formulaic pegs are hung the generalized lessons which are independent of the stories and are presented as the comment of Aesop or an anonymous narrator and not of the animals or characters of the stories. There is good reason for retelling the fables without these morals. The history of the collections pretty clearly indicates that the morals were not a necessary or standard accompaniment of the fables from the beginning. The fables are commonly arranged in the collections in an alphabetical order determined by the initial letter of the first word of each so that, for example, all fables beginning with the word *Fox* are grouped together. It is thus fairly easy to find most of the *Fox* fables but not so easy to find a fable to illustrate a particular point. It appears that the collectors began to give some help in this direction by adding brief *promythia,* or explanations, at the head of the fables. As the purpose of writing these shifted from that of indicating interest and point to one of interpretation, it was natural that the explanation should be made to follow rather than precede the fable it explained. As B. E. Perry, who has studied this history, puts it, the collectors "began to think of themselves no longer as mere compilers but somewhat as literary men speaking to the public in the capacity of interpreters and moral advisers."

The style of the fables is simple and direct. They are told in language that is unpretentious and free alike from high-flown verbiage and from colloquialism. When one stops to think that the fables are not all the product of the pen of a single author, he will realize that this feature of their style is one that had been fixed by convention and represents deliberate restraint rather than inept colorlessness. This restraint is in keeping with the general crispness and economy of narrative that is everywhere observed. Thesituation is usually described in a very few words, an incident is outlined with equal brevity, and a result indicated. The fable of *The Goose That Laid the Golden Eggs* (87) is a good example. It consists of three sentences. The first sets the stage: "Hermes was worshiped with unusual devotion by a

man, and as a reward he gave the man a goose that laid golden eggs." The second tells what the man did: "The man couldn't wait to reap the benefits gradually, but, without any delay, he killed the goose on the supposition that it would be solid gold inside." The third tells the result: "He found out that it was all flesh inside, and so the result was that he was not only disappointed in his expectations but he also lost the eggs."

Still, even with all this brevity, space may be found for a dramatic touch. Most fables end with the words of the principal character. They may simply be his last words, as in the fable of *The Crab and the Fox* (116), but very frequently they provide the fable with an epigrammatic climax, a punch line. This punch line can be seen in the fable of *The Pig and the Sheep* (85), which also shows the further dramatic refinement of miniature dialogue.

Effective character drawing is not to be expected in such brief scope. In the *Fables* of La Fontaine the individual animals often bear a stock character equivalent to some type or class of person in contemporary court society, but this is not so in the Aesopic fables. The fox may show some signs of being sly like his medieval counterpart Reynard or his more modern descendant Br'er Fox, as in the fable of *The Fox and the Leopard* (12), but he is so far from being consistently clever that he appears as a very prototype of stupidity combined with gluttony in the fable of *The Fox with the Swollen Belly* (24). The faithfulness of the dog, the long-suffering of the ass, and the timorousness of the deer are all recognized in the fables, but they are not so fixed as characteristics that these animals cannot be presented in other lights.

Arnold Clayton Henderson (essay date 1982)

SOURCE: "Medieval Beasts and Modern Cages: The Making of Meaning in Fables and Bestiaries," in *PMLA,* Vol. 97, No. 1, January 1982, pp. 40-49.

[*In the following essay, Henderson examines ways in which medieval fabulists freely modified Aesopic fables—sometimes adding elaborate morals to suit their needs—and looks critically at the rigidity of modern techniques for finding meaning in medieval works.*]

Not long ago, we were told that a poem should not mean but be. No one told the medieval author. He—or she—blithely layered meaning upon meaning. Noticing this difference between then and now, we have made meaning—the original meaning and the original reader'sprocess of getting at it—the central issue in most modern criticism of medieval literature. How are meanings wrapped up in a text? How did the original audience know what was there? Were some meanings hidden? We, certainly, have found many hidden meanings: historical allusions hiding behind the surface, pagan myths lingering beneath the surface, patristic exegesis glossing and transforming the surface. We have stripped the surface off entirely to find basic logical structures beneath. What we have not found is a method for testing the limits of our sometimes too universally successful methods.

Where ought we to start for an unobstructed view of authentically medieval moralizing? Some works spell their meanings out for us: the fables, the bestiaries, the sermons, and any other work with an explicit moral. Even if the moral is but an author's joke or a scribe's mistake, at least the joke or mistake is a medieval one; thus we have medieval commentary on medieval texts. Granted that authors may convey more than what they put in an explicit moral, even the partial meanings and misrepresentations reveal the mental processes of a medieval reader and suggest the kind of thing a meaning was expected to be. They are certified as conceivable and authentically medieval by the very scribes and authors who passed the works to us.

Beast fables are particularly useful as test cases, for they have oft-recycled plots, with each new author giving a meaning that may or may not be the same as that of his or her source. We catch the authors thinking aloud of what they have decided to do with their material. In the explicit moralizations to the fables, authors reveal their own perceptions, not of what the traditional material does mean or has meant (since we will find some of these authors consciously innovating), but of what potential for meaning they found. If we hope to extend the Nun's Priest's advice and take "the moralite" of not only his tale or works with explicit moralizations but all sorts of medieval works, we might well examine beforehand such a "control" as the relatively straightforward genre of fable.

When one follows the meanings explicit in fables and bestiaries from their entries into Christianity down through the close of the medieval period, one finds, to be sure, a good deal of mindless copying but also certain kinds of variety. The most innovative group seems to be a line of loosely related British and French fabulists working from the twelfth century on and creating variation in three major areas: (1) more specific social applications, (2) more elaborate moralizations that, in certain authors, resemble the point-for-point allegory of exegesis rather than the simple application more typical of fable, and (3) a style crackling with vividness and colloquial dialogue. Though many moralizations, even in these authors, remain copies of old moralizations, so much is new that we can be sure innovation was a sought-after good. The range of freedoms we find authors allowing themselves in their actual practice can help warn us when our modern methods of closing in on a meaning threaten to cage up our medieval authors.

The New Social Specificity

The first freedom of the fabulists is the freedom to shift a moral to a new specific application, often social, within a broad area suggested by the plot's inherent pattern. If a strong beast harms a weak one in the plot, then the moralization may provide a lesson about strength in general or else about the power of some specific social group—the rich, the bishops, the lords. Antique and most medieval collections before the later twelfth century preferred general ethical considerations to specific social satire. Generality was deep in the grain of fable collections. In imitating the antique collections of Phaedrus and Avianus, medieval collections copied a breadth of moralization that Phaedrus and Avianus had apparently themselves taken from earlier collections. As Ben Edwin Perry suggests, these earlier collections seem to have been intended as reference handbooks for orators; since orators intended rewriting the fables anyway to suit the circumstances of particular orations, the handbook needed to supply only brief headings to help locate appropriate fables—anything more precisely satirical was better left to the orator.[1] At least one quite late medieval fabulist, John Lydgate, still felt sufficiently in touch with his origins to give us with confidence Aesop's own intention—we are *supposed* to turn a fable to our own purposes: "Isopus . . . / Fonde out fables, þat men myght hem apply / To Sondry matyrs, yche man for hys party."[2] Toward the end of the twelfth century, such fabulists as Berechiah ben Natronai, Marie de France, and Odo of Cheriton began turning fables to new purposes right in the written moralization itself. They apply the ancient general lessons of weak and strong to specific classes in a real society: rich and poor, *seigneur* and *vilain*.[3]

One fable by Phaedrus, the first from the antique collection of greatest influence in the Middle Ages, is already about as specific in its social application as a fable of Phaedrus ever gets. A wolf and a lamb are drinking at a stream. The wolf claims the lamb fouls his water. No use for the lamb to point out that the water flows from the wolf to him, not the other way. The wolf eats him. The fable's application attacks those "who invent false charges by which to oppress the innocent."[4] "The innocent" and "false charges" are moral categories: villain and victim may be of any social class, though there is some indication that they meet at the lawcourts. Few other fables of Phaedrus are so specifically social in application. But this fable becomes much more specifically social from the end of the twelfth century on, as developed by Berechiah, Marie de France, Odo of Cheriton, and, in the fifteenth century, John Lydgate and Robert Henryson. It is still a fable of calumny and the innocent, but these later fabulists identify oppressive calumniators with the rich; they identify the innocent with the poor. Henryson cites even so specific a social class as tenant farmers.[5]

From the first, each fabulist of this new social specificity has his or her own concern, his or her own "party," to use Lydgate'sword. Within the power structure stands the courtly Marie de France; locked out of it stands the Jew Berechiah. Though they look on the same world of laymen, their perspectives are different. Odo of Cheriton prefers the ecclesiastical world—prefers it, that is, as a subject for satire. Odo looses a menagerie of snail bishops, spider bishops, and rector flies, of dog officials and crow officials picking the bones of the lesser clergy and, ultimately, of the poor. Though the three innovative fabulists often share the plots of fables, they each invent many new morals—morals that are not shared, not borrowed. Originality must have been valued, and we can sometimes hardly specify the "traditional meaning" of a fable after one of these writers has handled it.

Thus, from the late twelfth century on, fabulists were preparing for Robert Henryson's brilliant but not quite phoenixlike performance as social and philosophical fabulist. His work is not cold tradition suddenly enflamed by fiery genius, and we miss the essence when we set his fables alongside some dull old version he probably knew, like Walter of England's. What Henryson took from the tradition of social fabulists was not particular ideas but support for the process of being original. Such an urge to originality had its own tradition from Marie and Berechiah and Odo through the *Isopets:* Henryson rose from something other than his own ashes.[6]

The New, Point-for-Point Allegory

After the new social specificity, the second freedom of certain among these fabulists (Odo but not Marie) lies in their setting meanings forth more elaborately than before and by a method more at home with preachers and bestiarists than with traditional fabulists. As a preacher, Odo was, of course, familiar with the exegetical method of the Fathers and trained to use it in sermons, matching literal items in a text to their spiritual equivalents. This direct, detailed listing is a method no early fabulist would touch, at least not in collected fables. Fable collections, as distinct from isolated fables embedded in sermons or other texts, imitated a pagan literary tradition, retaining the air, as well as the plots, of Phaedrus and his peers. When Odo used a fable, anecdote, or other illustration in a sermon, he might naturally have felt that his genre was sermon, not fable collection, and he might naturally have moralized even the fable in a sermonlike style. When he did make his collection of fables—many of them, again, not classical fable but anecdotes or animal lore from varied sources—he perhaps continued to feel small allegiance to the tradition of Phaedrus. It is not surprising, then, that he continued his more exegetical style of moralizing right alongside morals of the older type. It is not surprising, but it is new, for his fables

circulated in collection form and could affect the expectations to be aroused by the genre of fable collection.

Most collections, even after Odo, retained the older sort of moralization in which the whole central act of the fable istransferred from beasts to human beings but in which the incidental properties and subsidiary characters of the fable are not each given their own meanings. So when we come to the detailed moralizations of John Lydgate and Robert Henryson, we must remember that the exegetical method, common in sermons and bestiaries, is not the method of fables. However little we credit Lydgate with originality and however much we suspect that the and Henryson had read their Odo or, perhaps more likely, had heard preachers influenced by Odo, still we must recognize that Lydgate and Henryson not only rediscover what was new in Odo but often surpass him in their energetic transformation of detail after detail.

One example, from Henryson, must suffice. A wolf overhears a plowman cursing his oxen, saying, "May the wolf take you!" The wolf demands that the promise be kept, the plowman refuses, and they ask a fox to act as judge. Accepting the plowman's bribe of chickens to get rid of the wolf, the fox leads the wolf off through darkening woods in search of a cheese the plowman supposedly offered in place of the oxen. They find a well whose water reflects the round, yellow moon, and the fox proclaims this reflection the cheese, ready for taking. But the wolf bids the fox go first, down in the well bucket. Once down, the fox calls for help lifting the too great cheese, and the wolf rides down in the other bucket, unaware that both buckets run on one pulley, so that as the wolf goes down, the fox goes up and runs off, leaving the wolf to bob alone in the well bottom. Whereas other fabulists moralize the act of trickery, Henryson moralizes both act and setting—the cheese of covetousness, the wood of wicked riches, even the chickens of good works.[7] Although elaborate allegory in sermons is said to have been distinctly the fashion in England in the late Middle Ages, with Holkot, Bromyard, and their followers, sermons are not fable collections.[8] Any fabulists who chose to adapt to their lesser genre the prestigious methods of the sermon would still have needed the freedom and will to innovate. The morals of Henryson's fables, or Lydgate's, are far harder to find in "sources" than are the plots. Once the authors had decided on a new fashion of moralization, they could hardly help finding "new meanings" in all the old fables that had never before had their entire plot and paraphernalia run through the great meaning machine of exegesis.

The New Colloquial Style

In pursuing the explicit meaning expressed in fables, we do not strictly need to examine style, whose meaning is implicit. But the stylistic shift that constitutes the third area of newness in late medieval fable appears sometimes linked to the shifts toward specific social meanings and more detailed allegories. The authors who innovated in other areas tended to do so in style, too, though not many passages show all three traits. Dialogue, formerly rare or restricted to making essential points, grows and becomes more flexible in fables from Marie and Berechiah on. Odo, the first we know to use the names of the *Renart* cycle, has at times the verve, too, of that great beast epic, then at peak popularity. Two centuries later, Henryson, when compared to Walter of England and the ordinary Romulus, seems an isolated genius at dialogue; but group him with the other innovators and you see these fabulists supporting one another in their invention of new, vivid dialogue as well as new moralizations. Once again Henryson may be the best, may be highly original, yet may still be nurtured by his tradition. Particular phrases need not be borrowed; inheriting the spirit and the sanction for invention suffices. For example, in Marie, *Isopet* I of Paris, or the Romulus of Trier, Henryson could have found his motif of the fox who wishes to break his Lenten vow to eat no meat and who, drowning a kid that he finds, calls the drowning a baptism and rechristens the kid a salmon, thus making his eating of the kid lawful. Henryson would have found there, too, a rather livelier style than in most old collections or, indeed, than in most of those still being copied and taught in the schools. But he did not find there the specific phrase by which he embodies this new zest for dialogue, the fox's joyous baptismal cry, "Ga doun, Schir Kid, cum up Schir Salmond agane!" What Henryson inherited was not a motif alone but a tradition of invention.

Medieval Invention—Turning Game into Earnest

For reasons, then, of social relevance or stylistic innovation, medieval fabulists sometimes varied the explicit meanings they assigned to the beasts and actions of their inherited, traditional fables. Were we to list all the extant meanings for every beast or for every role played by various beasts, we would still lack a medieval audience's sense of the process generating those meanings and making them acceptable. I suspect the sense was more nearly a spirit of fun than of obedience to some defined set of rules for moralization. I am certain it was not the process to which modern scholars are reduced: combing the analogues, the glosses, and the *Patrologia* for a known meaning one could try out on the work. Too many fable morals have unique elements; too many, particularly in Odo's collection, have been fitted to contemporary conditions.

Combing and cataloging do have interest and at least tell us some of the things a motif could have meant. Scholars seeking "the moralite" of the "Nun's Priest's Tale" have dug out many a fox and cock from works perhaps known to Chaucer and his audience. But the story antedates many such meanings and so need not mean what it might mean. If a fox, even a fox with Chaucer's Rossel for a name, satirizes friars in *Renart le nouvel,* the story of fox and cock does not itself depend on friars for its right to be told—it had circulated in the *Roman de Renart* and in Marie's fables for years before there were any orders of friars for authors to satirize.[9] On carved misericords and in manuscript margins of Chaucer's time one indeed finds the friar fox at his preachings, but he is flanked by other preaching foxes garbed as bishops or indeterminate ecclesiastics.[10] Friars, then, can have no exclusive right to ridicule in the guise of foxes. Similarly, cocks indeed represent priests in many an encyclopedia or a scriptural commentary, but the explicit meanings fabulists attached to the cock of this fable—as in Marie's version—or to the cock in most versions of another fable, the cock and the gem, show the cock only as the vainglorious fool. Preachy Chantecler may be, and we are free to compare him to the priest who tells his story or to the monk who has just finished telling of many another fall through fate and sin, but this sort of analogy making is not the same thing as discovering a code in which the cock *is* a priest. What are we to think of all the various works that do seem to equate cock and priest or fox and friar, or bishop, or devil, or wicked man, or anything else we have found in the explicit moralization of some particular fable or sermon exemplum? These equations must be, not the necessary meanings of the characters and plots in question, but possible meanings that the author chooses at the moment to develop.

"Traditional" meanings, the history of fable tells us, are potential in a given work, not necessary: the invention of new senses might itself be called a "traditional" pastime. Suppose, one long evening late in Chaucer's lifetime, that a group of medieval literati decided to indulge the half-playful spirit of such medieval literature-for-discussion forms as the *demande d'amour,* forms in which each member of the audience might, in turn, try his or her hand at supplying the conclusion or explanation for the work all have heard. Our group choose to hear the "Nun's Priest's Tale" and to expound their rival views of its true moral. We might well overhear from their conversation any or all of the interpretations of modern scholars, for each modern explanation has been drawn from some authentic find in the medieval texts. Yet would those idle chatterers about the fire have put forth their interpretations as exclusive truths or, rather, as playful—though meaningful—elaborations? We cannot know. We can, however, find in our simpler test genre of the moralized beasts evidence that wit, playfulness, and surprise were all available options.

Playful, surely, must be Richart de Fournival's *Bestiaire d'amour.* It amuses its obviously literate audience by packing the materials of a bestiary into the form of a love epistle.[11] The first speaker, the lover, junks most of the old religious senses and, evoking the approved methodology of exegesis, carefully explains just how every beast of the bestiary "means" that the lady should love him. But then the lady, accepting his facts of animal lore and taking up in her turn the method of exegesis, calmly shows how absolutely everything "means" quite the opposite of what he claimed. The very point of Richart's allegorizing is to make the result surprising and fantastical while preserving a straightforward, logical, and traditional mode of reasoning.

Place with Richart's dethcologized bestiary of love all the many hunts of love, chess games of love, and prisons of love. By method they are works of the old allegory; by application they are works of the new vogue of the literature of love. Were they, too, intended as playful? Even a sermon may be playful enough in its exegesis. Take a Latin text that says no one (*nemo*) can enter the kingdom of heaven without first doing such and such. Read thatsentence as if "no one" were a proper name. Collect all such sentences and you have the epic of *Nemo,* the hero who could indeed do all the things that no one could have done. Several sermons play this game with that most earnest of texts, the Bible. They amuse, yet along the way they remind the audience of much Scripture and doctrine; the resulting sermons take their place in serious orthodox collections.[12] Religious interpretations do not need even this jesting context to find the freedom to innovate: a bestiary somewhat later than Richart's discards standard meanings for the beasts but, unlike Richart's, turns all to the praise of Mary.[13]

That writers sought daring leaps rather than conventional echoes of the Fathers shows strikingly even in serious contexts by the transformation from secular to religious in two sermons on secular love songs written by a French preacher shortly before 1214, that is, a few years before Richart's bestiary. In the song "Sur la rive de la mer" we have the characters and properties of many a song, but they are now "explained." The maiden (*la pucelle*) is Saint Mary Magdalene, the stream (*la rive*) is the Virgin Mary, and the ill-matched wife (*la dame mal mariée*) is the soul, badly married in being tied to sin though called to be Christ's love. The preacher expects to surprise. He calls attention to the thoroughly secular frivolity of the songs and claims to be only "spoiling the Egyptians to enrich the Hebrews" in turning such light songs to a religious purpose.[14] We are clearly not to take these invented moralizations as evidence that all the songs of *la dame mal mariée* are "really" about the soul. In these religious as in secular contexts, one may preserve the *process* of allegorical thinking while making it generate surprising new meanings. Aware of what their materials meant, authors such as Richart or the anonymous preacher set about inventing meanings *not* anticipated by the audience yet recognizably possessed of a witty "rightness" once set forth.

Even an accident, a carelessly copied line, can seem to bear a new meaning, and authors may develop this supposed meaning into genuine new interpretations. In Phaedrus III.12, a cock finds a gem and, incapable of understanding its value, leaves it lying. This fable Phaedrus applies to those who do not understand him, that is, his book: "qui me non intellegunt" (Perry, p. 278). But in the ordinary Romulus the *me* dropped out: "qui non intelligunt" [sic] (Hervieux, II, 195). Now the fable seems to apply to those lacking understanding without reference to any particular thing misunderstood; the gem was accordingly later allegorized as, not one writer's book, but the quality of wisdom itself, and Henryson can plead eloquently for the pursuit of that wisdom which so many, like the cock, leave lying uncomprehended. Thus a copyist's slip, subjected to the same analogical process of reasoning that generates applications for genuine readings, produces a sensible, "original" passage, which must have seemed as "right" to the medieval audience as any original reading.

A new meaning becomes right by seeming a reasonable analogy. In *De Doctrina Christiana* (*On Christian Doctrine*), the handiest summary of what the medieval audience understood by "reasonable analogy," Augustine makes it clear that we should not memorize a set meaning for each beast or other item of the biblical text, a meaning that we would then transport to all the other entries for the same item. Rather, we should ask what things our item may resemble, without expecting the answer to be consistent from text to text: "but since things are similar to other things in a great many ways, we must not think it to be prescribed that what a thing signifies by similitude in one place must always be signified by that thing."[15] Augustine understands the useful watchword of modern structuralism, that not the actor but the role matters, not the beast named but the traits singled out and the function identified within a context.

Building similitudes in new ways can lead an author to discard one animal for another or to jam a new meaning up against an old one, yet without abandoning the basic method of reasoning. Nicole Bozon, a fabulist who otherwise follows Odo and Marie in many of his fables, manages to substitute a sheep for a wolf (in the fable of the well with two buckets) without changing the old moral.[16] The reason is simple: the point of the fable is that the wolf is stupid and easily hoodwinked by the rascally fox. A sheep can be as stupid as a wolf, so the moral does not change no matter which beast we choose. Nicole does not care about the other traits of wolves, however relevant they may be to the moral chosen by some other fabulist. In the bestiaries, one beast can normally mean various things. In a group of elephants one may be the Old Adam in every person, another may be Christ; a wild goat on a mountain may be Christ, a domestic goat lechery. The trait, the action, counts. Occasionally a bestiarist takes the trouble to explain how the meaning derives from the action. A sungazing eagle resembles a baptized soul and a farseeing goat on a mountain resembles God because they see clearly from on high. For clarity of vision, eagle and goat, with their superior physical vantage points or clear eyes, resemble the baptized soul or God, whose vision is spiritual. Guillaume le Clerc spells out the logic for us as he makes his claim that the goat, like Christ, sees from afar whatever people are doing: "Car Deu . . . / De loing esgarde e veit e sent / Quantque font ça e la la gent."[17] That word *car* ('because') is the key: Guillaume intends his allegories to ring with logic and not merely authority.

Reading through a few bestiaries, we soon find certain patterns of analogy becoming most familiar. Old and young may suggest the Old Adam and the new Christ, the person lost and saved (eagle, elephant, stag); high and low suggest spiritual and earthly (goat on a height); sleep and death suggest spiritual death through damnation (sirens, crocodile), while the contrasting arousal from sleep or death suggests either personal salvation or the historical resurrection of Christ (lion, pelican, phoenix). Each chapter of a bestiary, each fable in a collection, has a text and a meaning. A transforming boundary separates a bit of animal lore or a bit of a narrative about the beasts from the spiritual meaning that that material becomes as it passes to the moralization. The logical structure of the opening animal lore or opening narrative remains the structure of the moralization. If a fable is built on the contrast between an oppressive beast and its innocent victim, then the moralization will transform that opposition into some human opposition. No rule specifies which human opposition one must choose so long as the relative positions of the pair are comparable to those of the beasts. One may apply such a fable to the strong and the weak, the rich and the poor, the devil and the sinner, the landlord and the tenant farmer. This continuity of pattern between fable narrative and fable moral gives us a sense of reasonableness when our fabulists push a fable to new applications, from ethical to social, from lay to ecclesiastical. But we must be wary if we are to play this logical game of sensing the structural contrasts and attempting to predict their transformation from natural history to spiritual or social application. Sensing such a structural contrast as high-low, we might attempt to predict for the moral some sort of juxtaposition of spiritual and earthly. We would gain one thing, a sense of participating in a reading process something like that of the mystery-story reader. But, like the reader of that clue-laden genre, we, too, must expect some clues to be false. In many a bestiary the eagle dives into the water, descending, of course, from high to

low, yet not a single bestiary invokes the ready contrast of high and low in order to say something about a falling from spiritual to worldly levels. The fall was into water; its result was the renewal of the eagle. These traits suggest baptism. Baptism thus seems a reasonable moral, not because it is the ordinary moral (though it is), but because we can look back and see the logical pattern of old and new underlying both the animal lore and the rite of baptism, we can see the familiar washing motif in legend and moral alike.[18] Process, not inventory, generates new meanings and keeps the old alive and welcomed as reasonable. Use the old process on new elements of the narrative or on new realms of application in the world, and you produce new meanings, yet new meanings genuinely drawn from the old material by accepted methods. Augustine foresaw well enough such innovative potentials in his analogical method. Comparing things to one another, reader and author may select different pairs, but no harm arises if the reader's and author's final goals are compatible: "When, however, from a single passage in the Scripture not one but two or more meanings are elicited, even if what he who wrote the passage intended remains hidden, there is no danger if any of the meanings may be seen to be congruous with the truth taught in the passages of the Holy Scriptures" (Robertson, pp. 101-02).[19] Such is the thinking of our fable authors, our sportive bestiarists and allegorists of love, our earnest, jesting preachers: one may generate many a meaning from fable, song, or fleeting beast of the fields, provided only that the meaning is good and the method sound.

Conclusion (In Which Nothing is Concluded)

And now the moral of this search for explicit meanings. What do we learn from animal fables and from bestiaries and from works with explicit morals—what, that is, that would help us interpret all those other works without the morals? We learn that the fables and others surprise us, that we cannot quite predict the meaning until we see it. And what if there is no stated meaning to see? What if we are dealing with a genre that has no explicit *moralitas?* If there is such freedom with brief fables and bestiary chapters, what are we moderns to do, faced with the complex suggestiveness of *The Canterbury Tales,* the *Decameron,* or the *Commedia?* The possible meanings are all too possible. Perhaps the historical or exegetical critics can offer helpful suggestions, showing us what might be meant in our text because it was demonstrably meant in some other text. Perhaps structuralist analysis of the basic logical structures and movements in the text could suggest some chains of reasoning that might have been more habitual than others, giving us, as Roland Barthes puts it, not a new meaning so much as a new way of stating the old, of abstracting from the many senses that cultures have generated the inherent principles of generation.[20] Yet where the explicit moralizations of fable and bestiary allow us to detect authentic medieval meanings, we find that what was once meant need no longer be meant and that the process of reasoning may reason out many a surprise. We can catalog options known to be open to our authors, but we cannot predict their choices among options. Our medieval authors perhaps called this little mystery by the name of Free Will, and no "ism" seems of much use in pinning it down.

Inherent in each piece of animal lore or in each narrative of beasts are all the logical patterns that any writer has ever seen in it or any other patterns that one might reasonably—as the age defines reason—see in it. Each author reinterprets, and we, as critics, reinterpret too. Exegesis, as Morton W. Bloomfield argues, is a branch of the larger process of making the universe meaningful to ourselves.[21] We interpret everything. The message even of our eyes is only a stirring of nerve cells until our minds interpret the patterns—we call the process perception.[22] Poetry, supposed untranslatable, always is translated, not into a second language, but into the responses and interpretations by which we perceive the poem. Yet the second "language" takes its shape from the first, and the meaning we project has tests of reasonableness. Beast literature shows the universal process so clearly because it places the interpretations and their underlying logic so explicitly on the page; they record the living choices of living persons, choices drawn from the entire universe of meaning by available habits of reasoning. Our critical approaches to the past, if they are to avoid the wrong-way telescope that so often has made distant and "primitive" cultures seem simpler than our own, must keep before us not simply the inventory of medieval fact but the enduring process of mind at work.

Notes

[1] Perry, Introd., *Babrius and Phaedrus,* ed. and trans. Ben Edwin Perry, Loeb Classical Library (Cambridge: Harvard Univ. Press, 1965), pp. xi-xvi.

[2] Prologue to *Isopes Fabules,* vv. 9-14, in Part II (Secular Poems) of *The Minor Poems of John Lydgate,* ed. Henry Noble MacCracken, Early English Text Society, OS 192 (1934; rpt. London: Oxford Univ. Press, 1961), pp. 566-67.

[3] Arnold Clayton Henderson, "'Of Heigh or Lough Estat': Medieval Fabulists as Social Critics," *Viator,* 9 (1978), 265-90; the topic is treated more broadly in "Animal Fables as Vehicles of Social Protest and Satire: Twelfth Century to Henryson," *Niederdeutsche Studien,* 30 (1981). See also my "Moralized Beasts: The Development of Medieval Fable and Bestiary, Particularly from the Twelfth through the Fifteenth Centuries in England and France," Diss. Univ. of California, Berkeley, 1973.

Principal editions of fabulists with social content are Marie de France, *Die Fabeln der Marie de France,* ed. Karl Warnke, Bibliotheca Normannica 6 (Halle, 1898); *Recueil général des Isopets,* ed. Julia Bastin, Société des Anciens Textes Français No. 73, 2 vols. (Paris: H. Champion, 1929-30); Nicole Bozon, *Les Contes moralisés de Nicole Bozon,* ed. Lucy Toulmin Smith and Paul Meyer, Société des Anciens Textes Français No. 28 (Paris, 1889); Berechiah ben Natronai, *Fables of a Jewish Aesop,* trans. Moses Hadas (New York: Columbia Univ. Press, 1967)—but for biographical information, see the introduction to Hermann Gollancz, *The Ethical Treatises of Berachya Son of Rabbi Natronai ha-Nakdan* (London: David Nutt, 1902); John Lydgate, *Isopes Fabules* in *The Minor Poems* (n. 2, above); Robert Henryson, *Poems and Fables,* ed. Henry Harvey Wood, 2nd ed. (Edinburgh: Oliver and Boyd, 1958) (I have not yet used the new edition by Denton Fox); and Odo of Cheriton and John of Sheppey, both in Vol. IV of Léopold Hervieux, *Fabulistes latins,* 2nd ed. (Paris, 1899). Also social in part are two Latin collections related to Marie's, Robert's Romulus and the Romulus of Trier (Hervieux, II, 549-63, 564-652), and parts of the *Fabulae Rhythmicae* (Hervieux, II, 714-57).

For a discussion of *seigneur* and *vilain* in Marie de France, see Hans Robert Jauss, *Untersuchungen zur mittelalterlichen Tierdichtung* (Tübingen: Max Niemeyer, 1959), p. 49.

[4] "Haec propter illos scripta est homines fabula / qui fictis causis innocentes opprimunt," Perry, p. 193.

[5] The following treatments of this same fable all have social or political implications. Berechiah (n. 3, above) includes judge and bailiff among examples of "he that is stronger than his neighbor" (pp. 12-13). Marie de France (n. 3) applies the fable to feudal justice: "Ço funt li riche robeür, / li vescunte e li jugeür / de cels qu'il unt en lur justise" (fable 2). Accepting the reading *seignur* for *robeür,* after A. Ewart and R. C. Johnston (*Marie de France: Fables* [Oxford: Basil Blackwell, 1942]), these lines mean, "rich lords, viscounts, and judges behave this way towards those under their jurisdiction." Lydgate (n. 2) asserts that as dead lambs grace the king's table, so the poor go to heaven (MacCracken, p. 578). Henryson (n. 3) refers to *maill men,* or tenant farmers (pp. 93-95). There are analogues by Odo of Cheriton and his follower, John of Sheppey, in Hervieux, IV, 197-98, 417, and in anonymous Latin collections, where the fable is made an attack on *tyranni* (Hervieux, II, 565) or *principes potentes* who oppress *pauperes* (Hervieux, II, 715).

[6] For Henryson's probable use of a collection like the *Isopet* of Lyon, see John MacQueen, *Robert Henryson: A Study of the Major Narrative Poems* (Oxford:

Clarendon, 1967), pp. 200-07. But I am arguing something different from any specific debt. I am arguing that because Henryson wrote in a tradition that considered certain forms of originality as proper, even his original inventions may be seen as nourished by that tradition of originality.

[7] Henryson's version of the well story is in Wood, pp. 77-84. For this non-Phaedrine and apparently Jewish-Arabic story, Henryson draws most closely on Petrus Alphonsi in some version, possibly French. The Latin is edited by Alfons Hilka and Werner Söderhjelm, *Disciplina Clericalis* (Heidelberg: C. Winter, 1911), Exemplum 23, the English by W. H. Hulme (*Western Reserve University Bulletin,* NS 22, No. 3 [1919], 48-50), and the French *Chastoiement d'un père à son fils* by Edward D. Montgomery, Jr. (Univ. of North Carolina Studies in the Romance Languages and Literatures, No. 101 [Chapel Hill: Univ. of North Carolina Press, 1971], pp. 140-46). Like Henryson's version, the French has a full moon (v. 3642), where the others have a half-moon. Other principal versions, none with a moral quite like Henryson's, are these: the French *Roman de Renart* (Branches IV and IVa) is related to the English *Vox and the Wolf* (ed. Bruce Dickins and R. M. Wilson, *Early Middle English Texts,* rev. ed. [London: Bowes and Bowes, 1956], pp. 62-70), to several German versions (*Reinhart Fuchs,* ed. Jakob Grimm [Berlin, 1834], pp. 54-62; *Der Fuhs und der Wolf,* in Grimm, pp. 356-58; and *Reinke de vos,* ed. Friedrich Prien [Halle, 1887], pp. 202-04), to the later French *Renart le contrefait* (in A. C. M. Robert, *Fables inédites,* II [Paris, 1825], 300-07), and to allusions in the Flemish (O. Delepierre, trans., and Jan Frans Willems, ed., *Le Roman du Renard traduit . . . d'après un texte flamand du XIIe siècle* [Brussels, 1837], pp. 301-02) and Caxton's *The History of Reynard the Fox,* ed. Donald Sands (Cambridge: Harvard Univ. Press, 1960), Ch. xxxiii. Versions in fable, rather than epic, form include the *Kalila et Dimna,* in Hervieux, v, 755-56, which resembles Petrus; Odo of Cheriton (Hervieux, IV, 192-93); John of Sheppey (Hervieux, IV, 441-42); Nicole Bozon (n. 3, above), pp. 150-51, and Hervieux, IV, 261; Spanish versions derived from Odo (*Libro de los Exenplos, por A.B.C.,* ed. John Esten Keller [Madrid: Consejo Superior de Investigaciones Cientificas, 1961], No. 363, pp. 280-81, and *El Libro de los Gatos,* ed. John Esten Keller [Madrid: Consejo Superior de Investigaciones Cientificas, 1958], No. 14, pp. 55-56); Berechiah (n. 3), No. 117; and the ninth fable from "Alfonce" (i.e., Petrus Alphonsi) in Caxton's collection (1484), ed. Joseph Jacobs, as *The Fables of Aesop* (1889; rpt. New York: Burt Franklin, 1970), II, 276-78, and ed. Robert Thomas Lenaghan, as *Caxton's Aesop* (Cambridge: Harvard Univ. Press, 1967), pp. 205-07. Even this list does not exhaust the versions of this tale, and at least one of the folk versions, that retold by Joel Chandler Harris in *Uncle Remus* ([1880; rpt. New York: Schocken, 1965], pp.

78-79) has an exchange between fox and rabbit about "de way de worril [world] goes" that even in wording echoes Henryson's image of the wheel of Fortune (vv. 2418-19) and Caxton's image of the world's rise and fall (*History of Reynard,* Ch. xxxiii)!

[8] Joseph Albert Mosher, *The Exemplum in the Early Religious and Didactic Literature of England* (New York: Columbia Univ. Press, 1911), pp. 81-82, refers to Holkot's sermons. See also Gerald Robert Owst, *Preaching in Medieval England* (Cambridge: Cambridge Univ. Press, 1926), p. 304, for Bromyard and pp. 311-12 for the trend generally.

[9] There has been quite a debate about what medieval motifs may be traced in the Nun's Priest's Tale and how seriously to use them in reading the tale's meaning. See esp. Mortimer J. Donovan, "The 'Moralite' of the Nun's Priest's Sermon," *Journal of English and Germanic Philology,* 52 (1953), 498-508; Charles Dahlberg, "Chaucer's Cock and Fox," *Journal of English and Germanic Philology,* 53 (1954), 277-90; and Judson Boyce Allen, "The Ironic Fruyt: Chauntecleer as Figura," *Studies in Philology,* 66 (1969), 25-35. A late echo of the debate occurs in Nancy Dean, "Chaucerian Attitudes toward Joy with Particular Consideration of the *Nun's Priest's Tale,"* *Medium Aevum,* 44 (1975), 1-13. Robert A. Pratt presents evidence for Chaucer's combining primarily the versions in Marie de France, the *Roman de Renart,* and *Renart le contrefait* ("Three Old French Sources of the Nonnes Preestes Tale," *Speculum,* 47 [1972], 422-44, 646-68).

[10] Kenneth Varty, *Reynard the Fox: A Study of the Fox in Medieval English Art* (New York: Humanities Press, 1967), pp. 54-56.

[11] Richart de Fournival, *Li bestiaires d'amours di maistre Richart de Fornival e li response du bestiaire,* ed. Cesare Segre (Milan: R. Ricciardi, 1957).

[12] Gerald Robert Owst, *Literature and Pulpit in Medieval England,* II (Cambridge: Cambridge Univ. Press, 1933), 63-64.

[13] Paul Meyer, "Les Bestiaires," *Histoire littéraire de la France,* XXXIV (Paris: Imprimerie Nationale, 1914), 390; Gaston Raynaud, "Poème moralisé sur les propriétés des choses," *Romania,* 14 (1885), 443-84.

[14] "Debemus Hebraeos ditare et Ægyptios spoliare, prava in bonum exponere laborantes," quoted from Albert Lecoy de la Marche, *La Chaire française au moyen âge spécialement au XIIIe siècle,* 2nd ed. (Paris, 1886), p. 198. Taking Egyptian treasure to decorate the Tabernacle will also be Pierre Bersuire's image for his Christianizing interpretation of Ovid. See the prologue to *Reductorium morale Liber XV,* fol. lr, col. b 8-9, in Joseph Engels, ed., *Petrus Berchorius . . . Werkmateriaal,* III (Utrecht: Rijksuniversiteit, 1966), 2.

[15] "Sed quoniam multis modis res similes rebus apparent, non putemus esse praescriptum ut quod in aliquo loco res aliqua per similitudinem significaverit, hoc eam semper significare credamus," *De Doctrina Christiana,* 3.25.35, *Patrologia Latina,* Vol. XXXIV, Col. 78; trans. D. W. Robertson, Jr., *On Christian Doctrine* (New York: Liberal Arts Press, 1958), pp. 99-100.

[16] Toulmin Smith, pp. 150-51, and Hervieux, IV, 261.

[17] I translate the passage: "This beast, who sees so clearly, and who perceives from so far off his enemy who wickedly seeks him, is fitting as the example of God, for God looks from afar and sees and observes whatever people do here and there," *Le Bestiaire,* ed. Robert Reinsch (Leipzig, 1892), vv. 1749-56.

[18] Guillaume le Clerc's description of the eagle (Reinsch, vv. 657-80) follows the First Family Latin manuscript Royal 2C.xii of the British Library and its ancestor, the Greek *Physiologus* B, in allowing the eagle a three-fold plunge into water, suggesting baptism. Other bestiaries may lack the motifs of threeness or baptism while still suggesting some form of spiritual renewal.

Changes in the animal lore or "legend" portion of the bestiary often seem deliberate matchings of the legend to its intended allegory: Michael Curley shows the process operating long before Guillaume in the ancestral bestiary, the *Physiologus* (*Physiologus* [Austin: Univ. of Texas Press, 1979], Introd., p. XXV et passim).

[19] "Quando autem ex eisdem Scripturae verbis, non unum aliquid, sed duo vel plura sentiuntur, etiam si latet quid senserit ille qui scripsit, nihil periculi est, si quodlibet eoreum congruere veritati ex aliis locis sanctarum Scripturarum doceri potest," *De Doctrina Christiana* 3.27.38, *Patrologia Latina,* Vol. XXXIV, Col. 80 (Robertson, pp. 101-02). Cf. 1.36.41.

[20] Barthes, "L'Activité structuraliste," in *Essais critiques* (Paris: Editions du Seuil, 1964), pp. 218, 220.

[21] Bloomfield, "Allegory as Interpretation," *New Literary History,* 3 (1972), 301-18.

[22] Ernst H. Gombrich, *Art and Illusion: A Study in the Psychology of Pictorial Representation,* Bollingen Series No. 35, 2nd ed., v (New York: Pantheon, 1961), 3-30.

FURTHER READING

Biography

Goldsmith, Oliver. "The Life of Aesop." In *Bewick's Select Fables of Aesop,* pp. i-ix. New York: Cheshire House, 1932.

Reprints an eighteenth-century biographical essay which tries to separate fact from myth regarding the Greek fabulist's life.

Criticism

Allott, Terence. "John Ogilby, the British Fabulist—A Precursor of La Fontaine . . . And his Model?" *Papers on French Seventeenth Century Literature* XXII, No. 44 (1996): 105-14.

Speculated that the 1668 collection of fables by the French writer Jean de La Fontaine may have been based on the Aesopic fables of Scots publisher and printer Ogilby.

Bentley, Richard. "Dissertation upon the Fables of Aesop." In *Dissertations upon the Epistles of Phalaris, Themistocles, Socrates, Euripides, and the Fables of Aesop,* edited, with an introduction and notes, by Wilhelm Wagner, pp. 569-81. London: George Bell & Sons, 1883.

Bentley's late-seventeenth-century argument against the authenticity of the Aesopic fables is accompanied by an explanatory introduction from Wagner; contains numerous passages in Greek.

Berrigan, Joseph R. "The Latin Aesop of the Early Quattrocento: The Metrical Apologues of Leonardo Dati." *Manuscripta* XXVI, No. 1 (March 1982): 15-23.

Discusses the many Aesopic fables in Greek translated into Latin and thus made available to a wider audience during the fifteenth century.

Fahy, Everett. "Introduction." In *The Medici Aesop,* translated by Bernard McTigue, pp. 7-15. New York: Harry N. Abrams, Inc., Publishers, 1989.

Gives a physical description of the fifteenth-century "Medici" volume of Aesop's fables and speculates about the artist who illustrated the volume.

Fox, Denton. "Henryson and Caxton." *JEGP: Journal of English and Germanic Philology* LXVII (1968): 586-93.

Argues against assertions that William Caxton's Aesopic fables were the indisputable sources of Robert Henryson's fables.

Gopen, George D. "Introduction." In *The Moral Fables of Aesop by Robert Henryson,* translated by George D. Gopen, pp. 1-32. Notre Dame, Ind.: University of Notre Dame Press, 1987.

Discusses differences between Henryson's *Morall Fabillis* and other Aesopic fable collections, observing that Henryson devoted more attention to the moral aspects of the fables than most other translators or editors.

Hale, David G. "William Barret's *The Fables of Aesop.*" *The Papers of the Biographical Society of America* (1970):

283-94.

> Looks at aspects of the Aesopic fable collection of seventeenth-century Englishman William Barret, noting that Barret's undistinguished edition superseded Caxton's in popularity.

———. "Aesop in Renaissance England." *The Library* XXVII, No. 2 (June 1972): 116-25.

> Examines the extent of the Aesopic fable tradition in Renaissance England and its dependence on translations from the European continent.

Henryson, Robert. *The Moral Fables of Robert Henryson.* Reprinted from the edition of Andrew Hart. Edinburgh: The Maitland Club, 1832; New York: AMS Press, 1973, 98 p.

> A collection of Henryson's *Moral Fables of Aesop,* with an explanatory preface that focuses on Henryson's particular style and his interpretation of the fables.

Jacobs, Joseph. "A Short History of the Aesopic Fable." In *The Fables of Aesop,* edited by Joseph Jacobs and illustrated by Joseph Heighway, pp. xv-xxii. 1894. Reprint. Ann Arbor, Mich.: University Microfilms, Inc., 1966.

> Asserts that fables were used in Greece as covert political commentary beginning with Aesop.

Neugaard, Edward J. "Spanish and Catalan Aesopica." In *Essays in Honor of Josep M. Solà-Solé: Linguistic and Literary Relations of Catalan and Castilian,* edited by Suzanne S. Hintz, pp. 161-69. New York: Peter Lang, 1996.

> Examines sixteenth- and seventeenth-century Spanish and Catalan editions of Aesop.

Perry, B. E. *Studies in the Text History of the Life and Fables of Aesop.* Philological Monographs, No. VII, edited by L. Arnold Post. Haverford, PA: American Philological Association, 1936, 247p.

> Technical assessment of variations between editions of fables by and works about Aesop.

Shea, John S. "Introduction." In *Aesop Dress'd or a Collection of Fables Writ in Familiar Verse* by Bernard Mandeville, pp. i-xiii. 1704. The Augustan Reprint Society, no. 120. Los Angeles: William Andrews Clark Memorial Library.

> Indicates that Mandeville drew more directly from the fabular works in verse of French author Jean de La Fontaine than from the originals of Aesop.

Taylor, Archer. "Proverbs and Proverbial Phrases in Roger L'Estrange, *The Fables of Aesop.*" *Southern Folklore Quarterly* XXVI, No. 3 (September 1962): 232-45.

> Collection of proverbs from the Aesopic fables translated by L'Estrange.

Wolfgang, Lenora D. "Caxton's *Aesop:* The Origin and Evolution of a Fable, or, Do Not Believe Everything You Hear." *Proceedings of the American Philosophical Society* 135, No. 1 (March 1991): 73-83.

> Traces the sources of a medieval French poem and a similar fable attributed to Aesop.

Wooden, Warren W. "From Caxton to Comenius: The Origins of Children's Literature." *Fifteenth-Century Studies* 6 (1983): 303-23.

> Cites Caxton's illustrated *Fables of Aesop* as an important medieval children's book.

The English Realist Novel, 1740-1771

INTRODUCTION

The turning point in the development of the English novel is generally said to be 1740, the year Samuel Richardson published *Pamela*. Richardson claimed that this work represented a new fictional form, differing significantly from the novelistic works that had come before. Henry Fielding made a similar claim when he published *Joseph Andrews* in 1742. Subsequent critical opinion has concurred that these two works mark a departure in English fiction. Prose fiction in the early decades of the eighteenth century was a heterogeneous and experimental mix, containing many of the elements that would come to mark the realist novel and others that would eventually be discarded. The most significant development was a turn toward realism and away from the conventions and structures of the heroic romance. Fiction writers began to adopt a view of the relationship between reality and literature in which truth and art were found in ordinary experience and the development and assertion of the individual personality were paramount. As early as 1705, Delarivièr Manley had called for more realism, psychological detail, and natural dialogue in novelistic fiction. She and others, such as Aphra Behn, Mary Davys, Daniel Defoe, and Eliza Haywood, experimented with the techniques and forms that moved the novel closer to maturity, including the epistolary novel, characters drawn from all social levels, and depictions of contemporary life.

Richardson's *Pamela* was an unqualified and unprecedented success. Widely praised and enormously popular, it spawned a succession of imitations, parodies, and secondary scholarship. Richardson's aim in writing the novel had been didactic, and his effective blending of entertainment and ethical instruction was significant for the novel's success in an era when the genre itself was still considered morally suspect. Another striking achievement of that work was the detailed and nuanced portrait of the heroine and the rich attention to emotional life. With this attention to psychic depth, Richardson ushered in the novel of sensibility, wherein every act, gesture, and feeling is examined. *Pamela* marks a watershed in the development of the subjective point of view that is central to the modern novel. Fielding's contribution to the novel form was different, but equally important. *Joseph Andrews* is noted for its emphasis on naturalistic details of rural and domestic life, brilliantly evoking the particulars of setting and situation. Both of these works demonstrated a coherence of characterization, plot, and theme that had been missing in earlier novels. Richardson's and Fielding's later works continued to exemplify the mature novel, along with the works of Tobias Smollett, Laurence Sterne, and others. The striking success of Richardson's work led to increased production of popular novels, along with frequent plagiarism and the distribution of novels to a widening middle-class audience. The expansion of the audience moved the novel away from the category of great art and closer to that of a mass market entertainment. Popular fictions increasingly became commodities, disposable, serial pleasures, rather than timeless achievements.

Early novels had long been unesteemed and viewed as morally problematic. With the growing popularity of the genre, many worried that novels were dangerous and unwholesome, especially for younger readers and women. The increasing interest in realistic fiction heightened this anxiety, as the representations of immoral, unethical, or sexual behavior that had such a prominent place in the plots of many popular fictions were seen to be negative influences on impressionable readers. This issue, along with newly articulated questions of structure and genre definition, spurred critical debate. By the end of the eighteenth century, critical consensus held that the quality of novels had dropped off. The major genre at the end of the century, the Gothic romance, was considered inferior to the great works of the middle decades of the century. Novel-reading was regarded as a middle-brow activity, not suitable for the refined and highly educated. Jane Austen's *Northanger Abbey*, written at the end of the eighteenth century but not published until 1818, wittily satirizes its own genre by portraying a naive heroine who has formed her ideas of the world based on the sentimental and Gothic novels that she avidly reads.

REPRESENTATIVE WORKS

Thomas Amory
The Life and Opinions of John Buncle Esq.: Containing Various Observations and Reflections Made in Several Parts of the World and many Extraordinary Relations (novel) 1756-70

John Cleland
Memoirs of a Woman of Pleasure. 2 vols. (novel) 1748-49

Francis Coventry
Pompey the Little (novel) 1751

Mary Davys
The Reform'd Coquet; or the Memoirs of Amoranda
(novel) 1724
*The Accomplish'd Rake; or Modern Fine Gentleman.
Being an Exact Description of a person of Distinc-
tion* (novel) 1727

Henry Fielding
Joseph Andrews (novel) 1742
Tom Jones (novel) 1749

Oliver Goldsmith
The Vicar of Wakefield (novel) 1766

Samuel Richardson
Pamela; or Virtue Rewarded (novel) 1740
Clarissa (novel) 1748
Sir Charles Grandison (novel) 1753-54

Tobias George Smollett
The Adventures of Roderick Random (novel) 1748
The Adventures of a Peregrine Pickle (novel) 1751
The Expedition of Humphrey Clinker (novel) 1771

Laurence Sterne
Tristram Shandy. 9 vols. (novel) 1760-67
Sentimental Journey (novel) 1768

OVERVIEWS

Michael McKeon (essay date 1985)

SOURCE: "Generic Transformation and Social Change: Rethinking the Rise of the Novel" in *Cultural Critique*, Vol. 1, Fall, 1985, pp. 159-81.

[*In the following essay, McKeon analyzes the relationship between the instability of the novel as a genre and the growing instability of social categories during the eighteenth century.*]

Twenty-five years after its first appearance, Ian Watt's *The Rise of the Novel* continues to be the most attractive model we have of how to conduct the study of this crucial literary phenomenon.[1] The phenomenon is crucial because it is modern. If the novel originated in early modern Europe, it should be possible to observe and describe its emergence within a historical context whose richness of detail has no parallel in earlier periods. But of course this is no coincidence: it is the rise of an unprecedented historical consciousness, and of its institutional affiliates, that has both encouraged the preservation of historical detail, and legitimated contextual methods of study which use that detail as a

mode of understanding. Watt's book is attractive because it is fully responsive to the call for a historical and contextual method of study that seems somehow implicit in his subject. Thus his concern with the rise of a distinctive set of narrative procedures—"formal realism"—is informed by a concern with a parallel innovation in philosophical discourse, and these he connects, in turn, with a set of socioeconomic developments at whose center are the rise of the middle class, the growth of commercial capitalism, and the concomitant eclipse of feudal and aristocratic modes of intercourse. The analogy between these historical strands is most succinctly accounted for in their shared "individualism"—that is, in their common validation of individual experience—a term that allows Watt at various points to argue the importance to his subject of a fourth major strand of historical experience, the Protestant Reformation.

Watt's account of the unity of the historical context in which the novel arose is far more subtle, as all readers know, than this bald outline can suggest. And its general persuasiveness is evident in the fact that the sort of criticism to which it has seemed most vulnerable has aimed not to refute the relevance of historical context, but to complicate Watt's version of it. The problem is perhaps most notorious in the social strand of his context. Where is the evidence, critics have asked, for the dominance of the middle class in the early eighteenth century? How is it distinguished from the traditional social categories of the nobility and gentry, which clearly survive the rapid social mobility of the seventeenth century and persist into the eighteenth with considerable power and prestige? Don't the novels of Henry Fielding, an indispensable figure in the rise of the novel, evince a social attitude much closer to that of a middling gentry than to that of a putatively flourishing commercial middle class? But even in the literary realm, critics have also been preoccupied with a problem of persistence. The narrative procedures of Daniel Defoe, Samuel Richardson, and Fielding may explicitly subvert the idea and ethos of romance, but they also draw, without apparent irony, on many of its stock situations and conventions. Although Watt pays little attention to it, and then only as a superseded genre, romance can be seen to inhabit both the form and the content of these early eighteenth-century narratives. And once again it is Fielding who points the problem most acutely, since he has little use for several of those narrative procedures that have been advanced as the *sine qua non* of the new form.

From this brief summary it is clear that the two central problems with Watt's account of the rise of the novel are versions of each other. His treatment of the early modern historical context, because of its very richness, has sensitized us to what has been left out: the romance and the aristocracy. By the end of the eighteenth century, the conceptual categories of "the novel" and "the middle class" will be sufficiently stable to enjoy the stability of that nomenclature. But it is of course precisely in the period that we wish most definitively to understand—the period of crucial transformation—that such categories are most unstable and most resistant to being strictly identified either as what they are going to be, or as what they once were. What is required, then, is an understanding of how conceptual categories, whether "literary" or "social," exist at moments of historical change: how new forms first coalesce as tenable categories by being known in terms of, and against, more traditional forms that have thus far been taken to define the field of possibility. We must begin, in other words, with the very fact of categorial instability in the later seventeenth century.

Let me pause for a moment before entering my argument, in order to summarize it. What I have to say is based on a set of terms and relations that will recur from time to time throughout the essay. They are not particularly complicated, but I think it will be helpful to lay them out as quickly and clearly as possible. I plan to describe the two great instances of categorial instability that are central to the rise of the novel. The first sort of instability has to do with generic categories; the second, with social categories. The instability of generic categories registers an epistemological crisis, a major cultural transition in attitudes toward how to tell the truth in narrative. For convenience, I will call the set of problems associated with this epistemological crisis, "questions of truth." The instability of social categories registers a cultural crisis in attitudes toward how the external social order is related to the internal, moral state of its members. For convenience, I will call the set of problems associated with this social and moral crisis, "questions of virtue." Questions of truth and questions of virtue concern different realms of human experience, and they are likely to be raised in very different contexts. Yet in one central respect they are closely analogous. Questions of truth and virtue both pose problems of signification: What kind of authority or evidence is required of narrative to permit it to signify truth to its readers? What kind of social existence or behavior signifies an individual's virtue to others?

As we will see, the instability of generic and social categories is symptomatic of a change in attitudes about how truth and virtue are most authentically signified. But for both questions, we can observe the process of change only if we break it down into its component parts. Let me summarize this break-down: first, for questions of truth. At the beginning of the period of our concern, the reigning narrative epistemology involves a dependence on received authorities and a priori traditions; I will call this posture "romance idealism." In the seventeenth century, it is challenged and refuted by an empiricist epistemology that derives from many sources, and this I will call "naive empiricism." But

this negation of romance, having embarked on a journey for which it has no maps, at certain points loses its way. And it becomes vulnerable, in turn, to a counter-critique that has been generated by its own over-enthusiasm. I will call this counter-critique "extreme skepticism." As we will see, in refuting its empiricist progenitor, extreme skepticism inevitably recapitulates some features of the romance idealism which it is equally committed to opposing. For questions of virtue, the terms alter, but the two-part pattern of reversal is very much the same as for questions of truth. We begin with a relatively stratified social order, supported by a reigning world view which I will call "aristocratic ideology." Spurred by social change, this ideology is attacked and subverted by its prime antagonist, "progressive ideology." But at a certain point, progressive ideology gives birth to its own critique, which is both more radical than itself, and harks back to the common, aristocratic enemy. I will call this counter-critique "conservative ideology."

Needless to say, contemporaries did not articulate these several positions as consciously-formulated and coherent doctrines. I have abstracted these ideologies and epistemologies from a large body of early modern discourse, in order to isolate the principal stages in the process of historical change that we refer to when we speak of "the rise of the novel." By this means, I think, we may come closer to conceiving how change occurs: how the past can persist into the present, and help to mediate the establishment of difference through the perpetuation of similarity. Let me now proceed to fill in the spaces in my argument.

I

I will begin with questions of truth and the instability of the system of narrative genres in the seventeenth century. Evidence for the unstable usage of terminology lies everywhere, but it is most striking in explicit attempts to categorize the several genres of narrative. In 1672, the bookseller John Starkey advertised his list of publications in a catalogue divided into the following categories: Divinity; Physick; Law; History; Poetry and Plays; and Miscellanies. Under the heading of "history" he includes Suetonius, Rabelais, what he calls the "Novels" of Quevedo, biographies, travel narratives, and a contemporary work that we would be likely to see as a popular romance.[2] By modern standards, the most pressing problem raised by such usage is the absence of any will to distinguish consistently between "history" and "literature," "fact" and "fiction." But on the other hand, the catalogue of William London, printed fifteen years earlier, obligingly separates "History" from "Romances, Poems and Playes."[3]

What is most significant about this sort of usage is that it is not entirely foreign to us. Unlike traditional generic taxonomies, it evinces a real, but markedly inconsistent, commitment to comprehend its categories within a basic discrimination between the "factual" and the "fictional." Indeed, it is the inconsistent imposition of this recognizably "modern" concern on a more traditional system that makes the usage of this period look so chaotic. What it represents, I think, is a movement between opposed conceptions of how to tell the truth in narrative. Another sign of this movement is the transformation which the term "romance" has undergone in the past hundred years. Despite the neutral usage that I have just quoted, by the end of the seventeenth century the ascendant meaning of "romance" is both far broader, and far more pejorative, than before. Increasingly the idea of romance dominates the thought of the Restoration and early eighteenth century as a means of describing, and most often of discrediting, a particular, idealist way of knowing. Romance comes to stand for a species of deceit that undiscriminatingly includes lying and fictionalizing; and the category to which it is most often opposed is not "the novel," but "true history."

Many cultural movements contributed to the naive empiricist championing of "true history." Three of the most important are also closely intertwined: the scientific revolution, the typographical revolution, and the Protestant Reformation. Moreover in all three of these movements we can see both the dominant influence of naive empiricism, and the stealthy emergence of a subversive, extreme skepticism. I will begin with the new science. In his history of the founding institution of the new science, Thomas Sprat compares unfavorably the ancient mode of natural history with that of his fellow moderns: it "is not the true following of *Nature* . . . It is like *Romances,* in respect of *True History* . . ."[4] The new science was dedicated, of course, to objective observation, experiment, and related principles of empirical method. And it was deeply interested in trying to embody these principles in literary technique and form. According to the *Philosophical Transactions* of the Royal Society, "we have more need of severe, full and punctuall Truth, than of Romances or Panegyricks."[5] To this end, the Society even undertook to instruct foreign travellers in the best literary techniques for ensuring what we might call the "historicity" of their journals. It enlisted the aid of Robert Boyle and the mathematician Lawrence Rooke to formulate directions not only for how to keep a travel journal, but also for how to turn it into a narrative without diluting its crucial historicity.[6]

It is not too much to say that these directions amount to one of the most important, explicit bodies of literary theory composed in conjunction with the origins of the English novel. They prescribe a preferred style and rhetoric that correspond to a new type of the man of letters, the ethically and socially humble recorder of reality who is enabled to master the new knowledge by his very innocence of the old. In Sprat's words, the new breed are "plain, diligent, and laborious observers: such, who, though they bring not much knowledg [sic], yet bring their hands, and their eyes uncorrupted: such as have not their Brains infected by false Images . . ."[7] One such observer is described by the editors of the multi-volume collection of travel narratives in terms that might collectively be called the convention of the claim to historicity: "This Narrative has nothing of Art or Language, being left homely Stile, which it was not fit to alter, lest it might breed a Jealousy that something had been chang'd more than the bare Language."[8] According to another, equally conventional, traveller, "it would be no difficult Matter to embellish a Narrative with many Romantick Incidents, to please the unthinking Part of Mankind, who swallow every thing an artful Writer thinks fit to impose upon their Credulity, without any Regard to Truth or Probability. The judicious are not taken with such Trifles; . . . and they easily distinguish between Reality and Fiction."[9]

At the heart of the claim to historicity is the assertion that what one is describing really happened. And it is not hard to hear in these sober claims the naive empiricism of Defoe and Richardson, both of whom pretend to be only the editors of authentic documents whose plain and artless truth is above question. But if we permit the sobriety of the voices slightly to extend into self-parody, we also can detect the extreme skepticism of Swift and Fielding, subverting the claim to historicity by carrying it to absurdity. This is one example of how naive empiricism generates its own, radically skeptical, critique. Let me turn now to another example, one related not to the new science but to the new typography.

To a certain extent, we owe the very notion of comparative and competing accounts of the same event to the opportunity for comparison uniquely provided by print. Printing produces documentary objects that can be collected, categorized, collated, and edited. Like science, it promotes the norm of "objective" research, and it favors criteria of judgment that are appropriate to discrete and empirically apprehensible "objects": singularity, formal coherence, and self-consistency. Finally, print encourages a test of veracity that accords with the process itself of typographical reproduction: namely, the exact replication of objects or events in their external and quantitative dimensions.[10] Contemporaries were conscious of the epistemological powers of print. William Winstanley describes "some I have known (otherwise ingenious enough) apt to believe idle Romances, and Poetical Fictions, for Historical Varieties [i.e., verities], . . . and for this only reason, *Because they are Printed.*"[11] But only a slight extension of this awe brings us to the satiric stance of Cervantes, who has a great deal of fun at the expense of characters—including Sancho Panza—who naively believe everything they see in print. In fact much of the self-reflexive pleasure of Part II of *Don Quixote* lies in watching its characters compare the documentary objectivity of part I (which has already been printed) with the more fallible standard of truth upheld by private memory and experience.[12] Cervantes himself naively claims that his book is a "true history" dedicated to the critique of chivalric romance. But we know to read this affiliation, as well as his playful attitude toward print, as at least in part a skeptical critique of naive empiricism.

My third and final example concerns the contribution of Reformation thought to naive empiricism and its subversion. Protestantism, like the standard of "true history," elevates individual and closely observed experience over the a priori pronouncements of tradition. But Protestantism is also the religion of the Book, of the documentary object, and as such it inevitably tends to elevate the truth of Scripture as the truth of "true history." This documentary and empiricist emphasis is clear in the great works of the Protestant tradition. The central aim of John Foxe's *Acts and Monuments* (1563, 1570) is the documentation of the Protestant martyrs, and the task is achieved in an aura of scrupulous historicity and with a battery of editorial procedures that are dedicated to the critical authentication of every historical detail.[13] Such authenticating procedures may also be found in John Bunyan's *Life and Death of Mr. Badman* (1680), even though its protagonist is a palpable fiction. Bunyan claims that it is based on "True stories, that are neither *Lye,* nor *Romance . . .* All which are things either fully known by me, or being eye and ear-witness thereto, or that I have received from such hands, whose relation as to this, I am bound to believe."[14] By the same token, Protestant spirituality encouraged individual saints to a scrupulous documentation of their own "true histories." When Ralph Thoresby first went up to London, his father sent him a typical directive: "I would have you, in a little book, which you may either buy or make of two or three sheets of paper, take a little journal of any thing remarkable every day, principally as to yourself . . ."[15]

So from the beginning, Protestantism was deeply invested in the materialistically-oriented techniques of naive empiricism as a useful means to its spiritual and otherworldly ends. The potential contradiction between worldly means and otherworldly ends is most apparent in writings like the "apparition narratives" of the later seventeenth century; Defoe's *A True Relation Of the Apparition of one Mrs. Veal* (1706) is the best-known of them today. These narratives use the evidence of the senses in order to prove the extra-sensory world of spirit. They deploy an extraordinary arsenal of authenticating devices—names, places, dates, events, eye- and ear-witness testimony, etc.—in order to prove the reality of the invisible world. Richard Baxter explained his own important contribution to the form in terms that poignantly convey the dilemma of a culture divided between two competing standards of truth that still seem somehow reconcilable: "Apparitions, and other sensi-

ble Manifestations of the certain existence of Spirits of themselves Invisible, was a means that might do much with such as are prone to judge by Sense."[16] But it is a very short distance from Baxter's earnest and spiritualizing dependence on the evidence of the senses to the realm of conscious satire. Consider those moderns in Swift's early satires who mistake their own bodily wind for the spirit of intellect and divinity.[17] Once again, that is, the counter-critique of extreme skepticism is involuntarily extruded by naive empiricism itself as a form of subversive self-parody.

But over time, extreme skepticism emerges as a self-conscious and autonomous stance in its own right. Its premises are the same as those of the naive empiricism which it undertakes to negate. It is equally critical, that is, of "romance," but it is so thoroughly skeptical as to discredit empiricist skepticism itself as nothing more than a new, and artfully modernized, species of the old romance. It is this counter-critique that will issue eventually in Fielding's narrative form. Along the way we may observe certain milestones, narratives—like William Congreve's *Incognita* (1691)—which elegantly achieve the double negation that is characteristic of the form: first, of the fictions of romance, and then of naive empiricism itself. But like its antagonist, the counter-critique of extreme skepticism undergoes a considerable development; I have space only to offer several exemplary quotations.

Richard Steele is an important figure in the attack on naive empiricism. Echoing pamphleteers of the mid-seventeenth century, for example, he argued in one of his periodical letters that newspapers were to England what books of chivalry had been to Spain.[18] Steele was also critical of the claim to historicity in the genre of the secret memoir, which was especially popular among what he called "some merry gentlemen of the French nation." The secret memoir claimed, as Steele observed, to give the true history of military campaigns or court intrigues even though their mendacious authors had really been cowering behind the lines or scribbling in a drafty garret.[19] Writing of the same phenomenon, Pierre Bayle observed that thus "the new romances [that is, these supposedly historical memoirs] keep as far off as possible from the romantic way: but by this means true history is made extremely obscure; and I believe the civil powers will at last be forced to give these new romancers their option; either to write pure history, or pure romance . . ."[20] Henry Stubbe compared the natural histories of the Royal Society to "the story of *Tom Thumb,* and all the *Legends* or *falsifications of History,* which the *Papists* obtrude upon us."[21] The language is striking: whether implicitly or explicitly, over and over true history is discredited as the new romance. The skeptical critique of travel historicity was similarly acerbic. The dubious reader of a typically authenticated travel narrative of 1675 confuted the pamphlet's overheated claims by coolly writing on its title page: "By a new fashion'd Romancer."[22] The most thorough and trenchant critique of travel historicity was made by the Third Earl of Shaftesbury, who began, as Steele did, with the remark that "these are in our present Days, what *Books of Chivalry* were, in those of our Forefathers."[23] As the critique of naive empiricism gained momentum toward the end of the century, parodic impersonation seemed to offer itself as the most likely means of subversion. Another dubious reader of travel narratives wrote the following parody of a rival's fashionably plain style of objective narration: "*We cast Anchor: We made ready to Sail. The Wind took Courage. Robin is dead. We said Mass. We Vomited.* [Then he continues in his own, sarcastic voice.] Tho' they are poor Words any where else, yet in his Book, which is half compos'd of them, they are Sentences, and the worth of them is not to be told."[24]

But if this kind of extreme skepticism was to become more than an (admittedly liberating) act of subversion, it was obliged, like the subversive stance of naive empiricism before it, to elaborate an alternative, positive, and coherent conception of how to tell the truth in narrative. And here its position was quite as unstable as that of its opponent. For if the claim to historicity is naively posited as the negation of the negation of romance idealism, how tenuous must be that secret sanctuary of truth, distinct both from romance and from too confident a historicity, which is defined by the meta-critical act of double negation? With hindsight we might want to say that the counter-critique of extreme skepticism was groping toward a mode of narrative truthtelling which, through the very self-consciousness of its own fictionality, somehow detoxifies fiction of its error. But the ingenuity of this maneuver could itself look more like a mask for the stealthy recapitulation of romance lies. Consider Fielding's ostentatious indulgence in romance conventions, or Swift's obviously parabolic narratives. Indeed the sheer defensiveness of this counter-stance makes it parasitic upon, and reproductive of, the errors of the enemy. If naive empiricism is too sanguine regarding its own powers of negating romance fiction, its critique is too skeptical about that possibility, and it risks, through its reactive method of parodic impersonation, the effectual affirmation of what it is equally committed to replacing.

Both epistemologies, in other words, are unstable. I would argue that they attain stability not in themselves but in each other, in their dialectical relationship, as two competing versions of how to tell the truth in narrative, which, in their competition, constitute one part of the origins of the novel. The paradigmatic case is *Pamela* (1740) vs. *Shamela* (1741), since it is then that the conflict emerges into public consciousness and is institutionalized as a battle over whether it is Richardson or Fielding that is creating the "new species of writing." My argument is that it is, rather, the conjunc-

tion of the two. But I would also point out that the logic of our progress through the seventeenth century into the middle of the eighteenth argues against trying to pinpoint "the first novel," or even its first dialectical engagement. Before *Pamela* and *Shamela,* for example, there is the tacit but crucial confrontation between *Robinson Crusoe* (1719) and *Gulliver's Travels* (1726), a confrontation to which I will return. The novel rises not in the isolated emergence of a great text or two, but as an experimental process consisting of many different stages.

II

So far our attention has been focussed on epistemological instability, and the series of critiques by which questions of truth are propounded. We must now turn to the analogous questions of virtue, to the instability of socioeconomic categories, and to the interaction between what I have called the aristocratic, progressive, and conservative ideologies. In the seventeenth century, the traditional imprecision in the use of status categories is complicated by an unprecedented rate of social mobility. The effects of this mobility are suggested by the fact that it is at this time that attempts begin to be made to assess the population not according to a traditional, status stratification, but by annual income and expenditures. This amounts to the first, systematic emergence of the modern impulse to classify society according to the fundamentally economic criteria of class.

The form taken by these population tables is quite relevant to our purposes, because they provide the sort of evidence of instability, on the subject of social categories, that we found in publishers' book lists on the subject of generic categories. Gregory King's celebrated table of the 1690's ostensibly aims to give a continuous financial, and therefore quantitative; progression from the top to the bottom of English society. But he is obliged to work with both honorific and occupational categories, and around the middle of his table the two sorts of category become intermixed in a way that undermines the purpose of the project. For in several cases, King lists status categories above occupational ones, even though the crucial standard of average yearly income should reverse the orders. In other words, King's abiding respect for the traditional status hierarchy momentarily overrules his modernizing aim to create a hierarchy of incomes. The qualitative criteria of status infiltrate and disrupt the effort at a quantitative categorization.[25] Half a century later, in 1760, Joseph Massie carried over King's six traditional categories of elevated status to the top of his own table. But they repose there aloof and untouched, a kind of honorific gesture that has nothing to do with the real work of economic discrimination, for which Massie uses completely different categories in the rest of his table. In other words, status categories persist here as a vestigial remnant of a mode of thought which, however useless in the definitive description of contemporary English people by class, still appears indispensable.[26]

In both men, the instability of social categories owes to a discrepancy between two standards of classification, that of "status" and that of "class." It reflects what we might call a crisis of "status inconsistency," a divergence of power, wealth, and status widespread and persistent enough to resist the methods by which stable societies traditionally have accommodated the instances of non-correspondence that occasionally must arise. One such method is the traditional granting or selling of honors to newly enriched but ignoble families. To speak of "traditional" societies is also to speak of societies dominated by what I have called an "aristocratic" ideology. In aristocratic culture, it is not only that power, wealth, and honorific status most often accompany each other; honor also is understood to imply personal merit or virtue. Thus the social hierarchy is a great system of signification: the outward forms of genealogy and social rank are taken to signify an analogous, intrinsic moral order. The seventeenth-century crisis of status inconsistency therefore strikes at the moral foundations of aristocratic ideology. The sale of honors became, in Lawrence Stone's phrase, an "inflation," and the latent tension between honorific and monetary criteria became a glaring contradiction for contemporaries.[27] The word "honor" itself acquired a more complicated import. As a neutral term of description, its meaning was, in effect, internalized, changing from "title of rank" to "goodness of character."[28] But "honor" in the more traditional sense of the term, like "romance," had fallen on very hard times.

We can hear this in the genial contempt expressed by Bernard Mandeville. For Mandeville, honor "is only to be met with in People of the better sort, as some Oranges have kernels, and others not, tho' the outside be the same. In great Families it is like the Gout, generally counted Hereditary, and all Lords Children are born with it. . . . But there is nothing that encourages the Growth of it more than a Sword, and upon the first wearing of one, some People have felt considerable Shutes of it, in Four and twenty Hours."[29] The aristocratic system of signification held no illusions for Stephen Penton, either. For "if Merit were to be the Standard of Worldly Happiness, what great desert is there in being born Eldest Son and Heir to several Thousands a Year, when sometimes it falls out, that the Person is hardly able to Answer Two or Three the easiest Questions in the World wisely enough to save himself from being Begg'd?"[30] William Sprigge plausibly argued that "the younger Son is apt to think himself sprung from as Noble a stock, from the loyns of as good a Gentleman as his elder Brother, and therefore cannot but wonder, why fortune and the Law should make so great a difference between them that lay in the same wombe, that are formed of the same lumpe;

why Law or Custome should deny them an estate, whom nature hath given discretion to know how to manage it."[31] And Defoe draws the versified conclusion:

> What is't to us, what Ancestors we had?
> If Good, what better? or what worse, if Bad?

> . . . . .

> For Fame of Families is all a Cheat,
> *'Tis Personal Virtue only makes us great.*[32]

In the realm of social change, the idea of "personal virtue" occupies the place that "true history" does in epistemology. For progressive ideology, elevated birth is an arbitrary accident which should not be taken to signify worth. If it is, it becomes a fiction, an imaginary value, like "honor" a mere "romance." Thus Defoe observes that when gentlemen "value themselves as exalted in birth above the rest of the world . . . ," it is upon the basis of a strictly "imaginary honour."[33] *Real* honor, honor of *character,* attaches to personal virtue. And Defoe heartily approved of the assimilationist practice whereby the meritorious and newly-risen crowned their merit through the purchase of titles of rank.

But what were Swift's views on questions of virtue? Swift was as caustic as Defoe on the subject of aristocratic pretension. But he was far more inclined to see the ideas of inherited honor and gentle birth as useful fictions that had an instrumental social value. "Suppose there be nothing but *Opinion* in the Difference of Blood," he wrote. "Surely, that Difference is not wholly imaginary. . . . It should seem that the Advantage lies on the Side of Children, born from noble and wealthy Parents . . . [And] Ancient and honorable Birth[,] . . . whether it be of real or imaginary Value, hath been held in Veneration by all wise, polite States, both Ancient and Modern."[34] It may seem puzzling that men like Swift should return to half-embrace the very fiction they have rejected. But we already have seen this sort of movement in the return of extreme skepticism to a form of self-conscious romancing. For progressives like Defoe, aristocratic ideology was subverted and replaced by a brave new view of social signification. Virtue is signified not by the a priori condition of having been born with status and honor, but by the ongoing experience of demonstrated achievement and just reward. Thus the status inconsistency endemic to aristocratic culture is rectified, in this progressive view, by upward mobility through state service, private employment, or any other method of industrious self-application. To conservatives like Swift, this progressive model of the career open to talents was deeply repellant, as we will see. But the negation of both aristocratic and progressive ideology left conservative ideology without a positive and stable view of how the social injustice of status inconsistency ever might be overcome.

From the conservative point of view, progressive ideology only replaced the old social injustice by a new and more brutal version of it, unsoftened now by any useful fictions of inherited authority. At the heart of this new system was the naked cash nexus. For the conservative, the archetypal progressive upstart rose by exploiting the capitalist market, and especially the new mechanisms of financial investment and public credit which were established at the end of the seventeenth century. For men like Swift, only landed property had real value. All other property was, as he put it, "transient and imaginary," but most of all that of exchange value.[35] Defoe also recognized that the modern world of exchange value was ruled by, in his phrase, "the Power of Imagination."[36] And he perceived that in some mysterious sense, capitalist credit was only a secularization of aristocratic honor. But Defoe was convinced that the circulation of money and the opportunity for capital accumulation were essential if individual merit were to be dependably signified and rewarded. For Swift, the market exchange of commodities only established a new elite of the undeserving on the grounds of a new, and far more dangerous, species of corruption. That is, it only institutionalized a new form of status inconsistency: namely, wealth and power without virtue. As for honorific status, the situation had become hopelessly confused. To the conservative mentality, there was an obvious corruption in those progressive upstarts who sought to legitimate their rise by the purchase of a title. But the system of honors was itself corrupted, and many ancient landed families were as thoroughly indebted to the capitalist market for the improvement of their estates as anyone.

Here, as on questions of truth, the doubly-critical posture of men like Swift left very little ground for the affirmation of any positive social signifier of merit and virtue. With the triumph of Whig oligarchy in the eighteenth century, the aristocratic order seems to regain its stability after the rapid social mobility of the previous century. But the status category of "aristocracy" has altered considerably, even if the terminology has remained the same. The status orientation itself has been complicated by a class orientation—by individualistic and monetary criteria and by capitalist practices. The rise of the middle class, in other words, was not the rise of a discrete and determinate social entity, but a historical process in which traditional status groups were altered as much from within as from without. And the rise of the middle class is inseparable from the rise of a class orientation toward social relations. Men like Swift knew this; they knew that the enemy was not so easily distinguished as an ungentle, upstart invader from without. Nevertheless, for lack of a more dependable signifier, they retained in their minds the possession of land and gentle status as a self-consciously conventional signification of what seemed an increasingly embattled virtue.

Why should narrative, in particular, be suitable for the representation of progressive and conservative ideologies? The term "ideology" often is used to suggest a simplistic reduction of human complexity. But as I intend the term, "ideology" is discourse whose purpose is to mediate and explain apparently intractable social problems—in this case, the problematic questions of virtue. To explain the condition of status inconsistency is not to explain it away, but to render it intelligible. In fact, the very plausibility of ideological explanation depends on the degree to which it appears to do justice to the contradictory social reality that it seeks to explain. In the present context, ideological explanation works by telling stories. The question of how virtue is signified has an inherently narrative focus because it is concerned with genealogical succession and individual progress, with how human capacity is manifested in and through time. This concern can be seen in the "macro-narrative" of seventeenth-century history itself, which provided writers with an important model for their novelistic micronarratives. Seventeenth-century England was vitally concerned with the problem of political sovereignty and its sources. At the beginning of the century, sovereignty seemed to rest with the king and to be validated by, among other things, his genealogical inheritance of royalty. In 1642, Charles I warned that parliament's challenge to royal sovereignty threatened the very continuity of the historical succession. The great danger, he said, was that at last the common people would "destroy all rights and proprieties, all distinctions of families and merit, and by this means this splendid and excellently distinguished form of government end in a dark, equal chaos of confusion, and the long line of our many noble ancestors in a Jack Cade or a Wat Tyler."[37] Charles was not entirely wrong in this apocalyptic prophecy: seven years after it he was decapitated. And before the end of the century, the nation had joined together to depose another rightful monarch and to exclude the next fifty-seven prospective heirs to the throne. In their place was crowned a foreigner, and in the place of sovereignty by genealogical inheritance was affirmed sovereignty by achievement: the simple and pragmatic fact that a peaceful and stable settlement had been achieved.[38]

In the language of questions of virtue, the fall of Charles I is the most infamous instance of status inconsistency in the century. And after the Battle of Worcester in 1651, prince Charles wandered the land in disguise like nothing so much as a romance hero destined, after much travail, to be discovered and restored to his aristocratic patrimony.[39] But to readers of a progressive persuasion, the triumphs of Oliver Cromwell and William of Orange showed, in different ways, the superiority of industrious valor to mere lineage. Progressive ideology even entered into the making of Cromwell's New Model Army. In 1643 he declared: "I had rather have a plain russett-coated captain that knows what he fights for, and loves what he knows, than that which you call a gentleman and is nothing else . . . Better plain men than none, but best to have men patient of wants, faithful and conscientious in the employment . . ."[40]

Cromwell's language here reminds us that Calvinist Protestantism has an important relevance to progressive ideology, for God's mark of inner nobility was superior to any external social elevation. Speaking of divine election, Cromwell asked: "May not this stamp [of God] bear equal poise with any hereditary interest . . . ?"[41] And, as a coreligionist affirmed, "It is not the birth, but the new birth, that makes men truly noble."[42] If Calvinist election argued a new aristocracy alternative to that of birth, Calvinist discipline dictated a spirit of service and reform that worked both to glorify the works of God and to signify one's possession of grace. But what are the narrative implications of this dovetailing of Protestant belief and progressive ideology? As early as Foxe's *Acts and Monuments,* the apocalyptic battle between the Roman Catholic hierarchy and God's saints is colored by the progressive contest between corrupt noblemen and industrious commoners. Foxe's "Story of Roger Holland, Martyr," for example, is the tale of an apprentice who is idle and licentious until the moment of his Protestant conversion. Thereafter he prospers wonderfully as a merchant tailor. So when the reformed apprentice is finally called up before his papist inquisitor, he is able to manifest, through a spirited resistance and a serene martyrdom, that spiritual grace which already has been apparent in his labor discipline and his material prosperity.[43]

Calvinist doctrine encouraged in progressive narrative the self-serving conviction that divine grace could be internalized as virtue, and externalized once again as worldly achievement. But Calvinism also counselled against the proud sufficiency of human desire, and it sharpened the conservative critique of enthusiasm and the Protestant ethic. The adventures of Robinson Crusoe exemplify both the ethical obstacles to progressive ideology, and the power of that ideology to drive all before it. Robinson Crusoe is an industrious younger son whose worldly success at first signifies nothing more than acquisitiveness and ambition. But once he is shipwrecked, his island turns out to be a progressive utopia. Because it excludes all human society, it provides an arena in which the anti-social passions of avarice and domination can be indulged without suffering the consequences. Thus Robinson can accumulate goods without creating exchange value. He can exercise absolute sovereignty without incurring the wrath of a greater authority. And when human society finds him, and it comes time to leave the island, he is able to naturalize the artificial, laboratory conditions of his utopia because he has learned to internalize divinity, to identify his own passions with the will of God. A slighter version of this progressive, utopian

plot is given by Henry Neville, whose George Pine is an industrious city apprentice who happens to stumble into a travel narrative.[44] Stranded with four women on an Edenic desert island where productive labor is unneeded, Pine resourcefully proceeds to manifest his merit through reproductive labor, populating the island with offspring who then constitute a new genealogy and social order, of which he is the unquestioned sovereign.

But the progressive battle between aristocratic corruption and industrious virtue could of course be waged in a setting closer to home. Often it was embodied in plots that pitted aristocratic seducers, rapists, and dunderheads against chaste and canny young women of the middle and lower orders. The obvious exemplar is Richardson's *Pamela* (although it is by no means the rule that virtue should be so ostentatiously rewarded as hers is). Behind Pamela lies a succession of Pamela-like heroines, including the sister of Gabriel Harvey (Spenser's college friend), who left a manuscript account of her pert resistance to seduction.[45] The most important development of this particular progressive plot model was achieved by Aphra Behn, whose ingenious variations include a female aristocratic oppressor who is pathologically fixated on nobility of birth as the trigger of sexual desire, and who is finally reformed by falling in love with an apparent nobleman who turns out to be the son of a Dutch merchant.[46]

Whatever their differences, progressive plots have in common the aim to explain the meaning of the current crisis of status inconsistency, and, in the symbolic realm of fictional action, to overcome it. How do conservative plots manage this explanation so as to subvert progressive ideology itself? One method is by making the oppressor an aristocrat not by birth but by purchase, and his ruling corruption not sexual desire, but the lust for money and power. But the villains of conservative plots need not be aristocrats at all. Fielding's undeserving upstarts, like Shamela and Jonathan Wild, show an obvious debt to the assorted rogues, highwaymen, and pirates of criminal biography. When Charles Davenant undertook to describe the fall of English virtue under the Whigs, he cast his macro-history in the pseudo-autobiographical form of a micro-narrative about the rise of the rogue figure Mr. Double, "now worth Fifty thousand Pound, and 14 years ago I had not Shoes on my Feet." Mr. Double's story is that of a bad apprentice whose vice is not idleness but too much industry, and he ends his allegorical autobiography by comparing himself to "most of the Modern Whigs . . . Did they rise by Virtue or Merit? No more than my self."[47]

When conservative protagonists are sympathetic, they are victims of the modern world—either comically ingenuous innocents, or sacrifices to its corrupt inhumanity. One of the striking achievements of *Gulliver's*

Travels is that its protagonist is able to fill both of these conservative roles. Like Robinson Crusoe, Lemuel Gulliver begins as a naive and industrious younger son, a quantifying empiricist and an upwardly-mobile progressive. In Lilliput he falls into the role of the obsequious new man, hungry for royal favor and titles of honor (recall his assimilationist vanity at being made a Nardac, the highest honor in the land). But Gulliver in Lilliput is also a hardworking public servant who ruefully learns, like Lord Munodi later on, the conservative truth about modern courts and their disdain for true merit. However in his final voyage Gulliver so successfully assimilates upward that he goes native, believes he is a Houyhnhnm, and is forced to endure the comic rustication of an unsuccessful upstart, bloated with pride and uncomprehendingly indignant at his failure to make it.

In this final character of Gulliver (or in that of Shamela) we see the industrious virtue of the progressive protagonist pushed to its limits, so that it breaks open to reveal an ugly core of hypocritical opportunism. This technique of parodic impersonation is typical both of conservative ideology, and of its epistemological counterpart, extreme skepticism. It is the mark of a stance so intricately reactive as to be hard to pry loose, at times, from what it opposes. Moreover unlike progressive narrative, conservative plots are far from hopeful about the overcoming of the social injustice and status inconsistency which they explain with such passion. Their frequent pattern is a retrograde series of disenchantments with all putative resolutions, and conservative utopias tend to be, as Houyhnhnmland is and as Robinson Crusoe's island is not, hedged about with self-conscious fictionality, strictly unfulfillable and nowhere to be found.

Let me now briefly summarize this attempt to rethink the rise of the novel. In order to overcome some deficiencies in the reigning model of what this movement amounted to, I have isolated, as its central principle, two recurrent patterns of "double reversal." Naive empiricism negates romance idealism, and is in turn negated by a more extreme skepticism and a more circumspect approach to truth. Progressive ideology subverts aristocratic ideology, and is in turn subverted by conservative ideology. It is in these double reversals, and in their conflation, that the novel is constituted as a dialectical unity of opposed parts, an achievement that is tacitly acknowledged by the gradual stabilization of "the novel" as a terminological and a conceptual category in eighteenth-century usage. But we have also been concerned with a pattern of historical reversal that is of broader dimension than this movement, and from whose more elevated perspective the conflicts that are defined by our double reversals may even appear to dissolve into unity. For as we have seen over and over again, the origins of the English novel entail the positing of a "new" generic category as a dialecti-

cal negation of a "traditional" dominance—the romance, the aristocracy—whose character still saturates, as an antithetical but constitutive force, the texture of the category by which it is in the process of being replaced.

Of course the very capacity of seventeenth-century narrative to model itself so self-consciously on established categories bespeaks a detachment sufficient to imagine them *as* categories, to parody and thence to supersede them. And with hindsight we may see that the early development of the novel is our great example of the way that the birth of genres results from a momentary negation of the present so intense that it attains the positive status of a new tradition. But at the "first instant" of this broader dialectical reversal, the novel has a definitional volatility, a tendency to dissolve into its antithesis, which encapsulates the dialectical nature of historical process itself at a critical moment in the emergence of the modern world.

I have argued that the volatility of the novel at this time is *analogous* to that of the middle class. But it is clear that in a certain sense, the emerging novel also has *internalized* the emergence of the middle class in its preoccupation with the problem of how virtue is signified. From time to time we can observe the distinct questions of virtue and truth being raised simultaneously by writers of the most diverse aims and formal commitments. At such times we sense that writers wish to "make something" of the analogous relation between these questions, if only through their tacit juxtaposition. And occasionally the analogy will even be explicitly asserted. In this way, questions of truth and virtue begin to seem not so much distinct problems, as versions or transformations of each other, distinct ways of formulating and propounding a fundamental problem of what might be called epistemological, sociological, and ethical "signification." And the essential unity of this problem is clear from the fact that progressive and conservative positions on questions of virtue have their obvious corollary positions with respect to questions of truth. What this means is that epistemological choices come to have ideological significance, and a given account of the nature of social reality implies a certain formal commitment and procedure. Moreover we may conceive these correlations of truth and virtue also in terms of narrative form and content, so that the way the story is told, and what it is that is told, are implicitly understood to bear an integral relation to each other.

But I do not mean to suggest that the conflation of questions of truth and virtue occurred easily or quickly. On the contrary, it is the result of much thought and experimentation, a very small portion of which I have described here, expended over a considerable period of time. And the conflation itself begins to occur when writers begin to act—first gingerly, then systematically—upon the insight that the difficulties of one set of problems may be mediated and illuminated by the reflection of the other. This insight—the deep and fruitful analogy between questions of truth and questions of virtue—is the enabling foundation of the novel. And the genre of the novel can be understood comprehensively as an early modern cultural instrument designed to confront, on the level of narrative form and content, both intellectual and social crisis simultaneously. The novel emerges into consciousness when this conflation can be made with complete confidence. The conflict then comes to be embodied in a public controversy between Richardson and Fielding—writers who are understood to represent coherent, autonomous, and alternative methods for doing the same thing. At this point—in the mid-1740's, after the first confrontation between Richardson and Fielding—the novel has come to the end of its origins. And it begins then to enter new territory.

Notes

[1] *The Rise of the Novel: Studies in Defoe, Richardson and Fielding* (Berkeley: University of California Press, 1957). The following essay summarizes one central argument of my forthcoming book, *The Origins of the English Novel, 1600-1740* (Baltimore: Johns Hopkins University Press, 1986).

[2] *The Annals of Love, Containing Select Histories of the Amours of divers Princes Courts, Pleasantly Related* (1672), sig. Dd7ᵛ-Ee4ᵛ. Except where noted, place of publication of early modern works is London.

[3] *A Catalogve of The most vendible Books in England* . . . (1657).

[4] *The History of the Royal-Society of London* . . . (1667), 90-91.

[5] *Philosophical Transactions,* 11 (1676), 552.

[6] See *Philosophical Transactions,* 1 (1665-66), 141-43, 186-89. Boyle's instructions are excerpted from his *Some Considerations of the Usefulness of Experimental Natural Philosophy* (1663).

[7] *The History of the Royal-Society of London* . . . 72.

[8] Awnsham and John Churchill, eds., *A Collection of Voyages and Travels* . . . (1704), I, viii.

[9] Edward Cooke in ibid., II, xix.

[10] See in general Elizabeth L. Eisenstein, *The Printing Press as an Agent of Change: Communications and Cultural Transformations in Early Modern Europe* (Cambridge: Cambridge University Press, 1979), Chap. 2 and passim.

[11] *Histories and Observations Domestick and Foreign.* . . . (1683), sig. A5ᵛ, A6ʳ.

[12] E.g., see *Don Quixote,* II (1615), ii-iv.

[13] See the discussion of William Haller, *The Elect Nation: The Meaning and Relevance of Foxe's Book of Martyrs* (New York: Harper & Row, 1963), 122, 159-60, 213-14.

[14] Bunyan, *Life and Death,* 326, sig. A4ᵛ.

[15] *The Diary of Ralph Thoresby, FRS, Author of the Topography of Leeds (1677-1724),* ed. Rev. Joseph Hunter (1830), I, xv, quoted in George A. Starr, *Defoe and Spiritual Autobiography* (Princeton: Princeton University Press, 1965), 10.

[16] *The Certainty of the Worlds of Spirits* . . . (1691), sig. A4ʳ.

[17] E.g., *A Discourse concerning the Mechanical Operation of the Spirit.* . . . (1704).

[18] *Tatler,* No. 178, May 27-30, 1710.

[19] *Tatler,* No. 84, Oct. 22, 1709.

[20] *The Dictionary Historical and Critical of Mr Peter Bayle* (1697), 2nd ed. (1734-38), IV, "Nidhard," n. C, 366.

[21] *The Plus Ultra reduced to a Non Plus* . . . (1670), 11.

[22] See the copy of [Richard Head,] *O-Brazile, or the Inchanted Island* . . . (1675) reproduced in *Seventeenth-Century Tales of the Supernatural,* ed. Isabel M. Westcott, *Augustan Reprint Society,* No. 74 (1958).

[23] "*Soliloquy:* or Advice to an Author" (1714), in *Characteristicks of Men, Manners, Opinions, Times,* 2nd ed. (1714), I, 344.

[24] [François Misson,] *A New Voyage to the East-Indies, by Francis Leguat and His Companions.* . . . (London and Amsterdam, 1708), iv. The rival is the Abbot of Choisy.

[25] See the discussion in David Cressy, "Describing the Social Order of Elizabethan and Stuart England," *Literature and History,* No. 3 (March, 1976), 29-44.

[26] See Peter Matthias, "The Social Structure in the Eighteenth Century: A Calculation by Joseph Massie," in *The Transformation of England: Essays in the Economic and Social History of England in the Eighteenth Century* (New York: Columbia University Press, 1979), 176, 186, 188.

[27] See Lawrence Stone, *The Crisis of the Aristocracy, 1558-1641* (Oxford: Clarendon Press, 1965), Chap. 3. For a discussion of "status inconsistency" and reference-group theory in the context of seventeeth-century historiography, see Stone's *The Causes of the English Revolution, 1529-1642* (London: Routledge & Kegan Paul, 1972), Chap. 1.

[28] A generalization based on the use of the term in dramatic contexts: see C.L. Barber, *The Idea of Honor in the English Drama, 1591-1700,* Gothenburg Studies in English, 6 (Göteborg: Elanders, 1957), 330-31.

[29] *The Fable of the Bees* (1714), ed. Phillip Harth (Harmondsworth: Penguin, 1970), "Remark (R)," 212-13.

[30] *New Instructions to the Guardian . . .* (1694), 135-36.

[31] *A Modest Plea for an Equal Common-wealth Against Monarchy. . . .* (1659), 62-63.

[32] *The True-Born Englishman. A Satyr* (1700), 70-71.

[33] *The Compleat English Gentleman* (written 1728-29), ed. Karl D. Bülbring (London: David Nutt, 1890), 171.

[34] *Examiner,* No. 40, May 10, 1711; (Irish) *Intelligencer,* No. 9 (1728).

[35] *Examiner,* No. 34, Mar. 29, 1711.

[36] *Review,* III, No. 126, Oct. 22, 1706.

[37] "Answer to the Nineteen Propositions," June 18, 1642, in J.P. Kenyon, ed., *The Stuart Constitution, 1603-1688: Documents and Commentary* (Cambridge: Cambridge University Press, 1966), 23.

[38] See Gerald M. Straka, *Anglican Reaction to the Revolution of 1688,* State Historical Society of Wisconsin (Madison, Wi.: University of Wisconsin Press, 1962).

[39] See *Charles II's Escape from Worcester: A Collection of Narratives Assembled by Samuel Pepys,* ed. William Matthews (Berkeley: University of California Press, 1966), 40, 42, 44, 50, 74, 96.

[40] To Suffolk County Committee, Aug. 29, Sept. 28, 1643, in *The Writings and Speeches of Oliver Cromwell,* ed. Wilbur C. Abbott (Cambridge, Ma.: Harvard University Press, 1937), I, 256, 262.

[41] Quoted in Michael Walzer, *The Revolution of the Saints: A Study in the Origins of Radical Politics* (Cambridge, Ma.: Harvard University Press, 1965), 266.

[42] Thomas Edwards, "The Holy Choice," in *Three Sermons* (1625), 63-64, quoted in *ibid.,* 235.

[43] See *Acts and Monuments,* ed. S.R. Cattley (London: Seeley and Burnside, 1839), VIII, 473-74.

[44] See *The Isle of Pines . . .* (1668).

[45] See "A Noble Mans Sute to a Cuntrie Maide," in *Letter-Book of Gabriel Harvey, 1573-1580,* ed. Edward J.L. Scott, Camden Society, N. S. 33 (London: Nichols and Sons, 1884), 144-58.

[46] See *The Fair Jilt: or, the History of Prince Tarquin, and Miranda* (1696), in *The Histories and Novels Of the Late Ingenious Mrs Behn . . .* (1696).

[47] *The True Picture of a Modern Whig . . . ,* "6th ed." (1701), 14, 32.

William Warner (essay date 1994)

SOURCE: "Licensing Pleasure: Literary History and the Novel in Early Modern Britain," in *The Columbia History of the British Novel,* edited by John Richetti, Columbia University Press, 1994, pp. 1-22.

[*In this essay, Warner discusses social and critical attitudes toward the novel during the decades of its development.*]

The Scandal of Novel Reading

Novels have been a respectable component of culture for so long that it is difficult for twentieth-century observers to grasp the unease produced by novel reading in the eighteenth century. Long before it became an issue for debate in literary studies, a quantum leap in the number, variety, and popularity of novels provoked cultural alarm in England during the decades following 1700. The flood of novels on the market, and the pleasures they incited, led many to see novels as a catastrophe for book-centered culture. While the novel was not clearly defined or conceptualized, the targets of the anti-novel campaign were quite precise: seventeenth-century romances, novellas of Continental origin, and those "novels" and "secret histories" written by Behn, Manley, and Haywood in the decades following 1680. The central themes of this debate may be culled from several texts: Samuel Johnson's 1750 *Rambler No. 4* essay on the new fiction of Richardson, Fielding, and Smollett; Francis Coventry's enthusiastic pamphlet in support of Fielding, "An Essay on the New Species of Writing Founded by Mr. Fielding: With a Word or Two upon the Modern State of Criticism" (1751); and in *The Progress of Romance,* a literary history in dialogue form by Clara Reeve published in 1785.

These texts mobilize criticism and alarm, praise and prescription in an attempt to modulate the comparatively new vogue for novel reading. Francis Coventry mocks the unreflected "emulation" produced in readers by the French romances of an earlier day: "This [vogue] obtain'd a long Time. Every Beau was an *Orondates,* and all the Belles were *Stariras.*" Though Samuel Johnson could not account for the fashion for romance, his *Rambler No. 4* essay describes the more powerful identification that recent "familiar histories" like *Clarissa* and *Tom Jones* induce in their readers: "If the power of example is so great, as to take possession of the memory by a kind of violence, and produce effects almost without the intervention of the will, care ought to be taken that . . . the best examples only should be exhibited." If novels produce effects "almost without the intervention of the [reader's] will," then readers are at risk of becoming automatons, and the author must assume responsibility for the novel's moral effects.

The power and danger of novels, especially to young women not exposed to classical education, arose from the pleasures they induced. In *The Progress of Romance,* Clara Reeve's leading character, Euphrasia, remembers "my mother and aunts being shut up in the parlour reading *Pamela,* and I took it very hard that I was excluded." Closeted with a novel, some are included, and others excluded, from the circle of pleasure. Coventry remarks upon the tenacity with which readers clung to their pleasures: "For tho' it was a folly, it was a pleasing one: and if sense could not yield the pretty creatures greater pleasure, dear nonsense must be ador'd." Opposing this pleasure "lecture would lose it's force; and ridicule would strive in vain to remove it."

But what is so pernicious about reading novels? *The Progress of Romance* ends with a staged debate between the woman scholar Euphrasia and a high-culture snob named Hortensius. Hortensius develops a wide-ranging indictment of novel reading. First, novels turn the reader's taste against serious reading: "A person used to this kind of reading will be disgusted with every thing serious or solid, as a weakened and depraved stomach rejects plain and wholesome food." Second, novels incite the heart with false emotions: "The seeds of vice and folly are sown in the heart,—the passions are awakened,—false expectations are raised.—A young woman is taught to expect adventures and intrigues. . . . If a plain man addresses her in rational terms and pays her the greatest of compliments,—that of desiring to spend his life with her,—that is not sufficient, her vanity is disappointed, she expects to meet a Hero in Romance." Finally, novels induce a dangerous autonomy from parents and guardians: "From this kind of reading, young people fancy themselves capable of judging of men and manners, and . . . believe themselves wiser than their parents and guardians, whom they treat with contempt and ridicule." Hortensius indicts novels for transforming the cultural function of reading from providing solid moral nourishment to catering to exotic tastes; from preparing a woman for the ordinary rational address of a plain good man to leading her to expect a proposal from a hero out of romance; and from reinforcing reliance upon parents and guardians to promoting a belief in the subject's autonomy. Taken together, novels have disfigured the reader's body: the taste, passions, and judgment of stomach, heart, and mind. Here, as so often in the polemics that surround novels, the reader is characterized as a susceptible female whose moral life is at risk. By strong implication, she is most responsible for transmitting the virus of novel reading.

From the vantage point of the late twentieth century, and after nearly nine decades of film and five of television, the alarm provoked by novel reading may seem hyperbolic or even quaint. But a condescendingly modernist "pro-pleasure" position renders the alarm with novel reading, and its effects on early modern culture, unintelligible. Though it is difficult to credit the specific object of the alarm of the eighteenth-century critics of novels—after all, we recommend to students some of the very novels these early modern critics inveighed against—given our current anxieties about the cultural effects of slasher films, rap music, MTV, and soap operas, it seems contradictory to dismiss those who worried about the effects of novels when they were new. But there are fundamental obstacles to deciphering the eighteenth century's anxious discourse on the pleasures of novels. After psychoanalysis, most concede the difficulty of knowing why one experiences pleasure; it is even more difficult to define the content or cause of the pleasure of eighteenth-century novel readers. However, we can trace certain clear effects of the campaign against these unlicensed pleasures. First, cultural critics sketched the profile of the culture-destroying pleasure seeker who haunts the modern era: the obsessive, unrestrained, closeted consumer of fantasy. Then, novelists like Richardson and Fielding, accepting the cogency of this critique, developed replacement fictions as a cure for the novel-addicted reader. In doing so, they aimed to deflect and reform, improve and justify the pleasures of a new species of elevated novel.

Since Plato's attack on the poets, philosophers and cultural critics had worried the effects of an audience's absorption in fictional entertainment. During the early eighteenth century the market gave this old cultural issue new urgency. Although there had been a trade in books for centuries, several developments gave the circulation of novels unprecedented cultural force. At a time when state censorship in England was subsiding and technological advances were making all printed matter more affordable, the market in printed books offered a site for the production and consumption of a very broad spectrum of entertainment. Published anonymously, or by parvenu authors supported by no patron of rank, novels appeared as anonymous and irresponsible creations, conceived with only one guiding intention: to pander to any desire that would produce a sale. Novels not only violated the spirit of seriousness expected of readers of books like *The Pilgrim's Progress* or *Paradise Lost;* they made no pretense to making any lasting contribution to culture. Novels were the first "disposable" books, written in anticipation of their own obsolescence and in acceptance of their own transient function as part of a culture of serial entertainments. Although only a small part of print culture in the early decades of the eighteenth century, novels appear to have been the most high-profile, fashionable, and fast-moving segment of the market. The vogue for novels helped to constitute a market culture—in the modern sense of commodities for purchase by the individual. In short, novels desanctified the book. Little wonder that novels were figured as an uncontrollable menace to culture.

Many of the vices attributed to the novel are also characteristics of the market: both breed imitation, gratify desire, and are oblivious to their moral effects. The market appears as a machine evidencing an uncanny automatism. Once they had become "the thing," nothing could stop novels on the market. In critiquing novels, cultural critics deplored the market's powerful, autonomous effect upon culture. Coventry's description of the imitations provoked by the success of Fielding's novels develops a general rule about success and emulation in a market-driven culture: "It is very certain, that whenever any thing new, of what kind soever, is started by one man, and appears with great success in the world, it quickly produces several in the same taste." Producers for the market have become mere factors of the market. Using the by now clichéd terms for describing the Grub Street hacks, Clara Reeve emphasizes how the accelerating multiplicity of novels complicates her own efforts at the classification and criticism of romances and novels. Rampant production also allows bad imitations to proliferate and engenders new institutions to deliver novels indiscriminately into the hands of every reader: "The press groaned under the weight of Novels, which sprung up like mushrooms every year. . . . [Novels] did but now begin to increase upon us, but ten years more multiplied them tenfold. Every work of merit produced a swarm of imitators, till they became a public evil, and the institution of Circulating libraries, conveyed them in the cheapest manner to every bodies hand." An uncontrolled multiplicity threatens to metastasize culture. For the scholar surveying the production of many ages, the market has the effect of blurring the distinctness and expressive readability of culture. Thus in his *History of Fiction* (1814) John Dunlop complains that while earlier epochs developed "only one species of fiction," which could then be read as "characteristic" of the age, more

recently "different kinds have sprung up at once; and thus they were no longer expressive of the taste and feelings of the period of their composition." The critical histories of the novel by Reeve and Dunlop aim to restore the character to culture.

If, according to a formula developed in the writings of the French cultural critic Michel Foucault, power operates less by repressing or censoring than by producing new "reality," new "domains of objects and rituals of truth," then the success of novels on the market changed culture by producing a need to read. Clara Reeve describes this newly incited desire: "People must read something, they cannot always be engaged by dry disquisitions, the mind requires some amusement." Between uncritical surrender to novel reading and a wholesale rejection of novels in favor of "serious" reading, Richardson and Fielding traced a third pathway for the novel. In Reeve's words, the strategy was to "write an antidote to the bad effects" of novels "under the disguise" of being novels. This requires a cunning pharmacology. When Lady Echlin, Richardson's most morally exacting correspondent, warns that "the best instruction you can give, blended with love intrigue, will never answer your good intention," Richardson replies with a celebrated reformulation of the old demand that art should both amuse and instruct: "Instruction, Madam, is the Pill; Amusement is the Gilding. Writings that do not touch the Passions of the Light and Airy, will hardly ever reach the heart." Coventry describes the manner in which Fielding, "who sees all the little movements by which human nature is actuated," intervenes in the market for novels. "The disease became epidemical, but there were no hopes of a cure, 'till Mr. Fielding endeavour'd to show the World, that pure Nature could furnish out as agreeable entertainment, as those airy non-entical forms they had long ador'd, and persuaded the ladies to leave this extravagance to their Abigails with their cast cloaths." Thus the "disease" of romance, associated with the craze for new fashions, can be "cured" only by cutting new paths toward pleasure. Then the old novels, with their corrupting pleasures, can be passed on, along with old dresses, to the lady's servant.

It is beyond the scope of this chapter to give a detailed account of how the popularity of the "histories" published by Richardson and Fielding in the 1740s effected an upward revaluation of the novel in Britain. However, the key elements of their successful strategy are implicit in the metaphors of the antidote, the vaccine, and the gilded pill. First, a broad spectrum of earlier writings—romances, novellas, and secret histories written on the Continent and in Britain—are characterized as essentially equivalent. Deemed licentious, fantasy-ridden, and debased, they are decried as a cultural disease. Next, Richardson and Fielding produce substitute fictions to absorb the reader. Although Richardson and Fielding wrote antinovels, they didn't write non-novels. Just as a vaccine can achieve its antidotal function only by introducing a mild form of a disease into the body of the patient, their novels incorporated many elements of the dangerous old novels of Behn, Manley, and Haywood into this "new species" of fiction. By including improving discourse familiar from conduct books, spiritual autobiography, and the periodical essay, the "histories" of Richardson and Fielding could appear radically "new."

Cervantes' *Don Quixote* (1605/1615) and Lafayette's *Princess de Cleves* (1678) had demonstrated the power of a modern fiction composed on the textual "grounds" of the earlier romance. Those who elevated the novel in England pursued a similar strategy by appropriating elements from the earlier novel—such as the female libertine, or the intricate seduction scheme—and articulating (by connecting together, and thus "speaking") them in a new way, with a new meaning, as part of a new form of novel. Thus, within Richardson's *Clarissa,* the rake Lovelace, by using disguise and manipulation to pursue seduction, upholds the old novel's ethos of amorous intrigue within the plot lines of the new. The bad old obsession with sex and passion is still there, but through Clarissa's resistance and its attendant critical discourse, sex is sublimated to the virtuous sentiments of the new and improving novel. Incorporated into a new species of novel, the old novel gilds the pill from within, helping to insure the popularity of the new novel. To secure the enlightening cultural address of their novels, Richardson and Fielding disavowed rather than assumed their debt to those popular novels whose narrative resources they incorporated and whose cultural space they sought to occupy. They simultaneously absorbed and erased the novels they would supplant.

The new novel reorients rather than banishes spontaneous reader identification; now a morally improving emulation is promoted. When, in *The Progress of Romance,* Hortensius complains that Richardson's epistolary novels "have taught many young girls to wiredraw their language, and to spin always long letters out of nothing," Euphrasia defends the cultural value of studying and imitating Richardson over the "studies" of an earlier generation: "Let the young girls . . . copy Richardson, as often as they please, and it will be owing to the defects of their understandings, or judgments, if they do not improve by him. We could not say as much of the reading Ladies of the last age. . .

No truly, for their studies were the French and Spanish Romances, and the writings of Mrs. Behn, Mrs. Manly, and Mrs. Heywood [*sic*]." In order to serve as an antidotal substitute for the poison of novels, the elevated novels of Richardson and Fielding had to be founded in an antagonistic critique and overwriting of the earlier novels of Behn, Manley, and Haywood. This elevating novel brought a new disposition of pleasure and value to its readers. But the novel's rise is not a spontaneous or organic development. On the contested cultural site of novel reading at mid-century, it is, as the Marxist critic John Frow suggests in a different context, not so much the old that has died, but the new that has killed.

Sublimating the Novel by Telling Its History

The successes of *Pamela* (1740), *Joseph Andrews* (1742), *Clarissa* (1747-1748), and *Tom Jones* (1749), as well as the many imitations they provoked on the market, helped to countersign the elevated novel as a significant new cultural formation. But such validation also depended upon those critics who grasped the possibilities of this new kind of fiction and sought to describe its signal features, cultural virtues, and history. This project often required inventive critical strategies. By rescuing the elevated novel from the general cultural indictment of novels, the early literary critics and historians I have cited—Samuel Johnson, Francis Coventry, Clara Reeve, and John Dunlop—made their texts supplements to the project of elevating the novel.

For Johnson, a critical intervention on behalf of the new novel meant arguing, by way of response to the recent popularity of *Tom Jones* and *Roderick Random,* in favor of the "exemplary" characters of Richardson over the more true-to-life "mixed" characters of Fielding and Smollett. In a pamphlet published anonymously, "An Essay on the New Species of Writing Founded by Mr. Fielding" (1751), Coventry follows the basic procedure Fielding had devised in the many interpolated prefaces to *Joseph Andrews* and *Tom Jones*: he transports critical terms and ideas developed earlier for poetry, epic, and drama to the novel. But Coventry goes farther. Just as Aristotle modeled the "rules" of tragedy upon Sophocles, and early modern French and English critics defined the rules for epic through criticism of Homer, Coventry made Fielding's work the template for the "species" of writing he had "founded." As the "great Example" and "great original" for "future historians of this kind," Fielding's work provides the terms for a new inventory of neoclassical "laws": "As Mr. Fielding first introduc'd this new kind of Biography, he restrain'd it with Laws which should ever after be deem'd sacred by all that attempted his Manner; which I here propose to give a brief account of." In his "word or two on the modern state of criticism," Coventry bewails the decline of criticism from earlier epochs (from Horace to Pope), quotes and corrects the modern scorn for critics, and inveighs against the partisanship discernible in the reception of new plays. Coventry's way of posturing as a critic—he is unctuous, defensive, and yet arrogant—is the very antithesis of the imperious law-givings and definitive pronouncements characteristic of Fielding's narrators. But both styles of address suggest there is as yet no preestablished cultural vantage point or institutionalized discourse for the criticism of novels.

But such an anchor for the articulation of the novel was developing. Written thirty-five years later than Johnson's or Coventry's criticism, Reeve's *Progress of Romance* (1785) composes what seems to be the first scholarly literary history of novels in English. Within the term *romance* Reeve comprehends not only the Greek romance, the medieval romances (in both verse and prose), and the seventeenth-century heroic romance; she also goes backward to the epics of Homer and forward to the "modern novels" of France and England. The inclusion of Homeric epic in the category of romance is a classification dubious enough to have been rejected by virtually every subsequent literary historian of the novel; but it gives Reeve's protagonist, Euphrasia, a way to refute the high-culture bias of her polemical antagonist, Hortensius. In addition, by developing the term *romance* into a global category inclusive of fictional entertainments produced over a vast expanse of "times, countries, and manners," she uses the historicist horizon of her study to develop an indulgence that protects the now unfashionable romances as well as the modern novels under contemporary attack. The literary history and criticism of the English novel that has developed over the two hundred years since Reeve's text—from John Dunlop and Hippolyte Taine to Ian Watt and Michael McKeon—inevitably comes to be implicated in the task Richardson and Fielding seemed to set going in England: that of securing an elevated cultural address for the novel.

We can begin to grasp the broader cultural uses of literary history by attending to the way John Dunlop introduces his ambitious three-volume *History of Fiction: Being a Critical Account of the Most Celebrated Prose Works of Fiction, from the Earliest Greek Romances to the Novels of the Present Age* (1815). In order to articulate the general cultural value of fiction over history Dunlop quotes Lord Bacon:

> Fiction gives to mankind what history denies, and, in some measure, satisfies the mind with shadows when it cannot enjoy the substance: . . . Fiction strongly shows that a greater variety of things, a more perfect order, a more beautiful variety, than can any where be found in nature, is pleasing to the mind. And as real history gives us not the success of things according to the deserts of vice and virtue, Fiction corrects it, and presents us with the fates and fortunes of persons rewarded or punished according to merit. And as real history disgusts us with a familiar and constant similitude of things, Fiction relieves us by unexpected turns and changes, and thus not only delights, but inculcates morality and nobleness of soul. It raises the mind by accommodating the images of things to our desires, and not like history and reason, subjecting the mind to things."

By appealing to Bacon on the value of fiction, Dunlop not only invokes the authority of a major British thinker but also neatly hurdles almost two hundred years of wrangling over the morally dubious effects of taking pleasure from fiction. By using the general term *fiction* for his history of romances and novels, Dunlop encompasses the polemical terms of the debate he would nonetheless inflect and recast. Eighteenth-century defenses of the novel (from Congreve and Richardson to Fielding and Reeve) usually engage a set of polar oppositions still familiar to us: the novel is to the romance as the "real" is to the "ideal," as fact is to fantasy, as the probable is to the amazing, as the commonplace is to the exotic, and so on. Fiction is developed by Dunlop as a third term that can at once finesse and reconcile these polar oppositions. Fiction does this by becoming art, delivering "a more perfect order, a more beautiful variety" than "nature."

Through Dunlop's use of Bacon, Renaissance and Romantic aesthetics meet in a justification of fiction that is, finally, psychological. Through fiction, the reader is no longer "subject" to things, nor disgusted with "a familiar and constant similitude of things." Instead, fiction "relieves" and "delights," and "raises the mind by accommodating the images of things to our desires." The cultural efficacy of fiction comes from its successful gratification of the reader's pleasure. Dunlop's translation of Bacon assumes yet reverses the anxiety about the reader's pleasure that had motivated earlier condemnations of the novel. When Dunlop glosses Bacon's emphasis upon "delight," it becomes apparent that the pleasure Dunlop promotes is quite different from the pleasure that novel readers had been accused of indulging. Instead of obsessive, personal, deluded, erotic pleasures, we are called to soft and social ones: "How much are we indebted to [fiction] for pleasure and enjoyment! it sweetens solitude and charms sorrow. . . . " These pleasures improve and uplift the reader, by taking him or her into an elevated social and emotive space: "The rude are refined by an introduction, as it were, to the higher orders of mankind, and even the dissipated and selfish are, in some degree, corrected by those paintings of virtue and simple nature, which must ever be employed by the novelist if he wish to awaken emotion or delight." Having confirmed its beneficial effect, Dunlop can confirm the novel's rise from its earlier disreputable cultural position:

> This powerful instrument of virtue and happiness, after having been long despised, on account of the purposes to which it had been made subservient, has gradually become more justly appreciated, and more highly valued. Works of Fiction have been produced, abounding at once with the most interesting details, and the most sagacious reflections, and which differ from treatises of abstract philosophy only by the greater justness of their views, and the higher interest which they excite.

Dunlop's description of his project helps us to apprehend the broader purpose of his literary history: to sublimate the novel so as to produce a new disposition, or arrangement, of the pleasure of novel reading. With his title, which neither exiles all novels from culture in favor of drama, epic, sermons, or conduct books, nor favors the simple, uncritical acceptance of all novels into his narrative of the history of fiction, Dunlop announces that his history is to be "critical"—that is, it will judge works according to their quality so as to focus upon only "the most celebrated" prose fiction. What results, in both Reeve and Dunlop as well as in every subsequent literary history, is a chronological panorama, a certain spectacular sequential cinematography of culture in which selected cultural practices and productions are narrated as significant and valuable. By this means literary history (selectively) licenses (sublimated) pleasures. Through this literary history, novels produced in the market can be inserted into a (more or less) continuous narrative and turned toward higher cultural purposes: for example, serving as an expression of "the voice of the people" (Taine) or being part of "the Great Tradition" (Leavis).

Dunlop writes as though the culturally elevating role for fiction were already achieved. In fact, his own literary history is designed to promote that end. To argue the centrality of fiction to culture, Dunlop begins his introduction with an elaborate analogy between gardening and fiction making, which quickly implicates his own literary history. The analogy also indexes what we might call the necessary violence of literary history. Just as the "savage" has gathered, and placed around his dwelling, plants that please him, so too have men lived events "which are peculiarly grateful, and of which the narrative at once pleases himself, and excites in the minds of his hearers a kindred emotion." What are gathered are "unlooked-for occurrences, successful enterprise, or great and unexpected deliverance from signal danger and distress." A gardener learns that one must not just collect but also weed out the

> useless or noxious, and [those] which weaken or impair the pure delight which he derives from others . . . the rose should no longer be placed beside the thistle, as in the wild, but that it should flourish in a clear, and sheltered, and romantic situation, where its sweets may be undiminished, and where its form can be contemplated without any attending circumstances of uneasiness or disgust. The collector of agreeable facts finds, in like manner, that the sympathy which they excite can be heightened by removing from their detail every thing that is not interesting, or which tends to weaken the principal emotion, which it is his intention to raise. He renders, in this way, the occurrences more unexpected, the enterprises more successful, the deliverance from danger and distress more wonderful.

The same process that describes the "fine arts" of gardening and fiction making—selecting, weeding, and intensifying with an eye toward pleasure—applies also

to the literary history Dunlop composes. Dunlop's "critical" history of fiction becomes an improving and enlightening cultivation of fiction for culture. By using the fiction of widely different epochs to survey the variety of cultural achievements, literary history makes novels more than instruments of private (kinky, obsessive) gratification. They are drawn into the larger tableau of cultural accomplishment—which Dunlop calls "the advance of the human mind"—until a certain disinterested moral and aesthetic pleasure appears to be the telos of all fiction making.

But the gardening metaphor insinuates certain assumptions into the project of this literary history. Literary history as cultivation spatializes time, so that the successive conflicts between the often antagonistic types of fiction written in England over the course of a century by, for example, Behn, Richardson, Fielding, and Radcliffe, are arranged to appear as one harmoniously balanced array of species that can be surveyed in one leisurely stroll, as one wanders through a garden. However, it proves as implausible to have a literary history without a literary historian as it is to have a garden without a gardener. It is the valuative role of the literary historian—the critic holding the scales over each text read—that produces the synchronic moment of judgment through which a narrative of the progress or history of romance, novel, and fiction can be grasped and told. Then, the way in which that story is told has a feedback effect: which writers are included and excluded, which are brought into the foreground, cast into the shade, or weeded away, determines what kinds of writing and authorship will come to count as "tradition" that grounds subsequent value judgments. This is the ironic terminus of a hegemonic literary history. Literary history can easily become tautological and self-confirming, a garden wall to protect specimens collected against the very factors it might have interpreted: history, change, difference.

A Vortex Mis-seen as an Origin

Once Dunlop's literary history gets under way, it becomes apparent that civilizing the novel requires a certain calculated violence. In a chapter entitled "Sketch of the Origin and Progress of the English Novel," Dunlop offers a typology of the elevated novel: novels are divided into the "serious" (Richardson, Sheridan, Godwin), the "comic" (Fielding, Smollett), and the "romantic" (Walpole, Reeve, Radcliffe). But before offering this schematic overview of what we would now call the eighteenth-century novel, Dunlop does some weeding by giving cursory negative treatment to the novels of Behn, Manley, and the early Haywood. Behn's novels, we are informed, "have not escaped the moral contagion which infected the literature of that age." Though Dunlop merely alludes to "the objections which may be charged against many" of Behn's novels, he ends the passage describing the "faults in points of morals" of Behn's "imitator," Eliza Haywood, in this fashion: "Her male characters are in the highest degree licentious, and her females are as impassioned as the Saracen princesses in the Spanish romances of chivalry."

By orientalizing these early novels and by characterizing them as inappropriately erotic—too feminine, too European, and too immoral—Dunlop relegates to the margins of *The History of Fiction* some of the most popular novels published in England between 1683 and 1730. How is the eclipse of an influential strain of popular fiction to be understood? Dunlop's dismissal of Behn, Manley, and Haywood from his history confirms a judgment that critics of the early amorous novel had been making since the 1730s. This negative judgment might be attributed to changes in sensibility, taste, or style, or to the idea that a certain formula has exhausted its appeal. But these words merely relabel rather than explain the cultural change we are trying to interpret. It is, no doubt, correct to argue that the novels of amorous intrigue are an integral expression of the culture of the Restoration, with the zeal of Charles II's court for sexual license, its eschewal of the dour asceticism of the Commonwealth, and its enthusiastic translation of French cultural forms. Such a historical placement of the early novel allows one to align its passing with the reaction, after 1688, against the excesses of the Restoration. Pleasures disowned become discomforting, and through embarrassment, a kind of unpleasure.

Some feminist literary historians have attributed the devaluation of Behn, Manley, and Haywood to their gender. However, even before Richardson and Fielding won ascent from the market for their novels of the 1740s, the moral improvement of the novel of amorous intrigue was undertaken by Elizabeth Rowe, Jane Barker, and Penelope Aubin. Explanations based upon taste, political history, and gender fail to come to terms with the particular way in which the novels of Behn, Manley, and Haywood were devalued and overwritten in the 1740s.

The erasure or forgetting of earlier cultural formations is an obscure process. Unlike material objects, cultural ideas and forms do not become used up or out of date. Cultural forms—from letters and love stories to national constitutions—can be rejuvenated by new technology, foreign transplants, and political strife. In other words, recycling seems to be the rule rather than the exception in culture. Thus, for example, the novel of amorous intrigue, developed in the late Restoration by Behn under strong influence from the Continental novella and the aristocratic literature of love, was exploited for politically motivated scandal and satire by Delariviere Manley in the *New Atalantis* (1709). Then, following the spectacular success of *Love in Excess* (1719-1720), this species of novel was turned into

repeatable "formula fiction" on the market by Eliza Haywood in the 1720s. To remove elements from culture one must understand "forgetting" as, in Nietzsche's words, "an active and in the strictest sense positive faculty of repression." The incorporation of the novel of amorous intrigue within the elevated novel of the 1740s is one of the means by which old pleasures are disowned and effaced. As I have noted above, novelists like Richardson and Fielding promote this forgetting, first by defacing the novel of amorous intrigue and then by providing their own novels as replacements for the novels they characterize as degraded and immoral. These new novels overwrite—disavow but appropriate, waste but recycle—the novels they spurn.

Reeve and Dunlop do not commit their literary histories to exercising a "good memory." Unlike certain late-twentieth-century counterhegemonic literary histories—whether feminist, African-American, or gay and lesbian—the works of Reeve and Dunlop do not set out to counteract a biased cultural memory. Instead they are constrained by the protocols of a culturally elevating literary history to be critical and selective, and thus forgetful. In the introduction to *The Progress of Romance,* Reeve tells her readers that she seeks "to assist according to my best judgment, the reader's choice, amidst the almost infinite variety it affords, in a selection of such as are most worthy of a place in the libraries of readers of every class, who seek either for information or entertainment." The effacement of Behn's novels from those literary histories written in the wake of the novel's elevation does not depend upon the good will of the literary historian. Thus, while Reeve is generous with Behn—"let us cast a veil of compassion over her faults"—and Dunlop is severe, both ignore all her novels except *Oroonoko.* By contrast, the novels of Richardson and Fielding are given positions of special priority in both accounts of the novel's rise. The success of the elevated novel in the 1740s—its appearance in culture as the only novel worthy of reading, cultural attention, and detailed literary history—means the early novels of Behn, Manley, and Haywood will be pushed into the margins of literary histories, where they nonetheless never quite disappear but serve—as they do in Richardson and Fielding's texts—as an abject trace or degraded "other" needed to secure the identity of the "real" (i.e., legitimate) novel.

From Reeve forward, scholarly literary history develops a paradoxical relationship to the forgotten texts of the past. It retrieves from the archival memory of culture and reads again what its contemporary culture has almost completely forgotten. This activity pushes Reeve toward a certain regret about the shifts in cultural value that can look quite arbitrary to one who has looked long enough down the "stream of time."

> Romances have for many ages past been read and
> admired, lately it has been the fashion to decry and

ridicule them; but to an unprejudiced person, this will prove nothing but the variations of times, manners, and opinions.—Writers of all denominations,—Princes and Priests,—Bishops and Heroes,—have their day, and then are out of date.—Sometimes indeed a work of intrinsic merit will revive, and renew its claim to immortality: but this happiness falls to the lot of few, in comparison of those who roll down the stream of time, and fall into the gulph of oblivion.

This passage naturalizes the process of disappearance and forgetting—by its reference to the wheel of fortune that gives "princes and priests, bishops and heroes . . . their day" and then takes it away, as well as by its metaphorical characterization of the movement of a "work of . . . merit" down "the stream of time" into "the gulph of oblivion." These analogies obscure the particular cultural strife at work within shifts in cultural memory. Thus the differences of gender, politics, and class that separate Behn and Richardson, casting the first down into "oblivion" while the second is raised up into prominence, are conducted through the literary histories that translate them for a later age. Though literary historians attempt to be "unprejudiced" (Reeve) and embrace an ethos of "judgment, candour, and impartiality" (Coventry), and though their histories aspire to secure general moral or universal aesthetic grounds for critical judgment, the actual practice of literary history does not occlude but instead reflects cultural division.

Since one of the meanings of *gulf* is a "whirlpool, or absorbing eddy," I can accommodate my thesis about the novel's rise to Reeve's metaphor. The elevation of the new novel over the old novel of amorous intrigue produces a vortex or whirlpool within the land/seascape of eighteenth-century British culture. Where one kind of reading is thrown up, another is thrown down; where one kind of pleasure is licensed, another is discredited. This turbulent vortex of reciprocal appearance and disappearance is mis-seen as the origin of the novel. But in order for the elevated novel to appear, the novel of amorous intrigue must be made to disappear into a gulf of oblivion. Thus birth requires a burial, but only after the murder of the other novel. While this vortex first appears in the cultural strife of the 1740s, it is also readable in every subsequent literary history devised to tell of the novel's rise.

To apprehend "the rise of the novel" as a vortex of cultural conflict helps to refocus the way gender difference and strife crosscut the expansion of novel reading in early modern culture. In aligning romances with French fashions and insisting that both are distinctly female addictions, Coventry was repeating one of the clichés of his age. The romance was associated with women because of its popularity with women readers. Reeve, by casting *The Progress of Romance* in the form of a series of salon-like lectures and debates between Hortensius and Euphrasia (with Sophronia acting the role of a nonpartisan judge), inscribes the debate about romance and its value within a battle of the sexes. Euphrasia rejects Hortensius's sweeping critique of romances, first by asking how Hortensius can banish all "fiction" of questionable moral standards—for this would mean indicting the classical authors boys study in their youth—and then by rejecting any double standard by which novels might receive sweeping censure because they are the favorite reading of women. By exfoliating her account of the novel's progress in a series of lessons that finally wins the willing conversion of a skeptical male, Reeve's text acquires the shape and feel of a seduction. Hortensius seems to relent in his opposition to romance because of his high regard for Euphrasia. But the resolution of this staged debate does not overcome the deeper resonances of the gendered contest around romances and novels. The pejorative terms applied to romance (*fanciful, wishful, out of touch with reality,* etc.) are also applied to women. The favorable terms applied to novels (*realistic, rational, improving*) are congruent with those that describe the male as a politically responsible member of the public sphere.

Within the context of the debate about novels, it is not surprising that male and female critics offer different pathways toward the novel's elevation. In elevating the novel, Coventry follows Fielding's attempt to splice classical knowledge and criticism into the reading of the novel. Although John Dunlop, like Reeve, applies a modern, historicist, more or less tolerant horizon of scholarship to the novel, his appeal to philosophical grounds for evaluating fiction helps push the novel toward a monumental cultural role. In elevating the novel, Clara Reeve (like Mary Wollstonecraft and Laetitia Barbauld later) turns the novel into a form for transmitting social knowledge. Reeve ends her literary history by offering two lists to parents, guardians, and tutors, "intended chiefly for the female sex": "Books for Children" and "Books for Young Ladies." This two-stage course of reading includes fables, spellers, conduct books, periodical essays, and only one item on the second list we would describe as a novel—"Richardson's Works." Following this curriculum prepares young female minds for an informed and critical reading of the romances and novels Reeve has described in *The Progress of Romance.* Literary history acquires the pedagogical function it still serves in literary studies: it becomes a reading list with its entries contextualized by narrative.

The gendered divide that expresses itself throughout the course of the institutionalization of the novel in England and in the various accounts of its "rise" is only one instance, though perhaps the most pervasive and important one, of the partisanship David Perkins has detected in much literary history. Given the way literary history is used to shape pleasure and define value, how could it be different? Thus the various positions upon what constitutes the first novel, and implicitly, what is the most valuable paradigm of novelistic authorship, work within the earliest literary histories of the elevated novel, and are reflected in the divergent critical valuations of Richardson and Fielding. In this way, the rivalry of Richardson and Fielding on the market during the 1740s was reproduced in the earliest literary criticism and history of the novel. Coventry ignores Richardson in proclaiming Fielding's unheralded achievements, while Johnson's prescription for the novel's cultural role is rigged to favor Richardson's fictional practice. The antagonism of Richardson and Fielding expresses itself through the writings of Hazlitt, Coleridge, Scott, and every subsequent literary historian of their differences. This antagonism shows little sign of dissipating in our own day. It is not just that different values reflect themselves in divergent accounts of our cultural repertoire. There are also always different agendas for the future dispositions of pleasure and value. Thus recent feminist critics have found Richardson most useful in their critical work, but Fielding *not.*

The elevation of the novel and its countersigning by literary history is neither simply right nor wrong, good nor bad. New discursive formations——like the elevated novel—incite new and valuable cultural production. Thus, however unfair or tendentious its judgments about the early novels of Behn, Manley, and Haywood, literary history's sublimation of "the novel" enables the ambitious novelistic projects of the nineteenth and twentieth centuries. One example is the quixotic ambition to write "the Great American Novel." Literary history does not have to be fair, or oriented toward the categories we would now credit, in order for it to bear its effects into culture. Yet its judgments are also always—and interminably—open to revision. The appeals court of culture is always in session. The recent feminist revaluation of the women novelists of the early eighteenth century seems to depend upon a contemporary reinterpretation of what is happening in the novels of Behn, Manley, and Haywood: explicit treatments of gender, sexuality, and power that have critical currency in our own time.

The Rise of Debate about the Rise of the English Novel

This chapter's account of the cultural scandal of novel reading, and of the inventive responses of novelists and literary historians to that scandal, suggests a signal tendency of most literary histories of the novel. Like a museum, literary history turns the strife of history into a repertoire of forms. It does so by taking differences that may have motivated the writing or reading of novels within specific historical contexts—differences of religion, politics, class, social propriety, or ethical design, to name a few—and converts them into differences of kind. Thus, for example, the polemic between Rich-

ardson and Fielding about the sorts of narrative and character fiction should possess comes to represent, within literary history, two species of novel: the Richardson novel of psychology and sentiment, and the Fielding novel of social panorama and critique. The novels of amorous intrigue written by Behn and the early Haywood have a bad difference that puts them entirely outside the frame of literary history of the elevated novel.

Notice the reversal of vision that literary history effects. If we interpret the writings of Behn, Richardson, and Fielding as part of the cultural history of Britain, we can find complex patterns of antagonism and detect the conscious and unconscious efforts of each author to distinguish his or her writing from its antecedents. By differentiating his novels from Behn's, Richardson engenders many of the differences evident between their novels. By contrast, literary history "finds," upon the archival table of its investigations, different novels, which it then attempts to distinguish and classify. Differences among novels are no longer effects of history, but the initial data for literary classification. Thus the category "novel" acquires a paradoxical role: pregiven and yet belated in its arrival, "the novel" is made to appear ready at hand, but it is actually that which the literary history of the novel defines. Often presented as the humble, minimal, and preliminary axiom of a literary history, the idea of the novel operates within the literary history of canonical texts as a kind of law. Changes in the idea of the novel during the nineteenth century were a necessary precondition for the belated emergence of the novel's origins as a compelling enigma.

Through the nineteenth and twentieth centuries, the novel keeps rising, and *The Columbia History of the British Novel* is one more symptom of that movement. Space does not permit a full genealogy of the evolution of the question of the novel's origins. But I can offer a brief sketch of those changes whereby the question becomes one of the Gordian knots of literary studies. Over the course of the nineteenth and twentieth centuries, novels are collected, edited, reviewed, and taught in schools and universities. Three basic shifts in the category of "the novel" are concomitants of this modern institutionalization of the novel as an object of knowledge in literary studies. First the novel is nationalized. Novels were once considered the type of writing most likely to move easily across linguistic and national boundaries. The critics and literary historians I have quoted in this chapter found the romances and novels of different nations on the same shelves. Reeve and Dunlop discuss the novels of Cervantes, Marivaux, and Rousseau within the same conceptual coordinates as the novels of Richardson and Fielding. But in the nineteenth century, novels come to be understood as a type of writing particularly suited to representing the character, mores, landscape, and spirit of the nation. At its most significant, a novel is, in the phrase of the French literary historian Hippolyte Taine, an expression of "the voice of the people."

In the wake of this idea, a thesis develops that would never have occurred to Reeve or Dunlop: that the modern English novel has little or nothing to do with earlier novellas and romances, and thus it does not develop out of Italian, Spanish, or French precursors. Instead the novel is said to derive from distinctly English discourses: the journalism of Addison and Steele, the party writers of the reign of Queen Anne, the new Science, religious autobiography like Bunyan's, writers of travel and adventure, and so on. This position was first clearly enunciated by the nineteenth-century professor of English at Glasgow, Walter Raleigh, in his book *The English Novel* (1894). It has been developed much more fully in recent books by Michael McKeon and J. Paul Hunter. While Reeve's "progress of romance" and Dunlop's "history of fiction" are inclusively multinational, extending backward to ancient and medieval times and across the channel to include Continental romance and novella, national literary histories cut these temporal and spatial links. Traits of the British culture—empiricism, protestant individualism, moral seriousness, and a fondness for eccentric character—are promoted from secondary characteristics of novels which happened to have been written in England to primary radicals of the novel's generic identity.

By narrowing the vortex of the novel's formation, a nationalist British literary history produces a new object of cultural value now dubbed "the English novel." The English novel becomes the subject and eponymous protagonist in a series of literary histories written by Walter Raleigh (1894), George Saintsbury (1913), and Walter Allen (1954). The phrase appears again in the titles of William Lyon Phelps's *Advance of the English Novel* (1916), Ernest Baker's *History of the English Novel* (1924-1936), and Arnold Kettle's *Introduction to the English Novel* (1951). Within these literary histories, Richardson and Fielding and Smollett and Sterne become the "dream team" of eighteenth-century fiction, and, in Saintsbury's famous metaphor, they are the four wheels of that carriage of English fiction that, with its full modern development into a repeatable "formula" by Austen and Scott, is "set a-going to travel through the centuries." After Saintsbury, Defoe is added as a fifth early master of the English novel. With Ian Watt's *Rise of the Novel* (1957), the modifier "English" is implied but erased. Now the rise of "the English novel" marks the rise of "the" novel, that is, *all* novels. A synecdoche wags the dog. In this way a national literary history overcomes what has always worried the earliest promoters and elevators of the novel in Britain: the belatedness and indebtedness of English fiction.

The claim for the priority of the English novel made by this group of literary historians involves a shift in the novel's distinct identity: instead of consisting in its moral coherence, the novel's identity comes to derive from its adherence to some sort of realism. Although the kernel of this thesis is at least as old as the distinction between romance and novella defined by Congreve, Reeve, and others, the nineteenth century contributes an arduous and subtle development to the idea of what constitutes realism. With the development of the idea of society as an organic totality, the novel becomes—for Balzac, Dickens, and Eliot—uniquely appropriate for its study and analysis. Novelistic realism is complicated and enriched by those novelists—especially Flaubert and James—who undertake to aestheticize the novel. As art, the novel realizes its equality with poetry, and prepares itself for entrance into the "Great Tradition" (Leavis's 1948 title) of Western literature. The idea of the novel as art means that novel studies, and literary histories of the novel, come to privilege the novel's "form." Claims for the novel's formal coherence are not fatal to the idea of the novel's realistic imitation of social or psychic life. Instead the two ideas work together in literary histories from Ernest Baker's ten-volume *History of the English Novel* to Ian Watt's *Rise of the Novel* (1957). For Ian Watt "formal realism" becomes the distinctive characteristic of the novel and the crucial invention necessary for its "rise" to being the most influential linguistic vehicle of subjective experience.

With the idea of the novel's nationalism, its realism, and its power to express a personal interiority emerge three questions that have preoccupied scholarly study of the early British novel for at least one hundred years. Out of the concept of the novel's Englishness emerges a new question: how, where, and why does the *English* novel begin, originate, arise? This question is framed so as to assure that its answer will come from within the study of British culture. Once the novel is given a modern, relatively scientific epistemological mission—to be realistic in its representation of social and psychological life—one must ask, what constitutes realism? What form of writing should serve as the paradigm for novelistic mimesis? These are not so much questions that can be answered as a terrain for interminable negotiation and invention. Finally, how is the Englishness and realism of the novel implicated in the invention of the modern subject? With Watt, and those many critics and literary historians who have followed in his wake, the notion that the novel is a fully actualized form of a nation's literature, characterized by realism, is brought into alignment with two relatively new ideas about the novel's beginnings: its sudden birth and its distinctive modernity. Recently, new work on the novel's rise, influenced by Marxism, feminism, and poststructuralism, has sought to contest and complicate this classic interpretation of the rise of the novel.

Instead of trying to summarize this rich vein of work, I will close with an observation. The themes of the novel's modernity and sudden birth, its realism and aesthetic greatness, its expression of nationhood or moral guidance to the reader—whether formulated early or late in the novel's "progress"—all these themes serve to update the cultural project that unfolded in the eight decades after 1740, and that this essay has explored: the impulse to elevate the novel and to sublimate the pleasures it incites

---

FROM ROMANTICISM TO REALISM

Arnold Kettle (essay date 1951)

SOURCE: "Realism and Romance," in his *An Introduction to the English Novel*, 2d ed., Vol. 1, Hutchinson University Library, 1967, pp. 25-38.

[*In the following chapter from his history of the English novel, Kettle locates the origins of the novel in the traditions of the literary romance.*]

The moment we found ourselves, a few pages back, asking, by implication, the question, 'Why were the first novels written?' we had to begin thinking in terms of history, and it is essential that we should not run away from history. The rise and development of the English novel, like any other phenomenon in literature, can only be understood as a part of history.

History is not just something in a book; history is men's actions. History is life going on, changing, developing. We, too, are characters in history. Men make history. Every action of every man, consciously or not, is directed, satisfactorily or not, towards the solving of the myriad problems, gigantic and trivial, complex and random, first of keeping alive and then of 'living', with all that the word, after centuries of experience, implies. Living alters. It alters according to the degree to which man masters his problems, wins new battles with nature, solves the countless difficulties and possibilities of existing alongside other men. History is the process of change in living.

It is not by chance that the English novel dates from the eighteenth century. This does not mean, of course, that nothing like a novel existed before the year 1700 and then someone—Defoe presumably—waved a wand and there it was. We have already taken a glance at some of the writing on which the eighteenth-century novelists could draw. Nothing will come of nothing, and even the most original artist starts off from what has gone before.

The eighteenth-century novelists had on the one hand

the medieval romance and its successors, the courtly novels of Italy and France, and the English stories which in the sixteenth and seventeenth centuries had grown out of these two main sources: Lyly's *Euphues,* Sidney's *Arcadia,* Greene's *Menaphon,* Ford's *Ornatus and Artesia,* Congreve's *Incognita,* the stories of Mrs Aphra Behn, to mention only a few of the best known. And they had on the other hand the 'rogue' novels, the picaresque tradition which we have already briefly noticed. They had also translations from the classics (not to mention their originals) like *Daphnis and Chloe* and the *Golden Ass* and the *Satyricon* of Petronius. They had Boccaccio. They had Rabelais (Urquhart and Motteux' translation appearing between 1653 and 1694). They had the Authorised Version of the Bible. They had Cervantes. They had Bunyan.

It may appear pedantic to try to decide which of these writers should be called novelists. Certainly from many points of view it is of no importance what they are called, and certainly one does not wish to fall into a formalistic approach, than which there is little more futile. And yet, to avoid unnecessary confusion of terms, one or two definitions are inevitable.

The novel—as I use the term in this book—is a realistic prose fiction, complete in itself and of a certain length. Any such definition of a term so loosely and variously used over a long period is bound to be somewhat arbitrary. The question of length I leave, deliberately, vague. The point, I think, is that the novel is more than an anecdote and more than the exploration of one particular, more or less isolated, episode. Peacock's *Nightmare Abbey,* for instance, I take to be a novel, though a short one, while Conrad's *Heart of Darkness,* which is a little longer, I would class as a long short story; but such borderline problems are not really important.

The adjective 'realistic' is likely to need more justification. The words 'realism' and 'realistic' are used throughout this book in a very broad sense, to indicate 'relevant to real life' as opposed to 'romance' and 'romantic', by which are indicated escapism, wishful thinking, unrealism. The distinction is not, it must be insisted, between the photographic on the one hand and the fantastic and imaginative on the other. All art involves fantasy. A highly fantastic and superficially unlifelike story like *Gulliver's Travels* I class as realistic because it has to do with the actual problems and values of life. Mrs Radcliffe's *Udolpho* or P. C. Wren's *Beau Geste,* although presented as lifelike, are romance.

Clearly in both categories degree is important. Mrs Radcliffe's stories have more relevance to life than Mr Wren's, and it is not implied that a romance can have *no* serious value, merely that in it unrealism predominates. Similarly, nearly all fundamentally realistic novels have their romantic tint; some—like *Jane Eyre* and *Adam Bede*—are so shot through with romantic colouring as almost to cease to be serious works of art at all.

I do not pretend that either word is fully satisfactory: realism or romance. Realism has too many suggestions of mere photographic naturalism: Zola, Arnold Bennett and James T. Farrell. Romance is an even more dangerous word, on the one hand because of its connections with Romance (as opposed to Teutonic or Slav or Celtic) languages, on the other because of all the associations of the Romantic Movement, the fashionable denigrations of which one would not wish to support. But unfortunately no happier terms suggest themselves, and I therefore use realism and romance in the way I have indicated, conscious of the dangers involved, yet conscious also of the real and essential distinction underlying the terms.

If a novel is a realistic prose fiction, complete in itself and of a certain length, none of the books that have been mentioned as the store upon which the eighteenth-century writer had to draw—the fund of experience with which he began—is, with the exception of *Don Quixote* and, with certain reservations, *The Pilgrim's Progress,* a novel.

Apart from the picaresque stories, the *Satyricon,* Rabelais and the Bible, none of them is, in the sense I have indicated, realistic, though a number have realistic elements. While of the realistic stories none has the self-completeness, the unity of organisation and the length which we shall find to be characteristic of the novel. *The Unfortunate Traveller* is a series of episodes, a diary almost, with no beginning and no end. The *Satyricon,* as it has come down to us, is fragmentary. The Bible is only partially, in such books as *Esther, Ruth* and *Job,* written in the terms we are discussing. And even *Gargantua and Pantagruel,* superb, incredible masterpiece that it is, is less a novel than a gigantic chunk of novel-matter, the clay of half a dozen never quite organised novels.

Only Cervantes—the case of Bunyan is rather different—of all the prose writers to whom Defoe and Fielding and Richardson had access, was, in the sense we have come to give the term, a novelist. And Cervantes is indeed, with Rabelais, the great genius and architect of the modern novel. We shall see how direct and yet how subtle was his influence on Fielding and we shall see what it was that gave that influence its potency. But we cannot, in a book of this length, deal, even if we should wish to, with the question of formal 'influences'. The time has come to pose explicitly our first essential problem: why did the modern novel arise at all?

The answer can be put in a number of ways. The novel, we may say, arose as a realistic reaction to the medieval romance and its courtly descendants of the sixteenth and seventeenth centuries; the great eighteenth-century novels are nearly all anti-romances. Or the novel, we may say, arose with the growth for the first time of a large, widely distributed reading public; with the increase of literacy the demand for reading material naturally rose and the demand was greatest among well-to-do women who were the insatiable novel-readers of the time. For such a public, spread all over England in country houses, the theatre was not a feasible form of entertainment, but the novel was perfection. Hence the length of the novels (for their readers had only too much time on their hands), hence their tone, hence their number, hence (by the end of the eighteenth century) the circulating libraries. Or the novel, we may say, grew with the middle class, a new art-form based not on aristocratic patronage but on commercial publishing, an art-form written by and for the now-powerful commercial bourgeoisie.

These answers are all a part of the truth, but they are less than the whole of it. The whole answer cannot be condensed into a sentence and is as hard to grasp as history itself. We shall not understand the rise of the English novel unless we understand the meaning and importance of the English revolution of the seventeenth century.

Great revolutions in human society change men's consciousness and revolutionise not only their social relationships, but their outlook, their philosophy and their art. Feudalism, the society of the Middle Ages, had as its principal characteristic a peculiar rigidity of human relationships and ideas which sprang inevitably from the social structure.

The basic activity of feudal society was agriculture, the basic social unit the feudal estate or manor. Towns, though they gradually grew in importance, were the exception, not the rule. The governing class, that small minority who alone had the leisure, the education, the wherewithal to develop a sophisticated art (as opposed to the unwritten folk-culture of the unlettered), owed their social superiority to their ownership of the land and their virtual ownership of their serfs. Their chief concern, inevitably, was to maintain that ownership. Since their wealth and power did not depend on technical advances, they could have no deep interest in scientific experiment or widespread education. On the contrary, their whole interest, their very existence as the kind of people they were, demanded the preservation (with whatever sanctions, spiritual and physical, that might be necessary) of the *status quo.*

All summaries and simplifications inevitably do violence to the infinitely rich and complex processes of social and cultural change. One cannot hope to do justice in a few sentences to the whole vast complicated medieval culture. What one would emphasise here (without suggesting for a moment that there is no more to be said) is the social rigidity and intellectual conservatism of the feudal order. Such an order was bound to produce art of a particular kind and its characteristic product in the realm of prose literature was the romance.

Romance* was the non-realistic, aristocratic literature of feudalism. It was non-realistic in the sense that its underlying purpose was not to help people cope in a positive way with the business of living but to transport them to a world different, idealised, *nicer* than their own. It was aristocratic because the attitudes it expressed and recommended were precisely the attitudes the ruling class wished (no doubt usually unconsciously) to encourage in order that their privileged position might be perpetuated. And romance performed, as it performs to this day, the double function of entertainment through titillation and the conveying in palatable form of a particular kind of philosophy of life.

Romance grew in popularity in the Middle Ages as social relationships and class differences under feudalism became increasingly rigid. The connection between the emergence of a leisured ruling class and the growth of romance is very significant. It is not, of course, that only the leisured read or listen to romantic literature; on the contrary its quality of 'substitute-living' (the evocation of a kinder, more glamorous world) especially recommends it to the unleisured, those who most need the consolations of an escape from a cruel or humdrum reality.

The important point is that as division of labour increases and classes become as a consequence more stratified the rulers come to adopt a way of life very different from that of the majority. They have long, by virtue of their ownership, lived better; now they come to live differently. The ruling-class men no longer actually till their own fields and sell their own chattels at market, but pay someone else (not necessarily in money) to do it. The ruling-class women, in particular, become less and less like the women of the people in activity and even in appearance. And so the ideas and attitudes of the ruling class inevitably become different. Their culture, in all its many forms, changes.

The directions in which it changes—as far as literature is concerned—all lead away from realism, the frank and uninhibited representation and consideration of the experiences and potentialities of the community as a whole.[9] For how can such complete frankness exist? Not only do the rulers have their own way of life and therefore their own standards and values which the people do not, cannot—except in their dreams and fantasies—share; the rulers also have their secrets, secrets they are not prepared to share with the people or even to express quite frankly and openly to themselves. And what now primarily interests the ruling class is not the people's way of life (the word 'vulgar', originally connoting simply 'of the people' takes on new overtones), but the achievement of a culture which not merely pleases but actually strengthens and defends their class. Such a culture relies, is bound to rely, not on realism (even though the occasional realistic and—to that extent—revolutionary artist, like Chaucer, appears) but on romance.

Romance, in the first place, delights and entertains the rulers without bringing them face to face with realities they would sooner put behind them. The wimpled lady of the feudal court and her modern counterpart who steps out of her limousine to ask the attendant at the circulating library for a 'nice book' are one and the same. In the second place it builds, for the edification and pleasure of those unfortunate enough to find themselves outside the privileged *élite,* a fantasy, a pseudo-world, seductive or sad, delightful or horrible, which has one unfailing quality: that, however remote it may be from reality, the values and attitudes it incorporates are such as are least likely to undermine the theories and practice of class society.

Closely connected with, indeed inseparable from, the escapist nature of romance is its function as a form of titillation, a function that has had a profound influence on the modern novel. The bulk of medieval romances did not enlarge the consciousness of their audience in any helpful way, neither does *The Blue Lagoon;* but they did give their audience a kick, so does *The Postman Always Rings Twice.* The aim of such literature is not to sum up experience, not to enlarge the imagination, and not merely to provide an escape from the sordid (in many modern cases it is rather an escape *to* the sordid), but to provide sensation for sensation's sake. It thrives on the boredom and cynicism, the blasé and jaded unfulfilment of people who have too little to do or too little purpose and satisfaction in what they do do. Its crudest form is pornography: but it has many other forms less crude though scarcely more desirable.

The world to which medieval romance transported its audience was a world of chivalry and exciting adventures, of gallant men and charming women, of bad magicians and Christian gentlemen *sans peur et sans reproche,* above all of idealised love. It is not sufficient to label this world escapist and imagine one has explained it away. All art is, in an important sense, an escape. Nor is it enough to refer to romance's idealised picture of the world as though idealisation were a form of original sin and needed no more explicit condemnation. There is a sense in which the capacity to escape from his present experience, to use his accumulated consciousness of the past to project a vision of the future, is man's greatest and distinguishing ability. We must not forget the force of Aristotle's argument that poetry is valuable precisely because it shows men not simply as they are, but as they ought to be or (in terms more sympathetic to us today) as they are capable of becoming. This fantastic quality of art, that it takes us out of the real world so that, as Shelley put it, it 'awakens and enlarges the mind itself by rendering it the receptacle of a thousand unapprehended combinations of thought', this quality is not a trivial or accidental by-product but the very essence of the value of art. If art did in fact—as the ultra-naturalistic school tends to assume—merely paint a picture of what is, it would be a much less valuable form of human activity, for it would not alter men's consciousness but merely confirm it.

What we should remember, then, about romance, is not that it involves an escape, but a particular kind of escape. Medieval romance makes no attempt to give an impression of life in the lands and times it is dealing with, but it does attempt 'to use its subject matter as a means of conveying a new philosophy'. Dr Vinaver, in the Introduction to his monumental edition of *The Works of Thomas Malory,* writes: 'Whatever the subject of the narrative (of the courtly romance) its primary function . . . was to serve as the expression of the thoughts and emotions inspired by courtly idealism, to translate in terms of actions and characters the subtle varieties of courtly sentiment and the highly sophisticated code of courtly behaviour.'[10] And this is as true of the seventeenth-century prose romances like *Ornatus and Artesia* as it is of the twelfth-and thirteenth-century poets to whom Dr Vinaver is here referring.

The didactic element in romance is important. The picture of gallant knights and their ladies (usually married to somebody else) told a story which not merely elevated the feudal idea of chivalry, but as often as not had a religious sanction too. One of the principal results of the Christian world-picture in medieval romance (a world-picture generally superimposed upon an older, pagan mythology) was to emphasise a tendency to the over-simplification of ethical questions. Life becomes a battle between Good and Evil. Characters, instead of being realistic, that is to say human, that is to say neither wholly good nor wholly bad, tend to become entirely black or white. This is the effect of imposing a static, idealist moral code upon the actual movement and complexity of human behaviour. A static pattern imposed upon a changing, developing object is bound to be inadequate. The best of the romances, of course (much of Malory for instance), avoid these crudities and come thereby that much nearer realism and life.

The impulse towards realism in prose literature was part and parcel of the breakdown of feudalism and of the revolution that transformed the feudal world. Because today the term bourgeois is connected in our minds with people well-established, comfortable, conservative, it is not easy for us to think of the bourgeoisie as a revolutionary class. But we must recall that this was the very class which in seventeenth-century England organised the remarkable, democratic New Model Army, cut off the King's head and established the republican Commonwealth. The commercial bourgeoisie were revolutionaries against the feudal order because the feudal order denied them freedom. It denied them freedom, physically, legally, spiritually, to do what they wanted to do, to develop the way they needs must develop.

The feudal world, based on static property-relationships, exalting an unchanging, God-ordained hierarchy in Church and State, was a prison to the rising commercial class and to their artists and thinkers.' Freedom to trade, freedom to explore, freedom to investigate, freedom to invent, freedom to evolve an adequate philosophy, these were the supreme, undeniable needs of the men of the new society, and for them they were prepared, as men always must be for their necessary freedoms, to die. They were prepared to risk death on the high seas or on the battlefields; they were prepared, in full consciousness and with the black horror of the medieval hell as the reward of error, to go to the block or to the fire. And the bourgeois writers, exalted by their vision of

> a world of profit and delight,
>   Of power and honour and omnipotence,

were revolutionaries too, prepared like Faustus to play for the very highest and most desperate stakes in their task of forging a new literature adequate and helpful to the revolutionary consciousness of their age.

In the late sixteenth and the seventeenth centuries, the critical period of revolutionary transformation, the main emphasis and achievement in literature was in poetry. In the eighteenth century it is in prose. The shift corresponds to the changing needs and spirit of society.

Most of us tend to assume, until we think more carefully about it, that prose is simpler, more 'natural' and therefore probably older than poetry. But we now know from anthropologists that poetry is almost certainly a more primitive and historically an earlier development than prose. Because early literature is oral and not written down it is hard to get to know very much about it, and only slowly are we beginning to delve into the fascinating problems of the origins of literature. Such a study is not, however, an academic one in the narrow sense, indeed it is one from which the pedants tend to sheer off because it brings them up against too many inconvenient questions (the whole issue is therefore too often shelved on the grounds that we have not sufficient objective material).

The basic questions involved are: what is the *purpose* of poetry and prose? What functions do they perform in primitive society and why therefore do they arise? Clearly in the light of such questions many of the stock 'theories' of literature, that it is 'self-expression', that it gives delight, that it has something to do with the eternal verities, are hopelessly inadequate. Obviously literature expresses the self of the author (though when we recall that in primitive art there is often no one 'author' the problem becomes less simple); obviously it gives delight (or no one would like reading it); obviously it has something to do with long-term truths (or we would get nothing out of Homer today); the important questions are, why? In what way? How does literature work?

It seems reasonably certain that while the earliest poetry in primitive society is connected with ritual and work and is, in Christopher Caudwell's words, 'the language of collective speech and public emotion',[11] prose or non-rhythmical speech is the language of private persuasion. Poetry arises before prose not only because (in a period when writing is not yet practised) it is easier to remember and hand on (that is a consequence rather than a cause), but because it helps the people in their necessary common rituals through which they achieve their collective ability to master nature. The primitive affinity of poetry is with magic.

Prose arises later as science gradually supersedes magic and conscious control replaces instinctive emotion. Prose is a later, more sophisticated use of language than primitive poetry precisely because it presupposes a more objective, controlled and conscious view of reality. Stories—'images of men's changing lives organised in time'—can only come into existence as men become conscious, however imperfectly, of social processes and man's complicated, unending struggle against nature. This *objective* quality of prose, that it makes coherent some facet of outer reality already apprehended, is very significant. It explains, for instance, why it is more possible to translate a novel than a poem. And it explains why in eighteenth-century England there should have been a particular impulse towards prose-writing. For literature to the bourgeois writers of this period was, above all, a means of taking stock of the new society. A medium which could express a realistic and objective curiosity about man and his world, this was what they were after. It was the search for such a medium that led Fielding to describe *Joseph Andrews* as a 'comic epic poem in prose'. Their task was not so much to adapt themselves to a revolutionary situation as to cull and examine what that revolution had produced. They were themselves revolutionaries only in the sense that they participated in the consequences of a revolution; they were more free and therefore more realistic than their predecessors to just

the extent and in just those ways that the English bourgeois revolution involved in fact an increase in human freedom.

We must not push too far this distinction between prose and poetry because in practice the two interpenetrate and it would be disastrous to underestimate the degree to which *all* modern novelists use language poetically. But we will do well, nevertheless, to bear in mind some of the fundamental problems involved in this difficult subject. Two points in particular are worth emphasising.

In the first place I think it is as well to approach the study of a great body of prose literature, such as the English novel, with the realisation that prose is not just poetry's plain sister, a haphazard, prosaic (how significant the word is!), inferior, easy alternative to verse, but that it is a great and wonderful field of human activity and experiment. I think it is good to realise that the development of prose-writing is not a mean or humdrum part of man's history, but that it is linked close to his continuous, infinitely rich and various struggle to control his world and transform it, to evolve a philosophy adequate to his necessities and a society adequate to his desires. And particularly it is worth bearing in mind that prose is an advanced, subtle, precise form of human expression, presupposing a formidable self-consciousness, a delicacy of control which it has taken human beings untold centuries to acquire.

Secondly, I believe even this superficial glance at the origins of literature gives us a clue to our question: why did the novel arise when it did? Why did the medieval romance not continue to satisfy the needs of the men and women of the bourgeois revolution?

The answer, at bottom, is that the bourgeoisie, in order to win its freedom from the feudal order, had to tear the veil of romance from the face of feudalism. To the bourgeois man, as we have seen, feudal society was not satisfying but frustrating. And so he felt no impulse to defend that society and no sympathy with a literature designed to recommend its values and conceal its limitations. On the contrary his every need and instinct urged him to expose and undermine feudal standards and sanctities. Unlike the feudal ruling class he did not feel himself immediately threatened by revelations of the truth about the world and so he was not afraid of realism.

Notes

* I should make quite clear that I am not referring to the great medieval epics—such as the *Niebelungenlied* or the *Chanson de Roland*—which are not romance in the sense I use the word.

Ian Watt (essay date 1957)

SOURCE: "Realism and the Novel Form," in his *The Rise of the Novel*, University of California Press, 1957, pp. 9-34.

[*In the following excerpt, Watt maintains that a naturalistic or realistic literary technique, rather than subnect matter, is the esential defining characteristic of the realist novel of the eighteenth century.*]

There are still no wholly satisfactory answers to many of the general questions which anyone interested in the early eighteenth-century novelists and their works is likely to ask: Is the novel a new literary form? And if we assume, as is commonly done, that it is, and that it was begun by Defoe, Richardson and Fielding, how does it differ from the prose fiction of the past, from that of Greece, for example, or that of the Middle Ages, or of seventeenth-century France? And is there any reason why these differences appeared when and where they did?

Such large questions are never easy to approach, much less to answer, and they are particularly difficult in this case because Defoe, Richardson and Fielding do not in the usual sense constitute a literary school. Indeed their works show so little sign of mutual influence and are so different in nature that at first sight it appears that our curiosity about the rise of the novel is unlikely to find any satisfaction other than the meagre one afforded by the terms 'genius' and 'accident', the twin faces on the Janus of the dead ends of literary history. We cannot, of course, do without them: on the other hand there is not much we can do with them. The present inquiry therefore takes another direction: assuming that the appearance of our first three novelists within a single generation was probably not sheer accident, and that their geniuses could not have created the new form unless the conditions of the time had also been favourable, it attempts to discover what these favourable conditions in the literary and social situation were, and in what ways Defoe, Richardson and Fielding were its beneficiaries.

For this investigation our first need is a working definition of the characteristics of the novel—a definition sufficiently narrow to exclude previous types of narrative and yet broad enough to apply to whatever is usually put in the novel category. The novelists themselves do not help us very much here. It is true that both Richardson and Fielding saw themselves as founders of a new kind of writing, and that both viewed their work as involving a break with the old-fashioned romances; but neither they nor their contemporaries provide us with the kind of char-acterisation of the new genre that we need; indeed they did not even canonise the changed nature of their fiction by a change in nomenclature—our usage of the term 'novel' was not fully established until the end of the eighteenth century.

With the help of their larger perspective the historians of the novel have been able to do much more to determine the idiosyncratic features of the new form. Briefly, they have seen 'realism' as the defining characteristic which differentiates the work of the early eighteenth-century novelists from previous fiction. With their picture—that of writers otherwise different but alike in this quality of 'realism'—one's initial reservation must surely be that the term itself needs further explanation, if only because to use it without qualification as a defining characteristic of the novel might otherwise carry the invidious suggestion that all previous writers and literary forms pursued the unreal.

The main critical associations of the term 'realism' are with the French school of Realists. 'Réalisme' was apparently first used as an aesthetic description in 1835 to denote the 'vérité humaine' of Rembrandt as opposed to the 'idéalité poétique' of neo-classical painting; it was later consecrated as a specifically literary term by the foundation in 1856 of *Réalisme,* a journal edited by Duranty.[1]

Unfortunately much of the usefulness of the word was soon lost in the bitter controversies over the 'low' subjects and allegedly immoral tendencies of Flaubert and his successors. As a result, 'realism' came to be used primarily as the antonym of 'idealism', and this sense, which is actually a reflection of the position taken by the enemies of the French Realists, has in fact coloured much critical and historical writing about the novel. The prehistory of the form has commonly been envisaged as a matter of tracing the continuity between all earlier fiction which portrayed low life: the story of the Ephesian matron is 'realistic' because it shows that sexual appetite is stronger than wifely sorrow; and the fabliau or the picaresque tale are 'realistic' because economic or carnal motives are given pride of place in their presentation of human behaviour. By the same implicit premise, the English eighteenth-century novelists, together with Furetière, Scarron and Lesage in France, are regarded as the eventual climax of this tradition: the 'realism' of the novels of Defoe, Richardson and Fielding is closely associated with the fact that Moll Flanders is a thief, Pamela a hypocrite, and Tom Jones a fornicator.

This use of 'realism', however, has the grave defect of obscuring what is probably the most original feature of the novel form. If the novel were realistic merely because it saw life from the seamy side, it would only be an inverted romance; but in fact it surely attempts to portray all the varieties of human experience, and not merely those suited to one particular literary perspective: the novel's realism does not reside in the kind of life it presents, but in the way it presents it.

This, of course, is very close to the position of the French Realists themselves, who asserted that if their novels tended to differ from the more flattering pictures of humanity presented by many established ethical, social, and literary codes, it was merely because they were the product of a more dispassionate and scientific scrutiny of life than had ever been attempted before. It is far from clear that this ideal of scientific objectivity is desirable, and it certainly cannot be realised in practice: nevertheless it is very significant that, in the first sustained effort of the new genre to become critically aware of its aims and methods, the French Realists should have drawn attention to an issue which the novel raises more sharply than any other literary form—the problem of the correspondence between the literary work and the reality which it imitates. This is essentially an epistemological problem, and it therefore seems likely that the nature of the novel's realism, whether in the early eighteenth century or later, can best be clarified by the help of those professionally concerned with the analysis of concepts, the philosophers.

I

By a paradox that will surprise only the neophyte, the term 'realism' in philosophy is most strictly applied to a view of reality diametrically opposed to that of common usage—to the view held by the scholastic Realists of the Middle Ages that it is universals, classes or abstractions, and not the particular, concrete objects of sense-perception, which are the true 'realities'. This, at first sight, appears unhelpful, since in the novel, more than in any other genre, general truths only exist *post res;* but the very unfamiliarity of the point of view of scholastic Realism at least serves to draw attention to a characteristic of the novel which is analogous to the changed philosophical meaning of 'realism' today: the novel arose in the modern period, a period whose general intellectual orientation was most decisively separated from its classical and mediaeval heritage by its rejection—or at least its attempted rejection—of universals.[2]

Modern realism, of course, begins from the position that truth can be discovered by the individual through his senses: it has its origins in Descartes and Locke, and received its first full formulation by Thomas Reid in the middle of the eighteenth century.[3] But the view that the external world is real, and that our senses give us a true report of it, obviously does not in itself throw much light on literary realism; since almost everyone, in all ages, has in one way or another been forced to some such conclusion about the external world by his own experience, literature has always been to some extent exposed to the same epistemological naïveté. Further, the distinctive tenets of realist epistemology, and the controversies associated with them, are for the most part much too specialised in nature to have much

bearing on literature. What is important to the novel in philosophical realism is much less specific; it is rather the general temper of realist thought, the methods of investigation it has used, and the kinds of problems it has raised.

The general temper of philosophical realism has been critical, anti-traditional and innovating; its method has been the study of the particulars of experience by the individual investigator, who, ideally at least, is free from the body of past assumptions and traditional beliefs; and it has given a peculiar importance to semantics, to the problem of the nature of the correspondence between words and reality. All of these features of philosophical realism have analogies to distinctive features of the novel form, analogies which draw attention to the characteristic kind of correspondence between life and literature which has obtained in prose fiction since the novels of Defoe and Richardson.

(a)

The greatness of Descartes was primarily one of method, of the thoroughness of his determination to accept nothing on trust; and his *Discourse on Method* (1637) and his *Meditations* did much to bring about the modern assumption whereby the pursuit of truth is conceived of as a wholly individual matter, logically independent of the tradition of past thought, and indeed as more likely to be arrived at by a departure from it.

The novel is the form of literature which most fully reflects this individualist and innovating reorientation. Previous literary forms had reflected the general tendency of their cultures to make conformity to traditional practice the major test of truth: the plots of classical and renaissance epic, for example, were based on past history or fable, and the merits of the author's treatment were judged largely according to a view of literary decorum derived from the accepted models in the genre. This literary traditionalism was first and most fully challenged by the novel, whose primary criterion was truth to individual experience—individual experience which is always unique and therefore new. The novel is thus the logical literary vehicle of a culture which, in the last few centuries, has set an unprecedented value on originality, on the novel; and it is therefore well named.

This emphasis on the new accounts for some of the critical difficulties which the novel is widely agreed to present. When we judge a work in another genre, a recognition of its literary models is often important and sometimes essential; our evaluation depends to a large extent on our analysis of the author's skill in handling the appropriate formal conventions. On the other hand, it is surely very damaging for a novel to be in any sense an imitation of another literary work: and the reason for this seems to be that since the novelist's primary task is to convey the impression of fidelity to human experience, attention to any pre-established formal conventions can only endanger his success. What is often felt as the formlessness of the novel, as compared, say, with tragedy or the ode, probably follows from this: the poverty of the novel's formal conventions would seem to be the price it must pay for its realism.

But the absence of formal conventions in the novel is unimportant compared to its rejection of traditional plots. Plot, of course, is not a simple matter, and the degree of its originality or otherwise is never easy to determine; nevertheless a broad and necessarily summary comparison between the novel and previous literary forms reveals an important difference: Defoe and Richardson are the first great writers in our literature who did not take their plots from mythology, history, legend or previous literature. In this they differ from Chaucer, Spenser, Shakespeare and Milton, for instance, who, like the writers of Greece and Rome, habitually used traditional plots; and who did so, in the last analysis, because they accepted the general premise of their times that, since Nature is essentially complete and unchanging, its records, whether scriptural, legendary or historical, constitute a definitive repertoire of human experience.

This point of view continued to be expressed until the nineteenth century; the opponents of Balzac, for example, used it to deride his preoccupation with contemporary and, in their view, ephemeral reality. But at the same time, from the Renaissance onwards, there was a growing tendency for individual experience to replace collective tradition as the ultimate arbiter of reality; and this transition would seem to constitute an important part of the general cultural background of the rise of the novel.

It is significant that the trend in favour of originality found its first powerful expression in England, and in the eighteenth century; the very word 'original' took on its modern meaning at this time, by a semantic reversal which is a parallel to the change in the meaning of 'realism'. We have seen that, from the mediaeval belief in the reality of universals, 'realism' had come to denote a belief in the individual apprehension of reality through the senses: similarly the term 'original' which in the Middle Ages had meant 'having existed from the first' came to mean 'underived, independent, first-hand'; and by the time that Edward Young in his epoch-making *Conjectures on Original Composition* (1759) hailed Richardson as 'a genius as well moral as original',[4] the word could be used as a term of praise meaning 'novel or fresh in character or style'.

The novel's use of non-traditional plots is an early and probably independent manifestation of this emphasis. When Defoe, for example, began to write fiction he took little notice of the dominant critical theory of the day, which still inclined towards the use of traditional plots; instead, he merely allowed his narrative order to flow spontaneously from his own sense of what his protagonists might plausibly do next. In so doing Defoe initiated an important new tendency in fiction: his total subordination of the plot to the pattern of the autobiographical memoir is as defiant an assertion of the primacy of individual experience in the novel as Descartes's *cogito ergo sum* was in philosophy.

After Defoe, Richardson and Fielding in their very different ways continued what was to become the novel's usual practice, the use of non-traditional plots, either wholly invented or based in part on a contemporary incident. It cannot be claimed that either of them completely achieved that interpenetration of plot, character and emergent moral theme which is found in the highest examples of the art of the novel. But it must be remembered that the task was not an easy one, particularly at a time when the established literary outlet for the creative imagination lay in eliciting an individual pattern and a contemporary significance from a plot that was not itself novel.

(b)

Much else besides the plot had to be changed in the tradition of fiction before the novel could embody the individual apprehension of reality as freely as the method of Descartes and Locke allowed their thought to spring from the immediate facts of consciousness. To begin with, the actors in the plot and the scene of their actions had to be placed in a new literary perspective: the plot had to be acted out by particular people in particular circumstances, rather than, as had been common in the past, by general human types against a background primarily determined by the appropriate literary convention.

This literary change was analogous to the rejection of universals and the emphasis on particulars which characterises philosophic realism. Aristotle might have agreed with Locke's primary assumption, that it was the senses which 'at first let in particular ideas, and furnish the empty cabinet' of the mind.[5] But he would have gone on to insist that the scrutiny of particular cases was of little value in itself; the proper intellectual task of man was to rally against the meaningless flux of sensation, and achieve a knowledge of the universals which alone constituted the ultimate and immutable reality.[6] It is this generalising emphasis which gives most Western thought until the seventeenth century a strong enough family resemblance to outweigh all its other multifarious differences: similarly when in 1713 Berkeley's Philonous affirmed that 'it is an universally received maxim, that *everything which exists is particular*',[7] he was stating the opposite modern tendency which in turn gives modern thought since Descartes a certain unity of outlook and method.

Here, again, both the new trends in philosophy and the related formal characteristics of the novel were contrary to the dominant literary outlook. For the critical tradition in the early eighteenth century was still governed by the strong classical preference for the general and universal: the proper object of literature remained *quod semper quod ubique ab omnibus creditum est.* This preference was particularly pronounced in the neo-Platonist tendency, which had always been strong in the romance, and which was becoming of increasing importance in literary criticism and aesthetics generally. Shaftesbury, for instance, in his *Essay on the Freedom of Wit and Humour* (1709), expressed the distaste of this school of thought for particularity in literature and art very emphatically: 'The variety of Nature is such, as to distinguish every thing she forms, by a *peculiar* original character; which, if strictly observed, will make the subject appear unlike to anything extant in the world besides. But this effect the good poet and painter seek industriously to prevent. They hate *minuteness,* and are afraid of *singularity.* '[8] He continued: 'The mere Face-Painter, indeed, has little in common with the Poet; but, like the mere Historian, copies what he sees, and minutely traces every feature, and odd mark'; and concluded confidently that ''Tis otherwise with men of invention and design'.

Despite Shaftesbury's engaging finality, however, a contrary aesthetic tendency in favour of particularity soon began to assert itself, largely as a result of the application to literary problems of the psychological approach of Hobbes and Locke. Lord Kames was perhaps the most forthright early spokesman of this tendency. In his *Elements of Criticism* (1762) he declared that 'abstract or general terms have no good effect in any composition for amusement; because it is only of particular objects that images can be formed';[9] and Kames went on to claim that, contrary to general opinion, Shakespeare's appeal lay in the fact that 'every article in his descriptions is particular, as in nature'.

In this matter, as in that of originality, Defoe and Richardson established the characteristic literary direction of the novel form long before it could count on any support from critical theory. Not all will agree with Kames that 'every article' in Shakespeare's descriptions is particular; but particularity of description has always been considered typical of the narrative manner of *Robinson Crusoe* and *Pamela.* Richardson's first biographer, indeed, Mrs. Barbauld, described his genius in terms of an analogy which has continually figured in the controversy between neoclassical generality and realistic particularity. Sir Joshua Reynolds, for example, expressed his neo-

classical orthodoxy by preferring the 'great and general ideas' of Italian painting to the 'literal truth and . . . minute exactness in the detail of nature modified by accident' of the Dutch school;[10] whereas the French Realists, it will be remembered, had followed the 'vérité humaine' of Rembrandt, rather than the 'idéalité poétique' of the classical school. Mrs. Barbauld accurately indicated Richardson's position in this conflict when she wrote that he had 'the accuracy of finish of a Dutch painter . . . content to produce effects by the patient labour of minuteness'.[11] Both he and Defoe, in fact, were heedless of Shaftesbury's scorn, and like Rembrandt were content to be 'mere facepainters and historians'.

The concept of realistic particularity in literature is itself somewhat too general to be capable of concrete demonstration: for such demonstration to be possible the relationship of realistic particularity to some specific aspects of narrative technique must first be established. Two such aspects suggest themselves as of especial importance in the novel—characterisation, and presentation of background: the novel is surely distinguished from other genres and from previous forms of fiction by the amount of attention it habitually accords both to the individualisation of its characters and to the detailed presentation of their environment.

(c)

Philosophically the particularising approach to character resolves itself into the problem of defining the individual person. Once Descartes had given the thought processes within the individual's consciousness supreme importance, the philosophical problems connected with personal identity naturally attracted a great deal of attention. In England, for example, Locke, Bishop Butler, Berkeley, Hume and Reid all debated the issue, and the controversy even reached the pages of the *Spectator.*[12]

The parallel here between the tradition of realist thought and the formal innovations of the early novelists is obvious: both philosophers and novelists paid greater attention to the particular individual than had been common before. But the great attention paid in the novel to the particularisation of character is itself such a large question that we will consider only one of its more manageable aspects: the way that the novelist typically indicates his intention of presenting a character as a particular individual by naming him in exactly the same way as particular individuals are named in ordinary life.

Logically the problem of individual identity is closely related to the epistemological status of proper names; for, in the words of Hobbes, 'Proper names bring to mind one thing only; universals recall any one of many'.[13] Proper names have exactly the same function in social life: they are the verbal expression of the particular identity of each individual person. In literature, however, this function of proper names was first fully established in the novel.

Characters in previous forms of literature, of course, were usually given proper names; but the kind of names actually used showed that the author was not trying to establish his characters as completely individualised entities. The precepts of classical and renaissance criticism agreed with the practice of their literature in preferring either historical names or type names. In either case, the names set the characters in the context of a large body of expectations primarily formed from past literature, rather than from the context of contemporary life. Even in comedy, where characters were not usually historical but invented, the names were supposed to be 'characteristic', as Aristotle tells us,[14] and they tended to remain so until long after the rise of the novel.

Earlier types of prose fiction had also tended to use proper names that were characteristic, or non-particular and unrealistic in some other way; names that either, like those of Rabelais, Sidney or Bunyan, denoted particular qualities, or like those of Lyly, Aphra Behn or Mrs. Manley, carried foreign, archaic or literary connotations which excluded any suggestion of real and contemporary life. The primarily literary and conventional orientation of these proper names was further attested by the fact that there was usually only one of them—Mr. Badman or Euphues; unlike people in ordinary life, the characters of fiction did not have both given name and surname.

The early novelists, however, made an extremely significant break with tradition, and named their characters in such a way as to suggest that they were to be regarded as particular individuals in the contemporary social environment. Defoe's use of proper names is casual and sometimes contradictory; but he very rarely gives names that are conventional or fanciful—one possible exception, Roxana, is a pseudonym which is fully explained; and most of the main characters such as Robinson Crusoe or Moll Flanders have complete and realistic names or aliases. Richardson continued this practice, but was much more careful and gave all of his major characters, and even most of his minor ones, both a given name and a surname. He also faced a minor but not unimportant problem in novel writing, that of giving names that are subtly appropriate and suggestive, yet sound like ordinary realistic ones. Thus the romance-connotations of Pamela are controlled by the commonplace family name of Andrews; both Clarissa Harlowe and Robert Lovelace are in many ways appropriately named; and indeed nearly all Richardson's proper names, from Mrs. *Sin*clair to Sir Charles *Grand*ison, sound authentic and are yet suited to the personalities of the bearers.

Fielding, as an anonymous contemporary critic pointed out, christened his characters 'not with fantastic high-sounding Names, but such as, tho' they sometimes had some reference to the Character, had a more modern termination'.[15] Such names as Heartfree, Allworthy and Square are certainly modernised versions of the type name, although they are just credible; even Western or Tom Jones suggest very strongly that Fielding had his eye as much on the general type as on the particular individual. This, however, does not controvert the present argument, for it will surely be generally agreed that Fielding's practice in the naming, and indeed in the whole portrayal of his characters, is a departure from the usual treatment of these matters in the novel. Not, as we have seen in Richardson's case, that there is no place in the novel for proper names that are in some way appropriate to the character concerned: but that this appropriateness must not be such as to impair the primary function of the name, which is to symbolise the fact that the character is to be regarded as though he were a particular person and not a type.

Fielding, indeed, seems to have realised this by the time he came to write his last novel, *Amelia:* there his neo-classical preference for type-names finds expression only in such minor characters as Justice Thrasher and Bondum the bailiff; and all the main characters— the Booths, Miss Matthews, Dr. Harrison, Colonel James, Sergeant Atkinson, Captain Trent and Mrs. Bennet, for example—have ordinary and contemporary names. There is, indeed, some evidence that Fielding, like some modern novelists, took these names somewhat at random from a printed list of contemporary persons—all the surnames given above are in the list of subscribers to the 1724 folio edition of Gilbert Burnet's *History of His Own Time,* an edition which Fielding is known to have owned.[16]

Whether this is so or not, it is certain that Fielding made considerable and increasing concessions to the custom initiated by Defoe and Richardson of using ordinary contemporary proper names for their characters. Although this custom was not always followed by some of the later eighteenth-century novelists, such as Smollett and Sterne, it was later established as part of the tradition of the form; and, as Henry James pointed out with respect to Trollope's fecund cleric Mr. Quiverful,[17] the novelist can only break with the tradition at the cost of destroying the reader's belief in the literal reality of the character concerned.

(d)

Locke had defined personal identity as an identity of consciousness through duration in time; the individual was in touch with his own continuing identity through memory of his past thoughts and actions.[18] This lo-cation of the source of personal identity in the repertoire of its memories was continued by Hume:

'Had we no memory, we never should have any notion of causation, nor consequently of that chain of causes and effects, which constitute our self or person'.[19] Such a point of view is characteristic of the novel; many novelists, from Sterne to Proust, have made their subject the exploration of the personality as it is defined in the interpenetration of its past and present self-awareness.

Time is an essential category in another related but more external approach to the problem of defining the individuality of any object. The 'principle of individuation' accepted by Locke was that of existence at a particular locus in space and time: since, as he wrote, 'ideas become general by separating from them the circumstances of time and place',[20] so they become particular only when both these circumstances are specified. In the same way the characters of the novel can only be individualised if they are set in a background of particularised time and place.

Both the philosophy and the literature of Greece and Rome were deeply influenced by Plato's view that the Forms or Ideas were the ultimate realities behind the concrete objects of the temporal world. These forms were conceived as timeless and unchanging,[21] and thus reflected the basic premise of their civilisation in general that nothing happened or could happen whose fundamental meaning was not independent of the flux of time. This premise is diametrically opposed to the outlook which has established itself since the Renaissance, and which views time, not only as a crucial dimension of the physical world, but as the shaping force of man's individual and collective history.

The novel is in nothing so characteristic of our culture as in the way that it reflects this characteristic orientation of modern thought. E. M. Forster sees the portrayal of 'life by time' as the distinctive role which the novel has added to literature's more ancient preoccupation with portraying 'life by values';[22] Spengler's perspective for the rise of the novel is the need of 'ultrahistorical' modern man for a literary form capable of dealing with 'the whole of life';[23] while more recently Northrop Frye has seen the 'alliance of time and Western man' as the defining characteristic of the novel compared with other genres.[24]

We have already considered one aspect of the importance which the novel allots the time dimension: its break with the earlier literary tradition of using timeless stories to mirror the unchanging moral verities. The novel's plot is also distinguished from most previous fiction by its use of past experience as the cause of present action: a causal connection operating through time replaces the reliance of earlier narratives on disguises and coincidences, and this tends to give the novel a much more cohesive structure. Even more important, perhaps, is the effect upon characterisation of the novel's insistence on the time process. The most obvious and extreme example of this is the stream of consciousness novel which purports to present a direct quotation of what occurs in the individual mind under the impact of the temporal flux; but the novel in general has interested itself much more than any other literary form in the development of its characters in the course of time. Finally, the novel's detailed depiction of the concerns of everyday life also depends upon its power over the time dimension: T. H. Green pointed out that much of man's life had tended to be almost unavailable to literary representation merely as a result of its slowness;[25] the novel's closeness to the texture of daily experience directly depends upon its employment of a much more minutely discriminated time-scale than had previously been employed in narrative.

The role of time in ancient, mediaeval and renaissance literature is certainly very different from that in the novel. The restriction of the action of tragedy to twenty-four hours, for example, the celebrated unity of time, is really a denial of the importance of the temporal dimension in human life; for, in accord with the classical world's view of reality as subsisting in timeless universals, it implies that the truth about existence can be as fully unfolded in the space of a day as in the space of a lifetime. The equally celebrated personifications of time as the winged chariot or the grim reaper reveal an essentially similar outlook. They focus attention, not on the temporal flux, but on the supremely timeless fact of death; their role is to overwhelm our awareness of daily life so that we shall be prepared to face eternity. Both these personifications, in fact, resemble the doctrine of the unity of time in that they are fundamentally a-historical, and are therefore equally typical of the very minor importance accorded to the temporal dimension in most literature previous to the novel.

Shakespeare's sense of the historical past, for example, is very different from the modern one. Troy and Rome, the Plantagenets and the Tudors, none of them are far enough back to be very different from the present or from each other. In this Shakespeare reflects the view of his age: he had been dead for thirty years before the word 'anachronism' first appeared in English,[26] and he was still very close to the mediaeval conception of history by which, whatever the period, the wheel of time churns out the same eternally applicable *exempla*.

This a-historical outlook is associated with a striking lack of interest in the minute-by-minute and day-to-day temporal setting, a lack of interest which has caused the time scheme of so many plays both by Shakespeare and by most of his predecessors from Aeschylus onwards, to baffle later editors and critics. The attitude to time in early fiction is very similar; the sequence of events is set in a very abstract continuum of time and space, and allows very little importance to time as a factor in human relationships. Coleridge noted the 'marvellous independence and true imaginative absence of all particular space or time in the "Faerie Queene"';[27] and the temporal dimension of Bunyan's allegories or the heroic romances is equally vague and unparticularised.

Soon, however, the modern sense of time began to permeate many areas of thought. The late seventeenth century witnessed the rise of a more objective study of history and therefore of a deeper sense of the difference between the past and the present.[28] At the same time Newton and Locke presented a new analysis of the temporal process;[29] it became a slower and more mechanical sense of duration which was minutely enough discriminated to measure the falling of objects or the succession of thoughts in the mind.

These new emphases are reflected in the novels of Defoe. His fiction is the first which presents us with a picture both of the individual life in its larger perspective as a historical process, and in its closer view which shows the process being acted out against the background of the most ephemeral thoughts and actions. It is true that the time scales of his novels are sometimes both contradictory in themselves, and inconsistent with their pretended historical setting, but the mere fact that such objections arise is surely a tribute to the way the characters are felt by the reader to be rooted in the temporal dimension. We obviously could not think of making such objections seriously to Sidney's *Arcadia* or *The Pilgrim's Progress*; there is not enough evidence of the reality of time for any sense of discrepancies to be possible. Defoe does give us such evidence. At his best, he convinces us completely that his narrative is occurring at a particular place and at a particular time, and our memory of his novels consists largely of these vividly realised moments in the lives of his characters, moments which are loosely strung together to form a convincing biographical perspective. We have a sense of personal identity subsisting through duration and yet being changed by the flow of experience.

This impression is much more strongly and completely realised in Richardson. He was very careful to locate all his events of his narrative in an unprecedentedly detailed time-scheme: the superscription of each letter gives us the day of the week, and often the time of the day; and this in turn acts as an objective framework for the even greater temporal detail of the letters themselves—we are told, for example, that Clarissa died at 6.40 P.M. on Thursday, 7th September. Richardson's use of the letter form also induced in the reader a continual sense of actual participation in the action which was until then unparalleled in its completeness and intensity. He knew, as he wrote in the 'Preface' to *Clarissa,* that it was 'Critical situations . . . with what

may be called *instantaneous* descriptions and reflections' that engaged the attention best; and in many scenes the pace of the narrative was slowed down by minute description to something very near that of actual experience. In these scenes Richardson achieved for the novel what D. W. Griffith's technique of the 'close-up' did for the film: added a new dimension to the representation of reality.

Fielding approached the problem of time in his novels from a more external and traditional point of view. In *Shamela* he poured scorn on Richardson's use of the present tense: 'Mrs. Jervis and I are just in bed, and the door unlocked; if my master should come—Odsbobs! I hear him just coming in at the door. You see I write in the present tense, as Parson William says. Well, he is in bed between us . . .'[30] In *Tom Jones* he indicated his intention of being much more selective than Richardson in his handling of the time dimension: 'We intend . . . rather to pursue the method of those writers who profess to disclose the revolutions of countries, than to imitate the painful and voluminous historian, who, to preserve the regularity of his series, thinks himself obliged to fill up as much paper with the detail of months and years in which nothing remarkable happened, as he employs upon those notable eras when the greatest scenes have been transacted on the human stage'.[31] At the same time, however, *Tom Jones* introduced one interesting innovation in the fictional treatment of time. Fielding seems to have used an almanac, that symbol of the diffusion of an objective sense of time by the printing press: with slight exceptions, nearly all the events of his novel are chronologically consistent, not only in relation to each other, and to the time that each stage of the journey of the various characters from the West Country to London would actually have taken, but also in relation to such external considerations as the proper phases of the moon and the time-table of the Jacobite rebellion in 1745, the supposed year of the action.[32]

(e)

In the present context, as in many others, space is the necessary correlative of time. Logically the individual, particular case is defined by reference to two co-ordinates, space and time. Psychologically, as Coleridge pointed out, our idea of time is 'always blended with the idea of space'.[33] The two dimensions, indeed, are for many practical purposes inseparable, as is suggested by the fact that the words 'present' and 'minute' can refer to either dimension; while introspection shows that we cannot easily visualise any particular moment of existence without setting it in its spatial context also.

Place was traditionally almost as general and vague as time in tragedy, comedy and romance. Shakespeare, as Johnson tells us, 'had no regard to distinction of time or place';[34] and Sidney's *Arcadia* was as unlocalized as the Bohemian limbos of the Elizabethan stage. In the picaresque novel, it is true, and in Bunyan, there are many passages of vivid and particularised physical description; but they are incidental and fragmentary. Defoe would seem to be the first of our writers who visualised the whole of his narrative as though it occurred in an actual physical environment. His attention to the description of milieu is still intermittent; but occasional vivid details supplement the continual implication of his narrative and make us attach Robinson Crusoe and Moll Flanders much more completely to their environments than is the case with previous fictional characters. Characteristically, this solidity of setting is particularly noticeable in Defoe's treatment of movable objects in the physical world: in *Moll Flanders* there is much linen and gold to be counted, while Robinson Crusoe's island is full of memorable pieces of clothing and hardware.

Richardson, once again occupying the central place in the development of the technique of narrative realism, carried the process much further. There is little description of natural scenery, but considerable attention is paid to interiors throughout his novels. Pamela's residences in Lincolnshire and Bedfordshire are real enough prisons; we are given a highly detailed description of Grandison Hall; and some of the descriptions in *Clarissa* anticipate Balzac's skill in making the setting of the novel a pervasive operating force—the Harlowe mansion becomes a terrifyingly real physical and moral environment.

Here, too, Fielding is some way from Richardson's particularity. He gives us no full interiors, and his frequent landscape descriptions are very conventionalised. Nevertheless *Tom Jones* features the first Gothic mansion in the history of the novel:[35] and Fielding is as careful about the topography of his action as he is about its chronology; many of the places on Tom Jones's route to London are given by name, and the exact location of the others is implied by various other kinds of evidence.

In general, then, although there is nothing in the eighteenth-century novel which equals the opening chapters of *Le Rouge et le noir* or *Le Père Goriot,* chapters which at once indicate the importance which Stendhal and Balzac attach to the environment in their total picture of life, there is no doubt that the pursuit of verisimilitude led Defoe, Richardson and Fielding to initiate that power of 'putting man wholly into his physical setting' which constitutes for Allen Tate the distinctive capacity of the novel form;[36] and the considerable extent to which they succeeded is not the least of the factors which differentiate them from previous writers of fiction and which explain their importance in the tradition of the new form.

(f)

The various technical characteristics of the novel described above all seem to contribute to the furthering of an aim which the novelist shares with the philosopher—the production of what purports to be an authentic account of the actual experiences of individuals. This aim involved many other departures from the traditions of fiction besides those already mentioned. What is perhaps the most important of them, the adaptation of prose style to give an air of complete authenticity, is also closely related to one of the distinctive methodological emphases of philosophical realism.

Just as it was the Nominalist scepticism about language which began to undermine the attitude to universals held by the scholastic Realists, so modern realism soon found itself faced with the semantic problem. Words did not all stand for real objects, or did not stand for them in the same way, and philosophy was therefore faced with the problem of discovering their rationale. Locke's chapters at the end of the third Book of the *Essays Concerning Human Understanding* are probably the most important evidence of this trend in the seventeenth century. Much of what is said there about the proper use of words would exclude the great bulk of literature, since, as Locke sadly discovers, 'eloquence, like the fair sex', involves a pleasurable deceit.[1] On the other hand, it is interesting to note that although some of the abuses of language which Locke specified, such as figurative language, have been a regular feature of the romances, they are much rarer in the prose of Defoe and Richardson than in that of any previous writer of fiction.

The previous stylistic tradition for fiction was not primarily concerned with the correspondence of words to things, but rather with the extrinsic beauties which could be bestowed upon description and action by the use of rhetoric. Heliodorus's *Aethiopica* had established the tradition of linguistic ornateness in the Greek romances and the tradition had been continued in the Euphuism of John Lyly and Sidney, and in the elaborate conceits, or 'Phebus', of La Calprenede and Madeleine de Scudery. So even if the new writers of fiction had rejected the old tradition of mixing poetry with their prose, a tradition which has been followed even in narratives as completely devoted to the portrayal of low life as Petronius's *Satyricon*, there would still have remained a strong literary expectation that they would use language as a source of interest in its own right, rather than as a purely referential medium.

In any case, of course, the classical critical tradition in general has no use for the unadorned realistic description which such a use of language would imply. When the 9th *Tatler* (1709) introduced Swift's 'Description of the Morning' as a work where the author has 'run into a way perfectly new, and described things as they happen', it was being ironical. The implicit assumption of educated writers and critics was that an author's skill was shown, not in the closeness with which he made his words correspond to their objects, but in the literary sensitivity with which his style reflected the linguistic decorum appropriate to its subject. It is natural, therefore, that it is to writers outside the circle of wit that we should have to turn for our earliest examples of fictional narrative written in a prose which restricts itself almost entirely to a descriptive and denotative use of language. Natural, too, that both Defoe and Richardson should have been attacked by many of the better educated writers of the day for their clumsy and often inaccurate way of writing.

Their basically realistic intentions, of course, required something very different from the accepted modes of literary prose. It is true that the movement towards clear and easy prose in the late seventeeth century had done much to produce a mode of expression much better adapted to the realistic novel than had been available before; while the Lockean view of language was beginning to be reflected in literary theory–John Dennis, for example, proscribed imagery in certain cirmstances on the ground that it was unrealistic: 'No sort of imagery can ever be the language of grief. If a man complains in simile, I either laugh or sleep'. Nevertheless the prose norm of the Augustan period remained much too literary to be the natural voice of Moll Flanders or Pamela Andrews: and although the prose of Addison, for example, or Swift, is simple and direct enough, its ordered economy tends to suggest an acute summary rather than a full report of what it describes.

It is therefore likely that we must regard the break which Defoe and Richardson made with the accepted canons of prose style, not an incidental blemish, but rather as the price they had to pay for achieving the immediacy and closeness of the text to what is being described. With Defoe, this closeness is mainly physical, with Richardson mainly emotional, but in both we feel that the writer's exclusive aim is to make the words bring his object closer to us in all its concrete particularity, whatever the cost in repetition or parenthesis, or verbosity. Fielding, of course, did not break with the traditions of Augustan prose style or outlook. But it can be argued that this detracts from the authenticity of his narratives. Reading *Tom Jones* we do not imagine that we are eavesdropping on a new exploration of reality; the prose immediately informs us that exploratory operations have long since been accomplished, that we are to be spared that labour, and presented instead with a sifted and clarified report of the findings.

There is a curious antinomy here. On the one hand, Defoe and Richardson make an uncompromising application of the realist point of view in language and prose structure, and thereby forfeit other literary values. On the other hand, Fielding's stylistic virtues tend to interfere with his technique as a novelist, because a patent selectiveness of vision destroys our belief in the reality of report, or at least diverts our attention from the content of the report to the skill of the reporter. There would seem to be some inherent contradiction between the ancient and abiding literary values and the distinctive narrative technique of the novel.

That this may be so is suggested by a parallel with French fiction. In France, the classical critical outlook, with its emphasis on elegance and concision, was not fully challenged until the coming of Romanticism. It is perhaps partly for this reason that French fiction from *La Princesse de Clèves* to *Les Liaisons dangereuses* stands outside the main tradition of the novel. For all its psychological penetration and literary skill, we feel it is too stylish to be authentic. In this Madame de La Fayette and Choderlos de Laclos are the polar opposites of Defoe and Richardson, whose very diffuseness tends to act as a guarantee of the authenticity of their report, whose prose aims exclusively at what Locke defined as the proper purpose of language, 'to convey the knowledge of things',[38] and whose novels as a whole pretend to be no more than a transcription of real life—in Flaubert's words, 'le réel écrit'.

It would appear, then, that the function of language is much more largely referential in the novel than in other literary forms; that the genre itself works by exhaustive presentation rather than by elegant concentration. This fact would no doubt explain both why the novel is the most translatable of the genres; why many undoubtedly great novelists, from Richardson and Balzac to Hardy and Dostoevsky, often write gracelessly, and sometimes with downright vulgarity; and why the novel has less need of historical and literary commentary than other genres—its formal convention forces it to supply its own footnotes.

II

So much for the main analogies between realism in philosophy and literature. They are not proposed as exact; philosophy is one thing and literature is another. Nor do the analogies depend in any way on the presumption that the realist tradition in philosophy was a cause of the realism of the novel. That there was some influence is very likely, especially through Locke, whose thought everywhere pervades the eighteenth-century climate of opinion. But if a causal relationship of any importance exists it is probably much less direct: both the philosophical and the literary innovations must be seen as parallel manifestations of larger change—that vast transformation of Western civilisation since the Renaissance which has replaced the unified world picture of the Middle Ages with another very different one—one which presents us, essentially, with a developing but unplanned aggregate of particular individuals having particular experiences at particular times and at particular places.

Here, however, we are concerned with a much more limited conception, with the extent to which the analogy with philosophical realism helps to isolate and define the distinctive narrative mode of the novel. This, it has been suggested, is the sum of literary techniques whereby the novel's imitation of human life follows the procedures adopted by philosophical realism in its attempt to ascertain and report the truth. These procedures are by no means confined to philosophy; they tend, in fact, to be followed whenever the relation to reality of any report of an event is being investigated. The novel's mode of imitating reality may therefore be equally well summarised in terms of the procedures of another group of specialists in epistemology, the jury in a court of law. Their expectations, and those of the novel reader coincide in many ways: both want to know 'all the particulars' of a given case—the time and place of the occurrence; both must be satisfied as to the identities of the parties concerned, and will refuse to accept evidence about anyone called Sir Toby Belch or Mr. Badman—still less about a Chloe who has no surname and is 'common as the air'; and they also expect the witnesses to tell the story 'in his own words'. The jury, in fact, takes the 'circumstantial view of life', which T. H. Green[39] found to be the characteristic outlook of the novel.

The narrative method whereby the novel embodies this circumstantial view of life may be called its formal realism; formal, because the term realism does not here refer to any special literary doctrine or purpose, but only to a set of narrative procedures which are so commonly found together in the novel, and so rarely in other literary genres, that they may be regarded as typical of the form itself. Formal realism, in fact, is the narrative embodiment of a premise that Defoe and Richardson accepted very literally, but which is implicit in the novel form in general: the premise, or primary convention, that the novel is a full and authentic report of human experience, and is therefore under an obligation to satisfy its reader with such details of the story as the individuality of the actors concerned, the particulars of the times and places of their actions, details which are presented through a more largely referential use of language than is common in other literary forms.

Formal realism is, of course, like the rules of evidence, only a convention; and there is no reason why the report on human life which is presented by it should be in fact any truer than those presented through the very different conventions of other literary genres. The novel's air of total authenticity, indeed, does tend to authorise confusion on this point: and the tendency of some Realists and Naturalists to forget that the accurate transcription of actuality does not necessarily produce a work of any real truth or enduring literary value is no doubt partly responsible for the rather widespread distaste for Realism and all its works which is current today. This distaste, however, may also promote critical confusion by leading us into the opposite error; we must not allow an awareness of certain shortcomings in the aims of the Realist school to obscure the very considerable extent to which the novel in general, as much in Joyce as in Zola, employs the literary means here called formal realism. Nor must we forget that, although formal realism is only a convention, it has, like all literary conventions, its own peculiar advantages. There are important differences in the degree to which different literary forms imitate reality; and the formal realism of the novel allows a more immediate imitation of individual experience set in its temporal and spatial environment than do other literary forms. Consequently the novel's conventions make much smaller demands on the audience than do most literary conventions; and this surely explains why the majority of readers in the last two hundred years have found in the novel the literary form which most closely satisfies their wishes for a close correspondence between life and art. Nor are the advantages of the close and detailed correspondence to real life offered by formal realism limited to assisting the novel's popularity; they are also related to its most distinctive literary qualities, as we shall see.

In the strictest sense, of course, formal realism was not discovered by Defoe and Richardson; they only applied it much more completely than had been done before. Homer, for example, as Carlyle pointed out,[40] shared with them that outstanding 'clearness of sight' which is manifested in the 'detailed, ample and lovingly exact' descriptions that abound in their works; and there are many passages in later fiction, from *The Golden Ass* to *Aucassin and Nicolette,* from Chaucer to Bunyan, where the characters, their actions and their environment are presented with a particularity as authentic as that in any eighteenth-century novel. But there is an important difference: in Homer and in earlier prose fiction these passages are relatively rare, and tend to stand out from the surrounding narrative; the total literary structure was not consistently oriented in the direction of formal realism, and the plot especially, which was usually traditional and often highly improbable, was in direct conflict with its premises. Even when previous writers had overtly professed a wholly realistic aim, as did many seventeenth-century writers, they did not pursue it wholeheartedly. La Calprenède, Richard Head, Grimmelshausen, Bunyan, Aphra Behn, Furetière,[41] to mention only a few, had all asserted that their fictions were literally true; but their prefatory asseverations are no more convincing than the very similar ones to be found in most works of mediaeval hagiography. The aim of verisimilitude had not been deeply enough assimilated in either case to bring about the full rejection of all the non-realistic conventions that governed the genre.

For reasons to be considered in the next chapter, Defoe and Richardson were unprecedentedly independent of the literary conventions which might have interfered with their primary intentions, and they accepted the requirements of literal truth much more comprehensively. Of no fiction before Defoe's could Lamb have written, in terms very similar to those which Hazlitt used of Richardson,[1] 'It is like reading evidence in a court of Justice'.[2] Whether that is in itself a good thing is open to question; Defoe and Richardson would hardly deserve their reputation unless they had other and better claims on our attention. Nevertheless there can be little doubt that the development of a narrative method capable of creating such an impression is the most conspicuous manifestation of that mutation of prose fiction which we call the novel; the historical importance of Defoe and Richardson therefore primarily depends on the suddenness and completeness with which they brought into being what may be regarded as the lowest common denominator of the novel genre as a whole, its formal realism.

Notes

[1] See Bernard Weinberg, *French Realism: the Critical Reaction 1830-1870* (London, 1937), p. 114.

[2] See R. I. Aaron, *The Theory of Universals* (Oxford, 1952), pp. 18-41.

[3] See S. Z. Hasan, *Realism* (Cambridge, 1928), chs. 1 and 2.

[4] *Works* (1773), V, 125; see also Max Scheler, *Versuche zu einer Soziologie des Wissens* (München and Leipzig, 1924), pp. 104 ff.; Elizabeth L. Mann, 'The Problem of Originality in English Literary Criticism, 1750-1800', *PQ,* XVIII (1939), 97-118.

[5] *Essay Concerning Human Understanding* (1690), Bk. I, ch. 2, sect. xv.

[6] See *Posterior Analytics,* Bk. I, ch. 24; Bk. II, ch. 19.

[7] First *Dialogue between Hylas and Philonous,* 1713 (Berkeley, *Works,* ed. Luce and Jessop (London, 1949), II, 192).

[8] Pt. IV, sect. 3.

[9] 1763 ed., III, 198-199.

[10] *Idler,* No. 79 (1759). See also Scott Elledge, 'The Background and Development in English Criticism of the Theories of Generality and Particularity', *PMLA,* LX (1945), 161-174.

[11] *Correspondence of Samuel Richardson,* 1804, I, cxxxvii. For similar comments by contemporary French readers, see Joseph Texte, *Jean-Jacques Rousseau and the Cosmopolitan Spirit in Literature* (London, 1899), pp. 174-175.

[12] No. 578 (1714).

[13] *Leviathan* (1651), Pt. I, ch. 4.

[14] *Poetics,* ch. 9.

[15] *Essay on the New Species of Writing Founded by Mr. Fielding,* 1751, p. 18. This whole question is treated more fully in my 'The Naming of Characters in Defoe, Richardson and Fielding', *RES,* XXV (1949), 322-338.

[16] See Wilbur L. Cross, *History of Henry Fielding* (New Haven, 1918), I, 342-343.

[17] *Partial Portraits* (London, 1888), p. 118.

[18] *Human Understanding,* Bk. II, ch. 27, sects. ix, x.

[19] *Treatise of Human Nature,* Bk. I, pt. 4, sect. vi.

[20] *Human Understanding,* Bk. III, ch. 3, sect. vi.

[21] Plato does not specifically state that the Ideas are timeless, but the notion, which dates from Aristotle (*Metaphysics,* Bk. XII, ch. 6), underlies the whole system of thought with which they are associated.

[22] *Aspects of the Novel* (London, 1949), pp. 29-31.

[23] *Decline of the West,* trans. Atkinson (London, 1928), I, 130-131.

[24] 'The Four Forms of Fiction', *Hudson Review,* II (1950), 596.

[25] 'Estimate of the Value and Influence of Works of Fiction in Modern Times' (1862), *Works,* ed. Nettleship (London, 1888), III, 36.

[26] See Herman J. Ebeling, 'The Word Anachronism', *MLN,* LII (1937), 120-121.

[27] *Selected Works,* ed. Potter (London, 1933), p. 333.

[28] See G. N. Clark, *The Later Stuarts, 1660-1714* (Oxford, 1934), pp. 362-366; René Wellek, *The Rise of English Literary History* (Chapel Hill, 1941), ch. 2.

[29] See especially Ernst Cassirer, 'Raum und Zeit', *Das Erkenntnisproblem . . .* (Berlin, 1922-23), II, 339-374.

[30] Letter 6.

[31] Bk. II, ch. I.

[32] As was shown by F. S. Dickson (Cross, *Henry Fielding,* II, 189-193).

[33] *Biographia Literaria,* ed. Shawcross (London, 1907), I, 87.

[34] 'Preface' (1765), *Johnson on Shakespeare,* ed. Raleigh (London, 1908), pp. 21-22.

[35] See Warren Hunting Smith, *Architecture in English Fiction* (New Haven, 1934), p. 65.

[36] 'Techniques of Fiction', in *Critiques and Essays on Modern Fiction, 1920-1951,* ed. Aldridge (New York, 1952), p. 41.

[37] *Human Understanding,* Bk. III, ch. 10, sect. xxiii.

[38] 'Estimate', *Works,* III, 37.

[39] 'Burns', *Critical and Miscellaneous Essays* (New York, 1899), I, 276-277.

[40] See A.J. Tieje, 'A Peculiar Phase of the Theory of Realism in Pre-Richardsonian Prose-Fiction', *PMLA,* XXVII (1913), 213-252.

[41] 'He sets about describing every object and transaction, as if the whole had been given in on evidence by an eye-witness' (*Lectures on the English Comic Writers* (New York, 1845), p. 138).

[42] Letter to Walter Wilson, Dec. 16, 1822, printed in the latter's *Memoirs of the Life and Times of Daniel de Foe* (London, 1830, III, 428).

F. W. J. Hemmings (essay date 1974)

SOURCE: "Realism and the Novel: The Eighteenth-Century Beginnings," in *The Age of Realism,* Penguin, 1974, pp. 9-35.

[*Below, Hemmings discusses literary realism in the epistolary tradition and in particular in Henry Fielding's novel* Tom Jones.]

The Epistolary Novel

In due course the novelists came to realize that their business was not to hoax the reader with these elaborate and, finally, transparent confidence-tricks, but rather to persuade him that what he experiences when reading is as real as what he might experience in the ordinary transactions of life. Between childhood and the grave, we all of us come into contact with hundreds of our fellow beings; but our knowledge of most of them, and hence their reality for us, is for the most part sketchy, superficial, and monochrome. If we were honest with ourselves, we would have to admit that they are a good deal less real to us than many of the characters in the novels we read. How many unmarried girls can anyone of us say we have known as we know Emma Woodhouse or Natasha Rostov? For what young man's romantic aspirations and foolish daydreams can we be as indulgent as we are for Lucien Leuwen's or Frédéric Moreau's? All this is tantamount to saying that—reality being what the mind perceives as reality—these creations of Jane Austen or Tolstoy, Stendhal or Flaubert, which never had any 'real' existence, are possessed none the less of a superlative reality thanks to some mystery or other of the novelist's craft.

We may say that these authors compel us to respond to their creations, to sympathize, in extreme cases to identify with them in a way we should find it almost impossible to identify with a living man or woman of our private acquaintance. Possibly the first occasion in literary history when a novel achieved a widespread effect of this kind was when Richardson's *Clarissa* started to come off the press. Just as, a century later, his readers wrote to Dickens with passionate pleas to spare this or that doomed child-hero or stricken heroine, so after the appearance of the first volumes of Richardson's masterpiece the author was beset by anxious followers of Clarissa's fortunes begging him to have Lovelace relent and marry her as Mr B—had married Pamela. Even Fielding hoped this might happen; and Richardson's friend Laetitia Pilkington reported to him the wild lamentations that Colley Cibber had broken into when he learned what fearful fate lay in store for this latter-day virgin and martyr.

Clarissa was quickly and badly translated into French by Prévost, and was soon as well known to Parisians as to Londoners. Diderot waited till he could read it in the original and then penned his *Éloge de Richardson* (published 1762), an extravagant and highly emotional encomium which, translated into German in 1766 and praised by Herder, served to propagate the cult of Richardson still further afield. The essential passage in this essay, where Diderot analyses in glowing terms the English novelist's gift of enlisting the reader's sympathy for his characters, runs as follows:

> O Richardson! one cannot but act a part in thy works, intervene in the dialogues, approve, disapprove, admire, wax wrathful or indignant. How many times have I not caught myself, like children taken to see a play for the first time, exclaiming: *Do not believe him, he deceives you! If you go thither, you are lost.* My soul was held in a constant state of agitation . . . I had encountered in the space of a few hours a great number of situations such as the longest life scarcely offers in its fullest span. I had heard the true accents of the passions; I had seen the motive forces of self-interest and self-love

working in a hundred different ways; I had been the spectator of countless incidents, I felt I had acquired experience.

It would seem that Richardson's realism was valued by Diderot because it was a substitute for, or an augmentation of, 'real' experience. And, as he goes on to say, this realism was fortified by the very ordinariness of everyone and everything in the book:

> The world in which we live is his setting; the backcloth of his drama true; his characters have the greatest possible reality; his types are drawn from the middling part of society; his incidents are compatible with the way of life of any civilized nation; the passions he depicts are such as I experience myself; the same factors provoke them, they have the strength that I know them to have; the misfortunes and afflictions of his characters are of the sort that threatens me ceaselessly; he shows me the general course of the stream that bears me along.

That such banality should excite such enthusiasm is something that cries out for explanation. Partly it is that Richardson's novels were bound to strike Diderot as breaking quite new ground in literature. As he wrote at the very beginning of his essay: "By a novel, we have meant hitherto a string of fanciful and frivolous incidents, to read which was dangerous for one's taste and one's morals. I wish some other word could be found for the works of Richardson . . .' But the novelty did not lie simply in the absence of 'fanciful and frivolous incidents'. The impact of *Clarissa* on the contemporary reading public was due above all to the form in which Richardson had couched his story. *Pamela* had been a novel-in-letters; but since nearly all the letters in it had been written by the heroine, the book might as well have been presented entirely as her diary. Equally, it would have been conceivable as an autobiographical novel, presenting the memoirs of the servant-girl graduating to squire's lady—another *Paysanne parvenue*. But in *Clarissa* Richardson made far more extensive use of the resources of the epistolary novel, and in consequence the book is scarcely imaginable written in any other way. There are two principal sets of correspondence: the exchange of letters between Clarissa and her friend Miss Howe, and that between Lovelace and his fellow rake Belford. The same intrigue is thus seen under a double perspective and, with no sacrifice of plausibility, we are allowed greater insight into the heroine's predicament than she obtains herself—something the memoir-novel by its very nature can never give us. Moreover, Clarissa Harlowe could never have written her own confessions, since her story ends, and has to end, with her death. Here we touch on yet another of the drawbacks of the autobiographical novel: the reader is necessarily conscious that, whatever distressful circumstances may at any moment beset the writer, he must have survived them or he would not be relating them to us. If death

is the ultimate calamity, then the first-person novel can never achieve the ultimate in tragedy.

None of this altogether explains why Diderot, and others like him but less articulate about their reactions, should have experienced so overwhelming a sense of oneness with the rather silly girl that Clarissa was, if one considers her conduct in cold blood; nor why they should have followed her fortunes with bated breath and, at the end, with horror and compassion. It may be noted in passing that when, in 1761, Jean-Jacques ROUSSEAU (1712-78) brought out *La Nouvelle Héloïse,* which must count as the first entirely successful epistolary novel in France, it was greeted with similar excitement: the eagerness to read it was so great that booksellers found they could make more money renting the volumes at twelve sous an hour than by selling them to would-be purchasers. La Harpe commented with sardonic ambiguity that 'the ladies whiled away the nights reading it which they could not employ any better'. Rousseau himself was astonished to receive letters from all manner of good people who were evidently completely persuaded that Julie, Saint-Preux, Lord Bomston and Baron Wolmar were real people: there could have been no better proof of his success as a literary illusionist.

Both these novels, Richardson's and Rousseau's, were extremely long. Each provided the most detailed account of every scene in which the characters were involved, the most meticulous analysis too of their emotional reactions to each scene. Sometimes this verged on the ridiculous: Saint-Preux goes so far as to indite a letter to Julie, describing his state of rapturous anticipation, when he is actually in her bedroom waiting for her to come upstairs and fulfil her promise to give herself to him. Such exhaustiveness may jar with modern tastes, but the eighteenth-century reader had the delicious feeling that, for the first time, nothing was being kept from him. This was life itself in all its fullness, in all its dullness too, enlivened by apprehensive shudders; for in these novels the events, tiny and insignificant though they may appear to be, are relayed to us by those whom they touch most closely and who have no means of knowing, at the moment of writing, whither these events are tending and what the outcome will be. The emotional impact was bound to be more powerful than in the memoir-novel, where everything was presented through the lens of retrospective knowledge. Richardson himself took care to point out the difference, and the immense advantage of the epistolary form, in his preface to *Clarissa:*

> *Much more* lively and affecting . . . must be the style of those who write in the height of a *present* distress, the mind tortured by the pangs of uncertainty (the events then hidden in the womb of fate); than the dry, narrative, unanimated style of

a person relating difficulties and dangers surmounted, can be; the relater perfectly at ease; and if himself unmoved by his own story, not likely greatly to affect his reader.

After *Clarissa* and *La Nouvelle Héloïse* the epistolary novel had a brief vogue, culminating in *Les Liaisons dangereuses* (1782), the only work of fiction ever composed by the artillery officer Pierre Choderlos de LACLOS (1741-1803). The subject apart, which caused this work to be twice banned by the civil courts in France, *Les Liaisons dangereuses* represented the high-water mark of technical achievement in the genre. It is relatively short, and very few of the component letters are of any great length. Laclos avoided the trap of including letters which obviously serve only the purpose of giving the reader of the novel—as distinct from the intended recipient—information about the development of events: every one of the letters is prompted by a clear need on the part of the writer to communicate something or other of importance to the addressee. He made splendidly ironic use of the 'multiple viewpoint', by which the same event is reported by two or three different witnesses, each knowing a little more than the other about the true circumstances underlying the event. Letters are used not merely to disclose what has happened, but to instigate new happenings; there is, indeed, one letter that drives the woman who receives it mad. Finally, Laclos showed himself a past master in the art of revealing character through the quirks of style of each of his letter-writers: we gain a remarkable insight into their standard of education, maturity of outlook, and degree of sophistication not just by noting what they say, but by observing how they say it.

It was a virtuoso performance which perhaps discouraged any further exploitation of the genre. The example Laclos gave, of so triumphantly overcoming the difficulties inherent in the epistolary novel, incidentally demonstrated how formidable were those difficulties for a would-be realist. For to present a narrative entirely through the medium of private letters is, as one of Richardson's early biographers admitted, 'the most natural and the least probable way of telling a story'.[16] The most natural because, after all, people do write letters—or did, at all events, in the eighteenth century. The least probable because it is hard to believe that a multitude of connected events are likely to be found all duly chronicled in an assortment of letters from various writers, or that all these letters should by some happy chance have been preserved. To carry conviction, the novelist had so to arrange matters that letters were not exchanged between two people who could more conveniently meet and converse by word of mouth. He had, if he could, to dispense with the give-away device of the inactive confidant who has to be kept faithfully posted regarding every development. He had to arrange sufficient privacy and leisure to make letter-writing not just a possible but a plausible occu-pation even for persons in the thick of some highly charged emotional drama. And when he had done all this, he was still faced with the fundamentally unrealistic assumption lying at the very heart of this form of novel, that a man or a woman is ever likely confidently and candidly to set out on paper, for perusal by a friend, a relative or a lover, all that he thinks, all that he feels, all his anxieties and expectations.

Fielding: 'Tom Jones'

Little wonder that the epistolary novel fell so rapidly into disuse, even more completely than the fictional autobiography. Balzac's vast output includes only one novel-by-letters (*Mémoires de deux jeunes mariées*) and only one novel written in the first person (*Le Lys dans la vallée*). Nineteenth-century realism rejected both the forms that eighteenth-century fiction-writers had spent most of their time and energy in developing, and preferred instead to concentrate on a third type of novel, of which there had been only one really outstanding example, Fielding's *Tom Jones* (1749).

Henry Fielding (1707-54), unlike Richardson, had received the education of a gentleman (at Eton College), which meant that he was well-versed in the Greek and Latin classics and could read French. His first novel, *Joseph Andrews* (1742), which started as a satire on Richardson's *Pamela* but in its later stages developed a momentum of its own, owed something to *Gil Blas* and rather more than something to Marivaux's *Paysan parvenu*. But by the time he came to write *Tom Jones* he seems to have freed himself from the influence of the French authors of fictional memoirs, and of their anxious concern to maintain the pretence that their novels were not novels at all but authentic accounts of the actual experiences of real people. Fielding cast his eyes further back, and took as his models the sturdy story-tellers of antiquity, the authors of the old epics. One need not take too seriously the intention he proclaimed, in the preface to the second part of *Joseph Andrews,* to write 'a comic epic poem in prose': the two qualifications effectively cancel out the central concept. What does need to be seen is how Fielding grasped the artistic possibilities of a long narrative capable of being held together by its own internal logic, without needing to be buttressed by any claims to external authentication. As a classicist, he believed that the chief function of art was 'to copy nature'; in the prefatory chapters to the various component books of *Tom Jones,* the theme recurs constantly: 'our business is only to record truth'; 'it is our province to relate facts, and we shall leave causes to persons of much higher genius.' The common run of fertile story-tellers were denounced for the arbitrary subjectivity of their creations: 'truth distinguishes our writings from those idle romances which are filled with monsters, the productions not of nature, but of distempered brains.' The truth in question was, of course, the truth about human nature: psychology, as we should call it today, but psychology in breadth, not in depth. Here, life itself, multifarious contacts with all manner of men, could alone give the novelist his schooling. 'A true knowledge of the world is gained only by conversation, and the manners of every rank must be seen in order to be known.' The word *conversation,* in eighteenth-century English, meant more than just talk; it included 'the action of consorting with others', and clearly Mr Henry Fielding, the London magistrate, explayboy who was on familiar terms with the great as well as being in daily contact, professionally, with the riff-raff of the streets and the hardened criminal, was well-placed to write the first realist novel to mirror the whole range of English society, from the forelock-pulling rustic to the city fop and from the village hoyden to the luxurious lady of fashion. The mirror was, of course, angled: we are not given an entirely neutral account of the scene. Only a London-based Whig could have sketched the grotesque lineaments of the choleric, high-tory, sottish father of Sophia Western. Fielding, as Walter Allen has said, 'populated a whole world, but it exists as a considered criticism of the real world'.[17] But then, realism can never be altogether free of bias, and it is doubtful indeed whether a flatly photographic reproduction of human diversity should constitute the prime objective of art. Even at this time, the point had been taken by the greatest English critic of the age: 'If the world be promiscuously described, I cannot see of what use it can be to read the account; or why it may not be as safe to turn the eye immediately upon mankind, as upon a mirror which shows all that presents itself without discrimination.'[18]

Fielding exercised his discrimination not merely in his portraiture but in the formal organization of his work. To find a novel as carefully wrought as *Tom Jones* one needs to go back to *La Princesse de Clèves:* significantly, a product of classicism in its finest flowering. It has been suggested that in respect of the impeccable construction of his masterpiece Fielding may have been indebted to his earlier study of the French classical dramatists: he had started his literary career as a playwright. Only Sophocles' *Oedipus* and Ben Jonson's *Alchemist* seemed to Coleridge worthy to be compared to *Tom Jones* in point of structural perfection, while a professional novelist of a later generation (Thackeray) showed himself full of admiration for the 'literary providence' that Fielding displayed: 'Not an incident ever so trifling but advances the story, grows out of former incidents, and is connected with the whole.'[19] But, of course, such artifice, however well hidden, could be judged a distraction from the 'truth' that Fielding was aiming at. Life is not so tidy, and, as we have seen, the realist has to manage without providence, literary or divine.

This might seem an appropriate cautionary point with which to close this introductory chapter. All through

the 'age of realism' novelists will be faced with the same dilemma: social institutions, human relationships, the separate courses of individual lives, all these cannot be presented in a work of art without a certain measure of trimming and tailoring. An accurate reproduction of any 'slice of life' would be hopelessly unsatisfactory as literature: too formless, full of false trails and pointless anticlimaxes. However firm his allegiance to realism, a novelist has to impose his own peculiar vision on what he sees, partly because this vision is inseparable from his artistic consciousness, and partly because without it his work would lack shape and point and would finally prove unreadable. This underlying dilemma amounts to an internal contradiction at the very core of realism, one which was destined in the long run to discredit it, or at least to discredit its pretensions; but not before the struggle to achieve the impossible—a faithful representation of contemporary social reality which should yet be integrated into a smoothly consistent work of art—had resulted in the production of a series of striking literary masterpieces.

Notes

. . . [16] Anna Laetitia Barbauld, 'A Biographical Account of Samuel Richardson', introduction to the first volume of Richardson, *Correspondence* (1804). Quoted in Miriam Allott, *Novelists on the Novel* (London, 1959), p. 259.

[17] *The English Novel* (1954), Pelican Books edition, p. 63.

[18] S. Johnson, quoted in R. Wellek, *A History of Modern Criticism: the Later Eighteenth Century* (London, 1955), p. 85.

[19] Thackeray, *Critical Papers in Literature* (London, Macmillan, 1911), p. 207.

Clinton Bond (essay date 1994)

SOURCE: "Representing Reality: Strategies of Realism in the Early English Novel," in *Eighteenth Century Fiction,* Vol. 6, No. 2, January, 1994, pp. 121-40.

[*In the following excerpt, Bond analyzes realist techniques in the early novel, especially the work of Richardson.*]

> Some's fiction and some's not, and you can't be sure I wanted that feeling of when you're lying, people think you're telling the truth.[1]
>
> *Ken Kesey*

Alexander Pope read Samuel Richardson's *Pamela* "with great Approbation and Pleasure," and, according to Dr George Cheyne, commented that "it will do more good than a great many of the new Sermons."[2] However we read this comment, and I believe there are several layers of irony, Pope enjoyed the book well enough to make sure his appreciation and his understanding of it as a work of practical morality were forwarded to its author. His linking *Pamela* to the sermon would have won Richardson's gratitude, by placing it in that world of homiletic morality where Richardson consistently believed his works belonged. That *Pamela* was a fiction Pope did not doubt, but those features that make the text a novel for the modern reader apparently made little impression on him. He seems not to have responded to *Pamela*'s originality, nor did he recognize that the work's subtext attacked the world he had dedicated his life to defending.

Pope's sort of humanism, descended from the Roman Catholic thinkers of the sixteenth century, was in decline, and even though Pope would "not bear any faults to be mentioned in the story" of *Pamela*,[3] he was certainly willing to offer advice about the sequel, advice which Richardson could not or would not follow. Pope was so insensitive to the nature of the work that, according to Warburton, he suggested that Richardson turn the continuation of *Pamela* into a set of satirical "spy" letters, written by the naïve serving girl:

> Mr. Pope and I, talking over your work when the two last volumes came out, agreed, that one excellent subject of Pamela's letters in high life, would have been to have passed her judgment, on first stepping into it, on every thing she saw there, just as simple nature (and no one ever touched nature to the quick, as it were, more certainly and surely than you) dictated. The effect would have been this, that it would have produced, by good management, a most excellent and useful satire on all the follies and extravagancies of high life; which to one of Pamela's low station and good sense would have appeared as absurd and unaccountable as European polite vices and customs to an Indian. You easily conceive the effect this must have added to the entertainment of the book; and for the use, that is incontestable. And what could be more natural than this in Pamela, going into a new world, where every thing sensibly strikes a stranger.[4]

As a moral tale, Pope links *Pamela* to sermons and, as an epistolary tale, he links it to the *Lettres persanes* type of satirical comment—genres which, I argue below, were displaced and subverted by the novel.[5] Richardson, however, understood that what he had created was something very different and very new and, as we shall see, he sought to deflect Warburton's further solicitations when he readied *Clarissa* for publication.

As Pope's response to *Pamela* indicates, eighteenth-century novels were at first misunderstood; the tasks of the present essay are to explore the cultural fissures that separated authors and, more particularly, to discover what the unspoken and elusive claims of realistic fictions were. The novel's claim to be real, even—perhaps, particularly—while recognized as fiction, lies at the very heart of the genre, and should be seen less as a bizarre attempt to pass fiction as true than as a characteristic strategy built on the assertion that novels occupy exactly the same world—ideological and concrete—as their readers. Although they are preceded by a host of less successful attempts, *Pamela* and, more certainly, *Clarissa* stand out as probably the first texts in English which satisfactorily insert themselves into the world; as Edward Said remarks, such works insist "not only upon their circumstantial reality but also upon their status as *already* fulfilling a function, a reference, or a meaning in the world."[6] Because they already insist upon their "meaning" or particular function in the "real" world, it is clearly crucial to both the development of the genre and its place in the development of eighteenth-century culture that Richardson's first two novels operate as accomplices of other attempts to substantiate and revise a social and political world that had not yet come fully into being. This world, in many ways the one we call "modern," for the most part still holds ideological sway, but is beginning to be recognized as a "concept" to be penetrated and revealed as a creation of European humanism. Indeed, so powerful is the hold of eighteenth-century thought that even today, when "we have become uneasy about our whole way of constituting reality," many writers simply assume that in some way the Enlightenment represents transparent reality, and not merely the "age of realism."[7] Early novels, because they represented themselves as functioning parts of this world, anchoring themselves in realism, acted not only to refine but also to validate that connection between humanist ideology and "reality," which began in the Renaissance.

At the centre of the Richardsonian novel's relationship to the modern cultural formulation lies the claim that the world presented is the one true reality, a world that has moral meaning precisely because its patterns can be measured and reproduced as in the laboratory. Yet, at the same time, the concrete reality presented must be seen as peculiar and unique; that is, the "facts" of the novel should be specific and particular while simultaneously contributing to a general and repeatable pattern. On the general and repeatable, the early novelist seeks to impress a traditional pattern of morality. Richardson convinced himself that his primary goal was moral reformation, and he hoped that through *Clarissa* "the present age can be awakened and amended."[8] As I hope to show, however, the Richardsonian narrative never permits the sort of moral closure he sought, in part because the general pattern, as it was formulated by Richardson and other eighteenth-century novelists, is finally always subverted by the particular—the unique attributes characteristic of the "true History." I argue that it is the subversion of this mediation between particular moments and general notions that leads to the novel's "open" narrative flow, the feeling that the "novelist is drawn toward everything that is not yet completed."[9] At the conclusion of a novel, in spite of the author, we are left, not with a traditional homiletic pattern, but with something akin to the "lesson" Dr Johnson sought in biography: "to learn how a man 'was made happy; not how he lost the favour of his prince, but how he became discontented with himself.'"[10] Like Johnson's sort of biographical narrative, after much turmoil the novel eventually does forge a stable psychological acceptance of "reality," a psychic construct that is not merely an accommodation contained in traditional ideas about the world, but a limited and necessarily personal ordering and mastering.

Consequently, each time a reader seeks traditional patterns of coherence in a novel's action, more particulars intervene, forcing the acceptance of a character's (or narrator's) ever-changing psychological structuring.[11] This continuous restructuring of moral patterns—the constant subversion of stable or closed patterns by unstable or unanticipated incidents impossible to fit neatly into current constructions—parallels the novel's restructuring of traditional narrative patterns. Even though Richardson sought to place his novel within other, older, literary traditions—he speaks of *Clarissa* as "of the Tragic Kind" and as "the history (or rather dramatic narrative) of Clarissa"[12]—the actual experience of reading the book, the participation in its bewildering array of particularities, subverts his theorizing about the moral and formal goals of the novel.

In *Clarissa* the language rushes ever onward; the narrative is unquestionably "dramatic," but its world, unlike that of a drama compressed in time and space, seems sprawling and formless. Richardson uses literary techniques such as allusion and irony in his work, but they scarcely affect our perception of the narrative and operate essentially to provide his characters with poses struck only for the moment; they merely elucidate aspects of personality before the plunge back into the novel's relentlessly unfolding action. In some respects, of course, we can see that Clarissa is acting out the story of Job. This realization helps us later to understand some of the moral patterns in Richardson's mind, but we hardly stop to ponder the significance of the parallel as we read the novel. For Clarissa, in fact, the Bible only seems to come alive when she rearranges it in her meditations so that the scriptures more efficaciously reflect her peculiar case. Even Clarissa sacrifices the general moral pattern to the particular history, and its concomitant psychological reality.

Because the eighteenth-century novel stands in opposition to the "purer" artistry of the closed narrative and changes the ways fictions relate to readers and hence to society, it participates in a particularly crucial shift in the development of modern culture: the transformation of those habitual means and techniques for producing and disseminating ideologies that had, previously, largely been the province of political and ecclesiastical institutions. Novels, to my mind, subvert traditional representations and interpretations, rejecting what Foucault argues was the essential use of intellect in the sixteenth century: the "function proper to knowledge is not seeing or demonstrating; it is interpreting."[13] As Lennard Davis points out, this earlier "attitude toward reality diminishes the value of the literal train of events" because interpretation was meant to reinforce established institutions. Until the sixteenth century, discourse had been controlled, but humanism put into motion discourses which no one fully controlled or understood. Earlier, "Histories, stories, and news accounts . . . were important . . . only insofar as they clearly taught lessons and offered interpretations. If they were not new, if they were not accurate, or even if they were completely fabricated, they could still serve this purpose."[14] The closed narrative depends on interpretation and, hence, helps empower the institutional desire for social stability. The novel, on the contrary, is in the beginning at least a destabilizing force, relying first and foremost on the descriptive fact and in this way contributing to the establishment of a cultural reformulation that had been long in coming. According to Stephen Greenblatt, in the sixteenth century there was a shift "from the *consensus fidelium* embodied in the universal Catholic Church to the absolutist claims of the Book and the King";[15] but because, in Britain, the seventeenth century graphically and brutally declared the claim of "King" null and void and moved the "Book" from the absolutist claims of the church to the private, the individual, and the domestic, the shift from Church to King constitutes no more than a brief, although powerfully evoked, interlude. Only the shift to subjective representations of the Book created lasting changes. In addition to subverting the traditional structures of absolutism, this move inward paradoxically validates "the fact" and helps us trace a number of processes which we recognize as modern. The novel's appropriation of the fact and the individual's relation to it show how intimately connected it was to these cultural developments.[16] At the same time, the "new techniques of a minute parcellization and ordering of time, space and gesture," often remarked by Foucault,[17] create a new sort of openness. For example, in the developing economic structures of the seventeenth and eighteenth centuries, specificity reigned supreme; and yet so concrete an object as a contract, while binding particular individuals, could at the same time open the worlds of time and space. As Joyce Oldham Appleby remarks, "A single transaction could extend through the space of the globe and the lapse of a year, yet the connecting links were a letter dispatched, an instruction given, or two human beings engaged in a few minutes' negotiations."[18]

The novel at first seems to operate within a precise and traditional set of contraries, but the very execution of realistic particularity and psychological necessity generates new sets which demand new processes both for writing and reading these narratives. The early novelist claims that the work represents a "true History," singular and unreproducible, and yet the action (because the author asserts it is a "moral fiction") demands that it be interpreted as more than a particular history. As the novel grows, it changes (even while under the hand of the author) because the open narrative demands new and, in the early days of novelistic narratives, unanticipated sorts of formulations; new constructs appear because to a certain extent the author—even while striving to impose a moral pattern—is at the mercy of the forces unleashed: "fervent discussions around the gradually evolving Clarissa or Grandison, anguished contentions over their desirable destinies, became modes of ever finer ideological formulation, scrupulous probings of precise meanings. Transforming the production as well as consumption of his works into a social practice, Richardson half-converts himself from 'author' to the focal point of his readers' own writings."[19] Early novelists and readers discover that an open narrative continually resists the moral and coherent pattern, despite the author's attempt at control. The pre-eminence of realistic particularity and psychological realism distinguishes the works of Richardson and Defoe from those more traditional fictions derived from French prose, with their characteristically heavy doses of idealized incident and character; it was the treatment of realistic incident rather than the moral content which differentiated the early English masters of fiction from their French counterparts.[20] And this "treatment," by its own volition, created shifts which changed traditional structures; as these structures changed, the traditional ideological (and idealized) messages were invariably subverted.

As the new narrative form began the process of "becoming,"[21] it was rather roughly stitched together; no one saw the full scope of the enterprise. At those junctures where an author forced traditional patterns of morality onto the apparent patternlessness of realistic particularity without regard for his characters' developing perceptions, the seams between general and particular elements became obvious and disruptive. Defoe and Richardson are the first to produce seamless and realistic narratives, and even in their works ruptures occasionally occur. Some examples have been long noted; one celebrated incident occurs during Robinson Crusoe's musings while he ransacks the wrecked ship:

> I discover'd a Locker with Drawers in it, in one of which I found two or three Razors, and one Pair of large Sizzers, with some ten or a Dozen of good Knives and Forks; in another I found about Thirty six Pounds value in Money, some *European* Coin,

some *Brasil,* some Pieces of Eight, some Gold, some Silver.

> I smil'd to my self at the Sight of this Money, O Drug! Said I aloud, what art thou good for, Thou art not worth to me, no not the taking off of the Ground, one of those Knives is worth all this Heap, I have no Manner of use for thee, e'en remain where thou art, and go to the Bottom as a Creature whose Life is not worth saving. However, upon Second Thoughts, I took it away, and wrapping all this in a Piece of Canvas, I began to think of making another Raft.[22]

Here we see what happens when the essential struggle towards particularity becomes reversed, however briefly; in these paragraphs, Defoe permits the general moral platitude to efface Crusoe's habit of specificity. The traditional pattern of homiletic morality is so compelling for Defoe that the concrete situation is for a moment forgotten or ignored; it occupies such a different mental landscape that it no longer exists as a part of his visualization of the particular or as a characteristic habit of Crusoe's mind: this money, now abstracted in the moral imagination, is referred to in conventional terms as lying on the ground, whereas in the particulars of the story, it is in one of the locker's drawers. The platitude overwhelms the realist's artful habit of particularity; no matter how precisely the characters' inner shifts may be depicted during the course of the fiction, complete psychological coherence cannot be expected in early novels.

This passage has been crucial to arguments that Defoe's fictional narratives are intentionally ironic, but such a rupture can be thought of as intentional irony only by readers who come to it with interpretations forged by generations of more seamless narrative models. In fact, Defoe's passage represents a backward glance in novelistic discourse; it is a moment where the novel turns from the open narrative back towards an earlier form that had privileged textual interpretation in which particularity existed primarily as an opportunity for moral discourse. I do not wish to imply that the moral appeal of "natural law" did not exist for Defoe, but rather to argue that it was not finally what powered his narratives.[23] Even though the impulse towards general moral patterns seemed necessary to early novelists as they sought to square the world of realism with the world of natural moral law, their attempts were subverted by the methods of realism.

It was Richardson's genius to adapt epistolary techniques to the novel, and this adaptation enabled him to avoid many of the problems of coherency in earlier narratives. In some respects the epistolary novel constitutes the perfect metaphor for this developing form; the exchange of letters written "to the moment," with its point-counterpoint of ideas, and its potential for temporal confusion and intellectual contradiction, alleviates the need for seamless coherency while it emphasizes psychological development and realistic observation. Although the epistolary form, particularly when different letter writers are involved, creates the sort of "restless shifting of perspective" that has been associated with the dialogue and is increasingly recognized as a crucial component of the novel as a genre,[24] Richardson's use of the form demands that we attend to what is uppermost in the characters' minds, the physical implements for writing and the physical situations in which they write. The words themselves become objects to be perused with great care; at the same time the letters may seem ungraspable since they may be interpreted in ways that emphasize their open-endedness. They are at once concrete and infinitely changeable: "For writing . . . does indeed possess a body, a thick and violent material being: it is a matter of record and contract, seal and bond, tangible documentation which may be turned against its author, cited out of context, deployed as threat, testimony, blackmail."[25] Because they are open to such manipulations, and also because they are simply letters, often written in haste and with little thought for the morrow, they serve to separate the abstract idea from the deed described or the act observed: "letters lack the equilibrium of literature. They embody an emotional situation still in process; they are undetonated, on the brink."[26] In *Clarissa* the separation of the narrative into a group of writers exchanging letters with varying points of view further fragments our ability to grasp conceptually the actual progress of the narrative, and mirrors the sort of point-counterpoint of opinion which is characteristic of the novel. This fragmentation of perspective was consciously contrived by Richardson: "In this sort of writing, something, as I have hinted should be left (to the reader) to make out or debate upon. The whole story abounds with situations and circumstances debatable. It is not an unartful management to interest the readers so much in the story, as to make them differ in opinion as to the capital articles and by leading one, to espouse one, another, another, opinion, make them all, if not authors, carpers."[27] Moreover the very production of the novels themselves, throughout Richardson's life, involved seemingly endless discussions and obsessive revision: "The literary reception of his novels, as manuscripts pass from hand to hand and the flurry of letters increases, becomes an integral moment of their production, a constitutive force rather than retrospective response."[28] The link between a realistic discourse—the novel—and an actual social discourse concerning the unpublished text—its shape, its meaning, its relationship to reality—involves readers, authors, and characters in an extraordinary cultural matrix that, even after publication, defines the ways that authors, novels, and readers must interact.

Because these early novels, like the developing discourses of history and newspaper, demand that they be perceived as having real meaning in the world, they compel us to see the ideological pattern only as it is impressed on the fully realized world of the concrete, not the abstracted and allegorized world of the intellect. From the very beginning, the realistic novel has sought to secure its place in this particularized world—the only one we have, it argues. And thus even when acknowledging itself as fiction, it has refused to be designated as fiction: Richardson's "calculated hesitancy between fact and fiction is more than a generic muddle; it belongs to a fruitful crisis in the whole problem of literary representation. The term *fiction,* let alone the contemptible *novel,* is ideologically impermissible—not because of some puritan neurosis about lying, but because it would seem merely to devalue the reality of the issues at stake."[29] The novel came into the world insisting not only that it was already a part of that world but that the world it presented was already accomplished fact. It finally and firmly helped bind us to an apparently immutable culture that we have only now begun to perceive is, at least in part, a chosen fiction, made so to some extent unintentionally by a world powerless to withstand it. This is why we must attend to the novel's historical and social context, even though writers such as Jean-Marie Goulemot caution that as "literary historians, we know that the events related in fiction are not proper matter for sociological studies. First and foremost a novel yields information about novels: literary devices and their effects on the reader. To use fiction as a source from which to determine social and historical reality is risky and often misleading."[30] Risky and misleading, perhaps, but the literary historian has to recognize that our belief in "social and historical reality" depends, in part, on what novelists have taught us to see. For example, how do readers respond when Richardson asks them to draw precise conclusions about eighteenth-century social concerns, as he does in his footnote to letter 119 where Lovelace imagines his trial after the fantasy rape of Anna Howe? Richardson observes of Lovelace's wildly applauded—albeit imaginary—march from Newgate to the court-room of the Old Bailey: "Within these few years past, a passage has been made from the prison to the Sessions-house whereby malefactors are carried into court without going through the street. Lovelace's triumph on their supposed march shows the wisdom of this alteration" (2:423n). The novel claims to be true, and with that claim it turns an ideological construct into apparently unalterable fact. Thus when we are cautioned to separate "novel" from "society," we must respond that one of the forces which made our world was the realistic novel; even if we wish to read Lovelace's fantasy as Goulemot suggests, Richardson's note encourages us to slide not only to the margins of the text, but also to the margins of society.

Only when the characters themselves begin to grasp the significance of the novel's movement are they able to pause and read over the earlier letters which provide the keys to the novel's action, and finally comprehend their situations. Their comprehension, a necessary step towards the work's stability, is dependent on the immersion in particularity, not the withdrawal from it as in traditional interpretive gestures. After the moment of comprehension, a character may choose to withdraw from the social world, as Clarissa does, but this is a different sort of distancing, one still subject to the "law" of particularity and dependent on the understanding of characters and readers. So much that is contradictory or new is revealed before the novel arrives at its dénouement that we resist any design which simplifies the action or the characterizations. Notably, this resistance occurs in the footnotes which Richardson added to later editions of *Clarissa* to convince us that Lovelace's character is consistently base. We react to these notes with disbelief, refusing to acknowledge that the creator of Lovelace understands him any better than we. The evidence is before us; once the author appears to have relinquished his control, he cannot re-establish it. Richardson's notes on Lovelace simply reinforce our sense of the character's independence from authorial control, and, consequently, from any sort of "objective" control.[31]

Unlike history, then, the eighteenth-century novel represents the world experienced but not fully conceptualized, a world which because of its dependence upon a subjective grasp of reality is not capable of being wholly abstracted or moralized. The open narrative refuses to adhere fully to the patterns of the past, and in the process, begins to adhere to the dimly apprehendable patterns of the future. In Richardson's work, the events become internalized and the distance between character and audience is erased. So his novels create a new social, but not particularly moral, vision, one that in part grows out of the patterns of Protestantism but which no longer can be controlled by that ancestry. The Richardsonian character is too fully immersed in particularity, is too fully defined by his or her words, and no longer necessarily by the ideas which the words traditionally have been taken to mean. Although Richardson would not agree, his editorial revisions and additions of footnotes argue tellingly that his text subverts his moral purpose. Finally, in *Sir Charles Grandison,* he supplants individuality in the characterization of his hero almost entirely by abstract moral pattern.

The earliest English novels offer a particular, exclusive picture, which was intended to be a universal one, but the language of realistic fiction undermines obvious universality, forcing the ideal, as it were, out of the tower and into the streets, where it finds itself embattled by the world of money and power—the gritty world of economic and socio-sexual struggles—far removed from the intangible world of Platonic abstractions. After Defoe the novel, unlike those genres that seek explanations in the traditional loci of power, excludes the monarchy and other institutions traditionally associated with power; if they do appear, they are subordinated to the character's subjective valuation of them—as when Roxana entertains Charles II by dressing and dancing "in the Habit of *a Turkish Princess."* Although suitably overwhelmed by the encounter, she quickly subordinates her thoughts of the King to her own more pressing psychological needs: "This magnificent Doings equally both pleas'd and surpriz'd me, and I hardly knew where I was; but especially, that Notion of the King being the Person that danc'd with me, puff'd me up to that Degree, that I not only did not know any-body else, but indeed, was very far from knowing myself."[32]

In *Clarissa* the struggles for power within the family, as well as the battles between Clarissa and Lovelace, reveal the worldly struggles of money and land, class and sex. Richardson's moral point, dependent on the homiletic patterns of the past, is subverted by the subtle network of crushing forces all inscribed on the individual body of Clarissa.[33] This novel reveals the hidden sources of power in eighteenth-century society—less graspable than the concept of monarchy and court, church and bishops, but not less potent. Such delineations are variations of newly emerging awarenesses which, it seems to me, contribute immeasurably to the ideologies of Malthus and Gibbon, and in their turn, Darwin and Marx.

Thus by its very nature, the realistic novel depends on a rendering of the power structure in society and history; at its inception, however, it was discerned only as it functioned in more traditional patterns, and in ways quite similar to modern readings of these texts by literary scholars who seek to relate them to eighteenth-century ideas of manners and morality. Such readings have a value, but for most later readers, who have grown up reading open narratives, Robinson Crusoe's and Moll Flanders's spiritual quests are not merely counterpoised but overwhelmed by their quests for economic control and security—their acquisitiveness.[34] And it seems clear that this "naïve" response to the text is more in keeping with the ways realistic novels actually function; as we have seen, in these first tentative, but successful, renderings of realist fictions, the discrete but overwhelming array of facts become transmuted into more supple and complex patterns when placed against the traditional, closed narrative patterns of the past. The patterns are impressed on the world that the novel insists it shares with its audience, even though at first these forms were only dimly discerned in those novels which seemed so particular, so singular and unreproducible.

The novelist's claim of factuality lies at the heart of the genre's participation in this cultural transformation because it necessarily relies on those particulars which empower the subjective, thus reducing the claims of the shared ideal and subverting more general patterns of morality; in literature this includes the subverting of traditional genres such as tragedy, and the restructuring of those such as spiritual biography which depend on eschatologies external to the text (even when those patterns may be traced in the work).[35] Because the process of novel reading is more the "point" than any moral goal, the general audience does not necessarily grasp that peculiar truth which the author seeks to represent—the novel's point resists precise location. Thus truth becomes an ideological attitude dependent on individual subjectivity, and traditional morality finds itself fragmented and dependent on the subjective apprehension of potentially patternless factuality.

The subversion, then, of interpretation—the traditional reason for reading and writing—is a necessary consequence of knowingly accepting any fiction as "real" in the senses considered above, of consciously accepting, that is, the false claims of the author for the sake of participating more fully in the work's particularity. And it is a curious fact that this strange dialectic—the pretence that fictionality constitutes reality—born in the minds of these authors, is precisely what realistic fictions demand. Richardson emphasized this point in 1748 when he wrote to William Warburton, who had not tried to maintain the illusion of the work as a true history in the preface he provided for the first edition of volumes 3 and 4 of *Clarissa:*

> I could wish that the *Air* of Genuineness had been kept up, tho' I want not the letters to be *thought* genuine; only so far kept up, I mean, as that they should not prefatically be owned *not* to be genuine: and this for fear of weakening their Influence where any of them are aimed to be exemplary; as well as to avoid hurting that kind of Historical Faith which Fiction itself is generally read with, tho' we know it to be Fiction.[36]

Richardson makes two distinct points about realistic fictions: they are read with a "kind of Historical Faith" even when "we know [them] to be Fiction"; and, the "*Air* of Genuineness" should be maintained because this, he believes, contributes to their exemplary influences. At the same time he did not expect that his letters would be "*thought* genuine," but only that they should not be "*owned*" as fictions. Richardson's curious distinction is crucial to understanding the way realistic fictions work: one recognizes the fictionality, but dares not own it.[37]

Richardson failed to realize, however, that precisely the "Historical Faith" that he rightly understood to be so necessary to his fictions worked against those exemplary goals. Far from contributing to our acceptance of his moral, *Clarissa*'s particularity blurs the effect of these moral lessons. Once the claim to be "real" has

been made and the audience has acquiesced in the deception—as it must and as it desires to do—the novelist's moral designs (which depend on the willingness to interpret from a restrictive point of view no longer demanded of the audience or provided by the author) become far less important than the audience's participation in the "true History." Indeed, within a relatively few years, during which the ideological "lessons" of the novel were fully absorbed, this exact point was articulated by Samuel Taylor Coleridge, who asserted that when we pretend to read *Pilgrim's Progress* (or any realistic fiction) as if it were real, then because we know it to be in actuality, a fiction, the work's moral designs are subverted:

> in that admirable allegory, the first Part of *Pilgrim's Progress,* which delights every one, the interest is so great that [in] spite of all the writer's attempts to force the allegoric purpose on the reader's mind by his strange names—Old Stupidity of the Tower of Honesty, etc., etc.—his piety was baffled by his genius, and the Bunyan of Parnassus had the better of Bunyan of the conventicle; and with the same illusion as we read any tale known to be fictitious, as a novel, we go on with his characters as real persons, who had been nicknamed by their neighbors.[38]

Coleridge recognizes not only that the realistic story known to be fictional demands that its reader treat it and its characters as "real," but also that the reader simultaneously and without regret discounts the traditional moral impulse. Here indeed the moral pattern associated by Coleridge with Protestantism has been almost entirely discarded, because other, more compelling "illusions" are understood to be at stake. By Coleridge's time the factors that actually make up the novel's "truth"—moral or otherwise—had been assimilated. The means by which Richardson introduces reality diminish our willingness to accept his moral designs. Warburton—that heavy moralist—naturally recognized the unimportance of calling *Clarissa* a "fiction" if one wished to think of it primarily as a set of moral lessons.

The problems inherent in Richardson's twofold distinction regarding the nature of realistic fictions point towards a theoretical dilemma recently expressed by Lennard Davis: that "novelists had to claim that their works were true," because they sought to write works that were "morally verisimilar," but "factually realistic" works would be morally improbable. "If actual verisimilitude is then opposed to providence, and moral verisimilitude is antinovelistic in presenting the world as it should be and not as it is, then can we not say that the theory of the novel at this time was a reflexive or double one since it maintained two contradictory imperatives at once?"[39] In the minds of the writers, however, as Richardson's letter to Warburton makes clear, there was not so bald a contradiction; the moral and the realistic had always been split, even though they were assumed to be interdependent.

Richardson's enterprise was quite different from the foregoing model, and the author's understanding of it was a good deal more subtle. Richardson believed that the moral was, in some way, a function of history and that God's providence was operative in his world, but he also knew that such an understanding depended on the individual's moral valuation of factuality; at the same time, he recognized that realism was a technique that led readers to believe in the story's truth. Richardson did believe that a realistic fiction could have an exemplary effect. The fact that a more modern response to these texts, such as Coleridge's, repudiates this belief does not mean that eighteenth-century novelists did not firmly believe in the connection between, rather than the opposition of, verisimilitude and morality. For them, the claim to be truthful was a technique which they fully believed would lead to an appropriate moral response from the audience. Moreover, even from a more modern point of view, the immersion of the novel in the realistic does not lead to the "doubleness" that depends on the contradiction between moral verisimilitude and actual verisimilitude (which is merely a theoretical mirage, one perpetuated, it is true, by early writers and critics of the novel who did not fully understand or were unsympathetic to the genre's aims), but instead to the innumerable possibilities which emanate from the necessity for a subjective ordering of events. Arguing otherwise forces us to discount what I believe is a major effect of novels, the introduction to a more modern pattern of an individual's psychological comprehension and struggle for stability. This effect is emphatically not based on traditional Christian interpretive patterns, although it may be cast in a Christian light, depending on the character's predilections. The act of reading subverts the dialectic Davis proposes; it is the narrative's "openness" that powers the fiction.

In other words, only one element of Davis's dialectic—realistic verisimilitude—is necessary, even when the author seems to privilege the morally verisimilar, because the character-narrator's view of the world constantly reinvents, and thereby subverts, the traditional interpretive gesture. No author was fully aware of the consequences of realism, but as Richardson saw (and Davis's model does not), the claim to be factual was separate from the drive to be exemplary, although he believed the two to be complementary: what powered the novel was the open narrative, not the push towards "moral" verisimilitude. In other words, the crucial "fiction" of the novel is precisely the possibility that the relentless plot, immersed in seemingly aimless particularity, could lead anywhere, even to moral corruption, while at the same time the novel promises to provide a coherent view of the world, even though necessarily a subjective one. Thus, Richardson's nov-

els, to some degree, contain a strategy, a submerged discourse (perhaps not fully grasped by either reader or author), which inevitably finds itself reshaping the world, and this strategy depends on the work's appearing to be a true history, whether the audience realizes it is a fiction or not. When such works are read as "real" (even when the reader knows they are not), then they function in a far more revolutionary way than is possible for a fiction that announces itself as "art."

Like most authors, Richardson wrote in the belief his fictions could effect some change in the world he inhabited; and he understood that, for this, a realistic style was absolutely necessary. Irony and satire seemed more useful or acceptable styles to those eighteenth-century authors attached to or interested in defending the interests of the squirearchy as it then existed, however much they may have attacked specific instances of the abuse of power. Their works functioned to chastise the system but not to transform it. But for those, like Richardson, who participated—whether consciously or not—in changing the system in truly fundamental ways, realism was the discourse of necessity.

In the case of *Clarissa,* the fiction's power was fully established by the third edition (when Richardson's notes and Lovelace's letter fantasizing his trial for the abduction and rape of Anna Howe first appeared); *Clarissa* had become a cultural artifact—Angus Ross calls it "a story that became a myth to [Richardson's] own age, and remains so yet."[40] It was a realistic text so interwoven with the emerging ideologies of the culture that its characters' fantasies seem as real as the stones of Newgate and the streets of London. In thus embedding the idea in the concrete fact, the ideology in the stone, the novel inscribes the lessons of power on anyone who accepts its world as "real."

It was in the rejection of "artifice," the disdain for traditional rhetoric and the coupling of reportage to fact, where novelists found the power to help reshape the ideologies of the time. It is precisely this task of claiming factuality, of insisting on the "circumstantial reality" of the fictional text, which substantiates their version of the external world and largely differentiates the sort of writing we associate with Richardson and his precursors (such as Bunyan and Defoe) from other sorts of fictions.

One might advance the axiom that an author of fiction who appears to disdain literary artifice (however much it may exist in the text) does so, as Edward Said has said, out of a desire to make the fiction a part of the world, to demand that the world conform to the fiction, to supplant the current ideologies apparently in control of that world. Realistic narratives demand that the exterior world conform to their exclusive vision; they seek to transform reality by forcing that reality into a fiction where it can be judged only on the novel's terms. A new conceptualization of culture is what is at stake in early eighteenth-century novels.

The operation of ideology in the novel is the antithesis of what Greenblatt has discerned in *The Faerie Queene:* "Spenserean allegory . . . opens up an internal distance within art itself by continually referring the reader out to a fixed authority beyond the poem. Spenser's art does not lead us to perceive ideology critically, but rather affirms the existence and inescapable moral power of ideology as that principle of truth towards which art forever yearns. It is art whose status is questioned in Spenser, not ideology."[41] The Richardsonian novel, on the other hand, denies power to the structures which lie outside its scope; its realism is exclusive and subverts all that is external to it. Spenser's artifice affirms the power of what lies outside its scope, whereas the demand that a fiction be accepted as real points to the assumed power of the fiction and implies an entire set of relationships between book and culture, and an entire set of beliefs about the power of reality. In short, if one accepts the power of the real, one must accept the power of the fictional: "An art that displays its artfulness, that 'questions its own status,' as *The Faerie Queene* surely does, also undermines that status and, at the same time, 'protect[s] power from . . . questioning.'"[42] In *Clarissa* and to a lesser extent in *Pamela,* it is precisely the ideology of the world represented by Lovelace, Mr B., and the institution of the landed squirearchy and aristocracy that is being questioned.

Notes

[1] Interview, *San Francisco Examiner*, Sunday 26 October 1986, p. A29.

[2] Quoted in Maynard Mack, *Pope: A Life* (New York: W.W. Norton; New Haven: Yale University Press, 1985), p. 761; quoted in T.C. Duncan Eaves and Ben D. Kimpel, *Samuel Richardson: A Biography* (London: Oxford University Press, 1971), p. 124.

[3] Cheyne, quoted in Eaves and Kimpel, p. 124.

[4] Anna Laetitia Barbauld, *The Correspondence of Samuel Richardson*, 6 vols (New York: AMS Press, 1966) 1:134-35.

[5] In *Novels of the 1740s* (Athens: University of Georgia Press, 1982), Jerry C. Beasley remarks that Pamela, along with other "heroes and heroines of the major novels," bears a "resemblance to the moralizing spies of Marana and Montesquieu" which "may well have seemed more than just casual to the first readers of their stories" (p. 75). I believe, however, that A. D. McKillop's association of *Pamela* with "conduct-books and collections of commonplaces" is much closer to actuality. See *The Early Masters of English*

Prose Fiction (Lawrence: University of Kansas Press, 1956), p. 62.

[6] Edward W. Said, *The World, the Text, and the Critic* (Cambridge: Harvard University Press, 1983), p. 44. Said continues, "Cervantes and Cide Hamete come immediately to mind. More impressive is Richardson playing the role of 'mere' editor for *Clarissa*, simply placing those letters in successive order after they have done what they have done, arranging to fill the text with printer's devices, reader's aids, analytic contents, retrospective meditations, commentary, so that a collection of letters grows to fill the world and occupy all space, to become a circumstance as large and as engrossing as the reader's very understanding."

[7] Stephen Greenblatt, *Renaissance Self-Fashioning: From More to Shakespeare* (Chicago: University of Chicago Press, 1980), p. 174.

[8] *Selected Letters of Samuel Richardson*, ed. John Carroll (Oxford: Clarendon Press, 1964), p. 142.

[9] M.M. Bakhtin, "Epic and Novel: Toward a Methodology for the Study of the Novel," *The Dialogic Imagination*, ed. Michael Holquist (Austin: University of Texas Press, 1986), p. 27. Cf. Terry Eagleton, who, referring to the problem of Richardson's fictions, asks "how is a structural openness, the essential medium of transformed relations between producers and audiences, to be reconciled with a necessary doctrinal closure?" *The Rape of Clarissa: Writing, Sexuality and Class Struggle in Samuel Richardson* (Minneapolis: University of Minnesota Press, 1982), p. 22. I differ with Eagleton because I believe there is no real doctrinal closure for the reader, in spite of all the author's attempts.

[10] Quoted in W. Jackson Bate, *Samuel Johnson* (New York: Harcourt Brace Jovanovich, 1979), p. 122. I disagree with J. Paul Hunter about the relation of didacticism and moral pattern to the novel; in his valuable *Before Novels* (New York: W.W. Norton, 1990) Hunter asserts that "the didacticism of the early novel is central to the conception of the species. Its origins are so tied up with needs of contemporary readers and its early history is so dependent on the didactic assumptions in popular non-narrative forms that to miss— or excuse—its characteristic didacticism is to misappreciate its features and misdefine its nature" (p. 226). I believe, as I will suggest more fully below, that Hunter is too willing to take at face value authorial assertions of a work's moral end. The novel itself "excuses" or subverts "its characteristic didacticism." In spite of all his protestations to the contrary, in *Before Novels* Hunter seems to search for a "definition" of novel— albeit an inclusive one. For me the "novel" is far less stable than he implies.

[11] In *The Country and the City* (New York: Oxford University Press, 1973), Raymond Williams argues that this internalization makes the novel a less effective force for change. For example, he believes that no formal ideological "confrontation" occurs in *Clarissa*, a novel which dramatizes "the long process between economic advantage and other ideas of value," because "the action becomes internal, and is experienced and dramatised as a problem of character" (pp. 61-62).

[12] Carroll, *Selected Letters*, p. 99; Samuel Richardson, Postscript to *Clarissa, or, The History of a Young Lady*, 4 vols (London: Dent and New York: Dutton, 1932), 4:554. References are to this edition.

[13] Michel Foucault, *The Order of Things: An Archaeology of the Human Sciences* (New York: Pantheon, 1970), p. 40.

[14] Lennard Davis, *Factual Fictions: The Origins of the English Novel* (New York: Columbia University Press, 1983), p. 82.

[15] Greenblatt, p. 157.

[16] Foucault has attempted to chart the shifts from earlier "mechanisms of power" such as the French monarchy, which he characterizes as a "discontinuous, rambling, global system with little hold on detail," to those in the eighteenth century when "economic changes . . . made it necessary to ensure the circulation of effects of power through progressively finer channels, gaining access to individuals themselves, to their bodies, their gestures and all their daily actions." Michel Foucault, *Power/Knowledge*, ed. Colin Gordon (New York: Pantheon, 1980), pp. 151-52.

[17] Peter Dews, "Power and Subjectivity in Foucault," *New Left Review* 144 (March-April, 1984), 89.

[18] Joyce Oldham Appleby, *Economic Thought and Ideology in Seventeenth-Century England*, (Princeton: Princeton University Press, 1978), p. 206.

[19] Eagleton, p. 12.

[20] As John J. Richetti points out, the same is true of English scandal novels, which "possess none of the unity of theme or characterization that makes a narrative meaningful to us. There is in them no attempt to render that sense of a conditioning milieu, that biographical density and verisimilitude which make characterization possible and relevant. . . . There is . . . a deliberate and awkward artificiality." *Popular Fiction before Richardson* (Oxford: Clarendon Press, 1969), p. 121.

[21] Bakhtin, p. 22.

[22] Daniel Defoe, *Robinson Crusoe* (London and New York: Oxford University Press, 1972), p. 57. Ian Watt believes that the "discontinuities" in Defoe's fiction "strongly suggest that [he] did not plan his novel as a coherent whole, but worked piecemeal, very rapidly, and without any subsequent revision." *The Rise of the Novel* (Berkeley: University of California Press, 1964), p. 99. More pertinently, see Richetti's important recognition that "the various inconsistencies and contradictions that several generations of commentators have found in Defoe's narratives and tried to resolve by putting him on one side or another . . . are really . . . signs of the process of confrontation and mediation within the totality of perception and experience which mimetic fiction by its nature and tendency sets in motion." *Defoe's Narratives: Situations and Structures* (Oxford: Clarendon Press, 1975), p. 11.

[23] See for example, Maximillian E. Novak's questionable contention that all Defoe's "characters operate in a universe of unchanging natural law." *Defoe and the Nature of Man* (Oxford: Oxford University Press, 1963), p. 129.

[24] The phrase comes from Greenblatt's discussion of "the close equivalent at the verbal level" in Thomas More's *Utopia* "to the visual technique of anamorphosis, whose etymology itself suggests a back-and-forth movement, a constant forming and re-forming" (p. 23). Referring to the letters in *Clarissa*, John Preston points out that, "in the terms proposed by Frank Kermode" (*The Sense of an Ending,* p. 46), they "are deprived of 'plot,' of 'the sense of an ending,' which will bestow upon the whole duration and meaning." *The Created Self: The Reader's Role in Eighteenth-Century Fiction* (London: Heinemann, 1970), p. 40.

[25] Eagleton, p. 48.

[26] Preston, p. 39.

[27] Carroll, *Selected Letters,* p. 296.

[28] Eagleton, p. 12.

[29] Eagleton, p. 17.

[30] Jean-Marie Goulemot, "Sexual Imagination as Revealed in the *Traité des superstitions* of Abbé Jean-Baptiste Thiers," trans. Odile Wagner and Arthur Greenspan, in *Unauthorized Sexual Behavior during the Enlightenment*, ed. Robert P. Maccubbin, special issue of *Eighteenth-Century Life* 9, n.s. 3 (May, 1985), 22.

[31] G.A. Starr argues that Moll Flanders, as well as Defoe's other fictional characters, eludes precise definition; readers become ambivalent because the characters are ambiguous: Moll's "retractions never fully

'take back' whatever she has said or done; the process is always additive, so that what appear to be clarifying denials actually tend to make her position more ambiguous." *Defoe and Casuistry* (Princeton: Princeton University Press, 1971), p. 163.

[32] Daniel Defoe, *Roxana, The Fortunate Mistress,* ed. Jane Jack (London: Oxford University Press, 1964), pp. 173, 177.

[33] In *Clarissa's Ciphers: Meaning and Disruption in Richardson's "Clarissa"* (Ithaca: Cornell University Press, 1982), Terry Castle writes of "the tyranny of a sexual ideology that inscribes the female body itself" (p. 25), but this seems far too limited and limiting. More to the point is Foucault's assertion "that one of the primordial forms of class consciousness is the affirmation of the body; at least, this was the case for the bourgeoisie during the eighteenth century." *The History of Sexuality, Volume 1: An Introduction,* trans. Robert Hurley (New York: Pantheon, 1978), p. 126.

[34] I do not mean to imply that many people in the seventeenth and eighteenth centuries did not recognize the strength of economic motives; as Appleby remarks, "Acquisitiveness, long suffered as a barely repressible vice, shared in the respectability that naturalness acquired in seventeenth-century thought. . . . English economic commentators were articulating a new social reality in which the self-seeking drive appeared more powerful than institutional efforts to mold people's action" (p. 115).

[35] G.A. Starr and J. Paul Hunter have convincingly argued that patterns of spiritual autobiography do exist in Defoe's fiction. See Starr, *Defoe and Spiritual Autobiography* (Princeton: Princeton University Press, 1965); and Hunter, *The Reluctant Pilgrim* (Baltimore: Johns Hopkins University Press, 1966); but readers do not see Defoe's novels as essentially about spiritual regeneration.

[36] Carroll, *Selected Letters,* p. 85.

[37] As Michael McKeon puts it (although he does not accept it): "There has been considerable interest of late in the way *Clarissa* underscores, and is 'about,' the subjective powers of language and the letter form to render meaning radically indeterminate." *The Origins of the English Novel, 1600-1740* (Baltimore: Johns Hopkins University Press, 1988), p. 421.

[38] This passage from *Coleridge's Miscellaneous Criticism* is quoted in Stephen Knapp, *Personification and the Sublime: Milton to Coleridge* (Cambridge: Harvard University Press, 1985), p. 13.

[39] Davis, pp. 133, 112.

[40] Introduction to *Clarissa, or, The History of a Young Lady* (Harmondsworth: Penguin, 1985), p. 18.

[41] Greenblatt, p. 192.

[42] Barbara Leah Harman, review of Stephen Greenblatt, *Renaissance Self-Fashioning, diacritics* (Spring, 1984), 59.

April Alliston (essay date 1995)

SOURCE: "Female Sexuality and the Referent of Enlightenment Realisms," in *Spectacles of Realism: Body, Gender, Genre,* edited by Margaret Cohen and Christopher Prendergast, Cultural Politics, No. 10, University of Minnesota Press, 1995, pp. 11-27.

[*In the following essay, Alliston argues that there were several distinct types of realism at work in the early novel.*]

Twentieth-century historians of the novel generally distinguish the emerging genre from earlier (romance) narrative by its increased "realism," variously defined in terms of referentiality to the details of a quotidian experience shared by readers.[1] Judged by this standard, theorized as it is from the practice of nineteenth-century high realism, most eighteenth-century novels tend to appear underdeveloped, still uncomfortably close to the romance genre satirized in one of the first novels, *Don Quixote* (itself, of course, hardly "high realist"). Early novels may well be making a gesture of reference to something they identify as "the real," and in that sense it is appropriate to call them "realist." But it is not appropriate to assume that the logic of that gesture remains the same over the course of the novel's history, enabling critics to judge more and less successful expressions of the realist endeavor by a single, and often anachronistic, standard. The logics of referentiality at work in eighteenth-century fiction are multiple, and are based on conceptions of evidence that differ importantly from the one that came to dominate the later high realist tradition.

One effect of the normalized failure to recognize the multiplicity of realisms in eighteenth-century fiction is the marginalization of early women novelists. Accepted histories of the novel tend to associate women's work at the origins of the genre not with alternate concepts of how truth (or "reality") is evidenced, but with an underdeveloped execution of a singular model of realism. This critical judgment repeats the gesture of high realism itself in excluding alternate systems for representing reality from the literary canon, most often by adopting the very nineteenth-century metaphor of "natural" selection. After outlining a typology of the main varieties of eighteenth-century realism as I see them, I hope to open to debate the gender politics of various realist strategies, and then of twentieth-century criticism that describes the history of the novel in the rhetorical terms of biological evolution.

Three Types of Evidence, Three Types of Realism

The eighteenth-century novel differs starkly from later fiction in its frequent claims to factual truth, in the documentary forms of narration with which it evidences those truth claims, and in the wide acceptance of them by contemporary readers. The truth claimed was, generally speaking, a private truth (even when it concerned public figures, as in the "scandalous histories" of Delariviere Manley and Eliza Haywood). The documentary forms were therefore private documents or personal, eyewitness accounts: familiar letters, journals, memoirs, travelogues. Up to this point, I remain in agreement with Ian Watt's classic description of eighteenth-century realism. But where Watt constructs an ultimately unitary conception of "formal realism" as vacillating dialectically through the eighteenth century until it achieves synthesis in the novels of Austen, I would like to propose a nonhierarchical tripartite model of Enlightenment realisms.[2] I do not assert that three categories of realism exist by theoretical necessity, but that there were during the period at least three distinct types, representing three significantly different conventions for referring to reality, and that these intersected and competed with one another.

Watt refers to the "realism of representation" because these forms did not *represent* "reality" or events as much as, and except insofar as, they *presented* private testimony. But Watt conflates the technique of presentation with reliance upon a sense of plausibility for the construction of nontraditional plots. That is where I would like to draw an important distinction. More often than not, eighteenth-century novels presented reality as fantastic truth rather than plausible fiction.[3] Defoe's fictional *A Journal of the Plague Year* was initially read as a factual account, Diderot's reclusive friend actually made an effort to assist the fictive nun in distress, and Americans wept all the way through the nineteenth century at the grave of their first fictional heroine, Charlotte Temple (her tombstone still stands in New York's Trinity Churchyard).[4] These contemporary responses to eighteenth-century fiction do not by any means indicate that Defoe's remarkable episodes, the scenes of lesbian sex in a downright Gothic setting of incarceration and torture related by Diderot's nun, or the moral beatification of a young woman who "falls" and is abandoned as a result of her error corresponded to any Enlightenment sense of verisimilitude. What it does indicate is that the documents of private testimony, regardless of mechanical reproduction, were taken seriously as evidence of truth, and that such evidence was if anything supported by the implausibility of the events related.[5] Indeed, the idea of plausibility has always been accompanied by a certain awareness, more or less uneasy at different times, that its law is a law for narration, for the accounting for fact, and not for the facts themselves, which often seem to have no regard whatsoever for its dictates. What established the relationship of a text to the real for the eighteenth-century reader, then, was not the plausibility of a representation, but rather the presentation of documentary evidence of a firsthand or eyewitness account.[6] I shall refer to this form of realism as *evidentiary realism*.

If evidentiary realism prevailed during the first half of the eighteenth century, another type came to prominence with the works of Richardson and Rousseau, coexisting to the end of the century with "evidentiary" works like *Charlotte Temple,* but becoming increasingly important as the century proceeded. I shall distinguish this type from the first with the term *exemplary realism*. Whereas in evidentiary realism the (re)presentation of proof—documentation and eyewitness accounts—establishes the factuality of the account for the reading public, in exemplary realism the perceived exemplarity of the account begins to *create* factual truth according to its own model. In evidentiary realism, the text's status as presentation (of evidence) takes precedence over its status as representation (of what is proven by the evidence); in exemplary realism, the text's status as exemplum again takes precedence over its status as representation, so that it is read in terms of imitation rather than in terms of mimesis. That is, the text asks to be read as an example capable of generating real action through imitation, rather than as an imitation of real action. The church bells rang for Pamela's wedding and young men shot themselves in yellow vests that matched Werther's not because there was anything plausible about such representations (as Fielding so acidly observed), but because their perceived moral exemplarity generated its own imitative reality.[7]

Evidentiary and exemplary realism are in fact closely connected to one another in both conception and practice (especially Richardson's). Only a shift of emphasis differentiates them: the truth claim of exemplary realism no longer emphasizes as much the establishment of the exemplary person or event's individual and unique existence as fact; rather, it simultaneously asserts the exemplar's uniqueness and her existence, or at least her potential existence in multiple reproductions, by dint of imitation. Her "truth" as exemplar is supported by this double proof: she is unique (otherwise she would not be exemplary) and at the same time she is presented as worthy of imitation. This shift in emphasis also entails one from event to character. Not events, but characters, generally though not always female ones, are held up as examples. The emphasis on character remains in force for mimetic realism, and, like it, is very much alive to the present day.

The high realism of the nineteenth century takes the figure of example and turns it from the logic of imitation to that of mimesis. The characters of mimetic realism are presented as *examples,* like those of "exemplary" realism, but another shift of emphasis has occurred, this time in the meaning of the term *example.* The characters of mimetic realism are no longer examples in the sense that they are presented as models for imitation, but they are examples in the other, evidentiary sense: they are the particular instances that prove a maxim or precept—in this case an implicit statement of general truth about "reality"—by standing for it, representing it. What connects all three is the private nature of the truth in question, whether that truth be evidenced through documentation, presented as example, or mimetically represented. All the documentary forms mentioned above enact the public disclosure of private truth. When public truths are referred to (such as the actions of public figures in the early scandal chronicles or well-known historical events in mimetic realism), the gesture of the fiction is to involve those public truths within a private context that must remain a matter of public ignorance or doubt, unprovable by any but uncertain forms of evidence: that of private, unsubstantiated testimony; that of circumstantial evidence; or that of the authority of an omniscient narrator.

The Reality of Legitimacy

The truth-referent of realism, then, is historically a *private* truth. Eighteenth-century novels in England, France, and Germany come back obsessively to one private truth in particular: the truth about female sexuality and its conformity (or lack thereof) to patriline control. This preoccupation is so characteristic of fiction of the "longer eighteenth century" in Western Europe that it would almost be deceptive to describe it from a reading of specific instances.[8] The anxiety over woman's virtue and its corollary, man's legitimacy, is a preoccupation that the novel inherits from romance. Eighteenth-century realisms represent a search for new ways of either demonstrating or destabilizing the old romance truth about legitimacy of succession and transmission in terms of Enlightenment conceptions of evidence. In patriline terms, the question of female sexuality is identical with the question of legitimacy, and hence of legality; thus the logic of its demonstration historically follows changes in the dominant forms of legal evidence, culminating in the hegemony of mimetic realism's logic of verisimilitude.

The link between realism and patriline anxiety over legitimacy has its roots in classical aesthetics, where "recognition" as an essential aspect of mimetic representation is theorized by Aristotle from the praxis of tragic recognition. "Recognition" in Greek tragedy is generally recognition of a kinship relation; thus, I would trace it to the epic anxiety over recognition as evidence of patriline legitimacy.[9] "You must be, by your looks, Odysseus' boy?" says Athene (and Nestor, and Menelaos) to Telemachos, "Yes, how like him!" Telemachos replies, "thoughtfully": "My mother says I am his son; I know not/surely. Who has known his own engendering?"[10] A mother's word has never been, and by definition cannot be, adequate evidence to establish the legitimacy of a child in patriline terms. From this point of view, much of Western narrative since Homer has been an exercise in *not* simply taking women's words for it—a search for evidence that would establish the truth or falsehood of a mother's word on legitimacy without allowing her to remain the ultimate authority on the subject.

Michael McKeon describes the novel as a dialectical motion away from romance that negates it even while commemorating its ancient knowledge that "lineage existed to resolve questions of virtue and truth with a tacit simultaneity, making both a causal claim of genealogical descent attesting to an eminence of birth, hence worth, and a logical claim of testimonial precedent validating all present claims as true."[11] What is left out of this convincing account is that what most persists from that romance knowledge, and persists well through the period of mimetic realism's heyday, is the cultural value of patriline legitimacy, along with the anxious recognition, as represented by Telemachos's answer to the question of his lineage and his identity, of the very fragility of its own evidence.

Although anxiety about control over female sexuality and the evidence of legitimacy is as ancient as patriarchy, Enlightenment discourse moves the scene of recognition from the public theater of tragedy (or of Renaissance romance), itself originally modeled on the Athenian law court, to a domestic theater. *Clarissa* stages the "trial" of its heroine's virtue in the family sitting room, complete with pleading, testimony, material evidence (the letters), jury, judge, accuser, and incarceration of the defendant between sessions, in a kind of private theatricals taken seriously as courtroom drama (whereas playful private theatricals will become, for Jane Austen, a frivolous threat to the very feminine virtue these are staged to discover).[12] The real jury, of course, is not the Harlowe family, but the reading public. The members of the real jury are moved to sympathize with the defendant, not directly by her performance or by the pleadings of those who speak on her behalf, both of which fail to move the fictive jury, but rather by the evidence of their own senses, by the familiar letters, which they see as evidence of her sincerity. The letters are of course the very thing the Harlowe family, the jury in representation, views as evidence of her disobedience, regardless of their content.[13] What changes the perspective is an intersection of two things: the differing personal investments in the interpretation of the evidence for the jury of characters and the jury of readers, and the differing amounts and types of evidence presented to each. Only the readers see all the correspondence, with its several perspectives that tend further to verify the heroine's sincerity. To complement the presentation of evidence, a sympathetic response *outside* the situation of the courtroom drama is inscribed within the text in the mother-daughter relation.

Richardson takes advantage of the readers' lack of personal (i.e., *private*) investment in Clarissa's acting according to the will of her family—despite the fact that the same readers are likely to be so invested when it comes to real daughters in their own families—to present the more comprehensive evidence that proves Clarissa's virtue. Thus, he creates the illusion of having proved that Clarissa's word can be taken for her own virtue, and also demonstrates the narrowness and bias of the familial perspective. In placing the question, not only of a heroine's virtue, but moreover of her sincerity, of whether her own word can be taken for the truth of her virtue, within the play of difference between readers' and characters' evidence and interpretation of the evidence, Richardson is working (to his own different ends) with a feminine strategy of resistance to the norms of verisimilitude that points back to Marie de Lafayette's *La Princesse de Clèves*.[14]

Virtue and Verisimilitude

In *La Princesse de Clèves* as in *Clarissa,* a woman's statements about her own fidelity to patriarchal norms of female sexual conduct are judged by a fictive audience that possesses only the partial evidence of the senses (the Harlowes' of Clarissa's performance and her partial correspondence; the prince of Clèves's of his manservant's glimpse of Nemours going over the garden wall), as well as by readers of the novel, who are in possession of fuller evidence: a more complete correspondence in the case of *Clarissa,* and the omniscient narrator's presentation of the princess's private thoughts and actions in the other. Those private thoughts and actions include the princess's famous *aveu.* The *aveu* is a pledge of fidelity, of faithfulness to patriline law, but it is one whose evidence, for its fictive judge, consists in nothing other than its own status as a free, unforced confession.[15] It is thus paradoxical, because the confession of female desire inherently threatens the very law to which it pledges fidelity. Such an act of confession already constitutes a transgression, for both fictive and actual readers, of the law of verisimilitude, which prescribes that women maintain the *appearances* of female fidelity, as interpreted and judged by an authoritative male viewer or male-dominated community of viewers.[16] Writers throughout the eighteenth century, most of them women, imitated and transformed the "inimitable" strategy of the princess of Clèves for resistance to the normative hegemony of verisimilitude as an unstable category whose interpretation would always be manipulated in the service of

the ruling hierarchy.[17] The princess's strategy for resistance to the demand for the evidence of plausibility, for the appearances that would prove, according to the evidentiary logic particular to the law of verisimilitude, the truth of the narrative of female virtue, is to attempt to keep the scene of that narration entirely within the realm of the private. The princess is unsuccessful in this project, and has to relinquish desire in order to become mistress of her own private state, estate, status, and story.

Rather than expose, like Richardson, the trials of woman's virtue to the reading public on its domestic bench, eighteenth-century women novelists often attempt to circumvent the trial scenario altogether, by turning the nonfictional private documentary forms and the perceived instability of history in relation to verisimilitude (the recognition, referred to above, that plausibility is a category of narrative and not of reality) into forms of evidence that would force *the reader's recognition,* and hence legitimation, of the authority of the woman as narrator to determine the truth value of her own narrative.[18] Even when they do stage the heroine's trial of virtue, thereby conforming to a law of verisimilitude for what women authors might publish, they quite often undercut the reader's ability to judge of that trial on any evidence but that of the heroine's own word. They do so by writing the trial in the form of a letter- or memoir-novel that includes no masculine or skeptical demand for corroborating evidence, except where the heroine's own testimony portrays that skepticism as mistaken and its demand as silencing.

As I have said, the ultimate private truth, the truth that would always lack authoritative testimony and have to be judged by the standards of plausibility, was identified by Mme de Lafayette in *La Princesse de Clèves* as the truth about female sexual conduct and its conformity (or lack thereof) to the reproduction of patriline legitimacy. This indeed remains the ultimate truth for fiction in France and England, at least through the time of Dickens and Collins, for example, or of Balzac, whose work consistently explores questions of legitimacy and legitimate transmission. Lafayette and the writers who followed her (many of them women or "feminocentric" writers like Richardson) authorized private testimony in opposition both to traditional received authority and to the new logic of plausibility. Private testimony was identified with feminine narration through the linkage of the domestic sphere with femininity, and its truth value was evidenced not by plausibility, but by the very implausibility of the act of *free* "confession" of female desire, which constituted an inherently transgressive act in its potential threat to patriline legitimacy. Throughout the eighteenth century this strategy of free feminine narration—a hallmark of sentimentalism—competed in fiction with the authority of plausibility, which quickly came to dominate legal and historical proof (*Northanger Abbey* itself, a parodic commentary on the implausibility of Gothic romance, is a good example of this conflict). The logic of plausibility eventually won out in fiction, too, in the mimetic realism of the nineteenth century. This conflict and its resolution accounts for the shift from the immense popularity of epistolary fiction in the eighteenth century as a form of private documentary testimony to the use of letters in nineteenth-century fiction more exclusively as material evidence: conclusions drawn from the material evidence of the letter supersede the authority of its text as testimony.

The period between the publication of Richardson's novels and the triumph of mimetic realism saw the production of a strong body of fiction by women that presents the history of a heroine's virtue strictly through the private documentation of the heroine's own letters and their sympathetic reception by a female confidante. This form limits the evidence of virtue, and the force of its example, to the woman's own word for her history and conduct. Given the long history of literary anxiety over how the reality of a woman's sexual fidelity can be faithfully represented, it cannot be a matter of pure chance or pure aesthetic value that this pattern of evidence is *not* the one to be found in the canonical works of the same period that also present the exemplary history, in letters, of a virtuous heroine.[19] Neither Richardson, Rousseau, Burney, Laclos (whose skepticism about female virtue and its evidence is only more extreme than the others), nor Austen limits the evidence of the heroine's virtue to her own account, so that Austen, on the verge of high realism, at last drops the letters altogether in favor of a skeptical, omniscient narrator. In doing so, she demands of any heroine who is to prove her virtue the utmost fidelity to the principles of verisimilitude.

Conclusion: The Legitimacy of Reality

Although evidentiary and exemplary realisms, the realisms of Defoe and Richardson, may seem clunky and archaic when viewed, as they tend to be, as Cro-Magnons in the "evolution" of the novel as the genre of transcendent mimetic realism, contemporary women's fiction, whenever it has been subjected to the same standard of comparison, comes out looking like a horde of Neanderthals. Were they capable of speech? critics seem to be asking of early novels by women. Were their brains as big? Were these strange-looking texts the ancestors of the novel as well, did they contribute equally to the genesis of the genre of realism, or do they simply constitute a dead-end freak mutation?

The rhetoric of the "evolution" of *the* realist novel turns out to be identical with the discourse of mimetic realism itself; it is no accident that this metaphor is borrowed from the period of mimetic realism's heyday. One emphasizes the formal "perfection" of the representation, the other the "reality" that is to be

perfectly represented, but both discourses locate the value of the representation or the represented in terms of a logic akin to that of patriline legitimacy. If the idea of plausibility is based upon the fiction of a consensus of likelihood, centered on and originating in a masculine, first aristocratic and then bourgeois consensus about the likelihood of female sexual conduct and of the truth of a woman's word about it, the idea of evolution similarly devalues the production that it labels as indeterminate (for plausibility, the reality of paternity and the truth of a woman's word; for evolution, mutation or the production of new forms) by judging it according to the criterion of "selection." The logic of natural selection, like that of patriline descent, ascribes a higher value to that which it designates as "fit" or "legit" by distinguishing it from and opposing it to a field of other possibilities defined as an indiscriminate chaos of production (or reproduction). In so doing, both allay potential anxieties about the reality of indeterminacy by creating a legible line of descent, whether of the "fit" or of the "legit," that cuts through what would otherwise be, it seems, not a history but a cacophony.

Some individual historians of the novel overtly emphasize or even insist on an evolutionary metaphor, but even when they overtly reject it, some version of it often pervades their language, an inevitable connotation of words such as *development* and *rise*. John J. Richetti's main objection to Watt's *The Rise of the Novel,* for example, is what he identifies as the latter's "teleological bias," which "imposes an untenable pattern of growth and development upon the history of prose fiction. This preconception reduces any study of the material in question to the rather thankless, and to my mind meaningless, task of pointing out small 'advances' in realistic technique in various otherwise hapless hacks." I could not agree more with this critique of the evolutionary conception of literary history. Yet Richetti, too, in his epilogue, significantly titled "The Relevance of the Unreadable," leaves his hacks, most of them female hacks, as haplessly unread and unredeemed as ever—and for the same reason. He, too, is trying to read them through the dark glasses of late realism: "Defoe's narratives are often garrulous and disjointed *by modern standards of narrative coherence;* his imitators are merely diffuse or incoherent without any of his *saving realism.*"[20] Richetti is willing to give Defoe the benefit of his historical difference on the score of "narrative coherence" because his "realism" is *at times* more akin than others' to the mimetic realism, with its logic of plausibility, that has since been codified as the transparent representation of a reality that can never be diffuse or incoherent.[21]

I have just argued that the metaphor of literary evolution so pervasive in writing about the history of the novel as a genre, like all metaphors of descent in a patriarchal culture, masks the indeterminacy inherent in relations of patriline descent, in much the same way that Athene, Nestor, Helen, and Menelaos reassure Telemachos about the undecidability of Penelope's honesty by telling him that he looks just like his father. Those who use the metaphor most self-consciously, however, do emphasize the role of indeterminacy in evolutionary processes. English Showalter writes: "The evolutionary analogy describes quite well how progress emerged from *such chaos*" (i.e., the diversity of fictional forms produced in eighteenth-century Europe). Chaos exists, the chaos of diverse possibility, as Telemachos would be the last to deny; indeed, it is only the acknowledgment of the indeterminate as *all too real* that creates the anxious necessity of social and symbolic systems to devalue it. What emerges from the reality of chaos through these processes of selection, we must reassure ourselves, is at once *natural* (as implied by the rhetorical force of the evolutionary analogy) and representative of "progress."

Showalter continues:

> Given the literary situation, ranging from the tastes of potential readers to the mechanics of publishing, certain elements had greater fitness for survival than others. Whenever such an element occurred, it *naturally* seemed outstandingly successful, and was therefore imitated by subsequent writers, most of whom added nothing to it, but a few of whom perhaps advanced the genre one more evolutionary step by some new idea or device. During these prehistoric days, many offshoots of the original genre were headed for extinction; the gigantic romances of the seventeenth century resemble dinosaurs in more ways than one. At the same time, the early ancestors of the modern novel were toiling away in obscurity, profiting from their insignificance to adapt better and faster to new conditions.[22]

I have included the above passage because it vividly describes, with the detail of a *National Geographic* artist's rendition, two recurrent aspects of the evolutionary analogy that might seem to clear it of the present critique: the fittest literary forms (and their authors) are originally "insignificant" and "obscure" (although, apparently, also outstandingly successful from the outset), laboring in the shadow of such "dinosaurs" as the *roman de longue haleine,* a strongly *feminine*-identified genre. When this strategy of representation is examined, the outlines of romance emerge: what we have in the evolutionary analogy taken at its word is a romance of the novel, in which the genre-hero begins in an orphaned obscurity of unidentifiable lineage, but, recognized in time by its own inherently superior merits, ends by becoming fully legitimated, its ancient lineage seen to stretch back, finally, to the heroic epic. The evolutionary discourse modifies this implicit romance narrative, to be sure, by shifting the evidence mark of superiority from "nobility" (in its full sense, in which the ideas of "best" and "purest" include and occlude that of class superiority) to "fitness," a term that im-

plies a more relative sense of superiority, not necessarily absolute superiority, but one determined by environmental necessity.

One of the most recent, and certainly the most rigorous, of the proponents of the evolutionary analogy for the history of the novel repeats the twin moves just described in Showalter's work. Franco Moretti more strongly insists upon the role of indeterminacy in producing literary forms in the eighteenth century, and on that of "social necessity" in selecting from among them the fittest genre for survival into the nineteenth: the *Bildungsroman,* which he also identifies as the "most bastard" genre.[23] Thus he repeats and develops further perhaps not so much a romance as a *Bildungsroman* of the novel's development: in his Marxist adaptation of natural selection he is careful to de-emphasize strictly aesthetic values ("saving realism" or "pleasing readers") in favor of social norms as the determining factors, just as, he argues, the *Bildungsroman* abandons the romance interest in the inherently extraordinary or noble to mark the "normal" as worthy of interest.[24]

In any case, like the orphaned nobles of romance or the obscurely normal heroes of *Bildungsromane,* the "bastard genre" ends by becoming ligitimated. As Moretti writes, "The most bastard of these forms [i.e., of the various novelistic forms competing for survival at the end of the eighteenth century] became—the dominant genre of Western narrative."[25] It became so, as always, at the expense of the other bastards who remain bastards, thereby maintaining the meaningfulness of the opposition between the bastard and the legitimate. If the *Bildungsroman* is a "bastard" genre because it is a *hybrid* (a term more in keeping with the evolutionary rhetoric, whereas *bastard* evokes romance), then the women's novels of the eighteenth century described in the preceding sections might fairly contest with it for the title of "most bastard," for they actually undo the opposition of "classification" to "transformation," which, according to Moretti, finds its compromise position in the *Bildungsroman,* thus giving it the flexibility to survive the conflict between the two.[26] They combine the marriage plot identified with "classification" with the open-ended form identified with "transformation," and they do it through an embedded repetition of similar narratives that combine differing, multiple versions of "classificatory" endings, resisting the prioritization of any one of them, and thus resisting classification itself by creating an undecidable, open-ended form. They, too, are bastard forms, but they have remained the bastards of literary history as well, instead of becoming "the dominant genre of Western narrative."

What is the reason for the difference in the histories of these two bastards? Moretti identifies the selective factor, in keeping with his adaptation of the evolutionary metaphor to a Marxist literary history, as "social necessity."[27] "Social" it indubitably is; "necessity"—there's the rub. What Moretti's most evolved species of the evolutionary analogy allows us to see is that it does indeed provide an accurate representation of the processes of modern literary history, though not an absolute standard for judging the value, the perfection, or the readability of literary works. Insofar as the former—the accurate representation of what happened in literary history—was the project of all of the critics I have just mentioned, as I believe it was, they are right. The problem is that to represent the social in terms of a discourse of natural necessity is to perform, if inadvertently, a rhetorical gesture parallel to that of mimetic realism: one of its effects is to mask the social contingency and the constructedness of reality—whether of an individual's or of a genre's history—as something *natural* (or real), and hence unquestionably necessary. Romance becomes biology—or perhaps biology is simply post-Enlightenment romance. We need (which, as usual, means *some of us* need; it has now become "socially necessary") to question the investment of such critical moves, for of course the representation of literary history retrospectively affects the readability of literary works. In order to reread early women's novels, we will have to rethink literary tradition.

A feminist reconsideration of fiction judged as archaic and unreadable by the standards of mimetic realism—which are the standards promoted and perpetuated by the discourse of literary evaluation—allows not only for a more informed appreciation of early women's novels through an understanding of the political differences in their epistemology and referentiality, but also for a greater awareness of the politics of epistemology and referentiality concealed in mainstream Enlightenment evidentiary and exemplary realisms, in the mimetic realism that succeeded them in the nineteenth century, and in contemporary constructions of the history of the novel.

Notes

[1] See, for example, Robert A. Day, *Told in Letters: Epistolary Fiction before Richardson* (Ann Arbor: University of Michigan Press, 1966); J. Paul Hunter, *Before Novels: The Cultural Contexts of Eighteenth-Century English Fiction* (New York: W. W. Norton, 1990); John J. Richetti, *Popular Fiction before Richardson: Narrative Patterns 1700-1739* (Oxford: Clarendon, 1992 [1969]); English Showalter, *The Evolution of the French Novel, 1641-1782* (Princeton, N.J.: Princeton University Press, 1972); Ian Watt, *The Rise of the Novel: Studies in Defoe, Richardson, and Fielding* (Berkeley: University of California Press, 1957).

[2] Watt, *The Rise of the Novel*, 295-97.

[3] Delariviere Manley's preface to *The Secret History of Queen Zarah* (London, 1711) clarifies the latter distinction: "He that writes a True History ought to place the Accidents as they Naturally happen, without endeavouring to sweeten them for to procure a greater Credit, because he is not obliged to answer for their Probability; but he that composes a History to his Fancy, . . . is obliged to Write nothing that is improbable"; "To the Reader," n.p. See also Hunter, *Before Novels,* 193-96.

[4] Cathy N. Davidson, "Introduction," in Susanna Rowson, *Charlotte Temple* (New York: Oxford University Press, 1986), xiii; Robert Mauzi, "Preface," in Denis Diderot, *La Religieuse* (Paris: Gallimard, 1972), 9-13. I am grateful to Paula R. Backscheider for this information about Defoe's work.

[5] As David Hume lamented in 1748, "When anything is affirmed utterly absurd and miraculous, [the mind] rather the more readily admits of such a fact, upon account of that very circumstance, which ought to destroy all its authority." *Of Miracles,* ed. Antony Flew (La Salle, Ill.: Open Court, 1985), 35.

[6] This is in contrast to the later turn taken by both legal evidence and fictional representation, as Alexander Welsh argues in *Strong Representations: Narrative and Circumstantial Evidence in England* (Baltimore: Johns Hopkins University Press, 1992), 8: "By strong representations, I mean those of the later eighteenth and nineteenth centuries that openly distrust direct testimony, insist on submitting witnesses to the test of corroborating circumstances, and claim to know many things without anyone's having seen them at all."

[7] See also Robert Darnton on *Julie:* "Reader and writer communed across the printed page, each of them assuming the ideal form envisioned in the text." "Readers Respond to Rousseau: The Fabrication of Romantic Sensitivity," in *The Great Cat Massacre and Other Episodes in French Cultural History* (New York: Vintage, 1985 [1984]), 248-49.

[8] To illustrate from well-known examples, however, one might mention *Clarissa, Tom Jones, Corinne, La Nouvelle Héloïse, La Princessè de Clèves, The Castle of Otranto* (and indeed the Gothic in general, notably the works of Radcliffe and Lee), *Die Marquise von O; Geschichte des Fräuleins von Sternheim.*

[9] See Sheila Murnaghan, *Disguise and Recognition in the Odyssey* (Princeton, N.J.: Princeton University Press, 1987); Marylin Katz, *Penelope's Renoun: Meaning and Indeterminacy in the Odyssey* (Princeton, N.J.: Princeton University Press, 1991).

[10] Homer, *The Odyssey,* trans. Robert Fitzgerald (Garden City, N.Y.: Anchor/Doubleday, 1961), 20.

[11] Michael McKeon, *The Origins of the English Novel, 1600-1750* (Baltimore: Johns Hopkins University Press, 1987), 420.

[12] I refer to *Mansfield Park,* of course. The word *trial* appears on every other page of *Clarissa;* both the legal and religious senses of the word are played upon throughout the novel. See Watt, *The Rise of the Novel,* 34. See also Susan Pepper Robbins, "Jane Austen's Epistolary Fiction," in *Jane Austen's Beginnings: The Juvenilia and "Lady Susan,"* ed. J. David Grey (Ann Arbor: University of Michigan Research Press, 1989). Robbins notes that Jane Austen "knew that Clarissa's letters were documents in the case against Lovelace" (219).

[13] Samuel Richardson, *Clarissa; or, The History of a Young Lady,* ed. Angus Ross (Harmondsworth, England: Penguin, 1985 [1747-48]). See, for example, 364-65.

[14] Although Richardson, too, is resisting verisimilitude (as Fielding noticed), his "different ends" may be those identified by Paula Backscheider in "'The Woman's Part': Richardson, Defoe, and the Horrors of Marriage," *Eighteenth-Century Studies* 26 (Spring 1994); or by Nancy Armstrong in *Desire and Domestic Fiction: A Political History of the Novel* (New York: Oxford University Press, 1987): *to place women at the center of domestic ideology* rather than to have them threaten patrilineage by controlling the meaning of their own words.

[15] See Joan DeJean, "Lafayette's Ellipses: The Privileges of Anonymity," *PMLA* 99 (October 1984): 896-97.

[16] See my *Virtue's Faults; or, Women's Correspondence in Eighteenth-Century Fiction* (Stanford, Calif.: Stanford University Press, forthcoming); on the relation between female "fidelity" and verisimilitude, see, again, DeJean, "Lafayette's Ellipses"; and Nancy Miller, *Subject to Change: Reading Feminist Writing* (New York: Columbia University Press, 1988), 25-46.

[17] On the instability of plausibility in the history of legal argument, see Welsh, *Strong Representations:* "Thus circumstances typically told against the individual brought to trial as Johnson's definition of the word implies" (15). "[By the mid-Victorian period, when] defendants were fully represented, the weaknesses of circumstantial evidence could be advertised to the jury" (18).

[18] This is the case in Eliza Haywood's *The British Recluse* (London, 1724 [1722]), Mme Riccoboni's *Histoire de Miss Jenny Revel* (Paris, 1764), Sophie von La Roche's *Geschichte des Fräuleins von Sternheim* (Stuttgart: Philipp Reclam jun., 1983 [Leipzig, 1771]), and Sophia Lee's *The Recess* (London, 1783-85), to name only a few. On the instability of the relations among history, fiction, and verisimilitude in seventeenth-century France, see Showalter, *The Evolution of the French Novel,* 15-16, 53-56.

[19] See, for example, the works by Riccoboni and Lee mentioned in note 18. For a full account and bibliography of this fiction, see my *Virtue's Faults.*

[20] Richetti, *Popular Fiction before Richardson,* 5-6, 262; emphasis added.

[21] Though Crusoe may infer plausibility from circumstantial evidence, as Welsh argues (*Strong Representations,* 3-6), Defoe relies precisely on the force of the forms of eyewitness testimony to persuade his audience of Crusoe's truth.

[22] Showalter, *The Evolution of the French Novel,* 5-6; emphasis added.

[23] Franco Moretti, *Signs Taken for Wonders: Essays in the Sociology of Literary Forms* (London: Verso, 1988 [1983]), 264; Franco Moretti, *The Way of the World: The* Bildungsroman *in European Culture* (London: Verso, 1987), 10. Moretti emphasizes chance as that which distinguishes his Darwinian version of the metaphor from a Lamarckian one that would see formal variations as "'oriented' and 'preferentially inclined towards variations'" (*Signs Taken for Wonders,* 262).

[24] Richetti, *Popular Fiction before Richardson,* 262; Showalter, *The Evolution of the French Novel,* 349; Moretti, *The Way of the World,* 10-13.

[25] Moretti, *The Way of the World,* 10.

[26] Moretti borrows the terms *classification* and *transformation* from Yuri Lotman: the former "establishes a classification different from the original one but nevertheless perfectly clear and stable"; under the latter, "the opposite is true: what makes a story meaningful is its narrativity, its being an open-ended process" (*The Way of the World,* 7-9). On narrative structure in eighteenth-century women's epistolary fiction, see Alliston, *Virtue's Faults.*

[27] Moretti, *Signs Taken for Wonders,* 263.

WOMEN AND THE NOVEL

Katherine Sobba Green (essay date 1991)

SOURCE: "The Courtship Novel: Textual Liberation for Women," in her *The Courtship Novel 1740-1820: A Feminized Genre,* Lexington, University Press of Kentucky, 1991, pp. 11-24.

[*In this essay, Green discusses early courtship novels written by women within their literary, cultural, and historical contexts.*]

However enlightened our understanding of patriarchy, when we thumb back through eighteenth-century conduct books we expect to find a language of containment and circumscription that preempts female hopes and desires—the monitory gesture, uplifted forefinger, and glowering brow, usually belonging to male conduct writers. A line from the Reverend John Bennet's *Letters to a Young Lady* (1792) conveys the stereotypic patriarchal attitude: "If I was called upon to write the history of a woman's trials and sorrows, I would date it from the moment when nature pronounces her *marriageable.*"[1] Addressing boarding-school students, Bennet outlines a bleak prospectus for a woman's life—coextensive with her body, woman's history begins with puberty. Ominously, a woman becomes eligible for heroinization in the male-authored text only when she is objectified, when nature "pronounces her" an object of choice ("marriageable"). Writing as late as 1792, Bennet can still obscure the happier prospects of choice and love by adopting traditional cautionary tones. The future he predicts for his young female audience is dismal, and his advice for them is nothing more than passive acceptance. Against the essentializing "when nature pronounces her marriageable" there can be no recourse.

Bennet's easy assumption of the writerly pose stands in contrast to the authorial difficulties contemporary women faced. His "history of a woman's trials and sorrows" will begin at an emblematic moment of sexual differentiation, a biological rite of passage associated with woman's quietism. Ironically, a woman scripting such a story could never leave her body behind, never speak or write without admitting her gender, and yet to admit her womanhood would be to raise the question of her culpability. This gender-specific association between textual and sexual availability began, Ann Rosalind Jones conjectures, in the Renaissance: "The link between loose language and loose living arises from a basic association of women's bodies with their speech: a woman's accessibility to the social world beyond the household through speech was seen as intimately connected to the scandalous openness of her body."[2]

In fact, both somatic/semantic oppression and its ancillary trope recede into history as they are pursued, leaving modern readers to wonder whether the female writer has ever escaped the collocation text = body.[3] As far back as the autobiography of Chaucer's contemporary Margery Kempe, for instance, one may find a well articulated oral example. Seized for public preaching, Margery Kempe was taken before the archbishop, whose first question pressed to the patriarchal heart of the matter: "Why goest thou in white? Art thou a maiden?"[4] To whom does her body belong? The somatic test, which seeks to place her within the age-old masculinist tale of pursuit and conquest, would not have been applied to a male evangelist. Required to give her oath not to "teach or challenge the people" in the archbishop's diocese, Margery Kempe evasively defines a less public, less professional semantic position that resembles the subterfuges of the Renaissance poets Jones discusses. "I preach not, sir, I come in no pulpit. I use but communication and good words, and that will I do while I live."[5] Doughty Margery Kempe would speak, even if she could not usurp patrilogial space ("no pulpit") or the universal authority which that space defined. Her accommodations of cultural norms were nothing short of exemplary: wearing white garments that signed her body unavailable, she would not pretend to male prerogatives of speech ("preach") but instead use those available to her as a woman ("communication and good words"). When it actually came to writing her book, Kempe had another problem. She was illiterate. But, daughter to a mayor and wife to a tax collector, she could afford to employ scribes. Her father's and husband's status were essential determinants of her limited access to written expression.

For the increasing numbers of women producing public texts in the early 1700s, the somatic/semantic trope that had forced circumspection on Kempe and her Renaissance successors still held as one of the material conditions within and against which they wrote. This much one can guess from their anomalous and usually defensive prefaces. Aphra Behn, Delariviere Manley, Eliza Haywood, and others told risqué stories even while their prefaces persistently claimed moral purposes. Eliza Haywood's dedication of *The Rash Resolve* (1724) rehearses a common demur: "The Misfortunes of her who is the subject of it . . . cannot fail of exciting compassion in a generous Mind: and how blameable soever her Conduct may appear . . . the Train of Woes it drew on her, prevail to soften the severity of Censure."[6] Haywood's prose is conflicted, shifting unsteadily between two requirements: making the expected denunciation of the fallen woman's conduct and attempting to enlist reader sympathy or identification with her heroine.

Finally, such circumspection did not protect Haywood from Alexander Pope's censure in the *Dunciad*. Representing her as whore/writer, Pope insisted on the physical proximity of her biological and literary products. "See in the circle next, Eliza plac'd, / Two babes of love close clinging to her waist; / Fair as before her works she stands confessed."[7] "Babes of love" and "works," he implied, were interchangeable effects of sexual/textual depravity. It is not clear from what we know of her personal history whether Haywood was merely daunted or altogether converted by her public humiliation; the demonstrable fact is that she retreated to writing anonymously, eventually turning to genteel courtship plots. Beyond standing as an example of how the somatic/semantic trope affected women, Eliza Haywood's mid-career conversion, her definitive shift from masculine plots of pursuit, seduction, and betrayal to feminine ones of courtship and marriage, illustrates how early women novelists feminized their genre, avoiding or ameliorating the deleterious association between their bodies and their works.[8]

Because its domestic setting and linear plot easily accommodated not only conventional wisdom about women's roles but also incipient resistant ideologies, the courtship novel was an ideal medium for expressing middle-class women's values and issues. If they did not always adopt what we would recognize as feminist strategies or feminist causes, courtship novelists nonetheless feminized the genre in several important ways. First, they valorized the experience of the middle-class "proper lady" by making her the central figure in the plot while reducing male characters to minor roles.[9] Second, they brought the reader into the ordinary sphere of women, typically using domestic settings—country houses, with their dining rooms, closets, sitting rooms, groves, carriages, grounds, tenants' houses, and neighboring estates; or London houses, with their similar interiors and nearby parks, shops, and theaters. Third, by the nature of their heroines, settings, and issues, courtship novelists rendered their works gender-specific, appealing selectively to a community of identificatory readers, women of the middle and upper classes. Fourth, unlike many contemporary writers, these novelists did not usually include in their works prolonged scenes of sexual pursuit, machinations that, in any case, were never successful with their prudent heroines. Finally, courtship novels were didactic; they theorized overtly on women's conduct—at times replicating the repressive views of male-authored conduct books, and at other times expressing the incipient feminism that had begun to question received roles for women. They exposed threats to women's peace: authoritarian parents, rakish suitors, and even fashionable London. On the two issues of education and marriage, especially, courtship novelists sought to raise women's expectations.

It is important to recognize that the feminization of the novel was not an isolated phenomenon but part of a general shift in consciousness in eighteenth-century England. Among the circumstances that shaped receptivity to the new novelistic form, two were particularly important. The first was that, as a result of the currents of sensibility running through England, the courtship novel was part of a broader social imperative to legitimize women's self-actualization as affective individuals. The second, related circumstance that prepared the way was that courtship novels were aligned in their redefinition of feminine roles with two other textual forms that similarly expressed the tensions of ideological change—conduct books and periodicals. Each of

these developments in the history of ideas, given adequate scope, would provide matter for a book-length study. The following is necessarily an abbreviated and partial summary of the climate that fostered the growth of women's courtship novels.

Any discussion of sensibility and affective individualism must begin with Lawrence Stone's *Marriage, Sex and Family in England, 1500-1800* and give some account of the heated debate that followed Stone's assertion that human affections underwent a major course correction in the 1700s. According to Stone, *affective individualism* originated in a complex of social change toward greater freedom for children and more equal partnerships between spouses, toward increased separation of the nuclear family from the community, toward more affectionate relations between parents and children and husband and wife.[10] Notwithstanding the large amount of textual evidence Stone amassed, certain vexing questions about the verifiability of changes in marriage patterns continue to stimulate debate among historians: precisely whose lives were actually affected? how can the alteration in marriage patterns be documented? But while such questions are germane to historical study, I suggest that they do not shape the most fertile ground for literary inquiry. On the contrary, it is precisely the change in conceptualization and representation, the field of ideology, that must interest the literary scholar, and in this regard the evidence is both extensive and persuasive. Whether or not the British population actually changed its nuptial practices, historians have demonstrated that, at least within the realm of ideas—that is, within period texts—companionate marriage made a substantial impact on eighteenth-century England.[11]

Among the studies that have followed and clearly been influenced by Stone's, three merit special attention here for their elucidation of the relationship between affective individualism and literature: Jean Hagstrum's *Sex and Sensibility: Ideal and Erotic Love from Milton to Mozart* (1980), Edmund Leites's *The Puritan Conscience and Modern Sexuality* (1986), and Nancy Armstrong's *Desire and Domestic Fiction: A Political History of the Novel* (1987). Writing from somewhat different perspectives, Hagstrum and Leites are in general agreement in tracing a causal relationship between seventeenth-century Puritan beliefs and the subsequent upwelling into eighteenth-century literature of a new interest in affective individualism. Nancy Armstrong, on the other hand, observes that the Puritans had tried to replace a monarchy with a meritocracy in the seventeenth century, and that their theories continued to be useful in contesting the dominant political order, which, in this case, "depended . . . on representing women as economic and political objects."[12] In Armstrong's view, the new interest in affective individualism was merely a new way of achieving the old goal of domesticity. Within the domestic scene, merit and affect displaced the old system of status considerations as a means of determining relationships.

In *Sex and Sensibility,* Jean Hagstrum observes that, while the relationship between social change and the arts is never simple enough to permit us to chart cause and effect, it seems likely that some literary event conditioned Restoration and eighteenth-century receptiveness to changes in familial relations. Seventeenth-century Puritanism, then, was an important root of affective individualism. According to Hagstrum, it was the prelapsarian love between Milton's Adam and Eve that served as the literary model for new domestic relationships. Such writers as Steele, Addison, Thomson, and Fielding were disciples of the Puritan Milton, "who regarded marriage as satisfying the demands of body, mind, and spirit in a union more total than any that had been hitherto conceived of as realistically possible."[13] Thus, after Milton, love came to mean a fusion between sex and sensibility—more specifically, of three essential terms, *body, mind,* and *spirit.*

Hagstrum neglects to mention, however, that it was not until the mid-eighteenth century advent of the courtship novel that women finally mythologized the new reality for themselves. Moreover, when it came to literary expression, the textual interpretation of women's experience of love—the fusion of sex and sensibility, or body, mind, and spirit—was substantially different from men's. Sensibility largely devalued or displaced libidinal sexual passion, supplying instead the term "esteem," and in women's courtship novels the suppression of physical passion was still more rigorous, with *body* (Hagstrum's first term) finding only the most covert expression or being relegated to minor characters. To an even greater extent than in male-authored or male-centered fiction, blushings, faintings, tremblings, and other signs of the sensible body largely replaced "youthful dalliance," the passion and conjugal union Milton specifies. No doubt this absence of overt sexuality in courtship heroines marked the beginning of what Hagstrum, Sandra Gilbert and Susan Gubar, Mary Poovey, Edmund Leites, and Nancy Armstrong have variously referred to as a spiritualization of the domestic scene, or *angelisme.*[14]

Another reason why sexuality was displaced in women's texts may have been the novelists' desire to distinguish their texts from contemporary romances. In this light, one can read the omission of *body* as an attempt to differentiate woman's history from masculinist representations, which depended heavily on the conventions of male libido—pursuit/prey/objectification. Avoiding these patterns (which were later revived in the Gothics), women centered their novels on the limited space provided for female autonomy within courtship. If overt references to *body,* to sexual passion, are absent in female-authored courtship novels, this was not the case for Hagstrum's second and third

terms, *mind* and *spirit.* The ideology of affective individualism included the notion that men and women were to be intellectual companions, an ideal that naturally raised questions about women's mental preparation for marriage. At the same time, some period writers, no longer believing in accomplishments and domestic arts, exhorted daughters and parents to view education more as a method of self-actualization than as a narrow means to an end.

The third term in Hagstrum's taxonomy, *spirit*—which may have provided the strongest impetus behind the move toward affective individualism and companionate marriage—appears only sporadically in courtship novels. After Milton, who represented Adam and Eve's prelapsarian love as a spiritual experience that enforced their relationship with God, seventeenth- and eighteenth-century writers encouraged marriage for love and inveighed against arranged marriages as spiritually corruptive. Thus Hagstrum emphasizes, as does Leites, that the new literary topos of spousal love was indebted to Puritan ideals.

One of the more common criticisms of Stone's work has been the charge that he obscures the complicitous relationship between liberal humanism and patriarchy.[15] On the whole, the vogue for interrogating so-called liberal tendencies (in this case, the move toward more egalitarian relationships within the family) has been a valuable strategy in the postmodern quest to dismantle ideological monoliths. But such strategies also produce their own systemic oversimplifications. Just as we now recognize that the concept *patriarchy* must be read complexly, with historical specificity, so we must also acknowledge the same principle for the range of human experience (marriage, conjugal love, divorce, and so forth) associated with the term *affective individualism.*

Writing in this vein, Edmund Leites warns, in *The Puritan Conscience,* that in attempting to correct earlier historical naiveté, revisionist historians may go too far. Arguing against the practice of simplistically labeling liberal humanist ideals as cooptive strategies, he points out that conjugal love, in particular, has its own complex history—a genealogy that bears significantly on its implementation. Leites suggests that the new appreciation for married love in the eighteenth century was a natural development from the earlier Puritan desire to avoid an oscillating temperament. He locates as a motive force behind individualism John Locke's view that, while children must give ultimate allegiance to their parents, adults owe that ultimate allegiance "to no other person; they must not find other 'mothers' and 'fathers.' Their knowledge of law alone should command their obedience to civil authorities."[16]

Leites's theory is that the two complementary ideas—the Puritan interest in moral constancy and Locke's view of marriage as a contract between two autonomous beings—cohered as part of the concept of affective individualism that subsequently became so important for eighteenth-century England. Leites suggests further that the valorization of moral constancy led inevitably to a reciprocal hierarchy between the sexes—"a new set of complementary potencies": "The purity of women made them dependent upon men, for men, unlike women, could be commanding and animal without violating their place in the hierarchy. Inasmuch as women needed animality and a forceful, dominating power in their own lives, they had to get it exclusively from men. And men, in their animality and amoral will to power, needed the civilizing presence of women." Thus, while hc acknowledges that seventeenth- and eighteenth-century English culture was formed largely by men, Leites emphasizes that gains made through gender role definition were reciprocal and denies that "the idea of female purity answered only masculine interests."[17]

Leites's theoretical perspective is especially relevant to a study of women's literature in this period because it problematizes the male/female dichotomy in relation to affective individualism. While finding inherent disadvantages for both sexes in their socialization according to a reciprocal hierarchy pattern, Leites also acknowledges that this pattern to some degree empowered each sex. Thus, while he avoids the tendency of altogether reducing affective individualism to masculinist propaganda, he provides a groundwork for understanding why in this period women suddenly began writing courtship stories. In effect, one can argue on the basis of Leites's reciprocal hierarchy theory that women's new charge of maintaining domestic calm and civility gave them an empowering space from which to speak and to write.

Like Hagstrum and Leites, Nancy Armstrong acknowledges that there were significant changes in gender role definition during the eighteenth century, but for her purposes the more interesting question is how domestic fiction served the rising middle class in its power struggle with the aristocracy. She theorizes in *Desire and Domestic Fiction* that popular novels, by presenting a decontextualized, depoliticized surface, and by valorizing affective individualism, forwarded a middle-class power quest. Armstrong's point is that desire was reconstituted so that "language, which once represented the history of the individual as well as the history of the state in terms of kinship relations, was dismantled to form the masculine and feminine spheres that characterize modern culture." The gendered conflict that provides so much of the material for the domestic novel Armstrong consistently reads as a displacement of class conflict. She argues convincingly, for example, that in the domestic novel, the male party to an exchange usually approximates Richardson's Mr. B. "He is likely to bear certain features of the ruling

class that inhibit the operations of genuine love." Then, in the course of the novel, he will be remade in the image of a new ruling class, one that, like the gentry, is permeable—a class one could enter through marriage.[18]

Such a reading of the domestic novel has its drawbacks, however. One of these, inherent in any systematization, is the difficulty of accommodating widely divergent texts written over a considerable period of time. In fact, the weakest aspect of Armstrong's study is that, while she offers a complexly developed theory, she includes relatively few discussions of literary texts. There is something basically suspect, moreover, in the way such a Marxist reading first recognizes the artificiality of dividing human culture along gendered lines (e.g., domestic vs. political) and then implicitly assumes the traditionally masculinist, politically-invested, class-conscious view of history as a basis from which to describe domestic fiction. In effect, Armstrong reenacts the marginalization of the female, reducing once more precisely those voices and texts that historically have been labelled "minor," not representative of hegemonic views. Thus, while she constructs an interesting hypothesis for the largely unconscious process by which affective individualism and class struggle integrate within eighteenth- and nineteenth-century texts, Armstrong does not sufficiently credit and explain the more or less conscious resistances so many women authors expressed through their domestic novels. It is with this question that I will be primarily concerned. In other words, this study of the courtship novel largely confines itself to a purview of the community of women writers and readers whom affective individualism brought together in the domestic sphere.

A second circumstance that conditioned the reception of courtship novels was the presence of similar themes in women's conduct books and periodicals. If women were to be responsible for choosing in a new matrimonial game of chance with higher stakes, it followed that they had to be educated about how to weigh the odds, how to play their hands, and how to read the faces opposite theirs. Roles as well as rules had to be redefined. Jean Hagstrum observes that such a milieu of changing social patterns, where those patterns are inadequately expressed in literature, normally evokes new literary "filiations": "It would be surprising if . . . alternations of the magnitude that [Lawrence] Stone investigates—a truly profound reorientation of human desires and habits—were not also accompanied by linguistic enrichment and a body of internally related literature and art—by works, that is, that possess the power to mythologize reality."[19] Granted, the relationship between actual experience and ideology is more complex than Hagstrum's words would suggest, for, as Paul Smith's *Discerning the Subject* reminds us, the question whether lived experience or ideological representation comes first nearly always remains unanswered.[20] Nonetheless it is important to observe about the contemporary eighteenth-century milieu that among the texts a young woman would have had available to her from mid-century on were two "nonliterary" forms calculated to be especially accessible to female readers and specifically meant to inspire their imitation: conduct books and periodicals written for women.[21]

Valued for their didacticism, conduct books like John Burton's were so similar in content and purpose to novels written for women that one could well argue, as Joyce Hemlow does in a 1960 article, for using the term *courtesy novel* to describe some period fiction. Hemlow remarks that Fanny Burney was one among several writers who "attempted to justify and dignify their new art by including the reputable and useful matter of the courtesy books."[22] To read Burney's novel and others of its kind, then, is to discover "the books of laws and customs *a-la-mode*" that the embarrassed Evelina wished for when caught in her first social faux pas. But the question of where Evelina gets her advice raises a gender issue that both Joyce Hemlow and Mary Poovey neglect—an issue that bears complexly on the history of women's novels. For any discussion of the tandem development of women's novels and conduct books, it is crucial to recall that it was only late in the history of conduct literature that the conduct books ostensibly written for women really began serving as a means of *self*-definition for them.[23] By and large, it was men rather than women themselves who advised and, by extension, defined women, and no doubt male-authored conduct books for women were as suspiciously self-serving as many of those written for servants by their masters, for the simple reason that the group being addressed was not given the prerogative of self-definition. Nonetheless, Mary Poovey is largely correct in linking the general run of conduct books with ideologies one might broadly term bourgeois and patriarchal; it was literally the case that Evelina and other women had few alternatives to the law of the Father until the last quarter of the eighteenth century.

I mean, however, neither to argue that male-authored conduct literature was universally exploitative and repressive nor that there was a coherent and invariable patriarchal line. We know, for example, that Burney's contemporaries were reading both François de Salignac de la Mothe Fénelon's *Traité de l'éducation des Filles* (reprinted in translation five times during the 1700s) and the Marquis de Halifax's *New-Year's Gift: Advice to a Daughter* (which achieved sixteen editions by 1765). In fact, these two very popular books express quite different male attitudes toward women. But whether Fénelon encourages women intellectually or Halifax reminds them they are inferior in nature and in station, the salient fact is that as a group women were still being defined by men—a situation that was not to improve significantly until quite late in the century.

Granted, among the more benevolent male advisers was Samuel Richardson, whose involvement with conduct literature had begun with his printing of Fénelon's *Traité* (1721) and Defoe's *Religious Courtship* (1729). Richardson had written his own conduct book for apprentices, *The Apprentice's Vade Mecum* (1733). Interestingly, one of his last authorial efforts records in its title the kinship he took for granted between conduct literature and the novel: *A Collection of the Moral and Instructive Sentiments, Maxims, Cautions, and Reflexions Contained in the Histories of Pamela, Clarissa, and Sir Charles Grandison* (1755). Richardson, however, sympathetic though he proved himself, was merely another man who chose to advise women.[24] More remarkable than any advice he himself gave women was the fact that his large and shifting female coterie included early women writers both of conduct books and of novels. His friends Hester Mulso Chapone and Jane Collier wrote conduct books; Charlotte Lennox, several courtship novels.

Beyond Samuel Richardson's works and coterie, the most important collective sources of texts written for women in this period were two distinct literary communities, each of which contributed both female-authored conduct books and courtship novels to what one might broadly call the feminist cause. First, there was the select group of men and women who met for informal conversation and who quickly became known as the Bluestockings. Among early members were prominent society figures: Elizabeth Vesey, wife of a member of the Irish parliament; Elizabeth Montagu, wife of the wealthy Edward Montagu (whose grandfather was the first Earl of Sandwiche). Also attending were men of artistic and literary renown—David Garrick, Edmund Burke, Sir Josuah Reynolds, and Samuel Johnson—and literary women, several of whom became famous for their achievements—Elizabeth Carter, Fanny Burney, Hannah More, Anna Laetitia Barbauld, Fanny Boscawen, and Hester Chapone.

This elite company could be termed radical only insofar as they imported a new social custom from France: they exchanged the two-parlor system of entertaining company—which relegated women to gossip, cards, and tea while it favored men with more rational conversation, cigars, and sherry—for the salon, which brought together intellects of both sexes. For this real and symbolic divergence from somatic/semantic strictures, the English *bas bleu* were deservedly famous. In addition, a number of female Bluestockings devoted themselves to advising other women, producing works that were relatively progressive and feminist for the times.[25] Hester Chapone's *Letters on the Improvement of the Mind* (1797) and Hannah More's *Strictures on Female Education* (1799) were popular conduct books promoting better education for women. Anna Laetitia Barbauld, capitalizing on her teaching experiences, also flourished as a writer of children's books. More's

Coelebs in Search of a Wife (1808), though undeserving of comparison with even the least of Fanny Burney's novels, belongs with *Evelina* (1778), *Cecilia* (1782), and *Camilla* (1796) among novels of courtship advice. No doubt it was this textual legacy of the first English salon, along with the later radicalization of women's issues during the French Revolution, that subsequently converted the term *bluestocking,* originally applied to both sexes, into a gender-specific label of approbrium for the female pedant.

The "Feminist Controversy," the second feminist movement to yield an important body of conduct books and courtship novels, evolved during the heady period of the Revolution, when even equality between the sexes seemed possible. Preceded by the socially acceptable blues but perceived as being much more dangerous, Mary Wollstonecraft was the central figure of this movement.[26] After everything revolutionary began appearing suspect, the women in the "Feminist Controversy" were attacked for their association with the excesses of Revolutionary France. Meeting at the house of publisher Joseph Johnson, Wollstonecraft's circle was, in fact, comprised of radicals—sympathizers with the Revolution, brilliant but erratic people such as Swiss painter Henry Fuseli and poet and artist William Blake. Neither her early conduct book, *Thoughts on the Education of Daughters* (1786), nor the novel that followed two years later, *Mary, a Fiction* (1788), was particularly inflammatory. But in 1792, fired by Talleyrand's report on public education, which ignored questions of equality between the sexes, Wollstonecraft published her most provocative feminist statement, *A Vindication of the Rights of Women.* Whether her contemporaries agreed with her works, were inspired by the *Zeitgeist,* or wrote in outraged response to the brutal frankness of William Godwin's biography of her life, the decade of the nineties saw prolific publication of conduct books and courtship novels, many of which evoked Wollstonecraft's name in their prefaces.[27]

As I have briefly outlined it, then, the relationship among women's conduct books and their novels is much more complex than either Mary Poovey or Nancy Armstrong would allow. It is true that proper women novelists accepted and incorporated without question most traditional ideals of female decorum included in male-authored conduct books—in regard, for example, to choosing friends wisely, refusing clandestine correspondence, and treating servants kindly while maintaining the proper distance from them. In all probability male and female writers alike unconsciously served hegemonic interests by the kinds of advice they gave young women. But to read conduct literature as doing no more than this is to oversimplify its complex and often contradictory messages. On some matters—improving women's education and marrying for love,

for instance—female novelists and female conduct writers alike took unusually liberal and feminist positions.

Not surprisingly, at the same time that conduct books were being feminized, parallel changes were taking place in some periodicals. A few instances will suffice to illustrate the accommodations magazines began making for their growing female readership. Too well known to need recapitulating, Addison's and Steele's early efforts at domestic reform were succeeded by such women's journals as the *Female Tatler,* which echoed their incipient feminism, blaming parents who forced their daughters into marriage.[28] By mid-century, women's issues and interests, especially advice on choosing husbands, were spilling into Eliza Haywood's *Female Spectator* (1744-46) and Frances Brooke's *Old Maid* (1755)—whose editors, coincidentally, also wrote courtship novels. Beyond providing marriage guidance, Haywood was an especially enthusiastic advocate of improved education, claiming that she hoped "to bring learning into fashion among women" by promoting studies in philosophy, geography, history, and mathematics.[29]

Meanwhile, the *Ladies Magazine* (1749-53), one of the more entertaining publications for women, included not only a course of history by question and answer and a detailed account of contemporary crimes but also "verse, riddles and puzzles, a diary of events at home and abroad, play reviews, and short discourses on topics of general interest."[30] "Jasper Goodwill" is known to have borrowed most of his material from other periodicals, yet in one section of the magazine he made a signal change, to all appearances a calculated appeal to his female readers. His marriage announcements were not the customary baldly financial accounts, particularly of the young women's fortunes, which had long been the mainstay of such columns in the *London Magazine* and the *Chronicle.* Instead of quantifying the bride's fortune or listing the pound valuation of both spouses, Goodwill merely mentioned the respective families of bride and groom (as in the first two examples below). On the rare occasions on which he made reference to fortune at all (as in the last announcement), Goodwill did so only in the context of providing other "reasons" for the young woman's desirability in marriage:

MARRIAGES, Sir William Baird, Bart. at Edinburgh to Miss Gardener, one of the Daughters of the brave Col. Gardener, killed at the Battle of Preston-l'ans.——Peter Neville, Esq. to Miss Wilson, Daughter of the late John Wilson, of Chichester, Esq.;——Mr. William Halstead, a Gentleman of Estate, and Merchant of London, in Merton Chapel, Oxford, by the Rev. Dr. Leybourne, Principal of Alban-Hall, to his Niece, Miss Caswall, a young Lady of 6000£. Fortune. Particularly admired for her skill in Musick, and the Sweetness of her Voice; her Good Humour, good Sense, and every Accomplishment requisite to make a Husband most happy.[31]

Although, the phrases "a Gentleman of Estate" and "a young Lady of 6000£. Fortune" convey the idea that in simple pecuniary terms both families would have been content with the Halstead-Caswall marriage, there remains some inequity in the specificity with which Miss Caswall's fortune is listed. One may, however, read trends of broader social significance in Goodwill's treatment of Miss Caswall's personal qualities ("particularly admired for her . . ."): the growing claims of affective individualism and an increasing consciousness of a female audience. In making an effort to edit out or at least to diminish the language of the marketplace, Goodwill is accommodating the designated audience for his *Ladies Magazine.*

Another indication that journal editors were becoming increasingly conscious of female readers is that by 1751 even such decidedly male-oriented journals as the *London Magazine* (1732-83) were attempting to appeal to them. In the July 1751 issue, for instance— along with transcripts of Parliamentary debates, abstracts of books, accounts of trials, descriptions and maps of various cities, and mathematical questions—subscribers were offered an essay entitled "Cautions concerning Marriage, with a remarkable Story." Two summers later, in July 1753, the magazine was largely taken up by the Parliamentary news and contemporary debate surrounding Lord Hardwicke's "Act for the better preventing of Clandestine Marriage," a contretemps, as I will demonstrate later, that bears on the representation of heroines, and consequently on the understanding of female role definition in this period.

Notes

[1] John Bennet, *Letters to a Young Lady, on a Variety of Useful and Interesting Subjects; Calculated to Improve the Heart, Form the Manners, and Enlighten the Understanding* (Newburyport: John Mycall, 1792), 2:101.

[2] Ann Rosalind Jones, "Surprising Fame: Renaissance Gender Ideologies and Women's Lyric," in *The Poetics of Gender,* ed. Nancy K. Miller (New York: Columbia Univ. Press, 1986), 76.

[3] Kauffman, in *Discourses of Desire,* traces the influence of amorous epistolary discourse from the earliest extant textual example, Ovid's *Heroides,* through the modern novel. Kauffman argues that a heroine's simultaneously incorporating and responding to her passionate lover's letter, her prose record of frustrated desire, becomes part of the novel's dialogicity. Text implies, becomes, an alternative sign for body.

[4] Margery Kempe, *The Book of Margery Kempe,* in *The Norton Anthology of English Literature,* ed. M.H. Abrams et al. (New York: Norton, 1986), 1:375.

[5] Ibid., 1:377.

[6] Eliza Haywood, *The Rash Resolve* (1724; reprint, New York: Garland, 1973), viii-ix.

[7] Alexander Pope, *The Dunciad,* in *The Poems of Alexander Pope,* ed. John Butt (New Haven: Yale Univ. Press, 1963), bk. 2, lines 149-51.

[8] The term *feminization* is variously used to describe literature of this period by Stone, *Family, Sex and Marriage;* Eagleton, *Rape of Clarissa;* Goldberg, *Sex and Enlightenment;* and Armstrong, *Desire and Domestic Fiction.*

[9] Mary Poovey develops the theory that the idealization of female behavior influenced women writers, in *The Proper Lady and the Woman Writer* (Chicago: Univ. of Chicago Press, 1984), 3-47.

[10] Stone, *Family, Sex and Marriage,* 225-28.

[11] See note 3 to the Introduction, above.

[12] Armstrong, *Desire and Domestic Fiction,* 15.

[13] Jean Hagstrum, *Sex and Sensibility: Ideal and Erotic Love from Milton to Mozart* (Chicago: Univ. of Chicago Press, 1980), 160.

[14] For discussions of the spiritualization of the domestic scene, see Gilbert and Gubar, *Madwoman in the Attic,* 17-27; Poovey, *Proper Lady,* 26-30; and Hagstrum, *Sex and Sensibility,* 152-53.

[15] See, for example, Zillah R. Eisenstein, *The Radical Future of Liberal Feminism* (New York: Long-man, 1981), and Linda J. Nicholson, *Gender and History: The Limits of Social Theory in the Age of the Family* (New York: Columbia Univ. Press, 1986).

[16] Leites, *Puritan Conscience,* 48.

[17] Ibid., 134, 139.

[18] Armstrong, *Desire and Domestic Fiction,* 14, 112.

[19] Hagstrum, *Sex and Sensibility,* 2.

[20] Smith, *Discerning the Subject,* chapter 1.

[21] Paula Backscheider makes this association between courtship novels and other contemporary texts in "I Died for Love," in *Fettr'd or Free? British Women Novelists, 1670-1815,* ed. Mary Anne Schofield and

Cecilia Macheski (Athens: Ohio Univ. Press, 1986), 153.

22 Joyce Hemlow, "Fanny Burney and the Courtesy Books," *PMLA* 65 (1960): 755. See Goldberg, *Sex and Enlightenment*, 24-65, for a discussion of the relationships between conduct books and the novel.

23 John E. Mason, *Gentlefolk in the Making* (1935; reprint, New York: Octagon Press, 1971), develops the idea that a work of conduct literature defines a discrete group (4).

24 On the relationship between Richardson's novels and conduct books, see Margaret Anne Doody, *A Natural Passion: A Study of the Novels of Samuel Richardson* (Oxford: Clarendon Press, 1974), 32-77; Goldberg, *Sex and Enlightenment*, 24-65; and Sylvia Kasey Marks, *Sir Charles Grandison: The Compleat Conduct Book* (Lewisburg: Bucknell Univ. Press, 1986).

25 See Chauncey Brewster Tinker, *The Salon and English Letters: Chapters on the Interrelations of Literature and Society* (New York: Macmillan, 1915), and Joyce M. Horner, *The English Women Novelists and Their Connections with the Feminist Movement (1688-1797)*, Smith College Studies in Modern Languages, no. 11 (Northampton, Mass., 1929-30).

26 Irene Tayler and Gina Luria, "Gender and Genre: Women in British Romantic Literature," in *What Manner of Woman*, ed. Marlene Springer (New York: New York Univ. Press, 1977), treat the literature of the "Feminist Controversy" as precursor to that of the Romantic period, making the connection between Jane Austen and the turbulence of the 1790s.

27 Among conduct writers who must have felt Wollstonecraft's presence were John Bennet, Mrs. Bonhote, John Burton, Hester Chapone, Erasmus Darwin, Maria and Edward Edgeworth, James Fordyce, William Duff, Mary Hays, Catherine Macaulay, and J. Hamilton Moore. And then there were the courtship novelists of the eighties and nineties: Fanny Burney, Susannah Minifie Gunning, Mary Ann Hanway, Mary Hays, Elizabeth Inchbald, Thomas Holcroft, Charlotte Smith, Jane West, and Helen Maria Williams.

28 For more on this topic, see Michael G. Ketcham, *Transparent Designs: Reading, Performance, and Form in the "Spectator" Papers* (Athens: Univ. of Georgia Press, 1985).

29 Quoted in Cynthia L. White, *Women's Magazines, 1769-1968* (London: Michael Joseph, 1970), 28.

30 The *Ladies Magazine*, Dec. 30, 1749-Jan. 13, 1750.

31 Ibid.

Deborah Ross (essay date 1991)

SOURCE: "Introduction: A Secret History of the English Novel," in her *The Excellence of Falsehood: Romance, Realism, and Women's Contribution to the Novel*, Lexington, University Press of Kentucky, 1991, pp. 1-15.

[*In the following excerpt, Ross traces the early development of women's novels against the mainstream categories and especially the label of "romance."*]

> The only excellence of falsehood . . . is its resemblance to truth.
>
> —Charlotte Lennox

A student in an introductory literature course put a plain brown cover on his copy of Willa Cather's *My Ántonia* because he was afraid the feminine title and woman author would make everyone on the bus think he was reading a "romance novel." The cover was meant to prevent attacks on his taste and, more important, on his masculinity. How did "romance," a category that includes works as serious and carefully wrought as Spenser's *Faerie Queene*, come to suggest something both trivial and feminine?

Triviality, or "vanité," was a basis for attacks on romance almost from its first appearance in the Middle Ages (Douglas Kelly 79-80).[1] It was "feminine" in the sense that it chronicled a cultural shift of interest from war to love, and so contained important female characters.[2] During the Renaissance romances were increasingly designed for women readers; Sir Philip Sidney wrote his *Arcadia*, which he called a "trifle," for his sister (Nelson 57). Yet the word and the dedication seem more an excuse for not writing a learned treatise in Latin than a denial of artistic purpose. Not until the late seventeenth century were triviality and femininity linked in serious critical condemnations of the romance.

To understand this development, we will have to go back, briefly, to the fourteenth century, when the word "romance" first came into use in English to denote vernacular, and particularly French, narratives. These stories—at first usually in verse and by the late Renaissance in prose—had two main ingredients: adventure and love.[3] Love became the more prominent theme during the seventeenth century. From the beginning, the religious establishment considered these writings "vain" because, unlike the Bible, they were untrue. According to William Nelson, the early Church fathers criticized writers of the classical period for carelessness in separating fact and fiction (6-7). During the Renaissance this criticism became increasingly severe from both Puritan and counter-Reformation quarters (92), culminating in the late sixteenth century in what critics have called a "historical revolution"— a demand for truth about the past.[4] This concern could be difficult to reconcile with enthusiasm for newly re-discovered classical texts such as Aristotle's *Poetics;* for although Aristotle did distinguish "historical truth" from "poetic truth," he accorded more importance to the latter (Chapter IX). In contrast, sixteenth-century critics valued Greek epics, especially over contemporary romances such as Aristo's, because they were supposed to be based on historical events (Parker 44-45).[5]

To parry accusations of falsehood, romance writers such as Ronsard, Ariosto, and Tasso were driven to one of two defensive postures to gain respect for their art (Nelson 55): they could avoid lying by not pretending to historical truth—deriving dignity from the Greek tradition and its reverence for poetic invention—or they could assert their truthfulness, in either a historical or an allegorical sense (12-13). Somewhere between these two choices was a third: they could make their romances unverifiable and hence possibly true, like the Apocrypha. One way to do that was to set the stories in the distant past and in faraway lands (43-45); another was to write about presentday, ordinary people whose lives were not a matter of public record (107).[6] This latter category roughly corresponds to what we now think of as the "novel," a form of prose narrative that began to be distinguished from the romance in the later seventeenth century and that gradually, over the next hundred years—in theory, at least—came to replace it.

In France the term "nouvelle" began to be used instead of "roman" (though not consistently) to denote shorter works of fiction dealing with more recent times, written in plainer style (Davis 33-34); in English the cognates "novel" and "novella" also had associations with "news," or current events.[7] "Novels" (even when still called romances) established their veracity through expressed contrast with older romances, which now appeared false in a new way—in their lack of immediacy.[8] When, in the 1660s, the immensely influential critic Nicolas Boileau attacked the French romances of his century, he condemned them for inaccuracy about both the past and the present—for making old Roman warriors self-analytical and love-sick and for turning "excessively ugly" real contemporary figures into perfect beauties (*Dialogue des Héros de Roman* 444-45).[9] English critics of this period and after tended to swallow Boileau's pronouncements whole; his judgments are implicit in William Congreve's attempt, in 1692, to define "romance" and "novel" to emphasize the superior truth, or at least verisimilitude, of the latter.[10]

Such was the official evaluation of romances in the late seventeenth century. Yet often their most severe detractors—including Boileau (444) and, later, Samuel Johnson, who blamed his boyhood habit of reading romances for "that unsettled turn of mind which prevented his ever fixing in any profession" (Boswell 36)—confessed, off the record, to a guilty fondness for them

as children. From Shakespeare's time through the eighteenth century, romance maintained a "subliterary" life and popularity, and among its most faithful adherents were women.[11] During the seventeenth century women's enthusiasm for romance grew to such a pitch that they began to write them as well as read them, in more or less open defiance of antiromantic criticism that was becoming increasingly anti-feminist as well.

Romance appealed to seventeenth-century women of the upper classes, and gradually to women of the middle class as well, for many reasons—most obviously because it provided an imaginative escape from what for most of them, in a time of arranged marriages, must have been an emotionally dreary life. Romance was associated with imagination by later writers such as Joseph and Thomas Warton, Richard Hurd, and Clara Reeve, who felt their favorite literature had been nearly killed off in the late seventeenth century by an epidemic of "good sense" (Hurd 120).[12] Even then there were those who stated openly that the move away from romance was not a sign of progress toward scientific clarity, or of return to the clean Attic prose of the Greeks, but of cultural decline, the triumph of ugly old merchants over ideally beautiful nymphs and swains. But imagination and reality are not necessarily opposites; it was not at all clear to women readers that romances were any less true than what was normally called reality.

To understand how this could be so, we must examine some of the assumptions behind the critical distinction between romance and novel, particularly the meaning of the "resemblance to truth" that was supposed to separate them. "Novel" and "romance" overlapped during this period in more than terminology, for the claim to exclusive truth in narrative could never be met. It was easy enough for the critic to call a romance false, but it was the romance writer or novelist who then had to try to find out what would make a narrative true; their solutions were many and various, and all unsatisfactory.

As far back as Chrétien de Troyes, romance writers were claiming a degree of historical truth, usually a greater degree than their relatively "false" predecessors.[13] Even verisimilitude (or "vraisemblance") had a number of contradictory meanings in both romances and novels. It might mean observing probability—that is, omitting miracles or coincidences that obscure the workings of natural law, most often what is now meant by "realism."[14] Or it might mean observing laws of moral order, a concept relating to "bienséance" or decorum, usually associated with romance (Davis 32-33)—although the "bad morality" of romance was one of Boileau's chief objections to it (445). Or it might mean failing to observe either set of laws and thus including the fantastic coincidences and unfinished justice of "real life," a commonly stated intention of early novels such as Aphra Behn's *Oroonoko,* which she called a "history." Both romance and novel writers sometimes claimed that their works were literally true while expecting the reader to know that they were fictional; both were also capable of claiming that their stories were fictional while expecting the reader to recognize in them references to current events.[15]

Critical definitions were therefore bound to be simpler and cleaner than the works they were supposed to describe, and no fiction writer completely escaped romance.[16] Male writers generally took greater care than women to avoid the style and themes of seventeenth-century French romance, its pastoral settings and preoccupation with love, but in doing so they simply went back to the earlier, less feminine quest romance and reserved love for the comic ending. Some, such as Richardson, studiously avoided the external trappings of both older and more recent romance, "a hermit and a wood, a battle and a shipwreck" (Samuel Johnson 3:20); but many did not (Fielding's hermits and Smollett's shipwrecks immediately come to mind). None avoided the romance's basic ingredients—adventure and love.

"Romance" and "novel" were difficult to separate, not only because every narrative wound up being a "falsehood," but because the "truth" that "excellent" fiction was supposed to resemble was neither absolute nor universal. Whether truth meant history or current events, women, as members of a subculture, were equally removed from it. History could seem to them a rather boring study, as Jane Austen's Catherine Morland would later remark, with "the men all so good for nothing, and hardly any women at all" (*NA* 108). Nor did women frequent the coffee houses that J. Paul Hunter describes as important centers for the dissemination of "news" ("News" 501).[17] In a sense, official truth was merely verisimilitude for women, something lived second hand.[18]

Romance, however, could seem true to women in several ways. "Adventure" literally denotes events that come to one from without, and therefore the lives of the unempowered are full of it. Though real women were probably not carried off as often as they were in stories, they were commonly given or sold into matrimony—a trend that only became worse as the class of romance writers and readers shifted down from the French nobility to the English bourgeoisie. As for the other main ingredient of romance, love, in "reality" women were supposed not to feel it, for it was a manifestation of self-will that could only be obstructive in a patriarchal courtship system. The marriage for love that by this time formed the standard ending of romance, though "unreal" in the sense that it rarely happened to actual women, was accurate to women's emotional life.

The concentration on love in seventeenth-century French romances made them especially appealing to the female reader; one romance in particular, Honoré d'Urfé's *L'Astrée* (1610-1627), was an important source of inspiration for Madeleine de Scudéry, and hence an important text in the history of women's fiction. This romance puts forth a morality of love, one of the key tenets of which is that a lady by rights belongs to the man who loves her most. Yet, surprisingly, it does not teach the female reader to see herself as a mere object; that was rather the lesson of her experience. In *L'Astrée* the feelings she was not supposed to have are the basis of a whole world and a topic of endless metaphysical discussion.

The intensity of male love in the story endows the female will with a sort of divinity: Astrée and Queen Galathée are immensely powerful, and even the hero, Céladon, is powerless until he dresses in women's clothes. The rampant cross-dressing in *L'Astrée,* according to Louise K. Horowitz, represents an important step in a historical "feminization" process in fiction: "once knights, then shepherds, now transvestites" (254). Céladon spends a considerable portion of the story as the heroine's "female" friend, and when he casts off his disguise his behavior toward her changes very little. Friendship between women is thus a model for romantic love, and the differences between the sexes, both physical and psychological, are minimized.[19] This feature mitigates the effects of the symbolic "otherness" of the romance heroine; it became an important creed in women's "anti-anti-romantic" fiction later in the century.

Of course, the powerful women and sensitive men of *L'Astrée* must have been an escape fantasy for seventeenth-century women readers—and thus, like other romances, it has been seen as a tool used by the patriarchal establishment to support the status quo by "mak[ing] the lives of the dispossessed seem fulfilled" (Perry x).[20] Identifying with the heroine as beloved could be self-defeating, as feminists from Mary Wollstonecraft onward have noted.[21] Exceptional rather than commonplace, above the rest of her sex, the romance heroine competes with her reader, and in imitating her, readers compete with each other rather than joining forces to bring about social change. In any case the heroine cannot be imitated, for as a symbol she has no real character to imitate. Because she is supposed to be unconscious of her beauty and power, the reader, who displays her own consciousness in the act of reading, cannot resemble her.[22] Nevertheless, this heroine could be turned into somebody who would be useful in bringing about gradual improvement in women's lives. When women began writing instead of only reading romances, they were able to make this woman-as-beloved embody their own feelings and perceptions—a necessary step if those feelings were ever to form the basis for action.[23]

When Scudéry took up the pen, she wrote romances that women readers could enter—both literally, in veiled portraits, and through imaginative projection. Scudéry herself appears as Sappho in *Artamenes, or the Grand Cyrus,* thus becoming one of a long line of female "moderns" who, for better or for worse, would bear that classical nickname.[24] Even the heroines of her romances, while retaining their symbolic perfection, possess a consciousness not unlike that of the author, or of the reader, thus opening up new possibilities for "friendship" among the women inside and outside the text.

Clelia, for example, like her male-created predecessors, rarely initiates action (though she does swim the Tiber, an act of heroism that is later disastrously imitated by Charlotte Lennox's Female Quixote); but she does see, and what she sees is her romance's reality. In fact, not being able to act gives her the vantage point that makes her perception reliable, and that makes the male view of reality look skewed. Clelia's father is a Roman despot (not unlike a French or English bourgeois papa) who claims total authority to dispose of his daughter in marriage. She is pursued by two men but obediently refrains from encouraging either. Yet her father blames her for their attention, casting on her all the responsibility for "adventures" over which she has no control (1:46). This tendency to blame the victim was one of the most persistently exposed injustices in women's fiction for more than a century afterward as women writers revealed their own, alternative truth.

Because the heroine does not control the events of her life, the plot of *Clelia* lacks the "realism" of cause and effect that novel readers later came to require. Instead, it is loosely held together by the heroine's feelings and perceptions, as presented in the allegorical picture of her heart, the famous Map of Tender—a highly detailed representation of the psychology of a woman trying to preserve her dignity under the pressures of a patriarchal courtship system. The map assumes, as Clelia's father does not, that her suitors want her real regard and not just her hand and person. Thus it shows how a man may reach the most honored place in Clelia's heart: tender friendship; "for those I beautifie [beatify?] with the title of tender friends, they are but few in number, and they are before so firmly seated in my heart, that they can hardly make any farther progress" (1:41).[25]

As Clelia's friend Celeres interprets the allegory: "You see she hath imagined tenderness may proceed from three different causes, either from a great Esteem, Recognizance or Inclination, which hath obliged her to establish three Cities of Tender upon three Rivers, which derive their names from them, and to make three different ways to go thither, so as we say, Cumes on the Ionian, and Cumes on the Tyrrhene Sea, she makes us say, Tender on Inclination, Tender on Esteem, and Tender on Recognizance" (1:42).[26] The routes to Tender on Esteem and Tender on Recognizance are dotted with villages, as the progress is by slow stages, requiring, for Esteem, "pleasing verses, amorous and gallant Letters . . . Sincerity, Great Heart, Honesty, Generosity, Respect, Exactness, and Goodness," and for Recognizance, "complaisance," "Submission," "small cares," "Assiduity," "Empressement," "great services," "Sensibility," "Divine [obedience]," and "constant friendship" (1:42).[27] A wrong turn leads either to the "Lake of Indifference . . . which by its calm streams without doubt lively presents the thing of which it bears the name in this place," or to the "Sea of Enmity . . . which by the agitation of its waves, fitly agrees with that impetuous passion" (1:42)[28]

To reach Tender on Inclination, on the other hand, one simply proceeds down a river "which runs with such a rapid course, that there can be no lodging along the shore to go to [from] new Amity to Tender" (1:42).[29] "Inclination," then, is a shortcut to Clelia's highest and fondest regard. But the map also makes a contrary statement, for Celeres cites her intention "to describe to us in the Map that she never had love, nor would ever have any thing but tenderness in her heart." She "makes the River of Inclination cast it self into the Sea which is called the dangerous Sea, because it is dangerous for a woman to exceed the limits of friendship, and she makes in pursuit that beyond this Sea is that we call unknown Lands, because in effect we know not what they are . . . to make us understand in a peculiar manner, that she never yet loved, nor could ever receive any" (1:42).[30] Inclination may lead to tender friendship, but it is mysterious and threatening because it may lead beyond it. Its sexual meaning is clearly hinted, both by the danger and by the rapidity of the current, which flows into areas of Clelia's mind which no one, including herself, has explored. By claiming to want friendship rather than love, Clelia sets a limit to the power and importance of sex and hints that she may be happier without it.

But inclination means more than sex; in contrast to tenderness, a passive receptivity that also has sexual overtones, inclination is an active "leaning toward."[31] Though potentially self-destructive, it is paradoxically an expression of will. By refusing to surrender to her own inclinations—like George Eliot's Maggie Tulliver when she refuses to go any further down the Floss with Stephen Guest—Clelia means to avoid being conquered. But in the end, despite her denials, she marries for love, and therefore for inclination, choosing the man whose respect allows these various aspects of her will to harmonize. Aronces's inclination, though strong, is subdued by his even greater tenderness; in contrast, the villain Horatius believes he loves Clelia more because he feels compelled to carry her off by force.

As in *L'Astrée,* the heroine is awarded to the man who loves her most; but the man who wins her must be above regarding her as a prize.

The Map of Tender helps to show how the marriage that ends romance could assert the existence and importance of the feminine will. Feminist criticism often points out that the denouement of romance promulgated a myth of romantic love that prevented women from rebelling against matrimony.[32] But since romance heroines marry by their own inclination, often in direct opposition to parental authority, fathers had reason to complain about their daughters' reading habits. Clelia's map could be interpreted as recommending cooperation in arranged marriage, for if a woman is obliged to "recognize" or repay the attentions of her suitors, then the parentally selected candidate was bound to succeed in time, with a little effort. But what Clelia does makes a stronger impression than what she says, and the reader who wished to imitate her by marrying only for love might well oppose her father's plans—or she might imitate Scudéry herself and decline to marry at all. Though known to her friends as the "Princess of Esteem, Lady of Recognizance, Inclination, and Adjacent Lands," Scudéry rejoiced in her "strong propensity against marriage," as she had one of her characters comment in *Artamenes:* "I know quite well that there are many decent men, but when I think of them as husbands I also think of them as masters, and since masters have a tendency to become tyrants, I can, from that moment, only hate them" (Aronson 43-45).

The subversive tendency of Scudéry's romance caused Boileau, who disapproved of romances in general, to single hers out for special censure. In his *Satire X,* he describes what happens to the would-be Clelia in real life:

> At first you will see her, as in *Clelia,*
> Receiving her lovers under the soft title of
>   friends,
> Holding herself back with them to small,
>   permissible attentions:
> Then, soon in high water on the River of
>   Tender,
> Sail where she will, say everything, hear
>   (understand) everything.
> And do not presume that Venus, or Satan
> Will let her remain within the terms of the
>   romance.[33]

[67]

Boileau here helps to establish the French romance's smutty reputation for future generations of English critics. Although Scudéry wrote about love in the chastest and most platonic manner—and although Boileau, kinder to her than later English critics would be to English women novelists, admitted that she was personally untainted by "the bad morality taught in her romances" (445)—he warns that the young girl following her directions in *Clelia* would find Venus only in the form of Satan: looking for love, she would find sex.[34] This cynical reduction of love to sex was common in much male anti-romantic writing and continually elicited romantic opposition from the women writers in this study. Attacks such as this surprised Scudéry, who thought her version of love too obviously idealized for anyone to try for it (Aronson 146). But as we have seen, Boileau was right to sense danger in that "say everything, and understand everything," in the power of the Map of Tender to give form to women's vague desires and discontents.

Further satire of Scudéry in this poem suggests that she threatened more than male domestic authority. For Scudéry was not only a romance writer but a précieuse, a prominent member of several salons in which women as well as men set up for critics and judged the merits of literary works, both ancient and modern. The affected "Belle" of the tenth satire, for example,

> Laughs at the vain amateurs of Greek and of
>   Latin;
> Places Aristotle and Cotin in a scale;
> Then, with a hand still more delicate and
>   more skilful
> Coldly weighs Chappelain and Virgil;
> Points out many weaknesses in the latter;
> However admitting he has some merit.[35]

[74]

The précieuses are condemned for being on what Boileau considers the wrong side of the "ancients vs. moderns" controversy; although they praise the ancients, they prove themselves deplorably modern by presuming to weigh ancient and modern works in the same balance—an error they cannot help because the ancients were available to most women only in modern translations. On the same grounds romance writers were also deplorably modern, for however much they invoked classical ancestors, their own works were written in the vernacular.[36] Scudéry's claim that her works imitated Virgil's epics (Aronson 55-56) was therefore doubly discounted. Yet if she had avoided this criticism by learning Greek and Latin, she would have resembled the female pedant who is also condemned in Boileau's satire. Thus, Boileau permitted women neither to seize the keys to the magic kingdom of criticism by force, nor to earn them by hard work.

As we have seen, romance had long been considered trivial, and it was increasingly being considered feminine; but it was Boileau's satire that first damned both women and romance by mutual association. His attack on Scudéry marks the beginning of a long struggle between male critics and female romance writers and novelists that has yet to be fully resolved—a struggle that will be chronicled in the following chapters.[37] Of course, gender aside, it is arguably the theorist's job to create distinctions and the practitioner's job to blur them.[38] But this particular battle was clearly, in part, a battle of the sexes, a continued attempt to fortify serious literature against the encroachment of women's writings, which were becoming ever more abundant and popular. When novels were the preferred form, writers such as Henry Fielding scornfully classed Eliza Haywood's productions with French romances. And later, when romance was enjoying a new respectability, writers such as Sir Walter Scott wrote patronizingly of the "realist" Jane Austen. The need to draw and redraw lines that would keep women on the wrong side added zest to critics' attempts to use "resemblance to truth" to separate "romance" from "novel." For their part, women writers often accepted the critical categories in theory; but in practice they showed themselves more interested in combining and harmonizing than in separating and excluding.

The women in this study never fully severed their connection with the d'Urfé-Scudéry tradition. Their works cross categories, not only because romance and novel were not really separable, nor only because, to them, romance had a kind of reality, but because by maintaining some allegiance to a discredited style they could set alternative realities side by side in their fictions and permit them to comment on each other. As a result they revealed large gaps between what women wanted, what they had a right to demand, and what they were likely to receive—especially in love and marriage.[39] The attempt to depict in fiction a believable world in which women may love and be respected encouraged readers to claim their basic human right to choose, or not choose, a husband. Thus fiction affected life; and life in turn affected fiction. For as the conditions of women's lives improved, romance and realism could more fully coalesce, creating more consistent narratives. Jane Austen's works may strike readers of today as "modern" in a way those of her foremothers do not, not only because of her own talent, but because the struggles of the previous century created the conditions that permitted her talent to operate.

In the following chapters I will discuss the interplay of romance and realism in selected texts, not to give a comprehensive history of romance during this period, nor of women's fiction, nor even of English women's fiction, but to mark important stages of development. In the earlier works, the relationship between romance and realism is simplest. An ideal romance hero or heroine is brought into contact with the real world and is destroyed by its corruption. The romance world provides love, which the real world tries to kill, and the result is adventure—that is, suffering. Thus Aphra Behn's Oroonoko and Imoinda perish at the hands of European capitalists, and women in Delarivière Manley's romantic-satiric allegories

sacrifice their reputations and lives to love in a world dominated by heartless, power-seeking men.

By the mid-eighteenth century, tragedy begins to give way to comedy as heroines such as Eliza Haywood's Betsy Thoughtless and Charlotte Lennox's Harriot Stuart attempt to succeed at life by renouncing love and romance. But tragedy nearly overtakes them as they learn that love is essential to their happiness and goodness. Thus an ambivalence about the romance emerges. These novels, along with Lennox's *The Female Quixote,* are partly anti-romances; they endorse love while warning against the adventure it brings. Haywood's and Lennox's objection to the romance is moral as well as practical; the heroines' desire for attention—their willingness to *be* heroines—stems from the sin of vanity. In Fanny Burney's novels, the sin seems even greater: there romance becomes a symbol of the selfish individualism that threatened to destroy the social order. Burney almost recommends the sacrifice of love to prevent painful and wicked adventure; but in the end she too gives her heroines their romantic denouement.

Burney ultimately found that, despite her literary and moral objections to the romance, she was unable to describe the isolated and adventure-filled lives of her heroines, or to reward them as they deserve, without it. Like Alice's Looking-Glass House, romance was there to greet her at the end of every path that seemed to lead away from it. Each of her novels is more romantic than the one before, so that Ann Radcliffe was able to build a Gothic romance, *The Italian,* on a plot very similar to that of Burney's *Cecilia.* Though Radcliffe rejected the realistic novel of manners, her message is similar to Burney's: both novels associate love and adventure, passion and imagination, with insanity. Yet realism seemed less necessary to Radcliffe because in the later eighteenth century critics were showing a renewed interest in older romances, particularly those of the Elizabethan period. This change in the critical climate also affected the novels of Jane Austen by reminding readers that romance, though superficially "false," had once been used to express sacred truths. Austen both satirized and welcomed romance elements in her realistic fictions, using them to describe the relationship between the real lives of ordinary individuals and the encompassing romance, or religious allegory, that to a Christian gave that life meaning.

The progression I will describe is not exactly a "female tradition" of the novel. Most of the writers in this study were less interested in literary sisterhood or daughterhood than in trying to make their own separate peace with critical authority. Haywood renounced the novel as practiced by Manley (and by herself in the first half of her career), Lennox attacked Haywood's morals, and Burney named only men as her literary ancestors in the preface to *Evelina*. When Radcliffe took up romance instead of the Burneyan novel of manners, Austen responded with a novel of manners that satirized Radcliffean Gothic. Often these writers denied the romance aspects of their writing in order to win intellectual respect as rational creatures, unable to anticipate that once they were finally believed they would simply be dismissed on new grounds. Nevertheless, in affecting and being affected by the conditions of life, these women writers (along with others too numerous to include in this study) did create an important line of development not traced in standard courses and texts on the history of the novel. Despite the efforts of feminist criticism, those courses and texts still mainly consider Defoe, Fielding, Richardson, Smollett, and Sterne, though the stretches that are often required to lead students from one to the next should suggest that something important has been left out of the picture.

In contrast, the line of development I see, though it moves the canonical novelists to the periphery, has a logic of its own. I have called the work a "secret history" of the novel in this introductory chapter in part to pay my respects to the popular women writers of romans à clef—Scudéry, Behn, Manley, and Haywood—but also to borrow something of their self-consciously different, perhaps even perverse, "feminine" angle on reality. Just as Behn would describe Monmouth's rebellion in terms of the Duke's affairs of the heart, and just as Manley would characterize the Duke of Marlborough by his amours rather than his campaigns, I have chosen here to describe the history of the novel through the works of a few women novelists. The result is no more comprehensive than male-centered studies—but neither is it less so. Furthermore, whereas women's novels rarely fit well into the theoretical structures designed to explain male novelists, the structure of my own study leaves room for the inclusion of the more standard "major" works in all their complexity. In that sense it is a step toward the more complete, integrative history of the novel that still needs to be written.

One would think that that history would have been written already, given the new availability of editions of neglected women's novels, the proliferation of scholarly discussion of those novels, and the dazzling historicist criticism of the last decade. Studies by Lennard Davis, J. Paul Hunter, and Michael McKeon, for example, subtly and convincingly show the novel rising, or being born, out of social and ideological instabilities of the early eighteenth century. All, reacting against Northrop Frye's archetypal approach (among other approaches), distinguish the novel sharply from the romance; Davis even questions whether romances such as Scudéry's were a substantial influence on the novel at all (25, 41). Yet the social and intellectual currents each of these critics describes did not affect women in the same way that they affected men; nor do the novels of Aphra Behn, a woman who is sometimes called the first novelist, depart as radically from the French tradition as those of Daniel Defoe, the man who is usually called the first novelist.[40] These studies break down generic barriers by showing the interrelatedness of novels and other kinds of writing, and other manifestations of popular culture; but while exhaustively explicating one period in history, they play down connections with the past, the similarity between the impulses toward truth and verisimilitude that produced what they call novels and those that affected the earliest romance writers.[41] (A broader historical sweep may be found in Nelson's *Fact or Fiction,* and in Adams's *Travel Literature and the Evolution of the Novel*.) And though all these writers make serious efforts to include women novelists, they continue to make theoretical distinctions that do not accurately describe those novelists' practices.

That these and other "mainstream" studies do not fully incorporate the work of feminist scholarship may be due in part to assumptions inherent in some of that scholarship. Since the days of Mary Wollstonecraft, heightened awareness of the impossible conditions under which women artists attempted to create has led to the almost inescapable conclusion that their works must be seriously flawed—especially, as John Stuart Mill believed, with respect to originality.[42] Since the 1970s, many writers have been pointing out that women have not been completely powerless—though to prove this they have sometimes had to redefine "power" in some very tricky ways (Newton xiii-xv). Today, as Janet Todd notes in her survey, many branches of feminist criticism denigrate or simply ignore the works of early women writers because they inhabited an unenlightened age, or failed to illustrate Lacan's version of Freudian mythology, or belonged to a privileged class. The American style of feminist literary analysis, best illustrated by Sandra Gilbert and Susan Gubar, favors nineteenth-century novels such as Brontë's *Villette,* which can be made to reveal subtexts containing something like current feminist awareness, but this "double text" approach works less well with earlier authors whose values are more alien to our own (*Feminist Literary History* 29).[43] By regarding these early women's novels with "double vision," some critics conclude that romance elements are a sign of the crushing effects of patriarchy and so perpetuate the sense of their unoriginality, their "minor" status, and their marginality.[44]

Notes

Note: Unless otherwise indicated, all translations from French to English are mine.

Epigraph: Lennox, *The Female Quixote,* 418.

[1] There were ancient Greek and Latin stories that are now called romances, but the word in English originally denoted a modern language phenomenon.

[2] See D. Kelly 78; E. Auerbach 141.

[3] See Frye, *Secular Scripture,* 26.

[4] Nelson is quoting the title of a book by F.S. Fussner (41). See also Adams 12.

[5] See also Nelson 53

[6] Adams notes that all artists were considered liars in the late seventeenth century (82). He discusses several of the fiction writer's defenses against charges of falsehood (88-93).

[7] Hunter, "Novels," 480; Davis 45ff. Both McKeon and Hunter place the taste for "news" in the early eighteenth century, though McKeon sees something like it in the previous century; see, for example, McKeon 47-48, 54-55; Hunter, "Young," 261. This shift in taste has been compared to the change in sixteenth-century Spain that produced *Don Quixote;* see Harry Sieber, "The Romance of Chivalry in Spain from Rodriguez de Montalvo to Cervantes," in Brownlee, 214-17; see also McKeon 292-94.

[8] As the encyclopedist Bayle phrased it, "The new Romances keep as far off as possible from the Romantick Way" (Nelson 109; and Davis 38).

[9] Not all Scudéry's characters are beautiful; the ugly, satirical Aricidia in *Clelia* is an example of the psychological realism often overlooked in Scudéry's work. See Schofield, *Masking,* 21.

[10] Hurd shows that even Boileau's own words found their way into the writings of English critics—including Shaftesbury and Addison—who were sympathetic to the romance (79-86).

[11] See Nelson (76-77) on ambivalence in Shakespeare; in Spenser's *The Faerie Queene* (77ff.). In England romance sometimes migrated to the stage; Scudéry's romances were sources for Dryden's heroic dramas. By the 1690s that genre was also largely taken over by women such as Delarivière Manley (Hook, intro. to *The Female Wits,* ii).

[12] See Trowbridge, intro. to Hurd, vi.

[13] See D. Kelly 77, 87; Nelson 93; Uitti 137, 141. These early claims of truth, which resemble the "naïve empiricism" McKeon attributes to readers in the early eighteenth century, show that one cannot simply distinguish "romance" from "novel" along the lines of Bakhtin's distinction between "truth of idea" and "experiential actual." See Zimbardo 48.

[14] The first listing for "realism" in the *OED* is from Ruskin, 1856; Davis suggests that the concept as well as the term did not quite exist before then either (177-78).

[15] See Nelson on Scudéry, 100; Adams notes her accuracy in details about foreign countries, drawn from travel literature (113).

[16] On theorists' attempts to simplify the novel, see Davis 113; McKeon 88; and Hunter, "Novels," 498. Beasley counts the persistence of romance elements as one of the defining characteristics of the novel ("Life's Episodes" 21).

[17] Hunter notes that the "larger cultural embracing of the present moment as a legitimate subject . . . for serious discourse" opened the way for women writers such as Fanny Burney ("News" 495, 504); but a personal diary is hardly "news" in the same way that politics is. See Gardiner 205.

[18] If one accepts McKeon's theory that the novel appeared only after a painstaking process whereby readers became able to understand a work of fiction as "realistic" rather than true or false, then women's position may have given them a shortcut to this understanding.

[19] See Horowitz 257. This "unisex" romance convention runs counter to that noted by Boone (32-33, 40-42), who also refers to texts that show resemblance between the sexes as anti-romantic (12).

[20] See Jane Spencer xi.

[21] See Kirkham 37, 165.

[22] See Warren's argument that men considered romance reading and writing a desirable hobby for women (368).

[23] See Frye on the "revolutionary" potential of romance (*Secular Scripture* 178). Brownstein notes how easily the heroine of male romances could become conscious, since she had nothing to do and therefore had plenty of time to think (35-37).

[24] See Spencer 28.

[25] Passages from *Clelia* have been taken from the translation by John Davies, the version known to most seventeenth- and eighteenth-century English readers. I suspect that this translation was responsible for Scudéry's bad reputation among some English readers. The original French appears in notes, with only minor changes to conform to modern printing; accents remain unchanged. "Tenderness" and "Inclination" are "Tendre"

and "Inclination" in *Clélie*. For a discussion of the Map of Tender, see Brownstein 38; Aronson 93-95; and Doody, *A Natural Passion,* 294-97; the map is reprinted in Doody's book.

"Mais pour ceux que je mets au rang de mes tendres Amis, ils sont en fort petit nombre; & ils sont si avant dans mon coeur, qu'on n'y peut jamais faire plus de progrés" (1:391).

[26] "vous verrez qu'elle a imaginé qu'on peut avoir de la tendresse par trois causes differentes; ou par une grande estime, ou par reconnoissance, ou par inclination; & c'est ce qui l'a obligée d'establir ces trois Villes de Tendre, sur trois Rivieres qui portent ces trois noms, & de faire aussi trois routes differents pour y aller. Si bien que comme on dit Cumes sur la Mer d'Ionie, & Cumes sur la Mer Thyrrene, elle fait qu'on dit Tendre sur Inclination, Tendre sur Estime, & Tendre sur Reconnoissance" (1:399-400).

[27] "de jolis Vers, de Billet galant, & de Billet doux, . . . Sincerité, Grand Coeur, Probité, Generosité, Respect, Exactitude, & Bonté"; "Complaisance," "Soumission," "Petits Soins," "Assiduité," "Empressement," "Grands Services," "Sensibilité," "Obeïssance," "Constante Amitié" (1:400-403).

[28] "Lac d'Indifference . . . qui par ses eaux tranquiles, represente sans doute fort juste, la chose dont il porte le nom en cét endroit"; "mer d'Inimitié, . . . qui par l'agitation de ses Vagues, convient sans doute fort juste, avec cette impetueuse passion, que Clelie veut representer" (1:404).

[29] "qui va si viste, qu'on n'a que faire de logement le long de ses Rives, pour aller de Nouvelle Amitié à Tendre" (1:400).

[30] "faire connoistre sur cette Carte, qu'elle n'avoit jamais eu d'amour, & qu'elle n'auroit jamais dans le coeur que de la tendresse, fait que la Riviere d'Inclination se jette dans une Mer qu'on apelle la Mer dangereuse; parce qu'il est assez dangereux à une Femme, d'aller un peu au delà des dernieres Bornes de l'amitié; & elle fait en suitte qu'au delà de cette Mer, c'est ce que nous apellons Terres inconnuës, parce qu'en effet nous ne scavons point ce qu'il y a . . . de faire entendre d'une maniere particuliere, qu'elle n'a point eu d'amour, & qu'elle n'en peut avoir" (1:405). Note the mistranslation of the last clause above.

[31] Sex can even be against inclination, for one can lust against one's will. See Manley, *NAt,* 2:102; qtd. in Richetti 151.

[32] See Newton 8-9, 11, 21; Poovey 241; Schofield, *Masking,* 27; Boone 2, 7-10. Boone does note that the

marriage for *love* (37), especially between equal partners, as in Spenser and Shakespeare (56-57), could be subversive.

[33] "D'abord tu la verras, ainsi que dans Clélie / Recevant ses Amans sous le doux nom d'Amis, / S'en tenir avec eux aux petits soins permis: / Puis, bien-tost en grande eau sur le fleuve de Tendre, / Naviguer à souhait, tout dire, et tout entendre. / Et ne présume pas que Venus, ou Satan / Souffre qu'elle en demeure aux Termes du Roman" (67).

[34] Boileau claimed to have abstained from publishing or even writing down the *Dialogue des Héros de Roman* while Scudéry was alive out of respect (445); but the dates do not bear out this explanation. See notes to the *Dialogue* in the *Oeuvres Complètes* and White, *Nicolas de Boileau* (NY: Twayne, 1969), 19, 77-78. Boileau made other satiric references to Scudéry during her lifetime: in *Satire X,* as we have seen, and in Canto V, the Battle of the Books, in *Le Lutrin* (White 76).

[35] "Rit des vains amateurs du Grec et du Latin; / Dans la balance met Aristote et Cotin; / Puis, d'une main encor plus fine et plus habile / Peze sans passion Chappelain et Virgile; / Remarque en ce dernier beaucoup de pauvretez; / Mais pourtant confessant qu'il a quelques beautez" (74).

[36] Davis (27) emphasizes that the word "romance" suggests its Roman ancestry; see M.S. Brownlee 220. There is a class issue here: the "moderns" were associated with the middle class, and Boileau's criticism of the précieuses and of romances had something to do with their vulgarity. This may surprise readers of our own time, accustomed to regarding Scudéry and her circle as aristocratic, but it is an important reminder that class is no more reliable as a means of distinguishing romance from novel than any of the other criteria of criticism; see McKeon 268. Frye sees romance as a periodically recurring "proletarian" reaction against elitist literature (*Secular Scripture* 23).

[37] Attacks on Scudéry herself in England were not always anti-feminist because not everyone knew how many of the works published under her brother's name were really hers.

[38] See El Saffar's comments on Cervantes (249-50).

[39] See Poovey xv.

[40] On the issue of who was "first," see Gardiner. Although Davis questions the "firstness" of Defoe in the light of Behn's contribution, he misses the fact that she, not Fielding, was the first English novelist to include an account of a contemporary historical event,

in *Love Letters from a Nobleman to his Sister*—which, though in many respects close to French romance, thus also fits his definition of the novel (see 201).

[41] For example: Davis distinguishes novels from romances by noting that novels claim to be true (36) and distinguishes romantic from novelistic verisimilitude (30-33), yet writes later about novels that are avowed fictions (Henry Fielding's, 200) and about something like romantic "bienséance" in the novel (111). He admits that the roman à clef has characteristics he attributes to the novel, but does not include Scudéry in this category although she wrote them (36). McKeon writes about the gradual evolution of realism, the ability to read something that is neither strictly true nor false, through dialectical struggles with the nature of truth; yet Nelson shows that there was a way of doing this earlier, with the Apocrypha (21-22, 35). Hunter writes that male and female young people needed realistic novels to help them understand their daily lives in the early eighteenth century ("Young" 271-72), but I do not see why Scudéry's romances could not have been read for similar reasons, though by a different group of readers. Adams' premise is that from an international point of view romance and novel are impossible to distinguish; yet even he makes the curious distinguishing statement that "no important dramatist in the seventeenth century wrote fiction of any significance" (31), momentarily and uncharacteristically forgetting Behn. His emphasis on travel in both romance and novel also presents a problem for women, who traveled less as the eighteenth century progressed, and whose travel in earlier fiction is more part of the ravishers' quests than their own. Even Clelia's map (which he discusses, 271) mostly points out routes to male travelers; Clelia is the destination.

[42] See *The Subjection of Women* [1869]: *Essays on Sex Equality,* ed. Alice Rossi (Cambridge, MA: MIT Press, 1970), 69.

[43] Todd criticizes the separate *Norton Anthology* for women writers because of this nineteenth-century bias (*Feminist Literary History* 48). Schofield applies the Gilbert and Gubar type of reading to eighteenth-century novels (*Masking* 9). Other examples of "double" studies: Goreau (5) writes of two Aphra Behns; Schofield refers to Haywood's "double writing" (*Eliza Haywood* 5-6); Straub has entitled her study of Burney *Divided Fictions;* the introduction to *Fetter'd or Free?* calls eighteenth-century women novelists "Janus-like" (1).

[44] Conversely, realism is seen as a sign of originality and rebellion. See Simons 24, 32; Spender 21; Figes 16. See also Hunter on the present narrowness of the canon ("Contexts" 128-29, 133-34).

THE NOVEL AND OTHER LITERARY FORMS

Terry Castle (essay date 1986)

SOURCE: "Literary Transformations: The Masquerade in English Fiction," in *Masquerade and Civilization: The Carnivalesque in Eighteenth-Century English Culture and Fiction*, Stanford University Press, 1986, pp. 110-29.

[*In this excerpt from a study of the carnivalesque, Castle examines the relationship between the masquerade and English fiction in the eighteenth century.*]

The literary history of the masquerade in England could be said to begin, not with a novelist at all, but with John Dryden. The following dialogue from *Marriage à la Mode* (1673) celebrates the birth of a topos:

> PALAMEDE. We shall have noble sport tonight, Rhodophil; this masquerading is a most glorious invention.
>
> RHODOPHIL. I believe it was invented first by some jealous lover to discover the haunts of his jilting mistress, or perhaps by some distressed servant to gain an opportunity with a jealous man's wife.
>
> PALAMEDE. No, it must be the invention of a woman: it has so much of subtlety and love in it.
>
> RHODOPHIL. I am sure 'tis extremely pleasant, for to go unknown is the next degree to going invisible.
>
> PALAMEDE. What with our antique habits and feigned voices—do you know me? and I know you?—methinks we move and talk just like so many overgrown puppets.
>
> RHODOPHIL. Masquerade is only vizor-mask improved, a heightening of the same fashion.
>
> PALAMEDE. No, masquerade is vizor-mask in debauch, and I like it the better for't: for with a vizor-mask we fool ourselves into courtship for the sake of an eye that glanced or a hand that stole itself out of a glove sometimes to give us a sample of the skin. But in masquerade there is nothing to be known; she's all *terra incognita* and the bold discoverer leaps ashore and takes his lot among the wild Indians and savages without the vile consideration of safety to his person or of beauty or wholesomeness in his mistress. (IV, i, 121-45)

Here, in the form of a cosmogony, are all the later themes of the masquerade: pleasure, women, sex, the unknown. Likewise the scene that follows is archetypical enough—a comic imbroglio involving mistaken identity and transvestism, erotic and political intrigue, deceit, commotion, and badinage. With Dryden, the "glorious invention" of the masquerade, that terra incognita at the heart of civilized life, becomes part of the scenery of English literature.

But Dryden is merely a symbolic point of origin, and a somewhat distant one at that. To be sure, *Marriage à la Mode* directly influenced the eighteenth-century literature of the carnivalesque in at least one respect. The play was produced in original form until 1700; adaptations by Colley Cibber and others gave it continued life through the 1750's. It is likely that Dryden's masquerade scene provided a model for similar episodes in eighteenth-century comic drama. A century of masquerade plays, farces, and operas—from Shadwell's *The Virtuoso* (1676) to Sheridan's *The Duenna* (1773) and Cowley's *The Belle's Stratagem* (1781)— bear witness to the prototype.[1] In each play we find the same exploration of the masquerade's comic potential, the same identification of the scene with error and plot complication, fantasia and laughter. The masquerade seemed made for dramatic representation, and its "intrigues of the night" a perfect metaphor for the playful mystifications of the eighteenth-century comic theater itself.

What Dryden did not anticipate, however, were subsequent changes in the nature of masquerading, and the pressing ideological issues that came to surround the institution in the first decades of the eighteenth century. *Marriage à la Mode* re-creates the masquerade in its primeval, late-seventeenth-century English form— that of ornate, imitative, somewhat enigmatic court entertainment. Dryden's idealized Sicilians resemble members of the court of Charles II, and their travesties the characteristic pleasures of a newly liberated aristocracy. These merry "frolics," mentioned in the chronicles of Gilbert Burnet and others, themselves imitated of course the lavish masked fêtes of Paris and Versailles.[2] In a large sense the Restoration masquerade belonged to the art world of the European courts, and Dryden appropriately stresses the aesthetic and aristocratic context. True, there are hints in *Marriage à la Mode* of quasi-democratic possibilities in the masquerade: Melantha and Palamede participate despite any official court connection; Melantha, in particular, here attempts to efface her status as a mere "town" lady. Masquerading coincides at least implicitly with the subversive theme of social climbing. But Dryden's main emphasis is on the masquerade as "heightened" fashion, a shimmering imago of high life.

What occurred during the early 1700's, however, was a basic change in the place the masquerade occupied in society, and its popularization as a form of public commercial entertainment. No longer strictly the predilection of royalty and hangers-on, the masquerade was transformed, in the second decade of the century, into a public event, a diversion of the "Town"—accessible, like Vauxhall or the theater or the opera, to anyone with aspirations after fashionability. It became a part of a new and burgeoning industry of public pleasures.[3] This democratization of the masquerading impulse, on which Heidegger and others capitalized so adroitly, had a critical significance in the literary history of the carnivalesque. For as the "Midnight Masque" became more and more deeply lodged in eighteenth-century popular consciousness, so too its tremendous symbolic potential, for both good and bad, emerged. The masquerade entered the repertoire of cultural emblems. This process, as we have seen, resulted in a wealth of moralizing literature—an anti-masquerade complaint of considerable proportions. But the masquerade's new visibility also led to its most significant literary manifestation: its representation in contemporary fiction.

It was fitting that one form of entertainment should be absorbed into another—that the masquerade should find a place within the new genre of eighteenth-century realistic fiction. Both were the products of an increasingly self-conscious, novelty-seeking public. Yet the masquerade was ripe for fictional exploitation for other reasons too. Early on, Addison had intimated the narrative potential of the carnivalesque: in his *Remarks on Italy* (1718), following descriptions of the Italian carnival and the pleasures of dressing "as a false personage," he commented with prescience that "the secret history of a carnival would make a collection of very diverting novels."[4] Because of the masquerade's classic association with mystification and intrigue, masquerade scenes in fiction, as in the drama, provided diverting opportunities for plot development. Early works such as Haywood's *The Masqueraders; or, Fatal Curiosity* (1724) exploited the melodramatic possibilities of the occasion. But at the same time the masquerade's characteristic themes—social mutability and sexuality, luxury, pleasure, and transgression—mirrored some of the early novel's deeper moral and ideological concerns. By mid-century, not surprisingly, the masquerade set piece had become a commonplace in English fiction. Notable masquerade scenes appear in Defoe's *Roxana* (1724), Richardson's *Pamela*, Part 2 (1741) and *Sir Charles Grandison* (1753), Fielding's *Tom Jones* (1749) and *Amelia* (1751), Cleland's *Memoirs of a Woman of Pleasure* (1749), Smollett's *Adventures of Peregrine Pickle* (1751), Burney's *Cecilia* (1782), Inchbald's *A Simple Story* (1791), and Edgeworth's *Belinda* (1801). In addition, significant references to the world of public travesty occur in Smollett's *Roderick Random* (1748), Goldsmith's *The Vicar of Wakefield* (1766), Burney's *Evelina* (1778), Radcliffe's *The Mysteries of Udolpho* (1794), and a host of minor works of the period.[5] In the guise of presenting a faithful record of modern manners, English novelists had fortuitously revivified the ancient literary imagery of the carnivalesque, and found in the process a way of giving life to certain compelling, specifically novelistic imaginative concerns.

Which is not to say that the masquerade did not make a paradoxical addition to the scenery of the novel. All the contradictions surrounding the masquerade in eighteenth-century culture, where it was seen as both delightful and pernicious, are replicated in contemporary fiction. Indeed, the intense cultural ambivalence regarding the carnivalesque is displayed perhaps more prominently here than anywhere else. Eighteenth-century novelists responded to the institution of the masquerade with moral concern—the scene is usually presented as part of a stereotypical urban topography of vice or dissipation—yet they drew upon it, sometimes disingenuously, for a host of provocative and memorable effects.

The topos exposed certain fundamental tensions at the heart of the genre itself. The novel, as Tony Tanner has brilliantly demonstrated in *Adultery in the Novel,* has always dramatized a larger cultural conflict between moralistic and transgressive imperatives, equanimity and adventure, the desire for bourgeois stability and the subversive human fascination with change and novelty. For Tanner the prescriptive moral and ideological elements of English fiction have been profoundly at odds with those currents of rebelliousness and disorder that from the beginning have implicitly animated the genre. While acknowledging the eighteenth- and nineteenth-century novel's overt celebration of the bourgeois values of marriage, social stability, and "the securing of genealogical continuity," he also notes how the genre "gains its particular narrative urgency from an energy that threatens to contravene the stability of the family on which society depends." The orphans, prostitutes, and adventurers of early fiction incarnate for Tanner "a potentially disruptive or socially unstabilized energy that may threaten, directly or implicitly, the organization of society, whether by the indeterminacy of their origin, the uncertainty of the direction in which they will focus their unbonded energy, or their attitude to the ties that hold society together and that they may choose to slight or break." So potent and interesting are these destabilizing forces that the novel "becomes a paradoxical object in society, by no means an inert adjunct to the family décor, but a text that may work to subvert what it seems to celebrate."[6]

Eighteenth-century novels often represent the conflict spatially. Early realistic fiction often seems to value the organized and stable realm of the bourgeois household; the family or domestic space is typically both the starting point and the end point in eighteenth-century narrative. But plot itself depends on less stable and predictable realms: the Garden, the Road, the City. It is necessary to leave the unchanging, endlessly self-regulating world of the home—to move beyond the boundaries of order and rectitude—in order to precipitate interesting stories. Thus the picaresque tradition, and the eighteenth-century novel's obsession with wayfaring, wandering, journeys to the city, and so on.

Narrative begins with the transgressive step, the journey out of the *maison paternelle,* the house of the father.[7]

It should be clear right away how the novel of masquerade fits, loosely, into this picaresque tradition. To get to the masquerade in the first place, one must journey out of ordinary existence, away from the patterns of everyday life, into a world of strangeness, transformation, and mystery. In eighteenth-century fiction the masquerade is literally a topos, or place, somewhere out there, waiting to be discovered. It may be associated with a larger educational confrontation with chaotic urbanity: in several eighteenth-century novels the scene takes its place, in the manner of a set piece, as part of the classic theme of initiation—the hero or heroine's introduction to the "Town." Sometimes it is part of a series of topoi—one (though usually the last) in a number of unusual adventures. In *Tom Jones* and Smollett's *Adventures of Peregrine Pickle,* for example, the masquerade room is one among several urban sites the hero visits in his peregrinations; we see the underlying serial structure quite clearly.*

Yet given the particularly complex part the masquerade played in eighteenth-century life, the scene is never without special ambiguities. It crystallizes the conflicting imperatives at the heart of contemporary fiction.[8] Just as the actual masquerade brought to light certain underlying and problematic impulses in eighteenth-century English society, so the fictional masquerade scene could be said to unleash those transgressive forces present just under the ordinarily decorous surface of eighteenth-century narrative.

One might call the masquerade topos a master trope of destabilization in contemporary fiction. Its role is never merely static or emblematic. True, images of mask and masquerade can always be made to carry fixed emblematic meanings in eighteenth-century literature. As we have seen, contemporary satirists, drawing upon ancient iconographic traditions, reinscribed the masquerade's conventional association with the themes of deception and inauthenticity. Within the fluid world of contemporary prose fiction, however, the occasion has a more dynamic significance. It is associated with the disruption, rather than the stabilization, of meaning. Befitting its deeper link with the forces of transformation and mutability, the masquerade typically has a catalytic effect on plot. It is often connected with the working out of comic or providential narrative patterns. Yet this plot-engendering function almost invariably undermines whatever emblematic meaning the episode might otherwise be expected to carry. The scene prompts larger ideological and thematic inconsistencies. Almost invariably, the fictional masquerade escapes any kind of moral reducibility, just as the eighteenth-century novel itself moves away from the formulaic didactic content of satire and moral allegory.

Since these subversive effects will be described in more detail in later chapters, I will merely sketch them here. They are often veiled at the start by a certain conventional fictional rhetoric. Aware of readers' moral expectations, English novelists of the period usually preface the masquerade episode with some sort of didactic gloss. Thus even before the masquerade occurs, the heroine may be warned against it; or a character invested with special moral prestige, often a guardian or clergyman, may inveigh against its voluptuousness and excess. Virtuous characters, forced into attending a masquerade by the less pristine, may articulate vague anxieties about what dangers the event will hold—as when Pamela, in Richardson's sequel, wishes she did not have to go to the Haymarket with her husband, or when Harriet Byron, in *Sir Charles Grandison,* fears the masquerade she is to attend will be "the last diversion of this kind I shall ever be at" (Vol. I, p. 116). And sometimes the narrator himself locates the occasion within a larger satiric or moralizing context, as in *Amelia.* As one might expect, the danger the masquerade poses is primarily sexual (and threatens heroines far more than heroes), though the event is associated with all kinds of malignity and vice. In advance of any actual representation of the scene, the contemporary novelist, like the satirist, may attempt to limit the role of the masquerade to that of moral emblem.

We see in this effort a superficial connection with the programmatic didactic literature of the period and the familiar attacks of the anti-masquerade writers. As in those works, the reader is invited to comprehend the masquerade as a transparent epitome of vice, part of the moralized topography of the corrupt Town. The masquerade itself masquerades. Ostensibly the scene of pleasure, it is actually the scene of snares—a region of manipulation, disequilibrium, and sexual threat. This conventional opening critique often coincides, particularly in Fielding's novels, with a larger fictional attack on the deceptive and hypocritical nature of human society in general. Besides being the icon of a debauched world of fashion, or the allegory of urban disorder, the masquerade may intimate a global dysphoria: a universal inauthenticity, obfuscation, and brutality. The embedded moral condemnation of the masquerade scene confirms the fictional work's didactic pretensions and establishes, at least for a time, the quintessentially virtuous persona of the eighteenth-century English novelist, the unmasker of vice.

Yet such transparency is obscured by the scene itself. Despite the moralistic warnings, characters do, as though by a strange narrative compulsion, end up at masquerades. Indeed, one may take it as a rule that if the possibility of attending a masquerade is raised in an eighteenth-century novel, someone—and usually the heroine—will go. This turn toward the carnival world may make little sense in terms of didactic economy; the reader may feel the perniciousness of the occasion has already been sufficiently established. The shift into saturnalia is frequently an irrational-seeming plot development. In *Pamela,* for example, one cannot quite grasp why a reformed B. should force his pregnant wife to attend this scene of riot against her will, but he does. And similarly in *Amelia,* though Booth has strenuously protested his wife's acceptance of masquerade tickets from the sinister Noble Peer, he later insists that she accept a second set of tickets from the equally devious Colonel James. The crucial move from domestic salon to assembly room—from the predictable scenery of everyday life to the estranging realm of the carnivalesque—is almost always accompanied by a logical discontinuity, an incursion of irrationalism into the ordered cosmos of eighteenth-century psychological as well as topographic representation.

How to explain the curious attraction the scene exerts? Like its real prototype, the fictional masquerade must be considered a kind of pleasure-mechanism for author and reader alike. There is first the simple pleasure of local color. Eighteenth-century masquerade episodes generally convey the specular delights of the occasion—the exquisite visual incongruities of the costumed crowd. The fictional diversion conventionally diverts by adding an element of spectacle, in the ancient sense, to the otherwise quotidian landscape of the realistic novel. Thus in Burney's *Cecilia,* for instance, the reader may take vicarious pleasure in the rich and marvelous entertainment depicted there, where men turn into "Spaniards, chimney-sweepers, Turks, watchmen, conjurers, and old women," and women into "shepherdesses, orange girls, Circassians, gipseys, haymakers, and sultanas" (Vol. I, p. 169).

But the masquerade diverts in a second, more important sense. The verbal rendering of this beautiful and various phenomenological realm, the space of endless enchanting metamorphosis, typically coincides with an even more gratifying transformation: the proliferation of intrigue itself. The masquerade episode serves as a point for narrative transformation—the privileged site of plot. Above all, the masquerade is the place where significant events "take place." It is a classic locale in which the requisite mysteries of the story itself may be elaborated. This plot-producing function follows from the nature of the diversion. In life as in fiction, as we have seen, the eighteenth-century masquerade was a cultural locus of intimacy. There persons otherwise rigidly segregated by class and sex distinctions might come together in unprecedented and sometimes disruptive combinations. Masquerading substituted randomness and novelty—prerequisites of imbroglio—for the highly stylized patterns of everyday public and private exchange.

The open-endedness introduced into the system of human relations by the masquerade is perfectly suited to the elaboration of plot, which as Tzvetan Todorov has pointed out, depends on an initial destabilization of the ordinary—a disequilibrium at the heart of things. In his study of the fantastic, Todorov defines the minimum requirement for narrative, that "nucleus without which we cannot say there is any narrative at all," as "a movement between two equilibriums which are similar but not identical." In the genre of the fantastic—including fantastic tales of the eighteenth century like Walpole's *The Castle of Otranto* and Beckford's *Vathek*—that which precipitates movement, the necessary catalyst for narrative, is usually the supernatural intervention, a mysterious or extra-logical incursion that radically disrupts the stable modes of ordinary fictional existence. "Habitually linked to the narrative of an action," the marvelous element, Todorov writes, "proves to be the narrative raw material which best fills this specific function: to afford a modification of the preceding situation, and to break the established equilibrium" of the fantastic text. Social and literary operations here coincide, for "in both cases we are concerned with a transgression of the law."[9]

A comparison might be made between the role of the supernatural in fantastic literature and that of the masquerade in certain putatively realistic or secularized eighteenth-century narratives. The masquerade episode is likewise a transgression of the law, albeit a nontranscendental one; it deranges the orderly system of human relations intimated elsewhere in eighteenth-century English fiction. The masquerade engenders a set of *liaisons dangereuses* by throwing characters into proximity who would never meet if an exhaustive sociological decorum were truly the goal: the high and the low, the virtuous and the vicious, the attached and the unattached. And by the same token, the episode may bring about, for a time at least, the alienation of characters who *should* be together in the fictional world by virtue of established conjugal or familial ties: husbands and wives, parents and children, guardians and wards. Out of the masquerade's surplus of scandalous dialectical transactions, a multitude of intrigues may develop. True to its magical-seeming, transformational nature, the carnivalesque episode characteristically provides the mimetic disequilibrium on which plot itself depends.

This analogy with the supernatural event is not as arbitrary as it might seem. In several masquerade scenes a literal association with marvelous agency is inscribed atavistically in the imagery of costume. Important characters either come under the influence of others disguised as supernatural beings, or disguise themselves as such. Tom Jones meets the "Queen of the Fairies" (Lady Bellaston) and falls as though by magic under her sexual and economic sway; in *Cecilia* the heroine's sinister suitor, Mr. Monckton, appears before her in the shape of Lucifer. In Inchbald's *A Simple Story* Miss Milner dresses as the goddess Diana, transfixing all who see her. Since each of these distinctively costumed characters either perpetrates masquerade intrigue

or is instrumental in later plot developments, the sartorial hints of supernatural power might be taken as allegories of narrative power. And just as the actual masquerade gave people in the increasingly secularized eighteenth century a way of acting out memories of the traditional world of magic and folk belief—as witches, conjurers, devils, and the like—so the masquerade set piece gave vestigial fantastic and marvelous literary elements a paradoxical second life in realistic eighteenth-century English fiction.[10]

Characteristically, then, the masquerade episode precipitates plot. More often than not—and this will be a crux in my argument—it precipitates a comic plot in particular. It engenders a rewarding or euphoric pattern of narrative transformation, even for characters, like the beleaguered heroines of contemporary fiction, whom one would not expect to benefit from its disarming travesties. Granted, the beneficent instrumentality of the occasion may not be immediately obvious: the narrative repercussions of the masquerade can seem painful or melodramatic on the surface. But it is important to notice how frequently the episode's ostensibly disastrous "consequences" (to use Fielding's term) turn out to be a necessary prelude to something else: the amelioration of a central character's fortunes, the providential rewarding of the heroine. Like the Fortunate Fall (with which it has strong symbolic resonances), the masquerade stands out in eighteenth-century English narrative as an indispensable event—as that temporary plunge into enigma and difficulty without which the comic destiny of characters could not be realized.

Consider, for example, the situation in *Sir Charles Grandison*. The "cursed masquerade" early in that novel bears all the conventional marks of evil narrative agency: Harriet Byron is abducted from it by the odious Sir Hargrave Pollexfen, and her sexual ruin seems inevitable. After the "fatal news" of her kidnapping, her distraught Uncle Selby exclaims that while he formerly believed public masquerades "more silly than wicked," he now declares them "the most profligate of all diversions" (I, 119). The reader soon learns, however, that Harriet has miraculously escaped the expected fate: in a timely piece of action, the paragon Sir Charles hears muffled screams coming from Sir Hargrave's coach, and liberates her from her abductor.

Such is the happy accidental meeting on which Richardson's romance plot depends, for Harriet and Sir Charles later fall in love and marry. Yet, one could argue, it is Harriet's initial movement into the world of sexual danger, represented by the masked assembly, that diverts her toward her ultimate sexual reward. Without the masquerade she would neither be absorbed, as she is, into the beatific Grandison household (where she is taken after her ordeal) nor come to know her "god-like" benefactor so intimately. The masquerade excursion is paradoxically responsible for all her subsequent happiness and the essential erotic comedy of Richardson's novel. Again, this quasi-magical plot function is obscured on the surface of the fiction: Harriet's relieved relations afterward revile the occasion that has caused such "barbarous" suffering. But it is inscribed subliminally, in comments like those of Mr. Reeves, who suggests that Harriet's experience represents "a common case" heightened into "the marvelous" (I, 137). Harriet too has the sense of wondrous agency: "How shall I bear this goodness!" she exclaims after her adventure. "This is indeed bringing good out of evil! Did I not say, my cousin, that I was fallen into the company of angels?" (I, 145).

One might multiply cases in which the heroine's masquerade venture results in an affirmation or a reconstitution of the comic plot of the heterosexual romance. Roxana meets her most powerful patron, the Duke of M——, at the masquerade, attracting him with her lubricious "Turkish dance." In a somewhat more sedate manner, Burney's Cecilia also attracts a lover at the masquerade, her future husband, Delvile. In Inchbald's *A Simple Story,* though the masquerade episode appears at first to estrange Miss Milner and Dorriforth, it is a necessary preliminary to that ecstatic reconciliation scene during which Dorriforth marries his ward on the spot. And as we shall see shortly, even in Richardson's highly moralistic sequel to *Pamela,* Mr. B.'s masquerade flirtation with the Countess is not the disaster for the heroine it seems to be: it too sets up a transporting moment of "éclaircissement" later, when B. renounces his would-be paramour, begs his wife's forgiveness, and reaffirms his love for her.

Not only is the masquerade episode, then, a dense kernel of relations out of which plot in general develops, but it is specifically implicated in the larger comic patterns of eighteenth-century English fiction. Without it many of the providential-seeming turns of contemporary narrative are difficult to imagine. Yet such instrumentality also undermines the conventional moral significance of the topos, and threatens the didactic coherence of the work in which the masquerade occurs. By its very comic agency, the carnivalesque episode contradicts its superficial negative inscription within the eighteenth-century text, and reveals itself instead as part of the hidden, life-giving machinery of narrative pleasure. It ceases to be merely an emblem—of hypocrisy or anything else—at the moment it facilitates, like a kind of covert deus ex machina, the ultimate reward of characters and readers alike.

This scrambling of emblematic meaning, it turns out, is often paradigmatic; it can signal a general collapse of didactic account-ability in the masquerade novel. The scene typically leaves in its wake what I will call, borrowing from the ancient thematics of reversal and chaos, a World-Upside-Down effect.[11] Following the characters' carnivalesque excursion, the ordinary social or metaphysical hierarchies of the fiction may suddenly weaken or show signs of being overthrown altogether. Masquerade scandal is contagious: it spills over into everyday life. The reader experiences a sense of ideological topsy-turvydom, as though the ambiguous transformations on the narrative level had somehow precipitated thematic changes too. In Bakhtin's term, the fictional world itself is carnivalized.

I will offer specific examples of this phenomenon in subsequent chapters—particularly in the discussion of Fielding's *Amelia,* a novel in which the upside-down effect is especially pronounced. Suffice it to say here that the masquerade is typically linked to three kinds of ideological reversal in eighteenth-century English fiction. First, true to its traditional association with the power of women, the masquerade threatens patriarchal structures. Normative sexual relations in the fictional world may be overthrown, and female characters accede here to new kinds of sexual, moral, or strategic control over male associates. At the same time the obscure and the "low" find new kinds of status at the masquerade; servants challenge masters, and complex scenarios involving social mutability and the exchange of public roles may develop. Class as well as sexual arrangements are modified. And finally, somewhat more abstractly, the scene may be linked with patterns of characterological or moral reversal, particularly in novels like Fielding's, in which a highly dichotomized, even allegorical typology of character ordinarily prevails. Otherwise lucid moral types suddenly behave in a fashion conspicuously unlike themselves: ostensibly good characters (such as the reformed B., Tom Jones, and Amelia) act in peculiarly compromising or questionable ways, while stereotypically villainous characters are equally strangely rehabilitated.

The carnivalization of eighteenth-century English fiction is thus a multifaceted phenomenon. If the process begins with a localized or strictly anecdotal representation of the masquerade—the discrete scene or set piece—it does not end there. The invocation of the conventional topos almost always coincides with an elaboration of plot, and in particular the comic plots of sexual consummation and social mobility. At the same time the scene injects an enigmatic and destabilizing energy into the ordinarily polite and reactionary world of eighteenth-century representation. The literary artifact is transformed as a consequence: the masquerade novel seldom retains its claim to didactic purity, following the representation of this least purifying of diversions. It may suddenly seem a contradictory or hybrid imaginative structure—double in potential significance, unrecuperable according to any straightforward didactic logic. With the turn toward the irrational world of carnival, the eighteenth-century English novel becomes unlike itself: it diverges from its putative moral project and reshapes itself as phantasmagoria and dream.

For the novelist the masquerade topos satisfies diverse conscious and unconscious imperatives. In discussing specific works I will consider matters of intentionality, and examine to what degree the subversive effects of individual masquerade scenes may reflect larger, explicitly premeditated authorial designs. Certainly the pervasiveness of the topos in eighteenth-century fiction suggests a general ambivalence on the part of writers regarding the didactic project itself. For contemporary novelists, caught between the contradictory imperatives of the new genre, representing the masquerade may be a way of indulging in the scenery of transgression while seeming to maintain an aspect of moral probity. The occasion can be framed in the conventional negative manner, yet its very representation permits the novelist, like his characters, to differ from himself: to cast off the persona of the moralist and turn instead to the pleasures of "Intrigue." Seductive fantasies quickly take the place of staid instruction. For writers like Richardson and Fielding, in whom the imaginative conflict between moralism and subversion is intense, the masquerade may function as a figure for ambiguous authorial intentions—the textual sign of an inward tension regarding the novelist's conventional role.

Throughout this part of my study I draw upon Bakhtin's notion of the carnivalesque, a concept he developed most memorably in *Rabelais and His World*. Bakhtin used the term mainly to indicate a thematic— that traditional body of festive imagery preserved in European literature in various forms from the Middle Ages through the Romantic period. But it can also suggest a process of generic destabilization. The carnivalized work, he argues, resists formal classification, and instead, like Rabelais's *Pantagruel,* combines a multiplicity of literary modes in an increasingly mixed or "polyphonic" form.[12] It is worth noting finally that eighteenth-century novels containing masquerade scenes often display a notable generic instability. At times the masquerade scene may even prompt a formal shift in the work in which it occurs. In *Amelia* the scene coincides with a general shift from the satiric to the mimetic mode. In Richardson's sequel to *Pamela* there is even more generic instability. After the masquerade scene the text becomes a true hodgepodge of discourses—a mixture of embedded exempla, "table talk" (the symposia of the B. and Darnford households), and miscellaneous non-narrative items, such as Pamela's lengthy commentary on Locke's *Education.* Just as the masquerade episode precipitates narrative transformations, it also prompts generic transformation—instigating, in the classic Bakhtinian mode, lapses in consistency on every literary stratum. . . .

For the space of a century the culture of the masquer-

ade institutionalized dreams of disorder. While contemporary satirists complained of too much whirl, too much metamorphosis, in the masquerade—"So many various changes to impart, / Would tire an Ovid's or a Proteus' art," wrote the poet Christopher Pitt—novelists turned with relish to the occasion's exemplary reversals.[13] This "World painted in Miniature" became the emblem of an endless and fascinating mutability.[14] True, the mercurial imagery of the carnivalesque gave shape to a fantasy of change that, in one form or another, always lies at the heart of narrative. But the masquerade novel also had a compelling historical specificity. By embracing the spectacular, secretive figures of the carnival world, eighteenth-century English writers reenacted a larger contemporary flight into irony and illusion. The fiction of the masquerade was an epitome of the imaginative regime in which it flourished—and a mark of the eighteenth century's own ambivalent escape from consistency, transparency, and the claims of a pervasive decorum.

Notes

[*] On the thematic affinity between the picaresque and the scenery of masking and carnival, see Babcock, "Liberty's a Whore," pp. 109-10. Granted, the more a work approximates what Babcock calls the "antidevelopmental narrative" of the true picaresque, the less instrumental the impact a masquerade scene may have on plot per se. The scene becomes simply one among many disconnected adventures, as with the first masquerade episode in *Peregrine Pickle.* There, the masquerade in chapter 44 is merely an excuse for obscene comedy, when Peregrine's painter friend, disguised as a woman, is forced to urinate among gentlemen masqueraders. The episode leads nowhere in particular; it is simply followed by other disparate events. In a more structured work such as *Pamela,* though the masquerade initially seems part of a picaresque sequence, it has a narrative importance outweighing other episodes. Here the plot "takes": following B.'s masquerade liaison with the Countess, one thing does lead to another, and a more complex action involving the heroine evolves.

[1] Other masquerade plays are Aphra Behn's *The Emperour of the Moon* (1687), Susannah Centlivre's *The Perjur'd Husband; or, The Adventures of Venice* (1700), Benjamin Griffin's *The Masquerade; or, An Evening's Intrigue* (1717), Charles Johnson's *The Masquerade* (1719), the anonymous *The Masquerade; or, The Devil's Nursery* (1732), Fielding's *Miss Lucy in Town* (1742), Francis Gentleman's *The Pantheonites* (1773), and Hugh Kelly's *School for Wives* (1773). The masquerade scene gradually lost its appeal for English playwrights in the late eighteenth century, though it was preserved for a time on the Continent in the works of the Sturm und Drang writers, and among later Romantic dramatists and opera librettists. Archibald

MacLaren's *The Masquerade; or, Folly Exposed!* (1820) and Thomas Egerton Wilks's *The Black Domino; or, The Masqued Ball* (1838) are among the few self-consciously Romantic English masquerade dramas. A more memorable treatment is Schiller's *Die Verschwörung des Fiesco zu Genua* (1783). There is also an interesting masquerade reference in Act I of *Don Carlos* (1787). Lermontov's *The Masquerade* (1842) is another Romantic adaptation of the eighteenth-century theme. On the treatment of the masquerade in nineteenth-century opera, see chap. 8 [of Terry Castle, *Masquerade and Civilization: The Carnivalesque in Eighteenth-Century English Culture and Fiction*, Stanford University Press, 1986]. In twentieth-century drama the masquerade topos has had an ironic reworking in the plays of Pirandello and Frisch.

[2] For descriptions of masquerading at the court of Charles II, see Burnet, I, 292. Burnet is cited by the anonymous author of a "Historical Account of Masquerades" in *Lady's Magazine,* May 1775. The nineteenth-century chronicler William Connor Sydney provides additional information on Restoration masquerades in *Social Life in England,* pp. 367-72. On the fêtes of the French court, see the memoirs of Saint-Simon; and Pilon & Saisset.

[3] On this commercialization of public entertainment, see Brewer, McKendrick & Plumb.

[4] Addison, *Remarks on Italy,* in Addison, *Works,* II, 39.

[5] See, for example, Davys's *The Accomplished Rake*; the anonymous epistolary novel *The Masquerade; or, The History of Lord Avon and Miss Tameworth;* or Lee, "The Two Emilys." In the last work, the female protagonist woos her lover at a masquerade while dressed as an Italian peasant. For a Continental example, see Sophie von La Roche's *Geschichte des Fräuleins von Sternheim* (1771).

[6] Tanner, pp. 3-4.

[7] *Ibid.,* p. 120.

[8] Only two critics have looked in detail at particular masquerade scenes: David Blewett, in his chapter on *Roxana,* and Robert Folkenflik, in his article on *Tom Jones.* Both take a somewhat limited approach, however, confining themselves to speaking of the masquerade's emblematic significance. Taylor uses the concept of masquerading metaphorically, to discuss authorial personae in Defoe and Richardson, but is not concerned with actual masquerades.

[9] Todorov, pp. 163, 165-66. For a related discussion of narrative turning points and their association with *aporia,* or disorientation, see M. Brown.

[10] See Kalpakgian for a discussion of supernatural elements in Fielding's fiction. On the general waning of folk belief and magic practices in eighteenth-century England, see Thomas.

[11] On the history of the World-Upside-Down topos, see Curtius, pp. 94-98.

[12] The important concept of polyphony, or heteroglossia, occurs throughout Bakhtin's writings in various contexts too numerous and rich to summarize here. But see in particular *Rabelais,* introduction, and chap. 3, "Popular-Festive Forms and Images in Rabelais." The stylistic implications of heteroglossia are drawn out in the essay "Discourse in the Novel" in *Dialogic Imagination,* pp. 259-422.

[13] Pitt, *On the Masquerades* (1727; ll. 19-21).

[14] The phrase is from an anonymous essay on masquerades in *Universal Spectator,* April 5, 1729.

Robert James Merrett (essay date 1991-92)

SOURCE: "Natural History and the Eighteenth-Century Novel," *Eighteenth Century Studies*, Vol. 25, No. 2, Winter, 1991-1992, pp. 145-70.

[*In the following essay, Merrett analyzes the inter-related nature of the eighteenth-century passions for the study of natural history and for novel-reading and -writing.*]

In a compelling bibliographical examination of natural history's rise to a popularity rivaling the novel's by the end of the eighteenth century, G. S. Rousseau demonstrates the genre's broad social appeal and stresses its impact on the English language.[1] In applying this genre's popularity and linguistic power to the history of eighteenth-century novels, Serge Soupel stresses the involvement of scientific and literary language: he argues that, if scientific words informed fictional procedures, poetic diction predetermined scientific expression because natural philosophers forewent neither "genteel vocabulary" nor tropes but personified natural objects. Soupel's sense of the reciprocity of literary and scientific diction challenges literary history's equation of science with the plain style and the novel with empiricism.[2]

Natural history, considered both as a literary genre and as a scientific pursuit, not only revises traditional views about novelistic procedures but sheds light on current endeavors to remake the novel's history. Besides exploring the concept and generic influence of natural history to celebrate fiction's experimental variability, the present article explores Michael McKeon's sense of natural history as a narrative model in order to qualify his contention that by the 1740s the novel was a stable "conceptual category."[3]

Rousseau's documentation of natural history's overwhelming popularity in the 1770s helps us recognize that, from the time of Defoe, novelists largely defined their fictional techniques in the face of this rival form and that the tensions in novels, and among novelists, between admiration for and rejection of natural history continued well after 1740. The generic rivalry involving the novel and natural history in the eighteenth century obliges us to confront a plurality of fictional models and to adopt a flexible stance toward literary and cultural history. When he published *The Natural History of Selbourne* in 1788, Gilbert White offered the digest of twenty years of fieldwork and epistolary correspondence with leading naturalists. But this opus embodies more than a system of empirical observation; it is the acme of a genre invented partly by novelists and travel-writers and of a dialectic involving social hierarchy, economic progress, and spiritual mediation. For, despite his contributions to the Royal Society and closeness to the advanced ideas of Linnaeus and Buffon, his book draws on the theological view of nature found in John Ray's *Wisdom of God manifested in the Works of the Creation* (1691) and in William Derham's *Physico-Theology, or a Demonstration of the Being and Attributes of God from his Works of Creation* (1713). No less than Ray and Derham, White observed and described plants and animals so as to celebrate providential order and confirm the reciprocity of scientific observation and meditation. The tension between material fact and spirituality in *The Natural History of Selbourne* matches the social dialectic which Keith Thomas finds in natural history.[4] Thomas shows that, while natural history permeated all ranks of society, it was inherently aristocratic. Although McKeon insists aristocratic ideals were transformed by bourgeois ideology in the seventeenth century, Thomas avers that the social and theological themes of natural histories inscribe aristocratic values in ways that reveal these values to have been more enduring and flexible than literary historians have cared to admit.

The presence of physico-theology in natural histories defies single-minded notions of development in the novel and society. For the perpetual impulse to detect providential design and spiritual order upholds hierarchical principles and reconciles economic progress with social stability. Apologies for natural history opposed to aristocratic ideology make plain the traditional political values arising from the genre's dialectical methods. Take Joseph Priestley, the radical unitarian, and Frances Brooke, the orthodox anglican. In 1769, shortly after White began to record his observations in his journals, these authors, in defending physico-theology, exposed the lack of tension between tradition and progress in bourgeois thinking. In Priestley's mind, "Natural history exhibits a boundless variety of scenes"

that are "infinitely analogous to one another." Yet, he reduces natural history's meditative dialectic, its "contemplation of uniformity and variety," to material progress: the "new plants, new animals, and new fossils" collected by naturalists, which testify to the "unbounded power, wisdom, and goodness of God," also prove that "every object in Nature" is "rising in due degree to its maturity and perfection."[5] Sharing Priestley's dislike for the status quo, Brooke demeans the tensions in natural history to uphold a gentrified nostalgia. The sentimental heroine of *The History of Emily Montague* is a "little natural philosopher" who reads "Ray, Derham, and fifty other strange old fellows that one never heard of" and "eternally" pores "through a microscope to discover the wonders of creation." Brooke reduces physico-theology to a genteel, feminine pursuit, equating it with domestic retreat from economic progress and aristocratic ideology.[6]

But, since her novel's denouement validates colonial wealth and imperial power, Brooke's reduction of physico-theology evades the dialectic inherent in natural history, as does Priestley's. Their subordination of physico-theology to either tradition or progress implies that middle-class ideology refuses to integrate intellectual and social tensions in the generic manner of natural history and that this ideology is unstable. By contrast, White's trust in aristocratic ideology enabled him to bring the genre's dialectic to its acme in *The Natural History of Selbourne*. Analysis of the formal eclecticism and social philosophy in this work not only evinces the creative flexibility of aristocratic ideology but uncovers the conceptual instability of the novel in the 1740s. White's methods and social attitudes clarify the rivalry between natural history and novel, as well as that between earlier and later fictional models. He integrates linguistic and literary invention with science and reconciles social hierarchy to economic progress, delimiting a context vital to judging how well fictional images of plants and animals represent social dialectic. Since it relied on the taxonomic procedures and physico-theology of its rival, the novel was marked by natural history's aristocratic ideology. That it was not simply governed by a stable, progressive bourgeois ideology is clear from the various ways in which fiction of the 1740s anticipates White's work. A survey of natural analogies, fables, and hierarchical motifs in novels reveals the coexistence of figurative and inductive modes and explains why the novel imitated the social dialectic of its rival genre in ways that demand a revision of narrative history.

The Natural History of Selbourne is the acme of natural history, because it self-consciously integrates literary and scientific methods.[7] Its epistolary mode, its compilation of correspondence with other naturalists, and its digest of voluminous journals that advance observation and classification testify to White's coherent attitude to collaborative study, social discourse, and humane letters. His allusions to Virgil, in addressing the educated elite, embody a dialectical esteem for poetry and science: the allusions show that natural history employs deduction as well as induction, and that verbal and empirical reference is reciprocal.[8] Whether Virgil describes a dove haunting a cave (112), a swallow nesting among rafters (163), or frozen Italian rivers (127), White treats the Roman poet's diction as offering phenomenal evidence. If he grants that Virgil and the "ancients" did not "attend to specific differences" like "modern naturalists" (168-69), White is comfortable deducing information about species from classical texts. He reads general epithets in Virgil about birdsong, plumage, and nests as specifying swallows rather than martins (168), in the process confirming that both philology and classical poetry are major aspects of natural history.

Besides addressing the "classic reader" (172), White draws on vernacular poetry to substantiate his eclecticism and illustrate his dialectical methods. On the one hand, he asserts that the black-cap's "wild sweetness" reminds him of the song in *As You Like It* about the merry human voice tuning itself to the "wild bird's throat" (122), while, on the other, he differentiates between the ecological and theological views of Milton and Thomson. He belittles Milton's vagueness about how birds migrate (137) and mocks his refusal to admit "mutual fellowship" between birds and animals (187), but he heralds Thomson as a "nice observer of natural occurrences" (25). If Milton's similes help describe the world (279), the naturalist rejects the epic poet's scorn for converse between species, preferring Thomson's view of nature's systems. When Thomson explains how cows bedung the water they drink and introduce into streams and lakes the insects which feed fish, White lauds this image of creaturely interdependence, showing that, in his view, literary judgment, as well as associations, should break down single-minded attitudes about the distinctiveness of mankind.

White's biblical allusions express his wish to extend analogical relations between the species and between the animal and human worlds in the tradition of Derham's *Physico-Theology*. For White, providential design comprehends and relates all species. So, he applies Isaiah's verse about the gratitude of ox and ass to their keeper to the tortoise (146): that this "torpid" and "abject" reptile is grateful to man emblematizes God's systematization of nature.[9] He also extends Job's image of the ostrich's callousness to the cuckoo (124) and adapts Psalms 78:19 to declare that winter insects "furnish" the wheat-ear and win-chat "with a plentiful table in the wilderness" (186). From the stance of physico-theology's conjunction of empiricism and meditation, White's respect for and adaptation of biblical words matches his paradoxical view of the theological distinctiveness and comparability of animals and humans.

The extent of White's literary and allusive self-consciousness cannot be gauged until his political aim for developing the tensions between empiricism and spirituality is detected. In his mind, natural history inevitably defends social hierarchy. Scornful of the "want of a liberal education" in the "lower people" (194), he is sure that natural history has placed him in a "circle of gentlemen" (2). Social hierarchy lies behind his confidence that the agrarian revolution has reached a "pitch of perfection" and that enclosure is totally enlightened (211). He further naturalizes hierarchy by attacking the press for blaming grain shortages on "combinations" of landowners (169): such rabid journalism forgets that improvements in husbandry have minimized starvation. White sees himself as the equal of those he defends: he, too, owns "extensive shrubberies" and employs retainers to protect ornamental plants from killing frosts (267).[10] He regards the aristocratic advancement of horticulture and landscape design as an ultimate emblem of hierarchy (212 and 277): the gardens of aristocrats are major elements of natural geography for White (108).[11]

His commitment to social hierarchy is instrumental because it enables him to reconcile methodical doubt with ecological system. Stressing that "candour and openness" in destroying false analogies are the "life of natural history" (72), White still constructs analogies that figuratively embody the tensions between the hierarchy of creation and the logos in all creatures.[12] If he dissects a cuckoo to refute the "idle notion" that this bird does not incubate (200), his wish to study the "life and conversation of animals" (141) requires him to explain a cat's liking for a leveret, its natural enemy, by the myth of Romulus and Remus (205). His belief in the "chain of beings" (19) means that he applies imperial myth to animals while treating them as scientific objects. When he compares the owl's voice to man's and cooing doves to moaning lovers (227), his sense of birds' "ancient" and "elliptical" language equates them with mankind. White's fusion of empiricism with traditional emblem reaches an acme in his account of barnyard fowl: hens warn chicks about birds of prey, chicks twitter when fed flies, and, in giving a "favourite concubine" food, "gallant chanticleer" utters "amorous phrases" because he has a "considerable vocabulary" (229). By humanizing as well as objectifying animals, White shows how traditional social hierarchy accommodates ecological interdependence.[13]

The conceptual and political tensions between observation and meditation and between tradition and progress lead White to further the instrumentality of language and analogy to natural history. Conscious of the limitations of scientific classification and of the need to designate plants and animals by plural names, he makes polysemy and metaphor instrumental to such designation. Spurning "bare descriptions" and "few synonyms" (141), he employs correlative terms. Thus, the beech has "smooth rind or bark" and "glossy foliage, or graceful pendulous boughs" (3). Polysemy being exploratory, he records plural names: for example, "greater brambling, or snow fleck" (75); "house-swallow" or "chimney-swallow" (162); "heathcock, blackgame, or grouse" (19). To give "common birds" English names (31), he invents metaphors. He replaces Pliny's term for the long-legged plover, *Himantopus,* finding the image of a leather thong inapt, with Brisson's *l'échasse* (244) which he adapts to "stilt-plover" (244). While complaining that the "bane" of "our science is the comparing one animal to the other from memory" (87), he insists on analogies from the belief that naming creatures entails deductive similes. Thus, stone-curlews run from the egg like partridges (47), have manners "analogous to the bustard" and take flight like herons (89); bats drink, like swallows, on the wing (35); and the brown owl regurgitates fur and feathers like hawks while hiding food like dogs (34). His analogical observations tend to merge into mental association: the snipe's "ventriloquous hum" is like the turkey's, if perhaps made by its wings (49); the red-start wags its tail like fawning dogs; and the wagtail moves its like a jaded horse (101). The fusion of empirical and figurative description is complete in his human analogies. In saying that sparrow-hawks living in a crow's nest keep a "good house" and ample "larder" (109), that a snake in a "good humour" is "sweet" in its "person" (73), that a field-mice nest, "the size of a cricket ball," is a "wonderful procreant cradle," that cornricks are their "grand rendezvous" (36-37), and that a tortoise hates rain as much as a lady in "her best attire" (145), he boldly transfers the human realm into natural observation. When he claims that *OEdicnemus,* the latin name of the curlew, is aptly expressive since the bird's legs seem "swoln like those of a gouty man" (47), he confirms his willingness to admit anthropocentrism as well as metaphorical invention into scientific classification.

His fusion of empirical observation and analogical ideas shows that, far from viewing natural history systematically, White stresses physico-theology's pluralism by adopting dialectical or contrary stances to creation. Thus, if a bat is a "wonderful quadraped," its movement on the ground is "ridiculous and grotesque" (35); if the frog's limbs are a wonderful example of providence's economy, it is still "so vile a reptile" (52); if instinct drives most birds to nest wisely but forces martins to build stupidly, it is both "above" and "below" reason (156). The biblical, political, and rhetorical forces thwarting systematic empiricism are epitomized when, in urging botanists to advance the study of grasses, he insists that "to raise a thick turf on naked soil would be worth volumes of systematic knowledge" (220). Here White validates natural science by the humanist, aristocratic terms of Swift's King of Brobdingnag.[14]

Tensions between empiricism and meditation arising from natural history's debt to physico-theology evidence how much White's middle-class contemporaries upheld social hierarchy. The diaries of Thomas Turner, the grocer, and James Woodeforde, the parson, show that both defended the aristocracy because they valued natural history's speculative and economic benefits. Eager to observe exhibits of a raccoon, chamaleon, and salamander, Turner enthusiastically read Tournefort's travelogue, especially this writer's account of coral, sponges, sea mushrooms, and lithophytes.[15] But interest in Tournefort's systematic exposition of the vegetative life of stones coexists with respect for Derham's *Physico-Theology* (204): like White, Turner examines the world for signs of the "all-wise creator" (183). At the same time, his diary exposes the economic and social bases of natural history: the need to produce food makes him study the viability of vegetable seeds (54), and to produce cider from apples (66) and perry from pears (110) he learns the latest methods in arboriculture. An ultimate concern is the communal sharing of game, fish, and produce: garnering the fruits of the earth tightens traditional social bonds. An admirer of the Duke of Newcastle's cultural techniques, Turner, on receiving pears and melons from the Duke's estate, regards such gifts as a desirable form of benevolence.

With a similarly mixed curiosity and meditation, Woodeforde pays to view a Madagascan mongoose and a learned pig, and praises God when a peacock fans its tail.[16] That he operates on his cat's broken ribs (53), keeps a spider as a pet (99), measures the growth of oaks (402) and scotch firs (566) long after planting them, and records bird-sightings manifests a sensitive and learned empiricism. Yet, typically ambivalent about natural history, he is cruel and superstitious: he shoots an old woodpecker for pulling reeds from his thatch (219), and to cure a swollen eyelid he rubs it with a black cat's tail (396). If, being richer than the grocer, he farmed cash crops such as turnips (299), his diary, like Turner's, confirms natural history's ideology. Exchanging apple-trees, shrubs, and laurels with friends (332), he gives his parishioners pears (310), while accepting trout and pike from his landlord (132). Social hierarchy is firmly maintained by Woodeforde's pursuit of natural history.

Natural history's perpetuation of hierarchy in the middle-classes makes this genre an essential context to the novel. This is even more so because natural history shaped travelogues as well as diaries, and these latter genres informed the novel's evolution before and after 1740. White, in alluding to travelogues, recognizes that they mediate natural history.[17] Travelogues show the involved development of natural history and novel, proving this literary evolution to be dialectical. The travelogues of Defoe, Fielding, Johnson, and Smollett reveal that these writers were precursors of White, and, conversely, this influence serves to illustrate the novel's unstable generic identity.

The coexistence of social hierarchy and economic progress in the works of White, Turner, and Woodeforde is promoted by Defoe in *A Tour Through the Whole Island of Great Britain* (1724-27). Animals and plants denote to him not only food and scientific knowledge but also commerce and rank: he understands that naturalists compete for specimens with investment-conscious landlords and poor peasants.[18] His view that animals are economic and social signs is clear when pheasants in Norwich fields make him realize this city has more tradesmen than gentlemen (I, 72) and when, on the accidental killing of an eagle in a duckoy, he notes the landlord's anger at not being able to capitalize on showing the rare bird or selling it to gentlemen "curious in such things" (I, 210). In *A Tour,* the lists of birds and fish sold at markets symbolize natural plenitude, national wealth, and local civility. Anticipating White, Defoe is happy that that wheatears or "English ortolans" cost more at Tunbridge than nearby towns; such consumer demand means that the resort is economically healthy (I, 127).[19] Like White, he will not regard natural history in purely empirical terms. So, leaving naturalists to decide what migration says about avian intelligence, he insists, inspired by a flock of departing swallows, that our "summer friends" think (I, 56). Narrative experimentation as well as social ideology governs his empiricism, as in his account of how duckoys operate (I, 98). Fascinated that ducks are trained to lure foreign birds to slaughter, he enters the heads of the "naturalised" ducks, giving them powerful rhetoric and elaborate ideas: they fly abroad to betray their fellows, reporting easy living conditions in England and reaffirming this message when the newcomers reach the duckoy. He then impersonates the thoughts of both sets of ducks, conveying the victims' terror and the well-rewarded cunning of the Englishmen's servants (I, 100).

Divided sympathy for the ducks—the clever ones are "traytors" too and the "guests" willing victims—suggests that Defoe's narrative experiments gather dialectical energy from his divergent attitudes to natural history. He enjoys treating naturalists' methods satirically by laughing at their anthropocentric narrowness. Thus, he sneers at Leigh, Cotton, and Hobbes for championing the "wonderless wonders" of the Derbyshire peaks (II, 168). His account of Soland geese, seasonal visitors to the Firth of Forth, best exemplifies this ironic ambivalence (II, 293). Mixing direct and reported evidence, he expresses the contrary view that the birds' migration is and is not explained by the herring schools: the geese come with the herring but do not follow the fish. Denying the relevance of causal analysis, he humorously creates a set of analogies by which he links the geese, the fish the birds eat, and the locals who think the geese a "dainty." Since the birds have the "coarse, rank, ill-relish'd" taste of the fish, the locals' taste is compared to the Egyptians' notorious love of garlic and onions. He further mocks the categorical modes of natural history by stressing the tensions between classification and analogy when he specifies the characteristics of the Soland goose:

> It is a large fowl, rather bigger than an ordinary goose; 'tis duck-footed, and swims as a goose; but the bill is long, thick, and pointed like a crane, or heron, only much thicker, and not above five inches long. Their laying but one egg, which sticks to the rock, and will not fall off, unless pull'd off by force, and then not to be stuck on again; though we thought them fictions, yet, being there at the season, we found true; as also their hatching, by holding the egg fast in their foot. What Nature meant by giving these singularities to a creature, that has nothing else in it worth notice, we cannot determine.

If comically, this passage anticipates White's sense that natural science does not exclude rhetorical amplification and fanciful analogies and that tensions between specific and generic names involve empirical fact with imagination.

While his practice of travel writing let Defoe see that natural history lends itself to literary invention and narrative experimentation, Fielding's moral sense of fiction led him to reject travel writing and natural history as mediators of the novel. In *The Journal of a Voyage to Lisbon* (1755), his refusal to harmonize physico-theology and empiricism makes him fiercely spurn both genres. He charges that natural historians lie "for the lying sake" and report "monstrous improbabilities and absurdities."[20] Pliny offers "facts contrary to the honour of God, to the visible order of the creation, to the known laws of nature, to the histories of former ages, and to the experience of our own" (9). To Fielding, the exploitation of nature by empirical study and social ideology is pernicious. Unlike Defoe, he will not celebrate the social fact that some species are dainties: he refuses to see food in terms of status. He mockingly says that, were ortolans as big and cheap as "bustards," the rich would turn the common sparrow into a dainty (105). Angry that London markets sell expensive "john doree" and not whiting and sole that the poor can afford, he is disgusted that the rich enjoy food less for its inherent quality than for its costly exclusiveness (102). Outraged by the economic and social differentiation of animals, he distances himself from travelogues and natural histories. Observing the capture of a shark on the voyage, he only briefly describes the event because he will not conform "to the rules and practice of voyage-writing" (116). His support of Derham's *Physico-Theology* clarifies his contempt for natural history. Citing Derham's view that wasps warn those they sting and that the rattlesnake "never meditates a human prey without giving warning of his approach" to the "most venemous" of "human insects," Fielding insists that the animal serves the human world by providential design and that natural analogies are valid only if they emblematize providence's supervisory power. Fielding uses Derham's sense of vicious insects to subsume biological taxonomy under the religious trust that vicious humans are harmless since they wear their "dispositions in their countenances" (71).

The divergent reactions to natural history in the travelogues of Defoe and Fielding are mirrored in the works of Johnson and Smollett. Johnson comes to natural history with intellectual curiosity and moral flexibility, Smollett comes to it with dismissive, ulterior motives. In *A Journey to the Western Islands of Scotland* (1775), which White admired, Johnson promotes empiricism, confident that it illuminates moral issues.[21] Aware that natural science was a favorite study in Scotland and that naturalists tended to generalize instead of being "rigidly philosophical," he urges the Scots to determine whether Loch Ness stays unfrozen in winter (23). His own observations explore categorical problems for what they say about natural dialectic. He finds Hebrides geese "to be of a middle race": domestic enough to "own a home" yet wild enough "to fly quite away" (41). Assuming the otter's foot specifically "formed" for swimming, he finds it similar to the spaniel's (46). Undiscouraged by natural history's problems, he derives ecological concepts from them. Surprised no naturalist has proposed that the world must have once been as empty of animals as of men, he holds that the absence of creatures accounts for the growth of forests and argues that men and beasts share the environment (105). He warns that, if species are vanishing, animals being no match for guns, man too is at risk: no creature, certainly not humans, may live in barren regions (62).

Far from turning natural history's problems into an informative dialectic, Smollett, in *Travels Through France and Italy* (1766), develops a polemic which subjects its categorical and semantic aspects to satire of French and English culture. So, he chides the Benedictines of Boulogne for calling the wild duck they eat a species of fish and mocks English prudery for translating *cul-blanc* as "wheatear" rather than *"white-a—e."*[22] If visiting France obliges him to damn its culinary habits, he lauds its natural plenitude to demean England.[23] Since the *"becca ficas, grieves, or thrushes,"* served in French inns, are raw or overcooked (75 and 152), he offers a recipe for making them tender and crisp, which opposes his culinary skill to French waste of natural resources. Yet he appreciates such resources: France has more varieties of fish; its partridges are bigger; its flowers have a stronger aroma than in England (118); standard fruit trees at Nice are unrivaled by English wall-fruit, producing peaches more "solid and tasty" than English ones (160). His travelogue turns natural history into cultural ideology somewhat like Defoe, but with an opposite sense of nationalism and without Defoe's narrative playfulness. Nor does he regard humans ecologically like Johnson or promote physico-theology like Fielding. Unlike Defoe and Johnson but like Fielding, Smollett resists writing natural history on its own terms. But he differs from Fielding in making it serve political rather than moral and theological aims.

The plural stances to natural history adopted by novelists in travelogues imply that the novel had not attained a stable identity by the appearance of *The Natural History of Selbourne*. For these stances clarify the variability of novelistic models and ideologies. This variability may be illustrated and defined by analyzing how novels both appropriate and resist natural history.

Defoe exploits the procedures of natural history by converting problems of classification into sources of provocative narrative ambivalence, as evidenced best when the adventurers cross Africa in *Captain Singleton*.[24] He gives the African flora and fauna a teasing contrariness: he depicts them as strange and familiar, creating thereby a dialectic between experience and imagination. In the "horrid Desart," the adventurers find a "moist and nourishing root" which their beasts of burden eat, a root "not much unlike a Pasnip [sic]" (85). The animals also forage on a "kind of Herb like a Broad flat Thistle, tho' without any Prickle" (86). A setting fearful because of its unclassifiable life-forms sustains beast and man. The desert nurtures as well as alienates: apparently endless, it is "pretty full of green Stuff, of one sort or another" (91), and the men consume "great Quantities of Roots" and "Things like Pumpkins" (107). Nominal imprecision effects a dialectic proving nature trustworthy. When the men eat "a Root like Carrots, tho' of quite another Taste, but not unpleasant neither, and some *Guiney* Fowls whose Names we did not know" (129), tensions between word and thing, between general and specific names, create but quickly dissolve problems. Fusing analogy and classification, Defoe invents competing viewpoints which are paradoxically reassuring. When Singleton compares the "Wild-Fowl" to the kinds "we have in *England,*" namely "Duck, Teal, Widgeon," yet admits seeing "some kinds that we had not seen before" (102), the issue of natural classification is disorienting as well as comforting.

The African animals, like the plants specific and indeterminate, disturb the adventurers, upsetting their view of the world but confirming creation's beneficence. Eating "a creature like a Goat," they enjoy its meat but it is "no Goat" (92). Natives give them "three living Creatures as big as Calves, but not of that Kind" (107). Categorically frustrated, the Europeans invent analogies only to find them inapplicable: they trap hares "of a kind something different from ours in *England,* larger, and not so swift of Foot, but very good Meat" (113).

Baffled classification pushes them toward legend, as in the case of the animals which are "between the Kind of a Buffloe and a Deer, but indeed resembled neither; for they had no Horns, and had great Legs like a Cow, with a fine Head, and the Neck like a Deer" (112). Recalling Pliny, this passage makes the boundary between empiricism and invention uncertain. It is a boundary Singleton often traverses with anthropocentric complacency. Though Africa has a "Collection of fierce, ravenous, and devouring Creatures" (86), he says his band grew to not "much mind them" (114). When he calls fearful events "pleasant Adventures with the wild Creatures" (88) and ferocious beasts "Gentle-folks" at a "general Rendezvous" (102), his posturing is suspicious.[25] Singleton's failure to grasp the dialectic of natural history is clear in his views of elephants. Besides detailing their herbivorous habits (89), he sees them as terrifying yet compares them to a harmless "Drove of Cattel" raising dust on England's summer roads (82). Such a polarity confirms the irony that Defoe generates from natural history: tensions between admitting and denying the elephant's specific distinctness alert readers to Singleton's evasion of physico-theology, prompting them to meditate on its perspective.

Rather than appropriating natural history by ambivalently dramatizing its methods, Fielding's novels get narrative energy from defying the rival genre. His observation and classification of animals are often single-minded devices of satire. In *Joseph Andrews,* when Lady Booby calls her servant "a reptile of a lower order, a weed that grows in the common garden of creation," and Mrs. Slipslop laments that her mistress thinks servants not "born of the Christian *specious*," he makes natural history emblematize aristocratic complacency.[26] A traditional concern with satiric typology reduces bad characters to animals and devalues empiricism. In calling Slipslop a cow, tigress, and pike (51-52) and Parson Trulliber a goose and pig (163), Fielding's animal analogies sever human dignity from vice by trivializing the latter. When a would-be ravisher of Fanny is presented as a gamecock toying amorously with a hen till he spies a rival (142), the simile offsets the threat of sexual violence by debunking the rapist and creates the antithesis by which Parson Adams is seen to be "no chicken." Good characters are rarely associated with animals. Birds and dogs revere Joseph as a sign of his compatibility with Fanny (42): both see animals as fellow creatures. But those who compare people to animals are often evil. The squire who uses "dogs of his own species" to hunt men (231) is a barbarian when he treats Adams like "large jack rabbit" (227), and, on account of his view that the poor need clothes no more the [sic] a "horse or any other animal" (259), Peter Pounce is damned for lacking Christian charity. His analogy is the grossest rationalization of economic greed and social hierarchy.

In *Tom Jones,* concern for animals usually signals hypocrisy. Blifil's freeing of Sophia's bird, which sees it snatched by a hawk, stems from envy of Tom.[27] When Blifil views Sophia as a "human Ortolan" (263), the baseness of his sexual appetite is stressed. Neither meditative nor scientific concerns for animals escape Fielding's satire because he thinks they abuse human value. The Man of the Hill's physico-theology is spurned since he holds that, whereas no insect or vegetable is so low as not to be "honoured with bearing Marks of the Attributes of its Great Creator" (368), man has lost this favor. Fielding is as critical of the Royal Society's "laws of Animal OEconomy." He jeers at the Society's likely reaction to the "Bird with a Letter in his Maw," by which Tom writes to Sophia, to criticize its confusion of empirical and hypothetical procedures and its scorn for common sense (649). The abuse of natural history explains why Fielding resorts to fables. In fitting the story of Grimalkin to Mrs. Partridge when she attacks her husband (67) and to Squire Western when he stops following his daughter (477), Fielding renders the fable transparent by a comic ambivalence which employs the motif of the interdependence of animals and mankind for strictly moral aims. The jealous wife who is ferocious tiger and ignoble cat and the obsessive hunter who becomes an untransformable mouser are bathetic images stressing that animal analogies to humans must be governed by the tenet that conscience divides the two orders of creation (130). His fables confirm that Fielding rejects systematic concern for the animal realm and that he subordinates it to comic and ironic ambivalences, which fortify his religious creed that humanity is distinct and paramount in creation.

The fables that Richardson, a translator of Aesop, uses in his novels tend to establish positive analogies between animals and humans, because he stresses his heroines' pathos by joining empirical detail to biblical allusion in a way looking ahead to White. Fear impels Pamela to liken herself to weak animals. Mr. B. forces her to view herself as a bird: he makes her heart flutter "like a Bird in a Cage new caught" and causes her to think of living on hips, haws, pignuts, potatoes, and turnips.[28] She compares her victimizers to dangerous beasts: Mrs. Jewkes is a *"Wolfkin"* (121) and "inhuman Tygress" (155). If she charges herself with superstition when she thinks Mr. B. and Mrs. Jewkes turn the bull upon her (137), Pamela does not question the validity with which she fuses observations and judgments of animals. She remains certain that "Bulls, and Bears, and Lions, and Tygers," as well as wicked humans, are her enemies (148). The fables by which she examines herself confirm her analogical sense: she judges her lack of prudence in terms of the grasshopper and the ants (77), defines her timidity in terms of the town and country mice (78), and pictures her vulnerability in terms of the sheep accused by the wolf and tried by the vulture (162). By coming to natural history through fables and the Bible, she gives her life coherence: she feels marriage will prove her a pliant willow, not a rigid oak (370), and, citing 1 Samuel 17:37, thanks God for delivering her from the "Paw of the Lion and the Bear" (100).[29] This mixed narrative typology is clarified by the garden imagery. If the Lincolnshire garden is advanced, as its nectarines attest (151), Richardson, far from stressing the social implications of horticulture, emphasizes Pamela's pretended ignorance about beans and sunflowers as an epistolary stratagem (113). Her disgust with a "great nasty Worm" (118) tells less about her gardening ideas than about her self-dramatizing faith, epitomized by her belief that marriage renders her an undeservedly exalted worm (303). The typology within which Richardson frames natural history is most apparent when Pamela leaves the Lincolnshire estate only to scrutinize her exodus by likening herself to the Israelites in their longing after the onions and garlic of Egypt (211).

The greater attention to the social aspects of natural history in *Clarissa* permits Richardson to realize more fully physico-theology's dialectic. The Harlowe estate's "rambling Dutch-taste garden" (164), its filbert walk and yew hedge (327), its plantations of oaks, elms, and limes (352), and its phyllirea hedge (437) symbolize the Harlowes' endorsement of horticultural and political progress.[30] Their attitude heightens the allegorical uses to which Clarissa puts horticultural ideas. Seeing herself as a fallen blossom (1349), she puts on her coffin a lily emblem, together with a verse from Psalm 103 that values flowers as signs of transitoriness (1306). Imagining her seduction in terms of buds in spring being nipped by severe frost and blighted by the east wind (1106), she makes Lovelace the epitome of garden pests: he is the caterpillar eating the fair leaf of virgin fame, the eastern blast, the mildew thwarting the husbandman, and the canker-worm turning the damask rose yellow (892). Her transcendent faith is summed up in her trust that her spiritual hopes, being better rooted than her earthly ones, will bring forth more fruit (1121).

The many ornithological observations in *Clarissa* are instrumental to its characterization, since they convey the struggle between secular and religious values through contrary stances to natural history. Her bantams, pheasants, and pea-hens, a legacy from her grandfather, Clarissa visits twice a day (66): watching them, she enjoys their "inspiriting liveliness" (283). They heighten her sense of analogy. So, she challenges her brother's claim that sons, not daughters, are chickens produced for the home table by asking when their necks are wrung (77), but sees herself as a bird caught in her brother's snare (119). Her critical yet pathetic analogies are validated by Lovelace's merely selfish and secular attitudes. He stirs his fantasies by picturing her as a trapped bird. His physical knowledge of how a bird gradually accepts entrapment feeds his wish for

sexual control of Clarissa (557). To belittle her resistance in his fantasy, he details the mating of poultry: he observes how the strutting cock invites his favorite mistress to take a barley-corn in an affectedly meek prelude to mounting her exultantly (449). While he imagines the cowering hen to fantasize about sexual power, Clarissa treats birds as social and religious symbols. Stating that parental wings must protect young girls from vultures, hawks, kites, and other birds of prey (480), she meditates her relation to the pelican, owl, and sparrow, scriptural emblems of spiritual exile (1221). Her allegorizing is validated by Lovelace's histrionic and erratic analogies. In addition to thinking himself an eagle which preys, not on wrens, phil-tits, or wag-tails, but on the noblest of quarries (559), and modeling himself on the strutting villain of a bird who feathers lady after lady in imperial fashion and abandons them to hatch the "genial product" (917), he sees Clarissa as an innocent chicken whom he may capture only with aid of fellow rakes (659).

Lovelace's analogic inconsistency, arising from a libertinism that aims to debase Clarissa's physico-theology, also extends to animals. If he grants her nobility by calling her lion-hearted (647), when opposed by her family he sees himself as a lion like James II (165). Forgetting that this monarch fled the throne, Lovelace reveals that he is as vulnerable to Jacobite prejudices as to sexual fantasies: his natural images recoil on him because he lacks Clarissa's tropical discipline. The prospect of violating her makes him compare himself precariously to a hungry but bashful hound with froth on its vermilion jaws, an elephant attempting to snuff up the moon (473), and a fly buzzing round a taper (492). To Clarissa, such analogies are part of his rattle: alluding to Derham, she claims that Lovelace warns people that he is a snake (439). His histrionic abuse of natural history means that he never integrates ecology and spirituality. While he alludes to David's remorse about the lamb to flatter himself for not violating Rosebud (541), Clarissa, even in the trauma of rape, applies to herself the fable of the wild animal that turns into a dangerous lap-dog (891). Such self-criticism gives her a Johnsonian perspective: like Richardson's friend, she fortifies her case against Lovelace by arguing that, having destroyed other species, man attacks the weaker of his own (1126).

The characterization of Lovelace and Clarissa depends on opposing views of natural history: secular empiricism and anarchic libertinism are vanquished by appreciation of natural environment, social order, and spiritual transcendence. Besides illuminating the contrasting ways in which natural history stimulated Defoe to build paradoxes into narrative exposition and Fielding to endorse an outlook sympathetic only to traditional tropes, the conflict between Lovelace and Clarissa helps define the variable ideological reaction to natural history in subsequent novels. For instance, it clarifies the dialectic in *Rasselas,* showing that Johnson enlivens his story by embedding into it opposing stances to natural history.[31] Rasselas defines his discontent with the Happy Valley by contrasting himself to the birds and beasts (43), yet his awareness that he needs a goal comes from observing the lambs and kids (45). In his failure to escape the valley, he learns that plants and animals are infinitely engrossing subjects (49). If he criticizes simple-minded analogies between animals and man, Johnson nonetheless promotes them dialectically. The artist who models wings on the bat's fails not because of the inherent folly of the attempt but because he forgets his model, deluding himself that bat-wings will carry him beyond the eagle and the vulture (53). In making the upward, oblique line of conies' burrows lead to Rasselas's escape (70), Johnson implies that reason and common sense must rely on animal instinct. By the same token, he implies the necessary coexistence of empirical observation and traditional fable.

While Johnson derives an intellectual dialectic from Rasselas's contrary reactions to the animal world, Sterne in *A Sentimental Journey* makes Yorick react to it as erratically as possible in order to experiment comically with the tensions between sensibility and satire. Yorick's pretensions to identify with myrtles, cypresses, and the starling do not maintain traditional ritual: they are merely self-indulgent. Instead of heightening his consciousness by addressing the trees and the bird, Yorick converts them into rhetorical and heraldic emblems, exposing through his paradoxically 'fine but coarse awareness Sterne's ironical view that empirical precision and subjective rationalization are inextricable.[32] The recoil of his wish to cultivate his sensibility by eschewing the usual experiences of the Grand Tour is a histrionic materialism like Lovelace's. Yorick's response to the dead ass is slow and mechanical by contrast to his pony's intuition (38), and his citation of Bevoriskius's words on copulating sparrows (81) manifests a confused prurience as far removed from scientific observation as conceivable. Setting out to be close to nature and his heart, Yorick meets the contraries of life and writing with only momentary comprehension. If the dead ass creates anxiety in him one second, the next he falls asleep; if the starling's notes arouse him to the Bastille's horrors, he expresses his gratitude by selling the bird to unfeeling and insensitive lords and reducing its memory to a sign of conventional heraldic prestige.

The degree to which Yorick's sensitive declarations about natural history mask an uncritical acceptance of the status quo is the degree to which Sterne applies his experimental satire to attack the complex of economic progress and social hierarchy remarkable in Defoe and fulfilled by White. Smollett, partly since he was uninterested in Sterne's literary experimentation, promoted this complex. The allusions to natural history in

Humphry Clinker, for example, promote a dialectical ideology of tradition and progress.[33] Some allusions are typically comic, as when Matt. sees himself and fellow old-timers at Bath as "Chinese gudgeons" in a punch bowl (94) and Jery jokes about the marriage partners as widgeons about to find themselves in a duckoy (392). But most champion social hierarchy, ecology, and agricultural and financial innovation, showing that Smollett reconciles apparently incompatible ideas systematically. When Matt. calls lower-class women seeking rich husbands "shovel-nosed sharks" preying on the "blubber" of "uncouth whales of fortune" (66), natural history defies change to the social structure. As a landowner, Matt. upholds ecology to deflate London's economic centrality and to honor the rural gentry: while he boasts that his bread and poultry are products of natural soil and moderate cultivation (150), he derides London's artificial soil and the diseases of its force-fed poultry (152-53). Like White, Matt. promotes enclosure as a way of boosting productivity (252) and stresses the new modes of cultivating turnips, apricots, nectarines, pineapples, and grapes (260). He defends with enthusiasm the notion that the earth's fruits strengthen economic and political culture. At the end of the novel, he expounds the virtue of capitalizing land: families thereby become self-sufficient and able to finance their own mortgages. After hearing of the restoration of one estate according to the modern principles of enclosure, drainage, and shelter-belts (369), Matt. renews a friend's estate (385): he turns a shrubbery and pleasure grounds into corn fields and pasture, besides planting clumps of firs intermixed with beech and chestnut to make a windbreak that will both yield fuel and make the fields more productive.

If disgust with the invasion of rural life by urban fashion also motivated Goldsmith, Mackenzie, and Day, these novelists neither shared Smollett's ideas about the agrarian revolution nor reconciled social hierarchy with economic progress. The use of the names Thornhill, Primrose, and Burchell in *The Vicar of Wakefield* is a clue to Goldsmith's reactionary view of natural history.[34] When libertine Thornhill, after killing a stag on the Primroses' land, gives them the venison (55) and when his chaplain shoots a blackbird that her mother forces Sophia to accept as a gift (88), Goldsmith concedes that ownership of wild life symbolizes social power, while stressing that gifts of food from the upper classes fortify privilege by compromising recipients like the Primroses. Although they enjoy an idyllic life on their farm, their relative ignorance about natural history makes them vulnerable to the landlord who traps them in the political and legal systems. For example, Primrose sells "old Blackberry" cheaply because he is persuaded that the healthy horse is diseased (92). The lures of urban fashion, greed, and vanity ensnare the Primroses because their rural idealism is not informed by the concept of natural history embodied in Burchell, the true landlord. His love of children, ballads, and folk ways and his Augustan scorn of finance and high life make him an ideal land-owner.

More than Goldsmith, Mackenzie disjoins rural idyll and narrative realism in order to attack the social dialectic associated with natural history. The hero of *The Man of Feeling* rejects both urban and rural modes. Thus, Harley compares in disgust the profit a keeper of a London asylum makes from charging people to watch his "fierce and unmanageable" inmates with the money earned by those who display wild beasts.[35] He equally spurns landscape gardening and the "sacrilege of the plough" in the belief that modern design and agriculture displace the rural population (194). An ideal land-owner, he works the soil by hand and houses a displaced tenant farmer, giving him the means to subsistence and an environment suited to contemplation. To Mackenzie, the economic and social gap between landlord and tenant is bridged by their sharing a fellow feeling with trees, the servant regarding the trees near his original farm as family members (188) and the master being buried in the churchyard under the old tree he had so long loved (227).[36] The sentimental ecology in *The Man of Feeling* signals the author's dogmatic wish to evade natural history's complex of scientific classification, agricultural innovation, and aristocratic power.

In *The History of Sandford and Merton,* the last part of which appeared just after *The Natural History of Selbourne,* Day attempts to naturalize sentimental ecology even more dogmatically than Mackenzie, in the process exemplifying how hard middle-class ideology seeks to evade but is touched by natural history's methodological and social dialectic. Thus, Harry Merton, a middle-class boy, is innately sympathetic; he gives his supper to robins and avoids stepping on worms.[37] Forgetting that robins eat worms, Day presents Harry as both eager to learn plants' names and properties and certain that the rich alone destroy hedges, poultry, dogs and cattle (237). Tommy Sandford, an upper-class child, is inevitably cruel to animals, confirming Harry's prejudice. Because Harry naturally believes in utility and work, he lectures Tommy about reindeer and laplanders (278) and about the deadly nightshade (252). The dubious relevance of these lectures is matched by the inconsistency the boys' teacher manifests toward animals' rights. He urges that larks not be shot for eating farmers' turnips and that hares ought simply to be fenced out of gardens (277), yet he upholds the utility and propriety of singeing cats that attack caged birds, on the grounds they will be changed for ever (275). Day avoids the tension between adapting and accepting animal nature, like that between the ecological and utilitarian stances to natural history. This doctrinaire evasiveness is underscored by his use of fables. Harry not only compares himself

to ants as against flies by way of declaring his work ethic (251), but also employs the fable of the ass dressed in a lion's skin to demean aristocratic manners and rationalize his ignorance of dancing and polite manners (304). Paradoxically, traditional fables justify Harry's scorn for cultural tradition: reactionary emblems supposedly conform natural history to innate principle with ease.

The resistance by Goldsmith, Mackenzie, and Day to both social hierarchy and scientific and economic progress testifies to the mutual definition of the novel and natural history. By century's end, as Edgeworth's *Castle Rackrent* shows, it was the novel's reaction against natural history that allowed it to equate aristocratic manners with ecological ignorance and to argue that most landlords were absentees who extorted money from estates and abused tenants.[38] In its ideological variability, however, the novel still relied on its rival, as the less schematic and more optimistic treatment of natural history by Jane Austin witnesses. *Mansfield Park* uses natural history far more dialectically than do the radical sentimentalists.[39] In appreciating the cultural symbolism of the rural estate, Fanny Price is a natural historian: she collects plants (173), studies "inanimate nature" (110), and identifies with trees rather than tolerate Repton's design for improving Sotherton (87). Her distaste for the fashionable reshaping of landscape reflects a more radical physico-theological interest in nature's plentitude than Harley's or Harry Merton's. She deplores the excessive regularity of the planting and pruning of larches, laurels, and beeches at Sotherton (119); the natural forms of plants mediate knowledge to her. From the thriving evergreens in Mrs. Grant's shrubbery, she learns that her vicarage's soil is better than Mansfield Park's. Beautiful in themselves, the trees are more so because they impel her to contemplate nature's variety. She finds it spiritually inspiring that the law governing evergreens varies from that ruling deciduous trees. Like Rasselas, she sees that the commonest species and the multiplicity of botanical principles satisfy and develop her "rambling fancy" (223). Unlike the Man of the Hill, her love of nature is not anti-social. At Portsmouth she misses Mansfield Park's springtime vegetation but misses its people more: physico-theology develops her sociability (421). Austen stresses Fanny's social and moral maturity by contrasting her with mere pretenders to natural history. When Tom placates his father by telling of the numerous pheasants in the woods, he also masks his filial callousness (197). On taking a specimen of health and some pheasants' eggs from the gardener at Sotherton, Mrs. Norris says the birds will console her loneliness (133). But she is just grasping. Her claim to have improved the vicarage by planting one apricot tree is absurd (86). Her avarice is reminiscent of Tabitha Bramble: it is an avarice that heightens the eclecticism of Fanny's empirical, cultural, and spiritual concern with natural history.

That Fanny heightens esthetic with scientific ideas and develops a keen social sense from exploring physico-theology illustrates how much the novel's reaction to natural history advanced narrative modes and themes throughout the eighteenth century. A systemic relation with natural history both influenced the novel's formal experiments and obliged it to face its rival's aristocratic codes. Viewing the world with a shared language involving science and poetry, the novel, in facing natural history's dialectic of empirical and spiritual ideas, could not dismiss its emphasis on social hierarchy. Natural history's plural forms and eclectic techniques stress that its border with the novel is not closed, and this indeterminate boundary confirms that the novel does not possess a uniform ideology: satire of aristocracy and of economic change does not mean that the novel is governed by a middle-class outlook. In promoting social hierarchy and economic progress and in applying cultural and spiritual perspectives to empiricism, natural history made it impossible for the novel to avoid dialectical modes and concepts. Novelistic ideology is more involved than literary history claims because of the novel's co-existence with natural history: the novel documents the emergence of the middle-class in no stable or straightforward way; it attacks as much as promotes social evolution because natural history obliges it to see that social evolution is a complex matter. By the same token, fiction gains from the empirical and social strategies of natural history: scientific classification with its problems and dependence on philology and literary tropes together with the promotion of agrarian reform, and new forms of capitalism enrich story-forms and narrative procedures. By alluding to and appropriating natural history's forms, if but to subvert them, eighteenth-century novels realized the ideology of the landowning classes: in extending literacy and giving a wider readership cultural identity, the novel, in the face of natural history's intellectual and social strength, informed itself deeply with a genre that values theology and poetry and that welcomes social change by upholding political tradition. Natural history endowed the novel less with conceptual stability than with experimental variability.

Notes

[1] From publication records Rousseau shows that, by 1770, titles in natural history outnumbered all other science books and that its linguistic impact was greater than that of natural philosophy: "Science books and their readers in the eighteenth century," in Isabel Rivers (ed.), *Books and their Readers in Eighteenth-Century England* (New York: St. Martin's, 1982), pp. 202, 220, 225. Cf. Rousseau, "John Hill, Universal Genius *Manqué:* Remarks on His Life and Times, with a Checklist of his Works," *The Renaissance Man in the Eighteenth Century* (Los Angeles: Clark Memorial Library, 1978), pp. 45-129.

[2] Serge Soupel, "Science and Medicine and the Mid-Eighteenth-Century Novel: Literature and the Language of Science," *Literature and Science and Medicine* (Los Angeles: Clark Memorial Library, 1982), pp. 10, 24-25, 30.

[3] Michael McKeon, *The Origins of the English Novel 1600-1740* (Baltimore: Johns Hopkins University Press, 1987), "'Natural History' As A Narrative Model," pp. 68-73 and "Introduction," especially pp. 19-22.

[4] Richard Mabey, *Gilbert White: A Biography of the Author of "The Natural History of Selbourne"* (London: Century, 1986), explains White's indebtedness to Ray and Derham (pp. 11-12). White names these titles: *The Natural History of Selbourne*, ed. R. M. Lockley (London: Dent, 1949), pp. 51 and 105. All further references are to this edition. Keith Thomas, *Man and the Natural World: Changing Attitudes in England 1500-1800* (Harmondsworth: Penguin, 1984), links natural history to aristocratic power: pp. 13, 133, 184, 209, 227, 283. He says biological classification reinforced social hierarchy: pp. 40, 61.

[5] John A. Passmore (ed.), *Priestley's Writings on Philosophy, Science, and Politics* (New York: Collier), pp. 318-19.

[6] Mary Jane Edwards (ed.), *The History of Emily Montague* (Ottawa: Carleton University Press, 1985), p. 383.

[7] W. J. Keith, *The Rural Tradition: A Study of the Non-fiction Prose Writers of the English Countryside* (Toronto: Univ. of Toronto Press, 1974), pp. 50-57, gives a fine analysis of White's literary techniques.

[8] Lucy B. Maddox, "Gilbert White and the Politics of Natural History," *Eighteenth-Century Life,* vol. 10, no. 2 (May, 1986), 45-57, says White's focus on upper class Anglicans was sharpened by opposition to the French Revolution. Thomas's claim that White saw the natural world in a "direct, unstylized" way assumes the new science was "totally hostile to symbolic thinking": *Man and the Natural World*, pp. 266, 67. Raymond Williams makes the same assumption: *The Country And The City* (London: Chatto & Windus, 1973), pp. 118-19.

[9] For White's interest in the viewpoint of animals, see Lansing V. Hammond, "Gilbert White, Poetizer of the Commonplace" in *The Age of Johnson*, ed. Frederick W. Hilles (New Haven: Yale University Press, 1949), p. 377-83.

[10] On White as a landowner, see Mabey, *Gilbert White*, pp. 26-32.

[11] Defoe anticipates White's view of country houses: *A Tour through the Whole Island of Great Britain*, ed. G. D. H. Cole and D. C. Browning (London: Dent, 1974), Vol. 1, pp. 167-68.

[12] White's stance is analyzed by Hoyt Trowbridge, "White of Selbourne: The Ethos of Probabilism" in *Probability, Time, and Space in Eighteenth-Century Literature*, ed. Paula Backscheider (New York: AMS Press, 1979), pp. 79-109, and by S. E. G. Curtis, "A Comparison Between Gilbert White's *Selbourne* and William Bartram's *Travels*" in *Actes du VIIe congrès de Littérature Comparée*, ed. Milan Dimi and Juan Ferrate (Stuttgart: Erich Bieber, 1979), pp. 137-41.

[13] White's diction for the "father of the flock" resembles Lovelace's: Samuel Richardson, *Clarissa*, ed. Angus Ross (Harmondsworth: Penguin, 1985), p. 449. All references are to this edition.

[14] The King says that he who makes "two blades of grass" grow "where only one grew before" deserves "better of mankind . . . than the whole race of politicians put together": *Gulliver's Travels and Other Writings*, ed. Louis A. Landa (Boston: Houghton Mifflin, 1960), p. 109.

[15] *The Diary of Thomas Turner 1754-1765*, ed. David Vaisey (Oxford: Oxford University Press, 1985), pp. 164, 173, 6.

[16] *The Diary of a Country Parson 1758-1802*, ed. John Beresford (Oxford: Oxford University Press, 1978), pp. 230, 261, 50.

[17] See *The Natural History of Selbourne*, pp. 39, 42, 151, 189, 192, 219, 249, 262, for White's knowledge of travelogues. Cf. Maddox, "Gilbert White and the Politics of Natural History," p. 47.

[18] Defoe also anticipates White in criticizing Pliny (I, 248), esteeming "physick" gardens and exotic plants (I, 47), and viewing wildlife as a capital return (I, 79) and as a source of exclusive gifts (II, 269).

[19] White notes that at Tunbridge wheat-ears "appear at the tables of all the gentry that entertain with any degree of elegance": *The Natural History of Selbourne*, p. 161.

[20] *The Journal of a Voyage to Lisbon*, ed. Austin Dobson (London: Oxford University Press, 1907), p. 9. H. R. Hays, *Birds, Beasts, and Men: A Humanist History of Zoology* (Baltimore: Penguin, 1972), p. 28, says Pliny created an "anthropology of the absurd."

[21] Samuel Johnson, *A Journey to the Western Islands of Scotland* and James Boswell, *The Journal of a Tour to the Hebrides with Samuel Johnson, LL.D.*, ed. Allan Wendt (Boston: Houghton Mifflin, 1965). Citations are to this edition. For White's admiration of Johnson, see Mabey, *Gilbert White*, p. 153.

[22] Tobias Smollett, *Travels Through France and Italy*, ed. Frank Felsenstein (Oxford: Oxford University Press, 1981), pp. 17, 30.

[23] Smollett lists the fish and fruit for sale at Boulogne and Nice to imply the superior plenitude of France: see *Travels*, pp. 23, 153.

[24] *Captain Singleton*, ed. Shiv. K. Kumar (London: Oxford University Press, 1969). References are to this edition.

[25] Besides here anticipating White's anthropocentric analogies, Defoe shows his narrative hand when, in *A Tour*, he says amusingly that cartographers ignorant about northern Scotland "fill it up with hills and mountains, as they do the inner parts of Africa, with lyons and elephants, for want of knowing what else to place there" (II, 410).

[26] *Joseph Andrews*, ed. R. F. Brissenden (Harmondsworth: Penguin, 1977), pp. 159, 280.

[27] *Tom Jones*, ed. Sheridan Baker (New York: Norton, 1973), p. 120. Note, however, that Fielding, citing Philip Miller's *The Gardener's Dictionary*, stresses that natural classification must be based on experience (p. 373).

[28] *Pamela*, ed. T. C. Duncan Eaves and Ben D. Kimpel (Boston: Houghton Mifflin, 1971), pp. 43, 81.

[29] Note that Pamela refers to Mrs. Jewkes "huge Paw" on p. 121. See Numbers 11:5 for the reference to onions and garlic.

[30] Phyllirea, an ornamental evergreen from the Mediterranean, was imported into England in the seventeenth century.

[31] *The History of Rasselas, Prince of Abissinia*, ed. D. J. Enright (Harmondsworth: Penguin, 1976). References are to this edition.

[32] Albert J. Kuhn (ed.), *Three Sentimental Novels: A Sentimental Journey, The Man of Feeling, The History of Sandford and Merton* (New York: Holt Rinehart, 1970), pp. 26-27, 67.

[33] *Humphry Clinker*, ed. Angus Ross (Harmondsworth: Penguin, 1967). References are to this edition.

[34] *The Vicar of Wakefield*, ed. Stephen Coote (Harmondsworth: Penguin, 1982). References are to this edition.

[35] *Three Sentimental Novels*, p. 139.

[36] On the worship of trees, see *Man and the Natural World*, pp. 212-23.

[37] *Three Sentimental Novels*, p. 232-33.

[38] See *Castle Rackrent*, ed. George Watson (Oxford: Oxford University Press, 1980), pp. 14, 17.

[39] *Mansfield Park*, ed. Tony Tanner (Harmondsworth: Penguin, 1966). References are to this edition.

Laurie Fitzgerald (essay date 1995)

SOURCE: "Reconsidering the Late Eighteenth-Century Novel," in her *Shifting Genres, Changing Realities: Reading the Late Eighteenth-Century Novel*, Vol. 8 of The Age of Revolution and Romanticism: Interdisciplinary Studies, Peter Lang, 1995, pp. 1-15.

[*In this excerpt Fitzgerald discusses the nature of the novel and its relationships to other genres.*]

Novels of the late eighteenth century have, until recently, been largely ignored by twentieth-century scholars and critics. In the traditional view of the history of the novel that I learned as an undergraduate, there were the "Big Four" novelists—Richardson, Fielding, Sterne, and Smollett—who "invented" the British novel in a remarkably short period of time. Daniel Defoe and Oliver Goldsmith merited some attention for *Moll Flanders, Robinson Crusoe,* and *The Vicar of Wakefield;* they might therefore be regarded as alternate members of the "Big Four" Club. Then, nothing of note seemed to have happened until Jane Austen's novels miraculously appeared on the scene in the early nineteenth century. Although there were certainly some interesting blips on the literary seismograph—Radcliffe's *Mysteries of Udolpho,* in particular, and also perhaps Godwin's *Caleb Williams,* MacKenzie's *Man of Feeling,* and Burney's *Evelina,* novels published between 1770 and 1811 (the year *Sense and Sensibility* appeared) received very little critical or scholarly attention. If a student wanted to delve a bit more deeply into this period in novel history—in order to prepare for preliminary examinations for a doctoral degree in eighteenth-century British literature, for example—she resorted to the categories supplied by the few literary historians who had bothered to discuss late eighteenth-century novels: the Gothic novel *(Castle of Otranto,* The *Mysteries of Udolpho, The Monk, Vathek);* the sentimental novel *(The Man of Feeling, The Memoirs of Miss Sidney Biddulph);* the doctrinaire, philosophical or Jacobin novel *(Anna St. Ives, Nature and Art, Caleb Williams, Hermsprong).* Each "type" was viewed to be of some historical interest because of the authors' willingness to experiment with unusual content or stylistic innovations of various kinds. The main point, however, was to set these novels apart, into convenient categories, as a way of isolating what was new about them rather than in an attempt to incorporate them into the mainstream tradition of the novel. We used to assume that almost no one (and certainly no intelligent, well educated people) read those novels, even at the time they were published; they were, according to received opinion, amateurish, sloppy, primitive, and embarrassingly inept. Their badness at least could provide the sophisticated modern reader with a laugh or two. Because we concluded, from our superior vantage point, that these were bad novels, we assumed also that the next wave of "great" novelists—Austen, Dickens, and Eliot—probably dismissed them as well. Austen and Dickens couldn't possibly have learned anything from writers like Robert Bage and Charlotte Smith.

Recently, our understanding of the eighteenth-century novel has changed dramatically. The hegemony of the "Big Four" is being reexamined, and novelists who worked before and after them are getting fresh readings. Even so, as J. Paul Hunter observes in *Before Novels,* the formalist mind set is hard to shake:

> Traditional novelistic theory, based as it is on analogies with more traditional and more conservative literary forms and the structures that support them, does not like to hear the multiple discourses in novels or recognize the presence of competing modes within individual works. Recent narrative theory has been more receptive to odd, lumpy, and unexpected features, but most criticism of novels retains its *arriviste* snootiness, remaining intolerant of features that do not meet preconceived standards. Definitions remain high-minded, novels recalcitrant. (29) . . .

Genre Theory and Realism

By stressing that formal realism is just one mode of representation available to the novelist, genre theory provides an approach for revising our understanding of the late eighteenth-century novel, especially novels that encompass a broad panorama of genres and styles. Genre theorists have discussed the fluid quality of the novel, its elusive structural principles, and its incorporation of many different genres. Ralph Cohen argues, in rebuttal of the idea that eighteenth-century writers and critics were guided by a rigid code of decorum and rules, that writers freely explored the possibilities inherent in the interrelationships of genre, particularly with regard to the didactic function of literature, which, since the Renaissance, had gradually become elevated in importance ("On the Interrelations of Eighteenth-Century Literary Forms" 76-77). More recently, Cohen has stated that genre theory can provide "the most effective procedure for dealing with change in literary history . . . We need a new literary history, and I believe that genre theory can provide it" ("Genre Theory" 113).

Cohen's statement that referential and nonreferential truth can coexist in a given literary work is compatible with recent critical reassessments of the notion of realism by Elizabeth Deeds Ermarth, Taylor Stoehr, Paul Coates, and Robert Alter. Robert Alter has noted that there are two types of mimetic procedure for the novel: realism, in which the novelist seeks to maintain a relatively consistent illusion of reality, in that what is written refers exactly to some phenomenon of the real world; and a self-conscious approach that "systematically flaunts its own necessary condition of artifice, pointing at the relationship between art and reality" (13). Alter observes further that the relationships between novels and the world are far more complex than "the sturdy moral realism of Anglo-American novel criticism, from James to Leavis to Ian Watt" (21). Roland Barthes takes this view even further by suggesting that no truth is referential in literature, that what we have instead is the "referential illusion" (148).

Ian Watt would certainly agree with Alter's view that early critics of the novel failed to grasp the complexity of realism. In "Serious Reflections on *The Rise of the Novel*," Watt wrote that his concept that "realism of presentation" and "realism of assessment" could be separated was far too simplistic, for "some form of evaluation is always inextricably connected with any writer's presentation" (214). Watt also mentions a second problem with his definition of realism in *The Rise of the Novel:* in assuming that the novel rose in opposition to the traditional social and literary establishment of the time, he overlooked the ways in which the novel was a conservative didactic tool, based on a world view primarily "Augustan," which is "an elite outlook based on the defense of a civilized social order." Although the major eighteenth-century novelists, along with Jane Austen and Sir Walter Scott, criticized society, they did so in "ways and accents which suggest that the Augustan norms seemed to them to have universal validity, and these norms surely encouraged some of the special literary features which their novels had in common" (216). Watt concludes that this "Augustan" world view tended to emphasize "masculine" and "adult" rather than "feminine" and "adolescent" values; the feminine and the adolescent point of view was to receive greater attention later in the history of the novel. (We might squirm today at this linking of "feminine and adolescent"; however, Watt's implicit allusion to novels by women in his reassessment of *The Rise of the Novel* should be taken as a positive gesture). Watt's observations provide a useful introduction to my approach to late eighteenth-century novels, for many of them do explore the experiences of young people, particularly with regard to the selection of marriage partners and the question of the individual's obligation to his or her family. However, what Watt identifies as "feminine and adolescent values" in these novels might more precisely be described as an interest in the individual personality (both feminine and masculine) and the conflict between private desires and public expectations in the face of the gradual erosion of the family's power over the individual.

Many critics have analyzed the late-eighteenth-century novel's emphasis on feminine experience. Nancy Armstrong's *Desire and Domestic Fiction* traces the novel's "rise" by suggesting that the novel helped to create the domestic model for feminine experience. The novel rose not so much to chronicle middle-class experience, but to bring about a change in the way people perceived the individual's role in society: "Thus, what began chiefly as writing that situated the individual within the poles of nature and culture, self and society, sex and sexuality, only later became a psychological reality, and not the other way around" (13). Oddly, as Robert Folkenflik has observed, Armstrong spends little time discussing the works of eighteenth-century women writers, choosing to anchor her analysis of the formulation of domestic fiction on Richardson's *Pamela* (211). Important studies of eighteenth-century women writers abound, including those by Janet Todd, Jane Spencer, Dale Spender, Katherine Sobba Green, Mary Poovey, Elizabeth Bergen Brophy, and Mona Scheuermann.

Women's experiences are extremely important themes, but at the same time they are embedded in the changing condition of the family as a whole as depicted in novels at the end of the eighteenth century. Young men like Mortimer Delvile in *Cecilia* and Orlando Somerive in *The Old Manor House* are also severely affected by changes in their families' social and economic status. Many late eighteenth-century novels explore conflicts between individual desires and the expectations of the older generation and society in general. These conflicts are resolved, but at great cost to individual young women and young men. In such novels, therefore, the young person's ultimate integration into the accepted social structure is viewed as problematic; in contrast to the situation of Tom Jones or John Moore's Edward Evilen, social integration is not entirely a blessing for characters like Cecilia Beverley and Orlando Somerive. Their problem is not to learn to obey the rules of social conduct, but rather how to survive in a society that limits individuals because of conventional expectations that they marry certain people and not others, and get and spend money only in certain ways.

M. M. Bakhtin has suggested that the novel represents reality through the interplay of the many points of view embedded in a group of genres; there is no central, identifiable novel structure, and the "novel" is simply a loose shell surrounding a combination of components derived from different genres (321). This observation is particularly germane to many eighteenth-century novels, with their emphasis on epistemological investigations of the world in order to arrive at a didactic message, a feature that today's readers find difficult to appreciate. The vehicle for didacticism is the speech and action of the characters, or more specifically, in Bakhtin's analysis, the dialogue between the speeches and actions of all the characters, a dialogue based on allusions to many different genres. Thus, the dialogue between the real world and the artificial world of the novel, and between realistic and self-conscious representation within the novel itself, is re-enacted within the speech and actions of individual characters.

In some eighteenth-century novels, the freewheeling mixture of genres results in structural arrangements that defy the modern reader, conditioned to expect a linear sequence of events placed in a continuous temporal framework. Temporal logic, the foundation of formal realism, is a radical departure from earlier literature; as Elizabeth Deeds Ermarth observes, "The *Morte d'Arthur* or the *Song of Roland* baffles modern readers, who assume that a narrative of events is a *temporal* sequence without realizing that there are other kinds of sequence, such as rhetorical ones" (8). Modern readers are similarly unable to perceive the structural logic of eighteenth-century novels.

One rhetorical arrangement that is possible in the eighteenth-century novel, as Eric Rothstein has shown, is based on systems of analogical relationships. The characters are linked, not by a series of plausibly motivated actions, but by virtue of their respective positions with regard to a primary epistemological problem. Even characters who are introduced into a novel by the flimsiest imaginable threads of plot participate in the central epistemological pattern. Rothstein's term "positional," based on Roman Jakobson's description of metonymy, is also useful in describing this analogical tendency in eighteenth-century novels. Although he uses the term to define the style of eighteenth-century poetry, Rothstein states that a similar process is at work in the novel. Positional style is

> the linguistic placing of an object within a context. The context may be something more comprehensive than the object (table: furniture, house), another member of the same group (table: chair), or something connected to the object by nature or logic (table: banquet). Jakobson opposes metonymy, in his expanded sense of "positioning faculty" or "contextual focus," to metaphor, which governs relationships of similarity and identity. He postulates that the mental functions typical of "metonymy" and "metaphor" are fundamental to the way we comprehend the world: the essence of individual objects ("metaphor") on the one hand, the contextual classifications for those objects ("metonymy") on the other. *(Restoration and Eighteenth-Century Poetry 49-50)*

"Positional style" requires readers to compare and contrast sets of characters and ideas with one another,

even though individual scenes of the novel vary widely in tone and content. Just as readers arrange individual images in a poem within a context, proficient readers of eighteenth-century novels arrange and rearrange individual scenes, which can be described as self-contained chunks of novel material—the allusive fragments and predictable formulas from a broad range of genres that are woven again and again into novels of this period. The individual scene is meant to call up associations in the reader's mind, suggesting a general observation about the human condition that the particular moment in the novel typifies. The resulting novelistic world, created of allusions to a variety of literary genres and completed by the reader's experience and imaginative participation, may be more "realistic" than the much tidier worlds of linearly plotted novels. . . .

Philosophy, History, and Romance

A novel is not only a composite of fictional and non-fictional literary sources and various levels of self-consciousness or realism, but also, in Avrom Fleishman's words, "the supplement of historical and philosophical writing," with the result that "one cannot glory in its uniqueness without frequent forays into other ways of knowing and writing the world" (22). Michael McKeon would agree with this statement, for he amends Bakhtin's analysis of the discourse of genre by noting that it "accounts for only one of the two major postures whose interaction constitutes the epistemological origins of the novel" (118). Bakhtin, according to McKeon, neglects to take into account the novel's engagement with "naive empiricism" or questions of truth; he sees only the literary influences on the novel, when a dialogue between history and various literary genres is actually in effect. McKeon argues that the novel emerged in the Restoration and early eighteenth century from a dialectic between romance and history, a dialectic that is not a conflict between the demands of the two forms, but rather an interpenetration of the two.

> The empiricism of "true history" opposes the discredited idealism of romance, but it thereby generates a countervailing, extreme skepticism, which in turn discredits true history as a species of naive empiricism or "new romance." Once in motion, however, the sequence of action and reaction becomes a cycle: the existence of each opposed stance becomes essential for the ongoing negative definition of its antithesis. (88)

In McKeon's paradigm for the development of the eighteenth-century novel, romance casts doubt on history, even ridicules it; history's attempt to get at the "truth" of events undermines the imaginative world of romance. Both endeavors are undermined by skepticism, and the novel keeps working through these cycles over and over again.

McKeon also views the novel as a manifestation of what he terms the crisis in status consistency, the war between the classes, enacted in a dialectic between virtue as an inherited characteristic of the aristocrat, and virtue as an innate quality of the lower and middle classes, earning them upward mobility. The persistence of aristocratic romance forms in the portrayal of the lives of aristocratic characters in novels of the early eighteenth century is therefore not a "problem" with the eighteenth-century novel, but rather a vital component in its development:

> For the traditional categories do not really "persist" into the realm of the modern as an alien intrusion from without. Now truly abstracted and constituted as categories, they are incorporated within the very process of the emergent genre and are vitally functional in the finely articulated mechanism by which it establishes its own domain. (21)

In McKeon's view, the novel grew out of the revolutionary clash in early modern England between "status and class orientations and the attendant crisis in status inconsistency" (173-174). McKeon describes two competing ideologies: progressive ideology laments the social injustice of aristocratic rule, which equates hereditary power and status with virtue; conservative ideology, while agreeing that the aristocracy commits injustices, at the same time fears that a "'new aristocracy' of the undeserving," presumably based only on wealth, might be just as likely to commit and condone social injustice as the old aristocracy (174).

McKeon concentrates on the history of the novel up to the mid eighteenth-century, but his discussion of the social conflicts that were enacted in the dialectic between romance and history has direct applications to the late eighteenth-century novel as well. McKeon identifies two important eighteenth-century novel plots: stories of disinherited younger sons, and stories of conflicts between aristocratic seducers and lower- or middle-class women. Both of these plots are tied to questions of how wealth and status are transferred to young people within a society that assumes that individuals who already possess money and power are more deserving of additional rewards than those who possess virtue and integrity only. The two plots that McKeon discusses in detail are certainly prominent in the mid eighteenth century, but other plots become important later in the century. Two examples would be stories of young women who attempt to establish themselves in society by managing their inheritances independently of the wishes of a guardian or spouse and stories of deserving but poor young men who attempt to survive financially and socially on the basis of their virtue and ability (these young men were never disinherited because they never had anything to inherit in the first place). The five novels in my study are all versions of the romance plot of young people assum-

ing their proper places in society through suitable marriages or the acquisition of inherited wealth, or both. Nor are McKeon's questions of truth and virtue the only issues raised in the plots of these novels. Attention is also directed to questions about the role of the family in influencing an individual's decision to marry or not to marry a particular partner, with greater value placed on marriage for affection than marriage for economic convenience. The place of women in society is also considered, particularly in *Cecilia* and *Mount Henneth,* often as part of a more general question about the degree to which individual happiness is contingent upon conformity to social expectations. Stories of outsiders, persons like Schedoni in *The Italian* or Mr. Albany in *Cecilia,* who defy social expectations to either good or evil effect, are sometimes introduced as extreme versions of this theme.

McKeon's study, while extremely valuable, is necessarily selective in its scope. The interplay of genres in the novel is much more riotous and haphazard than McKeon's carefully controlled paradigm allows. The tension between romance and history is just one dialectic in the complicated blend of generic voices that produced novels in the early eighteenth century, and continues to produce them, as evidenced by Umberto Eco's *Foucault's Pendulum,* an amazing compendium of genres, including, among many other components, a computer manual, a history of the Knights Templars, and a reference guide to the occult. Our awareness of the many different genres incorporated into the early English novel is expanding at a rapid pace. Lennard Davis' *Factual Fictions,* an examination of the novel's relationship to the newspaper, is an early study of the novel's ability to absorb other types of prose writing. J. Paul Hunter's *Before Novels* is an excellent introduction to the eighteenth-century novel, and provides a thorough discussion of the most important genres that contributed to its development. More recently, Nancy Armstrong and Leonard Tennenhouse have suggested that American captivity narratives were a source for Richardson's *Pamela* and *Clarissa.* Other critics have begun to explore the relationship between the novel and writing about science and natural history; valuable studies have been published by Robert James Merrett, Serge Soupel, and Ann Jessie Van Sant. . . .

FURTHER READING

Criticism

Baker, Ernest A. *The History of the English Novel,* vols. III-V. New York: Barnes & Noble, Inc. 10 vols., 1950.
    Selection from a comprehensive history of the novel. The volumes cited focus on the late seventeenth through the early nineteenth centuries, discussing the

romance, the development of realism, the novel of sentiment, and the Gothic novel.

Butt, John. *The Mid-Eighteenth Century*. Oxford: Clarendon Press, 1979.
> Survey of English literature after 1740, with chapters on major novelists and other prose fiction.

Cruse, Amy. *The Shaping of English Literature and the Reader's Share in the Development of its Forms*. New York: Thomas Y. Crowell Co. nd.
> Studies the development of English literature by focusing on reader responses to contemporary authors. Included a chapter on books and authors read and discussed by Fanny Burney.

Elton, Oliver. *A Survey of English Literature 1730-1780*. 2 vols. London: Edward Arnold & Co., 1928.
> Comprehensive review of the period, with chapters on Richardson, Fielding, Smollett, Sterne and others.

Görtschacher, Wolfgang and Klein, Holger. *Narrative Strategies in Early English Fiction*. Salzburg: The Edwin Mellen Press, 1995, 365 p.
> Collection of essays on topics ranging from transformations of the romance to epistolary fiction.

Hill, Mary K. *Bath and the Eighteenth Century Novel*. Bath: Bath University Press, 1989, 76 p.
> Historical study of representations of the city of Bath in works of fiction by Defoe, Fielding, Smollett, and others.

Mayo, Robert D. *The English Novel in Magazines 1740-1815*. Evanston: Northwestern University Press, 1962, 421.
> History of the magazine tradition of prose fiction including serial novels and miscellanies.

McNeil, David. *The Grotesque Depiction of War and the Military in Eighteenth-Century English Fiction*. Newark: University of Delaware Press, 1990, 229 p.
> Study of eighteenth-century literary representations of war, with chapters on Smollett, Fielding, and Sterne.

Petit, Alexander, Ed. *Studies in the Novel, Special Number: Making Genre: Studies in the Novel or Something Like it, 1684-1762*, Vol. 30, No. 2, Summer, 1998.
> Eleven essays on the development of the novel genre, with an introductory overview. Includes essays on women's amatory fiction, Fielding's *Tom Jones,* and responses to Richardson's *Clarissa*.

Relihan, Constance C. *Fashioning Authority: The Development of Elizabethan Novelistic Discourse*. Kent, Ohio: The Kent State University Press, 1994, 162 p.
> Traces the history of the English novel to the Elizabethan period.

Richetti, John, Ed. *The Columbia History of the British Novel*. New York: Columbia University Press, 1994.
> Extensive collection of critical essays with selections on women's novels, Fielding, Smollet, Sterne, and Richardson.

Rogers, Katherine M. "Fantasy and Reality in Fictional Convents of the Eighteenth Century" in *Comparative Literature Studies*, Vol. 22, No. 3, Fall, 1985, 297-316.
> Discusses representations of convents in eighteenth-century fiction; includes commentary on Richardson's *Sir Charles Grandison*.

Spacks, Patricia Meyer. "Ev'ry Woman is at Heart a Rake" in *Eighteenth-Century Studies*, Vol. 8, No. 1, Fall, 1974, 27-46.
> Discusses gender relations in eighteenth-century life and literature.

Williams, Ioan. *Novel and Romance 1700-1800: A Documentary Record*. London: Routledge & Kegan Paul, 1970, 451 p.
> A collection of prefatory material and novel criticism from 1691-1798 with an introductory overview.

The Levellers

INTRODUCTION

The Levellers were a group of political activists that emerged in the mid-1640s, during the tumultuous period of England's Civil Wars. Often credited with being the first organized political party, the Levellers created or popularized such modern political tactics as mass demonstrations, large-scale petitioning, polemical pamphleteering, and lobbying members of Parliament. The party grew out of the Independent coalition and was led by John Lilburne, Richard Overton, and William Walwyn. While the Levellers did not advocate the "levelling" or elimination of property rights, as their opponents accused (thereby dubbing them the "Levellers"), they did seek to divorce wealth and property from political privilege. In addition to seeking economic and political freedom, the Levellers also sought religious tolerance.

The 1640s were a time of revolution in England. King Charles I in 1637 had attempted to impose Anglicanism in Scotland. At the same time, Puritans in England and especially in Parliament grew increasingly concerned about the influence of the Anglican Church on the King. King Charles demanded that Parliament raise funds to support his war against the Presbyterian Scots, who had gathered an army against him. Parliament, in turn, insisted that the King grant reforms in exchange for such funding—a demand that the King refused. By 1642 armed conflict between the King's army and Parliament had broken out, and in 1645, Oliver Cromwell, a military leader of Parliament, destroyed the King's army. The war was officially over in 1646, the King having been captured by Cromwell's army. However, Charles rejected the conditions Parliament set for his return to the throne, and he later escaped to form an alliance with the Scots. The second civil war began in 1648, with Cromwell leading his army against and defeating the forces of the King and of Scotland. Cromwell then purged Parliament of its Presbyterian members, leaving only those who favored the execution of Charles. The King was put to death by Parliament in 1649. Parliament and Cromwell then abolished both the monarchy and the House of Lords, declaring England a Commonwealth, which it remained until the restoration of King Charles II in 1660.

Against this historical backdrop, Lilburne, Overton, and Walwyn, among others, began to gain notice for their religious and political pamphlets. Lilburne is often described as the most religious of the Levellers, as well as the group's charismatic leader; Overton is usually considered the most rational, and Walwyn the most philosophical of the three. Each had significant pamphleteering experience when they came together, and each realized that given the unsettled state of England's political affairs, they had a chance to influence the contemporary political system. They envisioned freely elected representatives to the House of Commons with power equal to that of the House of Lords and the King. Another important component of their platform was that of complete freedom to practice any religion.

Modern critics have examined the individual contributions of the Leveller leaders to the party's ideology as well as the ways in which that ideology developed and was disseminated. M. A. Gibb has highlighted Lilburne's role as the leader of the movement, noting that the party did not officially organize until 1647, when the Commons rejected petitions presented for the release of Lilburne and Overton from prison. That year, Lilburne and Overton wrote *The Outcryes of the Oppressed Commons,* in which they presented their intention to appeal to the common people against the oppression of Parliament. Additionally, Gibb has discussed Lilburne's appeal to the soldiers in the New Model Army and the manner in which this support helped further the Leveller cause. Nigel Smith has examined a series of pamphlets by Overton, known as the "Marpriest" tracts, which emphasize his concern with religious and political toleration. Margot Heinemann has noted that Overton's prose is skillfully satirical and influenced by his theatrical connections. In contrast, T. B. Tomlinson has observed that William Walwyn's writing is characterized by his direct and "exceptionally unadorned" style. Tomlinson has examined Walwyn's pamphlets *The Power of Love* (1643) and *The Compassionate Samaritane* (1644) for their attacks on political and economic inequality.

The most significant Leveller documents include the three versions of their *Agreement of the People,* in which their demands as a party are presented to Parliament. Perez Zagorin has described the Leveller program as "a lower-middle-class utopia"; he suggests that the third version of the *Agreement,* entitled *An Agreement of the Free People of England* (1649), contians the clearest statement of the Leveller platform. D. B. Robertson has stated that in *A Manifestation* (1649), Leveller party leaders responded to accusations of atheism and anti-Scripturalism made by their opponents. Yet the religious statements made in this pamphlet, Robertson has argued, demonstrate the conflicting beliefs held by the leaders, and the way Lilburne's religious beliefs in particular seem to clash with his views regarding the equality of men. While the relationship between the sinful nature of man and the need for limited government may be inferred from Leveller writings, including the first two *Agreements,* Robertson has maintained that the third *Agreement* represents a more realistic conception of human nature and political life—a view emphasizing more limits on power than called for in the first two *Agreements.*

Another area of critical study is that of Leveller philosophy concerning the idea of natural law: the theory that moral laws are derived from human nature. Richard A. Gleissner has examined the role of this philosophical doctrine in Leveller political ideology. Specifically, Gleissner has analyzed how this concept was presented in 1647 in debates between Leveller leaders and such Parliamentary military leaders as Oliver Cromwell.

Despite their efforts to shape the existing political structures into an egalitarian, democratic form of government, the Levellers did not achieve their goals. As the government became increasingly centered under Cromwell's rule, the Levellers recognized that the inequalities and injustices that had existed under the King's rule still remained, although in a different guise. For this reason, they pushed strongly in their third *Agreement* for a system of government that would safeguard individual rights and prevent the consolidation of power in the hands of a single group as well as in the hands of an individual. In the 1650s the Levellers were denounced by Cromwell and government propagandists as subversives seeking to eliminate both law and property. At this time, too, Leveller leadership began to disappear: Lilburne, exiled by Cromwell in 1652, died in prison in 1657. Walwyn left politics to assume a medical practice. The Levellers, without strong leadership, soon lost all effectiveness as a group. F. D. Dow has commented that some weaknesses of the essential Leveller program doomed them from their start: Leveller ideology may have frightened the rich, neglected the poor, and been "too innovative in its assumptions to embrace all the godly 'middling sort'" of people.

REPRESENTATIVE WORKS

John Lilburne
Innocency and Truth Justified (pamphlet) 1645
The Freeman's Freedom Vindicated (pamphlet) 1646
Regall Tyranny Discovered (pamphlet) 1647

Richard Overton
Vox Borealis or the Northern Discovery (pamphlet) 1640-41
The Araignement of Mr. Persecution (pamphlet) 1645

Appeale from the Degenerate Representative Body the Commons of England, Assembled at Westminster, to the Body Represented (pamphlet) 1647

William Walwyn
The Power of Love (pamphlet) 1643
The Compassionate Samaritane (pamphlet) 1644
England's Lamentable Slaverie (pamphlet) 1645

John Lilburne and Richard Overton
The Outcryes of Oppresed Commons (pamphlet) 1647

John Lilburne, Richard Overton, Thomas Prince, and William Walwyn
A Manifestation (pamphlet) 1649
An Agreement of the Free People of England (petition) 1649

OVERVIEWS

F. D. Dow (essay date 1985)

SOURCE: "The Levellers," in *Radicalism in the English Revolution, 1640-1660,* pp. 30-56. Oxford: Basil Blackwell, 1985.

[*In the following essay, Dow studies the political factors leading to the emergence of the Leveller party. He also discusses various intellectual, religious, and philosophical influences on Leveller ideology, examines the primary goals of the party, and reviews the strengths and weaknesses of Leveller organization.*]

In recent times the Levellers have enjoyed a diminishing reputation among historians of seventeenth-century England. Once hailed as the champions of a democratic revolution who were defeated only by the political turncoats in the New Model Army, and still referred to by some present-day politicans as the founding fathers of the working-class movement, the Levellers have been severely cut down to size by the current triumph of the revisionists. Their significance in the English Revolution, it is now claimed, has been seriously overestimated by writers such as H. N. Brailsford and Christopher Hill. Marxist as well as conservative historians would now question the extent of their support, their impact on events (especially in the heady days of the army revolt in 1647), and the true nature of their apparently radical and democratic programme. None the less, despite the reservations about the movement which many historians now share, it is hard to deny that, in comparison with the parliamentarians and republicans whom we have examined so far, the Levellers broke new ground in several ways. They went farther than other groups in tackling the problem of building a new constitution instead of merely tinkering with the balance of institutions in the old. They sought to extend active political rights well beyond the charmed circle of the elite, and to develop new mechanisms for enforcing the accountability of the governors to the governed. They grounded their programme on a new ideological basis by developing arguments based on the doctrines of natural rights and of popular sovereignty. And they mobilized support for their movement by employing sophisticated modern techniques of propaganda and organization.

Disagreement among historians on the essential nature of the movement has been compounded by ambiguities in its composition and in its ideology, which in turn spring from the circumstances in which the Leveller party was formed and the way in which its policy was formulated. Rising out of the immediate political and religious turmoil of 1646-9, but tapping also longer-term social and economic grievances, the Leveller movement throve on the very fact that it had a multi-faceted appeal and could for a brief period represent many things to many men. Both ideologically and socially it was, as the Baptist Henry Denne described it, a very heterogeneous body. Its rapid rise and fall, its relatively short life, the fact that the leaders and their followers were thrown together by the crisis of the moment, all this meant that intellectual coherence suffered at the hands of an urgent need to hammer out a programme. The Levellers were not like a revolutionary party which had had a long period in opposition or in exile during which to assimilate and integrate various strands in its political thinking. Some historians have chosen to see a fundamental distinction between, on the one hand, those allegedly more moderate or 'constitutional' Levellers who concentrated on political reform and were less interested in social and economic restructuring and, on the other hand, the more radical wing of the movement, the 'true Levellers', which concerned itself with social democracy and economic problems and which had real affinities with the Diggers (Hill, 1975). This distinction seems much too arbitrary, and tends to obscure the rather more confused reality of the Leveller movement, where there was great internal flux and issues were seized upon and then abandoned as the political climate demanded. Changing external circumstances, especially relations with the New Model Army, dictated that policies (for example, on the franchise) should be modified and altered on grounds of expediency; and the individual concerns of particular leaders (such as Lilburne's interest in London's affairs or Overton's concern with social problems) might lead to specific issues being aired for a time without being fully and clearly integrated into the main platform. Policy documents designed to enlist mass support—the major petitions to parliament in March 1647 and September 1648 and the three Agreements of the People in November 1647, December 1648 and May 1649, for example—are a sure guide to the Leveller programme, but are not necessarily the fullest statements of Leveller views. To

these must be added the writings of a veritable host of prominent figures in the movement: Lilburne himself was the author of eighty pamphlets, and Richard Overton wrote forty between September 1645 and July 1649 alone (Greaves and Zaller, 1983).

The embarrassment of riches which this vast outpouring of pamphlet literature presents to the student of Leveller ideology raises a further difficulty about the composition and membership of the movement. The presentation of such a wide range of issues, together with the mass propagandist techniques which were used to procure subscriptions to petitions and a large turnout at demonstrations, makes it tempting to overestimate the strength of the party as such. As we shall see, expressions of sympathy with the attitudes the Levellers struck were numerous and vocal, especially in parts of London and the south-east, but it is not certain that this generalized sympathy was translated into widespread committed, consistent and sustained support for all the details of the party programme. Even in London, active party membership was probably much smaller than the numbers who turned out to Leveller spectacles, such as Lilburne's trial or Rainsborough's funeral, would suggest. Identification with the grievances the Levellers articulated was undoubtedly more widespread than active support for the remedies they espoused. Conservative historians would particularly demur at the suggestion that the radical ideology of the Leveller leaders was typical even of those social groups from which most support for the movement came. Clubmen, not Levellers (or Diggers), were arguably the true representatives of the wishes of the middling sort. . . . The Levellers' failure to build up solid grassroots commitment to the party and its official programme outside a limited section of the population of the south-east was, as we shall see, one of the main reasons for the downfall of the movement.

None the less, the difficulty of determining the nature of the Leveller programme or the extent of its support should not blind us to an appreciation of just how remarkable a phenomenon the Leveller movement of mid-seventeenth-century England was. 'Nowhere else', G. E. Aylmer writes, 'before the 1760s, or even perhaps before 1789, do we find the combination of radical journalism and pamphleteering, ideological zeal, political activism, and mass organization that prevailed in England from 1646 to 1649' (Aylmer, 1975, p. 9).

Origins and Influences

In explaining the background to and the origins of the Leveller movement we can look at three main sets of factors. First, there were particular grievances which the Levellers could exploit and which provided them with the issues on which to focus: these grievances encompassed both long- and short-term economic and social factors, the exceptional political conditions of the mid-1640s, and the religious disputes into which the nation had been plunged by the dismantling of episcopacy. Secondly, there was the intellectual heritage on which the Levellers could draw to establish the ideological underpinning for their programme of reform: this included the legacy of radical Protestantism; the doctrines of natural law and popular consent, which were ripe for extension into theories of natural rights and popular sovereignty; and particular interpretations of the course of English history since 1066. And third, there were models of popular participation, examples drawn from the actual political and religious experiences of Leveller leaders and supporters, which could inspire the party as it strove to develop practical solutions to the ills of the time.

The socio-economic preconditions for the rise of a movement like the Levellers had been created by long-term changes in landholding and in manufacturing. Those changes which had adversely affected the status and prosperity of the urban and rural 'middling sort of people' were especially important in providing potential supporters for the Levellers, who were to become principally the spokesmen for the 'industrious sort'. Pressure on the smaller peasant farmer who lacked the resources of his larger neighbour to benefit from an expanding market and rising prices; the discontent of the insecure copyholder subject to rack-renting; and the fear of the small cottager or husbandman at the prospect of enclosure, produced dissatisfaction which the Levellers could tap and issues on which they could take a stand. Of even greater significance were the problems of the small craftsmen and tradesmen, particularly in the towns, whose independence seemed threatened by large-scale merchants and entrepreneurs. The existence of such problems in London was crucially important, for the capital was to provide the core of the Leveller movement. Here a large pool of discontent existed among journeymen unable, because of changes in the structure of manufacturing, to find the resources to set up as masters in their own right. Anger smouldered among small tradesmen and merchants chafing at the alleged oppression of the guilds, the livery companies and, above all, the Merchant Adventurers; and indignation reigned among all those London householders who felt their economic rights and political interests threatened by corruption and oligarchy in the municipal government itself.

Many of these long-term economic grievances were felt throughout the early seventeenth century, but discontent was seriously exacerbated by the particular distress of the years from 1646 to 1649. The dislocations of war had seriously disrupted trade, unemployment increased, prices rose but wages failed to keep pace and at the end of the decade harvests were extremely poor. To add to this distress, parliament's imposition of taxes to pay for the army, especially the hated excise, had raised the price of consumable goods

even further, again to the particular annoyance of the London tradesmen. In January 1648 a pro-Leveller pamphlet entitled *The Mournfull Cryes of many thousand poor Tradesmen, who are ready to famish through decay of Trade* gave vent to this collection of grievances:

> Its your Taxes, Customs, and Excize, that compells the Countrey to raise the price of food, and to buy nothing from us but meer absolute necessaries; and then you of the City that buy our Work, must have your Tables furnished, and your Cups overflow; and therefore will give us little or nothing for our Work, even what you please, because you know we must sell for moneys to set our Families on work, or else we famish: Thus our Flesh is that whereupon you Rich men live, and wherewith you deck and adorn yourselves. (quoted in Shaw, 1968, p. 118)

London was, therefore, important to the Levellers because it was the scene of much economic distress for the small trader and artisan, but it was also significant because it was the focus of political and religious debate.

By 1646 the fighting in the Civil War had ended, but peace brought its problems no less profound than war. Between 1646 and 1649 the fundamental question of what to do with the King and what sort of political settlement to erect in the wake of parliamentary victories had to be resolved. An important consideration in all this was not simply how to preserve the gains made against the King, but also how to reach a settlement which would justify the sacrifices of ordinary people. Fears that these gains and sacrifices might be abandoned by parliament formed an essential backdrop to Leveller activities. As a developing issue, the quest for a settlement, coupled with radical suspicions of parliament's intentions, played a key part in determining the Levellers' relations with the officers and soldiers of the New Model Army. These relations in turn were crucial in determining how much influence the Levellers could exercise on the course of political events. In time it was to become very clear, not least in the Putney Debates of October-November 1647 and the Whitehall Debates of December 1648, that the Levellers and the Grandees (or senior officers) of the army differed on the nature of the political and religious settlement that should be reached with the King, and on the distribution of political power that should obtain in the new order. But in the immediate aftermath of the war it was also clear that both sides had good reason to fear and distrust the intentions of the dominant Presbyterian faction in parliament, that they shared a belief that a generous, compromise agreement should not be concluded with the King, and that by mid-1647 the Levellers had recognized that the army should have a large say in shaping the eventual settlement. The possibility of collaboration between the Levellers and the army Grandees would probably not have been seriously mooted, however, had it not been that the grievances and aspirations of the Levellers found such echoes among the rank and file that the Grandees had to take note in order to preserve the discipline and unity of the army. The radicalization of sections of the rank and file did not happen solely, or even directly, because of Leveller influence; it happened because the soldiers' perception of their own ill-treatment at the hands of the Presbyterian majority produced a political consciousness on which the Levellers could capitalize. The Levellers thus acted as a catalyst in forcing the soldiers to recognize and articulate their own role in producing a political settlement, but they were never powerful enough to make the Grandees dance entirely to the Leveller tune (Kishlansky, 1979a, 1979b). However, the Presbyterians' treatment of the army had provided the Levellers with an additional issue to exploit, an extra source of support on which to draw, and a lever with which to propel themselves into the political spotlight.

Integral to the confused politics of 1646-9 was the fact that a religious settlement also had to be hammered out in the wake of the destruction of episcopacy. In 1646 this issue came to a head when parliament prepared to erect a presbyterian system of church government. This attempt to set up a national church, to preserve the links between church and state and to impose discipline and unity on the godly, spurred into action those who wished to see a more tolerant system developed, with freedom for separatist churches and a loosening of the bonds between church and state. Many future Leveller supporters and leaders had already become convinced of the case for religious toleration in the early 1640s, and their desire to advance this cause was a key factor in the formation of the Leveller movement. The relationship between political and religious radicalism was very close, especially in London. Many separatist congregations or gathered churches had been formed in the very suburbs of the city where craftsmen and traders of the middling sort were suffering under the prevailing economic conditions. Each of the major Leveller spokesmen, including Richard Overton, William Walwyn and John Lilburne, had been involved in the struggle for religious freedom and had several years of pamphleteering and agitation behind them before they came together as a group in 1645. Religious toleration was a major issue in the Leveller campaign and occupied a vital position in their programme throughout the life of the party. The movement was crucially dependent for its strength on support from the gathered churches, and its appeal to radical elements in the army was likewise based in part on shared beliefs in toleration and liberty of conscience. In some ways the Leveller policy of political and social reform 'amounted to an expression of the aspirations of the sectarian community at large' (Tolmie, 1977, p. 149). Although the withdrawal of much sectarian support was eventually to cripple the Leveller movement, in its

early days the large coincidence of views and the overlap in personnel between Levellers and religious radicals was crucially important in promoting and shaping the party.

Economic and social distress, concern over the political settlement with the King, and anxiety about the imposition of an oppressive religious system, provided both the context for the emergence of the Leveller movement and the issues on which its programme could focus. But the definition and elaboration of that programme did not only depend on the immediate practical concerns of its supporters. Its ideological content and its political language reflected the intellectual heritage of the leaders of the movement. Leveller ideology was based on three principal sets of ideas. Each of these had been prefigured in the parliamentarian ideology we examined in chapter 2, but whereas the parliamentarians had interpreted these notions in a restrictive, conservative manner, the Levellers developed and extended them in a liberal, radical and democratic direction.

The first major strand in Leveller thinking was the influence of radical Protestantism, which some writers would wish to define more narrowly as the influence of Calvinistic Puritanism. Certainly the Levellers owed a great debt to Puritanism, but by 1646 their leaders and many of their supporters had abandoned an orthodox Calvinist position. None the less some Calvinist notions were eminently transferrable, psychologically as much as theologically, from the religious to the secular sphere, and the ambiguities inherent in Calvinism could be exploited in a variety of ways (Woodhouse, 1974). The doctrine of predestination, for example, with its distinction between the elect and the reprobate, might immediately suggest an elitist, hierarchical view of society, but in Leveller hands a stress on equality *within* the elect could be used to support more egalitarian notions. Similarly, the Puritan emphasis on inner spiritual worth and godly virtue suggested new criteria for the exercise of power: the challenge to traditional notions of leadership and rank could be transmuted into a demand for the monopoly of the elite on political power to be broken. The Puritan belief in a person's direct relationship with God and individual responsibility in biblical interpretation and other matters, linked to the intensely personal experience of knowledge of one's own salvation, undoubtedly influenced the highly in-dividualistic temper of the Leveller movement. So too did the Puritan stress on activism, on the duty of the godly to act out God's purposes in the world, which encouraged a belief in the ability and right of the common people to control their own destiny through active political participation. Furthermore, the voluntarist principle, which enjoined the godly to gather together in separate congregations, not only led to demands for religious toleration, but influenced the Levellers' concept of self-government.

The Levellers' propensity to develop the doctrines of radical Protestantism in a liberal direction was extended and reinforced by the second major influence on their thought: this was a cluster of ideas stemming from what G.E. Aylmer calls the 'rationalist, optimistic temper of the Renaissance, and more specifically the neoclassical idea of Natural Law' (1975, p. 12). The Levellers built on doctrines of natural law to produce a radical theory of the natural rights of man. The idea of 'natural law' (which had been used by Henry Parker) implied a set of principles implanted in nature by God which were knowable by and consonant with reason; since man himself was a rational creature he could discern these principles which, the Levellers now claimed, included certain natural rights. In 1646, in *The Free Man's Freedom Vindicated,* John Lilburne expressed this concept thus: 'All and every particular and individual man and woman, that ever breathed in the world, are by nature all equal and alike in their power, dignity, authority and majesty, none of them having (by nature) any authority, dominion or magisterial power one over and above another' (Shaw, 1968, p. 100).

The principle of reason and the belief in equal natural rights led the Levellers to espouse theories of popular consent and popular sovereignty (they believed in fact that only consent could give scope to reason). Hence also their emphasis on 'trust', that is their belief that those who governed did so on the basis of trust between themselves and the people to whom they were accountable. Where the Levellers differed radically from theorists like Henry Parker was in their insistence that sovereignty resided in the people and had not been delegated to parliament, and in their consequent desire to establish active political rights for the people and to restrict the powers of the legislature (Frank, 1955; Tuck, 1979; Woodhouse, 1974; Zagorin, 1954).

The third major intellectual influence on Leveller ideology was a set of ideas about English history and English law. Like the 'ancient constitution' theorists before them, the Levellers relied on a historical myth to defend their claim to be restoring chosen liberties, but in their case it was the rights of the people, not the privileges of parliament, which principally concerned them. Their attitudes here were in some ways highly ambivalent. On the one hand they appealed to Magna Carta, statute law and the principles of the common law to defend their claims about the legal rights of the individual, yet at the same time they subscribed to the historical myth of the 'Norman Yoke'. In their view, far from the principles of the law and the constitution having been handed down in an unbroken line since time immemorial, the Norman Conquest of 1066 had marked a decisive break in English history: for them the Conquest represented the enslavement of a free English people and the repression of Anglo-Saxon representative institutions. They regarded the law itself as part of the Norman bondage, and despite appeals to Magna Carta and other enactments they believed the mainstream of the common law had been corrupted and that wide-ranging legal as well as political reform would be necessary to restore the lost rights and liberties of the people. Arguments based on the notion of lost liberties were not entirely consistent with those based on natural rights; the first argument focused on the recovery of rights which used to exist, the second on the pursuit of rights because they ought to exist (Hill, 1958). This reflects the transitional nature of much Leveller thinking, and their Janus-like use of extant political theories to point in new radical and even progressive directions.

The Levellers certainly did combine an appeal to history with an appeal to reason, but the emphasis lay most heavily on the latter. They had therefore moved away from using an adherence to tradition or a reliance on precedent as legitimizing arguments in themselves, and in their use of rationalist arguments they looked forward to Locke and Paine rather than back to the parliamentarians. Overall, indeed, the Levellers had made significant leaps forward in the development of a radical political ideology. It was a major advance to move from the spiritual equality of the elect to the equal political rights of saints and sinners alike, and from the rights of the godly to the liberties of all Englishmen, just as it was of crucial importance to progress from an appeal to precedent towards an appeal to reason. Perhaps not surprisingly, the Levellers do not always score highly in terms of logic and intellectual coherence. But as political activists and innovators, they pushed forward the frontiers of political debate, expressed the aspirations and grievances of sections of the population who had been ignored by many parliamentarian writers, and prefigured the radical agitators of the later eighteenth century.

It must also be remembered that the Leveller programme was the result not only of thought, but also of experience. This was certainly true of the leaders, especially John Lilburne. The issues on which the Levellers focused reflected almost exactly the problems of Lilburne's own career. Like John Wilkes in the 1760s, Lilburne managed to establish his personal history as a paradigm of national injustice and oppression. He had a boundless capacity for identifying his own sufferings with the cause of liberty: his tirades against the Merchant Adventurers' trading monopoly, the corruption of the government of London, and arbitrary methods of trial and imprisonment reflected his own personal disasters as well as matters of general concern. In particular, he was able to use his repeated arrest and imprisonment by the authorities to generalize about oppression in a way which struck a responsive chord among his listeners, and provided a focus for agitation by the London crowd. Economic disaster, religious persecution and legal oppression: Lilburne had suffered them all. For this reason he was the ideal leader of a movement which reflected the grievances of the middling sort (Greaves and Zaller, 1983; Gregg, 1961).

Another type of experience also found its expression in the Leveller creed. The solutions they propounded to remedy their grievances were rooted in and inspired by actual models of popular participation. Many writers have noted that not merely the ideology of Puritanism but also the practice of the separatist churches influenced the Levellers in their ideal view of state and society: the actual experience of a small, relatively democratic and egalitarian religious community produced perhaps a more powerful image of society for many Leveller supporters than did intellectual theorizing. Likewise there were some practical precedents for political participation by the middling orders. Keith Thomas has drawn attention to the model of local government, with its opportunities for service as constable, churchwarden and juryman, and to the extension of the franchise to some of the middling sort before 1640, and has argued that such participation at 'village level' was 'a familiar enough experience to make its extension to the parliamentary sphere seem by no means unreasonable' (1972, p. 61). The expansion of the electorate in the early seventeenth century, the increase in contested elections in 1640, and the existence of a few constituencies like Westminster with a fairly broad franchise certainly meant that the Levellers' vision of wider political participation had something on which to build. But the most forceful model of popular action was surely the involvement of the common people in the Civil War: not merely their contribution to the fighting (although service in the New Model Army was clearly for some an energizing and radicalizing experience), but also their involvement with and influence upon political debate and decision-making, especially in London. It was not the Levellers but the parliamentarian preachers who first encouraged the belief that the common people should act out God's purposes and shift from a passive to an active role. It was not the Levellers who first brought the crowds on to the streets of London: there was precedent aplenty for the expression of popular opinion in the demonstrations outside parliament in 1641-2 and in the continuing pressure from all kinds of petitioners (including massive peace demonstrations) since the outbreak of war. Heightened political expectations and heightened political activity were as much the cause as the consequence of the formation of the Leveller movement in London; and it was in part to make sense of and ensure some gains from this degree of popular participation that the Leveller programme arose.

Beliefs and Programme

The Levellers' intellectual heritage combined with the fruits of practical experience to produce a political programme which had as its main theme a belief in the rights and liberties of the individual. Their concept of freedom, however, was cast in terms of 'freedom from restraint' as well as 'freedom to act'. Therefore, although they put forward positive claims for active political rights to be granted to the people, the thrust of many of their proposals had a more negative aspect. They certainly supported the liberty of the people, but this was cause and consequence of the fact that they were against the power of oligarchy and monopoly in government, in the economy, in the legal system and in religion. This combination of the positive and the negative was well expressed by Lilburne. In 1648 he wrote that those 'nicknamed Levellers are the supporters and true defenders of liberty and propriety, or anti-grandees, anti-imposters, anti-monopolists, anti-arbitrarians and anti-[economic] Levellers' (quoted in Greaves and Zaller, 1983).

The Levellers' political and constitutional proposals were designed to express their belief that government originated in a social contract, that the actions of government required the consent of the people, and that ultimate sovereignty resided in the people. They argued that in England in the later 1640s legitimate government had in effect been dissolved: parliament had so denied the liberties of the people that it had forfeited its right to govern. Therefore government (and indeed society) would have to be reconstituted by a new social contract. Hence the Levellers espoused an 'Agreement of the People' which all citizens would subscribe and which would both reconstitute political society and define the fundamental principles of the new political system (Frank, 1955; Zagorin, 1954). Those printed manifestos entitled on 'Agreement of the People' (published in November 1647, December 1648 and May 1649) are therefore to be construed literally: they were conceived as mechanisms for establishing the consent of the people to a new form of government which could ultimately be endorsed by all citizens. In setting out what that new form of government should be, whether in the Agreements themselves or in other declarations of policy, the Levellers addressed themselves to two main questions. First, given the inherent sovereignty of the people, how could that sovereignty be actively and continuously expressed; and second, who exactly, for political purposes, were 'the people'? The first question was answered by designing a series of devices to ensure the accountability of parliament to the electorate, and by proposals to 'reserve' certain crucial powers to the people, to curtail executive power and to achieve a large measure of decentralization in government. The second problem, which was probably less important to Levellers than was the first, produced proposals for the extension of the franchise.

The Levellers wanted a parliament which could be made frequently and easily responsive to the popular will. For this reason they were hostile to the political power of the monarchy and the House of Lords, and were confirmed in this belief by their view that the King and the aristocracy had been the chief beneficiaries of that Norman Yoke which had been placed on the necks of the common people in 1066. Some Leveller writings did contain a theoretical defence of republicanism, and calls were clearly made for the abolition of monarchy and the House of Lords. Other spokesmen, however, were prepared to retain these institutions so long as neither had a 'negative voice' (or veto) over legislation. The real aim of policy on this issue was to ensure that popular sovereignty should be reflected, untrammelled by any other body, in a one-chamber assembly which exercised the sole legislative power in the state. To ensure the accountability of this assembly to the electorate, the Levellers also demanded frequent elections (either every one or every two years) and measures to reduce patronage and oligarchical influence both at elections and in the Commons itself. In this vein they wished to exclude lawyers from the Commons and to award MPs a modest salary to free them from economic dependence on rich patrons. A redistribution of parliamentary seats and an extension of the franchise would promote the same end.

These checks on the power of parliament were not deemed sufficient in themselves to translate the sovereignty of the people into a continuous political reality. The Levellers' experience gave them ample reason to be suspicious of men once they were in power and to fear the growth of corrupt, self-interested faction in the legislature. Their bitterness was vividly expressed in this *cri de coeur* in 1649: 'we have', they wrote 'by wofull experience found the prevalence of corrupt interests powerfully inclining most men once entrusted with authority, to pervert the same to their own domination, and to the prejudice of our Peace and Liberties' (quoted in Aylmer, 1975, p. 164). To counteract this they proposed that certain powers should be forever 'reserved' to the people; that is, certain subjects were declared to be so fundamental to the liberties of the people that they were put beyond the normal legislative competence of parliament. How decisions could be taken on these subjects if the need arose was never clearly spelled out, but probably the Levellers envisaged that the people would voice an opinion through some sort of referendum. The number and nature of these reserved powers varied according to the circumstances in which the Levellers found themselves. There were only five in the first Agreement of the People in November 1647, including religious toleration and equality before the law, both of which remained fundamental to this part of the Leveller programme; but by the third Agreement in May 1649, the number of reserved powers had been considerably expanded to include other matters of a less important legal and fiscal nature.

The Levellers' antagonism to those who held the reins of power also led to a desire to limit the executive in

their new system of government. This is most noticeable in their pronouncements in 1649, after they had been bitterly humiliated by the army Grandees. In late 1648 the Leveller leaders had been outwardly courted by Cromwell and Ireton and invited to talks at Whitehall, but after the execution of the King in January 1649 it was clear that they had outlived their usefulness to the army command and could be summarily disposed of. Realizing this, and believing that the new republican regime was no more a friend to liberty than the old, the Levellers published bitter attacks on their new masters in *Englands New Chains Discovered* (two parts, February and March 1649), and in *The Hunting of the Foxes* (21 March 1649). They were also led to make more explicit their hostility to executive power as such. The Levellers seem to have assumed that when parliament was actually sitting, it would exercise full executive authority, subject to the checks which would normally operate on the competence of the legislature. When parliament was not in session other arrangements would have to be made: either a Council of State would be formed which would include MPs, or else a committee of MPs would exercise authority 'limited and bounded with express instructions, and accountable to the next section [session]' (Shaw, 1968, p. 79). The Levellers were clearly concerned to prevent the concentration of power in a few hands, and therefore did not wish to have an executive either powerful in itself or with the independent resources to fill parliament with its own supporters.

In various ways, then, Leveller insistence on the sovereignty of the people had led them to rethink the details of the political structure at national level. But equally important to their belief in government by popular consent was their keen interest in the local structure of authority and the decentralization of power. Indeed, there is no doubt that the Levellers imagined that, once their new system was in operation, power in the provinces would be much more important than government at the centre. Their demand for the election of officeholders by local communities was therefore crucial: in this way, public officials could be made responsible and responsive to the popular will in communities small enough to make that democratic control effective. The Levellers' proposals here overlapped with their demands for legal and judicial reform, for, in common with general opinion, the administration of justice and the enforcement of the law was in their view a large part of the work of government (Manning, 1976). Hence the desire for locally elected judicial officals and locally based law courts. The Earnest Petition of January 1648 demanded that 'some chosen Representatives of every Parish proportionally may be the Electors of the Sheriffs, Justices of the Peace, Committeemen, Grandjury men, and all ministers of Justice whatsoever' (Wolfe, 1944, p. 269). Decentralization was a consistent theme in many parts of the Leveller programme: it also influenced their demands for a locally trained and recruited militia in place of a centralized professional army, and it was reflected in their espousal of the independent rights of 'local' congregations. The revitalization of the small community—whether it be parish, borough, guild or church—was deemed essential to curb the power of oligarchy in law, politics, trade and religion. Decentralization was not merely as important as democracy: it was the indispensable condition for the democratization of the whole political system in church and state.

Among historians, Leveller plans for the devolution of power have received comparatively little emphasis compared with the close attention that has been given to the Leveller debate on the franchise. Despite various attempts to impose a spurious consistency on Leveller pronouncements on this subject, most writers would prefer simply to accept that the movement gave different answers at different times to the question 'who are the people?', and that there was always internal division on this issue. Therefore apparent shifts in opinion in the Levellers' public pronouncements are most usefully taken at face value. The logic of the Levellers' belief in the equal natural rights of every man and woman ought in theory to have impelled them towards the advocacy of universal suffrage. No one followed this path to the extent of calling for votes for women, but some Levellers clearly did demand universal *manhood* suffrage, although even this most radical group would have temporarily excluded men such as 'delinquents' (or former royalists). At the other end of the spectrum some moderate Levellers would have settled for a franchise restricted in the main to male heads of households owning modest amounts of property. In between, a case could be made for the exclusion of various types of working people. In *The Case of the Armie Truly Stated* (15 October 1647) Leveller influence in the army had produced the demand that 'all the freeborn at the age of 21 years and upwards, be the electors'. A few weeks later, however, when the Levellers came to debate the first Agreement of the People with the army Grandees at Putney, it was clear that there was a significant internal difference in the movement between those who believed that literally 'every man that is to live under a government ought first by his own consent to put himself under that government', and those who felt that only those 'that have not lost their birthright' ought to vote in elections (Woodhouse, 1974, p. 53). The notion of loss of birthright could open the way to some far-reaching exclusions from the franchise. The demands of political expediency and pressure from the Grandees also began to erode the case for universal manhood suffrage. In December 1648, in the second Agreement of the People (entitled *Foundations of Freedom*), the Levellers would have limited the franchise to 'Natives or Denizens of England, such as have subscribed this Agreement; not persons receiving Alms but such as are assessed ordinarily towards the relief of the poor; not servants to, or receiving

wages from any particular person' (Wolfe, 1944, p. 297). This was a considerable, and perhaps untypical, retreat from the public position the Levellers had held in 1647, but by May 1649 the third Agreement restored the franchise to all men over 21 'not being servants, or receiving Alms, or having served the late King in Arms or voluntary Contributions' (Aylmer, 1975, p. 162).

The Marxist historian C. B. Macpherson has argued that even during the Putney Debates the Levellers wanted to deny the vote to all types of wage-earners and anyone who had ever had to rely on poor relief. He believes that the Levellers deemed a man to have lost his birthright when he alienated his labour, as all wage-earners, alms-takers, servants and beggars had done; and that when a man lost his birthright he forfeited his right to vote (1964). Keith Thomas, on the other hand, has argued more plausibly that the Levellers did not, on the whole, take the extreme view that to alienate one's labour was to lose one's birthright, nor did they assume that wage-earners and servants were synonymous categories (1972). Many writers would now accept that when the Levellers excluded 'servants' they meant only living-in servants and apprentices, not wage-earners with their own homes, and when they mentioned 'alms-takers' they intended that only those permanently in receipt of alms would be excluded from the vote. What is clear, however, is that Levellers set great store by independence, both economic and political, and that their interest lay in enabling a man to cast an *independent* vote. For this reason, they were prepared to stop short of the logical consequence of their belief in equal natural rights and to retreat from the position of universal manhood suffrage. Here the Levellers showed that they had not transcended traditional patriarchal assumptions about the role of male heads of household, and that their basic desire was to protect the small producer against the power of 'great men'. Their willingness to exclude beggars and servants, for example, could be reconciled with their more radical claims by maintaining that such men could be 'represented in the votes of their masters', and by recognizing Ireton's claim at Putney that those 'who depended on the will of other men' might be incapable of exercising the vote in their own right. To enfranchise dependent men might in these circumstances do more to entrench the power of great men than to restrict it. Such a policy would not enable the small craftsman, artisan, trader or farmer to challenge the power of oligarchy in politics and ensure the election of a representative body responsive to the interests and wishes of the 'middle sort of people' (Manning, 1976; Thompson, 1980).

The Levellers' constitutional and political proposals were detailed and wide-ranging, but they were not the only means by which the movement sought to advance the liberties of the people. Of great importance for the protection of the individual's rights in society were their plans for the reform of the law and the legal system. Full equality before the law, Levellers believed, was the chief protection for the individual's right to life, liberty and property, and the main guarantee that his 'self-propriety' (as Overton called it) would not be invaded by others. The health of the nation depended on swift legal reform, Lilburne had argued in 1645, and 'the Reformation of Courts of Justice, is a worke of absolute necessitye, without which . . . you shall have no Peace' (*Englands Birth-Right Justified,* quoted in Aylmer, 1975, p. 60). As well as plans for the local election of justices of the peace and magistrates, calls were made for the simplification of legal procedure so that it might be cheaper and easier to understand. English should be used in legal proceedings, the Levellers demanded, instead of Latin and law French. The Levellers wanted every plain man to be able to defend his interests at law without the help of professional lawyers, whom Lilburne especially detested, likening them to locusts who swarmed over the land devouring and impoverishing it. Mindful of the leadership's personal experience at the hands of various tribunals, the Levellers demanded that every individual should be free from arbitrary arrest, from imprisonment without trial, and from interrogation which might incriminate him. No man was to have special privileges at law because of birth and status. Great emphasis was laid on the role of the jury, an essential institution in Leveller thinking. The jury was the embodiment of the freeborn men of England, men of independent mind who would judge a situation by the light of reason and reject the corrupting influence of faction. The right to trial by jury became a reserved power; and in March 1649 Lilburne bitterly criticized the new regime because the erection of the High Court of Justice meant that 'that great and strong hold of our preservation, the way of tryal by 12 sworn men of the Neighbourhood is infringed' (*Englands New Chains Discovered,* quoted in Aylmer, 1975, p. 143). The Levellers also wanted the reform of specific laws. Here their most urgent demand was for a change in the laws of debt. This would help, above all, the small trader who was often caught between the burden of defaulting or non-existent customers and the demands of suppliers clamouring to be paid. His 'cash flow' problems could easily land him in gaol, where he had no hope of earning anything to recoup his losses or meet his debts.

The individual's rights at law were crucial. So too was his right to liberty of conscience and worship. The involvement of individual Levellers in the campaign for religious toleration both predated and post-dated the emergence of the Leveller movement; indeed, as we have seen, it was this very issue which had brought several of the leading figures in the movement together for the first time. During its life, the movement's appeal to the sectarian interest was vital to its success, and although many sectarians in the end parted compa-

ny with and repudiated Leveller ideals for a secular state, many Leveller supporters continued to identify themselves with the cause of radical religion in the 1650s. By 1647, a demand for religious toleration and the abolition of compulsory tithes had been incorporated into the Leveller platform; some Levellers, including Lilburne, had also begun to demand a complete separation of church and state. In the Large (or comprehensive) Petition of March 1647 the Levellers, operating as a mass political movement for the first time, argued that the suppression of allegedly heretical opinions should be stopped lest 'the most necessary truths, and sincere professions thereof may be suppressed'. They also demanded that tithes be abolished and not replaced by any other form of compulsory state maintenance for the clergy. In the first Agreement of the People, of November 1647, religious toleration became a reserved power; thereafter it maintained its clear status as one of the fundamental laws which no mere statute law could infringe. Religious toleration also provided the issue over which the Levellers broke with the Grandees in the Whitehall Debates of December 1648. Cromwell and the officers professed to accept that the state had no power to coerce a man's conscience, but they wished to retain the power to restrict the practices of so-called idolatry or atheism (in effect Roman Catholicism and the 'lunatic fringe' of radical religion). The Levellers felt that even this power was an infringement of religious toleration. None the less, in both the first and second Agreements of the People some kind of state church and non-compulsory form of public worship was still envisaged: in 1647 they were prepared to grant a future parliament 'the publike way of instructing the Nation (so it be not compulsive)'. By the time of the third Agreement in 1649 the Levellers had refined their position: they demanded a complete separation of church and state with no established church, no tithes and no other form of state maintenance for ministers. However, they now recognized a distinction between liberty of conscience and worship, on the one hand, and civil equality on the other. In this way Catholics were to be allowed to worship freely but could not hold public office. In its advocacy of such a broad degree of religious toleration—truly limitless for some Levellers, and including Jews and Muslims as well as Catholics—the movement was shown at its most egalitarian and humanitarian.

In the area of social and economic reform, the Levellers were less united and more ambiguous in their public pronouncements. Specific proposals for schemes of social welfare and for penal reform were popular among some sections of the movement, but they tended to be elaborated more in the writings of individuals than as an integrated part of collaborative policy documents. In 'Certain Articles' appended to an *Appeale from the Degenerate Representative Body* (1647), for example, Richard Overton argued the case for establishing schools and hospitals for the poor. The economic issues which figured in the Leveller programme tended to be those which particularly affected the urban middling sort. Overall, Levellers assumed that the system of private property would be retained, and officially they were quick to repudiate the notion that they were in the strict sense 'economic Levellers'. In the second and third Agreements, the powers reserved to the people were extended to include this very subject: the future Representative was expressly forbidden to 'levell mens Estates, destroy Propriety, or make all things common' (Wolfe, 1944, p. 301; Aylmer, 1975, p. 167). Here again, the Levellers were shown to be more concerned with the destruction of monopoly than the creation of equality. Mirroring faithfully the grievances of their 'middling' supporters, especially in London, they were content to press for the abolition of those privileged groups like the Merchant Adventurers who had caused so much hardship to the 'industrious people' in the nation, including tradesmen and seafarers. More radically, they were also prepared on occasion to advocate the destruction of enclosures, the return of common lands to the people, and the abolition of 'base' or copyhold tenures. This would have benefited the smaller tenant farmer in the countryside faced with exploitation by a grasping landlord. Economic burdens on the people were also to be relieved by the abolition of the excise tax and by replacing it with more equitable forms of direct taxation. Beyond this, it is clear that only some members of the movement were prepared to countenance more egalitarian economic measures. William Walwyn was certainly one of those who had consistently condemned economic inequality. *The Power of Love* in 1643 was a particularly compelling statement of his views, but when he wrote *A Manifestation* in May 1649 on behalf of the other Leveller leaders, he conceded that economic levelling could not be forced on people against their will.

On the whole the individualistic liberal ideology of the Leveller movement encouraged their belief that political reform, not economic or social reform, would be the fount from which all other blessings for the common people would flow. Just as they believed that the source of the people's suffering was intrinsically political (in the long term the Norman Conquest, in the short term the corruption of parliament), so they believed that the remedies for these ills lay essentially in the political sphere. The economic issues which concerned them were principally those which affected the middling sort, the people to whom all Levellers would have given the franchise. In truth their economic and political thinking was all of a piece. They were against the agglomeration of wealth in a few hands, just as they opposed the concentration of political power in a few hands; conversely, they came out against complete equality of wealth just as they retreated from universal manhood suffrage. As Brian Manning concludes, if the Levellers hated the exorbitantly rich they also feared the very poor. Theirs was the 'characteristic doctrine

of men of an intermediate status in society', the 'industrious' people or the middling sort (Manning, 1976, p. 315).

The Strengths and Weaknesses of the Movement

In attempting to build up the strength of their movement and win support for their programme, the Levellers showed themselves to be shrewd publicists and propagandists. They were very soon able to whip up demonstrations of pro-Leveller feeling in the capital, establish links with aggrieved elements in the counties, and tap feelings of discontent in the army. The use of the press, the organization of petitions and demonstrations, the development of a party structure, and the skilful deployment of the charismatic appeal of its leaders, quickly built up the impression of a mass political movement, especially in London.

The Levellers contributed in no small measure to the vast outpouring of pamphlets, tracts, treatises and other forms of printed polemic which marked the intellectual and emotional ferment of the 1640s. Although many of their tracts tackled complex issues in considerable detail and often with elaborate citation of biblical and other references, the Levellers also took care to speak directly to the ordinary people in a pungent, witty and cogent manner. Their rhetoric 'intensified the strengths of common speech', and its form was influenced by sources as diverse as plain preaching and popular drama (Heinemann, 1978). Whether it was the witty, vituperative style of Richard Overton's *The Baiting of the Great Bull of Bashan* (July 1649) or the histrionic appeal of Lilburne's account of his trial in 1649, *The Trial of Lieut. Collonel John Lilburne,* the Levellers showed they could play to an audience (Erskine-Hill and Storey, 1983). From June 1648 until September 1649 Leveller ideas also found their way into *The Moderate,* a weekly newsbook run by Gilbert Mabbott which circulated in London and the provinces. Other newsbooks which briefly favoured the Leveller cause were the *Perfect Occurrences* of Henry Walker, and the short-lived *Mercurius Militaris* of John Harris, a former professional actor turned printer to the army radicals (Brailsford, 1976).

The drawing up and presentation of petitions to parliament was another tactic shrewdly employed by the Levellers to organize and mobilize public opinion. The circulation of petitions like the Large Petition of March 1647, the Earnest Petition of January 1648, and the Humble Petition of September 1648 (as well as others on single issues like the arrest and imprisonment of the party leaders), enabled the movement to reach out and embrace large sections of public opinion and provided an essential focus and rallying-point for Leveller supporters. These petitions were often publicized and circulated for signature through the gathered churches in London and the provinces. *The Mod-*

erate also helped to make their existence known. The act of presenting a petition to parliament became an occasion for mass crowd demonstrations in the streets of London. Likewise the arrest and trial of prominent members and the funerals of leading supporters afforded opportunities for shows of strength as well as for consciousness-raising. The funeral of Colonal Thomas Rainsborough on 14 November 1648 was the scene of much emotional drama. Crowds of supporters, many of them women, turned out sporting sea-green colours, which henceforth became a badge of the movement. In April 1649, the funeral of Robert Lockyer, an army Leveller who had been shot for taking part in a mutiny, provoked similar outbursts. Something of a personality cult was indeed an important element in the appeal of the movement. The quality of its leadership, particularly the charismatic appeal of John Lilburne, helps to account for the swift rise in the party's fortunes and its ability to draw large crowds of sympathizers to witness its public acts. Lilburne was well-suited to the role of 'populist and martyr', and his battles with authority provided a focus of identity for ordinary people. The resilience of the leadership after arrest and imprisonment, and their refusal to be silenced, also provided their followers with a model for popular action (Greaves and Zaller, 1983).

Partly to control the organization of public opinion through petitions and demonstrations, a party structure had grown up in London, and to a more limited extent in parts of the Home Counties. The City was divided up into wards, each of which sent representatives to a committee of the parish; in addition, twelve commissioners or agents were elected to act as a central executive committee for the party. Party subscriptions were levied according to a member's means, to support the cost of Leveller publications and other activities, and two treasurers were appointed to look after the party coffers. Various City taverns acted as party meeting-places: the party headquarters was situated in the Whale-bone Tavern, and other favoured haunts were the Saracen's Head in Friday Street and the Windmill Tavern.

One method which, on the whole, the Levellers did not espouse was the use of organized violence or armed rebellion. For most of its life the party stuck to its belief in the power of man to judge things by the light of reason and did not abandon its faith in rational argument. Few contemplated the violent overthrow of the regime by an armed citizenry, or even by the New Model Army. Of course, the Levellers sought to influence the army, and radical supporters in the rank and file provoked mutinies, notably at Ware in 1647 and Burford in 1649, but this did not amount to an overall plan for the armed take-over of the regime. A few 'physical force' Levellers did exist, such as Major White and Captain Bray, and one ex-soldier William Thompson advocated armed risings in 1649; but when the

party machine did come out in favour of mass armed rebellion in *The Remonstrance of Many Thousands of the Free People of England* (September 1649), it was merely the last fling of a dying movement (Aylmer, 1975; Hill, 1975).

The shrewd manipulation of issues and the mobilization of public opinion allowed the Levellers to build up support among apprentices, journeymen, small traders, craftsmen and artisans, and among some sections of the rural middling orders. Membership of a separatist congregation and, especially, residence in and around London, were factors which predisposed men towards Leveller ideas. For much of the party's history, a 'typical' Leveller might be a small craftsman, perhaps in the textile trade, who had contacts with a gathered church and lived in one of the poorer suburbs of the capital. Levellers claimed to be able to call on 10,000 supporters in the metropolis and could produce several thousand signatures for a petition in London fairly quickly. But outside this area, and outside the 'middling' social groups, support for the movement was probably much less firm. There were organized Leveller groups in Buckinghamshire, Hertfordshire and Kent, and sympathy for Leveller agitation was expressed in petitions which arrived from much farther afield including at various times Somerset, Yorkshire, Oxfordshire, Leicestershire, Berkshire and Wiltshire. The monster petition, *The Remonstrance of Many Thousands of the Free People of England,* claimed to have 98,064 signatures. In addition, Leveller views attracted considerable attention in the army.

However, it would be misleading to infer from this that England was full of committed party supporters. The superficial strength of the Leveller movement during its petitioning campaigns masked underlying weaknesses. Sympathy with the grievances to which the Levellers gave voice was greater than support for the solutions to those problems which the Levellers advocated. Not all those who shared the Levellers' hostility to the 'powers that be' were prepared to translate their antagonism into demands for radical change; and of those who were prepared to countenance a radical solution, not all agreed that it should be the Leveller one. This last point was crucial to the party's fortunes: the Leveller movement rose in part because it fed on, inspired and became part of a radical coalition of interests in London, in the army and in the counties; when deserted by and isolated from the other elements in this radical coalition, its weaknesses were exposed. The weaknesses were both organizational and ideological. Organizationally, the Levellers were too dependent on the gathered churches; they had not built up their own representative machinery among the rank and file of the army; and they had done little to mobilize the peasantry as opposed to the urban middling orders. Ideologically, their programme was too frightening to the rich, too neglectful of the poor, and too innovative in its assumptions to embrace all the godly 'middling sort'. A closer look at some key episodes in Leveller history will illustrate these points.

First, it is clear that in 1647 the Levellers failed to capture the lasting support of the 'honest radicals' in the counties, although for a time support for the army against parliament was a unifying issue. The 'honest radicals' were the 'godly party' in the counties, the connection between honesty and godliness being universally assumed (Underdown, 1978). The rank and file of those radicals for a while espoused a 'proto-Leveller' or Leveller-inclined position. Between March and June 1647, 'honest radicals' petitioned in support of the army. The first 'Leveller' petition came from Buckinghamshire and Hertfordshire and was presented to parliament along with a request for the release of Lilburne and Overton, who were at that time in prison. Other petitions to Fairfax followed in June from Buckinghamshire, Hertfordshire, Essex, Norfolk and Suffolk, with Essex making explicit reference to the Norman Yoke and Hertfordshire calling for the abolition of tithes and the relief of copyholders from arbitrary fines. But these proto-Leveller documents revealed two major weaknesses from the Leveller point of view: they did not have the backing of the upper echelons of the godly party, the 'establishment' radicals who might hold power in the county committees which had grown up to administer parliament's war effort in the localities, and geographically their spread was very uneven. The Levellers' appeal clearly diminished the farther from London one went, and in Underdown's opinion Bristol was the only place any distance from London from which 'genuinely Leveller' petitions have survived from 1647 (1978, p. 198). Later in the year, when Levellers embarked on a countrywide campaign to collect signatures for the first Agreement of the People, they were unable to build up a truly national organization. Despite reports of proselytization as far away as Nottinghamshire and Rutland, only in places close to London like Dartford in Kent were Leveller cells established.

In September 1648 the Levellers had another opportunity to canvass a wide spectrum of the radical interest. Their Humble Petition of 11 September reputedly had 40,000 signatures and sparked off responses from the tin-miners of Cornwall, the grand jury of Somerset, some farmers in the north, citizens in Newcastle, Bristol, Hull and York and the counties of Yorkshire, Oxfordshire, Leicestershire, Berkshire and Wiltshire (Brailsford, 1976, p. 355). As has been indicated, these petitions demonstrated support for the Levellers in a negative rather than a positive sense: they were engendered by the fear that a personal treaty would be concluded with the King (the Newport negotiations were currently taking place) and that all the gains of the war would be lost. They were not necessarily motivated by a strong commitment to all the details of the Leveller programme (Tolmie, 1977). Once the problem of the

King was disposed of, there was no guarantee that other radicals would subscribe to a Leveller future. As David Underdown has remarked, the events of late 1648 and early 1649 were to show 'how few of the honest party were committed Levellers' (1978, p. 203).

The loss of support among the leaders of the sectarian community was extremely serious for the Levellers. The Levellers' stand on religious toleration had been an important part of their appeal to other radical groups, but not all sectarians were prepared to go further along the road towards accepting the secular state as a 'legitimate sphere of moral action in its own right' (Tolmie, 1977, p. 144). They were not willing to make the full transition from Christian liberty and virtue to equal natural rights. As early as the autumn of 1647, although the movement had already gained the allegiance of many individual sectarians and much organizational help from some of the gathered churches in London (including Particular and General Baptists), the enemies of the Levellers in the 'generality of congregations' publicly declared themselves. *A Declaration by Congregational societies in and about the City of London* argued against the Levellers' alleged attempt to make all men 'equal in power'. It was supported by several pastors, like the Baptists William Kiffin and Hanserd Knollys whom Lilburne had counted among his associates. None the less, throughout 1648 Levellers and sectaries continued to make common cause. But by 1649 a great rift had opened up between the Levellers and the Baptist pastors. The latter had decided to come to terms with the new regime in return for toleration, and formally dissociated themselves from the Levellers in March. Meanwhile the presence of the army in London had allowed the Grandees to win access to the separatist churches and to gain the loyalty of many religious radicals. Thereafter, it was difficult for the Levellers, reeling from other blows, to assume the role of political spokesmen for the godly (Tolmie, 1977).

The attitude of the sectaries was also vital for the all-important question of Leveller strength in the New Model Army. On this topic the work of Mark Kishlansky has recently commanded much attention (1978, 1979a, 1979b). Kishlansky argues that at its formation the New Model Army was not inherently radical. Its entry into politics and its espousal of radical causes in and after 1647 arose from its own material grievances, and from the desire to vindicate its own honour *vis-à-vis* parliament, not principally because of Leveller agitation and influence. Although by the beginning of the summer of 1647 the concerns of the army and of the Levellers were strikingly similar, Kishlansky maintains that the two movements had not yet made common cause. This probably did not reflect any reluctance on the Levellers' part. On 18 April a pamphlet entitled *A New Found Stratagem,* probably written by Richard Overton, had called on the army to rescue the people 'from sudden vassalage and slavery'. Around the same time contacts were made between individuals in the army and Levellers in London. Edward Sexby, a trooper in Lord General Fairfax's regiment of horse, had already been in touch with Lilburne, and other soldiers who were to become the elected agents or Agitators of their regiments had Leveller connections. By June, the Levellers had increased their pleas to the army and by late July, Kishlansky surmises, Leveller ideas were beginning to have some impact on the soldiery. This is not to say, however, that when the General Council of the Army met during the summer the Levellers were really pulling the strings, or even that all Agitators were necessarily Levellers. The Levellers may have lent to army radicals a certain brand of political rhetoric, but their capacity to infiltrate and organize the rank and file was much more limited.

In September and October, however, the Levellers made a further effort. New Agitators were elected who were closer to the Leveller cause, and they agreed to recommend to the rank and file that the Leveller-inspired *The Case of the Armie Truly Stated* be accepted as a true statement of the army's grievances. *The Case* was redrafted in shortened form as an Agreement of the People, and it was this document which was then debated in the General Council of the Army at Putney between Grandees, Agitators and specially invited Leveller spokesmen. At first glance, the Putney Debates may seem to mark the high-water mark of Leveller influence, with the Grandees forced on to the defensive, their arguments subjected to close scrutiny by the radicals, and a high-ranking officer, Colonel Thomas Rainsborough, lending his passionate advocacy to the Leveller cause. Yet the Levellers lost at least some of the argument at Putney, and most of the action afterwards. They were outwitted at various points by Henry Ireton's intellectual skill (Tuck, 1979), and forced to concede ground on the franchise. Afterwards, their attempts to adopt direct action failed miserably and their inability seriously to disrupt army discipline was revealed. A small mutiny at Corkbush Field near Ware in Hertfordshire on 15 November was easily suppressed, and the Grandees reasserted their control over the army. The Grandees were helped in this by a split between the Levellers and the sectarian interest in the army, which mirrored the growing estrangement between the two movements in London. At Ware sectarian officers, especially the Particular Baptists, supported the Grandees and continued to do so throughout 1648 and 1649 wherever Leveller agitation threatened. Leveller ideas in general did not lose their impact among the rank and file, but, as we have seen, organizationally the Levellers were seriously weak. They had relied too much on the efforts of sectarians to organize the lower ranks (it was they who were behind the election of the first Agitators), instead of building up their own network;

therefore when Leveller and sectarian interests diverged, the Levellers were denied this support and were unable to build up an organization of their own (Tolmie, 1977).

The suppression of the Ware mutiny may have marked the end of a chapter in the history of the army Levellers, but it did not entirely destroy their influence. In November 1648, when attempts to reach a settlement with Charles I had come to naught, Cromwell and Ireton again made overtures to Lilburne, but, as we have seen, despite the closeness of the two sides on some issues, the negotiations on a new joint Agreement of the People foundered on the question of religious toleration. The Levellers' next chance came when unrest in the army once again opened up the possibility of direct action. Mutinies were started in April-May 1649, the first of them in London resulting in the execution of Robert Lockyer. In May further mutinies which had started at Banbury (involving 1,000-2,000 men) and at Salisbury (involving two regiments) failed to make contact with each other. The Salisbury men tried to make their way along the Thames valley but were defeated at Burford. Thereafter, civilian Levellers still continued their agitation in London, but in truth the heart had gone out of the movement. Its best and perhaps only chance of gaining political power, support from the army, had completely disappeared. The protests over Lilburne's trial in London in 1653 could not revive these chances, and in 1659 when the collapse of the Republic was imminent, those Levellers who were still active (Lilburne had died in 1657) adopted a position very similar to the Harringtonian republicans. The Leveller programme as a whole was not relaunched: although religious toleration and equality before the law were still demanded, the franchise issue was dropped, and Levellers now put greatest stress on respect for law and order, the sanctity of property rights and on hostility to arbitrary rule (Hill, 1984).

In their heyday, then, it is clear that the Levellers exhibited great flair in exciting the popular imagination and dramatizing public events, but ideologically and organizationally their movement was severely flawed. The Levellers alienated key groups above them in the political and social structure (the ruling classes generally, the Grandees of the army, and the establishment radicals of the 'honest party'). They failed to consolidate their appeal to the middling orders whose interests they especially represented (they could not hold on to the allegiance of the godly party, and they did not capitalize on the grievances of the middling peasants). They also neglected or were actively hostile to those below them in the social scale (those without property were to be excluded from the franchise and social and economic reforms were limited). The Levellers both went too far and not far enough in their espousal of a new political and social order: in the end, their ideological and organizational base proved too narrow to achieve political success.

The historical significance of the Levellers must, however, be recognized. It is true that far from envisaging a completely democratic or egalitarian paradise, they were anxious to retain property, patriarchy and hierarchy. Their creed was that of liberalism and individualism, not socialism or equality. They wished to make the world safe for the people of the middling order, whose economic and political independence was their prime goal. Their economic and social vision was in some ways reactionary rather than progressive: they wanted to protect a vanishing world of small independent proprietors and traders, rather than look forward to the burgeoning of the middle class in a capitalist society. Their ideal of small communities and of a glorious Anglo-Saxon past were also symptoms of emotional nostalgia.

Nevertheless, they made significant ideological advances. Unlike other parliamentarians and republicans who were also wrestling with questions of sovereignty and trust, the Levellers developed their doctrines of popular sovereignty and trusteeship into a claim for the broad extension of active political rights. They went far beyond the doctrine of parliamentary sovereignty to place real and continuing power in the hands of the 'people', if not the 'poor'. Their stress on decentralization, and the individualistic emphasis of many of their social, economic and legal proposals, were deeply threatening to the ongoing concentration of wealth, status and power in the hands of a small elite. To support their programme, the Levellers advanced a radical theory of natural rights which looked forward to the later eighteenth century. Their political ideology was also notable for its rationalist and secularist aspects. Their appeal to reason was innovative, for although they combined this with a vision of the past as the locus of lost rights, they did not have the same view of history-as-precedent or of the sanctity of tradition as their more conservative contemporaries. Finally, although they made heavy use of religious arguments and sanctions for their views, their anticlericalism, their desire to separate church and state and to treat saints and sinners alike as equal citizens gave political theory 'a push . . . in the direction of avowed secularism' (Frank, 1955, p. 246). In sum, the Levellers' contribution to the political and religious ferment of the 1640s was immense.

References

Aylmer, G.E. 1975: *The Levellers in the English Revolution.* London.

Brailsford, H.N. 1976: *The Levellers and the English Revolution.* Edited by Christopher Hill. London.

Frank, Joseph 1955: *The Levellers.* New York.

Greaves, Richard L. and Zaller, Robert (eds) 1983: *Biographical Dictionary of British Radicals in the Seventeenth Century,* vol. II: G-O. Brighton.

Heinemann, Margot 1978: 'Popular Drama and Leveller Style—Richard Overton and John Harris'. In Maurice Cornforth (ed.), *Rebels and their Causes,* London.

Hill, Christopher 1958: 'The Norman Yoke'. In his *Puritanism and Revolution,* London.

Hill, Christopher 1975: *The World Turned Upside Down* (Penguin edn). London.

Kishlansky, Mark 1978: 'The case of the army truly stated: The creation of the New Model Army'. *Past and Present,* 81, 51-75.

Kishlansky, Mark 1979a: 'The Army and the Levellers: The Roads to Putney'. *Historical Journal,* 22, 795-824.

Kishlansky, Mark 1979b: *The Rise of the New Model Army.* Cambridge.

Macpherson, C.B. 1964: *The Political Theory of Possessive Individualism* (paperback edn). Oxford.

Manning, Brian 1976: *The English People and the English Revolution.* London.

Shaw, Howard 1968: *The Levellers.* London.

Thomas, Keith 1972: 'The Levellers and the franchise'. In G.E. Aylmer (ed.), *The Interregnum: The Quest for Settlement 1646-1660,* London.

Tolmie, Murray 1977: *The Triumph of the Saints.* Cambridge.

Tuck, Richard 1979: *Natural Rights Theories.* Cambridge.

Underdown, David 1978: ' "Honest" radicals in the counties, 1642-1649'. In Donald Pennington and Keith Thomas (eds), *Puritans and Revolutionaries,* Oxford.

Wolfe, Don M. (ed.) 1944: *Leveller Manifestoes of the Puritan Revolution.* New York.

Woodhouse, A.S.P. 1974: *Puritanism and Liberty* (2nd edn with a preface by Ivan Roots). London.

Zagorin, Perez 1954: *A History of Political Thought in the English Revolution.* London.

Maurice Goldsmith (essay date 1986)

SOURCE: "Levelling by Sword, Spade and Word: Radical Egalitarianism in the English Revolution," in *Politics and People in Revolutionary England: Essays in Honor of Ivan Roots,* edited by Colin Jones, Malyn Newitt, and Stephen Roberts, pp. 65-80. Oxford: Blackwell, 1986.

[*In the following essay, Goldsmith maintains that despite the emphasis many modern critics place on the differences between the Levellers, the Diggers, and the Ranters, all three radical groups used the same type of rhetoric to argue for mankind's equality and freedom.*]

Despite, or because of, much recent work on the radicals of the English Revolution, there are many disagreements about the meaning of their views and proposals. The prevailing orthodoxy tends to emphasize the distinctions among various sorts of radicals, spreading them out along a spectrum from left to right. On this view, the Levellers, or some of them, turn out to be petit bourgeois, not-quite democrats, and their clash with the Grandees at Putney in 1647 a squabble over the enfranchisement of a few thousand voters.[1] However, notwithstanding differences in style and programme, Levellers, Diggers and Ranters shared a core of basic values and spoke a common language.

All these radicals agree that men are by nature equal and free. One of the clearest statements of this principle is in Richard Overton's *An Arrow Against All Tyrants:*

> For by naturall birth, all men are equally and alike born to the like propriety, liberty and freedome, and as we are delivered of God by the hand of nature into this world, every one with a naturall innate freedome and propriety (as it were writ in the table of every mans heart, never to be obliterated) even so are we to live, every one equally and alike to enjoy his Birth-right and priviledge; even all whereby God by nature hath made him free.[2]

Overton takes this principle to imply substantively equal treatment, for he enjoins Henry Marten and the Commons' committee to be impartial and to 'be no respector of persons, let not the *greatest peers* in the Land, be more respected with you, than so many *old Bellowesmenders, Broom men, Coblers, Tinkers or Chimneysweepers, who are all equally Free borne,* with the *hudgest men,* and *loftiest Anachims* in the Land'.[3]

That the Levellers, and not just Overton, generally adhered to this principle is easily illustrated. In *The Case of the Armie Truly Stated,* probably mainly by John Wildman, the rights and liberties of the free-born commoners to be insisted on include that, in the elections for the annual parliaments, 'all the free born at the age of 21 yeares and upwards, be the electors, excepting those that have or shall deprive themselves of that their freedome, either for some years or wholly by delinquency'.[4] Unless we suppose that Overton and Wildman, notwithstanding their being political allies, used the term 'free born' with two quite different meanings, then the freeborn who are to be equally respected must be the same freeborn (with the exception of those who are fighting against parliament) who are to be electors.

The same principle may be discovered in John Lilburne's *Regall Tyranny Discovered.* His argument against the House of Lords' tyranny relies upon the equality of men under God and by nature; thus all are equally under both the negative and the positive versions of the Golden Rule:

> And again seeing nature teacheth me to defend my self and preserve my life; reason teaches me in the negative, that it is but just that I should not do that to another, which I would not have another doe to me; but that in the affirmative I should do as I would be done unto.[5]

From this basic equality, Lilburne infers both that 'it is not lawfull for any man to subject himself to be a slave' and that among those 'that live in mutual society amongst one another in nature and reason, there is none above or over another against mutual consent and agreement'.[6]

Similar views are put forward in *The True Levellers Standard Advanced;* although the governing powers have committed themselves to reform and 'to bring in liberty, every man in his place', yet those who pursue this end are oppressed: 'And all because they stand to maintain an universal liberty and freedom, which is not only our birthright which our maker gave us, but which thou has sworn to restore unto us.'[7] They are also to be found in *Light Shining in Buckinghamshire,* in which it is argued that man, being created after God's image, embodies a pure spirit, reason, that implies right and conscience and so the Golden Rule. From this there follows men's equality:

> and the creature Man was priviledged with being Lord over the inferior creatures, but not over his own kinde; for all men being a like priviledged by birth, so all men were to enjoy the creatures a like without proprietie one more than the other, all men by the grant of God are a like free, and every man individuall, that is to say, no man was to Lord or command over his own kinde.[8]

Again in *The Law of Freedom in a Platform,* Gerrard Winstanley relies on a basic principle of equality; common action has recovered land and liberties from the oppressor, they having been 'recovered by a joint consent of the commoners, therefore it is all equity, that the commoners who assisted you should be set free from the conqueror's power with you'.[9]

Equity, or equality, is according to 'Reason' which is frequently identified with God; as it applies to human conduct it stipulates action according to one of the versions of the Golden Rule, that one should not treat others as one would not be treated or that one should treat others as one would be treated. In *The Law of Freedom,* this principle becomes the first root of law: 'The first root you see is common preservation, when there is a principle in everyone to seek the good of others as himself, without respecting persons.'[10] All must have equal privileges, equal rights, equal freedoms. Thus the Diggers employ the same words as the Levellers. Winstanley, like Overton, asserts that men by nature possess an equal natural right which implies equal treatment without respect for persons. Winstanley differed from the Levellers in believing that such a right immediately implied equality of property. In fact that inference was so natural that it formed the basis of many arguments used by 'conservatives' in opposing the popular and apparently democratic rhetoric used by parliamentarians early in the Civil War. Sir Simonds D'Ewes asserted in 1642 that:

all right and property, all *meum and tuum,* must cease in a civil war, and we know not what advantage the meaner sort also may take to divide the spoils of the rich and noble among them, who begin already to allege that all being of one mould there is no reason that some should have so much and others so little.[11]

Similarly the king's *Answer to the Nineteen Propositions* warned that parity and independence would be called liberty, and thereby social distinctions destroyed.[12]

The principle that all must have equal rights had earlier been applied by Overton even to papists and Jews. Lilburne and others used it to denounce the arbitrary actions of the House of Lords (and later the Commons) in imprisoning offenders for no offence against known law and without trial and for demanding that individuals answer questions about their activities on oath. Thus the notion that men are equal is expressed by pointing to the Golden Rule—which is taken to mean that men ought to conform their actions to a rule that holds for themselves as well as others and that there should be no special respect for supposedly superior persons.

The first implication drawn from this principle of equality is that just authority can only be derived from the consent of those who are subject to it. No man is naturally superior to another; equal freedom precludes natural or divinely arranged subordination. This notion lies behind the Levellers' rejection of the authority of the House of Lords and the assertion that only the

Commons, as elected representatives of the people, have been entrusted with governing power. It is expressed in the Levellers' dislike of the army officers' proceedings in purging parliament and trying and executing the king before, rather than after, the convening of a truly legitimate assembly, representative of the people. It lies behind their promotion of an 'agreement of the people' as the foundation of government. It rings out in Rainborough's statement at Putney:

> For really I think that the poorest he that is in England hath a life to live as the greatest he; and therefore truly, sir, I think it's clear, that every man that is to live under a government ought first by his own consent to put himself under that government; and I do think that the poorest man in England is not at all bound in a strict sense to that government that he hath not had a voice to put himself under.[13]

And it is equally sharply put by Winstanley's distinction between kingly government and commonwealth government. The first is tyrannical and oppressive—it makes men slaves. The second makes men free—a freedom that Winstanley, like the Levellers, would implement in annually elected parliaments.[14]

But it was not merely inequality of civil, religious or political rights that was deplored. The Levellers were not merely accused of principles which would produce 'utter confusion' politically; they were accused of principles which would 'deny all property too' and which therefore tended to anarchy.[15] Although these allegations were made against the Levellers generally, and at Putney against such supposed moderate, constitutionalist Levellers as Wildman, they are particularly plausible charges against William Walwyn—who is sometimes therefore hailed as further 'left' than the others.

Undoubtedly Walwyn is the most obvious candidate for this charge. It was put forcefully by John Price:

> This Mr. Walwyn, to work upon the indigent and poorer sort of people, and to raise up their spirits in discontents and clamours, &c. did one time professe, he could wish with all his heart that there was neither Pale, Hedge nor Ditch in the whole Nation, and that it was an unconscionable thing that one man should have ten thousand pounds, and another more deserving and usefull to the Common-wealth, should not be worth two pence, or to that purpose.

> At another time discoursing of the inequality and disproportion of the estates and conditions of men in the world, had words to this purpose, That it was a sad and miserable thing that it should so continue, and that it would never be well untill all things were common; and it being replyed, will that be ever? Answered, we must endeavour it: It being said, That this would destroy all Govern-ment; Answered, That then there would be lesse need of

Government, for then there would be no theeves, no covetous persons, no deceiving and abusing of one another, and so no need of Government, &c. but if in such a case they have a form and rule of government to determine cases, as may fall out, yet there will be no need of standing Officers in a Common-wealth, no need of Judges, &c. but if any difference arise, or any criminall fact be committed, take a Cobler from his Seat, or a Butcher from his Shop, or any other Tradesman that is an honest and just man, and let him hear the case, and determine the same, and then betake himself to his work again.[16]

Price clearly accuses Walwyn not merely of rabble-rousing among the lowest class, but of being in favour of equality of both political and property rights. Indeed it is difficult to tell if he is more scandalized by Walwyn's advocacy of community of property or by his willingness to allow the vulgar, even those so notoriously crude as butchers, to perform civic duties. On this account, Walwyn was no respecter of persons; he was prepared to take as much notice of a cobbler or a chimney sweep as he did of the well-off.

Significantly, neither Humphrey Brooke, Walwyn's son-in-law, in his defence of Walwyn, nor Walwyn himself in *Walwyn's Just Defence,* denied the charge that Walwyn favoured much greater equality of wealth and even community of property. Brooke excused his father-in-law by passing off the offending words as 'old expressions in the heat of Discourses'.[17] Nor did Walwyn repudiate these positions. In fact he goes further than merely avoiding a categorical denial. Having cited a few well-known passages in Scripture which castigate the rich, he reiterates his egalitarianism and refers his detractors to the Levellers' common programme, the *Agreement of the People:*

> And where you charge me, that I find fault that some abound whil'st others want bread; truly I think it a sad thing, in so fruitfull a land, as through God's blessing, this is; and I do think it one main end of Government, to provide, that those who refuse not labour, should eat comfortably; and if you think otherwise, I think it your errour, and your unhappinesse: But for my turning the world upside down, I leave it to you, it's not a work I ever intended, as all my actions, and the Agreement of the People, do sufficiently evince, and doth indeed so fully answer all your remaining rambling scandals, that I shall pray the courteous Reader hereof to read it, and apply it, and then shall not doubt my full and clear vindication: so far as that is, am I for plucking up of all the pales and hedges in the Nation; so far, for all things common.[18]

Yet the view that extremes of rich and poor were at least objectionable had already been expressed by Walwyn as early as 1643 in *The Power of Love:*

> Consider our Saviour saith, He that hath this worlds goods, and seeth his brother lack, how dwelleth the love of God in him? Judge then by this rule who are of Gods family; looke about and you will finde in these woefull dayes thousands of miserable, distressed, starved, imprisoned Christians: see how pale and wan they looke: how coldly, raggedly, & unwholsomely they are cloathed; live one week with them in their poore houses, lodge as they lodge, eate as they eate, and no oftner, and bee at the same passe to get that wretched food for a sickly wife, and hunger-starved children; (if you dare doe this for feare of death or diseases) then walke abroad, and observe the generall plenty of all necessaries, observe the gallant bravery of multitudes of men and women abounding in all things that can be imagined: observe likewise the innumerable numbers of those that have more than sufficeth. Neither will I limit you to observe the inconsiderate people of the world, but the whole body of religious people themselves, and in the very Churches and upon solemne dayes: view them well, and see whether they have not this worlds goods; their silkes, their beavers, their rings, and other divises will testifie they have; I, and the wants and distresses of the poore will testifie that the love of God they have not. What is aimed at? (sayes another) would you have all things common? for love seeketh not her owne good, but the good of others. You say very true, it is the Apostles doctrine: and you may remember the multitude of beleevers had all things common: that was another of their opinions, which many good people are afraid of. But (sayes another) what would you have? would you have no distinction of men, nor no government? feare it not: nor flye the truth because it suites not with your corrupt opinions or courses.[19]

Thus Walwyn's religious views and his account of Christian love lead to his accepting a greater amount of communal sharing than his opponents wished. It also led to his concern for the poor. Expressions of concern for the poor—not simply those not well-off, but those whose children might go hungry, who may not eat very often, who may be reduced to begging—are not confined to Walwyn, who is usually regarded as the most 'left' of the Levellers. Similar concerns may be found in the other, supposedly more moderate, Levellers. For example, take John Lilburne's views, put in very similar words:

> Therefore when I seriously consider how many men in the Parliament, and else-where of their associates (that judge themselves the onely Saints and godly men upon earth) that have considerable (and some of them vast) estates of their owne inheritance, and yet take five hundred, one, two, three, four, five, six thousand pounds *per annum* salaries, and other comings in by their places, and that out of the too much exhausted publick Treasury of the Nation, when thousands, not onely of the people of the world, as they call them, but also of the precious and redeemed Lambs of Christ, are ready to sterve

for want of bread, I cannot but wonder with my self, whether they have any conscience within them or no, and what they think of that saying of the Spirit of God: That whoso hath this worlds good, and seeth his brother hath need, and shutteth up his bowels of compassion from him, (which he absolutely doth, that any way takes a little of his little from him) how dwelleth the love of God in him? I John 3.17[20]

Richard Overton was another Leveller not unmindful of the condition of the poor; in *The Arraignement of Mr. Persecution,* he contrasts the situation of the Presbyterian ministers, who are making a good thing of their inheritance of the state church, with that of those who have to pay for it: 'poor men, that have not bread to still the cry of their children, must either pay or goe in person to the wars, while those devouring Church-lubbers live at ease, feed on dainties, neither pay nor goe themselves, but preach out our very hearts.'[21]

Nevertheless, these Leveller expressions of solicitude may be no more than a few words in passing and the implication that they are speaking on behalf of those who are pale, wan and hungry and who have no bread for a crying child may be mere rhetorical exaggeration. How far are these concerns part of the Levellers' programme? How far is *The Agreement of the People* for making all things common?

It is usually held that the Levellers were individualists who based freedom on property in one's person and favoured the liberty of small enterprisers to acquire external possessions; they had a notion of community, but it was inconsistent with their conception of individual freedom. They did not reject capitalism; they rejected Winstanley's communism.[22]

Certainly there is evidence which appears to support this view of the Levellers. In the petition of 11 September 1648, a document frequently cited by the Levellers themselves as an authoritative statement of their programme, they list a number of things which they had 'long expected' from the House of Commons. Among these things are that the House 'would have bound your selves and all future Parliaments from abolishing propriety, Levelling mens Estats, or making all things common'.[23] Did not Lilburne repudiate the tenets of the 'poor misguided Diggers'?[24]

Nevertheless, it is worth examining the Levellers' actual words in *A Manifestation,* a collective repudiation by Lilburne, Overton, Walwyn and Prince of the calumnies against them.

> First, Then it will be requisite that we express our selves concerning Levelling, for which we suppose is commonly meant an equalling of mens estates, and taking away the proper right and Title that every

man has to what is his own. This as we have formerly declared against, particularly in our petition of the 11 of Sept. so do we again professe that to attempt an inducing the same is most injurious, unlesse there did precede an universall assent thereunto from all and every one of the People. Nor doe we, under favour, judge it within the Power of a Representative it selfe, because although their power is supreame, yet it is but deputative and of trust, and consequently must be restrained expresly or tacitely, to some particulars essential as well to the Peoples safety and freedom as to the present Government.[25]

Thus the Levellers' repudiation of levelling is far from absolute. Let the existing House of Commons repudiate it, for no government possesses more than a limited jurisdiction. Nevertheless there is nothing intrinsically sacred about private property; it is not enjoined by God's law. Common property was voluntary among the primitive Christians.[26] It must be equally voluntary for seventeenth-century Englishmen. There would be nothing wrong in their abolishing it. But while the Leveller programme did not call for the abolition of private property, it always demanded some sort of effective action so that no one would have to beg.

Levelling and Digging are often contrasted. Yet on this matter, Gerrard Winstanley's views are not far from those of the Levellers: 'I do not say, nor desire, that every one shall be compelled to practise this common-wealth's government; for the spirits of some will be enemies at first, though afterwards will prove the most cordial and true friends thereunto.'[27] Apparently for Winstanley, as for the Levellers, true community could only be established voluntarily.

For the Levellers and for the Diggers a Christian society was not just a society outwardly professing Christianity. It was especially not a society imposing a public form of Christian worship. It was, however, a society expressing its Christianity in its actions. For the conscientious Christian in the sixteenth and seventeenth centuries, some concern about the poor was required. Indeed, many thought true Christianity incompatible with extremes of wealth and poverty. Given the views they published, it was hardly surprising that the Levellers were compared with those they called the 'falsely maligned' Anabaptists of Munster. But even quite conservative divines could denounce the evils of private property and excessive wealth. Robert Crowley felt called upon to denounce 'gredie cormorauntes' who oppressed the poor (as well as rebellious peasants) and preach natural equality:

> Which of you can laye for hym selfe any naturall cause whye he shoulde possesse the treasure of this wor[l]de, but *that* the same cause may be founde in hym also whom you make your slave? By nature (therefore) you claime no thynge but that whiche

you shall get with the swet of your faces . . . . The whole earth therfor (by byrth right) belongeth to the chyldren of men. They are all inheritours therof indifferently by nature.[28]

Crowley also felt it necessary to deny that he favoured making all things common—although he did think that true Christians ought to sell all and give the proceeds to be common as in the primitive church.[29] But Crowley only preached equality to remind well-off Christians that they had duties toward the less well-off.

For the picture of a commonwealth constructed with Christian principles in mind, we may turn to another sixteenth-century thinker, Thomas More. His *Utopia* is not a society in which men profess Christianity but one in which they act according to its principles. Utopians do believe in a form of natural religion which is consistent with Christian doctrine: they believe in a single, omnipotent god; most believe in rewards and punishments after death. Their society is constructed to promote virtuous conduct and the cultivation of the soul. They despise and reject the enjoyments beloved of wordly men: wealth they treat with contempt; all must work and all who work eat; silver, gold and jewels are the ornaments of criminal slaves. All necessary wants are catered for but property is communal. Power is accorded only to the virtuous by election and brings no overweening position but rather responsibilities to others. Sensual and sexual pleasure are both foreign to Utopians. Thus it is a Christian-like society which does not know that it is Christian. Its tastes and institutions accord with Christianity but it lacks revelation.[30]

The society advocated by Gerrard Winstanley in his last major work, *The Law of Freedom,* is very similar to More's Utopia. Both propose to exclude private ownership of land, the enclosing and dividing of the earth's common treasury. Both do without buying and selling, and in both it is less the profession of Christian doctrine that is emphasized than the acting of the precept to love one's neighbour as oneself. (Both muster the whole society's repressive force to ensure that this shall be the case.) Of course there are differences: for Winstanley equality means equality of rights as well as equality of wealth; More's society is an aristocracy, ruled by the virtuous (those noble by nature). For the Diggers all forms of inequality are forms of 'kingly power', usurped tyrannical power of one man over another, power not legitimized by consent. So, it is not surprising that Winstanley should have seen the execution of the king and the proclamation of a commonwealth as something to be taken quite literally as the extirpation of all lordly usurped power.[31]

Like the Levellers, Winstanley proposed to bring about the changes he advocated by agreement or consent. The Digger communities were gathered out of those who wished to adhere. Even in *The Law of Freedom,* which sketched a whole commonwealth rather than a gathered community, Winstanley suggested that the landlords would wither away from lack of those to work for hire, not be forcibly expropriated. In all his works he relied on voluntary adherence.

Thus *The Law of Freedom* presents us with a communistic society as disciplined as More's Utopia. It is a society governed by officers elected annually by universal manhood suffrage, excluding from those eligible for election and from the electorate those who have supported the king by arms or money and those who have purchased confiscated lands. The officers are to be forty years old or older; and Winstanley also suggests that 'uncivil livers, as drunkards, quarrellers, fearful ignorant men', pleasure-seekers and windbags are not fit to be chosen.[32] But it is not a secular society: it is a 'platform of commonwealth's government unto you, wherein I have declared a full commonwealth's freedom according to the rule of righteousnesse, which is God's Word'.[33] It cannot be seen as a secular ideal—the point of having a commonwealth is to follow God's rule. For those who believe that God is all in all there can hardly be a distinction between what is religious and what is secular. Winstanley's religious commitment was never repudiated; he announced no conversion to a new belief, but shifted from preaching directed at individuals to proposals aimed at a communal reform. Indeed his first five religious pamphlets were reprinted in 1650.[34] Both Levellers and Diggers adhered to a principle of men's equality which was both natural and in accord with their conception of Christianity; in their writings they supported these views by citing over and over again the same passages, for example, the Golden Rule and the requirement of charity from I John.

Among the adherents of the principle of equality who expounded their views using the same rhetoric must be counted the Ranters as well as the Levellers and the Diggers. Abiezer Coppe, for example, exhibits the acceptance of the principle of equality in his words and actions. While proclaiming that God's principle was as far from 'sword levelling, or digging-levelling' as 'the East is from the West, or the Heavens from the Earth', he prophesied:

> Behold, behold, behold, I the eternall God, the Lord of Hosts, who am that mighty Leveller, am comming (yea even at the doores) to Levell in good earnest, to Levell to some purpose, to Levell with a witnesse, to Levell the Hills with the Valleyes, and to lay the Mountaines low.[35]

What is to be flattened is all forms of social hierarchy: 'And as I live, I will plague your Honour, Pompe, Greatnesse, Superfluity, and confound it into parity, equality, community; that the neck of horrid pride, murder, malice and tyranny, &c. may be chopt off at one blow.'[36]

Disagreeing with the proposals of Levellers and Diggers, Coppe calls upon all to share what they have, obeying the Biblical injunctions:

> you will find the Dominicall letter to be G. and there are many words that begin with G. at this time GIVE begins with G. give, give, give, give up, give up your houses, horses, goods, gold, Lands, give up, account nothing on your own, have ALL THINGS common, or els the plague of God will rot and consume all that you have.[37]

He himself does so; resisting the temptation to restrict to two pence his charity to a 'poor wretch', 'a most strange deformed man, clad with patcht clouts', he decides to give him six pence. He then 'pulling out a shilling, said to the poor wretch, give me six pence, heer's a shilling for thee'. But the man has no change: 'I have never a penny.' Coppe then expresses a pious wish to have given him something, for which he receives the poor man's blessing. But he cannot ride away; first he turns back to bid him call for some money at a house in the next town, then 'the rust of my silver did so rise up in judgement against me, and burnt my flesh like fire: and the 5. of James thundered such an alarm in mine ears, that I was fain to cast all I had into the hands of him, whose visage was more marr'd than any mans that I ever saw.' Riding away again he feels 'sparkles of a great glory', so he once again accosts the poor wretch, puts off his hat, bows seven times and tells him, 'because I am a King, I have done this, but you need not tell any one.'[38] The story, true in the history, is also true in the mystery; it symbolizes the proper relation between those who have this world's goods and those who do not.

Coppe's conception of true religion is not confined to individual actions. It extends to social relations: 'The true Communion amongst men, is to have all things common, and to call nothing one hath, one's own.' True religion is giving one's bread to those without bread and telling them that it is their bread. Vain religion is exclusive, distinguishing the saints from the worldly.

> But take this hint before I leave thee.
>
> He that hath this worlds goods, and seeth his brother in want, and shutteth up the bowels of com-passion from his, the love of God dwelleth not in him; this mans Religion is in vain.

So Coppe called neither for levelling by the sword nor by the spade, but for *'Bloud-Life-Spirit levelling'*, which is presumably to be accomplished by God's spirit working in men.[39]

Ranters, like the Levellers and the Diggers, advocated levelling. Indeed, Lawrence Clarkson in his spiritual pilgrimage passed from the Levellers to the Ranters. While a Leveller, Clarkson wrote a pamphlet in which he chided the communality for choosing oppressors to represent it: 'for who are the oppressors, but the Nobility and Gentry; and who are the oppressed, if not the Yeoman, the Farmer, the Tradesman, and the Labourer?'[40] He retained his radical social views while a Ranter:

> for I apprehended there was no such thing as theft, cheat or a lie, but as man made it so: for if the creature had brought this world into no propriety, as *Mine* and *Thine,* there had been no such title as theft, cheat, or a lie; for the prevention hereof *Everard* and *Gerrard Winstanley* did dig up the Commons, that so all might have to live of themselves, then there had been no need of defrauding but unity with one another . . . .

But Clarkson perceived in Winstanley 'a self-love and vain-glory nursed in his heart, that if possible, by digging to have gained people to him, by which his name might become great among the poor Commonalty of the Nation'.[41] Still, it is clear that, at that time, his interpretation of the social arrangements implicit in true religion was consistent with that of the Diggers.

Thus for all these radicals, Levellers, Diggers and Ranters, adherence to a fundamental principle of equality implied a rejection of social privilege. This adherence was grounded in a common conception of the meaning of true Christianity. These views were expressed in a rhetoric common to all these radicals, frequently citing the same natural rights and relying on the same Scriptual passages and drawing the same implications from them. That conception implied different social arrangements from those prevalent in seventeenth-century England. Whatever their differences, they also agreed that an egalitarian society would be brought about voluntarily.

Notes

[1] C. B. Macpherson, *The Political Theory of Possessive Individualism: Hobbes to Locke* (Oxford, 1962), pp. 107-59, holds that 'the Levellers consistently excluded from their franchise proposals two substantial categories of men, namely servants or wage earners, and those in receipt of alms or beggars' (p. 107, n. 4). Thus they proposed to enfranchise only c. 205,000 additional electors, a mere 42,000 more than the Grandees. Christopher Hill in *The World Turned Upside Down: radical ideas during the English Revolution* (London, 1972), pp. 46-58, 86-103, apparently wishes to retain Macphersons's rejection of the Levellers as democrats while linking them to True Levellers and Diggers. He postulates differences between the Level-

ler leaders and distinctions between a moderate, civilian official leadership and several types of more radical Levellers. But although they may have been a heterogenous party, the Levellers' unity is impressive: the principal Levellers continued to co-operate with each other until the movement was crushed. Moreover, to support the theory, *The Moderate,* which treated the Diggers with sympathy, must be regarded as 'unofficial'.

Macpherson's views, although widely accepted, have been subjected to considerable critical scrutiny; see Peter Laslett, 'Market society and political theory', *Historical Journal,* 7 (1964); Keith Thomas, 'The Levellers and the franchise', in *The Interregnum: the quest for Settlement 1646-60,* ed. G. E. Aylmer (London, 1972); J. C. Davis, 'The Levellers and Christianity', in *Politics, Religion and the Civil War* (London, 1973); Iain Hampsher-Monk, 'The political theory of the Levellers: Putney, property and Professor Macpherson', *Political Studies,* 24 (1976), who shows that the Grandees, who were willing to go well beyond the existing franchise, consistently supposed the Levellers to be advocating manhood suffrage at Putney and that the arguments cannot be read as a debate, especially about whether four out of five were to be mere hewers of wood and drawers of water, on Macpherson's interpretation; and Christopher Thompson, 'Maximilian Petty and the Putney debate on the franchise', *Past and Present,* no. 88 (1980), pp. 63-9, who contends that Petty's position is misinterpreted by Macpherson. See also Brian Manning, *The English People and the English Revolution* (Harmondsworth, 1978), who piles up quotations which emphasize the Levellers' concern for those who sweat, who work with their hands, whose payments of tithes and taxes come out of their bellies, but then suggests that the Leveller leaders were of the 'middle', or even better, sort and their followers more radical, concluding that the Levellers stood for small propertied merchants and farmers.

[2] Richard Overton, *An Arrow Against All Tyrants* (London, 1646; repr. The Rota, Exeter, 1976), p. 3.

[3] Ibid., pp. 19-20.

[4] *The Case of the Armie Truly Stated* (London, 1647), in *Leveller Manifestoes of the Puritan Revolution,* ed. D. M. Wolfe (London, 1967), p. 212.

[5] John Lilburne, *Regall Tyranny Discovered* (London, 1647), p. 10.

[6] Ibid., p. 11.

[7] *The True Levellers Standard Advanced* (London, 1649), in *Winstanley: The Law of Freedom and other writings,* ed. Christopher Hill (Harmondsworth, 1973), p. 82.

[8] *Light Shining in Buckinghamshire* (London, 1648), in *The Works of Gerrard Winstanley,* ed. George H. Sabine (New York, 1965), p. 611.

[9] *The Law of Freedom* (London, 1652) in Hill, *Winstanley,* pp. 275-6.

[10] Ibid., p. 315.

[11] Quoted in Hill, *World Turned Upside Down,* p. 19, from P. Zagorin, *The Court and the Country* (London, 1969), p. 323.

[12] *His Majesties Answer to the XIX Propositions* (London, 1642); excerpts are included in Andrew Sharp, *Political Ideas of the English Civil Wars 1641-9* (London, 1983), pp. 40-3.

[13] A. S. P. Woodhouse (ed.), *Puritanism and Liberty: being the Army Debates (1647-9) from the Clarke manuscripts with supplementary documents,* 2nd edn (London, 1950), p. 53.

[14] *The Law of Freedom,* in Hill, *Winstanley,* p. 338.

[15] These accusations were voiced at Putney by Cromwell and Ireton; see Woodhouse, *Puritanism and Liberty,* pp. 7-8, 57-9.

[16] John Price, *Walwyns Wiles* (London, 1649), in *The Leveller Tracts,* ed. William Haller and Godfrey Davies (New York, 1944), pp. 302-3.

[17] Humphrey Brooke, *The Charity of Churchmen* (London, 1649), in Haller and Davies, *Leveller Tracts,* p. 346.

[18] William Walwyn, *Walwyns Just Defence* (London, 1649), in Haller and Davies, *Leveller Tracts,* p. 384.

[19] William Walwyn, *The Power of Love* (London, 1643), sigs. A3-A5 (italics reversed) in *Tracts on Liberty in the Puritan Revolution, 1638-47,* ed. William Haller (3 vols, New York, 1934), pp. 274-5. Walwyn goes on to urge that men and women be distinguished only as 'you see the love of God abound in them toward their brethren' and to argue that government is entrusted to rulers by common agreement.

[20] John Lilburne, *The Legall Fundamentall Liberties of the People of England* (London, 1649), in Haller and Davies, *Leveller Tracts,* p. 435.

[21] Richard Overton, *The Arraignement of Mr. Persecution* (London, 1645), p. 36, in Haller, *Tracts on Liberty,* III, p. 246.

[22] See Macpherson, *Possessive Individualism,* pp. 154-9; Hill, *World Turned Upside Down,* p. 99. Or at least,

for Hill, this is true of the 'constitutional Levellers' if not for 'unofficial Levellers' or 'True Levellers', although he notes Walwyn's views and Overton's proposal that former common ground, now enclosed, be opened to the poor, pp. 95-6. Overton's proposal is in *An Appeale from the Degenerate Representative Body, the Commons at Westminster* (London, 1647), in Wolfe, *Leveller Manifestoes,* p. 194.

23 Wolfe, *Leveller Manifestoes,* p. 288.

24 In *Legall Fundamentall Liberties,* in Haller and Davies, *Leveller Tracts,* p. 449.

25 *A Manifestation* (April 1649), in Haller and Davies, *Leveller Tracts,* p. 279.

26 Ibid.

27 *The Law of Freedom,* in Hill, *Winstanley,* pp. 289-90.

28 Robert Crowley, *An Informacion and Petition agaynst the Oppressours of the pore Commons of this Realme,* in *The Select Works of Robert Crowley,* ed. J. M. Cowper, Early English Text Society (London, 1872), pp. 163-4.

29 Ibid., pp. 156-8.

30 Thomas More, *Utopia,* ed. Edward Surtz, S.J. and J. H. Hexter, in *The Complete Works of Thomas More,* IV, (New Haven and London, 1965); see 'Introduction, Part I' by J. H. Hexter; see also J. C. Davis, *Utopia and the Ideal Society: a study of English utopian writing 1516-1700* (Cambridge, 1981), pp. 41-61.

31 See G. E. Aylmer, *'England's Spirit Unfould'd, or an Incouragement to take the Engagement:* A newly discovered pamphlet by Gerrard Winstanley', *Past and Present,* no. 40 (1968), esp. pp. 9-10.

32 *The Law of Freedom,* in Hill, *Winstanley,* pp. 321-4.

33 Ibid., p. 285.

34 See *Several Pieces Gathered into one volume* (London, 1650). (I owe this point to Barry Smith.) For a contrary view, arguing that Winstanley developed from a religious to a secular thinker, see George Juretic, 'Digger no millenarian: the revolutionizing of Gerrard Winstanley', *Journal of the History of Ideas,* 36 (1975). The extent of secularization of political ideas during the Interregnum is sometimes overestimated, partly because of the editing of republican views for late seventeenth-and eighteenth-century consumption; see Edmund Ludlow, *A Voyce from the Watch Tower: Part Five, 1660-62,* ed. A. B. Worden, Camden Society

Fourth Series, 21 (London, 1978), esp. introduction, pp. 1-13.

35 Abiezer Coppe, *A Fiery Flying Roll* (London, 1649; repr. The Rota, Exeter, 1973), p. 2.

36 Ibid., p. 4.

37 Ibid., Part II, pp. 3-4.

38 Ibid., pp. 4-6.

39 Ibid., pp. 21-2.

40 Lawrence Clarkson, *A Generall Charge or Impeachment of High-Treason* (London, 1647), p. 11.

41 Idem, *The Lost Sheep Found* (London, 1660; repr. The Rota, Exeter, 1974), p. 27.

Christopher Hill (essay date 1994)

SOURCE: "The First Losers, 1649-1651: Levellers, True Levellers, From Ranters to Muggletonians," in *The Experience of Defeat: Milton and Some Contemporaries,* pp. 27-47. London: Bookmarks, 1994.

[*In the following essay, Hill discusses the Leveller party's political aims and outlines the decline of the party.*]

1 Levellers

The Levellers have some claim to be regarded as the first organised political party, as opposed to religious groupings pursuing political ends. They came into existence in London in 1645-6 as the radical wing of the Independent coalition. They invented or popularised many modern political techniques—mass demonstrations, collecting signatures to petitions, pamphleteering, leafleting, lobbying MPs. They won support in the Army, especially among its lower ranks. They were always a heterogeneous body, with minimal formal links and organisation: no party cards, no membership tests, no local branches. So their views were correspondingly varied. A Leveller wanted a democratic republic in which the House of Commons was superior to the House of Lords (if there was one); he wanted redistribution and extension of the franchise, legal and economic reforms on behalf of men of small property—artisans, yeomen, small merchants—but not communism: though communist views were attributed to the Leveller William Walwyn, and the communist Diggers called themselves True Levellers. Levellers advocated democratisation of the gilds and City government of London, decentralisation of justice, election of local governors, stability of tenure for copyholders. Some Levellers wanted enclosures to be thrown open.

But the strength of the movement lay mainly in London and other towns—and in the Army. Here they took up the problem of pauperism, not exclusively from the point of view of the poor. 'Thousands of men and women', declared *The Large Petition* of March 1647, 'are permitted to live in beggary and wickedness all their life long, and to breed their children to the same idle and vicious course of life, and no effectual means used to reclaim either, or to reduce them to any virtue or industry.'[1] One or two Levellers—Walwyn, Prince—opposed the reconquest of Ireland on the ground that 'the cause of the Irish natives in seeking their just freedoms . . . was the very same with our cause here in endeavouring our own rescue and freedom from the power of oppressors.[2]

The Levellers were democrats who could never have been returned to power by any possible electorate—or only after a long period of freedom to propagate their views, to educate a democratic electorate. As they became aware of this problem, so they tried to find constitutional devices for getting round it. The draft constitution produced in 1647, the Agreement of the People, assumed that the English state had broken down in the civil war and must be refounded. Certain fundamental 'native rights' were safeguarded even from a sovereign Parliament—religious toleration, no tithes, no conscription, indemnity for actions committed in the war, equality before the law. 'As the laws ought to be equal, so they must be good and not evidently destructive to the safety and well-being of the people.' Some at least of these 'good laws' were spelt out in later versions of the Agreement. They included biennial Parliaments, responsibility of ministers to Parliament, franchise reform; only those who contracted in to the new state by accepting the Agreement were to have the vote.[3]

The Levellers had no distinctive religious policy, apart from wanting toleration and abolition of tithes. They drew support from diverse radical religious groups, though after 1649 leading Independents and Baptists repudiated them.[4] Individual Leveller leaders had very heretical views: Richard Overton was a mortalist, Walwyn a sceptical antinomian; Wildman may have been something like a deist.[5] Walwyn's *The Compassionate Samaritane* (1644), with its early plea for toleration, particularly annoyed the Presbyterian clergy. It was attacked in three Fast Sermons in 1644-5.[6] In 1647 John Trapp joined the critics in his *Commentary on the New Testament.*[7]

Levellers could have put their policies into effect only if they had captured control of the Army. They failed to accomplish this through the Agitators and the Army Council in the summer of 1647; the generals outmanoeuvred and outwitted them. Again in the winter of 1648-9 the generals needed the support of the Levellers until Parliament had been purged and the King

executed: a new Agreement of the People was negotiated. But it was never taken seriously by the Army leaders or the Rump. Leveller influence on Army rank and file had been due in great part to their call for arrears of wages and indemnity for actions committed during the civil war. After Pride's Purge in December 1648 these ceased to be problems, and it was revealed that the hold of the political and constitutional ideas of the Levellers was less strong. In March 1649 Cromwell told the Council of State, 'You must break these men or they will break you';[8] by May 1649 both civilian and Army Levellers had been broken.

Once they had lost their base in the Army, the Levellers had to find new political approaches. In 1649 they laid greater emphasis on opposition to enclosure and support for stability of tenure for copyholders. These had long figured in the Leveller programmes, and in suitable areas—in Buckinghamshire, for instance—Levellers encouraged attacks on enclosure in 1647-9.[9] In 1650-1 Lilburne and Wildman were in the Isle of Axholme supporting the commoners' opposition to fen drainage. It does not appear, however, that they did the fenmen much good; their activities certainly did not help to lay the basis for a mass movement.[10] The Levellers suffered a crisis of leadership.

Lilburne was notoriously volatile, and had thriven on his personal popularity in London. He was not at his best in defeat. In October 1649 he offered to emigrate with his adherents to the West Indies if the government would finance them[11] Lilburne, like Winstanley, recommended taking the Engagement to be true and faithful to the Commonwealth, and in 1650 he was again on good terms with Cromwell. But in 1651 he was advising the Presbyterian Christopher Love at his trial for treason against the Commonwealth.[12] In 1652 he was exiled. Next year he returned to face a spectacular trial in which his popularity in London was reaffirmed; but it was his last political appearance. He was illegally detained in prison until his death in 1657.[13] In 1655 he 'troubled and offended' his 'old and familiar friends' by turning Quaker. Typically, Lilburne outdid the Quakers at this date by renouncing 'carnal weapons of any kind whatsoever'.[14]

During his exile Lilburne had been in contact with royalists, though he protested vehemently that he had not plotted for a restoration of monarchy.[15] Wildman, Sexby and Overton had no such scruples. They may have entered into negotiations with exiled royalists only in order to deceive them, to take royalist (or Spanish) money in order to forward their own schemes.[16] But by this date it is doubtful whether they represented any significant organisation in England. It appears that Overton and Wildman at least were double agents, taking money from Thurloe as well as from royalists.[17] What alternative was there for such men if they wished to continue political activity and not—like Walwyn,

Winstanley and Coppe—withdraw into passivity?

The ex-Agitator Edmund Sexby, after being cashiered from the Army in 1651,[18] was for a short time the Commonwealth's agent with French rebels in Bordeaux, where he had the Agreement of the People translated into French.[19] After the establishment of the Protectorate, Sexby advocated Cromwell's assassination in Killing No Murder, and plotted with another ex-Leveller, Miles Sindercombe, to kill the Protector, 'it being certain,' Sindercombe was reported as saying, 'that the great ones of the King would never agree who should succeed, but would fall together by the ears about it, and then in that disorder the people would rise and so things might be brought to a commonwealth again'.[20] It is a hope with which many terrorists since have consoled themselves. Sexby died in gaol in 1657.

Walwyn took up medicine in the last thirty years of his life, defending the practice of professional secrecy from which he profited.[21] Wildman combined conspiracy with making money by land speculation.[22] One reason for his agreeing to act as a spy for Thurloe in 1656 may have been to recover extensive estates in Lancashire which had been sequestrated after his arrest for conspiracy in 1655.[23] Wildman spent the rest of his long life plotting against every regime from Cromwell to William III. In 1659 he was a member of Harrington's Rota Club. He had meanwhile established contacts with the Duke of Buckingham which lasted until well after the restoration: Pepys called Wildman 'a great creature of the Duke of Buckingham' in December 1667.[24] Wildman was involved in numerous plots against Charles II and James II, as well as in William of Orange's invasion in 1688.[25] In 1689 he advocated giving power to the people: failing that, he accepted a knighthood in 1692.[26]

So, lacking leadership, Leveller activity dwindled in the 1650s. There were rumours of Levellers in Cheshire in 1652,[27] of an 'insurrection' in Bedfordshire in 1653.[28] Lilburne's trial in the latter year produced an outburst of support in London, including demonstrations and over twenty pamphlets.[29] By now many former Leveller supporters seem to have come to think that Charles Stuart might be preferable to the Army.[30] There was indeed some logic in this. The Army dominated the state, and once the Leveller bid to capture control over the Army had failed, a weak monarchy balancing diverse interests might be less burdensome than the very expensive military rule.[31]

In the 1650s Levellers were attacked as subversives who would overthrow law and property. They were often deliberately confused with the Diggers or True Levellers. Cromwell denounced Levellers as 'a despicable and contemptible generation of men', who despised magistracy; their principles tended 'to make the tenant as liberal a fortune as the landlord'.[32] The idea that Levellers were 'bad men', 'robbers', was echoed by preachers and government propagandists, by James Harrington and later by Samuel Butler.[33]

When open propaganda was possible once more, in 1659, the surviving Levellers tried to refurbish their image by stressing their devotion to legality and property, their hostility to arbitrary rule. This made them virtually indistinguishable from Harringtonian republicans, with whom Wildman was associated in 1659-60, perhaps earlier, certainly later.[34] Most of the Leveller pamphlets published in these years were low-key and defensive, like *The Leveller: Or, the Principles and Maxims Concerning Government and Religion, which are asserted by those commonly called, Levellers,* possibly by Wildman.[35] It was directed mainly against military rule, stressing the Levellers' concern with legality, their defence of 'our liberties and properties'. Magna Carta was no longer the 'beggarly thing' that Overton had seen in it. Two-chamber government was advocated, though on Harringtonian rather than traditional lines. Toleration and equality before the law were demanded, but there is nothing about the franchise or about economic or legal reform.[36] Other tracts revived bits of the former Leveller programme, but 'none of them restated that programme in anything like its entirety.'[37]

We get a glimpse of Leveller reunion with middle-of-the-road republicans in a letter of 1656 to Charles II, signed by William Howard and eight others, offering him their services. The signatories, Howard told the King in a separate note, were Levellers, neither 'of great families or great estates'. This letter seems to represent an analysis and a programme on which the signatories had agreed to unite. They start from the experience of defeat. 'It is our lot . . . to be embarked in a shipwrecked commonwealth', thanks to 'the dark and mysterious effects of Providence'. These events 'command an (unwilling) silence upon our (sometimes mutinous and over-enquiring) hearts, resolving all into the good-will and pleasure of that all-disposing One whose wisdom is unsearchable and whose ways are past finding out'. There is no point in presumptuously kicking 'against the irresistible decrees of heaven'.[38] (Eternal Providence must be asserted, even if God's ways are not clearly justifiable.)

How has this state of affairs arisen? Under Charles I, great though his private virtues were, 'the whole commonwealth was faint, the whole nation sick . . . There were many errors, many defects, many irregularities, many illegal and eccentrical proceedings, . . . blots and stains upon the otherwise good government of the late King.' Charles had had to be rescued from 'evil councillors . . . who did every day thrust him into actions prejudicial to himself and destructive to the common good and safety of the people'.[39] In 1642 'we went out in the simplicity of our souls', the letter claims, motivated by 'the sure, safe, sound and unerring maxims of law, justice, reason and righteousness'. If they were deceived, it was by 'that grand imposter, that loathesome hypocrite, that detestable traitor [etc.] . . . who now calls himself our Protector'.[40] After much discussion, the writers had decided that a restoration of Charles II would be best for the 'common good, public safety, the honour, peace, welfare and prosperity of these nations'. Yet, 'lest we should seem to be altogether negligent of that first good though since dishonoured Cause, which God has so eminently owned us in', they offered conditions, whose acceptance by the King would win their support for his restoration.[41] These conditions were far indeed from the Leveller programme: restoration of both Houses of Parliament as they existed before Pride's Purge; confirmation of all concessions made by Charles I in the Isle of Wight Treaty of 1648; acceptance of legislation (or the repeal of existing legislation) by Parliament 'for the better securing of the just and natural rights and liberties of the people, for the obviating and preventing all dangerous and destructive excesses of government for the future'. There was to be religious toleration, tithes were to be replaced by some other means of financing the national ministry; there was to be an act of oblivion.[42]

In a covering note, and later in a personal interview with Charles II, Howard suggested that some of the demands in this letter might be modified. He also asked for £2,000 to be going on with—a sum which the King was in no position to provide even if he had been willing.[43] This was not untypical of Howard, who came of a 'great family' himself even if not of 'great estate'. Son of a peer who had taken the Parliamentarian side in the civil war, Howard was an unstable personality— a great preacher' among the Anabaptists and 'of special trust amongst the Levellers'. He was a friend of Wildman's and 'very intimate with Sindercombe', the man who tried to assassinate Cromwell in 1657.[44] After the restoration Howard plotted with the Dutch against Charles II, was frequently imprisoned and ended as a double agent, helping to get Lord Russell and Algernon Sidney convicted after the Rye House Plot.[45]

The name 'Leveller' was used to describe rioters in Worcestershrire in 1670,[46] and at various places in the 1720s and 1730s.[47] Levellers were discussed in the House of Commons in 1673;[48] in 1708 the French prophets were believed to be reviving 'Levelling principles'.[49]

Lilburne in 1649 looked to posterity which, 'we doubt not, shall reap the benefit of our labours, whatever shall become of us'.[50] His cause was lost when he wrote those words. But one Leveller left a more enduring message. Richard Rumbold was one of the guards at the scaffold when Charles I was executed. In February 1649—the month when Lilburne was looking to posterity—Rumbold petitioned for the re-establishment of the Council of Agitators. After the restoration he was the owner of Rye House, and seems to have played a leading part in the Rye House Plot of 1683, after which he fled to Holland. In 1685 he joined Argyll's invasion of Scotland, was captured and executed. On the scaffold he uttered words which long survived him: 'None comes into the world with a saddle upon his back, neither any booted and spurred to ride him.[51] Defoe used part of this phrase, without acknowledgement, in 1705; and it was often repeated.[52] It was probably a well-known Leveller phrase when Rumbold used it; it gained its apotheosis when Jefferson quoted it in 1826.[53]

2 True Levellers

The True Levellers or Diggers established a colony in April 1649 to cultivate in common the waste land of St George's Hill, Surrey, and later of the nearby Cobham Heath. They claimed that commons and waste land belonged to the people, not to lords of manors. The poor had borne the burden of fighting, taxation and free quarter in the civil war: they had a right to share in the freedom which Parliament had promised to establish.

> God's shaking nations, trying men,
> And changing times and customs,

Gerrard Winstanley had written in 1648. 'By the law of righteousness', he said later, 'the poorest man hath as true a title and just right to the land as the richest man.[54] Cultivation of commons and wastes would solve England's food problems and abolish poverty and begging.

Within a year, at least ten Digger colonies had been started in central and southern England, with more anticipated.[55] But they were all small affairs, harassed by local landowners and parsons; when the government withdrew Army protection they were swiftly broken up. By April 1650 all was over. After defeat, Winstanley in *The Law of Freedom in a Platform* (1652) worked out a programme for the introduction of a communist society by state action, example having failed. Winstanley's ideas are too rich to be briefly summarised. I must refer to what I have written elsewhere,[56] and here list only some of aspects of his thought which are relevant for our purposes.

Winstanley used Scripture language, but gave his own sense to the biblical stories. Whether the Crucifixion, the Resurrection and the Ascension were historical events 'it matters not much'[57]: he uses them as metaphors for psychological transformations within men and women. The Christ who lived at Jerusalem matters less than the Christ within. The rise of private property had been the Fall of Man: Its abolition, and that of wage labour, would allow a return to the innocence of Adam and Eve in the Garden of Eden. Winstanley's God is not to be found above the skies after we are dead, but within each one of us, here on earth. There is no heaven or hell after death, no personal immortality. Heaven, hell, Satan, are all within us. The universe—as Milton thought too—had been created out of the substance of God. The Second Coming of Jesus Christ is the rising of Reason within sons and daughters, and Reason teaches us the need for cooperation. Winstanley used the word Reason in preference to God. As Christ rises, so all men and women will come to see the necessity of cooperation. There is no other Second Coming.[58] Ultimately all mankind will be saved—ie brought into the haven of peace and rest on earth—not by the descent of a Saviour from the clouds but by the rising of communal consciousness within them. All men shall become Sons of God united by the Christ within.[59] Universalism was of course highly unorthodox when Winstanley began to preach it in 1648[60]; in his final version it was hardly Christian at all.

Winstanley saw the clergy as his main adversaries because they made a handsome living out of persuading the poor to accept their poverty on earth and look for their reward in heaven after death. The Diggers expected their heaven on earth. In Winstanley's ideal commonwealth there would be no state church; preaching for hire (i.e. an endowed ministry) would be as illegal as buying and selling, or lawyers taking fees. Winstanley rejected all church ordinances—prayer, preaching, baptism, holy communion, Sabbath observance. What mattered was 'the anointing' by the spirit of God. Winstanley believed that 'all the inward bondages of the mind' are 'occasioned by the outward bondage that one sort of people lay upon another', and will disappear in an equal society.[61]

Winstanley had accepted that England was a nation chosen as a model to the world. *The Law of Freedom* is analogous to *Paradise Lost* in that it attempts to explain how this hope had been frustrated.[62] Large excerpts from the pamphlet appeared in February 1652 in Daniel Border's newspaper *The Faithful Scout,* even before *The Law of Freedom* was published. Professor Woolrych points out that Border may have been taking his material at second hand, since three contemporary tracts also printed matter from *The Law of Freedom.*[63]

Winstanley's last pamphlet thus attracted some contemporary attention. But by 1652 Winstanley himself was exhausted and bitterly disillusioned. The dedication of *The Law of Freedom* to Oliver Cromwell may have been more than a device for winning publicity: like the Quakers later, Winstanley may still have had hopes of the Army. God, he said, had honoured Cromwell 'with the highest honour of any man since Moses's time'; Cromwell had not yet revealed himself as the lost leader of radical mythology. The Parliament which had proclaimed the Commonwealth might be persuaded to remove some of the burdens which afflicted the people. 'You have power in your hand', he told Cromwell, 'to act for common freedom if you will: I have no power.'[64] But by the time he had reached the end of his pamphlet Winstanley seems to have realised that his hopes were vain.

> O power where art thou, that must mend
> things amiss?
> Come change the heart of man, and make him
> truth to kiss.
> O death where art thou? Wilt thou not tidings
> send?
> I fear thee not, thou art my loving friend.[65]

Winstanley did not in fact die for another twenty-four years, but so far as we know he abandoned political activity and writing. In 1654 he visited Edward Burrough and told him that the Quakers were 'sent to perfect that work which fell in their hands'.[66] Or so Burrough said: Winstanley may not have spoken quite so strongly. Twenty-two years later he was buried as a Quaker, but there is no evidence in between that he played any active role in the Society of Friends. On the contrary: he held various parish offices at Cobham between 1659 and 1668, and in 1671 and 1672 he was one of two chief constables of Elmbridge Hundred. This would suggest that he conformed to the state church during those years.[67]

His influence may have been greater in the seventeenth century than used to be thought. Contemporaries indeed noted similarities between the ideas of Winstanley and the early Quakers which were obscured by developments of Quaker theology after 1660.[68] More than one later seventeenth-century author regarded Winstanley as the originator of the Quakers.[69] A more direct influence can be seen on the pamphlets of William Covell of Enfield, where in 1650 there had been a Digger colony. In 1649 and again in 1659 there were riots against the enclosure of Enfield Chase, from which purchasers expected to make comfortable profits. It was sold tithe-free, and improvements suggested by the surveyors would have increased the value by nearly 150 per cent—for example by evicting thirty-four squatters who had built cottages without leave.[70] The former Agitator, Cornet George Joyce, now Colonel Joyce, was one intending purchaser.[71]

Covell spoke of having had eight years service with the Army,[72] and was careful to describe himself as a 'gentleman' (as Winstanley was), and to deny being 'a Leveller who would destroy property'. Nevertheless, he proposed a return to the 'good ancient laws and customs which were before the Norman Yoke'. He wanted to abolish an endowed clergy: 'if any will have parish ministers, let them that will have them pay them.' Tithes, together with delinquents' estates and the lands of Inns of Court, Chancery and universities should be confiscated and used to pay public debts. All commons and waste lands should be settled on the poor for ever. 'The patents and grants by the kings to lords of manors may be well searched into, for they are encroachments upon the people.' Cooperative communities were to be established, which differed from those of the Diggers in that they were to be financed by some rich men. Within these communities there was to be no buying and selling. The rich were to be taxed in proportion to their estates to maintain the impotent and aged poor and to provide work for all the unemployed. A remarkable concluding provision was that all other laws were to be null for ever.[73] The whole pamphlet might have been written by Winstanley in his 'possibilist' mood of 1652. Covell believed that every man was king, priest and governor in, to and over himself. The people had a *right* to choose their own officers.[74] Covell's last publication was *The True Copy of a Letter* sent to Charles II in 1660, in which he addressed the King as 'thou'. (Enfield was to become a Quaker stronghold.) As late as 1666 there were rumours of a Fifth Monarchist conspiracy based on Epping Forest and Enfield Chase.[75] Echoes of Winstanley, as well as of *Areopagitica,* may also be heard in two pamphlets which Peter Cornelius Plockhoy published in 1659, not least in their fierce anti-clericalism: Great Antichrist (Bishop and King) had been succeeded by little Antichrists (priests). At least one Digger appears to have become a Harringtonian.[76]

It used to be thought that after the seventeenth century Winstanley was unknown until he was re-discovered at the end of the nineteenth century. But Benjamin Furley (1636-1714), Quaker friend of Algernon Sidney and Locke, owned Winstanley's writings.[77] In the mid-eighteenth century the radical Whig Thomas Hollis (who was interested in the mortalism of Richard Overton) gave a copy of *The Law of Freedom* to Henry Fielding.[78] In the 1790s ministers in the parish of Llangyfelach near Swansea were reading and discussing Winstanley's works.[79] A. F. Villemain's *Histoire de Cromwell d'apres les memoires du temps et les recueils parliamentaires* (1819) devoted a paragraph to the Diggers.[80] Now that historians have started to look out for it, more evidence will almost certainly be forthcoming.[81]

Notes

[1] In Haller, *Tracts on Liberty in the Puritan Revolution* (Columbia UP, 1933), III, p. 401. Attributed to Walwyn.

[2] See now my '17th Century English radicals and Ireland' in *Radicals, Rebels and Establishments* (ed P. J. Corish, *Historical Studies,* XV, Belfast, 1985)

[3] See *WTUD* [C. Hill, *The World Turned Upside Down,* Penguin edn., 1975] pp 66, 271-3

[4] See p. 322 below

[5] *Puritanism and Liberty ed.* A. S. P. Woodhouse (1938), pp. 107-8, 128, 161; *WTUD*), pp. 165-6. But contrast K. V. Thomas, Religion and the Decline of Magic (1971), pp. 236-7 (on Wildman and magic).

[6] Matthew Newcomen, *A Sermon* (1644), p. 38; Lazarus Seaman, *Solomons Choice* (1644),

[7] P. 41; A. Burgess, *Publike Affections* (1646), p. 16. Op cit. (1958 reprint) p. 515.

[8] See p. 182 below

[9] I owe this point to A. M. Johnson, 'Buckinghamshire 1640-60: A Study in County Politics' (unpubl. MA Thesis, University of Wales, 1963), pp. 261-2.

[10] J. Hughes, 'The Drainage Disputes in the Isle of Axholme', *The Lincolnshire Historian,* II (1954), pp. 13-34; C. Holmes, *Seventeenth-Century Lincolnshire* (Lincoln, 1980), pp. 210-11; K Lindley, *Fenland Riots and the English Revolution* (1982) pp. 194-6, 204-5, 211, 258 Lilburne and Wildman also agitated on behalf of a democratic party in City politics in 1650 (M. Ashley, *John Wildman, Plotter and Postmaster* 1947, p. 76).

[11] Lilburne, *The Innocent Mans Second Proffer* (1649). Many radicals emigrated to the West Indies after defeat (*WTUD, pp.* 254-5).

[12] G. D. Owen, 'The Conspiracy of Christopher Love,' *Trans. Hon. Soc. of Cymmrodorion* (1964), p. 97.

[13] C. J. Rolle was inclined to allow him a habeas corpus (W. Style, *Narrationes Modernae, or Modern Reports Begun in the now Upper Bench at Westminster* (1658), pp. 397-8).

[14] *The Resurrection of John Lilburne, now a Prisoner in Dover-Castle* (1656), pp. 1-5, 9-13, 21.

[15] P. Gregg, *Freeborn John: a Biography of John Lilburne* (1961), Chapter 27; H. N. Brailsford, *The Levellers and the English Revolution* (1961), p. 623; D. Underdown, *Royalist Conspiracy in England, 1649-60* (Yale UP, 1960), pp. 24-5.

[16] *A Collection of Original Letters and Papers Concerning the Affairs of England,* ed. T. Carte (1739), II, p. 103, cf. HMC *Portland MSS,* I pp. 591, 601; *Thurloe State Papers,* ed. T. Birch (1742), IV, pp. 161, 698, 743; cf. ibid., V, pp. 37, 100, and Underdown, op. cit., pp. 192-4,

[17] Brailsford, op. cit., p. 624; Underdown, op. cit., pp. 123-4, 135, 172; Ashley, op. cit., Chapters 7-10; Marie

Gimelfarb-Brack, *Liberte, Egalite, Fraternite, Justice: la vie et l'oeuvre de Richard Overton, Niveleur* (Berne, 1979), pp. 287-304. Ashley argues that Wildman's intention throughout was to work for an English republic.

[18] G. E. Aylmer, *The State's Servants* (1973), p. 135.

[19] *Clarke Papers,* ed. C. H. Firth, III (1899), p. 189; P. A. Knachel, *England and the Fronde: the Impact of the English Civil War and Revolution on France* (Cornell UP, 1967), pp. 161-3, 197-214, 269.

[20] *Thurloe State Papers,* V, p. 775; *Mercurius Politicus,* No. 348, 5-17 February 1657, pp. 7587-92, 7604-8. Sindercombe had been one of the mutineers of 1649. He was a mortalist and believed in universal redemption.

[21] See my *Change and Continuity in Seventeenth-Century England,* pp. 173-7.

[22] Ashley, op. cit., pp. 103, 237, 253-4; A. Fletcher, *A County Community in Peace and War: Sussex, 1600-1660* (1975), pp. 332-3 (Wildman rack-renting); cf. Lucy Hutchinson, *Memoirs of the Life of Colonel Hutchinson* (Oxford UP, 1973), p. 198; *Seventeenth-Century Economic Documents,* ed. J. Thirsk and J. Cooper (Oxford UP, 1972), pp. 282-3.

[23] *Thurloe State Papers,* IV, pp. 179, 215, 333, 340; V. p. 241.

[24] Ashley, op. cit., pp. 103, 184, 207, 217; *State Papers Collected by Edward Earl of Clarendon* III (1786), pp. 219-20; Pepys, Diary, 6 December 1667. Pepys called Wildman 'the Fifth Monarchy Man', which is hardly accurate. On 12 December 1667 and 4 November 1668 he called him a Commonwealthsman.

[25] See Sir Robert Southwell's Diary, in *Diary of the Popish Plot,* ed. D. C. Greene (New York 1977), pp. 57, 60 1, 68, 99; cf. *Portland MSS,* II, p. 49.

[26] Ashley, op. cit., pp. 277, 299.

[27] J S. Morrill, *Cheshire, 1630-1660* (Oxford UP, 1974), p. 275.

[28] T. Gataker, *His Vindication of the Annotations by him published* (1653), p. 12

[29] Woolrych, *Commonwealth to Protectorate* (Oxford UP, 1982), pp. 130, 250.

[30] [Anon.], *The Levellers (Falsly so called) Vindicated* (1649), in *Freedom in Arms. A Selection of Leveller Writings,* ed. A. L. Morton (1975), pp. 314, 316. This pamphlet was signed by six troopers of regiments involved in the mutiny which ended at Burford in May 1649.

[31] See eg. Carte, op. cit., I, pp. 332-3; II, p. 69; cf. *Clarendon State Papers,* III, pp. 272-3. 'Their intention is a free Parliament', which would recall the King to rule as 'administrator and not master of laws'; cf. pp. 315, 431.

[32] W. C. Abbott, *Writings and Speeches of Oliver Cromwell* (Harvard UP, 1937-47), III pp. 435-6; cf. IV, p. 267. See p. 187 below.

[33] E.g. *Mercurius Politicus,* No. 354, 19-26 March, 1657, pp. 7674-5, cf. 9-16 October, 1656 p. 7315; W. Hughes, *Magistracy Gods Ministry* (1652), To the Reader (assise sermon preached at Abingdon); ed. G. F. Nuttall, *Early Quaker Letters from the Swarthmore MSS. to 1660* (1952, duplicated), p. 150; *The Political Works of James Harrington,* ed. J. G. A. Pocock (Cambridge UP, 1977), p. 292; Samuel Butler, *Prose Observations,* ed. H. de Quehen (Oxford UP, 1979), p. 74; cf. pp. 226, 283.

[34] Ashley, op. cit., pp. 133, 218.

[35] Ibid., pp. 128, 136; Woolrych, 'Last Quests for Settlement, 1659-1660', in *The Interregnum the Quest for Settlement, 1656-1660,* ed. G. E. Aylmer (1972), p. 193.

[36] *The Leveller* is reprinted in *Harleian Miscellany* IV (1744-6), pp. 515-21. Cf. *A Plea for the Peoples Good Old Cause* (October 1659) and *A Plea for the Peoples Fundamental Lib-erties and Parliaments* (1660 written autumn 1659).

[37] Woolrych, 'Last Quests', pp. 193-4, lists many of these pamphlets. He notes their lack of interest in the franchise.

[38] Edward, Earl of Clarendon, *The History of the Rebellion and Civil Wars in England,* ed. W. D. Macray (Oxford UP, 1888), VI, pp. 67-8.

[39] Ibid., pp. 69, 75-6.

[40] Ibid., p. 70. One recalls later revolutionaries who were deceived by Stalin, solely guilty of everything that had gone wrong.

[41] Ibid., pp. 71-3.

[42] Ibid., pp. 73-4.

[43] Ibid., pp. 75-8.

[44] Ibid., pp. 66-7, *Thurloe State Papers,* V, p. 395; Underdown, op. cit., pp. 193-4, 198.

[45] K. H. D. Haley, *William of Orange and the English Opposition, 1672-4* (Oxford UP, 1953), pp 28, 35-7, 70-1, 78-83, 116, 174, 194, 201-2; *Haley, The First Earl of Shaftesbury* (Oxford UP, 1968), pp. 314, 714-20.

[46] *VCH [Victoria County History], Worcestershire,* IV, p. 192.

[47] Nicholas Tindal's *Continuation of Rapin's History of England* (1744-5), IV, p. 682 (enthusiastic Levellers who pulled down enclosures and sought equality in 1724); E. P. Thompson, *Whigs and Hunters* (1975), p. 256 (Ledbury, 1735); Thompson, 'The Moral Economy of the English Crowd in the 18th Century', *P. and P. [Past and Present],* 50 (1971), p 126 (Newcastle in 1740); cf. P.J. Corfield, *The Impact of the English Towns* (Oxford UP, 1982), p 65; and my 'From Lollards to Levellers', in my *Religion and Politics in 17th Century England* (Brighton, 1986).

[48] J. Stoughton, *History of Religion in England* (1881), III, p. 411.

[49] M. C. Jacob, *The Newtonians and the English Revolution, 1689-1720* (Cornell UP, 1976), pp. 262, 268.

[50] *Englands New Chains Discovered,* in Haller and Davies, op. cit., p. 166.

[51] *State Trials* (1811), pp. 873-81; James Wellwood, *Memoirs of the Most Material Transactions in England for the Last Hundred Years* (1700), p. 173. Wellwood claimed to have been present when Rumbold uttered these words.

[52] Daniel Defoe, *The Consolidator,* printed with *The History of the Plague in London in 1665* (1840), p. 216. Partridge echoed it in 1708 (B. S. Capp, *Astrology and the Popular Press: English Almanacs, 1500-1800,* 1979, p. 229).

[53] D. M. Wolfe, *The Image of Man in America* (Dallas, 1957), p. 19.

[54] Winstanley, *The Law of Freedom and Other Writings,* p. 131.

[55] K. V. Thomas, 'Another Digger Broadside', *P. and P.,* 42 (1969), pp. 57-61.

[56] *WTUD,* esp. Chapters 7 and 8; Introduction to Winstanley, *The Law of Freedom;* 'The Religion of Gerrard Winstanley', in my *Religion and Politics in 17th century England* (Brighton 1986).

[57] *The Law of Freedom,* p. 232.

[58] *Religion and Politics,* pp. 3-10, 17-18, 29-37, 47; cf pp. 230 and 306 below.

[59] Ibid., pp. 5-6, 10; see p. 306 below.

[60] But cf. pp. 84, 88-9 below—Erbery.

[61] Ibid., pp. 5-6, 8, 28-9, 33, 48. For the anointing see pp. 304-9 below.

[62] I owe this point to Sheila Reynolds, 'Gerrard Winstanley: his Search for Peace' (unpubl. MA thesis, McGill University, 1976), pp. 54, 61.

[63] Woolrych, *Commonwealth to Protectorate,* p. 39.

[64] Winstanley, *The Law of Freedom,* pp. 275, 278-85

[65] Ibid., p. 389.

[66] *The Religion of Gerrard Winstanley,* p. 51.

[67] J. Alsop, 'Gerrard Winstanley's Later Life', *P. and P.,* 82 (1979), pp. 73-81; cf. R. T. Vann, 'The Later Life of Gerrard Winstanley', *Journal of the History of Ideas,* XXVI (1965), pp. 133-6, D. C. Taylor, Gerrard Winstanley in Elmsbridge (1982), pp. 4-5; Barry Reay, 'Early Quaker Activity and Reactions to it, 1652-1664' (unpubl. Oxford DPhil. thesis, 1979), p. 5.

[68] See for example F. H. Higginson, *A Brief Relation of the preaching of the Northern Quakers* (1653), p. 26; Francis Harris, *Some Queries* (1655), p. 23. I owe both these references to the kindness of Dr Barry Reay.

[69] Thomas Comber, *Christianity no Enthusiasm* (1678), pp. 92, 181; Thomas Tenison, *An Argument for Union* (1683), p. 8. I owe this last reference too to Dr Reay.

[70] S. J. Madge, 'Rural Middlesex under the Commonwealth', *Transactions of the London and Middlesex Archeological Societies,* N.S., IV, pp. 432-43; cf. [Anon.], *A Relation of the Cruelties and Barbarous Murthers . . . committed* [at] . . . *Enfield* (1659).

[71] For Joyce see *Harleian Miscellany,* VIII (1744-6), pp. 293-6 and Woolrych, Commonwealth to Protectorate, p. 259. Joyce was cashiered in September 1653, allegedly for saying that he wished the pistol pointed at Cromwell on Triploe Heath in 1647 had gone off. Joyce on the contrary claimed that the charge of treason resulted from a dispute over land purchase between himself and Richard Cromwell.

[72] A Captain Covell was cashiered in October 1650 in Scotland (eight years after enlisting in 1642?) for allegedly saying 'sin was no sin' and denying the humanity of Christ (C. H. Firth and G. Davies, *Regimental History of Cromwell's Army* (Oxford UP, 1940), I, pp. 69-70. But this Covell's Christian name

is given as Christopher.

[73] Covell, *A Declaration unto the Parliament* (1659), pp. 8, 17-22.

[74] W. Covell, *A Proclamation to all, of all sorts, high and low* (n.d.,?1654), single sheet. See also J. M. Patrick, 'William Covell and the Troubles at Enfield in 1659: A Sequel of the Digger Movement', *University of Toronto Quarterly,* XIV (1944).

[75] Rogers, *Life and Opinions of a Fifth-Monarchy Man,* pp. 328-9.

[76] Cornelius Plockhoy, *The Way to the Peace and Settlement of these Nations* (March 1659) and *A Way propounded to make the poor in these and other Nations happy* (May 1659), esp. p. 21. For *Areopagitica* see O. Lutaud, *Les Deux Revolutions d'Angleterre: documents politiques, sociaux, religieux* (Paris, 1978), p. 439. For the Harringtonians see pp. 194-9 below.

[77] M. C. Jacob, *The Radical Enlightenment: Pantheists, Freemasons and Republicans* (1981), p. 161.

[78] C. Robbins, 'Library of Liberty', *Harvard Library Bulletin,* 5 (1951), p. 17, quoted by J. R. Jacob, *Henry Stubbe: Radical Protestantism and the Early Enlightenment in England* (1983), p. 161.

[79] Philip Jenkins, A Social and Political History of the Glamorgan Gentry, c. 1650-1720 (unpubl. Cambridge Ph.D. thesis, 1978), p. 298. 1 am grateful to Dr Jenkins for permission to quote from this thesis, and to M. C. Jacob for drawing my attention to it.

[80] O. Lutaud, op. cit., p. 161.

[81] Professor Linebaugh pointed out that an 18th-century song, 'Property must be, Save the Queen, save the Queen' appears to be written to the tune of the Diggers' song ('All the Atlantic Mountains Shook': paper delivered at a conference on Radicalism in England and America in the Seventeenth and Eighteenth Centuries, Philadelphia, 14 November 1981). . . .

PRINCIPAL FIGURES

M. A. Gibb (essay date 1947)

SOURCE: "Leader of the Levellers," in *John Lilburne the Leveller: A Christian Democrat,* pp. 160-86. London: Lindsay Drummond, 1947.

[*In the following essay, Gibb analyzes John Lilburne's leading role in the Leveller movement. In examining the petitions and pamphlets Lilburne authored or co-authored with other prominent Leveller figures, Gibb asserts Lilburne's influence on the party's ideology.*]

> '*I am confident that it must be the poor, the simple and mean things of the earth, that must confound the mighty and the strong*'.
>
> RICHARD OVERTON.

'Well boys, you have done your work, and may go play, unless you will go fall out amongst yourselves', remarked old Sir Jacob Astley good-humouredly to the Parliamentary soldiers who had taken him prisoner at Stow-in-the-Wold early in 1646. It was a shrewd comment.

The New Model had proved its worth; after the victory at Naseby, Fairfax and Cromwell, in a brilliant series of battles and sieges in the West country, had reduced the last strongholds of the Royalist cause, and the capture of Astley marked the final destruction of the King's last field force. Early in May the King fled to the Scots, and in June, with the surrender of Oxford, the first civil war was over.

Nevertheless, the appeal to the arbitrament of force had proved as inconclusive as ever; the questions at issue were not such as could be settled by the sword. The effect of the first Civil War had been the transference of power to the men who had forced the struggle, with this end in view: the bourgeois squires in Parliament, and in so far as it had clipped Charles's wings the Civil War would seem to have been fought not altogether in vain. Parliament's difficulty now lay in the fact that its first appeals for support, issued in 1642-3, were capable of wide interpretation; that they had indeed thrown up concepts of popular power in a sense at present highly inconvenient. The present conduct of Parliament certainly did not approximate very closely to that of a body which had just vindicated the cause of liberty. So far the only liberty secured would seem to be that of the Presbyterian oligarchy in Parliament and City to impose its will, while popular petitions were burned and popular spokesmen thrown into prison. It now seemed to men who had entered the war in the spirit of crusaders for liberty against a tyrant that they had been betrayed; that one despotism had been exchanged for another, while none could say whether the new might not prove worse than the old. To many—men such as Lilburne and Overton—it was apparent that under cover of ideologies they had been asked to fight for the power of a particular class; that never had the common liberty been intended, or indeed conceived as anything save Edwards' 'anarchy of the promiscuous multitude', to be avoided at all costs. Nevertheless, Parliament was now to suffer for the over-simplification of its own philosophy in the war's early stages. 'If I be called a state heretic', asserted Lilburne, 'I answer for myself that the Parliament's own declarations hath made me so, and if I be deluded and deceived, they are the men that have done it'.[1] Whatever the treatment the Long Parliament might mete out to Lilburne, it could not escape the fact that he had never swerved from his adherence to the principles for which the war had ostensibly been fought, principles actually formulated by its own declarations at the outbreak of hostilities. True, the spirit of Pym found no counterpart in such men as Holles and Stapleton, who now led the Commons; yet even Pym would have shrunk from Lilburne's logical application of his premises. No understanding was possible between Lilburne and the present Parliament; their concepts of liberty were fundamentally opposed. That such a Parliament should seek to crush John and his friends was inevitable; it was, however, its capital blunder. 'By its injudicious treatment of the most popular man in England', writes Dr. Gooch, 'Parliament was arraying against itself a force which only awaited an opportunity to sweep it away'.[2]

To a dispassionate observer it would have appeared obvious that Lilburne's and Overton's recent appeals to the House of Commons to assume the place they assigned it as supreme power in the constitution were destined to failure. That they continued such efforts is evidence of their desire to work through traditional channels, and their reluctance to recognize that as a representative institution the present Parliament was totally inadequate. Final conviction, however, was forced upon them, by the Commons' treatment of the petitions drawn up during the early months of 1647, probably by Walwyn, which aimed at educating public opinion in the programme so far pursued by the radicals. With Lilburne and Overton behind bars, outside pressure must be brought to bear upon the House of Commons. It is significant that there was still no attempt to act save through Parliamentary channels, and that at first the party which was gradually being welded into a unity by the sympathy evoked for Lilburne and Overton, did not appeal to the only other power in the state which had the force to back its demands—the Army. This very reasonable attitude, in the early stages of the Leveller Movement, is sig-nificant evidence of the probable influence of William Walwyn.[3] Believing all things capable of settlement by argument, if only one could argue long enough, he did not despair of effecting his purpose through present institutions of government. Eschewing always the appeal to force, and sensible, as an older man and reputable citizen, of the desirability of keeping on the right side of the law, he went quietly about the process of attempting to convince his opponents by reasoned exposition. Moreover, he shunned personal publicity when possible, so that it is consistent with his methods that the influence behind these early petitions is rather obscure.

The Leveller party[4] was born in these early months of 1647, when the Commons rejected petition after petition expressing sympathy with Lilburne and Overton, demanding their release and practical reform on the lines indicated in their pamphlets. The 'large' petition, the most important, was brought prematurely before the House on 15th March; a second in support of this, was condemned; while on 20th May the Commons' answer to the formal presentation of the 'large' petition was to order it to be burned at the hand of the common hangman. A few days later appeared a pamphlet, *Gold Tried in the Fire,* defending the recent petitions and recounting their fate. Not until the following year was the 'large' petition actually published.[5]

The petition was undoubtedly, as Professor Pease remarks, a party manifesto. It opened with expressions of disappointment in the outcome of the Civil War; true, Star Chamber, the Court of High Commission and Episcopacy had been swept away, and ship money and other illegal patents abolished, but the old oppressions had only disappeared to give place to new. 'We still find the nation oppressed with grievances of the same destructive nature as formerly, though under other notions'. Condemning the claim of the Lords to criminal jurisdiction over commoners as against popular sovereignty, and comparable to the tyranny of Star Chamber, it further attacked the monopoly of the Merchant Adventurers, tithes, imprisonments for debt, the extortions of prison-keepers and gaolers, and the great social scandal that 'thousands of men and women are permitted to live in beggary and wickedness all their life long, and to breed their children in the same idle and vicious course of life'. A final condemnation was reserved for the spirit of religious intolerance which stalked the land, and the House of Commons was besought to fulfil its purpose in taking a leading part for 'freedom and deliverance from all kinds of grievances and oppressions'.

The positive programme whereby this might be effected forms the basic policy of the Leveller party. The Commons must free themselves from the 'negative voice' of King and Lords; all sentences, fines or imprisonments imposed otherwise than by 'due course of law' must be revoked; no one is to be imprisoned for refusing to answer interrogatories; all statutes, oaths or covenants establishing penalties for non-conformity in religion must be abolished and no man be punished as a 'sectary' for preaching his opinion 'lest the most necessary truths and sincere professions thereof may be suppressed'; the Merchant Adventurers must be dissolved; and the laws translated into English in a form accessible to all. Furthermore, tithes and imprisonment for debt should be removed, the character of prisonkeepers more carefully inquired into and their extortions checked, while some scheme be set on foot whereby vagrancy might be cured. The lofty tone of the pamphlet is maintained in the final exhortation to the Commons:

"We trust the God of your good success will manifest the sincerity of our intentions therein, and that our humble desires are such, as tend not only to our own particular, but to the general good of the Commonwealth, and proper for this honourable house to grant, without which this nation cannot be safe or happy; and that he will bless you with true Christian fortitude, suitable to the trust and greatness of the work you have undertaken, and make the memory of this Parliament blessed to all succeeding generations".

Insisting thus upon the abolition of prerogative rights in government and in commerce, upon liberty of conscience and of speech, upon judicial reform, prison reform, and a more searching treatment for the problem of vagrancy, the large petition epitomizes the Leveller agitation to date. That it was a pro-gramme not for one Parliament, but for three hundred years, is self-evident; and there can be no doubt that any attempt to impose such a scheme, ready made, upon the England of 1647 must have been foredoomed to failure. Lilburne, Walwyn and Overton do, it is true, show in their pamphlets a sound recognition of the necessity for far-reaching educational reforms before democracy is possible, and it would be absurd to deny the value of their proposals.[6] Lilburne was quite right when he placed the success or failure of the petition as secondary to its propaganda value: 'the promoting of it would beget understanding and knowledge in the people, when they would hear it and read it and discourse upon it; and if nothing but that were effected, our labour would not be totally lost, for nothing did more instate tyrants in the secure possession of tyranny than ignorance and blindness in the people'.[7] All this is true; but the Levellers are, perhaps, over-optimistic of the social and moral effects of education, a defect they hold in common with many enthusiasts of the 'left'. In envisaging the public enlightenment that must of necessity precede any democratic settlement, they think of the public as infinitely impressionable, open to conviction by reason and persuasion, capable of their own high idealism and perfectionism. Divine reason, they believe, is present in each and every individual; educate the people, and theirs is the voice of God. 'Vox populi, vox Dei'. They never came to power, but had they done so they would have been forced to realize the necessity in social relationships of the contingent decision, they would have been forced to grapple with the problem of human moral weakness, the baser practices of the ugly struggle for survival soon to be depicted by Hobbes. At present it seemed to the Levellers that only ignorance prevented the people from assuming their heritage; there was a certain amount of truth in this, of course, but when they chose to ignore the moral problem they approached the deep issues of human destiny in the fatal spirit of 'Renaissance Man'.

The radicalism of the present pamphlet was certainly a shock for the existing House of Commons, and when it came before them in the petition of May their displeasure was manifest in the terse and unsatisfactory comment 'the House doth mislike this petition'. A certain Browne was committed to prison for agitating for a more explicit reply.[8] When the petitioners became so importunate as to try to force the Commons' hand the latter showed their attitude in ordering the burning of the large petition by the common hangman. By so doing, declared Overton, they burned the Great Charter itself; to Walwyn it would no doubt appear that they had burned even more.[9]

Lilburne and his followers now developed the theory that since the House of Commons had violated the trust reposed in it by burning the petition and failing to 'free' the nation, it had lost the power originally vested in it by the people, to whom that power now reverted. The kingdom, they said, was thus in a state of nature. This idea was elaborated by Lilburne and Overton in a pamphlet significantly entitled *The Outcryes of Oppressed Commons*. Announcing their intention to appeal to the people against Parliament, the authors made serious charges against the present House of Commons which, they declared, was 'more studious and industrious in unjustly dividing amongst themselves hundred thousands of pounds of the Commonwealth's money, than in actual doing to us (in whom all and every the Commons of England are concerned . . .) either justice or right, according to their duty and their often sworne oaths'.[10] The right to petition Parliament was one of the fundamental rights and privileges of the people; to support this contention they quoted the Parliamentary declaration of 2nd November, 1642, which declared that 'it is the liberty and privilege of the people, to petition unto them (Parliament) for the ease and redress of their grievances and oppressions'. A statute of Edward III was somewhat irrelevantly dragged in, while a further appeal to Coke's *Institutes* more cogently supported the case. Yet far from studying the distress of the people, or making any effort to alleviate their miseries, the present House of Commons seemed, to Lilburne and Overton, rather 'to study ways how to increase mischief and grievances, and to involve the generality of the people in an everlasting case of confusion, by making their wills and lusts a law, their envy and malice a law, their covetousness and ambition a law, for we for our parts are necessitated to declare (with anxiety of spirit) that we can obtain no justice nor right at their hands'.[11] The activities of those who petitioned on their behalf, and the fate of their petitions, were recalled; and the pamphlet ended by referring to the fundamental law, which existed for the benefit of 'every particular individual man in the kingdom', and which Parliament was bound to observe, or forfeit its power. By an appeal to this law, concluded the authors, had Parliament justified its resistance to the King; by the same principle they would now resist Parliament.[12]

In July Overton restated and elaborated the theory of the sovereignty of the people in his *Appeale from the degenerate Representative Body the Commons of England, assembled at Westminster, to the Body represented*. A firm and logical statement of the new theories of individualism, this pamphlet advanced such premises as that 'all betrusted powers, if forfeit, fall into the hands of the betrusters, as their proper centre, and where such a forfeit is committed, there it disobligeth from obedience and warranteth an appeal to the betrusters, without any contempt or disobedience to the powers in the least', and again, 'that all authority is fundamentally seated in the office, and but ministerially in the persons; therefore, the persons in their ministrations degenerating from safety to tyranny their authority ceaseth and is only to be found in the fundamental original, rise and situation thereof, which is the people, the body represented'. The law of nature and of necessity demanded this power in the individual to resume the authority delegated by him, if used against him. It was the law of self-preservation. Ending with a direct and stirring appeal to the people, the pamphlet besought them to rise with the Army, and evict the present Parliament: 'Come, come, now is no time to sit thrumming of caps. If they will not give us leave to use our tongues and our pens to present and make known our grievances, we must take leave to make use of our hands and swords for the defence and redemption of our lives, our laws and our liberties'. This was a more radical, and more carefully considered, analysis of the foundations of political power in England than had previously appeared in Leveller pamphlets; its two main premises, the idea of contract and of the fundamental law are basic to Leveller theory, and their formulation becomes more exact until they culminate in the *Agreement of the People*. Some further examination of these concepts becomes essential if we are to understand the significance of what follows.

The contract theory advanced in *England's Birthright, The Outcryes,* and, more definitely, in Overton's *Appeale . . .* is quite clearly the *gesellschaftsvertag* or *pacte d'association.*[13] This is the contract theory proper, which pre-supposes a number of individuals living together in a state of nature, agreed together to form an organized society. It is primarily an act of association establishing the body politic, and is viewed throughout in abstract terms. It is not intended to be interpreted as an historical act. Tacitly admitted and recognized, this social compact is probably conceived by the Levellers as in some form the basis of all societies. Originating in the rational faculty of man, which impels him to seek security and personal fulfilment through co-operation with his fellows, it naturally postulates the welfare of society as the end of good government. Hence its insistence upon the public weal: *salus populi, suprema lex*. Issuing in a definite, though mythically rather than historically conceived, act, it envisages law as the bond which binds the society thus established by con-

sent. In the first instance this law is the law of reason. Only later can the law be conceived, in Lilburne's sense, as an admixture of this rational law and the empirical law of custom which has grown up in the course of historical evolution. It will be appreciated that the arguments of the contract theory are, throughout, essentially artificial. But reason, the public weal and safety, expressed in concrete terms of law, are the recurrent themes.

Government is an expression of the general will, and restrains individual liberty by the application of force in the interest of the whole. This must be the test of every application of force. What place, then, has liberty in the contract idea? The individual is free in the civil sense if his natural liberty is only restricted by laws made for the common weal, for the aim of society is not to destroy individual liberty but to take it and to give it back in a better form. This idea is perfectly consonant with the idea of liberty because it operates when (and only when) the individual has freely consented to this arrangement. So the genesis of government by consent. We shall meet it soon in the famous words of Colonel Rainborough: 'Every man that is to live under a government ought first by his own consent to put himself under that government'. This is the best form of freedom attainable in human society; for it is recognized that liberty is relative, not absolute, and must be bounded by the terms of the contract and guarded by law.

Now arises the real test of the contract idea, and, incidentally, of that of democracy. It is abundantly invoked in the disputes which follow, so it is worth while to consider it in advance. Obviously a basic assumption lies hidden in the above theorizing: that if the people is consulted in the proper way we may implicitly trust its judgement on the question of the general good. This idea is presumably founded upon the premise that the state, being composed of individuals banded together for the preservation of their rights, cannot have any interests contrary to those rights. As an abstraction this would seem a reasonable supposition, for in every collective act the community ought to act to its own advantage. How to explain the fact that historically communities do not so act on all occasions, is the problem posed by Leveller opponents throughout. Lilburne, as we have seen, finds his most effective solution in the empirical arguments of historical fact. Hence his references to the 'Norman Yoke', the false laws brought in at the Conquest, and his systematic idealization of the Anglo-Saxon system. 'Our ancestors of old lived in the highest pitch of perfect liberty, and we now in dejected servility; we are not used as free men but as abjects, yea, as mere slaves'. The idea is frequently encountered in Parliamentary declarations of 1642-3 and finds expression in many Leveller pamphlets.[14] This exposition of a supposed mistake made by the people in bargaining away their true liberties and submitting themselves to an artificial bondage, points the way to the remedy, which again is central to Leveller theory and is extraordinarily penetrating. The public must be educated; by which is meant something over and above a general cultural education. Education in the nature of their liberties is the sense intended and the medium to be employed is propaganda. Lilburne was always quick to reiterate that while the people are not easily corrupted, they are peculiarly subject to deception. Here we have at once the strength and the weakness of democracy.

Lilburne's 'General Proposition' appended as postscript to *The Freeman's Freedom Vindicated* gives his clearest explanation of his views on the creation of man, man's fall from perfection, corruption, and entrance into society. It is worth quotation in full:

> "God, the absolute sovereign Lord and King of all things in heaven and earth, the original fountain and cause of all causes, who is circumscribed, governed and limited by no rules, but doth all things merely and only by his sovereign will and unlimited good pleasure, who made the world and all things therein for his own glory, by his own will and pleasure gave man, his mere creature, the sovereignty (under himself) over all the rest of his creatures (Gen. I, 26, 28, 29) and endued him with a rational understanding, and thereby created him after his own image. (Gen. I, 26-7 and 9-6). The first of which was Adam . . . made out of the dust or clay, out of whose side was taken a rib, which by the sovereign and absolute mighty creating power of God was made a female . . . called Eve. Which two are the earthly original fountain . . . of all and every particular and individual man and woman . . . in the world since, who are, and were, by nature all equal and alike in power, dignity, authority, and majesty, none of them having by nature any authority, dominion or magisterial power one over or above another; neither have they, or can they exercise any, but merely by institution or donation, that is to say, by mutual agreement or consent, given, derived, or assumed by mutual consent and agreement, for the good benefit and comfort each of other, and not for the mischief, hurt or damage of any; it being unnatural, irrational . . . wicked and unjust, for any man or men whatsoever to part with so much of their power as shall enable any of their Parliament men, commissioners, trustees, deputies . . . or servants, to destroy and undo them therewith. And unnatural, irrational, sinful, wicked, unjust, devilish and tyrannical it is for any man whatsoever, spiritual or temporal, clergyman or layman, to appropriate and assume unto himself a power, authority and jurisdiction, to rule, govern or reign over any sort of men in the world without their free consent, and whosoever doth it . . . do thereby, as much as in them lies, endeavour to appropriate and assume unto themselves the office and sovereignty of God (who alone doth, and is to, rule by his will and pleasure), and to be like their Creator, which was the sin of the devils, who not being content with their first station, but would be like God, for which sin they were thrown down into hell, reserved in everlasting chains under darkness, into the judgement of the great day (Jude, ver. 6). And Adam's sin it was, which brought the curse upon him and all his posterity, that he was not content with the station and condition that God created him in, but did aspire unto a better and more excellent, namely, to be like his Creator, which proved his ruin, yea, and indeed had been the everlasting ruin and destruction of him and all his, had not God been the more merciful unto him in the promised Messiah".[15]

Here is a theological version of the contract theory, the common form under which it appeared in contemporary writings, for the seventeenth century was still largely theocentric. The idea of contract blends well with the idea of the Fall; it also appears as a perfectly rational action. Faith and Reason are synthesized. Reformation theology and Renaissance humanism give the twofold religious and rational sanction for the establishment of democratic government. This philosophy reappears in *Regall Tyrannie Discovered,* and is presented in rather similar phraseology in Overton's *Arrow Against Tyrants.* In *London's Liberty in Chains* Lilburne also declares:

> "The Omnipotent God, creating Man in his own Image (which principally consisted in his reason and under-understanding) . . . made him Lord over the earth. . . . But made him not Lord, or gave him dominion over the individuals of mankind no further than by free consent, or agreement."[16]

While the idea of a *pacte d'association* is implicit in the sentence:

> All lawfull powers reside in the people, for whose good, welfare and happiness, all government and just policies were ordained."[17]

Characteristically Lilburnian is the idea of a partial transfer of original liberty in the social contract. This foreshadows the important reservations in the Agreement of the People, over which much dispute was to arise: it also links Lilburne in the direct line of Locke and the liberal theorists. We may note also Lilburne's version of the Fall, in man's pride, his aspiration for domination, his sin of self-aggrandizement, an interpretation very close to Milton's and, indeed, to Biblical tradition. Here Lilburne differs characteristically from Gerrard Winstanley, who saw the institution of property as evidence of the Fall, deducing therefrom a philosophy more akin to modern socialism than to modern democracy. In Lilburne tyranny and abject submission are alike viewed as wickedness, and implicit is the Miltonian aphorism 'none can love freedom heartily but good men.'[18]

In one important respect Lilburne goes further than Milton, and I am inclined to think it no mere accident of phraseology but evidence of a very interesting view. I refer to his inclusion of woman in his charter of freedom. Note his phrase 'every individual man and woman', and the implication that man and woman are 'equal in power, dignity, authority and majesty'. If this be so, it follows that woman has political rights on an equal footing with man, a by-product of the democratic theory already perceived by Lilburne's opponents with some considerable horror. It is consonant with Lilburne's actions to think that he did entertain this idea of the equal partnership of man and woman in civic affairs. Witness the part played by Elizabeth Lilburne in the struggle on hand. Further, the Petition of Women, presented by her in 1648 to which reference will later be made, once again advances similar views. It is, of course, extremely improbable that the women wrote it, and more likely that it expresses Lilburne's particular opinions. The preamble states: 'Since we are assured of our creation in the image of God, and of an interest in Christ equal unto men, as also of a proportionate share in the free-dom of this commonwealth'. Here is a clear assertion of spiritual and political equality, a contrast to Milton's frequent subjection of woman to man, as passion to reason, 'He for God only, she for God in him'. Lilburnian democracy becomes modern indeed if it be that it so included the idea of political parity between the sexes.

The events of the spring of 1647 played admirably into the hands of Lilburne and his associates, and made possible the Leveller approach to the Army. The challenge to the Presbyterian oligarchy came not merely from the Levellers—to whom they could reply by burning their petitions and imprisoning their spokesmen—but from the victorious New Model itself. Indeed, the moment forecast by Sir Jacob Astley had arrived: divided among themselves, the victors now began to argue with each other. The dispute concerned the residence of sovereignty, and on one point all parties were more or less agreed—it must never again be allowed to rest with the King.

How to achieve this, and where the sovereignty thus wrested from the monarchy should be placed, were problems more difficult of solution. Combined with the religious questions still at issue, they presented a formidable obstacle to all hopes of settlement.

In the perplexing quarrel which ran its tortuous course from 1647 until after the execution of the King, four main groups are discernible: the three broad divisions of the Puritan party—the Presbyterians, the more moderate Independents, represented by Cromwell and Ireton, and the radical Independents, represented by Lilburne, Walwyn, Overton and their disciples. Outside these three groups stood the Erastians.[19]

The edges of the three Puritan divisions tended to blur; in particular the party of the centre—as the more moderate Independents may be designated[20]—shared some of the characteristics of both right and left, and could even, to a certain extent evoke the sympathy and support of the Erastians. The Pres-byterians were the most conservative of the Puritans: their chief interests being in the religious sphere the establishment of a Presbyterian system of Church government on the lines of that laid down by the Westminster Assembly, and the suppression of all other doctrines. Opposed to liberty, they sought only reform according to the Presbyterian pattern: in one noteworthy respect their system differs from Scottish Presbyterianism, in that the Church so established is to be controlled by the State. In this aim the Presbyterian party could, and did, count on the support of the Erastians. In the civil government it upheld the supremacy of Parliament (which it had so far managed to control), the sanctity of private property (the Bishops' and the King's alone excepted!) and a very limited monarchy—'an assurance', writes Professor Woodhouse, 'that the revolution had not been so very revolutionary after all'.

The moderate Independents were sympathetic with the Presbyterian aims in civil government, sharing in particular their respect for private property. Their religious settlement, however, they could only regard with disfavour, and demanded toleration, even while appearing to agree with the proposal for a state-controlled Presbyterian Church. This advocacy of toleration inevitably allied them to some extent with Lilburne and the parties of the left, whose radical theories they nevertheless feared as tending to the overthrow of established government and existing property rights. In the army debates the fundamental divergence between these two is evidenced in the clash of Ireton and Rainborough, both excellent orators and both clear thinkers. The one stands for property rights and existing engagements, the other for natural rights and government by consent. There was no real hope of compromise, but the policy of the existing Parliament drove the two into an uneasy alliance; against the tyranny of the Presbyterian oligarchy which controlled both Lords and Commons, and extended further into the City government itself, which had established its influence in the commercial life of London, and which threatened everywhere to set up a despotism of its own selfish interests, the Independents of the centre combined with 'the one genuinely democratic party thrown up by the Puritan revolution, the Levellers'.[21] The partnership was in the first place brought into being by the Parliamentary plans to get rid of the New Model army, plans whose injustice created in the army a quickened sense of its corporate unity, and furnished soil in which the seeds of Lilburne's ideas could germinate with remarkable fertility. The Levellers, for their part, were by now convinced of the futility of expecting justice from the present Parliament, and in their appeal to the people found the army an excellent medium through which to act.

As its declarations so frequently assert, this army was in truth no ordinary one:

> "Our army, made up chiefly of volunteers, have amongst them many men, both officers and men, of considerable birth, breeding and education, some scholars and university men, and many of them of approved piety and men of parts, who out of pity have engaged themselves in scattering the knowledge of God in the dark and ignorant parts of the kingdom. . . . We were not merely mercenary soldiers, brought together by the hopes of pay and the fortunes of wars".[22]

Since the withdrawal of the Presbyterian generals, the leading officers were created partly by promotion from the ranks, partly by recruitment from the propertied classes. Between such men would obviously be differences of opinion, but at first they worked in harmony. The common enemy was the present Parliament, compound of landed and great burgher interests, who, now that the King had been reduced to military impotence, had little affection for the men whose sacrifice and effort had made their victory possible. A year's pay was owing to the army, and Parliament had no mind to furnish the arrears. Hence its fatal effort at disbandment, a capital blunder. By furnishing the soldiers with tangible material grievances, Parliament gave the army a common platform which enabled officers and men to work in unison.

Around its camp fires in the winter of 1646-7 this extraordinary army debated politics and religion; the pamphlets of Lilburne, Walwyn and Overton were eagerly bought, passed round and discussed, and found a sympathetic audience. By the teaching of its unlicensed preachers the army was already predominantly Independent in religion: in its ranks were to be found representatives both of the centre party and of the left. Moreover, with the spread of Leveller theories there was a perceptible drift towards more radical views. Soon after Naseby Baxter had visited the camp, and discovered an 'undreamed of' state of affairs; the revolutionary spirit was spreading: 'I found many honest men of ignorance and weak judgements, seduced into a disputing vein, to talking for Church democracy or State democracy'. He attributed the phenomenon largely to the reading of Leveller pamphlets: 'a great part of the mischief was caused by the distribution of the pamphlets of Overton and Lilburne and others, against the King and the ministry and for liberty of conscience; and the soldiers in their quarters had such books to read when they had none to contradict them'.[23] By the spring of 1647, commented one newswriter, with some exaggeration, the army was 'one Lilburne throughout', and quoted his books as statute law.[24]

Lilburne and Overton, for their part, were not slow to recognize the importance of their new ally, now, as it were, a fifth estate of the realm. Such was his influence over the common soldier that Lilburne could, according to his own version, have broken prison and led an armed revolt against Parliament: 'I could have got so many to have followed me as would have enabled me with my sword in my hand to have done justice and execution upon those grand treacherous fellows and tyrants at Westminster',[25] he told Fairfax. Preferring, however, to work through constitutional channels, he did not put his military capacity to the test, but decided instead to play his part in the events whereby the army was becoming an articulate body, with an organization capable of expressing and enforcing its demands.

This development began with the putting into operation of the Parliamentary scheme for disbanding the army. The Civil War over, some reduction of the New Model was obviously necessary: it was proposed, however, to retain a force for the reconquest of Ireland. The plan included no provisions for arrears of pay, nor was there to be an Act of Indemnity covering deeds committed in the recent war; furthermore, there was no guarantee against being pressed for service outside England. Parliament's uncompromising attitude towards the soldiers' protests provided the force which welded the hitherto diverse and inarticulate revolutionary elements in the army into a solid whole, capable of resistance, and outside the power of Parliament to quell. 'Never were the spirits of men more embittered than now', was Cromwell's comment to Fairfax.[26]

Officers and men were bound by a common cause, and the latter at first looked to their leaders for guidance. Towards the end of March the army officers drew up a petition to Parliament demanding merely indemnity, payment of arrears, with provision for the widows and children of those who had fallen in the war, and studiously avoiding all reference to wider issues.[27] At the same time there is the first hint of action by the common soldiers: 'as for the petition', wrote one of Ireton's company, 'they now speak it openly that they will send it up with two out of every troop'.[28] This is clearly a foreshadowing of the appointment of the Agitators.[29]

The petition, moderate though it was, provoked a storm of opposition in the House of Commons. Robert Lilburne, John's brother and one of the leading radical spirits among the army officers, together with Pride, Ireton and the two Hammonds, were summoned before the bar of the House as chief signatories of the petition. The dispute continued far into the night, and as the meeting thinned out Denzil Holles hastily drew up a resolution declaring the promoters of the petition enemies to the state, and the document itself highly seditious.[30] Not before Holles and Ireton had come almost to the point of a duel were the five officers allowed to return to their regiments.

A Parliamentary commission sent down to army headquarters on 15th April met with no success, while the end of the month saw the establishment of what may be termed the democratic organ of the army. First eight cavalry regiments, then all the regiments, chose representatives according to the plan already indicated—two agents, or agitators, for each regiment. By these means the rank and file possessed their own leaders, and could enter into communication with their officers, with Parliament, and if necessary could appeal to the growing body of public opinion, especially in London and the surrounding counties.

The influence of Lilburne, and of Leveller ideals, is clearly discernible both in the conduct and in the manifestos of the Agitators. Men of unusual qualities, for the most part, they were capable of holding their own, whether in Council debate or before the bar of the House of Lords. 'We are most of us but young statesmen', said Allen on one occasion,[31] yet their grasp of politics, and their ability to state their case, are worthy of Lilburne himself. In such men as Sexby, Allen, or Lockyer, the Levellers found invaluable allies; in turn, the Agitators were able to profit by Leveller example.

The programme of the Agitators ran beyond that expressed in the first petition of the army. The soldiers' material grievances were again emphasized, but beyond these there was an attempt to lay down the lines for a settlement of the kingdom according to the principles of justice and freedom.[32] Moreover, a significant demand for liberty of conscience also makes its appearance; by its insistence on religious toleration, therefore, the army drew still closer to the Leveller party.

In May the Agitators' plans for action were complete; the organization was perfected, even to its secret code, and already the scheme was on foot whereby the army hoped to secure the person of the King[33]—a valuable card to play against Parliament. When Cornet Joyce appeared at Holmby House on 2nd June for this purpose, Charles, naturally suspicious, asked to see his commission, and was told significantly by Joyce (pointing to his 500 troopers), 'Here is my commission.'[34] As Professor Woodhouse has remarked, a dozen years of military rule were heralded in the Cornet's reply. Whether his action had been sanctioned by Cromwell or not must be for ever uncertain,[35] but that the movement suited the plans of the Lieutenant-General is beyond doubt. It had, however, indicated the potential power of the common soldier to act without the officers' control; some means, therefore, must be devised for preserving discipline and co-ordinating the diverse elements in the ranks.

The first step was taken in the 'Solemn Engagement of the Army', signed by both officers and men in a general rendezvous at Newmarket on 5th June. Avowing their intention to promote 'such an establishment of common and equal right and freedom to the whole, as all might equally partake of', they bound themselves in a sort of covenant with the generality of the people. Further, they now created the famous General Council of the Army consisting of the general officers, and two officers and two soldiers from each regiment.[36]

Consolidating and amplifying the 'Solemn Engagement', the New Model issued a declaration on 14th June, which has gone down to history as the classic statement of its aims and character:

> "We were not a mere mercenary army, hired to serve any arbitrary power of a state, but called forth and conjured by the several declarations of Parliament, to the defence of our own and the people's just rights and liberties".[37]

Already, however, the beginning of a cleavage between the army officers and the forces of the left is visible, and this declaration, drawn up by Ireton, seems to make a determined effort to steer away from the theories of Lilburne and the Levellers. Parliament is accorded its proper constitutional position, the House of Commons entrusted only with the people's *interest* in the supreme power of the common-wealth, and, after due provision has been made for new elections, the observance of the Triennial Act, and the protection of Parliament against the King's right to arbitrary dissolution, the King is to be restored to limited power; and, says Ireton, speaking now for the people, 'we shall hereby, for our part, freely and cheerfully commit our stock or share of interest in this Kingdom, into this common bottom of Parliaments'. Unfortunately, the common bottom was to spring many leaks, while those with no stock or share of interest in the kingdom were also demanding a right to be heard. The battle between 'interest' and 'right' was about to begin.

From his captivity in the Tower Lilburne was following events with close attention. News came to him from Leveller agents in the army of 'divers great ones' who hoped to 'cool the business on foot'; it was his special effort, therefore, to fan it once more into flame. Sending his long-suffering wife to the army headquarters at St. Alban's, together with the Leveller agents, he stimulated the radical elements to demand decisive action. At the same time, he was not averse to including a pressing request that steps should be taken to secure his own liberty.[38]

His activities bore fruit. Urged forward by the Agitators, the officers consented to more stringent measures. On 16th June the Army Council preferred charges against eleven leading Presbyterian members of Parliament, including Holles, Stapleton, Lewes, Clothworthy and Waller. On the 26th further pressure was brought to bear on the House by the army's march towards London, which 'put the Parliament and City into a shrewd fright'.[39] The eleven members thereupon withdrew from the House, the City submitted, and the army retreated from Uxbridge to Reading. It was to prove a premature retirement, but the power of the New Model had been forcibly demonstrated.

At Reading Commissioners tried to effect an agreement between Parliament and Army, while Ireton began the preliminary draft of his *Heads of the Proposals,* founded on his declaration of 14th June. The reactionary forces seized their chance, and the purging of the Independents from the London militia was effected. The story goes that one Lieutenant-Colonel, told by the City authorities that 'he must fight against all malignants, sects and sectaries and *all godly persons* that shall come to oppose the City', professed extreme bewilderment, answering: 'Gentlemen, I had thought you all of you professed godliness. For my part, I do, and therefore I shall not engage against any godly man'. Alderman Gibbs qualified his statement by explaining that 'if any, out of pretence of godliness should come to oppose them, that he should fight against such'.[40] The tale affords an amusing example of the humourless Presbyterian mind.

As soon as the news reached Reading the Agitators petitioned the General for an immediate march on the capital. The influence of the Leveller party is seen in the accompanying demand for the release of Lilburne, Overton and others imprisoned for the publication of the unlicensed pamphlets.[41] A more direct appeal was made by Lilburne personally to Cromwell, in a letter warning him dramatically that the effect of delay might be to 'involve the Kingdom in a large effusion of blood', and begging him 'immediately to march with a declaration of peace of love to the body of the city; the doing of which will enable your friends here, I confidently hope, to do your work for you in sequestering the eleven members'.[42]

On 16th July the Army Council debated the Agitators' petition. Fearing to use a force which might grow beyond their control, Cromwell and Ireton hesitated to play too much into the Levellers' hands; they had no wish to destroy the Parliament which gave them their legal authority by its commission, and set up the (to them) unknown quantity of the Levellers' 'Representative'. The Army's aim, they urged, should be rather to unite with the Independent—or 'honest'!—element in the House of Commons: 'it hath been in most of our thoughts that this Parliament might be a reformed and purged Parliament, that we might see there men looking at public and common interests only', said Cromwell, with Pride's purge already in his mind. Urging that time should be given to drawing up a plan of settlement, that more could be gained by 'treaty' than

by force, Cromwell finally carried the day by an appeal to Providence, which had, he said, brought them so far and would, no doubt, point the way for the future. Cromwell, it will be noted, is here as always, realist first, man of religion second.

Professing his satisfaction in Cromwell's proposal of a four days' delay, Lieutenant Chillenden felt the imprisonment of Lilburne and his fellows 'weighty upon his spirit', and besought that the problem of their release should be given special attention. Meanwhile, from his 'watch tower in the Tower of London', John reinforced these demands in a letter to Fairfax, which declared passionately:

> "What you shall resolve to do for me, do it speedily and vigorously, for perish I can not and will not, if I can help it, and if nothing will serve the two Houses but my causeless destruction I am necessitated like a plain dealer . . . to protest unto your Excellency that if speedily they will not do me justice I will appeal to all the Commons of England, and the private soldiers of your Army, and do the best I can to set them about the ears, to cut their tyrannical throats, though I perish with them".[43]

He was spared the necessity of substantiating his threats by the rapid and dramatic developments which followed.

On 26th July the Houses were invaded by the London mob, who held down the Speaker in his chair, forced a vote for the immediate invitation of the King to London, and the repeal of the militia ordinance. Next morning, when Parliament assembled, it was found that both Speakers, eight peers, and fifty-seven members of the Commons were absent, having fled to the army, while the eleven sequestered members had miraculously reappeared. The remaining body proceeded to elect new Speakers, and made preparations for the defence of the City. It was the signal for action by the army. On 6th August Fairfax and Cromwell entered the capital 'in most martial and triumphant equipage'.[44]

The Presbyterians in the Commons remained intransigent. On 9th August they voted down a resolution that all business transacted in the Speaker's absence was null and void; and on the following day rejected a resolution approving the army's action. To Cromwell only one course was clear, at which he had already hinted in the recent debate: 'These men will never leave till the army pull them out by the ears', he is reported to have said.[45] At this point he was met with the startling and unexpected opposition of Fairfax, whose sudden and unwonted self-assertion may have been partly due to the influence of his Presbyterian wife and friends, but more to his aversion to an action which could not be defended on any constitutional grounds. Fearing the prospect of military rule, which he saw clearly foreshadowed in this proposal, he hoped, by refusing his assent 'to divert this humour of the army from being statesmen to their more proper duty as soldiers'.[46] It was a singularly vain hope.

Achieving his object by the show of force, without its use, Cromwell marshalled a body of troops in Hyde Park on 29th August—a reminder of the power at his disposal—and stationed more soldiers outside Westminster, while he himself strode into the House of Commons, forced the passage of an ordinance sanctioning all actions committed since the military occupation of the City, and took steps to secure the Independent control of Parliament. Seven of the eleven members had fled the country; one was placed under arrest.

The Independents were, for the moment, the supreme political power in the State, but the dissensions in their ranks were becoming more open. Lilburne had taught the common soldier to distrust the aims of his officers—or Grandees, as they were now more commonly called—while the Grandees, for their part, dreaded the radicalism of the Levellers and their agents in the army. Nevertheless, their majority was not yet secure enough to enable them to dispense with their allies of the Left; common necessity drove the two into hesitant contacts and uneasy alliances. In their meetings and debates, to the recorder of which posterity must be for ever grateful, is seen the quality of the Puritan mind as it tacked its problems; in particular the Leveller idea that most problems are capable of settlement by discussion. The struggle was between two rival fundamental conceptions of the State, between government by privilege and government by consent. Was the State to be controlled by a propertied minority in the interests of wealth, or was it to be animated by the ideal of the common weal, even to the extent of the subordination of the claims of property and privilege? In the divergence between these viewpoints may be measured the whole extent of the chasm which yawned between Cromwell and his 'gentlemen Independents', and 'Freeborn John' and his Leveller associates.

Notes

[1] *A Whip for the present House of Lords,* p. 15.

[2] *English Democratic Ideas in the Seventeenth Century,* p. 124.

[3] See Haller, *Tracts on Liberty,* I, p. 115; Pease, *Leveller Movement,* p. 158.

[4] The term 'Leveller', usually used in a wholly derogatory sense, appears to have owed its currency to either Charles I or Cromwell. By Heath the Levellers were credited with a 'devilish intention' to 'invade all property and by a wild parity to lay all things in common!' *Chronicle* (1676), p. 131. *The Oxford Dictionary* gives the first example of the use of the word as 1644, and quotes Nedham: *The Case of the Commonwealth* (1650) as the source. In this pamphlet Nedham traces the origin of the term to the party's democratic proposals: 'because all persons have an equality of right to choose and be chosen . . . the promoters of this way are not improperly called Levellers', p. 2. Lilburne and his friends resented the term, and repeatedly denied the charge of levelling.

[5] Under the title: *'To the Right Honble. and Supreme Authority of this nation, the Commons in Parliament Assembled'.* It is reproduced in Haller, *Tracts,* III, p. 397.

[6] Cf. 'Certain Articles for the good of the Commonwealth' in Overton's *Appeale:* 'That all ancient donations for the maintenance and continuance of free schools, which are . . . converted to any private use, and all such free schools which are destroyed . . . may be restored and erected again, and that all parts or counties . . . destitute of free schools for the due nurture and education of children, may have a competent number of such schools founded, erected and endowed at the public charge of those respective countics and places so destitute, that few or none of the freemen of England may for the future be ignorant of reading and writing'.

[7] *A Whip for the present House of Lords,* p. 13.

[8] *Commons' Journals,* V, p. 162; *Gold Tried in the Fire,* p. 9.

[9] *Commons' Journals,* V, pp. 179-80; Overton, *An Appeale . . . ,* p. 14.

[10] *The Outcryes . . . ,* p. 3.

[11] Ibid., p. 8.

[12] Ibid., p. 12.

[13] See J. W. Gough, *The Social Contract* (Oxford, 1936).

[14] In Lilburne's writings there is an alternation between ideas based on the contract theory proper, and those derived from the contract of government—the *herrschaftsvertag,* or *pacte de gouvernement,* which presupposes a society already formed. In *Legal Fundamental Liberties* (1649) he speaks of a pact between King and People rather on the lines of the Old Testament compacts: 'the King's irregular government, in the violating of the laws of England, the compact betwixt him and his people, which he in my judge-ment had then notably violated', and also 'it could not be rational for any man to appoint a compact to be betwixt two parties, but to bind both equally alike, King

as well as people; and not to keep the people bound to the express letter of the King's part, or any other, when the King, or that other, shall break his or theirs'. *L.F.L.,* p. 22. Lilburne would meet the idea often in his researches among Parliamentary literature of the Revolution, and he cites now this, now the more radical, contract theory as occasion demands. Overton, on the other hand, adheres more closely and logically to the idea of a *pacte d'association.* Further, it is not always possible to know how far Overton collaborated with Lilburne in the production of the 1646-9 political pamphlets. Overton relies far less upon documentation than does Lilburne, and is always inclined to argue rationally rather than empirically.

[15] *The Freeman's Freedom Vindicated: A Postscript containing a General Proposition.* Printed in Woodhouse, *Puritanism and Liberty,* p. 317.

[16] *London's Liberty in Chains,* p. 17.

[17] Ibid., p. 2.

[18] In *The Tenure of Kings and Magistrates* (1649) where these words appear occurs a passage strikingly similar to the one I have quoted from Lilburne's *Freeman's Freedom* . . . . The thought is marshalled in a more orderly fashion, but the ideas are virtually the same

> '. . . all men naturally were born free, being the image and resemblance of God Himself, and were, by privilege above all the creatures, born to command and not to obey: and that they lived so, till from the root of Adam's transgression falling among themselves to do wrong and violence, and foreseeing that such courses must needs tend to the destruction of them all, they agreed by common league to bind each other from mutual injury, and jointly to defend themselves against any that gave disturbance or opposition to such agreement. Hence came cities, towns, and commonwealths. And because no faith in all was found sufficiently binding, they saw it needful to ordain some authority that might restrain by force and punishment what was violated against peace and common right'.
>
> *Prose Works,* II, pp. 8-10.

[19] I follow Professor Woodhouse, who makes this division in his illuminating introduction to *Puritanism and Liberty* (1938).
[20] This is not to be identified with Cromwell's use of the term 'middle party', when speaking of the Erastian and other elements in the House of Commons. See *Puritanism and Liberty,* p. 16 ff.

[21] Woodhouse, *Puritanism and Liberty,* p. 17.

[22] *Vox Militaris.*

[23] *Reliquiae Baxterianae,* p. 53.

[24] Gardiner, *Great Civil War,* III, pp. 237, 245.

[25] *The Juglers Discovered* (1647), p. 4.

[26] Carlyle, *Letters and Speeches,* I, p. 260.

[27] *Clarke Papers,* I, pp. x-xi.

[28] Woodhouse, p. 21 ff; Gardiner, III, pp. 236-7.

[29] See below.

[30] *Commons' Journals,* V, p. 128; *Clarke Papers,* I, p. 2.

[31] Woodhouse, *Puritanism and Liberty,* p. 421.

[32] See *Advertisements for managing the councels of the Army,* ibid., p. 398.

[33] Woodhouse, *Puritanism and Liberty,* pp. 400, 401.

[34] Rushworth, *Historical Collections,* VI, p. 513.

[35] See *Clarke Papers,* I, pp. xxvi-xxx.

[36] Rushworth, VI, pp. 510-12.

[37] *A Representation from Sir Thomas Fairfax and the army under his command,* ibid., 564-70.

[38] *The Juglers Discovered,* p. 4.

[39] *Clarke Papers,* I, p. 132.

[40] Ibid., I, p. 152; Woodhouse, p. 26.

[41] The petition is printed in Woodhouse, pp. 409-10, with the debate which followed, pp. 410-20.

[42] *Jonah's Cry out of the Whale's Belly* (1647), p. 7.

[43] *The Juglers Discovered,* p. 8.

[44] *Seria Exercitus Series,* (1647).

[45] Ludlow, *Memoirs,* I, p. 189.

[46] Fairfax, *Short Memorial,* in *Arber's English Garner,* VIII, p. 570.

Margot Heinemann (essay date 1978)

SOURCE: "Popular Drama and Leveller-Style— Richard Overton and John Harris," in *Rebels and Their Causes: Essays in Honour of A. L. Morton,* pp. 69-92. London: Lawrence and Wishart, 1978.

[*In the essay that follows, Heinemann suggests that Richard Overton's involvement with the theater had an influence on his writing style once he began writing political pamphlets as a Leveller.*]

I

> They [the Levellers] wrote effectively not merely because they were exceptionally gifted or technically well equipped, though this can fairly be claimed at least for Overton and Walwyn, but because they wrote with a purpose clearly understood and deeply felt, and for an audience which they knew to be close and immediately responsive . . . . They stand near the head of one of the great streams of English prose, the stream which later was to include such mighty figures as Bunyan, Defoe, Paine, Cobbett and Shaw (A. L. Morton, 'The Leveller Style', in *The Matter of Britain,* 1966, p. 82).

Leveller rhetoric intensifies the strengths of common speech. Like the prose of Shakespeare's characters, it is packed with proverbs and colloquial sayings, using concrete and sometimes coarse images from everyday life for vividness and wit. It is rhythmic, energetic, irreverent, as well as weighty and dignified when the occasion requires.

One of the main influences on Leveller style was of course the Bible—the only book many of the rank and file will have known well—and the plain preaching based on it. I want to suggest that some of the most effective writers were also inspired by the other great source of instruction and culture open to ordinary Londoners, the theatres and the published texts of their plays. This seems pretty clear from the evidence of style alone; but it can also be shown that these men had personal links with the theatre which must have helped to form them and their writings.

That Parliamentary Puritans of every shade were united in hatred of the theatre—or at least its popular forms—is now recognized by most seventeenth-century historians to be a myth, though it still survives in many literary discussions. Prynne, who really was a committed opponent of plays, was typical not of Parliamentary Puritanism as a whole, but of the most rigid and dogmatic Presbyterian section within it, with which both Cromwellian Independents and Levellers later came into collision. Certainly he cannot be taken as a typical representative of the Puritan outlook in the 1630s among the masses of ordinary Londoners who later formed the basis of support for Lilburne.[1] While a considerable section of Puritan clergy (and of non-Puritan clergy for that matter)[2] and many Puritan merchants and businessmen opposed the theatre as a moral snare and a waste of precious time, Parliamentary-Puritan groups among the aristocracy included some of the best-known patrons of the drama, and among the more plebeian supporters of Parliament there must have been many, especially of the apprentices, who went to the popular playhouses.

Indeed many influential people with Puritan views in the twenty years before the civil war used or wished to use the theatre as a medium to influence wider opinion. Middleton's *Game at Chess* (1624), favoured by the Pembroke circle, is the most famous example. But even when the censorship tightened up further, and the companies were increasingly becoming 'royal slaves', many of the leading opposition peers, like the Earls of Essex, Warwick, Holland, Manchester and Pembroke, all interested in the drama, seem to have patronised the authors of plays with an obvious political reference (for instance Arthur Wilson, Massinger and Glapthorne).

Meanwhile the popular playhouses, such as the Red Bull and Fortune, from time to time put on plays which dramatised the criticisms and grievances of Londoners against the prerogative government. Most of these play-texts have disappeared, either destroyed by the censor or considered too 'low' and dangerous for printing; and we know of many only by the scattered records of their suppression. But enough remains to show that there was a large and profitable audience for 'opposition' drama: otherwise the companies would hardly have risked staging it. Thus there were anti-Spanish plays about foreign affairs, rousing sympathy for intervention on the Protestant side in Europe;[3] plays praising Magna Carta;[4] satirising bishops who went in for altars and ceremonies; libelling the ecclesiastical courts and their officers, and the rich citizens who ran the wine monopoly; criticising kings who raise taxes at their pleasure; and dealing (this in 1640) with Charles's unpopular Scottish expedition. It is a comprehensive list.[5]

When Parliament closed the theatres after the outbreak of war (September 1642) this did indeed gratify the anti-theatre lobby; but it was also an obvious security measure to prevent riotous assemblies and forestall possible Royalist propaganda (and, for that matter, the dramatising of popular grievances). Entertainment was held to be unsuitable anyway in a time of civil war, which called rather for discipline and prayer. Those dependent on the theatres as actors, musicians, theatre staff and dramatists faced disaster, and some of the best regular playwrights, we are told a year or so later, were 'for mere necessity compelled to get a living by writing contemptible penny pamphlets' (*The Actor's Remonstrance,* January 1643-4).

Judging by the number of anti-Laudian, anti-Strafford satires in semi-dramatic form printed around 1642, some of these hard-up dramatists were aiming at a Parliamentary-Puritan city audience rather than a Royalist one. These lively tracts return again and again to the same grievances, against the bishops and their Courts, against the persecution of Puritan ministers and the harrying of Puritan laymen, against rich Churchmen greedy for tithes and monopolists who squeeze money out of the poor. What made them saleable was the variety of forms, incidents, satirical images and semi-dramatic burlesques through which the same argument was presented so as to seem new and entertaining. Among these pamphlets are a number attributed to the most humorous and inventive of later Leveller pamphleteers, Richard Overton.[6]

II

The suggestion that Overton was at one time involved in the drama is supported by a good deal of varied evidence, none of it decisive in isolation, but convincing if one looks at it as a whole.

Little has hitherto been known about Overton's early life, but it has now been effectively shown that he was younger than earlier biographers supposed.[7] There is strong reason to believe that he was that Richard Overton who matriculated at Queens' College, Cambridge in 1631. His known work contains plenty of evidence that he was an educated man (if not necessarily University-educated), and Cambridge in the 1630s was a centre of Puritan scholarship and preaching. Nor was it only the gentry who went there. The town grammar schools, mostly non-fee-paying and often under strong Puritan influence, were sending boys in growing numbers in the early seventeenth century, who might come from families of farmers, craftsmen or small traders.[8] If we assume Overton *cannot* have had a University education, we then have to explain how he came by the Latin quotations and other signs of learning in his work. It seems more likely on the face of it that he did.[9]

In the same year that he matriculated (1631-32) Overton acted in a Latin comedy called *Versipellis* (meaning *The Turncoat*), the whole cast being Queens' men. One would dearly like to know more about this play. Unfortunately the text has disappeared; we know only that it was set in Antwerp, and that the author was probably Thomas Pestell (among whose papers it was found), who was a Leicestershire clergyman and chaplain to the Earl of Essex, and whose son, another Thomas Pestell, was one of the student actors.[10]

The elder Pestell was patronised by (and wrote flattering poems to or about) many of the Puritan peers who opposed the Laudian regime, notably Essex, Holland, Manchester, Warwick and Mandeville. He was summoned and fined by Laud's Court of High Commission in 1633 for scandalous behaviour, and especially for making insulting remarks and puns about Laud's Commissary Sir John Lambe:[11] so it seems not unlikely that' *Versipellis* had a satirical irreverent tone like that of many of Pestell's surviving poems.[12]

Cambridge in the 1630s was indeed a centre of religious conflict; for Laud was set on forcing the University, by tradition much more Puritan than Oxford, to conform to his rulings on doctrine, preaching and ceremonies. In 1636 he finally succeeded in establishing his own supremacy and right of visitation there, against strong opposition led by the Chancellor Lord Holland.[13] The leaders of the Laudians in Cambridge were Matthew (afterwards Bishop) Wren and John (later Bishop) Cosin, successively Masters of Peterhouse (next door to Overton's college of Queens'). Both figure much later in satirical pamphlets ascribed to Overton,[14] who seems to have kept an interest in Cambridge politics. His deep commitment to liberty of speech and discussion and religious toleration could well have been formed in the bigot-ridden University of that time.

The small world of college drama reflected these tensions. Though college plays were traditionally partly exercises in classical translation or imitation, partly slapstick, bawdy and schoolboy jokes, they might have topical local or social satire thrown in. The most gifted and popular Cambridge playwright of the time, Thomas Randolph, a young Fellow of Trinity somewhat over-inclined to drink and debt, was a protégé of Holland and patronised by the Puritan and anti-Laudian gentry.[15] His less gifted rival, Peter Hausted of Queens', after preaching over-zealously at the University Church in 1634 against nonconformity, was dragged from the pulpit, arrested and mobbed by the Puritan townsfolk. Randolph's most popular play, *Aristippus* (shown both at Cambridge and later in London), included anti-Spanish and pro-Parliament satirical references, which had to be cut out when it was printed and several times reprinted from 1630 to 1635 (the year in which Randolph died).[16]

Randolph's general line is to balance mockery of 'Spanish' Arminians and high-flyers with mockery of narrow Puritan sectaries. This was about as far as one could hope to go with safety in the 1630s, and perhaps as far as he or his Puritan-Anglican Court patrons wanted to go. But it's noticeable, even so, that the anti-Puritan satire is much less sharp than, say, Jonson's in *The Alchemist;* Randolph's sectaries are good-natured comics who can be won over to approve of plays with the right moral.[17]

Randolph, perhaps through Holland's influence,[18] apparently became regular dramatist at the Salisbury Court playhouse in London around 1629-31, and had two plays produced there, though he was back in Cambridge soon afterwards.[19] Overton is very likely to have known him, since Thomas Pestell of Queens', his fellow-actor in *Versipellis,* must have been at least acquainted with Randolph.[20]

We do not know what Overton was doing in the later 1630s, before we hear of him late in 1640 as printer and pamphleteer, nor whether he ever had any links with the professional theatre, though Southwark, where he was living about that time, was one of the main centres of the popular theatre. All we can say is that he was connected with Cambridge dramatic circles, especially with anti-Laudian ones, and that some contemporary college playwrights certainly did become London theatre poets. Moreover, his pamphleteering activity begins around the time when the theatres were in difficulties in 1640 and increases after they closed. It would not be surprising, however, if Overton later kept quiet about any theatre link, since his opponents among the right-wing Parliamentarians would certainly have used it against him. John Harris was never allowed by the Royalist newswriters to forget that he had once been a 'player's boy'.

III

Vox Borealis or the Northern Discovery, a left-Parliamentarian pamphlet-cum-newsbook of late 1640 or early 1641, is probably the earliest of Overton's writings that we have. Like some of his better-known tracts of 1645-6, this bears the bogus imprint of Marprelate:[21]

> Printed by Margery Mar-prelat, in Thwackcoat Lane, at the Sign of the Crab-tree Cudgel; without any privilege of the Cater-Caps, the year coming on 1641.

And even more than the original Marprelate tracts it is full of references to the theatre. In form it is a colloquial dialogue, supposed to take place in the English camp at Berwick, between Jamie, a dialect-speaking Scotsman recently returned from London bringing the political news, and Willie, who has been with the English army during the disastrous Scottish expedition. They both hate the Bishops; believe the English were defeated because the Scots had a good cause and they had not; and complain bitterly against the officers for their treatment of private soldiers, and especially for discharging them to find their own way home with 'but four or five shillings apiece to travel three hundred miles'.[22] At the end they look forward to seeing the Long Parliament, which is about to meet, bring down the power and pride of the Bishops when they get home.

After a brief run-down on the foreign and general news, Jamie describes several incidents where the Bishops have interfered with the London actors and put down their plays. The writer evidently knew a good deal about what was actually going on in the theatre world.

> In the meantime let me tell you a lamentable Tragedy, acted by the prelacy, against the poor players at the Fortune playhouse. . . . For they having gotten a new old play, called *The Cardinal's*

Conspiracy, whom they brought upon the stage in as great state as they could, with altars, images, crosses, crucifixes, and the like, to set forth his pomp and pride. But woeful was the sight to see how in the midst of all their mirth, the pursuivants came and seized upon the poor Cardinal, and all his consorts, and carried them away. And when they were questioned for it, in the High Commission Court, they pleaded ignorance, and told the Archbishop *that they took those examples of their altars, images,* and the like, *from heathen authors.* This did somewhat assuage his anger, that they did not bring him on the stage; but yet they were fined for it, and after a little imprisonment got their liberty. And having nothing left them but a few old swords and bucklers, they fell to act the *Valiant Scot,* which they played five days with great applause, which vexed the Bishops worse than the other, insomuch, as they were forbidden playing it any more, and some of them prohibited ever playing again.

Some details here may well have been added for satiric effect, such as the title *The Cardinal's Conspiracy* (referring to the common Puritan charge that Archbishop Laud expected to be made Roman Catholic Cardinal of England) and the reference to *The Valiant Scot,* a real play-title but intended here to recall to readers the defeat of the English by the Scottish Presbyterians in the Bishops' War, which in fact occurred much later than the players' fine.[23] But the attack on the play really happened, as we know from a letter of 8 May 1639 from Edmund Rossingham to Viscount Conway (C.S.P.D., 639, pp. 140-41).

> Thursday last (2 May) the players of the Fortune were fined £1000 for setting up an altar, a bason, and two candle-sticks, and bowing down before it upon the stage, and although they allege it was an old play revived, and an altar to the heathen gods, yet it was apparent that this play was revived on purpose in contempt of the ceremonies of the church.

Thus the actors had personally confronted Laud in the Court of High Commission, and had to argue their way out of it or risk losing their ears. We usually think of Laud now as the persecutor of Puritan preachers and theorists. But he was equally the terror of actors and dramatists who dared to criticise or satirise the regime or the Church, and this may be one reason why he is such a favourite personal target for Overton's satire in the early 1640s.

Vox Borealis goes on to recount another more recent incident of censorship and prosecution of players, though this time the reference is less clear Jamie says:

> There has been brave branding amongst the boys there [at London] upon this business, and they have divided themselves into three companies, the

Princes', the Queen's and the Duke of York's; the first were called the English, the second the French, and the Duke of York's were called the Scots company, who like brave blades were like to beat both the other two. And I can tell thee, that there has been such hot service amongst them, that some of their youngest soldiers have been fain to be carried home out of the field: whereupon it was blabbed abroad, that boys had done more than men durst do here at Berwick.

Probably what's being discussed here is the recent prosecution of William Beeston and his boys' company, who in the spring of 1640 had produced a play commenting on the King's expedition against the Scots and not licensed by the Master of the Revels.

On Monday the 4 May 1640 William Beeston was taken by a messenger and committed to the Marshalsea by my Lord Chamberlain's warrant for playing a play without licence. The same day the company at the Cockpit was commanded by my Lord Chamberlain's warrant to forbear playing, for playing when they were forbidden by me and for other disobedience. . . .

The play I called for and, forbidding the playing of it, keep the book because it had relation to the passages of the King's journey into the North and was complained of by his Majesty to me with command to punish the offenders. (*Dramatic Records of Sir Henry Herbert,* ed. J. Quincy Adams, 1917, p. 66.)

The issue was red-hot, and it was bold indeed of Beeston to risk handling it on the stage—perhaps he thought the feeling against the Scottish expedition was so strong that he could get away with it. If so he was wrong. He was imprisoned for some time in the Marshalsea, ousted from his position as manager of the King and Queen's Young Company, and replaced there by the courtier Davenant. The Court persecution of anti-bishop theatre was thus on a level with that of anti-bishop preaching: in both cases people lost their jobs and their means of influencing opinion.

This is not the last theatre reference in *Vox Borealis,* however. For good measure, in attacking the 'carpet knights' who came to the camp 'for fashion not for fighting', Willie singles out Sir John Suckling, leader of the 'précieux' court dramatists, as the type of these elegant idlers: 'but if it had once come to knocks, then you must have expected a tragedy instead of a comedy, as *The Loss of a Loyal Subject, The Prodigal's Repentance, The Suckling's Succour, The Last Lover,* or some such pretty piece.'[24]

Whether or not Overton was reporting the army's grievances from first-hand experience (as Wolfe suggests),[25]

the amount of factual detail he gives about theatres and censorship suggests inside knowledge.

Two of the anti-Laud pamphlets of 1642 Overton actually signed: *Articles of High Treason Against Cheapside Cross* (1642), a dialogue between Mr Papist and Mr News, describing the pulling down of the 'popish' cross by 'the rabble rout', and concluding with the Cross' last will and testament ('Item, I bequeath the iron about me to make a clapper for his Holiness passing bell. Item, I give and bequeath all the lead that is about me, to the hostile Catholics in Ireland, to make bullets to confound that cursed crew of heretics'). The will is signed (a zany Overtonian touch!):

'The Cross + her mark.'

The other signed pamphlet, *New Lambeth Fair* (1642), describes the selling-off of the bishops' now useless stock of accessories—lawn sleeves, robes, caps and beads—as fairings for children. References to these two in other contemporary tracts, repetition of particular devices, and stylistic echoes help to identify many other examples of Overton's work.[26]

The pamphlet which most strikingly shows the *dramatic* influence on Overton's writing is *Canterbury His Change of Diet* (1641), a six-page playlet satirising Laud (by this time a prisoner in the Tower), which refers in the text to 'Lambeth great Fair', and seems pretty certain to be his.[27]

The playlet is thus summarised on the title page:

1. Act. The Bishop of Canterbury having variety of dainties, is not satisfied till he be fed with tippets of men's ears.

2. Act. He hath his nose held to the grindstone.

3. Act. He is put into a bird-cage with the Confessor.

4. Act. The jester tells the King the story.

The humour is visual, slapstick and brutal, rather like that of *Ubu-Roi* (or of Marlowe's *Tamburlaine*). Thus in the first scene the Archbishop at table petulantly rejects a banquet of twenty-four dainty dishes, including cock and pheasant, quail and partridge. He demands something 'rare', like a carbonadoed cheek.[28] And when the pious divine wants to ask a blessing on the meat, Laud roars 'ho, ho' (like the Devil in the old interludes). 'He knocking there enter divers Bishops with muskets on their necks, bandoliers and swords by their sides.' Doctor, divine and lawyer are pinioned by this grotesque guard, while Laud cuts off their ears 'to be dressed for his supper' and departs 'after a low curtesy'— a burlesque staging of the vicious martyrdom of Bastwick (doctor), Burton (divine) and Prynne (lawyer).

The rest of the play is a fantasy of revenge. An honest carpenter, asked by Laud for the use of his grindstone to whet his knife, instead ties the Archbishop's nose to it; and when his 'Jesuit confessor' (who looks like Bishop Wren in the illustration) arrives to poultice his wounds, Carpenter and Carpenter's wife put both these 'cormorants' into a bird-cage ('They that have cut off ears at the first bout, God knows what they may cut off next'). A spirited wood-cut shows the prisoners in the cage, 'and a fool standing by, and laughing at them, Ha, ha, ha, ha, who is the fool now'.[29] In the final Act the jester (represented in the illustration with the traditional cap and bells) roars with laughter as he reports all this to the King.

> *Jester* I waited long to hear them sing, at last they began to chatter' . . .
>
> *King* What was the Song?
>
> *Jester* One sung thus: I would I was at Court again for me. Then the other answered: I would I was at Rome again with thee.
>
> *King* Well sirrah, you will never leave your flouts.
>
> *Jester* If I should, my liege, I were no Jester.

The King fails to appreciate the joke; but though, like Lear, he reprimands the fool, calling him 'Sirrah', he does not threaten him with the whip.

The epilogue is a 'jig'—the traditional song-and-dance finale of so many Elizabethan plays—between a Parator (Apparitor, or summoner of the Ecclesiastical Court) and the fool, in which the Parator agrees, since his master is fallen and he can make no more profit, that in future 'We'll wear tippet fool—caps, and never undo men.'

The *form* of the satire may have been suggested by the famous feast given by Laud for the King and Queen at Oxford in 1636, costing over £2,000, and followed by a play, Strode's *Floating Island,* parodying the mutilated Prynne in the play-hating Puritan Malevole ('Locks which I have scorned / Must hide my ear-stumps'.)[30]

Canterbury His Change of Diet is described by G. E. Bentley as a tract 'in the form of closet drama'. But the kind of play whose language and style it uses as model is utterly unlike the 'closet drama' of Fulke Greville and other aristocratic writers. The idiom is obviously that of the live theatre with its sharply-caricatured character types, its jigs, its snatches of folk-song, and its jesters who mix in serious matters and dare answer back to the king. Indeed it is not impossible that in these crisis years performances of this sort of show went on in private houses or barns. Whether this is so or not, the satire is obviously aimed to reach people who ordinarily go to plays, and by someone who knows the theatre well, if he hasn't actually been writing for it. Most of the funny parts would be unintelligible to an audience not familiar with acted plays, since they depend so much on visual effects and slapstick.

The Proctor and the Parator of May 1641, also ascribed by Wolfe to Overton, sounds very close to the actual play staged by the King's Company at the Red Bull in 1639, and suppressed by the Privy Council as

> a scandalous and libellous [play in which] they have audaciously reproached and in a libel personated not only some of the aldermen of the [City of London] and some other persons of quality, but also scandalised and libelled the whole profession of proctors belonging to the Court of Probate, and reflected upon the present Government.

And in *The Whore New Vamped,* also complained of in the same entry, Alderman William Abell, the wine monopolist, was called 'a base, drunken, sottish knave':[31] he too is a frequent target in Overton's satires.

Overton's dialogue between Mr Sponge the Proctor and Mr Hunter the Parator reveals an unholy conspiracy between them to search out offenders against the canon law and either fine them or get bribes from them to avoid prosecution.

> Country wenches would sell their petticoats rather to pay us than to endure a white sheet.' '(I) have gotten good booty from transgressors against holy-days, of chandlers, ale-houses, taverns, tobacco shops, butchers, comfit makers, gun-smiths, bakers, brokers, cooks, weavers and divers other malefactors against our terrible Canons and jurisdiction.' . . . 'I got no small trading by the Brownists, Anabaptists and Familists, who love a Barn better than a Church, and would come off roundly and secretly . . .'

They do well out of

> lecturers, who would be silenced because they supplied their places too diligently; nay, I have got well too by some of their auditors for leaving their own parish churches and minsters, and gadding after strangers . . .

Zealous honest ministers who preach twice a day, and refuse to wear surplices or christen children with the sign of the cross, are a steady source of profit.

> We do usually receive some bribe for a New Year's gift, and the Judge he expects a good piece of plate for his favour showed in ending causes according to the proctor's desire.

The broad popular alliance of godly ministers, sectaries, shopkeepers and ordinary sinners is thus evoked to rejoice at the downfall of these rogues, who have fallen on evil times with the decline of prerogative courts and the endless profitable legal business they involved. 'This certainty of the Triennial Parliament cuts our combs for ever doing any great exploits for after times.'

IV

A favourite device of Overton's, from these early tracts onwards, is to write in the name either of real public figures (Laud, Lord Justice Finch, Strafford, Attorney-General Noy)[33] or of caricatures resembling morality-play characters or Jonsonian 'humours' (Sir John Presbyter, Sir Simon Synod, Gaffer Christian). Essentially this is a dramatic technique.

Thus *A Letter from John Lord Finch, late Lord Keeper, to his Friend Dr Cozens, with a Commemoration of favours Dr Cozens showed him in his Vice-Chancellorship,* (1642) is written deadpan to mimic the pompous tones of the judge himself. Finch, a Cambridge man and the Star Chamber persecutor of Prynne, solemnly compliments the high-flying Laudian Cozens for having set up altars, crucifixes and holy pictures in Cambridge chapels; laments his ejection from office; and congratulates himself on his own brilliance in running away:

> Does the triple crown which you erected in St Mary's illustrate still the vulgar speculation? Sir, if the tumultuary imprecations of the vulgar do oppose you, yet macerate not yourself.

In *Old News Newly Revived,* another 1641 pamphlet-dialogue attributed to Overton, Finch is described on the run, in terms that suggest a comic actor playing the part: 'a brother of the blade, with a tilting feather, a flaunting periwig, buff doublet, scarlet hose, and sword as broad as a lath, he looked as like a Dammee newly come out of the North as could be imagined.'[34] Sir John Suckling too has fled, and 'the Blackfriars Actors have a foul loss of him . . . His coat of mail would not keep out their (the Scots') bullets, though it would Sir John Digby's rapier in the play-house.'[35]

In *Canterbury's Dream* Laud tells how his slumbers in prison are broken by the apparition of Cardinal Wolsey, who compares their relative skill as extortioners; cites himself as an awful warning ('The ruin of us both was indeed in our times the joy and voice of the people'); and finally departs in a manner recalling Hamlet's father ('Much more I have to say, but this is the third summons of the cock, and to fill the number up, I must return unto the children of the night').

In *The Bishop's Potion,* a spoof dialogue between Laud and his physician, the doctor diagnoses 'certain raw crudities' lying on his patient's stomach. An emetic is prescribed and the Archbishop vomits up the symbols of all his transgressions, including the tobacco patent; the Book of Sports; a parchment with the Star Chamber Order against Prynne, Burton and Bastwick; a bundle of papers presenting livings to dumb-dog clergy and suspending preaching ministers; and finally, after a supreme convulsion, up comes the Mitre ('I had almost broken my lungs!'). As a farcical image this harks right back to the 'Mar-Martin' plays of the 1590s, where the ape Martin was purged on stage, and indeed to Spenser; but the comic doctor with his grotesque cures goes back even earlier to the Mummers' plays, and is a stock figure in college drama like Randolph's *Aristippus.* It's not exactly what one thinks of as Puritan in tone, but the symbolism is impeccable.

The most vivid example of this black humour at its cruellest is *A Description of the Passage of Thomas Lord Strafford over the River of Styx,* which again is full of theatre stuff.[36] Strafford is ferried across Styx by Charon, who complains that he's a very heavy ghost, having 'devoured three kingdoms'. Strafford is deposited on the opposite bank in the waiting arms of Attorney-General Noy, who has already devised a fine new money-raising project for the Hades regime: Charon, whose fare is only ½d. per ghost, is to be made to pay a penny a passenger 'as a gratification or ventage to great Pluto'. As Strafford describes to Noy the fall of himself and Laud, the style changes from burlesque to serious, and he speaks in straight and reasonably effective blank verse, using the traditional metaphor of shipwreck much as Clarence does in *Richard III.*

> And thus adventured while my bark touched
>   heaven,
> Seas upon waves, and waves surmounting
>   seas,
> They danced me down into a vast abyss
> Where I lay docked in quicksands to embrace
> A certain ruin.

He goes on to compare Laud's dejection in prison to that of Antony after Actium, in terms which suggest the writer may have known Shakespeare's play.[37]

> He like the Roman Antony, when he
> Tried his last fortunes in sad Actium's fight
> And left the grappling Eagles and his honour
> To fly in's beauteous Cleopatra's boat,
> And quite ashamed that anyone but he
> Should own that fame to conquer Antony,
> His heart quite broken, and his head
>   bowed low,
> Whiles eightscore minutes wear in number out
> Their measured sands in the just glass of time,

Durst not look up towards Heaven, nor tempt
  her eyes,
Her eyes to him ten thousand thousand
  heavens
More dear than thousand conquests;
Just so his Grace, his faded head being laid
On both his hands, his elbows on his knees,
Will silent lean two or three hours together;
And in that posture, sad he now must leave
  her,
Stoops to his idol, greatness.

These early pamphlets show no interest in Laud's theology; there's nothing about Arminianism or predestination. The attack is on the riches of a Church which exploits the poor; spending of ordinary people's money on 'trinkets' and frivolities of ceremony; the luxurious life-style of bishops, who live like lords and eat like gluttons, a complaint familiar since Chaucer and the Lollards; above all the persecution not only of Prynne, Burton and Bastwick but of all manner of ordinary men and women. It's the democratic aspect of the case that already interests Overton. Though he was not as yet in contact with Lilburne and Walwyn, the Levelling note is already apparent.

Overton's known and much more famous pamphlets after 1645 are largely monologue or narrative rather than dramatic; but one of the best of all, *The Arraignment of Mr Persecution,* is in semi-dramatic form, and is believed to have served as the model for Bunyan when he wrote the trial of Faithful in *Pilgrim's Progress.* A. L. Morton has written finely of this tract in *The Leveller Style.*[38] It is far more ambitious than the brief squibs of 1641-42, with a large cast of persecutors and tolerationists, judges and jurymen, powerfully suggesting the *mass* involvement at the peak of the Leveller movement. Moreover while the earlier pamphlets are bent on punishment for the persecutors, cruel in their exultation over the fallen and crude in their anti-Popery, by 1645 the stress is on ending *all* persecution for religion, including that of Catholics and Jews, although the arch-persecutors (now personifications in the manner of the morality plays, Sir John Presbyter and Sir Simon Synod, rather than actual people) are still consigned to everlasting flames, as responsible for most of the wars and civil wars in the world. This tract shows the rapid growth in Overton's thought, under the impact of Presbyterian and right-wing Parliamentarian persecution of sectaries like Lilburne, and of his own involvement with the Leveller movement and with Anabaptism.

The success of Overton's dialogues and monologues also influenced other Leveller writers. Walwyn was already working closely with Overton in 1646 when he wrote *A Prediction of Master Edwards his Conversion and Recantation,* a spoof dramatic monologue by the embittered Presbyterian author of *Gangraena,* and *A Parable or Consultation of Physicians upon Master Edwards,* a complete allegory in which the doctors Love, Justice, Patience and Truth operate to remove the abscess which has poisoned Edwards' brain. So popular was Overton's semi-dramatic style that opponents too seem to have imitated it in the hope of appealing to his public. Thus in 1649 we find two play-pamphlets on *Newmarket Fair,* coarsely satirising Cromwell and Fairfax and their wives, mourning martyred Leveller soldiers like Private Arnold and showing the crowds brandishing the Agreement of the People as they mob Fairfax and bring back the King.[39] The writer is clearly aiming at a pseudo-radical appeal to the now disaffected and disillusioned among the Leveller rank and file.

All in all, Overton's writing is something new in English prose. Although many of his most brilliant pamphlets (for instance a series on tithes) are presented as monologues by 'Martin Mar-Priest', I cannot agree with Joseph Frank[40] that they are 'traditional and conformist' in style, merely repeating the achievements of Martin and anti-Martinists like Nashe fifty years before. In spite of the similarities, Overton is far more vivid, swift-moving and readable. He has more skill in sustained narrative and dramatisation, he is more consistently interesting and makes his meaning much clearer. It's here that the example of popular spoken drama must have been important.

V

A Leveller writer known to have been directly connected with the stage is John Harris, one time professional actor. In 1634 he performed as a boy player in Norwich, probably on tour with the King's Revels,[41] the London company for whom Randolph had worked, which in that same year borrowed a church robe from a pawnbroker 'to present Flamen, a priest of the heathens'—clearly a bit of deliberate anti-Laudian satire.[42] After the theatres closed Harris became a printer at Oxford.[43]

Harris can be reckoned among the leading Levellers. Under the anagram pseudonym of Sirrahniho, in 1647, he wrote two propaganda pamphlets demanding the release of Lilburne, Wildman and Sir John Maynard[44] (*The Grand Design* and *The Royal Quarrel*), and in 1648 he was one of a deputation of fifteen of Lilburne's friends (including Overton) who protested to Cromwell against his ill-treatment.[45] Harris was the craftsman on whom the Army Agitators relied to print their tracts and petitions during the revolt of 1647, and thereafter became for a time the Army's official printer, marching with his press in the rear of headquarters. As well as editing other newsbooks, he set out late in 1648 to produce an uncensored Leveller newspaper, *Mercurius Militaris or the Army's Scout,* lively and humorous in style and full of dramatic allusions; it ran for five numbers before the censor's harassment forced him to stop printing it.

Harris is one of the most radical and sceptical of the Leveller journalists, catching, as Brailsford says, 'the authentic tone of voice in which the agitators would address the New Model. Here are the clichés, the epigrams, the jokes which formed the common stock of their speeches.'[46] In *Mercurius Militaris* he mocks not only Parliament's proposed treaty with the King, but the institution of monarchy itself. Arguing that Parliament should get rid of the King altogether, he adapts Cassius's republican attack on Caesar, basing his rhetoric on Shakespeare's as naturally as on the soldiers' meetings, and bringing out with remarkable clarity the dislike of the parliamentarian right for the revolutionary situation in which their victories had placed them.

> What doth Parliament but mock his sacred Majesty in proposing anything to him to be confirmed? . . . I wonder what strength it would add, or what goodness to the propositions if he should sign them; can a single man compel 300,000 men to observe them when they are laws? Or can he compel them to break them? What virtue unknown is in this name Carolus Rex? Why is this name adored more than another? Write that and Denzil Holles together, is not this as fair a name? Weigh them, is it not as heavy? Conjure with them, Denzil Holles will start a spirit as soon as the name Carolus Rex: and yet this mere puff of breath, this powerless name King Charles set so high in the vulgar hearts, that what would be vice in others his name like richest alchemy change to virtue and worthiness and the subscribing this name to that which he can neither help nor hinder, must set him above his masters and conquerors, and permit him to bestride this narrow world like a colossus, when you victors must walk like petty slaves, and peep about under his huge legs to find yourselves dishonourable graves: *premoniti premuniti* (*Mercurius Militaris* No. 1, 10 October 1648, p. 5. BM E 467).

Harris' writings are full of these quick, easy references to the plays he must have known so well, and usually to Shakespeare—though Jonson comes in too. Thus in the same *Mercurius* he draws on Jonson's *Alchemist,* telling how Parliament has promised that the King may come to London in safety, freedom and honour:

> This makes me think that the King is an Alchemist, and the Lords are his Mercury; they are his crude and his sublimate, his precipitations and his unctions; he can make them dance the philosophical circle four or five times in an hour, like an Ape through a hoop, or a dog in a wheel.

And the servility Parliament may be expected to show to the returning King is described a few lines later in phrases that echo those of Kent about the sycophant Oswald (*King Lear,* Act II, scene 2, ll. 76-80):

> Most of the members, through fear or hopes, will become his apes, and shall laugh or weep, be hot or cold, change ever the garb, mode or habits as he varies (*Mercurius Militaris,* No. 3 October 24-31 1648, p. 17).[47]

The connection with *Lear,* is, I believe, not just a matter of phrasing, but of the whole line of thought. In the same issue of *Militaris* Harris is also writing:

> What work of the people does he for his wages? What good do they receive from him? He can neither make nor execute the laws, nor distribute any justice amongst them . . . But is it reason that a poor man shall be hanged for stealing 14d. and that a great man shall confess he sent his compeers to break houses, plunder and murder, and that thousands of families have been undone by them, and yet not so much as some reparations to be given them out of his lands.

I am not suggesting that Harris here is directly echoing *Lear:*

> Plate sin with gold,
> And the strong lance of justice hurtless
>   breaks:
> Arm it in rags, a pigmy's straw does pierce it.

But when he is writing at high speed about the pretensions and folly of kings and the injustice of courts, at deeper levels Shakespeare works on his thinking, supplies language and precedents.

In *Militaris* No. 2 (10 October-17 October 1648) Harris notes that 'every tyrant and his sycophants are pretended worshippers of that demi-god Authority' (p. 12). Angelo in *Measure for Measure* seems an appropriate character for a journalist exposing the hypocrisy of the Scottish Jack Presbyters (as Harris is here) to have in mind. As usual one Shakespearean reference triggers another: this time to *Henry VI:*

> He is the Lord's anointed . . . was anybody witness to his anointing? Or must we trust him upon his word only? If so, why might not Jack Cade be as well believed to have been Mortimer and rightful heir to the crown? Surely Jack Cade's tongue was never more double than his (p. 13).

Interestingly, Jack Cade comes in here not as a peasant revolutionary hero but (in Shakespeare's manner) as an impostor, a pretend-King. On the next page Judge-Advocate Whalley is described as Falstaff does Bardolph in *Henry IV:*[48]

with his face like an ignis fatuus . . . the gentleman had been quenching the fire in his face, and the liquor proved too strong (p. 14).

It is hardly a question here of Harris sharing theatrical injokes with his readers. Few New Model soldiers in 1648 would have much experience of plays, as readers of Overton's pamphlets would in 1641-43. Simply, like the playwrights before him, Harris stole freely what served his purpose, thereby strengthening both style and ideas. What the dramatists, Shakespeare especially, provide is not of course any kind of programme or scheme of political thought, but images and metaphors of great power and relevance.

VI

Cavalier culture could not inherit the rich and complex traditions of Jacobean theatre. For even though they required Court patronage and lived under the threat of Court censorship, the players' livelihood (at least in the public theatres) depended on their appeal to a popular audience. It was indeed a well-known charge against the 'common player' that his need for approval by the multitude made him a subversive force. 'Howsoever he pretends to have a royal master or mistress, his wages and dependance prove him to be the servant of the people.'[49] In Elizabethan and Jacobean drama the common people have a voice (even if what they say is not always enforced by the play as a whole), and often provide a sceptical commentary on the main heroic and royal action. One thinks of Henry V's soldiers before Agincourt, the gravediggers in *Hamlet,* the plebeian gibing of Lear's Fool. In the courtly Cavalier plays of the 1630s this voice is silent, and the structural use of contrast has gone.

Undoubtedly it was primarily the 'low' side of Shakespeare that led to his declining reputation in cultured court circles under Charles I.[50] By the time the Beaumont and Fletcher Folio was published in 1647 (during a brief interval of the wars), Sir John Berkenhead, the leading Royalist newsbook writer, in his commendatory verses spoke patronisingly of Shakespeare's outdated 'trunk-hose wit' as the result of writing too much for the mob, and now surpassed by the more correct and elegant work of Fletcher; and William Cartwright dismissed Shakespeare altogether as obscene and unfunny.[51] And while both Royalist and Puritan pamphleteers were making use of playhouse allusions, it seems that the Parliamentarian writers did so more often—so that Berkenhead himself could jeer at a Puritan controversialist for closing the theatres 'very wisely, lest men should track him, and find where he pilfers all his best similes'.[52]

The many-sided, dialectical embodiment of contradictory social forces and ideas that we find in the greatest seventeenth century drama was no longer possible, given the deepening split in society, in audiences and within people's minds. But something of the dramatists' vitality and ease in reaching a popular audience passed to the Leveller writers.

Notes

[1] Prynne was feted by the crowds, along with Burton and Bastwick, but as a heroic martyr of Laudian repression, rather than for his anti-theatre principles.

[2] Lancelot Andrews did not approve of plays, though he did not make an issue of it at Court, probably because for him loyalty to the monarchy seemed the more important issue; and Laud himself seems to have had no great liking for them.

[3] E.g. Massinger, *Believe as You List;* Glapthorne, *Albertus Wallenstein.*

[4] R. Davenport, *King John and Matilda.*

[5] See e.g. G. E. Bentley, *The Profession of Dramatist in Shakespeare's Time,* 1971, pp. 145-96, for an account of plays censored; Glynne Wickham, *Early English Stages,* Vol. II, Part 1, 1963, p. 94, S. R. Gardiner, 'The Political Element in Massinger' in *Contemporary Review,* August 1876; the Malone Society edition of *Believe as You List,* ed. C. J. Sisson, 1927.

[6] Marie Gimmelfarb thinks he may have been imprisoned for debt around 1642 (cf. her forthcoming book on Overton). If he was a playwright this would be very plausible.

[7] E.g. J. Frank, *The Levellers,* 1955, pp. 39-40, and the article by C. H. Firth in *DNB.*

[8] This has been demonstrated in detail for Leicestershire schools by Joan Simon, *Town Estates and Schools in the Sixteenth and Early Seventeenth Centuries,* in B. Simon (ed.), *Education in Leicestershire 1540-1940,* 1968. Leicestershire was probably Overton's home county.

[9] My view on this is confirmed by that reached by a quite different route by Marie Gimmelfarb. She considers that he was about Lilburne's age (i.e. born 1610-15), and dates his Mennonite conversion and declaration of faith, written in Amsterdam, at around 1643. I have benefited greatly from the facts she has made available to me and from discussing parts of this article with her.

[10] G. C. Moore Smith, *College Plays Performed in the University of Cambridge,* 1923, p. 85, 109-10. The MS, was seen by J. Nichols, who recorded it in his *History and Antiquities of the County of Leicester,* III, 927, but is now lost.

[11] Lambe, along with Laud's other helpmate Dr Duck, is also a favourite target of jokes and puns in Overton's early pamphlets.

[12] See Hannah Buchan (ed.), *The Poems of Thomas Pestell,* 1940, which reprints the full report of the 1633 case.

[13] For the conflict in Cambridge see H. R. Trevor-Roper, *Archbishop Laud,* 1962, pp. 204-10.

[14] E.g. *Copy of a letter from John Lord Finch to his friend Mr Cosins* (1641); *Old News Newly Revived* (1641); *A Rent in the Lawn Sleeves* (1641); *Farewell Mitre* (1642).

[15] His father was steward to Lord Zouch, an anti-Spanish peer since Elizabeth's time, part of whose estates lay in Northamptonshire.

[16] What G. E. Bentley calls the 'surprising' popularity of this play must have been partly due to the satirical in-jokes. In the BM *MS* (presumably the original acting version) a quack doctor advertises his skills: 'If it had not been treason I had cured Gondomar of his fistula and England of a subsidy.' In the 1630 printed edition the Prologue conjures up the spirit of Show, who is only allowed to present the play if he promises to keep off personal satire, which has got him into trouble before. He swears:

> I will not touch such men as I know vicious,
> Much less the good: I will not dare to say
> That such a one paid for his fellowship
> And had no learning but in's purse; no officer
> Need fear the sling of my detraction . . .
> You need not fear this show, you that are bad,
> It is no Parliament

> (*Aristippus,* 1630, p. 3).

[17] Thus in *The Muses' Looking Glass* two godly playhouse hawkers who denounce plays change their minds after seeing Randolph's edifying one:

> Bird: Hereafter I will visit comedies
>   And see them oft: they are good
> exercises!
>   I'll teach devotion now a milder
>   temper;
>   Not that it shall lose any of her heat
>   Or purity, but henceforth shall be such
>   As shall beam bright, although not blaze
> so much.

The sharper anti-Parliamentarian and anti-Puritan references in *Hey for Honesty* have mainly been added

much later by 'F. J.', who revised Randolph's original long after his death, during or after the Civil War.

[18] Holland was an aristocrat of Puritan leanings, younger son of the Rich family, brother of the Earl of Warwick, and cousin of Essex. The whole family, headed by the old Countess of Leicester, were patrons of the drama (Arthur Wilson being the family's playwright), and staged plays in their own country houses. Holland was written to by Maw, Master of Trinity, to use his influence to help Thomas Randolph.

Holland's Puritanism was of a decidedly 'courtly' and complicated kind. A well-known anti-Laudian, he was intriguing with the Queen in the mid-1630s as a way to outflank the pro-Spanish and more aggressively pro-Catholic party at court. (It was through the Queen, to whose favour he remained loyal, that Thomas Pestell senior, another Holland client, eventually became a chaplain to Charles I.) He was in no sense a radical. Nevertheless he was a close associate of Pym and Hampden, and well-known as a patron and protector of Puritan ministers. At the outset of the Civil War he took the Parliament side, but deserted it once too often and eventually followed Charles I to the block (see Barbara Donagan, 'A Courtier's Progress: Greed and Consistency in the Life of the Earl of Holland', in *Historical Journal,* June 1976, and R. M. Smuts 'The Puritan Followers of Henrietta Maria in the 1630s', in *English Historical Review,* January 1978).

[19] G. E. Bentley, *Randolph's Praeludium and the Salisbury Court Theatre,* in J. MacManaway (ed.), *J. Quincy Adams Memorial Studies,* 1948. See also G. E. Bentley, *The Jacobean and Caroline Stage,* 19, Vol. V, pp. 964-93.

[20] The Pestells at Packington in Leicestershire lived only a few miles from the Randolphs at Houghton. They had a common friend in James Duport, a common patron in Lord Holland. One Thomas Pestell (senior or junior) answered Randolph's mock-elegy on his own finger cut off in a brawl with a 'Reply to Mr. Randolph's verses on the loss of his finger'. Plays by Randolph and Pestell were probably both acted at Cambridge in the same season: then as now, drama enthusiasts in different colleges were likely to know one another. Overton may indeed have come from the same district: Marie Gimelfarb traced Overtons living in Lea Grange Manor, near Twycross, and Pestell senior also held a living at Cole-Orton, otherwise known as Cold Overton, near Ashby de la Zouch (H. Buchan, loc. cit., p. XXXI).

[21] Don M. Wolfe, *Unsigned Pamphlets of Richard Overton, 1641-49,* (Huntingdon Library Quarterly, 1957), lists additional reasons for assigning it to Overton.

[22] The bad treatment of discharged soldiers was already a common theme in popular drama. See for example Dekker, *The Wonder of a Kingdom,* printed 1636.

[23] As G. E. Bentley points out in his account of the affair in *The Profession of Dramatist in Shakespeare's Time,* 1971, p. 181.

[24] A later pamphlet of Overton's, *Old News Newly Revived,* returns to gibes against Suckling.

[25] Don M. Wolfe, *Unsigned Pamphlets of Richard Overton,* Huntingdon Library Quarterly, XXI, 2 February 1958, p. 128.

[26] The pioneering work on these tracts was done by Don M. Wolfe twenty years ago in *Unsigned Pamphlets of Richard Overton,* op. cit. Although I would dispute some of his attributions, I am heavily indebted to this article and to Christopher Hill for drawing my attention to it.

[27] It is convincingly identified, on this and other grounds, by Don M. Wolfe, ibid. Wolfe had not noted the possibility that Overton was an actor or playwright and his attribution is not made with that in mind. The signed tract *New Lambeth Fair* (1642) incorporates large portions of the unsigned *Lambeth Fair* (1641), to which *Canterbury His Change of Diet* alludes.

[28] Prynne had been branded S. L. on the cheeks—Seditious Libeller.

[29] The immediate reference is to Archy Armstrong, official Court jester to James I and Charles I, who had just been expelled from Court by the Privy Council on Laud's instigation for gibing at him ('Who's the fool now?' were among the 'scandalous words of a high nature' complained of). When Laud was in the Tower, Archy, from retirement on his Cumberland estates, issued a volume *Archy's Dreams,* which includes a vision of Laud in hell, and other anti-prelatical fancies. Compared with Overton's semi-dramatic satires it is laboured and unimaginative, however. (See Enid Welsford, *The Fool, his Social and Literary History,* 1968, pp. 172-81.)

[30] H. R. Trevor-Roper, *Archbishop Laud,* 1962, p. 29.

[31] C.S.P.D. 1639, pp. 529-30. The offender who spoke these lines was Andrew Cane, leader of Prince Charles [II] company and a famous comic.

[32] Don M. Wolfe cites stylistic similarities with his known work as 'rather certain signs' of Overton's authorship.

[33] Middleton's *Game at Chess,* where Gondomar and the Fat Bishop de Dominis were impersonated on stage, showed how effective this could be.

[34] The lath dagger was the regular property of the Vice or comic devil in the old morality plays.

[35] Digby and Suckling had in fact fought over a lady, the honours going to Digby.

[36] Don M. Wolfe's evidence for ascribing this to Overton is purely internal, based on content and word use. It could equally well—perhaps better—be ascribed to John Harris (see below), in whose writing Shakespearean echoes are common.

[37] Direct use of Plutarch would not have provided this image: neither would various Antony plays by the Countess of Pembroke and others.

[38] See *The Matter of Britain,* 1966, and the introduction to *Freedom in Arms,* 1975.

[39] These tracts are assigned by Wolfe to Overton, but I find this unconvincing both in terms of content and style. Overton in his signed writings at this time shows no trace of Royalist sympathies. There were many Royalist pamphleteers capable of using such a form: the likeliest being perhaps either John Crouch or John Tatham, who in 1660 staged an actual play, *The Rump,* on very similar lines.

[40] *The Levellers,* 1955, p. 259.

[41] G. E. Bentley, *The Jacobean and Caroline Stage,* Vol. II, p. 462.

[42] *Dramatic Records of Sir Henry Herbert,* ed. J. Quincy Adams, op. cit., p. 64. The broker spent the night in prison. 'The employment of such a robe for "a priest of the heathens" cannot have been innocent in intent' (G. E. Bentley, *The Profession of Dramatist in Shakespeare's Time,* 1971, p. 179).

[43] H. N. Brailsford in *The Levellers and the English Revolution,* 1961, 1976 reprint, pp. 410-12, gives a good summary of what is known about Harris, drawing attention to the Shakespearean echoes in his writing. Further detail is given in Joseph Frank, *The Beginnings of the English Newspaper,* 1961, pp. 165, 166, 192 and *passim.*

[44] Maynard was a Presbyterian and near-Royalist MP, one of the eleven sequestered members, who became friendly with Lilburne while in prison. He was son-in-law of Sir Thomas Myddleton, formerly Puritan Lord Mayor of London, and had himself written a masque in his youth. His family continued to befriend Lilburne to the end of his life, according to Pauline Gregg, *Freeborn John,* 1961, p. 358.

[45] Lilburne, *Legal Fundamental Liberties,* 1649. Quoted W. Haller and G. Davies, *The Leveller Tracts,* 1944, p. 424.

[46] Brailsford, op. cit., p. 411.

[47] This does not, like the *Julius Caesar* extract, follow Shakespeare word for word; but the unusual use of 'garb' (see *Lear,* Act II, Scene 2, 1. 98) and 'vary' in this context makes it pretty certain that Harris had *King Lear* at the back of his mind.

[48] Act III, Scene 2, 1. 42.

[49] J. Cocke, *A Common Player,* cited E. K. Chambers, *Elizabethan Stage,* 1923, Vol IV, p. 256.

[50] See the analysis of the Beaumont and Fletcher verses and of Cavalier critical attitudes by P. W. Thomas, *Sir John Berkenhead,* 1969, pp. 135 ff.

[51] Among the many commendatory verses prefaced to this volume, the only Parliamentarian piece is by John Harris, who describes himself as too unknown and unlearned to praise Fletcher effectively, and goes on to do so for another 126 lines. He does not mention Shakespeare, but works in eulogies of Essex (recently dead), Parliament and Queen Elizabeth.

[52] John Berkenhead, *The Assembly Man,* written 1647; cited in E. Sirluck, 'Shakespeare and Jonson among the pamphleteers of the First Civil War' in *Modern Philology,* Vol. 53, 1955-6, pp. 88-99. Sirluck counts theatrical allusions on the two sides, and concludes that 'the Puritans used Shakespeare and Jonson approximately twice as often in political propaganda as the Royalists did'. He points out that earlier scholars have underestimated Shakespeare's reputation at this date because they failed to examine pamphlet literature.

Michael B. Levy (essay date 1983)

SOURCE: "Freedom, Property and the Levellers: The Case of John Lilburne," in *The Western Political Quarterly,* Vol. 36, No. 1, March 1983, pp. 116-33.

[In the following essay, Levy counters the historical view of the Levellers as class-conscious elitists and proto-capitalists put forth by C. B. Macpherson. Levy examines Lilburne's writings and maintains that Lilburne was concerned with equality for all and with protecting the common people from an absolutist political regime.]

The seventeenth century struggle between Parliament and Crown—and its attendant philosophical and ideological debates—is customarily said to initiate the English liberal tradition. The same received opinion has placed the Levellers, the left-wing of Cromwell's New Model Army, at the headwaters of liberalism's most democratic and egalitarian branch. Colonel Rainsborough's exclamation at the Putney Debates in 1647 has epitomized the Levellers for generations of historians and students of political thought. "The poorest he that is in England hath a life to live as the greatest he; . . . I think it is clear that every man that is to live under a government ought to first consent to put himself under that government." The Levellers' demand for a popular constitution and broad franchise, their aggressive use of mass organizing techniques and pamphleteering, and their popular democratic army all have impressed historians as familiarly modern (Firth, 1891; Gardiner, 1893; Wolfe, 1944; Haller and Davies, 1944; Hill, 1958). Despite their defeat at the hands of the less egalitarian Independents led by Cromwell and Ireton, the Levellers seemed secure in history as harbingers of the democratic revolutions of later centuries.

However, since C. B. Macpherson's seminal work, *The Theory of Possessive Individualism* (1964), the exact nature of the Leveller contribution has been in question. As is well known, Macpherson saw the Levellers as "radical whigs" instead of the egalitarian democrats described in earlier historigraphy. By this distinction Macpherson meant that while the Levellers would have increased the right to vote beyond the traditional landed classes, instituted a mechanistic constitution, and furthered the rule of law, they would not have democratized either state or society in order that all might have participated equally and meaningfully in the political community. Macpherson reinterpreted the Levellers as quintessential liberal or "possessive" individualists who conceived freedom to be a "function of possession," or "property" especially "property in one's labor" (1964: 3, 151). Freedom was limited to those who lived off their own accumulated wealth or worked for themselves rather than for an employer for wages. This interpretation, if correct, meant that the Levellers would have excluded most Englishmen from the status of "freemen."

To support his hypothesis, Macpherson contended that Leveller proposals for the franchise in various versions of their proposed constitution, the "Agreements of the People," were far more restrictive than previous writers had appreciated. The "Agreements," he concluded, barred all whose livliehoods—and thus wills—were dependent upon others. This stipulation necessarily excluded those poor who depended upon public support or charity, and also servants since they were "included in their masters." Macpherson greatly expanded this last point by arguing forcefully that the term "servant" in seventeenth century usage included apprentices and all who worked for wages, effectively excluding the working class from the suffrage. If one read the

Levellers in proper context, Macpherson maintained, he would discover a set of unspoken theoretical assumptions which were to plague later liberal thought: (1) the individual was "natural proprietor of his capacities, owing nothing to society for them"; (2) freedom was a "function of property, . . . property in one's labor," and was forfeited by those who alienated it in wage relationships in the labor market; and (3) "life and liberty" were "possessions rather than . . . social rights with correlative duties" (1964: 107, 145-46, 151, 154; 1973: 2-23). These beliefs, he reasoned, were largely unconscious abstractions from Leveller experiences as small proprietors in an emerging market system, and continued to taint all later liberal thinking, even as liberals encompassed formal democratic procedures.

Because this interpretation so radically revised received notions, much of the subsequent work on Leveller political thought concentrated on the extent of the franchise in each version of the "Agreements" and the related question of the scope and meaning of the term "servant" in seventeenth-century English (Laslett, 1964; Howell and Brewster, 1970; Thomas, 1972; Morton, 1973; Macpherson, 1973: 207-23).[1] However inevitable, focusing on the franchise shifted discussion away from Macpherson's primary conceptual argument about the unconsciously capitalist assumptions which gave birth to liberal thought. My essay returns to Macpherson's fundamental contention about Leveller thinking—that a man could only be free if he owned property, operationally defined as "working capital" (1964: 150) and therefore excluding the working class—and examines in depth the relationship between freedom and property in the writings of the most prolific and widely read Leveller leader, John Lilburne.[2]

Lilburne, I shall argue, was a possessive individualist in only the most attenuated sense. To reduce his liberalism to a simple unconscious abstraction of market processes misses his intention and the political experiences which informed it. This argument rests on three points:

1. Lilburne's discussion of property must be placed in the context of a larger constitutional debate over the origin and nature of rights—property rights included—waged between royalist and parliamentarian throughout the seventeenth century. This debate took place in response to very concrete *political* events and requires no recourse to theories about an emerging capitalism to be explicable. Moreover the debate employs language typical of pre-capitalist political discourse. Lilburne participates in this debate and extends its scope in an egalitarian fashion.

2. Lilburne used the word "property" in an extended sense, far broader than later formal eighteenth-century definitions or twentieth-century everyday usage. This meaning can not be reduced to land, capital, or material objects even though it may involve them. Similarly, "self-property"—the property one has in oneself—is not defined by labor that is self-employed. Accordingly, those who work for wages did not forfeit their property in self.

3. Finally, one can only fully appreciate the centrality of property in its narrow and extended meanings for Lilburne in the light of his apocalyptic and separatist religious views. From this perspective, his arguments about property become part of an instrumental political sociology of religious liberty, a necessary means to larger political and ultimately cosmic ends.

In short the John Lilburne portrayed here ceases to be an unconscious class spokesman for emergent capitalism[3] and appears instead as an egalitarian agitator and thinker concerned with protecting a dissenting minority from an absolutist political regime. Whatever capitalist concerns Lilburne might have manifested were contingent commitments aiming at transcendent ends.

I

That property or "propriety" was in some sense a requisite for civil liberty was a commonplace understanding among Englishmen who opposed Stuart absolutism.[4] The belief is clearest when held up against its foil, the patriarchal rhetoric and policies of the royalist opponent.

When Lilburne angrily asserted in *Innocency and Truth Justified* (1645: 59) that "Kings cannot be said to have unconditionate and high propriety in all our lives, liberties, and possessions . . . ," he expressed a view common to the parliamentary parties of the previous generation of the Petition of Right and the generation which would follow him in the Glorious Revolution. This argument reasserted the traditional rights of free Englishmen to a status higher than that of "vassals and slaves" and demanded that the engrossing claims of the King and court (including the right to levy taxes without parliamentary consent) be limited.[5] Parliamentary rhetoric, self-consciously rooted in Magna Carta, took aim at royalist theorists who had hoped to legitimate a power for the King over his subjects and their goods far greater than earlier English writers had deemed allowable. One of the earliest and most extreme of these royalists formulations came from John Cowell in his law dictionary, *The Interpreter* (1607):

> Propertie signifieth the highest right that a man hath or can have to anything; which is no way depending upon any other man's courtesie. And this none of our kingdom can be said to have in any lands, or tenements, but only the king in the right of his crown.
>
> (AYLMER, 1980: 89; McILWAIN, 1918: LXXXVII-LXXXIX.)[6]

Cowell's statement created a furor because the logical conclusion of this definition implied that no subject could truly own property. The exercise of a property right would be by privilege bestowed through the grace of the Crown.

Neither the Stuarts nor Bishop Laud (Kenyon, 1969: 168) could fully embrace so controversial a definition, but it remained a favorite for a variety of court spokesmen throughout the century. Manwaring upheld this position in a sermon and drew sharp rebuttal from Pym, who decried as "enslaving" the doctrine "that a subject had no propriety in his goods, but that all was at the King's pleasure" (Kenyon, 1969: 202). Similarly, the quintessential patriarchalist Sir Robert Filmer ascribed all property to the King as rightful heir to Adam, conceding to individuals only contingent rights of use held by the King's grace (Filmer, 1652: 187-88).[7] Hobbes, although far from patriarchalist, agreed with Filmer that property in both land and chattel was a donation which the "sovereign assigneth to everyman a portion . . ." (1972: 296; Filmer, 1652b: 239; Schlatter, 1951: 140).[8] Underscoring the significance of this debate, Filmer held that the search for an origin of property independent of sovereign denotation was "a fiction or fancy" held by those who could only search in vain for "an original of government as might promise them more liberty" (Filmer, 1652a: 188). Simply, the royalists held that property was a wholly conventional right created by the sovereign and used at his pleasure. Property had neither independent origin nor status and could not be used to ground individual rights held against the very sovereign power that granted rights.

In contrast, Lilburne employed typical parliamentary rhetoric when, in recalling Coke, he emphasized "that the Liberties and Franchises were not of Grace and donation but of Right and Inheritance." It was no coincidence that he and others of the parliamentary party emphasized their rights and status as "free-men" or "free-born" Englishmen and accused their opponents of seeking to reduce them to the opposite condition— "vassals" or "slaves" (1646a: 2; Morton, 1973: 200-204; Thomas, 1972: 73-75). The royalist contention implied an unfree tenure for all property and a corresponding base personal status even for freeholders. One must remember that in the history of English law the distinction between freeholder and copyholder had been great indeed. The former had status in the royal courts and was protected by common law, while the latter remained tenant to his Lord and was governed by the customs of the manor, which could be quite arbitrary. Indeed the vulnerability of those who were not freeholders had become all too apparent by the middle of the seventeenth century given enclosures of common land, draining of fens and expulsions of fensmen, and the general dislocation and suffering which followed from the redefinition of customary rights. Whole classes of people lost the security of their livelihoods as customary rights were redefined in ways which they could not control. Parliamentary forces simply would not accept a similar legal status for themselves. In effect the patriarchalist contention that property was contingent donation would have reduced the whole nation to a status of copyholder to the King, and placed the legal rights of citizens in jeopardy. This is not to suggest that most who opposed the Stuarts were concerned with the fate of actual copyholders, since many stood to gain from the elimination of customary rights. Instead, they were concerned lest their own legal status be no greater.

When Lilburne held that one becomes a vassal or slave if his person and property had no formal legal status under the law he simply stated what was axiomatic to the parliamentary side. There is little of capitalist ideology per se in this belief and much of the perspective that Ewart Lewis ascribed to feudal thought: "the control of land involved a certain control of persons" (1954: 92).[9] It was in this light that an anonymous Leveller writing in *The Moderate* railed against those who could maintain that "all Goods, chattels, possessions, and whatsoever else a man hath are the King's, and that the people have only the use thereof, without any propriety at all. . . ." This condition, he noted, perfectly matched Aristotle's definition of a slave.

> Aristotle saith that Freemen and slaves differ only in this, that slaves have only the use of things without property, or interest, and canst acquire or get to themselves any Dominion, or the true right in anything; for whatever they do get, it accrueth to their masters and not to themselves. (1648, #23: 201.)

The logic of the Stuart apologists seemed at odds with the traditional understanding of what constituted a freemen in both English law and classical philosophy. This constitutional debate was hardly over abstract principles since Stuart attempts to levy taxes and charter monopolies coupled with their use of Star Chamber threatened the control over self and dominion which English political classes had taken for granted (Lilburne, 1646a: 5). Lilburne's connection between freedom and property was consonant with the broad range of parliamentary opinion. Unlike more conservative opponents of the crown, however, he and his friends carried this line of reasoning further to apply it to classes which had been excluded from political life altogether, and continued to press their arguments after the Stuart reign had ended when they attacked the extralegal excesses of Cromwell and the Protectorate."[10]

Knowledge of the royalist argument is a necessary condition to understanding Lilburne's belief that freedom is tied to the security and independence of property. It is not however, sufficient. To place his statements in their proper linguistic context requires that we explore the plasticity and subtlety of the term property (and "propriety") in the middle seventeenth century. It is this expanded meaning which gives us insight into Lilburne's egalitarian intentions.

Property in everyday, twentieth-century language—if not in our courts—connotes an object which someone possesses, which he has the right to transfer or bequest, and from which he can exclude others (Donahue, 1980: 28-47). By the eighteenth century this set of criteria dominated Whig thought on the subject and was enshrined in Blackstone's definition of property as "sole and despotic dominion which one man claims and exercises over the external things of the world" (1979: II, 2). In the seventeenth century, however, property had not yet taken on so exclusive, personal and objective a character, although the philosophical arguments of Grotius and Pufendorf (Tully, 1981: 72-80, 91-95, 98-102) were moving in this direction. Iain Hampsher-Monk has persuasively argued that property as used in the Interregnum often carried with it an older meaning of a secure collection of rights to use of direct something, rather than the thing itself (1978: 407-9; Lewis, 1954: I, 88-89). Since property did not equal an object, it made sense to say that someone had or should have a *propriety in* or *to* an estate or goods in the sense that the individual had the right to direct use under the law. With this meaning in mind, we can also understand how it would make sense to claim that one had a "property in" common lands, fens, or the exercise of a trade without implying that the individual possessed an exclusive concrete object. Thus property as a term still included sets of private and common rights (Lilburne, 1651; Judson, 1964: 36-37).

It is clear that Lilburne used property in this sense and often creatively elevated sets of rights to the status of property in order to establish very egalitarian points. For example, when he asserted that "all the Commons of England have an equal interest and property in the law, being all of us free-born Englishmen" (1646b: 11),[11] he both described possession of rights under the law as a form of property, and the individual possessors of these rights as property-holders. In a similar vein he could discuss the "propriety of our estates, our subsistence" (1649a: 6), or accuse the King and later Cromwell of robbing the people of their "lives, estates, and properties" in ways which distinguished between the set of rights or legal claims, their functions, and any physical object.[12]

This conception of property gave the term a far more expansive quality than we might anachronistically read into it, and accordingly opened up a wide variety of properties which an individual might have held. For example, Lilburne charged that his jailors had taken away his "liberty," "trade and livliehood," and "disenfranchize[d] [him] without cause." All of this "Made a slave and beast of me, and so changed the *property* that God created in me" (1646b: 35). That which "God created" obviously was neither land nor chattal; it was the "property" right to exercise natural talents and capacities in a manner consistent with reason and God's will.[13] Obviously this was a form of property available to all. To prevent the exercise of these capacities was to violate one's property, Further, it is clear from Lilburne's statement that his self-propriety had been seized and thwarted from actualization by an arbitrary act of the state (in this case, the Protectorate) and not through the alienation of labor in a contractual wage relation as Macpherson had suggested. His property in self had been taken away by an arbitrary act of government, his freedom, by definition, along with it.

Given the wide variety of meanings available to property, it would seem that an interpretation of Lilburne which reduced his understanding of freedom to a dependence upon owning "working capital" is one which is too constraining. No doubt Lilburne believed that property needed to be respected if freedom were to flourish and arbitrary government be constrained. "I love and honor all those just boundaries that distinguish *meum* and *tuum,* that supports just magistracy, and teaches subjection her due bounds . . ." (1643: 13). But the property that one might possess was broad and diverse enough to include equal rights before the law, control over possessions or land, security of customary tenure, or freedom to exercise one's trade.[14] Defined this way the statement "freedom requires property" does not mean that "one needs working capital in order to be free," nor its corollary that one who works for a wage is unfree. Rather freedom requires only that what is yours remains so secured by law, free from the engrossing power of the state, the coercion of another man, or an unrepresentative institution.[15] "It is a miserable servitude or bondage where the law is uncertain or unknown" (1649c: 4-5). Thus in a free society regulated by law, what is yours can only be justly taken from you if you alienate it freely (personally or through representatives) or forfeit your rights through violation of another's.

This relationship moreover was reciprocal. Just as freedom required property, and was in part defined by the security of one's claims, so did the preservation of property require freedom. For "property cannot be maintained if liberty is destroyed" (1649b: 11-12). If all of one's basic political rights were not upheld, one could not expect estate and goods to be any more secure. As Rainsborough argued at Putney, the right to vote was a form of protection through which the weak could protect their claims or properties against those more powerful.[16] Lilburne argued this same point in *London's Liberties in Chains* when he blamed the increased poverty and unemployment of London's inhabitants on royally chartered "Monopolies and Patents," and "arbitrary laws and unlimited Power." His solution, "a timely restauration of you to your ancient and just freedomes in electing your own officers" (1646b: 6). Freedom thus took on two dimensions in this context: (1) the maintaining of personal, private rights under the law, or the right to control what is yours alone (consistent with reason and law), and (2) the right to participate in controlling what is yours in common with others (e.g., the law) through suffrage. In both instances, however, freedom was understood as a condition in need of defense, a "sphere" of reason—the "proper measure of [man's] liberty"—to be protected from attacks by "Arbitrary power" (Lilburne, 1653: 3-4). Property in the extended sense helped provide protection against arbitrary power while democratic insitutions in turn helped protect property.

II

Although Lilburne would not have described it in these terms, his discussion of property points toward a worthwhile if incomplete teleological or instrumental theory of property. Still, we miss the urgency of his attachment to property and his visceral understanding of its centrality to liberty, if we overlook Lilburne's image of himself as a Christian martyr who had suffered at the hands of a hostile, engrossing regime.

Looking back on the political and constitutional struggles of the 1640s, Lilburne could still maintain that no liberty was greater for him than Christian liberty, without which the benefits of all wordly freedoms had little value (1652a: 4). In the 1630s, well before his days as Leveller activist, he had experienced a powerful conversion which set his soul "at liberty" and delivered him to "rest and ease" (1639a: 5). For his efforts at spreading this new truth and for smuggling unlicensed theological tracts from the Netherlands, he had been imprisoned, beaten, and pilloried—following in the steps of his then heroes (later opponents) Bastwick, Burton, and Prynne (Lilburne, 1638; Gibb, 1947: 48-54). In his helplessness,[17] Lilburne had felt the sting of arbitrary power and came to see in a most direct way the precariousness of freedom exercised in its face. How to temper power and protect the exercise and experience of freedom, especially in its Christian form, became the unspoken object of most of his subsequent political writings and action.

Lilburne's religious intensity may seem odd to those only familiar with his writings from the Leveller period—1645 to 1650—since they are usually legalistic and secular, filled with quotes from Coke, statute law, Magna Carta and Petition of Right, and parliamentary speeches. One is therefore tempted to draw a severe line between his earlier theological works and his later polemics on fundamental rights and the organization of the polity. In his own mind, however, these

activities were parts of the same project. As late as 1649, Lilburne could look back on his conversion as the seminal event:

> I know before God none is righteous no not one, but only he that is clothed with the glorious righteousness of Jesus Christ, which I assuredly know my soul hath been, and now is clothed with, in the strength of which I have walked for about 12 years together. (1649d: 19).

Again in 1649, he remembered his great turning and the vow he had made: "I should not be the servant of men (to serve their lusts and wills) but entirely and solely the servant of God . . ." (1649b: 25).[18] Reconstructing his logic as far as the texts warrant, it appears that he made a conscious decision to find in the positive laws of the nation the grounds upon which he and the community of the elect could mark off the secular autonomy needed to secure their divine subjection. Lilburne came to recognize in the "clearest and most highly priz'd laws of this nation" (1643: 13-14)—while far less pure than God's Word in the Bible—a set of fundamental principles in which all could equally participate and use to define and secure what was justly their own. Accordingly in his *Just Defense,* Lilburne spoke of himself as part of a tradition of Protestant martyrs—"John Hus in Bohemia, Jerem of Prague, John Wickliff in England"—who like himself were defenders of "their native countries and to the laws and liberties thereof, which roughly understood give check to all such unjust and evil practices" (1652b: 2-3). Recovering native liberties thus was a religiously motivated enterprise; not simply an end in itself but part of a quest to secure the conditions of religious freedom and community.

Lilburne's early religious writings show the influence of a Puritan apocalyptic tradition which saw the "last days" of the Books of Daniel and Revelations unfolding before their eyes (Christianson, 165-77, 249-50; Robertson, 44-48; Hayes, 48). Foxe, Bale, Brightman, Alsted, Mede, Thomas Goodwin, and the anonymous author of a *Glimpse of Syon's Glory* in various ways had predicted the defeat of the "Beast"—usually Rome, or the Laudian Church, later Charles I—followed by the one thousand year reign of Christ on earth (Hayes, 5-7; Capp, Ch. 1; Robertson, 44-48). Using a tradition inherited from Joachim of Floris, these writers saw stages of spiritual rule intertwined with temporal history. By placing the drama of personal salvation in shared historical space and time and locating its final act in the impending future, these Puritans gave a highly political and social coloration to their theology.

Some scholars have distinguished between orthodox and radical apocalyptic theorists. The former were literalists who fully expected the physical reign of Christ on earth, while the latter interpreted each stage as metaphor. The metaphorists translated their own mystical experiences into political possibility, seeing Christ within them, and themselves as his agents in the active creation of the new era (Hayes, 12-13). Lilburne however fits neither category easily. It is clear that he saw the Church of England and later Presbyterian clergy like his former ally Prynne as the Beast or Anti-Christ and the state as its willing accomplice. Furthermore, his early writings show that he believed quite literally that the physical return of Christ was imminent (1638a; 1638b). Yet the "Great storm" (1638b; 16-17) would also be preceded by massive conversions similar to the one Lilburne himself had experienced (1638c: 8, 14; 1638b; 8). The macrocosm of the apocalypse required first the microcosm of individual turning. Therefore, by the time Lilburne wrote the *Work of the Beast* in 1638, he had become most concerned with establishing the conditions which would allow Christ to appear *within* men "that he should reign and rule in your hearts and lives" (1638c: 8-9).

The logic of this perspective could have led Lilburne to favor an elitism of the elect, yet his emphasis remained egalitarian and democratic. His theology was essentially, if perhaps unconsciously, Arminian. Christ's grace was available to all "that were laborous and studious to know him awright" (1638c: 19), especially to the poor and unlearned who would make up much of Lilburne's later constituency (1638b: 14). To prepare for Christ's return and to better open one's soul to the divine light, it required that men and women, "all his chosen ones," separate from the Church of England ("withdraw . . . obedience and subjection from it") (1638c: 17-18; 1638b: 6; 1639A) and form their own covenant churches.

It is at this point that the function of property again becomes important. Lilburne preached a radical Brownist or Separatist form of church government which he believed offered individuals an escape from the Beast of the state church, and alternatively created in each indpendent congregation the ties of a community of believers. He was impressed by the fragility of such a community and the vulnerability of its members in confronting a unified church-state establishment. The "redeemed ones of Jesus Christ" were easy to attack, like the Jews of Persia in the time of Queen Esther (1647b: 2). A state church seemed to these saints, often the middling man of the great cities, as a tithing religious monopoly which took a "tenth part, yea or rather the seventh part of all things a man hath." Lilburne saw the church as one of three interlocking, oppressive monopolies (the other two being state chartered trading monopolies and government control over printing) which threatened the freedom and survival of religious dissidents:

> As first the Patent of ingrossing the preaching of the Word . . . The second monopoly is the patent of Merchant Adventurers [to] . . . the sole trade of all wollen commodities that are to be sent into the Netherlands . . . The third monopoly is that insufferable, unjust, and tyrannical Monopoly of Printing . . . (1645b: 9-11).[19]

A combination of monopolies over trade, religion and communications could strangle the saints and prevent the future salvation of others.

> Thousands of tens of thousands of souls shall perish for want of knowledge, and so run headlong to hell eternally. (1646b: 36.)[20]

> Men that will not be conformible unto them and absolutely of their cut and fashion . . . shall never eat and drink beg nor sell amongst them . . . (1646b: 36; 1645a: 52.)[21]

Again Lilburne described the victims of monopoly as "vassals" and saw their economic slavery enforcing a more serious religious bondage. "Men's minds made poor and base, and their Liberties, lost and gone, they might be ready to let go their religion . . ." (1649b: 9). Accordingly, it is only natural that he saw property in its extended sense as the bulwark of true religious freedom. Monopolies must be destroyed while rights of property respected so that dissenters would be free to practice their trade and sustain themselves and their families. Wage earners needed to be free to sell their labor,[22] small producers free to sell their products, copyholders secured in their customary rights if individuals were to be independent enough to exercise their wills and reason without fear of coercion. Only if printers were free to publish could dissident theologians publish their tracts and the poor have access to inexpensive Bibles.[23] Furthermore, tithes which stole one's property to feed Anti-Christ had to be eliminated; restoration of true property would allow the saints to support their own churches as they saw fit.[24] And last and most obvious, everyone's property in themselves had to be respected if each was to be free to receive and act upon the divine light. While property, including economic rights, was not an end in itself for someone who was clothed in Christ, Lilburne understood its importance for the maintenance of a community of dissenters.

Lilburne's writings on property, pieced together and studied as a whole, are less a full theory than an integrated perspective. His most glaring omission is the lack of a theory of origins. Given the importance of the patriarchical argument that property originated as and remained a royal donation, a genetic theory should have been paramount for anyone seriously engaged in theory building. Filmer had been quite conscious of this weakness in the parliamentary case and noted in his attacks on Grotius the inability of rights theorists to convincingly explain the transition from God's grant of the earth to mankind in common to the individual possession of it in severalty (Tully, 1980: 92). His contention that Kings were heir in primogeniture to Adam, of course, remains even less convincing (Laslett, 1949: 12, 22, 24). A serious full-blown philosophical attempt at resolving this problem with results satisfactory to the parliamentary side came later with John Locke's labor theory of appropriation. For his part, Lilburne relied heavily on the argument that a variety of rights had been part of every Englishman's inheritance under an "Ancient Constitution" which had been frustrated and suppressed since the Norman Conquest. By this reckoning, quite common among opponents of the Stuarts, events such as Magna Carta and the Petition of Rights were moments in a long struggle to regain the past (Hill, 1958: Ch. 3; Pocock, 1957). Yet even Lilburne realized the limits of the "Norman Yoke" and Magna Carta as an adequate basis for defending rights, and late in his career he began to speak of reason and nature as the proper ground for positive law. This argument remained quite undeveloped, however, and resembled a gloss on St. Thomas Aquinas filtered through St. Germain rather than an anticipation of Locke (Gleissner, 1981; Robertson, 50-71). Quite simply, Lilburne was far too derivative a thinker to have resolved so complex a question in an original or systematic fashion. He was an activist and his writings were always tools or weapons in his struggles. His views on property follow this pattern. It is a instrumentalist or teleologist approach with a weak and shifting genetic component added for purposes of philosophical legitimacy.

The seeds of an alternative might have been found in Lilburne's belief that we all have a self-property, i.e., that we possess natural capacities which we have a right to exercise and develop, but it is noteworthy that he does not pursue this direction. One could project from self-property a theory of justifiable acquisition, with material property defined as an extension of self and thus an irreducible manifestation of one's free personality. This line of analysis would have been most compatible with a capitalist emphasis on accumulation, but Lilburne did not investigate its possibilities. Property was not, for Lilburne, merely material objects nor symbols exchangeable for those objects; and he valued it for its capacity to protect autonomous personality, not as an inextricable part of that personality.

Nevertheless—perhaps *because* of his indifference to genetic questions—Lilburne's perception of the functions which property performed in the struggle against Stuart absolutism reveals the skeleton of a liberal democratic political sociology. Property in estate, self-propriety, property in the law all established conditions which would allow individuals to create a political community, and communities within that community, while preserving their fundamental autonomy. One exercised freedom in secular society but for ends which reached beyond the individual and the secular realm. Temporal power could never adequately define these ends nor

should it circumscribe the pursuit of them. Everyone by virtue of their innate reason and potential had a *prima facie* right to their freedom and moreover a claim to participate in helping to create the environment in which it would be manifested.

The stress on individual reason and rights, and the material conditions which sustain diversity all place property—not the least of which is property in goods—at the heart of Lilburne's analysis of the requisites of freedom. Nevertheless, Macpherson is correct to see Lilburne's idea of freedom as a function of possession; but his operational definition of property as "working capital" is far too narrow to be true to Lilburne's words or meanings. Rather than constrain the experience of freedom, Lilburne's extended notion of property coupled with his faith in each individual's capacity to achieve grace made freedom available to all. He would have agreed that one's livelihood and goods had to be free from arbitrary control if freedom was to remain secure, but he nowhere hints that each person must own working capital to experience personal freedom or exercise it in a political forum. Neither, given his functionalism and egalitarianism, is there any reason to read into Lilburne an indirect defense of unlimited accumulation. While his views were reasonably consonant with the interests of the *petit bourgeoisie* it is unfair to reduce them to a simple class expression. Significantly, Lilburne's notion of *material* property was far broader than the private dominion which the courts were already developing as market ends came to define juristic practices.[25] A theory of property whose purpose was to rationalize the market, encourage accumulation, and maximize economic efficiency would have been quite agreeable to the elimination of most customary rights in use. However, Lilburne and other Levellers' attitudes about fensmen, common lands, and other customary rights (Lilburne, 1651; Petition, 1648: #12, 191) all point to support for a wide variety of property arrangements other than those of the individual capitalist proprietor. The common thread in these positions remains a political one—defending the weak against the strong and preventing relations of power which leave many open to arbitrary coercion.

To emphasize the unconscious experience of the market place as the key to Leveller thought is to understate the harsh experience of Stuart repression and to ignore the legitimating rhetoric of Stuart apologists. The latter better explain Lilburne's defensive approach to property *qua* barrier, and his desire to expand its meaning in order to include and protect all.

In the contemporary context, a similar teleological theory would be capable of including a wide variety of rights—collective bargaining, varieties of social insurance, forms of worker self-management, public education, employee equity plans, and more—as forms of property which helped promote opportunity, independence, and diversity. Similarly its logic would condemn any proposal that attempted to eliminate property in material goods, or any set of proposals which permanently abbrogated the market and all forms of private exchange in return for centralized state planning and ownership. From this perspective a command economy would fulfill the worst possibilities inherent in the absolutist model, rendering all dependent on state power and those who controlled it. Simply the logic of Lilburne's arguments neither supports pure capitalist property relations nor collectivist socialism. His words and his actions were supportive of a wide variety of economic institutions not easily captured by contemporary categories or ideologies. That the conditions of liberty could only be achieved in a capitalist proprietal system and liberty available only to those who owned capital is a claim that Lilburne never made nor considered. It is alien to the spirit of his liberalism and the events which informed them. Such an interpretation should not be read back into his words.

Notes

[1] More recently Iain Hampsher-Monk (1978) has looked at the question of property and its meaning for the Levellers during the Putney Debates. This work, in its desire to place Leveller meaning in context, is closer to and usually compatible with my own. See Macpherson (1979) for a rejoinder.

[2] As Howell and Brewster (1970) emphasized, it is foolish to attribute the views of each Leveller to every Leveller. They were a relatively heterogeneous party coalition. Nevertheless, Lilburne was the most famous Leveller of his day and has provided us with the largest corpus of Leveller writings.

[3] "What I suggest is that the Levellers had reached their concept of freedom by generalizing from the data of their own experience . . . the freedom of the independent producer who was free of the will of other men to the extent that he had energy and working capital" (Macpherson, 1964: 150, 153).

[4] For a preliminary discussion of Royalist approaches to property see Dickinson (1977: 13-24). Tully (1980) places Locke in the context of major philosophical antecedents and opponents, but ignores the equally important constitutional debates over the status of property. Richards et al. (1981) look at Locke's theory of property in the context of Whig and Royalist apologists, and see him as far more egalitarian than his contemporaries. For Lilburne's acknowledgment of his intellectual debt to the preceding generation of Parlamentary leaders see Lilburne (1652B: 67).

[5] Cf. "and if he had a propriety in his Kingdome, what would become of the Subjects propriety in their Lands throughout the Kingedome, or of their Liberties, if his Majestie had the same right in their persons . . . if his Majestie might sell them or give them away, or dispose of them at pleasure, as a particular man may do with his Goods" (Lilburne with Overton, 1647a: 34).

[6] See McIlwain (1918: 306-7) for James I's response to Cowell's definition and the ensuing uproar. Tully (1979) and Tully (1980: 72-80) treat the narrowing of the scope of property in Grotius and Pufendorf.

[7] Christopher Hill (1940) discusses the precarious status of copyholders in this period.

[8] " . . . the Sovereign assigneth to every man a portion, according as he, and not according as any subject, or any number of them shall judge agreeable to Equity and the common good" (Hobbes 1972: 296). See also Filmer (1652b) and Schlatter (1951: 140).

[9] "Put broadly the claim of the Crown disputed from 1603 to 1640 was a claim to disregard law whenever in the King's judgement it was in the general interest this should be done" (Allen, 1967: 13).

[10] In emphasizing that the Levellers took the arguments common to the broad coalition forces in Parlament beyond their more conservative colleagues, I am neither suggesting that they violated their own class interest nor that they actually fulfilled it. Rather their arguments are best understood as a reaction to Stuart absolutism and the arbitrary disregard for law and custom instead of through the prisim of capitalism and capitalist class or strate interest.

[11] Obviously the meaning of "free-men" and "free-born" presents a problem since Macpherson believes it is a very limited category. In the above passage Lilburne sees "Common Liberties and Lawes of the Kingdome" as that which "makes us indeed free men," without defining who is or is not a free man. However he defines "freeman" in a quite egalitarian fashion in the same year (1646c: 16) as "every man born in the Realm." Two contemporary attempts at broadening the definition of property for reasons which bear some resemblance to Lilburne's thinking are Charles Reich (1964) and C. B. Macpherson (1977). Michael Levy (1983) provides a critical discussion of "new property" theorists.

[12] Lilburne as well as most Commonwealthmen often used the phrases "propriety and estates" and "propriety in our estates." This usage implies that property and estate are not identical terms and that estates only can be understood as the object itself. See Hampsher-Monk (1978: 404, fn. 4) for a very useful discussion of "property" in seventeenth century English dictionaries.

[13] " . . . the greatest good I can do is to be readily obedient to the pleasure, will, or command of him that

is absolutely sovereign over my soul and body, although my body shall perish in my duty" (Lilburne, 1643: 14). " . . . all men whatsoever must and ought to be ruled by the Law of God, which in great part is engraven in Nature and demonstrated by reason . . ." (1647a: 9).

[14] Lilburne (1646b: 22) charged that the merchant adventures had "robbed me of my trade." Judson (1964: 363) explains the contention that a "trade" was property" in seventeenth-century English political discourse. Lilburne also charges that the Merchant Adventurers monopoly over shipping in the cloth trade had enslaved sailors: "none shall be imployed but that they will be their slaves, and be content with what wages they will give them, and observe such rules as they will have them . . ." (1645a: 48). Note how Lilburne assumes that had sailors been able to bargain freely for wages and working conditions in an open labor market they would have been free men, not slaves.

[15] "I never was no never to any man breathing owned" (Lilburne, 1645A: 48).

[16] Without the franchise, Rainsborough argued " . . . the one part shall make hewers of wood and drawers of water, of the other five and so the greatest part of the nation be enslaved" (Woodhouse, 1938: 67; Aylmer, 1975: 111).

[17] In both *A Work of the Beast,* 1638, and *Come Out of Her My People,* 1639, Lilburne spoke of the Crown as completely legitimate. His attack on policies and public officials had not yet matured into an analysis of existing constitutional arrangements. It would be naïve, however, to assume that Lilburne did not understand that his attacks on the established Church had political consequences.

[18] "[N]o indirect ends or wordly allurements have engaged him therein" (Elizabeth Lilburne (1649: 160).

[19] Other Leveller attacks on tithes and chartered monpolies include Overton (1647), "the 'Large' Petition of March 1647" (Wolfe, 1944) and Lilburne (1647b).

[20] For a discussion of the right to a free press and an end to licensing of printers see Lilburne (1645b: 10; 1948a: 2).

[21] Lilburne accused the Monarch of draining the resources of "the poor and middle sort of people" (1648b). His own experiences made it clear to him how economic dependency was a powerful condition aiding religious conformity. " . . . banished from my master's service . . . only because the Prelates know that I was a familar acquaintence and visitor to the noble and renowned P. Bastwick" (1639b: 1-2).

[22] See fn. 14 above.

[23] "[I]t deprives many, both poore servants and others of mean condition to buy any Bibles at all, . . . that they thereby might be instructed in the way to heaven and happiness and taught their duty also towards their Masters and Magistrates" (1645b: 42).

[24] For a defense of tithing and an attack on the Leveller position see Baylie (1645: 117-24) and Edwards (1646: I, 113-22). It is worth noting that Edwards hated Lilburne and viewed his as a thoroughgoing democrat— incompatible with Macpherson's later interpretation— in both civil and ecclesiastical government (p. 153).

[25] Pocock (1979) discusses the difference between "civic" and "juristic" views of property in early eighteenth-century English political thought. Pocock (1975) provides the fullest exposition of a seventeenth and eighteenth century classical republican theory of property which is at the same time anti-royalist, non-capitalist and anti-commercial. While sharing similar "defensive" characteristics with Lilburne's view, Pocock limits republican property to land in freehold and shares in permanent trading corporations. Lilburne's conception is far more egalitarian and accepting of emerging urban and commercial market institutions, even if not reducible to them, as long as they do not violate traditional rights. *Moderate* #59 and #64 offers a Leveller defense of the customary rights of the Miners of Derby against the Earl of Rutland, who had hoped to exercise a more complete proprietary right over his mines and transform the miners into wage laborers.

References

Allen, J. W. (1967). *English Political Thought: 1603-1644.* New York: Archon Books.

Alsted, J. H. (1627). *Distribe de Mille Annis Apocalypticis,* trans. William Burton, 1643, *The Beloved City.*

Archer, John (1651). *The Personall Reign of Christ Upon Earth.*

Aylmer, G. E., ed. (1975). *The Levellers in the English Revolution.* Ithaca, N.Y.: Cornell University Press.

—— (1980). "The Meaning and Definition of 'Property' in Seventeenth Century England." *Past and Present* 86.

Bale, John (1548, 1550, 1570). *Expositions of Revelation.*

Baylie, Robert (1645). *A Dissuasive for the Errors of Time.* McAlpin Collection.

Blackstone, William (1979). *Commentaries on the Laws of England.* Chicago: University of Chicago Press: facsimile reprint 1765, vol. II.

Brightman, Thomas (1609). *Apocalypsis Apocalypseos,* trans. 1615, *Revelation of Revelations.*

Capp, B. S. (1972). *Fifth Monarchy Men.* Totowa, N.J.: Rowman and Littlefield.

Christianson, Paul (1978). *Reformers and Babylon: Apocalyptic Visions in England from the Reformation to the Outbreak of the Civil War.* Toronto: University of Toronto Press.

Dickinson, H. T. (1977). *Liberty and Property.* London: Weidenfeld and Nicholson.

Donahue, Charles Jr. (1980). "The Future of the Concept of Property Predicted from its Past." In Pennock, J. Roland, and John W. Chapman, eds. (1980). *Property: Nomos XXII.* New York: New York University Press.

Edwards, Thomas (1646). *Gangrena,* vol. I. McAlpin Collection. Reprinted 1977, a new edition. Menston, England: The Rota at University of Exerter.

Filmer, Sir Robert (1652a). "Observations Upon Aristotle's Politiques." In Laslett, 1949.

———— (1652b). "Observations on Mr. Hobbes' Leviathan." In Laslett, 1949.

Firth, C. H. (1891). *The Clarke Papers.* London: Camden Society.

Foxe, John (n.d.). *Acts and Monuments of the Christian Church,* ed. Pratt. 8 vols.

Gardiner, S. R. (1893). *The History of the Great Civil War.* London: Longman and Green.

Gibb, M. A. (1947). *John Lilburne: The Leveller.* London: Lindsey Drummond Ltd.

Gleissner, Richard (1981). "The Levellers and Natural Law: The Putney Debates." *Journal of British Studies* 20: 1.

Haller, W., and G. Davies (1944). *The Leveller Tracts.* New York: Columbia University Press.

Hampsher-Monk, Iain (1978). "The Political Theory of the Levellers: Putney, Property and Professor Macpherson." *Political Studies* 34: 4.

Hayes, T. Wilson (1979). *Winstanley the Digger.* Cambridge: Harvard University Press.

Hill, Christopher (1958). *Puritanism and Revolution.* London: Secker and Warburg.

Hobbes, Thomas (1972). *Leviathan,* ed. C. B. Macpherson. Baltimore: Penguin Books.

Howell, R., and D. E. Brewster (1970). "Reconsidering the Levellers: The Evidence of the 'Moderate'." *Past and Present* 46.

Judson, Margaret (1964). *The Crisis of the Constitution: 1603-1645.* New York: Octagon Books.

James I (1609). "A Speech." In McIlwain (1918): 206-307.

Kenyon, J. P., ed. (1969). *The Stuart Constitution.* Cambridge: Cambridge University Press.

Lamont, William M. (1969). *Godly Rule: Politics and Religion 1603-1660.* London: Dent.

Laslett, Peter, ed. (1949). *Patriarcha and Other Political Works of Sir Robert Filmer.* Oxford: Basil Blackwell.

———— (1964). "Market Society and Political Theory." *Historical Journal* 7.

Laud, Bishop (1640). "Canons of 1640." In Kenyon (1969): 168.

Leighton, (1628). *An Appeal to Parlament or Zion's Plea Against Prelacy.* Reprint Edinburgh 1842.

Levy, Michael B. (1983). "Liberal Egalitarianism and 'New Property' Entitlements: Critical Reflections." In Abbott, Philip, and Michael B. Levy. *The Liberal Future in America.* Westport, Conn.: Greenwood Press, forthcoming.

Lilburne, Elizabeth (1649). *A Petition.* Printed in Clement Walker (1649).

Lilburne, John (1638a). *An Answer to Nine Arguments.* Reprinted 1645. Thomason Collection E 25/7.

———— (1638b). *Coppy of a letter Written by L. C. L.* Reprinted 1645 in *Innocency and Truth Justified.* McAlpin Collection.

———— (1638c). *A Worke of the Beast.* McAlpin Collection.

———— (1939a). *Come Out of Her My People.* Pallard and Redgrave S. T. C. 15596. Reprinted 1971. Menston, England: The Rota at University of Exeter.

———— (1639b). *To All Breve, Courageous and Valiant Apprentizes.* Reprinted 1648 in *Prisoner's Plea for Habeas Corpus.* McAlpin Collection, Thomason E434 (19).

———— (1943). *For the Honorable William Lenthall Esq.* Reprinted in Varax (Clement Walker) (1649).

———— (1645a). *Innocnecy and Truth Justified.* McAlpin Collection, Thomason E314/21.

———— (1645b). *England's Birthright Justified.* McAlpin Collection, Thomason E304/17.

———— (1646a). *Liberty Vindicated Against Slavery.* McAlpin Collection, Thomason E35½.

———— (1646b). *London's Liberty in Chaines Discovered.* McAlpin Collection, Thomason E359/17.

———— (1646c). *Lilburne's Sentance Refuted.* McAlpin Collection, Thomason E362/20.

———— (1647a). (with Overton) *Regall Tyranny Discovered.* McAlpin Collection, Thomason E370/2.

———— (1647b). *Jonah's Cry Out of the Whale's Belly.* McAlpin Collection, Thomason E400/5.

———— (1648a). *England's New Chaines.* McAlpin Collection, Thomason G455/27.

———— (1648b). (with others, anon.) *Humble Petition of 1648.* In Morton (1975); Haller and Davies (1944); Wolfe (1944).

———— (1649a). *A Preparative to a Hue and Cry After Sir Arthur Haselrig.* McAlpin Collection, Thomason E573/16.

———— (1649b). *The Legal Fundamental Liberties of the People of England.* McAlpin Collection, Thomason E567/1.

———— (1649c). *A Discourse Betwixt Lt. Colonel John Lilburne . . . and Mr. Hugh Peter.* McAlpin Collection, Thomason E556/26.

———— (1649d). *The Picture of the Councel of State.* McAlpin Collection.

———— (1651). *The Case of the Tenants of the Manor of Epworth.* McAlpin Collection, Thomason E644/8.

———— (1652a). *Lt. Colonel John Lilburne his Apologeticall Narration.* McAlpin Collection, Thomason E659/30.

———— (1652b). *A True Relation of the Material Passages of Lieutenant Colonel John Lilburne's Sufferings.* McAlpin Collection.

Macpherson, C. B. (1964). *The Theory of Possessive Individualism.* London: Oxford University Press.

———— (1973). *Democratic Theory: Essays in Retrieval.* Oxford: Clarendon Press.

———— (1977). "Human Rights as Property Rights." *Dissent* 24, Winter.

———— (1979). "Hampsher-Monk's Leveller." *Political Studies* 25, 4.

Mede, Joseph (1627). *Clavis Apocalpytica,* Trans. Richard More, 1627, *The Key to Revelation.*

McIlwain, C. H. (1918*). The Political Works of James I.* Cambridge: Harvard University Press.

Miller, William L. (1980). "Primogeniture, Entails and Endowments in English Classical Economics." *History of Political Economy* 12, 4.

Moderate (1648). #23, December 12-19.

———— (1649a). #32, February 13-20.

———— (1649b). #59, August 21-28.

———— (1649c). #64, September 4-11.

Morton, A. L. (1973) *The World of the Ranters.* London: Lawrence and Wishart.

———— ed. (1975). *Freedom in Arms.* New York: International Publishers.

Overton, Richard (1647). *The Large Petition of March 1647.* In Morton (1975).

———— (July 17, 1647). *An Appeal.* In Don M. Wolfe (1944).

Parel, Anthony, and Thomas Flanigan, eds. (1979). *Theories of Property: Aristotle to the Present.* Waterloo, Ontario: Wilfred Laurier University Press.

The Petition of September 11, 1648 (anon.). In Morton (1975).

Pocock, J. G. A. (1957). *The Ancient Constitution and Feudal Law.* Cambridge: Cambridge University Press.

———— (1975). *The Machiavellian Moment.* Princeton University Press.

———— (1979). "The Mobility of Property and the Rise of Eighteenth Century Sociology." In Parel and Flanigan (1979).

Pym, John (1641). "Speech on Grievances, 17 April

1641." In Kenyon (1969): 202.

Reich, Charles (1964). "The New Property." *Yale Law Journal* 73, April.

Richards, J., L. Mulligan, and J. K. Graham (1981). "Property' and 'People': Political Usages of Locke and Some Contemporaries." *Journal of History of Ideas* 42, 1.

Robertson, D. B. (1951). *The Religious Foundations of Leveller Democracy*. New York: King's Crown Press.

Schlatter, Richard (1951). *Private Property: The History of An Idea*. London: Allen and Unwin.

Thomas, Keith (1972). "The Levellers and the Franchise." In G. E. Aylmer, *The Search for a Settlement: 1646-1660*. London: Lawrence and Wishart, 1973.

Tully, James (1979). "The Framework of Natural Rights in Locke's Analysis of Property." In Parel and Flanigan, 1979.

Tully, James (1980). *A Discourse on Property: John Locke and His Adversaries*. London: Cambridge University Press.

Varax, Theodorus (1649). See Walker, Clement.

Walker, Clement (1649). *The Triall of Lieutenant Colonel John Lilburne*. McAlpin Collection, Thomason E584/9.

——— (1649). *The Second Part of the Triall of Lieut. John Lilburne*. McAlpin Collection, Thomason E598/12.

Wolfe, Don M. (1944). *Leveller Manifestoes of the Puritan Revolution*. New York: Nelson.

Woodhouse, A. S. P. (1950). *Puritanism and Liberty*. London: Dent.

Nigel Smith (essay date 1986)

SOURCE: "Richard Overton's Marpriest Tracts: Towards a History of Leveller Style," in *Prose Studies, Special Issue: The Literature of Controversy—Polemical Strategy from Milton to Junius*, Vol. 9, No. 2, September 1986, pp. 39-66.

[*In the following essay, Smith examines a series of pamphlets written by Richard Overton prior to the emergence of the Levellers as an organized political group. Smith suggests that the pamphlets, known as the Marpriest tracts, demonstrate Overton's efforts to generate a sense of religious tolerance among his* *readers. He also commends them as persuasive and cogent political documents.*]

I

The history of the origins and development of the Leveller movement in the 1640s is a much-explored topic in recent historical writing. Standing for the most extreme version of personal and political liberty in that decade, the Levellers braved persecution in order to criticise Parliament and the New Model Army leaders. At various points between 1646 and 1649, they had considerable influence among the radical Puritan churches and in the Army itself. Their ideas for franchise reform have been seen in this century as the foundations of modern political democracy. Now, however, there is a need for an equally complex account of the genesis and development of the writings by individual Levellers, and the joint compositions which accompanied the main Leveller campaigns. Each individual brought a particular style or styles of writing from different religious or secular roots, and made that writing part of the very fabric of the movement. Especially in the work of the three most famous Levellers, John Liburne, Richard Overton and William Walwyn, style changed in accordance with the changing conditions of freedom to which the writers were subject.

While we know increasingly more about the conditions of production of these writings as published pamphlets, and about the relationship between publication and the physical organisation of the movement, the persuasive and imaginative content of the pamphlets has taken second place. In the argument which follows, a series of pamphlets by Richard Overton, the Marpriest tracts, published in the year prior to the emergence of the Leveller party proper, are shown to reveal just such a persuasive attempt to inculcate toleration in the minds of the public by means of popular forms of symbolism and jest. At the same time, the pamphlets may be said to reveal a response to the violence of ecclesiastical persecution and religious difference, while articulating an early and unextended version of the Leveller theory of natural rights.

Richard Overton's role as one of the most outspoken leaders of the Leveller movement in the 1640s and the early 1650s is a familiar one to historians of the Civil War. More recently, Overton's reputation as a writer of satire and polemic has been mooted, though we are still far from a full appreciation of his worth. There have been several statements concerning the quality of Overton's writing, as well as a full-length biography, which deals with the delicate problem of attribution.[1] Despite Margot Heinemann's crisp insights on the dramatic element in Overton's pamphlets, we are still in need of an assessment of the various polemical techniques employed in those pamphlets, in terms of the political, religious and publishing context within which

Overton wrote.[2] There is insufficient space here to do full justice to the variety and complexity of Overton's writing, to compare Overton's arguments in detail with those of the participants in the same debates, or to substantiate the recent attempts to extend radically the Overton canon.[3] Rather, this article will consider the seven pamphlets (and three of these seven in particular) which Overton wrote and published in 1645 and 1646, the "Marpriest" pamphlets, in order to show how Overton saw his role as a polemicist, what materials he chose to use, and what his achievement amounted to in these tracts.

The Marpriest tracts, so-called because they are centred on the persona of Martin Marpriest, are important as examples of extremely fine polemical writing. In many ways highly-wrought and patterned, they make hilarious reading in a popular festive mode, which had been taken into the realms of ecclesiastical discourse. They also mark a transition in radical religious writing in which the tradition of Puritan anti-prelatical satire established in the late 1580s by "Martin Marprelate" merged with secular, perhaps drama-based, forms of representation, to express both religious satire and the potent, emergent theories of natural or fundamental rights. These theories were the ideological fuel of the Leveller movement at its height. The Marpriest tracts were produced just at that juncture where the individuals who were later to lead the Levellers, were beginning to join their hitherto individual protesting voices together in a single movement. The Marpriest pamphlets reveal that nexus between tradition, readerships and persuasion, at that very point where religious sectarianism came forward to assess its relationship with the state and with the public at large.

The key for making a reassessment of Overton's satires lies in an exploration of Overton's understanding of Marprelate's writings and the related "Martinist" tracts. Quite recently, Overton has been compared unfavourably with Marprelate in the following terms: "This sense of character [in Marprelate], which represents an emerging and markedly modern consciousness, sets the satires apart from the welter of contemporary prose tracts and warrants the attention given to their forms. While other writers such as Richard Overton . . . assume personae or interject witty jibes, their efforts do not rise above the *ad hoc* attack of animadversion."[4] This judgement both overestimates the degree of polish in the Marprelate tracts and underestimates the content of Overton's writings.

Very little is known of Overton's life. Born perhaps in 1615, he may have studied at Cambridge and performed in plays there. He may also have witnessed in some capacity the Bishops' War against the Scots in the late 1630s. None of this evidence can be used with certain-

ty. The first definite news we have of him is his publication of a series of short anti-episcopal, anti-Laud pamphlets in 1641 and 1642.[5] These are pseudo-dramatic in form, and contain many of the strategies of satire and inversion which feature in the later Marpriest tracts.[6] At this point, Overton's work was part of a fairly crude satirical and witty style, itself part of the general anti-episcopal furor of the very early 1640s. No religious or political radicalism was apparent in these publications beyond a ridicule of Bishops and King.

According to Marie Gimelfarb-Brack, Overton then disappeared from the pamphleteering scene in London during two periods in 1642 and 1643. The first was in April 1642, a silence of eight months, after which Overton reappeared in January 1643 to help publish a reprint of a tract associated with Marprelate entitled *The Character Of A Puritan.*[7] The second disappearance followed in 1643, when it seems that Overton went to Amsterdam and converted there to Mennonite Anabaptism. Returning to England, he published in January 1644 an argument for the mortality of the soul, *Mans Mortalitie,* a work written under Anabaptist influence.[8]

The increase in the Presbyterian persecution of sectarians led Overton to speak out against oppressive ecclesiastical powers, but this time not the Bishops. Parliament had established the Assembly of Divines to discuss and recommend a reformed church discipline for the country. This body consisted of clergymen of different parties. The Presbyterians had attempted to establish their own model of church discipline, based upon a national hierarchy of assemblies, by act of Parliament. This was against the preference for a less hierarchical structure of locally-governed congregations favoured by the Independents. In *A Sacred Decretall* (p. 12), Overton recounts how the Presbyterians had requested in the early 1640s that the separatists Green and Spencer suspend their open and public meetings in order to stop fears of the rise of heresy, and therefore to hasten the overthrow of the Bishops. Green and Spencer had been promised liberty to worship later on, but in 1645 the Presbyterians urged their suppression. Overton's voice was but one among many here, though he spoke on behalf of the more extreme sectarian and tolerationist positions, as opposed to the Independent ministers who sat in the Westminster Assembly. He addressed the central issues of complaint against the Presbyterians: the Ordinances for the ordination of ministers, tithes (compared to a soap monopoly and related to fluctuating prices), the Directory for Public Worship, and press censorship. Despite the considerable debate between Presbyterians and Independents within the Assembly, the Presbyterians did try to silence the opposition of the Independents, and those groups to the left of them, by censoring the anti-Presbyterian press.[9] Overton launched his own attack on the Presbyterians in the Marpriest tracts, starting on 8 April 1645 with *The Araignement Of Mr. Persecvtion.*

The Marpriest tracts had two objectives: to discredit the Presbyterian objection to the liberty of conscience in speech and in the press, and to attack the continued Presbyterian insistence upon an ordained ministry only, maintained by tithes. In so far as Overton attacks the idea of Presbyterianism existing *jure divino,* he could be said to agree with the Erastian party in Parliament, which argued that any reformed church should be subject to the civil power. However, Overton advocates a degree of toleration which most Erastians would not have permitted. The pamphlets themselves were printed on a press established by Overton and William Larner, another opponent of episcopacy who would become a Leveller. In the second half of 1645, this press published tracts by John Liburne, and Sir Henry Marten, the republican member of the Commons who was associated with the emergent Levellers at this time. Here, the first statements of the Leveller campaign for the establishment of fundamental political rights and equality were made.

The success of the Marpriest tracts is evident in the way that they scandalised the Presbyterians during the following months. Martin Marpriest became one of a series of stylistically distinct voices speaking in defence of the individual rights of citizens and the entire separation of church and state. Both of these ideals appealed at the time, though not permanently, to most of the radical religious groups in London, the milieu from which the Levellers drew much of their early support. Such was Overton's success in obscuring the real author of the Marpriest tracts that he was able to escape the attention of the authorities for several months. However, he was finally apprehended by two members of the Stationers Company hostile to him, and brought before the House of Lords in August 1646.

The works which offended the Lords were *An Alarum to the House of Lords* (31 July 1646), *The Last Warning* (20 March 1646), written by Lilburne and Overton together, and later on, *A Defiance Against All Arbitrary Usurpations* (17 August 1646), but the informers also said that they had found other books in Overton's house.[10] These books may have been copies of the Marpriest tracts. The Lords interrogated Overton, he refused to answer questions, and he was committed to Newgate. The publishing, however, continued, including appeals to the House of Commons by Overton for his release. In fact, the forms employed by Overton in his tracts changed as his conditions of personal liberty altered. Further imprisonments continued, including that of Overton's wife and his younger brother. This situation continued until the release of Overton on 16 September 1647, in the context of Army pressure upon

Parliament, including soldiers' petitions for the release of Lilburne and Overton. Lilburne, however, remained in prison, and this state of affairs was the point where Leveller activity began properly, with tensions between the Army and Parliament, and between agitators and commanding officers within the Army.[11]

II

By 1645, Overton was a very experienced pamphleteer. He had mastered a popular satirical form (which was not without its imitators), and he had penned one of the most potent statements of radical religious theology to appear during the century. His choice of strategy in April 1645 was itself a deliberate response to the context in which he found himself. There were seven pamphlets in the series: *The Araignement Of Mr. Persecvtion* (8 April 1645), *A Sacred Decretall* (31 May 1645, though the date mentioned in the text itself is 6 June), *Martin's Eccho* (27 June 1645), *The Nativity of Sir John Presbyter* (2 July 1645), *The Ordinance For Tythes Dismounted* (29 December 1645), *Divine Observations* (24 January 1646), and finally *An Arrow Against All Tyrants* (12 October 1646). Apart from their polemical purpose, the Marpriest tracts were also an attempt to refashion the tradition of Puritan writing founded by Martin Marprelate, in terms of the more overtly dramatic ridicule of Overton's earlier pamphlets. Overton clearly saw parallels between his own situation and that of Marprelate. He might also have known of the strategies of a pamphleteer like Thomas Scot, whose attacks on James I's Spanish marriage policy led to his persecution and eventual assassination, and who also employed dialogue techniques in his pamphlets.[12] All three pamphleteers owe a general debt to the traditions of Medieval complaint satire. In fact, one of the Marpriest tracts contains a comparison of the persecution of religious radicals by the Presbyterians in the 1640s with the intimidation of the Elizabethan nonconformists, Barrow, Greenwood and Penry, by the Bishops.[13] The Presbyterian faction in Parliament had tried to staunch the flow of sectarian literature with the 1643 Licensing Ordinance which sought to impose a censorship by requiring the licensing of all publications. This was immediately ignored by many radicals. Like Marprelate, Overton wrote against censorship, making that censorship a central issue in each pamphlet. To do this, Overton followed Marprelate in adopting a disguise, so hiding his true identity from the gaze of a censorious authority. This very strategy had a radical destabilising effect upon the accepted and expected notions of readership and the persuasive power of the author. Like Marprelate too, Overton was aware that the strategies he was using were abhorrent to most Puritans, even the radical ones.

In fact, Overton may have been connected with the republication of two Martinist tracts in 1640 and 1642 (*A Dialogue Wherein Is Plainly Laide Open the tyran-*

nicall dealing of L. Bishopps against Gods children [1589, 1640], issued again as *The Character Of A Puritan* in 1643, and *Reformation No Enemie* [1641], a retitled *Hay any worke for Cooper* [1589], published again under its original title in March 1642). Only the seventeenth-century versions of *A Dialogue* are signed by Martin Marprelate, though it is now argued that the author of the Marprelate tracts and of *A Dialogue* was the same man, Job Throckmorton.[14] Marprelate was taken in the 1640s, then, to be the author of a far more dialogue-oriented style, as well as the familiar jesting *persona* of Martin, and this too influenced Overton. Both tracts seem to have been reprinted in a general anti-episcopal cause. However, Marprelate could not be reproduced to attack the Presbyterians, since it would not be apt. Overton had to develop a different mode.

Most Puritans regarded Marprelate's techniques with horror. Using the pattern supplied by jest books, and elaborating upon methods of ridicule in humanist dialogue, Martin Marprelate had broken the codes of Puritan rectitude and plainness.[15] He took his rhetorical dictum of *decorum personae* from Horace and Erasmus, where the author impersonated the object of attack, in order to ridicule that object.[16] The degree of ridicule was determined by the extent of the impersonated target's guilt or immorality. Obviously, the satirist himself could determine entirely the seriousness of the crime. The rest of Marprelate was an explosive form of humour where Elizabethan Bishops, like John Bridges, were seen to degrade themselves, and lose the dignity associated with their role and status at the hands of jesting, teasing Martin. Throckmorton was familiar with comic forms through his humanist education.[17] Not being a member of the clergy or a very strict Puritan, he found no difficulty in producing a potent satire which was to have a resounding influence upon the literature of the 1590s and afterwards.

The Puritans were offended by Marprelate because they felt he had discredited their cause by using a literary form which was in direct contradiction to their moral and ethical programme. For instance, the Independent minister Sidrach Simpson expressed the view that the godly should be in the business of persuasion and exhortation, not the subversive techniques of Marprelate, to achieve their ends.[18] Simpson was writing in the 1640s, but his attitudes are representative of a view which prevailed when the Marprelate pamphlets were first published. In Puritan eyes, Marprelate stood for a kind of imaginative transgression, an engagement with the darker, devilish side of the human psyche and will. In his *Gangraena* (1646, I, p. 38), the outraged Thomas Edwards noted the blasphemy of Marpriest in showing how the Holy Ghost left Scotland for England in a "Cloak-bagge," and how a prayer in *The Araignement* scoffed at the "Passion, Death, Resurrection and Ascension of Christ." This mode of expression and observation defied the uncomplicated black and white vision of good and evil through which Puritans viewed the world. There is a more well-known example which can help there. When Bunyan published *The Pilgrim's Progress* (1678), he was reprimanded by some of his fellow dissenters for publishing an allegory which borrowed its form from popular heroic literature. The "carnal" imagination had been used to talk about a godly subject. Critics have for some time also supposed that Bunyan may have taken some of his allegorical form in *The Pilgrim's Progress,* and the trial scenes in *The Pilgrim's Progess* and *The Holy War,* from Overton's *The Araignement Of Mr. Persecvtion.*[19] If this was the case, then in some sense Bunyan was using an imaginative form which transgressed against the dominant frame of Puritan literary imperatives.

If the harshness of non-Martinist sixteenth-century Puritan writing is compared with the pyrotechnics of Martin, the shock which the latter must have had upon contemporary readers is apparent:

> To the ende then it may appeare what that reformation is which we seeke for, and which these men do account the enemie of our state; it is to be vnderstood, that by reformation we mean nothing els, but the remouing of all those vnlawful callings which are maintained in our Church and ministrie, contrarie vnto the reuealed will and written word of the Lord our God, and the restoring therunto of all such offices and ministries.

> Well fare old mother experience yet/the burnt childe dreads the fire: his grace will cary to his graue I warrant you/the blowes which M. Cartwright gave him in this cause: & therefore no maruell though he was loth to have any other so banged as he himselfe was to his woe.[20]

Marprelate's voice is astonishing for its direct colloquial tones and imitation of verbal gestures. Marprelate has the ability to anticipate the reader's response, and turn it to his own ends. The effect, when coupled with the painstaking quotation of sections from episcopal pamphlets, is overwhelming:

> Would you haue the naturall eies put out (as your brethren the bishops haue don in the church of England/ euer since John of Canterbury urged his wretched subscription) and unnatural squint gogled eies put in their steede: when the body cannot see with any eies? but with the natural eies thereof.[21]

This was an early example of *calumniation,* the distortion of the substance of one's opponents' arguments in the very process of controversial exchange. Significantly, this was to worry Puritans greatly in the 1640s, when Presbyterian and Independent battled in the Westminster Assembly of Divines, called by Parliament to settle the religious affairs of the kingdom. Here is Sidrach Simpson again:

> There are two too usuall errours in handling Controversies. One to make the difference voluminous and many-headed, that so it may appear more horrid, monstrous and irreconcileable: the other to make the Opposites odious, by charging their reall or supposed faults upon their Tenents; for every man is glad to heare something against those they hate, and ready to believe it without any, or on very slight examination.[22]

III

Overton built upon Marprelate not simply through a direct textual imitation. Rather, we see the transformation of a polemical *persona*. For Overton, it was first necessary to signal his relationship to Marprelate by constructing a genealogy. "MARTIN MAR-PRIEST" is son to "old MARTIN the Metropolitane."[23] "MARTIN MAR-PRIEST" promises something of the same, but with a slight difference. As with most controversial writing of this nature, the success of any one attack is based upon the tensions between identities. In *Martin's Eccho,* Martin speaks of himself in the third person, as if to aggrandise his status, as well as to parody this form of authority. The invisible author exploits the relationship between him or herself, the speaking *persona* in the text, and the reader. Martin is presented as a chip off the old block. This time, however, "Mar-Priest" is more distinctly a figure of Christian folly, the words on one title page actually invoking the relevant passage from 1 Cor. 1.20.[24] Martin takes on a number of roles and disguises in the pamphlets which are dependent upon this wise fool identity. Not surprisingly, these other roles are determined by the particular context, though we should also note that they are made quite distinctly. So, Martin becomes, in *A Sacred Decretall* (p. 17), a "Tell-tale," who perceives the truth with a greater clarity than most. He is a martin, according to his fictional opponent, the bird which sees more clearly than others. This is especially true with regard to the issue of whether ordination is necessary before an individual may preach. At the same time, Martin is, of course, more honest, in order to gain the maximum persuasive purchase (p. 18).

In the sequel pamphlet to *A Sacred Decretall,* entitled *Martin's Eccho,* Martin appears as the correct adviser for the reader, through his sarcastic expounding of Presbyterian aims: "cease not to possesse both Parliament and People, that all that oppose you by word or writing (*though never so conformable to Truth*) are unnaturall enemies and Rebells to their Countrey, and insufferable in a Common-Wealth."[25] In *The Araignement,* Liberty of Conscience speaks with a Martinist voice,

thereby enhancing the direction of the criticisms (p. 26). This voice is characterised by its ability to perceive absurd logic in its opponents' statements, from which iniquity arises. The Presbyterian heresiographer Thomas Edwards was the scourge of the sects. His arguments are here rendered thus: *"States-men must weare Bells about their neckes, because antient Divines say, Kings are but Packe-horses to the Clergie"* (p. 19). There is an irony here, as Martin is referred to as "Dr. Martin," though he is speaking on behalf of the unlearned lay preachers of the sectarians. This paradox points up Overton's claim for the spirit, but he makes it in terms of the ecclesiastical hierarchy being attacked. The result is a freeing of the reader's sense of play and fun, as Martin gains an imaginative victory, contrasting both what he stands for, with the terms, apparently, of his opponents. Yet ironically again, Martin appears in Presbyterian eyes as a Protestant emblem or icon. If he will join the Presbyterians, Martin will become a greedy, oppressive giant with St. Peter's keys and St. Paul's *"Back-sword,"* as well as *"Scotch-Dagger"* and a "Classical Club." This image of violent greed, a negative image of the real Martin, is juxtaposed with the genuine power of God's vengeance which will act in the name of liberty of conscience.[26]

By contrast, the reader is subjected to the excruciating characters of Sir Simon Synod and Sir John Presbyter, both of whom speak in the tracts, and are represented dramatically or pictorially. Using the title of knight was a way of ridiculing any foolish priest at the time, while the latter name as a whole might be an ironic parody of the revered figure of Prester John. The theatrical association of the Martinist pamphlets with the Shakesperian representation of the foolish priest, Sir Oliver Mar-text, is apparent. Indeed, the Presbyterians are seen to behave precisely as hedge-priests, from the *Commedia dell'Arte,* but in a negative way: "why did you your selves put to your hands with such violence to break down the HEDGE by pulling up the *Hedge-stakes* thereof, the Lord Bishops, &c. as was evident by your Petitioning and Preaching against them." This is especially so given the frequency with which Presbyterians referred to the vineyard as an image of the place which God's husbandmen, the Presbyters, had to cultivate. There may also be associations with genuine leading Presbyterians, like Simeon Ashe, though he is referred to in the tracts in his own right.[27]

As with Martin, the mutable nature of these characters is evident. They are both allegorical personifications of the Presbyterian movement, and vice characters, whose recognisable mannerisms figure forth the shortcomings of the Presbyterian ideal. The impression is one of fearful, miserly lowness, which is devilish in its gluttony: "O how we gloz'd and fawn'd upon them! were fit to stroake them on the heads, and call them our *white Boyes,* while neatly we flatter'd them out of their Liberties; (*O divine pollicy!*) and cozen'd the fooles of all, (*Hoh, hoh, hoh, The Divell he laugh'd aloud:*)."[28] Sir John appears as a *miles gloriosus* of sorts in *The Araignment Of Mr. Persecvtion* (p. 9), though in the following pamphlets, *A Sacred Decretall* and *Martin's Eccho,* he is made into a young baby with one of the chief English Presbyterians, John Bastwick, and the Scot, Jockey, as his godfathers, and the Whore of Babylon as his godmother, an inverse parallel to Martin Marpriest's own genealogy. He is given a *corall,* a teething ring, to stifle his miserable wailings, the *corall* standing for the Ordinance for Tithes passed by a Parliament in which the Presbyterians had considerable influence.[29] Again, a Swiftian disproportion of roles is apparent as the source of the comic effect, a ridiculing by diminishment, by describing Presbyterian motives in terms of another set of human relationships.[30] The ecclesiological and the political are transformed into the domestic. Presbyterian claims are made to appear as both selfish and helpless. Sir Simon Synod displays a hatred of the common people. There is also a sense of great power being wielded by dangerous and unbalanced immaturity. The restless child, Sir John, controls the City of London with its powerful levy of merchants and aldermen, many of whom were sympathetic to the Presbyterians. While Martin has a strong voice, Sir Simon Synod, who speaks throughout *A Sacred Decretall,* has a slimy voice which is superstitious and incapable of disguising or suppressing his evil intentions. His voice is vain, negative and marked by false incantatory phrases which are self-evidently hollow: "O that profane *Martin!* that cursed *Martin!* that wicked *Martin!* wring off his neck, for *ever and ever, And let all people say,* AMEN.*"[31]

What should be noted here is the flux of identities, not only as each character is metamorphosised for the sake of the satirical attack at any particular point, but also because of the way in which each character renames the others. Here, we see the calumniation process going on in front of us within the pamphlets. The author is making the reader aware that he knows what is going on, and that he wants the reader to be aware too. Martin successively enhances our sense of the real folly and knavery of Sir John, whose status is diminished by the lunacy of his judgements.[32] Sir Simon becomes *Simon Suck-egge,*[33] a reference to the Presbyterian greed for tithes, but paranomasia is also used to identify the Presbyterians with the notorious Cavalier poet, Sir John Suckling (see also *Vox Borealis* (1641, Sig. C2r)). Martin, though, is characterised by Sir Simon and Sir John as both a violent bull and a disease.

The animalising tendency is of course an attempt to reduce rational men to beasts. Martin is a dog whose bark is louder than the Presbyterians *"Blurting."* There is also a play of identities upon bulls here. If Martin is an angry bull in the china shop of Presbyterianism, the Presbyterians are likened unto the *"Bulls of Bason"* (Ps.22.12), the traditional symbol of an oppressor, lat-

er applied by Overton and others to Cromwell. The allegory is fastidiously precise as it is explained in the text: Martin's right horn is for tithes, and his left horn for the Directory. The Presbyterians become wolves or foxes, the identifications usually applied to Papists, and again a potent part of English Protestant propaganda. The Presbyterians are also cormorants or young cubs in their greed, unclean birds in their attitudes towards church discipline, or "croaking skip-jacke" toads as they had just been cast up from the stomach of the dragon. On the other hand, domestic or pastoral animals exist as an image of social harmony, though the final balance is an impression of threat rather than harmony as the martins, cuckoos and swallows are forced to migrate (go into exile) by "Church-owles," "Jack-Dawes" (Sir John Presbyters), "blinde *Batts*" and "Presbyterian *Wood-cocks.*"[34]

Who, though, is the more violent here? Martin has a justified *holy violence,* because he is exposing the weakness, evil and folly of that neo-Papist religion, Presbyterianism. The woodcut which prefaces *A Sacred Decretall* shows Martin as a bull, seated at table, writing a tract, and in the act of writing, tossing a Presbyter, perhaps Sir Simon or Sir John, over his head and into a fire. . . . It is all a big joke: the bull perhaps winks at the viewer, as if to confirm his descent from the jesting figure of Martin Marprelate. Moreover, there is, it can be argued, a visual insight into the conditions of surreptitious pamphleteering at this time. Martin the bull would seem to be sitting in a small room within just a few texts on a shelf above the table. The horns give Martin a superior power over the Presbyterians since they are associated with the horns of Moses, while the horns signify the jealousy of the cuckold, deprived by the Presbyterians of the true relationship with Christ. In *A Sacred Decretall* a hilarious parody of the Assembly of Divines is developed as an ironic parallel to Martin's horns and true Christian worship. From a reference in a sermon by Matthew Newcomen which refers to the Assembly waiting daily upon the Angel in the Mount, Overton develops the picture of the Assembly as the mount of dunces, on top of which the Earl of Holland, a leading Presbyterian aristocrat, waits like Moses. The angel is a Scotsman, the Kirk, with whom the Earl has wrestled in the past on the verges of the mount, presumably a reference to the Bishops' War. The joke returns to the issue of Scriptural interpretation: in Scotland, the mount is called *"Dunce-Hill,'* but in England it is deceitfully rendered as *"Mount-Sion,"* referring to its popular name, Sion College. There is a sense of modesty and secrecy, as though Overton were trying to show the state to which the censorship has pushed radical religious writers. There is also a visual impression of overthrowing, suggestive of the phrase *overturning* which was to become so popular with the radicals in the later 1640s and the 1650s.[35] Presbyterianism, Popery in disguise, is thrown over as part of the old order. Overton's name, a homonym of *overturning,* signifies his aptness for his active role in this usurpation.

In fact, the Marpriest tracts repeatedly enforce "God's Vengeance" as the apocalyptic power which passes final judgement upon the Presbyterians. Overton is possibly trying to make capital out of the emergent popular millennialism at this point.

On the other hand, Sir John Presbyter is violent not in terms of reformation, but in terms of consumption. In an earlier pamphlet, *A New Play Called Canterburie His Change of Diot* (1641, Sig. A2r), Overton had comically represented Laud's persecution by shewing the Archbishop and accomplices dining on the ears cut from the Puritans Bastwick, Burton and Prynne in 1637. Consumption both ridicules and makes more horrific the presence of tyrannical violence. Overton's works of 1645 locate the Presbyterians in the tradition of greedy materialist Papists, the representation of a corruption which goes back to the very roots of the Reformation. Sir John becomes a machine-like cannibal who threatens to gnash people between his teeth as the Presbyterian favouring of tithes deprives people of that which enables them merely to survive:

> O all ye holy ravenous Order of *Syon-Jesuites,* pluck off his feathers, teare him in pieces, rend his flesh, crush his bones with your great *Iron Teeth,* make no more of him then you would of a *Tith Pigge,* be sure to devoure him, but you must have a speciall care to chew him well, for he is a tough *Bitt.*[36]

Overton is in no doubt that such appropriations cause real hardship: poor widows and orphans cry out while Presbyters endow their wives with fine clothes. Overton notes that the Presbyterian ministers are well paid: Cornelius Burges was settled as lecturer in St. Paul's Cathedral at a rate of £400 per year. The very titles of *Sir* Simon and *Sir* John reveal the link made between Presbyterianism and the gentry, many of whom were in favour of keeping tithes since they were often impropriators, and were allowed to keep a portion of what they collected for themselves.[37] The champing teeth have to be pacified with a *corall,* a child's teething ring.[38] The *corall* is the Ordinance for Tithes of 8 November 1644 and it is given by Parliament.[39] This fit of consumption is marked by a repeated usage of keywords which emphasise the greed: the tithes are to be paid not only in money, but more traditionally as lambs, geese and pigs.[40] Presbyterians have huge bellies, so that the collective body of the Assembly of Divines, even though it was not purely Presbyterian, still has an insatiable appetite. Here, Overton falls back upon a version of the body politic metaphor, a habitual means of representing metaphorically the political process in this period. Persecution is seen as a means of the destruction of the body politic in "*dissentions, mutinies, tumults, insurrections, uproares,* and *divi-*

sions."[41] It is also another point at which the festive inversion can be made plain in these pamphlets. While Sir John and Sir Simon have *classicall clubs,* as if they were stock braggart warriors, they will be contested by the *Independent hammer* of the sectarians. Such figures become associated with the Philistines.[42] Here, ecclesiastical debate is portrayed as a kind of Punch and Judy show, with Sir John as a ridiculous Hercules with his club, or equally, like a version of the tyrant Nero.[43]

However, these metaphorical envisionings of dissention, disruption, want, suffering and disfigurement alternate with a descriptive register which blatantly sets out the effects of religious oppression and civil strife. Against a background of European-wide violence in the Thirty Years' War, Overton exposes the stupidity of mutually opposed enemies, Papist and Protestant, who will always torture and maim in order to force the consciences of each other. Human history becomes a list of horrendous punishments, a condensed Foxe:

> this *Savage Blood-thirsty* Wretch *Hangeth, Burneth, Stoneth, Tortureth, Saweth a sunder, Casteth into the fiery* Fornace, *into the Lions Denne, Teareth in peeces with* Wild Horses, *Plucketh out the eyes, Roasteth quicke, Bur[i]eth alive, Plucketh out the* Tongues, *Imprisoneth, Scourgeth, Revileth, Curseth, yea, with* Bell, Booke *and* Candle, *Belyeth, Cutteth the* Eares, *Slitte[t]h the* Nose.[44]

The expansion on p.44 of the second edition of *The Araignement* connects this violence specifically with Scotland and the Solemn League and Covenant, the agreement taken by Parliament upon which the Presbyterian party was staking its claim. In *A Sacred Decretall,* the two indexes are merged, mixing mockery and horrific violence when Sir Simon Synod says that "*rods in pisse*" have been laid for a future whipping of Cromwell.[45] This dense recounting of violence is a response to persecution as well as a means of rousing people against it.

The modes of inversion here extend from the body politic metaphor to a series of plays upon surface appearances. The organising principle here is metamorphosis, fantastic transformation or metempsychosis, but applied to a base material subject. A similar technique had already been used against episcopacy by Sir Edward Dering in 1642.[46] Thus, particular attention is paid to the changing appearance of Sir John. Inside, or beneath the surface, he still *is* an oppressive Roman power, or a Jesuit.[47] As Overton was to say later in the narrative of his arrest and imprisonment, he would stand up and oppose tyranny in whichever *form* it occurred. Sir John has simply changed his dress, so that he is now disguised as a Presbyter. In *The Araignement,* Persecution is shown to have moved through several forms of tyranny, while maintaining the presumption of the "median posture." Sir John now has the characteristic *blew capp* and the *cloak-bagge,* the marks of a Presbyter. This is a clear development from Marprelate, where Bishops are distinguished by the "catercaps."[48] From the *cloak-bagge,* all other disguises may come: you can never trust a Presbyter.[49] This is juxtaposed again with the simple, plain cassock of Martin.

Moreover, the metamorphosis motif is also applied to the linguistic and Scriptural procedures of the Presbyterians. They are guilty of perpetrating false glosses and sophistications in their writings, "Castles in the Ayre," as well as incorporating metamorphosis itself in their own language, something which is equivalent to the deceitful disguise exhibited in their dress. The opening passage of *The Araignement* traces Persecution through the name of Spanish Inquisition, the casting off of episcopal garments for the sake of Presbytery, jumping down from Scotland to England, disguised "with a Sylogisticall pair of Britches (saving your presence) in *Bocardo,* and snatching a Rhetoricall Cassok he girt up his loynes with a Sophisticall Girdle, and ran into the wildernesse of *Tropes,* and *Figures.*" Like quickfire spreading, the passage accelerates as the figures of sure perception and judgement follow Persecution through the churches of the land until he is cornered in the Assembly of Divines, but in self-defence, he turns himself into a *"reverend Imprimatur,"* silencing his critics. Such a highly wrought *peripeteia* serves to explain aptly, in its concentration upon the Presbyterian use of metaphor, the nature of the trial which follows, for the trial is none other than an allegory of the paper war in which the arguments for the liberty of conscience were put forward in the early 1640s.[50] It is, of course, a judgement and set of perceptions which is imposed by Overton: *decorum personae* had become *decorum rhetoricae* also. In a sense, Overton is also fighting for a truth-status which he knows will be challenged because of the very nature of his satirical strategy. In an attack upon the Marpriest pamphlets, John Vicars singled out the deceitful rhetoric and allegory which Overton uses in his own pamphlet as a figure for the transformation of persecution.[51]

These forms are organised in *The Araignement Of Mr. Persecvtion* by the appealing device of the trial. The trial was to have an influence upon Overton's writings after the overt usage which it received in *The Araignement.* For instance, the title page of *The Inditement of Tythes* (Feb., 1646) (perhaps assembled by Overton) has echoes of a trial document, so that the sense of the reader being invited to share with the author a judgment upon Presbyterianism is compounded. It is also made more effective by its juxtaposition with other recognisable voices of radical religious or Leveller complaint, and the general claim that the Presbyterians use the law to deceive the common people, who have no skill in legal tactics.[52]

The Araignement Of Mr. Persecvtion itself is a substantial success as a trial pamphlet. It is only from this strength that the sequel pamphlets gain their credibility. The voices of ridicule and good sense are built up carefully, sanctioning in the reader's mind, as it were, the more flamboyant strategies of the later pamphlets. Dialogues, including trials, were by 1645 very much part of the sub-genres which prevailed in popular pamphlets, though the way in which *The Araignement* talks about a religious subject in such depth, and incorporates skilfully so many radical religious standpoints and personalities, was something of an innovation. Like impersonation and disguise, trials allowed opponents to be denigrated and for those opponents to be seen to denigrate themselves, only with the impression of fairness or righteousness which the properly conducted trial gives.[53] In the dialogue, Overton can be seen writing in a deliberately popular mode, which draws from both religious and secular traditions. There might also be a dramatic influence in the manner in which the characters are laid out like a *dramatis personae* list (p. 3), while this list also resembles loosely the *schema* which were often attached to works of devotion. On this level, the pamphlet again conflates the sacred with the secular at a deliberately profane and popular level.[54]

The identities of the characters in the trial are established by the application of both allegorical and political names to the characters in a Court of Assizes. The prisoner, Persecution, may seem to receive a rough deal because the jury is composed almost wholly of *good* characters, while the persecutor is the apocalyptic *God's Vengeance.* However, during the trial, Sir Simon Synod tries to organise an alternative jury consisting of members abhorrent to the Independent and sectarian cause. So, the trial manifests the continuing deceit and unfairness of the Presbyterians, while being set in a moral context in which good and evil, white and black, are established *a priori* in the *dramatis personae* (pp. 2-3).

Above all, it is a tension between the juridical role of the characters and their allegorical significance, both political and religious, which bolsters the appeal of the pamphlet. In this, Overton reveals himself to be a not unsubtle witness to the make-up of English social fabric, and the way that fabric was perceived by contemporaries. Thus, the members of the committee for the Grand Inquest include Mr Nationall Strength, with a play on *notional,* to point up the way in which people are initially concerned only with forms, outsides, rather than insides, or substances. Accordingly, Mr Nationall Strength thinks in similitudes of the body politic. Persecution has ruptured the *naturall skin* of the *one politicke body,* ruining a model of harmonious behaviour in the country. It is not simply that Persecution has sought social disruption, but that he has wreaked havoc upon the way in which the people think about the peace and unity of the nation. Despite the concern with surfaces, this aspect of people's habitual ways of thinking is seen to be continuous with other, more material, modes of oppression.

So, in allegorically elaborate and complete terms, Persecution is indicted and tried. He is defended by Sir John Presbyter and Sir Simon Synod, who are prevented from rigging the jury by the presiding Justices, Reason and Humility. Persecution is testified against by Gaffars Christian, Martyrs and Liberty of Conscience. The last, Sir Simon tries to keep out of the courtroom, a dramatic representation of censorship. Despite a further alliance between the Knights of Presbytery and the third justice, Conformity, Persecution, Sir John and Sir Simon are eventually punished by being kept in custody by Parliament until the final pronouncements at the Day of Judgement.

The main body of the pamphlet falls into two parts. The first belongs to the festive technique, and is concerned with the play and transformation of identities in order to ridicule Presbytery at the expense of Independency and the sects. The second is the expounding of the arguments of the two sides within the context of the trial scene.

IV

The writing of inversion itself is a kind of endless, energetic stream which could be appropriated for any standpoint. As Terry Eagleton has noted, carnival, like inversion, stands for little itself in terms of content, an *empty semiotic flow* which signifies only *comradeship* in the barriers it breaks down between reader and speaking voice.[55] As *The Araignement Of Mr. Persecvtion* progresses, this element is reduced, to make way for the serious statement of the opposition to persecution.

If the exchanges in the pamphlet wars of the 1590s were characterised by men, like Thomas Nashe, who wrote for a living, and who would invent the next trope in order to gain a penny, then it could be argued that Overton's style in part derives from the attitudes behind this method. Like Marprelate, Overton adopted such a rhetoric for a religious purpose, though it should be said also that Marprelate is generally held to have had an influence upon exactly those pamphleteers, like Nashe, who were hired to attack him.[56] It is logical enough, given that Overton is posturing as someone *low* attacking something *high*. It is here that the assuring voice of Martin which we have heard elsewhere in the Marpriest tracts turns into a racy voice of condemnation, the accretive qualities of the style matching the trading habits of the Presbyters.[57] According to William Prynne, that unrelenting opponent of Independency, Marpriest was guilty of "unchristian, uncivill, ap-

probrious, Billingsgate tearmes, as (I am confident) no *Oxford Aulicus* or satyricall *cavaleere* is able to paralell." Prynne also disliked the belittling, instanced in the likening of Parliamentary Ordinances to toys.[58] This relies upon a hasty syntax, which exploits the typography of print, and defies a sense of reason in the swift connections of thought, and the repeated exclamations which seem to parody a sermon. Here, both Presbyterian braggadocios speak:

> Woe *unto those* Anabaptists, Brownists, &c. *those cursed Heretickes, for those* presbyterian Feinds *expect but the* word of command, *to devoure them up:* But Mr. William[s], *all this will come to nothing, if this Prisoner be put to death, you see those Sectaries have had such freedom of speech that my Son Iacke and I can doe no good; now, there being not such a considerable person in this County as your self to prevaile.*[59]

However, this is not a Presbyterian sermon. It does not fit with Abraham Wright's imitation of Presbyterian sermons,[60] and also, Martin derides implicitly those preachers who are trained at university. The syntax achieves here its own metamorphosis, paralleling that which is taking place in Persecution's change of clothes.[61] This particular style is taken on throughout the pamphlet by various other voices of good sense. Though in *A Sacred Decretall,* Sir Simon Synod talks in a deliberately oily fashion (p. 17), verisimilitude to the legal setting in *The Araignement* is enhanced by the cool manner in which Persecution speaks, the way that he tries, in a voice of reason, to smear the Grand Inquest and Gods-Vengeance, even in the light of equity. Here, Sir Simon adopts the same description of the metempsychosis of Persecution, from his own point of view, that we witness at the beginning of the pamphlet, from Overton's point of view. The sense of pattern makes the writing more persuasive, as we see the gap between reality and naming: "his true *and* proper name *is* Present Reformation, *which by Interpretation, is, Presbyterian Government."*[62]

In fact, the codes here reveal much about the context of pamphleteering in the period. Unlike in Marprelate, there is no studied attempt to create a *persona* through specific, especially colloquial, phrases. There is a limited use of these in Overton, such as the occasional Marprelate-like laughter, "Ha, ha, ha." However, Overton insists largely on the clash of different personal and public voices. The clash of different styles must have been intended to signal to readers a particular stance, or simply a distinct interest, perhaps of an iniquitous nature. This is brought out well in *A Sacred Decretall,* where the style becomes self-consciously one of conspiracy. There may be a case for believing that Overton may have played conspiratorial roles himself, beyond pamphleteering. We know that later in 1652 he engaged surreptitiously in negotiations with Royalists, and his references in *Vox Borealis* (1641) to the speakers of the tract as spies (*scouts*) may be related to his experiences.[63]

In establishing each coded speech, keywords are important, for they define the terms of political and religious debate. Gaffar Christian knows, for instance, by *woefull experience* what persecution has done, *experience* here referring to the Puritan word for spiritual knowledge of the divine and of saving grace for the individual.[64] Though the Presbyterians did not interrupt the meetings of the Independents and sectarians, where confessions of *experience* might have been given in front of a congregation as a requirement of joining that church, the echoes implicit in *experience* associate the Presbyterians with the sometimes brutal interruption of separatist conventicles by Laudian or episcopal authorities.[65] Tonally, this is supported by the repeated apostrophes. The *O*s can become tedious, though they are presumably directed towards gathering a popular appeal. They do not feature greatly in other writing associated with radical religious pamphlet controversy, apart from the sermon. But again, they operate to destroy the sense of reason, expounded in Presbyterian pamphlets, and to invite the reader to share in Martin's play. After all, we are not so much listening to Martin's arguments as enjoying the sense of power released for the speaking voice and the reader in the destruction or containment of Persecution, Sir John, and Sir Simon. This is compounded by the use of proverbs, which enhance the popular impulse of Martin. In proverbs, there is no immediate or sustained thought-out sense, but a nugget of inherited wisdom cast in crude gnomic grammar. Alluding to the Chinese story, Overton refers to the proverbial long spoon necessary to eat with the devil.[66] Again, it is an opportunity for us to appreciate the sheer rightness of Martin. The same is true of the extensive classical allusion. There may be republican overtones in the quotation of the lamentation from Horace's first *Epistle,* lines 1-2, "*O Cives, Cives, quarenda pecunia primum, / Virtus post nummos.*"[67] In a culture based upon the higher truth residing in ancient wisdom, and the decay implicit in all contemporary learning, the quotation of classical literature has the same effect as the use of proverbs, except in a higher mode, as it were. At the pinnacle of this method is Overton's ridicule of the Presbyterians by suggesting that they are superstitious conjurors. *A Sacred Decretall* begins with a page of Latin conjurations which call down divine power in order to reveal Martin Marpriest's true identity. All that Sir Simon reveals is the figure of the bull tossing Sir John Presbyter on his shoulders. As Martin notes later in *Martin's Eccho,* the significance of this is that the truth is always revealed through any process of divination. The accusations of blasphemy and profanity in Martin's works is really an account of Sir Simon himself: "*mutatio nomine de te fabula narratur.*"[68] The doctrine of *decorum personae* is again justified.

The process which is articulated by these techniques is part of Overton's presentation of the process of *calmuniation,* as we have seen already. To identify the Presbyterians with the Papists is to indulge in a form of metonymy, whereby the one is a part of the other, or rather, the Presbyterians are substituted for the Papists. In terms of the way Martin represents this, it is a process of metempsychosis or metamorphosis of the form of carnal Rome through Episcopacy into Presbyterianism. But underneath this, the terms of identity operate through metonymy. By the same token, Overton as Martin complains at the way in which Anabaptists, Brownists and other sectarians are lumped together and pejoratively condemned as one rebellious group.[69] In fact, the Anabaptists and Brownists, on the evidence of their own confessions, says Overton, are full of piety and sincerity. Such a perspective, which Overton presents as the way things are, seems to be the root of all things in the sphere of public debate: thus we see two versions of Scottish history throughout the Marpriest pamphlets, and appreciate the falseness of the Presbyterian view of Scottish history. Again, on the other side, the Scots (where Presbyterianism had taken its strongest hold) are ridiculed in terms of their accents, as *Jemmy* is spelt to imitate Scottish speech.[70]

These figures are nevertheless related closely to the reality of politics and religion. Overton finds the convenient example of the Jesuit Lysimachus Nicanor's (alias the Scottish anti-Presbyterian John Corbet) letter of congratulation to the Scottish Presbyterians.[71] Martin's logic of perception, incorporating this metonymy, sees the connection between worship and necessity, it being an issue which brings liberty of conscience to the foreground. The Presbyterians support the Ordinance for the ordination of all ministers because it will stifle the sectarian preachers in the Parliamentarian army (Cromwell's soldiers are named here). However, for Martin, the fact that the soldiers are responsible for the victory of Marston Moor makes liberty of conscience a pre-requisite for internal unity if the larger, external forces of royal tyranny are to be beaten.[72]

The effect of this metonymy (as it were) was not merely a technique of public persuasion. Rather, it was a part of the genuine political and religious situation of the 1640s, when differences arose between parties and factions over different interpretations of Scripture or legal agreements. Here, the Presbyterians are seen to be distorting the Solemn League and Covenant of 1643 in their attacks upon liberty of conscience.[73]

Each of the soon-to-be Levellers had a device here, however, which enabled them to override the balancing of perspectives which the *calumniation* effect had. This was to present themselves as martyrs, thereby focussing upon the very point where calumniation occurs. Lilburne was perhaps the master of martyrological self-presentation, but Overton was not untalented in this mode. Martin is identified with the persecuted among the Puritans in the 1630s: "my voyce is no other then the *cry of blood,* even of the Prophets and Martyrs of Iesus."[74] *"Synodean coales"* are recommended for Martin by Sir Simon Synod.[75] This, of course, was allied to Leveller philosophy concerning natural rights, and so aids the power of the strategy. Emerging from the sense of oppression, the self is presented as a free commoner, while expression is seen as part of an activity guaranteed in natural or fundamental law, which guarantees the status of the self.[76] The concern with the liberty of the subject, especially with regard to issues of religious toleration was, as Overton admitted, to lead naturally to the more fully articulated Leveller ideas of guaranteed rights. In 1645, Overton's insistence upon the subject's liberties and *salus populi* is rendered within the satire with great clarity. The argument for Presbyteries by divine right as opposed to *de jure humano* is seen as an essential problem, leading to the Presbyterian desire to appropriate land and wealth from the Irish. By setting themselves above the magistrate, the Presbyterians are not only alienating the principles of civil power, but also in spiritual terms, the royal prerogative of Christ.[77] In the 1630s and the 1640s, the individual literally was the object of oppression. Hence the concern with martyrology, a tradition which, when used by the Levellers, put them in line, of course, with the greatest Protestant account of the sufferings of the righteous at the hands of tyrants and the Papacy, Foxe's *Book of Martyrs.* So, using the apt metaphor of struggle, liberty of conscience is described as a building which may be pulled down by the oppressor.[78]

Part of this concern with oppression, suffered by the self, or the writer, put Overton as Marpriest directly in the Marprelate tradition. This was the issue of press censorship. The advent of the printing press had created a new context for criticism of princes and the church, and demanded new ways of controlling such printed material.[79] Marprelate was the first Elizabethan Puritan to make the issue of press freedom part of the content, and the satirical strategies, in his pamphlets. Overton carried on with this method. The Presbyterians had tried to silence the sectarian presses in an Ordinance of 14 June 1643, which demanded that all publications be licensed, a group of censors for different subjects being appointed.[80] The Martinist exposure of this iniquity starts with a pun, *"Pres-byters,"* while the Marpriest tracts are spotted with references to works speaking out for freedom of conscience, William Walwyn's *The Compassionate Samaritane* (1644), Roger Williams' *The Blovdy Tenent of Persecution* (1644), and Overton's previous works, including those in the Marpriest series.[81]

The Stationers Company had controlled the press by a royally-granted monopoly until the 1640s, so that Overton's anger is directed at tyranny and monopoly, in a manner similar to his attack upon the greed of the Presbyterians. Whether Milton's own plea for freedom of speech and of the press, *Areopagitica,* can be said to have influenced Overton, is a difficult matter to answer. What both Milton and Martin Marpriest have in common is a use of the very issue and language of the debate regarding press censorship as a central element in their arguments, thereby speaking out at the very point of repression, while using censorship, like disguise, as a means of avoiding the gaze of the censor. This is a form of the militant and hilarious subversion, instanced in Martin Marpriest's mimicry of imprimaturs: "This is Licensed, and printed according to Holy Order, but not Entered into the Stationers Monopole."[82] Here, Holy Order is the unlicensable spirit and religious conviction of the sectarian and Independent congregations, so putting the imprimatur in radical religious terms, but still in the form of episcopal, Presbyterian or legal phraseology. The refusal to enter it in the Stationers Monopole is a simple statement of what the liberty of the press and religious toleration should mean. Other forms of subverting *official* printed forms also occur in the Marpriest tracts: apart from the self-mocking tones of *The Epistle Dedicatorie* in *The Araignement* (sig. A4r), Martin provides a notice of appointment, such as the House of Commons would attach to Parliamentary sermons, authorising their appearance as printed books (sig. A4r). Here, dated Saturday, 6 April 1645, Martin has the Presbyterian divines Henry Roborough and Adoniram Byfield (demoted by Martin to the posts of *scribes*) sign an order from the Assembly of Divines. The order demands that the leading Presbyterian, Cornelius Burges, and the Presbyterian heresiographer, Thomas Edwards, thank Martin for his pious pamphlet, and stipulate that the pamphlet should be printed, as a *divine Hand-Maide* to the *Directory,* the Presbyterian rules for church discipline and public order authorised by Parliament. Through impersonation, Martin again takes control, and there is a final joke, for by seizing the reins here, Martin has the Assembly of Divines allow him to authorise whoever he wants to print *The Araignement.* After the command, Martin says that only Martin Claw-Clergie (possibly Overton's cousin, Henry Overton, or more possibly, William Larner) may print the tract. By calling Martin Claw-Clergie printer to the Assembly of Divines, Overton is saying that the Assembly need such a printer to cure them of the Presbyterian malaise.

It is not too out of place to raise here the significant role which the actual mentioning of texts performs in Overton's persuasive patterns. Again, because liberty of conscience and expression is at issue, any statement at all is bound to draw attention to the possibility of its own illegality. Such is the case with the quoting of passages from various hostile works, a strategy which is quite different from the Presbyterians' quoting of Martin in order to show what to them is self-evident error.[83] The ultimate manifestation of this is when the greatest statements for liberty of conscience made in the 1640s appear, with their authors, as actual characters in the trial of *The Araignement.*[84] At the same time, throughout the Marpriest tracts, Overton spares no effort in quoting directly, and in most cases accurately, from the works of opponents, both heresiography and sermons. The jesting voice of Martin or the foolish voice of the Presbyterian knights is vindicated precisely because of the presented quotations, while the hypocrisy of Presbyterian language here can also be exposed. By quoting a phrase from a 1641 anti-episcopal sermon by Cornelius Burges, Overton is able to show the inconsistency of the Presbyterians (who once railed against persecution but who now give it sanction), and to expose the very violence in their language, personalities and policies: *"those Whips of Scorpions, the back-breaking, heartsinking Courts, which are now broken downe and dissolved."*[85] In such a situation, the laments of Burges and Ephraim Pagitt for the wrecked vineyard of the Lord, the Church, become crocodile tears. The almost contradictory use made of quotation here is noticeable. On the one hand, a passage from a sermon by Matthew Newcomen inviting punishment from the people if the Presbyterians fail is quoted with the obvious point. On the other, without the same irony, the Ordinance for Tithes is ridiculed for being taken as a Scriptural text: "onely I shall presume . . . to ranck it for the present amongst the *Apocrypha Writings,* as *A Divine Appendix to the Famous* HISTORY *of* BELL *and the* DRAGON."[86] Working within the pervasive food frame of reference in these tracts, Presbyterian books and laws, like the Solemn League and Covenant, become bait on which to hook the people, large phrases with which to dupe the minds of the population: *"Huick discipline omnes orbis principes & Monarchas fasces suos submittere & parere necesse est."*[87]

There is a degree of anxiety on Overton's part even here, however, for he fears, as Martin says in *The Postscript,* that a "Synoddicall misconstruction" will distort some of his meanings.[88] Martin does not wish to defame the Parliament, the Scots or the union of peace between the two kingdoms. He is simply interested in attacking the Presbyterian operation in these areas. Also, his imitation of the Order of Parliament is only "to shew the ostentation, pride, and vaine glory of the boasting Presbyters."[89] The omission of the explanation of satirical principle and practice between the imitation of the Order and the effect Overton wishes to make is an admission, implicitly, of the comic tradition working here. It is habitual and therefore does not need to be explained. Still, censorship is, in terms of the metamorphosis of the spirit of Persecution, the last straw. The genesis of *The Araignement* (p. 2) itself is explained as the frustration with the last resting place of Persecution—in the Presbyterian control of the press—

leads tò the Independent press going underground ("privately"). Through *dangerous labour* and *through a deliverance,* Overton was able to bring Persecution to justice; which is to say, in the printing of the pamphlet, and the trial which it contains. Clearly, unlicensed printing is considered by Martin to be good for the people,[90] while the habit of challenging authority by printing it within one's own frames of reference is repeated in *An Arrow Against All Tyrants,* when the 1646 Ordinance for arresting Overton *for printing scandalous things against this House* is reprinted *in toto,* under the imprimatur *Rectat Justitia* (p. 18, Sig. Alr).

V

How significant and successful were the Marpriest tracts? It is, of course, difficult to be precise in determining just how widely these pamphlets were read, what sort of effects and responses they generated, and how they compared with other contemporary polemical and satirical writings. However, there is a certain amount of evidence which enables us to see the complex response which Overton's tracts evoked. This itself sheds new light upon the content of the tracts and upon 1640s Puritanism in general.

There was in fact nothing special about the jesting style, be it used by Royalists or Parliamentarians, though it should be remembered that Overton was a very distinctive stylist. The tradition of jesting as a means of commenting upon political or religious events was fairly commonplace. One such work was *The Cow-Ragiovs Castle-Combat* (1645) by James Fencer and William Wrastler, alias the Cambridge wit John Gower, a work which had already appeared under the title *Pyrgomachia; Vel potius Pygomachia* (1635). The Royalist news journal, *Mercurius Aulicus,* was run by Sir John Birkenhead, while the Parliament issued *Mercurius Britannicus.* Both employed techniques of jest and ridicule. All of these types of political writing were attempts to popularise particular points of view. It has been suggested recently that the forms of symbolic and ritual humour which are found in these pamphlets were borrowed from social rituals, like carnival and charivari, and that these rituals were a way for those not in the political nation of partaking in pervasive moral and political debates.[91] If this is the case, and such elements can be detected in the Marpriest tracts, then it is also the case that these symbolic forms had been adopted by a fairly sophisticated argumentative mode. They could not possibly be used simply as social gesture, since they are part of a different language, a much more complex and non-symbolic critical argument. Many satirical pamphlets do not employ such arguments. Instead, they rely upon their wit. What makes Overton remarkable is the mutually enhancing satirical strategies and the detailed and extended argument, very much akin to Marprelate.

There was a series of complaints by Presbyterians and other opponents of toleration in the two years following the first publication of *The Araignement of Mr. Persecvtion.* The first category of these were outraged remarks in the heresiography of Thomas Edwards and the Erastian William Prynne. There were also attempts to answer Martin in his own terms, but, of course, Martinist language for the Presbyterians was forbidden because it was profane. Instead, in two broadsheets, *Proper Persecution, or the Sandy Foundation of a general Toleration* (22 December 1646) and *Reall Persecution, or the Foundation of a general Toleration, Displained and Portrayed* (13 February 1646/47), as well as in the lengthier elaborations of Prynne, sections from the Marpriest tracts, especially *Martin's Eccho,* were reprinted under phrases which condemned them as "hellish, heathenish and cursed carnal practices."[92] Interestingly enough, the pictures of inversion could be used in this mode, and one woodcut does show Martin Marpriest being ridden by a fool in a sort of charivari procession, as if it were an inversion and punishment for the picture at the front of *A Sacred Decretall.* . . . It has not previously been noted, but Lilburne was erroneously thought by some to have been the author of the Marpriest tracts. The figure in *Reall Persecution* bears some resemblance to portraits of Lilburne in other pamphlets. Whether Lilburne was being pointed at here, or not, the identity of Martin remained as obscure as ever.[93]

Overton did spark off a range of imitators, including an entire sub-genre of Sir John Presbyter pamphlets, and he may also have contributed further pamphlets himself.[94] The figure of the anti-tolerationist as braggadocio caught on and was applied to Prynne personally in *The Falsehood Of Mr. William Pryn's Truth Triumphing* (8 May 1645, p. 6). However, it is unlikely that all of these were written by Overton himself, if only for the simple reason that they do not seem to carry the same types of argument as the Marpriest tracts proper, even though many of the jesting features are similar to Overton's, especially in respect of disguise. The Royalist John Crouch's use of Overton's style, his possible acquaintance with Overton, and his possible interference with one Overton tract, has been mapped out by Marie Gimelfarb-Brack.[95] One can say with more certainty that other Royalists, such as John Cleveland, and not Parliamentarians, were influenced by Marpriest's style. Cleveland's poem, "The Hue And Cry After Sir John Presbyter," though drawing a sophisticated picture of the Presbyter, seems at first to dwell upon the image on the front of *A Sacred Decretall,* especially the description of the moustache: "The *Negative* and *Covenanting* Oath,/ Like two Mustachoes issuing from his mouth." . . .[96] But then there is an unmistakeable reference to *Martin's Eccho* as it gives indigestion (the complaint of Sir Simon Synod) to the Assembly of Divines, which met first at King Henry VII's Chapel, here envisioned as a decayed abbey:

So by an Abbyes Scheleton of late,
I heard an Eccho supererogate
Through imperfection, and the voice restore
As if she had the hicop or'e and or'e.[97]

Martin's vulgarity "supererogates" the purpose of the Presbyterians in the Assembly of Divines. Cleveland makes no statement of affinity with Martin: he would not of course have held with liberty of conscience. Ironically, while Overton went on finally to different modes of expression (though he may have written Marpriest pamphlets later on in the 1640s), his influence in the Marpriest style seems largely to have been upon the greatest opponents of toleration, the Royalists.

A sensible objection to the analysis which has just been presented would be that the complex patterns of satire and manipulation present in the texts were simply not understood with that detail in the mid- to late 1640s. The Marpriest tracts scandalised their opponents but because of their very nature, they made an easy target for immediate dismissal as blasphemous. The method of satire did not matter. This is a worrying conclusion, since it leaves the effect of these pamphlets still largely unexplained. It seems, from their statements, that the Presbyterians and Prynne understood the danger of Marpriest's satire, and were sufficiently troubled by both the extreme statements for toleration and rights, to quote sections from the tracts, without stooping to Martin's level in order to answer back. It was impossible for them to put their arguments for tithes, ordination, censorship and so forth, into the jesting mode, in order to answer Martin in kind.

Martin was first of all a weaver of fictions by means of the associative anarchy of the mind: his argument was effected in the first instance through that. But simply by quoting Martin within a general frame of condemnation, the Presbyterians were allowing Martin further space in the entire body of published materials. Marpriest had outflanked his enemies in terms of strategy, thereby winning the battle for toleration through his method at least: certainly for the rest of the 1640s, liberty of the press remained to a large extent, even if tithes remained, and persecution was still a reality. Yet, just like his father, Martin Marprelate, Martin Marpriest was to have his greatest direct influence upon those who were the farthest away from him in terms of the political and religious stances of 1645.

Notes

I should like to thank Dr Thomas N. Corns, Professor William Lamont and Dr Blair Worden for reading and commenting upon earlier drafts of this essay.

[1] Joseph Frank, *The Levellers* (Camb., Mass.: Harvard U.P., 1955); H. N. Brailsford, *The Levellers and the English Revolution,* edited and prepared for publi-

cation by Christopher Hill (London: Cresset Press, 1961); G. E. Aylmer, ed., *The Levellers in the English Revolution* (London: Thames and Hudson, 1974); Marie Gimelfarb-Brack, *Liberté, Egalité, Fraternité, Justice! La vie et l'oeuvre de Richard Overton, Niveleur* (Berne: Peter Lang, 1979). I am greatly indebted to Dr. Gimelfarb-Brack's work in this article.

[2] Margot Heinemann, *Puritanism and Theatre: Thomas Middleton and Opposition Drama under the Early Stuarts* (Cambridge: C.U.P., 1980), pp. 239-52.

[3] Gimelfarb-Brack, pp. 337-436.

[4] Raymond A. Anselment, *"Betwixt Jest and Earnest." Marprelate, Milton, Marvell, Swift & the Decorum of Religious Ridicule* (Toronto: Toronto U.P., 1979), p. 160.

[5] See Gimelfarb-Brack, pp. 21-74. For an analysis of some these early works in the contexts of the drama, see Heinemann, pp. 239-52, and Martin Butler, *Theatre and Crisis 1632-1642* (Cambridge: C.U.P., 1984), pp. 238-42, 246-7, 280.

[6] For instance, in *Articles Of High Treason Exhibited against Cheap-Side Crosse* (London, 1642), p. 4, the cross is seen to crucify itself, a reference to its demolition, because it was seen as an idolatrous symbol: "Oh dismall doome, oh more accursed fate,/ The *Crosse* in *Cheap-side* quite *crost out of date.*" The self-performed denigration is typical of the behaviour of the Presbyterian *personae* in the Marpriest tracts.

[7] See Gimelfarb-Brack, pp. 123-4. The suggestion that Overton was involved in these reprints comes from the appearance of the Latin phrase, *"Angliae MARTINIS disce favere tuis,"* on both *The Character* and *The Araignement Of Mr. Persecvtion* (London, 1645). There is no conclusive proof here, and it may be that Overton was merely copying the Marprelate printer, again signalling his filiation.

[8] See Overton, *Mans Mortalitie* (Amsterdam, 1644), edited by Harold Fisch (Liverpool: Liverpool U.P., 1968); Gimelfarb-Brack, pp. 84-116.

[9] See Ernest Sirluck, "Introduction," *Complete Prose Works of John Milton,* II (New Haven: Yale U.P., 1959), pp. 53-136. For an explanation of the movement of the Independents in the Assembly of Divines to a tolerationist stance, and not one of "accommodation" (toleration for those Independents only), see Robert S. Paul, *The Assembly of the Lord. Politics and Religion in the Westminster Assembly and the "Grand Debate"* (Edinburgh: T. and T. Clark, 1985), pp. 32, 49-51, 262, 540, 466, and especially pp. 477-8.

[10] *Journals of the House of Lords,* VIII, 451, 457, 458, 491; John Vicars, *The Schismatick Sifted* (London, 1646), p. 26.

[11] *Journals of the House of Lords,* VIII, 648.

[12] See Christopher Hill, "Radical Prose in 17th Century England: From Marprelate to the Levellers," *Essays in Criticism,* 32 (1982), 95-118; for Scot, see S. L. Adams, "The Protestant Cause: Religious Alliance with West European Calvinist Communities as a political issue in England, 1585-1630" (unpublished D. Phil. thesis, University of Oxford, 1972), Appendix III, "Thomas Scot and Bohemian Propaganda," pp. 448-62.

[13] *Martin's Eccho* (London, 1645), p. 3.

[14] Leland H. Carlson, *Martin Marprelate, Gentleman. Master Job Throckmorton Laid Open In His Colors* (San Marino, Calif.: Huntington Library, 1981), especially pp. 158-209.

[15] I am grateful to John Benger for sharing with me his knowledge of 16th century Puritan literature.

[16] On *decorum personae,* see Marprelate, *Oh read ouer D. John Bridges* (East Molesey, 1588), p. 1; John S. Coolidge, "Martin Marprelate, Marvell, and *Decorum Personae* as a Satirical Theme," *PMLA,* 74 (1959), 526-32.

[17] Carlson, pp. 100-1.

[18] Sidrach Simpson, *The Anatomist Anatomis'd* (London, 1644), p. 3.

[19] William Haller, *Tracts on Liberty in the Puritan Revolution, 1638-47,* 3 vols. (New York: Columbia U.P., 1934), p. 97n.; Heinemann, p. 251. For Puritan ideas of style, see Harold Fisch, "Puritanism and the Reform of Prose Style," *ELH,* 19 (1952), 229-48.

[20] John Penry, *A Treatise Wherein Is Manifestlie Proved, That Reformation And Those that sincerely fauor the same, are vnjustly charged to be enemies, vnto hir Maiestie, and the state* (Edinburgh, 1590), Sig. B2v; Marprelate, *Oh read ouer D. John Bridges,* p. 2.

[21] *Hay any worke for Cooper* (Coventry, 1589), pp. 7-8.

[22] Simpson, p. 3. On the effects of calumniation, see John K. Graham, "'Independent' and 'Presbyterian'. A Study of Religious and Political Language and the Politics of Words During the English Civil War, c. 1640-1646" (unpublished Ph. D. dissertation, Washington University, 1978).

[23] *The Araignement Of Mr. Persecvtion,* Sig. A2r.

Margery Marpriest's *Vox Borealis* (London, 1641, ? 1639) has also been attributed to Overton (see Gimel-farb-Brack, pp. 124-6) but it awaits a full analysis of its ingenious satire on the Bishops' War in terms of Cavalier culture and the politics of drama in the late 1630s.

[24] *Divine Observations,* Sig. A1r.

[25] *Martin's Eccho,* p. 8.

[26] *A Sacred Decretall,* p. 24; *The Araignement,* pp. 9, 12-13. A "back-sword" is a broad sword with one cutting edge only.

[27] See Shakespeare's *As You Like It; Martin's Eccho,* p. 7; for vineyard images, see John Vicars, pp. 1, 4. For the connection with the erosion of the sense of parish boundary by enclosures, see David Underdown, *Revel, Riot and Rebellion. Popular Politics and Culture in England 1603-1660* (Oxford: Clarendon P., 1985), pp. 80-1.

[28] *A Sacred Decretall,* p. 13.

[29] Ibid., p. 21.

[30] *Martin's Eccho,* p. 3; *A Defiance Against All Arbitrary Usurpations* (London, 1646), p. 1.

[31] *A Sacred Decretall,* pp. 17, 5, 10, 13, 8.

[32] *The Araignement,* p. 19.

[33] *Martin's Eccho,* p. 5.

[34] *The Araignement,* Sig. A3v, pp. 15, 16; *A Sacred Decretall,* pp. 3, 9.

[35] The Biblical reference here is Ezek. 21.27. See N. Smith, "'The Interior Word': Aspects of the Use of Language and Rhetoric in Radical Puritan and Sectarian Literature, c. 1640-c. 1660" (unpublished D. Phil. thesis, University of Oxford, 1985), pp. 387-8.

[36] *A Sacred Decretall,* p. 8. In *The Araignement,* p. 43, Overton gives the Biblical root of this image in Dan. 7.7.

[37] *The Araignement,* p. 43.

[38] *The Araignement,* p. 21.

[39] See C.H. Firth and R.S. Rait, *Acts and Ordinances of the Interregnum, 1642-1660,* 2 vols. (London, HMSO, 1911), I, pp. 567-9.

[40] *The Araignement,* p. 18.

[41] *The Araignement,* p. 27.

[42] *The Araignement,* pp. 22, 31.

[43] *The Araignement,* p. 22; *Martin's Eccho,* p. 13.

[44] *The Araignement,* p. 10.

[45] *A Sacred Decretall,* p. 16.

[46] Sir Edward Derling, *A Consideration And A Resolution* (London, 1642), pp. 5-6, where the transfer of votes from convocation to synod is ridiculed by comparison with metamorphosis, metempsychosis and transubstantiation.

[47] *A Sacred Decretall,* p. 6.

[48] Martin Marprclate, *Oh read ouer D. John Bridges,* p. 50. Catercaps were four-cornered academic caps.

[49] *A Sacred Decretall,* p. 20; see also John Milton, *Paradise Lost,* III, *ll.* 474-97, for a comparison of this dress with the habits of those in limbo.

[50] *The Araignement,* pp. 1-2, 16-18. "Bocardo" is a singularly apt word because it meant both prison and a difficult stage in syllogistic argument. So, Presbyterians are trapped by their apparel, both in body and in mind.

[51] Vicars, pp. 2, 32.

[52] *Martin's Eccho,* p. 9.

[53] *The Araignement,* pp. 31, 33-34.

[54] The most famous and influential religious dialogue of the 17th century was Arthur Dent's *The Plain Mans Pathway to Heaven* (London, 1601).

[55] Terry Eagleton, *Walter Benjamin or Towards a Revolutionary Criticism* (London: Verso Editions, 1981), p. 146.

[56] See Sandra Clark, *The Elizabethan Pamphleteers. Popular Moralistic Pamphlets 1580-1640* (London: Athlone P., 1983), pp. 25-8.

[57] *The Araignement,* p. 36.

[58] William Prynne, *A Fresh Discovery* (London, 1645), p. 15.

[59] *The Araignement,* p. 41.

[60] Abraham Wright, *Five Sermons, In Five several Styles* (London, 1656), "The Fourth Sermon, Which is that in the Presbyterian Style, or Way of Preaching," pp. [67]-159.

[61] *The Araignement,* p. 1.

[62] *The Araignement*, p. 34.

[63] See Brailsford, p. 624, and for full details, Gimelfarb-Brack, pp. 287-304. Prior to his exile in Holland in the later part of 1654, Overton also offered his services to the Protectorate government, as he feared a conspiracy of those "of great abilities and interest agn.t the Governm.t": Bodleian Library, MS Rawl. A. 18, fol. 74.

[64] *The Araignement*, pp. 13-14.

[65] *The Araignement*, p. 2.

[66] *A Sacred Decretall*, p. 4.

[67] *The Araignement*, p. 45.

[68] *Martin's Eccho*, p. 15.

[69] *Divine Observations*, Sig. A1r.

[70] *A Sacred Decretall*, pp. 17-18.

[71] *A Sacred Decretall*, p. 19. See [John Corbet],*The Epistle Congratulatorie of Lysimachus Nicanor Of the Societie of Jesu, to the Covenanters in Scotland* (? London, 1640).

[72] *A Sacred Decretall*, p. 14. See also *The Araignement*, p. 42.

[73] *The Araignement*, p. 34.

[74] *The Araignement*, p. 17.

[75] *A Sacred Decretall*, p. 9.

[76] *The Araignement*, p. 34.

[77] *The Araignement*, p. 28.

[78] *Divine Observations*, p. 6.

[79] See F. S. Siebert, *Freedom of the Press in England 1476-1776* (Urbana, Ill., Univ. of Illinois P., 1952), pp. 21-233.

[80] Firth and Rait, I, 184-7.

[81] *The Araignement*, pp. 32, 41; *A Sacred Decretall*, pp. 1-2.

[82] *The Araignement*, Sig. A1r.

[83] *A Sacred Decretall*, pp. 6-7.

[84] *The Araignement*, p. 37.

[85] *Martin's Eccho*, p. 11.

[86] *The Ordinance For Tythes Dismounted*, p. 38.

[87] *A Sacred Decretall*, p. 7.

[88] *The Araignement*, p. 46.

[89] *The Araignement*, p. 46.

[90] *A Defiance Against All Arbitrary Usurpations* (London, 1646), p. 18.

[91] See Stuart Clark, "Inversion, Misrule and the Meaning of Witchcraft", *Past and Present*, 87 (1980), 98-127; Underdown, pp. 39, 55, 100-1, 178, 254.

[92] *Proper Persecution, or the Sandy Foundation of a general Toleration* (London, 1646).

[93] For the suggestion that Lilburne was the author of the Marpriest tracts, see William Prynne, *The Lyar Confounded* (London, 1645), pp. 6, 10.

[94] See especially *The Ghost Of Sr. John Presbjter* (London, 11 August 1647) and *The last Will and Testament, Of Sir Iohn Presbyter* (London, 22 July 1647).

[95] Gimelfarb-Brack, pp. 437-69.

[96] John Cleveland, *Poems*, edited by Brian Morris and Eleanor Whithington (Oxford: Clarendon P., 1967), p. 45. A date not earlier than 1646 is offered for this poem by Morris and Whithington: Cleveland, p. 167.

[97] Cleveland, p. 46.

T. B. Tomlinson (essay date 1989)

SOURCE: "Seventeenth-Century Political Prose: William Walwyn," in *The Critical Review*, No. 29, 1989, pp. 25-41.

[*In the following essay, Tomlinson reviews the political pamphlets of William Walwyn, commending his direct and unadorned style as an effective medium for attacking economic inequality, the power of Parliament, and the tenets of Calvinism.*]

Late-sixteenth to seventeenth-century political prose in English is not so much rare, or even very hard to find, as rarely studied at length in the main, or "core", courses in English Literature at undergraduate level. As long ago as 1938, William Haller, writing as Professor of English at Barnard College, said:

> Inevitably the Puritan preachers exercised an incalculable influence on the development of popular literary taste and expression, an influence no less great for having been ignored by critics and historians. (*The Rise of Puritanism*, p.21)

At this point of his book, Haller is concentrating on late sixteenth-century sermons. But of course he knows, and shows, how these sermons, together with later tracts, were at the time both political facts of life, and part of our literature. Some of them are rather dull; but the best are not in the least that. And certainly they should I think touch our day-to-day practices in the undergraduate teaching of English literature more than they now do.

In History Faculties and Departments, the position is very different now, and has been for some considerable time; but within English literary studies, not even Haller's earlier, influential and widely-known collection, *Tracts on Liberty* (Columbia, 1934; repr. Octagon Books, 1965), seems to have been used or very much referred to. Yet his claim that, during the 1640s and earlier, England produced a rich store of pamphlets and sermons is surely true. Haller finds a bit more life and popular appeal in some of the sixteenth-century preachers he discusses than I can. But even granted this, and especially if we take in the more overtly political prose he prints from the 1640s, he has presented, in these two books, a formidable case.

To take as an instance one of Haller's recommendations from the period about fifty years before Walwyn's own pamphlets began to appear, Richard Greenham (d.1594?) preached and wrote, mainly from Dry Drayton, just outside Cambridge; and both Greenham's practice and his sermons, which drew young men to him from Cambridge itself, his own university, proved a thorn in the side of the established church to which he nevertheless continued to belong. Though his name, even, is hardly known to most students of English, his prose (arranged and published by an admirer and friend in 1599) includes lively, idiomatic English that should have recommended itself to staff and students in departments of literature long ago. Some of Greenham's recommendations for the good, puritan family life are, admittedly, a bit daunting. For instance, his descriptions, in *A Treatise of the Sabboth,* could put one in mind of the full horrors of middle-class Victorian Sundays. Apart from some excellent advice to spend time "viewing the creatures of God", much of the rest sounds, to modern ears at least, discouragingly stern. There are endless sessions of prayer and discourse recommended; Sunday travelling is especially forbidden, and there is to be no escape from this commandment, even by sending servants to do what should properly be the business of the week; and, certainly, there shall be no "playing" (" . . . the ox so led to water, is not to play and friske on that day"!)

No doubt this sort of thing might have put later generations off reading anything that looked at all as if it might come from one of the separating sects (though Greenham himself was certainly not from one of those, few as they anyway were in his day). Yet this widespread conviction that all puritans were merely the depressingly solemn people the Jacobean dramatists often made them out to be is surely wrong. Their output, from the days before they were actually dubbed "puritaines" on, is in fact remarkably varied in tone, and so in outlook. Thus even the admittedly "sad" (in the sense, presumably, of "serious") Greenham can easily and frequently include a tang of folk-wisdom and idiom that must alert one to possibilities quite different from the duller kinds of puritan preaching and living. The pronouncement above about the ox not being allowed to "play and friske on that day" is one such—clearly it is in touch with some more simply enjoying and enjoyable life than the overt intention of the passage allows. And elsewhere, even in *Grave Counsels and Godlie Observations,* his warning about Satan being more dangerous now, because more subtle, than he used to be when known "only by colours, by a flaming breath, by a hollow voyce, by hornes and clawes; and such sensible things . . .", is lively Elizabethan prose that might have come from any one of a dozen writers at the time. And finally, from the same series of "Godlie Observations", there is this, about men unprepared to meet their God:

> . . . yea if God begin to reckon with them, every countenance of a godly man, every chirping of a bird, and drawing neere of the least and weakest creature towards them, every shaking of a leafe, moving of a shadow, every noyse of the ayre appaleth their courage, and maketh them more fearful cowards.

It seems to me that this sort of writing, despite the familiarly repetitive Elizabethan phrase-pattern, could make some stretches of much more famous writers—Hooker, for instance, or some of the later Bacon—look comparatively inert, because comparatively impersonal. As for the very different sort of prose you get in Donne and Lancelot Andrewes, this too is certainly lively and alert: though who would willingly sit down and read through the whole of Donne's published sermons again? There may well be something in the familiar puritan charge that this highly developed, expert prose is the result of minds and personalities in fact *over*-developed (a "flaunting wit" was one of the claims made against it).

In any case, the best of the puritan writers, up to and including William Walwyn's own day, stick to the plain, lively, direct prose they constantly advocated against that of University, Church and Royalist writers. A good deal of this, despite William Haller's plea in 1938, is still either out of print or, for other reasons, not readily available to students interested in literature. On the other hand, heartening signs of the times now include, for instance, the publication, in a literary journal, of

Christopher Hill's F.W. Bateson lecture, "Radical Prose in 17th Century England" (*Essays in Criticism,* XXXII, 1982); the emergence of the Cambridge English Prose series (e.g. esp., *Revolutionary Prose of the English Civil War,* ed. Howard Erskine-Hill and Graham Storey, Cambridge, 1983); Nigel Smith's *A Collection of Ranter Writings from the Seventeenth Century* (London, 1983); and others from a bit earlier. It looks as if there just may be a resurgence of interest in seventeenth-century political and religious prose of a kind that will make collections and informed comment more readily available to students of literature. In the hope that this may be so, I would like to single out William Walwyn. I believe there is still no collected, or even selected, edition of Walwyn's tracts, with or without those more doubtfully ascribed to him. Nevertheless, many of his pieces are reprinted in anthologies; and copies of the rest are available from the British Library's Thomason Tracts collection.

For a brief description of what is known with fair certainty about Walwyn, I think I cannot do better than refer to, and rely on, A.L. Morton's account in Chapter 6 of his book, *The World of the Ranters: Religious Radicalism in the English Revolution* (London, 1970). As A.L. Morton's account shows very clearly, Walwyn himself was not, in any conceivable sense of the word, a ranter. He was born about 1600 into a comfortably-off, but not rich, gentry family in Worcestershire. As a younger brother, William was appointed to a silk-merchant in London, and later, having served out his apprenticeship, he was admitted to the Merchant Adventurers and traded successfully in London for about twenty years before retiring from business and political life to become a medical practitioner. In *The Fountain of Slaunder Discovered* (1649), Walwyn himself adds the teasing detail (confirmed, in virtually the same phrase, by his son-in-law, the physician Humphrey Brooke, also writing in 1649): "I have been married 21 years, and have had almost 20 children." As a brief summary of what sort of man this was, and the kind of life he led, A. L. Morton's own words can hardly be improved:

> In an age of rhetoric and hyperbole, when men engaged in the fiercest controversy and claimed attention by trying to shout louder than all their neighbours, there was one man who followed exactly the opposite course. He sought and secured attention by lowering his voice so that only the most careful and attentive listener could catch it. One of the most thorough-going revolutionaries in an age of revolution, his main concern was the battle of ideas.

And then, in his next paragraph, Morton continues, again aptly and rightly: "Yet William Walwyn, this quiet, reasonable, contemplative man, while no doubt conquering many minds, was perhaps more hated and more vilified than any of his contemporaries."

Exactly so; and this is matter touching the heart of England's difficulties in the 1640s. I would like to begin a consideration of this by looking at some of Walwyn's best-known, and best, passages and arguments from *The Power of Love* (Sept., 1643: ascribed to Walwyn by Haller "with little hesitation": *Tracts,* I, 123). At this stage, Walwyn is still beginning his relatively brief writing career, though by now he is in his early forties. Here he is attacking the gross inequalities, evident to any casual inspection of the London scene, between rich and poor. Many, indeed, had done as much before; but Walwyn's prose in 1643 is exceptionally unadorned, unemphatic. Certainly it carries neither ornamentation nor documentation, whether from biblical or any other authorities. This, perhaps, is one reason why, in the 1640s, it immediately began to draw fire from all sides; but it is one reason why it should draw our attention now. In this passage, from the "Address to the Reader", Walwyn adopts the fiction— he refused actually to join any of the sects he defended—that he is one of the Family of Love, itself highly controversial because its relatively few members stoutly maintained that Christ was no more than an ordinary man like any one of the rest of us:

> . . . *Judge then by this rule who are of God's family; looke about and you will finde in these woefull dayes thousands of miserable, distressed, starved, imprisoned Christians: see how pale and wan they looke: how coldly, raggedly, and unwholesomely they are cloathed; live one weeke with them in their poore houses, lodge as they lodge, eate as they eate, and no oftner, and bee at the same passe to get that wretched food for a sickly wife, and hunger-starved children; (if you dare doe this for feare of death or diseases) then walk abroad, and observe the generall plenty of all necessaries . . . the whole body of religious people themselves . . . their silkes, their beavers, their rings, ... I, and the wants and distresses of the poore will testifie that the love of God they have not.* (Haller, *Tracts,* II, 274-5)

Dickens himself is rarely as direct, or as tellingly simple, as this. A year later, in *The Compassionate Samaritane,* Walwyn (whose authorship Haller argues for, *Tracts,* I, 123) has a still more controversial passage on another of his favourite themes: a proper liberty of belief and conscience is not merely desirable in itself, but it will show people that *all* authority, whether it is vested in bishops or in presbyters or in sects, thrives on its ability to foster fear and ignorance. If people could throw off or ignore these fears,

> They would then handle their Ministers familiarly, as they doe one an other, shaking off that timorousness and awe which they have of the Divines, with which they are ignorantly brought up. He that bade us try all things, and hold fast that which was good, did suppose that men have faculties and abilities wherewithall to try all things, or

else the counsell had beene given in vaine . . .
if the people would but take boldnes to themselves and not distrust their owne understandings, they would soon find that use and experience
is the only difference, and that all necessary
knowledge is easie to be had, and by themselves
acquirable . . . (Haller, *Tracts,* III, 77)

Many of these phrases, or ones very like them, are to
become familiar Walwyn territory: "He that bade us
try all things . . ."; " . . . use and experience is the only
difference"; "all necessarie knowledge is easie to be
had". And their frank simplicity points to ways in which
Walwyn was undermining, not only the display evident
in episcopal vestments and ornaments (by now a thing
of the past anyway), but, closer to home, any formal
doctrine or hierarchy of even a sectarian kind.

At the same time, and even though this is still early in
Walwyn's political career, it must be admitted that some
parts even of these tracts do give hints of insecurities
that may give trouble later on. This admirably lucid,
unaffected prose does nevertheless have a few passages of rather condescending, even self-justificatory,
writing that show some of the unfortunate effects that
a combination of familiar Puritan tendencies and the
gathering threats of the political situation in the mid-
1640s induced. I want to come back to this difficulty; but
a way of approaching it might be to develop further
the question that was in fact Walwyn's own complaint:
why *was* he so singled out, particularly by former
friends and allies, for attack? He himself claims, sometimes a shade insistently, that he writes in kindness and
charity to all men; yet his tracts seem to have been
among the most feared of any of the period, and especially by Presbyterian and some at least of the sectarians.

I suspect that the occasion for the bitterness against
him evident in, for instance, *Walwins Wiles* and
Gangraena was not any of his more accusatory,
defiant passages, but simply that ability of his to state,
in the most unemphatic and unadorned prose, beliefs
and arguments that should have been close to every protestant, and certainly to every puritan, heart. And in a
situation of civil war, with the parliamentary side by
now militarily fairly strong but increasingly threatened
by ideological divisions within itself, it is easy to see
that a "still and soft voice" could cause more offence
than even the most envenomed rhetoric. It is in this
political situation that *The Compassionate Samaritane,* quoted above, appeals, in the simplest terms, to
ordinary people to distrust all authority. And before
this, the introduction to *The Power of Love,* fore-
casting this appeal, invites people to begin by doubting all pronounced truths until they have tested and
tried these in their own, individual experience:

> . . . *but come, feare nothing, you are advised by
> the Apostle to try all things, and to hold fast that
> which is good: to prove the Spirits whether they*

*bee of God or not; 'tis your selfe must doe it, you
are not to trust to the authority of any man, or to
any mans relation: you will find upon tryall that
scarcely any opinion hath beene reported truly to
you: and though in every one of them you may finde
some things you cannot agree unto, you will yet be
a gainer, by discovering many ex-cellent things that
you as yet may be unsatisfied in, and by due
consideration of them all perfect your owne
judgement.* (*Tracts,* II, 277)

Admittedly, this appeal is connected with very widespread appeals for freedom by other people from at
least the 1630s on; but where many of these are perfectly proper, and powerful, attacks on oppression,
Walwyn puts his emphasis much more on the absolute
necessity for each to trust, finally, his *own* judgment,
and certainly not that of any of the clergy, Presbyterian
or otherwise. In a sense, this claim has been of
the essence of Protestantism since at least Luther's
day. But few in actual authority could ever have
liked it for long; and so one can see how such
clear, ungarnished prose must have cut very close to
the bone with both Presbyterians and sectarians in the
1640s.

Another cause of offence given by Walwyn, and differently by some others at the time, emerges in *The
Power of Love* itself. Apart from some slight wishful-
thinking early on about how easy and pleasant life was
before civilization ruined it (with unfortunately no
second thoughts from Walwyn about what part his own
Merchant Adventurers might have been playing in this),
most of this piece is much more forcefully written than
the initial "Address to the Reader". And particularly
since it is written in the form of a sermon preached, it
must have offended and alarmed most particularly those
who were then trying to rationalize obvious differences between the Old Testament and the New in the
matter of the proper behaviour towards enemies and
oppressors. This pamphlet tells readers and audience
not to feel—"no not in the least respect"—that they
are any longer under the old laws of Moses and the
Ten Commandments:

> I am not a preacher of the law, but of the gospell;
> nor are you under the law, but under grace: the law
> was given by *Moses,* whose minister I am not: but
> grace and truth came by Iesus Christ, whose minister
> I am . . . (*Tracts,* II, 288)

So again one can see why this virtually had to be attacked; particularly since it follows on from the quiet-
er, but equally firm-minded prose of the "Address",
which includes this injunction: "And for that great
mountain (in your understanding) government, 'tis but
a mole-hill if you would handle it familiarly, and be
bold with it . . .". In almost any situation, this sort of
writing would appear more potentially unsettling than,

for instance, the apparently fiercer prose of Roger Williams, or even that of the justly popular Lilburne.

The Compassionate Samaritane, from which I have already quoted, followed in the next year, 1644. It is mainly in Walwyn's quietist manner, but very firmly and closely reasoned. After noting that he has discovered the *Apologeticall Narration* to be no separatist document, Walwyn moves straight on to defend the separatists (though adding that he is none such himself), and to plead for freedom in less ringing, but more particular, and possibly more effective, terms that Milton himself did in the same year:

> . . . let all men now have other thoughts, and assure themselves that the Brownist and Anabaptist are rationall examiners of those things they hold for truth, milde discourseres, and abe [able?] to give an account of what they believe; they who are unsatisfied in that particular, may, if they please to visit their private Congregations which are open to all commers, have further satisfaction . . . (*Tracts,* III, 68)

Here, too, Walwyn is offending and challenging virtually all comers, the more particularly since he is *inviting* everyone to question received truths as, he claims, the best of these people do. Milton himself didn't do this, even in "I cannot praise a fugitive and cloistered virtue . . .". Milton's was a call to arms, and put very much in that tone of voice; he wanted Parliament and people to ride out and challenge whatever forms of popish, episcopalian or other evil could be found. Like Milton, Walwyn knew that censorship of any kind probably suppresses truth, rather than protects it; but his probably more arresting emphasis was on the fact that all "truths", even biblical truths and others good men believe, must be open to "mild discourse" and questioning. His *very* English prose is firm and sure-footed at such points as this because he, more clearly even than Milton, has seized instinctively on the crux of the matter of the 1640s: this Parliament has freed us from Charles, Laud, the Ecclesiastical Commission, etc.; and this freedom is now threatened by a new censorship, proposed by Parliament itself. As much was agreed by many writers at the time. But Walwyn's further point is that, unless people, including ministers, ask *themselves* about the nature of their own, personal sense of freedom and truth, these, along with all other freedoms, will be extinguished, whatever the present Parliament decides. Appropriately, Walwyn's piece draws towards its close with a change of key challenging even the best, and nowadays better-known, sections of *Areopagitica:*

> Truth was not used to feare, or to seeke shifts or strategems for its advancement! I should rather

> thinke that they who are assured of her should desire that all mens mouthes be open . . . they shunne the battell that doubt their strength. (*Tracts,* III, 94)

After this, in 1645 and 1646, Walwyn's interests move very quickly, as William Haller and later writers have noted, towards taking in a larger proportion of purely secular matters. Personally, I think his interests were always, and securely, secular. His view of the Gospels and of the New Testament generally was always that if you forget about the difficult and obscurely translated bits, they are sensible, clear advice that anyone at all can follow, simply by using ordinary rational understanding. The *iure divino* pretended by priests, and now by presbyters, is never necessary, and is in fact designed to obscure the original, Protestant, truth. From the mid-forties on, however, the political situation is such that Walwyn feels that he, and therefore of course his prose pamphlets, must become more actively involved: "they shunne the battell that doubt their strength." Thus 1645 gives us, in the open letter entitled *Englands Lamentable Slaverie,* his excellent defence of the once again imprisoned Lilburne.

Walwyn begins the letter by noting some disagreements he has had with Lilburne, especially about Magna Charta. Walwyn never believed Magna Charta to be as complete or sure a foundation for political and religious freedom as Lilburne continued to claim it. But now, Walwyn admits, it looks as if it's all we have, since Parliament, or a majority of it, has disappointed earlier hopes:

> See how busie they have been about the regulating of petty inferiour trades and exercises, about the ordering of hunting, who should keep Deere and who should not, who should keep a Greayhound, and who a Pigeon-house, what punishment for Deere stealing, what for every Pigeon killed . . . who should weare cloth of such a price, who Velvet, Gold, and Silver, what wages poore Labourers should have, and the like precious and rare businesse, being most of them put on of purpose to divert them from the very thoughts of freedome, suitable to the representative, body of so great a people. (*Tracts,* III, 314. Haller accepts this as Walwyn's: I, 125.)

Walwyn perhaps should have noted that this sort of regulation had a much earlier history, from long before the Long Parliament first met. Nevertheless, his prose is eloquent and firmly-written; and this because he has a very sharp eye on actual facts of the time, as well as on clear and simply-put matters of principle. And as with all his tracts claiming freedom of belief and conscience, so here his often tart comments need no dressing of rhetorical tropes or figures. In the following, he continues his argument against what he sees as the practices of Parliament against Lilburne:

Seeming goodnesse is more dangerous than open wickednesse. Kind deeds are easily discerned from faire and pleasing words. All the Art and Sophisterie in the world, will not availe to perswade you, that you are not in Newgate, much lesse that you are at libertie. (*Tracts,* III, 316.)

In this letter, and in most of his pamphlets to this date, Walwyn's defensive moves, whether on his own or on others' behalf, have always included strongly positive claims. I am not thinking simply of the easily summarizable themes in, for instance, *The Power of Love,* which include the claim that Christ's salvation is offered and manifested "to sinners, to the ungodly, to all the world". Rather, the important claim to be made on Walwyn's behalf is that this and other tracts depend also on their own cogency, and on the unforced clarity and common sense of the prose Walwyn writes. What I have in mind here is no simply stylistic matter, but rather the product of a mind unusually clear, observant and—at least when living up to its own announced principles—honest. John Lilburne, too, has, and always shows in his "rivers of words" as Haller rightly names them, an excep-tionally open and generous nature. He is, one might say, physically incapable of deception. Yet Lilburne's more impetuous frankness of spirit too often seems to lead him into merely repeating, again and again, the challenges he has already so strongly issued, frequently from one or another of London's prisons.

Walwyn's mind seems to me a firmer, and more con-sidering one than Lilburne's; as at the same time it is also perhaps a freer-ranging one than his, or even than that of their highly intelligent colleague, Richard Overton. On the other hand, it is precisely these qualities that are to be put to the test during the political power-struggles of 1646 and later, when Thomas Edwards makes his main onslaught on the In-dependents and their supporters, Walwyn very much included.

Edwards is obviously a bright man, and he can write very lively seventeenth-century prose, at least in short bursts. *Gangraena*'s final three parts, in 1646, seem to me each too long for its own good; they do, on the other hand, have quite enough journalistic flair, as well as some truth, however twisted, to have caught attention and to have demanded at least some reply from Walwyn. The following is not specifically about him, or indeed about any persons named, but it is typical:

> They have done and practised many strange things in reference to baptisme of children, dressing up a Cat like a childe for to be baptized . . . they have baptized many weakly antient women naked in rivers in winter . . . tempting young girls out and baptizing them . . . (*Gangraena,* 2nd edn., 1646, p. 67, Peter-borough collection.)

Charges that concerned Walwyn more closely are broadly speaking of two kinds. The first is put, very cunningly by Edwards, in language that is virtually Walwyn's own. The Independents claim, he says, "That Christ died for all men alike, for the reprobate as well as for the elect . . . for Judas as well as Peter . . ." (p.31). So indeed Walwyn, and increas-ingly others, did claim; but Edwards turns this simply into an unargued accusation. And he links it with his second charge, that is with his Presbyterian condemna-tion of Walwyn's and others' growing demands for toleration by Parliament in matters of conscience and belief:

> A *Toleration* is the grand designe of the Devil, his Masterpiece and chiefe Engine he works by at this time to uphold his tottering Kingdome; it is the most compendious, ready, sure way to destroy all Religion, lay all waste . . . it is a most transcendent, Catholique, and fundamental evill . . . (pp.153-4)

Nowadays, since the English church has long ago re-laxed its insistence on any doctrine of the "elect", and when few educated readers would take such a doctrine seriously anyway, Walwyn's straight denial of Calvin-ism seems hardly surprising: Christ indeed died "for all men alike". In the Presbyterian 1640s, how-ever, this was no doubt still an alarming statement. And the claims Walwyn and others made for toleration were, in consequence, seen as revolutionary. The reasons that may explain this have been well argued by A.S.P. Woodhouse in the Introduction to his *Puritanism and Liberty* (1938) and by others since. That is to say, once you admit any degree of liberty in state and religion, there may at least *seem* to be a danger that all will be open: liberty tends to beget liberty. Its own nature is to demand more freedom still; just as any Hobbesian alternative must rely quite posi-tively on restraint, and so on authority, leading ultimately to authoritarianism.

In the 1640s, this dilemma, together with the very real dangers that must have seemed to be there in Walw-yn's quiet prose, had already been foreseen. Thus Hobbes himself, according to Clarendon's account of Great Tew in the 1630s, had certainly been alarmed by them, long before the publication of *Leviathan.* And now, when Edwards raises them in his alarmist prose in 1646, Walwyn's (to then) generally calmer voice is, naturally, forced a bit on the defensive. England is through the first of its civil wars; but the world has indeed been, as Christopher Hill forcibly recalls by using that favourite phrase of the 1640s, "turned up-side down". And the point at stake is a very real one. Edwards (like Hobbes) has an argument when he claims that all innovators are, from the very nature of their enterprise, "changeable as the moon", and so they may endanger the stability of "Presbyterian Government" (*Gangraena,* pp.51, 188).

What, then, is the quality of Walwyn's reply to this, and later on to related charges published in *Walwins Wiles?* In the first place, he simply denies many of the accusations. For instance—and most fully in his *Just Defence* (1649)—he flatly denies that he and his friends are "Atheists, Non-Scripturists, Jesuites and any thing to render us odious"; or that he himself has been guilty of either "abusing my self with a lewd woman", or recommending "Butchers or Coblers" for places in government. And indeed, since most such accusations appear, in both Edwards and Price (*Gangraena* and *Walwins Wiles*) in the terms and tone of voice simply of scurrilous abuse and name-calling, I think the shortest and fairest way is to take Walwyn's word for it on these matters.

On the very much more serious charge, of advocating free "toleration" to all, Walwyn sounds occasionally a bit uneasy, perhaps because he senses this matter goes indeed to the very heart of growing impulses towards democracy in politics and religion alike. The run of his pamphlets against Edwards, in particular, does I think include some passages of self-justificatory prose of a kind and in a tone of voice that are in themselves suspicious, and that certainly becomes tiresome when repeated so many times. For instance, in *A Whisper in the Eare of Mr. Thomas Edwards Minister* (1646), there is this, a brief extract from a long opening passage:

> . . . for what ever you through want of an ex-perimentall knowledge of me, or upon mis-report may judge of me, I am one that do truly and heartily love all mankind, it being the unfeigned desire of my soul, that all men might be saved . . . it is my extream grief that any man is afflicted, molested, or punished . . . . there is no man weake, but I would strengthen; nor ignorant, but I would informe: nor erronious, but I would rectifie . . . (*Tracts,* III, 322-3)

Or, from *The Fountain of Slaunder Discovered* (written from the Tower, May, 1649):

> In all which time, I believe scarce any that ever knew me, will be so disingenuous as to spot me with any vice; and as little of infirmity as any other; having never heard ill of my selfe, untill my hopes of the Parliament encouraged me to engage in publique affairs; being then 40 years of age, 20 of which I had been a serious and studious reader and observer of things necessary. (p.2, Thomason coll., B.L.)

As A .L. Morton, in his splendid appraisal of Walwyn, is nevertheless forced to add:

> His piety, his universal benevolence and the unself-consciousness with which he proclaims them, are they not just too good to be entirely true? Is not this apparent candour a mask behind which something more may be concealed? "A man of all Religions, and yet what Religion he is of no man can tell." Is there not, at the least, a certain smugness, or, as Vicars puts it, self-flattery here? (*The World of the Ranters,* p.158)

Yet despite the unfortunate truth in this, the other, and main, part of the stand Walwyn takes in answer to Edwards, Kiffin, Price and the rest is in firm, idiomatic and alert prose. He is clearly aware of the dangers posed by, and in, his own and his friends' political and religious individualism: the more Protestanism itself, and certainly some of the puritan impulses within it, moved towards placing reliance on the single individual's reception of God and His Word, the less stable it had to become (thus Thomas Edwards: "A *Toleration* is the grand designe of the Devil . . ."). What Walwyn opposes to this threatening instability is a mind, and prose, solidly and instinctively aware of the world outside itself, and so aware too of the claims and needs of other people:

> . . . it is but a promised land, a promised good that I and my Friends seek, it is neither offices, honours nor preferments, it is only promised Freedom, and exemption from the burdens for the whole Nation, not only for our selves; we wish them peace, we repine not at any mans honour, preferment or advantage; give us but Common Right, some foundations, some boundaries, some certainty of Law, and a good Government; that now, when there is so high discourse of Freedom, we may be delivered from will, power, and meer arbitrary discretion . . . (*Walwyn's Just Defence,* in Haller and Davies, eds., *The Leveller Tracts,* repr. 1964, p.357.)

In these matters, Walwyn's basic, instinctive move is always to rely on readily available common sense; or, as he calls it in another context, "practicall Christianity". Interestingly, the same instinct is there also in the writings of the man whom Walwyn unfortunately came to single out as almost his chief enemy and betrayer, John Goodwin. Early on in their acquaintance, the two were friends; and in the prose of much of Goodwin's *Anti-Cavalierisme* (1642), for instance, one can see and feel what they shared. For Goodwin, as for Walwyn, there is no need for scholarly debate to see wrong actions for what, quite physically and palpably, they are. "Half an eye is sufficient provision", he says, for this. You don't need geometry, or even a rule and square, "to try either whether the bow be straight, or the string bent and crooked" (*Tracts,* II, 216-218). And his *Theomachia* is similarly inclined, preferring always examples from every-day life and living. (Thus Tenderton steeple is not the *cause* of Goodwin Sands simply because you see it before you see them: an example taken, apparently, from Latimer: *Tracts,* III, 35ff.)

The fact that two such men, sharing so much, broke apart is obviously one sign of the dangers in individualism, and so perhaps in Protestantism itself, that Walwyn I think sensed. So it may be for this reason that he carried the matter further, in at least a couple of places, by explicitly rejecting *mere* individualism. Such a rejection is indeed strongly implicit in each of his claims for toleration: Presbyterians and sectarians alike should recognize that other views besides their own exist, and must be allowed the freedom to continue while the holders remain genuinely convinced of their truth. A more explicit statement is there in the fictionally imagined Edwards's sermon at the end of *A Parable, or Consultation of Physitians upon Master Edwards* (October, 1646). In the course of this, though it is a rather stiffishly-written parody, Walwyn nevertheless has the following apt reminder of the dangers inherent in the then current Presbyterian and sectarian divisions:

> If I now shall be so unadvised, as to call him an heretique who differs from me, I doe but provoke him to call me so, for he is as confident of his, as I am of my judgement. . . . if one should revile and reproach another, with the names of Heretiques and schismatiques, Anabaptist, Brownist, Antinomian, Seeker, Sectarie, Presbyter, this tends to nothing but to devide the honest party, and to make way for your common enemy; for in whatever the true and evident rule of *Love* is broken, it tends to dissolution . . . (p.15, Thomason coll., B. L.)

But perhaps the most explicit arguments about the difficulties inherent in any plea for liberty, however strongly justified, are in a pamphlet almost certainly, though not quite certainly, from Walwyn's hand: *The Vanitie of the Present Churches* (1649). Haller and Davies, in their book *The Leveller Tracts, 1647-1653* (Columbia, 1944; repr. Peter Smith 1964), are persuaded that this is indeed from William Walwyn; all I can add is that I agree with their comment (p.252) that the "style and point of view" suggest Walwyn. Indeed, the very turn of phrase and mind seems clearly his:

> For Judge you, had they the spirit of God as you pretend? would they need, as they do; when they have resolved to speak to you from a Text of Scriptures, to go sit in their Studies, three or four dayes together, turning over those authors, that have written thereupon; and beating their own braines, to find out the meaning and true intent thereof; no certainly, had they the spirit of God, it could in an instant, in the twinkling of an eye, inform them the meaning of his own writings; they would not need to be studying, seven, ten, or twenty years, to understand the truth of the Gospel . . . (Haller and Davies, p.256-7)

William Walwyn, surely! And to this one should add the phrases from the same pamphlet: " . . . necessary

Doctrines are not at all hard to be understood, nor require long time to learne them". From here, it is easy for Walwyn's very direct prose to take up the vexed question of what, then, about people who insist that their own individual reading, or hearing, of God, or of the contemporary political situation, is all that matters or all that should matter? At its best, that claim can be hard to answer; in a way, it must have been part of the original Protestant claims for freedom from what they saw as a too rigid Catholic Church dominance in Europe. Walwyn's answer, itself a re-assertion of long-established puritan reliance on the Gospels, is interesting:

> Some of them crying up their owne experiences, and the teachings of God within them, affirming that they speak not from Books, or Scrip-tures, written in Inke and Paper, and in Letters and Sillables, but from the inward suggestion of the Spirit, induce multitudes to neglect the Scriptures, and to give credit onely to their wilde Notions and Opinions . . . (Haller and Davies, p.259)

For Walwyn's case, the key phrases here are "from Books, or Scriptures, written in Inke and Paper". In other words, and speaking as a man who has backed the notion of constant discussion (with other people than one's self), Walwyn is here affirming that there are, nevertheless, authorities beyond individual opinion: "Books . . . written in Inke and Paper". There is always something solid and tangible, outside the mere self, which must be taken into account. Here, Walwyn is referring directly to the Gospels, particularly that according to St John. But of course he was then, and is now, very well know as a man who relied, not just on the Gospels, but also on both pre-Christian and "Papist" authors: Montaigne, he said, was almost his favourite author. The people he is addressing here in *The Vanitie of the Present Churches* certainly included some who were used to quoting the Bible copiously. However, their emphasis was not so much on "Books . . . written in Inke and Paper", as on disputing individual interpretations of phrases quoted from the Old Testament and, where necessary, rationalized in terms of the (often very different) New Testament. Walwyn, I think, isn't interested in this sort of typology, but rather in the commanding authority of the written word, pagan, papist, or otherwise.

In any setting as full of contention as that of the 1640s, with various extremes of individualism being backed by a good many, Walwyn's belief in something established, because visibly there and written, is impressive; and certainly removes him from any accusation of simply believing in a self-affirming self.

In this argument, *Walwins Just Defence* (1649) must be a key document. This is, of course, undeniably

Walwyn's own; and again, bits of it do seem to suffer from the political pressures that had been operative on him then for some few years. But even these bits are strongly put and seem, at least on the face of it, to have sense and justice behind them: " . . . for they [Goodwin's men] are ever carefull to row with, or not long against the tide". One recognizes the type. And, some pages later, Walwyn turns very deftly to include, even in this pamphlet written in his own defence and against his enemies, some of his earlier claims, wholly positive in spirit, and based here on some well-known New Testament incidents and passages:

> He upbraids me, that I find fault, that riches, and estates, and the things of this world, should prefer men to offices, and places of trust: but say that virtue, though in poor men, should be more regarded, as in Butchers, or Coblers: And truly I know some Butchers, though not many, as fit as some in your Congregations; . . . And as for Coblers, there are trades more in credit, hardly so useful, and Mr. Price knows it well; . . . he who thought it no robbery to be equall with God, and yet despised not to be esteemed the Son of a Carpenter, and chose simple herdsmen for his Prophets, and poor fisher-rmen for his Apostles, did certainly judge otherwise than these Churchmen judge. (Haller and Davies, p.383)

Finally, the *Just Defence* has this, I think very fine, passage: again political prose that manages to be at once strongly accusatory, and clearly affirmative in spirit:

> And when you charge me, that I find fault that some abound, whil'st others want bread; truly I think it is a sad thing, in so fruitfull a land, as, through Gods blessing, this is; and I do think it one main end of Government, to provide, that those who refuse not labour, should eat comfortably: and if you think otherwise, I think it your errour, and your unhappinesse: But for my turning the world upside down, I leave it to you, it's not a work I ever intended, as all my actions, and the Agreement of the People, do sufficiently evince . . . so far as that is, am I for plucking up of all the pales and hedges in the Nation; so far, for all things common. (Haller and Davies, p.384)

The last bit of this ("so far as that is, am I . . .") is referring to charges made against Walwyn that, in conversation, he used to advocate things far beyond the average Leveller position; that is, he was said to have advocated upsetting all enclosures and returning the land so opened out to common use, and even ownership. Walwyn may well have said something like this, in conversation and debate. But if so, one can I think be pretty certain that such remarks would have been very much in the spirit of free inquiry that led him to invite all people to question even the certainties (e.g.,

and esp., the Gospels) to which he himself held firmly throughout his life. His firm statement here on these matters can I think be trusted: he is prepared publicly to back the Agreement of the People to which he refers, and which certainly has no crypto-communist, or even "Digger", principles in it. And hence his clear and simple affirmation here: "But for me turning the world upside down, it's not a work I ever intended, as all my Actions, and the Agreement of the People, do sufficiently evince . . ."

During the Restoration, to his death c.1681, Walwyn, having anyway decided to leave political writing and controversy behind in the early 1650s, apparently retired from business-life in London and became a local medical practitioner, using only the simplest and least harmful remedies he could find, and always trying these out on himself first (A.L. Morton, *The World of the Ranters,* pp.193-4). However, in the meantime, English political prose and thinking changed a lot, because of course the political and social situation itself had changed. It could be claimed that Walwyn was one of the last who could feel free to write so idiomatically, simply and directly about politics as he did. In 1660, Charles II was welcomed, probably mainly because anything, then, seemed better than the recent past: an England that had just experienced savage civil wars; and of course not merely that, but, even worse, the consequences of it, in particular the division between friends, between one branch of a family and another, and even between father and son, brother and brother (e.g. Sir Edmund Verney, the King's standard-bearer at Edgehill, and his eldest son Ralph; the D'Ewes brothers, Simonds and Richard). In addition, there had been unheard-of claims for political freedoms such as those put most forcefully, and indeed movingly, by Rainsborough and others at Putney in 1647:

> For really I think that the poorest he that is in England hath a life to live, as the greatest he; and therefore truly, sir, I think it's clear, that every man that is to live under a government ought first by his own consent to put himself under that government . . . (A. S. P. Woodhouse, *Puritanism and Liberty,* p.53)

Nowadays these claims seem fair, and openly put, with an immediacy and simplicity close to Walwyn's own on related matters. However, they must have seemed alarming to those about to seize power in 1647; and the memory of Putney, together with the memory of the trial and public execution of the king in 1649, clearly influenced the post-1660 generation, which immediately and instinctively took means to try to fend off any more such demands, and in particular any more such civil wars. One fairly clear, and inevitable, result was a "civilization" of English political thought, and so of English prose, and indeed verse. The prevailing Restoration feeling was: "Let us distance ourselves from the wild barbarism of, perhaps especially, Shakespeare, and also from anything as immediately personal as the civil wars, and their consequence in the political thinking and prose of men like Walwyn and Rainsborough."

Thus "Trimmer" Halifax—clearly one of the most intelligent men acting and writing in Restoration England:

> It must be more than an ordinary provocation that can tempt a man to write in an age over-run with scribblers, as Egypt was with flies and locusts; the worst vermin of small authors hath given the world such a surfeit, that instead of desiring to write, a man would be more inclined to wish, for his own ease, that he could not read. But there are some things which do so raise our passions, that our reason can make no resistance; and when madmen in two extremes shall agree to make common sense treason, and join to fix an ill character upon the only men in the nation who deserve a good one, I am no longer master of my better resolution to let the world along, and must break loose from my more reasonable thoughts, to expose these false coiners, who would make their copper wares pass upon us for good payment. ("The Character of a Trimmer", *Halifax: Complete Works*, Penguin Classics, ed. J. P. Kenyon, 1969, p.49)

I have chosen this piece, from the Preface to Halifax's best-known pamphlet, because it is one of the more direct and outspoken paragraphs in the work, and as such, it is closer to William Walwyn than is the prose and manner of most of the rest. Even so, the thinking here is much more balanced and poised than that in any Walwyn piece (let alone in any one of the more impetuous Lilburne's). Halifax is far too easily, and genuinely, civilized to impose any rigid patterning on either his mind or his prose rhythms; yet in the cadences of, for instance, "But there are some things which do so raise our passions, that our reason can make no resistance . . .", we have more the generation of Dryden to Addison and beyond than is at all perceptible in the pamphlets of the 1640s. And so the still more civilized first section of the Halifax (I. The Laws and Government) opens with: "Our Trimmer, as he hath a great veneration for laws in general, so he hath a more particular for our own." And the third paragraph of the same begins: "All laws flow from that of Nature, and where that is not the foundation, they may be legally imposed but they will be lamely obeyed." (Pelican Classics edn., p.51).

These cadential, balanced passages were first published in 1688. The change from any of the political prose from the 1640-1660 period is as remarkable as it was sudden. The only slightly later habits of mind do have an increased clarity and restraint: the civilizing influences of the Restoration had their advantages, and in Halifax's political life and prose, these were very real ones. But they come very much at the expense of the warmer feelings—also restrained—evident in most pieces from Walwyn, and cut down the open and free play of mind—"independent" indeed—that had been so easily possible to William Walwyn and others in the 1640s.

RELIGION, POLITICAL PHILOSOPHY, AND PAMPHLETEERING

D. B. Robertson (essay date 1951)

SOURCE: "Leveller Beliefs about God and Man: Doctrine of God, Doctrine of Man, Richard Overton, William Walwyn," in *The Religious Foundations of Leveller Democracy*, pp. 90-104. New York: King's Crown Press, 1951.

[*In the following essay, Robertson examines the religious views collectively expressed by the Leveller leaders in the 1649 pamphlet* A Manifestation, *and the relationship between religious and political beliefs of the Levellers. Robertson also studies the way in which their individual views differ, especially on such topics as the idea of original sin.*]

Doctrine of God

The Levellers, it is clear, had the sectarian distrust of finespun rationalizations, of complex theological formulations. One cannot, therefore, expect to find an elaborate systematic statement of their religious beliefs. But this does not mean, of course, that there are no theological statements. There are some elemental statements of doctrine in their writings, though most of the indications are scattered and often implicit rather than explicit. They are important, however, not as any special contribution to Christian thought, as such, for they shared their beliefs, traditional as most of them were, with many of their day. The important aspect is in Leveller application of these beliefs to state and society.

Lilburne and the other Leveller leaders usually stated their religious beliefs as a reply to enemies who accused them of atheism and anti-Scripturalism. Thus in *A Manifestation* (1649) the four imprisoned leaders wrote in self-defense: "we beleeve there is one eternall and omnipotent God, the Author and Preserver of all things in the world. To whose will and directions, written first in our hearts, and afterwards in his blessed Word, we ought to square our actions and conversations."[1] Lilburne, particularly, stated his beliefs about God in opposition to the "arbitrary" actions of men. For instance, tyrants, he said, were imitators of God.

Lilburne made his most complete statement of his doctrine of God in a postscript to *The Free-Mans Freedome Vindicated* (1646), and thereafter stated the same general belief a number of times.[2] "God, the absolute Soveraign Lord and King, of all things in heaven and earth, the originall fountain, and cause of all causes, who is circumscribed, governed, and limited by no rules, but doth all things meerly and onely by his soveraign will, and unlimited good pleasure, gave man (his meer creature) the soveraignty (under himselfe) over all the rest of his Creatures, Gen. 1.26.28.29."[3] He conceives his fight against tyranny as a religious duty to curb the tyranny of rulers on the one hand and to uphold the sovereignty of God on the other. His "just and righteous quarrel" with Cromwell and his faction is the championing of "The liberties of the land of my nativities against the apostacies and tyrannies of her most perfidious and treacherous professed friends," and also "the holding out of Gods Soveraignty amongst the sons of men, as being that one, single, individual ALONE (either in heaven or earth) that is to raign, rule, govern, and give a law by his will and pleasure to the sons of men."[4]

God alone is absolute. God alone acts by will—may take "arbitrary" action. This is, of course, good Calvinistic doctrine. How does this concept relate to the Leveller concept of natural law, of the importance of reason in state and society? Man was made in the image of God, "which principally consisted in his reason and understanding."[5] Logically speaking, this implies a rational God, bound by the same rules of reason which govern men, for the Creator's nature is revealed in his creation. Lilburne held, on the human level, that laws made by Parliament were conceived upon rational grounds "to be binding to the very Parliament themselves as well as others."[6] But the same reasoning does not follow through to the Divine Being. Overton, a more careful and consistent thinker, and also more secular in his thinking, conceived the world in more rationalistic terms. Speaking of "right reason" he said,

> Several are its degrees, but its perfection and fulness is only in God. And its several branches and degrees are only communicable and derivated from him, as several beams and degrees of heat from the body of the sun—yet all heat. So in reason there are different degrees, as from morality to divinity, and under those two heads several subordinate degrees, all derivated and conveyed from the Creator (the original fountain) to the creature, yet all one and the same in nature—the difference only lying in the degree of the thing . . . And so the gifts and graces of God are one radically, yet different in their species, and all from one and the same Spirit, which can act nothing contrary to its own nature. And God is not a God of irrationality and madness, or tyranny. Therefore all his communications are reasonable and just, and what is so is of God.[7]

Overton's point seems clear, but what is the meaning of Lilburne's statement? Woodhouse[8] sees it as an achievement of the "principle of segregation," whereby the rationalist standard is maintained in the "natural order," while in the "order of grace" the view of God is "purely voluntarist." In effect this may be the case. The fact of the matter is, however, that Lilburne probably had not thought the point through. Actually he is concerned with asserting the sovereignty of God—the absolute sovereignty of God—and at the same time establishing the equality of men. In insisting upon the absolute, unqualified, uncircumscribed sovereignty of God, he is simply following Calvin, but the use he made of it in political terms would not have met with Calvin's approval. Lilburne was always fighting "will" in human beings as a corrupted element in human nature, as a symptom of personal, private interest—as "unnatural" and "arbitrary." Only in Almighty God, not in sinful man, is there a possibility of arbitrariness and will-acting. God is not bound by rational and moral standards—man is. Tyranny is the sin of usurping the place of God. It was such pride which brought the curse upon Adam and all his kind. Arbitrary action, the will of the King, Council, Parliament, Cromwell, etc., were very much a part of the life of England in the first half of the seventeenth century. As unclear, and logically inconsistent as Lilburne's doctrine of God is, it is as though he feels it necessary to make an ultimate concession to this most obvious element (will) in his world, so that no mediate concessions are possible. Or is his view perhaps the reflection of a basic contempt for the rationalism which the law of nature implied in certain features of his thought?

Doctrine of Man

The Puritans in general accepted the traditional Christian doctrine of the Fall of Adam and the consequent corruption of all mankind. Book II of Calvin's *Institutes* was spread over the pages of their writings. In varying degrees, according to the writer, it was conceived that original sin left untouched the reason of man to the extent that he could know good from evil and maintain some degree of dignity and order in society. Even Calvin, conscious as he was of human debility—aware that the human mind "halts and staggers even when it appears to follow the right way"—nevertheless conceded that "some seeds of political order are sown in the minds of all." He went on to say that "this is a powerful argument, that in the constitution of this life no man is destitute of the light of reason."[9] It was generally believed that those who had never heard of Christ, or those before Christ, were to some degree aware of the presence of God's image in them. But man's will to deliver what conscience and reason demanded in the sight of God was another matter. Ames was not representative in his belief that the will of man survived the Fall partially competent to do the good which reason and conscience perceived. It was generally believed, after Calvin, that whatever good man was able to do was to the glory of God and not of man. Even "common grace" was a witness to God's spirit, for it was the mark of the Creator.

There are indications in the writings of the Leveller leaders that they accepted the usual view of man's fall and incompetence, though in Overton and Walwyn the awareness of it is often faint. The view is more evident in Lilburne than in the other leaders, that the doctrine of original sin is necessary to the understanding of the world in which he lived. Lilburne, arguing against "uncircumscribed authority" and the necessity of government by law, recognized as the basis of this necessity the fact that "man is naturally ambitious and apt to encroach and usurpe upon the liberty" of others.[10] It is certainly a tacit recognition of the fact, apparent in all Leveller writings, that man is not any longer in Adam's state and cannot therefore live without precept. All the Leveller writers believed in the implications of the Fall, for paramount precept or law, applicable to all men alike, was the be-all of their endeavours. But Lilburne does state the orthodox position more exactly, always with Augustinian emphasis upon pride and ambition as the chief basis of the Fall. "And Adams sin it was, which brought the curse upon him and all his posterity, that he was not content with the station and condition that God created him in, but did aspire unto a better, and more excellent (namely to be like his Creator), which proved his ruin, yea, and indeed had been the everlasting ruin and destruction of him and all his, had not God been the more mercifull unto him in the promised Messiah."[11] The part of reason which survived the Fall, according to Lilburne, was what we call the "Golden Rule." After the Fall, Lilburne said, almost using Parker's words, man became "tyrannical and beastly in his principles and actions." Where before there had been unity and amity, now there was a "devouring temper of spirit." But for the measure of God's mercy toward man, man would be no different from the beasts. But in His mercy, God "institutes a perpetuall, morall, unchangeable, and everlasting law; that is to say, That whosoever he was, that would be so beastly, bearish, and Woolvish, as to fall upon his neighbour, brother, or friend, and do unto him that, which he would not he should do to him by taking away his life and blood from him; God ordaines, and expressly saith he shall lose his life without mercy or compassion for so doing."[12] Thus man stood, in Milton's words, "Betwixt the world destroyed and world restored."[13]

The Leveller writers all traced the necessity of government itself to the corrupted will of man. Lilburne quotes with approval the Leveller "large Petition" to the effect that "whosoever meanes to settle good lawes, must proceed in them with a sinister opinion of all mankind, and suppose that whosoever is not wicked, it is for want only of opportunitie."[14] In his *The Engagement Vindicated,*[15] Lilburne says, "for my part I say Govern-

ment it self is from God, or the prime Lawes of nature, without which by reason of mans corruption by the fall, he cannot live as a rationall Creature." Indicating the relationship of reason and will in man's corrupted state (cf. Parker, Rutherford, and Hobbes), Lilburne says, answering Prideaux's question of "who shall be judge?", that "man being a reasonable creature, is Judge for himself." He goes on to say, however, that "by reason of his present corrupted estate, and want of perfection, he is something partial in his own case, and therefore wherein many are concerned, Reason tels him, Commissioners chosen out and tyed to such rational Instructions as the Chusers give them, are the most proper and equallest Judges."[16] Liburne was persistently concerned that men in government not be allowed a position where partiality in their "own case" encroached upon the common good.[17] Defending themselves against the charge of anarchy, of desiring no government, the four leaders (Lilburne, Overton, Walwyn and Prince) proclaimed that "we know very well the pravity and corruption of mans heart is such that there could be no living without (government)."[18] Yet, as is clear in the Leveller writings, the reason of man is conceived to be sufficiently intact so that the people could be trusted to lead to a right and just solution of any political problem. Here the interests of most men were recognized as identical. And the leaders devised means, in their *Agreement,* whereby the reason of the people might express in an orderly and peaceful manner their requirements and at the same time provide protection against selfish tendencies.

One cannot, however, fail to detect in Overton and Walwyn, particularly, a weakening of the idea of original sin. It is true that they at times recognized the defect. They, for instance, signed with Lilburne and Prince the statement in *A Manifestation* quoted above. Overton gave acknowledgement to it in his *An Appeale,*[19] where he says, "for if right reason be not the only being and bounder of the Law over the corrupt nature of man (that what is rationall, the which injustice and tyranny cannot be, may only and at all times be legall . . .)." He recognizes as valid the Pauline dictum that "magistracy is for the praise of them that do well, and for the punishment of those that do evil."[20] Overton and Walwyn, with their generation, claimed to be "Biblical" in their interpretation of life and the world, and hence to accept the Biblical truths, but, of course, the Bible served all appeals. Adam's fall seemed always to be slipping their minds. Even Lilburne, in his enthusiasm for freedom and justice appears often to forget the material with which he must work and thinks in terms of Christ's restoration of the Image of God. One might say that in Overton and Walwyn are visible the workings of what developed so clearly in the rationalists of the eighteenth century: "primitivism," while in Lilburne there is a suggestion of sectarian "perfectibilitarianism." Lilburne seems quite confident that the image of God in the Christian is "restored, confirmed, and inlarged."[21] And he claims personal "righteousness" in Christ.[22] In how far beyond the golden rule every man was conceived to be in harmony with God's purposes is not clear. Certainly the possibility of a general restoration was envisaged. There were those, like Henry Marten, who boldly affirmed general restoration and lost no time in exploiting the political implications of it. Said Marten, "As God created every man free in Adam: so by nature are all alike freemen born; and since made free in grace by Christ: no guilt of the parent being of sufficiency to deprive the child of this freedome. And although there was that wicked and unchristian-like custome of villany introduced by the Norman Conqueror; yet was it but a violent usurpation upon the Law of our Creation, Nature, and the ancient Lawes of this Kingdome: and is now, since the clearer light of the Gospel hath shined forth, by a necessary harmony of humane society; quite abolished, as a thing odious both to God and man in this our Christian Commonwealth."[23]

Richard Overton

Richard Overton was associated with "heresy" more than once in his lifetime. In 1644 he was connected with Milton in a Parliamentary order, saying that "the authors, printers, and publishers of pamphlets against immortality of the soul and concerning divorce should be diligently inquired for."[24] The order was the result of Milton's publication, *The Doctrine and Discipline of Divorce* (1643) and of Overton's *Mans Mortallitie; or, A Treatise Wherein 'tis Proved, Both Theologically and Phylosophically, that Whole Man (as a Rationall Creature), is a Compound Wholly Mortal, Contrary to that Common Distinction of Soule and Body* (Jan. 19, 1644). Overton holds that the soul and body are one, that "whole Man" comes into being, grows, and dies. Christ subjected Himself to these laws of life. By nature all men, therefore, share in his resurrection of the soul and body—unless they deliberately reject Christ's atonement for sin.[25] It is evident that Overton based his whole theory of death and resurrection on the Hebrew-Christian doctrine of the fall.

Upon occasion, Overton could confess that he was "a man full of Sin, and personal Infirmities,"[26] and that his life was "hid in Christ," but these feelings were apparently not basic and seemed to affect his total outlook very little. Reason told him that the real issue was "not how great a sinner I am, but how faithfull and reall to the Commonwealth; that's the matter concerneth my neighbour, and whereof my neighbour is only in this publick Controversie to take notice."[27] While he may have agreed with Calvin to some degree that man's reason "halts and staggers," he nevertheless did not attribute this difficulty, as Calvin did, to any congenital defect. Whatever account he took of human weakness, and there is considerable concern with it, it seemed to him in the historic fight of the moment to be

largely the accumulated evil in customs and institutions. Like Walwyn, he placed broad confidence in man's reasonableness, his sociableness, his brotherhood. What is reasonable is divine;[28] what is unreasonable is devilish, and man is able to distinguish the two and choose between them.[29] In his beliefs about man and the world he certainly suggests the beginnings of secular naturalism and rationalism, but his independence from "dogma" is not complete, though in him it is probably as nearly achieved as in any of the Leveller leaders. He does recognize the practical necessity of taking a somewhat "sinister opinion of all mankind" in his agreement with Leveller proposals in general. And his is an attempt to have reason confirm rather than replace "God's Word" as the basis of understanding life.[30]

In 1649 when Overton was arrested by the Council of State, along with Lilburne, Walwyn and Prince, the soldiers who ransacked his house, he says, took away "certain papers which were my former Meditations upon the works of Creation, intituled, *Gods Word Confirmed by His Works*: wherein I endeavoured the probation of a God, a Creation, a State of Innocencie, a Fall, a Resurrection, a Restorer, a Day of Judgment, &c. barely from the consideration of things visible and created."[31] Thus he proposed to state the whole predicament of man without revelation, or to confirm revelation by reason, as he put it. It is evident, then, that while Overton thought in terms of Christian categories, he was capable of exploring rational, philosophical interpretations. He apparently never thought through the relationship between revelation and reason. He appealed to both to support liberty and justice.

William Walwyn

William Walwyn was one of the most interesting characters of his time. A merchant by trade, he joined the Parliament in its fight with the King; and he turned his searching mind against the intolerance of the Presbyterians. He never left his parish church, as most of his associates did, to join any sectarian group.[32] He followed the practice of defending the right of all men of all groups to follow their own light. But his habit of trying to find out the reason of men's faith made him hated and feared by Presbyterians and sectarians alike. Like Socrates, Walwyn went about asking men questions about their faith, and he was just as firmly condemned by the "religious" people as a corrupter of men's minds.[33] Walwyn himself claimed his whole aim was "to understand how men are setled in their faith, and to help them therein."[34] He seemed firmly to believe that reason could defeat every superstition, ignorance or evil intention. Walwyn typifies the Leveller conviction that discussion and argument will lead, if men are serious, to the right answer and the right action. "Powers and principalities" seemed not so important, for he says that "All the war I have made, hath been to get victory on the understandings of men."[35] He believed persistently that the Levellers' ideal settlement of the national constitution could be made by argumentation, by convincing men's minds. "The giving, and hearing, and debating of reason," he held, is the most certain way of securing peace and harmony on all levels of society, whether family or nation.[36] And he felt bound by conscience to lead men to live according to their natures as rational beings. Walwyn found peace in anti-nomianism himself,[37] and he went about telling men they could be saved unless they rejected Christ and his atonement. He was indeed "a striking example of Protestant humanism on the vernacular level."[38] The Bible had been first in his reading, but he had also been "accustomed to the reading of humane authors" for many years. Seneca, Lucian and Montaigne were the chief ones. And he developed a spirit of charitableness and reasonableness not common in his day. From Montaigne and the other humanistic writers "he could have derived the ideal of society as a union of men with equal rights to well-being, working together peacefully in rational pursuit of the common good."[39] In the sects he apparently thought he saw the same spirit, the spirit which animated Christ's first followers. Walwyn thus effected a combination of Christian primitivism with the golden age of the "humane writers." His doctrine of man must, therefore, be looked at in these terms.

The state of innocency was conceived in terms of Montaigne's island of cannibals. It was a state of nature, a state wherein God had shown man his love even as he had shown it in the revelation in the Scriptures. It was a state of happiness, of peace and plenty. One might ask, as Walwyn did, why such a gift from God was not "sufficient to keep mankind in order and the world in quiet."[40] The answer was that man had fallen from this state. But "the fall" was hardly the Christian Fall of Man. The fall is retrievable, according to Walwyn, for it is largely a result of ignorance and the seeking after human "inventions." Man lost his righteousness and his rationality when he set out to improve upon nature, to seek out "inventions of superfluous subtilities and artificiall things, which have beene multiplied with the ages of the world, every age still producing new."[41] Presumably, therefore, man's basic rationality and goodness are still intact; if enough people will conscientiously seek to reinstate the spirit, as Walwyn says he has always tried to do, who knows but there may yet be hope for the world? Ignorance, intolerance, poverty, tyranny and human vanity, all remedial, are thus the evil to be fought in the world.[42]

Walwyn's belief in man's continuing rationality, or perhaps better, Walwyn's disbelief in the crippling effects of "the Fall," is related to his doctrine of the law of nature. The demands of the law are absolute; man is able to live rationally, equal and free in society. Sin cannot be pleaded in defense of oppressive and suppressive government. For Lilburne, sin was a more serious factor to engage in man, but its seriousness did not incapacitate man to live in a society "of the people, by the people, for the people." There is, then, in all the Levellers, a qualified doctrine of sin. For Augustine the doctrine justified slavery. For Aquinas, for Luther and for Calvin it justified strong government. But the emphasis of the sects and the Levellers upon an original perfection produced in the Levellers, as they came to understand man's sinful nature, the concomitant emphasis upon limited government. Democratic principles may grow out of a belief that all men are equal in that they are sinful as well as out of the belief that all men are good. There were shades of difference among the Levellers and other sectarians on the degree to which sin must be a factor in politics.

The Leveller leaders, in varying degrees, were able to learn from experience. "Experience" was, of course, not new in Puritan thought as a source of knowledge, for the religious literature of the period is full of the expression, "experiential." History taught the Levellers what reason denied, taught them perhaps even to a final disillusionment, that man's corruptness is more than ignorance and is not so easily contained by law and rational argument. Greater provision must be made for human nature in the structure of government itself. In how far they thought through systematically the implications of what experience taught them is another matter.

The year 1647 was an especially educational one for the Levellers. That was the year of the Putney Debates, the debates on the Leveller *Agreement* between the Independent leaders and the Leveller Agitators. It became clear that rational argument was not to be effective against entrenched interests, against the property-conscious Independents. Men of property and men of religion, too, stood squarely against what seemed to the Leveller leaders the clear demands of both the first and second tables of law. It became difficult, the Levellers thought, to tell friend from foe, and Lilburne cautioned the soldiers not even to trust their own representatives, the Agitators, too far. "Suffer not one sort of men too long to remaine adjetators, least they be corrupted."[43] Coming out against the House of Lords, Lilburne's reasoning is that legislative power is arbitrary to begin with, and if you place arbitrary power in the hands of a group for life, as is the case with the House of Lords, you simply invite slavery—"considering the corruption and deceitfulnesse of mans heart, yea the best of men."[44] It was his own experience with the Lords which prompted this statement. Cromwell, too, was instrumental in the education of Lilburne and his fellows. Lilburne had had great hopes that Cromwell would carry through the revolution to its conclusion, and he professed to trust Cromwell completely. But it became evident at Putney and afterwards that Cromwell and the Independents wanted to contain the revolution where it was, that they would not practice the democratic principles, the Christian principles, which they had professed. Lilburne says that

> after the grand and superlative Apostacie of so tall a Caedar as Lieut. Gen. Cromwell pretended to be, for the liberties and freedomes of the people of this nation: I shall never hereafter in state affaires, (for his sake) trust either my father, brother, or any other relations I have in the world, but shall always to all I converse with, inculcate the remembrance of that deare *experiented truth* or maxime, recorded in the margent of our . . . large Petition, which is, 'That it hath been a maxime amongst the wisest Legislators that whosoever meanes to settle good Lawes, must proceed in them with a sinister opinion of all mankind, and suppose that whosoever is not wicked, it is for want only of the opportun-itie.'[45]

Other leaders express similar sentiments.[46] From the same experience Overton remarked that "God hath in some measure opened our eyes . . . the burnt child dreads the fire."[47]

By 1649 the "realism" in Leveller documents is even more definite. The four leaders wrote from the tower (in *A Manifestation*) that whereas their enemies had said that if the Levellers themselves were to get power they would be just as tyrannical as any, they (the Leveller leaders) had learned to provide even against their own selfishness. They confess that the "experimentall defections" of so many who have come into authority have made them "even mistrust our own hearts, and hardly beleeve our own Resolutions of the contrary." And so they have proposed an instrument which will not depend for the public good upon the goodness of men's hearts, a goodness which is more and more questionable. "And therefore we have proposed such an Establishment, as supposing men to be too flexible and yeelding to worldly Temptations, they should not yet have a means or opportunity either to injure particulars, or prejudice the Publick, without extreme hazard, and apparent danger to themselves."[48] Their final *Agreement,* as Pease says, represented their "reluctant modification of their ideals in recognition of the depravity of human nature."[49]

The final *Agreement* represents a more realistic view of human nature and of the nature of political life. In it the Levellers contrived a greater limitation on power than they had thought necessary before. The Preamble contains the statements that "We the free People of England, to whom God hath given hearts, means and opportunity to effect the same, do with submission to his wisdom, in his name, and desiring the equity thereof may be to his praise and glory; Agree to ascertain our Government, to abolish all arbitrary Power, and to set bounds and limits both to our Supreme, and all Subordinate Authority . . ."[50] The new foundation of government, as ever, was to be an

"agreement" of the people, not a command of parliament. The army officers proposed to get their version approved by the Rump Parliament, but the Levellers knew that such an agreement could be undone by a later Parliament if it chose. They proposed that the basic rights of the individual be placed beyond the power of "interests" to touch. But it is questionable whether the Leveller leaders were finally willing to trust to the reasonableness of the agreement alone to get the people to accept it. They appeared willing to function behind the power of the Army, where they tried frantically to maintain influence, to get acceptance of their *Agreement.* And, the *Agreement* was apparently to be binding even upon those who had not assented to it.[51]

The contents of the *Agreement* itself had been decided upon by "wofull experience" and "sad experience," as they said.[52] Human frailty was noted in the provision that a representative, popularly elected, was to sit for only one year and not be eligible for reelection till one term had elapsed. Representatives were not to hold other offices, so that none should be allowed to "maintain corrupt interests." The basic rights of the people were to be placed beyond the touch of elected representatives. It is through and through an attempt to cabin and confine power, to prevent men from getting into a position to molest their neighbors. Ireton had insisted in the Army Debates that the burden of the revolution had been the settlement of power. The Levellers then put the chief emphasis on the revolution as a crusade to get justice and rights, but now a more "sinister opinion of all mankind" made them take the danger of power more seriously in terms of political organization. The consciousness of human depravity led right-wing Puritans to accept the authoritative rendering of the divine commands by the Assembly of Divines and to distrust the implications of individual judgment in both religion and politics. It could lead to the totalitarianism of Hobbes. It could on the other hand strengthen the democracy of the last *Agreement,* wherein man is given credit enough to know his best interests and the interest of the nation but is not trusted to preserve, without compulsion, the general interest.

Notes

[1] p. 6; Haller & Davies, *Leveller Tracts,* p. 281.

[2] In *Englands Miserie and Remedie* (1645) is a brief statement of the central idea. See p. 3. Also *Regall Tyrannie,* p. 9; *Legall Fundamentall Liberties,* pp. 73-74, pp. 19-20.

[3] pp. 11-12.

[4] *Legall Fundamentall Liberties,* p. 73.

[5] *Londons Liberty,* p. 17.

[6] *Englands Birth-Right Justified*, p. 3.

[7] Overton, *An Appeale* (1647), in Woodhouse, *Puritanism and Liberty*, p. 324.

[8] Woodhouse, p. (94).

[9] Calvin, *Institutes*, Bk. II, Ch. II, p. 295. John Allen tr.

[10] *Englands Miserie and Remedie* (1645), p. 3.

[11] *Free-Mans Freedome Vindicated*, p. 12.

[12] *Londons Liberty*, pp. 17-18; see also *Strength out of Weaknesse*, p. 14.

[13] *Paradise Lost*, XII, p. 3.

[14] *The Peoples Prerogative and Priviledges*, Proeme.

[15] p. 6.

[16] *Strength out of Weaknesse*, p. 14.

[17] See for instance *Englands Birth-Right Justified*, p. 31.

[18] *A Manifestation*, p. 5.

[19] Woodhouse, *op. cit.*, p. 324.

[20] *An Appeale*, Woodhouse, p. 332.

[21] *Londons Liberty*, p. 20; see also *Free-Mans Freedome*, p. 12.

[22] *Picture of the Councel of State*, p. 23.

[23] *Vox Plebis*, p. 4.

[24] *DNB*, Vol. XIV, 1279; see Masson, *Life of Milton*, Vol. III, p. 164.

[25] It might be noted that Milton held similar views regarding immortality and resurrection. See *Of the Christian Doctrine*, Ch. XIV, p. 35; Ch. XV, pp. 39-41; pp. 17-27, 219, 263, 307; also Barker, *Milton and the Puritan Dilemma*, pp. 318-19.

[26] *Picture of the Councel of State*, p. 43.

[27] *Ibid.*, p. 44.

[28] *An Appeale*, Woodhouse, *op. cit.*, pp. 323-24.

[29] But Overton could hardly be called a secular naturalist of the eighteenth-century variety. And it is probably not fair to say that he simply used orthodox Puritan terminology upon occasion for his own opposite purposes, as Woodhouse suggests, p. (55).

[30] See *DNB*, Vol. XIV, pp. 1279-80.

[31] *Picture of the Councel of State*, p. 28.

[32] Walwyn, *A Whisper*, p. 5.

[33] See *Walwyns Wiles*, reprinted in Haller & Davies, *op. cit.*, pp. 285 ff.

[34] *Ibid.*, p. 5.

[35] *A Whisper*, p. 3; also *The Fountain of Slaunder*, p. 10.

[36] *The Fountain of Slaunder*, pp. 15, 18; see Pease, *The Leveller Movement*, pp. 242 ff.

[37] *A Whisper*, p. 3; *Walwyns Just Defence*, p. 8.

[38] Haller & Davies, *op. cit.*, p. 22.

[39] Haller, *Tracts on Liberty*, Vol. I, p. 41.

[40] *The Fountain of Slaunder*, p. 1.

[41] *The Power of Love*, pp. 2-3.

[42] See Haller, *Tracts on Liberty*, Vol. I, Ch. v; Pease, *op. cit.*, pp. 242 ff.; Schenk, "A Seventeenth-Century Radical," *The Economic History Review*, Vol. 14, pp. 75-83, Jan., 1944; also article in *DNB*.

[43] *The Juglers Discovered* (1647), p. 10.

[44] *A Whip for the Present House of Lords* (1647), p. 17.

[45] *The Peoples Prerogative and Priviledge* (1647), Proeme.

[46] Cf. Wildman's supposed statement, in *A Declaration of Some Proceedings*, p. 16; Overton, *An Appeale*, pp. 187-88, in Wolfe reprints; and Overton's *Hunting of the Foxes*, Wolfe, *op. cit.*, p. 362.

[47] *Hunting of the Foxes*, Wolfe, p. 373.

[48] *A Manifestation*, p. 7.

[49] Pease, *op. cit.*, p. 311.

[50] Haller & Davies, *op. cit.*, p. 321.

[51] Pease makes much of the question of whether those who had not given assent were to be bound by the *Agreement*. See particularly p. 214. But

Liburne said more than once that it was his duty to prevent men from acting against their own interests. A drowning man must be saved whether he wants to be or not.

[52] See Articles IX and XXIX.

Perez Zagorin (essay date 1954)

SOURCE: "The Leveller Party Programme," in *A History of Political Thought in the English Revolution*, pp. 35-42. 1954. Reprint: New York: Humanities Press, 1966.

[*In the following essay, Zagorin analyzes the third and final version of* The Agreement of the People *as representative of the Leveller party platform . He includes commentary on thes evolution of this document between 1647 and 1649.*]

In the separate writings of the Leveller leaders, there had been formulated a conception of the social order which insisted that institutions justify themselves before the bar of reason. Whatever the past had been, the present must be shaped so as to allow every man's rational nature scope for expression. Only thus could the law of Christ and true religion be fulfilled. By the middle of 1647 there existed a movement of men who accepted this theory as the expression of their deepest, but hitherto inchoate, feelings. By means of it, local suffering elevated itself to a height from which it could gain a view of its relationship to the social order that had produced it. For the first time, a mass-movement gathered from the victims of miscellaneous oppressions did not stop with demands for partial and isolated changes, but went on to call for a programme of comprehensive reform. A sufferer from monopolies could find in the writings of the Leveller leaders the basis for perceiving the connection between his own problems and those of many other separate men. He could find, too, that his adversaries were not only in the great trading companies, but in Parliament. And he would discover that his demand for a free trade had better foundation then precedent, being grounded in his right as a man. Thus the theory of the Leveller leaders became a force rallying soldiers and civilians to the banner Lilburne and his fellows had raised. Hob-nailed boots and clouted shoes demanded a reckoning. ' . . . suffer us,' they cried, 'to free ourselves, and the whole commonalty of the Kingdome from . . . an intolerable burden and slavery; to shake and tumble downe that mountain of dishonour and oppression, that this Kingdome for so long time hath groaned under. . . . '[1]

From 1647 onward, these demands for a general justice were being given a local habitation and a name in official party statements. Beginning with a petition in the spring of 1647 which the Commons commanded to be burnt as insolent and seditious,[2] the Leveller programme evolved through two versions of *The Agreement of the People* and other petitions,[3] to culminate in a third and final version of the *Agreement* in 1649.[4] This last *Agreement,* issued by Lilburne, Overton, Walwyn, and a lesser Leveller figure, Thomas Prince, from captivity in the Tower, was the Levellers' finest legacy, and their conclusive word on the problems of their distracted country. It summed up the experience gained during intense political struggles, crystallized the chief aspirations of those parts of the community for which they spoke, and presented their maturest conception of what was necessary for the achievement of a peace based on the people's freedom. A study of it will illuminate the Leveller plan of settlement in detail at its highest point, and make clear what its social bearings were.

The third *Agreement* begins with a preamble in which the people declare their intention of ascertaining their government. Then follow a a series of articles laying down the powers and duties of the future representative. Supreme authority is to reside in a Representative of 400 persons, to which all men, twenty-one years and over, not servants or in receipt of alms, may elect and be elected. Those who have aided the royalist cause are disabled from this privilege for ten years. Members are to be paid a salary, and each constituency is to be represented in proportion to its population. While men are officers in the armed forces or treasurers of public moneys, they may not be members of the Representative; nor may lawyers who are members practise during their term of office. No man may be elected a member twice in succession. Elections are to be held annually, and no Representative is to sit for more than a year or less than four months. In adjournments, a committee of members elected by the Representative, and acting under its published instructions, is to manage affairs. The power of the Representative is to extend, without the concurrence of any persons, to the conservation of peace, the regulation of commerce, the preservation of the people's liberties and estates as declared in the Petition of Right of 1628, the raising of money, and to all other things conducive to freedom, the removal of grievances, and the commonwealth's prosperity.

Now comes a long list of subjects on which the Representative is denied power. It may not compel or restrain any person in matters of religion, nor impress men for military service, 'every mans Conscience being to be satisfied in the justness of that cause wherein he hazards his own life, or may destroy others'. In order to abolish the enmities created by the war, it may not, except in execution of the judgements of the last Parliament sitting before the *Agreement* takes effect,[5] question any person for his part in the wars. It may not exempt any person from the operation of the laws on the pretext of tenure, grant, charter, patent, degree, birth, residence, or parliamentary privilege. It may not have anything to do with the execution of laws, nor permit legal proceedings and the laws to be in any language but English. It may not continue laws abridging the freedom of foreign trade, and may not raise money by excise taxes or except by an equal rate levied upon real and personal estate. It may not make or continue laws imprisoning men for debt, nor may it continue the death penalty for any crime but murder. It may not continue tithes, though impropriators are to be compensated. It may not take away the liberty of each parish to elect its own ministers. It may not alter judgments in trials from being given by twelve jurors, dwelling in the neighbourhood, and freely elected by the people. It may prevent no one from holding office for religion except upholders of the papal or any other foreign supremacy. It may not impose officials on counties, hundreds, cities, or towns, the people of which are freely to elect their own officers annually.

There follows, finally, a list of miscellaneous provisions. Future representatives are to pay all just public debts. In order to assure the subordination of the armed forces to the civil power, each constituency shall raise its own military forces and elect its officers, reserving to the Representative, however, the naming of the general officers. Any member of the Representative, or any other person, endeavouring to destroy the *Agreement,* or to establish communism, shall incur the penalty of high treason and lesser penalties shall be incurred by persons disturbing the people's elections.

In this multiplicity of powers and reservations, the general scheme of reconstruction can be clearly seen. The popular franchise, most important of all, was clearly provided for, though it excluded servants and those living on charity, as well as women. The former classes were denied a vote because, a Leveller spokesman pointed out, they 'depend upon the will of other men and should be afraid to displease [them]',[6] and it may be imagined that in the prevailing family organization, the exclusion of women would be similarly justified by the Levellers. Supporters of the royal cause were deprived of political rights for ten years, but by preventing the Representative from questioning men for their part in the wars, it was hoped that the country would grow once more into unity, especially since the benefits of the *Agreement* were believed by the Levellers to affect all interests favourably. At the same time, in permitting the Parliament sitting before the *Agreement* became effective to give judgment on the chief instigators of the war, it was expected that the king and certain royalists would be punished.

The peers and the monarchy were stripped of all their privileges and powers, but neither was abolished If we are to accept Wildman's statement in 1647,[7] the Levellers did not object to a peerage as such. So far as

monarchy was concerned, there is no doubt that had not Cromwell established a military rule by the time the third *Agreement* was drawn up, it would have been done away with. Both Lilburne and Overton had expressed a desire for this,[8] and in February 1649 the former had attacked the plan of settlement of the Cromwellian group for omitting a reservation against the restoration of monarchy.[9] But Lilburne later declared, 'I had rather . . . live under a regulated and wel-bounded King . . . then under any Government with Tyrannie',[10] and the final *Agreement* did not ban monarchy because the Levellers wished to be prepared for the possibility that Cromwell might be overthrown and the king restored on condition of his acceptance of their principles.[11]

With the proposals for a popularly elected annual Parliament free from any negative voice and subject to definite rules, the Levellers gave a conclusive answer to the constitutional and political questions which they believed to be at the centre of the issues that the revolution had precipitated. Similarly, by removing all compulsion in matters of religious faith, they dealt definitively with the religious question. They laid down the principle that toleration was to extend to all professions. And, whereas in their first and second *Agreements* they had permitted Parliament at its discretion to establish a national church, provided it was voluntary, they gave the Representative no such power now. The religion of the country was to be as varied as the faiths that flourished in it, and even Catholics could practise their beliefs without disturbance.

Finally, the various grievances against which the Levellers had been protesting were to be redressed by depriving the Representative of power to continue the laws which sanctioned them. It is interesting, however, that certain demands which had been put forward earlier did not now appear. Reservations in the second Leveller *Agreement* prohibiting the rate of interest from being set higher than 6 per cent and exempting estates of less than £30 from all national taxation were omitted. So was a requirement in the second *Agreement* that a record office be erected in every county for the registration of all bills, bonds, and conveyances. These were probably oversights. Most important of all, the abolition of base tenures, which Lilburne had called for in a list of articles at the end of the second *Agreement,* was overlooked.[12]

We can best understand the Leveller programme in this, its greatest formulation, if we characterize it as a lower-middle-class utopia. Utopia it was—and no dishonour on this account to its framers—because the prevailing relationships of economic and political power offered no basis for its realization. Lower middle class we may call it because its every line expressed the aspirations of the small and middle sort of people who formed the backbone of the Leveller movement.

The *Agreement* portrayed an equalitarian order which aimed at dissociating wealth from privilege by granting the same political rights to all. Under its electoral programme, it was expected that small merchants, craftsmen, and yeomen would possess sufficient weight to balance the economic advantages of great merchants and wealthy landlords. The pronounced emphasis on decentralization and local elections was to have the result of curbing both the oligarchies of the towns and rural areas, and London's power over the rest of the country. No longer would the central government appoint the justices of the peace and the sheriffs. No longer would these and other posts be habitually occupied by the gentry and the men of substance who packed the town corporations. Thus, it was hoped, the commonalty of town and country would establish its participation in political power.

Economically, the *Agreement* secured the interests primarily of people of lesser means. The removal of excise would ease those upon whom a tax on food fell heaviest. Though foreign trade monopolies were to be taken away, nothing was said of the whole complex of regulations governing guild privileges, apprenticeships, and local trade and industry. These the Levellers had never assailed, for they were the barriers behind which small masters and craftsmen were often entrenched. Lilburne had always borne in mind the economic grievances of such men, and had pointed out, for example, how clothiers, cloth-workers, and spinners were victimized by the Merchant Adventurers Company.[13] It was on behalf of these, it would seem, that the Levellers wished the system of regulation to function, and hence they confined their attack to foreign trade monopolies alone.

In all these respects, therefore, the Leveller programme carries the imprint of the interests of those of intermediate status in economic life. Moreover, its outlook was predominantly urban. The *Agreement's* demands, of course, called for the removal of grievances that were general, and not limited only to urban groups. But its silence on the problem of copyholds and man-orial lords was more than an oversight. Despite the occasional mention of the abolition of base tenures,[14] the land question was never a critical issue in the Leveller programme, and, among agrarian elements, it reflected more the aims of the small freeholder and yeomanry than those of the poor peasantry. This was a fundamental defect. It was on the latter that much of the power of the landed gentry depended and to leave the basis of this power unaffected by reform was to contradict the equalitarian commonwealth for which the Levellers stood. Because their programme dealt so summarily with the agrarian problem, the great majority of the rural population remained indifferent to it, despite the considerable rural discontent and disturbance which occurred during the revolution.[15]

The Leveller movement was distinguished in general by its high humanitarianism and by the essential hope that it would win its way through persuading the minds of men. It expressed care for the poor, the aged, the sick, the imprisoned, the oppressed, the unemployed. What they would do for these, the Levellers believed, was only what the law of Christ and of reason evidently required. The Leveller leaders would have shunned the notion that their position expressed the outlook of any class. They believed their demands were inferences from reason, as illuminated by Christ's law, and reason was the same in one man as in a thousand. Their programme corresponded to a universal interest, they held, and only men who have become beastly or who are blind, they would have argued, could fail to see this fact. Perhaps this was why in none of their *Agreements* was any provision made for amending the rules upon which the new political order was to operate. As the Leveller commonwealth was created, so, apparently, was it to remain forever. Moreover, there can be no doubt whatever that in spite of the call of Lilburne and Overton in 1647 for the people to rise, and in spite of the mutinies of Leveller soldiers in the army, the Levellers did not regard force as a normal or a desirable method of effecting political change. They relied, they said, 'solely upon that inbred and perswasive power that is in all good and just things, to make their own way in the hearts of men, and so to procure their own Establishment'.[16] When Lilburne called for a rising, it was because he believed the country was in a state of nature. If he had really subscribed to violence as a tactic, his movement would have been far more dangerous to the Cromwellian government than it was.

The Leveller programme was the glorious hope of men who lacked all possibility of gaining power. While Lilburne led a revolution that failed, Cromwell led one that succeeded. While Lilburne strove unsuccessfully for a democratic republic, Cromwell created an oligarchic one. If Lilburne's tragedy lay in the powerlessness of his movement to achieve its ends, Cromwell's consisted in the doom of a Stuart restoration that fatally overhung him because of the narrow basis on which his power was erected. Yet with all their differences, the Levellers and Cromwell had important principles in common. Both desired liberty of conscience, though not in the same degree. They were alike also in fearing a strong central government as the source from which despotism would always arise. Many actions to which Cromwell resorted to retain power would have been left undone if his rule had been a stable one.[17] Like the men for whom the Levellers spoke, Cromwell wished to be finished forever with the tyranny he saw exemplified in the interfering government of Charles I and his ministers, Laud and Strafford. But however one limits the state's role, it will still retain positive functions which can affect either favourably or not the various interests in the community. And so while the circumscribed state of the Levellers would have enforced the equalitarian order outlined in their *Agreement,* Cromwell's discharged the task of securing the property and position of the gentry and great merchants who inherited power in revolutionary and restoration England.

The Levellers at the very birth of political democracy stated its full theoretical implications. They would tolerate no groups or orders in society with special political privileges. They required that Parliament be truly representative. And they extended the right of consent to every individual. They admitted no sovereignty anywhere, unless it was in every man's conscience. They seriously accepted the possibility of any man refusing obedience to commands incompatible with his idea of reason or justice. This may appear anarchic, but to them it was the ultimate guarantee of liberty. But they clearly believed that a representative non-sovereign Parliament, itself subject to the laws it enacted for the people, and restrained by the safeguards of the *Agreement,* would erect that which every individual conscience unbiased by an irrational selfishness would be likely to accept.

Their great objective was political reform, and in the occasional Leveller pamphlets that continued to appear through the 1650s this aspiration was still being given utterance. The declaration of London Levellers in 1653 insisted that 'The people cannot be . . . Free . . . while the Supream power . . . is wrested out of their hands . . . and the prime Badge and principle of their Freedom is, Their own Election'.[18] The anonymous author of *Englands Remembrancers* (1656) advised Cromwell's millenarian opponents not to boycott the elections to Parliament announced in June 1656, because despite Cromwell's tyranny, '(unlesse there could be a personall agreement of the people) an assemblie of the peoples Deputies, is the only visible means to settle justice . . . .'

> 'Dear Christians, it is by the choice of your Deputies only, that the whole body politick of this nation can consult together for their preservation . . . there is no other way consistent with the laws of God, or the nature of mankind, whereby our breaches can be healed, lawfull powers and authorities created, righteousnesse and justice exercised amongst us.'[19]

The unknown Leveller who wrote *The Parliaments Plea* in October 1659 when the breakdown of all effective government seemed near, told the soldiers in the army that a durable settlement could be made only by consent of the people in Parliament, and counselled them to choose representatives and effect the army's submission to a freely elected Parliament ruling without any king or peerage, under powers prescribed in an agreement of the people.[20] And in November 1659, some inhabitants of Hampshire were still demanding an agreement of the people providing for a supreme representative body and the separation of legislative and administrative functions.[21]

The programme the Levellers announced for their own day took more than two hundred and fifty years to achieve. Like Moses, they never dwelt in Canaan. Yet the beliefs they voiced did not die, and rose from the ashes into which the hopes of revolutionary England were consumed. Long afterwards, they were taken up by new forces, by the Chartists and the trade unions, to become the battle-cry of new struggles.

Notes

[1] *An alarum to the headquarters,* 1647, 4.

[2] *To the right honourable and supreme authority of this nation, the Commons . . . the humble petition of many thousands; Commons journals,* V, 179. This petition is reprinted in Lilburne's *Rash oaths unwarrantable,* 29-35. Thomason's copy is dated 19th September 1648.

[3] *An agreement of the people,* 3rd November 1647; *Foundations of freedom; or an agreement of the people,* 15th December 1648. The most important Leveller petition of 1648 was *To the right honourable the Commons . . . the humble petition of thousands wel-affected persons,* 15th September 1648.

[4] *An agreement of the free people of England,* 1st May 1649. There were a number of documents known as agreements of the people published between 1647-9. Only three are Leveller. A discussion of the relation between all of these may be found in J. W. Gough, 'The agreements of the people, 1647-1649', *History,* N. S., XV, 60. Mr. Gough was unaware that what he lists as the third agreement was composed by a private person, Lieut.-Col. John Jubbes, and should be supplemented here by Wolfe, *Leveller manifestoes,* 311-12, W. Schenk, *op. cit.,* Appendix B.

[5] The *Agreement* provided that the sitting Parliament should dissolve in August 1949.

[6] This is Petty's explanation in the debates of the army council at Putney, A. S. P. Woodhouse, *op. cit.,* 83.

[7] At the Putney debates, *Ibid.,* 109.

[8] See above, Ch. II.

[9] *Englands new chains discovered,* First part, 1649 [3]. Lilburne referred to the officers' *Agreement of the people,* submitted by the army to the purged Parliament on 20th January 1649.

[10] *A discourse betwixt Lieutenant Colonel John Lilburne . . . and Mr. Hugh Peter,* 1649, 8.

[11] In 1652, while exiled in Holland, Lilburne was in touch with various royalists on this basis; see Gibb, *op. cit.,* 307-8.

[12] The Leveller petition of September 1648 had asked that enclosures of fens and commons be laid open or enclosed solely for the benefit of the poor.

[13] *Innocency and truth justified,* 50.

[14] See above, 39. Lilburne's position was repeated in the London Levellers' statement of 1653, *The fundamental lawes and liberties of England claimed . . . by several peaceable persons . . . commonly called Levellers,* 1653, 4.

[15] See instances in E. Lipson, *The economic history of England,* 3 vols., 1929-31, II, 406-7, and M. James, *Social problems and policy during the Puritan revolution 1640-1660,* London, 1930, 90-106.

[16] *A manifestation,* 7.

[17] Cf. E. Barker, *Oliver Cromwell and the English people,* Cambridge, 1937, 47-62.

[18] *The fundamental lawes and liberties of England claimed . . . by several peaceable persons . . . commonly called Levellers,* 6.

[19] *Englands remembrancers,* 4, 1-2.

[20] *The parliaments plea,* 13, 15-17, 21-2.

[21] *The weekly post,* 22nd-29th November 1659.

A. L. Morton (essay date 1966)

SOURCE: "The Leveller Style," in *The Matter of Britain: Essays in a Living Culture,* pp. 73-82. London: Lawrence & Wishart, 1966.

[*In the essay that follows, Morton compares the writing styles of Leveller leaders John Lilburne, Richard Overton, and William Walwyn, as exhibited in the many political pamphlets penned by each.*]

Many of us, when we think of the pamphlet literature of the English Revolution, think first, and often think only, of the work of John Milton. This is natural, since Milton's place not only as a poet but as a master of polemical prose has long been established. Nevertheless it can lead us to a false estimate of the vast and rich pamphlet literature of the age, for Milton was as far from being unique as he was from being typical, and, if his work is a peak, it is a peak only of one range among several. It may also be said to be somewhat outside the main current of English prose. Milton

was a classical scholar, as much at home in Latin as in English, and even his English prose reads most often like the magnificent translation of a magnificent original. In so far as he is typical, he is typical of the learned writers who wrote for a limited audience similarly endowed, and whose work is heavily larded with Latin, Greek and even Hebrew, and weighted down with allusions and quotations from all the literatures of Europe.

But meanwhile a new reading public and a new kind of writer was arising, men with little or no knowledge of any language but their own. In the twenty years between 1640 and 1660 these men came to the front, and thousands of their books, pamphlets and news-sheets poured off the press. The *Catalogue of Thomason Tracts,* the great collection in the British Museum, which is yet very far from being complete, lists nearly 15,000 pamphlets from these years, of which certainly the majority are by writers of this vernacular type. Of all the popular pamphlets, those written on behalf of the Levellers are among the most brilliant as well as the most important.

The Levellers were the party of the most advanced revolutionary sections of the lower-middle class, the independent peasantry, the smaller tradesmen and artisans and perhaps the journeymen of the bigger cities. They drew support above all from the masses of London, then at least ten times the size of any other town in England, and from the army, Cromwell's New Model, the plain men who knew what they fought for and loved what they knew.[1] After the defeat of the Royalists in the Civil War the Levellers demanded a radical transformation of the political and social structure, and, in *The Agreement of the People*[2] put forward the first comprehensive programme of bourgeois democracy, including manhood suffrage, annual parliaments, full guarantees of civil and religious liberty, abolition of all feudal privileges and the reform and simplification of the legal code. Such a programme was not realisable in the existing conditions and the Levellers were defeated, and, after the middle of 1649, declined rapidly in influence.

For several years, however, they had been at the centre of the revolutionary struggle, and one of the most important achievements of progressive historians in Britain and the U.S.A. during the past few decades has been a re-estimation of their role and importance and the reprinting of many of the host of superb pamphlets which they produced in the course of their campaigns.[3] It so happened that three at least of the outstanding Leveller figures—John Lilburne, Richard Overton and William Walwyn[4]—were also pamphleteers of the first order, each with a highly individual and strongly contrasting style of work. A hostile writer refers to one of their productions: *A Manifestation from Lieutenant Col. John Lilburn, Mr. William Walwyn, Mr. Thomas Prince, and Mr. Richard Overton, (Now Prisoners in the Tower of London) And others, commonly (though unjustly) styled Levellers:*—'whose devout, specious, meek, self-denying, soft and pleasant lips favours much of the sligh, cunning and close subtlety of . . . Mr. William Walwyn, who (as the Serpent that deceived our first Parents was more subtle than any beast of the field which the Lord God made) is much more crafty than the rest of his bretheren, of whose curious spinning we have several reasons to presume this piece, for here is not the licentious provoking daringness of L.Col. Lilburns pen, nor yet the notorious profanness of Mr. Richard Overtons pen.'[5] Allowing for the obvious prejudice here displayed, this is a reasonably just and accurate comparison: from the point of view of an opponent these were their distinguishing features. What they did share, apart from their common social and political outlook, was their vernacular humanism. All three were educated, widely-read men who had not been through the traditional classical discipline of the universities, but had been apprenticed to trades in their middle teens and had henceforth completed their education in accordance with their own interests and needs. This, undoubtedly, was one of the main reasons for their closeness to and immediate influence over their audience, most of whom had a background closely similar.

Of the three Lilburne was as much the most significant as a political personality as he was the least gifted as a writer. 'Martyr, folk-hero and demagogue' as Professor Haller calls him,[6] he dramatised his struggles and wrongs in a flood of words that poured from him without respite and often, it would seem, almost without reflection. His enemies were fond of describing him as a 'man of a turbulent spirit, always opposing, striving, and flying in the faces of all authorities, restless, and never satisfied whoever is uppermost . . . and that therefore it is very requisite that I be taken off, and that otherwise England must never look to rest long in peace; yea, so turbulent, that if there were none in the world but John Lilburne, rather than want one to strive withall, forsooth, John would certainly quarrel with Lilburne.'[7] In all this there was some truth, but Lilburne was turbulent because he felt himself, as indeed he actually became, a symbolic figure. A pamphlet written in defence of his friend William Larner is entitled *Everymans Case:* Lilburne felt everyman's case to be his own and his own everyman's: he was the representative of the whole body of the oppressed people demanding justice and the restoration of their stolen birth-right.

It is this which gave his writing its force and dignity, and at his best he could write with an unstrained simplicity, as when he subscribes himself, with neither boastfulness nor false modesty as: 'JOHN LILBURNE, that never yet changed his principles from better to worse, nor could never be threatened out of them, nor courted from them, that never feared the rich nor mighty, nor

never despised the poor nor needy, but alwaies hath, and hopes by Gods goodness to continue, *semper idem.'*[8] At times he uses homely, familiar ideas and images to drive home his point, and a rhetoric which moves because it springs from the heart:

> But as the Water-men at *Queen-hive* doe usually cry, 'Westward hough, hough,' so according to the present current of the times, most honest men have more than cause to cry in the Water-mens language, 'AEgypt hough, hough, the house of Bondage, slavery, oppression, taxation, heavy and cruell, wee can no longer beare it, wee can no longer beare it, wee can no longer beare it, wee are as much provoked and forced to cast off all our yokes and crosses from our shoulders (except only that of Persecution) as ever any people or Nation, though no People or Nation under heaven have been more free, beneficiall and helpfull to those whom we intrusted to help and deliver us from Oppression, which saith the *Wise-man,* is enough to make wise men mad.'[9]

Finally, in writing of his own experiences, or of current political happenings, he can maintain a clear narrative style which puts the course of events plainly before his readers. It was partly for these qualities, but above all for the sense of leadership and authority that runs through them, that his pamphlets were eagerly bought and read by the soldiers in the army and the common citizens of London, circulating in thousands, and sometimes in tens of thousands of copies.

Unfortunately, much of his writing falls woefully below these levels. There is a great deal of legalistic argument, overloaded with quotations and references to legal and theological authorities as well as to the Scriptures. In these passages the style becomes angry and involved: often a single sentence will run on for pages, till its beginning has been lost before the end is in sight. Yet, whether he is writing badly or well, it is always an unmistakable man who writes. Lilburne's style has always, like his character, something of the grandeur as well as a little of the absurdity of a national monument.

If Lilburne was the born leader, the Tribune of the People, Richard Overton was the dedicated freelance, the exuberant individualist who finds both freedom and happiness in surrender to a great cause. Like most of the Leveller leaders he began his public career as a defender of religious liberty who progressed thence by inevitable stages to political radicalism. Among his earlier works was the brilliant tolerationist polemic, *The Araignment of Mr. Persecution,* from which there is good reason to think Bunyan may have borrowed something for the trial scene of *The Pilgrim's Progress.*

Overton's style could be almost as verbose as Lilburne's, but in an entirely different way and for quite other reasons. Where Lilburne's writing staggers under its own weight, Overton's rushes and soars, towering fantastically at one moment, falling into ruins the next. It has a quality of delighted swashbuckling which leads him always from defence to attack, rejoicing to find a gap in the opposing line of battle through which he can plunge. Something of this aggressive quality shows itself in the titles which Overton gave his pamphlets: *A Defiance Against All Arbitrary Usurpations, An Arrow Against All Tyrants and Tyranny, shot into the Prerogative Bowels of the House of Lords, The Hunting of the Foxes . . . by five small Beagles (late of the Armie)*[10], and *The Baiting of the Great Bull of Bashan.*[11]

When Overton was arrested in 1649 there was taken up with him a certain soldier of the house who was found in bed with his (the soldier's) wife and who was told that 'he must get a Certificate from his Captain that he was married to her'. This was enough to set Overton away in his happiest vein:

> Friends and Country-men where are you now? What shall you do that have no Captains to give you Certificates? sure you must have the banes of Matrimony re-asked at the Conventicle of Gallants at White-hall, or at least you must thence have a Congregationall Licence, (without offence be it spoken to true Churches) to lie with your wives, else how shall your wives be chast or the children Legitimate? they have now taken Cognizance over your wives and beds, whether will they next? Judgement is now come into the hands of the armed-fury Saints. My Masters have a care what you do, or how you look upon your wives, for the new-Saints Millitant are paramount to all Laws, King, Parliament, husbands, wives, beds &c.[12]

Much more is involved here than high spirits. With the Levellers, revolutionary politics were, for the first time, bursting through the religious forms in which they had hitherto been veiled. The Calvinists had stood for the concentration of power in the hands of the godly minority, the elect, which, in practice, meant the prosperous bourgeoisie. The Levellers stood for the rights of man, for the conception of politics as a continuous activity of the whole nation. 'The poorest he that is in England hath a life to live, as the greatest he', declared the Leveller Colonel Rainborough,[13] and by the same token, the greatest sinner as the greatest saint. This meant that politics must be secularised, and it was because he stood most conspicuously and outspokenly for this that his enemies found in Overton's pen the 'notorious profanness' of which they complained. To them he replied in a passage that shows that pen at its best:

> As I am in myself in respect to my own personall sins and transgressions; so I am to myself and to God and so I must give an account; the just

must stand by his own faith; But as I am in relation to the Commonwealth, that all men have cognizance of, because it concerns their own particular lives. . . . So that the businesse is, not how great a sinner I am, but how faithfull and reall to the Common-wealth; that's the matter concerneth my neighbour, and whereof my neighbour is only in this publick Controversie to take notice; and for my personal sins that are not of Civil cognizance or wrong unto him, to leave them to God, whose judgement is righteous and just.[14]

And in his last known pamphlet, written from prison in July 1649, he turns the tables completely upon his critics and puts into the most popular language that humanist rejection of the dogma of original sin without which no democratic political philosophy is really possible:

> Mirth to you is like a Shoulder of Mutton to a sick Horse. . . . And now (my tender friends) I pray tell me what spirit is this? 'tis a *foul spirit,* away with it for shame; go purge, goe purge; one penniworth of the *Agreement of the people* with a good resolution taken morning and evening will work out this corruption. . . .

> *Mirth* sure is of *Divine Instinct,* and, I think I may boldly say more naturall than Melancholy, and lesse savours of the Curse. Nature in its Creation was pure and good, void of corruption or anything obnoxious or destructive: all misery and mischief came in with the fall . . . in which number you may reckon Melancholy . . . and 'tis the root of the root of all wickedness, *Covetousnesse,* for when have you seen a Melancholy man that's not covetous? and a covetous man seldom proves a good Common-wealths man; yet this ill *Weed* is gotten into so religious esteem that all our *Religion* is turned into Melancholy.[15]

It is not surprising that Overton (who was also suspect of Atheism) was hated by the 'new-Saints Millitant'. What does seem strange at first sight is that his comrade William Walwyn was even more hated and more unscrupulously maligned. While Lilburne was the popular leader and Overton the outrageous pamphleteer, Walwyn seems to have combined the roles of organiser and philosopher. He avoided notice as far as possible, was an able committee-man, an adept at the drafting and promotion of petitions and manifestoes, while almost all his numerous pamphlets appeared anonymously, though the authorship of many of them must have been widely known. Their titles are just as characteristic as those chosen by Overton, and illustrate very clearly the difference of method between the two men—*The Power of Love, The Compassionate Samaritane, A Still and Soft Voice from the Scriptures, Walwyns Just Defence*—what could appear less aggressive or more disarming? Yet these and similar works aroused in Presbyterians and Independents alike a frenzy of rage both on account of their political and theological implications and because the smooth texture of their argument afforded so little with which an opponent could come to grips.

Like Lilburne and Overton Walwyn became a whole-hearted advocate of religious toleration. But his demand for toleration did not, like that of most tolerationists of his time, spring from a desire that his own sect should be tolerated, but from a detachment then rare. Often one can sense him passing tacitly from the position that all forms of religion are good to the position that none are *very* good after all. Thus he can write:

> I blush not to say, I have long been accustomed to read Montaigns *Essaies*. . . . And in his twentieth Chapter, pag:102, he saies, speaking of the Cannibals, the very words that import lying, falshood, treason, dissimulation, covetousness, envy, detraction, and pardon, were never heard of amongst them.

> These, and the like flowers, I think it lawfull to gather out of his Wildernesse, and to give them room in my Garden; yet this worthy Montaign was but a Romish Catholique: yet to observe with what contentment and full swoln joy he recites these cogitations, is wonderfull to consideration: And now what shall I say; Go to this honest Papist, or to these innocent Cannibals, ye Independent Churches, to learn civility, humanity, simplicity of heart; yea, charity and Christianity.[16]

He seems to have belonged to no sect, and if he had any marked leaning it was towards such quietist, non-institutional groups as the Familists or Seekers, though he denies belonging to either of these.[17] In *The Power of Love* he argues not merely that all men may be saved if they will, but, from the Calvinist standpoint, much more dangerously, that none will be damned, a doctrine with the most explosive political implications.

His practice appears to have been to go from Church to Church with his friends, hearing and afterwards criticising the sermons. This in itself would be regarded by the Ministers as a scandalous presumption on the part of a layman without a classical, university training. Walwyn's offence became greater when he elaborated a theoretical justification, advising the common man to trust to his own reason:

> He that bade us try all things, and hold fast that which was good, did suppose that men have faculties and abilities wherewithall to try all things, or else the counsell had been given in vaine. And therefore however the Minister may by reason of his continuall exercise in preaching, and discoursing, by his skill in Arts and Languages, by the conceit of the esteeme he hath with a great part of admiring people . . .

presume it easie to possesse us, that they are more divine than other men (as they style themselves) yet if the people would but take boldnes to themselves and not distrust their owne understandings, they would soon find that use and experience is the only difference, and that all necessary knowledge is easie to be had, and by themselves acquirable.[18]

He indulged freely in argument, and would infuriate the orthodox by such a question as 'How can you prove the Scriptures to be the Word of God?'[19] In politics his method was the same: every position was subjected to the test of reason and utility, every argument built upon first principles:

> I carry with me in all places a Touch-stone that tryeth all things, and labours to hold nothing but what upon plain grounds appeareth good and useful: I abandon all nicities and uselesse things: my manner is in all disputes, reasonings and discourses, to enquire what is the use: and if I find it not very materiall, I abandon it, there are plain usefull doctrines sufficient to give peace to my mind, direction and comfort to my life: and to draw all men to a consideration of things evidently usefull, hath been a special cause that I have applied my selfe in a friendly manner unto all.[20]

Where Lilburne was accustomed to make his appeal to the supposed ancient laws of England, to Magna Carta and the legendary Saxon past, and Overton to a sturdy common sense, Walwyn would build upon what he regarded as the universal laws of nature. And he made his appeal in a personal, almost a confidential tone, and in a smooth, easy-running and civilised prose which stands almost alone in the seventeenth century. Many things about him are, and probably always will be, uncertain, since the fullest picture we have of him is drawn by his enemies, and many of their accusations against him, such as being an advocate of Communism, can neither be proved nor refuted. Walwyn replied to his attackers in a passage which shows that the art of the witch hunt, with all the refinements of the smear and the principle of guilt by association, has made but little advance since the seventeenth century:

> If you observe any man to be of a publique and active spirit, (though he be no Independent or Separatist) he can never be friend to you in your work, and therefore you are to give him out, to be strongly suspected of whoredom, or drunkennesse, prophanenesse, an irreligious person . . . or say he is suspected to hold intelligence with Oxford,[21] or anything no matter what, somewhat will be believed. . . .

> If you see any such man but once talking with a Papist . . . you may give out that very honest men suspect him to be a Jesuit: if any one but demand of you or any other, how you can know the

Scriptures to be the word of God, give it out for certain that he denieth them, or if any put questions concerning *God* of *Christ,* or the *Trinity,* you have more than enough to lay accusations upon them, that shall stick by them as long as they live.[22]

What we can at least say is that enough of Walwyn's own work remains to enable us to recognise a writer and thinker of exceptional boldness and originality, and a mind extraordinarily mature and civilised.

Further, and this is true of the Levellers as a whole and especially of the three I have been considering, they were civilised in a new way. Whatever their limitations, they had reached a conception of man and his place in society, of the role of persuasion and the power of the written and spoken word, that was more accurate, more nearly a reflection of objective reality, than any other group of their time in any country. They wrote effectively not merely because they were exceptionally gifted or technically well equipped, though this can fairly be claimed at least for Overton and Walwyn, but because they wrote with a purpose clearly understood and deeply felt, and for an audience which they knew to be close and immediately responsive. These badly printed pamphlets, often printed illegally on little backstreet presses, strike home today as they did three hundred years ago because they are warm, generous and candid, because their authors knew exactly what they wanted to say and went to their work without hesitation or doubt or any pretension to the grand style. They stand near the head of one of the great streams of English prose, the stream which later was to include such mighty figures as Bunyan, Defoe, Paine, Cobbett and Shaw. They can fairly claim to be the fathers of the tradition of plain English writing dedicated to the service of the plain man.

Notes

1 Carlyle: *Letters and Speeches of Oliver Cromwell,* ed. Lomax, I, 154.

2 Four documents, differing in important respects, were issued under this name. Two are reprinted in Gardiner: *Constitutional Documents of the Puritan Revolution.* All four are in Don M. Wolfe: *Leveller Manifestoes.*

3 The pamphlets of the Levellers are extremely rare and only survive in a few copies, sometimes a single copy, in great libraries. They were therefore virtually inaccessible till comparatively recently. In 1933 Prof. W. Haller published a number in *Tracts on Liberty in the Puritan Revolution 1638-1647,* 3 vols., Columbia University Press. More material was printed in Prof. A. S. P. Woodhouse's *Puritanism and Liberty,* Dent, London 1938. In 1944 there appeared *The Leveller Tracts 1647-1653,* ed. by W. Haller and Godfrey Davies,

Columbia University Press, and *Leveller Manifestoes,* ed. Don M. Wolfe, Nelson. These volumes taken together provide an adequate selection from the works of the most important Leveller pamphleteers.

4 Other Leveller writers, whom it is not possible to discuss here, include John Wildman, Thomas Prince and Samuel Chidley.

5 *Walwins Wiles,* p. 2.

6 Haller: *Liberty and Reformation in the Puritan Revolution,* p. 262.

7 Lilburne: *The Just Defence of John Lilburne,* pp. 1-2.

8 Lilburne and others: *The Picture of the Councel of State,* p. 23.

9 Lilburne: *England's Birth-Right Justified,* pp. 43-4.

10 The Foxes are Cromwell, Ireton, etc. The Beagles, five troopers who had been cashiered from the Army for opposing them.

11 Satirists at this time were fond of alluding to Cromwell as a bull. For example *A Hue and Cry after Cromwell,* published only a week later than Overton's pamphlet, says: 'He was brought up in the *Isle of Ely,* where for his agility of body he was called *the Townbull;* which made his Parents keep him for a *Breeder,* and not accustome him to the Yoak.'

12 *The Picture of the Councel of State,* p. 31.

13 Woodhouse: *Puritanism and Liberty,* p. 53.

14 *The Picture of the Councel of State,* p. 44.

15 *The Baiting of the Great Bull of Bashan,* pp. 3-4.

16 *Walwyns Just Defence,* pp. 10-11.

17 Thomas Edwards: *The Second Part of Gangraena,* p. 25. Walwyn: *A Whisper in the Eare of Mr. Thomas Edwards,* pp. 6-7.

18 *The Compassionate Samaritane,* pp. 25-6.

19 *Walwins Wiles,* p. 5.

20 *A Whisper,* p. 6.

21 Oxford was at this time the headquarters of the Royalists.

22 Walwyn: *An Antidote to Master Edwards His Old and New Poyson,* pp. 8-9.

Richard A. Gleissner (essay date 1980)

SOURCE: "The Levellers and Natural Law: The Putney Debates of 1647," in *The Journal of British Studies,* Vol. XX, No. 1, Fall 1980, pp. 74-89.

[*In the following essay, Gleissner investigates the Levellers' understanding and application of the concept of natural law to their political agenda. Gleissner examines in particular the way this topic was addressed at the 1647 debates in Putney between Leveller leaders and key figures in the New Model Army, including Oliver Cromwell.*]

Natural law is one of the oldest concepts in Western philosophy. When the Psalmist asked Yahweh, "What is man that Thou art mindful of him," he was struggling with the same problem that occupied thoughtful men in Greece: the need to understand man as he is and in his potentiality. Unlike the unknown Biblical poet, however, Plato and Aristotle found an answer with the aid of reason rather than revelation. For them, man is an entity in process of becoming, possessing an essential, cognizable nature that gives rise to certain inclinations he must fulfill. Until the Enlightenment, the idea of man's nature and his need to realize it served as the focus of much of secular thought, out of which developed principles of government and a distinctive ethic. But ordinary people were touched only by the practical consequences of such things. The great law codes and the teachings of the church combined with philosophy to work out the individual's relationship to others according to a teleological conception of law rooted in the very nature of things. Understandably, the ontological theses and conclusions drawn from the theory of natural law remained irrelevant and unknown to common folk.

In the midst of the English Civil War, the concept appeared in the welter of disputes and conflicting plans for the revitalization of all aspects of English life, invoked by ordinary men who were neither philosophers nor theologians, neither jurists nor statesmen. This paper considers the use of natural law by one group, the Levellers, at a dramatic moment in the turbulent period following the king's imprisonment. It seeks to relate the Levellers' understanding of the concept to the traditional teaching about it, rather than to what one historian refers to as that later age when "Eternal Reason, autonomous and untrammeled, would hail every aspect of life to judgment at its bar and reduce to rubble the sanctuaries which the past had regarded with awe."[1]

Historians have generally recognized the importance of natural law to Leveller political attitudes and objectives, but have not established the connection between those attitudes and the fundamental precepts of the classical theory of the law. Thus, Joseph Frank has sketched the historical development of the concept, and showed how some, including the Levellers, accepted the idea that Magna Carta somehow "defined for England the actual meaning of a law of nature." H.N. Brailsford recalled that throughout history efforts have been made to give the law "an objective meaning," but they always ended in failure, so that when Levellers and others thought they had identified the exact content of the law they actually moved away from what Frank called the "protean and traditional idea of a law of nature." William Haller characterized as "unprecedented" the fact that the Levellers spoke and acted according to a definite "conception of the law of nature and the state which they had come to accept as truth." When considering the process by which John Lilburne adopted natural law theory, Haller named Christopher Saint-Germain, Henry Parker, and Sir Edward Coke as primary influences on him while at the same time causing him to confuse the divine law with the natural. Brian Manning has disputed this explanation, arguing instead on behalf of William Walwyn as both the source of Lilburne's belief in natural law and of his and other Levellers' confusion about the differences between divine and natural laws.[2]

By far the main concern of scholars has been to show the way that natural law fit into Leveller political philosophy as a whole, rather than to investigate how that philosophy may have arisen from the assumptions about man that have been historically associated with the theory. Theodore Pease, for example, explained how Leveller citation of natural law accorded with ideas about social compact and covenant, while Haller and Davies specifically disallowed the notion that the "abstract dialectical force" of the theory made any impression on the Levellers. What convinced the latter to employ natural law arguments was the presumption that the law sprang "directly from common belief and experience" and answered "immediately to common need." Speaking of the "very positive political program" of the Levellers, Austin Woolrych described it as being "largely secular" whereby they "sought to harness religious radicalism to political radicalism," such as in the case of Lilburne's claim that "all men were born to equal natural rights upon the assumption that God had bestowed sovereignty over all the rest of his creatures upon Adam and Eve."[3] The idea of natural rights is an especially prominent one in Leveller historiography and no more so than in C.B. MacPherson's work. MacPherson was interested in associating Leveller ideology to what he called possessive individualism, a theory of rights that he discovers emergent in the seventeenth century and responsible for subverting "Christian natural law tradition." Hence, he preferred comparing Lilburne and Richard Overton to Thomas Hobbes and John Locke, and not at all to Plato, Aristotle, Aquinas, and Richard Hooker.[4] In sum, while historians have admitted that the concept of the law of nature played a remarkable role in Leveller thought, none has lifted that role from the limitations of time and place and situated it in the mainstream of realist philosophy. An analysis of the Putney debates offers an invaluable insight into the Levellers' perception of man and the world, a perception that depended in a fundamental way upon teachings older than the ones Hobbes or even Walwyn or Parker offered to Englishmen; indeed, the Levellers drew from principles and precepts as old as Western philosophy and that originated in the writings of Plato and Aristotle and passed to the Levellers from Thomas Aquinas and Hooker.

When Sir Thomas Fairfax, commander-in-chief of the New Model Army, summoned the General Council of Officers to meet in Putney in late October 1647 and debate certain important issues, he did so amid growing dissension in several regiments. Radicals among officers and men had recently denounced the general council for negotiating a political settlement with King Charles I that included the latter's restoration, though with severe restrictions to be placed on the royal prerogative. Under the direction of Lt. General Oliver Cromwell, the second-in-command, and Commissary General Henry Ireton, his son-in-law, the talks proceeded with the clear intention of preserving the social order in England much as it had existed before the Civil War. But the radicals, or Levellers, wanted no part of Charles and demanded significant constitutional reform.

In a lengthy statement expressing their opposition to the negotiations, *The Case of the Army,* the Levellers had proposed a number of fundamental changes, perhaps the most revolutionary being the enfranchisement of all freeborn Englishmen over the age of twenty-one who were not servants, and regardless of property holdings. On the very eve of the meeting of the general council they drew up a more formal set of demands styled "An Agreement of the People," but which contained, for some reason, only an ambiguous reference to universal freeborn suffrage.[5] Whether they adopted a more circumspect attitude toward specific reforms in the Agreement for tactical reasons or because they genuinely meant to be conciliatory, nonetheless the Levellers' vocal opposition to any discussions with the king seriously jeopardized the discipline and internal unity of the Army.

The principal radical spokesmen in the debates were Colonel Thomas Rainborough, a member of parliament, and John Wildman, a young attorney who may have been the author of *The Case of the Army.*[6] Though neither was an especially profound thinker, both were obviously well educated, intelligent, and sensitive to the intellectual environment of the day. That they were also comfortable with ideas is reflected in Wildman's protest at one point in debate, "I could wish we should have recourse to principles and maxims of just government [instead of arguments of safety], which are as loose as can be."[7] Moreover, they were fully acquaint-

ed with the component theses of the classical theory of natural law and able to apply them to their own particular situation.

Although in the course of the debates, Rainborough and Wildman did not expressly define the ontological and ethical theses of which the theory consisted, enough was said by them to indicate the extent of their understanding. In sum, they presumed (1) that all men share an essential structure that determines certain fundamental human inclinations or tendencies; (2) that the good for all men is the realization or fulfillment of these inclinations; (3) that norms or moral laws are derived from man's nature and his efforts to achieve authentic fulfillment.[8] From these premises, they went on to argue for full participation in government of all freemen—even the propertyless—as a matter of justice, whereas Cromwell and Ireton continued to uphold the practical necessity of reserving the exercise of political authority to men of "permanent fixed interest" in the kingdom in order to assure internal stability and peace. On the one hand, therefore, the Levellers approached the question of a constitutional settlement, at least in part, as an ethical or moral one; on the other hand, conservatives treated it for the moment as a simple problem of making minor adjustments to established institutions, divorced from any larger considerations.

Radical interest in the concept of natural law had been evident for some time. Increasingly, men such as Overton and Lilburne invoked it in the presentation of their program for reform and in their criticism of parliament. Overton, for example, located the power of all governments in natural law and the rights of men rooted in that law. In *An Arrow Against All Tyrants,* published almost exactly a year before the debates, he warned the House of Lords that by this alone "are you instated into your sovereign capacity, for the free people of this nation, for their better being, discipline, government, propriety and safety, have each of them communicated so much unto you (their Chosen Ones) of their natural rights and powers, that you may become their . . . lawful deputies, but no more." To every person, he wrote, "is given an individual property by nature, not to be invaded, or usurped by any; for every one as he is himself, so he hath a self propriety, else could he not be himself, and on this no second may presume to deprive any of, without manifest violation and affront to the very principles of nature."[9]

Writing from the Tower of London in 1646, where he had been sent for denouncing parliament, Lilburne declared that "God, creating men for his own praise . . . made him [sic] not lord, or gave him dominion over the individuals of mankind, no further than by free consent, or agreement, by giving up their power, each to other, for their better being." Nature, he said, had engraved on the soul of man "this golden and everlasting principle, to do to another, as he would have another to do to him."[10]

That the concept of a law of nature was readily adopted by the radicals reflects its continued importance to thoughtful men of the seventeenth century. Joseph Frank calls it the "chief theoretical link" between the Levellers and the Renaissance. He says that they were attracted to the concept's "potentially utopian tradition" that had produced, in turn, a belief "that the doctrines of the common law judges had put on record various definite and basic rules about man's relationship to man."[11] Yet if natural law served as a bridge, the works of men like Richard Hooker and George Buchanan must have contributed something to the connection, for Hooker in particular did more than any late Renaissance thinker to establish the theory in the center of seventeenth-century English political philosophy.

There are echoes of Hooker's *The Laws of Ecclesiastical Polity* in these quotations of Overton and Lilburne. Despite the apparent references to a social contract as the root of government, the emphasis that both placed on the consensual element in the origins of government bears a close resemblance to Hooker's. In Book One of the *Ecclesiastical Polity,* for instance, he explained that men's "strifes and troubles would be endless, except they gave their common consent all to be ordered by some whom they should agree upon." He added that "without which consent there were no reason that one man should take upon him to be lord or judge over another."[12] W.D.J. Cargill Thompson has recently pointed out that although Hooker's views "undoubtedly foreshadowed those of the seventeenth-century social contract theorists, the idea of contract . . . plays no part in his thought, and it is, in fact entirely alien to his political philosophy."[13]

The words "better being" used by Overton and Lilburne clearly expressed Leveller faith in the distinctive view of man taught by all the great natural law philosophers from the Greeks to Hooker. The words signified something other than physical safety or a more comfortable existence or freedom from arbitrary or repressive laws. They referred to the potency of human nature, to the thrust toward existential fulfillment shared by all men, an idea first developed by Plato and Aristotle.[14] Hooker observed, "All other things besides [God] are somewhat in possibility which as yet they are not in act. And for this cause there is in all things an appetite or desire whereby they incline to something which they may be."[15] "Better being" was equivalent to the notion of incipient tendency produced by nature itself. Indeed, the idea of an inherent thrust toward authentic realization of human nature occurred again and again in the writings of Levellers. In another

tract written in 1646, titled *A Defiance Against All Arbitrary Usurpations,* Overton had stated, "Nature itself doth bind every man to do according to his power."[16] The radicals in several regiments wrote in a letter to Fairfax forwarding *The Case of the Army,* "God hath given no man a talent to be wrapped up in a napkin & not improved; but the meanest vassal in the eye of the Lord is equally obliged and accounted to God with the greatest prince or commander under the sun, in and for the use of that talent betrusted to him."[17] Though this obviously referred to the *parousia*-parable of the talents found in the gospels of Matthew (25,14-30) and Luke (19,12-27), the radicals had not cited it because of any expectation of the imminent second coming of Christ. Rather, several times in the letter they alluded to obligations arising from man's very nature, "written naturally by the finger of God in our hearts," grounded in the "very dictates of Divinity, Nature and Reason ingraven in our hearts." Overton had concluded *An Arrow* by stating that "by nature we are sons of Adam, and from him have legitimately derived a natural propriety, right and freedom. . . . It is but the just rights and prerogatives of mankind (whereunto the people of England are heirs apparent, as well as other nations) which we desire . . . that we may be men, and live like men."[18]

In such fashion did the Levellers define their belief that by nature all men tend toward completion. That they did not speak or write with the precision of Aristotle or Hooker need not surprise us since they were not, after all, philosophers. Nonetheless, they consciously appropriated the various theses of natural law philosophy, such as that of human inclination, incorporating them into their programs and adverting to them in argument so that they provided the Levellers with an encompassing perspective of the human condition in general and the particular situation facing all Englishmen at that moment.

Although all of the participants in the Putney debates assumed that divine law was normative in character, scarcely any mention was made of it by the radicals.[19] On the other hand, the Levellers' insistence that norms of equal authority were rooted in the law of nature became a pivotal issue. While the speeches of radicals and conservatives ranged far beyond it, the question always hovered within reach: did moral conduct for the citizen or subject rest solely upon the definition of positive law, or did it derive from the very nature of man? Cromwell first drew attention to possible conflict between positive and natural law. At the beginning of the debate on October 28, while giving generous credit to the sincerity of the Levellers in drafting the Agreement, he suggested that implementation of that document would pose insurmountable political obstacles and would violate the original "engagement" of the army for fighting the king. "He that departs from that that is a real engagement and a real tie upon him," he said, "I think he transgresses without faith; for faith will bear up a man in every honest obligation."[20]

Wildman immediately objected, saying the point was whether the "engagement were honest and just or no." If it were not, "it doth not oblige the persons [even] if it be an oath itself." Later, he criticized those who "look to prophecies" as the key to determining the morality of actions, and those who "judge the justness of a thing by the consequences." Right and wrong for him depended on neither of these. Rainborough said that everyone was bound "to God and his conscience" to refuse to do evil, thus alluding to an objective source of morality available to all men.[21]

Ireton would have none of this. Not overly concerned about ethical considerations except in so far as they served the interests of the property holding classes, nor especially disturbed by any conflict between the army's original engagement and the Agreement, he denied that justice and honesty were a vital part of the differences between the Levellers and the council. What was of paramount importance, according to him, was the matter of obedience to lawfully constituted authority, and the radicals' suggestion that anything could excuse a man from absolute subordination to it. Speaking of the subject's duty to obey his governors, he said, "Yet, if I have engaged that they shall bind me by law, though afterwards I find they do require me to [do] a thing that is not just or honest, I am bound so far to my engagement that I must submit and suffer, though I cannot act and do that which their laws do impose upon me." Whether or not he meant that through passive disobedience a man must bear the consequences imposed by civil law, nonetheless he maintained that anything less than absolute obedience "will take away all commonwealths."[22] From this principle he mounted his attack on the Levellers, insisting that to admit the prescriptive rule of a law of nature would threaten order and stability and in particular property rights.

To refer to justice and honesty as Wildman had, that is, as superior moral criteria for judging agreements among men, struck Ireton as the very source of societal dissolution. "Men of this principle," he declared, "would think themselves as little as may be [obliged by any law] if in their apprehensions it be not a good law. I think they would think themselves as little obliged . . . of standing to that authority that is proposed in this paper [that is, the Agreement]." Underlying his words was an admission that government did indeed result from the voluntary consent of the governed; but for him the consensual act was a once-for-all thing giving governments both independence from the people as well as perpetual tenure. "Covenants freely made, freely entered into, must be kept one with another." He agreed with the Levellers "that if a man

have engaged himself to a thing that is not just—to a thing that is evil—that is sin if he do it," such a man is not bound to carry out his promise. He did not or would not, however, see, as the Levellers did, that a man could engage himself for a just and honest purpose and later be confronted by that which was unjust and dishonest, and therefore must not act contrary to those norms rooted in his very nature. "But when we talk of just," said Ireton, "it is not so much of what is sinful before God . . . [but] of what is just according to the foundation of justice between man and man. And for my part I account that the great foundation of justice [is] that we should keep convenant one with another, without which I know nothing of justice betwixt man and man."[23]

Hence, Ireton assumed that covenant establishing government, being good in itself, ever after required the abject submission of the participants. This alone guaranteed justice and righteousness, for there could be "no other foundation of right . . . but this general justice and this general ground of righteousness, that we should keep covenant one with another." Relating this to his chief concern, he said, "I would very fain know what you gentlemen, or any other, do account the right you have to anything in England—anything of estate, land or goods that you have. . . . What right hath any man to anything if you lay not [down] that principle that we are to keep covenant?"[24]

Wildman had argued in effect that to do that which was unjust or dishonest even within the context of government by consent violated morality. But Ireton rejected that view, as well as its justification, which he understood to be natural law. He did not believe that the latter could coexist with positive law, that is, as imposing obligations on a man apart from civil law, without jeopardizing property rights. "If you will resort only to the law of nature," he warned, "by the law of nature you have no more right to this land, or anything else, than I have. I have as much right to take hold of anything that is for my sustenance, take hold of anything that I have a desire to for my satis-faction, as you." Only positive law, the product of government by consent and enjoying perpetuity, could protect property and ensure peace among men. What one man "may claim by the law of nature, of taking my goods, that which makes it mine really and civilly, is the law." Conversely, that which makes it unlawful for a man to take another's goods "originally and radically is only this: because that man is in covenant with me to live together in peace . . . and not to meddle with that which another is possessed of, but that each of us should enjoy, and make use of, and dispose of, that which by the course of law is in his possession, and [another] shall not by violence take it away from him."[25]

Interesting parallels exist between Ireton's position and Thomas Hobbes' in the matter of permanency of government by consent, and the absolute need to perform contracts. Whether Ireton had read Hobbes cannot be proved and it may be there was no more than a coincidental agreement between his ideas and those contained in *The Elements of Law* (1640) and *De Cive* (1642). Still, it is useful to compare the two in order to further underscore the differences separating conservatives like the Commissary and the Levellers, and to show the presence of ideas in midcentury in England at variance with the traditional teachings about natural law.

Hobbes believed in the "inevitability of conflict in the desires and actions of men and argues the necessity of imposing order by human contrivance." Thus, although "earlier writers had posited a hierarchy of values, Hobbes asserts a single goal, self-preservation, which man shares with all living beings."[26] Because of the unitary end of man and the condition of warfare that subsists in a state of nature, government becomes imperative for human survival. The actual origins of government are located in the "compacts which each single citizen or subject mutually makes with the other; but all contracts, as they receive their force from the contractors, so by their consent they lose it again and are broken.[27] Hobbes did not think that these compacts could ever be broken, however, because "it is not to be imagined that ever it will happen, that all the subjects together . . . will combine against the supreme power [of governors]."[28] As for a single citizen who dissents from the compact, "since it is supposed that each one hath obliged himself to each other, if any one of them shall refuse, whatsoever the rest shall agree to do, he is bound notwithstanding."[29]

Ireton's insistence on the performance of obligations under the original compact entirely accorded with this. The point of his arguments in the debates was that Leveller demands for reform of the constitution contradicted the permanence of the compact, and the purposes of government to safeguard peace and property. Hobbes, however, went further in *De Cive* by calling all actions that "violate covenants and betrothed faith" treason.[30] Though Ireton carefully refrained from any accusation of treachery on the radicals' part, he obviously suspected them of plotting mischief at the expense of property holders. Certainly he shared Hobbes' fundamentally pessimistic appraisal of human nature and the need to subordinate the lower classes to superior political force capable of circumscribing their violent temperaments. Without that, property rights would be vulnerable.

Unlike Hobbes, Ireton did not invoke natural law in defense of the status quo or as an adjunct to civil law in controlling society. Indeed, he misunderstood the idea of a law of nature and of rights inherent in human nature. Nor did he recognize the Hobbesian version of natural law as rational conclusions drawn from an es-

sentially negative evaluation of man. Hobbes' use of the concept had nothing to do with the teachings of Hooker, Aquinas, Aristotle, and Plato. For Hooker, "whose view carried immense authority in the seventeenth century, the laws of nature are the laws eternal originating 'in the bosom of God' self-evident and hence known to all reasonable men, and providing the foundation upon which positive civil law rests." But for Hobbes, "they are theorems of conduct for the ordering of men's lives in a commonwealth so as to ensure civil peace."[31] They were merely "the instrumental and hypothetical rules of reason regarding the best means to self-preservation."[32] Yet Ireton saw them as being even less important. To him natural law was neither normative in Hooker's sense, nor rational in Hobbes'. His references to such a law in debate suggest that he identified it with absence of government, anarchy, and destruction of property. The "great foundation of justice" to which he referred consisted entirely of human recognition of the inviolability of covenants. Simple, narrow, and leaving no room for change or modification of social and political institutions, the Commissary's political principles doubted man's ability to achieve any fulfillment except in the most selfish respect, and one that would utterly ruin order in a community painfully retrieved from savagery.

Rainborough and Wildman countered Ireton's position by denying that natural law threatened property anymore than it threatened peace and stability in the community. There could be no conflict between it and positive law except in so far as the state violated the law of nature. Rainborough dismissed all concerns about property rights by reminding his audience, "God hath set down . . . this law of his, *Thou shalt not steal.*"[33] Wildman preferred answering Ireton by showing the inconsistency of the Commissary's principles with the army's public stance that it "stood upon such principles of right and freedom, and the laws of nature and nations, whereby men were to preserve themselves though the persons to whom authority belonged should fail in it." He said that if "anything tends to the destruction of a people, because the thing is absolutely unjust, that tends to their destruction, they may preserve themselves by opposing it."[34]

But Wildman was not simply referring to physical destruction. A careful reading of his remarks indicates that he thought of destruction in a much broader sense, namely, of an act of injustice perpetrated by government that limited men in their pursuit of their natural end. It was because of injustice of this sort that the Levellers believed the war had been fought, and because of it they would have nothing further to do with the king, "him that intended our bondage and brought a cruel war upon us."[35]

Fearful of a repetition of the kind of oppressive government they identified with Charles I, the Levellers felt that the problem of abuse of power had greater immediacy than the conservatives' preoccupation with property rights. To the radicals, enfranchisement of all freemen seemed the best way of preventing such abuse. Only by that means would government truly respond to the needs of the people and their search for "better being." Only through enfranchisement would consent of the governed become a reality, instead of a constitutional fiction, and the original agreement of people to establish government become self-renewing. Always, however, the Levellers' purpose was to protect the individual's right to live a more fully human existence without hindrance. "I think that the poorest he that is in England hath a life to live as the greatest he," was the way Rainborough put it.[36]

Of course Ireton opposed enfranchisement, and although the Levellers did not openly lay claim to the suffrage by natural law, he believed they defended it on that basis. "Since you cannot plead to it," he said, "by anything but the law of nature . . . for the end of better being, and that better being is not certain . . . upon these grounds, if you do . . . hold up this law of nature, I would fain have any man show me their bounds?" To conservatives, the "fundamental constitution" of the kingdom not only bestowed and protected property rights but justly linked them to the exercise of political authority. Such men "comprehend the local interest of this kingdom, that is, the persons in whom all land lies, and those in corporations in whom all trading lies"; they were the guarantors of peace and stability.[37]

In spite of Ireton's assertion otherwise, it was too questionable a proposition to defend the right to vote as being rooted in natural law, and the Levellers did not do so. However, they seem to have concluded that the exclusion of great numbers of persons from parliamentary elections simply because they lacked a certain amount of land was, indeed, a violation of the law. Since government resulted from the voluntary consent of the people, the Levellers argued that it was wrong to deprive them of a voice in elections.[38] Moreover, property qualifications were but another example of a willful class of men who controlled the reins of power defining rights and exacting obedience from the poor to laws that said what constituted justice and injustice. In what seems to be a confused reference to the notion of men in a state of nature, a radical officer said that if "we were to begin a government," according to the conservatives only those who possessed the equivalent of a forty-shilling estate would be allowed to vote, whereas previously "every man had such a choice." Though he might also have been alluding to a utopian and romantic interpretation of life in pre-Conquest England popular among some Levellers, still he clearly meant to underscore the equality of persons in establishing government, and the unfair laws written thereafter making the majority of people "hewers of wood and drawers of water."[39]

The radicals also believed that participation of all freemen in government was in accord with man's natural tendency toward existential completion. One Leveller (designated Buff-Coat in the transcript) said, "But I understand that all these debates, if we shall agree upon any one thing, this is our freedom; this is our liberty; this liberty and freedom we are debarred of." Each man was born free and sought "by natural instinct . . . his safety and weale."[40] That they did so in communion with one another was due both to the frailty of man and to a natural need for the society of others. Hooker had written that men "covet" fellowship and society. Because of "mutual grievances, injuries, and wrongs," men realized "there was no way but only by growing unto composition and agreement amongst themselves, by ordaining some kind of government public, and by yielding themselves subject thereunto." Hooker recalled that in the opinion of "some very great and judicious men" a kind of natural right reposed in the "noble, wise and virtuous" to govern the masses of "servile" disposition. Though the Levellers did not admit the existence of such a right, nevertheless they agreed with Hooker's conclusion that "for manifestation of this their right, and men's more peaceable contentment on both sides, the assent of them who are to be governed seemeth necessary."[41]

Arguing that government's "chief end . . . is to preserve persons as well as estates," the Levellers took for granted that the individual was more valuable than property. Hence, "every man born in England cannot, ought not, neither by the law of God nor the law of nature, to be exempted from the choice of those who are to make laws for him to live under, and for him . . . to lose his life under."[42] In *The Case of the Army,* the radicals had charged their officers with faithlessness toward the people by failing to abide by promises "to stand for the national interest, freedoms and rights," and by ignoring the law of nature and nations. Everyone, Wildman declared, "hath as clear a right to elect his representatives as the greatest person in England." That, he said, was "the undeniable maxim of government: that all government is in the free consent of the people." To continue the traditional distribution of power would be acquiescence in a state of slavery stretching back to the Normans.[43]

Rainborough bitterly criticized a system whereby a lord could choose twenty burgesses and a gentlemen only two, whereas "a poor man shall choose none." He said that he found no reason or justification for this practice in natural law or the law of nations, but that it existed only according to English civil law. Thereby, an ordinary Englishman "must lose that which God and nature hath given him," that is, the right to consent to positive law or withhold his consent.[44]

The teleological view of man shared by the Levellers necessitated their emphatic demand for an extension of the franchise to all freemen. As a rational creature, man was capable of recognizing his own incompletion and his need to become more truly himself, to "perform his function well," as Aristotle put it.[45] As a rational being, too, he had recognized his need for the association of others and of providing for government as a means of reaching fulfillment. But if he was responsible for creating government for his own needs, he was also capable of sharing in the governing process, and it did not matter how much land he owned or how much tax he paid annually. What mattered was the fact that a government's purposes were directly tied to his natural well-being, that laws derived their justice from the extent to which they encouraged and contributed to his natural end. Therefore, the power to select his governors was not only logically implied but in strict accord with the origins of government and its ends. "We are now engaged for our freedom," Wildman said; "that's the end of parliaments [and] not to constitute what is already according to the just rules of [the old] government." Consequently, he said, the question before the council should be framed: "Whether any person can justly be bound by law who doth not give his consent that such persons shall make laws for him."[46] To that the radicals responded in the negative, whereas men like Ireton and Cromwell replied affirmatively.

Misunderstanding the concept of natural law, conservatives likewise misunderstood the intent of Leveller demands for constitutional reform. All they saw was a movement of the lower classes that imperiled the traditional social order and distribution of authority in the kingdom. Challenged, threatened, and profoundly fearful of the future if this defiance was not nipped, they offered counterarguments to the opposition's, thereby tacitly admitting that it was no longer sufficient for nobles and gentry to insist upon obedience to a given set of institutions and a political process merely because they claimed them to be right and proper and honored by time. Ireton might assert that while government originated in the voluntary agreement of the people, once the bargain was struck all men were bound to it and had to make the most of it; yet even he recognized the inadequacy of such a premise. So the conservatives had had to summon a complex set of ideas; power needed the support of reason to legitimize itself. It was not enough, however, because natural law philosophy allowed no room for the static conception of man and the world assumed by the conservatives' arguments. Although Ireton dismissed the radicals' concern for individual freedom as so much cant, Cromwell sensed in it something more ominous. "When every man shall come to this condition of mind," he said, "I think the state will come to desolation."[47]

The Levellers had no intention of despoiling property holders of their estates. Neither did they seek some kind of "permanent revolution" by which England would be cleansed or purged of the bondage they attributed to six hundred years of "Norman" rule.[48] They did not feel the kind of blind anger and jealousy that Ireton and the conservatives suspected lurked in their hearts and minds. Rather, they found in the concept of the law of nature an explanation of the human condition and man's experience of himself that verified their own. The generations of nameless men and women in England who left slight record that they ever systematically questioned the historical social division of the kingdom or the constitution, or ever dreamed of enjoying a full and equitable share in government, suddenly intruded into the councils of the governing class through the voices of the Levellers. Speaking for the common folk, because they themselves were not far removed from the lower orders, the radicals gave expression to the human quest for something more than bare survival. They revealed that quite ordinary men reached out beyond themselves in a relentless pursuit of self-fulfillment, not to destroy other men or property or peace in the community, but to "live like men." In this too the Levellers contributed the initial effort in formulating that broad libertarian platform of the commonwealthmen so vital to a later generation of Americans.[49] Whereas the Calvinism of the saints denied that man in his depravity ever sought the good from a natural desire or impetus, the radicals insisted that he did and discovered a cause for optimism about man in this very movement of his being. Natural law vindicated their hopefulness, acknowledging that the human entity's struggle to reach completion is finished when, in Aristotle's words, "it lacks no particle of its natural magnitude."[50]

Notes

[1] Perez Zagorin, *A History of Political Thought in the English Revolution* (London, 1954), p. 29.

[2] Joseph Frank, *The Levellers, A History of the Writings of Three Seventeenth-Century Social Democrats: John Lilburne, Richard Overton, William Walwyn* (New York, 1955), pp. 5-7. H.N. Brailsford, *The Levellers and the English Revolution,* Christopher Hill (ed.) (Stanford, 1961), pp. 280-82. *The Leveller Tracts, 1647-1653,* William Haller and Godfrey Davies, (eds.) (Gloucester, 1964), pp. 8, 41-48. Brian Manning, "The Levellers and Christianity," in *Politics, Religion and the English Civil War,* Brian Manning (ed.) (New York, 1973), pp. 232-33.

[3] Theodore C. Pease, *The Leveller Movement* (Washington, 1916), pp. 24, 46-47, 74-75, 84, 180-81, 358-59; Haller and Davies, p. 37; Austin Wollrych, "Puritanism, Politics and Society" in *The English Revolution, 1600-1660,* E.W. Ives (ed.) (New York, 1969), p. 96; see also Brian Manning, "The Levellers," pp. 144-57.

[4] C. B. MacPherson, *The Political Theory of Possessive Individualism,* (Oxford, 1962), pp. 1, 141-42, 154-56, 158-59. William Haller (ed.), *Tracts on Liberty in the Puritan Revolution, 1638-1647,* 3 vols. (New York, 1979), I, pp. 23-25, 111-14.

[5] *The Case of the Army,* in Haller and Davies, pp. 64-84. The first clause of the Agreement said, "That the people of England being at this day very unequally distributed by counties, cities and boroughs, for the election of their deputies in Parliament, ought to be more indifferently proportioned, according to the number of the inhabitants; the circumstances whereof, for number, place, and manner, are to be set down before the end of this present Parliament." G.E. Aylmer (ed.), *The Levellers in the English Revolution* (London, 1975), pp. 89-91 for the Agreement. Brailsford speculates that a forthright demand for universal suffrage in the Agreement "may have been omitted to appease the Grandees" on the general council, p. 261.

[6] Shorthand notes of the debates were kept by Captain William Clarke, secretary to the general council and first published in C. H. Firth (ed.), *The Clarke Papers,* 4 vols. (London, 1891-1901), I, pp. 226-418; Frank, pp. 132, 309-10. Maurice Ashley, *John Wildman* (New Haven, 1947).

[7] *Clarke Papers,* p. 403.

[8] See John Wild, *Plato's Modern Enemies and the Theory of Natural Law* (Chicago, 1953) for a particularly cogent treatment of the realist theory of natural law, and Jacques Maritain, "Natural Law and Moral Law," in *Challenges and Renewals,* Joseph W. Evans and Leo R. Ward (eds.) (Notre Dame, 1966), pp. 213-28.

[9] Richard Overton, *An Arrow Against All Tyrants,* in Aylmer, p. 69; Manning, "The Levellers," pp. 150-56; John Dykstra Eusden, *Puritans, Lawyers, and Politics in Early Seventeenth-Century England* (New Haven, 1958), pp. 126-41.

[10] John Lilburne, *A Postscript,* in Aylmer, p. 71. Leo F. Solt, *Saints in Arms, Puritanism and Democracy in Cromwell's Army* (Oxford, 1959), pp. 80-82.

[11] Frank, p. 6. He also says, "In contradistinction to Calvinism, the orientation of such a belief [in natural law] was, on the whole, political rather than religious, its initial impact synthetic rather than disintegrative." For additional discussion of the relationship of natural law to Calvinism, see Michael Walzer, *The Revolution of the Saints, A Study in the Origins of Radical Politics* (New York, 1969), pp. 31-32, 35-36, 154.

[12] Richard Hooker, *The Laws of Ecclesiastical Polity,* Book I, Chapter X, 4 in *The Works of Mr. Richard Hooker,* John Keble (ed.), 3 vols. (London, 1888), I, pp. 241-42.

[13] W. D. J. Cargill Thompson, "The Philosopher of the 'Politic Society'; Richard Hooker as a Political Thinker," in *Studies in Richard Hooker: Essays Preliminary to an Edition of His Works,* W. Speed Hill (ed.) (Cleveland, 1972), p. 43; E.T. Davies, *The Political Ideas of Richard Hooker* (New York, 1972), pp. 65-66, says that it is difficult to trace a coherent theory of the social contract in Hooker, and that "it is more correct to say that Hooker followed the Aritotelian conception of the 'natural' basis of society." Elsewhere he says that there "can be no doubt that the nearest approach in his writings to a definite basis for political authority lies in his teaching that the force of law is based on the consent of the governed." p. 69.

[14] Examples of Plato's treatment of the subject may be found in *Republic,* 352a, 433a, 490a, 586c; *Laws,* 631b-e, 782d, 927b; *Gorgias,* 478, 499, 503. For Aristotle, see *Physics,* 192b, 198b; *Nicomachean Ethics,* 1097a, 1106a. D.B. Robertson, *The Religious Foundations of Leveller Democracy* (New York, 1951), pp. 53-61.

[15] Hooker, *Ecclesiastical Polity,* I, p. 215.

[16] Richard Overton, *A Defiance Against All Arbitrary Usurpations,* quoted in Frank, p. 88.

[17] *A Copy of a Letter from the Agents of the Aforesaid Five Regiments of Horse, unto His Excellency Sir Thomas Fairfax,* in Haller and Davies, p. 85.

[18] *Ibid.,* pp. 85-86. The most authoritative recent discussion of the parable of the talents may be found in Joachim Jeremias, *Rediscovering the Parables* (New York, 1966), pp. 45-50, which is an abridgement of the author's magisterial study *The Parables of Jesus* (New York, 1963). Overton, *An Arrow,* in Aylmer, p. 70. One may also cite again his statement that "every one as he is himself, so he hath a self propriety, else could he not be himself," as referring to the tendential character of man. On the natural inclination of man, see Thomas Aquinas, *Summa Theologica,* Question 94, Article 2 and 4 as an example of the treatment of this subject by the greatest of the medieval successors to Plato and Aristotle. In turn, Hooker leaned heavily upon the Thomistic development and exposition of natural law philosophy.

[19] Pease, p. 217, says of the Levellers, "Like other men they could see in outward happenings evidence of divine approval of their work; but for guidance they ever looked to their principles and not to passing events. When contrasted in this respect with Cromwell and the Saints they are strangely modern."

[20] *Clarke Papers,* pp. 239-40. When possible I have used the updated version of the debates found in Charles Blitzer (ed.), *The Commonwealth of England, Documents of the English Civil War* (New York, 1963), pp.

49-51. See Cromwell's remark regarding the obstacles arising from the Agreement that it "does contain in it very great alterations of the very government of the kingdom. . . . There will be very great mountains in the way of this."

[21] *Clarke Papers,* pp. 240, 245, 317. Blitzer, pp. 52, 56. On the relationship of conscience to natural law as Aquinas confronted the problem, see *Summa,* Question 94, Article 1 and 2.

[22] *Ibid.,* pp. 241-42. Manning, "The Levellers," p. 151.

[23] *Ibid.,* pp. 242, 262, 263; Blitzer, pp. 53, 62-63. How far Ireton departed in his remarks from traditional notions of justice may be seen by comparing them with Cicero's comments in the *Laws,* Book I, Chapter XV: "But if justice is conformity to written laws and national customs, and if . . . everything is to be tested by the standard of utility, then anyone who thinks it will be profitable to him will, if he is able, disregard and violate the laws. It follows that justice does not exist at all, if it does not exist in nature." Virtues, said Cicero, "originate in our natural inclination to love our fellow-men, and this is the foundation of justice." *De Re Publica, De Legibus,* Clinton W. Keyes (trans.) (Cambridge, Mass., 1928).

[24] *Ibid.,* pp. 262, 263.

[25] *Ibid.,* p. 263.

[26] Paul E. Sigmund, *Natural Law in Political Thought* (Cambridge, Mass., 1971), p. 80.

[27] Thomas Hobbes, *De Cive,* in Bernard Gert (ed.), *Man and Citizen* (New York, 1972), VI, 20, p. 188. See also I, 2; I, 7; I, 9; I, 13; II, 3; III, 1.

[28] *Ibid.,* p. 189; III, 1.

[29] *Ibid.* Hobbes added further emphasis to the need to obey covenants by citing sacred scripture in *The Elements of Law: Natural and Politic,* Ferdinand Tonnies, (ed.) (New York, 1969), I, 18, p. 96. See also *De Cive,* III, 1; III, 2.

[30] *Ibid.,* XIV, 21, pp. 286-87.

[31] Samuel I. Mintz, *The Hunting of Leviathan: Seventeenth-Century Reactions to the Materialism and Moral Philosophy of Thomas Hobbes* (Cambridge, 1969), p. 26. Wild, pp. 123-27. *De Cive,* I, 15; II, 1. *The Elements of Law,* I, 15, 1-2.

[32] Sigmund, p. 77; Mintz, pp. 26-27. See the interesting contrast that was drawn by John Dewey between Hobbes and the Levellers in his essay, "The Motivation of Hobbes' Political Philosophy," in Ralph Ross,

Herbert W. Schneider, Theodore Waldman, *Thomas Hobbes In His Time* (Minneapolis, 1974), p. 15.

[33] *Clarke Papers,* p. 309. Blitzer, p. 72. Less than twenty-five years earlier, Grotius had upheld the superiority of natural law over positive law in *De iure belli ac pacis* (1625) saying, "the civil law cannot ordain anything which the natural law prohibits, nor prohibit what that ordains." *The Great Legal Philosophers: Selected Readings in Jurisprudence,* Clarence Morris (ed.) (Philadelphia, 1959), pp. 94-95.

[34] *Ibid.,* p. 260. Blitzer, p. 61. See *A Declaration, or Representation . . . of the Army,* for an example of the army's citation of natural law in a public pronouncement, Haller and Davies, pp. 52-63.

[35] "Agreement," Aylmer, p. 91. One Leveller, Edward Sexby, summed up the radicals, mistrust of the king and the current negotiations with him when he said, "We have labored to please a King, and I think, except we go about to cut all our [own] throats, we shall not please him." Blitzer, p. 45.

[36] *Clarke Papers,* p. 301; Blitzer, p. 65.

[37] *Ibid.,* pp. 302, 308; Blitzer, pp. 67, 71.

[38] The argument along these lines recalls what Aquinas said in Question 90, Article 3 of the *Summa:* "A law, properly speaking, regards first and foremost the order of the common good. Now to order anything to the common good, belongs either to the whole people, or to someone who is the viceregent of the whole people. And therefore the making of a law belongs either to the whole people or to a public personage who has care of the whole people: Since in all other matters the directing of anything to the end concerns him to whom the end belongs." *Treatise on Law* (South Bend, n.d.), p. 8. See the third "Agreement of the People," Aylmer, p. 162, for a later assertion that the right to vote arose from the law of nature.

[39] *Clarke Papers,* pp. 312, 320. For a discussion of the idea of a golden age in Anglo-Saxon times, see Brailsford, pp. 129-30, and Christopher Hill, *Puritanism and Revolution, The English Revolution of the 17th Century* (New York, 1967), Chapter 3. Christopher Hill, *The World Turned Upside Down, Radical Ideas During the English Revolution* (New York, 1975), pp. 158, 226, 272.

[40] *Ibid.,* p. 243. Richard Overton, "An Appeal," in *Leveller Manifestoes of the Puritan Revolution,* Don M. Wolfe (ed.) (New York, 1967), pp. 162-63.

[41] Hooker, *Ecclesiastical Polity,* I, X, 4, pp. 241-42. His reference to "great and judicious men" was to Aristotle, *Politics,* III, iv. See also I, X, 1, p. 239 in Hooker.

[42] *Clarke Papers,* pp. 305, 320; Blitzer, p. 69. J.G.A. Pocock, *The Machiavellian Moment, Florentine Political Thought and the Atlantic Republican Tradition* (Princeton, 1975), pp. 374-78, for a discussion of the debates from a different angle, especially the concern about property rights.

[43] *The Case of the Army,* Haller and Davies, p. 71; *Clarke Papers,* p. 318.

[44] *Clarke Papers,* pp. 304-05; Blitzer, pp. 68-69.

[45] J.A.K. Thomson, *The Ethics of Aristotle: The Nicomachean Ethics Translated* (Baltimore, 1975), II, 1106; see also I, 1197.

[46] *Clarke Papers,* p. 318.

[47] *Ibid.,* p. 370.

[48] Rainborough protested that Ireton's purpose was to identify the Levellers with anarchy. He said men like the Commissary "not only yourselves believe that men are inclining to anarchy, but you would make all men believe that. . . . I wish you would not make the world believe that we are for anarchy." *Ibid.,* pp. 308-09.

[49] See the discussion of Leveller influence on later generations of English dissenting Whigs in Caroline Robbins, *The Eighteenth Century Commonwealthman* (New York, 1968), pp. 3-5, and the connections with the American Revolution in Bernard Bailyn, *The Ideological Origins of the American Revolution* (Cambridge, Mass., 1967).

[50] Aristotle, *Metaphysics,* H. Tredennick (trans.) (Cambridge, Mass., 1933), V, xvi, 3a.

FURTHER READING

Arblaster, Anthony. "Revolution, the Levellers, and C. B. Macpherson." In *1642: Literature and Power in the Seventeenth Century,* edited by Francis Barker, Jay Bernstein, John Coombes, et al., pp. 220-37. Proceedings of the Essex Conference on the Sociology of Literature, July 1980, University of Essex, 1981.

Criticizes C. B. Macpherson's 1962 assessment of the Levellers as a "less radical and less democratic" organization than was previously believed.

Aylmer, G. E., ed. *The Levellers in the English Revolution.* Ithaca, N.Y.: Cornell University Press, 1975, 180 p.

Provides an overview of the Levellers' role in the political turmoil of the English Revolution. The source also reprints selected tracts and petitions written by Leveller leaders.

Carlin, Norah. "Leveller Organization in London." *The Historical Journa,* Vol. 27, No. 4, 1984, pp. 955-60.

Explores the view held by some commentators and historians that the Levellers were not a well organized, distinctive, and cohesive group, suggesting that there is little evidence to support this claim.

————. "The Levellers and the Conquest of Ireland in 1649." *The Historical Journal,* Vol. 30, No. 2, 1987, pp. 269-88.

Analyzes the nature and effectiveness of Leveller opposition to Oliver Cromwell's invasion of Ireland.

Frank, Joseph. *The Levellers: A History of the Writings of Three Seventeenth-Century Social Democrats: John Lilburne, Richard Overton, William Walwyn.* Cambridge, Mass.: Harvard University Press, 1955, 345 p.

Traces the growth, development, and decline of the Leveller party and its ideology. The source includes detailed chapters on Leveller leaders and their lives and works prior to the emergence of the party in the mid-1640s.

Gibbons, B. J. "Richard Overton and the Secularism of the Interregnum Radicals." *The Seventeenth Century*, Vol. X, No. 1, Spring 1995, pp. 63-75.

Stresses the importance of religion in Overton's thought, countering those twentieth-century commentators who argue that the Levellers, and Overton especially, were primarily interested in secular politics.

Gooch, G. P. "The Political Opinions of the Army." In *English Democratic Ideas in the Seventeenth Century.* Second edition, pp. 118-40. Cambridge: Cambridge University Press, 1954.

Examines the nature and degree of support the Levellers received from the New Model Army.

Gregg, Pauline. *Free-Born John: A Biography of John Lilburne.* London: George G. Harrap & Co. Ltd., 1961, 424 p.

Critical biography of Lilburne, emphasizing the events that molded him into a radical political leader. Gregg details Lilburne's involvement with the Leveller party.

Haller, William and Godfrey Davies, eds. *The Leveller Tracts, 1647-1653.* New York: Columbia University Press, 1944, 481 p.

Includes a detailed introduction to the political atmosphere and events of the 1640s and a review of the roles of key figures during this period of political revolution in England. Pamphlets and petitions by such Leveller leaders as John Lilburne, Richard Overton, and William Walwyn are reprinted in their entirety.

Hill, Christopher. *Intellectual Origins of the English*

Revolution Revisited. Oxford: Clarendon Press, 1997, 422 p.

> Explores various intellectual influences that came to bear on the English Revolution, including the fields of medicine, science, philosophy, and religion.

Hughes, Ann. "Gender and Politics in Leveller Literature." In *Political Culture and Cultural Politics in Early Modern England: Essays Presented to David Underdown,* edited by Susan D. Amussen and Mark A. Kishlansky, pp. 162-88. Manchester: Manchester University Press, 1995.

> Studies the role of women in the Leveller movement, examining their place in Leveller political ideology as well as their duties as messengers, fund raisers, and petitioners.

McMichael, Jack R. and Barbara Taft, eds. *The Writings of William Walwyn.* Athens: University of Georgia Press, 1989, 584p.

> Offers a critical introduction to the life and philosophy of Walwyn and reprints his religious and political petitions and pamphlets from 1641 through 1652.

Pease, Theodore Calvin. *The Leveller Movement: Study in the History and Political Theory of the English Great Civil War.* Washington, D.C.: American Historical Association, 1916, 406 p.

> A dissertation written in 1915 detailing the genesis and rise to prominence of the Leveller party.

Smith, Nigel. "Soapboilers Speak Shakespeare Rudely: Masquerade and Leveller Pamphleteering." *Critical Survey* Vol. 5, No. 3, 1993, pp. 235-43.

> Reviews the literary impact of Leveller tracts, noting that the style as well as the content of such pamphlets seemed to have been "a very new thing in English society."

Wootton, David. "From Rebellion to Revolution: The Crisis of the Winter of 1642/3 and the Origins of Civil War Radicalism." *The English Historical Review* Vol. CV, No. 416, July, 1990, pp. 654-69.

> Examines the role of the Levellers and other radical groups in the breakdown of England's political system in 1642-43.

The Revolutionary Astronomers

INTRODUCTION

Since the second century B.C., when Ptolemy wrote his astronomical manual, *The Almagest,* until the seventeenth century A.D., a geocentric conception of the universe prevailed in Europe under Ptolemy's authority, which was itself founded on Aristotle's fourth-century work, the *Physics.* No other cosmological model was considered by European astronomers until the late sixteenth century, so thoroughly had Ptolemaic astronomy permeated the European mind and imagination. Like Darwinian evolution in the twentieth century, Ptolemaic astronomy, and particularly the geocentric model of the universe, was accepted reflexively and informed the imaginations of professional astronomers and educated people throughout Europe. Aristotle's authority dominated European philosophy as well as the science of this period; even in the theology of the Church and Protestant sects Aristotle's profound influence was received through the adaptive work of St. Thomas Aquinas. To dislodge the geocentric conception of the universe would upset a good deal else in the intellectual framework of Europe.

Ptolemaic astronomy involved a complex geometry of explanations of the planetary and sidereal movements, of epicycles, deferents, and equants, many of which were unworkable. The discrepancies between the growing body of observational data and Ptolemy's calculations, as well as the many inclarities in his mathematics, became increasingly apparent to astronomers by the mid-fifteenth century. Though Ptolemy's authority was not questioned, it became necessary to clarify the mathematics of his system to make them more useful. It was this intense review of the Ptolemaic calculations that led to the work of Nicolaus Copernicus a century later. Copernicus is known as the father of heliocentrism, the new astronomy that set the sun, not the earth, at the center of the universe, but historians generally agree that his purpose was conservative, not revolutionary. Working conscientiously within the established tradition, Copernicus's aim was to simplify and clarify in the extremely complex Ptolemaic calculations what had become unworkable in applied astronomy. Although his *De revolutionibus orbium coelestium* fundamentally altered the accepted structure of the universe by supposing the earth to be in motion with the planets around the sun, it did so from very orthodox assumptions and is even dedicated to Pope Paul III. Copernicus's theory left unchallenged such fundamental assumptions of the old model

as the sphericity of the universe, the circular motion (with epicycles) and regularity of the planetary orbits, and the finiteness of the universe, being bound by the sphere of the fixed stars. Even the idea of the sun's centrality derives from the pythagorean-platonic tradition of sun-worship, which, in Copernicus's mind, was its chief virtue. Copernicus postulated the earth's orbiting the sun not because of the force of his observational data, but because, believing in the pythagorean idea that the sun belongs at the center of the cosmos, the earth's motion was a necessary corollary. The mathematics were then worked with little effort at making new observations, the result being a theory that was scarcely more accurate than Ptolemy's, which is why Copernicus himself did not publish it, trying until the end of his life to make it work.

Published after Copernicus's death in 1543, *De revolutionibus* was widely recognized as an important hypothesis. Twenty-five years later it was being enthusiastically promoted in England by a prominent mathematician, Leonard Digges, as a revolutionary theory describing the real physical character of the universe rather than as the purely abstract hypothetical mathematical theorem as it was thought to be. Digges even went so far as to insist that the Copernican theory allowed for an infinite universe, though Copernicus himself only suggested it was much larger than the Ptolemaic universe. This came at the same time as a certain constriction and solidification of opinion in conservative circles that necessarily reacted to Copernicanism as it was being interpreted and would have nothing to do with it. Opinion was divided and Copernicanism was now in the hands of the innovators of astronomy.

Now that a viable alternative to Ptolemaic astronomy existed, it became necessary for those astronomers who did not wholly dismiss it to make variations and adaptations to the Copernican theory. The Dutch astronomer Tycho Brahewas one of the most important of these. Still, he is less renowned for his own cosmological hypothesis than for his design and use of the most accurate and powerful astronomical instruments of the time. Tycho's observational data were methodically planned and recorded and remarkably accurate. They helped discredit Aristotelian physics and were material in producing the *Rudolphine Tables* (1627), published after his death, which established Copernicanism as a workable theory. Tycho observed and recorded a nova's appearance in 1572 and a widely discussed comet in 1577 and demonstrated that Aristotle (and Ptolemy who followed him) was wrong that such things only occur beneath the sphere of the moon, that is, between earth and moon, beyond which nothing changes. Tycho had carefully calculated that both nova and comet occurred at distances from the earth far beyond that of the moon. The work in which he set forth his observations and his own geocentric hypothesis, *De Mundi aetherei recentioribus phaenomenis,* was published in 1588.

The stage was set for the coming of Galileo Galilei, who in the 1590s, still early in his career, was already a confirmed opponent of Aristotelian physics and convinced that the Copernican theory was a physical reality. Galileo was perhaps the first modern scientist, for he was an empiricist, basing his conclusions, not upon ancient authorities and mere logic, but upon his own observations made with the best instruments available. In 1609 and 1610, using a telescope he redesigned with improvements, Galileo recorded several observations that would make several Ptolemaic assumptions about the universe indefensible. He observed the surface of the moon to be mountainous and not perfectly spherical as supposed; he saw four of Jupiter's moons, spots on the sun, and the phases of Venus. All of these observations were explainable by the Copernican model but not by the Ptolemaic, which fact sealed Galileo's confidence. Galileo first published his findings in his *Sidereus Nuncius* (1610), but this work had little effect on the debate as Galileo was then too politically cautious to press his convictions. His *Dialogo (Dialogues Between the Ptolemaic and Copernican World Systems),* published in 1628, late in his career, garnered the most attention. In this work he supported the heliocentric theory, but in an unconventional mock-socratic format that satirized the traditional view. The *Dialogo,* with its strong arguments and the force of the authors' reputation, did much to propagate the Copernican theory and, in the view of many historians, assured that it would ultimately supplantthe Ptolemaic-Aristotelean model of the universe. Galileo's subsequent trouble with the Vatican had to do with the theological implications of the theory as Galileo taught it.

The fate of the Ptolemaic theory alrcady scaled—at least among professional astronomers, Johannes Kepler's three laws dealt the coup de grace. It was Kepler, a contemporary of Tycho Brahe and his collaborator for some years, who would establish that the planetary orbits are neither circular nor regular, but elliptical and move faster when closer to the sun. The first two of Kepler's three laws exploded two Ptolemaic (and Copernican) assumptions about celestial motion: that it is necessarily circular, circularity being the perfect form of motion, and also necessarily regular for no irregularity can occur in the celestial regions. Both in the way of mathematical theory and speculation, Kepler's three laws of planetary motion and the *Rudolphine Tables* helped astronomers accept the Copernican model of a heliocentric universe as a physical fact by improving on its mathematical accuracy and thus, at the very least, a theory to contend with. In the fifty years after Kepler's death (1630), it was the ambition of many astronomers to either disprove or modify Kepler's principles. So much attention for so long inevitably made Copericanism a commonplace and thus so much the easier to accept. Kepler indeed did more than anyone to establish the Copernican model in the European mind. For he paved a direct path to Newton whose discovery of the law of universal gravitation—by applying Kepler's laws in the light of his own discoveries— introduced a new physics that forever laid to rest the physics of Aristotle and the astronomy of Ptolemy. Until the twentieth century, Newtonian physics stood in the place of Aristotle and Ptolemy, holding sway in its ability to explain observable astronomical phenomena.

REPRESENTATIVE WORKS

Tycho Brahe
  De nova stella 1573
  Astronomiae instauratae progymnasmata 1602

Nicolaus Copernicus
  De revolutionibus orbitum coelestium [*On the Revolution of the Heavenly Bodies*] 1543

Galileo Galilei
> *Sidereus nuncius* [*The Starry Messenger*] 1610
> *Dialogo* [*Dialogues Between the Ptolemaic and Copernican World Systems*] 1628

Johannes Keppler
> *Prodromus Dissertationum Mathematicarum Continens Mysterium Cosmographicum* [*The Forerunner of Dissertations on the Universe, containing the Mystery of the Universe*] 1597
> *De Fundamentis Astrologiae Certioribus* [*The More reliable Bases of Astrology*] 1601

OVERVIEWS

J. L. E. Dreyer (essay date 1906)

SOURCE: "Conclusion," in *A History of Astronomy from Thales to Kepler,* by J. L. E. Dreyer, revised by W. H. Stahl, 2d ed., Dover Publications, Inc., 1953, pp. 413-24.

[*In the following essay, originally published in 1906 and reprinted with minor changes in 1953, Dreyer sketches the progress of the heliocentric model of the universe with particular attention to the unsuccessful attempts up to Newton's time at salvaging the old geocentric model by means of ever more ingenious modifications.*]

The system of Copernicus had been perfected by Kepler, and all that remained to be done was to persuade astronomers and physicists that the motion of the earth was physically possible, and to explain the reason why the earth and planets moved in accordance with Kepler's laws. To give a detailed account of how the earth's motion was gradually accepted, and how Newton's great discovery of the law of universal gravitation accounted for Kepler's laws, would be to write the history of the whole science of astronomy during the seventeenth century and does not come within the plan of this book. We shall only in a few words sketch the progress of the belief in the earth's motion and the feeble attempts at proposing modifications of existing theories up to the time of Newton.

A few months before Kepler's book on Mars came out the newly-invented telescope had been directed to the stars, and in the spring of the following year (1610) Galileo published his *Sidereus Nuncius,* giving the first account of the wonderful discoveries made with the new instrument, especially of the mountains in the moon and the four satellites of Jupiter. At the end of the little book Galileo, who had already for many years been an adherent of the Copernican system[1], publicly declared in its favour, pointing out the analogy between the

Illustration of Ptolemy

earth and the celestial bodies, and remarking that the discovery of four moons attending Jupiter during its motion round the sun put an end to the difficulty of the moon alone forming an exception to the general rule by moving round a planet instead of round the sun. Before the end of the year 1610 the discovery of sunspots had supplied a new and very striking proof of the fallacy of the Aristotelean doctrine of the immutability of all things celestial, while the discovery of the phases of Venus deprived the opponents of Copernicus of a favourite weapon. But above all it was of the greatest importance that the fixed stars in the telescope appeared as mere luminous points, so that the apparent diameters of several minutes attributed to them by all previous observers were proved to have no existence. This swept away the very serious objection raised by Tycho that a star having no annual parallax and yet showing a considerable apparent diameter must be incredibly large.

No wonder that an old supporter of the Ptolemaic system, and hitherto a most determined opponent of Copernicus, Christopher Clavius, in the last edition of his commentary to Sacrobosco (1611) remarked that astronomers would have to look out for a system which would agree with the new discoveries, as the old one would not serve them any longer[2]. But the common objections referring to a stone dropped from a tower or a cannon ball fired in the direction north and south were still brought forward with confidence to disprove the rotation of the earth, and in refuting them Galileo rendered important service. The three laws of motion were not enunciated by him, as often assumed by popular writers, for he never fully grasped the principle of inertia and failed to realise the continued motion in a straight line of a body left to itself, while he supposed a body describing a circle to continue to do so for ever if not acted on by any force. Although he therefore never shook himself quite free from Aristotelean ideas, maintaining the perfection of circular motion and even letting a falling body describe an arc of a circle through the earth's centre, there can be no doubt that his popular explanations must have strongly impressed many a wavering reader. But his infatuation for circular motion went so far that he quite ignored the fact that the planets do not move round the sun in concentric orbits. In the whole of his celebrated *Dialogo sopra i due massimi sistemi del Mondo, Tolemaico e Copernicano,* there is no allusion to the elliptic orbits; he even says (near the end of the "fourth day") that we are not yet able to decide how the orbits of the single planets are constituted, "as a proof of which Mars may be mentioned which now-a-days gives astronomers so much trouble; even the theory of the moon has been set forth in very different ways after that Copernicus had considerably altered that of Ptolemy[3]."

Planetary theory was thus left altogether untouched by Galileo, nor was his opinion as regards the nature of comets what might have been expected from so determined an opponent of Aristotelean physics. Tycho had conclusively proved that they are celestial bodies, but Galileo does not seem altogether satisfied that they have no parallax, and believes them to be vapours originally risen from the earth and refracting the light in a peculiar manner. His opinion on this matter was therefore not very different from that of Scipione Chiaramonti, who in his book *Antitycho* (1621) had upheld the Aristotelean doctrine of the sublunary nature of comets; but on the other hand Galileo fully agreed with Tycho in pronouncing new stars to be celestial bodies. It was not until Hevelius had again shown from accurate observations that comets are much farther off than the moon that the opponents to their character of heavenly bodies were finally silenced some sixty years after Tycho's death, and not till 1681 that the parabolic form of their orbits with the sun at the focus was discovered by Dörfel.

The persecution of Galileo by the Pope and the Inquisition for having (notwithstanding a previous warning) discussed the motion of the earth in a manner favourable to Copernicus, has been described so often that there is no need to give an account of it in this place. It looks like an act of Nemesis, that the Roman authorities should have taken special umbrage at the curious and altogether erroneous theory of the tides which Galileo propounded in the fourth day of his *Dialogo,* rejecting the ancient idea that they are caused by the moon and maintaining that they are quite incompatible with the Ptolemaic system. Perhaps his adversaries feared that "there might be something in it" and became exasperated in consequence. On the other hand, Galileo had hardly dealt quite fairly with his opponents in pretending that the Ptolemaic system was the only alternative to that of Copernicus. In the whole book there is no allusion whatever to the Tychonic system, although it is scarcely too much to say that about the year 1630 nobody, whose opinion was worth caring about, preferred the Ptolemaic to the Tychonic system.

The Copernican system had from the beginning been viewed with extreme dislike by theologians, both Roman Catholic and Protestant. We have seen in a previous chapter how strongly Luther and Melanchthon expressed themselves about it, and from a letter written to Kepler in 1598 by Hafenreffer, Professor of Divinity at Tübingen, it appears that the theory of the earth's motion was not in good odour among the theologians there[4]. But as yet the theory had not been directly forbidden anywhere, probably because Osiander's preface to the book of Copernicus (supposed to have been written by the author himself) disarmed the opponents by representing the theory as a mere means of computation. The fate of Giordano Bruno can hardly have been influenced by his advocacy of the earth's motion, for he had set forth a sufficient number of startling ideas to provide stakes for many scores of heretics. But the invention of the telescope and the analogy it revealed between the earth and the planets made the question assume an entirely different aspect. From a mathematical hypothesis which did not concern mankind in general it became a question of the actual position in the created world of the dwelling-place of man, whether it was (as hitherto supposed) the most important part of Creation or a comparatively insignificant part thereof. In the course of a thousand years theologians had retreated step by step from the standpoint of the Fathers of the Church; the Babylonian system of the world favoured by them had given way to the Ptolemaic; antipodes and other abominations had been tolerated; but now when impious hands tried to push the earth out of its imposing place in the centre of the world and make it travel among the stars, though they were moved by angels and the earth had the devil as central occupant, the theologians turned fiercely to bay. Action was taken within a few years of the invention of the telescope; on February 24, 1616, the consultors of the Inquisition at Rome declared the doctrine of the earth's motion to be heretical, and on the 5th March following the "Sacred Congregation" solemnly suspended the book of Copernicus and the commentary to Job by Didacus a Stunica[5] "until they are corrected" (*donec corrigantur*), and altogether damned and forbade the recently published book by a Carmelite Father, Foscarini, in which an attempt was made to show that the motion of the earth is in accordance with Scripture[6]. This was followed in 1620 by the issue of a *Monitum Sacræ Congregationis ad Nicolai Copernici lectorem,* in which instructions are given about the alterations to be made in the book *De Revolutionibus* before it may be reprinted. These are not very numerous, and refer only to passages in which the motion of the earth is positively asserted, but the whole of chapter VIII. of the first book is to be omitted and likewise the disrespectful allusion to Lactantius[7]. But no editor was ever found to publish a mutilated edition of the book of Copernicus. As the decree of 1620 forbade "all other books teaching the same thing," the *Dialogo* was naturally also put on the *Index* in 1633. In the edition of 1758 of the *Index* the clause forbidding "all other books" was at last omitted, but the book of Copernicus, Kepler's *Epitome,* Galileo's *Dialogue* and some other books were not released till 1822, so that the edition of 1835 is the first in which they are not mentioned. By that time it had become the turn of geology to suffer from the *odium theologicum,* and after 1859 the theory of organic evolution came to occupy the place in the theological mind once held by the Copernican system.

In Protestant countries no serious attempt was made to put down the doctrine of the earth's motion, perhaps because it would not have looked well to imitate the action of the hated Inquisition; but wherever the power of the Roman Curia could reach, philosophers had to submit, though some of them did it very unwillingly. Among these was Pierre Gassendi (1592-1655), who in his numerous writings often praises the Copernican system, and says that he would have preferred it if it had not been pronounced contrary to Scripture, for which reason he was obliged to adopt the Tychonic system. He made the experiment of dropping a stone from the top of the mast of a ship in motion and concluded, justly enough, that the result neither proved nor disproved the earth's motion[8]. All the same he fell foul of his countryman, Morin, a very violent anti-Copernican, who devoted one of his polemical writings (*Alae telluris fractae,* Paris, 1643) to a refutation of Gassendi. Of another renowned astronomer of the same time, the Jesuit Giovanni Battista Riccioli (1598-1671), it is more difficult to say what his private opinion really was. In his great treatise on astronomy, *Almagestum Novum,* in two large folio volumes (Bologna, 1651), an invaluable work for the historian of astronomy, he gives twenty arguments (which he refutes) in favour of the earth's motion and seventy-seven against it, many of the objections being very trivial or referring to facts which have no bearing on the question at issue. He speaks very highly of Copernicus and the simplicity of his system, and the arguments from Scripture and the Fathers, as well as the action of the Curia, are evidently what has

most weight with him. Yet he produces an argument of his own to which he attributes great weight[9]. If a body falls from the top of a tower under the equator of the earth (standing still) it will in four seconds pass through spaces proportional to the figures 1, 3, 5, 7; but if the earth were rotating he makes out that the four spaces would be about equal and that the body would not strike the ground with more force than it would have done after one second; therefore the earth does not rotate. This argument was shown to be fallacious by a well-known mathematician, Stefano degli Angeli, and a lively controversy ensued between him, Borelli and Riccioli and the latter's advocates, Manfredi and Zerilli[10]. Riccioli adopted the Tychonic system with a slight modification; while he accepts the motion of Mercury, Venus and Mars round the sun, he lets Jupiter and Saturn move round the earth, because they have satellites of their own, those of Saturn being his "laterones" or appendages, i.e. the ring imperfectly seen and not yet recognized as such. The other three planets are satellites of the sun. He did not consider the first law of Kepler to have been proved, since agreement between theory and observation was no proof[11]!

There were of course some opponents of the Copernican system who did not reject it from fear of the Church. The only one of any distinction was Longomontanus (1562-1647), the principal disciple of Tycho Brahe, who wrote a treatise which he appropriately called *Astronomia Danica,* since it was mainly founded on the work of Tycho, whose system he adopted, though he admitted the rotation of the earth. He rejected the elliptic orbits of Kepler, and his standpoint was altogether that of the sixteenth century.

But the opposition of the Church did not retard the progress of astronomy, though no doubt it made it difficult for the Copernican system to become recognized outside the sphere of professional astronomers. Slowly but surely the idea of the earth's motion gained ground. There were, however, still not a few astronomers who, though followers of Copernicus, did not accept the planetary theories of Kepler altogether. Among these was Philip Lansberg (1561-1632), who published planetary tables, founded on an epicyclic theory, which were much used among astronomers, though they were very inferior to the Rudolphine Tables[12]. The second law of Kepler was objected to by Ismael Boulliaud (1605-1694), who, in his *Astronomia Philolaica* (Paris, 1645), substituted for it an extraordinary theory. He supposed the ellipse to be a section of an oblique cone, on the axis of which the focus not occupied by the sun is situated, while the angular velocity is uniform with regard to the axis of the cone, being measured in circular sections parallel to the base of the cone[13]. In addition to being utterly unreasonable (for why should the planets climb round imaginary cones?) the theory is a very poor substitute for Kepler's, as the true anomaly is very badly represented except when the excentricity is very small. Neither would it have been any advantage to astronomers to have adopted the theory of Seth Ward, Savilian Professor at Oxford (1617-1689), who in two little books criticised the geometry of Boulliaud, and (throwing his cones overboard) merely adopted uniform motion with regard to the second focus[14]. Until Newton proved that Kepler's second law is a necessary consequence of the law of gravitation, Ward's theory found some admirers in England, and it was apparently on account of its obvious defects that J. D. Cassini suggested that the orbit of a planet is not an ellipse but a curve like it, in which the rectangle of the distances of a point from two fixed points or foci is a constant quantity[15]. But this theory was as bad as the one it was to displace, and both of them soon became only historical curiosities. How sad it is to remember that the first astronomer of note who fully and unreservedly accepted the great results of Kepler's work, Jeremiah Horrox (1619-1641), only reached the age of twenty-two years.

While these various fruitless attempts were made to modify the planetary theory of Kepler, a great mathematician and philosopher set up a general theory of the constitution of the universe, which, owing to its author's celebrity, held its ground in his native land for upwards of a hundred years, much longer than it deserved. It had been the intention of Descartes to prepare a work "On the world," founded on the Copernican system; but when he heard of Galileo's trial and abjuration he gave up the idea, as he had no desire to get into conflict with the Church. But some years later he found what he considered to be a way out of the difficulty, since the earth in his system was not to move freely through space, but was to be carried round the sun in a vortex of matter without changing its place relatively to neighbouring particles, so that it might (by a stretch of imagination) be said to be at rest. His account of the origin and present state of the solar system is contained in his *Principia Philosophiæ,* which appeared at Amsterdam in 1644. He assumes space to be full of matter which in the beginning was set in motion by God, the result being an immense number of vortices of particles of various size and shape, which by friction have their corners rubbed off. Hereby two kinds of matter are produced in each vortex, small spheres which continue to move round the centre of motion with a tendency to recede from it, and fine dust which gradually settles at the centre and forms a star or sun, while some of it, the particles which have become channelled and twisted when making their way through the vortex, form sun-spots. These may either dissolve after a while, or they may gradually form a crust all over the surface of the star, which then may wander from one vortex to another as a comet, or may settle permanently in some part of the vortex which has a velocity equal to its own and form a planet. Sometimes feebler vortices are gathered in by neighbouring stronger ones, and in this way the origin of the moon and satellites is explained.

The vortex theory of Descartes does not account for any of the peculiarities of the planetary orbits, and is indeed pure speculation unsupported by any facts. It was an outcome of the natural desire to explain the motion of the planets round the sun, why they neither wander off altogether nor fall into the sun, but it could only with difficulty account for the non-circular form of the orbits, in which respect it was inferior to Kepler's magnetic vortex theory. Another attempt at a general theory of the solar system was made by Giovanni Alfonso Borelli (1608-1679) in a book which professes to deal with the satellites of Jupiter only, perhaps to avoid saying anything about the motion of the earth[16]. He assumes that the planets have a natural tendency to approach to the sun (and the satellites to their central body), while the circular motion gives them a tendency to fly away from it, and these opposing forces must to a certain extent counterbalance each other. The former is a constant force, the latter is inversely proportional to the distance. As to the motion in the orbit, Borelli, like Kepler, connects it with the rotation of the sun, as the rays of the sun's light catch the planet and drive it along; but in the case of Jupiter, which is not self-luminous, he merely calls them "moving rays." To explain the oval form of the orbit he can only say that at the aphelion the tendency to approach the sun gets the upper hand, so that the planet gradually comes nearer to the sun. Hereby its velocity is increased and also the centrifugal force, which is inversely proportional to the radius vector, until the two forces become equal, after which the centrifugal force makes itself most felt and again increases the distance from the sun until the aphelion is reached.

Both in the way of mathematical theory and in speculation men of science thus vainly tried during the fifty years following that of Kepler's death to improve or modify his results. When they tried to substitute other rules for his two first laws they failed utterly, and when they speculated on the origin and cause of planetary motion they only produced theories just as vague as his were. All the same they did not labour in vain, as they accustomed themselves and others to recognize the Copernican system as a physical fact, and helped it to become more and more accepted by educated people at large. An interesting proof of the gradual change of feeling as regards the earth's motion is afforded by the utterances of some prominent men in England in the beginning and middle of the century. In several places in his writings Francis Bacon speaks of the Copernican system without in any way doing justice to it, and as if it were of no greater authority than the notion of the Ionians, that the planets describe spirals from east to west[17]. On the other hand, we find that John Wilkins, afterwards a brother-in-law of Cromwell, and still later Bishop of Chester, in 1640 published "A Discourse concerning a New Planet, tending to prove that (it is probable) our earth is one of the planets"; while Milton in the *Paradise Lost* speaks sympathetically about the new system. In England, where no astronomer of any importance except the short-lived Horrox had yet arisen, the ground was thus by degrees being prepared for the man whose work was to confirm the truth of Kepler's laws, and show them not to be arbitrary freaks of Nature but necessary consequences of a great law binding the whole universe together. From Thales to Kepler philosophers had searched for the true planetary system; Kepler had completed the search; Isaac Newton was to prove that the system found by him not only agreed with observation, but that no other system was possible.

Notes

[1] When he wrote his *Sermones de motu gravium* (in Pisa, before 1592) he seems to have been an adherent of the Ptolemaic system, as he says that rest is more agreeable to the earth than motion. But on Aug. 4, 1597, he wrote to Kepler that he had "for many years" been a follower of Copernicus, though he had not hitherto dared to defend the new system in public. *Kepleri Opera,* I. p. 40.

[2] Kepler drew attention to this utterance in the preface to his *Epitome Op.* VI. p. 117. Clavius died in February, 1612.

[3] Galileo (just before making this statement) remarks that the angular velocity of the moon must be greater at new moon than at full moon, since the moon when nearer to the sun describes a smaller orbit with reference to the sun. He compares the sun to the point of suspension of a pendulum, and earth and moon to two weights attached to the rod of the pendulum, the one representing the moon being placed at different distances from the point of suspension. Just as this alters the period of vibration of the pendulum, so (he concludes) does the earth move slower at the time of full moon than at that of new moon. This is a curious anticipation of the idea of planetary perturbation.

[4] *Kepleri Opera,* I. p. 37.

[5] See [*A History of Astronomy from Thales to Kepler,* by J. L. E. Dreyer, 2d ed., revised by W. H. Stahl, Dover Publications, Inc., 1953] p. 353.

[6] The text of the *Decretum* is given by von Gebler, *Die Acten des Galilei'schen Processes,* Stuttgart, 1877, p. 50. The title of Foscarini's book is *Lettera del R. Padre Maestro Paolo Antonio Foscarini, Carmelitano, sopra l'opinione de' Pittagorici, e del Copernico, della mobilità della Terra, e stabilità del Sole e il nuovo Pittagorico Sistema del Mondo. In Napoli per Lazzaro Scorrigio,* 1615. An English translation is given in Salusbury's *Mathematical Collections and Translations,* Vol. I. (1661), pp. 471-503. This book also contains translations of Galileo's *Dialogue* and of his letter to the Grand Duchess Christina of Tuscany, an attempt to reconcile the Bible and the Fathers with the Copernican system.

[7] This document is printed by Riccioli, *Almag. Nov.* II. pp. 496-97.

[8] *De motu impresso a motore translato epistolæ duæ,* Paris, 1642. He says (p. 156) that it is only "some cardinals" who have declared the earth to be at rest, and this is not an *articulum fidei,* but it must all the same have the greatest weight with believers. In his book, *De proportione qua gravia decidentia accelerantur* (1646), he says: "Videlicet ego Ecclesiæ alumnus, ita me totum ipsi devoveo, ut quicquid illa improbat, ipse anathema conclamem" (p. 286).

[9] *Alm. Nov.* II. p. 409.

[10] For titles see the Catalogue of the Crawford Library of the Royal Observatory, Edinburgh.

[11] *Alm. Nov.* I. p. 529. Riccioli's own planetary theory is wonderfully complicated, the excentricity being variable in the direction of the line of apsides and the semidiameter of the epicycle varying in the same period.

[12] *Philippi Lansbergii Tabulæ cælestium motuum perpetuæ,* Middelburg, 1632. They probably owed a great deal of the good repute they enjoyed for some time to the circumstance that they by a fluke represented the transit of Venus in 1639 fairly well, while the Rudolphine Tables threw Venus quite off the sun's disc.

[13] "Ut omnibus æqualis motus partibus respondeant singulæ partes apparentes, ita tamen ut Aphelio minores circuli æqualis motus conveniant, Perihelio maiores." *Astron. Phil.* p. 26.

[14] *In Ismaelis Bullialdi Astronomiæ Philolaicæ Fundamenta Inquisitio brevis,* Oxford, 1653, and *Astronomia geometrica,* London, 1656. Boulliaud replied to the former in his *Astronomiæ Philolaicæ Fundamenta clarius explicata,* Paris, 1657. Ward became Bishop of Exeter in 1662, of Salisbury 1667.

[15] *De l'origine et du progrès de l'astronomie* (1693), *Mém. de l'Acad. R. des Sciences,* 1666-1699, T. VIII. p. 43. As a native of Italy Cassini was afraid to pronounce publicly in favour of the earth's motion, even after his removal to Paris. Pingré, *Cométographie,* I. p. 116.

[16] *Theoricae mediceorum planetarum,* Florentiæ, 1666, reviewed by E. Goldbeck in an essay, *Die Gravitationshypothese bei Galilei und Borelli,* Berlin, 1897.

[17] *Novum Organum,* II. 36, also other passages quoted

by Whewell, *Hist. Induct. Sc.* 3rd ed. Vol. I. pp. 296 and 388. Gilbert and Harvey were two other investigators of whom Bacon did not think much. He was ready to teach scientific men how to work, but he was singularly unlucky when laying down the law about the work done by those inferior creatures.

Hans Reichenbach (essay date 1942)

SOURCE: "The Copernican View of the World," in *From Copernicus to Einstein,* translated by Ralph B. Winn, Philosophical Library, Inc., 1942, pp. 11-28.

[*In the following excerpt, Reichenbach offers a brief overview of how the scientific treatment of the problems of space and time developed from Copernicus to Newton.*]

. . . Men have been forming ideas concerning space and time since times immemorial, and curiously enough, have been writing and fighting about these things with the greatest interest, even fanaticism. This has been a strange strife, indeed, having little to do with economic necessities; it has always dealt with abstract things, far removed from our daily life and with no direct influence upon our daily activities. Why do we need to know whether the sun revolves around the earth or vice versa? What business of ours is it, anyway? Can this knowledge be of any use to us?

No sooner have we uttered these questions than we become aware of their foolishness. It may not be of any use to us, but we want to know something about these problems. We do not want to go blindly through the world. We desire more than a mere existence. We need these cosmic perspectives in order to be able to experience a feeling for our place in the world. The ultimate questions as to the meaning of our actions and as to the meaning of life in general always tend to involve astronomical problems. Here lies the mystery surrounding astronomy, here lies the wonder we experience at the sight of the starry sky, the wonder growing in proportion to our understanding of immense distances of space and of the stars' inner nature. Here is the source of scientific as well as popular astronomy.

These two branches have diverged in the course of their development. Astronomy, as a science, has come to forget its primitive wonder: instead, it approaches the realm of stars with sober research and calculation. This disenchantment with its subject-matter, which scientific study invariably entails, has permeated astronomy to a greater degree than the layman realizes. In observing the astronomers of today, how they measure, take notes, calculate, how little attention they pay to mysterious speculations, one may be surprised to find the wonderful structure of learning so cut and dry

at a close range. Yet nothing is more wrong and more objectionable than the feeling of a heartbreaking loss, with which some people regard the vanishing mysticism of the skies. Although science may have destroyed a few naive fantasies, what she has put in their place is so immensely greater that we can well bear the loss.

It takes perseverance and energy, of course, to comprehend the discoveries of science; but whoever undertakes the study is bound to learn many more surprising things from it than a naive study of nature can disclose. Scientific astronomy has always exercised, in fact, a great influence upon everyday thinking and upon the popular conception of the universe. If it is difficult today to pronounce the name of Copernicus without thinking of a turning point of history, it is not only because the name is connected with a profound transformation in the science, but also because all our knowledge and thinking have been deeply affected by his discovery. The statement that the earth does not occupy the center of the world means more than an astronomical fact; we interpret it as asserting that man is not the center of the world, that everything which appears large and mighty to us is in reality of the smallest significance, when measured by cosmic standards. The statement has been made possible as a result of scientific development in the course of thousands of years, yet it definitely contradicts our immediate experience. It takes a great deal of training in thinking to believe in it at all. Nowadays we are no longer conscious of these things, because we have been brought up since childhood in the Copernican view of the world. However, it cannot be denied that the view belies the testimony of our senses, that every immediate evidence shows the earth as standing still while the heavens are moving. And who among us can declare in all seriousness that he is able to imagine the tremendous size of the sun or to comprehend the cosmic distances defying all earthly ways of measurement? The significance of Copernicus lies precisely in the fact that he broke with an old belief apparently supported by all immediate sensory experiences. He could do it only because he had at his disposal a considerable amount of accumulated scientific thought and scientific data, only because he himself had followed the road of disillusionment in knowledge before he glimpsed new and broader perspectives.

If we endeavor to trace . . . the development of the problems of space and time, beginning with the discovery of Copernicus and closing with the still less accessible theory of the Copernicus of our day, we have no other alternative than to apply hard scientific thought to every step of the way. We must add that the discoveries of modern science have been made possible only by the abundance of new scientific materials. Einstein's doctrines are by no means an outgrowth of astronomical reflections alone; they are grounded in the facts of the theory of electricity and light as well.

We are able to comprehend them only insofar as we get acquainted with all of their sources. This derivation from several sources is characteristic of the theory of relativity. While the modern source gave rise to the special theory of relativity, the older sources provided the material for the construction of the general theory of relativity, in which the old and new knowledge became blended in a magnificent unity. . . .

The world-picture found by Copernicus goes back to the ancient Greeks. It was systematized about 140 A.D. by Ptolemy Claudius of Alexandria and outlined in his famous work *Almagest*. The most important feature of the Ptolemaic scheme of the universe is the principle that the earth is the center of the world. The heavenly globe revolves around it; and Ptolemy knew full well that it has the same spherical shape below the horizon, which it assumes above the horizon. In fact, Ptolemy knew even that the earth is a sphere. His proofs to this effect reveal a great knowledge of astronomy. He shows, first of all, the existence of curvature from north to south. As the Polar Star stands higher in the north and lower in the south, the surface of the earth must be correspondingly curved. The proof of the existence of curvature from west to east reveals even better observation. When the clocks are set by the sun in two places located west and east, and when an eclipse of the moon is thus observed, it will be seen at different times. However, the eclipse is a single objective event and should be seen everywhere at the same time. Hence we conclude that the clocks at the two places are not in accord. This can be accounted for by the curvature of the earth in the west-east direction: the sun passes the line of the meridian at different moments in different places.

In spite of the recognition of the spherical shape of the earth, Ptolemy was far from admitting its movement. He contended, on the contrary, that it was impossible for the earth to be moving at all, either in a rotating or in a progressive manner. As far as the former is concerned, he admitted the possibility of such an opinion, as long as the movement of the stars was considered. However, when we take into consideration everything that happens around us and in the air, this view—so he argues—becomes obviously absurd. For the earth, during its rotation, would have to leave the air behind. Objects in the atmosphere, such as flying birds, not being able to follow the rotation, would have to be also left behind. A progressive motion of the earth is equally impossible for, in that case, the earth would leave the center of the heavenly sphere, and we would see by night a smaller part of the sphere and by day a larger one.

One can see from these arguments that the great astronomer has devoted much serious thought to the problem. In the light of his rather limited knowledge of mechanics and of the heavenly spaces, his reason-

ing must have seemed quite conclusive. As far as his last objection was concerned, he could not have suspected that the interstellar distances were so great as to make the lateral shift of the earth completely unnoticeable.

The planets are characterized, according to Ptolemy, by common movements. Their path, as observed in the sky, is determined by superimposed circular orbits. As a result, there arise the so-called "epicycles." One must admit that Ptolemy has deeply understood the nature of planetary movements. When one gets acquainted with the Copernican conception, one discovers the facts revealed behind Ptolemy's epicycles: the loop of the planets' course mirrors their double motion as regards the earth. In the first place, they move in a circle around the sun, and in the second place, this movement is observed from the earth which, in its turn, revolves around the sun.

The Ptolemaic conception of the universe dominated the learned people's minds for more than one thousand years. The man who undermined this firm tradition—Nicholas Copernicus—required great independence of thought as well as great scientific knowledge, for only an insight into the ultimate relations of nature could give him the ability to discern new approaches to truth.

The canon of Frauenburg was long known as a learned astronomer before his new ideas were presented; he had studied in Italy all branches of science, he had acted as doctor and church administrator in his home town, and his astronomic knowledge was so well recognized that in 1514 he was asked by the Lateran Council for his opinion on questions of calendar reform. His new ideas concerning the system of the universe were formed, in their essence, at the age of 33. However, he did not promulgate them at that time, but devoted the following years to a thorough elaboration and demonstration of his theories. Only excerpts of his doctrine were published during his lifetime. His main work entitled *Of the Rotation of Celestial Bodies* appeared only after his death in 1546. He read the proofs only on his death-bed and thus failed to notice that his friend Osiander supplied the work with a foreword which contained a cautious compromise with the opinions of the Church.

If we examine the proofs given by Copernicus of his new theory, we find them quite insufficient from the point of view of present-day knowledge. He was able, in fact, to cite as a distinct advantage only the greater simplicity of his system. He regards it as improbable that the stars move with great speed in their large orbits and finds it more likely that the earth rotates on its axis, so that the speed of motion in each particular point is considerably smaller. Against Ptolemy's objection to this he urges that Ptolemy considered the rotating movement of the earth as implying force, whereas it is simply natural; its laws differ completely from those of a sudden jerky movement. All of this is certainly inconclusive. We know today that Newton's theory contains the first real proof of the Copernican conception of the universe. But it seems that new ideas are able to gain foothold by the sheer power of their inherent truth long before their objective verification has been obtained.

On the other hand, it is very important to acknowledge that the Copernican theory offers a very exact calculation of the apparent movements of the planets and that the tabulations (the so-called "Ephemerides") accompanying it are far superior to the older ones. Here lies one of the reasons which led the scientists to accept the Copernican system, even though it must be conceded that, from the modern standpoint, practically identical results could be obtained by means of a somewhat revised Ptolemaic system. Furthermore, Copernicus calculated quite accurately the radii of the planetary orbits (within less than 1%). In fact, he knew already that the sun must be slightly off the center of the solar system, for an assumption to the contrary led to estimable discrepancies.

Yet there was still a long way from this discovery to the recognition of the elliptic shape of the orbits; any conclusive evidence to this effect required above all better astronomic instruments. In this important connection, we must consider Tycho Brahe who is less prominent as a theoretician than as a builder of outstanding instruments. Brahe was able to work for many decades under the protection of the Danish king. He built the castle Uranienburg on an island, to which was attached a large settlement where precise instruments were prepared for him in special plants. It is amazing how the precision of instruments was increased in this manner. For instance, Copernicus had to be satisfied with measurements within 10' of the arc. This corresponds approximately to an angle covered by a five-pence piece at a distance of six meters. Tycho increased the precision to within half a minute of the arc. This angle would be enclosed by the same coin at a distance of 120 meters. With the instruments of today, of course, angles can be measured within one hundredth of a second of the arc. The coin would have to be placed at a distance of 360 kilometers to enclose such a small angle.

This precision we owe mainly to the use of the telescope. Tycho had to work without a telescope. One of his sextants with which he conducted his observations of Mars still stands in the Prague observatory, where Tycho, exiled from Denmark, spent the last years of his life (c. 1600). . . .

. . . By means of such a crude-looking apparatus, Tycho found the data on which modern astronomy is historically resting.

The man who continued Tycho Brahe's work was his assistant Johann Kepler whose name surpasses by far that of his master. Kepler carried on his observations with the sextants of Tycho. He determined the course of the motion of Mars by means of so many individual observations that he was able to pronounce it with certainty as elliptical in shape. He discovered through mere measurement also other laws of planetary motion, called after him "the Kepler's laws." One must admire the strength of character of this man, which manifests itself in his zeal for factual accuracy. Kepler was at first a mystic and speculative dreamer, disinclined to sober observations. He concentrated in his early works on searching for strange mathematical 'harmonies' of nature, and such a goal inclines one to distort facts rather than to establish them. It remains true, however, that Kepler has accomplished much more for his own aim by his zeal for factual accuracy than by his speculations. He himself expresses this thought. In his work entitled *Harmony of the World,* which appeared in 1619, he writes concerning the discovery of his laws: "At last I have found it, and my hopes and expectations are proven to be true that natural harmonies are present in the heavenly movements, both in their totality and in detail—though not in a manner which I previously imagined, but in another, more perfect, manner . . . If you forgive me, I shall be glad; if you are angry, I shall endure it. Here I cast my dice and write a book to be read by my contemporaries or by the future generations. It may wait long centuries for its reader. But even God himself had to wait for six thousand years for those who contemplate his work."

We must not forget, however, that, though the astronomic picture of the universe was considerably advanced, in regard to precision, by Kepler's discoveries, nevertheless, that world-view, though basically Copernican, differed very considerably from our Copernican idea of the world. Copernicus as well as Kepler was of the opinion that the solar system virtually exhausted the space of the universe. The stars, according to them, were tiny dots in the sphere of heavenly matter, which circumscribed the whole of space. When Giordano Bruno expressed his thoughts on the infinity of the firmament and maintained that fixed stars were independent solar systems, Kepler proceeded immediately to combat the idea. How difficult it must have been to climb the stairs leading to our present-day knowledge!

Astronomy made its decisive advance over Kepler's knowledge again through an improvement in the means of observation—through the invention of the telescope. The great merit of having made the first serviceable telescope and of having used it for the observation of the sky belongs to Galileo; though not the original inventor of the telescope, he constructed it after hearing of such instruments. He directed his telescope toward the moon and recognized the spots on the moon, on account of their jagged outline and shifting illumination, as tremendous mountains (1610). He pointed it towards Venus and saw its sickle-like shape, similar to that of the moon, which it periodically assumes as a result of receiving light from the sun. He directed the telescope towards Saturn and saw its 'triple' figure the details of which he could not yet discern. He directed it towards Jupiter and saw its satellites (the four brighter ones) designated by him as "medizeic planets."

All these facts, with their enlargement and enrichment of the Copernican world, must have greatly astonished his contemporaries. It also provoked, to be sure, the opposition of the old school of scientists who saw their tenets grounded in Aristotle seriously endangered. Galileo's most precarious position can be best envisaged from a letter written by him to Kepler: "I am very grateful that you have taken interest in my investigations from the very first glance at them and thus have become the first and almost the only person who gives full credence to my contentions; nothing else could be really expected from a man with your keenness and frankness. But what will you say to the noted philosophers of our University who, despite repeated invitations, still refuse to take a look either at the moon or the telescope and so close their eyes to the light of truth? This type of people regard philosophy as a book like Aeneid or Odyssey and believe that truth will be discovered, as they themselves assert, through the comparison of texts rather than through the study of the world or nature. You would laugh if you could hear some of our most respectable university philosophers trying to argue the new planets out of existence by mere logical arguments as if these were magical charms." Galileo relates how another scientist refused to take a look through the telescope "because it would only confuse him." The tragic fate of Galileo, caused by such antagonism, is well known. He had to pay with many years of incarceration and imprisonment for his sponsorship of the Copernican theory.

Another achievement of Galileo had apparently no direct connection with astronomy; but this connection was discerned soon enough. Galileo was the first man to investigate the laws of falling bodies. He has thereby established the basic laws on which the science of mechanics was destined to grow. The apparatus he built was quite primitive. For instance, he had no watch in the modern sense of the word, but had to measure time by means of water running out of a vessel. In spite of everything, he was able to determine the relationship between the distance and the time of the fall, and also the law of acceleration. He also discovered the fact—a most surprising fact for his day—that all bodies fall equally fast. Finally, he formulated the basic law of motion, named after him: that every body unaffected by external forces moves in a straight line at a uniform speed, and that this motion can never stop by itself. Although these laws seem to be merely bits of factual

information, nevertheless they signify an extraordinary progress as compared to the preceding era. There was no inclination at that time to collect data. It was believed that all one wanted to learn could be disclosed by speculative thinking. Galileo's great achievement was that he resorted to direct investigation of nature. Moreover, the facts he discovered were destined to attain a significance far beyond their own realm, namely, when Newton constructed the mechanics of heavens on them.

Fate allotted to the English physicist Isaac Newton (1643-1727) an outstanding role in the history of the natural sciences of the described period. He was the great unifier who combined the individual discoveries of Copernicus, Kepler and Galileo into one magnificent system. His intellectual achievement cannot be estimated too highly. With the vision of a genius he realized that the power of gravitation perceived by Galileo in his doctrines concerning falling bodies had a significance far transcending the region of the earth, that this power of attraction constituted a property of all mass, and that it determined the planets' behavior across cosmic distances. This far-reaching insight into the nature of things was accompanied by Newton's great caution in scientific investigation. He started with the correct premise that the power of attraction must diminish with distance. He then calculated what the magnitude of this power, already estimated by Galileo on the surface of the earth, could be at the distance of the moon. Next he computed the length of time required for the revolution of the moon around the earth, if this gravitational power was indeed responsible for the motion of the moon. All this was a magnificent elaboration of the original idea. Unfortunately, luck was against Newton, and his investigations resulted in anything but agreement with facts. Yet nothing shows better the greatness of the scholar's character than his conduct in the face of failure: he put his calculations away in a closet without publishing a single word concerning his profound meditations (1666). Only twenty years later could the mistake be explained. The length of the earth's radius, taken by Newton as the basis of his calculations, had been inexact; new estimates on the astronomers' part gave a new measurement with which Newton's reflections about the moon proved to be in full accord.

The mechanics of Newton has thus received confirmation, and it must have seemed like a magic key to his contemporaries. His theory transformed the fundamental facts of the preceding centuries into a uniform system, including the Copernican theory of the heliocentric motion of the planets, Kepler's laws concerning their orbits, and Galileo's laws of falling bodies in a gravitational field. Kepler did not live to greet this triumph of thought; no doubt, he would have rejoiced over this proof of the harmony of cosmic motions. The Copernican conception of the universe was at last scientifically established, insofar as the laws underlying it stood revealed. Up to that time the Copernican conception of the universe, as compared to the Ptolemaic conception, could justify itself only by its claim of representing the world-picture in simpler terms. But now, with the addition of Newtonian mechanics, it became the only acceptable one. Its real merit was made explicit: the Copernican conception of the world provided an explanation of natural phenomena, a cosmic order governed by laws. It was the destiny of the Western mind to absorb this worldview which so much corresponded to its innate tendencies of thought.

Thus ends the first period of new physics; and with it has come a new method of inquiry to dominate the natural sciences ever since. The collection of facts is the starting point of investigation; but it does not mark its end. Only when an explanation comes like a bolt of lightning and melts separate ideas together in the fire of thoughtful synthesis, is that stage reached which we call understanding and which satisfies the seeking spirit. . . .

PRINCIPAL FIGURES

Pierre Rousseau (essay date 1959)

SOURCE: "The Four Great Names in the Conquest of the Skies," in *Man's Conquest of the Stars,* translated by Michael Bullock, W. W. Norton and Company, Inc., 1959, pp. 104-41.

[*In the following excerpt, Rousseau gives a detailed synopsis of the work and contribution of each of the major revolutionary astronomers after Copernicus to the establishment of the heliocentric theory. Rousseau begins with Tycho Brahe and ends with Galileo, placing special emphasis on their fresh observations of the stars and planets with new instruments and showing how these led to finally dismantling the old geocentric model of the universe.*]

The Church had fired a warning shot that reverberated over the whole of scientific research and astronomy in particular. All those who were tempted to philosophize knew the risks they were running, and outside the countries in which the Reformation had emerged victorious they confined themselves strictly to observation.

Observation of nature was precisely the task of physicians, and it is to their credit that, at this perilous epoch, they did not limit themselves to the domain of biology, but extended their curiosity to phenomena far removed from it. The French physician Jean Fernel (1497-1558), for example, measured a degree of the terrestrial meridian, an operation that had not been repeated since 988 in Bagdad; the Flemish physician

Gemma Frisius (1508-55) expounded the method of calculating longitudes by transfer of the time of day; the Calabrian physician Aloysius Lilius (d. 1576) worked to reform the calendar; the Czech physician Tadeas Hâjek (1525-1600) taught the determination of the position of a heavenly body by the time at which it passed the meridian; and we must mention again the English physician William Gilbert . . ., the Saxon physician Gaspar Peucer (1525-1602) and many others. Besides these practitioners, mention should also be made of geographers like the Portuguese Nonius (1492-1577), originator of the *Loxodromic curve or rhumb-line,*[1] the German Reinhold, author of the Prutenic Tables, the Englishman Thomas Digges (d. 1595), who first introduced the measurement of parallaxes, the Dutchman Snellius (1591-1626), one of the fathers of geodesy, and even that noted astronomer, the Landgrave William IV of Hesse (1532-92), whose observations extended over thirty years.

All these seem today, however, to be overshadowed by a German pastor and jurist named Johann Bayer (1572-1625). In 1603 this amateur astronomer published his *Uranometria* or chart of the heavens. He listed sixty constellations, each of them finely mapped out and represented, according to the custom of the day, by allegorical figures. These sixty constellations comprised the forty-eight asterisms universally recognized since Ptolemy, and the twelve new ones that had emerged from navigators' descriptions of the southern sky. But the great advance introduced by the *Uranometria* was the designation of each star by a letter, and no longer, as was previously done, by a periphrase such as 'the star that is at the tip of the tail of the Great Bear', or 'that which is beneath the right elbow of Hercules'. Bayer attached the Greek letter α to the brightest star of each constellation, the letter β to the next in brightness, γ to the next, and so on. In this way, the most beautiful stars of the Bull, for example—in order of decreasing brightness 'the southern eye', 'the tip of the left horn', 'the nostrils', and so on—became more simply α Tauri, β Tauri, γ Tauri, etc. Although a minor reform which was in no way comparable to the great innovations of Hipparchus, and yet it was of capital importance, since by simplifying charts of the heavens and making observation easier it clarified the celestial array and facilitated its scientific study.

It must be added that, even in the case of the most objective scientists among those quoted, astronomical observation was by no means untainted by astrology. In fact, as Boquet writes, 'astrology and astronomy were one and the same science'. The Church, which proved so touchy when doubt was cast on Aristotle or Ptolemy, gave every encouragement to the vagaries of those who sought to tell the future by the skies. This was the case, to give only one example, with the Neapolitan Bishop Gauricus (1476-1558), whose prophecies won the favour of four successive Popes. Among the devotees of astrology were to be found physicians, such as the Frenchman Jean-Baptiste Morin (1585-1656), who predicted the birth of Antichrist, and even true scientists, who could not offer as an excuse for their subservience to this miserable nonsense the need to earn a living. Who, on reading these fervent lines, 'By what bizarre injustice does this so noble and useful science (astrology) find so many unbelievers, when arithmetic and geometry have never met a single one?' would guess that they were written by Tycho Brahe, an astronomer of severely critical mind, who never recorded an observation without having scrutinized it from every angle?

Tycho Brahe, the lord of the skies

Such was the man who now takes his place in this story, a complex character, a rich and powerful nobleman whose proud nature forbade blind obedience to the rules of his caste; a scrupulous scientist, who nevertheless firmly believed in the influence of the heavenly bodies on human destiny; a scientific genius who, without knowing it, and even without wishing it, finally tilted the balance in favour of the heliocentric theory, and whose work outweighs on its own that of all the astronomers who filled the years between Hipparchus and himself.

The foregoing chapters have shown the burning interest men have always felt in the problem of the universe. Since the most remote times and in spite of the rigours of their everyday existence, men have speculated about the nature of the celestial vault, the luminaries suspended from it and the various phenomena that occur upon it. Deep thinkers of ancient Greece came within a hair's breadth of the solution. Aristarchus had an inkling of the vast organism that constitutes the solar system, with its circle of planets revolving round the Sun against the motionless background of the stars. But apprenticeship in the school of reason had already taught men not to rest content with intuition, but to demand proof for every explanation. This proof—the proper motion of the planets round the Sun—could be gained only by assiduous observation of these planets, by locating their changing places on the background of fixed stars. We know how Peurbach, Regiomontanus and Copernicus strove after it, and we also know why they failed: the real movement of the planets is so slow, so slight, so gradual that to attempt to show it with the instruments of the day was like trying to dissect a flea with a butcher's knife. Before tackling the problem, it was essential to improve the instruments.

Improvements of the instruments, of sights and divided circles, was a thankless task that in no way stirred the imagination. How much more exciting to forge a grandiose theory of the cosmos than to slave over graduations or try to gain one place of decimals! Yet the latter is a *sine qua non* of the former; unless supported upon impeccable observation, any theory is only a shaky scaffold unattached to reality. Copernicus's idea was correct in broad outline; nevertheless it collapsed because it was not founded on the rock of irrefutable observations. The final victory of the heliocentric theory had, therefore, to wait until it was buttressed by firmly established observations, which could not be obtained until considerable improvement had been made in the instruments employed.

This was a logical development, illustrated by the case of Tycho Brahe himself.

On 21 August, 1560, a partial eclipse of the Sun was visible at Copenhagen. It made a deep impression on a boy of fourteen, Tycho Brahe, the son of a noble family of Knudstrup, a village near Malmo in Southern Sweden which at that time belonged to Denmark. Young Tycho, who was born on 4 December, 1546, was particularly amazed that astronomers should have been able to foretell the eclipse and give its date in calendars. He was so struck by the accuracy of this forecast that he watched out for other celestial phenomena, curious to see whether they accorded equally well with the predictions. Thus, to the great displeasure of his family, began his study of astronomy.

The young man was now in possession of two astronomical almanacs giving details of the position of the planets: the Alphonsine Tables, based on the Ptolemaic system and more than three hundred years old, and the Prutenic Tables, based on the Copernican system and only a few years old. With a simple compass he measured the angular distance from each planet to the neighbouring stars, and checked this measurement against the figure in the tables. As a rule the figures did not agree. On 24 August, 1563, for instance, there occurred a conjunction of Jupiter and Saturn which the Prutenic Tables forecast with an error of several days, and the Alphonsine Tables with an error of one month! We are not surprised by this discrepancy, since we now know that the latter was several degrees out, while Copernicus and Reinhold strove to keep within ten minutes of the correct figure. Brahe quickly realized that in order to make valid predictions the first task must be to calculate the position of the stars in the sky with the greatest possible accuracy, so as to have immovable points of reference; then to determine the course of each planet in relation to these reference points with equal strictness. These two aims called for the use of large and perfectly constructed instruments.

The liberality of an intelligent and generous ruler, King Frederick II of Denmark, enabled him to put his plans into execution. This Maecenas presented him with an island, a grant of money with which to erect an observatory on it and a pension with which to maintain the staff, buildings and instruments. The island was Hven, some fourteen miles north of Copenhagen. Conscious of his talents, dealing with the sovereign on equal terms, ruling with a rod of iron the peasants who were there to do his bidding, and overflowing with money from taxation (he was also governor of Kullagaard, canon of Roskilde, and so on), Tycho embarked upon the extraordinary life of a wealthy nobleman and a scientist to whom nothing was barred.

In the centre of the island rose Uraniborg. This was a red-brick palace in the Renaissance style bristling with pointed turrets—the revolving towers from which observations were made. The bedrooms, libraries and laboratories housed a multitude of assistants and pupils, not to mention the family and servants. Farther south lay Stjerneborg—Star Burg—a subterranean observatory that protected the instruments from the action of the wind and whose domes alone rose above the ground.

A mass of evidence tells us of Tycho Brahe's life at the head of this little state. Spending money like water, terrorizing the rustics, so proudly anti-conformist that he broke with his family in order to devote himself to science, married a simple peasant girl, defied Aristotle when occasion arose and regarded religion with supreme indifference, he was by no means the lachrymose and grandiloquent visionary portrayed by Max Brod in *The Redemption of Tycho Brahe*. His methods and achievements show him to us rather as an exceptionally clear-thinking, level-headed man, who forced the most venerable traditions to bow to the facts and for whom the most ingenious hypotheses were untenable when they contradicted straightforward observation.

What instruments were sheltered beneath the pointed towers of Uraniborg and the domes of Stjerneborg? As always since Hipparchus and Ptolemy, there were quadrants, armillas and movable sextants. The latter were graduated bars along which slid alidades with sights, by means of which bearings could be taken on the stars. This enabled their co-ordinates to be found—either the azimuth and the altitude above the horizon, or the right ascension and the declination. The largest quadrant measured seven feet in radius and rotated on a vertical axis in such a way as to sweep across all azimuths. Another, of six feet, was permanently attached to a wall in the meridian. An armilla was constructed on the same principle as our present-day equatorial telescopes: a divided circle of four feet six inches radius pivoted on one of its diameters fixed parallel to the axis of the Earth. The declination could be read directly from this first circle, while the right ascensions were given by a second circle welded in the equatorial plane of the first.

The majority of these instruments were of metal, not wood. The divisions were engraved on copper. The *vernier* had not yet been invented, but to increase accuracy Tycho employed a supplementary graduation in *transversals,* which enabled him, in some cases, to read down to ten seconds of arc. How different from Copernicus's crude triquetrum, with degrees drawn in ink on pieces of wood! To appreciate the accuracy of Tycho's observations we must recall that the most exact of modern appliances, such as the transit instrument, are provided with circles two to four feet in diameter, divided every, say, two minutes of arc, and that it is only after repeated readings with the aid of micrometric microscopes that they give the second. The astronomer of Uraniborg was acquainted neither with the telescope, nor the microscope, nor the method of repetition, and his timing apparatus was not a quartz clock capable of running to the second for a year, but a mercury clepsydra. This did not prevent him from calculating the co-ordinates of a star, α Arietis, taken as a reference point, to within fifteen seconds; deducing from this, by proceeding step by step, the co-ordinates of eight other basic stars to within twenty-five seconds; and then completing a catalogue of 977 stars with a precision about ten times as great as Ptolemy's catalogue. It is not surprising that with such emphasis on accuracy Tycho discerned in all his observations a discrepancy of four minutes and spotted the effect of atmospheric refraction already discovered by Roger Bacon; nor that he noted new inequalities in the movement of the Moon; nor, especially, that in the course of twenty years devoted to following the movements of the planets he finally described them to within one minute.

This we may recall, was the aim of all his labours, as it had been of Regiomontanus and Copernicus. Like his two forerunners, the lord of Hven intended to extract from his findings an astronomical almanac that would replace the Alphonsine and Prutenic Tables. These new tables, the criterion of the reliability and permanence of his work, were to be its true crown, the justification of all the toil effected at Hven and the proof that Frederick II's generosity had not been in vain.

But Fate crossed Tycho's path. His intelligent sovereign died, his other patrons disappeared. The hostility and jealousy excited by his exceptional situation now broke their bonds. Forced to leave his island, the astronomer took refuge in Bohemia at the head of a vast train of staff, furniture and astronomical equipment whose passage terrified the population.

All that Fate left him time to extract from the material he had amassed was a cosmological theory—a hybrid theory in which Tycho, too well informed to remain a Ptolemist, could nevertheless not make up his mind to become a Copernican. In Tycho Brahe's system the planets moved round the Sun, and the Sun, Moon and planets round the Earth, which was motionless in the centre of the universe.

Pious Kepler establishes the plan of the solar system

Tycho Brahe was the greatest astronomer we have met in the course of this story since Hipparchus. He was also a man of haughty character, despotic, harsh towards his inferiors and exacting towards others, a man in whom the love of science took precedence over every other consideration. An individual of this stamp is respected and flattered as long as he is felt to be supported by the favour of the great, but as soon as this support is withdrawn he becomes the object of all the dammed-up hatred and envy inspired by his position. Tycho never recovered from his expulsion from Hven. He died at Prague on 24 October, 1601. His tomb may still be seen in the Teyn church, covered with a bas-relief in pink marble. Only four years had passed since his departure from Hven, yet Uraniborg and Stjerneborg were already in ruins. Through the greed of the prebendaries and the vengeance of his enemies they had been pillaged, laid waste and razed to the ground. A few years later, evidence that the palatial dwelling really existed was sought in vain. Not until 1951 did excavation uncover a few traces. . . . Even Tycho's magnificent instruments were destroyed during the Thirty Years War, when the scientist's widow had already died in poverty and want. Nothing was left of Tycho Brahe, nothing but a few bundles of paper which he passed to one of his assistants, with a nerveless hand, a few hours before he died. This heritage, his observations of the planets, he bequeathed with the request that they should be used to produce an astronomical almanac, to be called the *Rudolphine Tables* in honour of the Emperor Rudolf II.

Among his innumerable assistants, a few had occupied a particular place in his life. Tengnagel became his son-in-law; Longomontanus stayed at his side through hard times as well as good; and there was the absent-minded young mathematician who had come to join the team, then exiled in Bohemia, one misty morning in February 1600.

It was to this man that Tycho left his records. His name was Johann Kepler.

Tycho Brahe was a man of genius not only because his observations were superior to anything that could be expected at that period, but also because he was able to recognize and call to his side the only man in the world capable of turning them to account. Brahe's perspicacity and the consequent meeting of two brains made to complement one another strikes us as one of the most fortunate events for astronomy that occurred throughout the ages. It was totally unexpected, and in fact Brahe and Kepler seemed poles apart.

The former reigned in his princely abode at Prague, a celebrated scientist surrounded by the perpetual coming and going of admirers and the benevolence of the Emperor. Kepler was nothing but a poor professor at the University of Graz—an Austrian town 220 miles to the south—living on the verge of penury. Born at Weil, in Würtemberg, on 16 May, 1571, this sickly young man had been successively waiter, farmer and seminarist. A Protestant by religion, he studied at the University of Tübingen. Here, far more than theology, he was interested in mathematics and astronomy, which were taught by Michael Maestlin (1550-1631). The latter also deserves the gratitude of mankind; it was he who, in defiance of official injunctions, taught his pupil Kepler the heliocentric system. He is said also to have taught it to Galileo himself in the course of a trip to Italy.

Young Kepler was appointed professor of mathematics at Graz in 1596, and he had just published his first book. Like every eminent scientist, Tycho Brahe received a copy. He realized at once what promise the unknown author showed and wished to have his collaboration. How could Kepler refuse to work with the great astronomer of Hven? Burdened by a family of five children, he could 'make ends meet' only by casting horoscopes in which he may not have believed. Thus, in 1600, he arrived in Prague to collaborate in the project of the *Rudolphine Tables*.

Apart from his genius, which Tycho alone recognized, Kepler had nothing in common with the latter. He was ignorant of the ways of society and disdained good manners, which did not matter. His intelligence was as abstract and mystical as Tycho's was clear and practical, which was a more serious source of conflict. The ambition of the former lord of the island was to construct instruments graduated with such exactitude that their accuracy was beyond dispute. Kepler's tastes carried him towards Pythagorianism, religious exaltation, grandiose and baroque flights of the imagination. His first 'scientific' achievement was to demonstrate the harmony of the universe by comparing the number and arrangement of the planets with the five inscribable regular polyhedrons. His geometrical proofs were interspersed with lyrical apostrophes to the Creator, and he was firmly convinced that God had made the stars to help man take his bearings at night and that man was the centre of the universe.

This naïve finalism did not prevent him from giving wholehearted support to the heliocentric theory of Copernicus—another point of conflict with Tycho. Kepler knew his scientific superiority and he was a dreamer with a liking for vague theories; his host was a man filled with pride of birth and a meticulous investigator who could not imagine science otherwise than as the accumulation of carefully checked facts. Nevertheless, it was to this exasperating assistant, who stirred him to alternate admiration and annoyance, that he left his treasure of twenty years' observation.

His patron dead, Kepler became once more a wanderer, seeking a position with the Emperor, a post at the University or employment as astrologer with a military leader. He was now escorted by twelve children and showered with securities by the great, who forgot to pay him. But his wealth lay in this inheritance from Tycho, which it was his task to bring to fruition.

To bring Tycho's heritage to fruition meant to see whether the positions given for each planet really lay on the eccentric circular orbit ascribed to it by Ptolemy. Kepler considered the case of Mars, collated the observations and noted that they differed by eight minutes of arc from the predictions in the tables. The discrepancy could not arise from systematic errors, since Tycho's inaccuracies did not exceed one minute. Hence it must be the theory that was wrong, and the orbit could not be circular.

Kepler immediately adopted the Copernican hypothesis. He then saw that calculation agreed better with observation when the orbit was assumed to be oval. Finally he arrived at the first of the three major laws which posterity has christened 'Kepler's Laws': The orbit of a planet is an ellipse with the Sun situated at a focus.

The second law followed almost at once. It runs thus: The *radius vector,* joining the Sun to a planet, sweeps equal areas in equal times.

This means, for example, that the straight line joining the Earth to the Sun does not revolve at a constant speed, like the hand of a clock. . . . Consequently, the Earth travels faster at the moment of the winter solstice than at the moment of the summer solstice. This law explains the variations in the apparent speed of the Sun and planets that had so intrigued the ancient astronomers; just as the first law, regarding the eccentricity of the orbit, explains the variations in their luminosity.

These first two laws were published by Kepler in 1609 in his book *The New Astronomy, founded on the study of the motion of Mars.* The third did not appear until 1619, in his *Harmony of the World:* it was more complicated and cost him seventeen years of research. The third of the great laws governing the motion of the heavenly bodies is expressed as follows: The squares of the periodic times of any two planets are proportional to the cubes of the major axes of their orbits.

We will explain this statement by an example.

One revolution of the Earth takes 365 days, the square of which is 365 X 365 = 132,225. That of Mars takes 687 days, the square of which is 687 X 687 = 471,969.

The law in question states that these two numbers, 132,225 and 471,969, are proportional to the cubes of the major axes of the respective orbits of the Earth and Mars. From this it follows that the distance from Mars to the Sun and from the Earth to the Sun are to one another as the cube root of 471,969 is to the cube root of 132,225, that is to say in the proportion of 1·524 to 1.

The importance of this discovery is evident. Having found the path followed by the planets, the variable speed at which they travel along it, the distance—in relation to the duration of their revolution—they are from the Sun, Kepler had thereby established the final plan of the solar system. Henceforth there was no room for doubt. Not merely was it no longer possible to wonder whether Venus was or was not closer to the Earth than Mars: the precise dimensions of their respective orbits were determined with an exactitude hitherto known only to mathematics. Heracleides Ponticus, Aristarchus and Copernicus had formed a general idea of the organization as a whole, but this was only a qualitative interpretation, a painting sketched in without a model by brilliantly intuitive minds. For this pleasant picture, Kepler substituted a strict and accurate diagram; the circles demanded by Platonic aesthetics gave place to ellipses; uniform movements, to speeds that varied according to an inflexible formula. The planetary world ceased to be a vaguely defined aggregation obeying convenient rules; it became a coherent whole subject to inviolable natural laws, and the prediction of phenomena, instead of being a purely empirical matter, acquired the full rigour of geometry. Working with his laws, Kepler was able to state that on such and such a day, such and such a planet would be at such and such a point in the sky, on another day there would be an occultation and on yet another day an eclipse. Thus, in fulfilment of the promise he had made to the dying Tycho, he produced in 1627 the *Rudolphine Tables.*

These tables owed nothing to those of Hipparchus, nor to those of Ibn-Yunis or Ulugh Beigh, nor to the Alphonsine or Prutenic Tables, and they paid as little heed to Tycho Brahe's system as to Ptolemy's. In short, they were modern tables based on the same principles as the *Nautical Almanac* of our own day. Kepler did not omit to acknowledge his debt to Tycho. He could never have drawn up his tables without the material accumulated by the Danish astronomer.

The publication of this work heralded the triumph of the heliocentric view, and also the final burial of Kepler's hopes. Tycho's heirs demanded a share in the tables; Longomontanus added his calumnies to their claims; first the Emperor, then the Duke of Wallenstein, who employed him as an astrologer, ceased to pay him. Weighed down by too harsh a destiny, this profound genius, this sensitive and visionary mathematician, breathed his last at Ratisbon on 15 November, 1630.

A free mind: Galileo

We should be wrong in thinking that the discovery of Kepler's laws and the publication of the *Rudolphine Tables* aroused any considerable echo in Europe and immediately rallied the learned world to the heliocentric theory. Paradoxically, the opposing camp, apart from those instinctively drawn to it by their philosophical opinions and religious faith or scientific ignorance, also attracted scientists with a positivist outlook. The latter were suspicious of the extravagant hotchpotch of aesthetico-mysticism with which Kepler surrounded the enunciation of his laws. How could a pure geometer look favourably upon results which their author interlarded with statements about the music of the spheres and invocations to God? Thus, even mathematicians who maintained a personal correspondence with Kepler received his work with a reserve bordering on scepticism.

This was the case, in particular, with the professor of mathematics at the University of Padua, with whom Kepler had been exchanging letters since 1597. Although Kepler knew the professor to be a convinced Copernican, his reprimands and moving exhortations were of no avail: the professor remained icy. No doubt the esoteric impedimenta with which Kepler cluttered his proofs rendered them suspect in his eyes.

This professor of mathematics was called Galileo Galilei. Born at Pisa on 18 February, 1564, at the time when *The New Astronomy* appeared he was a man of forty-five, vigorous, with an unfettered mind and a happy disposition. There is nothing surprising about the fact that, while still young, he espoused the heliocentric theory, thus breaking with Ptolemy at the outset of his career: he was a child of the same Tuscany that gave birth to Dante, Giotto, Petrarch, Leonardo da Vinci and Michelangelo. A financial centre where huge fortunes were built up, Florence was better suited to the emancipation of intelligence than to introverted meditation. The capitalism that flourished there contributed to the development of more liberal and more realistic ideas than were current in other countries less stimulated by commerce and more tightly muzzled by the Inquisition.

What a difference there was between Galileo, a son of the new and luminous Alexandria that was Tuscany, and, say, Copernicus and Kepler, the offspring of countries that were more closed, more misty, graver and more respectful towards dogma and authority! By comparison with Copernicus, flaccidly taking the line of least resistance, determined at all costs to keep out of trouble, by comparison with Kepler, struggling in the midst of his poverty and a myriad astrological superstitions, Galileo stood out as a lucid scientist incapable of concealing the slightest particle of the truth. This truth, which horrified the partisans of scientific ortho-doxy, he confessed, taught and proclaimed. Not only did he shout it from the rooftops, but he assailed its opponents, drenched them in sarcasm, turned them over and over on the grill of his irony. Not until he was seventy, and under the threat of torture and death, did he finally pretend to see reason. It is understandable that a character like his, full of pride in his possession of the truth, should not have appealed to everyone and that one authority should have written, for example: 'A curious man, whose scientific ability compels respect, but whose character is unattractive: the more we study him, the more we admire and the less we like him.' This is a matter of taste: some people prefer darkness to light and the persecutor to his victim.

We can understand the hostility Galileo aroused from the outset when we recall that, while still a young lecturer of twenty-five, he did not hesitate to repudiate the authority of Aristotle. The latter declared that the heavier a body is, the faster it falls. Galileo had only to ascend to the top of the famous leaning tower of Pisa and drop two iron balls, one weighing 1 lb., the other 10 lb., and observe that they both touched the ground at the same time. Thus began a series of studies on weight, which were irrefutable because based on experiment. This was the first time the dogmatic rules of Aristotle had been opposed by concrete reality, and it is easy to imagine the howl raised by the Peripatetics.

The republic of Venice, which appointed the great man to a chair at the University of Padua in 1592 and paid him magnificently, was the most suitable place in the world to cultivate a science so intrepidly pursued. Far from censuring his audacities, the Senate applauded them: they increased the number of students and enriched the State!

To the lustre conferred upon him by his discoveries in mechanics Galileo added the merit of practical inventions—the thermometer, the hydrostatic scales, a new fortification technique. In 1609 came the momentous discovery of the astronomical telescope.

The first harvest of the telescope

Let us make it clear at once that Galileo did not invent the telescope. It had been known for at least a year under the name 'Holland glass', and specimens could be bought from spectacle-makers in the Hague, Brussels and Paris. Roger Bacon had an inkling of the magnifying effect of lenses in 1260; in about 1590, the Italian Giovanni Battista Porta (1538-1615) produced a combination of lenses that made distant objects appear closer, and Dutch opticians—Metius, Jansen, Lippershey—began making and selling these appliances in 1608. But none of them dreamed that the 'Holland glass' could be anything but a toy. It never occurred to any of them that it might be something more than a profitable article of sale. Galileo learned of the existence of this apparatus in 1609, through a letter from a correspondent in Paris. He tried out various arrangements of concave and convex lenses and had little difficulty in reconstructing the one employed by the Dutch opticians. He at once applied it to celestial observation and he may justly be said to have invented the *astronomical* telescope.

Two of Galileo's earliest telescopes may be seen today in the Physics Museum, Florence; they are modest tubes fitted at one end with a convex lens and at the other, the eye-piece, with a concave lens. They magnified, at most, some twenty times. Faced by these relics, the layman will smile, recalling the gigantic telescope of Mount Palomar of which the mirror is seventeen feet across, inside which the observer is housed like an insect and which magnifies a thousand times. But the man of science will be moved, for he knows that the latter is only the descendant of the former, and that the humble contrivance devised by Galileo produced an even more abundant harvest than the Californian colossus, although the latter has extended the dominion of thought several thousand million light-years.

Galileo began to reap this harvest during the early April evenings of 1609, with instruments the most powerful of which had a 2¼ inch objective and magnified thirty times. He trained it on the Moon and at one glance perceived an earth almost the same as our own, with mountains, valleys, shadows that lengthened as the Sun went down, and the pale 'earthshine' that dilutes with a discreet glimmer the dense lunar night. Aristotle asserted that the Moon was smooth, because a perfect spherical shape was the only one appropriate to the heavenly bodies; Galileo shrugged his shoulders.

He shrugged his shoulders again when, on directing his tube towards the Sun, he saw spots. Spots on the Sun, which the Stagirite had declared to be incorruptible! He might not have believed his eyes, if he had not known that a similar observation had already been made by the Dutchman John Fabricius (1587-1615), who used only an ordinary 'Holland glass'. The German Jesuit Christoph Scheiner (1575-1650) made the same discovery at about the same time, but his provincial's obstinate adherence to Aristotelian views prompted him to caution. It was not until 1626 that he began to publish his work, *Rosa Ursina,* in which he determined the duration of the Sun's rotation and the zones of appearance of the sunspots.

During this time Galileo was continuing his explorations at Padua. After the Moon and the Sun, the planet Venus entered the field of his object-glass. Slowly, evening after evening, its aspect changed. Since, according to Ptolemy, it revolved round the Earth and was lit from the side by the Sun, it was not surprising that it appeared as a crescent; but the crescent

grew, became a circle, the circle became indented, shrank and vanished, then the crescent reappeared—a sequence of phases exactly resembling those of the Moon. There could be no doubt about it. If Venus had phases, it meant this planet must revolve round the Sun as the Moon does round the Earth. Copernicus was right.

After Venus came Jupiter. At the first viewing the disc appeared tiny, and close to it were three little stars. The next day, these stars had changed position and there were four of them. Intrigued, Galileo observed them closely several days in succession and saw them shift from one evening to the next, eclipse one another and pass in front of the disc of the planet. The astronomer realized that these were four satellites rotating around Jupiter. The same discovery was made simultaneously by the German Simon Mayer, called Marius (1570-1624), who made himself a telescope 'the length of an arm' with an object-glass 'one and a half fingers in diameter'.

Intoxicated with the discoveries that filled his telescope every time he raised it towards the skies, Galileo moved on to Saturn. But the image was far smaller than that of Jupiter, and also more confused. The disc seemed to be extended on two sides by 'ears', unless these were two satellites. The perplexed scientist hid his mortification behind an anagram meaning 'I observed the highest planet (Saturn) and found it threefold'. Forty-six years later, Huygens solved the mystery by showing that the strange object was a ring that encircles Saturn.

And there were the stars. What a harvest the objective reaped in the still virgin fields of heaven where, for every known orb, a hundred rose up out of the depths of invisibility. Constellations ceased to be an allegorical assembly of a few stars; they multiplied, became a concourse, sometimes a seething mass, of dozens, of hundreds of stars unsuspected by the eye. Instead of the six stars of the Pleiades, Galileo discerned forty; he counted eighty instead of seven in Orion's Belt and Sword, forty instead of three in the asterism of Praesepe, while in the Milky Way the eye was confronted by a mass of luminous dust.

Behind the familiar stellar world, behind the visible face of the philosophical world of Aristotle, whose motions had been traced by Ptolemy, Galileo discovered another, incomparably richer and more mysterious. In his turn, the illustrious Pisan astronomer drew up an inventory of them in his *Siderius Nuncius* or 'Sidereal Messenger', eighteen months after constructing his first telescope. What a stir this caused among the learned and even among the merely educated! And naturally the astonishing revelation of such marvels aroused people's curiosity to see them for themselves, as well as to discover fresh ones.

While Galileo was being showered with favours by the Medici, congratulated by Rome, appointed professor at Pisa University and elected to the Accademia dei Lincei, the telescope came into the hands of innumerable emulators and everywhere spread a taste for astronomy. How many troops there were now for the conquest of the skies! We can understand this sudden craze. How much more attractive the exploration of the heavens was, when practised in this fashion, with the aid of an instrument that sounded the invisible depths, than the astronomy of yesterday with its divided circles, its mensurations and its trigonometrical formulae! Armed with the telescope, Galilean astronomy was a stimulus to the imagination, a spur to thought. It was a living, stirring and popular science, just as classical astronomy, so learned and so sterile, was austere, lofty and aristocratic.

No sooner had Galileo launched his attack, no sooner had his *Siderius Nuncius* indicated the objectives to be attained, than there was an outburst of discoveries. On 15 December, 1612, Simon Marius, who had already recovered from their obscurity the four satellites of Jupiter, reported the existence, close to the constellation of Andromeda, of a strange little luminescent cloud, 'like a candle seen at night through a sheet of horn', as he described it. This was the first appearance of the great nebula of Andromeda, a sister galaxy to our own, the vast proportions of which were not known until three centuries later. As early as 1610 Peiresc . . . had announced the presence of a similar cloud in the constellation of Orion: this was the nebula of Orion, studied in detail by Huygens in 1656. In 1620 the Belgian Charles Malapert discerned the phases of Mercury, which exactly resemble those of Venus. In 1630 the Italian Zucchi drew attention to the parallel belts that run across the disc of Jupiter.

Meanwhile, the primitive telescope had been improved. The first advance was due to Kepler. Galileo sent him his book; he made himself a telescope and came away dazzled by the multitude of stars it brought into view. But this telescope was incapable of great magnification and its field was very small. Kepler looked for another system of lenses that would obviate these two drawbacks. In 1611 he published the outline of an arrangement in which the concave eye-piece was replaced by a convex one, a major advance which was the starting point for the optical instruments employed in modern astronomy. Galileo's telescope remained in the form of the opera-glass and field-glass; Kepler's became the true astronomical refractor—the ancestor of the giant at the Yerkes Observatory, whose object-glass is a biconvex lens forty inches across.

Which astronomer first applied Kepler's suggestions and constructed this true 'astronomical' refractor? Perhaps, in 1613, the Jesuit Scheiner, who discovered the sunspots. Perhaps the Austrian Franciscan Schyrle of Rheita (1597-1660), whose surname, Rheita, long served as a common noun designating the telescope. In any case, it was a colleague of Scheiner's, the Italian Jesuit Nicola Zucchi (1586-1670) who, in 1616, created the reflecting telescope. In this instrument the ordinary object-glass is replaced by a concave mirror, by which the image is reflected into the eye-piece and magnified by it.

Galileo's telescope, Kepler's astronomical telescope, the reflecting telescope, celestial discoveries that echoed from one end of Europe to the other—this outburst of inventions, revelations and miracles was the cause and consequence of enthusiastic investigation of the sky, to whose new and fabulous riches the telescope provided the key.

Galileo's condemnation is his victory

This outburst overturned a great deal more than the existing conception of the firmament. It struck a violent blow at the teaching of Ptolemy and Aristotle and hence at the authority of the Scriptures. For, since Venus exhibited phases like the Moon, was it not evident that this planet revolved around the Sun? Did not the fact that there were four satellites circulating around Jupiter prove that not everything in the universe gravitated round the Earth? And did not the system of four globes rotating round the Jovian world illustrate what the system of planets revolving round the Sun must be like? And this illustration was all the more striking because Kepler's laws applied just as rigorously to the Jovian system as to the solar system, as was proved by the Belgian priest Godefroi Wendelen (1580-1667).

In short, the most ineluctable observations proved that the planets revolved around the Sun, not around the Earth, and therefore that Ptolemy was wrong. Galileo, who was not reticent by temperament and who liked to make truth heard, did not fail to shout it from the housetops and write it to all his friends. Naturally, the partisans of traditional astronomy were up in arms; some declared that the heavenly bodies seen by the telescope were only optical illusions created by the objective itself; others found it impossible to believe so many things that were not in Aristotle; finally, the Church refused to accept discoveries that contradicted certain passages in the Bible, for example the miracle of Joshua.

Conflict was inevitable between these two equally intransigent authorities, on the one hand the authority of observation and experiment, on the other that of faith and dogma. Seeing the world sliding farther and farther down the slope of heresy, the ecclesiastical authorities were led officially to take up a position. In 1616 they had the following two propositions examined by the Qualifiers, or experts of the Holy Office:

1. The Sun is the centre of the world and hence immovable of local motion;

2. The Earth is not the centre of the world, not immovable, but moves according to the whole of itself, also with a diurnal motion.

On 24 February the opinion of the Qualifiers was accepted by the Holy Office and the first proposition was declared 'foolish and absurd, philosophically and formally heretical', and the second was declared 'to receive the same censure in philosophy and, as regards theological truth, to be at least erroneous in faith'. Galileo was ordered to cease propaganda in favour of the heliocentric system.

It would be disregarding Galileo's impetuosity and his irresistible urge to scald his opponents with irony to imagine that he let matters rest there. In 1632 he published, in Italian, his major work, *Dialogues on the two great systems of the world, the Ptolemaic and the Copernican*. A masterpiece of ironic wit, it was nothing but a long plea for the heliocentric theory, disguised under protestations of respect for the Church. The latter ingenuously accorded the *imprimatur* and the Pope himself was not in the least shocked by the book. It took a little longer for the scandal to break. Then the supreme pontiff recognized himself in one of the characters drawn by the author, and entrusted with the task of defending Ptolemy, a picturesque individual of the type we might describe today as 'gormless'.

We know the sequel. Galileo was called to Rome, brought before the Holy Office and condemned, on 22 June, 1633, to recant the heresy that the Earth moved.

Tradition presents this grand old man to us as a pitiable victim of religious fanaticism. Let us not exaggerate: the scientist, who knew perfectly well the risk he was running, was treated as the law of the Church demanded, but with clemency. In the end it was he who emerged victorious from the debate, since his trial represented the last desperate rearguard action by the Peripatetics in flight before the rising tide of facts. Yet it took two centuries for the Vatican to admit its defeat, for Galileo's *Dialogues* were not removed from the Index until the beginning of the nineteenth century. And it was only in 1952, while receiving members of the congress of the International Astronomical Union meeting in Rome, that Pope Pius XII glorified 'the modern conception of astronomical science which was, in the past, the ideal of so many great men, Copernicus, Galileo, Kepler, Newton. . . .'

To tell the truth, though we may justly conclude that it was Galileo who delivered the death blow to the Ptolemaic system and ensured the final triumph of heliocentrism, his victory was certainly not recognized as such at the time. It looked more like a defeat of the Copernicans. As Protestants were no less geocentrically minded than the rest, the heliocentrists nowhere ventured to present the theory as anything but a hypothesis, and dispute between them and their opponents was more active than ever.

It seems pretty clear that, among astronomers, no one was now a Ptolemist at heart. They all proclaimed their loyalty to the Scriptures, but the majority paid only lip service to geocentrism.

The Italian Jesuit Giovanni Battista Riccioli (1598-1671), for example, the author of the first map of the Moon . . ., accepted the Ptolemaic theory only with regret and, commenting on the decree of the Holy Office, added: 'It is not an article of faith that the Sun moves and the Earth is at rest.' Wendelen, who has been referred to above, his compatriot Canon Martin-Etienne van Velden (1664-1724) and, among the French, the Minim Friar Marin Mersenne (1588-1648) and Abbés Picard (1620-82 or 1683) and Gassendi (1592-1655) were more or less overt heliocentrists. Naturally, this dual attitude did not facilitate scientific work. Joseph Bertrand relates that in 1746, the period of the Battle of Fontenoy, Diderot's *Pensées philosophiques,* the *Esprit des Lois* and the invention of the lightning conductor, the Italian Jesuit Ruggero Boscovich (1711-87), a distinguished astronomer and a disciple of Newton, sought to calculate the orbit of a comet according to three observations, 'a completely impossible problem,' explains Joseph Bertrand, 'if the Earth is supposed motionless'. Boscovich declared at the time: 'Full of respect for the Holy Scriptures and the decree of the Holy Inquisition, I regard the Earth as immovable.' Then, having put himself in order with his conscience, he hastened to add: 'Nevertheless, for simplicity of explanation, I shall act as though it revolved; for it has been proved that appearances are the same in the two hypotheses.'

Cruelly torn between the imperatives of science, which drew them towards the heliocentric system, and obedience to the Church, which held them down to geocentrism, some scientists compromised and rallied to Tycho Brahe's thesis. But this hybrid position was highly unstable, and in spite of the angry cries of theologians and Bossuet's majestic sermons,[2] belief in the motion of the Earth spread with gathering momentum.

France, England and the Low Countries provide arms for the conquest of the skies

It must be remembered that the first years of the seventeenth century were marked by a general retreat from her possessions by Spain. The chief causes of the progressive disintegration of her empire were the Spaniards' laziness, their voracity, which led them to prefer financial juggling to commercial activity, and the omnipotence of a fabulously wealthy aristocracy and priesthood in a ruined country. The main stages in this disintegration were the proclamation of the independence of the Netherlands (1579), the rout of the invincible Armada (1588), the Treaty of Vervins and the Edict of Nantes (1598).

The downfall of Spain meant a loss to the Church and a corresponding gain to liberty of conscience and scientific research. England and the Low Countries henceforth concentrated all their efforts on economic improvement and threw themselves wide open to technical progress, while France, thanks to Henry IV, liberated herself from religious intolerance and decreed freedom of worship. Spain and Italy were thus thrown out of circuit and continued to suffocate under the iron-collar of the Inquisition; as a result the conquest of the skies withered away in Italy while becoming more and more vigorous in the Netherlands, Britain and France.

In 1633, when Galileo's recantation echoed round the world, this state of affairs was already very much in evidence. On the scientific plane, Spain had long ceased to count. Italy also abdicated, strangled by her philosophical bonds. The spirit of free investigation had crossed the frontier and was now spreading in the South of France. The astronomical telescope here enjoyed a tremendous vogue, and around Aix-en-Provence a whole crop of astronomers worked enthusiastically to continue Galileo's wonderful achievements.

These stargazers were no longer men of letters or physicians; they were jurists, to whom the freedom afforded by the Edict of Nantes allowed intellectual audacities previously unthinkable. They deliberately rejected Aristotle and Ptolemy, made a point of valuing only concrete facts and logical reasoning, and set about the examination of celestial phenomena unencumbered by any prejudices. Such were Nicolas Fabri de Peiresc (1580-1637), counsellor in the parliament of Aix; Gassendi, the first to observe the passage of Mercury in front of the solar disc on 7 November, 1631; and a group of lawyers and clerics more sensitive to exact observation than to the taboos imposed by a philosopher of Stagira two thousand years earlier.

As partisans, acknowledged or otherwise, of the heliocentric system, it goes without saying that these people were simultaneously opposed to the Aristotelian conception of the cosmos. Aristotle had declared the Earth to be immovable at the centre of the universe, the stars to be moving round it with a circular and uniform motion, the planets to be imperishable and incorruptible. It was now notorious that the planetary orbits were ellipses, that the planets travelled along them at variable speeds, and that the pure countenance of the Sun might be corrupted by spots. New stars had even been observed in the reputedly unalterable skies, such as those noted in 1572 (by Tycho Brahe), in 1600 (by the Flemish astronomer Wilhelm Blaeu, 1571-1638) and in 1604.

Furthermore, and in more general terms, Aristotle had asserted that natural phenomena, since they were perceptible to us by quality rather than quantity, could not be expressed in a mathematical form. This assertion, too, was contradicted by the new discoveries. Not only had Kepler reduced planetary motions to a mathematical formula, but Galileo, in his early work, had similarly 'mathematized' the study of weight. These few mathematical relationships discerned in natural phenomena would, however, have had only limited application, if a philosopher of genius had not been led to generalize them and to interpret the universe as a whole in terms of a vast mechanism subject to strict material laws. Need we add that this was Descartes?

Galileo was thirty-two when René Descartes (1596-1650) was born. At the time of the 1633 trial, the latter was in Holland, whose liberal atmosphere, realistic mentality and commercial activity favoured a revolution in thinking. His major work appeared four years later. Applying the principles laid down in his *Discours sur la Méthode,* Descartes formulated a general theory of the world. He supposed it to be made up of an invisible substance called ether composed of very small particles in a continuous state of eddying movement, which accounted for all phenomena (the 'Vortex Theory'). He went back to the descriptions of Copernicus and Kepler, and, in addition, deduced new laws and facts in the fields of optics and mechanics.

The spiraloid shape of the galaxies restores a striking topicality to the great French thinker's views, which are for the most part now quite out of date. Outworn though they now appear to us, we cannot fail to see in them the first attempt at a truly scientific explanation of nature, the first effort to interpret nature not in purely deductive abstract terms, as the Scholastics and Aristotelians did, but on the basis of visible evidence treated according to the exigencies of reason.

The rise in the standard of living and the increased wealth of the middle classes in France, Britain and the Low Countries were largely due to technical progress. Technicians and financiers began to seem the authors of prosperity and they naturally relied upon those who, through their ability to interpret natural phenomena correctly, enabled them to improve their tools and augment profit and interest. In other words, scientists like Galileo and Descartes gradually thrust into the shadow the hair-splitting disciples of Aristotle with their contempt for concrete reality. The latter were reduced to the level of supernumeraries in the epic of civilization. It was the former who now occupied the centre of the stage. In the age of machines, whose advent they heralded, they were destined to create modern civilization.

Let us welcome this salutary interaction between the needs of economics (to be exact, of commercial navigation), which led Tycho Brahe and Kepler to improve the prediction of celestial movements; the mathematical form given to the latter by Kepler and Galileo, which induced them to state the great natural laws in the same stringent terms; and the effectiveness of these laws in enabling man to increase his power over things and so bring about the industrial revolution of the eighteenth century. Tycho Brahe's paternity in respect of this revolution is less remote than might be thought, since it was from the observations at Hven that Kepler extracted the laws of the planets, from these that Newton derived the discovery of universal gravitation and the general theorems of mechanics, and these theorems which, in turn, gave rise to the rational evolution of machines, the basis of the rapid advances in industry that took place from 1760 onwards.

At the time of the *Discours de la Méthode* (1637) Aristotelianism was no more to scientists than a dusty relic of the past. It was none the less the symbol of religious authority, and they were obliged to bow to it as the Swiss of William Tell's day had to bow to Gessler's hat. Even after Kepler's and Galileo's achievements, astronomical investigation remained permeated by an unpleasant metaphysical odour. This was because, even admitting that the planets described mathematically defined orbits, it remained to be discovered *why* they did so. What mysterious force compelled them to revolve around the Sun? Was it a 'motive virtue', sister to Molière's 'dormitive virtue'? Or was it an attraction derived from the properties of the *lodestone,* properties popularized in 1600 by William Gilbert?

Was it not possible to track down this hidden cause by the method of scientific investigation that had proved so successful in the hands of Kepler, Galileo and Descartes? This was precisely the task Galileo set himself when, after his recantation and house arrest at Arcetri, near Florence, where exploration of the firmament was forbidden him, he was able to devote himself entirely to meditation. In 1638 he published at Leyden his *Dialogues on Two New Sciences.*

This work has rightly been seen as the charter of dynamics. In it Galileo, thinking over experiments carried out during his youth at Pisa, deduced from them the basic laws of this science—the law of the falling of bodies, of the pendulum, of the inclined plane and of the rate of projectiles together with the distinction between an object's *mass* and its *weight;*[3] in it he also formulated the principle of inertia, according to which a body in motion that is free from the action of any force will continue to move indefinitely in a straight line and with constant velocity. These laws formed the basis of terrestrial mechanics. The adjective 'terrestrial' is important, because there existed another mechanics, that which governed planetary motion, whose laws had been discovered by Kepler. It is hardly necessary

to state that these two types of mechanics were as dissimilar as possible and that there seemed to be no common measure between Kepler's laws and, for example, the law of the fall of bodies discovered by Galileo?[4]

Kepler died in abject poverty in 1630. Galileo, now blind, passed away in his turn on 8 January, 1642. On 4 January of the following year Newton was born.

Newton, or unadulterated genius

Everything was known and nothing was known. For if the nature of the planetary paths was now established, if it was now possible, thanks to Kepler's laws, to draw up astronomical tables incomparably more accurate than any that had gone before, the mechanism behind it all was just as much a mystery as ever. Why did the planets revolve around the Sun? What mysterious influence compelled them to describe ellipses and not circles, or, more simply, prevented them from shooting off in a straight line?

This problem was hotly discussed, especially in London. The young astronomer Halley . . . , who had just made himself famous by predicting the return of a great comet, the frightful gnome Robert Hooke (1653-1703), as learned as he was irascible, and the architect Christopher Wren (1632-1723), who had previously been a professor of mathematics and astronomy, pursued endless investigations, convinced they were on the brink of a solution but unable to find the ultimate 'open sesame'.

Halley knew that if the orbits had been circular it would have been possible to invoke a force of attraction coming from the Sun and varying as the inverse square of the distance. But did this law apply to elliptical orbits? Halley strongly suspected that it did. Wren declared his inability to solve the problem. Hooke claimed to have solved it, but offered no proof. Perhaps he had solved it. This hunchbacked, sickly and deformed experimental philosopher appears to us now as one of the vastest brains in the history of science. Among his numerous inventions were the first screw-divided quadrant, an anemometer, a weather clock, the anchor escapement of clocks (put into practical effect later by William Clement . . .), and a universal joint; he was the first to apply the spring balance wheel to watches. He also evolved a theory of elasticity and it seems that he divined the true doctrine of universal gravitation, but failed to demonstrate his discovery through lack of mathematical knowledge.

In any case, no convincing and acceptable solution was forthcoming. All Wren could think of was to offer a prize of £1 (worth forty shillings) to anyone who could prove, within two months, that the path of a planet subject to the law of the inverse square was necessarily an ellipse. As this bait still produced no result, Halley decided in August 1684 to consult one of his friends, a Cambridge professor called Isaac Newton.

Newton was by then already one of the great names in optics. He was born on 4 January, 1643, in the little hamlet of Woolthorpe in Lincolnshire. His career as a schoolboy and as a student at Cambridge was undistinguished except by a very great experimental ingenuity. Not till he was twenty-one did he give Barrow, his favourite professor, cause to suspect the exceptional genius slumbering within him.

In 1669 Newton succeeded Barrow as Lucasian professor of mathematics at Cambridge. By this time Newton had made a name for himself by resolving white light into its constituent colours with the aid of a prism. Perfecting Zucchi's invention, he had also constructed a metal reflecting telescope. This instrument, now one of the most precious relics of the Royal Society, excited the most lively admiration, shared and expressed by the King himself. In 1672 Newton was elected a member of this erudite company. Since then, apart from a dispute with Hooke on the fall of bodies, Newton had won fame by his famous corpuscular theory of light.

In short, when Halley came to talk to him about the controversy that had arisen between himself, Hooke and Wren, Newton was one of the most celebrated opticians of the day, but there seemed no reason why he should be able to throw light on the question at issue. We may judge the young astronomer's amazement when his friend told him he had taken an interest in the problem, and indeed, found a complete solution to it. It was typical of Newton that he attached so little importance to his proof that, in spite of Halley's insistence, he was unable to lay his hands on it and had to reconstruct it from memory.

This carelessness is more significant than might appear. It shows that Newton's scale of values was not the same as ours. He devoted no more effort to his *Principia* than to two almost valueless works of mystic erudition, *The Chronology of Ancient Kingdoms amended* and *Observations upon the Prophecies of Daniel and the Apocalypse of St. John.* It also reveals that Newton, rather than provoke argument, preferred to let his memoranda sleep forgotten at the bottom of a drawer.

This great genius was, in fact, excessively touchy. Any expression of doubt regarding one of his results put him in a state of fury. History tells us of his quarrels with poor Flamsteed and we recall his unending polemic against Leibniz, against whom Newton continued to inveigh even after his adversary's death.

Sir Harold Spencer-Jones, a man we cannot suspect of

prejudice, has said of Newton: 'He was a bachelor, of retiring disposition, devoid of tact, unskilled in affairs and in the handling of men.'[5] It is difficult to believe that this description is entirely accurate, however, since he was highly successful as master of the Mint and left a pretty fortune to his heirs. As to his awkward character, it was undoubtedly of a purely pathological nature, since for two years Newton suffered from nervous depression bordering on madness.

But what does all this matter? Does its author's unsociable character prevent the law of gravity from being one of the loftiest conquests of human intelligence? And no matter how acrid his relations with his fellow men may have been, does not Newton deserve to be ranked with Einstein as the greatest scientific genius mankind has produced?

For this is our first opportunity of examining a being out of the common run, an unadulterated scientific genius—not a cool, clear, balanced brain like Galileo and Descartes, but a spirit resembling Kepler, fanciful, given to mysticism, fundamentally religious and lit by brilliant flashes of inspiration.

Although Newton showed himself, in optics, an experimenter without peer, although he displayed, in his *Principia,* inflexible logic, although he rejected the use of hypothesis, even the most legitimate—the type of hypothesis whose utility was later demonstrated by Poincaré—it would be wrong to see in him an example of the modern rationalistic scientist. 'Newton was not the first scientist of the age of reason,' writes Lord Keynes. 'He was the last of the magicians, the last of the Babylonians and Sumerians, the last great mind who looked out on the visible and intellectual world with the same eyes as those who began to build our intellectual inheritance rather less than 10,000 years ago.'[6] In short he was a man of highly unusual type, whose three great discoveries were made almost simultaneously, as though at the touch of a wand.

This takes us back to the year 1665, when a great outbreak of the plague compelled Cambridge University to close down. Newton, who had just passed his first degrees there, returned to his father's house at Woolsthorpe.[7] Here—but let us rather quote Newton himself:

'In the beginning of the year 1665 I found the method of approximating series and the Rule for reducing any dignity of any Binomial[8] into such a series. The same year in May I found the method of tangents of Gregory and Slusius, and in November had the direct method of Fluxions,[9] and the next year in January had the Theory of Colours, and in May following I had entrance into the inverse method of Fluxions.[10] And the same year I began to think of gravity extending to the orb of the Moon. . . .'

How Newton discovered universal gravitation

Thus these three months of concentrated meditation had been enough for Newton to evolve the theory of light and infinitesimal calculus and to discover universal gravitation. We can picture this young man of twenty-four roaming the countryside, immersed in thought, observing nature and applying to familiar things an incredibly acute analytical mind. We can imagine him sitting down one moonlit evening to dream beneath an apple-tree.[11] An apple detached itself and fell. Why did it fall? Why did the Moon, up there in the sky, not fall too? His Cambridge professor would have considered this question naïve—how could you compare the Moon to an apple? Was not the latter subject to weight, according to the laws of the fall of bodies and Galilean mechanics? And the former to an unknown force that kept it suspended above the Earth while it obeyed Kepler's laws?

The best proof that these two kinds of mechanics had nothing in common lay in the fact that Galileo's was governed by the principle of inertia, which did not seem to apply to Kepler's at all. Had it applied, the Moon would have travelled away in a straight line, instead of revolving around the Earth. . . .

Why, then, did the Moon not comply with this principle? What force held it to our globe? Was it not weight, whose centripetal action thus counterbalanced the planet's centrifugal tendency?

But was weight, which diminishes in proportion to the distance above the ground, still operative at the distance of the Moon? Newton knew this distance—60 terrestrial radii. At the surface of the Earth, that is to say at the distance of one radius, a falling body travels sixteen feet in the first second of its fall. If, as Newton suspected, the force of weight varies in inverse ratio to the square of the distance, the Moon, at a distance of 60 terrestrial radii ought to 'fall' 60 X 60 times less fast. That is to say it ought to fall only 0·00444 foot per second. Did the Moon really 'fall' at this rate?

This was easy to verify. The orbit followed by our satellite has a length of 2π X 60 terrestrial radii, and as its revolution takes 27 days 7 hours 43 minutes—i.e. 2,360,580 seconds—its speed comes to 0·0001597 of a terrestrial radius per second, and the distance it 'falls' in this time to 0·0000000021 of a terrestrial radius. Did this value agree with the figure of 0·00444 of a foot found above? For this we must know the number of feet in a terrestrial diameter. Now, at this period the value of the terrestrial radius was not yet known with much accuracy. The figure used by Newton was 18,437,000 feet (instead of the true figure of 21,120,000 feet). The true amount the Moon 'fell' in a second was therefore 0·00389 foot, which did not agree at all with the theoretical figure of 0·00444 foot.

When the young Newton found himself with this discrepancy at the end of his calculation he was undismayed. He was quite sure his intuition was correct. But he was less certain of his data, and particularly of the doubtful figure he had taken for the radius of the Earth. There was also a weak point in his reasoning: he had reckoned the distance from the Earth to the Moon from the centre of the Earth. This meant supposing that the force which kept the Moon revolving around our globe was situated at the very centre of the latter; in other words, that the attraction exercised by the Earth upon the Moon was the same as if the whole mass of the terrestrial sphere were concentrated at its centre. How could this be proved? While waiting to find some proof, Newton busied himself with other matters, with optics for example.

Not until sixteen years later, during the course of a meeting of the Royal Society, did he hear of the work executed by a French scientist, Abbé Jean Picard, who, in 1669-70, measured a meridian arc between Paris and Amiens. This measurement, obtained by the stringent method of geodetic triangulation, gave him 57,060 *toises* to one degree, say 3,269,297 *toises* for the radius of the Earth, or 21,250,430 feet. Newton quickly introduced this new figure into his old sum and discovered with profound emotion that it now worked out at his theoretical figure of 0·00444 foot, which, according to him, the Moon must 'fall' every second.

There remained the task of proving that the attraction exercised by a spherical mass is the same as though it were concentrated in the centre. He did not succeed in proving this until 1685, after Halley had been urging him for several months to communicate his discovery to the Royal Society. But to make his work known, to publish it, meant exposing himself to criticism and inviting discussion, something of which Newton had a horror. We must admire the devotion and generosity of Halley, a great-hearted man as well as a great scientist: having overcome his friend's objections he personally financed the printing of Newton's book, because the Royal Society had put all its capital into the publication of a *History of the Fishes*.

Newton's book, entitled *Philosophiae Naturalis Principia Mathematica,* 'Mathematical Principles of Natural Science', was published in July 1687. It has been termed the loftiest production of the human mind. There is no point in speculating on the justice of this assessment or in trying to decide what position Newton occupies in the history of science—in particular, whether he should be placed before or after Einstein. His claim to our admiration is unchallenged. No one has ever disputed the inscription engraved on the statue at

Trinity College, Cambridge: 'Who surpassed the human race by the power of his thought' (Lucretius).

This unanimous esteem is explained by the fact that his *Principia* constitutes a veritable key to the universe. Whereas the greatest astronomers—Aristarchus, Hipparchus, Ptolemy, Tycho Brahe, Kepler, Galileo—had merely accumulated data and formulated incomplete theories, Newton constructed a harmonious and logical synthesis. He showed that the mover of the universe was attraction, and from this starting-point he reconsidered and explained all the facts gathered together by observation over a period of two thousand years.

Attempts have been made to find forerunners to the discoverer of this fundamental law, from Anaxagoras, Plato and Aristotle to the Italian Borelli, the Frenchman Boulliaud and above all Hooke. It is true that the idea of an attraction varying in inverse ratio to the square of the distance had been 'in the air' ever since Kepler. But a gulf separates intuition from proof, and Newton stood in about the same relation to these pioneers as the engineer who realizes a project stands to the layman who puts forward an idea in the well-known form 'all you have to do is so and so'.

In his book, the author of the *Principia* began by creating mechanics, or, more accurately, dynamics. He based it on three axioms: the law of inertia, already propounded by Galileo; the law that the rate of change of the momentum of a body measures in direction and magnitude the force acting upon it, generalized as $F = mg$ and also adumbrated by the great Florentine; and, finally, the law that to every action there is an equal and opposite reaction.

Applying Kepler's laws in the light of these three principles, Newton arrived at the law of universal attraction. He showed that the force which kept the Moon revolving round the Earth and the planets round the Sun was none other than gravity, that is to say an attraction proportional to mass and to the inverse of the square of the distance. Under the action of this force, a material point necessarily describes a *conic* (ellipse, parabola or hyperbola). Armed with this law of gravitation, Newton cast increasingly bright light on the most controversial problems, illuminating the abysses before which human intelligence had previously recoiled in terror.

The satellites of Jupiter and Saturn docilely obeyed the Newtonian principle; the rapid rotation of the Jovian globe accounted for its flattening, so clearly visible through the telescope; that the Earth was likewise flattened then appeared as a deduction from the laws of the pendulum; and in the Earth's equatorial ridge, upon which the Moon exercises a particular attraction, Newton discerned the cause of the precession of the equi-noxes,' which had been known but remained unexplained for 1,800 years. By means of the gravitational pull of the planets on their satellites and of the Sun on the planets, it became possible to calculate the mass of these heavenly bodies and so trace to their source the inequalities in the motion of the Moon. Even comets, whose behaviour had formerly seemed so erratic, were now seen to be governed by the strict rule of universal attraction. The comet of 1680 arrived just in time for Newton to try his power over it. He determined its parabolic orbit and showed that such objects could no more escape from the inflexible laws of the skies than the planets or any other heavenly body. He also cast light on every single aspect of the tides. He found their cause in the attraction of the Moon and, partially, of the Sun, upon the section of the ocean closest to our satellite. He even succeeded in calculating the Moon's mass by studying spring tides and neap tides.

In short, reading the *Principia* was rather like seeing the solar system, hitherto a dark agglomeration of undisciplined bodies round which blew the eerie winds of astrology, suddenly lit up, the planets bending to inviolable laws and the mystery vanishing like an insubstantial shadow before the irresistible advance of scientific knowledge.

The heavenly bodies subject to scientific law

From a distance of nearly three hundred years and living in an age when wonders of science surround us on every side, it is difficult for us to appreciate the resolution with which Newton must have dedicated his faculties to the task of erecting, storey by storey, his brilliant synthesis. His aim was to make an ordered universe, governed by a single law, out of what had been a chaos of unproductive observations and bewildering theories. He achieved it by means of perpetual concentration, his mind soaring, as it were, above his body and forcing him to ignore the most ordinary needs of everyday life. After rising in the morning, he was liable to sit for hours motionless on the edge of his bed sunk in contemplation. One day a friend of the family, Dr. William Stukeley, came to dinner. On a table a chicken awaited the beginning of the meal. Newton was nowhere to be seen. Tired of waiting and ravenously hungry, Stukeley succumbed to temptation and ate the chicken. When his host finally appeared and sat down in front of the dish, on which there was nothing left but the bones, he declared with only a hint of surprise: 'Well, well, I thought I hadn't dined, but I see I was wrong!'

Publication of the *Principia* was the zenith of this exceptional career. In 1704 he published a volume on *Optics*, but after 1687 he was already one of the glories of Britain, a celebrity who was visited with respect and curiosity and whom the King had rewarded with the post of master of the Mint. Physically, he is described by Fontenelle as 'a man of medium height, somewhat stout during his latter years, with extremely lively and piercing eyes and a face that was both pleasant and venerable, especially when he removed his wig and revealed his pure white, thick and bushy hair. He never used spectacles and lost only one tooth during the whole of his life.'

He died on 20 March, 1727, and received the highest posthumous honours. 'The pall-bearers were the Lord Chancellor,' writes Fontenelle, 'the Dukes of Montrose and Roxborough, and the Earls of Pembroke, Sussex and Macclesfield.' Westminster Abbey, the sepulchre of the heroes of English history, was the last resting-place of the man who wrote: 'I do not know what I may appear to the world, but to myself I seem to have been only like a boy, playing on the sea-shore, and diverting myself, in now and then finding a smoother pebble or a prettier shell than ordinary, whilst the great ocean of truth lay all undiscovered before me.'

The diffusion of Newton's theories through the scientific world covered a period corresponding to the reign of James II in England and Louis XIV in France. On both sides of the Channel could be seen preludes to the coming industrial revolution—increase in manufactured goods, development of hydraulic power, expansion of trade, and strenuous commercial competition that quickly degenerated into open warfare between the two most important powers in the world.

It was naturally in Britain that the *Principia* had their initial impact, first in Edinburgh, then in Cambridge. The first edition, written in Latin, was out of print by 1691. Two more were printed between then and 1726, when the first English translation was issued. The Continent was much more difficult to conquer. It took its line from France, where Cartesianism reigned simultaneously with the Sun King. Fontenelle, Cassini, Réaumur, Huygens and Leibniz were horrified that anyone should dare to substitute for the rationalistic system of Descartes, who subjected even living beings to the mechanistic yoke, the Newtonian hypothesis of attraction, which they held—through a mental aberration that now seems to us astonishing—to be an occult and unscientific affair. Maupertuis wrote in 1731: 'It took more than half a century to win the academies over to the theory of attraction. It remained shut up within its island, or, if it did cross the sea, it was looked upon as merely the creation of a monster that had only recently been proscribed. People so congratulated themselves on having banished occult qualities from philosophy, they were so afraid that they might find their way in again, that anything which was believed to bear the slightest resemblance to them struck terror.'

Two years later Voltaire gave a witty description of the difference of outlook between the British Isles and the Continent:

A Frenchman arriving in London finds things very much changed, in philosophy as in everything else. He has left the world full, he finds it empty. In Paris we see the universe as composed of vortices of tenuous matter; in London they see none of that. With us, it is the pressure of the Moon that causes the flow of the sea; among the English, it is the sea which gravitates towards the Moon, so that when you believe the Moon ought to give us high tide, these gentlemen believe there ought to be low tide. . . . You will note, too, that the Sun, which in France has nothing to do with the matter, here contributes a quarter of the effect. . . . Among your Cartesians, everything is the result of a repulsion which is scarcely understood; with Mr. Newton it springs from an attraction, the cause of which is no better known. In Paris, you picture the Earth as shaped like a melon; in London, it is flat on two sides. Light, to a Cartesian, exists in the air; to a Newtonian, it comes from the Sun in six and a half minutes. Your chemistry operates entirely with acids, alkalis and tenuous matter: in Britain, even chemistry is dominated by the theory of attraction.[12]

But we know how the fiery polemicist took advantage of this opportunity to 'shake accepted ideas', as M. Cox puts it, and give the advocates of outworn traditions another piece of his mind. The most curious fact is that Voltaire's initiation in the Newtonian doctrine and its propagation were the work, before Maupertuis, of a woman, the Marquise Gabrielle-Emilie du Châtelet (1706-49). With her knowledge of Latin, Italian, English, Spanish and Flemish, and especially of mathematics, she was certainly of a very different stamp from the blue-stockings so cruelly castigated by Molière two-thirds of a century earlier.

We need not be too surprised to see a woman, whose position in the world might have brought her less austere successes, devoting herself to what is generally thought to be a rather forbidding science. We must recall that it was good form for 'persons of quality' to discuss scientific discoveries. Remember that Fontenelle chose a marquise to act as his interlocutor in his *Entretiens sur la Pluralité des Mondes* (1686). Moreover, even without going as far back as the unfortunate Hypatia of Alexandria, Voltaire's seductive friend had predecessors—the wife of Regiomontanus, who acted as his assistant, the Duchess of Ferrara, Renée of France (1510-75), Sophie Brahe (1556-1643), who collaborated with her illustrious brother, the learned German woman Maria Cunitz (1610-64), the author of astronomical tables that were easier to use than Kepler's, and a certain Jeanne Dumée, a manuscript by whom on Copernicus's theory is said to be housed in the French National Library, Paris.

Though retarded by the obstinacy of the Cartesians, Newton's triumph was all the greater when it came. And it was France that staged its grand finale, thanks to the most brilliant constellation of mathematicians the world has ever seen, from Clairaut to Laplace. It was France that turned the solar system into a battlefield upon which science has gained splendid victories.

Notes

[1] The loxodromic curve is one which cuts all the meridians at the same angle. It is much used in navigation.

[2] 'There is no course so impetuous that divine omnipotence cannot check it when it wishes; consider the Sun, with what impetuosity it travels across the vast arena opened up to it by Providence! Yet you are not unaware that God fixed it in olden times in the centre of the sky merely at the word of a man.' (Quoted by Joseph Bertrand, *Les Fondateurs de l'Astronomie moderne,* Paris, 1865).

[3] We know that the *weight* of a body (measured on the dynameter) is the product of its *mass* (measured on the scales) multiplied by gravity (9·81 m/s), which is expressed in the well-known equation: $F = mg$.

[4] Nowadays this law is expressed as $e = \frac{1}{2} gt^2$.

[5] *Ciel et Terre,* April-June 1947, p. 80.

[6] *Newton Tercentenary Celebrations* (Cambridge University Press, 1947).

[7] 'The house in which he was born is practically unchanged and is still owned by the family to which it was sold in Newton's lifetime.' (P. Doig, *op. cit.*).

[8] Newton's binomial, of course.

[9] Differential calculus.

[10] Integral calculus.

[11] Newton's apple-tree died in 1814, but grafts had been taken, so that it was possible to plant its shoots in various parts of the world. In 1954, one of them was planted in Newton's Garden at Trinity College, Cambridge.

[12] Quoted by J. F. Cox, 'Hommage à la marquise du Châtelet', in *Ciel et Terre,* January-February 1950.

Arthur Koestler (essay date 1959)

SOURCE: "Kepler and Galileo," in *The Sleepwalkers: A History of Man's Changing Vision of the Universe,* The Macmillan Company, 1959, pp. 352-78.

[*In the following excerpt, Koestler gives a frank and detailed account of Galileo's life and work, attempting to separate fact from legend. He gives particular attention to Galileo's professional relationship with Kepler and his struggle with the authorities of the Roman Catholic Church.*]

1. *A Digression on Mythography*

It was indeed a new departure. The range and power of the main sense organ of *homo sapiens* had suddenly started to grow in leaps to thirty times, a hundred times, a thousand times its natural capacity. Parallel leaps and bounds in the range of other organs were soon to transform the species into a race of giants in power—without enlarging his moral stature by an inch. It was a monstrously one-sided mutation—as if moles were growing to the size of whales, but retaining the instincts of moles. The makers of the scientific revolution were individuals who in this transformation of the race played the part of the mutating genes. Such genes are *ipso facto* unbalanced and unstable. The personalities of these "mutants" already foreshadowed the discrepancy in the next development of man: the intellectual giants of the scientific revolution were moral dwarfs.

They were, of course, neither better nor worse than the average of their contemporaries. They were moral dwarfs only in proportion to their intellectual greatness. It may be thought unfair to judge a man's character by the standard of his intellectual achievements, but the great civilizations of the past did precisely this; the divorce of moral from intellectual values is itself a characteristic development of the last few centuries. It is foreshadowed in the philosophy of Galileo, and became fully explicit in the ethical neutrality of modern determinism. The indulgence with which historians of science treat the Founding Fathers is based on precisely that tradition which the Fathers introduced—the tradition of keeping intellect and character as strictly apart as Galileo taught us to separate the "primary" and "secondary" qualities of objects. Thus moral assessments are thought to be essential in the case of Cromwell or Danton, but irrelevant in the case of Galileo, Descartes or Newton. However, the scientific revolution produced not only discoveries, but a new attitude to life, a change in the philosophical climate. And on that new climate, the personalities and beliefs of those who initiated it had a lasting influence. The most pronounced of these influences, in their different fields, were Galileo's and Descartes'.

The personality of Galileo, as it emerges from works of popular science, has even less relation to historic fact than Canon Koppernigk's. In his particular case, however, this is not caused by a benevolent indifference towards the individual as distinct from his achievement, but by more partisan motives. In works with a theological bias, he appears as the nigger in the woodpile; in rationalist mythography, as the Maid of Orleans of Science, the St. George who slew the dragon of the Inquisition. It is, therefore, hardly surprising that the fame of this outstanding genius rests mostly on discoveries he never made, and on feats he never performed. Contrary to statements in even recent outlines of science, Galileo did not invent the telescope; nor the microscope; nor the thermometer; nor the pendulum clock. He did not discover the law of inertia; nor the parallelogram of forces or motions; nor the sun spots. He made no contribution to theoretical astronomy; he did not throw down weights from the leaning tower of Pisa, and did not prove the truth of the Copernican system. He was not tortured by the Inquisition, did not languish in its dungeons, did not say *"eppur si muove";* and he was not a martyr of science.

What he *did* was to found the modern science of dynamics, which makes him rank among the men who shaped human destiny. It provided the indispensable complement to Kepler's laws for Newton's universe: "If I have been able to see farther," Newton said, "it was because I stood on the shoulders of giants." The giants were, chiefly, Kepler, Galileo and Descartes.

2. *Youth of Galileo*

Galileo Galilei was born in 1564 and died in 1642, the year Newton was born. His father, Vincento Galilei, was an impoverished scion of the lower nobility, a man of remarkable culture, with considerable achievements as a composer and writer on music, a contempt for authority, and radical leanings. He wrote, for instance (in a study on counter-point): "It appears to me that those who try to prove an assertion by relying simply on the weight of authority act very absurdly."[1]

One feels at once the contrast in climate between the childhoods of Galileo and our previous heroes. Copernicus, Tycho, Kepler, never completely severed the navel-cord which had fed into them the rich, mystic sap of the Middle Ages. Galileo is a second-generation intellectual, a second-generation rebel against authority; in a nineteenth century setting, he would have been the Socialist son of a Liberal father.

His early portraits show a ginger-haired, short-necked, beefy young man of rather coarse features, a thick nose and conceited stare. He went to the excellent Jesuit school at the Monastery of Vallombrosa, near Florence; but Galileo senior wanted him to become a merchant (which was by no means considered degrading for a patrician in Tuscany) and brought the boy home to Pisa; then, in recognition of his obvious gifts, changed his mind and at seventeen sent him to the local university to study medicine. But Vincento had five children to look after (a younger son, Michelangelo, plus three daughters), and the University fees were high; so he

tried to obtain a scholarship for Galileo. Although there were no less than forty scholarships for poor students available in Pisa, Galileo failed to obtain one, and was compelled to leave the University without a degree. This is the more surprising as he had already given unmistakable proof of his brilliance: in 1582, in his second year at the University, he discovered the fact that a pendulum of a given length swings at a constant frequency, regardless of amplitude.[2] His invention of the "pulsilogium", a kind of metronome for timing the pulse of patients, was probably made at the same time. In view of this and other proofs of the young student's mechanical genius, his early biographers explained the refusal of a scholarship by the animosity which his unorthodox anti-Aristotelian views raised. In fact, however, Galileo's early views on physics contain nothing of a revolutionary nature.[3] It is more likely that the refusal of the scholarship was due not to the unpopularity of Galileo's views, but of his person—that cold, sarcastic presumption, by which he managed to spoil his case throughout his life.

Back home he continued his studies, mostly in applied mechanics, which attracted him more and more, perfecting his dexterity in making mechanical instruments and gadgets. He invented a hydrostatic balance, wrote a treatise on it which he circulated in manuscript, and began to attract the attention of scholars. Among these was the Marchese Guidobaldo del Monte who recommended Galileo to his brother-in-law, Cardinal del Monte, who in turn recommended him to Ferdinand de Medici, the ruling Duke of Tuscany; as a result, Galileo was appointed a lecturer in mathematics at the University of Pisa, four years after that same University had refused him a scholarship. Thus at the age of twenty-five, he was launched on his academic career. Three years later, in 1592, he was appointed to the vacant Chair of Mathematics at the famous University of Padua, again through the intervention of his patron, del Monte.

Galileo remained in Padua for eighteen years, the most creative and fertile years of his life. It was here that he laid the foundations of modern dynamics, the science concerned with moving bodies. But the results of these researches he only published towards the end of his life. Up to the age of forty-six, when the *Messenger from the Stars* was sent into the world, Galileo had published no scientific work.[4] His growing reputation in this period, before his discoveries through the telescope, rested partly on treatises and lectures circulated in manuscript, partly on his mechanical inventions (among them the thermoscope, a forerunner of the thermometer), and the instruments which he manufactured in large numbers with skilled artisans in his own workshop. But his truly great discoveries—such as the laws of motion of falling bodies and projectiles—and his ideas on cosmology he kept strictly for himself and for his private correspondents. Among these was Johannes Kepler.

3. *The Church and the Copernican System*

The first contact between the two Founding Fathers took place in 1597. Kepler was then twenty-six, a professor of mathematics in Gratz; Galileo was thirty-three, a professor of mathematics in Padua. Kepler had just completed his *Cosmic Mystery* and, profiting from a friend's journey to Italy, had sent copies of it, among others, "to a mathematician named Galileus Galileus, as he signs himself".[5]

Galileo acknowledged the gift in the following letter:

> Your book, my learned doctor, which you sent me through Paulus Amberger, I received not a few days but merely a few hours ago; since the same Paulus informed me of his impending return to Germany, I would be ungrateful indeed not to thank you at once: I accept your book the more gratefully as I regard it as proof of having been found worthy of your friendship. So far I have only perused the preface of your work, but from this I gained some notion of its intent [The preface (and first chapter) proclaim Kepler's belief in the Copernican system and outline his arguments in favour of it.], and I indeed congratulate myself on having an associate in the study of Truth who is a friend of Truth. For it is a misery that so few exist who pursue the Truth and do not pervert philosophical reason. However, this is not the place to deplore the miseries of our century but to congratulate you on the ingenious arguments you found in proof of the Truth. I will only add that I promise to read your book in tranquility, certain to find the most admirable things in it, and this I shall do the more gladly as I adopted the teaching of Copernicus many years ago, and his point of view enables me to explain many phenomena of nature which certainly remain inexplicable according to the more current hypotheses. I have written [*conscripsi*] many arguments in support of him and in refutation of the opposite view—which, however, so far I have not dared to bring into the public light, frightened by the fate of Copernicus himself, our teacher, who, though he acquired immortal fame with some, is yet to an infinite multitude of others (for such is the number of fools) an object of ridicule and derision. I would certainly dare to publish my reflections at once if more people like you existed; as they don't, I shall refrain from doing so.

There follow more polite affirmations of esteem, the signature "Galileus Galileus", and the date: 4 August, 1597.[6]

The letter is important for several reasons. Firstly, it provides conclusive evidence that Galileo had become a convinced Copernican in his early years. He was thirty-three when he wrote the letter; and the phrase "many years ago" indicates that his conversion took place in his twenties. Yet his first explicit public pro-nouncement in favour of the Copernican system was only made in 1613, a full sixteen years after his letter to Kepler, when Galileo was forty-nine years of age. Through all these years he not only taught, in his lectures, the old astronomy according to Ptolemy, but expressly repudiated Copernicus. In a treatise which he wrote for circulation among pupils and friends, of which a manuscript copy, dated 1606, survives,[6a] he adduced all the traditional arguments against the earth's motion: that rotation would make it disintegrate, that clouds would be left behind, etc., etc.—arguments which, if the letter is to be believed, he himself had refuted many years before.

But the letter is also interesting for other reasons. In a single breath, Galileo four times evokes Truth: friend of Truth, investigating Truth, pursuit of Truth, proof of Truth; then apparently without awareness of the paradox, he calmly announces his intention to suppress Truth. This may partly be explained by the *mores* of late Renaissance Italy ("that age without a superego" as a psychiatrist described it); but taking that into account, one still wonders at the motives of his secrecy.

Why, in contrast to Kepler, was he so afraid of publishing his opinions? He had, at that time, no more reason to fear religious persecution than Copernicus had. The Lutherans, not the Catholics, had been the first to attack the Copernican system—which prevented neither Rheticus nor Kepler from defending it in public. The Catholics, on the other hand, were uncommitted. In Copernicus' own day, they were favourably inclined towards him—it will be remembered how Cardinal Schoenberg and Bishop Giese had urged him to publish his book. Twenty years after its publication, the Council of Trent re-defined Church doctrine and policy in all its aspects, but it had nothing to say against the heliocentric system of the universe. Galileo himself, as we shall see, enjoyed the active support of a galaxy of Cardinals, including the future Urban VIII, and of the leading astronomers among the Jesuits. Up to the fateful year 1616, discussion of the Copernican system was not only permitted, but encouraged by them—under the one proviso, that it should be confined to the language of science, and should not impinge on theological matters. The situation was summed up clearly in a letter from Cardinal Dini to Galileo in 1615: "One may write freely as long as one keeps out of the sacristy."[7] This was precisely what the disputants failed to do, and it was at this point that the conflict began. But nobody could have foreseen these developments twenty years earlier, when Galileo wrote to Kepler.

Thus legend and hindsight combined to distort the picture, and gave rise to the erroneous belief that to defend the Copernican system as a working hypothesis entailed the risk of ecclesiastical disfavour or persecution. During the first fifty years of Galileo's lifetime, no such risk existed; and the thought did not even occur to Galileo. What he feared is clearly stated in his letter: to share the fate of Copernicus, to be mocked and derided; *ridendus et explodendum*—"laughed at and hissed off the stage" are his exact words. Like Copernicus, he was afraid of the ridicule both of the unlearned and the learned asses, but particularly of the latter: his fellow professors at Pisa and Padua, the stuffed shirts of the peripatetic school, who still considered Aristotle and Ptolemy as absolute authority. And this fear, as will be seen, was fully justified.

4. *Early Quarrels*

Young Kepler was delighted with Galileo's letter. On the first occasion when a traveller left Gratz for Italy, he answered in his impulsive manner:

> Gratz, October 13, 1597.
>
> Your letter, my most excellent humanist, which you wrote on August 4, I received on September 1; it caused me to rejoice twice: first because it meant the beginning of a friendship with an Italian; secondly, because of our agreement on the Copernican cosmography. . . . I assume that if your time has permitted it, you have by now become better acquainted with my little book, and I ardently desire to know your critical opinion of it; for it is my nature to press all to whom I write for their unvarnished opinion; and believe me, I much prefer even the most acrimonious criticism of a single enlightened man to the unreasoned applause of the common crowd.
>
> I would have wished, however, that you, possessed of such an excellent mind, took up a different position. With your clever secretive manner you underline, by your example, the warning that one should retreat before the ignorance of the world, and should not lightly provoke the fury of the ignorant professors; in this respect you follow Plato and Pythagoras, our true teachers. But considering that in our era, at first Copernicus himself and after him a multitude of learned mathematicians have set this immense enterprise going so that the motion of the earth is no longer a novelty, it would be preferable that we help to push home by our common efforts this already moving carriage to its destination. . . . You could help your comrades, who labour under such iniquitous criticism, by giving them the comfort of your agreement and the protection of your authority. For not only your Italians refuse to believe that they are in motion because they do not feel it; here in Germany, too, one does not make oneself popular by holding such opinions. But there exist arguments which protect us in the face of these difficulties. . . . Have faith, Galilii, and come forward! If my guess is right, there are but few among the prominent mathematicians of Europe who would wish to secede from us: for such is the force of Truth. If your Italy seems less advantageous to you for

publishing [your works] and if your living there is an obstacle, perhaps our Germany will allow us to do so. But enough of this. Let me know, at least privately if you do not want to do it in public, what you have discovered in support of Copernicus. . . .

Kepler then confessed that he had no instruments, and asked Galileo whether he had a quadrant sufficiently precise to read quarter-minutes of arc; if so, would Galileo please make a series of observations to prove that the fixed stars show small seasonal displacements—which would provide direct proof of the earth's motion.

> Even if we could detect no displacement at all, we would nevertheless share the laurels of having investigated a most noble problem which nobody has attacked before us. *Sat Sapienti.* . . . Farewell, and answer me with a very long letter.[8]

Poor, naïve Kepler! It did not occur to him that Galileo might take offence at his exhortations, and regard them as an implied reproach of cowardice. He waited in vain for an answer to his exuberant overtures. Galileo withdrew his feelers; for the next twelve years, Kepler did not hear from him.

But from time to time unpleasant rumours reached him from Italy. Among Kepler's admirers was a certain Edmund Bruce, a sentimental English traveller in Italy, amateur philosopher and science snob, who loved to rub shoulders with scholars and to spread gossip about them. In August 1602, five years after Galileo had broken off their correspondence, Bruce wrote Kepler from Florence that Magini (the professor of astronomy at Bologna) had assured him of his love and admiration of Kepler, whereas Galileo had admitted to him, Bruce, having received Kepler's *Mysterium,* but had denied this to Magini.

> I scolded Galileo for his scant praise of you, for I know for certain that he lectures on your and his own discoveries to his pupils and others. I, however, act and shall always act in a manner which serves not his fame, but yours.[9]

Kepler could not be bothered to answer this busybody, but a year later—21 August, 1603—Bruce wrote again, this time from Padua:

> If you knew how often and how much I discuss you with all the savants of Italy you would consider me not only an admirer but a friend. I spoke with them of your admirable discoveries in music, of your studies of Mars, and explained to them your *Mysterium* which they all praise. They wait impatiently for your future works. . . . Galileo has your book and teaches your discoveries as his own. . . . [10]

This time Kepler did answer. After apologizing for the delay and declaring himself delighted with Bruce's friendship, he continued:

> But there is something about which I wish to warn you. Do not form a higher opinion of me, and do not induce others to do so, than my achievements are able to justify. . . . For you certainly understand that betrayed expectations lead eventually to contempt. I wish in no way to restrain Galileo from claiming, what is mine, as his own. My witnesses are the bright daylight and time.[11]

The letter ends with "Greetings to Magini and Galileo".

Bruce's accusations should not be taken seriously. In fact, the opposite is true: the trouble with Galileo was not that he appropriated Kepler's discoveries—but that he ignored them, as we shall see. But the episode nevertheless sheds some additional light on the relations between the two men. Though Bruce cannot be trusted on points of fact, the inimical attitude of Galileo to Kepler emerges clearly from Bruce's letters. It fits in with the fact that he broke off the correspondence, and with later events.

Kepler, on the other hand, who had good reason to be offended by Galileo's silence, could easily have been provoked by Bruce's scandal-mongering into starting one of those juicy quarrels between scholars which were the order of the day. He was suspicious and excitable enough, as his relations with Tycho have shown. But towards Galileo he always behaved in an oddly generous way. It is true that they lived in different countries and never met personally; but hatred, like gravity, is capable of action at a distance. The reason for Kepler's forbearingness was perhaps that he had no occasion to develop an inferiority complex towards Galileo.

The year after the Bruce episode, in October 1604, a bright new star appeared in the constellation Serpentarius. It caused even more excitement than Tycho's famous *nova* of 1572, because its appearance happened to coincide with a so-called great conjunction of Jupiter, Saturn and Mars in the "fiery triangle"—a gala performance that occurs only once in every eight hundred years. Kepler's book *De Stella Nova* (1606) was primarily concerned with its astrological significance; but he showed that the *nova,* like the previous one, must be located in the "immutable" region of the fixed stars, and thus drove another nail into the coffin of the Aristotelian universe. The star of 1604 is still called "Kepler's *nova*" [John Donne referred to Kepler's *nova* when he wrote (*To the Countesse of Huntingdon*): Who vagrant transitory Comets sees, [/] Wonders, because they are rare: but a new

starre [/] Whose motion with the firmament agrees, [/] Is miracle, for there no new things are].

Galileo, too, observed the new star, but published nothing about it. He gave three lectures on the subject, of which only fragments are preserved; he, too, seems to have denied the contention of the Aristotelians that it was a meteor or some other sublunary phenomenon, but could not have gone much further, since his lectures in defence of Ptolemy were still circulated two years later.[12]

Between 1600 and 1610, Kepler published his *Optics* (1604), the *New Astronomy* (1609) and a number of minor works. In the same period, Galileo worked on his fundamental researches into free fall, the motion of projectiles, and the laws of the pendulum, but published nothing except a brochure containing instructions for the use of the so-called military or proportional compass. This was an invention made in Germany some fifty years earlier,[13] which Galileo had improved, as he improved a number of other gadgets that had been known for a long time. Out of this minor publication[14] developed the first of the futile and pernicious feuds which Galileo was to wage all his life.

It began when a mathematician named Balthasar Capra in Padua published, a year after Galileo, another brochure of instructions for the use of the proportional compass.[15] Galileo's *Instructions* were in Italian, Capra's in Latin; both referred to the same subject, which interested only military engineers and technicians. It is very likely that Capra had borrowed from Galileo's *Instructions* without naming him; on the other hand, Capra showed that some of Galileo's explanations were mathematically erroneous, but again without naming him. Galileo's fury knew no bounds. He published a pamphlet *Against the Calumnies and Impostures of Balthasar Capra, etc.* (Venice 1607), in which that unfortunate man and his teacher[16] were described as "that malevolent enemy of honour and of the whole of mankind", "a venom-spitting basilisque", "an educator who bred the young fruit on his poisoned soul with stinking ordure", "a greedy vulture, swooping at the unborn young to tear its tender limbs to pieces", and so on. He also obtained from the Venetian Court the confiscation, on the grounds of plagiarism, of Capra's *Instructions.* Not even Tycho and Ursus had sunk to such fish-wife language; yet they had fought for the authorship of a system of the universe, not of a gadget for military engineers.

In his later polemical writings, Galileo's style progressed from coarse invective to satire, which was sometimes cheap, often subtle, always effective. He changed from the cudgel to the rapier, and achieved a rare mastery of it; while in the purely expository passages his lucidity earned him a prominent place in the development of Italian didactic prose. But behind the polished façade, the same passions were at work which had exploded in the affair of the proportional compass: vanity, jealousy and self-righteousness combined into a demoniac force, which drove him to the brink of self-destuction. He was utterly devoid of any mystical, contemplative leanings, in which the bitter passions could from time to time be resolved; he was unable to transcend himself and find refuge, as Kepler did in his darkest hours, in the cosmic mystery. He did not stand astride the watershed; Galileo is wholly and frighteningly modern.

5. *The Impact of the Telescope*

It was the invention of the telescope which brought Kepler and Galileo, each travelling along his own orbit, to their closest conjunction. To pursue the metaphor, Kepler's orbit reminds one of the parabola of comets which appear from infinity and recede into it; Galileo's as an eccentric ellipse, closed upon itself.

The telescope was, as already mentioned, not invented by Galileo. In September 1608, a man at the annual Frankfurt fair offered a telescope for sale which had a convex and a concave lens, and magnified seven times. On 2 October, 1608, the spectacle-maker Johann Lippershey of Middleburg claimed a licence for thirty years from the Estates General of the Netherlands for manufacturing telescopes with single and double lenses. In the following month, he sold several of these, for three hundred and six hundred gilders respectively, but was not granted an exclusive licence because in the meantime two other men had claimed the same invention. Two of Lippershey's instruments were sent as a gift by the Dutch Government to the King of France; and in April 1609, telescopes could be bought in spectacle-makers' shops in Paris. In the summer of 1609, Thomas Harriot in England made telescopic observations of the moon and drew maps of the lunar surface. In the same year, several of the Dutch telescopes found their way to Italy and were copied there.

Galileo himself claimed in the *Messenger from the Stars* that he had merely read reports of the Dutch invention, and that these had stimulated him to construct an instrument on the same principle, which he succeeded in doing "through deep study of the theory of refraction". Whether he actually saw and handled one of the Dutch instruments brought to Italy is a question without importance, for once the principle was known, lesser minds than Galileo's could and did construct similar gadgets. On 8 August, 1609, he invited the Venetian Senate to examine his spy-glass from the tower of St. Marco, with spectacular success; three days later, he made a present of it to the Senate, accompanied by a letter in which he explained that the instrument, which magnified objects nine times, would prove of utmost importance in war. It made it possible to see "sails and shipping that were so far off that it was two hours

before they were seen with the naked eye, steering full-sail into the harbour",[17] thus being invaluable against invasion by sea. It was not the first and not the last time that pure research, that starved cur, snapped up a bone from the warlords' banquet.

The grateful Senate of Venice promptly doubled Galileo's salary to a thousand scudi per year, and made his professorship at Padua (which belonged to the Republic of Venice) a lifelong one. It did not take the local spectacle-makers long to produce telescopes of the same magnifying power, and to sell in the streets for a few scudi an article which Galileo had sold the Senate for a thousand a year—to the great amusement of all good Venetians. Galileo must have felt his reputation threatened, as in the affair of the military compass; but, fortunately, this time his passion was diverted into more creative channels. He began feverishly to improve his telescope, and to aim it at the moon and stars, which previously had attracted him but little. Within the next eight months he succeeded, in his own words: "by sparing neither labour nor expense, in constructing for myself an instrument so superior that objects seen through it appear magnified nearly a thousand times, and more than thirty times nearer than if viewed by the natural powers of sight alone."

The quotation is from *Sidereus Nuncius,* the *Messenger from the Stars,* published in Venice in March 1610. It was Galileo's first scientific publication, and it threw his telescopic discoveries like a bomb into the arena of the learned world. It not only contained news of heavenly bodies "which no mortal had seen before"; it was also written in a new, tersely factual style which no scholar had employed before. So new was this language that the sophisticated Imperial Ambassador in Venice described the *Star Messenger* as "a dry discourse or an inflated boast, devoid of all philosophy".[18] In contrast to Kepler's exuberant baroque style, some passages of the *Sidereus Nuncius* would almost qualify for the austere pages of a contemporary "Journal of Physics".

The whole booklet has only twenty-four leaves in octavo. After the introductory passages, Galileo described his observations of the moon, which led him to conclude:

> that the surface of the moon is not perfectly smooth, free from inequalities and exactly spherical, as a large school of philosophers considers with regard to the moon and the other heavenly bodies, but that, on the contrary, it is full of irregularities, uneven, full of hollows and protuberances, just like the surface of the earth itself, which is varied everywhere by lofty mountains and deep valleys.

He then turned to the fixed stars, and described how the telescope added, to the moderate numbers that can be seen by the naked eye, "other stars, in myriads, which have never been seen before, and which surpass the old, previously known stars in number more than ten times." Thus, for instance, to the nine stars in the belt and sword of Orion he was able to add eighty others which he discovered in their vicinity; and to the seven in the Pleiades, another thirty-six. The Milky Way dissolved before the telescope into "a mass of innumerable stars planted together in clusters"; and the same happened when one looked at the luminous nebulae.

But the principal sensation he left to the end:

> There remains the matter which seems to me to deserve to be considered the most important in this work, namely, that I should disclose and publish to the world the occasion of discovering and observing four planets, never seen from the very beginning of the world up to our own times.

The four new planets were the four moons of Jupiter, and the reason why Galileo attributed to their discovery such capital importance he explained in a somewhat veiled aside:

> Moreover, we have an excellent and exceedingly clear argument to put at rest the scruples of those who can tolerate the revolution of the planets about the sun in the Copernican system, but are so disturbed by the revolution of the single moon around the earth while both of them describe an annual orbit round the sun, that they consider this theory of the universe to be impossible.

In other words, Galileo thought the main argument of the anti-Copernicans to be the impossibility of the moon's composite motion around the earth, and with the earth around the sun; and further believed that this argument would be invalidated by the composite motion of the four Jupiter moons. It was the only reference to Copernicus in the whole booklet, and it contained no explicit commitment. Moreover, it ignored the fact that in the Tychonic system *all* the planets describe a composite motion around the sun and with the sun around the earth; and that even in the more limited "Egyptian" system at least the two inner planets do this.

Thus Galileo's observations with the telescope produced no important arguments in favour of Copernicus, nor any clear committal on his part. Besides, the discoveries announced in the *Star Messenger* were not quite as original as they pretended to be. He was neither the first, nor the only scientist, who had turned a telescope at the sky and discovered new wonders with it. Thomas Harriot made systematic telescopic observations and maps of the moon in the summer of 1609, before Galileo, but he did not publish them. Even the Emperor Rudolph had watched the moon through a telescope before the he had heard of Galileo. Galileo's star maps were so inaccurate that the Pleiades group can only be identified on them with difficulty, the Orion

group not at all; and the huge dark spot under the moon's equator, surrounded by mountains, which Galileo compared to Bohemia, simply does not exist.

Yet when all this is said, and all the holes are picked in Galileo's first published text, its impact and significance still remain tremendous. Others had seen what Galileo saw, and even his priority in the discovery of the Jupiter moons is not established beyond doubt[18a]; yet he was the first to publish what he saw, and to describe it in a language which made everybody sit up. It was the cumulative effect which made the impact; the vast philosophical implications of this further prizing-open of the universe were instinctively felt by the reader, even if they were not explicitly stated. The mountains and valleys of the moon confirmed the similarity between heavenly and earthly matter, the homogeneous nature of the stuff from which the universe is built. The unsuspected number of invisible stars made an absurdity of the notion that they were created for man's pleasure, since he could only see them armed with a machine. The Jupiter moons did not prove that Copernicus was right, but they did further shake the antique belief that the earth was the centre of the world around which everything turned. It was not this or that particular detail, but the total contents of the *Messenger from the Stars* which created the dramatic effect.

The booklet aroused immediate and passionate controversy. It is curious to note that Copernicus' *Book of Revolutions* had created little stir for half a century, and Kepler's Laws even less at their time, while the *Star Messenger,* which had only an indirect bearing on the issue, caused such an outburst of emotions. The main reason was, no doubt, its immense readability. To digest Kepler's *magnum opus* required, as one of his colleagues remarked, "nearly a lifetime"; but the *Star Messenger* could be read in an hour, and its effect was like a punch in the solar plexus on those grown up in the traditional view of the bounded universe. And that vision, though a bit shaky, still retained an immense, reassuring coherence. Even Kepler was frightened by the wild perspective opened up by Galileo's spyglass: "The infinite is unthinkable," he repeatedly exclaimed in anguish.

The shock-waves of Galileo's message spread immediately, as far as England. It was published in March 1610; Donne's *Ignatius* was published barely ten months later,[19] but Galileo (and Kepler) are repeatedly mentioned in it:

> I will write [quoth Lucifer] to the Bishop of
>> Rome:
> He shall call Galileo the Florentine to him ...

But soon, the satirical approach yielded to the metaphysical, to a full realization of the new cosmic perspective:

Man has weav'd out a net, and this net
throwne
Upon the Heavens, and now they are his
owne . . .

Milton was still an infant in 1610; he grew up with the new wonders. His awareness of the "vast unbounded Deep" which the telescope disclosed, reflects the end of the medieval walled universe:

Before [his] eyes in sudden view appear
The secrets of the hoary Deep—a dark
Illimitable ocean, without bound,
Without dimension . . . [20]

6. *The Battle of the Satellites*

Such was the objective impact on the world at large of Galileo's discoveries with his "optick tube". But to understand the reactions of the small, academic world in his own country, we must also take into account the subjective effect of Galileo's personality. Canon Koppernigk had been a kind of invisible man throughout his life; nobody who met the disarming Kepler, in the flesh or by correspondence, could seriously dislike him. But Galileo had a rare gift of provoking enmity; not the affection alternating with rage which Tycho aroused, but the cold, unrelenting hostility which genius plus arrogance minus humility creates among mediocrities.

Without this personal background, the controversy which followed the publication of the *Sidereus Nuncius* would remain incomprehensible. For the subject of the quarrel was not the *significance* of the Jupiter satellites, but their *existence*—which some of Italy's most illustrious scholars flatly denied. Galileo's main academic rival was Magini in Bologna. In the month following the publication of the *Star Messenger,* on the evenings of 24 and 25 April, 1610, a memorable party was held in a house in Bologna, where Galileo was invited to demonstrate the Jupiter moons in his spy-glass. Not one among the numerous and illustrious guests declared himself convinced of their existence. Father Clavius, the leading mathematician in Rome, equally failed to see them; Cremonini, teacher of philosophy at Padua, refused even to look into the telescope; so did his colleague Libri. The latter, incidentally, died soon afterwards, providing Galileo with an opportunity to make more enemies with the much quoted sarcasm: "Libri did not choose to see my celestial trifles while he was on earth; perhaps he will do so now he has gone to Heaven."

These men may have been partially blinded by passion and prejudice, but they were not quite as stupid as it may seem. Galileo's telescope was the best available, but it was still a clumsy instrument without fixed mountings, and with a visual field so small that, as some-body has said, "the marvel is not so much that he found Jupiter's moons, but that he was able to find Jupiter itself." The tube needed skill and experience in handling, which none of the others possessed. Sometimes, a fixed star appeared in duplicate. Moreover, Galileo himself was unable to explain why and how the thing worked; and the *Sidereus Nuncius* was conspicuously silent on this essential point. Thus it was not entirely unreasonable to suspect that the blurred dots which appeared to the strained and watering eye pressed to the spectacle-sized lens, might be optical illusions in the atmosphere, or somehow produced by the mysterious gadget itself. This, in fact, was asserted in a sensational pamphlet, *Refutation of the Star Messenger,*[20] published by Magini's assistant, a young fool called Martin Horky. The whole controversy about optical illusions, haloes, reflections from luminous clouds, and about the unreliability of testimonies, inevitably reminds one of a similar controversy three hundred years later: the flying saucers. Here, too, emotion and prejudice combined with technical difficulties against clear-cut conclusions. And here, too, it was not unreasonable for self-respecting scholars to refuse to look at the photographic "evidence" for fear of making fools of themselves. Similar considerations may be applied to the refusal of otherwise open-minded scholars to get involved in the ambiguous phenomena of occult seances. The Jupiter moons were no less threatening to the outlook on the world of sober scholars in 1610, than, say, extra-sensory perception was in 1950.

Thus, while the poets were celebrating Galileo's discoveries which had become the talk of the world, the scholars in his own country were, with very few exceptions, hostile or sceptical. The first, and for some time the only, scholarly voice raised in public in defence of Galileo, was Johannes Kepler's.

7. *The Shield Bearer*

It was also the weightiest voice, for Kepler's authority as the first astronomer of Europe was uncontested—not because of his two Laws, but by virtue of his position as Imperial Mathematicus and successor to Tycho. John Donne, who had a grudging admiration for him, has summed up Kepler's reputation "who (as himselfe testifies of himselfe) ever since Tycho Brahe's death hath received it into his care, that no new thing should be done in heaven without his knowledge."[21]

The first news of Galileo's discovery had reached Kepler when Wackher von Wackenfeld called on him on or around 15 March, 1610. The weeks that followed he spent in feverish expectation of more definite news. In the first days of April, the Emperor received a copy of the *Star Messenger* which had just been published in Venice, and Kepler was graciously permitted "to have a look and rapidly glance through it". On 8 April, at last, he received a copy of his own from Galileo, accompanied by a request for his opinion.

Galileo had never answered Kepler's fervent request for an opinion on the *Mysterium,* and had remained equally silent on the *New Astronomy.* Nor did he bother to put his own request for Kepler's opinion on the *Star Messenger* into a personal letter. It was transmitted to Kepler verbally by the Tuscan Ambassador in Prague, Julian de Medici. Although Kepler was not in a position to verify Galileo's disputed discoveries, for he had no telescope, he took Galileo's claims on trust. He did it enthusiastically and without hesitation, publicly offering to serve in the battle as Galileo's "squire" or "shield bearer"—he, the Imperial Mathematicus to the recently still unknown Italian scholar. It was one of the most generous gestures in the sour annals of science.

The courier for Italy was to leave on 19 April; in the eleven days at his disposal Kepler wrote his pamphlet *Conversation with the Star Messenger* in the form of an open letter to Galileo. It was printed the next month in Prague, and a pirated Italian translation appeared shortly afterwards in Florence.

It was precisely the support that Galileo needed at that moment. The weight of Kepler's authority played an important part in turning the tide of the battle in his favour, as shown by Galileo's correspondence. He was anxious to leave Padua and to be appointed Court Mathematician to Cosimo de Medici, Grand Duke of Tuscany, in whose honour he had called Jupiter's planets "the Medicean stars". In his application to Vinta, the Duke's Secretary of State, Kepler's support figures prominently:

> Your Excellency, and their Highnesses through you, should know that I have received a letter— or rather an eight-page treatise—from the Imperial Mathematician, written in approbation of every detail contained in my book without the slightest doubt or contradiction of anything. And you may believe that this is the way leading men of letters in Italy would have spoken from the beginning if I had been in Germany or somewhere far away.[22]

He wrote in almost identical terms to other correspondents, among them to Matteo Carosio in Paris:

> We were prepared for it that twenty-five people would wish to refute me; but up to this moment I have seen only one statement by Kepler, the Imperial Mathematician, which confirms everything that I have written, without rejecting even an iota of it; which statement is now being reprinted in Venice, and you shall soon see it.[23]

Yet, while Galileo boasted about Kepler's letter to the Grand Duke and his correspondents, he neither thanked Kepler nor even acknowledged it.

Apart from its strategical importance in the cosmological battle, the *Conversation with the Star Messenger* is without much scientific value; it reads like a baroque arabesque, a pattern of amusing doodles around the hard core of Galileo's treatise. It starts with Kepler voicing his hope that Galileo, whose opinion matters to him more than anybody's, would comment on the *Astronomia Nova,* and thereby renew a correspondence "laid aside twelve years ago". He relates with gusto how he had received the first news of the discoveries from Wackher—and how he had worried whether the Jupiter moons could be fitted into the universe built around the five Pythagorean solids. But as soon as he had cast a glance at the *Star Messenger,* he realized that "it offered a highly important and wonderful show to astronomers and philosophers, that it invited all friends of true philosophy to contemplate matters of the highest import. . . . Who could be silent in the face of such a message? Who would not feel himself overflow with the love of the Divine which is so abundantly manifested here?" Then comes his offer of support "in the battle against the grumpy reactionaries, who reject everything that is unknown as unbelievable, and regard everything that departs from the beaten track of Aristotle as a desecration. . . . Perhaps I shall be considered reckless because I accept your claims as true without being able to add my own observations. But how could I distrust a reliable mathematician whose art of language alone demonstrates the straightness of his judgement? . . ."

Kepler had instinctively felt the ring of truth in the *Star Messenger,* and that had settled the question for him. However much he may have resented Galileo's previous behaviour, he felt committed "to throw himself into the fray" for Truth, Copernicus and the Five Perfect Solids. For, having finished the Promethean labours of the *New Astronomy,* he was again steeped in the mystic twilight of a Pythagorean universe built around cube, tetrahedra, dodecahedra, and so on. They are the *leitmotif* of his dialogue with the *Star Messenger;* neither the elliptical orbits, neither the First nor the Second Law, are mentioned even once. Their discovery appeared to him merely as a tedious detour in the pursuit of his *idée fixe.*

It is a rambling treatise, written by a hurried pen which jumps from one subject to another: astrology, optics, the moon's spots, the nature of the ether, Copernicus, the habitability of other worlds, interplanetary travel:

> There will certainly be no lack of human pioneers when we have mastered the art of flight. Who would have thought that navigation across the vast ocean is less dangerous and quieter than in the narrow, threatening gulfs of the Adriatic, or the Baltic, or the British straits? Let us create vessels and sails adjusted to the heavenly ether, and there will be plenty of people unafraid of the empty wastes. In

the meantime, we shall prepare, for the brave sky-travellers, maps of the celestial bodies—I shall do it for the moon, you Galileo, for Jupiter.

Living in an atmosphere saturated with malice, Professors Magini, Horky, and even Maestlin, could not believe their ears when they heard Kepler singing Galileo's praises, and tried to discover some hidden sting in the treatise. They gloated over a passage in which Kepler showed that the principle of the telescope had been outlined twenty years before by one of Galileo's countrymen, Giovanni Della Porta, and by Kepler himself in his work on optics in 1604. But since Galileo did not claim the invention of the telescope, Kepler's historical excursion could not be resented by him; moreover, Kepler emphasized that Della Porta's and his own anticipations were of a purely theoretical nature "and cannot diminish the fame of the inventor, whoever it was. For I know what a long road it is from a theoretical concept to its practical achievement, from the mention of the antipodes in Ptolemy to Columbus' discovery of the New World, and even more from the two-lensed instruments used in this country to the instrument with which you, O Galilee, penetrated the very skies."

In spite of this, the German envoy in Venice, Georg Fugger, wrote with relish that Kepler had "torn the mask off Galileo's face",[24] and Francis Stelluti (a member of the Lincean Academy) wrote to his brother: "According to Kepler, Galileo makes himself out to be the inventor of the instrument, but more than thirty years ago Della Porta described it in his *Natural Magic*. . . . And so poor Galileo will look foolish."[25] Horky also quoted Kepler in his much read pamphlet against Galileo, whereupon Kepler immediately informed Horky that "since the demands of honesty have become incompatible with my friendship for you, I hereby terminate the latter",[26] and offered Galileo to publish the rebuke; but when the youngster relented, he forgave him.

These reactions indicate the extent of dislike for Galileo in his native Italy. But whatever hidden irony the scholars had imputed to Kepler's *Dissertatio,* the undeniable fact was that the Imperial Mathematicus had expressly endorsed Galileo's claims. This persuaded some of Galileo's opponents, who had previously refused to take him seriously, to look for themselves through improved telescopes which were now becoming available. The first among the converts was the leading astronomer in Rome, the Jesuit Father Clavius. In the sequel, the Jesuit scholars in Rome not only confirmed Galileo's observations, but considerably improved on them.

8. *The Parting of the Orbits*

Galileo's reaction to the service Kepler had rendered him was, as we saw, complete silence. The Tuscan

Ambassador at the Imperial Court urgently advised him to send Kepler a telescope to enable him to verify, at least *post factum,* Galileo's discoveries which he had accepted on trust. Galileo did nothing of the sort. The telescopes which his workshop turned out he donated to various aristocratic patrons.

Four months thus went by, Horky's pamphlet was published, the controversy had reached its peak, and so far not a single astronomer of repute had publicly confirmed having seen the moons of Jupiter. Kepler's friends began to reproach him for having testified to what he himself had not seen; it was an impossible situation.[26a] On 9 August, he again wrote to Galileo:

> . . . You have aroused in me a great desire to see your instrument so that at last I too can enjoy, like yourself, the spectacle of the skies. For among the instruments at our disposal here the best magnifies only ten times, the others hardly thrice. . . . [27]

He talked about his own observations of Mars and the moon, expressed his indignation at Horky's knavery; and then continued:

> The law demands that everybody should be trusted unless the contrary is proven. And how much more is this the case when the circumstances warrant trustworthiness. In fact, we are dealing not with a philosophical but with a legal problem: did Galileo deliberately mislead the world by a hoax? . . .

> I do not wish to hide from you that letters have reached Prague from several Italians who deny that those planets can be seen through your telescope.

> I am asking myself how it is possible that so many deny [their existence], including those who possess a telescope. . . . Therefore I ask you, my Galileo, nominate witnesses for me as soon as possible. From various letters written by you to third persons I have learnt that you do not lack such witnesses. But I am un-able to name any testimony except your own. . . . [27a]

This time Galileo hurried to answer, evidently scared by the prospect of losing his most powerful ally:

> Padua, August 19, 1610.

> I have received both your letters, my most learned Kepler. The first, which you have already published, I shall answer in the second edition of my observations. In the meantime, I wish to thank you for being the first, and almost the only, person who completely accepted my assertions, though you had no proof, thanks to your frank and noble mind.[28]

Galileo went on to tell Kepler that he could not lend him his telescope, which magnified a thousandfold, because he had given it to the Grand Duke who wished "to exhibit it in his gallery as an eternal souvenir among his most precious treasures". He made various excuses about the difficulty of constructing instruments of equal excellence, ending with the vague promise that he would, as soon as possible, make new ones "and send them to my friends". Kepler never received one.

In the next paragraph, Horky and the vulgar crowd came in for some more abuse; "but Jupiter defies both giants and pygmies; Jupiter stands in the sky, and the sycophants may bark as they wish". Then he turned to Kepler's request for witnesses, but still could not name a single astronomer; "In Pisa, Florence, Bologna, Venice and Padua, a good many have seen [the Medicean stars] but they are all silent and hesitate." Instead, he named his new patron, the Grand Duke, and another member of the Medici family (who could hardly be expected to deny the existence of stars named after them). He continued:

> As a further witness I offer myself, who have been singled out by our University for a lifelong salary of a thousand florins, such as no mathematician has ever enjoyed, and which I would continue to receive forever even if the Jupiter moons were to deceive us and vanish.

After complaining bitterly about his colleagues "most of whom are incapable of identifying either Jupiter or Mars, and hardly even the moon", Galileo concluded:

> What is to be done? Let us laugh at the stupidity of the crowd, my Kepler. . . . I wish I had more time to laugh with you. How you would shout with laughter, my dearest Kepler, if you were to hear what the chief philosophers of Pisa said against me to the Grand Duke. . . . But the night has come and I can no longer converse with you. . . .

This is the second, and last, letter which Galileo ever wrote to Kepler.[29] The first, it will be remembered, was written thirteen years earlier, and its theme-song had been the perversity of philosophers and the stupidity of the crowd, concluding with the wistful remark "if only more people like Kepler existed". Now, writing for the first time after these thirteen years, he again singled out Kepler as a unique ally to laugh with him at the foolishness of the world. But concerning the quandary into which his loyal ally had got himself, the letter was as unhelpful as could be. It contained not a word on the progress of Galileo's observations, about which Kepler was burning to hear; and it made no mention of an important new discovery which Galileo had made, and which he had communicated, about a fortnight earlier, to the Tuscan Ambassador in Prague.[30] The communication ran as follows:

SMAISMRMILMEPOETALEUMIBUNENUGTTAURIAS.

This meaningless sequence of letters was an anagram made up from the words describing the new discovery. The purpose behind it was to safeguard the priority of the find without disclosing its content, lest somebody else might claim it as his own. Ever since the affair of the proportional compass, Galileo had been very anxious to ascertain the priority of his observations—even, as we shall hear, in cases where the priority was not his. But whatever his motives in general, they can hardly excuse the fact that he asked the Tuscan Ambassador to dangle the puzzle before the tantalized eyes of Kepler, whom he could not suspect of intending to steal his discovery.

Poor Kepler tried to solve the anagram, and patiently transformed it into what he himself called a "barbaric Latin verse": *"Salve umbistineum geminatum Martia proles"*—"Hail, burning twin, offspring of Mars."[31] He accordingly believed that Galileo had discovered moons around Mars, too. Only three months later, on 13 November, did Galileo condescend to disclose the solution—not, of course, to Kepler, but to Rudolph, because Julian de Medici informed him that the Emperor's curiosity was aroused.

The solution was: *"Altissimum planetam tergeminum observavi"*—"I have observed the highest planet [Saturn] in triplet form". Galileo's telescope was not powerful enough to disclose Saturn's rings (they were only seen half a century later by Heuygens); he believed Saturn to have two small moons on opposite sides, and very close to the planet.

A month later, he sent another anagram to Julian de Medici: *"Haec immatura a me jam frustra leguntouroy"*—"These immature things I am searching for now in vain". Once again Kepler tried several solutions, among them: *"Macula rufa in Jove est gyratur mathem, etc."* ["There is a red spot in Jupiter which rotates mathematically."] then wrote to Galileo in exasperation:

> I beseech you not to withhold from us the solution for long. You must see that you are dealing with honest Germans . . . consider what embarrassment your silence causes me.[32]

Galileo disclosed his secret a month later—again not directly to Kepler, but to Julian de Medici: *"Cynthiae figuras aemulatur mater amorum"*—"The mother of love [Venus] emulates the shapes of Cynthia [the moon]." Galileo had discovered that Venus, like the moon, showed phases—from sickle to full disc and back—a proof that she revolved around the sun. He also considered this as proof of the Copernican system—which it was not, for it equally fitted the Egyptian or the Tychonic system.

In the meantime, Kepler's dearest wish: to see for himself the new marvels, was at last fulfilled. One of Kepler's patrons, the Elector Ernest of Cologne, Duke of Bavaria, was among the select few whom Galileo had honoured with the gift of a telescope. In the summer of 1610, Ernest was in Prague on affairs of state, and for a short period lent his telescope to the Imperial Mathematicus. Thus from 3 August to 9 September, Kepler was able to watch the Jupiter moons with his own eyes. The result was another short pamphlet, *Observation-Report on Jupiter's Four Wandering Satellites,*[33] in which Kepler confirmed, this time from first-hand experience, Galileo's discoveries. The treatise was immediately reprinted in Florence, and was the first public testimony by independent, direct observation, of the existence of the Jupiter moons. It was also the first appearance in history of the term "satellite" which Kepler had coined in a previous letter to Galileo.[34]

At this point the personal contact between Galileo and Kepler ends. For a second time Galileo broke off their correspondence. In the subsequent months, Kepler wrote several more letters, which Galileo left unanswered, or answered indirectly by messages via the Tuscan Ambassador. Galileo wrote to Kepler only once during this whole period of the "meeting of their orbits": the letter of 19 August, 1610, which I have quoted. In his works he rarely mentions Kepler's name, and mostly with intent to refute him. Kepler's three Laws, his discoveries in optics, and the Keplerian telescope, are ignored by Galileo, who firmly defended to the end of his life circles and epicycles as the only conceivable from of heavenly motion.

Notes

[1] F. Sherwood Taylor, *Galileo and the Freedom of Thought* (London, 1938), p. 1.

[2] This is strictly true for small angles only, but sufficient for practical purposes of time-measurement. The correct law of the pendulum was discovered by huygens.

    The Candelabra still shown at the Cathedral of Pisa, whose oscillations are alleged to have given Galileo his idea, was only installed several years after the discovery.

[3] His manuscript treatise *De Motu*, written about 1590, and privately circulated, certainly deviates from Aristotelian physics, but by subscribing to the entirely respectable theory of impetus which had been taught by the Paris school in the fifteenth century and by several of Galileo's predecessors and contemporaries. Cf. A. Koyré, *Études Galileennes* (Paris, 1939).

[4] About his technical treatise on the proportional compass, see below.

[5] Letter to Maestlin, September 1597, G.W., Vol. XIII, p. 140 *seq.*

[6] G.W., Vol. XIII, p. 130 f.

[6a] *Trattato della Sfera, Opera, Ristampa della Ediz. Nazionale* (Florence, 1929-39), Vol. II, pp. 203-255. Henceforth "Opere" refers to this edition, except when marked "Ed. F. Flora", which refers to the handier selection of works and letters in one volume, published in 1953.

[7] Quoted by Sherwood Taylor, op. cit., p. 85.

[8] G.W., Vol. XIII, p. 144 *seq.*

[9] G.W., Vol. XIV, p. 256.

[10] Ibid., p. 441.

[11] Ibid., p. 444 f.

[12] It is surprising to read that Prof. Charles Singer attributes the discovery that the nova of 1604 had no parallax to galileo, and moreover, passing in silence over Tycho's classic book on the nova of 1572, writes:

> New stars when previously noticed had been considered to belong to the lower and less perfect regions near the earth. Galileo had thus attacked the incorruptible and interchangeable heavens and had delivered a blow to the Aristotelian scheme, wellnigh as serious as the experiment on the tower of Pisa (sic)." (Ch. Singer, *A Short History of Science to the Nineteenth Century*, Oxford, 1941, p. 206.)

Since that experiment is also legendary, Prof. Singer's comparison contains an ironic truth; but this triple misstatement is characteristic of the power of the Galileo myth over some eminent historians of science. Prof. Singer also seems to believe that Galileo invented the telescope (op. cit., 217), that in Tycho's system "the sun revolves round the earth in twenty-four hours carrying all the planets with it" (ibid., p. 183), that Kepler's Third Law was "enunciated in the *Epitome Astronomiae*" (ibid., p. 205), etc.

[13] Cf. Zinner, op. cit., p. 514.

[14] *Le Operazioni delle Compasso Geometrico e Militare*, Padova, 1606; *Opere* II, pp. 362-405.

[15] *Usus et Fabrica Ciriui Cuiusdam Proporziones*, Padova, 1607; *Opere* II, pp. 425-511.

[16] Capra's teacher was the distinguished astronomer Simon Marius (1573-1624), discoverer of the Andromeda Nebula, with whom Galileo later became involved in another priority quarrel. See [*The Sleepwalkers: A History of Man's Changing Vision of the Universe,* by Arthur Koestler, The Macmillan Company, 1959], p. 468.

[17] Letter to B. Landucci, quoted by [Karl von] Gebler, *Galileo Galilei and the Roman Curia*, London, 1879, p. 19.

[18] George Fugger (a member of the famous banker's family) in a letter to Kepler, 16.4.1610, G.W., Vol. XVI, p. 302.

[18a] Cf. Zinner, op. cit., p. 345 f.
[19] This refers to the first, Latin edition.

[20] *Paradise Lost*, book ii, l. 890.

[20a] *Peregrinatio còntra Nuncium Sydereum*, Mantua, 1610.

[21] *Ignatius his Conclave.*

[22] *Opere,* ed. F. Flora, Milano-Napoli, 1953, p. 887 *seq.*

[23] Ibid., p. 894 *seq.*

[24] 28.5.1610, G.W., Vol. XVI, p. 314.

[25] Quoted by E. Rosen, *The Naming of the Telescope*, New York, 1947.

[26] Letter to Horky, 9.8.1610, G.W., Vol. XVI, p. 323.

[26a] G.W., "Poor Kepler is unable to stem the feeling against Your Excellency, for Magini has written three letters, which were confirmed by 24 learned men from Bologna, to give effect that they had been present when you tried to demonstrate your discoveries . . . but failed to see what you intended to show them." M. Hasdale to Galileo, 15.4 and 28.4 1610, G.W., Vol. XVI, pp. 300 f, 308.

[27] G.W., Vol. XVI, p. 319 *seq.*

[27a] It was probably this letter which lead Prof. de Santillana to the erroneous statement: "It took even Kepler, always generous and open-minded, a whole five months before rallying to the cause of the telescope.... His first *Dissertatio cum Nuncio sidereo*, of April, 1610, is full of reservations." (*Dialogue on the Great World Systems*, Chicago, 1937, p. 98 n.) Kepler's reservations referred, as we saw, to the priority of the invention of the telescope, not to Galileo's discoveries with it.

[28] G.W., Vol. XVI, p. 327 *seq.*

[29] Except for a short note of introduction to Kepler, which Galileo gave a traveller seventeen years later, in 1627. *Opere* XIII, p. 374 f.

[30] [Karl von] Gebler, op. cit., p. 24.

[31] At least, that seems to be the meaning. The word *"umbistineum"* does not exist and may either be derived from *"ambustus"*, burnt up, or *"umbo"*=boss, projection.

[32] 9.1.1611, G.W., Vol. XVI, p. 356 *seq.*

[33] *Narratio de Observatis a se quatuor Iovis satteliti-bus erronibus.*
[34] 25.10.1610, G.W., Vol. XVI, p. 341.

Works Cited

. . . Kepler, Johannes. *Johannes Kepler, Gesammelte Werke.* Edited by W. van Dyck and Max Caspar. Munich, 1938-. . . .

Zinner, E. *Entstehung und Ausbreitung der Copernican-ischen Lehre.* Erlangen, 1943.

REVOLUTIONARY ASTRONOMICAL MODELS

S. K. Heninger, Jr. (essay date 1977)

SOURCE: "Copernicus and His Consequences," in *The Cosmographical Glass: Renaissance Diagrams of the Universe,* The Huntington Library, 1977, pp. 45-80.

[*In the following excerpt, Heninger gives a detailed explanation of each of the many cosmological models that the Copernican theory had spawned in the seventeenth century, thereby telling the story of the difficult transition to the new astronomy.*]

The geocentric system gives the appearance of neatness and accounts readily for the casually observed phenomena in the world around us. Nonetheless, it proved unwieldy to the professional astronomer. His job was to chart the actual movement of the planets, rather than construct a perfect model of the universe; and often, in order to provide information required by astrologers and physicians, he was obliged to predict the planets' positions at a given moment. Moreover, the practicing astronomer was aware of data accumulated from centuries of observations. These empirical data made it clear that when the Earth is taken as the fixed point of reference for plotting the movements of the planets, their courses are anything but simple. They do not move at constant speed, and retrograde motion must be accounted for as well as forward motion. Rather than being outrightly circular, . . . the orbits of the planets when plotted against the Earth are convoluted configurations that are recurrent, and therefore predictable, but outrageously cumbersome. The Ptolemaic system when put into practice depended upon a complicated geometry of deferents and epicycles and equants.

In order to clarify the mathematics of the Ptolemaic system, profesional astronomers in the mid-fifteenth century began to subject it to intensive review. Prominent among those who worked for improved exactness and greater ease in computation were Georg Peurbach, a professor of mathematics at the university of Vienna, and Johannes Regiomontanus (i.e., Johann Müller of Konigsberg), Peurbach's pupil and later a much respected mathematical practitioner among the affluent burghers of Nuremberg. Regiomontanus established his own printing house there and brought out a series of almanacs as well as Peurbach's major work, *Theoricae planetarum novae* (c. 1474). This textbook was a massive effort to bring Ptolemy up to date. It sought to explain the geocentric universe in terms of mathematics that was becoming increasingly sophisticated.

Nicolaus Copernicus, today highly touted as the father of heliocentrism, represents the culmination of this thrust to revise Ptolemaic astronomy. He should be seen, however, not as a radical innovator, one who struck out boldly in new directions, but rather as one who worked modestly and self-consciously within the established tradition. Copernicus' aim was to render plain what had become unmanageably clumsy in applied astronomy, and to reinstate a world-view that emphasized simplicity and wholeness. He wished to recognize as a primal force an inherent tendency in nature toward coherence and order—what he called "a certain natural appetency implanted in the parts by the divine providence of the universal Artisan, in order that they should unite with one another in their oneness and wholeness and come together in the form of a globe."[100]

No renaissance platonist could have stated the basic thesis of Timaean cosmology with greater fidelity. There is no doubt of Copernicus' deference to the traditional astronomy, a deference that stemmed not so much from fear of punishment by ecclesiastical authorities as from his own firm commitment to the revered principles of cosmos. In the *De revolutionibus orbium coelestium,* written in Frauenburg at a safe distance from controversy, Copernicus demonstrates his orthodoxy in a number of ways. First, in the dedicatory epistle to Pope Paul III he eagerly acknowledges his recourse to authorities, especially the pythagoreans who had proposed a central Sun with the Earth moving about it ([*]3ᵛ-[*]4). He also begins with the fundamental premise that the world is spherical, and bases his subsequent hypotheses upon this initial assumption.[101] Furthermore, he accepts as a donné that the courses of the heavenly bodies are circular or compounded of circular motions, and are therefore regular (a2ᵛ-a3). Finally, he never casts doubt upon the Ptolemaic assumption that the world is finite, bounded by a sphere of fixed stars (cı).

At the risk of verging upon the facetious, we might say that Copernicus did no more than a bit of tinkering with the existing world-view. At most he made a minor adjustment in the Ptolemaic system, which had held sway for two millenia. Copernicus merely made the Sun the center of the system instead of the Earth, and this done for the conservative reason of returning the universe to a state of mathematical simplicity. But he retained the sphericity and the regularity and the finiteness of the orthodox cosmology.

The conservatism of Copernicus is immediately evident when we compare his diagram of the universe with . . . a diagram from a text of Aristotle's *De caelo* printed for use in the schools. Copernicus' diagram . . . is manifestly at pains to reflect the tradition. And in his description of the diagram, Copernicus begins with the outermost sphere, the sphere of fixed stars, to emphasize the finiteness of his system:

> The first and highest of all is the sphere of the fixed stars, which comprehends itself and all things, and is accordingly immovable. In fact it is the place of the universe, *i.e.,* it is that to which the movement and position of all the other stars are referred. . . . Saturn, the first of the wandering stars follows; it completes its circuit in 30 years. After it comes Jupiter moving in a 12-year period of revolution. Then Mars, which completes a revolution every 2 years. The place fourth in order is occupied by the annual revolution in which we said the Earth together with the orbital circle of the moon as an epicycle is comprehended. In the fifth place, Venus, which completes its revolution in 7½ months. The sixth and final place is occupied by Mercury, which completes its revolution in a period of 88 days. In the center of all rests the sun.[102]

[Copernicus's] diagram repeats [Aristotle's] except for one detail: the Sun is placed at the center, and the Earth with the Moon revolving about it is placed between Venus and Mars. Thereby the orbit of the Moon is made an epicycle; but the orbits of the other planets, which heretofore had been described only by the use of intricate epicycles and eccentrics, are returned to simple circularity.[103]

The distance between the ambience of Copernicus and the scientism of modern heliocentrism is enormous, and the differences are far more significant than the similarities. For example, as a continuation of the passage quoted in the paragraph above, Copernicus offers his reason for placing the sun in the middle of the universe. Characteristically, he makes his statement in the form of a rhetorical question: "For who would place this lamp of a very beautiful temple in another or better place than this whereform it can illuminate everything at the same time?" The argument in this passage proceeds from the premise of cosmos, that the universe is beautiful and ordered, and from the dogma that the sphere is the perfect solid because all points on its surface are equidistant from its center. No support is offered from the actual observation of phenomena, and the indifference to empirical data is not an oversight. Copernicus consolidates his assertion by citing a string of well-known epithets for the sun:

> As a matter of fact, not unhappily do some call it the lantern; others, the mind and still others, the pilot of the world. Trismegistus calls it a "visible god"; Sophocles' Electra, "that which gazes upon all things." And so the sun, as if resting on a kingly throne, governs the family of stars which wheel around.[104]

This does not sound like someone who might change the course of intellectual history. Copernicus is looking backward, not forward. He is reflecting the age-old beliefs of the pythagorean-platonic tradition as it had often formulated itself in sun worship.

Of course, Copernicus did put forward proposals that had far-reaching effects in the work of later scientists. As a result of placing the sun at the center of the universe, he necessarily assigned motion to the earth as it revolved around the sun. This was an annual revolution of the earth. He also assigned to earth a diurnal rotation about its own axis, and this was a proposal of prime importance. If the earth spun around every twenty-four hours, then the heavens could cease their turning. Copernicus stopped the celestial spheres from their whirling about in daily circuit, and thereby prepared for new coordinates of astronomical calculation.

But Copernicus himself thought in terms of simplifying the old, not in terms of introducing the new. And the real break with Ptolemaic astronomy did not come until the ancient concept of cosmos was discarded— until the pythagorean dislike of the limitless was laid aside and the universe was proclaimed to be infinite. Kepler still actively propounded a mathematically ordered (and therefore limited) universe and circumscribed it within a clearly defined sphere, as we shall see. Galileo never publicly engaged with the question of whether our world is infinite.[105] In any case, the so-called Copernican revolution would have been anathema to the modest canon of Frauenburg Cathedral, and in any practical sense was delayed until the late seventeenth century, when Newton made it possible to explain the movements of the planets in terms of celestial mechanics. Only then did description of the universe break out of its sanctified mold of cosmos.

Certainly Copernicus was not seen by his contemporaries and immediate followers as a revolutionary, or even an adventurous innovator. They saw him more in the role of revivalist, as one who had resurrected and reasserted an ancient world-view first proposed by certain pythagoreans. Copernicus himself gave evidence toward this conclusion in his dedicatory epistle to Pope Paul III.[106] For Kepler, writing a foreword to the read-

er of his *Mysterium cosmographicum,* Copernicus was in direct line from Pythagoras—in the same mathematical tradition, though perhaps "a better observer of the universe."[107] For Galileo addressing the reader of his *Dialogo . . . sopra i due massimi sistemi del mondo,* Copernicus had expounded "the Pythagorean opinion of the mobility of the Earth."[108] It was the gradually solidifying opinion of reactionaries that eventually denounced a theory of terrestrial motion and drove Copernicus from the ranks of conservative thought. Increasing religious and intellectual orthodoxy in certain circles in time forced the adherents of Copernicanism to become more and more separatist. But only in retrospect does Copernicus assume the role of an intellectual radical.

Nonetheless, Copernicus' work was rapidly recognized as an important hypothesis that offered a viable alternative to Ptolemaic geocentrism. It was, in fact, largely the interest of Georg Joachim Rheticus, a young astronomer from the university of Wittenberg, that brought the *De revolutionibus orbium coelestium* into print. And after 1543, the date of its publication, it received immediate and widespread recognition. Already in 1556 Robert Recorde was referring to it in England,[109] and the interpid John Dee went so far as to be its advocate.[110]

The strongest advocate of Copernicanism in England was Thomas Digges, the talented son of Leonard Digges, one of the most respected mathematical practitioners in mid-sixteenth-century London. Since 1553, Leonard Digges had issued successive editions of a practical handbook of astrological lore entitled *A prognostication everlastinge of righte good effecte.* To the 1576 edition of his father's perennial almanac, and to the several subsequent editions, Thomas appended a lengthy exposition of the Copernican hypothesis, which he entitled rather aggressively: "A perfit description of the cælestiall orbes according to the most auncuente doctrine of the *Pythagoreans,* latelye revived by *Copernicus* and by geometricall demonstrations approved". . . .

As a prologue to this treatise, the first extended treatment of terrestrial mobility in English, Thomas Digges offered some comments to clarify his circumstance. He begins by recognizing the wide acceptance of the Ptolemaic system, which was taught in all universities in accordance with the authority of Aristotle. But soon he turns to Copernicus, a "rare witte" who has recently proposed that "the Earth resteth not in the Center of the whole world, but . . . is caried yearely rounde about the Sunne". . . . Digges then, echoing the very words of Copernicus, proceeds to extoll the sun: "which like a king in the middest of all raigneth and geeveth lawes of motion to the rest, sphærically dispearsing his glorious beames of light through al this sacred Cœlestiall Temple." Moreover, in addition to the annual motion of the earth, there is a daily motion, with the earth "tourning everye 24. houres rounde upon his owne Center." This hypothesis, Digges contends, has been proved by Copernicus, "with demonstrations Mathematicall most apparantly by him to the world delivered." Finally, with extraordinary audacity, Digges maintains that Copernicus intended for his proposal to be taken as an actual description of the physical arrangement of our universe, not merely as an abstract mathematical theorem as some had suggested:

> I thought it convenient together with the olde Theorick [of Ptolemy] also to publishe this, to the ende such noble English minds (as delight to reache above the baser sort of men) might not be altogether defrauded of so noble a part of Philosophy. And to the ende it might manifestly appeare that *Copernicus* mente not as some have fondly excused him to deliver these grounds of the Earthes mobility onely as Mathematicall principles, fayned & not as Philosophicall truly averred. . . . [111]

Digges is taking the heliocentric system out of the insubstantial realm of theoretical geometry and asking that we make it our physical reality.

The whole-hearted commitment of Thomas Digges to Copernicanism is boldly asserted in . . . a diagram of the universe which he placed as an extra-size foldout before the "Perfit description of the cælestiall orbes" appended to his father's perennial almanac. There we see the sun shining resplendently in the center of the diagram, the fixed point about which the earth and planets move. First among the celestial spheres is "the orbe of Mercury" with a period of revolution of 80 days. Next comes "the orbe of Venus," and it "rouleth round in 9 monethes." And then comes an orb for the earth, which is notably larger than the others because the moon travels around it in an epicyclic pattern with the sun as its center. The globe representing the earth is depicted in detail with each of the four elements included, and a label identifies its orb in terms recalling the mutability that characterizes it: "the great orbe carreinge this globe of mortalitye." The revolution of the earth—its "circular periode"—of course determines our year. Then follows in the usual sequence a sphere for each of the remaining three planets: "the orbe of Mars makinge his revolution in 2 yeares," "the orbe of Jupiter makinge his periode in 12 yeares," and "the orbe of Saturne makinge his revolution in 30 yeares."

The salient feature of Digges' diagram, however, is his treatment of the sphere of fixed stars. He recognizes this component of the traditional cosmology, but gives it a most daring interpretation. In the Ptolemaic system the fixed stars were placed on the underside of a single celestial sphere, so that all of them were equidistant from the center of the universe. Digges, however, without precedent for such an innovation, removes the lim-

it of a single sphere for the fixed stars. Instead, he proposes that the region of stars extends outward to infinity, and he illustrates this proposition by placing a large number of stars randomly in space beyond the boundary of the planetary orbs.

Digges came to a conclusion about the infiniteness of the heavens as a result of his belief in the earth's mobility. In his text, which is largely a redaction of Copernicus,[112] he reviews the arguments that aristotelians had made for thinking the earth rests immobile in the center of the heavenly spheres. . . . In the aristotelian arrangement of the elements, earth is absolutely heavy and naturally moves toward the center, so that our earth is central and fixed by virtue of its inherent heaviness. In such a system the heavens must be finite because they are the components in motion, and that which is infinite cannot move. When the earth is made the component of the system that moves in daily rotation, however—as it does in Copernicus' system—then the heavens stand still, and the heavens can be allowed to become infinite. The primum mobile is no longer necessary to provide motion from an extraneous source, and consequently it is discarded. With the removal of the primum mobile also goes the rigid demarcation between a finite cosmos and an empyrean representing a different and discontinuous order of being. The result is a system like Digges', with an outer sphere that defies confinement and consequently defies regular measured motion. As the label on Digges' diagram announces: "This orbe of starres fixed infinitely up extendeth hit selfe in altitude sphericallye, and therfore [is] immovable."

Digges' argument is basically scientific and doubtless his prime concern is to confirm the hypothesis of Copernicus. He concludes his treatise, in fact, with a confident *probatum est:* "So if it bee Mathematically considered and wyth Geometricall Mensurations every part of every *Theoricke* examined: the discreet Student shall fynde that *Copernicus* not without great reason did propone this grounde of the Earthes Mobility". . . . Nonetheless, there is another factor in his argument that we should note. Digges is working toward a premise that incorporates the abode of deity into the physical structure of the universe. In the orthodox pythagorean-platonic cosmology, with its unremitting dichotomy between the sense-perceptible world and an empyrean that does not submit to observation, the godhead was placed in a category beyond human knowledge, and at best we can infer his attributes by studying his creation, nature. In the aristotelian adaptation of that system, the deity was denied a suitable habitat: the heavens, though composed of the ethereal quintessence, were nevertheless finite and constantly moving. To Digges' mind, it is more appropriate to place God in an infinite and unmoving heaven. No other habitat suitably accords with His attributes of omnipotence and steadfastness. With a religious fervor, therefore, Digges continues his label for the outermost sphere of his diagram:

> ... the pallace of foelicitye garnished with perpetuall shininge glorious lightes innumerable, farr excellinge our sonne both in quantitye and qualitye the very court of coelestiall angelles devoyd of greefe and replenished with perfite endlesse joye. . . .

Digges is thankful for the insight that led him to this discovery, and with uplifted spirit he reports upon this divine mystery. With more than a tinge of Calvinism, he concludes his praise of the starry heavens with the most approbative of epithets: "the habitacle for the elect." But what Digges has done, of course, is to incorporate the blessed seat of divinity—"the very court of coelestiall angelles . . . [and] the habitacle for the elect"—into a physical system dependent upon mathematical laws. He has conflated the infinite and the finite into a single continuum. He did nto foresee that such naïveté would soon bring into conflict the scientists and the theologians.

The renaissance man who for us has come to symbolize the innocent victim in the life-and-death struggle between religion and science is Galileo Galilei. His fearless assertion of scientific discoveries and the resultant persecution by the Church have been legendized. His courage and wisdom as well as his sufferings are well known. The facts are somewhat different from the legend, but that is another matter. What concerns us here is Galileo's crucial role in gaining acceptance for the Copernican theory.

With some justification Galileo may be seen as the first thoroughgoing man of science who worked through his discoveries and hypotheses to arrive at a comprehensive world-view that we recognize as our own. He was an empiricist, reliant upon observation and experiment, and the subject of his inquiry was the measurable world about us. He sought to quantify and reduce to mathematical laws what had heretofore been explained largely by authority and logic. He showed no restrictive deference to the orthodox cosmology, as did Copernicus. He had no mystical inclinations, as did Kepler. Unlike Tycho, he was not induced to compromise in the face of political and theological pressures. His aim was to reveal truth by the scientific method, and to make knowledge available and understandable to all.

For Galileo the truth of the Copernican theory as physical reality became increasingly self-evident, and the major effort of his mature years was to establish this conviction as an accepted premise not only in the laboratories of science, but in educated circles everywhere. To this end, he worked for decades on a carefully reasoned defense of the heliocentric system, what eventually he published in 1632 as the *Dialogo . . . sopra i*

due massimi sistemi del mondo tolemaico, e copernicano. Galileo presented his opinions in the form of such a dialogue for several reasons. First, the new is often best delineated by contrasting it with the old, and Copernicanism is most clearly defined by pointing to its departures from Ptolemaic astronomy. Second, Galileo had cause to fear indictment by ecclesiastical authorities, and a dialogue allowed some pretense of offering a balanced argument, of presenting alternatives between which the reader can make his choice. Finally, the dialogue form gave opportunity for Galileo to display his considerable literary talent, and consequently to reach the largest number of his educated contemporaries. The *Dialogo* is a masterpiece on any terms: rhetorical, scientific, or literary. It is both informative and entertaining—urbane, artful, lively—the platonic dialogue in modern dress.

Already in the 1590s Galileo had accepted the Copernican hypothesis, a conclusion that he communicated to his distant colleague, Kepler, in 1597. Subsequent discoveries unalterably confirmed this early belief. When Galileo looked through his telescope in 1609, he could see that the surface of the moon is mountainous, not perfectly spherical, making the moon very much like our earth; and he could see four satellites revolving about Jupiter. These observed data render untenable the Ptolemaic assumptions about the unique quintessence that comprises the heavens, and they demonstrate that some point other than the earth can be the center of circular motion in our universe. Next year the discovery of spots on the sun contributed to rejecting the aristotelian distinction between a corruptible earth and the unchanging heavens. The observation that Venus went through phases similar to those of the moon also fitted with a heliocentric system. Everything pointed to the validity of Copernicus' theory, and Galileo was eager to propound it.

The *Dialogo* proceeds, in mock-platonic fashion, through four successive days, and involves three speakers: Filippo Salviati, a young friend of Galileo from Florence and an avowed Copernican; Giovanni Francesco Sagredo, a Venetian gentleman who professes neutrality but usually supports Salviati; and Simplicio, a fictional character with allegiance to the debased aristotelianism then taught in the schools. In the brief preface Galileo explains with a straight face that "Simplicio" comes from Simplicius, a well-known commentator on Aristotle— thereby demonstrating the sort of double-edged foolery that runs through most of the work. The argument itself, though, is serious, and only a simpleton more simple than Simplicio could miss Galileo's point. The earth and the heavens are bound together in one physical continuum, as Thomas Digges had argued; and the sun, not the earth, is the center of its motion.

The high point of the *Dialogo* comes on the third day when Salviati undertakes to demonstrate the annual motion of the earth about the sun. As so often in the conversation, Salviati sounds like a patient schoolmaster and Simplicio becomes an accomplice in his own refutation. Simplicio complains of difficulty in understanding such a complex configuration, so Salviati suggests that he take a sheet of paper and a pair of compasses, and they go through the construction of a diagram step by step. . . . [Simplicio] begins with . . . the terrestrial globe . . and . . . the sun. Then according to Simplicio's drawing—at Salviati's prompting—the circle . . . about the sun represents the orbit of Venus, and [another] circle . . . represents the orbit of Mercury. Next Simplicio draws a circle . . . to represent the orbit of Mars, and then follow two circles, . . . to represent the orbits of Jupiter and Saturn, respectively. Simplicio, now with very little help from Salviati, includes an orbit for the moon about the earth . . .; and though not mentioned in the text, the four satellites of Jupiter also appear in orbit about that center of motion. At this moment—with a barely suppressed "Ah, ha!"—Salviati triumphantly proclaims, "We have all this while, Simplicius, disposed the mundane bodies exactly according to the order of Copernicus."[113]

After publication of Galileo's *Dialogo,* the widespread acceptance of a heliocentric system was assured. Salviati's arguments, and the overweening respect for Galileo's scientific achievements, swept away all but the most stubborn opposition. Despite the immediate placement of the *Dialogo* on the index of prohibited books—the Church had earlier prohibited Copernicus' *De revolutionibus orbium coelestium* in 1616—there was no chance of keeping the earth fixed as the hub of a tidy universe. The earth moved, and the mechanical laws that govern its motion became the next concern of astronomers.

It should be noted again, however, that Galileo does not follow the Copernican hypothesis to its logical conclusion and advocate an infinite universe. He broaches the subject in a gingerly fashion at the end of the discussion . . . but ultimately begs the question. After Simplicio has constructed all of the planetary orbits and the orbit for the moon, Salviati asks pointedly:

> Now, Simplicius, what shall we do with the fixed stars? Shall we suppose them scattered through the immense abysses of the Universe, at different distances from one determinate point; or else placed in a surface spherically distended about a centre of its own, so that each of them may be equidistant from the said centre?

This is the question that Thomas Digges had asked himself. . . . He opted for the first alternative and scattered the stars through the immense abyss of space. But Digges was far ahead of his time—ahead, even, of Galileo. For Simplicio replies to Salviati's question with a colossal hedge:

> I would rather take a middle way and would assign them a circle described about a determinate centre and comprised within two spherical surfaces, to wit, one very high and concave, and the other lower, and convex, betwixt which I would constitute the innumerable multitude of stars, but yet at diverse altitudes. (page 339)

Simplicio allows for some variation in the distance of stars from the center of the universe, but not much; all of the stars are compressed between two fixed limits, between two concentric spheres. And there Galileo lets the matter drop. While insisting upon a heliocentric universe, he refuses to argue for its infinitude.

Once Copernicus had posited both a diurnal and an annual motion for the earth, there were others who suggested variations and adaptations of his theory. Most prominent among these was Tycho Brahe, a brilliant though contentious nobleman of Denmark who dominated the science of astronomy for the last few decades of the sixteenth century. Tycho's forte was the manufacture of measuring instruments and the recording of observations. His data were methodical and remarkably accurate, the result of thoughtful planning. His hypothesis about arranging the planets, however, is at best an expedient compromise.

Already in the 1570s Tycho had reason to discredit the aristotelian tenet that the celestial spheres are incorruptible, in contrast to the terrestrial realm of mutable elements. In 1572 he observed a nova in Cassiopeia, and in 1577 a widely discussed comet. Aristotelian physics decreed that such events be confined to the sublunary regions, which are variable. But both the nova and the comet, Tycho concluded after careful calculation, were considerably more distant from the earth than is the moon, and therefore transpired in what had previously been held to be the invariable realm of quintessential ether. Unquestionably the heavens are not immutable, as Aristotle and his followers had insisted.

Tycho inevitably inclined toward the Copernican hypothesis in lieu of the Ptolemaic, because Copernicus had introduced significant simplifications of utmost importance to the practicing astronomer. But there were two objections to the Copernican theory that Tycho could not ignore. First, the earth is manifestly ponderous, palpably heavy and steadfast, and not likely to move either at the speed or with the variety of motions that Copernicus requires. Second, since Tycho could detect no parallax in his observation of the stars, it would appear that the distance between the sphere of Saturn and the stars is enormous, thus leaving a vast and puzzling void in the system.[114] Therefore with doggedness—or should we say industry?—Tycho devised a world-system that accepted as much as possible of Copernicus' hypothesis, but nonetheless took into account these two objections.

Tycho sets forth the principles of his system in a book on the notorious comet of 1577, *De mundi aetherei recentioribus phaenomenis,* printed on his own press at Uraniborg in 1588. This volume reporting on "recent phenomena in the celestial world" was intended as part of a multi-volume series that considered the whole subject of astronomy in the light of recent discoveries. . . . Tycho had reached [a number of conclusions]. The earth is stationary in the center with the moon revolving about it. The sun also revolves about the earth in an annual movement, and its orbit is indicated by a circle. The other planets, however, revolve about the sun. Mercury and Venus revolve in orbits whose radii are shorter than the distance between the sun and earth; but the radii of the orbits of Mars, Jupiter, and Saturn are greater than the distance between the sun and earth. The orbit of Mars, in fact, intersects the orbit of the sun at two points, so that there is a possibility of collision. The whole system is firmly enclosed within a traditional sphere of fixed stars, thereby making it unequivocally finite. And since the earth is fixed without any motion of its own, the entire heavens must spin completely around every twenty-four hours to account for the diurnal changes that we see. While Tycho's hypothesis may seem a shameless compromise to us, a falling between two stools, it gained a large number of adherents in its own day by dint of its reasonableness and avoidance of controversy. For many, it replaced the Ptolemaic system as the most formidable rival to Copernicanism.

A world-system similar to Tycho's was proposed at about the same time by another practicing astronomer Nicolaus Raimarus, or Reymers, also known as Ursus (the Bear).[115] Reymers was a man of low birth who through intelligence and hard work made a name for himself as a man of learning. He rose to be professor of mathematics in Prague and a protegé of Emperor Rudolph II, and it required the combined efforts of Tycho and Kepler to impugn his authority. In 1588 at Strasbourg, Reymers published his remarkably competent *Fundamentum astronomicum,* a manual of advanced trigonometry, to which he appended *Hypotheses novae ac verae motuum corporum mundanorum* (fol. 37-40ᵛ). In this treatise, dedicated at least in part to John Dee, Reymers sets forth twenty original *theses astronomicae* and several annotations that clarify his "new and true hypotheses concerning the motions of cosmic bodies". . . . He claims to have derived his system from an ancient authority, Apollonius Pergaeus, and he dedicates it to that noble patron of astronomers, Wilhelm IV, Landgrave of Hesse.

According to Reymers, the earth is in the center of the universe, and it rotates diurnally on its own axis to produce night and day. Circling the earth is the moon, whose radius of revolution is quite short, and the sun, whose radius of revolution is considerably longer. The other planets, as in the system of Tycho, then circle around the sun. First come Mercury and Venus, whose radii of revolution are shorter than the distance from the sun to the earth; and next come Mars, Jupiter, and Saturn, whose radii of revolution are greater than twice the distance from the sun to the earth. The entire system is bounded by the familiar sphere of fixed stars, which is divided into twelve equal parts and identified with the zodiac. This outermost circle is also marked off in 360°. In addition, perpendicular lines crossing at the earth indicate the horizon—labeled *or*[iens] for "east" on the left and *oc*[cidens] for "west" on the right—when the sun is in its zenith at noon.

One particularly noteworthy feature of this diagram is the outer circle which delimits it. The stars are not imbedded in this sphere—that is, all stars are not equidistant from the earth. Some fall within the circle, and even more fall without. Furthermore, Reymers makes some effort to arrange the stars in constellations appropriate to each sign of the zodiac. Like Thomas Digges . . ., Reymers may be suggesting, however cautiously, that the universe is not firmly bounded by a single sphere of fixed stars. At least in his Thesis XVIII he is willing to entertain the possibility (fol. 38ᵛ).

Regardless of his conclusion about the finitude of the universe, there are two definite and highly significant differences between the system of Reymers and that of Tycho. First, the orbit of Mars is plotted so that it clears the orbit of the sun and does not intersect it, thereby removing the unsettling possibility of collision. Second, and even more important, Reymers argues for the daily rotation of the earth, and consequently does away with the need for the whole celestial apparatus to circle around each twenty-four hours. In this respect, Reymers' system comes closer to that of Copernicus than does the system of Tycho.

Egoist that he was, Tycho was infuriated by the publication of Reymers' hypothesis and determined to destroy its author. Tycho charged Reymers with having pilfered a manuscript while on a visit to Uraniborg in 1584, and Reymers indignantly lodged a counter-charge that Tycho had stolen the idea from him. The two men, the outstanding astronomers of Europe in the 1590s, carried on the acrimonious argument to their dying breaths. When Tycho was joined by Kepler at Prague in 1600, he set his young assistant the odious task of writing a definitive refutation of the hated rival. It is not a happy chapter in the history of astronomy.

Yet another world-system even closer to Tycho's was put forward by Helisaeus Röslin, a German doctor and sometime astronomer with a mystic bent. His hypothesis . . . was published in the *De opere dei creationis seu de mundo hypotheses* (Frankfurt, 1597), a curious little volume that well illustrates the inextricable fusion of science, religion, and occultism in the renaissance. Röslin places earth in the center of the universe, and like Tycho (but unlike Reymers) he deprives it of all motion, diurnal as well as annual. The moon and the sun revolve around the earth. The other five planets, however, revolve around the sun (though the orbits of Mars, Jupiter, and Saturn in some unexplained way are also conceived as concentric circles centering upon the earth). As in the system of Reymers, the orbit of Mars clears the path of the sun, but just barely. Reymers was utterly scornful of Röslin's hypothesis; and in the *De astronomicis hypothesibus seu systemate mundano tractatus astronomicus et cosmographicus* (Prague 1597), written when Reymers was at the height of his career, he disparages Tycho as well as Röslin, claiming that Röslin has followed Tycho like one monkey imitating another (C3).

To say the least, by the turn of the seventeenth century there were several alternative world-systems to choose among. Copernicus had been repeated, refined, and respected by many, not least of all by Englishmen. And Galileo was standing in the wings, ready for his entrance as the champion of heliocentrism. Although the Ptolemaic system itself was largely discredited, there were compromises that still preserved its salient features: the immobility of the earth and the delimiting fixity of the outermost sphere. Tycho and Reymers, and even Röslin, had argued their cases persuasively. Kepler just a few years before had published his startling *Mysterium cosmographicum* (Tübingen, 1596), in which he enhances the new mathematics at the same time he confirms the old notion of cosmic harmony by finding the key to the universal structure in the proportions between spheres circumscribing the five regular solids. . . . This was a harbinger of the curious alliance, yet contretemps, between science and religion that characterizes the early seventeenth century, an interaction between disparate disciplines that produced a mind as mercurially complex as that of Sir Thomas Browne.

For lesser men, however, confusion is an understandable result. And it is confusion that the prosaic Robert Burton professes:

> Nicholas Ramerus will have the Earth the Center of the World, but moveable [i.e., rotating on its axis], and the eighth sphere immoveable, the five upper Planets to move about the Sun, the Sun and Moon about the Earth. Of which Orbs, Tycho Brahe puts the Earth the Center immoveable, the stars immoveable, the rest with Ramerus, the Planets without Orbs to wander in the Air, keep time and distance, true motion, according to that virtue which God hath given them.[116] Helisæus Rœslin censureth both, with Copernicus (whose Hypothesis concerning the motion of the earth Philippus Lansbergius[117] hath lately vindicated, and demonstrated with solid arguments in a just volume . . .).[118]

Burton has obviously read widely in the raging debate about whether the earth is a moving or a stationary body. He is remarkably well informed, and continues to ruminate upon the possibilities:

> Rœslin (I say) censures all, and Ptolemy himself as unsufficient: one offends against natural Philosophy, another against Optick principles, a third against Mathematical, as not answering to Astronomical observations: one puts a great space betwixt Saturn's Orb and the eighth sphere,[119] another too narrow. In his own hypothesis he [Röslin] makes the Earth as before the universal Center, the Sun to the five upper Planets, to the eighth sphere he ascribes diurnal motion, Eccentricks and Epicycles to the seven Planets, which had been formerly exploded.

Despite his diligence, though, Burton can come to no conclusion, and his net response is annoyance with the astronomers: "The World is tossed in a blanket amongst them, they hoist the Earth up and down like a ball, make it stand and go at their pleasures."

As a result of this conflict in world-systems—proposals passionately formulated by zealous prophets—it proved necessary to compare one hypothesis with another. It became a frequent practice to line up diagrams of the possibilities, so that a reader could see at a glance the distinguishing features of each, or how many share a particular feature. The Ptolemaic system sits beside the Copernican, which in turn brings forward the Tychonic—and so on, for as many alternatives as the author can muster. The number of such comparative series during the seventeenth century bears witness to the interest in cosmology and to the uncertainty about it. This was a period not so much of doubt as of questioning—not so much of skepticism as of inquiry.

As early as 1573 Valentinus Nabodus, or Naiboda, had published in Venice a sequence of diagrams that compare world-systems in his *Primarum de coelo et terra institutionum quotidianarumque mundi revolutionum, libri tres.* Naiboda served as professor of mathematics at Cologne and later at Pauda, and called himself "physicus et astronomus" (fol. 1). In this volume, as the title indicates, he reviews the first principles of both the heavens and the earth, and the arguments for the daily rotation of the world. Clearly he is writing in the backwash of Copernicus. To illustrate his discussion, Naiboda provides three woodcuts: first, a diagram of the traditional geocentric system, then a diagram of the system described by Martianus Capella, and finally a diagram of the Copernican hypothesis.

Naiboda's diagram of the geocentric system . . . is largely conventional. As the caption announces, this is "a system of the major parts of the cosmos by which, authorities generally claim, everything in the entire universe is interconnected." The Earth, of course, is at the center, surrounded by a sphere for each of the seven planets, and by a sphere of fixed stars. This makes a total of only eight celestial spheres. Naiboda had omitted the cristalline sphere and the primum mobile, probably under the influence of Agostino Ricchi. In the *De motu octavae sphaerae, opus* (Trino, 1513), Ricchi had argued that no sphere should be given credence unless it carries a visible body, a condition not met by the thoroughly transparent cristalline sphere or the primum mobile. . . .

Naiboda's "System of the major parts of the universe from the writings of Martianus Capella" . . . puts in visual form the cosmology enunciated by this early fifth-century encyclopedist in his *De nuptiis Philologiae et Mercurii libri novem* (VIII. 853-55). The last seven books of this much-read school text are devoted one each to the seven liberal arts—the trivium and the quadrivium—as they had maintained their identity through the middle ages and well into the renaissance. In Book VIII, dealing with Astronomy, Martianus sets forth a world-system, and here is one of the few depictions of it. Earth is again the center, surrounded by a sphere of the four elements, our elementary world. Next comes the sphere of the Moon, which circles about the Earth, as does the Sun. The planets Mercury and Venus, however, circle about the Sun; and the radius of Venus' orbit is just a mite shorter than the distance between the sphere of the Moon and the sphere of the Sun, and also shorter than the distance between the sphere of the Sun and the sphere of Mars. Spheres for the three superior planets—Mars, Jupiter, and Saturn—then follow, and each of them centers on the Earth. Finally, the entire system is bounded by a sphere of fixed stars. Naiboda advances this system because Martianus had argued that the Sun is the center for the spheres of Mercury and Venus—in other words, some center other than the Earth is the hub for celestial motion. Copernicus had similarly cited Martianus to make the same point.[120] When Galileo reported on the moons of Jupiter after looking through his telescope, it was exactly this point, of course, that he incontrovertibly proved.

Naiboda's "System of the universe according to the opinion of the great man Nicolaus Copernicus of Thurn" . . . is evidently taken from the *De revolutionibus orbium coelestium. . . .* The sun is in the center, surrounded by orbits for Mercury, Venus, Earth, Mars, Jupiter, and Saturn, while the moon circles about the earth. A sphere of fixed stars determines the outer limit of this finite system.

Despite Naiboda's early example, publishing a methodical comparison of all recognized hypotheses really begins with Helisaeus Röslin in [his] slim quarto. . . . An appendix is given over to a series of diagrams for the universe according to various authorities. There are diagrams of the Ptolemaic system, the Copernican hypothesis, the hypothesis of Reymers, the hypothesis of Röslin himself, and the hypothesis of Tycho Brahe. . . .

"The system of the universe according to the hypotheses of Ptolemy and the ancient philosophers" . . . is fairly straightforward. The Earth presumably occupies the center, though it is not precisely designated, and the other seven planets revolve around it. An epicycle for the Moon is indicated, and also Mars is shown with an epicyclic orbit to account for its retrograde motion. Otherwise all is familiar, with a sphere of fixed stars coinciding with the primum mobile to give the system an outer limit.

In printing this volume, an error was made in the placement of diagrams. "The system of the universe according to the hypotheses of Nicolaus Copernicus" . . . was transposed with "The system of the universe according to the hypotheses of the noble Dane, Tycho Brahe" . . . as the printer confesses to his embarrassment. . . . But making the transposition that the printer requests, we see that the Copernican diagram closely repeats the heliocentric diagram in the *De revolutionibus orbium coelestium . . .*, while the Tychonic diagram is a reasonable reproduction of the diagram in Tycho's *De mundi aetherei recentioribus phaenomenis. . . .*

"The system of the universe according to the hypotheses of Reymers (the Bear) from Ditmarschen" . . . is somewhat simplified from the original diagram . . . , but accurate enough. And "The system of the universe according to Dr. Helisaeus Röslin" . . . we have already discussed. As in the other diagrams (except the Copernican), the earth is assumed to be the center of the system, but is not specifically indicated.

In the year before Galileo published his *Dialogo,* Jean-Baptiste Morin officiously offered a survey of the best-known theories about the motion or immobility of the earth up to that time: *Famosi et antiqui problematis de telluris motu, vel quiete; hactenus optata solutio* (Paris, 1631). Morin had trained as a physician, and in 1631 was the newly appointed professor of mathematics at the Collège de France, the celebrated institution in Paris that had been a center for scientific studies since Francis I had founded it a century earlier. For some time, however, Morin had pursued a lucrative career as an astrologer, and for forty years was eminently successful in catering to the rich and powerful in France. He was, for example, more than disinterestedly implicated in several maneuvers with Cardinal Richelieu—altogether a fascinating figure in this lively period of intrigue, though hardly a champion of truth and progress.

In astronomical matters, Morin was *au courant,* but adamantly conservative. Consequently, in his treatise, "A pleasant solution of the famous and ancient problem of whether the earth moves or is still," he concludes in favor of the latter alternative. The earth does *not* move, he argues, for the biblical and scientific reasons that had become commonplace among the orthodox. At best, Morin countenances the compromise of Tycho, which kept the earth at the center of the universe, although it made the sun the center of all the planetary spheres except that of the moon.

. . ."The system of the world according to Ptolemy" [in Morin's work] is wholly conventional except for one item: the cristalline sphere is omitted, and instead a large space intrudes between the sphere of Saturn and the sphere of the fixed stars, presumably to account for Tycho's inability to observe stellar parallax. . . . "The system of the world according to Copernicus" is honestly presented [by Morin] without distortion, though here again there is a large space between the sphere of Saturn and the sphere of fixed stars; and the primum mobile, distinctly present in the other two diagrams, does not appear. "The system of the world according to Tycho" is faithfully reproduced [by Morin] . . ., though the moons of Jupiter observed by Galileo are now inserted about that planet, and a separate sphere representing the primum mobile is drawn around the entire system to emphasize its finitude.

A Frenchman situated on the scale of respectability at the end opposite from Morin was Pierre Gassendi, an eminent philosopher and serious astronomer—a true savant. Known for his probity and deep thought, he was patronized by the highest men of the realm, including the king. As a reward for honest service, he garnered two honorable titles: Dean of the Cathedral Church in Digne and Regius Professor of Mathematics. Gassendi contributed to the anti-aristotelian movement of the seventeenth century, and through his reconstruction of Epicurus' philosophy provided groundswell for the cresting wave of empiricism. As an innovative thinker, he is worthy of sharing honors with Descartes, whom he often opposed in disputations of considerable consequence.

Gassendi was one of the first men to have a sense of science as a developing corpus of knowledge, a cumulative effort of the human spirit that involves generations of investigators. He was a *philosophe* with an interest in the history of science as a record of achievement rather than as an authority to be resurrected or a straw man to be demolished. In consequence, he wrote carefully researched biographies of several astronomers who had preceded him in the discipline, including Peiresc, Peurbach, Regiomontanus, Copernicus, and Tycho. Even more important, he published what may be considered the first history of astronomy, *Institutio astronomica juxta hypotheseis tam veterum quam Copernici, et Tychonis* (Paris, 1647).[121]

This exhaustive treatment of astronomical principles according to the major authorities was enormously influential in England as well as on the Continent. A revised reprinting was carried out in London in 1653,

and other editions appeared in the Netherlands. In the *Institutio astronomica* Gassendi, as the title suggests, deals in a fundamental way with the principles of astronomy. The first book is devoted to those definitions and propositions concerning the terrestrial and celestial globes that are necessary to making the following books intelligible. Gassendi then methodically discusses the hypotheses of the ancients (i.e., the geocentric system), of Copernicus, and of Tycho—the three world-systems that Morin had compared. But Gassendi is much more thorough. Furthermore, unlike Morin, Gassendi as a practicing astronomer sees the advantages of heliocentrism. By implication at least, he supports Copernicus. In the final analysis, however, he defers to the literal meaning of the Holy Scriptures, and grudgingly gives the nod to the Tychonic hypothesis. Joshua could not have commanded the sun to stand still unless it moves about the earth.

Scattered through this lengthy treatise are diagrams of each of the three world-systems that Gassendi has chosen to concentrate upon. . . . First comes the standard Ptolemaic diagram . . . with its "immobile empyreal heaven"—what poets after Milton refer to as "the empyrean." Only two things here are worthy of special note: the sphere of fixed stars is given a Greek name, [*Aplanes*], as well as a Latin name, *firmamentum;* and the cristalline sphere, to allow for what was known as "trepidation of the spheres," is divided into a "primary" and a "secondary" cristalline sphere. Otherwise, however, all is in proper place, with the four elements clearly in their central position and God in His *coelum empyreum immobile.* Appreciably later in the text comes the diagram for the Copernican proposal . . ., obviously taken from Galileo . . ., though Gassendi has cautiously enclosed it within a sphere of fixed stars. Finally, some fifty pages later comes the diagram for the Tychonic proposal . . ., copied directly from Tycho. . . .

Earlier, in 1642, Gassendi had published two letters to refute those who denied the movement of the earth. Morin, with the self-centered pomposity of a fool, took these letters as a personal attack, and proclaimed a vendetta. What saves this episode from rightful oblivion is a comic error. The fashionable astrologer ostentatiously predicted Gassendi's death in 1650—but to his own detriment. Gassendi, though in notoriously poor health, enjoyed a particularly good year and did not die until 1655.

More seriously, the two letters arguing against a stationary earth aroused the concern of Church authorities. When pressed on the matter, however, Gassendi discreetly chose to hedge. He had long been a friend of Galileo, and had written letters to aid in Galileo's defense as well as personal letters of condolence. In consequence, Gassendi was acutely aware of how an encounter with the Inquisition might go. Remembering these difficulties, he reserved final judgment about the motion of the earth.

Gassendi was helped in this by Giovanni-Battista Riccioli, a Jesuit who had lectured in philosophy and theology at Parma and Bologna for several decades. After the condemnation of Galileo, Father Riccioli was appointed by his superiors to counter the Copernicans on their own grounds—that is, according to principles of mathematics and astronomy, rather than Church doctrine. When discussing Gassendi, Father Riccioli fell back upon the time-tested sophistry—as old as Andreas Osiander, who had supplied the apologetic preface to Copernicus' *De revolutionibus orbium coelestium*—that Gassendi had presented his arguments as a theoretical hypothesis only, and not as a physical fact.[122] Father Riccioli, for his own purposes, was eager to retrieve Gassendi from the ranks of the Copernicans and claim him as an ally.

Father Riccioli's industry on behalf of the Holy Congregation is preserved in a magnificent two-volume work that stands as a major monument to seventeenth-century erudition: *Almagestum novum astronomiam veterum novamque complectens* (Bologna, 1651). Although later developments in astronomy have bypassed this colossal effort to provide "a new almagest comprising both the old and the new astronomy," it rises with indestructible grandeur like some baroque palace, outdated and visibly chipped, but secure in its very flamboyance. Later scientists have disagreed with Father Riccioli in most of his conclusions, but his graciousness and the fullness of his exposition remain intact.

. . . [An] engraved frontispiece of Father Riccioli's *Almagestum novum,* . . . appears before each of the two volumes. A few hints in the Preface (I.xvii) suggest a general outline of the elaborate allegory in this frontispiece, though it is largely self-evident. A winged figure identified as Astraea and representing Astronomy stands on the right. She wears a classical costume and buskins adorned with stars, and the zodiac serves as her belt. She assertively quotes Psalm 104: "[The foundations of the earth] should not be removed forever." In her left hand she carries an armillary sphere, though her attention is fixed upon the pair of scales held in her right hand. On these she carefully weighs the Copernican system against Father Riccioli's own . . ., which outweighs its adversary. Across the balancing beam is a Latin inscription: "Weighed in His scales."

Facing Astraea is another mythological figure identified as Argus of the hundred eyes, a denizen of allegory uniquely well qualified to practice astronomy. He is additionally identified as an astronomer by the telescope he holds. In the spirit of the engraving, Argus represents the astronomer in search of Divine Truth, since the light of the sun shines through his telescope. He is covered with eyes by which to see, and he casts his own eyes up towards heaven. Most tellingly, he

quotes Psalm 8: "When I consider thy heavens, the work of thy fingers. . . ."

Lying on the ground between these two figures is the ancient astronomer Claudius Ptolemaeus, who rapturously exclaims: "I am extolled and at the same time improved." Ptolemy is extolled by Father Riccioli in the sense that the Jesuit, like his Alexandrian predecessor, maintains the earth at the center of a finite universe, but Father Riccioli has also made adjustments to accord with the times. At Ptolemy's feet lies a diagram of his system, still prominent though evidently subordinate. His left hand rests upon a large coat-of-arms belonging to the Prince of Monaco, to whom the *Almagestum novum* is dedicated. His right hand rests upon another shield displaying two spheres, presumably a fanciful *impresa* for Ptolemy himself.

The upper third of this frontispiece is given over to an exposition of Father Riccioli's own world-system. At top center is the tetragrammaton, surrounded by an expansive aureole. Immediately below is a divine hand with three outstretched fingers, referring to the number, measure, and weight by which God created our universe. The product of that exercise is displayed by the cherubs who wing their self-conscious way toward the middle of the page from both margins. Those on the right bear the three planets that according to Father Riccioli revolve around the earth below: the moon, half of whose pock-marked surface is lit by beams reflected from the sun; Jupiter, surrounded by its four satellites; and Saturn, in its reported three-part form (the ring had not yet been described as such). Beneath these three planets a comet sweeps in from the right, still contained, as Aristotle had taught, within the orb of the moon. From the opposite side, a cherub bears the sun, which despite its brilliance nonetheless circles around the earth. Three other cherubs, however, carry the planets that according to Father Riccioli revolve about the sun: Mercury, Venus, and Mars. Mercury and Venus appear in their crescent form to indicate that they undergo phases, a recently observed phenomenon. Over this busy scene flutter two banners, which together comprise the second verse of Psalm 19: "Day unto day uttereth speech, and night unto night sheweth knowledge." The same injunction to study astronomy is operative here as at the beginning of the renaissance: by observing the heavens, we discern the attributes of our maker.

Copernicans such as Philippe van Lansberge had complained with justification that the Church opposed the heliocentric hypothesis on theological grounds alone, without examining the evidence and the scientific arguments in its support. In order to counter this complaint, Father Riccioli set himself a course of arduous study and mastered the science of astronomy. He scrupulously compiled the arguments in favor of Copernicus' system, and with the same care devised arguments to disprove it. With as much impartiality as he could manage, he conceded it to be the best unified and most beautiful of all the world-systems that had been proposed. He openly admired Copernicus' conception. He preferred it even to that of Tycho because of its elegant simplicity. Nonetheless, Father Riccioli felt compelled to uphold a literal reading of the Holy Scriptures, and therefore maintained the immobility of the earth in the center of a finite universe, an arrangement decreed and sustained by divine intention. No less than Milton, Father Riccioli asserted eternal providence; and in the process, he offered a painstaking critique of heliocentrism.

. . . Chapter vi of Book III bears the heading: "On the location of the sun and of the earth in the universe, upon which occasion the more notable world-systems are presented." Six separate diagrams then follow in rapid order, each with an explication and with a full list of authorities.

[The diagram labelled] "The system of Pythagoras, Ptolemy, etc." is the well-known geocentric system of the ancients. It had become customary by this time, however, to remove the cristalline sphere and the primum mobile, thereby constricting the system to eight celestial spheres. . . .

[The diagram labelled] "The system of Plato and the Platonists" is a representation of the geocentric system that derives from the *Timaeus* (38C-E). The Moon is of course the planet closest to Earth. But then, for some reason not given in the text, the sphere of the Sun is immediately adjacent to the sphere of the Moon. As further anomalies, after the sphere of the Sun come the spheres of Venus and Mercury in that order. Plato does not mention the other planets by name, but it is implied that the spheres of the three superior planets (Mars, Jupiter, and Saturn) follow in the usual order. Porphyry and other neoplatonists, however, differed from their master on at least one point, and reversed the arrangement of Venus and Mercury. For them, the order of the planets (ranging outward from Earth) comprised the Moon, the Sun, Mercury, and then Venus. Some later commentators, misinterpreting a passage in the *Timaeus* (34A), assumed that in this platonic hypothesis the Earth rotates upon its own axis.

[The diagram labelled] "The system of the Egyptians, Vitruvius, Martianus Capella, Macrobius, Bede, etc." [is] a system already discussed. . . . Vitrivius does indeed hint at such a system in the *De architectura* (IX.v-vi), while Macrobius in the *Commentarius in somnium Scipionis* is more explicit and ascribes it to the Egyptians (I.xix.1-6). Bede discusses the order of the planets in his *De natura rerum* (xiii), but does not place Mercury and Venus in orbit about the Sun, though one of the several scholia might suggest such an arrangement.

[These three diagrams] were the major hypotheses of those ages that derived their cosmologies without ben-

efit of extensive observational data. Coming into the renaissance, . . . [the fourth diagram,] "The system of Philolaus, Aristarchus, and Copernicus" [is] the heliocentric system that Copernicus was seen as having revived from the early pythagoreans, Philolaus and Aristarchus of Samos. The sun is of course in the center. Mercury comes next with a periodical revolution of eighty days, followed by Venus with a periodical revolution of nine months. Then comes the earth, circled by the moon, and the orbit of this combination is completed in one year. The amount of space required between the orbit of Venus and that of Mars to allow the moon to revolve about the earth is indicated by dotted circles. Beyond the earth and moon appear the three upper planets: Mars with a periodical revolution of two years, Jupiter with a periodical revolution of twelve years, and Saturn with a periodical revolution of thirty years. Finally, a sphere of fixed stars provides the outermost limit for the diagram.

[The fifth diagram] . . . presents "The system of Tycho," . . . by this time was commonplace. The diagram could have come directly from Tycho himself . . . , or perhaps from Gassendi. . . . But there is an innovation here: a relaxed concept of the sphere of fixed stars. This diagram allows for the stars to escape from the fixity of a sphere and to range at some varying distances between two limits, as Galileo had tentatively proposed . . . .

[The sixth diagram showing] . . . Father Riccioli's own system [is discussed next.] It is basically a geocentric system similar to Tycho's, with the moon and the sun revolving around the earth. Three planets—Mercury, Venus, and Mars—revolve about the sun, as in Tycho's system. The two uppermost planets, however, fix upon the earth as their center of motion. Father Riccioli argues that Jupiter and Saturn, since they have satellite bodies of their own, are planets of a different order from Mercury, Venus, and Mars, and therefore require the earth as an adequately steadfast point about which to wheel. He confirms his conservative view by placing a definite sphere of fixed stars around the circumference of his system.

Despite the steady formulation of important new theories, Father Riccioli's *Almagestum novum* remained a respected source-book of astronomy throughout the seventeenth century. Until the accumulation of a considerable body of fresh data, it was not likely to be replaced. Not surprisingly, the six diagrams of Father Riccioli reappear in the work of a fellow Jesuit, the equally erudite Athanasius Kircher. In 1656 Father Kircher published his account of an imaginary journey through the heavens which supposedly resulted from a dream, but which of course is a literary device as time honored as Cicero's report of Scipio's dream. On the journey Father Kircher has the benefit of two angelic guides, Cosmiel and Theodidactus, who proceed by dialogue to instruct him about the various regions of the universe. The author, like his friend Father Riccioli, is learned and up-to-date in his information, but more than the format of the work is conservative. His universe is basically aristotelian, comprising the four elements below and the quintessential spheres above, with an astrological overlay of planetary influences. The later editions of Father Kircher's *Iter exstaticum coeleste* contain [a seventh diagram][123] which is no more than an epitome of [the first six].

Across the Channel, Father Riccioli's diagrams received an extremely handsome redaction in a volume that stands as a landmark in English neoclassicism. In 1675 in London, Sir Edward Sherburne published his translation of Manilius' *The sphere*, dedicated to his benefactor, Charles II. As part of his learned critical apparatus, Sherburne added an appendix that includes a treatise entitled "The original and progress of astronomy" (pages 1-5) and also a lengthy "Catalogue of the most eminent astronomers, ancient & modern" (pages 6-126). Next comes an essay entitled "Of the cosmical system" (pages 127-37), in which, as Sherburne declares, he sets out "to explain and illustrate this Subject, by representing the several Opinions, as well of the *Ancients* as *Moderns,* touching the same" (page 127). Father Riccioli's *Almagestum novum* was undeniably open on Sherburne's study table as he wrote; it is gratefully cited on almost every page.

Illustrating Sherburne's historical survey of cosmology, the famous artist Wenceslaus Hollar supplied a large engraving for each of the six world-systems that Father Riccioli had distinguished. This series is the most beautiful as well as the easiest to study of all renaissance diagrams of the universe.[124] The best way to appreciate the completeness of this achievement is to see the pages whole . . . so that Hollar's engravings are enhanced by Sherburne's text.

Sherburne's essay on cosmology shows a comprehensiveness and depth of learning that is not unusual for his time. Such were the views of a cultivated Englishman when *Paradise Lost* was a recent addition to the growing library of cosmic speculation.

At the end of the seventeenth century, mathematical practitioners as active and current as William Leybourn were still using Father Riccioli as the point of reference. In 1690 Leybourn published in London his compendious textbook, *Cursus mathematicis. Mathematical sciences, in nine books.* There we find . . . essentially a repetition of the diagrams that Father Riccioli had set forth. Although the immediate source of Leybourn's page is Sherburne's discourse "Of the cosmical system" . . . —as Leybourn readily admits in his text (page 429)—the authority behind both these English cosmologists is unmistakably the Italian Jesuit who at mid-century had mounted the most sweeping arguments against the heliocentric theory.

What we find in the century and a half after Copernicus, then, is a fluid debate about the arrangement of the planets. This debate focused on the central issues of whether the earth or the sun moves, and whether the universe is infinite or delimited by an enclosing sphere. Gradually, the heliocentric hypothesis won acceptance. That the earth revolves daily around its own axis and moves in annual orbit about the sun was more easily conceded than the disturbing proposition that space is limitless. In any case, at the end of the seventeenth century the matter was far from settled in the public mind, despite fair agreement among the scientists. And the implications of heliocentrism had just begun to be explored.

Notes

. . . [100] . . . appetentiam quandam naturalem partibus inditam à divina providentia opificis universorum, ut in unitatem integritatemque suam sese conferant in formam globi coëuntes (*De revolutionibus orbium coelestium,* b3); translated by Charles Glenn Wallis (Chicago, 1952), p. 521.

[101] The title of the first chapter in Book I is "Quod mundus sit sphaericus" (a1).

[102] *De revolutionibus orbium coelestium,* c1-c1ᵛ; tr. Wallis, p. 526.

[103] In actual fact, some epicycles are still necessary to allow for circular rather than elliptical orbits for the planets, but their number is appreciably reduced. It was Kepler, of course, who early in the next century discovered that planetary orbits are ellipses, and thereby did away with the need for epicycles. . . .

[104] Tr. Wallis, pp. 527-28.

[105] The closest he comes is on the third day of the *Dialogo . . . sopra i due massimi sistemi del mondo. . . .* Cf. *Dialogue on the Great World Systems,* tr. Thomas Salusbury, ed. Giorgio de Santillana (Univ. of Chicago Press, 1953), p. 333, n. 25; also ibid., p. 23, n. 16.

[106] Tr. Wallis, p. 508.

[107] Melior Mundi speculator (*Mysterium cosmographicum* [Tübingen, 1596], A1ᵛ).

[108] *Dialogue,* tr. Salusbury, ed. Santillana, p. 5.

[109] *Castle of knowledge,* p. 165.

[110] See Dee's epistle prefixed to John Feild's *Ephemeris anni 1557. carrentis juxta Copernici et Reinhaldi canones* (London, 1556).

[111] Digges had in mind the foreword to the *De revolutionibus orbium coelestium,* which we now know to

have been inserted by a well-meaning but undistinguished theologian named Andreas Osiander in order to avert possible controversy.

[112] *De revolutionibus orbium coelestium,* I.vii-viii.

[113] Galileo, *Dialogue,* tr. Salusbury, ed. Santillana, pp. 336-39.

[114] Stellar parallax was first observed in 1838 by Friedrich Wilhelm Bessel.

[115] See Grant McColley, "Nicolas Reymers and the Fourth System of the World," *Popular Astronomy,* 46 (1938), 25-31.

[116] This statement has reference to the controversy over whether the planetary spheres are solid, or even material. In order to allow the orbit of Mars to intersect the orbit of the sun, Tycho was compelled to argue that the planetary spheres are "liquid," like air. Therefore in Tycho's system, as Burton says, the planets wander "without Orbs," and maintain their orderly courses only by virtue of divine providence. During Burton's century, Kepler and Newton were to define this virtue in mathematical terms as "gravity." . . .

[117] Philippe van Lansberge was a Flemish Protestant, an active clergyman as well as mathematician and cosmologist who strongly supported the Copernican hypothesis. His most important work in this respect is *Commentationes in motum terrae diurnum, et annuum, et in verum adspectabilis caeli typum* (Middelbourg, 1630).

[118] Burton, *The Anatomy of Melancholy,* ed. Floyd Dell and Paul Jordan-Smith (New York, 1929), p. 427. . . .

[120] *De revolutionibus orbium ˈcoelestium* [I.x], b4ᵛ.

[121] Gassendi later published a more concise and coherent history of astronomy as part of the preface to his *Tychonis Brahei . . . vita* et al. (Paris, 1654), ā4ēē1ᵛ. He covers astronomy from its legendary beginnings to his own time. Joseph Moxon printed an English translation of this text as an appendix to *A tutor to astronomie and geographie* (London, 1659), with the title "A discourse of the antiquity, progress, and augmentation of astronomie" (pp. 1-40).

[122] Riccioli, *Almagestum novum* (2 vols.; Bologna, 1651), II.489.

[123] The first edition of this work—*Itinerarium exstaticum* (Rome, 1656)—has no plates.

[124] A serious contender for this accolade is the splendid series of double-page engravings that adorns Andreas Cellarius' *Harmonia macrocosmica* (Amsterdam, 1661).

FURTHER READING

Criticism

Berry, Arthur. *A Short History of Astronomy: From the Earliest Times Through the Nineteenth Century.* New York: Dover Publications, 1961 (originally published in 1898), 440 p.

A broad overview of the history of astronomy from the Greeks through the nineteenth century, including biographical sketches.

Christianson, Gale E. *The Wild Abyss: The Story of the Men Who Made Modern Astronomy.* New York: The Free Press, 1978, 461p.

Covers the major themes and historical figures in the history of astronomy against a broader background of social and cultural developments.

Hall, A. Rupert. *From Galileo to Newton 1630-1720.* New York: Harper & Row, Publishers, 1963, 380p.

Explains the transition of the early seventeenth century, especially outside of Italy, from the dominance of the geocentric theory of the cosmos to that of the heliocentric theory.

King, Henry C. *The Background of Astronomy.* London: Watts, 1911, 254p.

Outlines the history of astronomy from its obscure beginnings in the Near East to the close of the sixteenth century in Europe.

Park, David. *The How and the Why: An Essay on the Origins and Development of Physical Theory.* Princeton: Princeton University Press, 1988, 459 p.

Explains the difficulties for the seventeenth-century astronomers of deducing from limited observational data fundamental mathematical principles that explain the whole structure and motion of the solar system.

Rapport, Samuel and Helen Wright, eds. *Astronomy.* New York: New York University Press, 1964, 354 p.

A brief introduction to the field of astronomy.

Taton, René and Curtis Wilson, eds. *Planetary Astronomy from the Renaissance to the Rise of Astrophysics, Part A: Tycho Brae to Newton in The General History of Astronomy,* Vol. 2. Cambridge: Cambridge University Press, 1989.

Deals with the history of the descriptive and theoretical astronomy of the solar system from the sixteenth century to the end of the nineteenth.

de Vaucouleirs, Gérard. *Discovery of the Universe: An Outline of the History of Astronomy from the Origins to 1956.* New York: Macmillan, 1957, 328 p.

Details the major developments in astronomy from antiquity to the immediate post-war era.

Literature Criticism from 1400 to 1800

Cumulative Indexes

How to Use This Index

Literary Criticism Series
Cumulative Author Index

20/1631
See Upward, Allen
A/C Cross
See Lawrence, T(homas) E(dward)
Abasiyanik, Sait Faik 1906-1954
See Sait Faik
See also CA 123
Abbey, Edward 1927-1989   **CLC 36, 59**
See also CA 45-48; 128; CANR 2, 41; MTCW 2
Abbott, Lee K(ittredge) 1947-   **CLC 48**
See also CA 124; CANR 51; DLB 130
Abe, Kobo 1924-1993**CLC 8, 22, 53, 81; DAM NOV**
See also CA 65-68; 140; CANR 24, 60; DLB 182; MTCW 1, 2
Abelard, Peter c. 1079-c. 1142   **CMLC 11**
See also DLB 115, 208
Abell, Kjeld 1901-1961   **CLC 15**
See also CA 111
Abish, Walter 1931-   **CLC 22**
See also CA 101; CANR 37; DLB 130
Abrahams, Peter (Henry) 1919-   **CLC 4**
See also BW 1; CA 57-60; CANR 26; DLB 117; MTCW 1, 2
Abrams, M(eyer) H(oward) 1912-   **CLC 24**
See also CA 57-60; CANR 13, 33; DLB 67
Abse, Dannie 1923-   **CLC 7, 29; DAB; DAM POET**
See also CA 53-56; CAAS 1; CANR 4, 46, 74; DLB 27; MTCW 1
Achebe, (Albert) Chinua(lumogu) 1930-**C L C 1, 3, 5, 7, 11, 26, 51, 75; BLC 1; DA; DAB; DAC; DAM MST, MULT, NOV; WLC**
See also AAYA 15; BW 2, 3; CA 1-4R; CANR 6, 26, 47; CLR 20; DLB 117; MAICYA; MTCW 1, 2; SATA 38, 40; SATA-Brief 38
Acker, Kathy 1948-1997   **CLC 45, 111**
See also CA 117; 122; 162; CANR 55
Ackroyd, Peter 1949-   **CLC 34, 52**
See also CA 123; 127; CANR 51, 74; DLB 155; INT 127; MTCW 1
Acorn, Milton 1923-   **CLC 15; DAC**
See also CA 103; DLB 53; INT 103
Adamov, Arthur 1908-1970 **CLC 4, 25; DAM DRAM**
See also CA 17-18; 25-28R; CAP 2; MTCW 1
Adams, Alice (Boyd) 1926-**CLC 6, 13, 46; SSC 24**
See also CA 81-84; CANR 26, 53, 75; DLBY 86; INT CANR-26; MTCW 1, 2
Adams, Andy 1859-1935   **TCLC 56**
See also YABC 1
Adams, Brooks 1848-1927   **TCLC 80**
See also CA 123; DLB 47
Adams, Douglas (Noel) 1952-   **CLC 27, 60; DAM POP**
See also AAYA 4; BEST 89:3; CA 106; CANR 34, 64; DLBY 83; JRDA; MTCW 1
Adams, Francis 1862-1893   **NCLC 33**
Adams, Henry (Brooks) 1838-1918 **TCLC 4, 52; DA; DAB; DAC; DAM MST**

See also CA 104; 133; CANR 77; DLB 12, 47, 189; MTCW 1
Adams, Richard (George) 1920-**CLC 4, 5, 18; DAM NOV**
See also AAYA 16; AITN 1, 2; CA 49-52; CANR 3, 35; CLR 20; JRDA; MAICYA; MTCW 1, 2; SATA 7, 69
Adamson, Joy(-Friederike Victoria) 1910-1980 **CLC 17**
See also CA 69-72; 93-96; CANR 22; MTCW 1; SATA 11; SATA-Obit 22
Adcock, Fleur 1934-   **CLC 41**
See also CA 25-28R; CAAS 23; CANR 11, 34, 69; DLB 40
Addams, Charles (Samuel) 1912-1988**CLC 30**
See also CA 61-64; 126; CANR 12, 79
Addams, Jane 1860-1945   **TCLC 76**
Addison, Joseph 1672-1719   **LC 18**
See also CDBLB 1660-1789; DLB 101
Adler, Alfred (F.) 1870-1937   **TCLC 61**
See also CA 119; 159
Adler, C(arole) S(chwerdtfeger) 1932-**CLC 35**
See also AAYA 4; CA 89-92; CANR 19, 40; JRDA; MAICYA; SAAS 15; SATA 26, 63, 102
Adler, Renata 1938-   **CLC 8, 31**
See also CA 49-52; CANR 5, 22, 52; MTCW 1
Ady, Endre 1877-1919   **TCLC 11**
See also CA 107
A.E. 1867-1935   **TCLC 3, 10**
See also Russell, George William
Aeschylus 525B.C.-456B.C.   **CMLC 11; DA; DAB; DAC; DAM DRAM, MST; DC 8; WLCS**
See also DLB 176
Aesop 620(?)B.C.-564(?)B.C.   **CMLC 24**
See also CLR 14; MAICYA; SATA 64
Affable Hawk
See MacCarthy, Sir(Charles Otto) Desmond
Africa, Ben
See Bosman, Herman Charles
Afton, Effie
See Harper, Frances Ellen Watkins
Agapida, Fray Antonio
See Irving, Washington
Agee, James (Rufus) 1909-1955 **TCLC 1, 19; DAM NOV**
See also AITN 1; CA 108; 148; CDALB 1941-1968; DLB 2, 26, 152; MTCW 1
Aghill, Gordon
See Silverberg, Robert
Agnon, S(hmuel) Y(osef Halevi) 1888-1970 **CLC 4, 8, 14; SSC 30**
See also CA 17-18; 25-28R; CANR 60; CAP 2; MTCW 1, 2
Agrippa von Nettesheim, Henry Cornelius 1486-1535   **LC 27**
Aherne, Owen
See Cassill, R(onald) V(erlin)
Ai 1947-   **CLC 4, 14, 69**
See also CA 85-88; CAAS 13; CANR 70; DLB 120

Aickman, Robert (Fordyce) 1914-1981 **C L C 57**
See also CA 5-8R; CANR 3, 72
Aiken, Conrad (Potter) 1889-1973**CLC 1, 3, 5, 10, 52; DAM NOV, POET; PC 26; SSC 9**
See also CA 5-8R; 45-48; CANR 4, 60; CDALB 1929-1941; DLB 9, 45, 102; MTCW 1, 2; SATA 3, 30
Aiken, Joan (Delano) 1924-   **CLC 35**
See also AAYA 1, 25; CA 9-12R; CANR 4, 23, 34, 64; CLR 1, 19; DLB 161; JRDA; MAICYA; MTCW 1; SAAS 1; SATA 2, 30, 73
Ainsworth, William Harrison 1805-1882   **NCLC 13**
See also DLB 21; SATA 24
Aitmatov, Chingiz (Torekulovich) 1928-**C L C 71**
See also CA 103; CANR 38; MTCW 1; SATA 56
Akers, Floyd
See Baum, L(yman) Frank
Akhmadulina, Bella Akhatovna 1937-   **C L C 53; DAM POET**
See also CA 65-68
Akhmatova, Anna 1888-1966**CLC 11, 25, 64; DAM POET; PC 2**
See also CA 19-20; 25-28R; CANR 35; CAP 1; MTCW 1, 2
Aksakov, Sergei Timofeyvich 1791-1859   **NCLC 2**
See also DLB 198
Aksenov, Vassily
See Aksyonov, Vassily (Pavlovich)
Akst, Daniel 1956-   **CLC 109**
See also CA 161
Aksyonov, Vassily (Pavlovich) 1932- **C L C 22, 37, 101**
See also CA 53-56; CANR 12, 48, 77
Akutagawa, Ryunosuke 1892-1927 **TCLC 16**
See also CA 117; 154
Alain 1868-1951   **TCLC 41**
See also CA 163
Alain-Fournier   **TCLC 6**
See also Fournier, Henri Alban
See also DLB 65
Alarcon, Pedro Antonio de 1833-1891**NCLC 1**
Alas (y Urena), Leopoldo (Enrique Garcia) 1852-1901   **TCLC 29**
See also CA 113; 131; HW 1
Albee, Edward (Franklin III) 1928-**CLC 1, 2, 3, 5, 9, 11, 13, 25, 53, 86, 113; DA; DAB; DAC; DAM DRAM, MST; DC 11; WLC**
See also AITN 1; CA 5-8R; CABS 3; CANR 8, 54, 74; CDALB 1941-1968; DLB 7; INT CANR-8; MTCW 1, 2
Alberti, Rafael 1902-   **CLC 7**
See also CA 85-88; DLB 108; HW 2
Albert the Great 1200(?)-1280   **CMLC 16**
See also DLB 115
Alcala-Galiano, Juan Valera y
See Valera y Alcala-Galiano, Juan

Alcott, Amos Bronson 1799-1888   NCLC 1
See also DLB 1
Alcott, Louisa May 1832-1888 NCLC 6, 58;
DA; DAB; DAC; DAM MST, NOV; SSC
27; WLC
See also AAYA 20; CDALB 1865-1917; CLR
1, 38; DLB 1, 42, 79; DLBD 14; JRDA;
MAICYA; SATA 100; YABC 1
Aldanov, M. A.
See Aldanov, Mark (Alexandrovich)
Aldanov, Mark (Alexandrovich) 1886(?)-1957
TCLC 23
See also CA 118
Aldington, Richard 1892-1962   CLC 49
See also CA 85-88; CANR 45; DLB 20, 36, 100,
149
Aldiss, Brian W(ilson) 1925- CLC 5, 14, 40;
DAM NOV
See also CA 5-8R; CAAS 2; CANR 5, 28, 64,
DLB 14; MTCW 1, 2; SATA 34
Alegria, Claribel 1924-CLC 75; DAM MULT;
PC 26
See also CA 131; CAAS 15; CANR 66; DLB
145; HW 1; MTCW 1
Alegria, Fernando 1918-   CLC 57
See also CA 9-12R; CANR 5, 32, 72; HW 1, 2
Aleichem, Sholom   TCLC 1, 35; SSC 33
See also Rabinovitch, Sholem
Alepoudelis, Odysseus
See Elytis, Odysseus
Aleshkovsky, Joseph 1929-
See Aleshkovsky, Yuz
See also CA 121; 128
Aleshkovsky, Yuz   CLC 44
See also Aleshkovsky, Joseph
Alexander, Lloyd (Chudley) 1924-   CLC 35
See also AAYA 1, 27; CA 1-4R; CANR 1, 24,
38, 55; CLR 1, 5, 48; DLB 52; JRDA;
MAICYA; MTCW 1; SAAS 19; SATA 3, 49,
81
Alexander, Samuel 1859-1938   TCLC 77
Alexie, Sherman (Joseph, Jr.) 1966- CLC 96;
DAM MULT
See also AAYA 28; CA 138; CANR 65; DLB
175, 206; MTCW 1; NNAL
Alfau, Felipe 1902-   CLC 66
See also CA 137
Alger, Horatio, Jr. 1832-1899   NCLC 8
See also DLB 42; SATA 16
Algren, Nelson 1909-1981CLC 4, 10, 33; SSC
33
See also CA 13-16R; 103; CANR 20, 61;
CDALB 1941-1968; DLB 9; DLBY 81, 82;
MTCW 1, 2
Ali, Ahmed 1910-   CLC 69
See also CA 25-28R; CANR 15, 34
Alighieri, Dante
See Dante
Allan, John B.
See Westlake, Donald E(dwin)
Allan, Sidney
See Hartmann, Sadakichi
Allan, Sydney
See Hartmann, Sadakichi
Allen, Edward 1948-   CLC 59
Allen, Fred 1894-1956   TCLC 87
Allen, Paula Gunn 1939-   CLC 84; DAM
MULT
See also CA 112; 143; CANR 63; DLB 175;
MTCW 1; NNAL
Allen, Roland
See Ayckbourn, Alan
Allen, Sarah A.

See Hopkins, Pauline Elizabeth
Allen, Sidney H.
See Hartmann, Sadakichi
Allen, Woody 1935- CLC 16, 52; DAM POP
See also AAYA 10; CA 33-36R; CANR 27, 38,
63; DLB 44; MTCW 1
Allende, Isabel 1942- CLC 39, 57, 97; DAM
MULT, NOV; HLC; WLCS
See also AAYA 18; CA 125; 130; CANR 51,
74; DLB 145; HW 1, 2; INT 130; MTCW 1,
2
Alleyn, Ellen
See Rossetti, Christina (Georgina)
Allingham, Margery (Louise) 1904-1966C L C
19
See also CA 5-8R; 25-28R; CANR 4, 58; DLB
77; MTCW 1, 2
Allingham, William 1824-1889   NCLC 25
See also DLB 35
Allison, Dorothy E. 1949-   CLC 78
See also CA 140; CANR 66; MTCW 1
Allston, Washington 1779-1843   NCLC 2
See also DLB 1
Almedingen, E. M.   CLC 12
See also Almedingen, Martha Edith von
See also SATA 3
Almedingen, Martha Edith von 1898-1971
See Almedingen, E. M.
See also CA 1-4R; CANR 1
Almodovar, Pedro 1949(?)-CLC 114; HLCS 1
See also CA 133; CANR 72; HW 2
Almqvist, Carl Jonas Love 1793-1866 N C L C
42
Alonso, Damaso 1898-1990   CLC 14
See also CA 110; 131; 130; CANR 72; DLB
108; HW 1, 2
Alov
See Gogol, Nikolai (Vasilyevich)
Alta 1942-   CLC 19
See also CA 57-60
Alter, Robert B(ernard) 1935-   CLC 34
See also CA 49-52; CANR 1, 47
Alther, Lisa 1944-   CLC 7, 41
See also CA 65-68; CAAS 30; CANR 12, 30,
51; MTCW 1
Althusser, L.
See Althusser, Louis
Althusser, Louis 1918-1990   CLC 106
See also CA 131; 132
Altman, Robert 1925-   CLC 16, 116
See also CA 73-76; CANR 43
Alvarez, A(lfred) 1929-   CLC 5, 13
See also CA 1-4R; CANR 3, 33, 63; DLB 14,
40
Alvarez, Alejandro Rodriguez 1903-1965
See Casona, Alejandro
See also CA 131; 93-96; HW 1
Alvarez, Julia 1950-   CLC 93; HLCS 1
See also AAYA 25; CA 147; CANR 69; MTCW
1
Alvaro, Corrado 1896-1956   TCLC 60
See also CA 163
Amado, Jorge 1912- CLC 13, 40, 106; DAM
MULT, NOV; HLC
See also CA 77-80; CANR 35, 74; DLB 113;
HW 2; MTCW 1, 2
Ambler, Eric 1909-1998   CLC 4, 6, 9
See also CA 9-12R; 171; CANR 7, 38, 74; DLB
77; MTCW 1, 2
Amichai, Yehuda 1924-   CLC 9, 22, 57, 116
See also CA 85-88; CANR 46, 60; MTCW 1
Amichai, Yehudah
See Amichai, Yehuda

Amiel, Henri Frederic 1821-1881   NCLC 4
Amis, Kingsley (William) 1922-1995CLC 1, 2,
3, 5, 8, 13, 40, 44; DA; DAB; DAC; DAM
MST, NOV
See also AITN 2; CA 9-12R; 150; CANR 8, 28,
54; CDBLB 1945-1960; DLB 15, 27, 100,
139; DLBY 96; INT CANR-8; MTCW 1, 2
Amis, Martin (Louis) 1949- CLC 4, 9, 38, 62,
101
See also BEST 90:3; CA 65-68; CANR 8, 27,
54, 73; DLB 14, 194; INT CANR-27; MTCW
1
Ammons, A(rchie) R(andolph) 1926-CLC 2, 3,
5, 8, 9, 25, 57, 108; DAM POET; PC 16
See also AITN 1; CA 9-12R; CANR 6, 36, 51,
73; DLB 5, 165; MTCW 1, 2
Amo, Tauraatua i
See Adams, Henry (Brooks)
Amory, Thomas 1691(?)-1788   LC 48
Anand, Mulk Raj 1905-   CLC 23, 93; DAM
NOV
See also CA 65-68; CANR 32, 64; MTCW 1, 2
Anatol
See Schnitzler, Arthur
Anaximander c. 610B.C.-c. 546B.C.CMLC 22
Anaya, Rudolfo A(lfonso) 1937-   CLC 23;
DAM MULT, NOV; HLC
See also AAYA 20; CA 45-48; CAAS 4; CANR
1, 32, 51; DLB 82, 206; HW 1; MTCW 1, 2
Andersen, Hans Christian 1805-1875NCLC 7;
DA; DAB; DAC; DAM MST, POP; SSC
6; WLC
See also CLR 6; MAICYA; SATA 100; YABC
1
Anderson, C. Farley
See Mencken, H(enry) L(ouis); Nathan, George
Jean
Anderson, Jessica (Margaret) Queale 1916-
CLC 37
See also CA 9-12R; CANR 4, 62
Anderson, Jon (Victor) 1940- CLC 9; DAM
POET
See also CA 25-28R; CANR 20
Anderson, Lindsay (Gordon) 1923-1994C L C
20
See also CA 125; 128; 146; CANR 77
Anderson, Maxwell 1888-1959TCLC 2; DAM
DRAM
See also CA 105; 152; DLB 7; MTCW 2
Anderson, Poul (William) 1926-   CLC 15
See also AAYA 5; CA 1-4R; CAAS 2; CANR
2, 15, 34, 64; DLB 8; INT CANR-15; MTCW
1, 2; SATA 90; SATA-Brief 39; SATA-Essay
106
Anderson, Robert (Woodruff) 1917-CLC 23;
DAM DRAM
See also AITN 1; CA 21-24R; CANR 32; DLB
7
Anderson, Sherwood 1876-1941 TCLC 1, 10,
24; DA; DAB; DAC; DAM MST, NOV;
SSC 1; WLC
See also AAYA 30; CA 104; 121; CANR 61;
CDALB 1917-1929; DLB 4, 9, 86; DLBD
1; MTCW 1, 2
Andier, Pierre
See Desnos, Robert
Andouard
See Giraudoux, (Hippolyte) Jean
Andrade, Carlos Drummond de   CLC 18
See also Drummond de Andrade, Carlos
Andrade, Mario de 1893-1945   TCLC 43
Andreae, Johann V(alentin) 1586-1654LC 32
See also DLB 164

Andreas-Salome, Lou 1861-1937 **TCLC 56**
See also DLB 66
Andress, Lesley
See Sanders, Lawrence
Andrewes, Lancelot 1555-1626 **LC 5**
See also DLB 151, 172
Andrews, Cicily Fairfield
See West, Rebecca
Andrews, Elton V.
See Pohl, Frederik
Andreyev, Leonid (Nikolaevich) 1871-1919
TCLC 3
See also CA 104
Andric, Ivo 1892-1975 **CLC 8**
See also CA 81-84; 57-60; CANR 43, 60; DLB
147; MTCW 1
Androvar
See Prado (Calvo), Pedro
Angelique, Pierre
See Bataille, Georges
Angell, Roger 1920- **CLC 26**
See also CA 57-60; CANR 13, 44, 70; DLB 171,
185
Angelou, Maya 1928-**CLC 12, 35, 64, 77; BLC
1; DA; DAB; DAC; DAM MST, MULT,
POET, POP; WLCS**
See also AAYA 7, 20; BW 2, 3; CA 65-68;
CANR 19, 42, 65; CDALBS; CLR 53; DLB
38; MTCW 1, 2; SATA 49
Anna Comnena 1083-1153 **CMLC 25**
Annensky, Innokenty (Fyodorovich) 1856-1909
TCLC 14
See also CA 110; 155
Annunzio, Gabriele d'
See D'Annunzio, Gabriele
Anodos
See Coleridge, Mary E(lizabeth)
Anon, Charles Robert
See Pessoa, Fernando (Antonio Nogueira)
Anouilh, Jean (Marie Lucien Pierre) 1910-1987
**CLC 1, 3, 8, 13, 40, 50; DAM DRAM; DC
8**
See also CA 17-20R; 123; CANR 32; MTCW
1, 2
Anthony, Florence
See Ai
Anthony, John
See Ciardi, John (Anthony)
Anthony, Peter
See Shaffer, Anthony (Joshua); Shaffer, Peter
(Levin)
Anthony, Piers 1934- **CLC 35; DAM POP**
See also AAYA 11; CA 21-24R; CANR 28, 56,
73; DLB 8; MTCW 1, 2; SAAS 22; SATA 84
Anthony, Susan B(rownell) 1916-1991 **TCLC
84**
See also CA 89-92; 134
Antoine, Marc
See Proust, (Valentin-Louis-George-Eugene-)
Marcel
Antoninus, Brother
See Everson, William (Oliver)
Antonioni, Michelangelo 1912- **CLC 20**
See also CA 73-76; CANR 45, 77
Antschel, Paul 1920-1970
See Celan, Paul
See also CA 85-88; CANR 33, 61; MTCW 1
Anwar, Chairil 1922-1949 **TCLC 22**
See also CA 121
Apess, William 1798-1839(?)**NCLC 73; DAM
MULT**
See also DLB 175; NNAL
Apollinaire, Guillaume 1880-1918**TCLC 3, 8,**

51; **DAM POET; PC 7**
See also Kostrowitzki, Wilhelm Apollinaris de
See also CA 152; MTCW 1
Appelfeld, Aharon 1932- **CLC 23, 47**
See also CA 112; 133
Apple, Max (Isaac) 1941- **CLC 9, 33**
See also CA 81-84; CANR 19, 54; DLB 130
Appleman, Philip (Dean) 1926- **CLC 51**
See also CA 13-16R; CAAS 18; CANR 6, 29,
56
Appleton, Lawrence
See Lovecraft, H(oward) P(hillips)
Apteryx
See Eliot, T(homas) S(tearns)
Apuleius, (Lucius Madaurensis) 125(?)-175(?)
CMLC 1
See also DLB 211
Aquin, Hubert 1929-1977 **CLC 15**
See also CA 105; DLB 53
Aquinas, Thomas 1224(?)-1274 **CMLC 33**
Scc also DLB 115
Aragon, Louis 1897-1982 **CLC 3, 22; DAM
NOV, POET**
See also CA 69-72; 108; CANR 28, 71; DLB
72; MTCW 1, 2
Arany, Janos 1817-1882 **NCLC 34**
Aranyos, Kakay
See Mikszath, Kalman
Arbuthnot, John 1667-1735 **LC 1**
See also DLB 101
Archer, Herbert Winslow
See Mencken, H(enry) L(ouis)
Archer, Jeffrey (Howard) 1940- **CLC 28;
DAM POP**
See also AAYA 16; BEST 89:3; CA 77-80;
CANR 22, 52; INT CANR-22
Archer, Jules 1915- **CLC 12**
See also CA 9-12R; CANR 6, 69; SAAS 5;
SATA 4, 85
Archer, Lee
See Ellison, Harlan (Jay)
Arden, John 1930-**CLC 6, 13, 15; DAM DRAM**
See also CA 13-16R; CAAS 4; CANR 31, 65,
67; DLB 13; MTCW 1
Arenas, Reinaldo 1943-1990 **CLC 41; DAM
MULT; HLC**
See also CA 124; 128; 133; CANR 73; DLB
145; HW 1; MTCW 1
Arendt, Hannah 1906-1975 **CLC 66, 98**
See also CA 17-20R; 61-64; CANR 26, 60;
MTCW 1, 2
Aretino, Pietro 1492-1556 **LC 12**
Arghezi, Tudor 1880-1967 **CLC 80**
See also Theodorescu, Ion N.
See also CA 167
Arguedas, Jose Maria 1911-1969**CLC 10, 18;
HLCS 1**
See also CA 89-92; CANR 73; DLB 113; HW 1
Argueta, Manlio 1936- **CLC 31**
See also CA 131; CANR 73; DLB 145; HW 1
Ariosto, Ludovico 1474-1533 **LC 6**
Aristides
See Epstein, Joseph
Aristophanes 450B.C.-385B.C.**CMLC 4; DA;
DAB; DAC; DAM DRAM, MST; DC 2;
WLCS**
See also DLB 176
Aristotle 384B.C.-322B.C. **CMLC 31; DA;
DAB; DAC; DAM MST; WLCS**
See also DLB 176
Arlt, Roberto (Godofredo Christophersen)
1900-1942**TCLC 29; DAM MULT; HLC**
See also CA 123; 131; CANR 67; HW 1, 2

Armah, Ayi Kwei 1939- **CLC 5, 33; BLC 1;
DAM MULT, POET**
See also BW 1; CA 61-64; CANR 21, 64; DLB
117; MTCW 1
Armatrading, Joan 1950- **CLC 17**
See also CA 114
Arnette, Robert
See Silverberg, Robert
**Arnim, Achim von (Ludwig Joachim von
Arnim)** 1781-1831 **NCLC 5; SSC 29**
See also DLB 90
Arnim, Bettina von 1785-1859 **NCLC 38**
See also DLB 90
Arnold, Matthew 1822-1888**NCLC 6, 29; DA;
DAB; DAC; DAM MST, POET; PC 5;
WLC**
See also CDBLB 1832-1890; DLB 32, 57
Arnold, Thomas 1795-1842 **NCLC 18**
See also DLB 55
Arnow, Harriette (Louisa) Simpson 1908-1986
CLC 2, 7, 18
See also CA 9-12R; 118; CANR 14; DLB 6;
MTCW 1, 2; SATA 42; SATA-Obit 47
Arouet, Francois-Marie
See Voltaire
Arp, Hans
See Arp, Jean
Arp, Jean 1887-1966 **CLC 5**
See also CA 81-84; 25-28R; CANR 42, 77
Arrabal
See Arrabal, Fernando
Arrabal, Fernando 1932- **CLC 2, 9, 18, 58**
See also CA 9-12R; CANR 15
Arrick, Fran **CLC 30**
See also Gaberman, Judie Angell
Artaud, Antonin (Marie Joseph) 1896-1948
TCLC 3, 36; DAM DRAM
See also CA 104; 149; MTCW 1
Arthur, Ruth M(abel) 1905-1979 **CLC 12**
See also CA 9-12R; 85-88; CANR 4; SATA 7,
26
Artsybashev, Mikhail (Petrovich) 1878-1927
TCLC 31
See also CA 170
Arundel, Honor (Morfydd) 1919-1973**CLC 17**
See also CA 21-22; 41-44R; CAP 2; CLR 35;
SATA 4; SATA-Obit 24
Arzner, Dorothy 1897-1979 **CLC 98**
Asch, Sholem 1880-1957 **TCLC 3**
See also CA 105
Ash, Shalom
See Asch, Sholem
Ashbery, John (Lawrence) 1927-**CLC 2, 3, 4,
6, 9, 13, 15, 25, 41, 77; DAM POET; PC 26**
See also CA 5-8R; CANR 9, 37, 66; DLB 5,
165; DLBY 81; INT CANR-9; MTCW 1, 2
Ashdown, Clifford
See Freeman, R(ichard) Austin
Ashe, Gordon
See Creasey, John
Ashton-Warner, Sylvia (Constance) 1908-1984
CLC 19
See also CA 69-72; 112; CANR 29; MTCW 1,
2
Asimov, Isaac 1920-1992 **CLC 1, 3, 9, 19, 26,
76, 92; DAM POP**
See also AAYA 13; BEST 90:2; CA 1-4R; 137;
CANR 2, 19, 36, 60; CLR 12; DLB 8; DLBY
92; INT CANR-19; JRDA; MAICYA;
MTCW 1, 2; SATA 1, 26, 74
Assis, Joaquim Maria Machado de
See Machado de Assis, Joaquim Maria
Astley, Thea (Beatrice May) 1925- **CLC 41**

See also CA 65-68; CANR 11, 43, 78

Aston, James
See White, T(erence) H(anbury)

Asturias, Miguel Angel 1899-1974 **CLC 3, 8, 13; DAM MULT, NOV; HLC**
See also CA 25-28; 49-52; CANR 32; CAP 2; DLB 113; HW 1; MTCW 1, 2

Atares, Carlos Saura
See Saura (Atares), Carlos

Atheling, William
See Pound, Ezra (Weston Loomis)

Atheling, William, Jr.
See Blish, James (Benjamin)

Atherton, Gertrude (Franklin Horn) 1857-1948 **TCLC 2**
See also CA 104; 155; DLB 9, 78, 186

Atherton, Lucius
See Masters, Edgar Lee

Atkins, Jack
See Harris, Mark

Atkinson, Kate **CLC 99**
See also CA 166

Attaway, William (Alexander) 1911-1986 **CLC 92; BLC 1; DAM MULT**
See also BW 2, 3; CA 143; DLB 76

Atticus
See Fleming, Ian (Lancaster); Wilson, (Thomas) Woodrow

Atwood, Margaret (Eleanor) 1939- **CLC 2, 3, 4, 8, 13, 15, 25, 44, 84; DA; DAB; DAC; DAM MST, NOV, POET; PC 8; SSC 2; WLC**
See also AAYA 12; BEST 89:2; CA 49-52; CANR 3, 24, 33, 59; DLB 53; INT CANR-24; MTCW 1, 2; SATA 50

Aubigny, Pierre d'
See Mencken, H(enry) L(ouis)

Aubin, Penelope 1685-1731(?) **LC 9**
See also DLB 39

Auchincloss, Louis (Stanton) 1917- **CLC 4, 6, 9, 18, 45; DAM NOV; SSC 22**
See also CA 1-4R; CANR 6, 29, 55; DLB 2; DLBY 80; INT CANR-29; MTCW 1

Auden, W(ystan) H(ugh) 1907-1973 **CLC 1, 2, 3, 4, 6, 9, 11, 14, 43; DA; DAB; DAC; DAM DRAM, MST, POET; PC 1; WLC**
See also AAYA 18; CA 9-12R; 45-48; CANR 5, 61; CDBLB 1914-1945; DLB 10, 20; MTCW 1, 2

Audiberti, Jacques 1900-1965 **CLC 38; DAM DRAM**
See also CA 25-28R

Audubon, John James 1785-1851 **NCLC 47**

Auel, Jean M(arie) 1936- **CLC 31, 107; DAM POP**
See also AAYA 7; BEST 90:4; CA 103; CANR 21, 64; INT CANR-21; SATA 91

Auerbach, Erich 1892-1957 **TCLC 43**
See also CA 118; 155

Augier, Emile 1820-1889 **NCLC 31**
See also DLB 192

August, John
See De Voto, Bernard (Augustine)

Augustine 354-430 **CMLC 6; DA; DAB; DAC; DAM MST; WLCS**
See also DLB 115

Aurelius
See Bourne, Randolph S(illiman)

Aurobindo, Sri
See Ghose, Aurabinda

Austen, Jane 1775-1817 **NCLC 1, 13, 19, 33, 51; DA; DAB; DAC; DAM MST, NOV; WLC**

See also AAYA 19; CDBLB 1789-1832; DLB 116

Auster, Paul 1947- **CLC 47**
See also CA 69-72; CANR 23, 52, 75; MTCW 1

Austin, Frank
See Faust, Frederick (Schiller)

Austin, Mary (Hunter) 1868-1934 **TCLC 25**
See also CA 109; DLB 9, 78, 206

Autran Dourado, Waldomiro
See Dourado, (Waldomiro Freitas) Autran

Averroes 1126-1198 **CMLC 7**
See also DLB 115

Avicenna 980-1037 **CMLC 16**
See also DLB 115

Avison, Margaret 1918- **CLC 2, 4, 97; DAC; DAM POET**
See also CA 17-20R; DLB 53; MTCW 1

Axton, David
See Koontz, Dean R(ay)

Ayckbourn, Alan 1939- **CLC 5, 8, 18, 33, 74; DAB; DAM DRAM**
See also CA 21-24R; CANR 31, 59; DLB 13; MTCW 1, 2

Aydy, Catherine
See Tennant, Emma (Christina)

Ayme, Marcel (Andre) 1902-1967 **CLC 11**
See also CA 89-92; CANR 67; CLR 25; DLB 72; SATA 91

Ayrton, Michael 1921-1975 **CLC 7**
See also CA 5-8R; 61-64; CANR 9, 21

Azorin **CLC 11**
See also Martinez Ruiz, Jose

Azuela, Mariano 1873-1952 **TCLC 3; DAM MULT; HLC**
See also CA 104; 131; HW 1, 2; MTCW 1, 2

Baastad, Babbis Friis
See Friis-Baastad, Babbis Ellinor

Bab
See Gilbert, W(illiam) S(chwenck)

Babbis, Eleanor
See Friis-Baastad, Babbis Ellinor

Babel, Isaac
See Babel, Isaak (Emmanuilovich)

Babel, Isaak (Emmanuilovich) 1894-1941(?) **TCLC 2, 13; SSC 16**
See also CA 104; 155; MTCW 1

<indexbod**Babits, Mihaly** 1883-1941 **TCLC 14**
See also CA 114

Babur 1483-1530 **LC 18**

Bacchelli, Riccardo 1891-1985 **CLC 19**
See also CA 29-32R; 117

Bach, Richard (David) 1936- **CLC 14; DAM NOV, POP**
See also AITN 1; BEST 89:2; CA 9-12R; CANR 18; MTCW 1; SATA 13

Bachman, Richard
See King, Stephen (Edwin)

Bachmann, Ingeborg 1926-1973 **CLC 69**
See also CA 93-96; 45-48; CANR 69; DLB 85

Bacon, Francis 1561-1626 **LC 18, 32**
See also CDBLB Before 1660; DLB 151

Bacon, Roger 1214(?)-1292 **CMLC 14**
See also DLB 115

Bacovia, George **TCLC 24**
See also Vasiliu, Gheorghe

Badanes, Jerome 1937- **CLC 59**

Bagehot, Walter 1826-1877 **NCLC 10**
See also DLB 55

Bagnold, Enid 1889-1981 **CLC 25; DAM DRAM**
See also CA 5-8R; 103; CANR 5, 40; DLB 13,

160, 191; MAICYA; SATA 1, 25

Bagritsky, Eduard 1895-1934 **TCLC 60**

Bagrjana, Elisaveta
See Belcheva, Elisaveta

Bagryana, Elisaveta **CLC 10**
See also Belcheva, Elisaveta
See also DLB 147

Bailey, Paul 1937- **CLC 45**
See also CA 21-24R; CANR 16, 62; DLB 14

Baillie, Joanna 1762-1851 **NCLC 71**
See also DLB 93

Bainbridge, Beryl (Margaret) 1933- **CLC 4, 5, 8, 10, 14, 18, 22, 62; DAM NOV**
See also CA 21-24R; CANR 24, 55, 75; DLB 14; MTCW 1, 2

Baker, Elliott 1922- **CLC 8**
See also CA 45-48; CANR 2, 63

Baker, Jean H. **TCLC 3, 10**
See also Russell, George William

Baker, Nicholson 1957- **CLC 61; DAM POP**
See also CA 135; CANR 63

Baker, Ray Stannard 1870-1946 **TCLC 47**
See also CA 118

Baker, Russell (Wayne) 1925- **CLC 31**
See also BEST 89:4; CA 57-60; CANR 11, 41, 59; MTCW 1, 2

Bakhtin, M.
See Bakhtin, Mikhail Mikhailovich

Bakhtin, M. M.
See Bakhtin, Mikhail Mikhailovich

Bakhtin, Mikhail
See Bakhtin, Mikhail Mikhailovich

Bakhtin, Mikhail Mikhailovich 1895-1975 **CLC 83**
See also CA 128; 113

Bakshi, Ralph 1938(?)- **CLC 26**
See also CA 112; 138

Bakunin, Mikhail (Alexandrovich) 1814-1876 **NCLC 25, 58**

Baldwin, James (Arthur) 1924-1987 **CLC 1, 2, 3, 4, 5, 8, 13, 15, 17, 42, 50, 67, 90; BLC 1; DA; DAB; DAC; DAM MST, MULT, NOV, POP; DC 1; SSC 10, 33; WLC**
See also AAYA 4; BW 1; CA 1-4R; 124; CABS 1; CANR 3, 24; CDALB 1941-1968; DLB 2, 7, 33; DLBY 87; MTCW 1, 2; SATA 9; SATA-Obit 54

Ballard, J(ames) G(raham) 1930- **CLC 3, 6, 14, 36; DAM NOV, POP; SSC 1**
See also AAYA 3; CA 5-8R; CANR 15, 39, 65; DLB 14, 207; MTCW 1, 2; SATA 93

Balmont, Konstantin (Dmitriyevich) 1867-1943 **TCLC 11**
See also CA 109; 155

Baltausis, Vincas
See Mikszath, Kalman

Balzac, Honore de 1799-1850 **NCLC 5, 35, 53; DA; DAB; DAC; DAM MST, NOV; SSC 5; WLC**
See also DLB 119

Bambara, Toni Cade 1939-1995 **CLC 19, 88; BLC 1; DA; DAC; DAM MST, MULT; WLCS**
See also AAYA 5; BW 2, 3; CA 29-32R; 150; CANR 24, 49; CDALBS; DLB 38; MTCW 1, 2

Bamdad, A.
See Shamlu, Ahmad

Banat, D. R.
See Bradbury, Ray (Douglas)

Bancroft, Laura
See Baum, L(yman) Frank

Banim, John 1798-1842 **NCLC 13**

See also DLB 116, 158, 159
Banim, Michael 1796-1874   **NCLC 13**
See also DLB 158, 159
Banjo, The
See Paterson, A(ndrew) B(arton)
Banks, Iain
See Banks, Iain M(enzies)
Banks, Iain M(enzies) 1954-   **CLC 34**
See also CA 123; 128; CANR 61; DLB 194;
INT 128
Banks, Lynne Reid   **CLC 23**
See also Reid Banks, Lynne
See also AAYA 6
Banks, Russell 1940-   **CLC 37, 72**
See also CA 65-68; CAAS 15; CANR 19, 52,
73; DLB 130
Banville, John 1945-   **CLC 46, 118**
See also CA 117; 128; DLB 14; INT 128
Banville, Theodore (Faullain) de 1832-1891
NCLC 9
Baraka, Amiri 1934-**CLC 1, 2, 3, 5, 10, 14, 33,
115; BLC 1; DA; DAC; DAM MST, MULT,
POET, POP; DC 6; PC 4; WLCS**
See also Jones, LeRoi
See also BW 2, 3; CA 21-24R; CABS 3; CANR
27, 38, 61; CDALB 1941-1968; DLB 5, 7,
16, 38; DLBD 8; MTCW 1, 2
Barbauld, Anna Laetitia 1743-1825**NCLC 50**
See also DLB 107, 109, 142, 158
Barbellion, W. N. P.   **TCLC 24**
See also Cummings, Bruce F(rederick)
Barbera, Jack (Vincent) 1945-   **CLC 44**
See also CA 110; CANR 45
Barbey d'Aurevilly, Jules Amedee 1808-1889
NCLC 1; SSC 17
See also DLB 119
Barbour, John c. 1316-1395   **CMLC 33**
See also DLB 146
Barbusse, Henri 1873-1935   **TCLC 5**
See also CA 105; 154; DLB 65
Barclay, Bill
See Moorcock, Michael (John)
Barclay, William Ewert
See Moorcock, Michael (John)
Barea, Arturo 1897-1957   **TCLC 14**
See also CA 111
Barfoot, Joan 1946-   **CLC 18**
See also CA 105
Barham, Richard Harris 1788-1845**NCLC 77**
See also DLB 159
Baring, Maurice 1874-1945   **TCLC 8**
See also CA 105; 168; DLB 34
Baring-Gould, Sabine 1834-1924   **TCLC 88**
See also DLB 156, 190
Barker, Clive 1952-   **CLC 52; DAM POP**
See also AAYA 10; BEST 90:3; CA 121; 129;
CANR 71; INT 129; MTCW 1, 2
Barker, George Granville 1913-1991 **CLC 8,
48; DAM POET**
See also CA 9-12R; 135; CANR 7, 38; DLB
20; MTCW 1
Barker, Harley Granville
See Granville-Barker, Harley
See also DLB 10
Barker, Howard 1946-   **CLC 37**
See also CA 102; DLB 13
Barker, Jane 1652-1732   **LC 42**
Barker, Pat(ricia) 1943-   **CLC 32, 94**
See also CA 117; 122; CANR 50; INT 122
Barlach, Ernst 1870-1938   **TCLC 84**
See also DLB 56, 118
Barlow, Joel 1754-1812   **NCLC 23**
See also DLB 37

Barnard, Mary (Ethel) 1909-   **CLC 48**
See also CA 21-22; CAP 2
Barnes, Djuna 1892-1982**CLC 3, 4, 8, 11, 29;
SSC 3**
See also CA 9-12R; 107; CANR 16, 55; DLB
4, 9, 45; MTCW 1, 2
Barnes, Julian (Patrick) 1946- **CLC 42; DAB**
See also CA 102; CANR 19, 54; DLB 194;
DLBY 93; MTCW 1
Barnes, Peter 1931-   **CLC 5, 56**
See also CA 65-68; CAAS 12; CANR 33, 34,
64; DLB 13; MTCW 1
Barnes, William 1801-1886   **NCLC 75**
See also DLB 32
Baroja (y Nessi), Pio 1872-1956**TCLC 8; HLC**
See also CA 104
Baron, David
See Pinter, Harold
Baron Corvo
See Rolfe, Frederick (William Serafino Austin
Lewis Mary)
Barondess, Sue K(aufman) 1926-1977 **CLC 8**
See also Kaufman, Sue
See also CA 1-4R; 69-72; CANR 1
Baron de Teive
See Pessoa, Fernando (Antonio Nogueira)
Baroness Von S.
See Zangwill, Israel
Barres, (Auguste-) Maurice 1862-1923**TCLC
47**
See also CA 164; DLB 123
Barreto, Afonso Henrique de Lima
See Lima Barreto, Afonso Henrique de
Barrett, (Roger) Syd 1946-   **CLC 35**
Barrett, William (Christopher) 1913-1992
CLC 27
See also CA 13-16R; 139; CANR 11, 67; INT
CANR-11
Barrie, J(ames) M(atthew) 1860-1937 **TCLC
2; DAB; DAM DRAM**
See also CA 104; 136; CANR 77; CDBLB
1890-1914; CLR 16; DLB 10, 141, 156;
MAICYA; MTCW 1; SATA 100; YABC 1
Barrington, Michael
See Moorcock, Michael (John)
Barrol, Grady
See Bograd, Larry
Barry, Mike
See Malzberg, Barry N(athaniel)
Barry, Philip 1896-1949   **TCLC 11**
See also CA 109; DLB 7
Bart, Andre Schwarz
See Schwarz-Bart, Andre
Barth, John (Simmons) 1930-**CLC 1, 2, 3, 5, 7,
9, 10, 14, 27, 51, 89; DAM NOV; SSC 10**
See also AITN 1, 2; CA 1-4R; CABS 1; CANR
5, 23, 49, 64; DLB 2; MTCW 1
Barthelme, Donald 1931-1989**CLC 1, 2, 3, 5, 6,
8, 13, 23, 46, 59, 115; DAM NOV; SSC 2**
See also CA 21-24R; 129; CANR 20, 58; DLB
2; DLBY 80, 89; MTCW 1, 2; SATA 7;
SATA-Obit 62
Barthelme, Frederick 1943-   **CLC 36, 117**
See also CA 114; 122; CANR 77; DLBY 85;
INT 122
Barthes, Roland (Gerard) 1915-1980**CLC 24,
83**
See also CA 130; 97-100; CANR 66; MTCW
1, 2
Barzun, Jacques (Martin) 1907-   **CLC 51**
See also CA 61-64; CANR 22
Bashevis, Isaac
See Singer, Isaac Bashevis

Bashkirtseff, Marie 1859-1884   **NCLC 27**
Basho
See Matsuo Basho
Bass, Kingsley B., Jr.
See Bullins, Ed
Bass, Rick 1958-   **CLC 79**
See also CA 126; CANR 53; DLB 212
Bassani, Giorgio 1916-   **CLC 9**
See also CA 65-68; CANR 33; DLB 128, 177;
MTCW 1
Bastos, Augusto (Antonio) Roa
See Roa Bastos, Augusto (Antonio)
Bataille, Georges 1897-1962   **CLC 29**
See also CA 101; 89-92
Bates, H(erbert) E(rnest) 1905-1974**CLC 46;
DAB; DAM POP; SSC 10**
See also CA 93-96; 45-48; CANR 34; DLB 162,
191; MTCW 1, 2
Bauchart
See Camus, Albert
Baudelaire, Charles 1821-1867 **NCLC 6, 29,
55; DA; DAB; DAC; DAM MST, POET;
PC 1; SSC 18; WLC**
Baudrillard, Jean 1929-   **CLC 60**
Baum, L(yman) Frank 1856-1919   **TCLC 7**
See also CA 108; 133; CLR 15; DLB 22; JRDA;
MAICYA; MTCW 1, 2; SATA 18, 100
Baum, Louis F.
See Baum, L(yman) Frank
Baumbach, Jonathan 1933-   **CLC 6, 23**
See also CA 13-16R; CAAS 5; CANR 12, 66;
DLBY 80; INT CANR-12; MTCW 1
Bausch, Richard (Carl) 1945-   **CLC 51**
See also CA 101; CAAS 14; CANR 43, 61; DLB
130
Baxter, Charles (Morley) 1947- **CLC 45, 78;
DAM POP**
See also CA 57-60; CANR 40, 64; DLB 130;
MTCW 2
Baxter, George Owen
See Faust, Frederick (Schiller)
Baxter, James K(eir) 1926-1972   **CLC 14**
See also CA 77-80
Baxter, John
See Hunt, E(verette) Howard, (Jr.)
Bayer, Sylvia
See Glassco, John
Baynton, Barbara 1857-1929   **TCLC 57**
Beagle, Peter S(oyer) 1939-   **CLC 7, 104**
See also CA 9-12R; CANR 4, 51, 73; DLBY
80; INT CANR-4; MTCW 1; SATA 60
Bean, Normal
See Burroughs, Edgar Rice
Beard, Charles A(ustin) 1874-1948 **TCLC 15**
See also CA 115; DLB 17; SATA 18
Beardsley, Aubrey 1872-1898   **NCLC 6**
Beattie, Ann 1947-**CLC 8, 13, 18, 40, 63; DAM
NOV, POP; SSC 11**
See also BEST 90:2; CA 81-84; CANR 53, 73;
DLBY 82; MTCW 1, 2
Beattie, James 1735-1803   **NCLC 25**
See also DLB 109
Beauchamp, Kathleen Mansfield 1888-1923
See Mansfield, Katherine
See also CA 104; 134; DA; DAC; DAM MST;
MTCW 2
Beaumarchais, Pierre-Augustin Caron de 1732-
1799   **DC 4**
See also DAM DRAM
Beaumont, Francis 1584(?)-1616**LC 33; DC 6**
See also CDBLB Before 1660; DLB 58, 121
**Beauvoir, Simone (Lucie Ernestine Marie
Bertrand) de** 1908-1986**CLC 1, 2, 4, 8, 14,**

31, 44, 50, 71; DA; DAB; DAC; DAM MST, NOV; WLC
See also CA 9-12R; 118; CANR 28, 61; DLB 72; DLBY 86; MTCW 1, 2
Becker, Carl (Lotus) 1873-1945   TCLC 63
See also CA 157; DLB 17
Becker, Jurek 1937-1997   CLC 7, 19
See also CA 85-88; 157; CANR 60; DLB 75
Becker, Walter 1950-   CLC 26
Beckett, Samuel (Barclay) 1906-1989 CLC 1, 2, 3, 4, 6, 9, 10, 11, 14, 18, 29, 57, 59, 83; DA; DAB; DAC; DAM DRAM, MST, NOV; SSC 16; WLC
See also CA 5-8R; 130; CANR 33, 61; CDBLB 1945-1960; DLB 13, 15; DLBY 90; MTCW 1, 2
Beckford, William 1760-1844   NCLC 16
See also DLB 39
Beckman, Gunnel 1910-   CLC 26
See also CA 33-36R; CANR 15; CLR 25; MAICYA; SAAS 9; SATA 6
Becque, Henri 1837-1899   NCLC 3
See also DLB 192
Beddoes, Thomas Lovell 1803-1849 NCLC 3
See also DLB 96
Bede c. 673-735   CMLC 20
See also DLB 146
Bedford, Donald F.
See Fearing, Kenneth (Flexner)
Beecher, Catharine Esther 1800-1878 N C L C 30
See also DLB 1
Beecher, John 1904-1980   CLC 6
See also AITN 1; CA 5-8R; 105; CANR 8
Beer, Johann 1655-1700   LC 5
See also DLB 168
Beer, Patricia 1924-   CLC 58
See also CA 61-64; CANR 13, 46; DLB 40
Beerbohm, Max
See Beerbohm, (Henry) Max(imilian)
Beerbohm, (Henry) Max(imilian) 1872-1956 TCLC 1, 24
See also CA 104; 154; CANR 79; DLB 34, 100
Beer-Hofmann, Richard 1866-1945TCLC 60
See also CA 160; DLB 81
Begiebing, Robert J(ohn) 1946-   CLC 70
See also CA 122; CANR 40
Behan, Brendan 1923-1964 CLC 1, 8, 11, 15, 79; DAM DRAM
See also CA 73-76; CANR 33; CDBLB 1945-1960; DLB 13; MTCW 1, 2
Behn, Aphra 1640(?)-1689 LC 1, 30, 42; DA; DAB; DAC; DAM DRAM, MST, NOV, POET; DC 4; PC 13; WLC
See also DLB 39, 80, 131
Behrman, S(amuel) N(athaniel) 1893-1973 CLC 40
See also CA 13-16; 45-48; CAP 1; DLB 7, 44
Belasco, David 1853-1931   TCLC 3
See also CA 104; 168; DLB 7
Belcheva, Elisaveta 1893-   CLC 10
See also Bagryana, Elisaveta
Beldone, Phil "Cheech"
See Ellison, Harlan (Jay)
Beleno
See Azuela, Mariano
Belinski, Vissarion Grigoryevich 1811-1848 NCLC 5
See also DLB 198
Belitt, Ben 1911-   CLC 22
See also CA 13-16R; CAAS 4; CANR 7, 77; DLB 5
Bell, Gertrude (Margaret Lowthian) 1868-1926

TCLC 67
See also CA 167; DLB 174
Bell, J. Freeman
See Zangwill, Israel
Bell, James Madison 1826-1902   TCLC 43; BLC 1; DAM MULT
See also BW 1; CA 122; 124; DLB 50
Bell, Madison Smartt 1957-   CLC 41, 102
See also CA 111; CANR 28, 54, 73; MTCW 1
Bell, Marvin (Hartley) 1937-CLC 8, 31; DAM POET
See also CA 21-24R; CAAS 14; CANR 59; DLB 5; MTCW 1
Bell, W. L. D.
See Mencken, H(enry) L(ouis)
Bellamy, Atwood C.
See Mencken, H(enry) L(ouis)
Bellamy, Edward 1850-1898   NCLC 4
See also DLB 12
Bellin, Edward J.
See Kuttner, Henry
Belloc, (Joseph) Hilaire (Pierre Sebastien Rene Swanton) 1870-1953 TCLC 7, 18; DAM POET; PC 24
See also CA 106; 152; DLB 19, 100, 141, 174; MTCW 1; YABC 1
Belloc, Joseph Peter Rene Hilaire
See Belloc, (Joseph) Hilaire (Pierre Sebastien Rene Swanton)
Belloc, Joseph Pierre Hilaire
See Belloc, (Joseph) Hilaire (Pierre Sebastien Rene Swanton)
Belloc, M. A.
See Lowndes, Marie Adelaide (Belloc)
Bellow, Saul 1915-CLC 1, 2, 3, 6, 8, 10, 13, 15, 25, 33, 34, 63, 79; DA; DAB; DAC; DAM MST, NOV, POP; SSC 14; WLC
See also AITN 2; BEST 89:3; CA 5-8R; CABS 1; CANR 29, 53; CDALB 1941-1968; DLB 2, 28; DLBD 3; DLBY 82; MTCW 1, 2
Belser, Reimond Karel Maria de 1929-
See Ruysslinck, Ward
See also CA 152
Bely, Andrey   TCLC 7; PC 11
See Bugayev, Boris Nikolayevich
See also MTCW 1
Belyi, Andrei
See Bugayev, Boris Nikolayevich
Benary, Margot
See Benary-Isbert, Margot
Benary-Isbert, Margot 1889-1979   CLC 12
See also CA 5-8R; 89-92; CANR 4, 72; CLR 12; MAICYA; SATA 2; SATA-Obit 21
Benavente (y Martinez), Jacinto 1866-1954 TCLC 3; DAM DRAM, MULT; HLCS 1
See also CA 106; 131; HW 1, 2; MTCW 1, 2
Benchley, Peter (Bradford) 1940-   CLC 4, 8; DAM NOV, POP
See also AAYA 14; AITN 2; CA 17-20R; CANR 12, 35, 66; MTCW 1, 2; SATA 3, 89
Benchley, Robert (Charles) 1889-1945 T C L C 1, 55
See also CA 105; 153; DLB 11
Benda, Julien 1867-1956   TCLC 60
See also CA 120; 154
Benedict, Ruth (Fulton) 1887-1948 TCLC 60
See also CA 158
Benedict, Saint c. 480-c. 547   CMLC 29
Benedikt, Michael 1935-   CLC 4, 14
See also CA 13-16R; CANR 7; DLB 5
Benet, Juan 1927-   CLC 28
See also CA 143
Benet, Stephen Vincent 1898-1943 TCLC 7;

DAM POET; SSC 10
See also CA 104; 152; DLB 4, 48, 102; DLBY 97; MTCW 1; YABC 1
Benet, William Rose 1886-1950   TCLC 28; DAM POET
See also CA 118; 152; DLB 45
Benford, Gregory (Albert) 1941-   CLC 52
See also CA 69-72; 175; CAAE 175; CAAS 27; CANR 12, 24, 49; DLBY 82
Bengtsson, Frans (Gunnar) 1894-1954 T C L C 48
See also CA 170
Benjamin, David
See Slavitt, David R(ytman)
Benjamin, Lois
See Gould, Lois
Benjamin, Walter 1892-1940   TCLC 39
See also CA 164
Benn, Gottfried 1886-1956   TCLC 3
See also CA 106; 153; DLB 56
Bennett, Alan 1934-CLC 45, 77; DAB; DAM MST
See also CA 103; CANR 35, 55; MTCW 1, 2
Bennett, (Enoch) Arnold 1867-1931 TCLC 5, 20
See also CA 106; 155; CDBLB 1890-1914; DLB 10, 34, 98, 135; MTCW 2
Bennett, Elizabeth
See Mitchell, Margaret (Munnerlyn)
Bennett, George Harold 1930-
See Bennett, Hal
See also BW 1; CA 97-100
Bennett, Hal   CLC 5
See also Bennett, George Harold
See also DLB 33
Bennett, Jay 1912-   CLC 35
See also AAYA 10; CA 69-72; CANR 11, 42, 79; JRDA; SAAS 4; SATA 41, 87; SATA-Brief 27
Bennett, Louise (Simone) 1919-CLC 28; BLC 1; DAM MULT
See also BW 2, 3; CA 151; DLB 117
Benson, E(dward) F(rederic) 1867-1940 TCLC 27
See also CA 114; 157; DLB 135, 153
Benson, Jackson J. 1930-   CLC 34
See also CA 25-28R; DLB 111
Benson, Sally 1900-1972   CLC 17
See also CA 19-20; 37-40R; CAP 1; SATA 1, 35; SATA-Obit 27
Benson, Stella 1892-1933   TCLC 17
See also CA 117; 155; DLB 36, 162
Bentham, Jeremy 1748-1832   NCLC 38
See also DLB 107, 158
Bentley, E(dmund) C(lerihew) 1875-1956 TCLC 12
See also CA 108; DLB 70
Bentley, Eric (Russell) 1916-   CLC 24
See also CA 5-8R; CANR 6, 67; INT CANR-6
Beranger, Pierre Jean de 1780-1857NCLC 34
Berdyaev, Nicolas
See Berdyaev, Nikolai (Aleksandrovich)
Berdyaev, Nikolai (Aleksandrovich) 1874-1948 TCLC 67
See also CA 120; 157
Berdyayev, Nikolai (Aleksandrovich)
See Berdyaev, Nikolai (Aleksandrovich)
Berendt, John (Lawrence) 1939-   CLC 86
See also CA 146; CANR 75; MTCW 1
Beresford, J(ohn) D(avys) 1873-1947 T C L C 81
See also CA 112; 155; DLB 162, 178, 197
Bergelson, David 1884-1952   TCLC 81

Berger, Colonel
See Malraux, (Georges-)Andre
Berger, John (Peter) 1926-   **CLC 2, 19**
See also CA 81-84; CANR 51, 78; DLB 14, 207
Berger, Melvin H. 1927-   **CLC 12**
See also CA 5-8R; CANR 4; CLR 32; SAAS 2;
SATA 5, 88
Berger, Thomas (Louis) 1924-CLC 3, 5, 8, 11,
18, 38; DAM NOV
See also CA 1-4R; CANR 5, 28, 51; DLB 2;
DLBY 80; INT CANR-28; MTCW 1, 2
Bergman, (Ernst) Ingmar 1918- CLC 16, 72
See also CA 81-84; CANR 33, 70; MTCW 2
Bergson, Henri(-Louis) 1859-1941 TCLC 32
See also CA 164
Bergstein, Eleanor 1938-   **CLC 4**
See also CA 53-56; CANR 5
Berkoff, Steven 1937-   **CLC 56**
See also CA 104; CANR 72
Bermant, Chaim (Icyk) 1929-   **CLC 40**
See also CA 57-60; CANR 6, 31, 57
Bern, Victoria
See Fisher, M(ary) F(rances) K(ennedy)
Bernanos, (Paul Louis) Georges 1888-1948
TCLC 3
See also CA 104; 130; DLB 72
Bernard, April 1956-   **CLC 59**
See also CA 131
Berne, Victoria
See Fisher, M(ary) F(rances) K(ennedy)
Bernhard, Thomas 1931-1989 CLC 3, 32, 61
See also CA 85-88; 127; CANR 32, 57; DLB
85, 124; MTCW 1
Bernhardt, Sarah (Henriette Rosine) 1844-1923
TCLC 75
See also CA 157
Berriault, Gina 1926- CLC 54, 109; SSC 30
See also CA 116; 129; CANR 66; DLB 130
Berrigan, Daniel 1921-   **CLC 4**
See also CA 33-36R; CAAS 1; CANR 11, 43,
78; DLB 5
Berrigan, Edmund Joseph Michael, Jr. 1934-
1983
See Berrigan, Ted
See also CA 61-64; 110; CANR 14
Berrigan, Ted   **CLC 37**
See also Berrigan, Edmund Joseph Michael, Jr.
See also DLB 5, 169
Berry, Charles Edward Anderson 1931-
See Berry, Chuck
See also CA 115
Berry, Chuck   **CLC 17**
See also Berry, Charles Edward Anderson
Berry, Jonas
See Ashbery, John (Lawrence)
Berry, Wendell (Erdman) 1934- CLC 4, 6, 8,
27, 46; DAM POET
See also AITN 1; CA 73-76; CANR 50, 73; DLB
5, 6; MTCW 1
Berryman, John 1914-1972CLC 1, 2, 3, 4, 6, 8,
10, 13, 25, 62; DAM POET
See also CA 13-16; 33-36R; CABS 2; CANR
35; CAP 1; CDALB 1941-1968; DLB 48;
MTCW 1, 2
Bertolucci, Bernardo 1940-   **CLC 16**
See also CA 106
Berton, Pierre (Francis Demarigny) 1920-
CLC 104
See also CA 1-4R; CANR 2, 56; DLB 68; SATA
99
Bertrand, Aloysius 1807-1841   **NCLC 31**
Bertran de Born c. 1140-1215   **CMLC 5**
Besant, Annie (Wood) 1847-1933   **TCLC 9**

See also CA 105
Bessie, Alvah 1904-1985   **CLC 23**
See also CA 5-8R; 116; CANR 2, 80; DLB 26
Bethlen, T. D.
See Silverberg, Robert
Beti, Mongo   CLC 27; BLC 1; DAM MULT
See also Biyidi, Alexandre
See also CANR 79
Betjeman, John 1906-1984 CLC 2, 6, 10, 34,
43; DAB; DAM MST, POET
See also CA 9-12R; 112; CANR 33, 56; CDBLB
1945-1960; DLB 20; DLBY 84; MTCW 1,
2
Bettelheim, Bruno 1903-1990   **CLC 79**
See also CA 81-84; 131; CANR 23, 61; MTCW
1, 2
Betti, Ugo 1892-1953   **TCLC 5**
See also CA 104; 155
Betts, Doris (Waugh) 1932- CLC 3, 6, 28
See also CA 13-16R; CANR 9, 66, 77; DLBY
82; INT CANR-9
Bevan, Alistair
See Roberts, Keith (John Kingston)
Bey, Pilaff
See Douglas, (George) Norman
Bialik, Chaim Nachman 1873-1934 TCLC 25
<indexhSee also CA 170
Bickerstaff, Isaac
See Swift, Jonathan
Bidart, Frank 1939-   **CLC 33**
See also CA 140
Bienek, Horst 1930-   **CLC 7, 11**
See also CA 73-76; DLB 75
Bierce, Ambrose (Gwinett) 1842-1914(?)
TCLC 1, 7, 44; DA; DAC; DAM MST; SSC
9; WLC
See also CA 104; 139; CANR 78; CDALB
1865-1917; DLB 11, 12, 23, 71, 74, 186
Biggers, Earl Derr 1884-1933   **TCLC 65**
See also CA 108; 153
Billings, Josh
See Shaw, Henry Wheeler
Billington, (Lady) Rachel (Mary) 1942- C L C
43
See also AITN 2; CA 33-36R; CANR 44
Binyon, T(imothy) J(ohn) 1936-   **CLC 34**
See also CA 111; CANR 28
Bioy Casares, Adolfo 1914-1999CLC 4, 8, 13,
88; DAM MULT; HLC; SSC 17
See also CA 29-32R; CANR 19, 43, 66; DLB
113; HW 1, 2; MTCW 1, 2
Bird, Cordwainer
See Ellison, Harlan (Jay)
Bird, Robert Montgomery 1806-1854NCLC 1
See also DLB 202
Birkerts, Sven 1951-   **CLC 116**
See also CA 128; 133; CAAS 29; INT 133
Birney, (Alfred) Earle 1904-1995CLC 1, 4, 6,
11; DAC; DAM MST, POET
See also CA 1-4R; CANR 5, 20; DLB 88;
MTCW 1
Biruni, al 973-1048(?)   **CMLC 28**
Bishop, Elizabeth 1911-1979 CLC 1, 4, 9, 13,
15, 32; DA; DAC; DAM MST, POET; PC
3
See also CA 5-8R; 89-92; CABS 2; CANR 26,
61; CDALB 1968-1988; DLB 5, 169;
MTCW 1, 2; SATA-Obit 24
Bishop, John 1935-   **CLC 10**
See also CA 105
Bissett, Bill 1939-   **CLC 18; PC 14**
See also CA 69-72; CAAS 19; CANR 15; DLB
53; MTCW 1

Bissoondath, Neil (Devindra) 1955-CLC 120;
DAC
See also CA 136
Bitov, Andrei (Georgievich) 1937- **CLC 57**
See also CA 142
Biyidi, Alexandre 1932-
See Beti, Mongo
See also BW 1, 3; CA 114; 124; MTCW 1, 2
Bjarme, Brynjolf
See Ibsen, Henrik (Johan)
Bjoernson, Bjoernstjerne (Martinius) 1832-
1910   **TCLC 7, 37**
See also CA 104
Black, Robert
See Holdstock, Robert P.
Blackburn, Paul 1926-1971   **CLC 9, 43**
See also CA 81-84; 33-36R; CANR 34; DLB
16; DLBY 81
Black Elk 1863-1950 TCLC 33; DAM MULT
See also CA 144; MTCW 1; NNAL
Black Hobart
See Sanders, (James) Ed(ward)
Blacklin, Malcolm
See Chambers, Aidan
Blackmore, R(ichard) D(oddridge) 1825-1900
TCLC 27
See also CA 120; DLB 18
Blackmur, R(ichard) P(almer) 1904-1965
CLC 2, 24
See also CA 11-12; 25-28R; CANR 71; CAP 1;
DLB 63
Black Tarantula
See Acker, Kathy
Blackwood, Algernon (Henry) 1869-1951
TCLC 5
See also CA 105; 150; DLB 153, 156, 178
Blackwood, Caroline 1931-1996CLC 6, 9, 100
See also CA 85-88; 151; CANR 32, 61, 65; DLB
14, 207; MTCW 1
Blade, Alexander
See Hamilton, Edmond; Silverberg, Robert
Blaga, Lucian 1895-1961   **CLC 75**
See also CA 157
Blair, Eric (Arthur) 1903-1950
See Orwell, George
See also CA 104; 132; DA; DAB; DAC; DAM
MST, NOV; MTCW 1, 2; SATA 29
Blair, Hugh 1718-1800   **NCLC 75**
Blais, Marie-Claire 1939-CLC 2, 4, 6, 13, 22;
DAC; DAM MST
See also CA 21-24R; CAAS 4; CANR 38, 75;
DLB 53; MTCW 1, 2
Blaise, Clark 1940-   **CLC 29**
See also AITN 2; CA 53-56; CAAS 3; CANR
5, 66; DLB 53
Blake, Fairley
See De Voto, Bernard (Augustine)
Blake, Nicholas
See Day Lewis, C(ecil)
See also DLB 77
Blake, William 1757-1827 NCLC 13, 37, 57;
DA; DAB; DAC; DAM MST, POET; PC
12; WLC
See also CDBLB 1789-1832; CLR 52; DLB 93,
163; MAICYA; SATA 30
Blasco Ibanez, Vicente 1867-1928 TCLC 12;
DAM NOV
See also CA 110; 131; HW 1, 2; MTCW 1
Blatty, William Peter 1928-CLC 2; DAM POP
See also CA 5-8R; CANR 9
Bleeck, Oliver
See Thomas, Ross (Elmore)
Blessing, Lee 1949-   **CLC 54**

Blish, James (Benjamin) 1921-1975   **CLC 14**
See also CA 1-4R; 57-60; CANR 3; DLB 8;
MTCW 1; SATA 66

Bliss, Reginald
See Wells, H(erbert) G(eorge)

Blixen, Karen (Christentze Dinesen) 1885-1962
See Dinesen, Isak
See also CA 25-28; CANR 22, 50; CAP 2;
MTCW 1, 2; SATA 44

Bloch, Robert (Albert) 1917-1994   **CLC 33**
See also AAYA 29; CA 5-8R; 146; CAAS 20;
CANR 5, 78; DLB 44; INT CANR-5; MTCW
1; SATA 12; SATA-Obit 82

Blok, Alexander (Alexandrovich) 1880-1921
TCLC 5; PC 21
See also CA 104

Blom, Jan
See Breytenbach, Breyten

Bloom, Harold 1930-   **CLC 24, 103**
See also CA 13-16R; CANR 39, 75; DLB 67;
MTCW 1

Bloomfield, Aurelius
See Bourne, Randolph S(illiman)

Blount, Roy (Alton), Jr. 1941-   **CLC 38**
See also CA 53-56; CANR 10, 28, 61; INT
CANR-28; MTCW 1, 2

Bloy, Leon 1846-1917   **TCLC 22**
See also CA 121; DLB 123

Blume, Judy (Sussman) 1938-   **CLC 12, 30;**
DAM NOV, POP
See also AAYA 3, 26; CA 29-32R; CANR 13,
37, 66; CLR 2, 15; DLB 52; JRDA;
MAICYA; MTCW 1, 2; SATA 2, 31, 79

Blunden, Edmund (Charles) 1896-1974 **C L C
2, 56**
See also CA 17-18; 45-48; CANR 54; CAP 2;
DLB 20, 100, 155; MTCW 1

Bly, Robert (Elwood) 1926- **CLC 1, 2, 5, 10, 15,
38; DAM POET**
See also CA 5-8R; CANR 41, 73; DLB 5;
MTCW 1, 2

Boas, Franz 1858-1942   **TCLC 56**
See also CA 115

Bobette
See Simenon, Georges (Jacques Christian)

Boccaccio, Giovanni 1313-1375   **CMLC 13;**
SSC 10

Bochco, Steven 1943-   **CLC 35**
See also AAYA 11; CA 124; 138

Bodel, Jean 1167(?)-1210   **CMLC 28**

Bodenheim, Maxwell 1892-1954   **TCLC 44**
See also CA 110; DLB 9, 45

Bodker, Cecil 1927-   **CLC 21**
See also CA 73-76; CANR 13, 44; CLR 23;
MAICYA; SATA 14

Boell, Heinrich (Theodor) 1917-1985 **CLC 2,
3, 6, 9, 11, 15, 27, 32, 72; DA; DAB; DAC;
DAM MST, NOV; SSC 23; WLC**
See also CA 21-24R; 116; CANR 24; DLB 69;
DLBY 85; MTCW 1, 2

Boerne, Alfred
See Doeblin, Alfred

Boethius 480(?)-524(?)   **CMLC 15**
See also DLB 115

Bogan, Louise 1897-1970 **CLC 4, 39, 46, 93;**
DAM POET; PC 12
See also CA 73-76; 25-28R; CANR 33; DLB
45, 169; MTCW 1, 2

Bogarde, Dirk   **CLC 19**
See also Van Den Bogarde, Derek Jules Gaspard
Ulric Niven
See also DLB 14

Bogosian, Eric 1953-   **CLC 45**

See also CA 138

Bograd, Larry 1953-   **CLC 35**
See also CA 93-96; CANR 57; SAAS 21; SATA
33, 89

Boiardo, Matteo Maria 1441-1494   **LC 6**

Boileau-Despreaux, Nicolas 1636-1711 **LC 3**

Bojer, Johan 1872-1959   **TCLC 64**

Boland, Eavan (Aisling) 1944-   **CLC 40, 67,
113; DAM POET**
See also CA 143; CANR 61; DLB 40; MTCW
2

Boll, Heinrich
See Boell, Heinrich (Theodor)

Bolt, Lee
See Faust, Frederick (Schiller)

Bolt, Robert (Oxton) 1924-1995 **CLC 14; DAM
DRAM**
See also CA 17-20R; 147; CANR 35, 67; DLB
13; MTCW 1

Bombet, Louis-Alexandre-Cesar
See Stendhal

Bomkauf
See Kaufman, Bob (Garnell)

Bonaventura   **NCLC 35**
See also DLB 90

Bond, Edward 1934- **CLC 4, 6, 13, 23; DAM
DRAM**
See also CA 25-28R; CANR 38, 67; DLB 13;
MTCW 1

Bonham, Frank 1914-1989   **CLC 12**
See also AAYA 1; CA 9-12R; CANR 4, 36;
JRDA; MAICYA; SAAS 3; SATA 1, 49;
SATA-Obit 62

Bonnefoy, Yves 1923-   **CLC 9, 15, 58; DAM
MST, POET**
See also CA 85-88; CANR 33, 75; MTCW 1, 2

Bontemps, Arna(ud Wendell) 1902-1973 **C L C
1, 18; BLC 1; DAM MULT, NOV, POET**
See also BW 1; CA 1-4R; 41-44R; CANR 4,
35; CLR 6; DLB 48, 51; JRDA; MAICYA;
MTCW 1, 2; SATA 2, 44; SATA-Obit 24

Booth, Martin 1944-   **CLC 13**
See also CA 93-96; CAAS 2

Booth, Philip 1925-   **CLC 23**
See also CA 5-8R; CANR 5; DLBY 82

Booth, Wayne C(layson) 1921-   **CLC 24**
See also CA 1-4R; CAAS 5; CANR 3, 43; DLB
67

Borchert, Wolfgang 1921-1947   **TCLC 5**
See also CA 104; DLB 69, 124

Borel, Petrus 1809-1859   **NCLC 41**

Borges, Jorge Luis 1899-1986 **CLC 1, 2, 3, 4, 6,
8, 9, 10, 13, 19, 44, 48, 83; DA; DAB; DAC;
DAM MST, MULT; HLC; PC 22; SSC 4;
WLC**
See also AAYA 26; CA 21-24R; CANR 19, 33,
75; DLB 113; DLBY 86; HW 1, 2; MTCW
1, 2

Borowski, Tadeusz 1922-1951   **TCLC 9**
See also CA 106; 154

Borrow, George (Henry) 1803-1881 **NCLC 9**
See also DLB 21, 55, 166

Bosman, Herman Charles 1905-1951 **T C L C
49**
See also Malan, Herman
See also CA 160

Bosschere, Jean de 1878(?)-1953   **TCLC 19**
See also CA 115

Boswell, James 1740-1795 **LC 4, 50; DA; DAB;
DAC; DAM MST; WLC**
See also CDBLB 1660-1789; DLB 104, 142

Bottoms, David 1949-   **CLC 53**
See also CA 105; CANR 22; DLB 120; DLBY

83

Boucicault, Dion 1820-1890   **NCLC 41**

Boucolon, Maryse 1937(?)-
See Conde, Maryse
See also BW 3; CA 110; CANR 30, 53, 76

Bourget, Paul (Charles Joseph) 1852-1935
TCLC 12
See also CA 107; DLB 123

Bourjaily, Vance (Nye) 1922-   **CLC 8, 62**
See also CA 1-4R; CAAS 1; CANR 2, 72; DLB
2, 143

Bourne, Randolph S(illiman) 1886-1918
TCLC 16
See also CA 117; 155; DLB 63

Bova, Ben(jamin William) 1932-   **CLC 45**
See also AAYA 16; CA 5-8R; CAAS 18; CANR
11, 56; CLR 3; DLBY 81; INT CANR-11;
MAICYA; MTCW 1; SATA 6, 68

Bowen, Elizabeth (Dorothea Cole) 1899-1973
**CLC 1, 3, 6, 11, 15, 22, 118; DAM NOV;
SSC 3, 28**
See also CA 17-18; 41-44R; CANR 35; CAP 2;
CDBLB 1945-1960; DLB 15, 162; MTCW
1, 2

Bowering, George 1935-   **CLC 15, 47**
See also CA 21-24R; CAAS 16; CANR 10; DLB
53

Bowering, Marilyn R(uthe) 1949-   **CLC 32**
See also CA 101; CANR 49

Bowers, Edgar 1924-   **CLC 9**
See also CA 5-8R; CANR 24; DLB 5

Bowie, David   **CLC 17**
See also Jones, David Robert

Bowles, Jane (Sydney) 1917-1973 **CLC 3, 68**
See also CA 19-20; 41-44R; CAP 2

Bowles, Paul (Frederick) 1910- **CLC 1, 2, 19,
53; SSC 3**
See also CA 1-4R; CAAS 1; CANR 1, 19, 50,
75; DLB 5, 6; MTCW 1, 2

Box, Edgar
See Vidal, Gore

Boyd, Nancy
See Millay, Edna St. Vincent

Boyd, William 1952-   **CLC 28, 53, 70**
See also CA 114; 120; CANR 51, 71

Boyle, Kay 1902-1992 **CLC 1, 5, 19, 58; SSC 5**
See also CA 13-16R; 140; CAAS 1; CANR 29,
61; DLB 4, 9, 48, 86; DLBY 93; MTCW 1,
2

Boyle, Mark
See Kienzle, William X(avier)

Boyle, Patrick 1905-1982   **CLC 19**
See also CA 127

Boyle, T. C. 1948-
See Boyle, T(homas) Coraghessan

Boyle, T(homas) Coraghessan 1948- **CLC 36,
55, 90; DAM POP; SSC 16**
See also BEST 90:4; CA 120; CANR 44, 76;
DLBY 86; MTCW 2

Boz
See Dickens, Charles (John Huffam)

Brackenridge, Hugh Henry 1748-1816 **N C L C
7**
See also DLB 11, 37

Bradbury, Edward P.
See Moorcock, Michael (John)
See also MTCW 2

Bradbury, Malcolm (Stanley) 1932- **CLC 32,
61; DAM NOV**
See also CA 1-4R; CANR 1, 33; DLB 14, 207;
MTCW 1, 2

Bradbury, Ray (Douglas) 1920- **CLC 1, 3, 10,
15, 42, 98; DA; DAB; DAC; DAM MST,**

NOV, POP; SSC 29; WLC
See also AAYA 15; AITN 1, 2; CA 1-4R; CANR
2, 30, 75; CDALB 1968-1988; DLB 2, 8;
MTCW 1, 2; SATA 11, 64

Bradford, Gamaliel 1863-1932   **TCLC 36**
See also CA 160; DLB 17

Bradley, David (Henry), Jr. 1950-   **CLC 23,
118; BLC 1; DAM MULT**
See also BW 1, 3; CA 104; CANR 26; DLB 33

Bradley, John Ed(mund, Jr.) 1958-   **CLC 55**
See also CA 139

Bradley, Marion Zimmer 1930-**CLC 30; DAM
POP**
See also AAYA 9; CA 57-60; CAAS 10; CANR
7, 31, 51, 75; DLB 8; MTCW 1, 2; SATA 90

Bradstreet, Anne 1612(?)-1672**LC 4, 30; DA;
DAC; DAM MST, POET; PC 10**
See also CDALB 1640-1865; DLB 24

Brady, Joan 1939-   **CLC 86**
See also CA 141

Bragg, Melvyn 1939-   **CLC 10**
See also BEST 89:3; CA 57-60; CANR 10, 48;
DLB 14

Brahe, Tycho 1546-1601   **LC 45**

Braine, John (Gerard) 1922-1986**CLC 1, 3, 41**
See also CA 1-4R; 120; CANR 1, 33; CDBLB
1945-1960; DLB 15; DLBY 86; MTCW 1

Bramah, Ernest 1868-1942   **TCLC 72**
See also CA 156; DLB 70

Brammer, William 1930(?)-1978   **CLC 31**
See also CA 77-80

Brancati, Vitaliano 1907-1954   **TCLC 12**
See also CA 109

Brancato, Robin F(idler) 1936-   **CLC 35**
See also AAYA 9; CA 69-72; CANR 11, 45;
CLR 32; JRDA; SAAS 9; SATA 97

Brand, Max
See Faust, Frederick (Schiller)

Brand, Millen 1906-1980   **CLC 7**
See also CA 21-24R; 97-100; CANR 72

Branden, Barbara   **CLC 44**
See also CA 148

Brandes, Georg (Morris Cohen) 1842-1927
TCLC 10
See also CA 105

Brandys, Kazimierz 1916-   **CLC 62**

Branley, Franklyn M(ansfield) 1915-**CLC 21**
See also CA 33-36R; CANR 14, 39; CLR 13;
MAICYA; SAAS 16; SATA 4, 68

Brathwaite, Edward (Kamau) 1930-**CLC 11;
BLCS; DAM POET**
See also BW 2, 3; CA 25-28R; CANR 11, 26,
47; DLB 125

Brautigan, Richard (Gary) 1935-1984**CLC 1,
3, 5, 9, 12, 34, 42; DAM NOV**
See also CA 53-56; 113; CANR 34; DLB 2, 5,
206; DLBY 80, 84; MTCW 1; SATA 56

Brave Bird, Mary 1953-
See Crow Dog, Mary (Ellen)
See also NNAL

Braverman, Kate 1950-   **CLC 67**
See also CA 89-92

Brecht, (Eugen) Bertolt (Friedrich) 1898-1956
**TCLC 1, 6, 13, 35; DA; DAB; DAC; DAM
DRAM, MST; DC 3; WLC**
See also CA 104; 133; CANR 62; DLB 56, 124;
MTCW 1, 2

Brecht, Eugen Berthold Friedrich
See Brecht, (Eugen) Bertolt (Friedrich)

Bremer, Fredrika 1801-1865   **NCLC 11**

Brennan, Christopher John 1870-1932**TCLC
17**
See also CA 117

Brennan, Maeve 1917-1993   **CLC 5**
See also CA 81-84; CANR 72

Brent, Linda
See Jacobs, Harriet A(nn)

Brentano, Clemens (Maria) 1778-1842**NCLC
1**
See also DLB 90

Brent of Bin Bin
See Franklin, (Stella Maria Sarah) Miles
(Lampe)

Brenton, Howard 1942-   **CLC 31**
See also CA 69-72; CANR 33, 67; DLB 13;
MTCW 1

Breslin, James 1930-1996
See Breslin, Jimmy
See also CA 73-76; CANR 31, 75; DAM NOV;
MTCW 1, 2

Breslin, Jimmy   **CLC 4, 43**
See also Breslin, James
See also AITN 1; DLB 185; MTCW 2

Bresson, Robert 1901-   **CLC 16**
See also CA 110; CANR 49

Breton, Andre 1896-1966**CLC 2, 9, 15, 54; PC
15**
See also CA 19-20; 25-28R; CANR 40, 60; CAP
2; DLB 65; MTCW 1, 2

Breytenbach, Breyten 1939(?)-   **CLC 23, 37;
DAM POET**
See also CA 113; 129; CANR 61

Bridgers, Sue Ellen 1942-   **CLC 26**
See also AAYA 8; CA 65-68; CANR 11, 36;
CLR 18; DLB 52; JRDA; MAICYA; SAAS
1; SATA 22, 90

Bridges, Robert (Seymour) 1844-1930 **TCLC
1; DAM POET**
See also CA 104; 152; CDBLB 1890-1914;
DLB 19, 98

Bridie, James   **TCLC 3**
See also Mavor, Osborne Henry
See also DLB 10

Brin, David 1950-   **CLC 34**
See also AAYA 21; CA 102; CANR 24, 70; INT
CANR-24; SATA 65

Brink, Andre (Philippus) 1935- **CLC 18, 36,
106**
See also CA 104; CANR 39, 62; INT 103;
MTCW 1, 2

Brinsmead, H(esba) F(ay) 1922-   **CLC 21**
See also CA 21-24R; CANR 10; CLR 47;
MAICYA; SAAS 5; SATA 18, 78

Brittain, Vera (Mary) 1893(?)-1970 **CLC 23**
See also CA 13-16; 25-28R; CANR 58; CAP 1;
DLB 191; MTCW 1, 2

Broch, Hermann 1886-1951   **TCLC 20**
See also CA 117; DLB 85, 124

Brock, Rose
See Hansen, Joseph

Brodkey, Harold (Roy) 1930-1996   **CLC 56**
See also CA 111; 151; CANR 71; DLB 130

Brodskii, Iosif
See Brodsky, Joseph

Brodsky, Iosif Alexandrovich 1940-1996
See Brodsky, Joseph
See also AITN 1; CA 41-44R; 151; CANR 37;
DAM POET; MTCW 1, 2

Brodsky, Joseph 1940-1996 **CLC 4, 6, 13, 36,
100; PC 9**
See also Brodskii, Iosif; Brodsky, Iosif
Alexandrovich
See also MTCW 1

Brodsky, Michael (Mark) 1948-   **CLC 19**
See also CA 102; CANR 18, 41, 58

Bromell, Henry 1947-   **CLC 5**
See also CA 53-56; CANR 9

Bromfield, Louis (Brucker) 1896-1956**TCLC
11**
See also CA 107; 155; DLB 4, 9, 86

Broner, E(sther) M(asserman) 1930- **CLC 19**
See also CA 17-20R; CANR 8, 25, 72; DLB 28

Bronk, William (M.) 1918-1999   **CLC 10**
See also CA 89-92; CANR 23; DLB 165

Bronstein, Lev Davidovich
See Trotsky, Leon

Bronte, Anne 1820-1849   **NCLC 71**
See also DLB 21, 199

Bronte, Charlotte 1816-1855 **NCLC 3, 8, 33,
58; DA; DAB; DAC; DAM MST, NOV;
WLC**
See also AAYA 17; CDBLB 1832-1890; DLB
21, 159, 199

Bronte, Emily (Jane) 1818-1848**NCLC 16, 35;
DA; DAB; DAC; DAM MST, NOV, POET;
PC 8; WLC**
See also AAYA 17; CDBLB 1832-1890; DLB
21, 32, 199

Brooke, Frances 1724-1789   **LC 6, 48**
See also DLB 39, 99

Brooke, Henry 1703(?)-1783   **LC 1**
See also DLB 39

Brooke, Rupert (Chawner) 1887-1915 **TCLC
2, 7; DA; DAB; DAC; DAM MST, POET;
PC 24; WLC**
See also CA 104; 132; CANR 61; CDBLB
1914-1945; DLB 19; MTCW 1, 2

Brooke-Haven, P.
See Wodehouse, P(elham) G(renville)

Brooke-Rose, Christine 1926(?)-   **CLC 40**
See also CA 13-16R; CANR 58; DLB 14

Brookner, Anita 1928- **CLC 32, 34, 51; DAB;
DAM POP**
See also CA 114; 120; CANR 37, 56; DLB 194;
DLBY 87; MTCW 1, 2

Brooks, Cleanth 1906-1994 **CLC 24, 86, 110**
See also CA 17-20R; 145; CANR 33, 35; DLB
63; DLBY 94; INT CANR-35; MTCW 1, 2

Brooks, George
See Baum, L(yman) Frank

Brooks, Gwendolyn 1917- **CLC 1, 2, 4, 5, 15,
49; BLC 1; DA; DAC; DAM MST, MULT,
POET; PC 7; WLC**
See also AAYA 20; AITN 1; BW 2, 3; CA 1-
4R; CANR 1, 27, 52, 75; CDALB 1941-
1968; CLR 27; DLB 5, 76, 165; MTCW 1,
2; SATA 6

Brooks, Mel   **CLC 12**
See also Kaminsky, Melvin
See also AAYA 13; DLB 26

Brooks, Peter 1938-   **CLC 34**
See also CA 45-48; CANR 1

Brooks, Van Wyck 1886-1963   **CLC 29**
See also CA 1-4R; CANR 6; DLB 45, 63, 103

Brophy, Brigid (Antonia) 1929-1995 **CLC 6,
11, 29, 105**
See also CA 5-8R; 149; CAAS 4; CANR 25,
53; DLB 14; MTCW 1, 2

Brosman, Catharine Savage 1934-   **CLC 9**
See also CA 61-64; CANR 21, 46

Brossard, Nicole 1943-   **CLC 115**
See also CA 122; CAAS 16; DLB 53

Brother Antoninus
See Everson, William (Oliver)

The Brothers Quay
See Quay, Stephen; Quay, Timothy

Broughton, T(homas) Alan 1936-   **CLC 19**
See also CA 45-48; CANR 2, 23, 48

Broumas, Olga 1949-   **CLC 10, 73**

See also CA 85-88; CANR 20, 69

Brown, Alan 1950-   **CLC 99**
See also CA 156

Brown, Charles Brockden 1771-1810 **NCLC 22, 74**
See also CDALB 1640-1865; DLB 37, 59, 73

Brown, Christy 1932-1981   **CLC 63**
See also CA 105; 104; CANR 72; DLB 14

Brown, Claude 1937- **CLC 30; BLC 1; DAM MULT**
See also AAYA 7; BW 1, 3; CA 73-76

Brown, Dee (Alexander) 1908- **CLC 18, 47; DAM POP**
See also AAYA 30; CA 13-16R; CAAS 6; CANR 11, 45, 60; DLBY 80; MTCW 1, 2; SATA 5

Brown, George
See Wertmueller, Lina

Brown, George Douglas 1869-1902 **TCLC 28**
See also CA 162

Brown, George Mackay 1921-1996**CLC 5, 48, 100**
See also CA 21-24R; 151; CAAS 6; CANR 12, 37, 67; DLB 14, 27, 139; MTCW 1; SATA 35

Brown, (William) Larry 1951-   **CLC 73**
See also CA 130; 134; INT 133

Brown, Moses
See Barrett, William (Christopher)

Brown, Rita Mae 1944-**CLC 18, 43, 79; DAM NOV, POP**
See also CA 45-48; CANR 2, 11, 35, 62; INT CANR-11; MTCW 1, 2

Brown, Roderick (Langmere) Haig-
See Haig-Brown, Roderick (Langmere)

Brown, Rosellen 1939-   **CLC 32**
See also CA 77-80; CAAS 10; CANR 14, 44

Brown, Sterling Allen 1901-1989 **CLC 1, 23, 59; BLC 1; DAM MULT, POET**
See also BW 1, 3; CA 85-88; 127; CANR 26; DLB 48, 51, 63; MTCW 1, 2

Brown, Will
See Ainsworth, William Harrison

Brown, William Wells 1813-1884   **NCLC 2; BLC 1; DAM MULT; DC 1**
See also DLB 3, 50

Browne, (Clyde) Jackson 1948(?)-   **CLC 21**
See also CA 120

Browning, Elizabeth Barrett 1806-1861 **NCLC 1, 16, 61, 66; DA; DAB; DAC; DAM MST, POET; PC 6; WLC**
See also CDBLB 1832-1890; DLB 32, 199

Browning, Robert 1812-1889 **NCLC 19; DA; DAB; DAC; DAM MST, POET; PC 2; WLCS**
See also CDBLB 1832-1890; DLB 32, 163; YABC 1

Browning, Tod 1882-1962   **CLC 16**
See also CA 141; 117

Brownson, Orestes Augustus 1803-1876 **NCLC 50**
See also DLB 1, 59, 73

Bruccoli, Matthew J(oseph) 1931-   **CLC 34**
See also CA 9-12R; CANR 7; DLB 103

Bruce, Lenny   **CLC 21**
See also Schneider, Leonard Alfred

Bruin, John
See Brutus, Dennis

Brulard, Henri
See Stendhal

Brulls, Christian
See Simenon, Georges (Jacques Christian)

Brunner, John (Kilian Houston) 1934-1995

CLC 8, 10; DAM POP
See also CA 1-4R; 149; CAAS 8; CANR 2, 37; MTCW 1, 2

Bruno, Giordano 1548-1600   **LC 27**

Brutus, Dennis 1924- **CLC 43; BLC 1; DAM MULT, POET; PC 24**
See also BW 2, 3; CA 49-52; CAAS 14; CANR 2, 27, 42; DLB 117

Bryan, C(ourtlandt) D(ixon) B(arnes) 1936- **CLC 29**
See also CA 73-76; CANR 13, 68; DLB 185; INT CANR-13

Bryan, Michael
See Moore, Brian

Bryant, William Cullen 1794-1878 **NCLC 6, 46; DA; DAB; DAC; DAM MST, POET; PC 20**
See also CDALB 1640-1865; DLB 3, 43, 59, 189

Bryusov, Valery Yakovlevich 1873-1924 **TCLC 10**
See also CA 107; 155

Buchan, John 1875-1940   **TCLC 41; DAB; DAM POP**
See also CA 108; 145; DLB 34, 70, 156; MTCW 1; YABC 2

Buchanan, George 1506-1582   **LC 4**
See also DLB 152

Buchheim, Lothar-Guenther 1918-   **CLC 6**
See also CA 85-88

Buchner, (Karl) Georg 1813-1837 **NCLC 26**

Buchwald, Art(hur) 1925-   **CLC 33**
See also AITN 1; CA 5-8R; CANR 21, 67; MTCW 1, 2; SATA 10

Buck, Pearl S(ydenstricker) 1892-1973**CLC 7, 11, 18; DA; DAB; DAC; DAM MST, NOV**
See also AITN 1; CA 1-4R; 41-44R; CANR 1, 34; CDALBS; DLB 9, 102; MTCW 1, 2; SATA 1, 25

Buckler, Ernest 1908-1984   **CLC 13; DAC; DAM MST**
See also CA 11-12; 114; CAP 1; DLB 68; SATA 47

Buckley, Vincent (Thomas) 1925-1988**CLC 57**
See also CA 101

Buckley, William F(rank), Jr. 1925-**CLC 7, 18, 37; DAM POP**
See also AITN 1; CA 1-4R; CANR 1, 24, 53; DLB 137; DLBY 80; INT CANR-24; MTCW 1, 2

Buechner, (Carl) Frederick 1926-**CLC 2, 4, 6, 9; DAM NOV**
See also CA 13-16R; CANR 11, 39, 64; DLBY 80; INT CANR-11; MTCW 1, 2

Buell, John (Edward) 1927-   **CLC 10**
See also CA 1-4R; CANR 71; DLB 53

Buero Vallejo, Antonio 1916-   **CLC 15, 46**
See also CA 106; CANR 24, 49, 75; HW 1; MTCW 1, 2

Bufalino, Gesualdo 1920(?)-   **CLC 74**
See also DLB 196

Bugayev, Boris Nikolayevich 1880-1934 **TCLC 7; PC 11**
See also Bely, Andrey
See also CA 104; 165; MTCW 1

Bukowski, Charles 1920-1994**CLC 2, 5, 9, 41, 82, 108; DAM NOV, POET; PC 18**
See also CA 17-20R; 144; CANR 40, 62; DLB 5, 130, 169; MTCW 1, 2

Bulgakov, Mikhail (Afanas'evich) 1891-1940 **TCLC 2, 16; DAM DRAM, NOV; SSC 18**
See also CA 105; 152

Bulgya, Alexander Alexandrovich 1901-1956

TCLC 53
See also Fadeyev, Alexander
See also CA 117

Bullins, Ed 1935- **CLC 1, 5, 7; BLC 1; DAM DRAM, MULT; DC 6**
See also BW 2, 3; CA 49-52; CAAS 16; CANR 24, 46, 73; DLB 7, 38; MTCW 1, 2

Bulwer-Lytton, Edward (George Earle Lytton) 1803-1873   **NCLC 1, 45**
See also DLB 21

Bunin, Ivan Alexeyevich 1870-1953 **TCLC 6; SSC 5**
See also CA 104

Bunting, Basil 1900-1985   **CLC 10, 39, 47; DAM POET**
See also CA 53-56; 115; CANR 7; DLB 20

Bunuel, Luis 1900-1983   **CLC 16, 80; DAM MULT; HLC**
See also CA 101; 110; CANR 32, 77; HW 1

Bunyan, John 1628-1688   **LC 4; DA; DAB; DAC; DAM MST; WLC**
See also CDBLB 1660-1789; DLB 39

Burckhardt, Jacob (Christoph) 1818-1897 **NCLC 49**

Burford, Eleanor
See Hibbert, Eleanor Alice Burford

Burgess, Anthony**CLC 1, 2, 4, 5, 8, 10, 13, 15, 22, 40, 62, 81, 94; DAB**
See also Wilson, John (Anthony) Burgess
See also AAYA 25; AITN 1; CDBLB 1960 to Present; DLB 14, 194; DLBY 98; MTCW 1

Burke, Edmund 1729(?)-1797 **LC 7, 36; DA; DAB; DAC; DAM MST; WLC**
See also DLB 104

Burke, Kenneth (Duva) 1897-1993 **CLC 2, 24**
See also CA 5-8R; 143; CANR 39, 74; DLB 45, 63; MTCW 1, 2

Burke, Leda
See Garnett, David

Burke, Ralph
See Silverberg, Robert

Burke, Thomas 1886-1945   **TCLC 63**
See also CA 113; 155; DLB 197

Burney, Fanny 1752-1840   **NCLC 12, 54**
See also DLB 39

Burns, Robert 1759-1796 **LC 3, 29, 40; DA; DAB; DAC; DAM MST, POET; PC 6; WLC**
See also CDBLB 1789-1832; DLB 109

Burns, Tex
See L'Amour, Louis (Dearborn)

Burnshaw, Stanley 1906-   **CLC 3, 13, 44**
See also CA 9-12R; DLB 48; DLBY 97

<Burr, Anne 1937-   **CLC 6**
See also CA 25-28R

Burroughs, Edgar Rice 1875-1950 **TCLC 2, 32; DAM NOV**
See also AAYA 11; CA 104; 132; DLB 8; MTCW 1, 2; SATA 41

Burroughs, William S(eward) 1914-1997**CLC 1, 2, 5, 15, 22, 42, 75, 109; DA; DAB; DAC; DAM MST, NOV, POP; WLC**
See also AITN 2; CA 9-12R; 160; CANR 20, 52; DLB 2, 8, 16, 152; DLBY 81, 97; MTCW 1, 2

Burton, SirRichard F(rancis) 1821-1890 **NCLC 42**
See also DLB 55, 166, 184

Busch, Frederick 1941-   **CLC 7, 10, 18, 47**
See also CA 33-36R; CAAS 1; CANR 45, 73; DLB 6

Bush, Ronald 1946-   **CLC 34**
See also CA 136

Bustos, F(rancisco)
See Borges, Jorge Luis
Bustos Domecq, H(onorio)
See Bioy Casares, Adolfo; Borges, Jorge Luis
Butler, Octavia E(stelle) 1947-**CLC 38; BLCS; DAM MULT, POP**
See also AAYA 18; BW 2, 3; CA 73-76; CANR 12, 24, 38, 73; DLB 33; MTCW 1, 2; SATA 84
Butler, Robert Olen (Jr.) 1945-**CLC 81; DAM POP**
See also CA 112; CANR 66; DLB 173; INT 112; MTCW 1
Butler, Samuel 1612-1680   **LC 16, 43**
See also DLB 101, 126
Butler, Samuel 1835-1902 **TCLC 1, 33; DA; DAB; DAC; DAM MST, NOV; WLC**
See also CA 143; CDBLB 1890-1914; DLB 18, 57, 174
Butler, Walter C.
See Faust, Frederick (Schiller)
Butor, Michel (Marie Francois) 1926-**CLC 1, 3, 8, 11, 15**
See also CA 9-12R; CANR 33, 66; DLB 83; MTCW 1, 2
Butts, Mary 1892(?)-1937   **TCLC 77**
See also CA 148
Buzo, Alexander (John) 1944-   **CLC 61**
See also CA 97-100; CANR 17, 39, 69
Buzzati, Dino 1906-1972   **CLC 36**
See also CA 160; 33-36R; DLB 177
Byars, Betsy (Cromer) 1928-   **CLC 35**
See also AAYA 19; CA 33-36R; CANR 18, 36, 57; CLR 1, 16; DLB 52; INT CANR-18; JRDA; MAICYA; MTCW 1; SAAS 1; SATA 4, 46, 80
Byatt, A(ntonia) S(usan Drabble) 1936- **C L C 19, 65; DAM NOV, POP**
See also CA 13-16R; CANR 13, 33, 50, 75; DLB 14, 194; MTCW 1, 2
Byrne, David 1952-   **CLC 26**
See also CA 127
Byrne, John Keyes 1926-
See Leonard, Hugh
See also CA 102; CANR 78; INT 102
Byron, George Gordon (Noel) 1788-1824 **NCLC 2, 12; DA; DAB; DAC; DAM MST, POET; PC 16; WLC**
See also CDBLB 1789-1832; DLB 96, 110
Byron, Robert 1905-1941   **TCLC 67**
See also CA 160; DLB 195
C. 3. 3.
See Wilde, Oscar
Caballero, Fernan 1796-1877   **NCLC 10**
Cabell, Branch
See Cabell, James Branch
Cabell, James Branch 1879-1958   **TCLC 6**
See also CA 105; 152; DLB 9, 78; MTCW 1
Cable, George Washington 1844-1925 **T C L C 4; SSC 4**
See also CA 104; 155; DLB 12, 74; DLBD 13
Cabral de Melo Neto, Joao 1920-   **CLC 76; DAM MULT**
See also CA 151
Cabrera Infante, G(uillermo) 1929-**CLC 5, 25, 45, 120; DAM MULT; HLC**
See also CA 85-88; CANR 29, 65; DLB 113; HW 1, 2; MTCW 1, 2
Cade, Toni
See Bambara, Toni Cade
Cadmus and Harmonia
See Buchan, John
Caedmon fl. 658-680   **CMLC 7**

See also DLB 146
Caeiro, Alberto
See Pessoa, Fernando (Antonio Nogueira)
Cage, John (Milton, Jr.) 1912-1992 **CLC 41**
See also CA 13-16R; 169; CANR 9, 78; DLB 193; INT CANR-9
Cahan, Abraham 1860-1951   **TCLC 71**
See also CA 108; 154; DLB 9, 25, 28
Cain, G.
See Cabrera Infante, G(uillermo)
Cain, Guillermo
See Cabrera Infante, G(uillermo)
Cain, James M(allahan) 1892-1977**CLC 3, 11, 28**
See also AITN 1; CA 17-20R; 73-76; CANR 8, 34, 61; MTCW 1
Caine, Mark
See Raphael, Frederic (Michael)
Calasso, Roberto 1941-   **CLC 81**
See also CA 143
Calderon de la Barca, Pedro 1600-1681 **L C 23; DC 3; HLCS 1**
Caldwell, Erskine (Preston) 1903-1987**CLC 1, 8, 14, 50, 60; DAM NOV; SSC 19**
See also AITN 1; CA 1-4R; 121; CAAS 1; CANR 2, 33; DLB 9, 86; MTCW 1, 2
Caldwell, (Janet Miriam) Taylor (Holland) 1900-1985**CLC 2, 28, 39; DAM NOV, POP**
See also CA 5-8R; 116; CANR 5; DLBD 17
Calhoun, John Caldwell 1782-1850**NCLC 15**
See also DLB 3
Calisher, Hortense 1911-**CLC 2, 4, 8, 38; DAM NOV; SSC 15**
See also CA 1-4R; CANR 1, 22, 67; DLB 2; INT CANR-22; MTCW 1, 2
Callaghan, Morley Edward 1903-1990**CLC 3, 14, 41, 65; DAC; DAM MST**
See also CA 9-12R; 132; CANR 33, 73; DLB 68; MTCW 1, 2
Callimachus c. 305B.C.-c. 240B.C. **CMLC 18**
See also DLB 176
Calvin, John 1509-1564   **LC 37**
Calvino, Italo 1923-1985**CLC 5, 8, 11, 22, 33, 39, 73; DAM NOV; SSC 3**
See also CA 85-88; 116; CANR 23, 61; DLB 196; MTCW 1, 2
Cameron, Carey 1952-   **CLC 59**
See also CA 135
Cameron, Peter 1959-   **CLC 44**
See also CA 125; CANR 50
Campana, Dino 1885-1932   **TCLC 20**
See also CA 117; DLB 114
Campanella, Tommaso 1568-1639   **LC 32**
Campbell, John W(ood, Jr.) 1910-1971 **C L C 32**
See also CA 21-22; 29-32R; CANR 34; CAP 2; DLB 8; MTCW 1
Campbell, Joseph 1904-1987   **CLC 69**
See also AAYA 3; BEST 89:2; CA 1-4R; 124; CANR 3, 28, 61; MTCW 1, 2
Campbell, Maria 1940-   **CLC 85; DAC**
See also CA 102; CANR 54; NNAL
Campbell, (John) Ramsey 1946-**CLC 42; SSC 19**
See also CA 57-60; CANR 7; INT CANR-7
Campbell, (Ignatius) Roy (Dunnachie) 1901-1957   **TCLC 5**
See also CA 104; 155; DLB 20; MTCW 2
Campbell, Thomas 1777-1844   **NCLC 19**
See also DLB 93; 144
Campbell, Wilfred   **TCLC 9**
See also Campbell, William
Campbell, William 1858(?)-1918

See Campbell, Wilfred
See also CA 106; DLB 92
Campion, Jane   **CLC 95**
See also CA 138
Campos, Alvaro de
See Pessoa, Fernando (Antonio Nogueira)
Camus, Albert 1913-1960**CLC 1, 2, 4, 9, 11, 14, 32, 63, 69; DA; DAB; DAC; DAM DRAM, MST, NOV; DC 2; SSC 9; WLC**
<indeSee also CA 89-92; DLB 72; MTCW 1, 2
Canby, Vincent 1924-   **CLC 13**
See also CA 81-84
Cancale
See Desnos, Robert
Canetti, Elias 1905-1994**CLC 3, 14, 25, 75, 86**
See also CA 21-24R; 146; CANR 23, 61, 79; DLB 85, 124; MTCW 1, 2
Canfield, Dorothea F.
See Fisher, Dorothy (Frances) Canfield
Canfield, Dorothea Frances
See Fisher, Dorothy (Frances) Canfield
Canfield, Dorothy
See Fisher, Dorothy (Frances) Canfield
Canin, Ethan 1960-   **CLC 55**
See also CA 131; 135
Cannon, Curt
See Hunter, Evan
Cao, Lan 1961-   **CLC 109**
See also CA 165
Cape, Judith
See Page, P(atricia) K(athleen)
Capek, Karel 1890-1938 **TCLC 6, 37; DA; DAB; DAC; DAM DRAM, MST, NOV; DC 1; WLC**
See also CA 104; 140; MTCW 1
Capote, Truman 1924-1984**CLC 1, 3, 8, 13, 19, 34, 38, 58; DA; DAB; DAC; DAM MST, NOV, POP; SSC 2; WLC**
See also CA 5-8R; 113; CANR 18, 62; CDALB 1941-1968; DLB 2, 185; DLBY 80, 84; MTCW 1, 2; SATA 91
Capra, Frank 1897-1991   **CLC 16**
See also CA 61-64; 135
Caputo, Philip 1941-   **CLC 32**
See also CA 73-76; CANR 40
Caragiale, Ion Luca 1852-1912   **TCLC 76**
See also CA 157
Card, Orson Scott 1951-**CLC 44, 47, 50; DAM POP**
See also AAYA 11; CA 102; CANR 27, 47, 73; INT CANR-27; MTCW 1, 2; SATA 83
Cardenal, Ernesto 1925-   **CLC 31; DAM MULT, POET; HLC; PC 22**
See also CA 49-52; CANR 2, 32, 66; HW 1, 2; MTCW 1, 2
Cardozo, Benjamin N(athan) 1870-1938 **TCLC 65**
See also CA 117; 164
Carducci, Giosue (Alessandro Giuseppe) 1835-1907   **TCLC 32**
See also CA 163
Carew, Thomas 1595(?)-1640   **LC 13**
See also DLB 126
Carey, Ernestine Gilbreth 1908-   **CLC 17**
See also CA 5-8R; CANR 71; SATA 2
Carey, Peter 1943-   **CLC 40, 55, 96**
See also CA 123; 127; CANR 53, 76; INT 127; MTCW 1, 2; SATA 94
Carleton, William 1794-1869   **NCLC 3**
See also DLB 159
Carlisle, Henry (Coffin) 1926-   **CLC 33**
See also CA 13-16R; CANR 15
Carlsen, Chris

See Holdstock, Robert P.
Carlson, Ron(ald F.) 1947-   **CLC 54**
See also CA 105; CANR 27
Carlyle, Thomas 1795-1881   **NCLC 70; DA;**
DAB; DAC; DAM MST
See also CDBLB 1789-1832; DLB 55; 144
Carman, (William) Bliss 1861-1929 **TCLC 7;**
DAC
See also CA 104; 152; DLB 92
Carnegie, Dale 1888-1955   **TCLC 53**
Carossa, Hans 1878-1956   **TCLC 48**
See also CA 170; DLB 66
Carpenter, Don(ald Richard) 1931-1995 **C L C**
41
See also CA 45-48; 149; CANR 1, 71
Carpenter, Edward 1844-1929   **TCLC 88**
See also CA 163
Carpentier (y Valmont), Alejo 1904-1980 **CLC**
8, 11, 38, 110; DAM MULT; HLC
See also CA 65-68; 97-100; CANR 11, 70; DLB
113; HW 1, 2
Carr, Caleb 1955(?)-   **CLC 86**
See also CA 147; CANR 73
Carr, Emily 1871-1945   **TCLC 32**
See also CA 159; DLB 68
Carr, John Dickson 1906-1977   **CLC 3**
See also Fairbairn, Roger
See also CA 49-52; 69-72; CANR 3, 33, 60;
MTCW 1, 2
Carr, Philippa
See Hibbert, Eleanor Alice Burford
Carr, Virginia Spencer 1929-   **CLC 34**
See also CA 61-64; DLB 111
Carrere, Emmanuel 1957-   **CLC 89**
Carrier, Roch 1937- **CLC 13, 78; DAC; DAM**
MST
See also CA 130; CANR 61; DLB 53; SATA
105
Carroll, James P. 1943(?)-   **CLC 38**
See also CA 81-84; CANR 73; MTCW 1
Carroll, Jim 1951-   **CLC 35**
See also AAYA 17; CA 45-48; CANR 42
Carroll, Lewis   **NCLC 2, 53; PC 18; WLC**
See also Dodgson, Charles Lutwidge
See also CDBLB 1832-1890; CLR 2, 18; DLB
18, 163, 178; DLBY 98; JRDA
Carroll, Paul Vincent 1900-1968   **CLC 10**
See also CA 9-12R; 25-28R; DLB 10
Carruth, Hayden 1921- **CLC 4, 7, 10, 18, 84;**
PC 10
See also CA 9-12R; CANR 4, 38, 59; DLB 5,
165; INT CANR-4; MTCW 1, 2; SATA 47
Carson, Rachel Louise 1907-1964   **CLC 71;**
DAM POP
See also CA 77-80; CANR 35; MTCW 1, 2;
SATA 23
Carter, Angela (Olive) 1940-1992 **CLC 5, 41,**
76; SSC 13
See also CA 53-56; 136; CANR 12, 36, 61; DLB
14, 207; MTCW 1, 2; SATA 66; SATA-Obit
70
Carter, Nick
See Smith, Martin Cruz
Carver, Raymond 1938-1988 **CLC 22, 36, 53,**
55; DAM NOV; SSC 8
See also CA 33-36R; 126; CANR 17, 34, 61;
DLB 130; DLBY 84, 88; MTCW 1, 2
Cary, Elizabeth, Lady Falkland 1585-1639
LC 30
Cary, (Arthur) Joyce (Lunel) 1888-1957
TCLC 1, 29
See also CA 104; 164; CDBLB 1914-1945;
DLB 15, 100; MTCW 2

Casanova de Seingalt, Giovanni Jacopo 1725-
1798   **LC 13**
Casares, Adolfo Bioy
See Bioy Casares, Adolfo
Casely-Hayford, J(oseph) E(phraim) 1866-1930
TCLC 24; BLC 1; DAM MULT
See also BW 2; CA 123; 152
Casey, John (Dudley) 1939-   **CLC 59**
See also BEST 90:2; CA 69-72; CANR 23
Casey, Michael 1947-   **CLC 2**
See also CA 65-68; DLB 5
Casey, Patrick
See Thurman, Wallace (Henry)
Casey, Warren (Peter) 1935-1988   **CLC 12**
See also CA 101; 127; INT 101
Casona, Alejandro   **CLC 49**
See also Alvarez, Alejandro Rodriguez
Cassavetes, John 1929-1989   **CLC 20**
See also CA 85-88; 127
Cassian, Nina 1924-   **PC 17**
Cassill, R(onald) V(erlin) 1919-   **CLC 4, 23**
See also CA 9-12R; CAAS 1; CANR 7, 45; DLB
6
Cassirer, Ernst 1874-1945   **TCLC 61**
See also CA 157
Cassity, (Allen) Turner 1929-   **CLC 6, 42**
See also CA 17-20R; CAAS 8; CANR 11; DLB
105
Castaneda, Carlos (Cesar Aranha) 1931(?)-
1998   **CLC 12, 119**
See also CA 25-28R; CANR 32, 66; HW 1;
MTCW 1
Castedo, Elena 1937-   **CLC 65**
See also CA 132
Castedo-Ellerman, Elena
See Castedo, Elena
Castellanos, Rosario 1925-1974 **CLC 66; DAM**
MULT; HLC
See also CA 131; 53-56; CANR 58; DLB 113;
HW 1; MTCW 1
Castelvetro, Lodovico 1505-1571   **LC 12**
Castiglione, Baldassare 1478-1529   **LC 12**
Castle, Robert
See Hamilton, Edmond
Castro, Guillen de 1569-1631   **LC 19**
Castro, Rosalia de 1837-1885 **NCLC 3; DAM**
MULT
Cather, Willa
See Cather, Willa Sibert
Cather, Willa Sibert 1873-1947 **TCLC 1, 11,**
31; DA; DAB; DAC; DAM MST, NOV;
SSC 2; WLC
See also AAYA 24; CA 104; 128; CDALB 1865-
1917; DLB 9, 54, 78; DLBD 1; MTCW 1, 2;
SATA 30
Catherine, Saint 1347-1380   **CMLC 27**
Cato, Marcus Porcius 234B.C.-149B.C.
CMLC 21
See also DLB 211
Catton, (Charles) Bruce 1899-1978   **CLC 35**
See also AITN 1; CA 5-8R; 81-84; CANR 7,
74; DLB 17; SATA 2; SATA-Obit 24
Catullus c. 84B.C.-c. 54B.C.   **CMLC 18**
See also DLB 211
Cauldwell, Frank
See King, Francis (Henry)
Caunitz, William J. 1933-1996   **CLC 34**
See also BEST 89:3; CA 125; 130; 152; CANR
73; INT 130
Causley, Charles (Stanley) 1917-   **CLC 7**
See also CA 9-12R; CANR 5, 35; CLR 30; DLB
27; MTCW 1; SATA 3, 66
Caute, (John) David 1936-   **CLC 29; DAM**

NOV
See also CA 1-4R; CAAS 4; CANR 1, 33, 64;
DLB 14
Cavafy, C(onstantine) P(eter) 1863-1933
TCLC 2, 7; DAM POET
See also Kavafis, Konstantinos Petrou
See also CA 148; MTCW 1
Cavallo, Evelyn
See Spark, Muriel (Sarah)
Cavanna, Betty   **CLC 12**
See also Harrison, Elizabeth Cavanna
See also JRDA; MAICYA; SAAS 4; SATA 1,
30
Cavendish, Margaret Lucas 1623-1673 **LC 30**
See also DLB 131
Caxton, William 1421(?)-1491(?)   **LC 17**
See also DLB 170
Cayer, D. M.
See Duffy, Maureen
Cayrol, Jean 1911-   **CLC 11**
See also CA 89-92; DLB 83
Cela, Camilo Jose 1916- **CLC 4, 13, 59; DAM**
MULT; HLC
See also BEST 90:2; CA 21-24R; CAAS 10;
CANR 21, 32, 76; DLBY 89; HW 1; MTCW
1, 2
Celan, Paul   **CLC 10, 19, 53, 82; PC 10**
See also Antschel, Paul
See also DLB 69
Celine, Louis-Ferdinand CLC 1, 3, 4, 7, 9, 15,
47
See also Destouches, Louis-Ferdinand
See also DLB 72
Cellini, Benvenuto 1500-1571   **LC 7**
Cendrars, Blaise 1887-1961   **CLC 18, 106**
See also Sauser-Hall, Frederic
Cernuda (y Bidon), Luis 1902-1963 **CLC 54;**
DAM POET
See also CA 131; 89-92; DLB 134; HW 1
Cervantes (Saavedra), Miguel de 1547-1616
LC 6, 23; DA; DAB; DAC; DAM MST,
NOV; SSC 12; WLC
Cesaire, Aime (Fernand) 1913- **CLC 19, 32,**
112; BLC 1; DAM MULT, POET; PC 25
See also BW 2, 3; CA 65-68; CANR 24, 43;
MTCW 1, 2
Chabon, Michael 1963-   **CLC 55**
See also CA 139; CANR 57
Chabrol, Claude 1930-   **CLC 16**
See also CA 110
Challans, Mary 1905-1983
See Renault, Mary
See also CA 81-84; 111; CANR 74; MTCW 2;
SATA 23; SATA-Obit 36
Challis, George
See Faust, Frederick (Schiller)
Chambers, Aidan 1934-   **CLC 35**
See also AAYA 27; CA 25-28R; CANR 12, 31,
58; JRDA; MAICYA; SAAS 12; SATA 1, 69
Chambers, James 1948-
See Cliff, Jimmy
See also CA 124
Chambers, Jessie
See Lawrence, D(avid) H(erbert Richards)
Chambers, Robert W(illiam) 1865-1933
TCLC 41
See also CA 165; DLB 202; SATA 107
Chandler, Raymond (Thornton) 1888-1959
TCLC 1, 7; SSC 23
See also AAYA 25; CA 104; 129; CANR 60;
CDALB 1929-1941; DLBD 6; MTCW 1, 2
Chang, Eileen 1920-1995   **SSC 28**
See also CA 166

Chang, Jung 1952-   **CLC 71**
See also CA 142
Chang Ai-Ling
See Chang, Eileen
Channing, William Ellery 1780-1842 **NCLC 17**
See also DLB 1, 59
Chao, Patricia 1955-   **CLC 119**
<indexSee also CA 163
Chaplin, Charles Spencer 1889-1977 **CLC 16**
See also Chaplin, Charlie
See also CA 81-84; 73-76
Chaplin, Charlie
See Chaplin, Charles Spencer
See also DLB 44
Chapman, George 1559(?)-1634 **LC 22; DAM DRAM**
See also DLB 62, 121
Chapman, Graham 1941-1989   **CLC 21**
See also Monty Python
See also CA 116; 129; CANR 35
Chapman, John Jay 1862-1933   **TCLC 7**
See also CA 104
Chapman, Lee
See Bradley, Marion Zimmer
Chapman, Walker
See Silverberg, Robert
Chappell, Fred (Davis) 1936-   **CLC 40, 78**
See also CA 5-8R; CAAS 4; CANR 8, 33, 67; DLB 6, 105
Char, Rene(-Emile) 1907-1988 **CLC 9, 11, 14, 55; DAM POET**
See also CA 13-16R; 124; CANR 32; MTCW 1, 2
Charby, Jay
See Ellison, Harlan (Jay)
Chardin, Pierre Teilhard de
See Teilhard de Chardin, (Marie Joseph) Pierre
Charles I 1600-1649   **LC 13**
Charriere, Isabelle de 1740-1805   **NCLC 66**
Charyn, Jerome 1937-   **CLC 5, 8, 18**
See also CA 5-8R; CAAS 1; CANR 7, 61; DLBY 83; MTCW 1
Chase, Mary (Coyle) 1907-1981   **DC 1**
See also CA 77-80; 105; SATA 17; SATA-Obit 29
Chase, Mary Ellen 1887-1973   **CLC 2**
See also CA 13-16; 41-44R; CAP 1; SATA 10
Chase, Nicholas
See Hyde, Anthony
Chateaubriand, Francois Rene de 1768-1848 **NCLC 3**
See also DLB 119
Chatterje, Sarat Chandra 1876-1936(?)
See Chatterji, Saratchandra
See also CA 109
Chatterji, Bankim Chandra 1838-1894 **NCLC 19**
Chatterji, Saratchandra   **TCLC 13**
See also Chatterje, Sarat Chandra
Chatterton, Thomas 1752-1770 **LC 3; DAM POET**
See also DLB 109
Chatwin, (Charles) Bruce 1940-1989 **CLC 28, 57, 59; DAM POP**
See also AAYA 4; BEST 90:1; CA 85-88; 127; DLB 194, 204
Chaucer, Daniel
See Ford, Ford Madox
Chaucer, Geoffrey 1340(?)-1400 **LC 17; DA; DAB; DAC; DAM MST, POET; PC 19; WLCS**
See also CDBLB Before 1660; DLB 146

Chaviaras, Strates 1935-
See Haviaras, Stratis
See also CA 105
Chayefsky, Paddy   **CLC 23**
See also Chayefsky, Sidney
See also DLB 7, 44; DLBY 81
Chayefsky, Sidney 1923-1981
See Chayefsky, Paddy
See also CA 9-12R; 104; CANR 18; DAM DRAM
Chedid, Andree 1920-   **CLC 47**
See also CA 145
Cheever, John 1912-1982 **CLC 3, 7, 8, 11, 15, 25, 64; DA; DAB; DAC; DAM MST, NOV, POP; SSC 1; WLC**
See also CA 5-8R; 106; CABS 1; CANR 5, 27, 76; CDALB 1941-1968; DLB 2, 102; DLBY 80, 82; INT CANR-5; MTCW 1, 2
Cheever, Susan 1943-   **CLC 18, 48**
See also CA 103; CANR 27, 51; DLBY 82; INT CANR-27
Chekhonte, Antosha
See Chekhov, Anton (Pavlovich)
Chekhov, Anton (Pavlovich) 1860-1904 **TCLC 3, 10, 31, 55; DA; DAB; DAC; DAM DRAM, MST; DC 9; SSC 2, 28; WLC**
See also CA 104; 124; SATA 90
Chernyshevsky, Nikolay Gavrilovich 1828-1889 **NCLC 1**
Cherry, Carolyn Janice 1942-
See Cherryh, C. J.
See also CA 65-68; CANR 10
Cherryh, C. J.   **CLC 35**
See also Cherry, Carolyn Janice
See also AAYA 24; DLBY 80; SATA 93
Chesnutt, Charles W(addell) 1858-1932 **TCLC 5, 39; BLC 1; DAM MULT; SSC 7**
See also BW 1, 3; CA 106; 125; CANR 76; DLB 12; 50, 78; MTCW 1, 2
Chester, Alfred 1929(?)-1971   **CLC 49**
See also CA 33-36R; DLB 130
Chesterton, G(ilbert) K(eith) 1874-1936 **TCLC 1, 6, 64; DAM NOV, POET; SSC 1**
See also CA 104; 132; CANR 73; CDBLB 1914-1945; DLB 10, 19, 34, 70, 98, 149, 178; MTCW 1, 2; SATA 27
Chiang, Pin-chin 1904-1986
See Ding Ling
See also CA 118
Ch'ien Chung-shu 1910-   **CLC 22**
See also CA 130; CANR 73; MTCW 1, 2
Child, L. Maria
See Child, Lydia Maria
Child, Lydia Maria 1802-1880   **NCLC 6, 73**
See also DLB 1, 74; SATA 67
Child, Mrs.
<indexSee Child, Lydia Maria
Child, Philip 1898-1978   **CLC 19, 68**
See also CA 13-14; CAP 1; SATA 47
Childers, (Robert) Erskine 1870-1922 **TCLC 65**
See also CA 113; 153; DLB 70
Childress, Alice 1920-1994 **CLC 12, 15, 86, 96; BLC 1; DAM DRAM, MULT, NOV; DC 4**
See also AAYA 8; BW 2, 3; CA 45-48; 146; CANR 3, 27, 50, 74; CLR 14; DLB 7, 38; JRDA; MAICYA; MTCW 1, 2; SATA 7, 48, 81
Chin, Frank (Chew, Jr.) 1940-   **DC 7**
See also CA 33-36R; CANR 71; DAM MULT; DLB 206
Chislett, (Margaret) Anne 1943-   **CLC 34**
See also CA 151

Chitty, Thomas Willes 1926-   **CLC 11**
See also Hinde, Thomas
See also CA 5-8R
Chivers, Thomas Holley 1809-1858 **NCLC 49**
See also DLB 3
Choi, Susan   **CLC 119**
Chomette, Rene Lucien 1898-1981
See Clair, Rene
See also CA 103
Chopin, Kate **TCLC 5, 14; DA; DAB; SSC 8; WLCS**
See also Chopin, Katherine
See also CDALB 1865-1917; DLB 12, 78
Chopin, Katherine 1851-1904
See Chopin, Kate
See also CA 104; 122; DAC; DAM MST, NOV
Chretien de Troyes c. 12th cent. -   **CMLC 10**
See also DLB 208
Christie
See Ichikawa, Kon
Christie, Agatha (Mary Clarissa) 1890-1976 **CLC 1, 6, 8, 12, 39, 48, 110; DAB; DAC; DAM NOV**
See also AAYA 9; AITN 1, 2; CA 17-20R; 61-64; CANR 10, 37; CDBLB 1914-1945; DLB 13, 77; MTCW 1, 2; SATA 36
Christie, (Ann) Philippa
See Pearce, Philippa
See also CA 5-8R; CANR 4
Christine de Pizan 1365(?)-1431(?)   **LC 9**
See also DLB 208
Chubb, Elmer
See Masters, Edgar Lee
Chulkov, Mikhail Dmitrievich 1743-1792 **LC 2**
See also DLB 150
Churchill, Caryl 1938-   **CLC 31, 55; DC 5**
See also CA 102; CANR 22, 46; DLB 13; MTCW 1
Churchill, Charles 1731-1764   **LC 3**
See also DLB 109
Chute, Carolyn 1947-   **CLC 39**
See also CA 123
Ciardi, John (Anthony) 1916-1986 **CLC 10, 40, 44; DAM POET**
See also CA 5-8R; 118; CAAS 2; CANR 5, 33; CLR 19; DLB 5; DLBY 86; INT CANR-5; MAICYA; MTCW 1, 2; SAAS 26; SATA 1, 65; SATA-Obit 46
Cicero, Marcus Tullius 106B.C.-43B.C. **CMLC 3**
See also DLB 211
Cimino, Michael 1943-   **CLC 16**
See also CA 105
Cioran, E(mil) M. 1911-1995   **CLC 64**
See also CA 25-28R; 149
Cisneros, Sandra 1954- **CLC 69, 118; DAM MULT; HLC; SSC 32**
See also AAYA 9; CA 131; CANR 64; DLB 122, 152; HW 1, 2; MTCW 2
Cixous, Helene 1937-   **CLC 92**
See also CA 126; CANR 55; DLB 83; MTCW 1, 2
Clair, Rene   **CLC 20**
See also Chomette, Rene Lucien
Clampitt, Amy 1920-1994   **CLC 32; PC 19**
See also CA 110; 146; CANR 29, 79; DLB 105
Clancy, Thomas L., Jr. 1947-
See Clancy, Tom
See also CA 125; 131; CANR 62; INT 131; MTCW 1, 2
Clancy, Tom   **CLC 45, 112; DAM NOV, POP**
See also Clancy, Thomas L., Jr.
See also AAYA 9; BEST 89:1, 90:1; MTCW 2

Clare, John 1793-1864 **NCLC 9; DAB; DAM POET; PC 23**
See also DLB 55, 96

Clarin
See Alas (y Urena), Leopoldo (Enrique Garcia)

Clark, Al C.
See Goines, Donald

Clark, (Robert) Brian 1932- **CLC 29**
See also CA 41-44R; CANR 67

Clark, Curt
See Westlake, Donald E(dwin)

Clark, Eleanor 1913-1996 **CLC 5, 19**
See also CA 9-12R; 151; CANR 41; DLB 6

Clark, J. P.
See Clark, John Pepper
See also DLB 117

Clark, John Pepper 1935- **CLC 38; BLC 1; DAM DRAM, MULT; DC 5**
See also Clark, J. P.
See also BW 1; CA 65-68; CANR 16, 72; MTCW 1

Clark, M. R.
See Clark, Mavis Thorpe

Clark, Mavis Thorpe 1909- **CLC 12**
See also CA 57-60; CANR 8, 37; CLR 30; MAICYA; SAAS 5; SATA 8, 74

Clark, Walter Van Tilburg 1909-1971 **CLC 28**
See also CA 9-12R; 33-36R; CANR 63; DLB 9, 206; SATA 8

Clark Bekederemo, J(ohnson) P(epper)
See Clark, John Pepper

Clarke, Arthur C(harles) 1917- **CLC 1, 4, 13, 18, 35; DAM POP; SSC 3**
See also AAYA 4; CA 1-4R; CANR 2, 28, 55, 74; JRDA; MAICYA; MTCW 1, 2; SATA 13, 70

Clarke, Austin 1896-1974 **CLC 6, 9; DAM POET**
See also CA 29-32; 49-52; CAP 2; DLB 10, 20

Clarke, Austin C(hesterfield) 1934- **CLC 8, 53; BLC 1; DAC; DAM MULT**
See also BW 1; CA 25-28R; CAAS 16; CANR 14, 32, 68; DLB 53, 125

Clarke, Gillian 1937- **CLC 61**
See also CA 106; DLB 40

Clarke, Marcus (Andrew Hislop) 1846-1881 **NCLC 19**

Clarke, Shirley 1925- **CLC 16**

Clash, The
See Headon, (Nicky) Topper; Jones, Mick; Simonon, Paul; Strummer, Joe

Claudel, Paul (Louis Charles Marie) 1868-1955 **TCLC 2, 10**
See also CA 104; 165; DLB 192

Claudius, Matthias 1740-1815 **NCLC 75**
See also DLB 97

Clavell, James (duMaresq) 1925-1994 **CLC 6, 25, 87; DAM NOV, POP**
See also CA 25-28R; 146; CANR 26, 48; MTCW 1, 2

Cleaver, (Leroy) Eldridge 1935-1998 **CLC 30, 119; BLC 1; DAM MULT**
See also BW 1, 3; CA 21-24R; 167; CANR 16, 75; MTCW 2

Cleese, John (Marwood) 1939- **CLC 21**
See also Monty Python
See also CA 112; 116; CANR 35; MTCW 1

Cleishbotham, Jebediah
See Scott, Walter

Cleland, John 1710-1789 **LC 2, 48**
See also DLB 39

Clemens, Samuel Langhorne 1835-1910
See Twain, Mark

See also CA 104; 135; CDALB 1865-1917; DA; DAB; DAC; DAM MST, NOV; DLB 11, 12, 23, 64, 74, 186, 189; JRDA; MAICYA; SATA 100; YABC 2

Cleophil
See Congreve, William

Clerihew, E.
See Bentley, E(dmund) C(lerihew)

Clerk, N. W.
See Lewis, C(live) S(taples)

Cliff, Jimmy **CLC 21**
See also Chambers, James

Cliff, Michelle 1946- **CLC 120; BLCS**
See also BW 2; CA 116; CANR 39, 72; DLB 157

Clifton, (Thelma) Lucille 1936- **CLC 19, 66; BLC 1; DAM MULT, POET; PC 17**
See also BW 2, 3; CA 49-52; CANR 2, 24, 42, 76; CLR 5; DLB 5, 41; MAICYA; MTCW 1, 2; SATA 20, 69

<Clinton, Dirk
See Silverberg, Robert

Clough, Arthur Hugh 1819-1861 **NCLC 27**
See also DLB 32

Clutha, Janet Paterson Frame 1924-
See Frame, Janet
See also CA 1-4R; CANR 2, 36, 76; MTCW 1, 2

Clyne, Terence
See Blatty, William Peter

Cobalt, Martin
See Mayne, William (James Carter)

Cobb, Irvin S(hrewsbury) 1876-1944 **TCLC 77**
See also CA 175; DLB 11, 25, 86

Cobbett, William 1763-1835 **NCLC 49**
See also DLB 43, 107, 158

Coburn, D(onald) L(ee) 1938- **CLC 10**
See also CA 89-92

Cocteau, Jean (Maurice Eugene Clement) 1889-1963 **CLC 1, 8, 15, 16, 43; DA; DAB; DAC; DAM DRAM, MST, NOV; WLC**
See also CA 25-28; CANR 40; CAP 2; DLB 65; MTCW 1, 2

Codrescu, Andrei 1946- **CLC 46; DAM POET**
See also CA 33-36R; CAAS 19; CANR 13, 34, 53, 76; MTCW 2

Coe, Max
See Bourne, Randolph S(illiman)

Coe, Tucker
See Westlake, Donald E(dwin)

Coen, Ethan 1958- **CLC 108**
See also CA 126

Coen, Joel 1955- **CLC 108**
See also CA 126

The Coen Brothers
See Coen, Ethan; Coen, Joel

Coetzee, J(ohn) M(ichael) 1940- **CLC 23, 33, 66, 117; DAM NOV**
See also CA 77-80; CANR 41, 54, 74; MTCW 1, 2

Coffey, Brian
See Koontz, Dean R(ay)

Cohan, George M(ichael) 1878-1942 **TCLC 60**
See also CA 157

Cohen, Arthur A(llen) 1928-1986 **CLC 7, 31**
See also CA 1-4R; 120; CANR 1, 17, 42; DLB 28

Cohen, Leonard (Norman) 1934- **CLC 3, 38; DAC; DAM MST**
See also CA 21-24R; CANR 14, 69; DLB 53; MTCW 1

Cohen, Matt 1942- **CLC 19; DAC**

See also CA 61-64; CAAS 18; CANR 40; DLB 53

Cohen-Solal, Annie 19(?)- **CLC 50**

Colegate, Isabel 1931- **CLC 36**
See also CA 17-20R; CANR 8, 22, 74; DLB 14; INT CANR-22; MTCW 1

Coleman, Emmett
See Reed, Ishmael

Coleridge, M. E.
See Coleridge, Mary E(lizabeth)

Coleridge, Mary E(lizabeth) 1861-1907 **TCLC 73**
See also CA 116; 166; DLB 19, 98

Coleridge, Samuel Taylor 1772-1834 **NCLC 9, 54; DA; DAB; DAC; DAM MST, POET; PC 11; WLC**
See also CDBLB 1789-1832; DLB 93, 107

Coleridge, Sara 1802-1852 **NCLC 31**
See also DLB 199

Coles, Don 1928- **CLC 46**
See also CA 115; CANR 38

Coles, Robert (Martin) 1929- **CLC 108**
See also CA 45-48; CANR 3, 32, 66, 70; INT CANR-32; SATA 23

Colette, (Sidonie-Gabrielle) 1873-1954 **TCLC 1, 5, 16; DAM NOV; SSC 10**
See also CA 104; 131; DLB 65; MTCW 1, 2

Collett, (Jacobine) Camilla (Wergeland) 1813-1895 **NCLC 22**

Collier, Christopher 1930- **CLC 30**
See also AAYA 13; CA 33-36R; CANR 13, 33; JRDA; MAICYA; SATA 16, 70

Collier, James L(incoln) 1928- **CLC 30; DAM POP**
See also AAYA 13; CA 9-12R; CANR 4, 33, 60; CLR 3; JRDA; MAICYA; SAAS 21; SATA 8, 70

Collier, Jeremy 1650-1726 **LC 6**

Collier, John 1901-1980 **SSC 19**
See also CA 65-68; 97-100; CANR 10; DLB 77

Collingwood, R(obin) G(eorge) 1889(?)-1943 **TCLC 67**
See also CA 117; 155

Collins, Hunt
See Hunter, Evan

Collins, Linda 1931- **CLC 44**
See also CA 125

Collins, (William) Wilkie 1824-1889 **NCLC 1, 18**
See also CDBLB 1832-1890; DLB 18, 70, 159

Collins, William 1721-1759 **LC 4, 40; DAM POET**
See also DLB 109

Collodi, Carlo 1826-1890 **NCLC 54**
See also Lorenzini, Carlo
See also CLR 5

Colman, George 1732-1794
See Glassco, John

Colt, Winchester Remington
See Hubbard, L(afayette) Ron(ald)

Colter, Cyrus 1910- **CLC 58**
See also BW 1; CA 65-68; CANR 10, 66; DLB 33

Colton, James
See Hansen, Joseph

Colum, Padraic 1881-1972 **CLC 28**
See also CA 73-76; 33-36R; CANR 35; CLR 36; MAICYA; MTCW 1; SATA 15

Colvin, James
See Moorcock, Michael (John)

Colwin, Laurie (E.) 1944-1992 **CLC 5, 13, 23, 84**

See also CA 89-92; 139; CANR 20, 46; DLBY
80; MTCW 1

Comfort, Alex(ander) 1920-CLC 7; DAM POP
See also CA 1-4R; CANR 1, 45; MTCW 1

Comfort, Montgomery
See Campbell, (John) Ramsey

Compton-Burnett, I(vy) 1884(?)-1969 CLC 1,
3, 10, 15, 34; DAM NOV
See also CA 1-4R; 25-28R; CANR 4; DLB 36;
MTCW 1

Comstock, Anthony 1844-1915   TCLC 13
See also CA 110; 169

Comte, Auguste 1798-1857   NCLC 54

Conan Doyle, Arthur
See Doyle, Arthur Conan

Conde, Maryse 1937-   CLC 52, 92; BLCS;
DAM MULT
See Boucolon, Maryse
See also BW 2; MTCW 1

Condillac, Etienne Bonnot de 1714-1780 L C
26

Condon, Richard (Thomas) 1915-1996CLC 4,
6, 8, 10, 45, 100; DAM NOV
See also BEST 90:3; CA 1-4R; 151; CAAS 1;
CANR 2, 23; INT CANR-23; MTCW 1, 2

Confucius 551B.C.-479B.C.   CMLC 19; DA;
DAB; DAC; DAM MST; WLCS

Congreve, William 1670-1729 LC 5, 21; DA;
DAB; DAC; DAM DRAM, MST, POET;
DC 2; WLC
See also CDBLB 1660-1789; DLB 39, 84

Connell, Evan S(helby), Jr. 1924-CLC 4, 6, 45;
DAM NOV
See also AAYA 7; CA 1-4R; CAAS 2; CANR
2, 39, 76; DLB 2; DLBY 81; MTCW 1, 2

Connelly, Marc(us Cook) 1890-1980   CLC 7
See also CA 85-88; 102; CANR 30; DLB 7;
DLBY 80; SATA-Obit 25

Connor, Ralph   TCLC 31
See also Gordon, Charles William
See also DLB 92

Conrad, Joseph 1857-1924TCLC 1, 6, 13, 25,
43, 57; DA; DAB; DAC; DAM MST, NOV;
SSC 9; WLC
See also AAYA 26; CA 104; 131; CANR 60;
CDBLB 1890-1914; DLB 10, 34, 98, 156;
MTCW 1, 2; SATA 27

Conrad, Robert Arnold
See Hart, Moss

Conroy, Pat
See Conroy, (Donald) Pat(rick)
See also MTCW 2

Conroy, (Donald) Pat(rick) 1945-CLC 30, 74;
DAM NOV, POP
See also Conroy, Pat
See also AAYA 8; AITN 1; CA 85-88; CANR
24, 53; DLB 6; MTCW 1

Constant (de Rebecque), (Henri) Benjamin
1767-1830   NCLC 6
See also DLB 119

Conybeare, Charles Augustus
See Eliot, T(homas) S(tearns)

Cook, Michael 1933-   CLC 58
See also CA 93-96; CANR 68; DLB 53

Cook, Robin 1940-   CLC 14; DAM POP
See also BEST 90:2; CA 108; 111; CANR 41;
INT 111

Cook, Roy
See Silverberg, Robert

Cooke, Elizabeth 1948-   CLC 55
See also CA 129

Cooke, John Esten 1830-1886   NCLC 5
See also DLB 3

Cooke, John Estes
See Baum, L(yman) Frank

Cooke, M. E.
See Creasey, John

Cooke, Margaret
See Creasey, John

Cook-Lynn, Elizabeth 1930-   CLC 93; DAM
MULT
See also CA 133; DLB 175; NNAL

Cooney, Ray   CLC 62

Cooper, Douglas 1960-   CLC 86

Cooper, Henry St. John
See Creasey, John

Cooper, J(oan) California (?)- CLC 56; DAM
MULT
See also AAYA 12; BW 1; CA 125; CANR 55;
DLB 212

Cooper, James Fenimore 1789-1851NCLC 1,
27, 54
See also AAYA 22; CDALB 1640-1865; DLB
3; SATA 19

Coover, Robert (Lowell) 1932- CLC 3, 7, 15,
32, 46, 87; DAM NOV; SSC 15
See also CA 45-48; CANR 3, 37, 58; DLB 2;
DLBY 81; MTCW 1, 2

Copeland, Stewart (Armstrong) 1952-CLC 26

Copernicus, Nicolaus 1473-1543   LC 45

Coppard, A(lfred) E(dgar) 1878-1957 T C L C
5; SSC 21
See also CA 114; 167; DLB 162; YABC 1

Coppee, Francois 1842-1908   TCLC 25
See also CA 170

Coppola, Francis Ford 1939-   CLC 16
See also CA 77-80; CANR 40, 78; DLB 44

Corbiere, Tristan 1845-1875   NCLC 43

Corcoran, Barbara 1911-   CLC 17
See also AAYA 14; CA 21-24R; CAAS 2;
CANR 11, 28, 48; CLR 50; DLB 52; JRDA;
SAAS 20; SATA 3, 77

Cordelier, Maurice
See Giraudoux, (Hippolyte) Jean

Corelli, Marie 1855-1924   TCLC 51
See also Mackay, Mary
See also DLB 34, 156

Corman, Cid 1924-   CLC 9
See also Corman, Sidney
See also CAAS 2; DLB 5, 193

Corman, Sidney 1924-
See Corman, Cid
See also CA 85-88; CANR 44; DAM POET

Cormier, Robert (Edmund) 1925-CLC 12, 30;
DA; DAB; DAC; DAM MST, NOV
See also AAYA 3, 19; CA 1-4R; CANR 5, 23,
76; CDALB 1968-1988; CLR 12, 55; DLB
52; INT CANR-23; JRDA; MAICYA;
MTCW 1, 2; SATA 10, 45, 83

Corn, Alfred (DeWitt III) 1943-   CLC 33
See also CA 104; CAAS 25; CANR 44; DLB
120; DLBY 80

Corneille, Pierre 1606-1684   LC 28; DAB;
DAM MST

Cornwell, David (John Moore) 1931- CLC 9,
15; DAM POP
See also le Carre, John
See also CA 5-8R; CANR 13, 33, 59; MTCW
1, 2

Corso, (Nunzio) Gregory 1930-   CLC 1, 11
See also CA 5-8R; CANR 41, 76; DLB 5, 16;
MTCW 1, 2

Cortazar, Julio 1914-1984CLC 2, 3, 5, 10, 13,
15, 33, 34, 92; DAM MULT, NOV; HLC;
SSC 7
See also CA 21-24R; CANR 12, 32; DLB 113;

HW 1, 2; MTCW 1, 2

CORTES, HERNAN 1484-1547   LC 31

Corvinus, Jakob
See Raabe, Wilhelm (Karl)

Corwin, Cecil
See Kornbluth, C(yril) M.

Cosic, Dobrica 1921-   CLC 14
See also CA 122; 138; DLB 181

Costain, Thomas B(ertram) 1885-1965 C L C
30
See also CA 5-8R; 25-28R; DLB 9

Costantini, Humberto 1924(?)-1987 CLC 49
See also CA 131; 122; HW 1

Costello, Elvis 1955-   CLC 21

Costenoble, Philostene
See Ghelderode, Michel de

Cotes, Cecil V.
See Duncan, Sara Jeannette

Cotter, Joseph Seamon Sr. 1861-1949 T C L C
28; BLC 1; DAM MULT
See also BW 1; CA 124; DLB 50

Couch, Arthur Thomas Quiller
See Quiller-Couch, SirArthur (Thomas)

Coulton, James
See Hansen, Joseph

Couperus, Louis (Marie Anne) 1863-1923
TCLC 15
See also CA 115

Coupland, Douglas 1961-CLC 85; DAC; DAM
POP
See also CA 142; CANR 57

Court, Wesli
See Turco, Lewis (Putnam)

Courtenay, Bryce 1933-   CLC 59
See also CA 138

Courtney, Robert
See Ellison, Harlan (Jay)

Cousteau, Jacques-Yves 1910-1997   CLC 30
See also CA 65-68; 159; CANR 15, 67; MTCW
1; SATA 38, 98

Coventry, Francis 1725-1754   LC 46

Cowan, Peter (Walkinshaw) 1914-   SSC 28
See also CA 21-24R; CANR 9, 25, 50

Coward, Noel (Peirce) 1899-1973CLC 1, 9, 29,
51; DAM DRAM
See also AITN 1; CA 17-18; 41-44R; CANR
35; CAP 2; CDBLB 1914-1945; DLB 10;
MTCW 1, 2

Cowley, Abraham 1618-1667   LC 43
See also DLB 131, 151

Cowley, Malcolm 1898-1989   CLC 39
See also CA 5-8R; 128; CANR 3, 55; DLB 4,
48; DLBY 81, 89; MTCW 1, 2

Cowper, William 1731-1800   NCLC 8; DAM
POET
See also DLB 104, 109

Cox, William Trevor 1928-   CLC 9, 14, 71;
DAM NOV
See also Trevor, William
See also CA 9-12R; CANR 4, 37, 55, 76; DLB
14; INT CANR-37; MTCW 1, 2

Coyne, P. J.
See Masters, Hilary

Cozzens, James Gould 1903-1978CLC 1, 4, 11,
92
See also CA 9-12R; 81-84; CANR 19; CDALB
1941-1968; DLB 9; DLBD 2; DLBY 84, 97;
MTCW 1, 2

Crabbe, George 1754-1832   NCLC 26
See also DLB 93

Craddock, Charles Egbert
See Murfree, Mary Noailles

Craig, A. A.

See Anderson, Poul (William)

Craik, Dinah Maria (Mulock) 1826-1887
NCLC 38
See also DLB 35, 163; MAICYA; SATA 34

Cram, Ralph Adams 1863-1942 **TCLC 45**
See also CA 160

Crane, (Harold) Hart 1899-1932 **TCLC 2, 5,
80; DA; DAB; DAC; DAM MST, POET;
PC 3; WLC**
See also CA 104; 127; CDALB 1917-1929;
DLB 4, 48; MTCW 1, 2

Crane, R(onald) S(almon) 1886-1967**CLC 27**
See also CA 85-88; DLB 63

Crane, Stephen (Townley) 1871-1900 **TCLC
11, 17, 32; DA; DAB; DAC; DAM MST,
NOV, POET; SSC 7; WLC**
See also AAYA 21; CA 109; 140; CDALB 1865-
1917; DLB 12, 54, 78; YABC 2

Cranshaw, Stanley
See Fisher, Dorothy (Frances) Canfield

Crase, Douglas 1944- **CLC 58**
See also CA 106

Crashaw, Richard 1612(?)-1649 **LC 24**
See also DLB 126

Craven, Margaret 1901-1980 **CLC 17; DAC**
See also CA 103

Crawford, F(rancis) Marion 1854-1909**TCLC
10**
See also CA 107; 168; DLB 71

Crawford, Isabella Valancy 1850-1887**NCLC
12**
See also DLB 92

Crayon, Geoffrey
See Irving, Washington

Creasey, John 1908-1973 **CLC 11**
See also CA 5-8R; 41-44R; CANR 8, 59; DLB
77; MTCW 1

Crebillon, Claude Prosper Jolyot de (fils) 1707-
1777 **LC 1, 28**

Credo
See Creasey, John

Credo, Alvaro J. de
See Prado (Calvo), Pedro

Creeley, Robert (White) 1926-**CLC 1, 2, 4, 8,
11, 15, 36, 78; DAM POET**
See also CA 1-4R; CAAS 10; CANR 23, 43;
DLB 5, 16, 169; DLBD 17; MTCW 1, 2

Crews, Harry (Eugene) 1935- **CLC 6, 23, 49**
See also AITN 1; CA 25-28R; CANR 20, 57;
DLB 6, 143, 185; MTCW 1, 2

Crichton, (John) Michael 1942-**CLC 2, 6, 54,
90; DAM NOV, POP**
See also AAYA 10; AITN 2; CA 25-28R; CANR
13, 40, 54, 76; DLBY 81; INT CANR-13;
JRDA; MTCW 1, 2; SATA 9, 88

Crispin, Edmund **CLC 22**
See also Montgomery, (Robert) Bruce
See also DLB 87

Cristofer, Michael 1945(?)- **CLC 28; DAM
DRAM**
See also CA 110; 152; DLB 7

Croce, Benedetto 1866-1952 **TCLC 37**
See also CA 120; 155

Crockett, David 1786-1836 **NCLC 8**
See also DLB 3, 11

Crockett, Davy
See Crockett, David

Crofts, Freeman Wills 1879-1957 **TCLC 55**
See also CA 115; DLB 77

Croker, John Wilson 1780-1857 **NCLC 10**
See also DLB 110

Crommelynck, Fernand 1885-1970 **CLC 75**
See also CA 89-92

Cromwell, Oliver 1599-1658 **LC 43**

Cronin, A(rchibald) J(oseph) 1896-1981**C L C
32**
See also CA 1-4R; 102; CANR 5; DLB 191;
SATA 47; SATA-Obit 25

Cross, Amanda
See Heilbrun, Carolyn G(old)

Crothers, Rachel 1878(?)-1958 **TCLC 19**
See also CA 113; DLB 7

Croves, Hal
See Traven, B.

Crow Dog, Mary (Ellen) (?)- **CLC 93**
See also Brave Bird, Mary
See also CA 154

Crowfield, Christopher
See Stowe, Harriet (Elizabeth) Beecher

Crowley, Aleister **TCLC 7**
See also Crowley, Edward Alexander

Crowley, Edward Alexander 1875-1947
See Crowley, Aleister
See also CA 104

Crowley, John 1942- **CLC 57**
See also CA 61-64; CANR 43; DLBY 82; SATA
65

Crud
See Crumb, R(obert)

Crumarums
See Crumb, R(obert)

Crumb, R(obert) 1943- **CLC 17**
See also CA 106

Crumbum
See Crumb, R(obert)

Crumski
See Crumb, R(obert)

Crum the Bum
See Crumb, R(obert)

Crunk
See Crumb, R(obert)

Crustt
See Crumb, R(obert)

Cryer, Gretchen (Kiger) 1935- **CLC 21**
See also CA 114; 123

Csath, Geza 1887-1919 **TCLC 13**
See also CA 111

Cudlip, David 1933- **CLC 34**

Cullen, Countee 1903-1946**TCLC 4, 37; BLC
1; DA; DAC; DAM MST, MULT, POET;
PC 20; WLCS**
See also BW 1; CA 108; 124; CDALB 1917-
1929; DLB 4, 48, 51; MTCW 1, 2; SATA 18

Cum, R.
See Crumb, R(obert)

Cummings, Bruce F(rederick) 1889-1919
See Barbellion, W. N. P.
See also CA 123

Cummings, E(dward) E(stlin) 1894-1962**CLC
1, 3, 8, 12, 15, 68; DA; DAB; DAC; DAM
MST, POET; PC 5; WLC**
See also CA 73-76; CANR 31; CDALB 1929-
1941; DLB 4, 48; MTCW 1, 2

Cunha, Euclides (Rodrigues Pimenta) da 1866-
1909 **TCLC 24**
See also CA 123

Cunningham, E. V.
See Fast, Howard (Melvin)

Cunningham, J(ames) V(incent) 1911-1985
CLC 3, 31
See also CA 1-4R; 115; CANR 1, 72; DLB 5

Cunningham, Julia (Woolfolk) 1916-**CLC 12**
See also CA 9-12R; CANR 4, 19, 36; JRDA;
MAICYA; SAAS 2; SATA 1, 26

Cunningham, Michael 1952- **CLC 34**
See also CA 136

Cunninghame Graham, R(obert) B(ontine)
1852-1936 **TCLC 19**
See also Graham, R(obert) B(ontine)
Cunninghame
See also CA 119; DLB 98

Currie, Ellen 19(?)- **CLC 44**

Curtin, Philip
See Lowndes, Marie Adelaide (Belloc)

Curtis, Price
See Ellison, Harlan (Jay)

Cutrate, Joe
See Spiegelman, Art

Cynewulf c. 770-c. 840 **CMLC 23**

Czaczkes, Shmuel Yosef
See Agnon, S(hmuel) Y(osef Halevi)

Dabrowska, Maria (Szumska) 1889-1965**CLC
15**
See also CA 106

Dabydeen, David 1955- **CLC 34**
See also BW 1; CA 125; CANR 56

Dacey, Philip 1939- **CLC 51**
See also CA 37-40R; CAAS 17; CANR 14, 32,
64; DLB 105

Dagerman, Stig (Halvard) 1923-1954 **T C L C
17**
See also CA 117; 155

Dahl, Roald 1916-1990**CLC 1, 6, 18, 79; DAB;
DAC; DAM MST, NOV, POP**
See also AAYA 15; CA 1-4R; 133; CANR 6,
32, 37, 62; CLR 1, 7, 41; DLB 139; JRDA;
MAICYA; MTCW 1, 2; SATA 1, 26, 73;
SATA-Obit 65

Dahlberg, Edward 1900-1977 **CLC 1, 7, 14**
<iSee also CA 9-12R; 69-72; CANR 31, 62; DLB
48; MTCW 1

Daitch, Susan 1954- **CLC 103**
See also CA 161

Dale, Colin **TCLC 18**
See also Lawrence, T(homas) E(dward)

Dale, George E.
See Asimov, Isaac

Daly, Elizabeth 1878-1967 **CLC 52**
See also CA 23-24; 25-28R; CANR 60; CAP 2

Daly, Maureen 1921- **CLC 17**
See also AAYA 5; CANR 37; JRDA; MAICYA;
SAAS 1; SATA 2

Damas, Leon-Gontran 1912-1978 **CLC 84**
See also BW 1; CA 125; 73-76

Dana, Richard Henry Sr. 1787-1879**NCLC 53**

Daniel, Samuel 1562(?)-1619 **LC 24**
See also DLB 62

Daniels, Brett
See Adler, Renata

Dannay, Frederic 1905-1982 **CLC 11; DAM
POP**
See also Queen, Ellery
See also CA 1-4R; 107; CANR 1, 39; DLB 137;
MTCW 1

D'Annunzio, Gabriele 1863-1938**TCLC 6, 40**
See also CA 104; 155

Danois, N. le
See Gourmont, Remy (-Marie-Charles) de

Dante 1265-1321 **CMLC 3, 18; DA; DAB;
DAC; DAM MST, POET; PC 21; WLCS**

d'Antibes, Germain
See Simenon, Georges (Jacques Christian)

Danticat, Edwidge 1969- **CLC 94**
See also AAYA 29; CA 152; CANR 73; MTCW
1

Danvers, Dennis 1947- **CLC 70**

Danziger, Paula 1944- **CLC 21**
See also AAYA 4; CA 112; 115; CANR 37; CLR
20; JRDA; MAICYA; SATA 36, 63, 102;

SATA-Brief 30
Da Ponte, Lorenzo 1749-1838   **NCLC 50**
Dario, Ruben 1867-1916   **TCLC 4; DAM MULT; HLC; PC 15**
  See also CA 131; HW 1, 2; MTCW 1, 2
Darley, George 1795-1846   **NCLC 2**
  See also DLB 96
Darrow, Clarence (Seward) 1857-1938**TCLC 81**
  See also CA 164
Darwin, Charles 1809-1882   **NCLC 57**
  See also DLB 57, 166
Daryush, Elizabeth 1887-1977   **CLC 6, 19**
  See also CA 49-52; CANR 3; DLB 20
Dasgupta, Surendranath 1887-1952**TCLC 81**
  See also CA 157
Dashwood, Edmee Elizabeth Monica de la Pasture 1890-1943
  See Delafield, E. M.
  See also CA 119; 154
Daudet, (Louis Marie) Alphonse 1840-1897   **NCLC 1**
  See also DLB 123
Daumal, Rene 1908-1944   **TCLC 14**
  See also CA 114
Davenant, William 1606-1668   **LC 13**
  See also DLB 58, 126
Davenport, Guy (Mattison, Jr.) 1927-**CLC 6, 14, 38; SSC 16**
  See also CA 33-36R; CANR 23, 73; DLB 130
Davidson, Avram (James) 1923-1993
  See Queen, Ellery
  See also CA 101; 171; CANR 26; DLB 8
Davidson, Donald (Grady) 1893-1968**CLC 2, 13, 19**
  See also CA 5-8R; 25-28R; CANR 4; DLB 45
Davidson, Hugh
  See Hamilton, Edmond
Davidson, John 1857-1909   **TCLC 24**
  See also CA 118; DLB 19
Davidson, Sara 1943-   **CLC 9**
  See also CA 81-84; CANR 44, 68; DLB 185
Davie, Donald (Alfred) 1922-1995   **CLC 5, 8, 10, 31**
  See also CA 1-4R; 149; CAAS 3; CANR 1, 44; DLB 27; MTCW 1
Davies, Ray(mond Douglas) 1944-   **CLC 21**
  See also CA 116; 146
Davies, Rhys 1901-1978   **CLC 23**
  See also CA 9-12R; 81-84; CANR 4; DLB 139, 191
Davies, (William) Robertson 1913-1995 **CLC 2, 7, 13, 25, 42, 75, 91; DA; DAB; DAC; DAM MST, NOV, POP; WLC**
  See also BEST 89:2; CA 33-36R; 150; CANR 17, 42; DLB 68; INT CANR-17; MTCW 1, 2
Davies, W(illiam) H(enry) 1871-1940**TCLC 5**
  See also CA 104; DLB 19, 174
Davies, Walter C.
  See Kornbluth, C(yril) M.
Davis, Angela (Yvonne) 1944- **CLC 77; DAM MULT**
  See also BW 2, 3; CA 57-60; CANR 10
Davis, B. Lynch
  See Bioy Casares, Adolfo; Borges, Jorge Luis
Davis, Harold Lenoir 1894-1960   **CLC 49**
  See also CA 89-92; DLB 9, 206
Davis, Rebecca (Blaine) Harding 1831-1910   **TCLC 6**
  See also CA 104; DLB 74
Davis, Richard Harding 1864-1916 **TCLC 24**
  See also CA 114; DLB 12, 23, 78, 79, 189;

DLBD 13
Davison, Frank Dalby 1893-1970   **CLC 15**
  See also CA 116
Davison, Lawrence H.
  See Lawrence, D(avid) H(erbert Richards)
Davison, Peter (Hubert) 1928-   **CLC 28**
  See also CA 9-12R; CAAS 4; CANR 3, 43; DLB 5
Davys, Mary 1674-1732   **LC 1, 46**
  See also DLB 39
Dawson, Fielding 1930-   **CLC 6**
  See also CA 85-88; DLB 130
Dawson, Peter
  See Faust, Frederick (Schiller)
Day, Clarence (Shepard, Jr.) 1874-1935   **TCLC 25**
  See also CA 108; DLB 11
Day, Thomas 1748-1789   **LC 1**
  See also DLB 39; YABC 1
Day Lewis, C(ecil) 1904-1972 **CLC 1, 6, 10; DAM POET; PC 11**
  See also Blake, Nicholas
  See also CA 13-16; 33-36R; CANR 34; CAP 1; DLB 15, 20; MTCW 1, 2
Dazai Osamu 1909-1948   **TCLC 11**
  See also Tsushima, Shuji
  See also CA 164; DLB 182
de Andrade, Carlos Drummond 1892-1945
  See Drummond de Andrade, Carlos
Deane, Norman
  See Creasey, John
de Beauvoir, Simone (Lucie Ernestine Marie Bertrand)
  See Beauvoir, Simone (Lucie Ernestine Marie Bertrand) de
de Beer, P.
  See Bosman, Herman Charles
de Brissac, Malcolm
  See Dickinson, Peter (Malcolm)
de Chardin, Pierre Teilhard
  See Teilhard de Chardin, (Marie Joseph) Pierre
Dee, John 1527-1608   **LC 20**
Deer, Sandra 1940-   **CLC 45**
De Ferrari, Gabriella 1941-   **CLC 65**
  See also CA 146
Defoe, Daniel 1660(?)-1731 **LC 1, 42; DA; DAB; DAC; DAM MST, NOV; WLC**
  See also AAYA 27; CDBLB 1660-1789; DLB 39, 95, 101; JRDA; MAICYA; SATA 22
de Gourmont, Remy(-Marie-Charles)
  See Gourmont, Remy (-Marie-Charles) de
de Hartog, Jan 1914-   **CLC 19**
  See also CA 1-4R; CANR 1
de Hostos, E. M.
  See Hostos (y Bonilla), Eugenio Maria de
de Hostos, Eugenio M.
  See Hostos (y Bonilla), Eugenio Maria de
Deighton, Len   **CLC 4, 7, 22, 46**
  See also Deighton, Leonard Cyril
  See also AAYA 6; BEST 89:2; CDBLB 1960 to Present; DLB 87
Deighton, Leonard Cyril 1929-
  See Deighton, Len
  See also CA 9-12R; CANR 19, 33, 68; DAM NOV, POP; MTCW 1, 2
Dekker, Thomas 1572(?)-1632 **LC 22; DAM DRAM**
  See also CDBLB Before 1660; DLB 62, 172
Delafield, E. M. 1890-1943   **TCLC 61**
  See also Dashwood, Edmee Elizabeth Monica de la Pasture
  See also DLB 34
de la Mare, Walter (John) 1873-1956**TCLC 4,**

53; **DAB; DAC; DAM MST, POET; SSC 14; WLC**
  See also CA 163; CDBLB 1914-1945; CLR 23; DLB 162; MTCW 1; SATA 16
Delaney, Franey
  See O'Hara, John (Henry)
Delaney, Shelagh 1939-**CLC 29; DAM DRAM**
  See also CA 17-20R; CANR 30, 67; CDBLB 1960 to Present; DLB 13; MTCW 1
Delany, Mary (Granville Pendarves) 1700-1788   **LC 12**
Delany, Samuel R(ay, Jr.) 1942-**CLC 8, 14, 38; BLC 1; DAM MULT**
  See also AAYA 24; BW 2, 3; CA 81-84; CANR 27, 43; DLB 8, 33; MTCW 1, 2
De La Ramee, (Marie) Louise 1839-1908
  See Ouida
  See also SATA 20
de la Roche, Mazo 1879-1961   **CLC 14**
  See also CA 85-88; CANR 30; DLB 68; SATA 64
De La Salle, Innocent
  See Hartmann, Sadakichi
Delbanco, Nicholas (Franklin) 1942- **CLC 6, 13**
  See also CA 17-20R; CAAS 2; CANR 29, 55; DLB 6
del Castillo, Michel 1933-   **CLC 38**
  See also CA 109; CANR 77
Deledda, Grazia (Cosima) 1875(?)-1936   **TCLC 23**
  See also CA 123
Delibes, Miguel   **CLC 8, 18**
  See also Delibes Setien, Miguel
Delibes Setien, Miguel 1920-
  See Delibes, Miguel
  See also CA 45-48; CANR 1, 32; HW 1; MTCW 1
DeLillo, Don 1936- **CLC 8, 10, 13, 27, 39, 54, 76; DAM NOV, POP**
  See also BEST 89:1; CA 81-84; CANR 21, 76; DLB 6, 173; MTCW 1, 2
de Lisser, H. G.
  See De Lisser, H(erbert) G(eorge)
  See also DLB 117
De Lisser, H(erbert) G(eorge) 1878-1944   **TCLC 12**
  See also de Lisser, H. G.
  See also BW 2; CA 109; 152
Deloney, Thomas 1560(?)-1600   **LC 41**
  See also DLB 167
Deloria, Vine (Victor), Jr. 1933- **CLC 21; DAM MULT**
  See also CA 53-56; CANR 5, 20, 48; DLB 175; MTCW 1; NNAL; SATA 21
Del Vecchio, John M(ichael) 1947-   **CLC 29**
  See also CA 110; DLBD 9
de Man, Paul (Adolph Michel) 1919-1983   **CLC 55**
  See also CA 128; 111; CANR 61; DLB 67; MTCW 1, 2
De Marinis, Rick 1934-   **CLC 54**
  See also CA 57-60; CAAS 24; CANR 9, 25, 50
Dembry, R. Emmet
  See Murfree, Mary Noailles
Demby, William 1922-**CLC 53; BLC 1; DAM MULT**
  See also BW 1, 3; CA 81-84; DLB 33
de Menton, Francisco
  See Chin, Frank (Chew, Jr.)
Demijohn, Thom
  See Disch, Thomas M(ichael)
de Montherlant, Henry (Milon)

See Montherlant, Henry (Milon) de
Demosthenes 384B.C.-322B.C.   **CMLC 13**
   See also DLB 176
de Natale, Francine
   See Malzberg, Barry N(athaniel)
Denby, Edwin (Orr) 1903-1983   **CLC 48**
   See also CA 138; 110
Denis, Julio
   See Cortazar, Julio
Denmark, Harrison
   See Zelazny, Roger (Joseph)
Dennis, John 1658-1734   **LC 11**
   See also DLB 101
Dennis, Nigel (Forbes) 1912-1989   **CLC 8**
   See also CA 25-28R; 129; DLB 13, 15; MTCW
   1
Dent, Lester 1904(?)-1959   **TCLC 72**
   See also CA 112; 161
De Palma, Brian (Russell) 1940-   **CLC 20**
   See also CA 109
De Quincey, Thomas 1785-1859   **NCLC 4**
   See also CDBLB 1789-1832; DLB 110; 144
Deren, Eleanora 1908(?)-1961
   See Deren, Maya
   See also CA 111
Deren, Maya 1917-1961   **CLC 16, 102**
   See also Deren, Eleanora
Derleth, August (William) 1909-1971 **CLC 31**
   See also CA 1-4R; 29-32R; CANR 4; DLB 9;
   DLBD 17; SATA 5
Der Nister 1884-1950   **TCLC 56**
de Routisie, Albert
   See Aragon, Louis
Derrida, Jacques 1930-   **CLC 24, 87**
   See also CA 124; 127; CANR 76; MTCW 1
Derry Down Derry
   See Lear, Edward
Dersonnes, Jacques
   See Simenon, Georges (Jacques Christian)
Desai, Anita 1937-**CLC 19, 37, 97; DAB; DAM
   NOV**
   See also CA 81-84; CANR 33, 53; MTCW 1,
   2; SATA 63
Desai, Kiran 1971-   **CLC 119**
   See also CA 171
de Saint-Luc, Jean
   See Glassco, John
de Saint Roman, Arnaud
   See Aragon, Louis
Descartes, Rene 1596-1650   **LC 20, 35**
De Sica, Vittorio 1901(?)-1974   **CLC 20**
   See also CA 117
Desnos, Robert 1900-1945   **TCLC 22**
   See also CA 121; 151
Destouches, Louis-Ferdinand 1894-1961**CLC
   9, 15**
   See also Celine, Louis-Ferdinand
   See also CA 85-88; CANR 28; MTCW 1
de Tolignac, Gaston
   See Griffith, D(avid Lewelyn) W(ark)
Deutsch, Babette 1895-1982   **CLC 18**
   See also CA 1-4R; 108; CANR 4, 79; DLB 45;
   SATA 1; SATA-Obit 33
Devenant, William 1606-1649   **LC 13**
Devkota, Laxmiprasad 1909-1959 **TCLC 23**
   See also CA 123
De Voto, Bernard (Augustine) 1897-1955
   TCLC 29
   See also CA 113; 160; DLB 9
De Vries, Peter 1910-1993 **CLC 1, 2, 3, 7, 10,
   28, 46; DAM NOV**
   See also CA 17-20R; 142; CANR 41; DLB 6;
   DLBY 82; MTCW 1, 2

Dexter, John
   See Bradley, Marion Zimmer
Dexter, Martin
   See Faust, Frederick (Schiller)
Dexter, Pete 1943-   **CLC 34, 55; DAM POP**
   See also BEST 89:2; CA 127; 131; INT 131;
   MTCW 1
Diamano, Silmang
   See Senghor, Leopold Sedar
Diamond, Neil 1941-   **CLC 30**
   See also CA 108
Diaz del Castillo, Bernal 1496-1584   **LC 31;
   HLCS 1**
di Bassetto, Corno
   See Shaw, George Bernard
Dick, Philip K(indred) 1928-1982**CLC 10, 30,
   72; DAM NOV, POP**
   See also AAYA 24; CA 49-52; 106; CANR 2,
   16; DLB 8; MTCW 1, 2
Dickens, Charles (John Huffam) 1812-1870
   **NCLC 3, 8, 18, 26, 37, 50; DA; DAB; DAC;
   DAM MST, NOV; SSC 17; WLC**
   See also AAYA 23; CDBLB 1832-1890; DLB
   21, 55, 70, 159, 166; JRDA; MAICYA; SATA
   15
Dickey, James (Lafayette) 1923-1997 **CLC 1,
   2, 4, 7, 10, 15, 47, 109; DAM NOV, POET,
   POP**
   See also AITN 1, 2; CA 9-12R; 156; CABS 2;
   CANR 10, 48, 61; CDALB 1968-1988; DLB
   5, 193; DLBD 7; DLBY 82, 93, 96, 97, 98;
   INT CANR-10; MTCW 1, 2
Dickey, William 1928-1994   **CLC 3, 28**
   See also CA 9-12R; 145; CANR 24, 79; DLB 5
Dickinson, Charles 1951-   **CLC 49**
   See also CA 128
Dickinson, Emily (Elizabeth) 1830-1886
   **NCLC 21, 77; DA; DAB; DAC; DAM
   MST, POET; PC 1; WLC**
   See also AAYA 22; CDALB 1865-1917; DLB
   1; SATA 29
Dickinson, Peter (Malcolm) 1927-**CLC 12, 35**
   See also AAYA 9; CA 41-44R; CANR 31, 58;
   CLR 29; DLB 87, 161; JRDA; MAICYA;
   SATA 5, 62, 95
Dickson, Carr
   See Carr, John Dickson
Dickson, Carter
   See Carr, John Dickson
Diderot, Denis 1713-1784   **LC 26**
Didion, Joan 1934-**CLC 1, 3, 8, 14, 32; DAM
   NOV**
   See also AITN 1; CA 5-8R; CANR 14, 52, 76;
   CDALB 1968-1988; DLB 2, 173, 185;
   DLBY 81, 86; MTCW 1, 2
Dietrich, Robert
   See Hunt, E(verette) Howard, (Jr.)
Difusa, Pati
   See Almodovar, Pedro
Dillard, Annie 1945-   **CLC 9, 60, 115; DAM
   NOV**
   See also AAYA 6; CA 49-52; CANR 3, 43, 62;
   DLBY 80; MTCW 1, 2; SATA 10
Dillard, R(ichard) H(enry) W(ilde) 1937-
   CLC 5
   See also CA 21-24R; CAAS 7; CANR 10; DLB
   5
Dillon, Eilis 1920-1994   **CLC 17**
   See also CA 9-12R; 147; CAAS 3; CANR 4,
   38, 78; CLR 26; MAICYA; SATA 2, 74;
   SATA-Essay 105; SATA-Obit 83
Dimont, Penelope
   See Mortimer, Penelope (Ruth)

Dinesen, Isak   **CLC 10, 29, 95; SSC 7**
   See also Blixen, Karen (Christentze Dinesen)
   See also MTCW 1
Ding Ling   **CLC 68**
   See also Chiang, Pin-chin
Diphusa, Patty
   See Almodovar, Pedro
Disch, Thomas M(ichael) 1940-   **CLC 7, 36**
   See also AAYA 17; CA 21-24R; CAAS 4;
   CANR 17, 36, 54; CLR 18; DLB 8;
   MAICYA; MTCW 1, 2; SAAS 15; SATA 92
Disch, Tom
   See Disch, Thomas M(ichael)
d'Isly, Georges
   See Simenon, Georges (Jacques Christian)
Disraeli, Benjamin 1804-1881   **NCLC 2, 39**
   See also DLB 21, 55
Ditcum, Steve
   See Crumb, R(obert)
Dixon, Paige
   See Corcoran, Barbara
Dixon, Stephen 1936-   **CLC 52; SSC 16**
   See also CA 89-92; CANR 17, 40, 54; DLB 130
Doak, Annie
   See Dillard, Annie
Dobell, Sydney Thompson 1824-1874   **NCLC
   43**
   See also DLB 32
Doblin, Alfred   **TCLC 13**
   See also Doeblin, Alfred
Dobrolyubov, Nikolai Alexandrovich 1836-1861
   NCLC 5
Dobson, Austin 1840-1921   **TCLC 79**
   See also DLB 35; 144
Dobyns, Stephen 1941-   **CLC 37**
   See also CA 45-48; CANR 2, 18
Doctorow, E(dgar) L(aurence) 1931- **CLC 6,
   11, 15, 18, 37, 44, 65, 113; DAM NOV, POP**
   See also AAYA 22; AITN 2; BEST 89:3; CA
   45-48; CANR 2, 33, 51, 76; CDALB 1968-
   1988; DLB 2, 28, 173; DLBY 80; MTCW 1,
   2
Dodgson, Charles Lutwidge 1832-1898
   See Carroll, Lewis
   See also CLR 2; DA; DAB; DAC; DAM MST,
   NOV, POET; MAICYA; SATA 100; YABC 2
Dodson, Owen (Vincent) 1914-1983 **CLC 79;
   BLC 1; DAM MULT**
   See also BW 1; CA 65-68; 110; CANR 24; DLB
   76
Doeblin, Alfred 1878-1957   **TCLC 13**
   See also Doblin, Alfred
   See also CA 110; 141; DLB 66
Doerr, Harriet 1910-   **CLC 34**
   See also CA 117; 122; CANR 47; INT 122
Domecq, H(onorio) Bustos
   See Bioy Casares, Adolfo; Borges, Jorge Luis
Domini, Rey
   See Lorde, Audre (Geraldine)
Dominique
   See Proust, (Valentin-Louis-George-Eugene-)
   Marcel
Don, A
   See Stephen, SirLeslie
Donaldson, Stephen R. 1947- **CLC 46; DAM
   POP**
   See also CA 89-92; CANR 13, 55; INT CANR-
   13
Donleavy, J(ames) P(atrick) 1926-**CLC 1, 4, 6,
   10, 45**
   See also AITN 2; CA 9-12R; CANR 24, 49, 62,
   80; DLB 6, 173; INT CANR-24; MTCW 1,
   2

Donne, John 1572-1631 **LC 10, 24; DA; DAB; DAC; DAM MST, POET; PC 1; WLC**
  See also CDBLB Before 1660; DLB 121, 151
Donnell, David 1939(?)- **CLC 34**
Donoghue, P. S.
  See Hunt, E(verette) Howard, (Jr.)
Donoso (Yanez), Jose 1924-1996 **CLC 4, 8, 11, 32, 99; DAM MULT; HLC; SSC 34**
  See also CA 81-84; 155; CANR 32, 73; DLB 113; HW 1, 2; MTCW 1, 2
Donovan, John 1928-1992 **CLC 35**
  See also AAYA 20; CA 97-100; 137; CLR 3; MAICYA; SATA 72; SATA-Brief 29
Don Roberto
  See Cunninghame Graham, R(obert) B(ontine)
Doolittle, Hilda 1886-1961 **CLC 3, 8, 14, 31, 34, 73; DA; DAC; DAM MST, POET; PC 5; WLC**
  See also H. D.
  See also CA 97-100; CANR 35; DLB 4, 45; MTCW 1, 2
Dorfman, Ariel 1942- **CLC 48, 77; DAM MULT; HLC**
  See also CA 124; 130; CANR 67, 70; HW 1, 2; INT 130
Dorn, Edward (Merton) 1929- **CLC 10, 18**
  See also CA 93-96; CANR 42, 79; DLB 5; INT 93-96
Dorris, Michael (Anthony) 1945-1997 **CLC 109; DAM MULT, NOV**
  See also AAYA 20; BEST 90:1; CA 102; 157; CANR 19, 46, 75; DLB 175; MTCW 2; NNAL; SATA 75; SATA-Obit 94
Dorris, Michael A.
  See Dorris, Michael (Anthony)
Dorsan, Luc
  See Simenon, Georges (Jacques Christian)
Dorsange, Jean
  See Simenon, Georges (Jacques Christian)
Dos Passos, John (Roderigo) 1896-1970 **CLC 1, 4, 8, 11, 15, 25, 34, 82; DA; DAB; DAC; DAM MST, NOV; WLC**
  See also CA 1-4R; 29-32R; CANR 3; CDALB 1929-1941; DLB 4, 9; DLBD 1, 15; DLBY 96; MTCW 1, 2
Dossage, Jean
  See Simenon, Georges (Jacques Christian)
Dostoevsky, Fedor Mikhailovich 1821-1881 **NCLC 2, 7, 21, 33, 43; DA; DAB; DAC; DAM MST, NOV; SSC 2, 33; WLC**
Doughty, Charles M(ontagu) 1843-1926 **TCLC 27**
  See also CA 115; DLB 19, 57, 174
Douglas, Ellen **CLC 73**
  See also Haxton, Josephine Ayres; Williamson, Ellen Douglas
Douglas, Gavin 1475(?)-1522 **LC 20**
  See also DLB 132
Douglas, George
  See Brown, George Douglas
Douglas, Keith (Castellain) 1920-1944 **TCLC 40**
  See also CA 160; DLB 27
Douglas, Leonard
  See Bradbury, Ray (Douglas)
Douglas, Michael
  See Crichton, (John) Michael
Douglas, (George) Norman 1868-1952 **TCLC 68**
  See also CA 119; 157; DLB 34, 195
Douglas, William
  See Brown, George Douglas
Douglass, Frederick 1817(?)-1895 **NCLC 7, 55;**

BLC 1; **DA; DAC; DAM MST, MULT; WLC**
  See also CDALB 1640-1865; DLB 1, 43, 50, 79; SATA 29
Dourado, (Waldomiro Freitas) Autran 1926- **CLC 23, 60**
  See also CA 25-28R; CANR 34; DLB 145; HW 2
Dourado, Waldomiro Autran
  See Dourado, (Waldomiro Freitas) Autran
Dove, Rita (Frances) 1952- **CLC 50, 81; BLCS; DAM MULT, POET; PC 6**
  See also BW 2; CA 109; CAAS 19; CANR 27, 42, 68, 76; CDALBS; DLB 120; MTCW 1
Doveglion
  See Villa, Jose Garcia
Dowell, Coleman 1925-1985 **CLC 60**
  See also CA 25-28R; 117; CANR 10; DLB 130
Dowson, Ernest (Christopher) 1867-1900 **TCLC 4**
  See also CA 105; 150; DLB 19, 135
Doyle, A. Conan
  See Doyle, Arthur Conan
Doyle, Arthur Conan 1859-1930 **TCLC 7; DA; DAB; DAC; DAM MST, NOV; SSC 12; WLC**
  See also AAYA 14; CA 104; 122; CDBLB 1890-1914; DLB 18, 70, 156, 178; MTCW 1, 2; SATA 24
Doyle, Conan
  See Doyle, Arthur Conan
Doyle, John
  See Graves, Robert (von Ranke)
Doyle, Roddy 1958(?)- **CLC 81**
  See also AAYA 14; CA 143; CANR 73; DLB 194
Doyle, Sir A. Conan
  See Doyle, Arthur Conan
Doyle, Sir Arthur Conan
  See Doyle, Arthur Conan
Dr. A
  See Asimov, Isaac; Silverstein, Alvin
Drabble, Margaret 1939- **CLC 2, 3, 5, 8, 10, 22, 53; DAB; DAC; DAM MST, NOV, POP**
  See also CA 13-16R; CANR 18, 35, 63; CDBLB 1960 to Present; DLB 14, 155; MTCW 1, 2; SATA 48
Drapier, M. B.
  See Swift, Jonathan
Drayham, James
  See Mencken, H(enry) L(ouis)
Drayton, Michael 1563-1631 **LC 8; DAM POET**
  See also DLB 121
Dreadstone, Carl
  See Campbell, (John) Ramsey
Dreiser, Theodore (Herman Albert) 1871-1945 **TCLC 10, 18, 35, 83; DA; DAC; DAM MST, NOV; SSC 30; WLC**
  See also CA 106; 132; CDALB 1865-1917; DLB 9, 12, 102, 137; DLBD 1; MTCW 1, 2
Drexler, Rosalyn 1926- **CLC 2, 6**
  See also CA 81-84; CANR 68
Dreyer, Carl Theodor 1889-1968 **CLC 16**
  See also CA 116
Drieu la Rochelle, Pierre(-Eugene) 1893-1945 **TCLC 21**
  See also CA 117; DLB 72
Drinkwater, John 1882-1937 **TCLC 57**
  See also CA 109; 149; DLB 10, 19, 149
Drop Shot
  See Cable, George Washington
Droste-Hulshoff, Annette Freiin von 1797-1848

NCLC 3
  See also DLB 133
Drummond, Walter
  See Silverberg, Robert
Drummond, William Henry 1854-1907 **TCLC 25**
  See also CA 160; DLB 92
Drummond de Andrade, Carlos 1902-1987 **CLC 18**
  See also Andrade, Carlos Drummond de
  See also CA 132; 123
Drury, Allen (Stuart) 1918-1998 **CLC 37**
  See also CA 57-60; 170; CANR 18, 52; INT CANR-18
Dryden, John 1631-1700 **LC 3, 21; DA; DAB; DAC; DAM DRAM, MST, POET; DC 3; PC 25; WLC**
  See also CDBLB 1660-1789; DLB 80, 101, 131
Duberman, Martin (Bauml) 1930- **CLC 8**
  See also CA 1-4R; CANR 2, 63
Dubie, Norman (Evans) 1945- **CLC 36**
  See also CA 69-72; CANR 12; DLB 120
Du Bois, W(illiam) E(dward) B(urghardt) 1868-1963 **CLC 1, 2, 13, 64, 96; BLC 1; DA; DAC; DAM MST, MULT, NOV; WLC**
  See also BW 1, 3; CA 85-88; CANR 34; CDALB 1865-1917; DLB 47, 50, 91; MTCW 1, 2; SATA 42
Dubus, Andre 1936- **CLC 13, 36, 97; SSC 15**
  See also CA 21-24R; CANR 17; DLB 130; INT CANR-17
Duca Minimo
  See D'Annunzio, Gabriele
Ducharme, Rejean 1941- **CLC 74**
  See also CA 165; DLB 60
Duclos, Charles Pinot 1704-1772 **LC 1**
Dudek, Louis 1918- **CLC 11, 19**
  See also CA 45-48; CAAS 14; CANR 1; DLB 88
Duerrenmatt, Friedrich 1921-1990 **CLC 1, 4, 8, 11, 15, 43, 102; DAM DRAM**
  See also CA 17-20R; CANR 33; DLB 69, 124; MTCW 1, 2
Duffy, Bruce 1953(?)- **CLC 50**
  See also CA 172
Duffy, Maureen 1933- **CLC 37**
  See also CA 25-28R; CANR 33, 68; DLB 14; MTCW 1
Dugan, Alan 1923- **CLC 2, 6**
  See also CA 81-84; DLB 5
du Gard, Roger Martin
  See Martin du Gard, Roger
Duhamel, Georges 1884-1966 **CLC 8**
  See also CA 81-84; 25-28R; CANR 35; DLB 65; MTCW 1
Dujardin, Edouard (Emile Louis) 1861-1949 **TCLC 13**
  See also CA 109; DLB 123
Dulles, John Foster 1888-1959 **TCLC 72**
  See also CA 115; 149
Dumas, Alexandre (pere)
  See Dumas, Alexandre (Davy de la Pailleterie)
Dumas, Alexandre (Davy de la Pailleterie) 1802-1870 **NCLC 11; DA; DAB; DAC; DAM MST, NOV; WLC**
  See also DLB 119, 192; SATA 18
Dumas, Alexandre (fils) 1824-1895 **NCLC 71; DC 1**
  See also AAYA 22; DLB 192
Dumas, Claudine
  See Malzberg, Barry N(athaniel)
Dumas, Henry L. 1934-1968 **CLC 6, 62**
  See also BW 1; CA 85-88; DLB 41

du Maurier, Daphne 1907-1989 **CLC 6, 11, 59; DAB; DAC; DAM MST, POP; SSC 18**
See also CA 5-8R; 128; CANR 6, 55; DLB 191; MTCW 1, 2; SATA 27; SATA-Obit 60

Dunbar, Paul Laurence 1872-1906 **TCLC 2, 12; BLC 1; DA; DAC; DAM MST, MULT, POET; PC 5; SSC 8; WLC**
See also BW 1, 3; CA 104; 124; CANR 79; CDALB 1865-1917; DLB 50, 54, 78; SATA 34

Dunbar, William 1460(?)-1530(?) **LC 20**
See also DLB 132, 146

Duncan, Dora Angela
See Duncan, Isadora

Duncan, Isadora 1877(?)-1927 **TCLC 68**
See also CA 118; 149

Duncan, Lois 1934- **CLC 26**
See also AAYA 4; CA 1-4R; CANR 2, 23, 36; CLR 29; JRDA; MAICYA; SAAS 2; SATA 1, 36, 75

Duncan, Robert (Edward) 1919-1988 **CLC 1, 2, 4, 7, 15, 41, 55; DAM POET; PC 2**
See also CA 9-12R; 124; CANR 28, 62; DLB 5, 16, 193; MTCW 1, 2

Duncan, Sara Jeannette 1861-1922 **TCLC 60**
See also CA 157; DLB 92

Dunlap, William 1766-1839 **NCLC 2**
See also DLB 30, 37, 59

Dunn, Douglas (Eaglesham) 1942- **CLC 6, 40**
See also CA 45-48; CANR 2, 33; DLB 40; MTCW 1

Dunn, Katherine (Karen) 1945- **CLC 71**
See also CA 33-36R; CANR 72; MTCW 1

Dunn, Stephen 1939- **CLC 36**
See also CA 33-36R; CANR 12, 48, 53; DLB 105

Dunne, Finley Peter 1867-1936 **TCLC 28**
See also CA 108; DLB 11, 23

Dunne, John Gregory 1932- **CLC 28**
See also CA 25-28R; CANR 14, 50; DLBY 80

Dunsany, Edward John Moreton Drax Plunkett 1878-1957
See Dunsany, Lord
See also CA 104; 148; DLB 10; MTCW 1

Dunsany, Lord **TCLC 2, 59**
See also Dunsany, Edward John Moreton Drax Plunkett
See also DLB 77, 153, 156

du Perry, Jean
See Simenon, Georges (Jacques Christian)

Durang, Christopher (Ferdinand) 1949- **CLC 27, 38**
See also CA 105; CANR 50, 76; MTCW 1

Duras, Marguerite 1914-1996 **CLC 3, 6, 11, 20, 34, 40, 68, 100**
See also CA 25-28R; 151; CANR 50; DLB 83; MTCW 1, 2

Durban, (Rosa) Pam 1947- **CLC 39**
See also CA 123

Durcan, Paul 1944- **CLC 43, 70; DAM POET**
See also CA 134

Durkheim, Emile 1858-1917 **TCLC 55**

Durrell, Lawrence (George) 1912-1990 **CLC 1, 4, 6, 8, 13, 27, 41; DAM NOV**
See also CA 9-12R; 132; CANR 40, 77; CDBLB 1945-1960; DLB 15, 27, 204; DLBY 90; MTCW 1, 2

Durrenmatt, Friedrich
See Duerrenmatt, Friedrich

Dutt, Toru 1856-1877 **NCLC 29**

Dwight, Timothy 1752-1817 **NCLC 13**
See also DLB 37

Dworkin, Andrea 1946- **CLC 43**
See also CA 77-80; CAAS 21; CANR 16, 39, 76; INT CANR-16; MTCW 1, 2

Dwyer, Deanna
See Koontz, Dean R(ay)

Dwyer, K. R.
See Koontz, Dean R(ay)

Dwyer, Thomas A. 1923- **CLC 114**
See also CA 115

Dye, Richard
See De Voto, Bernard (Augustine)

Dylan, Bob 1941- **CLC 3, 4, 6, 12, 77**
See also CA 41-44R; DLB 16

Eagleton, Terence (Francis) 1943-
See Eagleton, Terry
See also CA 57-60; CANR 7, 23, 68; MTCW 1, 2

Eagleton, Terry **CLC 63**
See also Eagleton, Terence (Francis)
See also MTCW 1

Early, Jack
See Scoppettone, Sandra

East, Michael
See West, Morris L(anglo)

Eastaway, Edward
See Thomas, (Philip) Edward

Eastlake, William (Derry) 1917-1997 **CLC 8**
See also CA 5-8R; 158; CAAS 1; CANR 5, 63; DLB 6, 206; INT CANR-5

Eastman, Charles A(lexander) 1858-1939 **TCLC 55; DAM MULT**
See also DLB 175; NNAL; YABC 1

Eberhart, Richard (Ghormley) 1904- **CLC 3, 11, 19, 56; DAM POET**
See also CA 1-4R; CANR 2; CDALB 1941-1968; DLB 48; MTCW 1

Eberstadt, Fernanda 1960- **CLC 39**
See also CA 136; CANR 69

Echegaray (y Eizaguirre), Jose (Maria Waldo) 1832-1916 **TCLC 4; HLCS 1**
See also CA 104; CANR 32; HW 1; MTCW 1

Echeverria, (Jose) Esteban (Antonino) 1805-1851 **NCLC 18**

Echo
See Proust, (Valentin-Louis-George-Eugene-) Marcel

Eckert, Allan W. 1931- **CLC 17**
See also AAYA 18; CA 13-16R; CANR 14, 45; INT CANR-14; SAAS 21; SATA 29, 91; SATA-Brief 27

Eckhart, Meister 1260(?)-1328(?) **CMLC 9**
See also DLB 115

Eckmar, F. R.
See de Hartog, Jan

Eco, Umberto 1932- **CLC 28, 60; DAM NOV, POP**
See also BEST 90:1; CA 77-80; CANR 12, 33, 55; DLB 196; MTCW 1, 2

Eddison, E(ric) R(ucker) 1882-1945 **TCLC 15**
See also CA 109; 156

Eddy, Mary (Ann Morse) Baker 1821-1910 **TCLC 71**
See also CA 113; 174

Edel, (Joseph) Leon 1907-1997 **CLC 29, 34**
See also CA 1-4R; 161; CANR 1, 22; DLB 103; INT CANR-22

Eden, Emily 1797-1869 **NCLC 10**

Edgar, David 1948- **CLC 42; DAM DRAM**
See also CA 57-60; CANR 12, 61; DLB 13; MTCW 1

Edgerton, Clyde (Carlyle) 1944- **CLC 39**
See also AAYA 17; CA 118; 134; CANR 64; INT 134

Edgeworth, Maria 1768-1849 **NCLC 1, 51**

See also DLB 116, 159, 163; SATA 21

Edmonds, Paul
See Kuttner, Henry

Edmonds, Walter D(umaux) 1903-1998 **CLC 35**
See also CA 5-8R; CANR 2; DLB 9; MAICYA; SAAS 4; SATA 1, 27; SATA-Obit 99

Edmondson, Wallace
See Ellison, Harlan (Jay)

Edson, Russell **CLC 13**
See also CA 33-36R

Edwards, Bronwen Elizabeth
See Rose, Wendy

Edwards, G(erald) B(asil) 1899-1976 **CLC 25**
See also CA 110

Edwards, Gus 1939- **CLC 43**
See also CA 108; INT 108

Edwards, Jonathan 1703-1758 **LC 7; DA; DAC; DAM MST**
See also DLB 24

Efron, Marina Ivanovna Tsvetaeva
See Tsvetaeva (Efron), Marina (Ivanovna)

Ehle, John (Marsden, Jr.) 1925- **CLC 27**
See also CA 9-12R

Ehrenbourg, Ilya (Grigoryevich)
See Ehrenburg, Ilya (Grigoryevich)

Ehrenburg, Ilya (Grigoryevich) 1891-1967 **CLC 18, 34, 62**
See also CA 102; 25-28R

Ehrenburg, Ilyo (Grigoryevich)
See Ehrenburg, Ilya (Grigoryevich)

Ehrenreich, Barbara 1941- **CLC 110**
See also BEST 90:4; CA 73-76; CANR 16, 37, 62; MTCW 1, 2

Eich, Guenter 1907-1972 **CLC 15**
See also CA 111; 93-96; DLB 69, 124

Eichendorff, Joseph Freiherr von 1788-1857 **NCLC 8**
See also DLB 90

Eigner, Larry **CLC 9**
See also Eigner, Laurence (Joel)
See also CAAS 23; DLB 5

Eigner, Laurence (Joel) 1927-1996
See Eigner, Larry
See also CA 9-12R; 151; CANR 6; DLB 193

Einstein, Albert 1879-1955 **TCLC 65**
See also CA 121; 133; MTCW 1, 2

Eiseley, Loren Corey 1907-1977 **CLC 7**
See also AAYA 5; CA 1-4R; 73-76; CANR 6; DLBD 17

Eisenstadt, Jill 1963- **CLC 50**
See also CA 140

Eisenstein, Sergei (Mikhailovich) 1898-1948 **TCLC 57**
See also CA 114; 149

Eisner, Simon
See Kornbluth, C(yril) M.

Ekeloef, (Bengt) Gunnar 1907-1968 **CLC 27; DAM POET; PC 23**
See also CA 123; 25-28R

Ekelof, (Bengt) Gunnar
See Ekeloef, (Bengt) Gunnar

Ekelund, Vilhelm 1880-1949 **TCLC 75**

Ekwensi, C. O. D.
See Ekwensi, Cyprian (Odiatu Duaka)

Ekwensi, Cyprian (Odiatu Duaka) 1921- **CLC 4; BLC 1; DAM MULT**
See also BW 2, 3; CA 29-32R; CANR 18, 42, 74; DLB 117; MTCW 1, 2; SATA 66

Elaine **TCLC 18**
See also Leverson, Ada

El Crummo
See Crumb, R(obert)

Elder, Lonne III 1931-1996   **DC 8**
   See also BLC 1; BW 1, 3; CA 81-84; 152;
    CANR 25; DAM MULT; DLB 7, 38, 44
Elia
   See Lamb, Charles
Eliade, Mircea 1907-1986   **CLC 19**
   See also CA 65-68; 119; CANR 30, 62; MTCW
    1
Eliot, A. D.
   See Jewett, (Theodora) Sarah Orne
Eliot, Alice
   See Jewett, (Theodora) Sarah Orne
Eliot, Dan
   See Silverberg, Robert
Eliot, George 1819-1880 **NCLC 4, 13, 23, 41,**
    49; DA; DAB; DAC; DAM MST, NOV; PC
    20; WLC
   See also CDBLB 1832-1890; DLB 21, 35, 55
Eliot, John 1604-1690   **LC 5**
   See also DLB 24
   <indexbEliot, T(homas) S(tearns) 1888-1965
    CLC 1, 2, 3, 6, 9, 10, 13, 15, 24, 34, 41, 55,
    57, 113; DA; DAB; DAC; DAM DRAM,
    MST, POET; PC 5; WLC
   See also AAYA 28; CA 5-8R; 25-28R; CANR
    41; CDALB 1929-1941; DLB 7, 10, 45, 63;
    DLBY 88; MTCW 1, 2
Elizabeth 1866-1941   **TCLC 41**
Elkin, Stanley L(awrence) 1930-1995 **CLC 4,**
    6, 9, 14, 27, 51, 91; DAM NOV, POP; SSC
    12
   See also CA 9-12R; 148; CANR 8, 46; DLB 2,
    28; DLBY 80; INT CANR-8; MTCW 1, 2
Elledge, Scott   **CLC 34**
Elliot, Don
   See Silverberg, Robert
Elliott, Don
   See Silverberg, Robert
Elliott, George P(aul) 1918-1980   **CLC 2**
   See also CA 1-4R; 97-100; CANR 2
Elliott, Janice 1931-   **CLC 47**
   See also CA 13-16R; CANR 8, 29; DLB 14
Elliott, Sumner Locke 1917-1991   **CLC 38**
   See also CA 5-8R; 134; CANR 2, 21
Elliott, William
   See Bradbury, Ray (Douglas)
Ellis, A. E.   **CLC 7**
Ellis, Alice Thomas   **CLC 40**
   See also Haycraft, Anna
   See also DLB 194; MTCW 1
Ellis, Bret Easton 1964- **CLC 39, 71, 117; DAM**
    POP
   See also AAYA 2; CA 118; 123; CANR 51, 74;
    INT 123; MTCW 1
Ellis, (Henry) Havelock 1859-1939 **TCLC 14**
   See also CA 109; 169; DLB 190
Ellis, Landon
   See Ellison, Harlan (Jay)
Ellis, Trey 1962-   **CLC 55**
   See also CA 146
Ellison, Harlan (Jay) 1934-   **CLC 1, 13, 42;**
    DAM POP; SSC 14
   See also AAYA 29; CA 5-8R; CANR 5, 46; DLB
    8; INT CANR-5; MTCW 1, 2
Ellison, Ralph (Waldo) 1914-1994 **CLC 1, 3,**
    11, 54, 86, 114; BLC 1; DA; DAB; DAC;
    DAM MST, MULT, NOV; SSC 26; WLC
   See also AAYA 19; BW 1, 3; CA 9-12R; 145;
    CANR 24, 53; CDALB 1941-1968; DLB 2,
    76; DLBY 94; MTCW 1, 2
Ellmann, Lucy (Elizabeth) 1956-   **CLC 61**
   See also CA 128
Ellmann, Richard (David) 1918-1987**CLC 50**

   See also BEST 89:2; CA 1-4R; 122; CANR 2,
    28, 61; DLB 103; DLBY 87; MTCW 1, 2
Elman, Richard (Martin) 1934-1997 **CLC 19**
   See also CA 17-20R; 163; CAAS 3; CANR 47
Elron
   See Hubbard, L(afayette) Ron(ald)
Eluard, Paul   **TCLC 7, 41**
   See also Grindel, Eugene
Elyot, Sir Thomas 1490(?)-1546   **LC 11**
Elytis, Odysseus 1911-1996 **CLC 15, 49, 100;**
    DAM POET; PC 21
   See also CA 102; 151; MTCW 1, 2
Emecheta, (Florence Onye) Buchi 1944-**CLC**
    14, 48; BLC 2; DAM MULT
   See also BW 2, 3; CA 81-84; CANR 27; DLB
    117; MTCW 1, 2; SATA 66
Emerson, Mary Moody 1774-1863 **NCLC 66**
Emerson, Ralph Waldo 1803-1882 **NCLC 1,**
    38; DA; DAB; DAC; DAM MST, POET;
    PC 18; WLC
   See also CDALB 1640-1865; DLB 1, 59, 73
Eminescu, Mihail 1850-1889   **NCLC 33**
Empson, William 1906-1984**CLC 3, 8, 19, 33,**
    34
   See also CA 17-20R; 112; CANR 31, 61; DLB
    20; MTCW 1, 2
Enchi, Fumiko (Ueda) 1905-1986   **CLC 31**
   See also CA 129; 121; DLB 182
Ende, Michael (Andreas Helmuth) 1929-1995
    CLC 31
   See also CA 118; 124; 149; CANR 36; CLR
    14; DLB 75; MAICYA; SATA 61; SATA-
    Brief 42; SATA-Obit 86
Endo, Shusaku 1923-1996 **CLC 7, 14, 19, 54,**
    99; DAM NOV
   See also CA 29-32R; 153; CANR 21, 54; DLB
    182; MTCW 1, 2
Engel, Marian 1933-1985   **CLC 36**
   See also CA 25-28R; CANR 12; DLB 53; INT
    CANR-12
Engelhardt, Frederick
   See Hubbard, L(afayette) Ron(ald)
Enright, D(ennis) J(oseph) 1920-**CLC 4, 8, 31**
   See also CA 1-4R; CANR 1, 42; DLB 27; SATA
    25
Enzensberger, Hans Magnus 1929-   **CLC 43**
   See also CA 116; 119
Ephron, Nora 1941-   **CLC 17, 31**
   See also AITN 2; CA 65-68; CANR 12, 39
Epicurus 341B.C.-270B.C.   **CMLC 21**
   See also DLB 176
Epsilon
   See Betjeman, John
Epstein, Daniel Mark 1948-   **CLC 7**
   See also CA 49-52; CANR 2, 53
Epstein, Jacob 1956-   **CLC 19**
   See also CA 114
Epstein, Jean 1897-1953   **TCLC 92**
Epstein, Joseph 1937-   **CLC 39**
   See also CA 112; 119; CANR 50, 65
Epstein, Leslie 1938-   **CLC 27**
   See also CA 73-76; CAAS 12; CANR 23, 69
Equiano, Olaudah 1745(?)-1797 **LC 16; BLC**
    2; DAM MULT
   See also DLB 37, 50
ER   **TCLC 33**
   See also CA 160; DLB 85
Erasmus, Desiderius 1469(?)-1536   **LC 16**
Erdman, Paul E(mil) 1932-   **CLC 25**
   See also AITN 1; CA 61-64; CANR 13, 43
Erdrich, Louise 1954-**CLC 39, 54, 120; DAM**
    MULT, NOV, POP
   See also AAYA 10; BEST 89:1; CA 114; CANR

    41, 62; CDALBS; DLB 152, 175, 206;
    MTCW 1; NNAL; SATA 94
Erenburg, Ilya (Grigoryevich)
   See Ehrenburg, Ilya (Grigoryevich)
Erickson, Stephen Michael 1950-
   See Erickson, Steve
   See also CA 129
Erickson, Steve 1950-   **CLC 64**
   See also Erickson, Stephen Michael
   See also CANR 60, 68
Ericson, Walter
   See Fast, Howard (Melvin)
Eriksson, Buntel
   See Bergman, (Ernst) Ingmar
Ernaux, Annie 1940-   **CLC 88**
   See also CA 147
Erskine, John 1879-1951   **TCLC 84**
   See also CA 112; 159; DLB 9, 102
Eschenbach, Wolfram von
   See Wolfram von Eschenbach
Eseki, Bruno
   See Mphahlele, Ezekiel
Esenin, Sergei (Alexandrovich) 1895-1925
    TCLC 4
   See also CA 104
   <indexboEshleman, Clayton 1935- **CLC 7**
   See also CA 33-36R; CAAS 6; DLB 5
Espriella, Don Manuel Alvarez
   See Southey, Robert
Espriu, Salvador 1913-1985   **CLC 9**
   See also CA 154; 115; DLB 134
Espronceda, Jose de 1808-1842   **NCLC 39**
Esse, James
   See Stephens, James
Esterbrook, Tom
   See Hubbard, L(afayette) Ron(ald)
Estleman, Loren D. 1952-**CLC 48; DAM NOV,**
    POP
   See also AAYA 27; CA 85-88; CANR 27, 74;
    INT CANR-27; MTCW 1, 2
Euclid 306B.C.-283B.C.   **CMLC 25**
Eugenides, Jeffrey 1960(?)-   **CLC 81**
   See also CA 144
Euripides c. 485B.C.-406B.C.**CMLC 23; DA;**
    DAB; DAC; DAM DRAM, MST; DC 4;
    WLCS
   See also DLB 176
Evan, Evin
   See Faust, Frederick (Schiller)
Evans, Caradoc 1878-1945   **TCLC 85**
Evans, Evan
   See Faust, Frederick (Schiller)
Evans, Marian
   See Eliot, George
Evans, Mary Ann
   See Eliot, George
Evarts, Esther
   See Benson, Sally
Everett, Percival L. 1956-   **CLC 57**
   See also BW 2; CA 129
Everson, R(onald) G(ilmour) 1903- **CLC 27**
   See also CA 17-20R; DLB 88
Everson, William (Oliver) 1912-1994 **CLC 1,**
    5, 14
   See also CA 9-12R; 145; CANR 20; DLB 212;
    MTCW 1
Evtushenko, Evgenii Aleksandrovich
   See Yevtushenko, Yevgeny (Alexandrovich)
Ewart, Gavin (Buchanan) 1916-1995**CLC 13,**
    46
   See also CA 89-92; 150; CANR 17, 46; DLB
    40; MTCW 1
Ewers, Hanns Heinz 1871-1943   **TCLC 12**

See also CA 109; 149
Ewing, Frederick R.
See Sturgeon, Theodore (Hamilton)
Exley, Frederick (Earl) 1929-1992 **CLC 6, 11**
See also AITN 2; CA 81-84; 138; DLB 143;
DLBY 81
Eynhardt, Guillermo
See Quiroga, Horacio (Sylvestre)
Ezekiel, Nissim 1924- **CLC 61**
See also CA 61-64
Ezekiel, Tish O'Dowd 1943- **CLC 34**
See also CA 129
Fadeyev, A.
See Bulgya, Alexander Alexandrovich
Fadeyev, Alexander **TCLC 53**
See also Bulgya, Alexander Alexandrovich
Fagen, Donald 1948- **CLC 26**
Fainzilberg, Ilya Arnoldovich 1897-1937
See Ilf, Ilya
See also CA 120; 165
Fair, Ronald L. 1932- **CLC 18**
See also BW 1; CA 69-72; CANR 25; DLB 33
Fairbairn, Roger
See Carr, John Dickson
Fairbairns, Zoe (Ann) 1948- **CLC 32**
See also CA 103; CANR 21
Falco, Gian
See Papini, Giovanni
Falconer, James
See Kirkup, James
Falconer, Kenneth
See Kornbluth, C(yril) M.
Falkland, Samuel
See Heijermans, Herman
Fallaci, Oriana 1930- **CLC 11, 110**
See also CA 77-80; CANR 15, 58; MTCW 1
Faludy, George 1913- **CLC 42**
See also CA 21-24R
Faludy, Gyoergy
See Faludy, George
Fanon, Frantz 1925-1961 **CLC 74; BLC 2;**
DAM MULT
See also BW 1; CA 116; 89-92
Fanshawe, Ann 1625-1680 **LC 11**
Fante, John (Thomas) 1911-1983 **CLC 60**
See also CA 69-72; 109; CANR 23; DLB 130;
DLBY 83
Farah, Nuruddin 1945-**CLC 53; BLC 2; DAM**
MULT
See also BW 2, 3; CA 106; DLB 125
Fargue, Leon-Paul 1876(?)-1947 **TCLC 11**
See also CA 109
Farigoule, Louis
See Romains, Jules
Farina, Richard 1936(?)-1966 **CLC 9**
See also CA 81-84; 25-28R
Farley, Walter (Lorimer) 1915-1989 **CLC 17**
See also CA 17-20R; CANR 8, 29; DLB 22;
JRDA; MAICYA; SATA 2, 43
Farmer, Philip Jose 1918- **CLC 1, 19**
See also AAYA 28; CA 1-4R; CANR 4, 35; DLB
8; MTCW 1; SATA 93
Farquhar, George 1677-1707 **LC 21; DAM**
DRAM
See also DLB 84
Farrell, J(ames) G(ordon) 1935-1979 **CLC 6**
See also CA 73-76; 89-92; CANR 36; DLB 14;
MTCW 1
Farrell, James T(homas) 1904-1979**CLC 1, 4,**
8, 11, 66; SSC 28
See also CA 5-8R; 89-92; CANR 9, 61; DLB 4,
9, 86; DLBD 2; MTCW 1, 2
Farren, Richard J.

See Betjeman, John
Farren, Richard M.
See Betjeman, John
Fassbinder, Rainer Werner 1946-1982**CLC 20**
See also CA 93-96; 106; CANR 31
Fast, Howard (Melvin) 1914- **CLC 23; DAM**
NOV
See also AAYA 16; CA 1-4R; CAAS 18; CANR
1, 33, 54, 75; DLB 9; INT CANR-33; MTCW
1; SATA 7; SATA-Essay 107
Faulcon, Robert
See Holdstock, Robert P.
Faulkner, William (Cuthbert) 1897-1962**CLC**
1, 3, 6, 8, 9, 11, 14, 18, 28, 52, 68; DA; DAB;
DAC; DAM MST, NOV; SSC 1; WLC
See also AAYA 7; CA 81-84; CANR 33;
CDALB 1929-1941; DLB 9, 11, 44, 102;
DLBD 2; DLBY 86, 97; MTCW 1, 2
Fauset, Jessie Redmon 1884(?)-1961**CLC 19,**
54; BLC 2; DAM MULT
See also BW 1; CA 109; DLB 51
Faust, Frederick (Schiller) 1892-1944(?)
TCLC 49; DAM POP
See also CA 108; 152
Faust, Irvin 1924- **CLC 8**
See also CA 33-36R; CANR 28, 67; DLB 2,
28; DLBY 80
Fawkes, Guy
See Benchley, Robert (Charles)
Fearing, Kenneth (Flexner) 1902-1961 **CLC**
51
See also CA 93-96; CANR 59; DLB 9
Fecamps, Elise
See Creasey, John
Federman, Raymond 1928- **CLC 6, 47**
See also CA 17-20R; CAAS 8; CANR 10, 43;
DLBY 80
Federspiel, J(uerg) F. 1931- **CLC 42**
See also CA 146
Feiffer, Jules (Ralph) 1929- **CLC 2, 8, 64;**
DAM DRAM
See also AAYA 3; CA 17-20R; CANR 30, 59;
DLB 7, 44; INT CANR-30; MTCW 1; SATA
8, 61
Feige, Hermann Albert Otto Maximilian
See Traven, B.
Feinberg, David B. 1956-1994 **CLC 59**
See also CA 135; 147
Feinstein, Elaine 1930- **CLC 36**
See also CA 69-72; CAAS 1; CANR 31, 68;
DLB 14, 40; MTCW 1
Feldman, Irving (Mordecai) 1928- **CLC 7**
See also CA 1-4R; CANR 1; DLB 169
Felix-Tchicaya, Gerald
See Tchicaya, Gerald Felix
Fellini, Federico 1920-1993 **CLC 16, 85**
See also CA 65-68; 143; CANR 33
Felsen, Henry Gregor 1916- **CLC 17**
See also CA 1-4R; CANR 1; SAAS 2; SATA 1
Fenno, Jack
See Calisher, Hortense
Fenollosa, Ernest (Francisco) 1853-1908
TCLC 91
Fenton, James Martin 1949- **CLC 32**
See also CA 102; DLB 40
Ferber, Edna 1887-1968 **CLC 18, 93**
See also AITN 1; CA 5-8R; 25-28R; CANR 68;
DLB 9, 28, 86; MTCW 1, 2; SATA 7
Ferguson, Helen
See Kavan, Anna
Ferguson, Samuel 1810-1886 **NCLC 33**
See also DLB 32
Fergusson, Robert 1750-1774 **LC 29**

See also DLB 109
Ferling, Lawrence
See Ferlinghetti, Lawrence (Monsanto)
Ferlinghetti, Lawrence (Monsanto) 1919(?)-
CLC 2, 6, 10, 27, 111; DAM POET; PC 1
See also CA 5-8R; CANR 3, 41, 73; CDALB
1941-1968; DLB 5, 16; MTCW 1, 2
Fernandez, Vicente Garcia Huidobro
See Huidobro Fernandez, Vicente Garcia
Ferrer, Gabriel (Francisco Victor) Miro
See Miro (Ferrer), Gabriel (Francisco Victor)
Ferrier, Susan (Edmonstone) 1782-1854
NCLC 8
See also DLB 116
Ferrigno, Robert 1948(?)- **CLC 65**
See also CA 140
Ferron, Jacques 1921-1985 **CLC 94; DAC**
See also CA 117; 129; DLB 60
Feuchtwanger, Lion 1884-1958 **TCLC 3**
See also CA 104; DLB 66
Feuillet, Octave 1821-1890 **NCLC 45**
See also DLB 192
Feydeau, Georges (Leon Jules Marie) 1862-
1921 **TCLC 22; DAM DRAM**
See also CA 113; 152; DLB 192
Fichte, Johann Gottlieb 1762-1814 **NCLC 62**
See also DLB 90
Ficino, Marsilio 1433-1499 **LC 12**
Fiedeler, Hans
See Doeblin, Alfred
Fiedler, Leslie A(aron) 1917- **CLC 4, 13, 24**
See also CA 9-12R; CANR 7, 63; DLB 28, 67;
MTCW 1, 2
Field, Andrew 1938- **CLC 44**
See also CA 97-100; CANR 25
Field, Eugene 1850-1895 **NCLC 3**
See also DLB 23, 42, 140; DLBD 13; MAICYA;
SATA 16
Field, Gans T.
See Wellman, Manly Wade
Field, Michael 1915-1971 **TCLC 43**
See also CA 29-32R
Field, Peter
See Hobson, Laura Z(ametkin)
Fielding, Henry 1707-1754 **LC 1, 46; DA;**
DAB; DAC; DAM DRAM, MST, NOV;
WLC
See also CDBLB 1660-1789; DLB 39, 84, 101
Fielding, Sarah 1710-1768 **LC 1, 44**
See also DLB 39
Fields, W. C. 1880-1946 **TCLC 80**
See also DLB 44
Fierstein, Harvey (Forbes) 1954- **CLC 33;**
DAM DRAM, POP
See also CA 123; 129
Figes, Eva 1932- **CLC 31**
See also CA 53-56; CANR 4, 44; DLB 14
Finch, Anne 1661-1720 **LC 3; PC 21**
See also DLB 95
Finch, Robert (Duer Claydon) 1900- **CLC 18**
See also CA 57-60; CANR 9, 24, 49; DLB 88
Findley, Timothy 1930- **CLC 27, 102; DAC;**
DAM MST
See also CA 25-28R; CANR 12, 42, 69; DLB
53
Fink, William
See Mencken, H(enry) L(ouis)
Firbank, Louis 1942-
See Reed, Lou
See also CA 117
Firbank, (Arthur Annesley) Ronald 1886-1926
TCLC 1
See also CA 104; DLB 36

Fisher, Dorothy (Frances) Canfield 1879-1958 **TCLC 87**
See also CA 114; 136; CANR 80; DLB 9, 102; MAICYA; YABC 1

Fisher, M(ary) F(rances) K(ennedy) 1908-1992 **CLC 76, 87**
See also CA 77-80; 138; CANR 44; MTCW 1

Fisher, Roy 1930- **CLC 25**
See also CA 81-84; CAAS 10; CANR 16; DLB 40

Fisher, Rudolph 1897-1934 **TCLC 11; BLC 2; DAM MULT; SSC 25**
See also BW 1, 3; CA 107; 124; CANR 80; DLB 51, 102

Fisher, Vardis (Alvero) 1895-1968 **CLC 7**
See also CA 5-8R; 25-28R; CANR 68; DLB 9, 206

Fiske, Tarleton
See Bloch, Robert (Albert)

Fitch, Clarke
See Sinclair, Upton (Beall)

Fitch, John IV
See Cormier, Robert (Edmund)

Fitzgerald, Captain Hugh
See Baum, L(yman) Frank

FitzGerald, Edward 1809-1883 **NCLC 9**
See also DLB 32

Fitzgerald, F(rancis) Scott (Key) 1896-1940 **TCLC 1, 6, 14, 28, 55; DA; DAB; DAC; DAM MST, NOV; SSC 6, 31; WLC**
See also AAYA 24; AITN 1; CA 110; 123; CDALB 1917-1929; DLB 4, 9, 86; DLBD 1, 15, 16; DLBY 81, 96; MTCW 1, 2

Fitzgerald, Penelope 1916- **CLC 19, 51, 61**
See also CA 85-88; CAAS 10; CANR 56; DLB 14, 194; MTCW 2

Fitzgerald, Robert (Stuart) 1910-1985 **CLC 39**
See also CA 1-4R; 114; CANR 1; DLBY 80

FitzGerald, Robert D(avid) 1902-1987 **CLC 19**
See also CA 17-20R

Fitzgerald, Zelda (Sayre) 1900-1948 **TCLC 52**
See also CA 117; 126; DLBY 84

Flanagan, Thomas (James Bonner) 1923- **CLC 25, 52**
See also CA 108; CANR 55; DLBY 80; INT 108; MTCW 1

Flaubert, Gustave 1821-1880 **NCLC 2, 10, 19, 62, 66; DA; DAB; DAC; DAM MST, NOV; SSC 11; WLC**
See also DLB 119

Flecker, Herman Elroy
See Flecker, (Herman) James Elroy

Flecker, (Herman) James Elroy 1884-1915 **TCLC 43**
See also CA 109; 150; DLB 10, 19

Fleming, Ian (Lancaster) 1908-1964 **CLC 3, 30; DAM POP**
See also AAYA 26; CA 5-8R; CANR 59; CDBLB 1945-1960; DLB 87, 201; MTCW 1, 2; SATA 9

Fleming, Thomas (James) 1927- **CLC 37**
See also CA 5-8R; CANR 10; INT CANR-10; SATA 8

Fletcher, John 1579-1625 **LC 33; DC 6**
See also CDBLB Before 1660; DLB 58

Fletcher, John Gould 1886-1950 **TCLC 35**
See also CA 107; 167; DLB 4, 45

Fleur, Paul
See Pohl, Frederik

Flooglebuckle, Al
See Spiegelman, Art

Flying Officer X
See Bates, H(erbert) E(rnest)

Fo, Dario 1926- **CLC 32, 109; DAM DRAM; DC 10**
See also CA 116; 128; CANR 68; DLBY 97; MTCW 1, 2

Fogarty, Jonathan Titulescu Esq.
See Farrell, James T(homas)

Folke, Will
See Bloch, Robert (Albert)

Follett, Ken(neth Martin) 1949- **CLC 18; DAM NOV, POP**
See also AAYA 6; BEST 89:4; CA 81-84; CANR 13, 33, 54; DLB 87; DLBY 81; INT CANR-33; MTCW 1

Fontane, Theodor 1819-1898 **NCLC 26**
See also DLB 129

Foote, Horton 1916- **CLC 51, 91; DAM DRAM**
See also CA 73-76; CANR 34, 51; DLB 26; INT CANR-34

Foote, Shelby 1916- **CLC 75; DAM NOV, POP**
See also CA 5-8R; CANR 3, 45, 74; DLB 2, 17; MTCW 2

Forbes, Esther 1891-1967 **CLC 12**
See also AAYA 17; CA 13-14; 25-28R; CAP 1; CLR 27; DLB 22; JRDA; MAICYA; SATA 2, 100

Forche, Carolyn (Louise) 1950- **CLC 25, 83, 86; DAM POET; PC 10**
See also CA 109; 117; CANR 50, 74; DLB 5, 193; INT 117; MTCW 1

Ford, Elbur
See Hibbert, Eleanor Alice Burford

Ford, Ford Madox 1873-1939 **TCLC 1, 15, 39, 57; DAM NOV**
See also CA 104; 132; CANR 74; CDBLB 1914-1945; DLB 162; MTCW 1, 2

Ford, Henry 1863-1947 **TCLC 73**
See also CA 115; 148

Ford, John 1586-(?) **DC 8**
See also CDBLB Before 1660; DAM DRAM; DLB 58

Ford, John 1895-1973 **CLC 16**
See also CA 45-48

Ford, Richard 1944- **CLC 46, 99**
See also CA 69-72; CANR 11, 47; MTCW 1

Ford, Webster
See Masters, Edgar Lee

Foreman, Richard 1937- **CLC 50**
See also CA 65-68; CANR 32, 63

Forester, C(ecil) S(cott) 1899-1966 **CLC 35**
See also CA 73-76; 25-28R; DLB 191; SATA 13

Forez
See Mauriac, Francois (Charles)

Forman, James Douglas 1932- **CLC 21**
See also AAYA 17; CA 9-12R; CANR 4, 19, 42; JRDA; MAICYA; SATA 8, 70

Fornes, Maria Irene 1930- **CLC 39, 61; DC 10; HLCS 1**
See also CA 25-28R; CANR 28; DLB 7; HW 1, 2; INT CANR-28; MTCW 1

Forrest, Leon (Richard) 1937-1997 **CLC 4; BLCS**
See also BW 2; CA 89-92; 162; CAAS 7; CANR 25, 52; DLB 33

Forster, E(dward) M(organ) 1879-1970 **CLC 1, 2, 3, 4, 9, 10, 13, 15, 22, 45, 77; DA; DAB; DAC; DAM MST, NOV; SSC 27; WLC**
See also AAYA 2; CA 13-14; 25-28R; CANR 45; CAP 1; CDBLB 1914-1945; DLB 34, 98, 162, 178, 195; DLBD 10; MTCW 1, 2; SATA 57

Forster, John 1812-1876 **NCLC 11**
See also DLB 144, 184

Forsyth, Frederick 1938- **CLC 2, 5, 36; DAM NOV, POP**
See also BEST 89:4; CA 85-88; CANR 38, 62; DLB 87; MTCW 1, 2

Forten, Charlotte L. **TCLC 16; BLC 2**
See also Grimke, Charlotte L(ottie) Forten
See also DLB 50

Foscolo, Ugo 1778-1827 **NCLC 8**

Fosse, Bob **CLC 20**
See also Fosse, Robert Louis

Fosse, Robert Louis 1927-1987
See Fosse, Bob
See also CA 110; 123

Foster, Stephen Collins 1826-1864 **NCLC 26**

Foucault, Michel 1926-1984 **CLC 31, 34, 69**
See also CA 105; 113; CANR 34; MTCW 1, 2

Fouque, Friedrich (Heinrich Karl) de la Motte 1777-1843 **NCLC 2**
See also DLB 90

Fourier, Charles 1772-1837 **NCLC 51**

Fournier, Henri Alban 1886-1914
See Alain-Fournier
See also CA 104

Fournier, Pierre 1916- **CLC 11**
See also Gascar, Pierre
See also CA 89-92; CANR 16, 40

Fowles, John (Philip) 1926- **CLC 1, 2, 3, 4, 6, 9, 10, 15, 33, 87; DAB; DAC; DAM MST; SSC 33**
See also CA 5-8R; CANR 25, 71; CDBLB 1960 to Present; DLB 14, 139, 207; MTCW 1, 2; SATA 22

Fox, Paula 1923- **CLC 2, 8**
See also AAYA 3; CA 73-76; CANR 20, 36, 62; CLR 1, 44; DLB 52; JRDA; MAICYA; MTCW 1; SATA 17, 60

Fox, William Price (Jr.) 1926- **CLC 22**
See also CA 17-20R; CAAS 19; CANR 11; DLB 2; DLBY 81

Foxe, John 1516(?)-1587 **LC 14**
See also DLB 132

Frame, Janet 1924- **CLC 2, 3, 6, 22, 66, 96; SSC 29**
See also Clutha, Janet Paterson Frame

France, Anatole **TCLC 9**
See also Thibault, Jacques Anatole Francois
See also DLB 123; MTCW 1

Francis, Claude 19(?)- **CLC 50**

Francis, Dick 1920- **CLC 2, 22, 42, 102; DAM POP**
See also AAYA 5, 21; BEST 89:3; CA 5-8R; CANR 9, 42, 68; CDBLB 1960 to Present; DLB 87; INT CANR-9; MTCW 1, 2

Francis, Robert (Churchill) 1901-1987 **CLC 15**
See also CA 1-4R; 123; CANR 1

Frank, Anne(lies Marie) 1929-1945 **TCLC 17; DA; DAB; DAC; DAM MST; WLC**
See also AAYA 12; CA 113; 133; CANR 68; MTCW 1, 2; SATA 87; SATA-Brief 42

Frank, Bruno 1887-1945 **TCLC 81**
See also DLB 118

Frank, Elizabeth 1945- **CLC 39**
See also CA 121; 126; CANR 78; INT 126

Frankl, Viktor E(mil) 1905-1997 **CLC 93**
See also CA 65-68; 161

Franklin, Benjamin
See Hasek, Jaroslav (Matej Frantisek)

Franklin, Benjamin 1706-1790 **LC 25; DA; DAB; DAC; DAM MST; WLCS**
See also CDALB 1640-1865; DLB 24, 43, 73

Franklin, (Stella Maria Sarah) Miles (Lampe) 1879-1954 **TCLC 7**

See also CA 104; 164
Fraser, (Lady) Antonia (Pakenham) 1932-
CLC 32, 107
See also CA 85-88; CANR 44, 65; MTCW 1,
2; SATA-Brief 32
Fraser, George MacDonald 1925-   **CLC 7**
See also CA 45-48; CANR 2, 48, 74; MTCW 1
Fraser, Sylvia 1935-   **CLC 64**
See also CA 45-48; CANR 1, 16, 60
Frayn, Michael 1933-**CLC 3, 7, 31, 47; DAM
DRAM, NOV**
See also CA 5-8R; CANR 30, 69; DLB 13, 14,
194; MTCW 1, 2
Fraze, Candida (Merrill) 1945-   **CLC 50**
See also CA 126
Frazer, J(ames) G(eorge) 1854-1941**TCLC 32**
See also CA 118
Frazer, Robert Caine
See Creasey, John
Frazer, Sir James George
See Frazer, J(ames) G(eorge)
Frazier, Charles 1950-   **CLC 109**
See also CA 161
Frazier, Ian 1951-   **CLC 46**
See also CA 130; CANR 54
Frederic, Harold 1856-1898   **NCLC 10**
See also DLB 12, 23; DLBD 13
Frederick, John
See Faust, Frederick (Schiller)
Frederick the Great 1712-1786   **LC 14**
Fredro, Aleksander 1793-1876   **NCLC 8**
Freeling, Nicolas 1927-   **CLC 38**
See also CA 49-52; CAAS 12; CANR 1, 17,
50; DLB 87
Freeman, Douglas Southall 1886-1953 **TCLC
11**
See also CA 109; DLB 17; DLBD 17
Freeman, Judith 1946-   **CLC 55**
See also CA 148
Freeman, Mary Eleanor Wilkins 1852-1930
TCLC 9; SSC 1
See also CA 106; DLB 12, 78
Freeman, R(ichard) Austin 1862-1943 **T C L C
21**
See also CA 113; DLB 70
French, Albert 1943-   **CLC 86**
See also BW 3; CA 167
French, Marilyn 1929-**CLC 10, 18, 60; DAM
DRAM, NOV, POP**
See also CA 69-72; CANR 3, 31; INT CANR-
31; MTCW 1, 2
French, Paul
See Asimov, Isaac
Freneau, Philip Morin 1752-1832   **NCLC 1**
See also DLB 37, 43
Freud, Sigmund 1856-1939   **TCLC 52**
See also CA 115; 133; CANR 69; MTCW 1, 2
Friedan, Betty (Naomi) 1921-   **CLC 74**
See also CA 65-68; CANR 18, 45, 74; MTCW
1, 2
Friedlander, Saul 1932-   **CLC 90**
See also CA 117; 130; CANR 72
Friedman, B(ernard) H(arper) 1926- **CLC 7**
See also CA 1-4R; CANR 3, 48
Friedman, Bruce Jay 1930-   **CLC 3, 5, 56**
See also CA 9-12R; CANR 25, 52; DLB 2, 28;
INT CANR-25
Friel, Brian 1929- **CLC 5, 42, 59, 115; DC 8**
See also CA 21-24R; CANR 33, 69; DLB 13;
MTCW 1
Friis-Baastad, Babbis Ellinor 1921-1970**C L C
12**
See also CA 17-20R; 134; SATA 7

Frisch, Max (Rudolf) 1911-1991**CLC 3, 9, 14,
18, 32, 44; DAM DRAM, NOV**
See also CA 85-88; 134; CANR 32, 74; DLB
69, 124; MTCW 1, 2
Fromentin, Eugene (Samuel Auguste) 1820-
1876   **NCLC 10**
See also DLB 123
Frost, Frederick
See Faust, Frederick (Schiller)
Frost, Robert (Lee) 1874-1963**CLC 1, 3, 4, 9,
10, 13, 15, 26, 34, 44; DA; DAB; DAC;
DAM MST, POET; PC 1; WLC**
See also AAYA 21; CA 89-92; CANR 33;
CDALB 1917-1929; DLB 54; DLBD 7;
MTCW 1, 2; SATA 14
Froude, James Anthony 1818-1894 **NCLC 43**
See also DLB 18, 57, 144
Frov, Herald
See Waterhouse, Keith (Spencer)
Fry, Christopher 1907- **CLC 2, 10, 14; DAM
DRAM**
See also CA 17-20R; CAAS 23; CANR 9, 30,
74; DLB 13; MTCW 1, 2; SATA 66
Frye, (Herman) Northrop 1912-1991**CLC 24,
70**
See also CA 5-8R; 133; CANR 8, 37; DLB 67,
68; MTCW 1, 2
Fuchs, Daniel 1909-1993   **CLC 8, 22**
See also CA 81-84; 142; CAAS 5; CANR 40;
DLB 9, 26, 28; DLBY 93
Fuchs, Daniel 1934-   **CLC 34**
See also CA 37-40R; CANR 14, 48
Fuentes, Carlos 1928-**CLC 3, 8, 10, 13, 22, 41,
60, 113; DA; DAB; DAC; DAM MST,
MULT, NOV; HLC; SSC 24; WLC**
See also AAYA 4; AITN 2; CA 69-72; CANR
10, 32, 68; DLB 113; HW 1, 2; MTCW 1, 2
Fuentes, Gregorio Lopez y
See Lopez y Fuentes, Gregorio
Fugard, (Harold) Athol 1932-**CLC 5, 9, 14, 25,
40, 80; DAM DRAM; DC 3**
See also AAYA 17; CA 85-88; CANR 32, 54;
MTCW 1
Fugard, Sheila 1932-   **CLC 48**
See also CA 125
Fuller, Charles (H., Jr.) 1939-**CLC 25; BLC 2;
DAM DRAM, MULT; DC 1**
See also BW 2; CA 108; 112; DLB 38; INT 112;
MTCW 1
Fuller, John (Leopold) 1937-   **CLC 62**
See also CA 21-24R; CANR 9, 44; DLB 40
Fuller, Margaret   **NCLC 5, 50**
See also Ossoli, Sarah Margaret (Fuller
marchesa d')
Fuller, Roy (Broadbent) 1912-1991**CLC 4, 28**
See also CA 5-8R; 135; CAAS 10; CANR 53;
DLB 15, 20; SATA 87
Fulton, Alice 1952-   **CLC 52**
See also CA 116; CANR 57; DLB 193
Furphy, Joseph 1843-1912   **TCLC 25**
See also CA 163
Fussell, Paul 1924-   **CLC 74**
See also BEST 90:1; CA 17-20R; CANR 8, 21,
35, 69; INT CANR-21; MTCW 1, 2
Futabatei, Shimei 1864-1909   **TCLC 44**
See also CA 162; DLB 180
Futrelle, Jacques 1875-1912   **TCLC 19**
See also CA 113; 155
Gaboriau, Emile 1835-1873   **NCLC 14**
Gadda, Carlo Emilio 1893-1973   **CLC 11**
See also CA 89-92; DLB 177
Gaddis, William 1922-1998**CLC 1, 3, 6, 8, 10,
19, 43, 86**

See also CA 17-20R; 172; CANR 21, 48; DLB
2; MTCW 1, 2
Gage, Walter
See Inge, William (Motter)
Gaines, Ernest J(ames) 1933- **CLC 3, 11, 18,
86; BLC 2; DAM MULT**
See also AAYA 18; AITN 1; BW 2, 3; CA 9-
12R; CANR 6, 24, 42, 75; CDALB 1968-
1988; DLB 2, 33, 152; DLBY 80; MTCW 1,
2; SATA 86
Gaitskill, Mary 1954-   **CLC 69**
See also CA 128; CANR 61
Galdos, Benito Perez
See Perez Galdos, Benito
Gale, Zona 1874-1938**TCLC 7; DAM DRAM**
See also CA 105; 153; DLB 9, 78
Galeano, Eduardo (Hughes) 1940- **CLC 72;
HLCS 1**
See also CA 29-32R; CANR 13, 32; HW 1
Galiano, Juan Valera y Alcala
See Valera y Alcala-Galiano, Juan
Galilei, Galileo 1546-1642   **LC 45**
Gallagher, Tess 1943-   **CLC 18, 63; DAM
POET; PC 9**
See also CA 106; DLB 212
Gallant, Mavis 1922-   **CLC 7, 18, 38; DAC;
DAM MST; SSC 5**
See also CA 69-72; CANR 29, 69; DLB 53;
MTCW 1, 2
Gallant, Roy A(rthur) 1924-   **CLC 17**
See also CA 5-8R; CANR 4, 29, 54; CLR 30;
MAICYA; SATA 4, 68
Gallico, Paul (William) 1897-1976   **CLC 2**
See also AITN 1; CA 5-8R; 69-72; CANR 23;
DLB 9, 171; MAICYA; SATA 13
Gallo, Max Louis 1932-   **CLC 95**
See also CA 85-88
Gallois, Lucien
See Desnos, Robert
Gallup, Ralph
See Whitemore, Hugh (John)
Galsworthy, John 1867-1933**TCLC 1, 45; DA;
DAB; DAC; DAM DRAM, MST, NOV;
SSC 22; WLC**
See also CA 104; 141; CANR 75; CDBLB
1890-1914; DLB 10, 34, 98, 162; DLBD 16;
MTCW 1
Galt, John 1779-1839   **NCLC 1**
See also DLB 99, 116, 159
Galvin, James 1951-   **CLC 38**
See also CA 108; CANR 26
Gamboa, Federico 1864-1939   **TCLC 36**
See also CA 167; HW 2
Gandhi, M. K.
See Gandhi, Mohandas Karamchand
Gandhi, Mahatma
See Gandhi, Mohandas Karamchand
Gandhi, Mohandas Karamchand 1869-1948
TCLC 59; DAM MULT
See also CA 121; 132; MTCW 1, 2
Gann, Ernest Kellogg 1910-1991   **CLC 23**
See also AITN 1; CA 1-4R; 136; CANR 1
Garcia, Cristina 1958-   **CLC 76**
See also CA 141; CANR 73; HW 2
Garcia Lorca, Federico 1898-1936**TCLC 1, 7,
49; DA; DAB; DAC; DAM DRAM, MST,
MULT, POET; DC 2; HLC; PC 3; WLC**
See also CA 104; 131; DLB 108; HW 1, 2;
MTCW 1, 2
Garcia Marquez, Gabriel (Jose) 1928-**CLC 2,
3, 8, 10, 15, 27, 47, 55, 68; DA; DAB; DAC;
DAM MST, MULT, NOV, POP; HLC; SSC
8; WLC**

See also AAYA 3; BEST 89:1, 90:4; CA 33-36R; CANR 10, 28, 50, 75; DLB 113; HW 1, 2; MTCW 1, 2

Gard, Janice
See Latham, Jean Lee

Gard, Roger Martin du
See Martin du Gard, Roger

Gardam, Jane 1928-   **CLC 43**
See also CA 49-52; CANR 2, 18, 33, 54; CLR 12; DLB 14, 161; MAICYA; MTCW 1; SAAS 9; SATA 39, 76; SATA-Brief 28

Gardner, Herb(ert) 1934-   **CLC 44**
See also CA 149

Gardner, John (Champlin), Jr. 1933-1982
    CLC 2, 3, 5, 7, 8, 10, 18, 28, 34; DAM NOV, POP; SSC 7
See also AITN 1; CA 65-68; 107; CANR 33, 73; CDALBS; DLB 2; DLBY 82; MTCW 1; SATA 40; SATA-Obit 31

Gardner, John (Edmund) 1926-**CLC 30; DAM POP**
See also CA 103; CANR 15, 69; MTCW 1

Gardner, Miriam
See Bradley, Marion Zimmer

Gardner, Noel
See Kuttner, Henry

Gardons, S. S.
See Snodgrass, W(illiam) D(e Witt)

Garfield, Leon 1921-1996   **CLC 12**
See also AAYA 8; CA 17-20R; 152; CANR 38, 41, 78; CLR 21; DLB 161; JRDA; MAICYA; SATA 1, 32, 76; SATA-Obit 90

Garland, (Hannibal) Hamlin 1860-1940
    TCLC 3; SSC 18
See also CA 104; DLB 12, 71, 78, 186

Garneau, (Hector de) Saint-Denys 1912-1943
    TCLC 13
See also CA 111; DLB 88

Garner, Alan 1934-**CLC 17; DAB; DAM POP**
See also AAYA 18; CA 73-76; CANR 15, 64; CLR 20; DLB 161; MAICYA; MTCW 1, 2; SATA 18, 69

Garner, Hugh 1913-1979   **CLC 13**
See also CA 69-72; CANR 31; DLB 68

Garnett, David 1892-1981   **CLC 3**
See also CA 5-8R; 103; CANR 17, 79; DLB 34; MTCW 2

Garos, Stephanie
See Katz, Steve

Garrett, George (Palmer) 1929-**CLC 3, 11, 51; SSC 30**
See also CA 1-4R; CAAS 5; CANR 1, 42, 67; DLB 2, 5, 130, 152; DLBY 83

Garrick, David 1717-1779   **LC 15; DAM DRAM**
See also DLB 84

Garrigue, Jean 1914-1972   **CLC 2, 8**
See also CA 5-8R; 37-40R; CANR 20

Garrison, Frederick
See Sinclair, Upton (Beall)

Garth, Will
See Hamilton, Edmond; Kuttner, Henry

Garvey, Marcus (Moziah, Jr.) 1887-1940
    TCLC 41; BLC 2; DAM MULT
See also BW 1; CA 120; 124; CANR 79

Gary, Romain   **CLC 25**
See also Kacew, Romain
See also DLB 83

Gascar, Pierre   **CLC 11**
See also Fournier, Pierre

Gascoyne, David (Emery) 1916-   **CLC 45**
See also CA 65-68; CANR 10, 28, 54; DLB 20; MTCW 1

Gaskell, Elizabeth Cleghorn 1810-1865NCLC 70; DAB; DAM MST; SSC 25
See also CDBLB 1832-1890; DLB 21, 144, 159

Gass, William H(oward) 1924-**CLC 1, 2, 8, 11, 15, 39; SSC 12**
See also CA 17-20R; CANR 30, 71; DLB 2; MTCW 1, 2

Gasset, Jose Ortega y
See Ortega y Gasset, Jose

Gates, Henry Louis, Jr. 1950-**CLC 65; BLCS; DAM MULT**
See also BW 2, 3; CA 109; CANR 25, 53, 75; DLB 67; MTCW 1

Gautier, Theophile 1811-1872   **NCLC 1, 59; DAM POET; PC 18; SSC 20**
See also DLB 119

Gawsworth, John
See Bates, H(erbert) E(rnest)

Gay, John 1685-1732   **LC 49; DAM DRAM**
See also DLB 84, 95

Gay, Oliver
See Gogarty, Oliver St. John

Gaye, Marvin (Penze) 1939-1984   **CLC 26**
See also CA 112

Gebler, Carlo (Ernest) 1954-   **CLC 39**
See also CA 119; 133

Gee, Maggie (Mary) 1948-   **CLC 57**
See also CA 130; DLB 207

Gee, Maurice (Gough) 1931-   **CLC 29**
See also CA 97-100; CANR 67; CLR 56; SATA 46, 101

Gelbart, Larry (Simon) 1923-   **CLC 21, 61**
See also CA 73-76; CANR 45

Gelber, Jack 1932-   **CLC 1, 6, 14, 79**
See also CA 1-4R; CANR 2; DLB 7

Gellhorn, Martha (Ellis) 1908-1998 **CLC 14, 60**
See also CA 77-80; 164; CANR 44; DLBY 82, 98

Genet, Jean 1910-1986**CLC 1, 2, 5, 10, 14, 44, 46; DAM DRAM**
See also CA 13-16R; CANR 18; DLB 72; DLBY 86; MTCW 1, 2

Gent, Peter 1942-   **CLC 29**
See also AITN 1; CA 89-92; DLBY 82

Gentlewoman in New England, A
See Bradstreet, Anne

Gentlewoman in Those Parts, A
See Bradstreet, Anne

George, Jean Craighead 1919-   **CLC 35**
See also AAYA 8; CA 5-8R; CANR 25; CLR 1; DLB 52; JRDA; MAICYA; SATA 2, 68

George, Stefan (Anton) 1868-1933**TCLC 2, 14**
See also CA 104

Georges, Georges Martin
See Simenon, Georges (Jacques Christian)

Gerhardi, William Alexander
See Gerhardie, William Alexander

Gerhardie, William Alexander 1895-1977
    CLC 5
See also CA 25-28R; 73-76; CANR 18; DLB 36

Gerstler, Amy 1956-   **CLC 70**
See also CA 146

Gertler, T.   **CLC 34**
See also CA 116; 121; INT 121

Ghalib   **NCLC 39**
See also Ghalib, Hsadullah Khan

Ghalib, Hsadullah Khan 1797-1869
See Ghalib
See also DAM POET

Ghelderode, Michel de 1898-1962 **CLC 6, 11; DAM DRAM**

See also CA 85-88; CANR 40, 77

Ghiselin, Brewster 1903-   **CLC 23**
See also CA 13-16R; CAAS 10; CANR 13

Ghose, Aurabinda 1872-1950   **TCLC 63**
See also CA 163

Ghose, Zulfikar 1935-   **CLC 42**
See also CA 65-68; CANR 67

Ghosh, Amitav 1956-   **CLC 44**
See also CA 147; CANR 80

Giacosa, Giuseppe 1847-1906   **TCLC 7**
See also CA 104

Gibb, Lee
See Waterhouse, Keith (Spencer)

Gibbon, Lewis Grassic   **TCLC 4**
See also Mitchell, James Leslie

Gibbons, Kaye 1960-**CLC 50, 88; DAM POP**
See also CA 151; CANR 75; MTCW 1

Gibran, Kahlil 1883-1931   **TCLC 1, 9; DAM POET, POP; PC 9**
See also CA 104; 150; MTCW 2

Gibran, Khalil
See Gibran, Kahlil

Gibson, William 1914-   **CLC 23; DA; DAB; DAC; DAM DRAM, MST**
See also CA 9-12R; CANR 9, 42, 75; DLB 7; MTCW 1; SATA 66

Gibson, William (Ford) 1948-   **CLC 39, 63; DAM POP**
See also AAYA 12; CA 126; 133; CANR 52; MTCW 1

Gide, Andre (Paul Guillaume) 1869-1951
    TCLC 5, 12, 36; DA; DAB; DAC; DAM MST, NOV; SSC 13; WLC
See also CA 104; 124; DLB 65; MTCW 1, 2

Gifford, Barry (Colby) 1946-   **CLC 34**
See also CA 65-68; CANR 9, 30, 40

Gilbert, Frank
See De Voto, Bernard (Augustine)

Gilbert, W(illiam) S(chwenck) 1836-1911
    TCLC 3; DAM DRAM, POET
See also CA 104; 173; SATA 36

Gilbreth, Frank B., Jr. 1911-   **CLC 17**
See also CA 9-12R; SATA 2

Gilchrist, Ellen 1935-**CLC 34, 48; DAM POP; SSC 14**
See also CA 113; 116; CANR 41, 61; DLB 130; MTCW 1, 2

Giles, Molly 1942-   **CLC 39**
See also CA 126

Gill, Eric 1882-1940   **TCLC 85**

Gill, Patrick
See Creasey, John

Gilliam, Terry (Vance) 1940-   **CLC 21**
See also Monty Python
See also AAYA 19; CA 108; 113; CANR 35; INT 113

Gillian, Jerry
See Gilliam, Terry (Vance)

Gilliatt, Penelope (Ann Douglass) 1932-1993
    CLC 2, 10, 13, 53
See also AITN 2; CA 13-16R; 141; CANR 49; DLB 14

Gilman, Charlotte (Anna) Perkins (Stetson)
    1860-1935   **TCLC 9, 37; SSC 13**
See also CA 106; 150; MTCW 1

Gilmour, David 1949-   **CLC 35**
See also CA 138, 147

Gilpin, William 1724-1804   **NCLC 30**

Gilray, J. D.
See Mencken, H(enry) L(ouis)

Gilroy, Frank D(aniel) 1925-   **CLC 2**
See also CA 81-84; CANR 32, 64; DLB 7

Gilstrap, John 1957(?)-   **CLC 99**

See also CA 160
Ginsberg, Allen 1926-1997**CLC 1, 2, 3, 4, 6, 13, 36, 69, 109; DA; DAB; DAC; DAM MST, POET; PC 4; WLC**
See also AITN 1; CA 1-4R; 157; CANR 2, 41, 63; CDALB 1941-1968; DLB 5, 16, 169; MTCW 1, 2
Ginzburg, Natalia 1916-1991**CLC 5, 11, 54, 70**
See also CA 85-88; 135; CANR 33; DLB 177; MTCW 1, 2
Giono, Jean 1895-1970   **CLC 4, 11**
See also CA 45-48; 29-32R; CANR 2, 35; DLB 72; MTCW 1
Giovanni, Nikki 1943- **CLC 2, 4, 19, 64, 117; BLC 2; DA; DAB; DAC; DAM MST, MULT, POET; PC 19; WLCS**
See also AAYA 22; AITN 1; BW 2, 3; CA 29-32R; CAAS 6; CANR 18, 41, 60; CDALBS; CLR 6; DLB 5, 41; INT CANR-18; MAICYA; MTCW 1, 2; SATA 24, 107
Giovene, Andrea 1904-   **CLC 7**
See also CA 85-88
Gippius, Zinaida (Nikolayevna) 1869-1945
See Hippius, Zinaida
See also CA 106
Giraudoux, (Hippolyte) Jean 1882-1944 **TCLC 2, 7; DAM DRAM**
See also CA 104; DLB 65
Gironella, Jose Maria 1917-   **CLC 11**
See also CA 101
Gissing, George (Robert) 1857-1903**TCLC 3, 24, 47**
See also CA 105; 167; DLB 18, 135, 184
Giurlani, Aldo
See Palazzeschi, Aldo
Gladkov, Fyodor (Vasilyevich) 1883-1958 **TCLC 27**
See also CA 170
Glanville, Brian (Lester) 1931-   **CLC 6**
See also CA 5-8R; CAAS 9; CANR 3, 70; DLB 15, 139; SATA 42
Glasgow, Ellen (Anderson Gholson) 1873-1945 **TCLC 2, 7; SSC 34**
See also CA 104; 164; DLB 9, 12; MTCW 2
Glaspell, Susan 1882(?)-1948**TCLC 55; DC 10**
See also CA 110; 154; DLB 7, 9, 78; YABC 2
Glassco, John 1909-1981   **CLC 9**
See also CA 13-16R; 102; CANR 15; DLB 68
Glasscock, Amnesia
See Steinbeck, John (Ernst)
Glasser, Ronald J. 1940(?)-   **CLC 37**
Glassman, Joyce
See Johnson, Joyce
Glendinning, Victoria 1937-   **CLC 50**
See also CA 120; 127; CANR 59; DLB 155
Glissant, Edouard 1928- **CLC 10, 68; DAM MULT**
See also CA 153
Gloag, Julian 1930-   **CLC 40**
See also AITN 1; CA 65-68; CANR 10, 70
Glowacki, Aleksander
See Prus, Boleslaw
Gluck, Louise (Elisabeth) 1943-**CLC 7, 22, 44, 81; DAM POET; PC 16**
See also CA 33-36R; CANR 40, 69; DLB 5; MTCW 2
Glyn, Elinor 1864-1943   **TCLC 72**
See also DLB 153
Gobineau, Joseph Arthur (Comte) de 1816-1882   **NCLC 17**
See also DLB 123
Godard, Jean-Luc 1930-   **CLC 20**
See also CA 93-96

Godden, (Margaret) Rumer 1907-1998 **C L C 53**
See also AAYA 6; CA 5-8R; 172; CANR 4, 27, 36, 55, 80; CLR 20; DLB 161; MAICYA; SAAS 12; SATA 3, 36
Godoy Alcayaga, Lucila 1889-1957
See Mistral, Gabriela
See also BW 2; CA 104; 131; DAM MULT; HW 1, 2; MTCW 1, 2
Godwin, Gail (Kathleen) 1937- **CLC 5, 8, 22, 31, 69; DAM POP**
See also CA 29-32R; CANR 15, 43, 69; DLB 6; INT CANR-15; MTCW 1, 2
Godwin, William 1756-1836   **NCLC 14**
See also CDBLB 1789-1832; DLB 39, 104, 142, 158, 163
Goebbels, Josef
See Goebbels, (Paul) Joseph
Goebbels, (Paul) Joseph 1897-1945 **TCLC 68**
See also CA 115; 148
Goebbels, Joseph Paul
See Goebbels, (Paul) Joseph
Goethe, Johann Wolfgang von 1749-1832 **NCLC 4, 22, 34; DA; DAB; DAC; DAM DRAM, MST, POET; PC 5; WLC**
See also DLB 94
Gogarty, Oliver St. John 1878-1957**TCLC 15**
See also CA 109; 150; DLB 15, 19
Gogol, Nikolai (Vasilyevich) 1809-1852**NCLC 5, 15, 31; DA; DAB; DAC; DAM DRAM, MST; DC 1; SSC 4, 29; WLC**
See also DLB 198
Goines, Donald 1937(?)-1974**CLC 80; BLC 2; DAM MULT, POP**
See also AITN 1; BW 1, 3; CA 124; 114; DLB 33
Gold, Herbert 1924-   **CLC 4, 7, 14, 42**
See also CA 9-12R; CANR 17, 45; DLB 2; DLBY 81
Goldbarth, Albert 1948-   **CLC 5, 38**
See also CA 53-56; CANR 6, 40; DLB 120
Goldberg, Anatol 1910-1982   **CLC 34**
See also CA 131; 117
Goldemberg, Isaac 1945-   **CLC 52**
See also CA 69-72; CAAS 12; CANR 11, 32; HW 1
Golding, William (Gerald) 1911-1993**CLC 1, 2, 3, 8, 10, 17, 27, 58, 81; DA; DAB; DAC; DAM MST, NOV; WLC**
See also AAYA 5; CA 5-8R; 141; CANR 13, 33, 54; CDBLB 1945-1960; DLB 15, 100; MTCW 1, 2
Goldman, Emma 1869-1940   **TCLC 13**
See also CA 110; 150
Goldman, Francisco 1954-   **CLC 76**
See also CA 162
Goldman, William (W.) 1931-   **CLC 1, 48**
See also CA 9-12R; CANR 29, 69; DLB 44
Goldmann, Lucien 1913-1970   **CLC 24**
See also CA 25-28; CAP 2
Goldoni, Carlo 1707-1793**LC 4; DAM DRAM**
Goldsberry, Steven 1949-   **CLC 34**
See also CA 131
Goldsmith, Oliver 1728-1774 **LC 2, 48; DA; DAB; DAC; DAM DRAM, MST, NOV, POET; DC 8; WLC**
See also CDBLB 1660-1789; DLB 39, 89, 104, 109, 142; SATA 26
Goldsmith, Peter
See Priestley, J(ohn) B(oynton)
Gombrowicz, Witold 1904-1969**CLC 4, 7, 11, 49; DAM DRAM**
See also CA 19-20; 25-28R; CAP 2

Gomez de la Serna, Ramon 1888-1963**CLC 9**
See also CA 153; 116; CANR 79; HW 1, 2
Goncharov, Ivan Alexandrovich 1812-1891 **NCLC 1, 63**
Goncourt, Edmond (Louis Antoine Huot) de 1822-1896   **NCLC 7**
See also DLB 123
Goncourt, Jules (Alfred Huot) de 1830-1870 **NCLC 7**
See also DLB 123
Gontier, Fernande 19(?)-   **CLC 50**
Gonzalez Martinez, Enrique 1871-1952 **TCLC 72**
See also CA 166; HW 1, 2
Goodman, Paul 1911-1972   **CLC 1, 2, 4, 7**
See also CA 19-20; 37-40R; CANR 34; CAP 2; DLB 130; MTCW 1
Gordimer, Nadine 1923-**CLC 3, 5, 7, 10, 18, 33, 51, 70; DA; DAB; DAC; DAM MST, NOV; SSC 17; WLCS**
See also CA 5-8R; CANR 3, 28, 56; INT CANR-28; MTCW 1, 2
Gordon, Adam Lindsay 1833-1870 **NCLC 21**
Gordon, Caroline 1895-1981**CLC 6, 13, 29, 83; SSC 15**
See also CA 11-12; 103; CANR 36; CAP 1; DLB 4, 9, 102; DLBD 17; DLBY 81; MTCW 1, 2
Gordon, Charles William 1860-1937
See Connor, Ralph
See also CA 109
Gordon, Mary (Catherine) 1949- **CLC 13, 22**
See also CA 102; CANR 44; DLB 6; DLBY 81; INT 102; MTCW 1
Gordon, N. J.
See Bosman, Herman Charles
Gordon, Sol 1923-   **CLC 26**
See also CA 53-56; CANR 4; SATA 11
Gordone, Charles 1925-1995**CLC 1, 4; DAM DRAM; DC 8**
See also BW 1, 3; CA 93-96; 150; CANR 55; DLB 7; INT 93-96; MTCW 1
Gore, Catherine 1800-1861   **NCLC 65**
See also DLB 116
Gorenko, Anna Andreevna
See Akhmatova, Anna
Gorky, Maxim 1868-1936**TCLC 8; DAB; SSC 28; WLC**
See also Peshkov, Alexei Maximovich
See also MTCW 2
Goryan, Sirak
See Saroyan, William
Gosse, Edmund (William) 1849-1928**TCLC 28**
See also CA 117; DLB 57, 144, 184
Gotlieb, Phyllis Fay (Bloom) 1926-   **CLC 18**
See also CA 13-16R; CANR 7; DLB 88
Gottesman, S. D.
See Kornbluth, C(yril) M.; Pohl, Frederik
Gottfried von Strassburg fl. c. 1210- **CMLC 10**
See also DLB 138
Gould, Lois   **CLC 4, 10**
See also CA 77-80; CANR 29; MTCW 1
Gourmont, Remy (-Marie-Charles) de 1858-1915   **TCLC 17**
See also CA 109; 150; MTCW 2
Govier, Katherine 1948-   **CLC 51**
See also CA 101; CANR 18, 40
Goyen, (Charles) William 1915-1983**CLC 5, 8, 14, 40**
See also AITN 2; CA 5-8R; 110; CANR 6, 71; DLB 2; DLBY 83; INT CANR-6
Goytisolo, Juan 1931- **CLC 5, 10, 23; DAM**

MULT; HLC
See also CA 85-88; CANR 32, 61; HW 1, 2;
MTCW 1, 2
Gozzano, Guido 1883-1916 **PC 10**
See also CA 154; DLB 114
Gozzi, (Conte) Carlo 1720-1806 **NCLC 23**
Grabbe, Christian Dietrich 1801-1836 **N C L C 2**
See also DLB 133
Grace, Patricia 1937- **CLC 56**
Gracian y Morales, Baltasar 1601-1658 **LC 15**
Gracq, Julien **CLC 11, 48**
See also Poirier, Louis
See also DLB 83
Grade, Chaim 1910-1982 **CLC 10**
See also CA 93-96; 107 ·
Graduate of Oxford, A
See Ruskin, John
Grafton, Garth
See Duncan, Sara Jeannette
Graham, John
See Phillips, David Graham
Graham, Jorie 1951- **CLC 48, 118**
See also CA 111; CANR 63; DLB 120
Graham, R(obert) B(ontine) Cunninghame
See Cunninghame Graham, R(obert) B(ontine)
See also DLB 98, 135, 174
Graham, Robert
See Haldeman, Joe (William)
Graham, Tom
See Lewis, (Harry) Sinclair
Graham, W(illiam) S(ydney) 1918-1986 **C L C 29**
See also CA 73-76; 118; DLB 20
Graham, Winston (Mawdsley) 1910- **CLC 23**
See also CA 49-52; CANR 2, 22, 45, 66; DLB 77
Grahame, Kenneth 1859-1932 **TCLC 64; DAB**
See also CA 108; 136; CANR 80; CLR 5; DLB 34, 141, 178; MAICYA; MTCW 2; SATA 100; YABC 1
Granovsky, Timofei Nikolaevich 1813-1855 **NCLC 75**
See also DLB 198
Grant, Skeeter
See Spiegelman, Art
Granville-Barker, Harley 1877-1946 **TCLC 2; DAM DRAM**
See also Barker, Harley Granville
See also CA 104
Grass, Guenter (Wilhelm) 1927- **CLC 1, 2, 4, 6, 11, 15, 22, 32, 49, 88; DA; DAB; DAC; DAM MST, NOV; WLC**
See also CA 13-16R; CANR 20, 75; DLB 75, 124; MTCW 1, 2
Gratton, Thomas
See Hulme, T(homas) E(rnest)
Grau, Shirley Ann 1929- **CLC 4, 9; SSC 15**
See also CA 89-92; CANR 22, 69; DLB 2; INT CANR-22; MTCW 1
Gravel, Fern
See Hall, James Norman
Graver, Elizabeth 1964- **CLC 70**
See also CA 135; CANR 71
Graves, Richard Perceval 1945- **CLC 44**
See also CA 65-68; CANR 9, 26, 51
Graves, Robert (von Ranke) 1895-1985 **C L C 1, 2, 6, 11, 39, 44, 45; DAB; DAC; DAM MST, POET; PC 6**
See also CA 5-8R; 117; CANR 5, 36; CDBLB 1914-1945; DLB 20, 100, 191; DLBD 18; DLBY 85; MTCW 1, 2; SATA 45
Graves, Valerie

See Bradley, Marion Zimmer
Gray, Alasdair (James) 1934- **CLC 41**
See also CA 126; CANR 47, 69; DLB 194; INT 126; MTCW 1, 2
Gray, Amlin 1946- **CLC 29**
See also CA 138
Gray, Francine du Plessix 1930- **CLC 22; DAM NOV**
See also BEST 90:3; CA 61-64; CAAS 2; CANR 11, 33, 75; INT CANR-11; MTCW 1, 2
Gray, John (Henry) 1866-1934 **TCLC 19**
See also CA 119; 162
Gray, Simon (James Holliday) 1936- **CLC 9, 14, 36**
See also AITN 1; CA 21-24R; CAAS 3; CANR 32, 69; DLB 13; MTCW 1
Gray, Spalding 1941- **CLC 49, 112; DAM POP; DC 7**
See also CA 128; CANR 74; MTCW 2
Gray, Thomas 1716-1771 **LC 4, 40; DA; DAB; DAC; DAM MST; PC 2; WLC**
See also CDBLB 1660-1789; DLB 109
Grayson, David
See Baker, Ray Stannard
Grayson, Richard (A.) 1951- **CLC 38**
See also CA 85-88; CANR 14, 31, 57
Greeley, Andrew M(oran) 1928- **CLC 28; DAM POP**
See also CA 5-8R; CAAS 7; CANR 7, 43, 69; MTCW 1, 2
Green, Anna Katharine 1846-1935 **TCLC 63**
See also CA 112; 159; DLB 202
Green, Brian
See Card, Orson Scott
Green, Hannah
See Greenberg, Joanne (Goldenberg)
Green, Hannah 1927(?)-1996 **CLC 3**
See also CA 73-76; CANR 59
Green, Henry 1905-1973 **CLC 2, 13, 97**
See also Yorke, Henry Vincent
See also CA 175; DLB 15
Green, Julian (Hartridge) 1900-1998
See Green, Julien
See also CA 21-24R; 169; CANR 33; DLB 4, 72; MTCW 1
Green, Julien **CLC 3, 11, 77**
See also Green, Julian (Hartridge)
See also MTCW 2
Green, Paul (Eliot) 1894-1981 **CLC 25; DAM DRAM**
See also AITN 1; CA 5-8R; 103; CANR 3; DLB 7, 9; DLBY 81
Greenberg, Ivan 1908-1973
See Rahv, Philip
See also CA 85-88
Greenberg, Joanne (Goldenberg) 1932- **C L C 7, 30**
See also AAYA 12; CA 5-8R; CANR 14, 32, 69; SATA 25
Greenberg, Richard 1959(?)- **CLC 57**
See also CA 138
Greene, Bette 1934- **CLC 30**
See also AAYA 7; CA 53-56; CANR 4; CLR 2; JRDA; MAICYA; SAAS 16; SATA 8, 102
Greene, Gael **CLC 8**
See also CA 13-16R; CANR 10
Greene, Graham (Henry) 1904-1991 **CLC 1, 3, 6, 9, 14, 18, 27, 37, 70, 72; DA; DAB; DAC; DAM MST, NOV; SSC 29; WLC**
See also AITN 2; CA 13-16R; 133; CANR 35, 61; CDBLB 1945-1960; DLB 13, 15, 77, 100, 162, 201, 204; DLBY 91; MTCW 1, 2;

SATA 20
Greene, Robert 1558-1592 **LC 41**
See also DLB 62, 167
Greer, Richard
See Silverberg, Robert
Gregor, Arthur 1923- **CLC 9**
See also CA 25-28R; CAAS 10; CANR 11; SATA 36
Gregor, Lee
See Pohl, Frederik
Gregory, Isabella Augusta (Persse) 1852-1932 **TCLC 1**
See also CA 104; DLB 10
Gregory, J. Dennis
See Williams, John A(lfred)
Grendon, Stephen
See Derleth, August (William)
Grenville, Kate 1950- **CLC 61**
See also CA 118; CANR 53
Grenville, Pelham
See Wodehouse, P(elham) G(renville)
Greve, Felix Paul (Berthold Friedrich) 1879-1948
See Grove, Frederick Philip
See also CA 104; 141, 175; CANR 79; DAC; DAM MST
Grey, Zane 1872-1939 **TCLC 6; DAM POP**
See also CA 104; 132; DLB 212; MTCW 1, 2
Grieg, (Johan) Nordahl (Brun) 1902-1943 **TCLC 10**
See also CA 107
Grieve, C(hristopher) M(urray) 1892-1978 **CLC 11, 19; DAM POET**
See also MacDiarmid, Hugh; Pteleon
See also CA 5-8R; 85-88; CANR 33; MTCW 1
Griffin, Gerald 1803-1840 **NCLC 7**
See also DLB 159
Griffin, John Howard 1920-1980 **CLC 68**
See also AITN 1; CA 1-4R; 101; CANR 2
Griffin, Peter 1942- **CLC 39**
See also CA 136
Griffith, D(avid Lewelyn) W(ark) 1875(?)-1948 **TCLC 68**
See also CA 119; 150; CANR 80
Griffith, Lawrence
See Griffith, D(avid Lewelyn) W(ark)
Griffiths, Trevor 1935- **CLC 13, 52**
See also CA 97-100; CANR 45; DLB 13
Griggs, Sutton Elbert 1872-1930(?) **TCLC 77**
See also CA 123; DLB 50
Grigson, Geoffrey (Edward Harvey) 1905-1985 **CLC 7, 39**
See also CA 25-28R; 118; CANR 20, 33; DLB 27; MTCW 1, 2
Grillparzer, Franz 1791-1872 **NCLC 1**
See also DLB 133
Grimble, Reverend Charles James
See Eliot, T(homas) S(tearns)
Grimke, Charlotte L(ottie) Forten 1837(?)-1914
See Forten, Charlotte L.
See also BW 1; CA 117; 124; DAM MULT, POET
Grimm, Jacob Ludwig Karl 1785-1863 **NCLC 3, 77**
See also DLB 90; MAICYA; SATA 22
Grimm, Wilhelm Karl 1786-1859 **NCLC 3, 77**
See also DLB 90; MAICYA; SATA 22
Grimmelshausen, Johann Jakob Christoffel von 1621-1676 **LC 6**
See also DLB 168
Grindel, Eugene 1895-1952
See Eluard, Paul
See also CA 104

Grisham, John 1955- **CLC 84; DAM POP**
See also AAYA 14; CA 138; CANR 47, 69;
MTCW 2

Grossman, David 1954- **CLC 67**
See also CA 138

Grossman, Vasily (Semenovich) 1905-1964
CLC 41
See also CA 124; 130; MTCW 1

Grove, Frederick Philip **TCLC 4**
See also Greve, Felix Paul (Berthold Friedrich)
See also DLB 92

Grubb
See Crumb, R(obert)

Grumbach, Doris (Isaac) 1918-**CLC 13, 22, 64**
See also CA 5-8R; CAAS 2; CANR 9, 42, 70;
INT CANR-9; MTCW 2

Grundtvig, Nicolai Frederik Severin 1783-1872
NCLC 1

Grunge
See Crumb, R(obert)

Grunwald, Lisa 1959- **CLC 44**
See also CA 120

Guare, John 1938- **CLC 8, 14, 29, 67; DAM
DRAM**
See also CA 73-76; CANR 21, 69; DLB 7;
MTCW 1, 2

Gudjonsson, Halldor Kiljan 1902-1998
See Laxness, Halldor
See also CA 103; 164

Guenter, Erich
See Eich, Guenter

Guest, Barbara 1920- **CLC 34**
See also CA 25-28R; CANR 11, 44; DLB 5,
193

Guest, Judith (Ann) 1936- **CLC 8, 30; DAM
NOV, POP**
See also AAYA 7; CA 77-80; CANR 15, 75;
INT CANR-15; MTCW 1, 2

Guevara, Che **CLC 87; HLC**
See also Guevara (Serna), Ernesto

Guevara (Serna), Ernesto 1928-1967
See Guevara, Che
See also CA 127; 111; CANR 56; DAM MULT;
HW 1

Guicciardini, Francesco 1483-1540 **LC 49**

Guild, Nicholas M. 1944- **CLC 33**
See also CA 93-96

Guillemin, Jacques
See Sartre, Jean-Paul

Guillen, Jorge 1893-1984 **CLC 11; DAM
MULT, POET; HLCS 1**
See also CA 89-92; 112; DLB 108; HW 1

Guillen, Nicolas (Cristobal) 1902-1989 **C L C
48, 79; BLC 2; DAM MST, MULT, POET;
HLC; PC 23**
See also BW 2; CA 116; 125; 129; HW 1

Guillevic, (Eugene) 1907- **CLC 33**
See also CA 93-96

Guillois
See Desnos, Robert

Guillois, Valentin
See Desnos, Robert

Guiney, Louise Imogen 1861-1920 **TCLC 41**
See also CA 160; DLB 54

Guiraldes, Ricardo (Guillermo) 1886-1927
TCLC 39
See also CA 131; HW 1; MTCW 1

Gumilev, Nikolai (Stepanovich) 1886-1921
TCLC 60
See also CA 165

Gunesekera, Romesh 1954- **CLC 91**
See also CA 159

Gunn, Bill **CLC 5**

See also Gunn, William Harrison
See also DLB 38

Gunn, Thom(son William) 1929-**CLC 3, 6, 18,
32, 81; DAM POET; PC 26**
See also CA 17-20R; CANR 9, 33; CDBLB
1960 to Present; DLB 27; INT CANR-33;
MTCW 1

Gunn, William Harrison 1934(?)-1989
See Gunn, Bill
See also AITN 1; BW 1, 3; CA 13-16R; 128;
CANR 12, 25, 76

Gunnars, Kristjana 1948- **CLC 69**
See also CA 113; DLB 60

Gurdjieff, G(eorgei) I(vanovich) 1877(?)-1949
TCLC 71
See also CA 157

Gurganus, Allan 1947- **CLC 70; DAM POP**
See also BEST 90:1; CA 135

Gurney, A(lbert) R(amsdell), Jr. 1930- **C L C
32, 50, 54; DAM DRAM**
See also CA 77-80; CANR 32, 64

Gurney, Ivor (Bertie) 1890-1937 **TCLC 33**
See also CA 167

Gurney, Peter
See Gurney, A(lbert) R(amsdell), Jr.

Guro, Elena 1877-1913 **TCLC 56**

Gustafson, James M(oody) 1925- **CLC 100**
See also CA 25-28R; CANR 37

Gustafson, Ralph (Barker) 1909- **CLC 36**
See also CA 21-24R; CANR 8, 45; DLB 88

Gut, Gom
See Simenon, Georges (Jacques Christian)

Guterson, David 1956- **CLC 91**
See also CA 132; CANR 73; MTCW 2

Guthrie, A(lfred) B(ertram), Jr. 1901-1991
CLC 23
See also CA 57-60; 134; CANR 24; DLB 212;
SATA 62; SATA-Obit 67

Guthrie, Isobel
See Grieve, C(hristopher) M(urray)

Guthrie, Woodrow Wilson 1912-1967
See Guthrie, Woody
See also CA 113; 93-96

Guthrie, Woody **CLC 35**
See also Guthrie, Woodrow Wilson

Guy, Rosa (Cuthbert) 1928- **CLC 26**
See also AAYA 4; BW 2; CA 17-20R; CANR
14, 34; CLR 13; DLB 33; JRDA; MAICYA;
SATA 14, 62

Gwendolyn
See Bennett, (Enoch) Arnold

H. D. **CLC 3, 8, 14, 31, 34, 73; PC 5**
See also Doolittle, Hilda

H. de V.
See Buchan, John

Haavikko, Paavo Juhani 1931- **CLC 18, 34**
See also CA 106

Habbema, Koos
See Heijermans, Herman

Habermas, Juergen 1929- **CLC 104**
See also CA 109

Habermas, Jurgen
See Habermas, Juergen

Hacker, Marilyn 1942- **CLC 5, 9, 23, 72, 91;
DAM POET**
See also CA 77-80; CANR 68; DLB 120

Haeckel, Ernst Heinrich (Philipp August) 1834-
1919 **TCLC 83**
See also CA 157

Hafiz c. 1326-1389 **CMLC 34**

Hafiz c. 1326-1389(?) **CMLC 34**

Haggard, H(enry) Rider 1856-1925 **TCLC 11**
See also CA 108; 148; DLB 70, 156, 174, 178;

MTCW 2; SATA 16

Hagiosy, L.
See Larbaud, Valery (Nicolas)

Hagiwara Sakutaro 1886-1942 **TCLC 60; PC
18**

Haig, Fenil
See Ford, Ford Madox

Haig-Brown, Roderick (Langmere) 1908-1976
CLC 21
See also CA 5-8R; 69-72; CANR 4, 38; CLR
31; DLB 88; MAICYA; SATA 12

Hailey, Arthur 1920-**CLC 5; DAM NOV, POP**
See also AITN 2; BEST 90:3; CA 1-4R; CANR
2, 36, 75; DLB 88; DLBY 82; MTCW 1, 2

Hailey, Elizabeth Forsythe 1938- **CLC 40**
See also CA 93-96; CAAS 1; CANR 15, 48;
INT CANR-15

Haines, John (Meade) 1924- **CLC 58**
See also CA 17-20R; CANR 13, 34; DLB 212

Hakluyt, Richard 1552-1616 **LC 31**

Haldeman, Joe (William) 1943- **CLC 61**
See also CA 53-56; CAAS 25; CANR 6, 70,
72; DLB 8; INT CANR-6

Hale, Sarah Josepha (Buell) 1788-1879**NCLC
75**
See also DLB 1, 42, 73

Haley, Alex(ander Murray Palmer) 1921-1992
**CLC 8, 12, 76; BLC 2; DA; DAB; DAC;
DAM MST, MULT, POP**
See also AAYA 26; BW 2, 3; CA 77-80; 136;
CANR 61; CDALBS; DLB 38; MTCW 1, 2

Haliburton, Thomas Chandler 1796-1865
NCLC 15
See also DLB 11, 99

Hall, Donald (Andrew, Jr.) 1928- **CLC 1, 13,
37, 59; DAM POET**
See also CA 5-8R; CAAS 7; CANR 2, 44, 64;
DLB 5; MTCW 1; SATA 23, 97

Hall, Frederic Sauser
See Sauser-Hall, Frederic

Hall, James
See Kuttner, Henry

Hall, James Norman 1887-1951 **TCLC 23**
See also CA 123; 173; SATA 21

Hall, Radclyffe
See Hall, (Marguerite) Radclyffe
See also MTCW 2

Hall, (Marguerite) Radclyffe 1886-1943
TCLC 12
See also CA 110; 150; DLB 191

Hall, Rodney 1935- **CLC 51**
See also CA 109; CANR 69

Halleck, Fitz-Greene 1790-1867 **NCLC 47**
See also DLB 3

Halliday, Michael
See Creasey, John

Halpern, Daniel 1945- **CLC 14**
See also CA 33-36R

Hamburger, Michael (Peter Leopold) 1924-
CLC 5, 14
See also CA 5-8R; CAAS 4; CANR 2, 47; DLB
27

Hamill, Pete 1935- **CLC 10**
See also CA 25-28R; CANR 18, 71

Hamilton, Alexander 1755(?)-1804 **NCLC 49**
See also DLB 37

Hamilton, Clive
See Lewis, C(live) S(taples)

Hamilton, Edmond 1904-1977 **CLC 1**
See also CA 1-4R; CANR 3; DLB 8

Hamilton, Eugene (Jacob) Lee
See Lee-Hamilton, Eugene (Jacob)

Hamilton, Franklin

See Silverberg, Robert

Hamilton, Gail
See Corcoran, Barbara

Hamilton, Mollie
See Kaye, M(ary) M(argaret)

Hamilton, (Anthony Walter) Patrick 1904-1962 **CLC 51**
See also CA 113; DLB 191

Hamilton, Virginia 1936- **CLC 26; DAM MULT**
See also AAYA 2, 21; BW 2, 3; CA 25-28R; CANR 20, 37, 73; CLR 1, 11, 40; DLB 33, 52; INT CANR-20; JRDA; MAICYA; MTCW 1, 2; SATA 4, 56, 79

Hammett, (Samuel) Dashiell 1894-1961 **C L C 3, 5, 10, 19, 47; SSC 17**
See also AITN 1; CA 81-84; CANR 42; CDALB 1929-1941; DLBD 6; DLBY 96; MTCW 1, 2

Hammon, Jupiter 1711(?)-1800(?) **NCLC 5; BLC 2; DAM MULT, POET; PC 16**
See also DLB 31, 50

Hammond, Keith
See Kuttner, Henry

Hamner, Earl (Henry), Jr. 1923- **CLC 12**
See also AITN 2; CA 73-76; DLB 6

Hampton, Christopher (James) 1946- **CLC 4**
See also CA 25-28R; DLB 13; MTCW 1

Hamsun, Knut **TCLC 2, 14, 49**
See also Pedersen, Knut

Handke, Peter 1942- **CLC 5, 8, 10, 15, 38; DAM DRAM, NOV**
See also CA 77-80; CANR 33, 75; DLB 85, 124; MTCW 1, 2

Hanley, James 1901-1985 **CLC 3, 5, 8, 13**
See also CA 73-76; 117; CANR 36; DLB 191; MTCW 1

Hannah, Barry 1942- **CLC 23, 38, 90**
See also CA 108; 110; CANR 43, 68; DLB 6; INT 110; MTCW 1

Hannon, Ezra
See Hunter, Evan

Hansberry, Lorraine (Vivian) 1930-1965 **CLC 17, 62; BLC 2; DA; DAB; DAC; DAM DRAM, MST, MULT; DC 2**
See also AAYA 25; BW 1, 3; CA 109; 25-28R; CABS 3; CANR 58; CDALB 1941-1968; DLB 7, 38; MTCW 1, 2

Hansen, Joseph 1923- **CLC 38**
See also CA 29-32R; CAAS 17; CANR 16, 44, 66; INT CANR-16

Hansen, Martin A(lfred) 1909-1955 **TCLC 32**
See also CA 167

Hanson, Kenneth O(stlin) 1922- **CLC 13**
See also CA 53-56; CANR 7

Hardwick, Elizabeth (Bruce) 1916- **CLC 13; DAM NOV**
See also CA 5-8R; CANR 3, 32, 70; DLB 6; MTCW 1, 2

Hardy, Thomas 1840-1928 **TCLC 4, 10, 18, 32, 48, 53, 72; DA; DAB; DAC; DAM MST, NOV, POET; PC 8; SSC 8; WLC**
See also CA 104; 123; CDBLB 1890-1914; DLB 18, 19, 135; MTCW 1, 2

Hare, David 1947- **CLC 29, 58**
See also CA 97-100; CANR 39; DLB 13; MTCW 1

Harewood, John
See Van Druten, John (William)

Harford, Henry
See Hudson, W(illiam) H(enry)

Hargrave, Leonie
See Disch, Thomas M(ichael)

Harjo, Joy 1951- **CLC 83; DAM MULT**
See also CA 114; CANR 35, 67; DLB 120, 175; MTCW 2; NNAL

Harlan, Louis R(udolph) 1922- **CLC 34**
See also CA 21-24R; CANR 25, 55, 80

Harling, Robert 1951(?)- **CLC 53**
See also CA 147

Harmon, William (Ruth) 1938- **CLC 38**
See also CA 33-36R; CANR 14, 32, 35; SATA 65

Harper, F. E. W.
See Harper, Frances Ellen Watkins

Harper, Frances E. W.
See Harper, Frances Ellen Watkins

Harper, Frances E. Watkins
See Harper, Frances Ellen Watkins

Harper, Frances Ellen
See Harper, Frances Ellen Watkins

Harper, Frances Ellen Watkins 1825-1911 **TCLC 14; BLC 2; DAM MULT, POET; PC 21**
See also BW 1, 3; CA 111; 125; CANR 79; DLB 50

Harper, Michael S(teven) 1938- **CLC 7, 22**
See also BW 1; CA 33-36R; CANR 24; DLB 41

Harper, Mrs. F. E. W.
See Harper, Frances Ellen Watkins

Harris, Christie (Lucy) Irwin 1907- **CLC 12**
See also CA 5-8R; CANR 6; CLR 47; DLB 88; JRDA; MAICYA; SAAS 10; SATA 6, 74

Harris, Frank 1856-1931 **TCLC 24**
See also CA 109; 150; CANR 80; DLB 156, 197

Harris, George Washington 1814-1869 **NCLC 23**
See also DLB 3, 11

Harris, Joel Chandler 1848-1908 **TCLC 2; SSC 19**
See also CA 104; 137; CANR 80; CLR 49; DLB 11, 23, 42, 78, 91; MAICYA; SATA 100; YABC 1

Harris, John (Wyndham Parkes Lucas) Beynon 1903-1969
See Wyndham, John
See also CA 102; 89-92

Harris, MacDonald **CLC 9**
See also Heiney, Donald (William)

Harris, Mark 1922- **CLC 19**
See also CA 5-8R; CAAS 3; CANR 2, 55; DLB 2; DLBY 80

Harris, (Theodore) Wilson 1921- **CLC 25**
See also BW 2, 3; CA 65-68; CAAS 16; CANR 11, 27, 69; DLB 117; MTCW 1

Harrison, Elizabeth Cavanna 1909-
See Cavanna, Betty
See also CA 9-12R; CANR 6, 27

Harrison, Harry (Max) 1925- **CLC 42**
See also CA 1-4R; CANR 5, 21; DLB 8; SATA 4

Harrison, James (Thomas) 1937- **CLC 6, 14, 33, 66; SSC 19**
See also CA 13-16R; CANR 8, 51, 79; DLBY 82; INT CANR-8

Harrison, Jim
See Harrison, James (Thomas)

Harrison, Kathryn 1961- **CLC 70**
See also CA 144; CANR 68

Harrison, Tony 1937- **CLC 43**
See also CA 65-68; CANR 44; DLB 40; MTCW 1

Harriss, Will(ard Irvin) 1922- **CLC 34**
See also CA 111

Harson, Sley
See Ellison, Harlan (Jay)

Hart, Ellis
See Ellison, Harlan (Jay)

Hart, Josephine 1942(?)- **CLC 70; DAM POP**
See also CA 138; CANR 70

Hart, Moss 1904-1961 **CLC 66; DAM DRAM**
See also CA 109; 89-92; DLB 7

Harte, (Francis) Bret(t) 1836(?)-1902 **TCLC 1, 25; DA; DAC; DAM MST; SSC 8; WLC**
See also CA 104; 140; CANR 80; CDALB 1865-1917; DLB 12, 64, 74, 79, 186; SATA 26

Hartley, L(eslie) P(oles) 1895-1972 **CLC 2, 22**
See also CA 45-48; 37-40R; CANR 33; DLB 15, 139; MTCW 1, 2

Hartman, Geoffrey H. 1929- **CLC 27**
See also CA 117; 125; CANR 79; DLB 67

Hartmann, Sadakichi 1867-1944 **TCLC 73**
See also CA 157; DLB 54

Hartmann von Aue c. 1160-c. 1205 **CMLC 15**
See also DLB 138

Hartmann von Aue 1170-1210 **CMLC 15**

Haruf, Kent 1943- **CLC 34**
See also CA 149

Harwood, Ronald 1934- **CLC 32; DAM DRAM, MST**
See also CA 1-4R; CANR 4, 55; DLB 13

Hasegawa Tatsunosuke
See Futabatei, Shimei

Hasek, Jaroslav (Matej Frantisek) 1883-1923 **TCLC 4**
See also CA 104; 129; MTCW 1, 2

Hass, Robert 1941- **CLC 18, 39, 99; PC 16**
See also CA 111; CANR 30, 50, 71; DLB 105, 206; SATA 94

Hastings, Hudson
See Kuttner, Henry

Hastings, Selina **CLC 44**

Hathorne, John 1641-1717 **LC 38**

Hatteras, Amelia
See Mencken, H(enry) L(ouis)

Hatteras, Owen **TCLC 18**
See also Mencken, H(enry) L(ouis); Nathan, George Jean

Hauptmann, Gerhart (Johann Robert) 1862-1946 **TCLC 4; DAM DRAM**
See also CA 104; 153; DLB 66, 118

Havel, Vaclav 1936- **CLC 25, 58, 65; DAM DRAM; DC 6**
See also CA 104; CANR 36, 63; MTCW 1, 2

Haviaras, Stratis **CLC 33**
See also Chaviaras, Strates

Hawes, Stephen 1475(?)-1523(?) **LC 17**
See also DLB 132

Hawkes, John (Clendennin Burne, Jr.) 1925-1998 **CLC 1, 2, 3, 4, 7, 9, 14, 15, 27, 49**
See also CA 1-4R; 167; CANR 2, 47, 64; DLB 2, 7; DLBY 80, 98; MTCW 1, 2

Hawking, S. W.
See Hawking, Stephen W(illiam)

Hawking, Stephen W(illiam) 1942- **CLC 63, 105**
See also AAYA 13; BEST 89:1; CA 126; 129; CANR 48; MTCW 2

Hawkins, Anthony Hope
See Hope, Anthony

Hawthorne, Julian 1846-1934 **TCLC 25**
See also CA 165

Hawthorne, Nathaniel 1804-1864 **NCLC 39; DA; DAB; DAC; DAM MST, NOV; SSC 3, 29; WLC**
See also AAYA 18; CDALB 1640-1865; DLB

1, 74; YABC 2

Haxton, Josephine Ayres 1921-
See Douglas, Ellen
See also CA 115; CANR 41

Hayaseca y Eizaguirre, Jorge
See Echegaray (y Eizaguirre), Jose (Maria
Waldo)

Hayashi, Fumiko 1904-1951 **TCLC 27**
See also CA 161; DLB 180

Haycraft, Anna
See Ellis, Alice Thomas
See also CA 122; MTCW 2

Hayden, Robert E(arl) 1913-1980 **CLC 5, 9,
14, 37; BLC 2; DA; DAC; DAM MST,
MULT, POET; PC 6**
See also BW 1, 3; CA 69-72; 97-100; CABS 2;
CANR 24, 75; CDALB 1941-1968; DLB 5,
76; MTCW 1, 2; SATA 19; SATA-Obit 26

Hayford, J(oseph) E(phraim) Casely
See Casely-Hayford, J(oseph) E(phraim)

Hayman, Ronald 1932- **CLC 44**
See also CA 25-28R; CANR 18, 50; DLB 155

Haywood, Eliza (Fowler) 1693(?)-1756 **LC 1,
44**
See also DLB 39

Hazlitt, William 1778-1830 **NCLC 29**
See also DLB 110, 158

Hazzard, Shirley 1931- **CLC 18**
See also CA 9-12R; CANR 4, 70; DLBY 82;
MTCW 1

Head, Bessie 1937-1986 **CLC 25, 67; BLC 2;
DAM MULT**
See also BW 2, 3; CA 29-32R; 119; CANR 25;
DLB 117; MTCW 1, 2

Headon, (Nicky) Topper 1956(?)- **CLC 30**

Heaney, Seamus (Justin) 1939- **CLC 5, 7, 14,
25, 37, 74, 91; DAB; DAM POET; PC 18;
WLCS**
See also CA 85-88; CANR 25, 48, 75; CDBLB
1960 to Present; DLB 40; DLBY 95; MTCW
1, 2

Hearn, (Patricio) Lafcadio (Tessima Carlos)
1850-1904 **TCLC 9**
See also CA 105; 166; DLB 12, 78, 189

Hearne, Vicki 1946- **CLC 56**
See also CA 139

Hearon, Shelby 1931- **CLC 63**
See also AITN 2; CA 25-28R; CANR 18, 48

Heat-Moon, William Least **CLC 29**
See also Trogdon, William (Lewis)
See also AAYA 9

Hebbel, Friedrich 1813-1863 **NCLC 43; DAM
DRAM**
See also DLB 129

Hebert, Anne 1916- **CLC 4, 13, 29; DAC; DAM
MST, POET**
See also CA 85-88; CANR 69; DLB 68; MTCW
1, 2

Hecht, Anthony (Evan) 1923- **CLC 8, 13, 19;
DAM POET**
See also CA 9-12R; CANR 6; DLB 5, 169

Hecht, Ben 1894-1964 **CLC 8**
See also CA 85-88; DLB 7, 9, 25, 26, 28, 86

Hedayat, Sadeq 1903-1951 **TCLC 21**
See also CA 120

Hegel, Georg Wilhelm Friedrich 1770-1831
NCLC 46
See also DLB 90

Heidegger, Martin 1889-1976 **CLC 24**
See also CA 81-84; 65-68; CANR 34; MTCW
1, 2

Heidenstam, (Carl Gustaf) Verner von 1859-
1940 **TCLC 5**

See also CA 104

Heifner, Jack 1946- **CLC 11**
See also CA 105; CANR 47

Heijermans, Herman 1864-1924 **TCLC 24**
See also CA 123

Heilbrun, Carolyn G(old) 1926- **CLC 25**
See also CA 45-48; CANR 1, 28, 58

Heine, Heinrich 1797-1856 **NCLC 4, 54; PC 25**
See also DLB 90

Heinemann, Larry (Curtiss) 1944- **CLC 50**
See also CA 110; CAAS 21; CANR 31; DLBD
9; INT CANR-31

Heiney, Donald (William) 1921-1993
See Harris, MacDonald
See also CA 1-4R; 142; CANR 3, 58

Heinlein, Robert A(nson) 1907-1988 **CLC 1, 3,
8, 14, 26, 55; DAM POP**
See also AAYA 17; CA 1-4R; 125; CANR 1,
20, 53; DLB 8; JRDA; MAICYA; MTCW 1,
2; SATA 9, 69; SATA-Obit 56

Helforth, John
See Doolittle, Hilda

Hellenhofferu, Vojtech Kapristian z
See Hasek, Jaroslav (Matej Frantisek)

Heller, Joseph 1923- **CLC 1, 3, 5, 8, 11, 36, 63;
DA; DAB; DAC; DAM MST, NOV, POP;
WLC**
See also AAYA 24; AITN 1; CA 5-8R; CABS
1; CANR 8, 42, 66; DLB 2, 28; DLBY 80;
INT CANR-8; MTCW 1, 2

Hellman, Lillian (Florence) 1906-1984 **CLC 2,
4, 8, 14, 18, 34, 44, 52; DAM DRAM; DC 1**
See also AITN 1, 2; CA 13-16R; 112; CANR
33; DLB 7; DLBY 84; MTCW 1, 2

Helprin, Mark 1947- **CLC 7, 10, 22, 32; DAM
NOV, POP**
See also CA 81-84; CANR 47, 64; CDALBS;
DLBY 85; MTCW 1, 2

Helvetius, Claude-Adrien 1715-1771 **LC 26**

Helyar, Jane Penelope Josephine 1933-
See Poole, Josephine
See also CA 21-24R; CANR 10, 26; SATA 82

Hemans, Felicia 1793-1835 **NCLC 71**
See also DLB 96

Hemingway, Ernest (Miller) 1899-1961 **CLC
1, 3, 6, 8, 10, 13, 19, 30, 34, 39, 41, 44, 50,
61, 80; DA; DAB; DAC; DAM MST, NOV;
SSC 1, 25; WLC**
See also AAYA 19; CA 77-80; CANR 34;
CDALB 1917-1929; DLB 4, 9, 102, 210;
DLBD 1, 15, 16; DLBY 81, 87, 96, 98;
MTCW 1, 2

Hempel, Amy 1951- **CLC 39**
See also CA 118; 137; CANR 70; MTCW 2

Henderson, F. C.
See Mencken, H(enry) L(ouis)

Henderson, Sylvia
See Ashton-Warner, Sylvia (Constance)

Henderson, Zenna (Chlarson) 1917-1983 **SSC
29**
See also CA 1-4R; 133; CANR 1; DLB 8; SATA
5

Henkin, Joshua **CLC 119**
See also CA 161

Henley, Beth **CLC 23; DC 6**
See also Henley, Elizabeth Becker
See also CABS 3; DLBY 86

Henley, Elizabeth Becker 1952-
See Henley, Beth
See also CA 107; CANR 32, 73; DAM DRAM,
MST; MTCW 1, 2

Henley, William Ernest 1849-1903 **TCLC 8**
See also CA 105; DLB 19

Hennissart, Martha
See Lathen, Emma
See also CA 85-88; CANR 64

Henry, O. **TCLC 1, 19; SSC 5; WLC**
See also Porter, William Sydney

Henry, Patrick 1736-1799 **LC 25**

Henryson, Robert 1430(?)-1506(?) **LC 20**
See also DLB 146

Henry VIII 1491-1547 **LC 10**
See also DLB 132

Henschke, Alfred
See Klabund

Hentoff, Nat(han Irving) 1925- **CLC 26**
See also AAYA 4; CA 1-4R; CAAS 6; CANR
5, 25, 77; CLR 1, 52; INT CANR-25; JRDA;
MAICYA; SATA 42, 69; SATA-Brief 27

Heppenstall, (John) Rayner 1911-1981 **C L C
10**
See also CA 1-4R; 103; CANR 29

Heraclitus c. 540B.C.-c. 450B.C. **CMLC 22**
See also DLB 176

Herbert, Frank (Patrick) 1920-1986 **CLC 12,
23, 35, 44, 85; DAM POP**
See also AAYA 21; CA 53-56; 118; CANR 5,
43; CDALBS; DLB 8; INT CANR-5; MTCW
1, 2; SATA 9, 37; SATA-Obit 47

Herbert, George 1593-1633 **LC 24; DAB;
DAM POET; PC 4**
See also CDBLB Before 1660; DLB 126

Herbert, Zbigniew 1924-1998 **CLC 9, 43;
DAM POET**
See also CA 89-92; 169; CANR 36, 74; MTCW
1

Herbst, Josephine (Frey) 1897-1969 **CLC 34**
See also CA 5-8R; 25-28R; DLB 9

Hergesheimer, Joseph 1880-1954 **TCLC 11**
See also CA 109; DLB 102, 9

Herlihy, James Leo 1927-1993 **CLC 6**
See also CA 1-4R; 143; CANR 2

Hermogenes fl. c. 175- **CMLC 6**

Hernandez, Jose 1834-1886 **NCLC 17**

Herodotus c. 484B.C.-429B.C. **CMLC 17**
See also DLB 176

Herrick, Robert 1591-1674 **LC 13; DA; DAB;
DAC; DAM MST, POP; PC 9**
See also DLB 126

Herring, Guilles
See Somerville, Edith

Herriot, James 1916-1995 **CLC 12; DAM POP**
See also Wight, James Alfred
See also AAYA 1; CA 148; CANR 40; MTCW
2; SATA 86

Herrmann, Dorothy 1941- **CLC 44**
See also CA 107

Herrmann, Taffy
See Herrmann, Dorothy

Hersey, John (Richard) 1914-1993 **CLC 1, 2, 7,
9, 40, 81, 97; DAM POP**
See also AAYA 29; CA 17-20R; 140; CANR
33; CDALBS; DLB 6, 185; MTCW 1, 2;
SATA 25; SATA-Obit 76

Herzen, Aleksandr Ivanovich 1812-1870
NCLC 10, 61

Herzl, Theodor 1860-1904 **TCLC 36**
See also CA 168

Herzog, Werner 1942- **CLC 16**
See also CA 89-92

Hesiod c. 8th cent. B.C.- **CMLC 5**
See also DLB 176

Hesse, Hermann 1877-1962 **CLC 1, 2, 3, 6, 11,
17, 25, 69; DA; DAB; DAC; DAM MST,
NOV; SSC 9; WLC**
See also CA 17-18; CAP 2; DLB 66; MTCW 1,

2; SATA 50

Hewes, Cady
See De Voto, Bernard (Augustine)

Heyen, William 1940-   **CLC 13, 18**
See also CA 33-36R; CAAS 9; DLB 5

Heyerdahl, Thor 1914-   **CLC 26**
See also CA 5-8R; CANR 5, 22, 66, 73; MTCW
1, 2; SATA 2, 52

Heym, Georg (Theodor Franz Arthur) 1887-
1912   **TCLC 9**
See also CA 106

Heym, Stefan 1913-   **CLC 41**
See also CA 9-12R; CANR 4; DLB 69

Heyse, Paul (Johann Ludwig von) 1830-1914
TCLC 8
See also CA 104; DLB 129

Heyward, (Edwin) DuBose 1885-1940 **T C L C
59**
See also CA 108; 157; DLB 7, 9, 45; SATA 21

Hibbert, Eleanor Alice Burford 1906-1993
CLC 7; DAM POP
See also BEST 90:4; CA 17-20R; 140; CANR
9, 28, 59; MTCW 2; SATA 2; SATA-Obit 74

Hichens, Robert (Smythe) 1864-1950 **T C L C
64**
See also CA 162; DLB 153

Higgins, George V(incent) 1939-**CLC 4, 7, 10,
18**
See also CA 77-80; CAAS 5; CANR 17, 51;
DLB 2; DLBY 81, 98; INT CANR-17;
MTCW 1

Higginson, Thomas Wentworth 1823-1911
TCLC 36
See also CA 162; DLB 1, 64

Highet, Helen
See MacInnes, Helen (Clark)

Highsmith, (Mary) Patricia 1921-1995**CLC 2,
4, 14, 42, 102; DAM NOV, POP**
See also CA 1-4R; 147; CANR 1, 20, 48, 62;
MTCW 1, 2

Highwater, Jamake (Mamake) 1942(?)- **C L C
12**
See also AAYA 7; CA 65-68; CAAS 7; CANR
10, 34; CLR 17; DLB 52; DLBY 85; JRDA;
MAICYA; SATA 32, 69; SATA-Brief 30

Highway, Tomson 1951-**CLC 92; DAC; DAM
MULT**
See also CA 151; CANR 75; MTCW 2; NNAL

Higuchi, Ichiyo 1872-1896   **NCLC 49**

Hijuelos, Oscar 1951- **CLC 65; DAM MULT,
POP; HLC**
See also AAYA 25; BEST 90:1; CA 123; CANR
50, 75; DLB 145; HW 1, 2; MTCW 2

Hikmet, Nazim 1902(?)-1963   **CLC 40**
See also CA 141; 93-96

Hildegard von Bingen 1098-1179 **CMLC 20**
See also DLB 148

Hildesheimer, Wolfgang 1916-1991   **CLC 49**
See also CA 101; 135; DLB 69, 124

Hill, Geoffrey (William) 1932- **CLC 5, 8, 18,
45; DAM POET**
See also CA 81-84; CANR 21; CDBLB 1960
to Present; DLB 40; MTCW 1

Hill, George Roy 1921-   **CLC 26**
See also CA 110; 122

Hill, John
See Koontz, Dean R(ay)

Hill, Susan (Elizabeth) 1942-   **CLC 4, 113;
DAB; DAM MST, NOV**
See also CA 33-36R; CANR 29, 69; DLB 14,
139; MTCW 1

Hillerman, Tony 1925- **CLC 62; DAM POP**
See also AAYA 6; BEST 89:1; CA 29-32R;

CANR 21, 42, 65; DLB 206; SATA 6

Hillesum, Etty 1914-1943   **TCLC 49**
See also CA 137

Hilliard, Noel (Harvey) 1929-   **CLC 15**
See also CA 9-12R; CANR 7, 69

Hillis, Rick 1956-   **CLC 66**
See also CA 134

Hilton, James 1900-1954   **TCLC 21**
See also CA 108; 169; DLB 34, 77; SATA 34

Himes, Chester (Bomar) 1909-1984**CLC 2, 4,
7, 18, 58, 108; BLC 2; DAM MULT**
See also BW 2; CA 25-28R; 114; CANR 22;
DLB 2, 76, 143; MTCW 1, 2

Hinde, Thomas   **CLC 6, 11**
See also Chitty, Thomas Willes

Hindin, Nathan
See Bloch, Robert (Albert)

Hine, (William) Daryl 1936-   **CLC 15**
See also CA 1-4R; CAAS 15; CANR 1, 20; DLB
60

Hinkson, Katharine Tynan
See Tynan, Katharine

Hinton, S(usan) E(loise) 1950- **CLC 30, 111;
DA; DAB; DAC; DAM MST, NOV**
See also AAYA 2; CA 81-84; CANR 32, 62;
CDALBS; CLR 3, 23; JRDA; MAICYA;
MTCW 1, 2; SATA 19, 58

Hippius, Zinaida   **TCLC 9**
See also Gippius, Zinaida (Nikolayevna)

Hiraoka, Kimitake 1925-1970
See Mishima, Yukio
See also CA 97-100; 29-32R; DAM DRAM;
MTCW 1, 2

Hirsch, E(ric) D(onald), Jr. 1928-   **CLC 79**
See also CA 25-28R; CANR 27, 51; DLB 67;
INT CANR-27; MTCW 1

Hirsch, Edward 1950-   **CLC 31, 50**
See also CA 104; CANR 20, 42; DLB 120

Hitchcock, Alfred (Joseph) 1899-1980**CLC 16**
See also AAYA 22; CA 159; 97-100; SATA 27;
SATA-Obit 24

Hitler, Adolf 1889-1945   **TCLC 53**
See also CA 117; 147

Hoagland, Edward 1932-   **CLC 28**
See also CA 1-4R; CANR 2, 31, 57; DLB 6;
SATA 51

Hoban, Russell (Conwell) 1925-   **CLC 7, 25;
DAM NOV**
See also CA 5-8R; CANR 23, 37, 66; CLR 3;
DLB 52; MAICYA; MTCW 1, 2; SATA 1,
40, 78

Hobbes, Thomas 1588-1679   **LC 36**
See also DLB 151

Hobbs, Perry
See Blackmur, R(ichard) P(almer)

Hobson, Laura Z(ametkin) 1900-1986**CLC 7,
25**
See also CA 17-20R; 118; CANR 55; DLB 28;
SATA 52

Hochhuth, Rolf 1931-   **CLC 4, 11, 18; DAM
DRAM**
See also CA 5-8R; CANR 33, 75; DLB 124;
MTCW 1, 2

Hochman, Sandra 1936-   **CLC 3, 8**
See also CA 5-8R; DLB 5

Hochwaelder, Fritz 1911-1986**CLC 36; DAM
DRAM**
See also CA 29-32R; 120; CANR 42; MTCW 1

Hochwalder, Fritz
See Hochwaelder, Fritz

Hocking, Mary (Eunice) 1921-   **CLC 13**
See also CA 101; CANR 18, 40

Hodgins, Jack 1938-   **CLC 23**

See also CA 93-96; DLB 60

Hodgson, William Hope 1877(?)-1918 **T C L C
13**
See also CA 111; 164; DLB 70, 153, 156, 178;
MTCW 2

Hoeg, Peter 1957-   **CLC 95**
See also CA 151; CANR 75; MTCW 2

Hoffman, Alice 1952-   **CLC 51; DAM NOV**
See also CA 77-80; CANR 34, 66; MTCW 1, 2

Hoffman, Daniel (Gerard) 1923-**CLC 6, 13, 23**
See also CA 1-4R; CANR 4; DLB 5

Hoffman, Stanley 1944-   **CLC 5**
See also CA 77-80

Hoffman, William M(oses) 1939-   **CLC 40**
See also CA 57-60; CANR 11, 71

Hoffmann, E(rnst) T(heodor) A(madeus) 1776-
1822   **NCLC 2; SSC 13**
See also DLB 90; SATA 27

Hofmann, Gert 1931-   **CLC 54**
See also CA 128

Hofmannsthal, Hugo von 1874-1929**TCLC 11;
DAM DRAM; DC 4**
See also CA 106; 153; DLB 81, 118

Hogan, Linda 1947-   **CLC 73; DAM MULT**
See also CA 120; CANR 45, 73; DLB 175;
NNAL

Hogarth, Charles
See Creasey, John

Hogarth, Emmett
See Polonsky, Abraham (Lincoln)

Hogg, James 1770-1835   **NCLC 4**
See also DLB 93, 116, 159

Holbach, Paul Henri Thiry Baron 1723-1789
LC 14

Holberg, Ludvig 1684-1754   **LC 6**

Holden, Ursula 1921-   **CLC 18**
See also CA 101; CAAS 8; CANR 22

Holderlin, (Johann Christian) Friedrich 1770-
1843   **NCLC 16; PC 4**

Holdstock, Robert
See Holdstock, Robert P.

Holdstock, Robert P. 1948-   **CLC 39**
See also CA 131

Holland, Isabelle 1920-   **CLC 21**
See also AAYA 11; CA 21-24R; CANR 10, 25,
47; CLR 57; JRDA; MAICYA; SATA 8, 70;
SATA-Essay 103

Holland, Marcus
See Caldwell, (Janet Miriam) Taylor (Holland)

Hollander, John 1929-   **CLC 2, 5, 8, 14**
See also CA 1-4R; CANR 1, 52; DLB 5; SATA
13

Hollander, Paul
<indexSee Silverberg, Robert

Holleran, Andrew 1943(?)-   **CLC 38**
See also CA 144

Hollinghurst, Alan 1954-   **CLC 55, 91**
See also CA 114; DLB 207

Hollis, Jim
See Summers, Hollis (Spurgeon, Jr.)

Holly, Buddy 1936-1959   **TCLC 65**

Holmes, Gordon
See Shiel, M(atthew) P(hipps)

Holmes, John
See Souster, (Holmes) Raymond

Holmes, John Clellon 1926-1988   **CLC 56**
See also CA 9-12R; 125; CANR 4; DLB 16

Holmes, Oliver Wendell, Jr. 1841-1935**T C L C
77**
See also CA 114

Holmes, Oliver Wendell 1809-1894 **NCLC 14**
See also CDALB 1640-1865; DLB 1, 189;
SATA 34

Holmes, Raymond
  See Souster, (Holmes) Raymond
Holt, Victoria
  See Hibbert, Eleanor Alice Burford
Holub, Miroslav 1923-1998   **CLC 4**
  See also CA 21-24R; 169; CANR 10
Homer c. 8th cent. B.C.-   **CMLC 1, 16; DA;**
  DAB; DAC; DAM MST, POET; PC 23;
  WLCS
  See also DLB 176
Hongo, Garrett Kaoru 1951-   **PC 23**
  See also CA 133; CAAS 22; DLB 120
Honig, Edwin 1919-   **CLC 33**
  See also CA 5-8R; CAAS 8; CANR 4, 45; DLB
  5
Hood, Hugh (John Blagdon) 1928-CLC **15, 28**
  See also CA 49-52; CAAS 17; CANR 1, 33;
  DLB 53
Hood, Thomas 1799-1845   **NCLC 16**
  See also DLB 96
Hooker, (Peter) Jeremy 1941-   **CLC 43**
  See also CA 77-80; CANR 22; DLB 40
hooks, bell   **CLC 94; BLCS**
  See also Watkins, Gloria
  See also MTCW 2
Hope, A(lec) D(erwent) 1907-   **CLC 3, 51**
  See also CA 21-24R; CANR 33, 74; MTCW 1,
  2
Hope, Anthony 1863-1933   **TCLC 83**
  See also CA 157; DLB 153, 156
Hope, Brian
  See Creasey, John
Hope, Christopher (David Tully) 1944- **C L C**
  52
  See also CA 106; CANR 47; SATA 62
Hopkins, Gerard Manley 1844-1889 **N C L C**
  17; DA; DAB; DAC; DAM MST, POET;
  PC 15; WLC
  See also CDBLB 1890-1914; DLB 35, 57
Hopkins, John (Richard) 1931-1998   **CLC 4**
  See also CA 85-88; 169
Hopkins, Pauline Elizabeth 1859-1930 **T C L C**
  28; BLC 2; DAM MULT
  See also BW 2, 3; CA 141; DLB 50
Hopkinson, Francis 1737-1791   **LC 25**
  See also DLB 31
Hopley-Woolrich, Cornell George 1903-1968
  See Woolrich, Cornell
  See also CA 13-14; CANR 58; CAP 1; MTCW
  2
Horatio
  See Proust, (Valentin-Louis-George-Eugene-)
  Marcel
Horgan, Paul (George Vincent O'Shaughnessy)
  1903-1995   **CLC 9, 53; DAM NOV**
  See also CA 13-16R; 147; CANR 9, 35; DLB
  212; DLBY 85; INT CANR-9; MTCW 1, 2;
  SATA 13; SATA-Obit 84
Horn, Peter
  See Kuttner, Henry
Hornem, Horace Esq.
  See Byron, George Gordon (Noel)
Horney, Karen (Clementine Theodore
  Danielsen) 1885-1952   **TCLC 71**
  See also CA 114; 165
Hornung, E(rnest) W(illiam) 1866-1921
  TCLC 59
  See also CA 108; 160; DLB 70
Horovitz, Israel (Arthur) 1939-CLC **56; DAM**
  DRAM
  See also CA 33-36R; CANR 46, 59; DLB 7
Horvath, Odon von
  See Horvath, Oedoen von

See also DLB 85, 124
Horvath, Oedoen von 1901-1938   **TCLC 45**
  See also Horvath, Odon von
  See also CA 118
Horwitz, Julius 1920-1986   **CLC 14**
  See also CA 9-12R; 119; CANR 12
Hospital, Janette Turner 1942-   **CLC 42**
  See also CA 108; CANR 48
Hostos, E. M. de
  See Hostos (y Bonilla), Eugenio Maria de
Hostos, Eugenio M. de
  See Hostos (y Bonilla), Eugenio Maria de
Hostos, Eugenio Maria
  See Hostos (y Bonilla), Eugenio Maria de
Hostos (y Bonilla), Eugenio Maria de 1839-1903
  TCLC 24
  See also CA 123; 131; HW 1
Houdini
  See Lovecraft, H(oward) P(hillips)
Hougan, Carolyn 1943-   **CLC 34**
  See also CA 139
Household, Geoffrey (Edward West) 1900-1988
  CLC 11
  See also CA 77-80; 126; CANR 58; DLB 87;
  SATA 14; SATA-Obit 59
Housman, A(lfred) E(dward) 1859-1936
  TCLC 1, 10; DA; DAB; DAC; DAM MST,
  POET; PC 2; WLCS
  See also CA 104; 125; DLB 19; MTCW 1, 2
Housman, Laurence 1865-1959   **TCLC 7**
  See also CA 106; 155; DLB 10; SATA 25
Howard, Elizabeth Jane 1923-   **CLC 7, 29**
  See also CA 5-8R; CANR 8, 62
Howard, Maureen 1930-   **CLC 5, 14, 46**
  See also CA 53-56; CANR 31, 75; DLBY 83;
  INT CANR-31; MTCW 1, 2
Howard, Richard 1929-   **CLC 7, 10, 47**
  See also AITN 1; CA 85-88; CANR 25, 80; DLB
  5; INT CANR-25
Howard, Robert E(rvin) 1906-1936   **TCLC 8**
  See also CA 105; 157
Howard, Warren F.
  See Pohl, Frederik
Howe, Fanny (Quincy) 1940-   **CLC 47**
  See also CA 117; CAAS 27; CANR 70; SATA-
  Brief 52
Howe, Irving 1920-1993   **CLC 85**
  See also CA 9-12R; 141; CANR 21, 50; DLB
  67; MTCW 1, 2
Howe, Julia Ward 1819-1910   **TCLC 21**
  See also CA 117; DLB 1, 189
Howe, Susan 1937-   **CLC 72**
  See also CA 160; DLB 120
Howe, Tina 1937-   **CLC 48**
  See also CA 109
Howell, James 1594(?)-1666   **LC 13**
  See also DLB 151
Howells, W. D.
  See Howells, William Dean
Howells, William D.
  See Howells, William Dean
Howells, William Dean 1837-1920TCLC **7, 17,**
  41
  See also CA 104; 134; CDALB 1865-1917;
  DLB 12, 64, 74, 79, 189; MTCW 2
Howes, Barbara 1914-1996   **CLC 15**
  See also CA 9-12R; 151; CAAS 3; CANR 53;
  SATA 5
Hrabal, Bohumil 1914-1997   **CLC 13, 67**
  See also CA 106; 156; CAAS 12; CANR 57
Hroswitha of Gandersheim c. 935-c. 1002
  CMLC 29
  See also DLB 148

Hsun, Lu
  See Lu Hsun
Hubbard, L(afayette) Ron(ald) 1911-1986
  CLC 43; DAM POP
  See also CA 77-80; 118; CANR 52; MTCW 2
Huch, Ricarda (Octavia) 1864-1947TCLC **13**
  See also CA 111; DLB 66
Huddle, David 1942-   **CLC 49**
  See also CA 57-60; CAAS 20; DLB 130
Hudson, Jeffrey
  See Crichton, (John) Michael
Hudson, W(illiam) H(enry) 1841-1922 **T C L C**
  29
  See also CA 115; DLB 98, 153, 174; SATA 35
Hueffer, Ford Madox
  See Ford, Ford Madox
Hughart, Barry 1934-   **CLC 39**
  See also CA 137
Hughes, Colin
  See Creasey, John
Hughes, David (John) 1930-   **CLC 48**
  See also CA 116; 129; DLB 14
Hughes, Edward James
  See Hughes, Ted
  See also DAM MST, POET
Hughes, (James) Langston 1902-1967CLC **1,**
  5, 10, 15, 35, 44, 108; BLC 2; DA; DAB;
  DAC; DAM DRAM, MST, MULT, POET;
  DC 3; PC 1; SSC 6; WLC
  See also AAYA 12; BW 1, 3; CA 1-4R; 25-28R;
  CANR 1, 34; CDALB 1929-1941; CLR 17;
  DLB 4, 7, 48, 51, 86; JRDA; MAICYA;
  MTCW 1, 2; SATA 4, 33
Hughes, Richard (Arthur Warren) 1900-1976
  CLC 1, 11; DAM NOV
  See also CA 5-8R; 65-68; CANR 4; DLB 15,
  161; MTCW 1; SATA 8; SATA-Obit 25
Hughes, Ted 1930-1998   **CLC 2, 4, 9, 14, 37,**
  119; DAB; DAC; PC 7
  See also Hughes, Edward James
  See also CA 1-4R; 171; CANR 1, 33, 66; CLR
  3; DLB 40, 161; MAICYA; MTCW 1, 2;
  SATA 49; SATA-Brief 27; SATA-Obit 107
Hugo, Richard F(ranklin) 1923-1982 CLC **6,**
  18, 32; DAM POET
  See also CA 49-52; 108; CANR 3; DLB 5, 206
Hugo, Victor (Marie) 1802-1885NCLC **3, 10,**
  21; DA; DAB; DAC; DAM DRAM, MST,
  NOV, POET; PC 17; WLC
  See also AAYA 28; DLB 119, 192; SATA 47
Huidobro, Vicente
  See Huidobro Fernandez, Vicente Garcia
Huidobro Fernandez, Vicente Garcia 1893-
  1948   **TCLC 31**
  See also CA 131; HW 1
Hulme, Keri 1947-   **CLC 39**
  See also CA 125; CANR 69; INT 125
Hulme, T(homas) E(rnest) 1883-1917 **T C L C**
  21
  See also CA 117; DLB 19
Hume, David 1711-1776   **LC 7**
  See also DLB 104
Humphrey, William 1924-1997   **CLC 45**
  See also CA 77-80; 160; CANR 68; DLB 212
Humphreys, Emyr Owen 1919-   **CLC 47**
  See also CA 5-8R; CANR 3, 24; DLB 15
Humphreys, Josephine 1945-   **CLC 34, 57**
  See also CA 121; 127; INT 127
Huneker, James Gibbons 1857-1921TCLC **65**
  See also DLB 71
Hungerford, Pixie
  See Brinsmead, H(esba) F(ay)
Hunt, E(verette) Howard, (Jr.) 1918- **CLC 3**

See also AITN 1; CA 45-48; CANR 2, 47

Hunt, Kyle
See Creasey, John

Hunt, (James Henry) Leigh 1784-1859 **N C L C 1, 70; DAM POET**
See also DLB 96, 110, 144

Hunt, Marsha 1946-   **CLC 70**
See also BW 2, 3; CA 143; CANR 79

Hunt, Violet 1866(?)-1942   **TCLC 53**
See also DLB 162, 197

Hunter, E. Waldo
See Sturgeon, Theodore (Hamilton)

Hunter, Evan 1926- **CLC 11, 31; DAM POP**
See also CA 5-8R; CANR 5, 38, 62; DLBY 82; INT CANR-5; MTCW 1; SATA 25

Hunter, Kristin (Eggleston) 1931-   **CLC 35**
See also AITN 1; BW 1; CA 13-16R; CANR 13; CLR 3; DLB 33; INT CANR-13; MAICYA; SAAS 10; SATA 12

Hunter, Mollie 1922-   **CLC 21**
See also McIlwraith, Maureen Mollie Hunter
See also AAYA 13; CANR 37, 78; CLR 25; DLB 161; JRDA; MAICYA; SAAS 7; SATA 54, 106

Hunter, Robert (?)-1734   **LC 7**

Hurston, Zora Neale 1903-1960 **CLC 7, 30, 61; BLC 2; DA; DAC; DAM MST, MULT, NOV; SSC 4; WLCS**
See also AAYA 15; BW 1, 3; CA 85-88; CANR 61; CDALBS; DLB 51, 86; MTCW 1, 2

Huston, John (Marcellus) 1906-1987 **CLC 20**
See also CA 73-76; 123; CANR 34; DLB 26

Hustvedt, Siri 1955-   **CLC 76**
See also CA 137

Hutten, Ulrich von 1488-1523   **LC 16**
See also DLB 179

Huxley, Aldous (Leonard) 1894-1963 **CLC 1, 3, 4, 5, 8, 11, 18, 35, 79; DA; DAB; DAC; DAM MST, NOV; WLC**
See also AAYA 11; CA 85-88; CANR 44; CDBLB 1914-1945; DLB 36, 100, 162, 195; MTCW 1, 2; SATA 63

Huxley, T(homas) H(enry) 1825-1895 **N C L C 67**
See also DLB 57

Huysmans, Joris-Karl 1848-1907 **TCLC 7, 69**
See also CA 104; 165; DLB 123

Hwang, David Henry 1957- **CLC 55; DAM DRAM; DC 4**
See also CA 127; 132; CANR 76; DLB 212; INT 132; MTCW 2

Hyde, Anthony 1946-   **CLC 42**
See also CA 136

Hyde, Margaret O(ldroyd) 1917-   **CLC 21**
See also CA 1-4R; CANR 1, 36; CLR 23; JRDA; MAICYA; SAAS 8; SATA 1, 42, 76

Hynes, James 1956(?)-   **CLC 65**
See also CA 164

Ian, Janis 1951-   **CLC 21**
See also CA 105

Ibanez, Vicente Blasco
See Blasco Ibanez, Vicente

Ibarguengoitia, Jorge 1928-1983   **CLC 37**
See also CA 124; 113; HW 1

Ibsen, Henrik (Johan) 1828-1906 **TCLC 2, 8, 16, 37, 52; DA; DAB; DAC; DAM DRAM, MST; DC 2; WLC**
See also CA 104; 141

Ibuse, Masuji 1898-1993   **CLC 22**
See also CA 127; 141; DLB 180

Ichikawa, Kon 1915-   **CLC 20**
See also CA 121

Idle, Eric 1943-   **CLC 21**

See also Monty Python
See also CA 116; CANR 35

Ignatow, David 1914-1997   **CLC 4, 7, 14, 40**
See also CA 9-12R; 162; CAAS 3; CANR 31, 57; DLB 5

Ihimaera, Witi 1944-   **CLC 46**
See also CA 77-80

Ilf, Ilya   **TCLC 21**
See also Fainzilberg, Ilya Arnoldovich

Illyes, Gyula 1902-1983   **PC 16**
See also CA 114; 109

Immermann, Karl (Lebrecht) 1796-1840 **NCLC 4, 49**
See also DLB 133

Ince, Thomas H. 1882-1924   **TCLC 89**

Inchbald, Elizabeth 1753-1821   **NCLC 62**
See also DLB 39, 89

Inclan, Ramon (Maria) del Valle
See Valle-Inclan, Ramon (Maria) del

Infante, G(uillermo) Cabrera
See Cabrera Infante, G(uillermo)

Ingalls, Rachel (Holmes) 1940-   **CLC 42**
See also CA 123; 127

Ingamells, Reginald Charles
See Ingamells, Rex

Ingamells, Rex 1913-1955   **TCLC 35**
See also CA 167

Inge, William (Motter) 1913-1973 **CLC 1, 8, 19; DAM DRAM**
See also CA 9-12R; CDALB 1941-1968; DLB 7; MTCW 1, 2

Ingelow, Jean 1820-1897   **NCLC 39**
See also DLB 35, 163; SATA 33

Ingram, Willis J.
See Harris, Mark

Innaurato, Albert (F.) 1948(?)- **CLC 21, 60**
See also CA 115; 122; CANR 78; INT 122

Innes, Michael
See Stewart, J(ohn) I(nnes) M(ackintosh)

Innis, Harold Adams 1894-1952   **TCLC 77**
See also DLB 88

Ionesco, Eugene 1909-1994 **CLC 1, 4, 6, 9, 11, 15, 41, 86; DA; DAB; DAC; DAM DRAM, MST; WLC**
See also CA 9-12R; 144; CANR 55; MTCW 1, 2; SATA 7; SATA-Obit 79

Iqbal, Muhammad 1873-1938   **TCLC 28**

Ireland, Patrick
See O'Doherty, Brian

Iron, Ralph
See Schreiner, Olive (Emilie Albertina)

Irving, John (Winslow) 1942- **CLC 13, 23, 38, 112; DAM NOV, POP**
See also AAYA 8; BEST 89:3; CA 25-28R; CANR 28, 73; DLB 6; DLBY 82; MTCW 1, 2

Irving, Washington 1783-1859 **NCLC 2, 19; DA; DAB; DAC; DAM MST; SSC 2; WLC**
See also CDALB 1640-1865; DLB 3, 11, 30, 59, 73, 74, 186; YABC 2

Irwin, P. K.
See Page, P(atricia) K(athleen)

Isaacs, Jorge Ricardo 1837-1895   **NCLC 70**

Isaacs, Susan 1943-   **CLC 32; DAM POP**
See also BEST 89:1; CA 89-92; CANR 20, 41, 65; INT CANR-20; MTCW 1, 2

Isherwood, Christopher (William Bradshaw) 1904-1986   **CLC 1, 9, 11, 14, 44; DAM DRAM, NOV**
See also CA 13-16R; 117; CANR 35; DLB 15, 195; DLBY 86; MTCW 1, 2

Ishiguro, Kazuo 1954- **CLC 27, 56, 59, 110; DAM NOV**

See also BEST 90:2; CA 120; CANR 49; DLB 194; MTCW 1, 2

Ishikawa, Hakuhin
See Ishikawa, Takuboku

Ishikawa, Takuboku 1886(?)-1912 **TCLC 15; DAM POET; PC 10**
See also CA 113; 153

Iskander, Fazil 1929-   **CLC 47**
See also CA 102

Isler, Alan (David) 1934-   **CLC 91**
See also CA 156

Ivan IV 1530-1584   **LC 17**

Ivanov, Vyacheslav Ivanovich 1866-1949 **TCLC 33**
See also CA 122

Ivask, Ivar Vidrik 1927-1992   **CLC 14**
See also CA 37-40R; 139; CANR 24

Ives, Morgan
See Bradley, Marion Zimmer

Izumi Shikibu c. 973-c. 1034   **CMLC 33**

J. R. S.
See Gogarty, Oliver St. John

Jabran, Kahlil
See Gibran, Kahlil

Jabran, Khalil
See Gibran, Kahlil

Jackson, Daniel
See Wingrove, David (John)

Jackson, Jesse 1908-1983   **CLC 12**
See also BW 1; CA 25-28R; 109; CANR 27; CLR 28; MAICYA; SATA 2, 29; SATA-Obit 48

Jackson, Laura (Riding) 1901-1991
See Riding, Laura
See also CA 65-68; 135; CANR 28; DLB 48

Jackson, Sam
See Trumbo, Dalton

Jackson, Sara
See Wingrove, David (John)

Jackson, Shirley 1919-1965 **CLC 11, 60, 87; DA; DAC; DAM MST; SSC 9; WLC**
See also AAYA 9; CA 1-4R; 25-28R; CANR 4, 52; CDALB 1941-1968; DLB 6; MTCW 2; SATA 2

Jacob, (Cyprien-)Max 1876-1944   **TCLC 6**
See also CA 104

Jacobs, Harriet A(nn) 1813(?)-1897 **NCLC 67**

Jacobs, Jim 1942-   **CLC 12**
See also CA 97-100; INT 97-100

Jacobs, W(illiam) W(ymark) 1863-1943 **TCLC 22**
See also CA 121; 167; DLB 135

Jacobsen, Jens Peter 1847-1885   **NCLC 34**

Jacobsen, Josephine 1908-   **CLC 48, 102**
See also CA 33-36R; CAAS 18; CANR 23, 48

Jacobson, Dan 1929-   **CLC 4, 14**
See also CA 1-4R; CANR 2, 25, 66; DLB 14, 207; MTCW 1

Jacqueline
See Carpentier (y Valmont), Alejo

Jagger, Mick 1944-   **CLC 17**

Jahiz, al- c. 780-c. 869   **CMLC 25**

Jakes, John (William) 1932- **CLC 29; DAM NOV, POP**
See also BEST 89:4; CA 57-60; CANR 10, 43, 66; DLBY 83; INT CANR-10; MTCW 1, 2; SATA 62

James, Andrew
See Kirkup, James

James, C(yril) L(ionel) R(obert) 1901-1989 **CLC 33; BLCS**
See also BW 2; CA 117; 125; 128; CANR 62; DLB 125; MTCW 1

James, Daniel (Lewis) 1911-1988
 See Santiago, Danny
 See also CA 174; 125
James, Dynely
 See Mayne, William (James Carter)
James, Henry Sr. 1811-1882   **NCLC 53**
James, Henry 1843-1916 **TCLC 2, 11, 24, 40, 47, 64; DA; DAB; DAC; DAM MST, NOV; SSC 8, 32; WLC**
 See also CA 104; 132; CDALB 1865-1917; DLB 12, 71, 74, 189; DLBD 13; MTCW 1, 2
James, M. R.
 See James, Montague (Rhodes)
 See also DLB 156
James, Montague (Rhodes) 1862-1936 **T C L C 6; SSC 16**
 See also CA 104; DLB 201
James, P. D. 1920-   **CLC 18, 46**
 See also White, Phyllis Dorothy James
 See also BEST 90:2; CDBLB 1960 to Present; DLB 87; DLBD 17
James, Philip
 See Moorcock, Michael (John)
James, William 1842-1910   **TCLC 15, 32**
 See also CA 109
James I 1394-1437   **LC 20**
Jameson, Anna 1794-1860   **NCLC 43**
 See also DLB 99, 166
Jami, Nur al-Din 'Abd al-Rahman 1414-1492
 LC 9
Jammes, Francis 1868-1938   **TCLC 75**
Jandl, Ernst 1925-   **CLC 34**
Janowitz, Tama 1957- **CLC 43; DAM POP**
 See also CA 106; CANR 52
Japrisot, Sebastien 1931-   **CLC 90**
Jarrell, Randall 1914-1965 **CLC 1, 2, 6, 9, 13, 49; DAM POET**
 See also CA 5-8R; 25-28R; CABS 2; CANR 6, 34; CDALB 1941-1968; CLR 6; DLB 48, 52; MAICYA; MTCW 1, 2; SATA 7
Jarry, Alfred 1873-1907   **TCLC 2, 14; DAM DRAM; SSC 20**
 See also CA 104; 153; DLB 192
Jarvis, E. K.
 See Bloch, Robert (Albert); Ellison, Harlan (Jay); Silverberg, Robert
Jeake, Samuel, Jr.
 See Aiken, Conrad (Potter)
Jean Paul 1763-1825   **NCLC 7**
Jefferies, (John) Richard 1848-1887**NCLC 47**
 See also DLB 98, 141; SATA 16
Jeffers, (John) Robinson 1887-1962**CLC 2, 3, 11, 15, 54; DA; DAC; DAM MST, POET; PC 17; WLC**
 See also CA 85-88; CANR 35; CDALB 1917-1929; DLB 45, 212; MTCW 1, 2
Jefferson, Janet
 See Mencken, H(enry) L(ouis)
Jefferson, Thomas 1743-1826   **NCLC 11**
 See also CDALB 1640-1865; DLB 31
Jeffrey, Francis 1773-1850   **NCLC 33**
 See also DLB 107
Jelakowitch, Ivan
 See Heijermans, Herman
Jellicoe, (Patricia) Ann 1927-   **CLC 27**
 See also CA 85-88; DLB 13
Jen, Gish   **CLC 70**
 See also Jen, Lillian
Jen, Lillian 1956(?)-
 See Jen, Gish
 See also CA 135
Jenkins, (John) Robin 1912-   **CLC 52**

 See also CA 1-4R; CANR 1; DLB 14
Jennings, Elizabeth (Joan) 1926- **CLC 5, 14**
 See also CA 61-64; CAAS 5; CANR 8, 39, 66; DLB 27; MTCW 1; SATA 66
Jennings, Waylon 1937-   **CLC 21**
Jensen, Johannes V. 1873-1950   **TCLC 41**
 See also CA 170
Jensen, Laura (Linnea) 1948-   **CLC 37**
 See also CA 103
Jerome, Jerome K(lapka) 1859-1927**TCLC 23**
 See also CA 119; DLB 10, 34, 135
Jerrold, Douglas William 1803-1857**NCLC 2**
 See also DLB 158, 159
Jewett, (Theodora) Sarah Orne 1849-1909
 TCLC 1, 22; SSC 6
 See also CA 108; 127; CANR 71; DLB 12, 74; SATA 15
Jewsbury, Geraldine (Endsor) 1812-1880
 NCLC 22
 See also DLB 21
Jhabvala, Ruth Prawer 1927-**CLC 4, 8, 29, 94; DAB; DAM NOV**
 See also CA 1-4R; CANR 2, 29, 51, 74; DLB 139, 194; INT CANR-29; MTCW 1, 2
Jibran, Kahlil
 See Gibran, Kahlil
Jibran, Khalil
 See Gibran, Kahlil
Jiles, Paulette 1943-   **CLC 13, 58**
 See also CA 101; CANR 70
Jimenez (Mantecon), Juan Ramon 1881-1958
 TCLC 4; DAM MULT, POET; HLC; PC 7
 See also CA 104; 131; CANR 74; DLB 134; HW 1; MTCW 1, 2
Jimenez, Ramon
 See Jimenez (Mantecon), Juan Ramon
Jimenez Mantecon, Juan
 See Jimenez (Mantecon), Juan Ramon
Jin, Ha 1956-   **CLC 109**
 See also CA 152
Joel, Billy   **CLC 26**
 See also Joel, William Martin
Joel, William Martin 1949-
 See Joel, Billy
 See also CA 108
John, Saint 7th cent. -   **CMLC 27**
John of the Cross, St. 1542-1591   **LC 18**
Johnson, B(ryan) S(tanley William) 1933-1973
 CLC 6, 9
 See also CA 9-12R; 53-56; CANR 9; DLB 14, 40
Johnson, Benj. F. of Boo
 See Riley, James Whitcomb
Johnson, Benjamin F. of Boo
 See Riley, James Whitcomb
Johnson, Charles (Richard) 1948-**CLC 7, 51, 65; BLC 2; DAM MULT**
 See also BW 2, 3; CA 116; CAAS 18; CANR 42, 66; DLB 33; MTCW 2
Johnson, Denis 1949-   **CLC 52**
 See also CA 117; 121; CANR 71; DLB 120
Johnson, Diane 1934-   **CLC 5, 13, 48**
 See also CA 41-44R; CANR 17, 40, 62; DLBY 80; INT CANR-17; MTCW 1
Johnson, Eyvind (Olof Verner) 1900-1976
 CLC 14
 See also CA 73-76; 69-72; CANR 34
Johnson, J. R.
 See James, C(yril) L(ionel) R(obert)
Johnson, James Weldon 1871-1938 **TCLC 3, 19; BLC 2; DAM MULT, POET; PC 24**
 See also BW 1, 3; CA 104; 125; CDALB 1917-

 1929; CLR 32; DLB 51; MTCW 1, 2; SATA 31
Johnson, Joyce 1935-   **CLC 58**
 See also CA 125; 129
Johnson, Judith (Emlyn) 1936-   **CLC 7, 15**
 See also CA 25-28R, 153; CANR 34
Johnson, Lionel (Pigot) 1867-1902 **TCLC 19**
 See also CA 117; DLB 19
Johnson, Marguerite (Annie)
 See Angelou, Maya
Johnson, Mel
 See Malzberg, Barry N(athaniel)
Johnson, Pamela Hansford 1912-1981**CLC 1, 7, 27**
 See also CA 1-4R; 104; CANR 2, 28; DLB 15; MTCW 1, 2
Johnson, Robert 1911(?)-1938   **TCLC 69**
 See also BW 3; CA 174
Johnson, Samuel 1709-1784**LC 15; DA; DAB; DAC; DAM MST; WLC**
 See also CDBLB 1660-1789; DLB 39, 95, 104, 142
Johnson, Uwe 1934-1984   **CLC 5, 10, 15, 40**
 See also CA 1-4R; 112; CANR 1, 39; DLB 75; MTCW 1
Johnston, George (Benson) 1913-   **CLC 51**
 See also CA 1-4R; CANR 5, 20; DLB 88
Johnston, Jennifer 1930-   **CLC 7**
 See also CA 85-88; DLB 14
Jolley, (Monica) Elizabeth 1923-**CLC 46; SSC 19**
 See also CA 127; CAAS 13; CANR 59
Jones, Arthur Llewellyn 1863-1947
 See Machen, Arthur
 See also CA 104
Jones, D(ouglas) G(ordon) 1929-   **CLC 10**
 See also CA 29-32R; CANR 13; DLB 53
Jones, David (Michael) 1895-1974**CLC 2, 4, 7, 13, 42**
 See also CA 9-12R; 53-56; CANR 28; CDBLB 1945-1960; DLB 20, 100; MTCW 1
Jones, David Robert 1947-
 See Bowie, David
 See also CA 103
Jones, Diana Wynne 1934-   **CLC 26**
 See also AAYA 12; CA 49-52; CANR 4, 26, 56; CLR 23; DLB 161; JRDA; MAICYA; SAAS 7; SATA 9, 70
Jones, Edward P. 1950-   **CLC 76**
 See also BW 2, 3; CA 142; CANR 79
Jones, Gayl 1949-   **CLC 6, 9; BLC 2; DAM MULT**
 See also BW 2, 3; CA 77-80; CANR 27, 66; DLB 33; MTCW 1, 2
Jones, James 1921-1977   **CLC 1, 3, 10, 39**
 See also AITN 1, 2; CA 1-4R; 69-72; CANR 6; DLB 2, 143; DLBD 17; DLBY 98; MTCW 1
Jones, John J.
 See Lovecraft, H(oward) P(hillips)
Jones, LeRoi   **CLC 1, 2, 3, 5, 10, 14**
 See also Baraka, Amiri
 See also MTCW 2
Jones, Louis B. 1953-   **CLC 65**
 See also CA 141; CANR 73
Jones, Madison (Percy, Jr.) 1925-   **CLC 4**
 See also CA 13-16R; CAAS 11; CANR 7, 54; DLB 152
Jones, Mervyn 1922-   **CLC 10, 52**
 See also CA 45-48; CAAS 5; CANR 1; MTCW 1
Jones, Mick 1956(?)-   **CLC 30**
Jones, Nettie (Pearl) 1941-   **CLC 34**
 See also BW 2; CA 137; CAAS 20

Jones, Preston 1936-1979   **CLC 10**
   See also CA 73-76; 89-92; DLB 7
Jones, Robert F(rancis) 1934-   **CLC 7**
   See also CA 49-52; CANR 2, 61
Jones, Rod 1953-   **CLC 50**
   See also CA 128
Jones, Terence Graham Parry 1942- **CLC 21**
   See also Jones, Terry; Monty Python
   See also CA 112; 116; CANR 35; INT 116
Jones, Terry
   See Jones, Terence Graham Parry
   See also SATA 67; SATA-Brief 51
Jones, Thom 1945(?)-   **CLC 81**
   See also CA 157
Jong, Erica 1942- **CLC 4, 6, 8, 18, 83; DAM**
   NOV, POP
   See also AITN 1; BEST 90:2; CA 73-76; CANR
   26, 52, 75; DLB 2, 5, 28, 152; INT CANR-
   26; MTCW 1, 2
Jonson, Ben(jamin) 1572(?)-1637 **LC 6, 33;**
   DA; DAB; DAC; DAM DRAM, MST,
   POET; DC 4; PC 17; WLC
   See also CDBLB Before 1660; DLB 62, 121
Jordan, June 1936-**CLC 5, 11, 23, 114; BLCS;**
   DAM MULT, POET
   See also AAYA 2; BW 2, 3; CA 33-36R; CANR
   25, 70; CLR 10; DLB 38; MAICYA; MTCW
   1; SATA 4
Jordan, Neil (Patrick) 1950-   **CLC 110**
   See also CA 124; 130; CANR 54; INT 130
Jordan, Pat(rick M.) 1941-   **CLC 37**
   See also CA 33-36R
Jorgensen, Ivar
   See Ellison, Harlan (Jay)
Jorgenson, Ivar
   See Silverberg, Robert
Josephus, Flavius c. 37-100   **CMLC 13**
Josipovici, Gabriel 1940-   **CLC 6, 43**
   See also CA 37-40R; CAAS 8; CANR 47; DLB
   14
Joubert, Joseph 1754-1824   **NCLC 9**
Jouve, Pierre Jean 1887-1976   **CLC 47**
   See also CA 65-68
Jovine, Francesco 1902-1950   **TCLC 79**
Joyce, James (Augustine Aloysius) 1882-1941
   TCLC 3, 8, 16, 35, 52; DA; DAB; DAC;
   DAM MST, NOV, POET; PC 22; SSC 3,
   26; WLC
   See also CA 104; 126; CDBLB 1914-1945;
   DLB 10, 19, 36, 162; MTCW 1, 2
Jozsef, Attila 1905-1937   **TCLC 22**
   See also CA 116
Juana Ines de la Cruz 1651(?)-1695   **LC 5;**
   HLCS 1; PC 24
Judd, Cyril
   See Kornbluth, C(yril) M.; Pohl, Frederik
Julian of Norwich 1342(?)-1416(?)   **LC 6**
   See also DLB 146
Junger, Sebastian 1962-   **CLC 109**
   See also AAYA 28; CA 165
Juniper, Alex
   See Hospital, Janette Turner
Junius
   See Luxemburg, Rosa
Just, Ward (Swift) 1935-   **CLC 4, 27**
   See also CA 25-28R; CANR 32; INT CANR-
   32
Justice, Donald (Rodney) 1925- **CLC 6, 19,**
   102; DAM POET
   See also CA 5-8R; CANR 26, 54, 74; DLBY
   83; INT CANR-26; MTCW 2
Juvenal c. 60-c. 13   **CMLC 8**
   See also Juvenalis, Decimus Junius

See also DLB 211
Juvenalis, Decimus Junius 55(?)-c. 127(?)
   See Juvenal
Juvenis
   See Bourne, Randolph S(illiman)
Kacew, Romain 1914-1980
   See Gary, Romain
   See also CA 108; 102
Kadare, Ismail 1936-   **CLC 52**
   See also CA 161
Kadohata, Cynthia   **CLC 59**
   See also CA 140
Kafka, Franz 1883-1924**TCLC 2, 6, 13, 29, 47,**
   53; DA; DAB; DAC; DAM MST, NOV;
   SSC 5, 29; WLC
   See also CA 105; 126; DLB 81; MTCW 1, 2
Kahanovitsch, Pinkhes
   See Der Nister
Kahn, Roger 1927-   **CLC 30**
   See also CA 25-28R; CANR 44, 69; DLB 171;
   SATA 37
Kain, Saul
   See Sassoon, Siegfried (Lorraine)
Kaiser, Georg 1878-1945   **TCLC 9**
   See also CA 106; DLB 124
Kaletski, Alexander 1946-   **CLC 39**
   See also CA 118; 143
Kalidasa fl. c. 400-   **CMLC 9; PC 22**
Kallman, Chester (Simon) 1921-1975 **CLC 2**
   See also CA 45-48; 53-56; CANR 3
Kaminsky, Melvin 1926-
   See Brooks, Mel
   See also CA 65-68; CANR 16
Kaminsky, Stuart M(elvin) 1934-   **CLC 59**
   See also CA 73-76; CANR 29, 53
Kandinsky, Wassily 1866-1944   **TCLC 92**
   See also CA 118; 155
Kane, Francis
   See Robbins, Harold
Kane, Paul
   See Simon, Paul (Frederick)
Kane, Wilson
   See Bloch, Robert (Albert)
Kanin, Garson 1912-   **CLC 22**
   See also AITN 1; CA 5-8R; CANR 7, 78; DLB
   7
Kaniuk, Yoram 1930-   **CLC 19**
   See also CA 134
Kant, Immanuel 1724-1804   **NCLC 27, 67**
   See also DLB 94
Kantor, MacKinlay 1904-1977   **CLC 7**
   See also CA 61-64; 73-76; CANR 60, 63; DLB
   9, 102; MTCW 2
Kaplan, David Michael 1946-   **CLC 50**
Kaplan, James 1951-   **CLC 59**
   See also CA 135
Karageorge, Michael
   See Anderson, Poul (William)
Karamzin, Nikolai Mikhailovich 1766-1826
   NCLC 3
   See also DLB 150
Karapanou, Margarita 1946-   **CLC 13**
   See also CA 101
Karinthy, Frigyes 1887-1938   **TCLC 47**
   See also CA 170
Karl, Frederick R(obert) 1927-   **CLC 34**
   See also CA 5-8R; CANR 3, 44
Kastel, Warren
   See Silverberg, Robert
Kataev, Evgeny Petrovich 1903-1942
   See Petrov, Evgeny
   See also CA 120
Kataphusin

See Ruskin, John
Katz, Steve 1935-   **CLC 47**
   See also CA 25-28R; CAAS 14, 64; CANR 12;
   DLBY 83
Kauffman, Janet 1945-   **CLC 42**
   See also CA 117; CANR 43; DLBY 86
Kaufman, Bob (Garnell) 1925-1986 **CLC 49**
   See also BW 1; CA 41-44R; 118; CANR 22;
   DLB 16, 41
Kaufman, George S. 1889-1961**CLC 38; DAM**
   DRAM
   See also CA 108; 93-96; DLB 7; INT 108;
   MTCW 2
Kaufman, Sue   **CLC 3, 8**
   See also Barondess, Sue K(aufman)
Kavafis, Konstantinos Petrou 1863-1933
   See Cavafy, C(onstantine) P(eter)
   See also CA 104
Kavan, Anna 1901-1968   **CLC 5, 13, 82**
   See also CA 5-8R; CANR 6, 57; MTCW 1
Kavanagh, Dan
   See Barnes, Julian (Patrick)
Kavanagh, Julie 1952-   **CLC 119**
   See also CA 163
Kavanagh, Patrick (Joseph) 1904-1967 **C L C**
   22
   See also CA 123; 25-28R; DLB 15, 20; MTCW
   1
Kawabata, Yasunari 1899-1972 **CLC 2, 5, 9,**
   18, 107; DAM MULT; SSC 17
   See also CA 93-96; 33-36R; DLB 180; MTCW
   2
Kaye, M(ary) M(argaret) 1909-   **CLC 28**
   See also CA 89-92; CANR 24, 60; MTCW 1,
   2; SATA 62
Kaye, Mollie
   See Kaye, M(ary) M(argaret)
Kaye-Smith, Sheila 1887-1956   **TCLC 20**
   See also CA 118; DLB 36
Kaymor, Patrice Maguilene
   See Senghor, Leopold Sedar
Kazan, Elia 1909-   **CLC 6, 16, 63**
   See also CA 21-24R; CANR 32, 78
Kazantzakis, Nikos 1883(?)-1957 **TCLC 2, 5,**
   33
   See also CA 105; 132; MTCW 1, 2
Kazin, Alfred 1915-1998   **CLC 34, 38, 119**
   See also CA 1-4R; CAAS 7; CANR 1, 45, 79;
   DLB 67
Keane, Mary Nesta (Skrine) 1904-1996
   See Keane, Molly
   See also CA 108; 114; 151
Keane, Molly   **CLC 31**
   See also Keane, Mary Nesta (Skrine)
   See also INT 114
Keates, Jonathan 1946(?)-   **CLC 34**
   See also CA 163
Keaton, Buster 1895-1966   **CLC 20**
Keats, John 1795-1821**NCLC 8, 73; DA; DAB;**
   DAC; DAM MST, POET; PC 1; WLC
   See also CDBLB 1789-1832; DLB 96, 110
Keene, Donald 1922-   **CLC 34**
   See also CA 1-4R; CANR 5
Keillor, Garrison   **CLC 40, 115**
   See also Keillor, Gary (Edward)
   See also AAYA 2; BEST 89:3; DLBY 87; SATA
   58
Keillor, Gary (Edward) 1942-
   See Keillor, Garrison
   See also CA 111; 117; CANR 36, 59; DAM
   POP; MTCW 1, 2
Keith, Michael
   See Hubbard, L(afayette) Ron(ald)

Keller, Gottfried 1819-1890 **NCLC 2; SSC 26**
See also DLB 129

Keller, Nora Okja   **CLC 109**

Kellerman, Jonathan 1949-   **CLC 44; DAM POP**
See also BEST 90:1; CA 106; CANR 29, 51; INT CANR-29

Kelley, William Melvin 1937-   **CLC 22**
See also BW 1; CA 77-80; CANR 27; DLB 33

Kellogg, Marjorie 1922-   **CLC 2**
See also CA 81-84

Kellow, Kathleen
See Hibbert, Eleanor Alice Burford

Kelly, M(ilton) T(erry) 1947-   **CLC 55**
See also CA 97-100; CAAS 22; CANR 19, 43

Kelman, James 1946-   **CLC 58, 86**
See also CA 148; DLB 194

Kemal, Yashar 1923-   **CLC 14, 29**
See also CA 89-92; CANR 44

Kemble, Fanny 1809-1893   **NCLC 18**
See also DLB 32

Kemelman, Harry 1908-1996   **CLC 2**
See also AITN 1; CA 9-12R; 155; CANR 6, 71; DLB 28

Kempe, Margery 1373(?)-1440(?)   **LC 6**
See also DLB 146

Kempis, Thomas a 1380-1471   **LC 11**

Kendall, Henry 1839-1882   **NCLC 12**

Keneally, Thomas (Michael) 1935- **CLC 5, 8, 10, 14, 19, 27, 43, 117; DAM NOV**
See also CA 85-88; CANR 10, 50, 74; MTCW 1, 2

Kennedy, Adrienne (Lita) 1931- **CLC 66; BLC 2; DAM MULT; DC 5**
See also BW 2, 3; CA 103; CAAS 20; CABS 3; CANR 26, 53; DLB 38

Kennedy, John Pendleton 1795-1870 **NCLC 2**
See also DLB 3

Kennedy, Joseph Charles 1929-
See Kennedy, X. J.
See also CA 1-4R; CANR 4, 30, 40; SATA 14, 86

Kennedy, William 1928- **CLC 6, 28, 34, 53; DAM NOV**
See also AAYA 1; CA 85-88; CANR 14, 31, 76; DLB 143; DLBY 85; INT CANR-31; MTCW 1, 2; SATA 57

Kennedy, X. J.   **CLC 8, 42**
<indeSee also Kennedy, Joseph Charles
See also CAAS 9; CLR 27; DLB 5; SAAS 22

Kenny, Maurice (Francis) 1929-   **CLC 87; DAM MULT**
See also CA 144; CAAS 22; DLB 175; NNAL

Kent, Kelvin
See Kuttner, Henry

Kenton, Maxwell
See Southern, Terry

Kenyon, Robert O.
See Kuttner, Henry

Kepler, Johannes 1571-1630   **LC 45**

Kerouac, Jack   **CLC 1, 2, 3, 5, 14, 29, 61**
See also Kerouac, Jean-Louis Lebris de
See also AAYA 25; CDALB 1941-1968; DLB 2, 16; DLBD 3; DLBY 95; MTCW 2

Kerouac, Jean-Louis Lebris de 1922-1969
See Kerouac, Jack
See also AITN 1; CA 5-8R; 25-28R; CANR 26, 54; DA; DAB; DAC; DAM MST, NOV, POET, POP; MTCW 1, 2; WLC

Kerr, Jean 1923-   **CLC 22**
See also CA 5-8R; CANR 7; INT CANR-7

Kerr, M. E.   **CLC 12, 35**
See also Meaker, Marijane (Agnes)

See also AAYA 2, 23; CLR 29; SAAS 1

Kerr, Robert   **CLC 55**

Kerrigan, (Thomas) Anthony 1918- **CLC 4, 6**
See also CA 49-52; CAAS 11; CANR 4

Kerry, Lois
See Duncan, Lois

Kesey, Ken (Elton) 1935- **CLC 1, 3, 6, 11, 46, 64; DA; DAB; DAC; DAM MST, NOV, POP; WLC**
See also AAYA 25; CA 1-4R; CANR 22, 38, 66; CDALB 1968-1988; DLB 2, 16, 206; MTCW 1, 2; SATA 66

Kesselring, Joseph (Otto) 1902-1967 **CLC 45; DAM DRAM, MST**
See also CA 150

<indexbKessler, Jascha (Frederick)** 1929- **CLC 4**
See also CA 17-20R; CANR 8, 48

Kettelkamp, Larry (Dale) 1933-   **CLC 12**
See also CA 29-32R; CANR 16; SAAS 3; SATA 2

Key, Ellen 1849-1926   **TCLC 65**

Keyber, Conny
See Fielding, Henry

Keyes, Daniel 1927- **CLC 80; DA; DAC; DAM MST, NOV**
See also AAYA 23; CA 17-20R; CANR 10, 26, 54, 74; MTCW 2; SATA 37

Keynes, John Maynard 1883-1946 **TCLC 64**
See also CA 114; 162, 163; DLBD 10; MTCW 2

Khanshendel, Chiron
See Rose, Wendy

Khayyam, Omar 1048-1131 **CMLC 11; DAM POET; PC 8**

Kherdian, David 1931-   **CLC 6, 9**
See also CA 21-24R; CAAS 2; CANR 39, 78; CLR 24; JRDA; MAICYA; SATA 16, 74

Khlebnikov, Velimir   **TCLC 20**
See also Khlebnikov, Viktor Vladimirovich

Khlebnikov, Viktor Vladimirovich 1885-1922
See Khlebnikov, Velimir
See also CA 117

Khodasevich, Vladislav (Felitsianovich) 1886-1939   **TCLC 15**
See also CA 115

Kielland, Alexander Lange 1849-1906 **TCLC 5**
See also CA 104

Kiely, Benedict 1919-   **CLC 23, 43**
See also CA 1-4R; CANR 2; DLB 15

Kienzle, William X(avier) 1928-   **CLC 25; DAM POP**
See also CA 93-96; CAAS 1; CANR 9, 31, 59; INT CANR-31; MTCW 1, 2

Kierkegaard, Soren 1813-1855   **NCLC 34**

Kieslowski, Krzysztof 1941-1996   **CLC 120**
See also CA 147; 151

Killens, John Oliver 1916-1987   **CLC 10**
See also BW 2; CA 77-80; 123; CAAS 2; CANR 26; DLB 33

Killigrew, Anne 1660-1685   **LC 4**
See also DLB 131

Kim
See Simenon, Georges (Jacques Christian)

Kincaid, Jamaica 1949- **CLC 43, 68; BLC 2; DAM MULT, NOV**
See also AAYA 13; BW 2, 3; CA 125; CANR 47, 59; CDALBS; DLB 157; MTCW 2

King, Francis (Henry) 1923- **CLC 8, 53; DAM NOV**
See also CA 1-4R; CANR 1, 33; DLB 15, 139; MTCW 1

King, Kennedy
See Brown, George Douglas

<indexboKing, Martin Luther, Jr.** 1929-1968 **CLC 83; BLC 2; DA; DAB; DAC; DAM MST, MULT; WLCS**
See also BW 2, 3; CA 25-28; CANR 27, 44; CAP 2; MTCW 1, 2; SATA 14

King, Stephen (Edwin) 1947- **CLC 12, 26, 37, 61, 113; DAM NOV, POP; SSC 17**
See also AAYA 1, 17; BEST 90:1; CA 61-64; CANR 1, 30, 52, 76; DLB 143; DLBY 80; JRDA; MTCW 1, 2; SATA 9, 55

King, Steve
See King, Stephen (Edwin)

King, Thomas 1943-   **CLC 89; DAC; DAM MULT**
See also CA 144; DLB 175; NNAL; SATA 96

Kingman, Lee   **CLC 17**
See also Natti, (Mary) Lee
See also SAAS 3; SATA 1, 67

Kingsley, Charles 1819-1875   **NCLC 35**
See also DLB 21, 32, 163, 190; YABC 2

Kingsley, Sidney 1906-1995   **CLC 44**
See also CA 85-88; 147; DLB 7

Kingsolver, Barbara 1955- **CLC 55, 81; DAM POP**
See also AAYA 15; CA 129; 134; CANR 60; CDALBS; DLB 206; INT 134; MTCW 2

Kingston, Maxine (Ting Ting) Hong 1940- **CLC 12, 19, 58; DAM MULT, NOV; WLCS**
See also AAYA 8; CA 69-72; CANR 13, 38, 74; CDALBS; DLB 173, 212; DLBY 80; INT CANR-13; MTCW 1, 2; SATA 53

Kinnell, Galway 1927- **CLC 1, 2, 3, 5, 13, 29; PC 26**
See also CA 9-12R; CANR 10, 34, 66; DLB 5; DLBY 87; INT CANR-34; MTCW 1, 2

Kinsella, Thomas 1928-   **CLC 4, 19**
See also CA 17-20R; CANR 15; DLB 27; MTCW 1, 2

Kinsella, W(illiam) P(atrick) 1935- **CLC 27, 43; DAC; DAM NOV, POP**
See also AAYA 7; CA 97-100; CAAS 7; CANR 21, 35, 66, 75; INT CANR-21; MTCW 1, 2

Kinsey, Alfred C(harles) 1894-1956 **TCLC 91**
See also CA 115; 170; MTCW 2

Kipling, (Joseph) Rudyard 1865-1936 **TCLC 8, 17; DA; DAB; DAC; DAM MST, POET; PC 3; SSC 5; WLC**
See also CA 105; 120; CANR 33; CDBLB 1890-1914; CLR 39; DLB 19, 34, 141, 156; MAICYA; MTCW 1, 2; SATA 100; YABC 2

Kirkup, James 1918-   **CLC 1**
See also CA 1-4R; CAAS 4; CANR 2; DLB 27; SATA 12

Kirkwood, James 1930(?)-1989   **CLC 9**
See also AITN 2; CA 1-4R; 128; CANR 6, 40

Kirshner, Sidney
See Kingsley, Sidney

Kis, Danilo 1935-1989   **CLC 57**
See also CA 109; 118; 129; CANR 61; DLB 181; MTCW 1

Kivi, Aleksis 1834-1872   **NCLC 30**

Kizer, Carolyn (Ashley) 1925- **CLC 15, 39, 80; DAM POET**
See also CA 65-68; CAAS 5; CANR 24, 70; DLB 5, 169; MTCW 2

Klabund 1890-1928   **TCLC 44**
See also CA 162; DLB 66

Klappert, Peter 1942-   **CLC 57**
See also CA 33-36R; DLB 5

Klein, A(braham) M(oses) 1909-1972 **CLC 19;**

DAB; DAC; DAM MST
See also CA 101; 37-40R; DLB 68
Klein, Norma 1938-1989 **CLC 30**
See also AAYA 2; CA 41-44R; 128; CANR 15,
37; CLR 2, 19; INT CANR-15; JRDA;
MAICYA; SAAS 1; SATA 7, 57
Klein, T(heodore) E(ibon) D(onald) 1947-
CLC 34
See also CA 119; CANR 44, 75
Kleist, Heinrich von 1777-1811 **NCLC 2, 37;
DAM DRAM; SSC 22**
See also DLB 90
Klima, Ivan 1931- **CLC 56; DAM NOV**
See also CA 25-28R; CANR 17, 50
Klimentov, Andrei Platonovich 1899-1951
See Platonov, Andrei
See also CA 108
Klinger, Friedrich Maximilian von 1752-1831
NCLC 1
See also DLB 94
Klingsor the Magician
See Hartmann, Sadakichi
Klopstock, Friedrich Gottlieb 1724-1803
NCLC 11
See also DLB 97
Knapp, Caroline 1959- **CLC 99**
See also CA 154
Knebel, Fletcher 1911-1993 **CLC 14**
<indexSee also AITN 1; CA 1-4R; 140; CAAS 3;
CANR 1, 36; SATA 36; SATA-Obit 75
Knickerbocker, Diedrich
See Irving, Washington
Knight, Etheridge 1931-1991**CLC 40; BLC 2;
DAM POET; PC 14**
See also BW 1, 3; CA 21-24R; 133; CANR 23;
DLB 41; MTCW 2
Knight, Sarah Kemble 1666-1727 **LC 7**
See also DLB 24, 200
Knister, Raymond 1899-1932 **TCLC 56**
See also DLB 68
Knowles, John 1926- **CLC 1, 4, 10, 26; DA;
DAC; DAM MST, NOV**
See also AAYA 10; CA 17-20R; CANR 40, 74,
76; CDALB 1968-1988; DLB 6; MTCW 1,
2; SATA 8, 89
Knox, Calvin M.
See Silverberg, Robert
Knox, John c. 1505-1572 **LC 37**
See also DLB 132
<Knye, Cassandra
See Disch, Thomas M(ichael)
Koch, C(hristopher) J(ohn) 1932- **CLC 42**
See also CA 127
Koch, Christopher
See Koch, C(hristopher) J(ohn)
Koch, Kenneth 1925- **CLC 5, 8, 44; DAM
POET**
See also CA 1-4R; CANR 6, 36, 57; DLB 5;
INT CANR-36; MTCW 2; SATA 65
Kochanowski, Jan 1530-1584 **LC 10**
Kock, Charles Paul de 1794-1871 **NCLC 16**
Koda Shigeyuki 1867-1947
See Rohan, Koda
See also CA 121
Koestler, Arthur 1905-1983**CLC 1, 3, 6, 8, 15,
33**
See also CA 1-4R; 109; CANR 1, 33; CDBLB
1945-1960; DLBY 83; MTCW 1, 2
Kogawa, Joy Nozomi 1935- **CLC 78; DAC;
DAM MST, MULT**
See also CA 101; CANR 19, 62; MTCW 2;
SATA 99
Kohout, Pavel 1928- **CLC 13**

See also CA 45-48; CANR 3
Koizumi, Yakumo
See Hearn, (Patricio) Lafcadio (Tessima Carlos)
Kolmar, Gertrud 1894-1943 **TCLC 40**
See also CA 167
Komunyakaa, Yusef 1947-**CLC 86, 94; BLCS**
See also CA 147; DLB 120
Konrad, George
See Konrad, Gyoergy
Konrad, Gyoergy 1933- **CLC 4, 10, 73**
See also CA 85-88
Konwicki, Tadeusz 1926- **CLC 8, 28, 54, 117**
See also CA 101; CAAS 9; CANR 39, 59;
MTCW 1
Koontz, Dean R(ay) 1945- **CLC 78; DAM
NOV, POP**
See also AAYA 9; BEST 89:3, 90:2; CA 108;
CANR 19, 36, 52; MTCW 1; SATA 92
Kopernik, Mikolaj
See Copernicus, Nicolaus
Kopit, Arthur (Lee) 1937-**CLC 1, 18, 33; DAM
DRAM**
See also AITN 1; CA 81-84; CABS 3; DLB 7;
MTCW 1
Kops, Bernard 1926- **CLC 4**
See also CA 5-8R; DLB 13
Kornbluth, C(yril) M. 1923-1958 **TCLC 8**
See also CA 105; 160; DLB 8
Korolenko, V. G.
See Korolenko, Vladimir Galaktionovich
Korolenko, Vladimir
See Korolenko, Vladimir Galaktionovich
Korolenko, Vladimir G.
See Korolenko, Vladimir Galaktionovich
Korolenko, Vladimir Galaktionovich 1853-
1921 **TCLC 22**
See also CA 121
Korzybski, Alfred (Habdank Skarbek) 1879-
1950 **TCLC 61**
See also CA 123; 160
Kosinski, Jerzy (Nikodem) 1933-1991**CLC 1,
2, 3, 6, 10, 15, 53, 70; DAM NOV**
See also CA 17-20R; 134; CANR 9, 46; DLB
2; DLBY 82; MTCW 1, 2
Kostelanetz, Richard (Cory) 1940- **CLC 28**
See also CA 13-16R; CAAS 8; CANR 38, 77
Kostrowitzki, Wilhelm Apollinaris de 1880-
1918
See Apollinaire, Guillaume
See also CA 104
Kotlowitz, Robert 1924- **CLC 4**
See also CA 33-36R; CANR 36
Kotzebue, August (Friedrich Ferdinand) von
1761-1819 **NCLC 25**
See also DLB 94
<inKotzwinkle, William 1938-**CLC 5, 14, 35**
See also CA 45-48; CANR 3, 44; CLR 6; DLB
173; MAICYA; SATA 24, 70
Kowna, Stancy
See Szymborska, Wislawa
Kozol, Jonathan 1936- **CLC 17**
See also CA 61-64; CANR 16, 45
Kozoll, Michael 1940(?)- **CLC 35**
Kramer, Kathryn 19(?)- **CLC 34**
Kramer, Larry 1935-**CLC 42; DAM POP; DC
8**
See also CA 124; 126; CANR 60
Krasicki, Ignacy 1735-1801 **NCLC 8**
Krasinski, Zygmunt 1812-1859 **NCLC 4**
Kraus, Karl 1874-1936 **TCLC 5**
See also CA 104; DLB 118
Kreve (Mickevicius), Vincas 1882-1954**TCLC
27**

See also CA 170
Kristeva, Julia 1941- **CLC 77**
See also CA 154
Kristofferson, Kris 1936- **CLC 26**
See also CA 104
Krizanc, John 1956- **CLC 57**
Krleza, Miroslav 1893-1981 **CLC 8, 114**
See also CA 97-100; 105; CANR 50; DLB 147
Kroetsch, Robert 1927- **CLC 5, 23, 57; DAC;
DAM POET**
See also CA 17-20R; CANR 8, 38; DLB 53;
MTCW 1
Kroetz, Franz
See Kroetz, Franz Xaver
Kroetz, Franz Xaver 1946- **CLC 41**
See also CA 130
Kroker, Arthur (W.) 1945- **CLC 77**
<See also CA 161
Kropotkin, Peter (Alekseevich) 1842-1921
TCLC 36
See also CA 119
Krotkov, Yuri 1917- **CLC 19**
See also CA 102
Krumb
See Crumb, R(obert)
Krumgold, Joseph (Quincy) 1908-1980 **C L C
12**
See also CA 9-12R; 101; CANR 7; MAICYA;
SATA 1, 48; SATA-Obit 23
Krumwitz
See Crumb, R(obert)
Krutch, Joseph Wood 1893-1970 **CLC 24**
See also CA 1-4R; 25-28R; CANR 4; DLB 63,
206
Krutzch, Gus
See Eliot, T(homas) S(tearns)
Krylov, Ivan Andreevich 1768(?)-1844**N C L C
1**
See also DLB 150
Kubin, Alfred (Leopold Isidor) 1877-1959
TCLC 23
See also CA 112; 149; DLB 81
Kubrick, Stanley 1928- **CLC 16**
See also AAYA 30; CA 81-84; CANR 33; DLB
26
Kumin, Maxine (Winokur) 1925- **CLC 5, 13,
28; DAM POET; PC 15**
See also AITN 2; CA 1-4R; CAAS 8; CANR 1,
21, 69; DLB 5; MTCW 1, 2; SATA 12
Kundera, Milan 1929- **CLC 4, 9, 19, 32, 68,
115; DAM NOV; SSC 24**
See also AAYA 2; CA 85-88; CANR 19, 52,
74; MTCW 1, 2
Kunene, Mazisi (Raymond) 1930- **CLC 85**
See also BW 1, 3; CA 125; DLB 117
Kunitz, Stanley (Jasspon) 1905-**CLC 6, 11, 14;
PC 19**
See also CA 41-44R; CANR 26, 57; DLB 48;
INT CANR-26; MTCW 1, 2
Kunze, Reiner 1933- **CLC 10**
See also CA 93-96; DLB 75
Kuprin, Aleksandr Ivanovich 1870-1938
TCLC 5
See also CA 104
Kureishi, Hanif 1954(?)- **CLC 64**
See also CA 139; DLB 194
Kurosawa, Akira 1910-1998 **CLC 16, 119;
DAM MULT**
See also AAYA 11; CA 101; 170; CANR 46
Kushner, Tony 1957(?)-**CLC 81; DAM DRAM;
DC 10**
See also CA 144; CANR 74; MTCW 2
Kuttner, Henry 1915-1958 **TCLC 10**

See also Vance, Jack
See also CA 107; 157; DLB 8
Kuzma, Greg 1944-   **CLC 7**
See also CA 33-36R; CANR 70
Kuzmin, Mikhail 1872(?)-1936   **TCLC 40**
See also CA 170
Kyd, Thomas 1558-1594**LC 22; DAM DRAM;**
DC 3
See also DLB 62
Kyprianos, Iossif
See Samarakis, Antonis
La Bruyere, Jean de 1645-1696   **LC 17**
Lacan, Jacques (Marie Emile) 1901-1981
CLC 75
See also CA 121; 104
Laclos, Pierre Ambroise Francois Choderlos de
1741-1803   **NCLC 4**
La Colere, Francois
See Aragon, Louis
Lacolere, Francois
See Aragon, Louis
La Deshabilleuse
See Simenon, Georges (Jacques Christian)
Lady Gregory
See Gregory, Isabella Augusta (Persse)
Lady of Quality, A
See Bagnold, Enid
La Fayette, Marie (Madelaine Pioche de la
Vergne Comtes 1634-1693   **LC 2**
Lafayette, Rene
See Hubbard, L(afayette) Ron(ald)
Laforgue, Jules 1860-1887**NCLC 5, 53; PC 14;**
SSC 20
Lagerkvist, Paer (Fabian) 1891-1974 **CLC 7,**
10, 13, 54; DAM DRAM, NOV
See also Lagerkvist, Par
See also CA 85-88; 49-52; MTCW 1, 2
Lagerkvist, Par   **SSC 12**
See also Lagerkvist, Paer (Fabian)
See also MTCW 2
Lagerloef, Selma (Ottiliana Lovisa) 1858-1940
TCLC 4, 36
See also Lagerlof, Selma (Ottiliana Lovisa)
See also CA 108; MTCW 2; SATA 15
Lagerlof, Selma (Ottiliana Lovisa)
See Lagerloef, Selma (Ottiliana Lovisa)
See also CLR 7; SATA 15
La Guma, (Justin) Alex(ander) 1925-1985
CLC 19; BLCS; DAM NOV
See also BW 1, 3; CA 49-52; 118; CANR 25;
DLB 117; MTCW 1, 2
Laidlaw, A. K.
See Grieve, C(hristopher) M(urray)
Lainez, Manuel Mujica
See Mujica Lainez, Manuel
See also HW 1
Laing, R(onald) D(avid) 1927-1989   **CLC 95**
See also CA 107; 129; CANR 34; MTCW 1
Lamartine, Alphonse (Marie Louis Prat) de
1790-1869**NCLC 11; DAM POET; PC 16**
Lamb, Charles 1775-1834   **NCLC 10; DA;**
DAB; DAC; DAM MST; WLC
See also CDBLB 1789-1832; DLB 93, 107, 163;
SATA 17
Lamb, Lady Caroline 1785-1828   **NCLC 38**
See also DLB 116
Lamming, George (William) 1927- **CLC 2, 4,**
66; BLC 2; DAM MULT
See also BW 2, 3; CA 85-88; CANR 26, 76;
DLB 125; MTCW 1, 2
L'Amour, Louis (Dearborn) 1908-1988 **C L C**
25, 55; DAM NOV, POP
See also AAYA 16; AITN 2; BEST 89:2; CA 1-

4R; 125; CANR 3, 25, 40; DLB 206; DLBY
80; MTCW 1, 2
Lampedusa, Giuseppe (Tomasi) di 1896-1957
TCLC 13
See also Tomasi di Lampedusa, Giuseppe
See also CA 164; DLB 177; MTCW 2
Lampman, Archibald 1861-1899   **NCLC 25**
See also DLB 92
Lancaster, Bruce 1896-1963   **CLC 36**
See also CA 9-10; CANR 70; CAP 1; SATA 9
Lanchester, John   **CLC 99**
Landau, Mark Alexandrovich
See Aldanov, Mark (Alexandrovich)
Landau-Aldanov, Mark Alexandrovich
See Aldanov, Mark (Alexandrovich)
Landis, Jerry
See Simon, Paul (Frederick)
Landis, John 1950-   **CLC 26**
See also CA 112; 122
Landolfi, Tommaso 1908-1979   **CLC 11, 49**
See also CA 127; 117; DLB 177
Landon, Letitia Elizabeth 1802-1838 **N C L C**
15
See also DLB 96
Landor, Walter Savage 1775-1864 **NCLC 14**
See also DLB 93, 107
Landwirth, Heinz 1927-
See Lind, Jakov
See also CA 9-12R; CANR 7
Lane, Patrick 1939-   **CLC 25; DAM POET**
See also CA 97-100; CANR 54; DLB 53; INT
97-100
Lang, Andrew 1844-1912   **TCLC 16**
See also CA 114; 137; DLB 98, 141, 184;
MAICYA; SATA 16
Lang, Fritz 1890-1976   **CLC 20, 103**
See also CA 77-80; 69-72; CANR 30
Lange, John
See Crichton, (John) Michael
Langer, Elinor 1939-   **CLC 34**
See also CA 121
Langland, William 1330(?)-1400(?)   **LC 19;**
DA; DAB; DAC; DAM MST, POET
See also DLB 146
Langstaff, Launcelot
See Irving, Washington
Lanier, Sidney 1842-1881   **NCLC 6; DAM**
POET
See also DLB 64; DLBD 13; MAICYA; SATA
18
Lanyer, Aemilia 1569-1645   **LC 10, 30**
See also DLB 121
Lao-Tzu
See Lao Tzu
Lao Tzu fl. 6th cent. B.C.-   **CMLC 7**
Lapine, James (Elliot) 1949-   **CLC 39**
See also CA 123; 130; CANR 54; INT 130
Larbaud, Valery (Nicolas) 1881-1957**TCLC 9**
See also CA 106; 152
Lardner, Ring
See Lardner, Ring(gold) W(ilmer)
Lardner, Ring W., Jr.
See Lardner, Ring(gold) W(ilmer)
Lardner, Ring(gold) W(ilmer) 1885-1933
TCLC 2, 14; SSC 32
See also CA 104; 131; CDALB 1917-1929;
DLB 11, 25, 86; DLBD 16; MTCW 1, 2
Laredo, Betty
See Codrescu, Andrei
Larkin, Maia
See Wojciechowska, Maia (Teresa)
Larkin, Philip (Arthur) 1922-1985**CLC 3, 5, 8,**
9, 13, 18, 33, 39, 64; DAB; DAM MST,

POET; PC 21
See also CA 5-8R; 117; CANR 24, 62; CDBLB
1960 to Present; DLB 27; MTCW 1, 2
Larra (y Sanchez de Castro), Mariano Jose de
1809-1837   **NCLC 17**
Larsen, Eric 1941-   **CLC 55**
See also CA 132
Larsen, Nella 1891-1964   **CLC 37; BLC 2;**
DAM MULT
See also BW 1; CA 125; DLB 51
Larson, Charles R(aymond) 1938-   **CLC 31**
See also CA 53-56; CANR 4
Larson, Jonathan 1961-1996   **CLC 99**
See also AAYA 28; CA 156
Las Casas, Bartolome de 1474-1566   **LC 31**
Lasch, Christopher 1932-1994   **CLC 102**
See also CA 73-76; 144; CANR 25; MTCW 1,
2
Lasker-Schueler, Else 1869-1945   **TCLC 57**
See also DLB 66, 124
Laski, Harold 1893-1950   **TCLC 79**
Latham, Jean Lee 1902-1995   **CLC 12**
See also AITN 1; CA 5-8R; CANR 7; CLR 50;
MAICYA; SATA 2, 68
Latham, Mavis
See Clark, Mavis Thorpe
Lathen, Emma   **CLC 2**
See also Hennissart, Martha; Latsis, Mary J(ane)
Lathrop, Francis
See Leiber, Fritz (Reuter, Jr.)
Latsis, Mary J(ane) 1927(?)-1997
See Lathen, Emma
See also CA 85-88; 162
Lattimore, Richmond (Alexander) 1906-1984
CLC 3
See also CA 1-4R; 112; CANR 1
Laughlin, James 1914-1997   **CLC 49**
See also CA 21-24R; 162; CAAS 22; CANR 9,
47; DLB 48; DLBY 96, 97
Laurence, (Jean) Margaret (Wemyss) 1926-
1987 **CLC 3, 6, 13, 50, 62; DAC; DAM**
MST; SSC 7
See also CA 5-8R; 121; CANR 33; DLB 53;
MTCW 1, 2; SATA-Obit 50
Laurent, Antoine 1952-   **CLC 50**
Lauscher, Hermann
See Hesse, Hermann
Lautreamont, Comte de 1846-1870**NCLC 12;**
SSC 14
Laverty, Donald
See Blish, James (Benjamin)
Lavin, Mary 1912-1996**CLC 4, 18, 99; SSC 4**
See also CA 9-12R; 151; CANR 33; DLB 15;
MTCW 1
Lavond, Paul Dennis
See Kornbluth, C(yril) M.; Pohl, Frederik
Lawler, Raymond Evenor 1922-   **CLC 58**
See also CA 103
Lawrence, D(avid) H(erbert Richards) 1885-
1930 **TCLC 2, 9, 16, 33, 48, 61, 93; DA;**
DAB; DAC; DAM MST, NOV, POET; SSC
4, 19; WLC
See also CA 104; 121; CDBLB 1914-1945;
DLB 10, 19, 36, 98, 162, 195; MTCW 1, 2
Lawrence, T(homas) E(dward) 1888-1935
TCLC 18
See also Dale, Colin
See also CA 115; 167; DLB 195
Lawrence of Arabia
See Lawrence, T(homas) E(dward)
Lawson, Henry (Archibald Hertzberg) 1867-
1922   **TCLC 27; SSC 18**
See also CA 120

Lawton, Dennis
  See Faust, Frederick (Schiller)
Laxness, Halldor   **CLC 25**
  See also Gudjonsson, Halldor Kiljan
Layamon fl. c. 1200-   **CMLC 10**
  See also DLB 146
Laye, Camara 1928-1980 **CLC 4, 38; BLC 2;**
    DAM MULT
  See also BW 1; CA 85-88; 97-100; CANR 25;
    MTCW 1, 2
Layton, Irving (Peter) 1912-**CLC 2, 15; DAC;**
    DAM MST, POET
  See also CA 1-4R; CANR 2, 33, 43, 66; DLB
    88; MTCW 1, 2
Lazarus, Emma 1849-1887   **NCLC 8**
Lazarus, Felix
  See Cable, George Washington
Lazarus, Henry
  See Slavitt, David R(ytman)
Lea, Joan
  See Neufeld, John (Arthur)
Leacock, Stephen (Butler) 1869-1944**TCLC 2;**
    DAC; DAM MST
  See also CA 104; 141; CANR 80; DLB 92;
    MTCW 2
Lear, Edward 1812-1888   **NCLC 3**
  See also CLR 1; DLB 32, 163, 166; MAICYA;
    SATA 18, 100
Lear, Norman (Milton) 1922-   **CLC 12**
  See also CA 73-76
Leautaud, Paul 1872-1956   **TCLC 83**
  See also DLB 65
Leavis, F(rank) R(aymond) 1895-1978**CLC 24**
  See also CA 21-24R; 77-80; CANR 44; MTCW
    1, 2
Leavitt, David 1961-   **CLC 34; DAM POP**
  See also CA 116; 122; CANR 50, 62; DLB 130;
    INT 122; MTCW 2
Leblanc, Maurice (Marie Emile) 1864-1941
    TCLC 49
  See also CA 110
Lebowitz, Fran(ces Ann) 1951(?)-**CLC 11, 36**
  See also CA 81-84; CANR 14, 60, 70; INT
    CANR-14; MTCW 1
Lebrecht, Peter
  See Tieck, (Johann) Ludwig
le Carre, John   **CLC 3, 5, 9, 15, 28**
  See also Cornwell, David (John Moore)
  See also BEST 89:4; CDBLB 1960 to Present;
    DLB 87; MTCW 2
Le Clezio, J(ean) M(arie) G(ustave) 1940-
    CLC 31
  See also CA 116; 128; DLB 83
Leconte de Lisle, Charles-Marie-Rene 1818-
    1894   **NCLC 29**
Le Coq, Monsieur
  See Simenon, Georges (Jacques Christian)
Leduc, Violette 1907-1972   **CLC 22**
  See also CA 13-14; 33-36R; CANR 69; CAP 1
Ledwidge, Francis 1887(?)-1917   **TCLC 23**
  See also CA 123; DLB 20
Lee, Andrea 1953-   **CLC 36; BLC 2; DAM**
    MULT
  See also BW 1, 3; CA 125
Lee, Andrew
  See Auchincloss, Louis (Stanton)
Lee, Chang-rae 1965-   **CLC 91**
  See also CA 148
Lee, Don L.   **CLC 2**
  See also Madhubuti, Haki R.
Lee, George W(ashington) 1894-1976**CLC 52;**
    BLC 2; DAM MULT
  See also BW 1; CA 125; DLB 51

Lee, (Nelle) Harper 1926-   **CLC 12, 60; DA;**
    DAB; DAC; DAM MST, NOV; WLC
  See also AAYA 13; CA 13-16R; CANR 51;
    CDALB 1941-1968; DLB 6; MTCW 1, 2;
    SATA 11
Lee, Helen Elaine 1959(?)-   **CLC 86**
  See also CA 148
Lee, Julian
  See Latham, Jean Lee
Lee, Larry
  See Lee, Lawrence
Lee, Laurie 1914-1997   **CLC 90; DAB; DAM**
    POP
  See also CA 77-80; 158; CANR 33, 73; DLB
    27; MTCW 1
Lee, Lawrence 1941-1990   **CLC 34**
  See also CA 131; CANR 43
Lee, Li-Young 1957-   **PC 24**
  See also CA 153; DLB 165
Lee, Manfred B(ennington) 1905-1971**CLC 11**
  See also Queen, Ellery
  See also CA 1-4R; 29-32R; CANR 2; DLB 137
Lee, Shelton Jackson 1957(?)-   **CLC 105;**
    BLCS; DAM MULT
  See also Lee, Spike
  See also BW 2, 3; CA 125; CANR 42
Lee, Spike
  See Lee, Shelton Jackson
  See also AAYA 4, 29
Lee, Stan 1922-   **CLC 17**
  See also AAYA 5; CA 108; 111; INT 111
Lee, Tanith 1947-   **CLC 46**
  See also AAYA 15; CA 37-40R; CANR 53;
    SATA 8, 88
Lee, Vernon   **TCLC 5; SSC 33**
  See also Paget, Violet
  See also DLB 57, 153, 156, 174, 178
Lee, William
  See Burroughs, William S(eward)
Lee, Willy
  See Burroughs, William S(eward)
Lee-Hamilton, Eugene (Jacob) 1845-1907
    TCLC 22
  See also CA 117
Leet, Judith 1935-   **CLC 11**
Le Fanu, Joseph Sheridan 1814-1873**NCLC 9,**
    58; DAM POP; SSC 14
  See also DLB 21, 70, 159, 178
Leffland, Ella 1931-   **CLC 19**
  See also CA 29-32R; CANR 35, 78; DLBY 84;
    INT CANR-35; SATA 65
Leger, Alexis
  See Leger, (Marie-Rene Auguste) Alexis Saint-
    Leger
Leger, (Marie-Rene Auguste) Alexis Saint-
    Leger 1887-1975   **CLC 4, 11, 46; DAM**
    POET; PC 23
  See also CA 13-16R; 61-64; CANR 43; MTCW
    1
Leger, Saintleger
  See Leger, (Marie-Rene Auguste) Alexis Saint-
    Leger
Le Guin, Ursula K(roeber) 1929- **CLC 8, 13,**
    22, 45, 71; DAB; DAC; DAM MST, POP;
    SSC 12
  See also AAYA 9, 27; AITN 1; CA 21-24R;
    CANR 9, 32, 52, 74; CDALB 1968-1988;
    CLR 3, 28; DLB 8, 52; INT CANR-32;
    JRDA; MAICYA; MTCW 1, 2; SATA 4, 52,
    99
Lehmann, Rosamond (Nina) 1901-1990**CLC 5**
  See also CA 77-80; 131; CANR 8, 73; DLB 15;
    MTCW 2

Leiber, Fritz (Reuter, Jr.) 1910-1992 **CLC 25**
  See also CA 45-48; 139; CANR 2, 40; DLB 8;
    MTCW 1, 2; SATA 45; SATA-Obit 73
Leibniz, Gottfried Wilhelm von 1646-1716**LC**
    35
  See also DLB 168
Leimbach, Martha 1963-
  See Leimbach, Marti
  See also CA 130
Leimbach, Marti   **CLC 65**
  See also Leimbach, Martha
Leino, Eino   **TCLC 24**
  See also Loennbohm, Armas Eino Leopold
Leiris, Michel (Julien) 1901-1990   **CLC 61**
  See also CA 119; 128; 132
Leithauser, Brad 1953-   **CLC 27**
  See also CA 107; CANR 27; DLB 120
Lelchuk, Alan 1938-   **CLC 5**
  See also CA 45-48; CAAS 20; CANR 1, 70
Lem, Stanislaw 1921-   **CLC 8, 15, 40**
  See also CA 105; CAAS 1; CANR 32; MTCW
    1
Lemann, Nancy 1956-   **CLC 39**
  See also CA 118; 136
Lemonnier, (Antoine Louis) Camille 1844-1913
    TCLC 22
  See also CA 121
Lenau, Nikolaus 1802-1850   **NCLC 16**
L'Engle, Madeleine (Camp Franklin) 1918-
    CLC 12; DAM POP
  See also AAYA 28; AITN 2; CA 1-4R; CANR
    3, 21, 39, 66; CLR 1, 14, 57; DLB 52; JRDA;
    MAICYA; MTCW 1, 2; SAAS 15; SATA 1,
    27, 75
Lengyel, Jozsef 1896-1975   **CLC 7**
  See also CA 85-88; 57-60; CANR 71
Lenin 1870-1924
  See Lenin, V. I.
  See also CA 121; 168
Lenin, V. I.   **TCLC 67**
  See also Lenin
Lennon, John (Ono) 1940-1980   **CLC 12, 35**
  See also CA 102
Lennox, Charlotte Ramsay 1729(?)-1804
    NCLC 23
  See also DLB 39
Lentricchia, Frank (Jr.) 1940-   **CLC 34**
  See also CA 25-28R; CANR 19
Lenz, Siegfried 1926-   **CLC 27; SSC 33**
  See also CA 89-92; CANR 80; DLB 75
Leonard, Elmore (John, Jr.) 1925-**CLC 28, 34,**
    71, 120; DAM POP
  See also AAYA 22; AITN 1; BEST 89:1, 90:4;
    CA 81-84; CANR 12, 28, 53, 76; DLB 173;
    INT CANR-28; MTCW 1, 2
Leonard, Hugh   **CLC 19**
  See also Byrne, John Keyes
  See also DLB 13
Leonov, Leonid (Maximovich) 1899-1994
    CLC 92; DAM NOV
  See also CA 129; CANR 74, 76; MTCW 1, 2
Leopardi, (Conte) Giacomo 1798-1837**NCLC**
    22
Le Reveler
  See Artaud, Antonin (Marie Joseph)
Lerman, Eleanor 1952-   **CLC 9**
  See also CA 85-88; CANR 69
Lerman, Rhoda 1936-   **CLC 56**
  See also CA 49-52; CANR 70
Lermontov, Mikhail Yuryevich 1814-1841
    NCLC 47; PC 18
  See also DLB 205
Leroux, Gaston 1868-1927   **TCLC 25**

See also CA 108; 136; CANR 69; SATA 65
Lesage, Alain-Rene 1668-1747   **LC 2, 28**
Leskov, Nikolai (Semyonovich) 1831-1895
      NCLC 25; SSC 34
Lessing, Doris (May) 1919-**CLC 1, 2, 3, 6, 10,**
      15, 22, 40, 94; DA; DAB; DAC; DAM MST,
      NOV; SSC 6; WLCS
      See also CA 9-12R; CAAS 14; CANR 33, 54,
      76; CDBLB 1960 to Present; DLB 15, 139;
      DLBY 85; MTCW 1, 2
Lessing, Gotthold Ephraim 1729-1781   **LC 8**
      See also DLB 97
Lester, Richard 1932-   **CLC 20**
Lever, Charles (James) 1806-1872 **NCLC 23**
      See also DLB 21
Leverson, Ada 1865(?)-1936(?)   **TCLC 18**
      See also Elaine
      See also CA 117; DLB 153
Levertov, Denise 1923-1997 **CLC 1, 2, 3, 5, 8,**
      15, 28, 66; DAM POET; PC 11
      See also CA 1-4R; 163; CAAS 19; CANR 3,
      29, 50; CDALBS; DLB 5, 165; INT CANR-
      29; MTCW 1, 2
Levi, Jonathan   **CLC 76**
Levi, Peter (Chad Tigar) 1931-   **CLC 41**
      See also CA 5-8R; CANR 34, 80; DLB 40
Levi, Primo 1919-1987   **CLC 37, 50; SSC 12**
      See also CA 13-16R; 122; CANR 12, 33, 61,
      70; DLB 177; MTCW 1, 2
Levin, Ira 1929-   **CLC 3, 6; DAM POP**
      See also CA 21-24R; CANR 17, 44, 74; MTCW
      1, 2; SATA 66
Levin, Meyer 1905-1981   **CLC 7; DAM POP**
      See also AITN 1; CA 9-12R; 104; CANR 15;
      DLB 9, 28; DLBY 81; SATA 21; SATA-Obit
      27
Levine, Norman 1924-   **CLC 54**
      See also CA 73-76; CAAS 23; CANR 14, 70;
      DLB 88
Levine, Philip 1928-**CLC 2, 4, 5, 9, 14, 33, 118;**
      DAM POET; PC 22
      See also CA 9-12R; CANR 9, 37, 52; DLB 5
Levinson, Deirdre 1931-   **CLC 49**
      See also CA 73-76; CANR 70
Levi-Strauss, Claude 1908-   **CLC 38**
      See also CA 1-4R; CANR 6, 32, 57; MTCW 1,
      2
Levitin, Sonia (Wolff) 1934-   **CLC 17**
      See also AAYA 13; CA 29-32R; CANR 14, 32,
      79; CLR 53; JRDA; MAICYA; SAAS 2;
      SATA 4, 68
Levon, O. U.
      See Kesey, Ken (Elton)
Levy, Amy 1861-1889   **NCLC 59**
      See also DLB 156
Lewes, George Henry 1817-1878 **NCLC 25**
      See also DLB 55, 144
Lewis, Alun 1915-1944   **TCLC 3**
      See also CA 104; DLB 20, 162
Lewis, C. Day
      See Day Lewis, C(ecil)
Lewis, C(live) S(taples) 1898-1963**CLC 1, 3, 6,**
      14, 27; DA; DAB; DAC; DAM MST, NOV,
      POP; WLC
      See also AAYA 3; CA 81-84; CANR 33, 71;
      CDBLB 1945-1960; CLR 3, 27; DLB 15,
      100, 160; JRDA; MAICYA; MTCW 1, 2;
      SATA 13, 100
Lewis, Janet 1899-1998   **CLC 41**
      See also Winters, Janet Lewis
      See also CA 9-12R; 172; CANR 29, 63; CAP
      1; DLBY 87
Lewis, Matthew Gregory 1775-1818**NCLC 11,**

62
      See also DLB 39, 158, 178
Lewis, (Harry) Sinclair 1885-1951 **TCLC 4,**
      13, 23, 39; DA; DAB; DAC; DAM MST,
      NOV; WLC
      See also CA 104; 133; CDALB 1917-1929;
      DLB 9, 102; DLBD 1; MTCW 1, 2
Lewis, (Percy) Wyndham 1882(?)-1957**TCLC**
      2, 9; SSC 34
      See also CA 104; 157; DLB 15; MTCW 2
Lewisohn, Ludwig 1883-1955   **TCLC 19**
      See also CA 107; DLB 4, 9, 28, 102
Lewton, Val 1904-1951   **TCLC 76**
Leyner, Mark 1956-   **CLC 92**
      See also CA 110; CANR 28, 53; MTCW 2
Lezama Lima, Jose 1910-1976**CLC 4, 10, 101;**
      DAM MULT; HLCS 1
      See also CA 77-80; CANR 71; DLB 113; HW
      1, 2
L'Heureux, John (Clarke) 1934-   **CLC 52**
      See also CA 13-16R; CANR 23, 45
Liddell, C. H.
      See Kuttner, Henry
Lie, Jonas (Lauritz Idemil) 1833-1908(?)
      TCLC 5
      See also CA 115
Lieber, Joel 1937-1971   **CLC 6**
      See also CA 73-76; 29-32R
Lieber, Stanley Martin
      See Lee, Stan
Lieberman, Laurence (James) 1935- **CLC 4,**
      36
      See also CA 17-20R; CANR 8, 36
Lieh Tzu fl. 7th cent. B.C.-5th cent. B.C.
      CMLC 27
Lieksman, Anders
      See Haavikko, Paavo Juhani
Li Fei-kan 1904-
      See Pa Chin
      See also CA 105
Lifton, Robert Jay 1926-   **CLC 67**
      See also CA 17-20R; CANR 27, 78; INT
      CANR-27; SATA 66
Lightfoot, Gordon 1938-   **CLC 26**
      See also CA 109
Lightman, Alan P(aige) 1948-   **CLC 81**
      See also CA 141; CANR 63
Ligotti, Thomas (Robert) 1953-**CLC 44; SSC**
      16
      See also CA 123; CANR 49
Li Ho 791-817   **PC 13**
Liliencron, (Friedrich Adolf Axel) Detlev von
      1844-1909   **TCLC 18**
      See also CA 117
Lilly, William 1602-1681   **LC 27**
Lima, Jose Lezama
      See Lezama Lima, Jose
Lima Barreto, Afonso Henrique de 1881-1922
      TCLC 23
      See also CA 117
Limonov, Edward 1944-   **CLC 67**
      See also CA 137
Lin, Frank
      See Atherton, Gertrude (Franklin Horn)
Lincoln, Abraham 1809-1865   **NCLC 18**
Lind, Jakov   **CLC 1, 2, 4, 27, 82**
      See also Landwirth, Heinz
      See also CAAS 4
Lindbergh, Anne (Spencer) Morrow 1906-
      CLC 82; DAM NOV
      See also CA 17-20R; CANR 16, 73; MTCW 1,
      2; SATA 33
Lindsay, David 1878-1945   **TCLC 15**

See also CA 113
Lindsay, (Nicholas) Vachel 1879-1931 **T C L C**
      17; DA; DAC; DAM MST, POET; PC 23;
      WLC
      See also CA 114; 135; CANR 79; CDALB
      1865-1917; DLB 54; SATA 40
Linke-Poot
      See Doeblin, Alfred
Linney, Romulus 1930-   **CLC 51**
      See also CA 1-4R; CANR 40, 44, 79
Linton, Eliza Lynn 1822-1898   **NCLC 41**
      See also DLB 18
Li Po 701-763   **CMLC 2**
Lipsius, Justus 1547-1606   **LC 16**
Lipsyte, Robert (Michael) 1938-**CLC 21; DA;**
      DAC; DAM MST, NOV
      See also AAYA 7; CA 17-20R; CANR 8, 57;
      CLR 23; JRDA; MAICYA; SATA 5, 68
Lish, Gordon (Jay) 1934-   **CLC 45; SSC 18**
      See also CA 113; 117; CANR 79; DLB 130;
      INT 117
Lispector, Clarice 1925(?)-1977   **CLC 43;**
      HLCS 1; SSC 34
      See also CA 139; 116; CANR 71; DLB 113;
      HW 2
Littell, Robert 1935(?)-   **CLC 42**
      See also CA 109; 112; CANR 64
Little, Malcolm 1925-1965
      See Malcolm X
      See also BW 1, 3; CA 125; 111; DA; DAB;
      DAC; DAM MST, MULT; MTCW 1, 2
Littlewit, Humphrey Gent.
      See Lovecraft, H(oward) P(hillips)
Litwos
      See Sienkiewicz, Henryk (Adam Alexander
      Pius)
Liu, E 1857-1909   **TCLC 15**
      See also CA 115
Lively, Penelope (Margaret) 1933- **CLC 32,**
      50; DAM NOV
      See also CA 41-44R; CANR 29, 67, 79; CLR
      7; DLB 14, 161, 207; JRDA; MAICYA;
      MTCW 1, 2; SATA 7, 60, 101
Livesay, Dorothy (Kathleen) 1909-**CLC 4, 15,**
      79; DAC; DAM MST, POET
      See also AITN 2; CA 25-28R; CAAS 8; CANR
      36, 67; DLB 68; MTCW 1
Livy c. 59B.C.-c. 17   **CMLC 11**
      See also DLB 211
Lizardi, Jose Joaquin Fernandez de 1776-1827
      NCLC 30
Llewellyn, Richard
      See Llewellyn Lloyd, Richard Dafydd Vivian
      See also DLB 15
Llewellyn Lloyd, Richard Dafydd Vivian 1906-
      1983   **CLC 7, 80**
      See also Llewellyn, Richard
      See also CA 53-56; 111; CANR 7, 71; SATA
      11; SATA-Obit 37
Llosa, (Jorge) Mario (Pedro) Vargas
      See Vargas Llosa, (Jorge) Mario (Pedro)
Lloyd, Manda
      See Mander, (Mary) Jane
Lloyd Webber, Andrew 1948-
      See Webber, Andrew Lloyd
      See also AAYA 1; CA 116; 149; DAM DRAM;
      SATA 56
Llull, Ramon c. 1235-c. 1316   **CMLC 12**
Lobb, Ebenezer
      See Upward, Allen
Locke, Alain (Le Roy) 1886-1954 **TCLC 43;**
      BLCS
      See also BW 1, 3; CA 106; 124; CANR 79; DLB

51

Locke, John 1632-1704   **LC 7, 35**
  See also DLB 101
Locke-Elliott, Sumner
  See Elliott, Sumner Locke
Lockhart, John Gibson 1794-1854   **NCLC 6**
  See also DLB 110, 116, 144
Lodge, David (John) 1935-**CLC 36; DAM POP**
  See also BEST 90:1; CA 17-20R; CANR 19,
  53; DLB 14, 194; INT CANR-19; MTCW 1,
  2
Lodge, Thomas 1558-1625   **LC 41**
Lodge, Thomas 1558-1625   **LC 41**
  See also DLB 172
Loennbohm, Armas Eino Leopold 1878-1926
  See Leino, Eino
  See also CA 123
Loewinsohn, Ron(ald William) 1937-**CLC 52**
  See also CA 25-28R; CANR 71
Logan, Jake
  See Smith, Martin Cruz
Logan, John (Burton) 1923-1987   **CLC 5**
  See also CA 77-80; 124; CANR 45; DLB 5
Lo Kuan-chung 1330(?)-1400(?)   **LC 12**
Lombard, Nap
  See Johnson, Pamela Hansford
London, Jack   **TCLC 9, 15, 39; SSC 4; WLC**
  See also London, John Griffith
  See also AAYA 13; AITN 2; CDALB 1865-
  1917; DLB 8, 12, 78, 212; SATA 18
London, John Griffith 1876-1916
  See London, Jack
  See also CA 110; 119; CANR 73; DA; DAB;
  DAC; DAM MST, NOV; JRDA; MAICYA;
  MTCW 1, 2
Long, Emmett
  See Leonard, Elmore (John, Jr.)
Longbaugh, Harry
  See Goldman, William (W.)
Longfellow, Henry Wadsworth 1807-1882
    NCLC 2, 45; DA; DAB; DAC; DAM MST,
    POET; WLCS
  See also CDALB 1640-1865; DLB 1, 59; SATA
  19
Longinus c. 1st cent. -   **CMLC 27**
  See also DLB 176
Longley, Michael 1939-   **CLC 29**
  See also CA 102; DLB 40
Longus fl. c. 2nd cent. -   **CMLC 7**
Longway, A. Hugh
  See Lang, Andrew
Lonnrot, Elias 1802-1884   **NCLC 53**
Lopate, Phillip 1943-   **CLC 29**
  See also CA 97-100; DLBY 80; INT 97-100
Lopez Portillo (y Pacheco), Jose 1920-**CLC 46**
  See also CA 129; HW 1
Lopez y Fuentes, Gregorio 1897(?)-1966**CLC
  32**
  See also CA 131; HW 1
Lorca, Federico Garcia
  <See Garcia Lorca, Federico
Lord, Bette Bao 1938-   **CLC 23**
  See also BEST 90:3; CA 107; CANR 41, 79;
  INT 107; SATA 58
Lord Auch
  See Bataille, Georges
Lord Byron
  See Byron, George Gordon (Noel)
Lorde, Audre (Geraldine) 1934-1992**CLC 18,
  71; BLC 2; DAM MULT, POET; PC 12**
  See also BW 1, 3; CA 25-28R; 142; CANR 16,
  26, 46; DLB 41; MTCW 1, 2
Lord Houghton

  See Milnes, Richard Monckton
Lord Jeffrey
  See Jeffrey, Francis
Lorenzini, Carlo 1826-1890
  See Collodi, Carlo
  See also MAICYA; SATA 29, 100
Lorenzo, Heberto Padilla
  See Padilla (Lorenzo), Heberto
Loris
  See Hofmannsthal, Hugo von
Loti, Pierre   **TCLC 11**
  See also Viaud, (Louis Marie) Julien
  See also DLB 123
Louie, David Wong 1954-   **CLC 70**
  See also CA 139
Louis, Father M.
  See Merton, Thomas
Lovecraft, H(oward) P(hillips) 1890-1937
    TCLC 4, 22; DAM POP; SSC 3
  See also AAYA 14; CA 104; 133; MTCW 1, 2
Lovelace, Earl 1935-   **CLC 51**
  See also BW 2; CA 77-80; CANR 41, 72; DLB
  125; MTCW 1
Lovelace, Richard 1618-1657   **LC 24**
  See also DLB 131
Lowell, Amy 1874-1925   **TCLC 1, 8; DAM
  POET; PC 13**
  See also CA 104; 151; DLB 54, 140; MTCW 2
Lowell, James Russell 1819-1891   **NCLC 2**
  See also CDALB 1640-1865; DLB 1, 11, 64,
  79, 189
Lowell, Robert (Traill Spence, Jr.) 1917-1977
  **CLC 1, 2, 3, 4, 5, 8, 9, 11, 15, 37; DA; DAB;
  DAC; DAM MST, NOV; PC 3; WLC**
  See also CA 9-12R; 73-76; CABS 2; CANR 26,
  60; CDALBS; DLB 5, 169; MTCW 1, 2
Lowenthal, Michael (Francis) 1969-**CLC 119**
  See also CA 150
Lowndes, Marie Adelaide (Belloc) 1868-1947
  TCLC 12
  See also CA 107; DLB 70
Lowry, (Clarence) Malcolm 1909-1957**TCLC
  6, 40; SSC 31**
  See also CA 105; 131; CANR 62; CDBLB
  1945-1960; DLB 15; MTCW 1, 2
Lowry, Mina Gertrude 1882-1966
  See Loy, Mina
  See also CA 113
Loxsmith, John
  See Brunner, John (Kilian Houston)
Loy, Mina   **CLC 28; DAM POET; PC 16**
  See also Lowry, Mina Gertrude
  See also DLB 4, 54
Loyson-Bridet
  See Schwob, Marcel (Mayer Andre)
Lucan 39-65   **CMLC 33**
  See also DLB 211
Lucas, Craig 1951-   **CLC 64**
  See also CA 137; CANR 71
Lucas, E(dward) V(errall) 1868-1938   **TCLC
  73**
  See also DLB 98, 149, 153; SATA 20
Lucas, George 1944-   **CLC 16**
  See also AAYA 1, 23; CA 77-80; CANR 30;
  SATA 56
Lucas, Hans
  See Godard, Jean-Luc
Lucas, Victoria
  See Plath, Sylvia
Lucian c. 120-c. 180   **CMLC 32**
  See also DLB 176
Ludlam, Charles 1943-1987   **CLC 46, 50**
  See also CA 85-88; 122; CANR 72

Ludlum, Robert 1927-**CLC 22, 43; DAM NOV,
  POP**
  See also AAYA 10; BEST 89:1, 90:3; CA 33-
  36R; CANR 25, 41, 68; DLBY 82; MTCW
  1, 2
Ludwig, Ken   **CLC 60**
Ludwig, Otto 1813-1865   **NCLC 4**
  See also DLB 129
Lugones, Leopoldo 1874-1938   **TCLC 15;
  HLCS 1**
  See also CA 116; 131; HW 1
Lu Hsun 1881-1936   **TCLC 3; SSC 20**
  See also Shu-Jen, Chou
Lukacs, George   **CLC 24**
  See also Lukacs, Gyorgy (Szegeny von)
Lukacs, Gyorgy (Szegeny von) 1885-1971
  See Lukacs, George
  See also CA 101; 29-32R; CANR 62; MTCW 2
Luke, Peter (Ambrose Cyprian) 1919-1995
    CLC 38
  See also CA 81-84; 147; CANR 72; DLB 13
Lunar, Dennis
  See Mungo, Raymond
Lurie, Alison 1926-   **CLC 4, 5, 18, 39**
  See also CA 1-4R; CANR 2, 17, 50; DLB 2;
  MTCW 1; SATA 46
Lustig, Arnost 1926-   **CLC 56**
  See also AAYA 3; CA 69-72; CANR 47; SATA
  56
Luther, Martin 1483-1546   **LC 9, 37**
  See also DLB 179
Luxemburg, Rosa 1870(?)-1919   **TCLC 63**
  See also CA 118
Luzi, Mario 1914-   **CLC 13**
  See also CA 61-64; CANR 9, 70; DLB 128
Lyly, John 1554(?)-1606**LC 41; DAM DRAM;
  DC 7**
  See also DLB 62, 167
L'Ymagier
  See Gourmont, Remy (-Marie-Charles) de
Lynch, B. Suarez
  See Bioy Casares, Adolfo; Borges, Jorge Luis
Lynch, David (K.) 1946-   **CLC 66**
  See also CA 124; 129
Lynch, James
  See Andreyev, Leonid (Nikolaevich)
Lynch Davis, B.
  See Bioy Casares, Adolfo; Borges, Jorge Luis
Lyndsay, Sir David 1490-1555   **LC 20**
Lynn, Kenneth S(chuyler) 1923-   **CLC 50**
  See also CA 1-4R; CANR 3, 27, 65
Lynx
  See West, Rebecca
Lyons, Marcus
  See Blish, James (Benjamin)
Lyre, Pinchbeck
  See Sassoon, Siegfried (Lorraine)
Lytle, Andrew (Nelson) 1902-1995   **CLC 22**
  See also CA 9-12R; 150; CANR 70; DLB 6;
  DLBY 95
Lyttelton, George 1709-1773   **LC 10**
Maas, Peter 1929-   **CLC 29**
  See also CA 93-96; INT 93-96; MTCW 2
Macaulay, Rose 1881-1958   **TCLC 7, 44**
  See also CA 104; DLB 36
Macaulay, Thomas Babington 1800-1859
    NCLC 42
  See also CDBLB 1832-1890; DLB 32, 55
MacBeth, George (Mann) 1932-1992**CLC 2, 5,
  9**
  See also CA 25-28R; 136; CANR 61, 66; DLB
  40; MTCW 1; SATA 4; SATA-Obit 70
MacCaig, Norman (Alexander) 1910-**CLC 36;**

DAB; DAM POET
See also CA 9-12R; CANR 3, 34; DLB 27
MacCarthy, Sir(Charles Otto) Desmond 1877-
1952　　　　　　　　　　　　　**TCLC 36**
See also CA 167
MacDiarmid, Hugh **CLC 2, 4, 11, 19, 63; PC 9**
See also Grieve, C(hristopher) M(urray)
See also CDBLB 1945-1960; DLB 20
MacDonald, Anson
See Heinlein, Robert A(nson)
Macdonald, Cynthia 1928-　　　　**CLC 13, 19**
See also CA 49-52; CANR 4, 44; DLB 105
MacDonald, George 1824-1905　　　　**TCLC 9**
See also CA 106; 137; CANR 80; DLB 18, 163,
178; MAICYA; SATA 33, 100
Macdonald, John
See Millar, Kenneth
MacDonald, John D(ann) 1916-1986 **CLC 3,
27, 44; DAM NOV, POP**
See also CA 1-4R; 121; CANR 1, 19, 60; DLB
8; DLBY 86; MTCW 1, 2
Macdonald, John Ross
See Millar, Kenneth
Macdonald, Ross　　　　**CLC 1, 2, 3, 14, 34, 41**
See also Millar, Kenneth
See also DLBD 6
MacDougal, John
See Blish, James (Benjamin)
MacEwen, Gwendolyn (Margaret) 1941-1987
CLC 13, 55
See also CA 9-12R; 124; CANR 7, 22; DLB
53; SATA 50; SATA-Obit 55
Macha, Karel Hynek 1810-1846　　　**NCLC 46**
Machado (y Ruiz), Antonio 1875-1939 **T C L C
3**
See also CA 104; 174; DLB 108; HW 2
Machado de Assis, Joaquim Maria 1839-1908
TCLC 10; BLC 2; HLCS 1; SSC 24
See also CA 107; 153
Machen, Arthur　　　　　　　**TCLC 4; SSC 20**
See also Jones, Arthur Llewellyn
See also DLB 36, 156, 178
Machiavelli, Niccolo 1469-1527 **LC 8, 36; DA;
DAB; DAC; DAM MST; WLCS**
MacInnes, Colin 1914-1976　　　　**CLC 4, 23**
See also CA 69-72; 65-68; CANR 21; DLB 14;
MTCW 1, 2
MacInnes, Helen (Clark) 1907-1985 **CLC 27,
39; DAM POP**
See also CA 1-4R; 117; CANR 1, 28, 58; DLB
87; MTCW 1, 2; SATA 22; SATA-Obit 44
Mackay, Mary 1855-1924
See Corelli, Marie
See also CA 118
Mackenzie, Compton (Edward Montague)
1883-1972　　　　　　　　　　　　**CLC 18**
See also CA 21-22; 37-40R; CAP 2; DLB 34,
100
Mackenzie, Henry 1745-1831　　　　**NCLC 41**
See also DLB 39
Mackintosh, Elizabeth 1896(?)-1952
See Tey, Josephine
See also CA 110
MacLaren, James
See Grieve, C(hristopher) M(urray)
Mac Laverty, Bernard 1942-　　　　**CLC 31**
See also CA 116; 118; CANR 43; INT 118
MacLean, Alistair (Stuart) 1922(?)-1987 **C L C
3, 13, 50, 63; DAM POP**
See also CA 57-60; 121; CANR 28, 61; MTCW
1; SATA 23; SATA-Obit 50
Maclean, Norman (Fitzroy) 1902-1990　**C L C
78; DAM POP; SSC 13**

See also CA 102; 132; CANR 49; DLB 206
MacLeish, Archibald 1892-1982 **CLC 3, 8, 14,
68; DAM POET**
See also CA 9-12R; 106; CANR 33, 63;
CDALBS; DLB 4, 7, 45; DLBY 82; MTCW
1, 2
MacLennan, (John) Hugh 1907-1990　**CLC 2,
14, 92; DAC; DAM MST**
See also CA 5-8R; 142; CANR 33; DLB 68;
MTCW 1, 2
MacLeod, Alistair 1936- **CLC 56; DAC; DAM
MST**
See also CA 123; DLB 60; MTCW 2
Macleod, Fiona
See Sharp, William
MacNeice, (Frederick) Louis 1907-1963 **C L C
1, 4, 10, 53; DAB; DAM POET**
See also CA 85-88; CANR 61; DLB 10, 20;
MTCW 1, 2
MacNeill, Dand
See Fraser, George MacDonald
Macpherson, James 1736-1796　　　　　**LC 29**
See also Ossian
See also DLB 109
Macpherson, (Jean) Jay 1931-　　　　**CLC 14**
See also CA 5-8R; DLB 53
MacShane, Frank 1927-　　　　　　　**CLC 39**
See also CA 9-12R; CANR 3, 33; DLB 111
Macumber, Mari
See Sandoz, Mari(e Susette)
Madach, Imre 1823-1864　　　　　　**NCLC 19**
Madden, (Jerry) David 1933-　　　　**CLC 5, 15**
See also CA 1-4R; CAAS 3; CANR 4, 45; DLB
6; MTCW 1
Maddern, Al(an)
See Ellison, Harlan (Jay)
Madhubuti, Haki R. 1942- **CLC 6, 73; BLC 2;
DAM MULT, POET; PC 5**
See also Lee, Don L.
See also BW 2, 3; CA 73-76; CANR 24, 51,
73; DLB 5, 41; DLBD 8; MTCW 2
Maepenn, Hugh
See Kuttner, Henry
Maepenn, K. H.
See Kuttner, Henry
Maeterlinck, Maurice 1862-1949　　　**TCLC 3;
DAM DRAM**
See also CA 104; 136; CANR 80; DLB 192;
SATA 66
Maginn, William 1794-1842　　　　　　**NCLC 8**
See also DLB 110, 159
Mahapatra, Jayanta 1928-　　　　**CLC 33; DAM
MULT**
See also CA 73-76; CAAS 9; CANR 15, 33, 66
Mahfouz, Naguib (Abdel Aziz Al-Sabilgi)
1911(?)-
See Mahfuz, Najib
See also BEST 89:2; CA 128; CANR 55; DAM
NOV; MTCW 1, 2
Mahfuz, Najib　　　　　　　　　　**CLC 52, 55**
See also Mahfouz, Naguib (Abdel Aziz Al-
Sabilgi)
See also DLBY 88
Mahon, Derek 1941-　　　　　　　　**CLC 27**
See also CA 113; 128; DLB 40
Mailer, Norman 1923- **CLC 1, 2, 3, 4, 5, 8, 11,
14, 28, 39, 74, 111; DA; DAB; DAC; DAM
MST, NOV, POP**
See also AITN 2; CA 9-12R; CABS 1; CANR
28, 74, 77; CDALB 1968-1988; DLB 2, 16,
28, 185; DLBD 3; DLBY 80, 83; MTCW 1,
2
Maillet, Antonine 1929-　**CLC 54, 118; DAC**

See also CA 115; 120; CANR 46, 74, 77; DLB
60; INT 120; MTCW 2
Mais, Roger 1905-1955　　　　　　　　**TCLC 8**
See also BW 1, 3; CA 105; 124; DLB 125;
MTCW 1
Maistre, Joseph de 1753-1821　　　　**NCLC 37**
Maitland, Frederic 1850-1906　　　　**TCLC 65**
Maitland, Sara (Louise) 1950-　　　　**CLC 49**
See also CA 69-72; CANR 13, 59
Major, Clarence 1936- **CLC 3, 19, 48; BLC 2;
DAM MULT**
See also BW 2, 3; CA 21-24R; CAAS 6; CANR
13, 25, 53; DLB 33
Major, Kevin (Gerald) 1949-　　**CLC 26; DAC**
See also AAYA 16; CA 97-100; CANR 21, 38;
CLR 11; DLB 60; INT CANR-21; JRDA;
MAICYA; SATA 32, 82
Maki, James
See Ozu, Yasujiro
Malabaila, Damiano
See Levi, Primo
Malamud, Bernard 1914-1986 **CLC 1, 2, 3, 5,
8, 9, 11, 18, 27, 44, 78, 85; DA; DAB; DAC;
DAM MST, NOV, POP; SSC 15; WLC**
See also AAYA 16; CA 5-8R; 118; CABS 1;
CANR 28, 62; CDALB 1941-1968; DLB 2,
28, 152; DLBY 80, 86; MTCW 1, 2
Malan, Herman
See Bosman, Herman Charles; Bosman, Herman
Charles
Malaparte, Curzio 1898-1957　　　　**TCLC 52**
Malcolm, Dan
See Silverberg, Robert
Malcolm X　　　**CLC 82, 117; BLC 2; WLCS**
See also Little, Malcolm
Malherbe, Francois de 1555-1628　　　**LC 5**
Mallarme, Stephane 1842-1898 **NCLC 4, 41;
DAM POET; PC 4**
Mallet-Joris, Francoise 1930-　　　　**CLC 11**
See also CA 65-68; CANR 17; DLB 83
Malley, Ern
See McAuley, James Phillip
Mallowan, Agatha Christie
See Christie, Agatha (Mary Clarissa)
Maloff, Saul 1922-　　　　　　　　　**CLC 5**
See also CA 33-36R
Malone, Louis
See MacNeice, (Frederick) Louis
Malone, Michael (Christopher) 1942- **CLC 43**
See also CA 77-80; CANR 14, 32, 57
Malory, (Sir) Thomas 1410(?)-1471(?) **LC 11;
DA; DAB; DAC; DAM MST; WLCS**
See also CDBLB Before 1660; DLB 146; SATA
59; SATA-Brief 33
Malouf, (George Joseph) David 1934- **CLC 28,
86**
See also CA 124; CANR 50, 76; MTCW 2
Malraux, (Georges-)Andre 1901-1976 **CLC 1,
4, 9, 13, 15, 57; DAM NOV**
See also CA 21-22; 69-72; CANR 34, 58; CAP
2; DLB 72; MTCW 1, 2
Malzberg, Barry N(athaniel) 1939-　　**CLC 7**
See also CA 61-64; CAAS 4; CANR 16; DLB 8
Mamet, David (Alan) 1947- **CLC 9, 15, 34, 46,
91; DAM DRAM; DC 4**
See also AAYA 3; CA 81-84; CABS 3; CANR
15, 41, 67, 72; DLB 7; MTCW 1, 2
Mamoulian, Rouben (Zachary) 1897-1987
CLC 16
See also CA 25-28R; 124
Mandelstam, Osip (Emilievich) 1891(?)-1938(?)
TCLC 2, 6; PC 14
See also CA 104; 150; MTCW 2

Mander, (Mary) Jane 1877-1949 **TCLC 31**
See also CA 162

Mandeville, John fl. 1350- **CMLC 19**
See also DLB 146

Mandiargues, Andre Pieyre de **CLC 41**
See also Pieyre de Mandiargues, Andre
See also DLB 83

Mandrake, Ethel Belle
See Thurman, Wallace (Henry)

Mangan, James Clarence 1803-1849 **NCLC 27**

Maniere, J.-E.
See Giraudoux, (Hippolyte) Jean

Mankiewicz, Herman (Jacob) 1897-1953
TCLC 85
See also CA 120; 169; DLB 26

Manley, (Mary) Delariviere 1672(?)-1724 **L C
1, 42**
See also DLB 39, 80

Mann, Abel
See Creasey, John

Mann, Emily 1952- **DC 7**
See also CA 130; CANR 55

Mann, (Luiz) Heinrich 1871-1950 **TCLC 9**
See also CA 106; 164; DLB 66, 118

Mann, (Paul) Thomas 1875-1955 **TCLC 2, 8,
14, 21, 35, 44, 60; DA; DAB; DAC; DAM
MST, NOV; SSC 5; WLC**
See also CA 104; 128; DLB 66; MTCW 1, 2

Mannheim, Karl 1893-1947 **TCLC 65**

Manning, David
See Faust, Frederick (Schiller)

Manning, Frederic 1887(?)-1935 **TCLC 25**
See also CA 124

Manning, Olivia 1915-1980 **CLC 5, 19**
See also CA 5-8R; 101; CANR 29; MTCW 1

Mano, D. Keith 1942- **CLC 2, 10**
See also CA 25-28R; CAAS 6; CANR 26, 57;
DLB 6

Mansfield, Katherine **TCLC 2, 8, 39; DAB; SSC
9, 23; WLC**
See also Beauchamp, Kathleen Mansfield
See also DLB 162

Manso, Peter 1940- **CLC 39**
See also CA 29-32R; CANR 44

Mantecon, Juan Jimenez
See Jimenez (Mantecon), Juan Ramon

Manton, Peter
See Creasey, John

Man Without a Spleen, A
See Chekhov, Anton (Pavlovich)

Manzoni, Alessandro 1785-1873 **NCLC 29**

Map, Walter 1140-1209 **CMLC 32**

Mapu, Abraham (ben Jekutiel) 1808-1867
NCLC 18

Mara, Sally
See Queneau, Raymond

Marat, Jean Paul 1743-1793 **LC 10**

Marcel, Gabriel Honore 1889-1973 **CLC 15**
See also CA 102; 45-48; MTCW 1, 2

Marchbanks, Samuel
See Davies, (William) Robertson

Marchi, Giacomo
See Bassani, Giorgio

Margulies, Donald **CLC 76**

Marie de France c. 12th cent. - **CMLC 8; PC
22**
See also DLB 208

Marie de l'Incarnation 1599-1672 **LC 10**

Marier, Captain Victor
See Griffith, D(avid Lewelyn) W(ark)

Mariner, Scott
See Pohl, Frederik

Marinetti, Filippo Tommaso 1876-1944 **TCLC**

10
See also CA 107; DLB 114

Marivaux, Pierre Carlet de Chamblain de 1688-
1763 **LC 4; DC 7**

Markandaya, Kamala **CLC 8, 38**
See also Taylor, Kamala (Purnaiya)

Markfield, Wallace 1926- **CLC 8**
See also CA 69-72; CAAS 3; DLB 2, 28

Markham, Edwin 1852-1940 **TCLC 47**
See also CA 160; DLB 54, 186

Markham, Robert
See Amis, Kingsley (William)

Marks, J
See Highwater, Jamake (Mamake)

Marks-Highwater, J
See Highwater, Jamake (Mamake)

Markson, David M(errill) 1927- **CLC 67**
See also CA 49-52; CANR 1

Marley, Bob **CLC 17**
See also Marley, Robert Nesta

Marley, Robert Nesta 1945-1981
See Marley, Bob
See also CA 107; 103

Marlowe, Christopher 1564-1593 **LC 22, 47;
DA; DAB; DAC; DAM DRAM, MST; DC
1; WLC**
See also CDBLB Before 1660; DLB 62

Marlowe, Stephen 1928-
See Queen, Ellery
See also CA 13-16R; CANR 6, 55

Marmontel, Jean-Francois 1723-1799 **LC 2**

Marquand, John P(hillips) 1893-1960 **CLC 2,
10**
See also CA 85-88; CANR 73; DLB 9, 102;
MTCW 2

Marques, Rene 1919-1979 **CLC 96; DAM
MULT; HLC**
See also CA 97-100; 85-88; CANR 78; DLB
113; HW 1, 2

Marquez, Gabriel (Jose) Garcia
See Garcia Marquez, Gabriel (Jose)

Marquis, Don(ald Robert Perry) 1878-1937
TCLC 7
See also CA 104; 166; DLB 11, 25

Marric, J. J.
See Creasey, John

Marryat, Frederick 1792-1848 **NCLC 3**
See also DLB 21, 163

Marsden, James
See Creasey, John

Marsh, (Edith) Ngaio 1899-1982 **CLC 7, 53;
DAM POP**
See also CA 9-12R; CANR 6, 58; DLB 77;
MTCW 1, 2

Marshall, Garry 1934- **CLC 17**
See also AAYA 3; CA 111; SATA 60

Marshall, Paule 1929- **CLC 27, 72; BLC 3;
DAM MULT; SSC 3**
See also BW 2, 3; CA 77-80; CANR 25, 73;
DLB 157; MTCW 1, 2

Marshallik
See Zangwill, Israel

Marsten, Richard
See Hunter, Evan

Marston, John 1576-1634 **LC 33; DAM DRAM**
See also DLB 58, 172

Martha, Henry
See Harris, Mark

Marti (y Perez), Jose (Julian) 1853-1895
NCLC 63; DAM MULT; HLC
See also HW 2

Martial c. 40-c. 104 **PC 10**
See also DLB 211

Martin, Ken
See Hubbard, L(afayette) Ron(ald)

Martin, Richard
See Creasey, John

Martin, Steve 1945- **CLC 30**
See also CA 97-100; CANR 30; MTCW 1

Martin, Valerie 1948- **CLC 89**
See also BEST 90:2; CA 85-88; CANR 49

Martin, Violet Florence 1862-1915 **TCLC 51**

Martin, Webber
See Silverberg, Robert

Martindale, Patrick Victor
See White, Patrick (Victor Martindale)

Martin du Gard, Roger 1881-1958 **TCLC 24**
See also CA 118; DLB 65

Martineau, Harriet 1802-1876 **NCLC 26**
See also DLB 21, 55, 159, 163, 166, 190; YABC
2

Martines, Julia
See O'Faolain, Julia

Martinez, Enrique Gonzalez
See Gonzalez Martinez, Enrique

Martinez, Jacinto Benavente y
See Benavente (y Martinez), Jacinto

Martinez Ruiz, Jose 1873-1967
See Azorin; Ruiz, Jose Martinez
See also CA 93-96; HW 1

Martinez Sierra, Gregorio 1881-1947 **TCLC 6**
See also CA 115

Martinez Sierra, Maria (de la O'LeJarraga)
1874-1974 **TCLC 6**
See also CA 115

Martinsen, Martin
See Follett, Ken(neth Martin)

Martinson, Harry (Edmund) 1904-1978 **C L C
14**
See also CA 77-80; CANR 34

Marut, Ret
See Traven, B.

Marut, Robert
See Traven, B.

Marvell, Andrew 1621-1678 **LC 4, 43; DA;
DAB; DAC; DAM MST, POET; PC 10;
WLC**
See also CDBLB 1660-1789; DLB 131

Marx, Karl (Heinrich) 1818-1883 **NCLC 17**
See also DLB 129

Masaoka Shiki **TCLC 18**
See also Masaoka Tsunenori

Masaoka Tsunenori 1867-1902
See Masaoka Shiki
See also CA 117

Masefield, John (Edward) 1878-1967 **CLC 11,
47; DAM POET**
See also CA 19-20; 25-28R; CANR 33; CAP 2;
CDBLB 1890-1914; DLB 10, 19, 153, 160;
MTCW 1, 2; SATA 19

Maso, Carole 19(?)- **CLC 44**
See also CA 170

Mason, Bobbie Ann 1940- **CLC 28, 43, 82; SSC
4**
See also AAYA 5; CA 53-56; CANR 11, 31,
58; CDALBS; DLB 173; DLBY 87; INT
CANR-31; MTCW 1, 2

Mason, Ernst
See Pohl, Frederik

Mason, Lee W.
See Malzberg, Barry N(athaniel)

Mason, Nick 1945- **CLC 35**

Mason, Tally
See Derleth, August (William)

Mass, William
See Gibson, William

Master Lao
See Lao Tzu

Masters, Edgar Lee 1868-1950 **TCLC 2, 25;
DA; DAC; DAM MST, POET; PC 1;
WLCS**
See also CA 104; 133; CDALB 1865-1917;
DLB 54; MTCW 1, 2

Masters, Hilary 1928- **CLC 48**
See also CA 25-28R; CANR 13, 47

Mastrosimone, William 19(?)- **CLC 36**

Mathe, Albert
See Camus, Albert

Mather, Cotton 1663-1728 **LC 38**
See also CDALB 1640-1865; DLB 24, 30, 140
<indMather, Increase 1639-1723 **LC 38**
See also DLB 24

Matheson, Richard Burton 1926- **CLC 37**
See also CA 97-100; DLB 8, 44; INT 97-100

Mathews, Harry 1930- **CLC 6, 52**
See also CA 21-24R; CAAS 6; CANR 18, 40

Mathews, John Joseph 1894-1979 **CLC 84;
DAM MULT**
See also CA 19-20; 142; CANR 45; CAP 2;
DLB 175; NNAL

Mathias, Roland (Glyn) 1915- **CLC 45**
See also CA 97-100; CANR 19, 41; DLB 27

Matsuo Basho 1644-1694 **PC 3**
See also DAM POET

Mattheson, Rodney
See Creasey, John

Matthews, Greg 1949- **CLC 45**
See also CA 135

Matthews, William (Procter, III) 1942-1997
CLC 40
See also CA 29-32R; 162; CAAS 18; CANR
12, 57; DLB 5

Matthias, John (Edward) 1941- **CLC 9**
See also CA 33-36R; CANR 56

Matthiessen, Peter 1927-**CLC 5, 7, 11, 32, 64;
DAM NOV**
See also AAYA 6; BEST 90:4; CA 9-12R;
CANR 21, 50, 73; DLB 6, 173; MTCW 1, 2;
SATA 27

Maturin, Charles Robert 1780(?)-1824**NCLC
6**
See also DLB 178

Matute (Ausejo), Ana Maria 1925- **CLC 11**
See also CA 89-92; MTCW 1

Maugham, W. S.
See Maugham, W(illiam) Somerset

Maugham, W(illiam) Somerset 1874-1965
**CLC 1, 11, 15, 67, 93; DA; DAB; DAC;
DAM DRAM, MST, NOV; SSC 8; WLC**
See also CA 5-8R; 25-28R; CANR 40; CDBLB
1914-1945; DLB 10, 36, 77, 100, 162, 195;
MTCW 1, 2; SATA 54

Maugham, William Somerset
See Maugham, W(illiam) Somerset

Maupassant, (Henri Rene Albert) Guy de 1850-
1893**NCLC 1, 42; DA; DAB; DAC; DAM
MST; SSC 1; WLC**
See also DLB 123

Maupin, Armistead 1944-**CLC 95; DAM POP**
See also CA 125; 130; CANR 58; INT 130;
MTCW 2

Maurhut, Richard
See Traven, B.

Mauriac, Claude 1914-1996 **CLC 9**
See also CA 89-92; 152; DLB 83

Mauriac, Francois (Charles) 1885-1970 **C L C
4, 9, 56; SSC 24**
See also CA 25-28; CAP 2; DLB 65; MTCW 1,
2

Mavor, Osborne Henry 1888-1951
See Bridie, James
See also CA 104

Maxwell, William (Keepers, Jr.) 1908-**CLC 19**
See also CA 93-96; CANR 54; DLBY 80; INT
93-96

May, Elaine 1932- **CLC 16**
See also CA 124; 142; DLB 44

Mayakovski, Vladimir (Vladimirovich) 1893-
1930 **TCLC 4, 18**
See also CA 104; 158; MTCW 2

Mayhew, Henry 1812-1887 **NCLC 31**
See also DLB 18, 55, 190

Mayle, Peter 1939(?)- **CLC 89**
See also CA 139; CANR 64

Maynard, Joyce 1953- **CLC 23**
See also CA 111; 129; CANR 64

Mayne, William (James Carter) 1928-**CLC 12**
See also AAYA 20; CA 9-12R; CANR 37, 80;
CLR 25; JRDA; MAICYA; SAAS 11; SATA
6, 68

Mayo, Jim
See L'Amour, Louis (Dearborn)

Maysles, Albert 1926- **CLC 16**
See also CA 29-32R

Maysles, David 1932- **CLC 16**

Mazer, Norma Fox 1931- **CLC 26**
See also AAYA 5; CA 69-72; CANR 12, 32,
66; CLR 23; JRDA; MAICYA; SAAS 1;
SATA 24, 67, 105

Mazzini, Guiseppe 1805-1872 **NCLC 34**

McAuley, James Phillip 1917-1976 **CLC 45**
See also CA 97-100

McBain, Ed
See Hunter, Evan

McBrien, William Augustine 1930- **CLC 44**
See also CA 107

McCaffrey, Anne (Inez) 1926-**CLC 17; DAM
NOV, POP**
See also AAYA 6; AITN 2; BEST 89:2; CA 25-
28R; CANR 15, 35, 55; CLR 49; DLB 8;
JRDA; MAICYA; MTCW 1, 2; SAAS 11;
SATA 8, 70

McCall, Nathan 1955(?)- **CLC 86**
See also BW 3; CA 146

McCann, Arthur
See Campbell, John W(ood, Jr.)

McCann, Edson
See Pohl, Frederik

McCarthy, Charles, Jr. 1933-
See McCarthy, Cormac
See also CANR 42, 69; DAM POP; MTCW 2

McCarthy, Cormac 1933- **CLC 4, 57, 59, 101**
See also McCarthy, Charles, Jr.
See also DLB 6, 143; MTCW 2

McCarthy, Mary (Therese) 1912-1989**CLC 1,
3, 5, 14, 24, 39, 59; SSC 24**
See also CA 5-8R; 129; CANR 16, 50, 64; DLB
2; DLBY 81; INT CANR-16; MTCW 1, 2

McCartney, (James) Paul 1942- **CLC 12, 35**
See also CA 146

McCauley, Stephen (D.) 1955- **CLC 50**
See also CA 141

McClure, Michael (Thomas) 1932-**CLC 6, 10**
See also CA 21-24R; CANR 17, 46, 77; DLB
16

McCorkle, Jill (Collins) 1958- **CLC 51**
See also CA 121; DLBY 87

McCourt, Frank 1930- **CLC 109**
See also CA 157

McCourt, James 1941- **CLC 5**
See also CA 57-60

McCourt, Malachy 1932- **CLC 119**

McCoy, Horace (Stanley) 1897-1955**TCLC 28**
See also CA 108; 155; DLB 9

McCrae, John 1872-1918 **TCLC 12**
See also CA 109; DLB 92

McCreigh, James
See Pohl, Frederik

McCullers, (Lula) Carson (Smith) 1917-1967
**CLC 1, 4, 10, 12, 48, 100; DA; DAB; DAC;
DAM MST, NOV; SSC 9, 24; WLC**
See also AAYA 21; CA 5-8R; 25-28R; CABS
1, 3; CANR 18; CDALB 1941-1968; DLB
2, 7, 173; MTCW 1, 2; SATA 27

McCulloch, John Tyler
See Burroughs, Edgar Rice

McCullough, Colleen 1938(?)- **CLC 27, 107;
DAM NOV, POP**
See also CA 81-84; CANR 17, 46, 67; MTCW
1, 2

McDermott, Alice 1953- **CLC 90**
See also CA 109; CANR 40

McElroy, Joseph 1930- **CLC 5, 47**
See also CA 17-20R

McEwan, Ian (Russell) 1948- **CLC 13, 66;
DAM NOV**
See also BEST 90:4; CA 61-64; CANR 14, 41,
69; DLB 14, 194; MTCW 1, 2

McFadden, David 1940- **CLC 48**
See also CA 104; DLB 60; INT 104

McFarland, Dennis 1950- **CLC 65**
See also CA 165

McGahern, John 1934- **CLC 5, 9, 48; SSC 17**
See also CA 17-20R; CANR 29, 68; DLB 14;
MTCW 1

McGinley, Patrick (Anthony) 1937- **CLC 41**
See also CA 120; 127; CANR 56; INT 127

McGinley, Phyllis 1905-1978 **CLC 14**
See also CA 9-12R; 77-80; CANR 19; DLB 11,
48; SATA 2, 44; SATA-Obit 24

McGinniss, Joe 1942- **CLC 32**
See also AITN 2; BEST 89:2; CA 25-28R;
CANR 26, 70; DLB 185; INT CANR-26

McGivern, Maureen Daly
See Daly, Maureen

McGrath, Patrick 1950- **CLC 55**
See also CA 136; CANR 65

McGrath, Thomas (Matthew) 1916-1990**CLC
28, 59; DAM POET**
See also CA 9-12R; 132; CANR 6, 33; MTCW
1; SATA 41; SATA-Obit 66

McGuane, Thomas (Francis III) 1939-**CLC 3,
7, 18, 45**
See also AITN 2; CA 49-52; CANR 5, 24, 49;
DLB 2, 212; DLBY 80; INT CANR-24;
MTCW 1

McGuckian, Medbh 1950- **CLC 48; DAM
POET**
See also CA 143; DLB 40

McHale, Tom 1942(?)-1982 **CLC 3, 5**
See also AITN 1; CA 77-80; 106

McIlvanney, William 1936- **CLC 42**
See also CA 25-28R; CANR 61; DLB 14, 207

McIlwraith, Maureen Mollie Hunter
See Hunter, Mollie
See also SATA 2

McInerney, Jay 1955-**CLC 34, 112; DAM POP**
See also AAYA 18; CA 116; 123; CANR 45,
68; INT 123; MTCW 2

McIntyre, Vonda N(eel) 1948- **CLC 18**
See also CA 81-84; CANR 17, 34, 69; MTCW
1

McKay, ClaudeTCLC 7, 41; BLC 3; DAB; PC
2
See also McKay, Festus Claudius

See also DLB 4, 45, 51, 117
McKay, Festus Claudius 1889-1948
See McKay, Claude
See also BW 1, 3; CA 104; 124; CANR 73; DA;
DAC; DAM MST, MULT, NOV, POET;
MTCW 1, 2; WLC
McKuen, Rod 1933- **CLC 1, 3**
See also AITN 1; CA 41-44R; CANR 40
McLoughlin, R. B.
See Mencken, H(enry) L(ouis)
McLuhan, (Herbert) Marshall 1911-1980
CLC 37, 83
See also CA 9-12R; 102; CANR 12, 34, 61;
DLB 88; INT CANR-12; MTCW 1, 2
McMillan, Terry (L.) 1951- **CLC 50, 61, 112;
BLCS; DAM MULT, NOV, POP**
See also AAYA 21; BW 2, 3; CA 140; CANR
60; MTCW 2
McMurtry, Larry (Jeff) 1936-**CLC 2, 3, 7, 11,
27, 44; DAM NOV, POP**
See also AAYA 15; AITN 2; BEST 89:2; CA 5-
8R; CANR 19, 43, 64; CDALB 1968-1988;
DLB 2, 143; DLBY 80, 87; MTCW 1, 2
McNally, T. M. 1961- **CLC 82**
McNally, Terrence 1939- **CLC 4, 7, 41, 91;
DAM DRAM**
See also CA 45-48; CANR 2, 56; DLB 7;
MTCW 2
McNamer, Deirdre 1950- **CLC 70**
McNeal, Tom **CLC 119**
McNeile, Herman Cyril 1888-1937
See Sapper
See also DLB 77
McNickle, (William) D'Arcy 1904-1977 **C L C
89; DAM MULT**
See also CA 9-12R; 85-88; CANR 5, 45; DLB
175, 212; NNAL; SATA-Obit 22
McPhee, John (Angus) 1931- **CLC 36**
See also BEST 90:1; CA 65-68; CANR 20, 46,
64, 69; DLB 185; MTCW 1, 2
McPherson, James Alan 1943- **CLC 19, 77;
BLCS**
See also BW 1, 3; CA 25-28R; CAAS 17;
CANR 24, 74; DLB 38; MTCW 1, 2
McPherson, William (Alexander) 1933- **C L C
34**
See also CA 69-72; CANR 28; INT CANR-28
Mead, George Herbert 1873-1958 **TCLC 89**
Mead, Margaret 1901-1978 **CLC 37**
See also AITN 1; CA 1-4R; 81-84; CANR 4;
MTCW 1, 2; SATA-Obit 20
Meaker, Marijane (Agnes) 1927-
See Kerr, M. E.
See also CA 107; CANR 37, 63; INT 107;
JRDA; MAICYA; MTCW 1; SATA 20, 61,
99
Medoff, Mark (Howard) 1940- **CLC 6, 23;
DAM DRAM**
See also AITN 1; CA 53-56; CANR 5; DLB 7;
INT CANR-5
Medvedev, P. N.
See Bakhtin, Mikhail Mikhailovich
Meged, Aharon
See Megged, Aharon
Meged, Aron
See Megged, Aharon
Megged, Aharon 1920- **CLC 9**
See also CA 49-52; CAAS 13; CANR 1
Mehta, Ved (Parkash) 1934- **CLC 37**
See also CA 1-4R; CANR 2, 23, 69; MTCW 1
Melanter
See Blackmore, R(ichard) D(oddridge)
Melies, Georges 1861-1938 **TCLC 81**

Melikow, Loris
See Hofmannsthal, Hugo von
Melmoth, Sebastian
See Wilde, Oscar
Meltzer, Milton 1915- **CLC 26**
See also AAYA 8; CA 13-16R; CANR 38; CLR
13; DLB 61; JRDA; MAICYA; SAAS 1;
SATA 1, 50, 80
Melville, Herman 1819-1891**NCLC 3, 12, 29,
45, 49; DA; DAB; DAC; DAM MST, NOV;
SSC 1, 17; WLC**
See also AAYA 25; CDALB 1640-1865; DLB
3, 74; SATA 59
Menander c. 342B.C.-c. 292B.C. **CMLC 9;
DAM DRAM; DC 3**
See also DLB 176
Mencken, H(enry) L(ouis) 1880-1956 **T C L C
13**
See also CA 105; 125; CDALB 1917-1929;
DLB 11, 29, 63, 137; MTCW 1, 2
Mendelsohn, Jane 1965(?)- **CLC 99**
See also CA 154
Mercer, David 1928-1980**CLC 5; DAM DRAM**
See also CA 9-12R; 102; CANR 23; DLB 13;
MTCW 1
Merchant, Paul
See Ellison, Harlan (Jay)
Meredith, George 1828-1909 **TCLC 17, 43;
DAM POET**
See also CA 117; 153; CANR 80; CDBLB 1832-
1890; DLB 18, 35, 57, 159
Meredith, William (Morris) 1919-**CLC 4, 13,
22, 55; DAM POET**
See also CA 9-12R; CAAS 14; CANR 6, 40;
DLB 5
Merezhkovsky, Dmitry Sergeyevich 1865-1941
TCLC 29
See also CA 169
Merimee, Prosper 1803-1870**NCLC 6, 65; SSC
7**
See also DLB 119, 192
Merkin, Daphne 1954- **CLC 44**
See also CA 123
Merlin, Arthur
See Blish, James (Benjamin)
Merrill, James (Ingram) 1926-1995**CLC 2, 3,
6, 8, 13, 18, 34, 91; DAM POET**
See also CA 13-16R; 147; CANR 10, 49, 63;
DLB 5, 165; DLBY 85; INT CANR-10;
MTCW 1, 2
Merriman, Alex
See Silverberg, Robert
Merriman, Brian 1747-1805 **NCLC 70**
Merritt, E. B.
See Waddington, Miriam
Merton, Thomas 1915-1968 **CLC 1, 3, 11, 34,
83; PC 10**
See also CA 5-8R; 25-28R; CANR 22, 53; DLB
48; DLBY 81; MTCW 1, 2
Merwin, W(illiam) S(tanley) 1927- **CLC 1, 2,
3, 5, 8, 13, 18, 45, 88; DAM POET**
See also CA 13-16R; CANR 15, 51; DLB 5,
169; INT CANR-15; MTCW 1, 2
Metcalf, John 1938- **CLC 37**
See also CA 113; DLB 60
Metcalf, Suzanne
See Baum, L(yman) Frank
Mew, Charlotte (Mary) 1870-1928 **TCLC 8**
See also CA 105; DLB 19, 135
Mewshaw, Michael 1943- **CLC 9**
See also CA 53-56; CANR 7, 47; DLBY 80
Meyer, June
See Jordan, June

Meyer, Lynn
See Slavitt, David R(ytman)
Meyer-Meyrink, Gustav 1868-1932
See Meyrink, Gustav
See also CA 117
Meyers, Jeffrey 1939- **CLC 39**
See also CA 73-76; CANR 54; DLB 111
Meynell, Alice (Christina Gertrude Thompson)
1847-1922 **TCLC 6**
See also CA 104; DLB 19, 98
Meyrink, Gustav **TCLC 21**
See also Meyer-Meyrink, Gustav
See also DLB 81
Michaels, Leonard 1933- **CLC 6, 25; SSC 16**
See also CA 61-64; CANR 21, 62; DLB 130;
MTCW 1
Michaux, Henri 1899-1984 **CLC 8, 19**
See also CA 85-88; 114
Micheaux, Oscar (Devereaux) 1884-1951
TCLC 76
See also BW 3; CA 174; DLB 50
Michelangelo 1475-1564 **LC 12**
Michelet, Jules 1798-1874 **NCLC 31**
Michels, Robert 1876-1936 **TCLC 88**
Michener, James A(lbert) 1907(?)-1997 **C L C
1, 5, 11, 29, 60, 109; DAM NOV, POP**
See also AAYA 27; AITN 1; BEST 90:1; CA 5-
8R; 161; CANR 21, 45, 68; DLB 6; MTCW
1, 2
Mickiewicz, Adam 1798-1855 **NCLC 3**
Middleton, Christopher 1926- **CLC 13**
See also CA 13-16R; CANR 29, 54; DLB 40
Middleton, Richard (Barham) 1882-1911
TCLC 56
See also DLB 156
Middleton, Stanley 1919- **CLC 7, 38**
See also CA 25-28R; CAAS 23; CANR 21, 46;
DLB 14
Middleton, Thomas 1580-1627 **LC 33; DAM
DRAM, MST; DC 5**
See also DLB 58
Migueis, Jose Rodrigues 1901- **CLC 10**
Mikszath, Kalman 1847-1910 **TCLC 31**
See also CA 170
Miles, Jack **CLC 100**
Miles, Josephine (Louise) 1911-1985**CLC 1, 2,
14, 34, 39; DAM POET**
See also CA 1-4R; 116; CANR 2, 55; DLB 48
Militant
See Sandburg, Carl (August)
Mill, John Stuart 1806-1873 **NCLC 11, 58**
See also CDBLB 1832-1890; DLB 55, 190
Millar, Kenneth 1915-1983 **CLC 14; DAM
POP**
See Macdonald, Ross
See also CA 9-12R; 110; CANR 16, 63; DLB
2; DLBD 6; DLBY 83; MTCW 1, 2
Millay, E. Vincent
See Millay, Edna St. Vincent
Millay, Edna St. Vincent 1892-1950 **TCLC 4,
49; DA; DAB; DAC; DAM MST, POET;
PC 6; WLCS**
See also CA 104; 130; CDALB 1917-1929;
DLB 45; MTCW 1, 2
Miller, Arthur 1915-**CLC 1, 2, 6, 10, 15, 26, 47,
78; DA; DAB; DAC; DAM DRAM, MST;
DC 1; WLC**
See also AAYA 15; AITN 1; CA 1-4R; CABS
3; CANR 2, 30, 54, 76; CDALB 1941-1968;
DLB 7; MTCW 1, 2
Miller, Henry (Valentine) 1891-1980**CLC 1, 2,
4, 9, 14, 43, 84; DA; DAB; DAC; DAM
MST, NOV; WLC**

See also CA 9-12R; 97-100; CANR 33, 64;
  CDALB 1929-1941; DLB 4, 9; DLBY 80;
  MTCW 1, 2
Miller, Jason 1939(?)-   **CLC 2**
  See also AITN 1; CA 73-76; DLB 7
Miller, Sue 1943-   **CLC 44; DAM POP**
  See also BEST 90:3; CA 139; CANR 59; DLB
  143
Miller, Walter M(ichael, Jr.) 1923-**CLC 4, 30**
  See also CA 85-88; DLB 8
Millett, Kate 1934-   **CLC 67**
  See also AITN 1; CA 73-76; CANR 32, 53, 76;
  MTCW 1, 2
Millhauser, Steven (Lewis) 1943-**CLC 21, 54,**
  109
  See also CA 110; 111; CANR 63; DLB 2; INT
  111; MTCW 2
Millin, Sarah Gertrude 1889-1968   **CLC 49**
  See also CA 102; 93-96
Milne, A(lan) A(lexander) 1882-1956**TCLC 6,**
  88; DAB; DAC; DAM MST
  See also CA 104; 133; CLR 1, 26; DLB 10, 77,
  100, 160; MAICYA; MTCW 1, 2; SATA 100;
  YABC 1
Milner, Ron(ald) 1938-**CLC 56; BLC 3; DAM**
  MULT
  See also AITN 1; BW 1; CA 73-76; CANR 24;
  DLB 38; MTCW 1
Milnes, Richard Monckton 1809-1885 **NCLC
  61**
  See also DLB 32, 184
Milosz, Czeslaw 1911- **CLC 5, 11, 22, 31, 56,**
  82; DAM MST, POET; PC 8; WLCS
  See also CA 81-84; CANR 23, 51; MTCW 1, 2
Milton, John 1608-1674 **LC 9, 43; DA; DAB;**
  DAC; DAM MST, POET; PC 19; WLC
  See also CDBLB 1660-1789; DLB 131, 151
Min, Anchee 1957-   **CLC 86**
  See also CA 146
Minehaha, Cornelius
  See Wedekind, (Benjamin) Frank(lin)
Miner, Valerie 1947-   **CLC 40**
  See also CA 97-100; CANR 59
Minimo, Duca
  See D'Annunzio, Gabriele
Minot, Susan 1956-   **CLC 44**
  See also CA 134
Minus, Ed 1938-   **CLC 39**
Miranda, Javier
  See Bioy Casares, Adolfo
Mirbeau, Octave 1848-1917   **TCLC 55**
  See also DLB 123, 192
Miro (Ferrer), Gabriel (Francisco Victor) 1879-
  1930   **TCLC 5**
  See also CA 104
Mishima, Yukio 1925-1970**CLC 2, 4, 6, 9, 27;**
  DC 1; SSC 4
  See also Hiraoka, Kimitake
  See also DLB 182; MTCW 2
Mistral, Frederic 1830-1914   **TCLC 51**
  See also CA 122
Mistral, Gabriela   **TCLC 2; HLC**
  See also Godoy Alcayaga, Lucila
  See also MTCW 2
Mistry, Rohinton 1952-   **CLC 71; DAC**
  See also CA 141
Mitchell, Clyde
  See Ellison, Harlan (Jay); Silverberg, Robert
Mitchell, James Leslie 1901-1935
  See Gibbon, Lewis Grassic
  See also CA 104; DLB 15
Mitchell, Joni 1943-   **CLC 12**
  See also CA 112

Mitchell, Joseph (Quincy) 1908-1996**CLC 98**
  See also CA 77-80; 152; CANR 69; DLB 185;
  DLBY 96
Mitchell, Margaret (Munnerlyn) 1900-1949
  TCLC 11; DAM NOV, POP
  See also AAYA 23; CA 109; 125; CANR 55;
  CDALBS; DLB 9; MTCW 1, 2
Mitchell, Peggy
  See Mitchell, Margaret (Munnerlyn)
Mitchell, S(ilas) Weir 1829-1914   **TCLC 36**
  See also CA 165; DLB 202
Mitchell, W(illiam) O(rmond) 1914-1998**CLC
  25; DAC; DAM MST**
  See also CA 77-80; 165; CANR 15, 43; DLB
  88
Mitchell, William 1879-1936   **TCLC 81**
Mitford, Mary Russell 1787-1855   **NCLC 4**
  See also DLB 110, 116
Mitford, Nancy 1904-1973   **CLC 44**
  See also CA 9-12R; DLB 191
Miyamoto, (Chujo) Yuriko 1899-1951 **T C L C
  37**
  See also CA 170, 174; DLB 180
Miyazawa, Kenji 1896-1933   **TCLC 76**
  See also CA 157
Mizoguchi, Kenji 1898-1956   **TCLC 72**
  See also CA 167
Mo, Timothy (Peter) 1950(?)-   **CLC 46**
  See also CA 117; DLB 194; MTCW 1
Modarressi, Taghi (M.) 1931-   **CLC 44**
  See also CA 121; 134; INT 134
Modiano, Patrick (Jean) 1945-   **CLC 18**
  See also CA 85-88; CANR 17, 40; DLB 83
Moerck, Paal
  See Roelvaag, O(le) E(dvart)
Mofolo, Thomas (Mokopu) 1875(?)-1948
  TCLC 22; BLC 3; DAM MULT
  See also CA 121; 153; MTCW 2
Mohr, Nicholasa 1938-**CLC 12; DAM MULT;**
  HLC
  See also AAYA 8; CA 49-52; CANR 1, 32, 64;
  CLR 22; DLB 145; HW 1, 2; JRDA; SAAS
  8; SATA 8, 97
Mojtabai, A(nn) G(race) 1938- **CLC 5, 9, 15,**
  29
  See also CA 85-88
Moliere 1622-1673**LC 10, 28; DA; DAB; DAC;**
  DAM DRAM, MST; WLC
Molin, Charles
  See Mayne, William (James Carter)
Molnar, Ferenc 1878-1952   **TCLC 20; DAM**
  DRAM
  See also CA 109; 153
Momaday, N(avarre) Scott 1934- **CLC 2, 19,**
  85, 95; DA; DAB; DAC; DAM MST,
  MULT, NOV, POP; PC 25; WLCS
  See also AAYA 11; CA 25-28R; CANR 14, 34,
  68; CDALBS; DLB 143, 175; INT CANR-
  14; MTCW 1, 2; NNAL; SATA 48; SATA-
  Brief 30
Monette, Paul 1945-1995   **CLC 82**
  See also CA 139; 147
Monroe, Harriet 1860-1936   **TCLC 12**
  See also CA 109; DLB 54, 91
Monroe, Lyle
  See Heinlein, Robert A(nson)
Montagu, Elizabeth 1720-1800   **NCLC 7**
Montagu, Mary (Pierrepont) Wortley 1689-
  1762   **LC 9; PC 16**
  See also DLB 95, 101
Montagu, W. H.
  See Coleridge, Samuel Taylor
Montague, John (Patrick) 1929- **CLC 13, 46**

See also CA 9-12R; CANR 9, 69; DLB 40;
  MTCW 1
Montaigne, Michel (Eyquem) de 1533-1592
  LC 8; DA; DAB; DAC; DAM MST; WLC
Montale, Eugenio 1896-1981**CLC 7, 9, 18; PC
  13**
  See also CA 17-20R; 104; CANR 30; DLB 114;
  MTCW 1
Montesquieu, Charles-Louis de Secondat 1689-
  1755   **LC 7**
Montgomery, (Robert) Bruce 1921-1978
  See Crispin, Edmund
  See also CA 104
Montgomery, L(ucy) M(aud) 1874-1942
  TCLC 51; DAC; DAM MST
  See also AAYA 12; CA 108; 137; CLR 8; DLB
  92; DLBD 14; JRDA; MAICYA; MTCW 2;
  SATA 100; YABC 1
Montgomery, Marion H., Jr. 1925-   **CLC 7**
  See also AITN 1; CA 1-4R; CANR 3, 48; DLB
  6
Montgomery, Max
  See Davenport, Guy (Mattison, Jr.)
Montherlant, Henry (Milon) de 1896-1972
  CLC 8, 19; DAM DRAM
  See also CA 85-88; 37-40R; DLB 72; MTCW
  1
Monty Python
  See Chapman, Graham; Cleese, John
  (Marwood); Gilliam, Terry (Vance); Idle,
  Eric; Jones, Terence Graham Parry; Palin,
  Michael (Edward)
  See also AAYA 7
Moodie, Susanna (Strickland) 1803-1885
  NCLC 14
  See also DLB 99
Mooney, Edward 1951-
  See Mooney, Ted
  See also CA 130
Mooney, Ted   **CLC 25**
  See also Mooney, Edward
Moorcock, Michael (John) 1939-**CLC 5, 27, 58**
  See also Bradbury, Edward P.
  See also AAYA 26; CA 45-48; CAAS 5; CANR
  2, 17, 38, 64; DLB 14; MTCW 1, 2; SATA
  93
Moore, Brian 1921-1999**CLC 1, 3, 5, 7, 8, 19,**
  32, 90; DAB; DAC; DAM MST
  See also CA 1-4R; 174; CANR 1, 25, 42, 63;
  MTCW 1, 2
Moore, Edward
  See Muir, Edwin
Moore, G. E. 1873-1958   **TCLC 89**
Moore, George Augustus 1852-1933**TCLC 7;**
  SSC 19
  See also CA 104; DLB 10, 18, 57, 135
Moore, Lorrie   **CLC 39, 45, 68**
  See also Moore, Marie Lorena
Moore, Marianne (Craig) 1887-1972**CLC 1, 2,**
  4, 8, 10, 13, 19, 47; DA; DAB; DAC; DAM
  MST, POET; PC 4; WLCS
  See also CA 1-4R; 33-36R; CANR 3, 61;
  CDALB 1929-1941; DLB 45; DLBD 7;
  MTCW 1, 2; SATA 20
Moore, Marie Lorena 1957-
  See Moore, Lorrie
  See also CA 116; CANR 39
Moore, Thomas 1779-1852   **NCLC 6**
  See also DLB 96, 144
Morand, Paul 1888-1976   **CLC 41; SSC 22**
  See also CA 69-72; DLB 65
Morante, Elsa 1918-1985   **CLC 8, 47**
  See also CA 85-88; 117; CANR 35; DLB 177;

MTCW 1, 2

Moravia, Alberto 1907-1990**CLC 2, 7, 11, 27, 46; SSC 26**
See also Pincherle, Alberto
See also DLB 177; MTCW 2

More, Hannah 1745-1833   **NCLC 27**
See also DLB 107, 109, 116, 158

More, Henry 1614-1687   **LC 9**
See also DLB 126

More, Sir Thomas 1478-1535   **LC 10, 32**

Moreas, Jean   **TCLC 18**
See also Papadiamantopoulos, Johannes

Morgan, Berry 1919-   **CLC 6**
See also CA 49-52; DLB 6

Morgan, Claire
See Highsmith, (Mary) Patricia

Morgan, Edwin (George) 1920-   **CLC 31**
See also CA 5-8R; CANR 3, 43; DLB 27

Morgan, (George) Frederick 1922-   **CLC 23**
See also CA 17-20R; CANR 21

Morgan, Harriet
See Mencken, H(enry) L(ouis)

Morgan, Jane
See Cooper, James Fenimore

Morgan, Janet 1945-   **CLC 39**
See also CA 65-68

Morgan, Lady 1776(?)-1859   **NCLC 29**
See also DLB 116, 158

Morgan, Robin (Evonne) 1941-   **CLC 2**
See also CA 69-72; CANR 29, 68; MTCW 1; SATA 80

Morgan, Scott
See Kuttner, Henry

Morgan, Seth 1949(?)-1990   **CLC 65**
See also CA 132

Morgenstern, Christian 1871-1914   **TCLC 8**
See also CA 105

Morgenstern, S.
See Goldman, William (W.)

Moricz, Zsigmond 1879-1942   **TCLC 33**
See also CA 165

Morike, Eduard (Friedrich) 1804-1875**NCLC 10**
See also DLB 133

Moritz, Karl Philipp 1756-1793   **LC 2**
See also DLB 94

Morland, Peter Henry
See Faust, Frederick (Schiller)

Morley, Christopher (Darlington) 1890-1957
TCLC 87
See also CA 112; DLB 9

Morren, Theophil
See Hofmannsthal, Hugo von

Morris, Bill 1952-   **CLC 76**

Morris, Julian
See West, Morris L(anglo)

Morris, Steveland Judkins 1950(?)-
See Wonder, Stevie
See also CA 111

Morris, William 1834-1896   **NCLC 4**
See also CDBLB 1832-1890; DLB 18, 35, 57, 156, 178, 184

Morris, Wright 1910-1998**CLC 1, 3, 7, 18, 37**
See also CA 9-12R; 167; CANR 21; DLB 2, 206; DLBY 81; MTCW 1, 2

Morrison, Arthur 1863-1945   **TCLC 72**
See also CA 120; 157; DLB 70, 135, 197

Morrison, Chloe Anthony Wofford
See Morrison, Toni

Morrison, James Douglas 1943-1971
See Morrison, Jim
See also CA 73-76; CANR 40

Morrison, Jim   **CLC 17**

See also Morrison, James Douglas

Morrison, Toni 1931-**CLC 4, 10, 22, 55, 81, 87; BLC 3; DA; DAB; DAC; DAM MST, MULT, NOV, POP**
See also AAYA 1, 22; BW 2, 3; CA 29-32R; CANR 27, 42, 67; CDALB 1968-1988; DLB 6, 33, 143; DLBY 81; MTCW 1, 2; SATA 57

Morrison, Van 1945-   **CLC 21**
See also CA 116; 168

Morrissy, Mary 1958-   **CLC 99**

Mortimer, John (Clifford) 1923-   **CLC 28, 43; DAM DRAM, POP**
See also CA 13-16R; CANR 21, 69; CDBLB 1960 to Present; DLB 13; INT CANR-21; MTCW 1, 2

Mortimer, Penelope (Ruth) 1918-   **CLC 5**
See also CA 57-60; CANR 45

Morton, Anthony
See Creasey, John

Mosca, Gaetano 1858-1941   **TCLC 75**

Mosher, Howard Frank 1943-   **CLC 62**
See also CA 139; CANR 65

Mosley, Nicholas 1923-   **CLC 43, 70**
See also CA 69-72; CANR 41, 60; DLB 14, 207

Mosley, Walter 1952-   **CLC 97; BLCS; DAM MULT, POP**
See also AAYA 17; BW 2; CA 142; CANR 57; MTCW 2

Moss, Howard 1922-1987   **CLC 7, 14, 45, 50; DAM POET**
See also CA 1-4R; 123; CANR 1, 44; DLB 5

Mossgiel, Rab
See Burns, Robert

Motion, Andrew (Peter) 1952-   **CLC 47**
See also CA 146; DLB 40

Motley, Willard (Francis) 1909-1965   **CLC 18**
See also BW 1; CA 117; 106; DLB 76, 143

Motoori, Norinaga 1730-1801   **NCLC 45**

Mott, Michael (Charles Alston) 1930-**CLC 15, 34**
See also CA 5-8R; CAAS 7; CANR 7, 29

Mountain Wolf Woman 1884-1960   **CLC 92**
See also CA 144; NNAL

Moure, Erin 1955-   **CLC 88**
See also CA 113; DLB 60

Mowat, Farley (McGill) 1921-**CLC 26; DAC; DAM MST**
See also AAYA 1; CA 1-4R; CANR 4, 24, 42, 68; CLR 20; DLB 68; INT CANR-24; JRDA; MAICYA; MTCW 1, 2; SATA 3, 55

Mowatt, Anna Cora 1819-1870   **NCLC 74**

Moyers, Bill 1934-   **CLC 74**
See also AITN 2; CA 61-64; CANR 31, 52

Mphahlele, Es'kia
See Mphahlele, Ezekiel
See also DLB 125

Mphahlele, Ezekiel 1919-1983   **CLC 25; BLC 3; DAM MULT**
See also Mphahlele, Es'kia
See also BW 2, 3; CA 81-84; CANR 26, 76; MTCW 2

Mqhayi, S(amuel) E(dward) K(rune Loliwe) 1875-1945**TCLC 25; BLC 3; DAM MULT**
See also CA 153

Mrozek, Slawomir 1930-   **CLC 3, 13**
See also CA 13-16R; CAAS 10; CANR 29; MTCW 1

Mrs. Belloc-Lowndes
See Lowndes, Marie Adelaide (Belloc)

Mtwa, Percy (?)-   **CLC 47**

Mueller, Lisel 1924-   **CLC 13, 51**
See also CA 93-96; DLB 105

Muir, Edwin 1887-1959   **TCLC 2, 87**

See also CA 104; DLB 20, 100, 191

Muir, John 1838-1914   **TCLC 28**
See also CA 165; DLB 186

Mujica Lainez, Manuel 1910-1984   **CLC 31**
See also Lainez, Manuel Mujica
See also CA 81-84; 112; CANR 32; HW 1

Mukherjee, Bharati 1940-**CLC 53, 115; DAM NOV**
See also BEST 89:2; CA 107; CANR 45, 72; DLB 60; MTCW 1, 2

Muldoon, Paul 1951-**CLC 32, 72; DAM POET**
See also CA 113; 129; CANR 52; DLB 40; INT 129

Mulisch, Harry 1927-   **CLC 42**
See also CA 9-12R; CANR 6, 26, 56

Mull, Martin 1943-   **CLC 17**
See also CA 105

Muller, Wilhelm   **NCLC 73**

Mulock, Dinah Maria
See Craik, Dinah Maria (Mulock)

Munford, Robert 1737(?)-1783   **LC 5**
See also DLB 31

Mungo, Raymond 1946-   **CLC 72**
See also CA 49-52; CANR 2

Munro, Alice 1931-   **CLC 6, 10, 19, 50, 95; DAC; DAM MST, NOV; SSC 3; WLCS**
See also AITN 2; CA 33-36R; CANR 33, 53, 75; DLB 53; MTCW 1, 2; SATA 29

Munro, H(ector) H(ugh) 1870-1916
See Saki
See also CA 104; 130; CDBLB 1890-1914; DA; DAB; DAC; DAM MST, NOV; DLB 34, 162; MTCW 1, 2; WLC

Murdoch, (Jean) Iris 1919-**CLC 1, 2, 3, 4, 6, 8, 11, 15, 22, 31, 51; DAB; DAC; DAM MST, NOV**
See also CA 13-16R; CANR 8, 43, 68; CDBLB 1960 to Present; DLB 14, 194; INT CANR-8; MTCW 1, 2

Murfree, Mary Noailles 1850-1922   **SSC 22**
See also CA 122; DLB 12, 74

Murnau, Friedrich Wilhelm
See Plumpe, Friedrich Wilhelm

Murphy, Richard 1927-   **CLC 41**
See also CA 29-32R; DLB 40

Murphy, Sylvia 1937-   **CLC 34**
See also CA 121

Murphy, Thomas (Bernard) 1935-   **CLC 51**
See also CA 101

Murray, Albert L. 1916-   **CLC 73**
See also BW 2; CA 49-52; CANR 26, 52, 78; DLB 38

Murray, Judith Sargent 1751-1820   **NCLC 63**
See also DLB 37, 200

Murray, Les(lie) A(llan) 1938-**CLC 40; DAM POET**
See also CA 21-24R; CANR 11, 27, 56

Murry, J. Middleton
See Murry, John Middleton

Murry, John Middleton 1889-1957   **TCLC 16**
See also CA 118; DLB 149

Musgrave, Susan 1951-   **CLC 13, 54**
See also CA 69-72; CANR 45

Musil, Robert (Edler von) 1880-1942   **TCLC 12, 68; SSC 18**
See also CA 109; CANR 55; DLB 81, 124; MTCW 2

Muske, Carol 1945-   **CLC 90**
See also Muske-Dukes, Carol (Anne)

Muske-Dukes, Carol (Anne) 1945-
See Muske, Carol
See also CA 65-68; CANR 32, 70

Musset, (Louis Charles) Alfred de 1810-1857

NCLC 7
See also DLB 192
My Brother's Brother
See Chekhov, Anton (Pavlovich)
Myers, L(eopold) H(amilton) 1881-1944
TCLC 59
See also CA 157; DLB 15
Myers, Walter Dean 1937-   **CLC 35; BLC 3;**
DAM MULT, NOV
See also AAYA 4, 23; BW 2, 3; CA 33-36R;
CANR 20, 42, 67; CLR 4, 16, 35; DLB 33;
INT CANR-20; JRDA; MAICYA; MTCW 2;
SAAS 2; SATA 41, 71; SATA-Brief 27
Myers, Walter M.
See Myers, Walter Dean
Myles, Symon
See Follett, Ken(neth Martin)
Nabokov, Vladimir (Vladimirovich) 1899-1977
CLC 1, 2, 3, 6, 8, 11, 15, 23, 44, 46, 64;
DA; DAB; DAC; DAM MST, NOV; SSC
11; WLC
See also CA 5-8R; 69-72; CANR 20; CDALB
1941-1968; DLB 2; DLBD 3; DLBY 80, 91;
MTCW 1, 2
Nagai Kafu 1879-1959   **TCLC 51**
See also Nagai Sokichi
See also DLB 180
Nagai Sokichi 1879-1959
See Nagai Kafu
See also CA 117
Nagy, Laszlo 1925-1978   **CLC 7**
See also CA 129; 112
Naidu, Sarojini 1879-1943   **TCLC 80**
Naipaul, Shiva(dhar Srinivasa) 1945-1985
CLC 32, 39; DAM NOV
See also CA 110; 112; 116; CANR 33; DLB
157; DLBY 85; MTCW 1, 2
Naipaul, V(idiadhar) S(urajprasad) 1932-
CLC 4, 7, 9, 13, 18, 37, 105; DAB; DAC;
DAM MST, NOV
See also CA 1-4R; CANR 1, 33, 51; CDBLB
1960 to Present; DLB 125, 204, 206; DLBY
85; MTCW 1, 2
Nakos, Lilika 1899(?)-   **CLC 29**
Narayan, R(asipuram) K(rishnaswami) 1906-
CLC 7, 28, 47; DAM NOV; SSC 25
See also CA 81-84; CANR 33, 61; MTCW 1,
2; SATA 62
Nash, (Frediric) Ogden 1902-1971 **CLC 23;**
DAM POET; PC 21
See also CA 13-14; 29-32R; CANR 34, 61; CAP
1; DLB 11; MAICYA; MTCW 1, 2; SATA 2,
46
Nashe, Thomas 1567-1601(?)   **LC 41**
See also DLB 167
Nashe, Thomas 1567-1601   **LC 41**
Nathan, Daniel
See Dannay, Frederic
Nathan, George Jean 1882-1958   **TCLC 18**
See also Hatteras, Owen
See also CA 114; 169; DLB 137
Natsume, Kinnosuke 1867-1916
See Natsume, Soseki
See also CA 104
Natsume, Soseki 1867-1916   **TCLC 2, 10**
See also Natsume, Kinnosuke
See also DLB 180
Natti, (Mary) Lee 1919-
See Kingman, Lee
See also CA 5-8R; CANR 2
Naylor, Gloria 1950-CLC 28, 52; BLC 3; DA;
DAC; DAM MST, MULT, NOV, POP;
WLCS

See also AAYA 6; BW 2, 3; CA 107; CANR 27,
51, 74; DLB 173; MTCW 1, 2
Neihardt, John Gneisenau 1881-1973CLC 32
See also CA 13-14; CANR 65; CAP 1; DLB 9,
54
Nekrasov, Nikolai Alekseevich 1821-1878
NCLC 11
Nelligan, Emile 1879-1941   **TCLC 14**
See also CA 114; DLB 92
Nelson, Willie 1933-   **CLC 17**
See also CA 107
Nemerov, Howard (Stanley) 1920-1991CLC 2,
6, 9, 36; DAM POET; PC 24
See also CA 1-4R; 134; CABS 2; CANR 1, 27,
53; DLB 5, 6; DLBY 83; INT CANR-27;
MTCW 1, 2
Neruda, Pablo 1904-1973CLC 1, 2, 5, 7, 9, 28,
62; DA; DAB; DAC; DAM MST, MULT,
POET; HLC; PC 4; WLC
See also CA 19-20; 45-48; CAP 2; HW 1;
MTCW 1, 2
Nerval, Gerard de 1808-1855NCLC 1, 67; PC
13; SSC 18
Nervo, (Jose) Amado (Ruiz de) 1870-1919
TCLC 11; HLCS 1
See also CA 109; 131; HW 1
Nessi, Pio Baroja y
See Baroja (y Nessi), Pio
Nestroy, Johann 1801-1862   **NCLC 42**
See also DLB 133
Netterville, Luke
See O'Grady, Standish (James)
Neufeld, John (Arthur) 1938-   **CLC 17**
See also AAYA 11; CA 25-28R; CANR 11, 37,
56; CLR 52; MAICYA; SAAS 3; SATA 6,
81
Neville, Emily Cheney 1919-   **CLC 12**
See also CA 5-8R; CANR 3, 37; JRDA;
MAICYA; SAAS 2; SATA 1
Newbound, Bernard Slade 1930-
See Slade, Bernard
See also CA 81-84; CANR 49; DAM DRAM
Newby, P(ercy) H(oward) 1918-1997 **CLC 2,**
13; DAM NOV
See also CA 5-8R; 161; CANR 32, 67; DLB
15; MTCW 1
Newlove, Donald 1928-   **CLC 6**
See also CA 29-32R; CANR 25
Newlove, John (Herbert) 1938-   **CLC 14**
See also CA 21-24R; CANR 9, 25
Newman, Charles 1938-   **CLC 2, 8**
See also CA 21-24R
Newman, Edwin (Harold) 1919-   **CLC 14**
See also AITN 1; CA 69-72; CANR 5
Newman, John Henry 1801-1890   **NCLC 38**
See also DLB 18, 32, 55
Newton, (Sir)Isaac 1642-1727   **LC 35**
Newton, Suzanne 1936-   **CLC 35**
See also CA 41-44R; CANR 14; JRDA; SATA
5, 77
Nexo, Martin Andersen 1869-1954 TCLC 43
Nezval, Vitezslav 1900-1958   **TCLC 44**
See also CA 123
Ng, Fae Myenne 1957(?)-   **CLC 81**
See also CA 146
Ngema, Mbongeni 1955-   **CLC 57**
See also BW 2; CA 143
Ngugi, James T(hiong'o)   **CLC 3, 7, 13**
See also Ngugi wa Thiong'o
Ngugi wa Thiong'o 1938-   **CLC 36; BLC 3;**
DAM MULT, NOV
See also Ngugi, James T(hiong'o)
See also BW 2; CA 81-84; CANR 27, 58; DLB

125; MTCW 1, 2
Nichol, B(arrie) P(hillip) 1944-1988 **CLC 18**
See also CA 53-56; DLB 53; SATA 66
Nichols, John (Treadwell) 1940-   **CLC 38**
See also CA 9-12R; CAAS 2; CANR 6, 70;
DLBY 82
Nichols, Leigh
See Koontz, Dean R(ay)
Nichols, Peter (Richard) 1927- CLC 5, 36, 65
See also CA 104; CANR 33; DLB 13; MTCW
1
Nicolas, F. R. E.
See Freeling, Nicolas
Niedecker, Lorine 1903-1970   **CLC 10, 42;**
DAM POET
See also CA 25-28; CAP 2; DLB 48
Nietzsche, Friedrich (Wilhelm) 1844-1900
TCLC 10, 18, 55
See also CA 107; 121; DLB 129
Nievo, Ippolito 1831-1861   , NCLC 22
Nightingale, Anne Redmon 1943-
See Redmon, Anne
See also CA 103
Nightingale, Florence 1820-1910   **TCLC 85**
See also DLB 166
Nik. T. O.
See Annensky, Innokenty (Fyodorovich)
Nin, Anais 1903-1977 CLC 1, 4, 8, 11, 14, 60;
DAM NOV, POP; SSC 10
See also AITN 2; CA 13-16R; 69-72; CANR
22, 53; DLB 2, 4, 152; MTCW 1, 2
Nishida, Kitaro 1870-1945   **TCLC 83**
Nishiwaki, Junzaburo 1894-1982   **PC 15**
See also CA 107
Nissenson, Hugh 1933-   **CLC 4, 9**
See also CA 17-20R; CANR 27; DLB 28
Niven, Larry   **CLC 8**
See also Niven, Laurence Van Cott
See also AAYA 27; DLB 8
Niven, Laurence Van Cott 1938-
See Niven, Larry
See also CA 21-24R; CAAS 12; CANR 14, 44,
66; DAM POP; MTCW 1, 2; SATA 95
Nixon, Agnes Eckhardt 1927-   **CLC 21**
See also CA 110
Nizan, Paul 1905-1940   **TCLC 40**
See also CA 161; DLB 72
Nkosi, Lewis 1936-   **CLC 45; BLC 3; DAM**
MULT
See also BW 1, 3; CA 65-68; CANR 27; DLB
157
Nodier, (Jean) Charles (Emmanuel) 1780-1844
NCLC 19
See also DLB 119
Noguchi, Yone 1875-1947   **TCLC 80**
Nolan, Christopher 1965-   **CLC 58**
See also CA 111
Noon, Jeff 1957-   **CLC 91**
See also CA 148
Norden, Charles
See Durrell, Lawrence (George)
Nordhoff, Charles (Bernard) 1887-1947
TCLC 23
See also CA 108; DLB 9; SATA 23
Norfolk, Lawrence 1963-   **CLC 76**
See also CA 144
Norman, Marsha 1947-CLC 28; DAM DRAM;
DC 8
See also CA 105; CABS 3; CANR 41; DLBY
84
Normyx
See Douglas, (George) Norman
Norris, Frank 1870-1902   **SSC 28**

See also Norris, (Benjamin) Frank(lin, Jr.)
See also CDALB 1865-1917; DLB 12, 71, 186
Norris, (Benjamin) Frank(lin, Jr.) 1870-1902
TCLC 24
See also Norris, Frank
See also CA 110; 160
Norris, Leslie 1921-   **CLC 14**
See also CA 11-12; CANR 14; CAP 1; DLB 27
North, Andrew
See Norton, Andre
North, Anthony
See Koontz, Dean R(ay)
North, Captain George
See Stevenson, Robert Louis (Balfour)
North, Milou
See Erdrich, Louise
Northrup, B. A.
See Hubbard, L(afayette) Ron(ald)
North Staffs
See Hulme, T(homas) E(rnest)
Norton, Alice Mary
See Norton, Andre
See also MAICYA; SATA 1, 43
Norton, Andre 1912-   **CLC 12**
See also Norton, Alice Mary
See also AAYA 14; CA 1-4R; CANR 68; CLR
50; DLB 8, 52; JRDA; MTCW 1; SATA 91
Norton, Caroline 1808-1877   **NCLC 47**
See also DLB 21, 159, 199
Norway, Nevil Shute 1899-1960
See Shute, Nevil
See also CA 102; 93-96; MTCW 2
Norwid, Cyprian Kamil 1821-1883 **NCLC 17**
Nosille, Nabrah
See Ellison, Harlan (Jay)
Nossack, Hans Erich 1901-1978   **CLC 6**
See also CA 93-96; 85-88; DLB 69
Nostradamus 1503-1566   **LC 27**
Nosu, Chuji
See Ozu, Yasujiro
Notenburg, Eleanora (Genrikhovna) von
See Guro, Elena
Nova, Craig 1945-   **CLC 7, 31**
See also CA 45-48; CANR 2, 53
Novak, Joseph
See Kosinski, Jerzy (Nikodem)
Novalis 1772-1801   **NCLC 13**
See also DLB 90
Novis, Emile
See Weil, Simone (Adolphine)
Nowlan, Alden (Albert) 1933-1983   **CLC 15;**
DAC; DAM MST
See also CA 9-12R; CANR 5; DLB 53
Noyes, Alfred 1880-1958   **TCLC 7**
See also CA 104; DLB 20
Nunn, Kem   **CLC 34**
See also CA 159
Nye, Robert 1939- **CLC 13, 42; DAM NOV**
See also CA 33-36R; CANR 29, 67; DLB 14;
MTCW 1; SATA 6
Nyro, Laura 1947-   **CLC 17**
Oates, Joyce Carol 1938-**CLC 1, 2, 3, 6, 9, 11,**
15, 19, 33, 52, 108; DA; DAB; DAC; DAM
MST, NOV, POP; SSC 6; WLC
See also AAYA 15; AITN 1; BEST 89:2; CA 5-
8R; CANR 25, 45, 74; CDALB 1968-1988;
DLB 2, 5, 130; DLBY 81; INT CANR-25;
MTCW 1, 2
O'Brien, Darcy 1939-1998   **CLC 11**
See also CA 21-24R; 167; CANR 8, 59
O'Brien, E. G.
See Clarke, Arthur C(harles)
O'Brien, Edna 1936- **CLC 3, 5, 8, 13, 36, 65,**

116; **DAM NOV; SSC 10**
See also CA 1-4R; CANR 6, 41, 65; CDBLB
1960 to Present; DLB 14; MTCW 1, 2
O'Brien, Fitz-James 1828-1862   **NCLC 21**
See also DLB 74
O'Brien, Flann   **CLC 1, 4, 5, 7, 10, 47**
See also O Nuallain, Brian
O'Brien, Richard 1942-   **CLC 17**
See also CA 124
O'Brien, (William) Tim(othy) 1946- **CLC 7,**
19, 40, 103; DAM POP
See also AAYA 16; CA 85-88; CANR 40, 58;
CDALBS; DLB 152; DLBD 9; DLBY 80;
MTCW 2
Obstfelder, Sigbjoern 1866-1900   **TCLC 23**
See also CA 123
O'Casey, Sean 1880-1964**CLC 1, 5, 9, 11, 15,**
88; DAB; DAC; DAM DRAM, MST;
WLCS
See also CA 89-92; CANR 62; CDBLB 1914-
1945; DLB 10; MTCW 1, 2
O'Cathasaigh, Sean
See O'Casey, Sean
Ochs, Phil 1940-1976   **CLC 17**
See also CA 65-68
O'Connor, Edwin (Greene) 1918-1968**CLC 14**
See also CA 93-96; 25-28R
O'Connor, (Mary) Flannery 1925-1964 **C L C**
1, 2, 3, 6, 10, 13, 15, 21, 66, 104; DA; DAB;
DAC; DAM MST, NOV; SSC 1, 23; WLC
See also AAYA 7; CA 1-4R; CANR 3, 41;
CDALB 1941-1968; DLB 2, 152; DLBD 12;
DLBY 80; MTCW 1, 2
O'Connor, Frank   **CLC 23; SSC 5**
See also O'Donovan, Michael John
See also DLB 162
O'Dell, Scott 1898-1989   **CLC 30**
See also AAYA 3; CA 61-64; 129; CANR 12,
30; CLR 1, 16; DLB 52; JRDA; MAICYA;
SATA 12, 60
Odets, Clifford 1906-1963**CLC 2, 28, 98; DAM**
DRAM; DC 6
See also CA 85-88; CANR 62; DLB 7, 26;
MTCW 1, 2
O'Doherty, Brian 1934-   **CLC 76**
See also CA 105
O'Donnell, K. M.
See Malzberg, Barry N(athaniel)
O'Donnell, Lawrence
See Kuttner, Henry
O'Donovan, Michael John 1903-1966**CLC 14**
See also O'Connor, Frank
See also CA 93-96
Oe, Kenzaburo 1935- **CLC 10, 36, 86; DAM**
NOV; SSC 20
See also CA 97-100; CANR 36, 50, 74; DLB
182; DLBY 94; MTCW 1, 2
O'Faolain, Julia 1932-   **CLC 6, 19, 47, 108**
See also CA 81-84; CAAS 2; CANR 12, 61;
DLB 14; MTCW 1
O'Faolain, Sean 1900-1991 **CLC 1, 7, 14, 32,**
70; SSC 13
See also CA 61-64; 134; CANR 12, 66; DLB
15, 162; MTCW 1, 2
O'Flaherty, Liam 1896-1984**CLC 5, 34; SSC 6**
See also CA 101; 113; CANR 35; DLB 36, 162;
DLBY 84; MTCW 1, 2
Ogilvy, Gavin
See Barrie, J(ames) M(atthew)
O'Grady, Standish (James) 1846-1928**T C L C**
5
See also CA 104; 157
O'Grady, Timothy 1951-   **CLC 59**

See also CA 138
O'Hara, Frank 1926-1966 **CLC 2, 5, 13, 78;**
DAM POET
See also CA 9-12R; 25-28R; CANR 33; DLB
5, 16, 193; MTCW 1, 2
O'Hara, John (Henry) 1905-1970**CLC 1, 2, 3,**
6, 11, 42; DAM NOV; SSC 15
See also CA 5-8R; 25-28R; CANR 31, 60;
CDALB 1929-1941; DLB 9, 86; DLBD 2;
MTCW 1, 2
O Hehir, Diana 1922-   **CLC 41**
See also CA 93-96
Okigbo, Christopher (Ifenayichukwu) 1932-
1967 **CLC 25, 84; BLC 3; DAM MULT,**
POET; PC 7
See also BW 1, 3; CA 77-80; CANR 74; DLB
125; MTCW 1, 2
Okri, Ben 1959-   **CLC 87**
See also BW 2, 3; CA 130; 138; CANR 65; DLB
157; INT 138; MTCW 2
Olds, Sharon 1942- **CLC 32, 39, 85; DAM**
POET; PC 22
See also CA 101; CANR 18, 41, 66; DLB 120;
MTCW 2
Oldstyle, Jonathan
See Irving, Washington
Olesha, Yuri (Karlovich) 1899-1960   **CLC 8**
See also CA 85-88
Oliphant, Laurence 1829(?)-1888 **NCLC 47**
See also DLB 18, 166
Oliphant, Margaret (Oliphant Wilson) 1828-
1897   **NCLC 11, 61; SSC 25**
See also DLB 18, 159, 190
Oliver, Mary 1935-   **CLC 19, 34, 98**
See also CA 21-24R; CANR 9, 43; DLB 5, 193
Olivier, Laurence (Kerr) 1907-1989 **CLC 20**
See also CA 111; 150; 129
Olsen, Tillie 1912-**CLC 4, 13, 114; DA; DAB;**
DAC; DAM MST; SSC 11
See also CA 1-4R; CANR 1, 43, 74; CDALBS;
DLB 28, 206; DLBY 80; MTCW 1, 2
Olson, Charles (John) 1910-1970**CLC 1, 2, 5,**
6, 9, 11, 29; DAM POET; PC 19
See also CA 13-16; 25-28R; CABS 2; CANR
35, 61; CAP 1; DLB 5, 16, 193; MTCW 1, 2
Olson, Toby 1937-   **CLC 28**
See also CA 65-68; CANR 9, 31
Olyesha, Yuri
See Olesha, Yuri (Karlovich)
Ondaatje, (Philip) Michael 1943-**CLC 14, 29,**
51, 76; DAB; DAC; DAM MST
See also CA 77-80; CANR 42, 74; DLB 60;
MTCW 2
Oneal, Elizabeth 1934-
See Oneal, Zibby
See also CA 106; CANR 28; MAICYA; SATA
30, 82
Oneal, Zibby   **CLC 30**
See also Oneal, Elizabeth
See also AAYA 5; CLR 13; JRDA
O'Neill, Eugene (Gladstone) 1888-1953**TCLC**
1, 6, 27, 49; DA; DAB; DAC; DAM DRAM,
MST; WLC
See also AITN 1; CA 110; 132; CDALB 1929-
1941; DLB 7; MTCW 1, 2
Onetti, Juan Carlos 1909-1994   **CLC 7, 10;**
DAM MULT, NOV; HLCS 1; SSC 23
See also CA 85-88; 145; CANR 32, 63; DLB
113; HW 1, 2; MTCW 1, 2
O Nuallain, Brian 1911-1966
See O'Brien, Flann
See also CA 21-22; 25-28R; CAP 2
Ophuls, Max 1902-1957   **TCLC 79**

See also CA 113

Opie, Amelia 1769-1853 **NCLC 65**
See also DLB 116, 159

Oppen, George 1908-1984 **CLC 7, 13, 34**
See also CA 13-16R; 113; CANR 8; DLB 5, 165

Oppenheim, E(dward) Phillips 1866-1946
TCLC 45
See also CA 111; DLB 70

Opuls, Max
See Ophuls, Max

Origen c. 185-c. 254 **CMLC 19**

Orlovitz, Gil 1918-1973 **CLC 22**
See also CA 77-80; 45-48; DLB 2, 5

Orris
See Ingelow, Jean

Ortega y Gasset, Jose 1883-1955 **TCLC 9;**
DAM MULT; HLC
See also CA 106; 130; HW 1, 2, MTCW 1, 2

Ortese, Anna Maria 1914- **CLC 89**
See also DLB 177

Ortiz, Simon J(oseph) 1941- **CLC 45; DAM**
MULT, POET; PC 17
See also CA 134; CANR 69; DLB 120, 175;
NNAL

Orton, Joe **CLC 4, 13, 43; DC 3**
See also Orton, John Kingsley
See also CDBLB 1960 to Present; DLB 13;
MTCW 2

Orton, John Kingsley 1933-1967
See Orton, Joe
See also CA 85-88; CANR 35, 66; DAM
DRAM; MTCW 1, 2

Orwell, George **TCLC 2, 6, 15, 31, 51; DAB;**
WLC
See also Blair, Eric (Arthur)
See also CDBLB 1945-1960; DLB 15, 98, 195

Osborne, David
See Silverberg, Robert

Osborne, George
See Silverberg, Robert

Osborne, John (James) 1929-1994 **CLC 1, 2, 5,**
11, 45; DA; DAB; DAC; DAM DRAM,
MST; WLC
See also CA 13-16R; 147; CANR 21, 56;
CDBLB 1945-1960; DLB 13; MTCW 1, 2

Osborne, Lawrence 1958- **CLC 50**

Osbourne, Lloyd 1868-1947 **TCLC 93**

Oshima, Nagisa 1932- **CLC 20**
See also CA 116; 121; CANR 78

Oskison, John Milton 1874-1947 **TCLC 35;**
DAM MULT
See also CA 144; DLB 175; NNAL

Ossian c. 3rd cent. - **CMLC 28**
See also Macpherson, James

Ossoli, Sarah Margaret (Fuller marchesa d')
1810-1850
See Fuller, Margaret
See also SATA 25

Ostrovsky, Alexander 1823-1886 **NCLC 30, 57**

Otero, Blas de 1916-1979 **CLC 11**
See also CA 89-92; DLB 134

Otto, Rudolf 1869-1937 **TCLC 85**

Otto, Whitney 1955- **CLC 70**
See also CA 140

Ouida **TCLC 43**
See also De La Ramee, (Marie) Louise
See also DLB 18, 156

Ousmane, Sembene 1923- **CLC 66; BLC 3**
See also BW 1, 3; CA 117; 125; MTCW 1

Ovid 43B.C.-17 **CMLC 7; DAM POET; PC 2**
See also DLB 211

Owen, Hugh

See Faust, Frederick (Schiller)

Owen, Wilfred (Edward Salter) 1893-1918
TCLC 5, 27; DA; DAB; DAC; DAM MST,
POET; PC 19; WLC
See also CA 104; 141; CDBLB 1914-1945;
DLB 20; MTCW 2

Owens, Rochelle 1936- **CLC 8**
See also CA 17-20R; CAAS 2; CANR 39

Oz, Amos 1939- **CLC 5, 8, 11, 27, 33, 54; DAM**
NOV
See also CA 53-56; CANR 27, 47, 65; MTCW
1, 2

Ozick, Cynthia 1928- **CLC 3, 7, 28, 62; DAM**
NOV, POP; SSC 15
See also BEST 90:1; CA 17-20R; CANR 23,
58; DLB 28, 152; DLBY 82; INT CANR-
23; MTCW 1, 2

Ozu, Yasujiro 1903-1963 **CLC 16**
See also CA 112

Pacheco, C.
See Pessoa, Fernando (Antonio Nogueira)

Pa Chin **CLC 18**
See also Li Fei-kan

Pack, Robert 1929- **CLC 13**
See also CA 1-4R; CANR 3, 44; DLB 5

Padgett, Lewis
See Kuttner, Henry

Padilla (Lorenzo), Heberto 1932- **CLC 38**
See also AITN 1; CA 123; 131; HW 1

Page, Jimmy 1944- **CLC 12**

Page, Louise 1955- **CLC 40**
See also CA 140; CANR 76

Page, P(atricia) K(athleen) 1916- **CLC 7, 18;**
DAC; DAM MST; PC 12
See also CA 53-56; CANR 4, 22, 65; DLB 68;
MTCW 1

Page, Thomas Nelson 1853-1922 **SSC 23**
See also CA 118; DLB 12, 78; DLBD 13

Pagels, Elaine Hiesey 1943- **CLC 104**
See also CA 45-48; CANR 2, 24, 51

Paget, Violet 1856-1935
See Lee, Vernon
See also CA 104; 166

Paget-Lowe, Henry
See Lovecraft, H(oward) P(hillips)

Paglia, Camille (Anna) 1947- **CLC 68**
See also CA 140; CANR 72; MTCW 2

Paige, Richard
See Koontz, Dean R(ay)

Paine, Thomas 1737-1809 **NCLC 62**
See also CDALB 1640-1865; DLB 31, 43, 73,
158

Pakenham, Antonia
See Fraser, (Lady) Antonia (Pakenham)

Palamas, Kostes 1859-1943 **TCLC 5**
See also CA 105

Palazzeschi, Aldo 1885-1974 **CLC 11**
See also CA 89-92; 53-56; DLB 114

Paley, Grace 1922- **CLC 4, 6, 37; DAM POP;**
SSC 8
See also CA 25-28R; CANR 13, 46, 74; DLB
28; INT CANR-13; MTCW 1, 2

Palin, Michael (Edward) 1943- **CLC 21**
See also Monty Python
See also CA 107; CANR 35; SATA 67

Palliser, Charles 1947- **CLC 65**
See also CA 136; CANR 76

Palma, Ricardo 1833-1919 **TCLC 29**
See also CA 168

Pancake, Breece Dexter 1952-1979
See Pancake, Breece D'J
See also CA 123; 109

Pancake, Breece D'J **CLC 29**

See also Pancake, Breece Dexter
See also DLB 130

Panko, Rudy
See Gogol, Nikolai (Vasilyevich)

Papadiamantis, Alexandros 1851-1911 **TCLC**
29
See also CA 168

Papadiamantopoulos, Johannes 1856-1910
See Moreas, Jean
See also CA 117

Papini, Giovanni 1881-1956 **TCLC 22**
See also CA 121

Paracelsus 1493-1541 **LC 14**
See also DLB 179

Parasol, Peter
See Stevens, Wallace

Pardo Bazan, Emilia 1851-1921 **SSC 30**

Pareto, Vilfredo 1848-1923 **TCLC 69**
See also CA 175

Parfenie, Maria
See Codrescu, Andrei

Parini, Jay (Lee) 1948- **CLC 54**
See also CA 97-100; CAAS 16; CANR 32

Park, Jordan
See Kornbluth, C(yril) M.; Pohl, Frederik

Park, Robert E(zra) 1864-1944 **TCLC 73**
See also CA 122; 165

Parker, Bert
See Ellison, Harlan (Jay)

Parker, Dorothy (Rothschild) 1893-1967 **CLC**
15, 68; DAM POET; SSC 2
See also CA 19-20; 25-28R; CAP 2; DLB 11,
45, 86; MTCW 1, 2

Parker, Robert B(rown) 1932- **CLC 27; DAM**
NOV, POP
See also AAYA 28; BEST 89:4; CA 49-52;
CANR 1, 26, 52; INT CANR-26; MTCW 1

Parkin, Frank 1940- **CLC 43**
See also CA 147

Parkman, Francis, Jr. 1823-1893 **NCLC 12**
See also DLB 1, 30, 186

Parks, Gordon (Alexander Buchanan) 1912-
CLC 1, 16; BLC 3; DAM MULT
See also AITN 2; BW 2, 3; CA 41-44R; CANR
26, 66; DLB 33; MTCW 2; SATA 8

Parmenides c. 515B.C.-c. 450B.C. **CMLC 22**
See also DLB 176

Parnell, Thomas 1679-1718 **LC 3**
See also DLB 94

Parra, Nicanor 1914- **CLC 2, 102; DAM**
MULT; HLC
See also CA 85-88; CANR 32; HW 1; MTCW
1

Parrish, Mary Frances
See Fisher, M(ary) F(rances) K(ennedy)

Parson
See Coleridge, Samuel Taylor

Parson Lot
See Kingsley, Charles

Partridge, Anthony
See Oppenheim, E(dward) Phillips

Pascal, Blaise 1623-1662 **LC 35**

Pascoli, Giovanni 1855-1912 **TCLC 45**
See also CA 170

Pasolini, Pier Paolo 1922-1975 **CLC 20, 37,**
106; PC 17
See also CA 93-96; 61-64; CANR 63; DLB 128,
177; MTCW 1

Pasquini
See Silone, Ignazio

Pastan, Linda (Olenik) 1932- **CLC 27; DAM**
POET
See also CA 61-64; CANR 18, 40, 61; DLB 5

Pasternak, Boris (Leonidovich) 1890-1960
 **CLC 7, 10, 18, 63; DA; DAB; DAC; DAM
 MST, NOV, POET; PC 6; SSC 31; WLC**
 See also CA 127; 116; MTCW 1, 2
Patchen, Kenneth 1911-1972 **CLC 1, 2, 18;
 DAM POET**
 See also CA 1-4R; 33-36R; CANR 3, 35; DLB
 16, 48; MTCW 1
Pater, Walter (Horatio) 1839-1894 **NCLC 7**
 See also CDBLB 1832-1890; DLB 57, 156
Paterson, A(ndrew) B(arton) 1864-1941
 TCLC 32
 See also CA 155; SATA 97
Paterson, Katherine (Womeldorf) 1932-**C L C
 12, 30**
 See also AAYA 1; CA 21-24R; CANR 28, 59;
 CLR 7, 50; DLB 52; JRDA; MAICYA;
 MTCW 1; SATA 13, 53, 92
Patmore, Coventry Kersey Dighton 1823-1896
 NCLC 9
 See also DLB 35, 98
Paton, Alan (Stewart) 1903-1988 **CLC 4, 10,
 25, 55, 106; DA; DAB; DAC; DAM MST,
 NOV; WLC**
 See also AAYA 26; CA 13-16; 125; CANR 22;
 CAP 1; DLBD 17; MTCW 1, 2; SATA 11;
 SATA-Obit 56
Paton Walsh, Gillian 1937-
 See Walsh, Jill Paton
 See also CANR 38; JRDA; MAICYA; SAAS 3;
 SATA 4, 72
Patton, George S. 1885-1945 **TCLC 79**
Paulding, James Kirke 1778-1860 **NCLC 2**
 See also DLB 3, 59, 74
Paulin, Thomas Neilson 1949-
 See Paulin, Tom
 See also CA 123; 128
Paulin, Tom **CLC 37**
 See also Paulin, Thomas Neilson
 See also DLB 40
Paustovsky, Konstantin (Georgievich) 1892-
 1968 **CLC 40**
 See also CA 93-96; 25-28R
Pavese, Cesare 1908-1950 **TCLC 3; PC 13;
 SSC 19**
 See also CA 104; 169; DLB 128, 177
Pavic, Milorad 1929- **CLC 60**
 See also CA 136; DLB 181
Pavlov, Ivan Petrovich 1849-1936 **TCLC 91**
 See also CA 118
Payne, Alan
 See Jakes, John (William)
Paz, Gil
 See Lugones, Leopoldo
Paz, Octavio 1914-1998**CLC 3, 4, 6, 10, 19, 51,
 65, 119; DA; DAB; DAC; DAM MST,
 MULT, POET; HLC; PC 1; WLC**
 See also CA 73-76; 165; CANR 32, 65; DLBY
 90, 98; HW 1, 2; MTCW 1, 2
p'Bitek, Okot 1931-1982 **CLC 96; BLC 3;
 DAM MULT**
 See also BW 2, 3; CA 124; 107; DLB 125;
 MTCW 1, 2
Peacock, Molly 1947- **CLC 60**
 See also CA 103; CAAS 21; CANR 52; DLB
 120
Peacock, Thomas Love 1785-1866 **NCLC 22**
 See also DLB 96, 116
Peake, Mervyn 1911-1968 **CLC 7, 54**
 See also CA 5-8R; 25-28R; CANR 3; DLB 15,
 160; MTCW 1; SATA 23
Pearce, Philippa **CLC 21**
 See also Christie, (Ann) Philippa

See also CLR 9; DLB 161; MAICYA; SATA 1,
 67
Pearl, Eric
 See Elman, Richard (Martin)
Pearson, T(homas) R(eid) 1956- **CLC 39**
 See also CA 120; 130; INT 130
Peck, Dale 1967- **CLC 81**
 See also CA 146; CANR 72
Peck, John 1941- **CLC 3**
 See also CA 49-52; CANR 3
Peck, Richard (Wayne) 1934- **CLC 21**
 See also AAYA 1, 24; CA 85-88; CANR 19,
 38; CLR 15; INT CANR-19; JRDA;
 MAICYA; SAAS 2; SATA 18, 55, 97
Peck, Robert Newton 1928- **CLC 17; DA;
 DAC; DAM MST**
 See also AAYA 3; CA 81-84; CANR 31, 63;
 CLR 45; JRDA; MAICYA; SAAS 1; SATA
 21, 62
Peckinpah, (David) Sam(uel) 1925-1984 **C L C
 20**
 See also CA 109; 114
Pedersen, Knut 1859-1952
 See Hamsun, Knut
 See also CA 104; 119; CANR 63; MTCW 1, 2
Peeslake, Gaffer
 See Durrell, Lawrence (George)
Peguy, Charles Pierre 1873-1914 **TCLC 10**
 See also CA 107
Peirce, Charles Sanders 1839-1914 **TCLC 81**
Pena, Ramon del Valle y
 See Valle-Inclan, Ramon (Maria) del
Pendennis, Arthur Esquir
 See Thackeray, William Makepeace
Penn, William 1644-1718 **LC 25**
 See also DLB 24
PEPECE
 See Prado (Calvo), Pedro
Pepys, Samuel 1633-1703 **LC 11; DA; DAB;
 DAC; DAM MST; WLC**
 See also CDBLB 1660-1789; DLB 101
Percy, Walker 1916-1990**CLC 2, 3, 6, 8, 14, 18,
 47, 65; DAM NOV, POP**
 See also CA 1-4R; 131; CANR 1, 23, 64; DLB
 2; DLBY 80, 90; MTCW 1, 2
Percy, William Alexander 1885-1942**TCLC 84**
 See also CA 163; MTCW 2
Perec, Georges 1936-1982 **CLC 56, 116**
 See also CA 141; DLB 83
Pereda (y Sanchez de Porrua), Jose Maria de
 1833-1906 **TCLC 16**
 See also CA 117
Pereda y Porrua, Jose Maria de
 See Pereda (y Sanchez de Porrua), Jose Maria
 de
Peregoy, George Weems
 See Mencken, H(enry) L(ouis)
Perelman, S(idney) J(oseph) 1904-1979 **C L C
 3, 5, 9, 15, 23, 44, 49; DAM DRAM; SSC
 32**
 See also AITN 1, 2; CA 73-76; 89-92; CANR
 18; DLB 11, 44; MTCW 1, 2
Peret, Benjamin 1899-1959 **TCLC 20**
 See also CA 117
Peretz, Isaac Loeb 1851(?)-1915 **TCLC 16;
 SSC 26**
 See also CA 109
Peretz, Yitzhok Leibush
 See Peretz, Isaac Loeb
Perez Galdos, Benito 1843-1920 **TCLC 27;
 HLCS 1**
 See also CA 125; 153; HW 1
Perrault, Charles 1628-1703 **LC 2**

See also MAICYA; SATA 25
Perry, Brighton
 See Sherwood, Robert E(mmet)
Perse, St.-John
 See Leger, (Marie-Rene Auguste) Alexis Saint-
 Leger
Perutz, Leo(pold) 1882-1957 **TCLC 60**
 See also CA 147; DLB 81
Peseenz, Tulio F.
 See Lopez y Fuentes, Gregorio
Pesetsky, Bette 1932- **CLC 28**
 See also CA 133; DLB 130
Peshkov, Alexei Maximovich 1868-1936
 See Gorky, Maxim
 See also CA 105; 141; DA; DAC; DAM DRAM,
 MST, NOV; MTCW 2
Pessoa, Fernando (Antonio Nogueira) 1888-
 1935**TCLC 27; DAM MULT; HLC; PC 20**
 See also CA 125
Peterkin, Julia Mood 1880-1961 **CLC 31**
 See also CA 102; DLB 9
Peters, Joan K(aren) 1945- **CLC 39**
 See also CA 158
Peters, Robert L(ouis) 1924- **CLC 7**
 See also CA 13-16R; CAAS 8; DLB 105
Petofi, Sandor 1823-1849 **NCLC 21**
Petrakis, Harry Mark 1923- **CLC 3**
 See also CA 9-12R; CANR 4, 30
Petrarch 1304-1374 **CMLC 20; DAM POET;
 PC 8**
Petrov, Evgeny **TCLC 21**
 See also Kataev, Evgeny Petrovich
Petry, Ann (Lane) 1908-1997 **CLC 1, 7, 18**
 See also BW 1, 3; CA 5-8R; 157; CAAS 6;
 CANR 4, 46; CLR 12; DLB 76; JRDA;
 MAICYA; MTCW 1; SATA 5; SATA-Obit 94
Petursson, Halligrimur 1614-1674 **LC 8**
Peychinovich
 See Vazov, Ivan (Minchov)
Phaedrus c. 18B.C.-c. 50 **CMLC 25**
 See also DLB 211
Philips, Katherine 1632-1664 **LC 30**
 See also DLB 131
 <indexboPhilipson, Morris H.** 1926-**CLC 53**
 See also CA 1-4R; CANR 4
Phillips, Caryl 1958- **CLC 96; BLCS; DAM
 MULT**
 See also BW 2; CA 141; CANR 63; DLB 157;
 MTCW 2
Phillips, David Graham 1867-1911 **TCLC 44**
 See also CA 108; DLB 9, 12
Phillips, Jack
 See Sandburg, Carl (August)
Phillips, Jayne Anne 1952-**CLC 15, 33; SSC 16**
 See also CA 101; CANR 24, 50; DLBY 80; INT
 CANR-24; MTCW 1, 2
Phillips, Richard
 See Dick, Philip K(indred)
Phillips, Robert (Schaeffer) 1938- **CLC 28**
 See also CA 17-20R; CAAS 13; CANR 8; DLB
 105
Phillips, Ward
 See Lovecraft, H(oward) P(hillips)
Piccolo, Lucio 1901-1969 **CLC 13**
 See also CA 97-100; DLB 114
Pickthall, Marjorie L(owry) C(hristie) 1883-
 1922 **TCLC 21**
 See also CA 107; DLB 92
Pico della Mirandola, Giovanni 1463-1494**LC
 15**
Piercy, Marge 1936- **CLC 3, 6, 14, 18, 27, 62**
 See also CA 21-24R; CAAS 1; CANR 13, 43,
 66; DLB 120; MTCW 1, 2

Piers, Robert
See Anthony, Piers
Pieyre de Mandiargues, Andre 1909-1991
See Mandiargues, Andre Pieyre de
See also CA 103; 136; CANR 22
Pilnyak, Boris   **TCLC 23**
See also Vogau, Boris Andreyevich
Pincherle, Alberto 1907-1990   **CLC 11, 18;**
   DAM NOV
See also Moravia, Alberto
See also CA 25-28R; 132; CANR 33, 63;
MTCW 1
Pinckney, Darryl 1953-   **CLC 76**
See also BW 2, 3; CA 143; CANR 79
Pindar 518B.C.-446B.C.   **CMLC 12; PC 19**
See also DLB 176
Pineda, Cecile 1942-   **CLC 39**
See also CA 118
Pinero, Arthur Wing 1855-1934   **TCLC 32;**
   DAM DRAM
See also CA 110; 153; DLB 10
Pinero, Miguel (Antonio Gomez) 1946-1988
   CLC 4, 55
See also CA 61-64; 125; CANR 29; HW 1
Pinget, Robert 1919-1997   **CLC 7, 13, 37**
See also CA 85-88; 160; DLB 83
Pink Floyd
See Barrett, (Roger) Syd; Gilmour, David; Mason, Nick; Waters, Roger; Wright, Rick
Pinkney, Edward 1802-1828   **NCLC 31**
Pinkwater, Daniel Manus 1941-   **CLC 35**
See also Pinkwater, Manus
See also AAYA 1; CA 29-32R; CANR 12, 38;
CLR 4; JRDA; MAICYA; SAAS 3; SATA 46,
76
Pinkwater, Manus
See Pinkwater, Daniel Manus
See also SATA 8
Pinsky, Robert 1940-**CLC 9, 19, 38, 94; DAM**
   POET
See also CA 29-32R; CAAS 4; CANR 58;
DLBY 82, 98; MTCW 2
Pinta, Harold
See Pinter, Harold
Pinter, Harold 1930-**CLC 1, 3, 6, 9, 11, 15, 27,**
   58, 73; DA; DAB; DAC; DAM DRAM,
   MST; WLC
See also CA 5-8R; CANR 33, 65; CDBLB 1960
to Present; DLB 13; MTCW 1, 2
Piozzi, Hester Lynch (Thrale) 1741-1821
   NCLC 57
See also DLB 104, 142
Pirandello, Luigi 1867-1936**TCLC 4, 29; DA;**
   DAB; DAC; DAM DRAM, MST; DC 5;
   SSC 22; WLC
See also CA 104; 153; MTCW 2
Pirsig, Robert M(aynard) 1928-**CLC 4, 6, 73;**
   DAM POP
See also CA 53-56; CANR 42, 74; MTCW 1,
2; SATA 39
Pisarev, Dmitry Ivanovich 1840-1868 **NCLC**
   25
Pix, Mary (Griffith) 1666-1709   **LC 8**
See also DLB 80
Pixerecourt, (Rene Charles) Guilbert de 1773-
   1844   **NCLC 39**
See also DLB 192
Plaatje, Sol(omon) T(shekisho) 1876-1932
   TCLC 73; BLCS
See also BW 2, 3; CA 141; CANR 79
Plaidy, Jean
See Hibbert, Eleanor Alice Burford
Planche, James Robinson 1796-1880**NCLC 42**

Plant, Robert 1948-   **CLC 12**
Plante, David (Robert) 1940-   **CLC 7, 23, 38;**
   DAM NOV
See also CA 37-40R; CANR 12, 36, 58; DLBY
83; INT CANR-12; MTCW 1
Plath, Sylvia 1932-1963 **CLC 1, 2, 3, 5, 9, 11,**
   14, 17, 50, 51, 62, 111; DA; DAB; DAC;
   DAM MST, POET; PC 1; WLC
See also AAYA 13; CA 19-20; CANR 34; CAP
2; CDALB 1941-1968; DLB 5, 6, 152;
MTCW 1, 2; SATA 96
Plato 428(?)B.C.-348(?)B.C.   **CMLC 8; DA;**
   DAB; DAC; DAM MST; WLCS
See also DLB 176
Platonov, Andrei   **TCLC 14**
See also Klimentov, Andrei Platonovich
Platt, Kin 1911-   **CLC 26**
See also AAYA 11; CA 17-20R; CANR 11;
JRDA; SAAS 17; SATA 21, 86
Plautus c. 251B.C.-184B.C. **CMLC 24; DC 6**
See also DLB 211
Plick et Plock
See Simenon, Georges (Jacques Christian)
Plimpton, George (Ames) 1927-   **CLC 36**
See also AITN 1; CA 21-24R; CANR 32, 70;
DLB 185; MTCW 1, 2; SATA 10
Pliny the Elder c. 23-79   **CMLC 23**
See also DLB 211
Plomer, William Charles Franklin 1903-1973
   CLC 4, 8
See also CA 21-22; CANR 34; CAP 2; DLB
20, 162, 191; MTCW 1; SATA 24
Plowman, Piers
See Kavanagh, Patrick (Joseph)
Plum, J.
See Wodehouse, P(elham) G(renville)
Plumly, Stanley (Ross) 1939-   **CLC 33**
See also CA 108; 110; DLB 5, 193; INT 110
Plumpe, Friedrich Wilhelm 1888-1931**TCLC**
   53
See also CA 112
Po Chu-i 772-846   **CMLC 24**
Poe, Edgar Allan 1809-1849 **NCLC 1, 16, 55;**
   DA; DAB; DAC; DAM MST, POET; PC
   1; SSC 34; WLC
See also AAYA 14; CDALB 1640-1865; DLB
3, 59, 73, 74; SATA 23
Poet of Titchfield Street, The
See Pound, Ezra (Weston Loomis)
Pohl, Frederik 1919-   **CLC 18; SSC 25**
See also AAYA 24; CA 61-64; CAAS 1; CANR
11, 37; DLB 8; INT CANR-11; MTCW 1, 2;
SATA 24
Poirier, Louis 1910-
See Gracq, Julien
See also CA 122; 126
Poitier, Sidney 1927-   **CLC 26**
See also BW 1; CA 117
Polanski, Roman 1933-   **CLC 16**
See also CA 77-80
Poliakoff, Stephen 1952-   **CLC 38**
See also CA 106; DLB 13
Police, The
See Copeland, Stewart (Armstrong); Summers,
Andrew James; Sumner, Gordon Matthew
Polidori, John William 1795-1821 **NCLC 51**
See also DLB 116
Pollitt, Katha 1949-   **CLC 28**
See also CA 120; 122; CANR 66; MTCW 1, 2
Pollock, (Mary) Sharon 1936-**CLC 50; DAC;**
   DAM DRAM, MST
See also CA 141; DLB 60
Polo, Marco 1254-1324   **CMLC 15**

Polonsky, Abraham (Lincoln) 1910- **CLC 92**
See also CA 104; DLB 26; INT 104
Polybius c. 200B.C.-c. 118B.C.   **CMLC 17**
See also DLB 176
Pomerance, Bernard 1940-   **CLC 13; DAM**
   DRAM
See also CA 101; CANR 49
Ponge, Francis (Jean Gaston Alfred) 1899-1988
   CLC 6, 18; DAM POET
See also CA 85-88; 126; CANR 40
Pontoppidan, Henrik 1857-1943   **TCLC 29**
See also CA 170
Poole, Josephine   **CLC 17**
See also Helyar, Jane Penelope Josephine
See also SAAS 2; SATA 5
Popa, Vasko 1922-1991   **CLC 19**
See also CA 112; 148; DLB 181
Pope, Alexander 1688-1744 **LC 3; DA; DAB;**
   DAC; DAM MST, POET; PC 26; WLC
See also CDBLB 1660-1789; DLB 95, 101
Porter, Connie (Rose) 1959(?)-   **CLC 70**
See also BW 2, 3; CA 142; SATA 81
Porter, Gene(va Grace) Stratton 1863(?)-1924
   TCLC 21
See also CA 112
Porter, Katherine Anne 1890-1980**CLC 1, 3, 7,**
   10, 13, 15, 27, 101; DA; DAB; DAC; DAM
   MST, NOV; SSC 4, 31
See also AITN 2; CA 1-4R; 101; CANR 1, 65;
CDALBS; DLB 4, 9, 102; DLBD 12; DLBY
80; MTCW 1, 2; SATA 39; SATA-Obit 23
Porter, Peter (Neville Frederick) 1929-**CLC 5,**
   13, 33
See also CA 85-88; DLB 40
Porter, William Sydney 1862-1910
See Henry, O.
See also CA 104; 131; CDALB 1865-1917; DA;
DAB; DAC; DAM MST; DLB 12, 78, 79;
MTCW 1, 2; YABC 2
Portillo (y Pacheco), Jose Lopez
See Lopez Portillo (y Pacheco), Jose
Post, Melville Davisson 1869-1930 **TCLC 39**
See also CA 110
Potok, Chaim 1929-   **CLC 2, 7, 14, 26, 112;**
   DAM NOV
See also AAYA 15; AITN 1, 2; CA 17-20R;
CANR 19, 35, 64; DLB 28, 152; INT CANR-
19; MTCW 1, 2; SATA 33, 106
Potter, (Helen) Beatrix 1866-1943
See Webb, (Martha) Beatrice (Potter)
See also MAICYA; MTCW 2
Potter, Dennis (Christopher George) 1935-1994
   CLC 58, 86
See also CA 107; 145; CANR 33, 61; MTCW 1
Pound, Ezra (Weston Loomis) 1885-1972**CLC**
   1, 2, 3, 4, 5, 7, 10, 13, 18, 34, 48, 50, 112;
   DA; DAB; DAC; DAM MST, POET; PC
   4; WLC
See also CA 5-8R; 37-40R; CANR 40; CDALB
1917-1929; DLB 4, 45, 63; DLBD 15;
MTCW 1, 2
Povod, Reinaldo 1959-1994   **CLC 44**
See also CA 136; 146
Powell, Adam Clayton, Jr. 1908-1972**CLC 89;**
   BLC 3; DAM MULT
See also BW 1, 3; CA 102; 33-36R
Powell, Anthony (Dymoke) 1905-**CLC 1, 3, 7,**
   9, 10, 31
See also CA 1-4R; CANR 1, 32, 62; CDBLB
1945-1960; DLB 15; MTCW 1, 2
Powell, Dawn 1897-1965   **CLC 66**
See also CA 5-8R; DLBY 97
Powell, Padgett 1952-   **CLC 34**

See also CA 126; CANR 63

Power, Susan 1961- **CLC 91**

Powers, J(ames) F(arl) 1917-**CLC 1, 4, 8, 57; SSC 4**

See also CA 1-4R; CANR 2, 61; DLB 130; MTCW 1

Powers, John J(ames) 1945-

See Powers, John R.

See also CA 69-72

Powers, John R. **CLC 66**

See also Powers, John J(ames)

Powers, Richard (S.) 1957- **CLC 93**

See also CA 148; CANR 80

Pownall, David 1938- **CLC 10**

See also CA 89-92; CAAS 18; CANR 49; DLB 14

Powys, John Cowper 1872-1963**CLC 7, 9, 15, 46**

See also CA 85-88; DLB 15; MTCW 1, 2

Powys, T(heodore) F(rancis) 1875-1953 **TCLC 9**

See also CA 106; DLB 36, 162

Prado (Calvo), Pedro 1886-1952 **TCLC 75**

See also CA 131; HW 1

Prager, Emily 1952- **CLC 56**

Pratt, E(dwin) J(ohn) 1883(?)-1964 **CLC 19; DAC; DAM POET**

See also CA 141; 93-96; CANR 77; DLB 92

Premchand **TCLC 21**

See also Srivastava, Dhanpat Rai

Preussler, Otfried 1923- **CLC 17**

See also CA 77-80; SATA 24

Prevert, Jacques (Henri Marie) 1900-1977 **CLC 15**

See also CA 77-80; 69-72; CANR 29, 61; MTCW 1; SATA-Obit 30

Prevost, Abbe (Antoine Francois) 1697-1763 **LC 1**

Price, (Edward) Reynolds 1933-**CLC 3, 6, 13, 43, 50, 63; DAM NOV; SSC 22**

See also CA 1-4R; CANR 1, 37, 57; DLB 2; INT CANR-37

Price, Richard 1949- **CLC 6, 12**

See also CA 49-52; CANR 3; DLBY 81

Prichard, Katharine Susannah 1883-1969 **CLC 46**

See also CA 11-12; CANR 33; CAP 1; MTCW 1; SATA 66

Priestley, J(ohn) B(oynton) 1894-1984**CLC 2, 5, 9, 34; DAM DRAM, NOV**

See also CA 9-12R; 113; CANR 33; CDBLB 1914-1945; DLB 10, 34, 77, 100, 139; DLBY 84; MTCW 1, 2

Prince 1958(?)- **CLC 35**

Prince, F(rank) T(empleton) 1912- **CLC 22**

See also CA 101; CANR 43, 79; DLB 20

Prince Kropotkin

See Kropotkin, Peter (Alekseievich)

Prior, Matthew 1664-1721 **LC 4**

See also DLB 95

Prishvin, Mikhail 1873-1954 **TCLC 75**

Pritchard, William H(arrison) 1932- **CLC 34**

See also CA 65-68; CANR 23; DLB 111

Pritchett, V(ictor) S(awdon) 1900-1997 **C L C 5, 13, 15, 41; DAM NOV; SSC 14**

See also CA 61-64; 157; CANR 31, 63; DLB 15, 139; MTCW 1, 2

Private 19022

See Manning, Frederic

Probst, Mark 1925- **CLC 59**

See also CA 130

Prokosch, Frederic 1908-1989 **CLC 4, 48**

See also CA 73-76; 128; DLB 48; MTCW 2

Propertius, Sextus c. 50B.C.-c. 16B.C.**C M L C 32**

See also DLB 211

Prophet, The

See Dreiser, Theodore (Herman Albert)

Prose, Francine 1947- **CLC 45**

See also CA 109; 112; CANR 46; SATA 101

Proudhon

See Cunha, Euclides (Rodrigues Pimenta) da

Proulx, Annie

See Proulx, E(dna) Annie

Proulx, E(dna) Annie 1935- **CLC 81; DAM POP**

See also CA 145; CANR 65; MTCW 2

Proust, (Valentin-Louis-George-Eugene-) Marcel 1871-1922 **TCLC 7, 13, 33; DA; DAB; DAC; DAM MST, NOV; WLC**

See also CA 104; 120; DLB 65; MTCW 1, 2

Prowler, Harley

See Masters, Edgar Lee

Prus, Boleslaw 1845-1912 **TCLC 48**

Pryor, Richard (Franklin Lenox Thomas) 1940- **CLC 26**

See also CA 122; 152

Przybyszewski, Stanislaw 1868-1927**TCLC 36**

See also CA 160; DLB 66

Pteleon

See Grieve, C(hristopher) M(urray)

See also DAM POET

Puckett, Lute

See Masters, Edgar Lee

Puig, Manuel 1932-1990**CLC 3, 5, 10, 28, 65; DAM MULT; HLC**

See also CA 45-48; CANR 2, 32, 63; DLB 113; HW 1, 2; MTCW 1, 2

Pulitzer, Joseph 1847-1911 **TCLC 76**

See also CA 114; DLB 23

Purdy, A(lfred) W(ellington) 1918- **CLC 3, 6, 14, 50; DAC; DAM MST, POET**

See also CA 81-84; CAAS 17; CANR 42, 66; DLB 88

Purdy, James (Amos) 1923- **CLC 2, 4, 10, 28, 52**

See also CA 33-36R; CAAS 1; CANR 19, 51; DLB 2; INT CANR-19; MTCW 1

Pure, Simon

See Swinnerton, Frank Arthur

Pushkin, Alexander (Sergeyevich) 1799-1837 **NCLC 3, 27; DA; DAB; DAC; DAM DRAM, MST, POET; PC 10; SSC 27; WLC**

See also DLB 205; SATA 61

P'u Sung-ling 1640-1715 **LC 49; SSC 31**

Putnam, Arthur Lee

See Alger, Horatio, Jr.

Puzo, Mario 1920-1999 **CLC 1, 2, 6, 36, 107; DAM NOV, POP**

See also CA 65-68; CANR 4, 42, 65; DLB 6; MTCW 1, 2

Pygge, Edward

See Barnes, Julian (Patrick)

Pyle, Ernest Taylor 1900-1945

See Pyle, Ernie

See also CA 115; 160

Pyle, Ernie 1900-1945 **TCLC 75**

See also Pyle, Ernest Taylor

See also DLB 29; MTCW 2

Pyle, Howard 1853-1911 **TCLC 81**

See also CA 109; 137; CLR 22; DLB 42, 188; DLBD 13; MAICYA; SATA 16, 100

Pym, Barbara (Mary Crampton) 1913-1980 **CLC 13, 19, 37, 111**

See also CA 13-14; 97-100; CANR 13, 34; CAP

1; DLB 14, 207; DLBY 87; MTCW 1, 2

Pynchon, Thomas (Ruggles, Jr.) 1937-**CLC 2, 3, 6, 9, 11, 18, 33, 62, 72; DA; DAB; DAC; DAM MST, NOV, POP; SSC 14; WLC**

See also BEST 90:2; CA 17-20R; CANR 22, 46, 73; DLB 2, 173; MTCW 1, 2

Pythagoras c. 570B.C.-c. 500B.C. **CMLC 22**

See also DLB 176

Q

See Quiller-Couch, SirArthur (Thomas)

Qian Zhongshu

See Ch'ien Chung-shu

Qroll

See Dagerman, Stig (Halvard)

Quarrington, Paul (Lewis) 1953- **CLC 65**

See also CA 129; CANR 62

Quasimodo, Salvatore 1901-1968 **CLC 10**

See also CA 13-16; 25-28R; CAP 1; DLB 114; MTCW 1

Quay, Stephen 1947- **CLC 95**

Quay, Timothy 1947- **CLC 95**

Queen, Ellery **CLC 3, 11**

See also Dannay, Frederic; Davidson, Avram (James); Lee, Manfred B(ennington); Marlowe, Stephen; Sturgeon, Theodore (Hamilton); Vance, John Holbrook

Queen, Ellery, Jr.

See Dannay, Frederic; Lee, Manfred B(ennington)

Queneau, Raymond 1903-1976 **CLC 2, 5, 10, 42**

See also CA 77-80; 69-72; CANR 32; DLB 72; MTCW 1, 2

Quevedo, Francisco de 1580-1645 **LC 23**

Quiller-Couch, SirArthur (Thomas) 1863-1944 **TCLC 53**

See also CA 118; 166; DLB 135, 153, 190

Quin, Ann (Marie) 1936-1973 **CLC 6**

See also CA 9-12R; 45-48; DLB 14

Quinn, Martin

See Smith, Martin Cruz

Quinn, Peter 1947- **CLC 91**

Quinn, Simon

See Smith, Martin Cruz

Quiroga, Horacio (Sylvestre) 1878-1937 **TCLC 20; DAM MULT; HLC**

See also CA 117; 131; HW 1; MTCW 1

Quoirez, Francoise 1935- **CLC 9**

See also Sagan, Francoise

See also CA 49-52; CANR 6, 39, 73; MTCW 1, 2

Raabe, Wilhelm (Karl) 1831-1910 **TCLC 45**

See also CA 167; DLB 129

Rabe, David (William) 1940- **CLC 4, 8, 33; DAM DRAM**

See also CA 85-88; CABS 3; CANR 59; DLB 7

Rabelais, Francois 1483-1553**LC 5; DA; DAB; DAC; DAM MST; WLC**

Rabinovitch, Sholem 1859-1916

See Aleichem, Sholom

See also CA 104

Rabinyan, Dorit 1972- **CLC 119**

See also CA 170

Rachilde 1860-1953 **TCLC 67**

See also DLB 123, 192

Racine, Jean 1639-1699 **LC 28; DAB; DAM MST**

Radcliffe, Ann (Ward) 1764-1823**NCLC 6, 55**

See also DLB 39, 178

Radiguet, Raymond 1903-1923 **TCLC 29**

See also CA 162; DLB 65

Radnoti, Miklos 1909-1944 **TCLC 16**

See also CA 118

Rado, James 1939-   CLC 17
  See also CA 105
Radvanyi, Netty 1900-1983
  See Seghers, Anna
  See also CA 85-88; 110
Rae, Ben
  See Griffiths, Trevor
Raeburn, John (Hay) 1941-   CLC 34
  See also CA 57-60
Ragni, Gerome 1942-1991   CLC 17
  See also CA 105; 134
Rahv, Philip 1908-1973   CLC 24
  See also Greenberg, Ivan
  See also DLB 137
Raimund, Ferdinand Jakob 1790-1836 NCLC 69
  See also DLB 90
Raine, Craig 1944-   CLC 32, 103
  See also CA 108, CANR 29, 51; DLB 40
Raine, Kathleen (Jessie) 1908-   CLC 7, 45
  See also CA 85-88; CANR 46; DLB 20; MTCW 1
Rainis, Janis 1865-1929   TCLC 29
  See also CA 170
Rakosi, Carl 1903-   CLC 47
  See also Rawley, Callman
  See also CAAS 5; DLB 193
Raleigh, Richard
  See Lovecraft, H(oward) P(hillips)
Raleigh, Sir Walter 1554(?)-1618   LC 31, 39
  See also CDBLB Before 1660; DLB 172
Rallentando, H. P.
  See Sayers, Dorothy L(eigh)
Ramal, Walter
  See de la Mare, Walter (John)
Ramana Maharshi 1879-1950   TCLC 84
Ram****n y Cajal, Santiago 1852-1934
     TCLC 93
Ramon, Juan
  See Jimenez (Mantecon), Juan Ramon
Ramos, Graciliano 1892-1953   TCLC 32
  See also CA 167; HW 2
Rampersad, Arnold 1941-   CLC 44
  See also BW 2, 3; CA 127; 133; DLB 111; INT 133
Rampling, Anne
  See Rice, Anne
Ramsay, Allan 1684(?)-1758   LC 29
  See also DLB 95
Ramuz, Charles-Ferdinand 1878-1947 TCLC 33
  See also CA 165
Rand, Ayn 1905-1982 CLC 3, 30, 44, 79; DA;
  DAC; DAM MST, NOV, POP; WLC
  See also AAYA 10; CA 13-16R; 105; CANR 27, 73; CDALBS; MTCW 1, 2
Randall, Dudley (Felker) 1914- CLC 1; BLC 3;
  DAM MULT
  See also BW 1, 3; CA 25-28R; CANR 23; DLB 41
Randall, Robert
  See Silverberg, Robert
Ranger, Ken
  See Creasey, John
Ransom, John Crowe 1888-1974 CLC 2, 4, 5,
  11, 24; DAM POET
  See also CA 5-8R; 49-52; CANR 6, 34; CDALBS; DLB 45, 63; MTCW 1, 2
Rao, Raja 1909-   CLC 25, 56; DAM NOV
  See also CA 73-76; CANR 51; MTCW 1, 2
Raphael, Frederic (Michael) 1931- CLC 2, 14
  See also CA 1-4R; CANR 1; DLB 14
Ratcliffe, James P.

  See Mencken, H(enry) L(ouis)
Rathbone, Julian 1935-   CLC 41
  See also CA 101; CANR 34, 73
Rattigan, Terence (Mervyn) 1911-1977 CLC 7;
  DAM DRAM
  See also CA 85-88; 73-76; CDBLB 1945-1960;
  DLB 13; MTCW 1, 2
Ratushinskaya, Irina 1954-   CLC 54
  See also CA 129; CANR 68
Raven, Simon (Arthur Noel) 1927-   CLC 14
  See also CA 81-84
Ravenna, Michael
  See Welty, Eudora
Rawley, Callman 1903-
  See Rakosi, Carl
  See also CA 21-24R; CANR 12, 32
Rawlings, Marjorie Kinnan 1896-1953 TCLC 4
  See also AAYA 20; CA 104; 137; CANR 74;
  DLB 9, 22, 102; DLBD 17; JRDA; MAICYA;
  MTCW 2; SATA 100; YABC 1
Ray, Satyajit 1921-1992   CLC 16, 76; DAM MULT
  See also CA 114; 137
Read, Herbert Edward 1893-1968   CLC 4
  See also CA 85-88; 25-28R; DLB 20, 149
Read, Piers Paul 1941-   CLC 4, 10, 25
  See also CA 21-24R; CANR 38; DLB 14; SATA 21
Reade, Charles 1814-1884   NCLC 2, 74
  See also DLB 21
Reade, Hamish
  See Gray, Simon (James Holliday)
Reading, Peter 1946-   CLC 47
  See also CA 103; CANR 46; DLB 40
Reaney, James 1926-   CLC 13; DAC; DAM MST
  See also CA 41-44R; CAAS 15; CANR 42; DLB 68; SATA 43
Rebreanu, Liviu 1885-1944   TCLC 28
  See also CA 165
Rechy, John (Francisco) 1934- CLC 1, 7, 14,
  18, 107; DAM MULT; HLC
  See also CA 5-8R; CAAS 4; CANR 6, 32, 64;
  DLB 122; DLBY 82; HW 1, 2; INT CANR-6
Redcam, Tom 1870-1933   TCLC 25
Reddin, Keith   CLC 67
Redgrove, Peter (William) 1932- CLC 6, 41
  See also CA 1-4R; CANR 3, 39, 77; DLB 40
Redmon, Anne   CLC 22
  See also Nightingale, Anne Redmon
  See also DLBY 86
Reed, Eliot
  See Ambler, Eric
Reed, Ishmael 1938- CLC 2, 3, 5, 6, 13, 32, 60;
  BLC 3; DAM MULT
  See also BW 2, 3; CA 21-24R; CANR 25, 48,
  74; DLB 2, 5, 33, 169; DLBD 8; MTCW 1, 2
Reed, John (Silas) 1887-1920   TCLC 9
  See also CA 106
Reed, Lou   CLC 21
  See also Firbank, Louis
Reeve, Clara 1729-1807   NCLC 19
  See also DLB 39
Reich, Wilhelm 1897-1957   TCLC 57
Reid, Christopher (John) 1949-   CLC 33
  See also CA 140; DLB 40
Reid, Desmond
  See Moorcock, Michael (John)
Reid Banks, Lynne 1929-
  See Banks, Lynne Reid

  See also CA 1-4R; CANR 6, 22, 38; CLR 24;
  JRDA; MAICYA; SATA 22, 75
Reilly, William K.
  See Creasey, John
Reiner, Max
  See Caldwell, (Janet Miriam) Taylor (Holland)
Reis, Ricardo
  See Pessoa, Fernando (Antonio Nogueira)
Remarque, Erich Maria 1898-1970 CLC 21;
  DA; DAB; DAC; DAM MST, NOV
  See also AAYA 27; CA 77-80; 29-32R; DLB 56; MTCW 1, 2
Remington, Frederic 1861-1909   TCLC 89
  See also CA 108; 169; DLB 12, 186, 188; SATA 41
Remizov, A.
  See Remizov, Aleksei (Mikhailovich)
Remizov, A. M.
  See Remizov, Aleksei (Mikhailovich)
Remizov, Aleksei (Mikhailovich) 1877-1957
     TCLC 27
  See also CA 125; 133
Renan, Joseph Ernest 1823-1892   NCLC 26
Renard, Jules 1864-1910   TCLC 17
  See also CA 117
Renault, Mary   CLC 3, 11, 17
  See also Challans, Mary
  See also DLBY 83; MTCW 2
Rendell, Ruth (Barbara) 1930- CLC 28, 48;
  DAM POP
  See also Vine, Barbara
  See also CA 109; CANR 32, 52, 74; DLB 87;
  INT CANR-32; MTCW 1, 2
Renoir, Jean 1894-1979   CLC 20
  See also CA 129; 85-88
Resnais, Alain 1922-   CLC 16
Reverdy, Pierre 1889-1960   CLC 53
  See also CA 97-100; 89-92
Rexroth, Kenneth 1905-1982 CLC 1, 2, 6, 11,
  22, 49, 112; DAM POET; PC 20
  See also CA 5-8R; 107; CANR 14, 34, 63;
  CDALB 1941-1968; DLB 16, 48, 165, 212;
  DLBY 82; INT CANR-14; MTCW 1, 2
Reyes, Alfonso 1889-1959 TCLC 33; HLCS 1
  See also CA 131; HW 1
Reyes y Basoalto, Ricardo Eliecer Neftali
  See Neruda, Pablo
Reymont, Wladyslaw (Stanislaw) 1868(?)-1925
     TCLC 5
  See also CA 104
Reynolds, Jonathan 1942-   CLC 6, 38
  See also CA 65-68; CANR 28
Reynolds, Joshua 1723-1792   LC 15
  See also DLB 104
Reynolds, Michael Shane 1937-   CLC 44
  See also CA 65-68; CANR 9
Reznikoff, Charles 1894-1976   CLC 9
  See also CA 33-36; 61-64; CAP 2; DLB 28, 45
Rezzori (d'Arezzo), Gregor von 1914-1998
     CLC 25
  See also CA 122; 136; 167
Rhine, Richard
  See Silverstein, Alvin
Rhodes, Eugene Manlove 1869-1934 TCLC 53
Rhodius, Apollonius c. 3rd cent. B.C.- CMLC 28
  See also DLB 176
R'hoone
  See Balzac, Honore de
Rhys, Jean 1890(?)-1979 CLC 2, 4, 6, 14, 19,
  51; DAM NOV; SSC 21
  See also CA 25-28R; 85-88; CANR 35, 62;
  CDBLB 1945-1960; DLB 36, 117, 162;

Author Index

MTCW 1, 2

Ribeiro, Darcy 1922-1997   **CLC 34**
See also CA 33-36R; 156

Ribeiro, Joao Ubaldo (Osorio Pimentel) 1941-
CLC 10, 67
See also CA 81-84

Ribman, Ronald (Burt) 1932-   **CLC 7**
See also CA 21-24R; CANR 46, 80

Ricci, Nino 1959-   **CLC 70**
See also CA 137

Rice, Anne 1941-   **CLC 41; DAM POP**
See also AAYA 9; BEST 89:2; CA 65-68; CANR
12, 36, 53, 74; MTCW 2

Rice, Elmer (Leopold) 1892-1967 **CLC 7, 49;**
DAM DRAM
See also CA 21-22; 25-28R; CAP 2; DLB 4, 7;
MTCW 1, 2

Rice, Tim(othy Miles Bindon) 1944- **CLC 21**
See also CA 103; CANR 46

Rich, Adrienne (Cecile) 1929-**CLC 3, 6, 7, 11,**
18, 36, 73, 76; DAM POET; PC 5
See also CA 9-12R; CANR 20, 53, 74;
CDALBS; DLB 5, 67; MTCW 1, 2

Rich, Barbara
See Graves, Robert (von Ranke)

Rich, Robert
See Trumbo, Dalton

Richard, Keith   **CLC 17**
See also Richards, Keith

Richards, David Adams 1950- **CLC 59; DAC**
See also CA 93-96; CANR 60; DLB 53

Richards, I(vor) A(rmstrong) 1893-1979**C L C**
14, 24
See also CA 41-44R; 89-92; CANR 34, 74; DLB
27; MTCW 2

Richards, Keith 1943-
See Richard, Keith
See also CA 107; CANR 77

Richardson, Anne
See Roiphe, Anne (Richardson)

Richardson, Dorothy Miller 1873-1957**TCLC**
3
See also CA 104; DLB 36

Richardson, Ethel Florence (Lindesay) 1870-
1946
See Richardson, Henry Handel
See also CA 105

Richardson, Henry Handel   **TCLC 4**
See also Richardson, Ethel Florence (Lindesay)
See also DLB 197

Richardson, John 1796-1852 **NCLC 55; DAC**
See also DLB 99

Richardson, Samuel 1689-1761**LC 1, 44; DA;**
DAB; DAC; DAM MST, NOV; WLC
See also CDBLB 1660-1789; DLB 39

Richler, Mordecai 1931-**CLC 3, 5, 9, 13, 18, 46,**
70; DAC; DAM MST, NOV
See also AITN 1; CA 65-68; CANR 31, 62; CLR
17; DLB 53; MAICYA; MTCW 1, 2; SATA
44, 98; SATA-Brief 27

Richter, Conrad (Michael) 1890-1968**CLC 30**
See also AAYA 21; CA 5-8R; 25-28R; CANR
23; DLB 9, 212; MTCW 1, 2; SATA 3

Ricostranza, Tom
See Ellis, Trey

Riddell, Charlotte 1832-1906   **TCLC 40**
See also CA 165; DLB 156

Ridgway, Keith 1965-   **CLC 119**
See also CA 172

Riding, Laura   **CLC 3, 7**
See also Jackson, Laura (Riding)

Riefenstahl, Berta Helene Amalia 1902-
See Riefenstahl, Leni

See also CA 108

Riefenstahl, Leni   **CLC 16**
See also Riefenstahl, Berta Helene Amalia

Riffe, Ernest
See Bergman, (Ernst) Ingmar

Riggs, (Rolla) Lynn 1899-1954   **TCLC 56;**
DAM MULT
See also CA 144; DLB 175; NNAL

Riis, Jacob A(ugust) 1849-1914   **TCLC 80**
See also CA 113; 168; DLB 23

Riley, James Whitcomb 1849-1916**TCLC 51;**
DAM POET
See also CA 118; 137; MAICYA; SATA 17

Riley, Tex
See Creasey, John

Rilke, Rainer Maria 1875-1926**TCLC 1, 6, 19;**
DAM POET; PC 2
See also CA 104; 132; CANR 62; DLB 81;
MTCW 1, 2

Rimbaud, (Jean Nicolas) Arthur 1854-1891
NCLC 4, 35; DA; DAB; DAC; DAM MST,
POET; PC 3; WLC

Rinehart, Mary Roberts 1876-1958**TCLC 52**
See also CA 108; 166

Ringmaster, The
See Mencken, H(enry) L(ouis)

Ringwood, Gwen(dolyn Margaret) Pharis
1910-1984   **CLC 48**
See also CA 148; 112; DLB 88

Rio, Michel 19(?)-   **CLC 43**

Ritsos, Giannes
See Ritsos, Yannis

Ritsos, Yannis 1909-1990   **CLC 6, 13, 31**
See also CA 77-80; 133; CANR 39, 61; MTCW
1

Ritter, Erika 1948(?)-   **CLC 52**

Rivera, Jose Eustasio 1889-1928   **TCLC 35**
See also CA 162; HW 1, 2

Rivers, Conrad Kent 1933-1968   **CLC 1**
See also BW 1; CA 85-88; DLB 41

Rivers, Elfrida
See Bradley, Marion Zimmer

Riverside, John
See Heinlein, Robert A(nson)

Rizal, Jose 1861-1896   **NCLC 27**

Roa Bastos, Augusto (Antonio) 1917-**CLC 45;**
DAM MULT; HLC
See also CA 131; DLB 113; HW 1

Robbe-Grillet, Alain 1922-**CLC 1, 2, 4, 6, 8, 10,**
14, 43
See also CA 9-12R; CANR 33, 65; DLB 83;
MTCW 1, 2

Robbins, Harold 1916-1997   **CLC 5; DAM**
NOV
See also CA 73-76; 162; CANR 26, 54; MTCW
1, 2

Robbins, Thomas Eugene 1936-
See Robbins, Tom
See also CA 81-84; CANR 29, 59; DAM NOV,
POP; MTCW 1, 2

Robbins, Tom   **CLC 9, 32, 64**
See also Robbins, Thomas Eugene
See also BEST 90:3; DLBY 80; MTCW 2

Robbins, Trina 1938-   **CLC 21**
See also CA 128

Roberts, Charles G(eorge) D(ouglas) 1860-1943
TCLC 8
See also CA 105; CLR 33; DLB 92; SATA 88;
SATA-Brief 29

Roberts, Elizabeth Madox 1886-1941   **T C L C**
68
See also CA 111; 166; DLB 9, 54, 102; SATA
33; SATA-Brief 27

Roberts, Kate 1891-1985   **CLC 15**
See also CA 107; 116

Roberts, Keith (John Kingston) 1935-**CLC 14**
See also CA 25-28R; CANR 46

Roberts, Kenneth (Lewis) 1885-1957**TCLC 23**
See also CA 109; DLB 9

Roberts, Michele (B.) 1949-   **CLC 48**
See also CA 115; CANR 58

Robertson, Ellis
See Ellison, Harlan (Jay); Silverberg, Robert

Robertson, Thomas William 1829-1871**NCLC**
35; DAM DRAM

Robeson, Kenneth
See Dent, Lester

Robinson, Edwin Arlington 1869-1935**T C L C**
5; DA; DAC; DAM MST, POET; PC 1
See also CA 104; 133; CDALB 1865-1917;
DLB 54; MTCW 1, 2

Robinson, Henry Crabb 1775-1867**NCLC 15**
See also DLB 107

Robinson, Jill 1936-   **CLC 10**
See also CA 102; INT 102

Robinson, Kim Stanley 1952-   **CLC 34**
See also AAYA 26; CA 126

Robinson, Lloyd
See Silverberg, Robert

Robinson, Marilynne 1944-   **CLC 25**
See also CA 116; CANR 80; DLB 206

Robinson, Smokey   **CLC 21**
See also Robinson, William, Jr.

Robinson, William, Jr. 1940-
See Robinson, Smokey
See also CA 116

Robison, Mary 1949-   **CLC 42, 98**
See also CA 113; 116; DLB 130; INT 116

Rod, Edouard 1857-1910   **TCLC 52**

Roddenberry, Eugene Wesley 1921-1991
See Roddenberry, Gene
See also CA 110; 135; CANR 37; SATA 45;
SATA-Obit 69

Roddenberry, Gene   **CLC 17**
See also Roddenberry, Eugene Wesley
See also AAYA 5; SATA-Obit 69

Rodgers, Mary 1931-   **CLC 12**
See also CA 49-52; CANR 8, 55; CLR 20; INT
CANR-8; JRDA; MAICYA; SATA 8

Rodgers, W(illiam) R(obert) 1909-1969**CLC 7**
See also CA 85-88; DLB 20

Rodman, Eric
See Silverberg, Robert

Rodman, Howard 1920(?)-1985   **CLC 65**
See also CA 118

Rodman, Maia
See Wojciechowska, Maia (Teresa)

Rodriguez, Claudio 1934-   **CLC 10**
See also DLB 134

Roelvaag, O(le) E(dvart) 1876-1931**TCLC 17**
See also CA 117; 171; DLB 9

Roethke, Theodore (Huebner) 1908-1963**CLC**
1, 3, 8, 11, 19, 46, 101; DAM POET; PC 15
See also CA 81-84; CABS 2; CDALB 1941-
1968; DLB 5, 206; MTCW 1, 2

Rogers, Samuel 1763-1855   **NCLC 69**
See also DLB 93

Rogers, Thomas Hunton 1927-   **CLC 57**
See also CA 89-92; INT 89-92

Rogers, Will(iam Penn Adair) 1879-1935
TCLC 8, 71; DAM MULT
See also CA 105; 144; DLB 11; MTCW 2;
NNAL

Rogin, Gilbert 1929-   **CLC 18**
See also CA 65-68; CANR 15

Rohan, Koda   **TCLC 22**

See also Koda Shigeyuki
Rohlfs, Anna Katharine Green
See Green, Anna Katharine
Rohmer, Eric   **CLC 16**
See also Scherer, Jean-Marie Maurice
Rohmer, Sax   **TCLC 28**
See also Ward, Arthur Henry Sarsfield
See also DLB 70
Roiphe, Anne (Richardson) 1935- **CLC 3, 9**
See also CA 89-92; CANR 45, 73; DLBY 80;
INT 89-92
Rojas, Fernando de 1465-1541**LC 23; HLCS 1**
Rolfe, Frederick (William Serafino Austin
Lewis Mary) 1860-1913   **TCLC 12**
See also CA 107; DLB 34, 156
Rolland, Romain 1866-1944   **TCLC 23**
See also CA 118; DLB 65
Rolle, Richard c. 1300-c. 1349   **CMLC 21**
See also DLB 146
Rolvaag, O(le) E(dvart)
See Roelvaag, O(le) E(dvart)
Romain Arnaud, Saint
See Aragon, Louis
Romains, Jules 1885-1972   **CLC 7**
See also CA 85-88; CANR 34; DLB 65; MTCW
1
Romero, Jose Ruben 1890-1952   **TCLC 14**
See also CA 114; 131; HW 1
Ronsard, Pierre de 1524-1585 **LC 6; PC 11**
Rooke, Leon 1934- **CLC 25, 34; DAM POP**
See also CA 25-28R; CANR 23, 53
Roosevelt, Franklin Delano 1882-1945**T C L C**
93
See also CA 116; 173
Roosevelt, Theodore 1858-1919   **TCLC 69**
See also CA 115; 170; DLB 47, 186
Roper, William 1498-1578   **LC 10**
Roquelaure, A. N.
See Rice, Anne
Rosa, Joao Guimaraes 1908-1967   **CLC 23;**
HLCS 1
See also CA 89-92; DLB 113
Rose, Wendy 1948-**CLC 85; DAM MULT; PC**
13
See also CA 53-56; CANR 5, 51; DLB 175;
NNAL; SATA 12
Rosen, R. D.
See Rosen, Richard (Dean)
Rosen, Richard (Dean) 1949-   **CLC 39**
See also CA 77-80; CANR 62; INT CANR-30
Rosenberg, Isaac 1890-1918   **TCLC 12**
See also CA 107; DLB 20
Rosenblatt, Joe   **CLC 15**
See also Rosenblatt, Joseph
Rosenblatt, Joseph 1933-
See Rosenblatt, Joe
See also CA 89-92; INT 89-92
Rosenfeld, Samuel
See Tzara, Tristan
Rosenstock, Sami
See Tzara, Tristan
Rosenstock, Samuel
See Tzara, Tristan
Rosenthal, M(acha) L(ouis) 1917-1996 **C L C**
28
See also CA 1-4R; 152; CAAS 6; CANR 4, 51;
DLB 5; SATA 59
Ross, Barnaby
See Dannay, Frederic
Ross, Bernard L.
See Follett, Ken(neth Martin)
Ross, J. H.
See Lawrence, T(homas) E(dward)

Ross, John Hume
See Lawrence, T(homas) E(dward)
Ross, Martin
See Martin, Violet Florence
See also DLB 135
Ross, (James) Sinclair 1908- **CLC 13; DAC;**
DAM MST; SSC 24
See also CA 73-76; DLB 88
Rossetti, Christina (Georgina) 1830-1894
NCLC 2, 50, 66; DA; DAB; DAC; DAM
MST, POET; PC 7; WLC
See also DLB 35, 163; MAICYA; SATA 20
Rossetti, Dante Gabriel 1828-1882 **NCLC 4,**
77; DA; DAB; DAC; DAM MST, POET;
WLC
See also CDBLB 1832-1890; DLB 35
Rossner, Judith (Perelman) 1935-**CLC 6, 9, 29**
See also AITN 2; BEST 90:3; CA 17-20R;
CANR 18, 51, 73; DLB 6; INT CANR-18;
MTCW 1, 2
Rostand, Edmond (Eugene Alexis) 1868-1918
TCLC 6, 37; DA; DAB; DAC; DAM
DRAM, MST; DC 10
See also CA 104; 126; DLB 192; MTCW 1
Roth, Henry 1906-1995   **CLC 2, 6, 11, 104**
See also CA 11-12; 149; CANR 38, 63; CAP 1;
DLB 28; MTCW 1, 2
Roth, Philip (Milton) 1933-**CLC 1, 2, 3, 4, 6, 9,**
15, 22, 31, 47, 66, 86, 119; DA; DAB; DAC;
DAM MST, NOV, POP; SSC 26; WLC
See also BEST 90:3; CA 1-4R; CANR 1, 22,
36, 55; CDALB 1968-1988; DLB 2, 28, 173;
DLBY 82; MTCW 1, 2
Rothenberg, Jerome 1931-   **CLC 6, 57**
See also CA 45-48; CANR 1; DLB 5, 193
Roumain, Jacques (Jean Baptiste) 1907-1944
TCLC 19; BLC 3; DAM MULT
See also BW 1; CA 117; 125
Rourke, Constance (Mayfield) 1885-1941
TCLC 12
See also CA 107; YABC 1
Rousseau, Jean-Baptiste 1671-1741   **LC 9**
Rousseau, Jean-Jacques 1712-1778**LC 14, 36;**
DA; DAB; DAC; DAM MST; WLC
Roussel, Raymond 1877-1933   **TCLC 20**
See also CA 117
Rovit, Earl (Herbert) 1927-   **CLC 7**
See also CA 5-8R; CANR 12
Rowe, Elizabeth Singer 1674-1737   **LC 44**
See also DLB 39, 95
Rowe, Nicholas 1674-1718   **LC 8**
See also DLB 84
Rowley, Ames Dorrance
See Lovecraft, H(oward) P(hillips)
Rowson, Susanna Haswell 1762(?)-1824
NCLC 5, 69
See also DLB 37, 200
Roy, Arundhati 1960(?)-   **CLC 109**
See also CA 163; DLBY 97
Roy, Gabrielle 1909-1983 **CLC 10, 14; DAB;**
DAC; DAM MST
See also CA 53-56; 110; CANR 5, 61; DLB 68;
MTCW 1; SATA 104
Royko, Mike 1932-1997   **CLC 109**
See also CA 89-92; 157; CANR 26
Rozewicz, Tadeusz 1921-   **CLC 9, 23; DAM**
POET
See also CA 108; CANR 36, 66; MTCW 1, 2
Ruark, Gibbons 1941-   **CLC 3**
See also CA 33-36R; CAAS 23; CANR 14, 31,
57; DLB 120
Rubens, Bernice (Ruth) 1923-   **CLC 19, 31**
See also CA 25-28R; CANR 33, 65; DLB 14,

207; MTCW 1
Rubin, Harold
See Robbins, Harold
Rudkin, (James) David 1936-   **CLC 14**
See also CA 89-92; DLB 13
Rudnik, Raphael 1933-   **CLC 7**
See also CA 29-32R
Ruffian, M.
See Hasek, Jaroslav (Matej Frantisek)
Ruiz, Jose Martinez   **CLC 11**
See also Martinez Ruiz, Jose
Rukeyser, Muriel 1913-1980**CLC 6, 10, 15, 27;**
DAM POET; PC 12
See also CA 5-8R; 93-96; CANR 26, 60; DLB
48; MTCW 1, 2; SATA-Obit 22
Rule, Jane (Vance) 1931-   **CLC 27**
See also CA 25-28R; CAAS 18; CANR 12; DLB
60
Rulfo, Juan 1918-1986   **CLC 8, 80; DAM**
MULT; HLC; SSC 25
See also CA 85-88; 118; CANR 26; DLB 113;
HW 1, 2; MTCW 1, 2
Rumi, Jalal al-Din 1297-1373   **CMLC 20**
Runeberg, Johan 1804-1877   **NCLC 41**
Runyon, (Alfred) Damon 1884(?)-1946**T C L C**
10
See also CA 107; 165; DLB 11, 86, 171; MTCW
2
Rush, Norman 1933-   **CLC 44**
See also CA 121; 126; INT 126
Rushdie, (Ahmed) Salman 1947-**CLC 23, 31,**
55, 100; DAB; DAC; DAM MST, NOV,
POP; WLCS
See also BEST 89:3; CA 108; 111; CANR 33,
56; DLB 194; INT 111; MTCW 1, 2
Rushforth, Peter (Scott) 1945-   **CLC 19**
See also CA 101
Ruskin, John 1819-1900   **TCLC 63**
See also CA 114; 129; CDBLB 1832-1890;
DLB 55, 163, 190; SATA 24
Russ, Joanna 1937-   **CLC 15**
See also CANR 11, 31, 65; DLB 8; MTCW 1
Russell, George William 1867-1935
See Baker, Jean H.
See also CA 104; 153; CDBLB 1890-1914;
DAM POET
Russell, (Henry) Ken(neth Alfred) 1927-**C L C**
16
See also CA 105
Russell, William Martin 1947-   **CLC 60**
See also CA 164
Rutherford, Mark   **TCLC 25**
See also White, William Hale
See also DLB 18
Ruyslinck, Ward 1929-   **CLC 14**
See also Belser, Reimond Karel Maria de
Ryan, Cornelius (John) 1920-1974   **CLC 7**
See also CA 69-72; 53-56; CANR 38
Ryan, Michael 1946-   **CLC 65**
See also CA 49-52; DLBY 82
Ryan, Tim
See Dent, Lester
Rybakov, Anatoli (Naumovich) 1911-1998
CLC 23, 53
See also CA 126; 135; 172; SATA 79
Ryder, Jonathan
See Ludlum, Robert
Ryga, George 1932-1987**CLC 14; DAC; DAM**
MST
See also CA 101; 124; CANR 43; DLB 60
S. H.
See Hartmann, Sadakichi
S. S.

See Sassoon, Siegfried (Lorraine)
Saba, Umberto 1883-1957   **TCLC 33**
    See also CA 144; CANR 79; DLB 114
Sabatini, Rafael 1875-1950   **TCLC 47**
    See also CA 162
Sabato, Ernesto (R.) 1911-**CLC 10, 23; DAM MULT; HLC**
    See also CA 97-100; CANR 32, 65; DLB 145; HW 1, 2; MTCW 1, 2
Sa-Carniero, Mario de 1890-1916 **TCLC 83**
Sacastru, Martin
    See Bioy Casares, Adolfo
Sacher-Masoch, Leopold von 1836(?)-1895 **NCLC 31**
Sachs, Marilyn (Stickle) 1927-   **CLC 35**
    See also AAYA 2; CA 17-20R; CANR 13, 47; CLR 2; JRDA; MAICYA; SAAS 2; SATA 3, 68
Sachs, Nelly 1891-1970   **CLC 14, 98**
    See also CA 17-18; 25-28R; CAP 2; MTCW 2
Sackler, Howard (Oliver) 1929-1982 **CLC 14**
    See also CA 61-64; 108; CANR 30; DLB 7
Sacks, Oliver (Wolf) 1933-   **CLC 67**
    See also CA 53-56; CANR 28, 50, 76; INT CANR-28; MTCW 1, 2
Sadakichi
    See Hartmann, Sadakichi
Sade, Donatien Alphonse Francois, Comte de 1740-1814   **NCLC 47**
Sadoff, Ira 1945-   **CLC 9**
    See also CA 53-56; CANR 5, 21; DLB 120
Saetone
    See Camus, Albert
Safire, William 1929-   **CLC 10**
    See also CA 17-20R; CANR 31, 54
Sagan, Carl (Edward) 1934-1996**CLC 30, 112**
    See also AAYA 2; CA 25-28R; 155; CANR 11, 36, 74; MTCW 1, 2; SATA 58; SATA-Obit 94
Sagan, Francoise   **CLC 3, 6, 9, 17, 36**
    See also Quoirez, Francoise
    See also DLB 83; MTCW 2
Sahgal, Nayantara (Pandit) 1927-   **CLC 41**
    See also CA 9-12R; CANR 11
Saint, H(arry) F. 1941-   **CLC 50**
    See also CA 127
St. Aubin de Teran, Lisa 1953-
    See Teran, Lisa St. Aubin de
    See also CA 118; 126; INT 126
Saint Birgitta of Sweden c. 1303-1373**CMLC 24**
Sainte-Beuve, Charles Augustin 1804-1869 **NCLC 5**
Saint-Exupery, Antoine (Jean Baptiste Marie Roger) de 1900-1944 **TCLC 2, 56; DAM NOV; WLC**
    See also CA 108; 132; CLR 10; DLB 72; MAICYA; MTCW 1, 2; SATA 20
St. John, David
    See Hunt, E(verette) Howard, (Jr.)
Saint-John Perse
    See Leger, (Marie-Rene Auguste) Alexis Saint-Leger
Saintsbury, George (Edward Bateman) 1845-1933   **TCLC 31**
    See also CA 160; DLB 57, 149
Sait Faik   **TCLC 23**
    See also Abasiyanik, Sait Faik
Saki   **TCLC 3; SSC 12**
    See also Munro, H(ector) H(ugh)
    See also MTCW 2
Sala, George Augustus   **NCLC 46**
Salama, Hannu 1936-   **CLC 18**

Salamanca, J(ack) R(ichard) 1922-**CLC 4, 15**
    See also CA 25-28R
Sale, J. Kirkpatrick
    See Sale, Kirkpatrick
Sale, Kirkpatrick 1937-   **CLC 68**
    See also CA 13-16R; CANR 10
Salinas, Luis Omar 1937-   **CLC 90; DAM MULT; HLC**
    See also CA 131; DLB 82; HW 1, 2
Salinas (y Serrano), Pedro 1891(?)-1951 **TCLC 17**
    See also CA 117; DLB 134
Salinger, J(erome) D(avid) 1919-**CLC 1, 3, 8, 12, 55, 56; DA; DAB; DAC; DAM MST, NOV, POP; SSC 2, 28; WLC**
    See also AAYA 2; CA 5-8R; CANR 39; CDALB 1941-1968; CLR 18; DLB 2, 102, 173; MAICYA; MTCW 1, 2; SATA 67
<indSalisbury, John
    See Caute, (John) David
Salter, James 1925-   **CLC 7, 52, 59**
    See also CA 73-76; DLB 130
Saltus, Edgar (Everton) 1855-1921 **TCLC 8**
    See also CA 105; DLB 202
Saltykov, Mikhail Evgrafovich 1826-1889 **NCLC 16**
Samarakis, Antonis 1919-   **CLC 5**
    See also CA 25-28R; CAAS 16; CANR 36
Sanchez, Florencio 1875-1910   **TCLC 37**
    See also CA 153; HW 1
Sanchez, Luis Rafael 1936-   **CLC 23**
    See also CA 128; DLB 145; HW 1
Sanchez, Sonia 1934-   **CLC 5, 116; BLC 3; DAM MULT; PC 9**
    See also BW 2, 3; CA 33-36R; CANR 24, 49, 74; CLR 18; DLB 41; DLBD 8; MAICYA; MTCW 1, 2; SATA 22
Sand, George 1804-1876**NCLC 2, 42, 57; DA; DAB; DAC; DAM MST, NOV; WLC**
    See also DLB 119, 192
Sandburg, Carl (August) 1878-1967**CLC 1, 4, 10, 15, 35; DA; DAB; DAC; DAM MST, POET; PC 2; WLC**
    See also AAYA 24; CA 5-8R; 25-28R; CANR 35; CDALB 1865-1917; DLB 17, 54; MAICYA; MTCW 1, 2; SATA 8
Sandburg, Charles
    See Sandburg, Carl (August)
Sandburg, Charles A.
    See Sandburg, Carl (August)
Sanders, (James) Ed(ward) 1939-   **CLC 53; DAM POET**
    See also CA 13-16R; CAAS 21; CANR 13, 44, 78; DLB 16
Sanders, Lawrence 1920-1998**CLC 41; DAM POP**
    See also BEST 89:4; CA 81-84; 165; CANR 33, 62; MTCW 1
Sanders, Noah
    See Blount, Roy (Alton), Jr.
Sanders, Winston P.
    See Anderson, Poul (William)
Sandoz, Mari(e Susette) 1896-1966   **CLC 28**
    See also CA 1-4R; 25-28R; CANR 17, 64; DLB 9, 212; MTCW 1, 2; SATA 5
Saner, Reg(inald Anthony) 1931-   **CLC 9**
    See also CA 65-68
Sankara 788-820   **CMLC 32**
Sannazaro, Jacopo 1456(?)-1530   **LC 8**
Sansom, William 1912-1976 **CLC 2, 6; DAM NOV; SSC 21**
    See also CA 5-8R; 65-68; CANR 42; DLB 139; MTCW 1

Santayana, George 1863-1952   **TCLC 40**
    See also CA 115; DLB 54, 71; DLBD 13
Santiago, Danny   **CLC 33**
    See also James, Daniel (Lewis)
    See also DLB 122
Santmyer, Helen Hoover 1895-1986 **CLC 33**
    See also CA 1-4R; 118; CANR 15, 33; DLBY 84; MTCW 1
Santoka, Taneda 1882-1940   **TCLC 72**
Santos, Bienvenido N(uqui) 1911-1996 **C L C 22; DAM MULT**
    See also CA 101; 151; CANR 19, 46
Sapper   **TCLC 44**
    See also McNeile, Herman Cyril
Sapphire
    See Sapphire, Brenda
Sapphire, Brenda 1950-   **CLC 99**
Sappho fl. 6th cent. B.C.-   **CMLC 3; DAM POET; PC 5**
    See also DLB 176
Saramago, Jose 1922-   **CLC 119; HLCS 1**
    See also CA 153
Sarduy, Severo 1937-1993**CLC 6, 97; HLCS 1**
    See also CA 89-92; 142; CANR 58; DLB 113; HW 1, 2
Sargeson, Frank 1903-1982   **CLC 31**
    See also CA 25-28R; 106; CANR 38, 79
Sarmiento, Felix Ruben Garcia
    See Dario, Ruben
Saro-Wiwa, Ken(ule Beeson) 1941-1995**C L C 114**
    See also BW 2; CA 142; 150; CANR 60; DLB 157
Saroyan, William 1908-1981**CLC 1, 8, 10, 29, 34, 56; DA; DAB; DAC; DAM DRAM, MST, NOV; SSC 21; WLC**
    See also CA 5-8R; 103; CANR 30; CDALBS; DLB 7, 9, 86; DLBY 81; MTCW 1, 2; SATA 23; SATA-Obit 24
Sarraute, Nathalie 1900-**CLC 1, 2, 4, 8, 10, 31, 80**
    See also CA 9-12R; CANR 23, 66; DLB 83; MTCW 1, 2
Sarton, (Eleanor) May 1912-1995 **CLC 4, 14, 49, 91; DAM POET**
    See also CA 1-4R; 149; CANR 1, 34, 55; DLB 48; DLBY 81; INT CANR-34; MTCW 1, 2; SATA 36; SATA-Obit 86
Sartre, Jean-Paul 1905-1980**CLC 1, 4, 7, 9, 13, 18, 24, 44, 50, 52; DA; DAB; DAC; DAM DRAM, MST, NOV; DC 3; SSC 32; WLC**
    See also CA 9-12R; 97-100; CANR 21; DLB 72; MTCW 1, 2
Sassoon, Siegfried (Lorraine) 1886-1967**CLC 36; DAB; DAM MST, NOV, POET; PC 12**
    See also CA 104; 25-28R; CANR 36; DLB 20, 191; DLBD 18; MTCW 1, 2
Satterfield, Charles
    See Pohl, Frederik
Saul, John (W. III) 1942-**CLC 46; DAM NOV, POP**
    See also AAYA 10; BEST 90:4; CA 81-84; CANR 16, 40; SATA 98
Saunders, Caleb
    See Heinlein, Robert A(nson)
Saura (Atares), Carlos 1932-   **CLC 20**
    See also CA 114; 131; CANR 79; HW 1
Sauser-Hall, Frederic 1887-1961   **CLC 18**
    See also Cendrars, Blaise
    See also CA 102; 93-96; CANR 36, 62; MTCW 1
Saussure, Ferdinand de 1857-1913 **TCLC 49**
Savage, Catharine

See Brosman, Catharine Savage

Savage, Thomas 1915-   **CLC 40**
See also CA 126; 132; CAAS 15; INT 132

Savan, Glenn 19(?)-   **CLC 50**

Sayers, Dorothy L(eigh) 1893-1957 **TCLC 2, 15; DAM POP**
See also CA 104; 119; CANR 60; CDBLB 1914-1945; DLB 10, 36, 77, 100; MTCW 1, 2

Sayers, Valerie 1952-   **CLC 50**
See also CA 134; CANR 61

Sayles, John (Thomas) 1950- **CLC 7, 10, 14**
See also CA 57-60; CANR 41; DLB 44

Scammell, Michael 1935-   **CLC 34**
See also CA 156

Scannell, Vernon 1922-   **CLC 49**
See also CA 5-8R; CANR 8, 24, 57; DLB 27; SATA 59

Scarlett, Susan
See Streatfeild, (Mary) Noel

Scarron
See Mikszath, Kalman

Schaeffer, Susan Fromberg 1941- **CLC 6, 11, 22**
See also CA 49-52; CANR 18, 65; DLB 28; MTCW 1, 2; SATA 22

Schary, Jill
See Robinson, Jill

Schell, Jonathan 1943-   **CLC 35**
See also CA 73-76; CANR 12

Schelling, Friedrich Wilhelm Joseph von 1775-1854   **NCLC 30**
See also DLB 90

Schendel, Arthur van 1874-1946   **TCLC 56**

Scherer, Jean-Marie Maurice 1920-
See Rohmer, Eric
See also CA 110

Schevill, James (Erwin) 1920-   **CLC 7**
See also CA 5-8R; CAAS 12

Schiller, Friedrich 1759-1805 **NCLC 39, 69; DAM DRAM**
See also DLB 94

Schisgal, Murray (Joseph) 1926-   **CLC 6**
See also CA 21-24R; CANR 48

Schlee, Ann 1934-   **CLC 35**
See also CA 101; CANR 29; SATA 44; SATA-Brief 36

Schlegel, August Wilhelm von 1767-1845 **NCLC 15**
See also DLB 94

Schlegel, Friedrich 1772-1829   **NCLC 45**
See also DLB 90

Schlegel, Johann Elias (von) 1719(?)-1749 **LC 5**

Schlesinger, Arthur M(eier), Jr. 1917- **CLC 84**
See also AITN 1; CA 1-4R; CANR 1, 28, 58; DLB 17; INT CANR-28; MTCW 1, 2; SATA 61

Schmidt, Arno (Otto) 1914-1979   **CLC 56**
See also CA 128; 109; DLB 69

Schmitz, Aron Hector 1861-1928
See Svevo, Italo
See also CA 104; 122; MTCW 1

Schnackenberg, Gjertrud 1953-   **CLC 40**
See also CA 116; DLB 120

Schneider, Leonard Alfred 1925-1966
See Bruce, Lenny
See also CA 89-92

Schnitzler, Arthur 1862-1931 **TCLC 4; SSC 15**
See also CA 104; DLB 81, 118

Schoenberg, Arnold 1874-1951   **TCLC 75**
See also CA 109

Schonberg, Arnold
See Schoenberg, Arnold

Schopenhauer, Arthur 1788-1860   **NCLC 51**
See also DLB 90

Schor, Sandra (M.) 1932(?)-1990   **CLC 65**
See also CA 132

Schorer, Mark 1908-1977   **CLC 9**
See also CA 5-8R; 73-76; CANR 7; DLB 103

Schrader, Paul (Joseph) 1946-   **CLC 26**
See also CA 37-40R; CANR 41; DLB 44

Schreiner, Olive (Emilie Albertina) 1855-1920 **TCLC 9**
See also CA 105; 154; DLB 18, 156, 190

Schulberg, Budd (Wilson) 1914- **CLC 7, 48**
See also CA 25-28R; CANR 19; DLB 6, 26, 28; DLBY 81

Schulz, Bruno 1892-1942 **TCLC 5, 51; SSC 13**
See also CA 115; 123; MTCW 2

Schulz, Charles M(onroe) 1922-   **CLC 12**
See also CA 9-12R; CANR 6; INT CANR-6; SATA 10

Schumacher, E(rnst) F(riedrich) 1911-1977 **CLC 80**
See also CA 81-84; 73-76; CANR 34

Schuyler, James Marcus 1923-1991 **CLC 5, 23; DAM POET**
See also CA 101; 134; DLB 5, 169; INT 101

Schwartz, Delmore (David) 1913-1966 **CLC 2, 4, 10, 45, 87; PC 8**
See also CA 17-18; 25-28R; CANR 35; CAP 2; DLB 28, 48; MTCW 1, 2

Schwartz, Ernst
See Ozu, Yasujiro

Schwartz, John Burnham 1965-   **CLC 59**
See also CA 132

Schwartz, Lynne Sharon 1939-   **CLC 31**
See also CA 103; CANR 44; MTCW 2

Schwartz, Muriel A.
See Eliot, T(homas) S(tearns)

Schwarz-Bart, Andre 1928-   **CLC 2, 4**
See also CA 89-92

Schwarz-Bart, Simone 1938- **CLC 7; BLCS**
See also BW 2; CA 97-100

Schwob, Marcel (Mayer Andre) 1867-1905 **TCLC 20**
See also CA 117; 168; DLB 123

Sciascia, Leonardo 1921-1989   **CLC 8, 9, 41**
See also CA 85-88; 130; CANR 35; DLB 177; MTCW 1

Scoppettone, Sandra 1936-   **CLC 26**
See also AAYA 11; CA 5-8R; CANR 41, 73; SATA 9, 92

Scorsese, Martin 1942-   **CLC 20, 89**
See also CA 110; 114; CANR 46

Scotland, Jay
See Jakes, John (William)

Scott, Duncan Campbell 1862-1947 **TCLC 6; DAC**
See also CA 104; 153; DLB 92

Scott, Evelyn 1893-1963   **CLC 43**
See also CA 104; 112; CANR 64; DLB 9, 48

Scott, F(rancis) R(eginald) 1899-1985 **CLC 22**
See also CA 101; 114; DLB 88; INT 101

Scott, Frank
See Scott, F(rancis) R(eginald)

Scott, Joanna 1960-   **CLC 50**
See also CA 126; CANR 53

Scott, Paul (Mark) 1920-1978   **CLC 9, 60**
See also CA 81-84; 77-80; CANR 33; DLB 14, 207; MTCW 1

Scott, Sarah 1723-1795   **LC 44**
See also DLB 39

Scott, Walter 1771-1832   **NCLC 15, 69; DA; DAB; DAC; DAM MST, NOV, POET; PC 13; SSC 32; WLC**

See also AAYA 22; CDBLB 1789-1832; DLB 93, 107, 116, 144, 159; YABC 2

Scribe, (Augustin) Eugene 1791-1861 **NCLC 16; DAM DRAM; DC 5**
See also DLB 192

Scrum, R.
See Crumb, R(obert)

Scudery, Madeleine de 1607-1701   **LC 2**

Scum
See Crumb, R(obert)

Scumbag, Little Bobby
See Crumb, R(obert)

Seabrook, John
See Hubbard, L(afayette) Ron(ald)

Sealy, I. Allan 1951-   **CLC 55**

Search, Alexander
See Pessoa, Fernando (Antonio Nogueira)

Sebastian, Lee
See Silverberg, Robert

Sebastian Owl
See Thompson, Hunter S(tockton)

Sebestyen, Ouida 1924-   **CLC 30**
See also AAYA 8; CA 107; CANR 40; CLR 17; JRDA; MAICYA; SAAS 10; SATA 39

Secundus, H. Scriblerus
See Fielding, Henry

Sedges, John
See Buck, Pearl S(ydenstricker)

Sedgwick, Catharine Maria 1789-1867 **NCLC 19**
See also DLB 1, 74

Seelye, John (Douglas) 1931-   **CLC 7**
See also CA 97-100; CANR 70; INT 97-100

Seferiades, Giorgos Stylianou 1900-1971
See Seferis, George
See also CA 5-8R; 33-36R; CANR 5, 36; MTCW 1

Seferis, George **CLC 5, 11**
See also Seferiades, Giorgos Stylianou

Segal, Erich (Wolf) 1937- **CLC 3, 10; DAM POP**
See also BEST 89:1; CA 25-28R; CANR 20, 36, 65; DLBY 86; INT CANR-20; MTCW 1

Seger, Bob 1945-   **CLC 35**

Seghers, Anna **CLC 7**
See also Radvanyi, Netty
See also DLB 69

Seidel, Frederick (Lewis) 1936-   **CLC 18**
See also CA 13-16R; CANR 8; DLBY 84

Seifert, Jaroslav 1901-1986   **CLC 34, 44, 93**
See also CA 127; MTCW 1, 2

Sei Shonagon c. 966-1017(?)   **CMLC 6**

Sejour, Victor 1817-1874   **DC 10**
See also DLB 50

Sejour Marcou et Ferrand, Juan Victor
See Sejour, Victor

Selby, Hubert, Jr. 1928- **CLC 1, 2, 4, 8; SSC 20**
See also CA 13-16R; CANR 33; DLB 2

Selzer, Richard 1928-   **CLC 74**
See also CA 65-68; CANR 14

Sembene, Ousmane
See Ousmane, Sembene

Senancour, Etienne Pivert de 1770-1846 **NCLC 16**
See also DLB 119

Sender, Ramon (Jose) 1902-1982 **CLC 8; DAM MULT; HLC**
See also CA 5-8R; 105; CANR 8; HW 1; MTCW 1

Seneca, Lucius Annaeus c. 1-c. 65 **CMLC 6; DAM DRAM; DC 5**
See also DLB 211

Senghor, Leopold Sedar 1906- **CLC 54; BLC**

3; DAM MULT, POET; PC 25
See also BW 2, 3; CA 116; 125; CANR 47, 74;
MTCW 1, 2

Senna, Danzy 1970-   **CLC 119**
See also CA 169

Serling, (Edward) Rod(man) 1924-1975 **C L C
30**
See also AAYA 14; AITN 1; CA 162; 57-60;
DLB 26

Serna, Ramon Gomez de la
See Gomez de la Serna, Ramon

Serpieres
See Guillevic, (Eugene)

Service, Robert
See Service, Robert W(illiam)
See also DAB; DLB 92 ᛁ

Service, Robert W(illiam) 1874(?)-1958**TCLC
15; DA; DAC; DAM MST, POET; WLC**
See also Service, Robert
See also CA 115; 140; SATA 20

Seth, Vikram 1952-**CLC 43, 90; DAM MULT**
See also CA 121; 127; CANR 50, 74; DLB 120;
INT 127; MTCW 2

Seton, Cynthia Propper 1926-1982   **CLC 27**
See also CA 5-8R; 108; CANR 7

Seton, Ernest (Evan) Thompson 1860-1946
TCLC 31
See also CA 109; CLR 58; DLB 92; DLBD 13;
JRDA; SATA 18

Seton-Thompson, Ernest
See Seton, Ernest (Evan) Thompson

Settle, Mary Lee 1918-   **CLC 19, 61**
See also CA 89-92; CAAS 1; CANR 44; DLB
6; INT 89-92

Seuphor, Michel
See Arp, Jean

**Sevigne, Marie (de Rabutin-Chantal) Marquise
de** 1626-1696   **LC 11**

Sewall, Samuel 1652-1730   **LC 38**
See also DLB 24

Sexton, Anne (Harvey) 1928-1974**CLC 2, 4, 6,
8, 10, 15, 53; DA; DAB; DAC; DAM MST,
POET; PC 2; WLC**
See also CA 1-4R; 53-56; CABS 2; CANR 3,
36; CDALB 1941-1968; DLB 5, 169;
MTCW 1, 2; SATA 10

Shaara, Jeff 1952-   **CLC 119**
See also CA 163

Shaara, Michael (Joseph, Jr.) 1929-1988**C L C
15; DAM POP**
Scc also AITN 1; CA 102; 125; CANR 52;
DLBY 83

Shackleton, C. C.
See Aldiss, Brian W(ilson)

Shacochis, Bob   **CLC 39**
See also Shacochis, Robert G.

Shacochis, Robert G. 1951-
See Shacochis, Bob
See also CA 119; 124; INT 124

Shaffer, Anthony (Joshua) 1926-   **CLC 19;
DAM DRAM**
See also CA 110; 116; DLB 13

Shaffer, Peter (Levin) 1926-**CLC 5, 14, 18, 37,
60; DAB; DAM DRAM, MST; DC 7**
See also CA 25-28R; CANR 25, 47, 74; CDBLB
1960 to Present; DLB 13; MTCW 1, 2

Shakey, Bernard
See Young, Neil

Shalamov, Varlam (Tikhonovich) 1907(?)-1982
CLC 18
See also CA 129; 105

Shamlu, Ahmad 1925-   **CLC 10**

Shammas, Anton 1951-   **CLC 55**

Shange, Ntozake 1948-**CLC 8, 25, 38, 74; BLC
3; DAM DRAM, MULT; DC 3**
See also AAYA 9; BW 2; CA 85-88; CABS 3;
CANR 27, 48, 74; DLB 38; MTCW 1, 2

Shanley, John Patrick 1950-   **CLC 75**
See also CA 128; 133

Shapcott, Thomas W(illiam) 1935-   **CLC 38**
See also CA 69-72; CANR 49

Shapiro, Jane   **CLC 76**

Shapiro, Karl (Jay) 1913-**CLC 4, 8, 15, 53; PC
25**
See also CA 1-4R; CAAS 6; CANR 1, 36, 66;
DLB 48; MTCW 1, 2

Sharp, William 1855-1905   **TCLC 39**
See also CA 160; DLB 156

Sharpe, Thomas Ridley 1928-
See Sharpe, Tom
See also CA 114; 122; INT 122

Sharpe, Tom   **CLC 36**
See also Sharpe, Thomas Ridley
See also DLB 14

Shaw, Bernard   **TCLC 45**
See also Shaw, George Bernard
See also BW 1; MTCW 2

Shaw, G. Bernard
See Shaw, George Bernard

Shaw, George Bernard 1856-1950**TCLC 3, 9,
21; DA; DAB; DAC; DAM DRAM, MST;
WLC**
See also Shaw, Bernard
See also CA 104; 128; CDBLB 1914-1945;
DLB 10, 57, 190; MTCW 1, 2

Shaw, Henry Wheeler 1818-1885   **NCLC 15**
See also DLB 11

Shaw, Irwin 1913-1984   **CLC 7, 23, 34; DAM
DRAM, POP**
See also AITN 1; CA 13-16R; 112; CANR 21;
CDALB 1941-1968; DLB 6, 102; DLBY 84;
MTCW 1, 21

Shaw, Robert 1927-1978   **CLC 5**
See also AITN 1; CA 1-4R; 81-84; CANR 4;
DLB 13, 14

Shaw, T. E.
See Lawrence, T(homas) E(dward)

Shawn, Wallace 1943-   **CLC 41**
See also CA 112

Shea, Lisa 1953-   **CLC 86**
See also CA 147

Sheed, Wilfrid (John Joseph) 1930-**CLC 2, 4,
10, 53**
See also CA 65-68; CANR 30, 66; DLB 6;
MTCW 1, 2

Sheldon, Alice Hastings Bradley 1915(?)-1987
See Tiptree, James, Jr.
See also CA 108; 122; CANR 34; INT 108;
MTCW 1

Sheldon, John
See Bloch, Robert (Albert)

Shelley, Mary Wollstonecraft (Godwin) 1797-
1851**NCLC 14, 59; DA; DAB; DAC; DAM
MST, NOV; WLC**
See also AAYA 20; CDBLB 1789-1832; DLB
110, 116, 159, 178; SATA 29

Shelley, Percy Bysshe 1792-1822   **NCLC 18;
DA; DAB; DAC; DAM MST, POET; PC
14; WLC**
See also CDBLB 1789-1832; DLB 96, 110, 158

Shepard, Jim 1956-   **CLC 36**
See also CA 137; CANR 59; SATA 90

Shepard, Lucius 1947-   **CLC 34**
See also CA 128; 141

Shepard, Sam 1943- **CLC 4, 6, 17, 34, 41, 44;
DAM DRAM; DC 5**

See also AAYA 1; CA 69-72; CABS 3; CANR
22; DLB 7, 212; MTCW 1, 2

Shepherd, Michael
See Ludlum, Robert

Sherburne, Zoa (Lillian Morin) 1912-1995
CLC 30
See also AAYA 13; CA 1-4R; CANR 3, 37;
MAICYA; SAAS 18; SATA 3

Sheridan, Frances 1724-1766   **LC 7**
See also DLB 39, 84

Sheridan, Richard Brinsley 1751-1816**N C L C
5; DA; DAB; DAC; DAM DRAM, MST;
DC 1; WLC**
See also CDBLB 1660-1789; DLB 89

Sherman, Jonathan Marc   **CLC 55**

Sherman, Martin 1941(?)-   **CLC 19**
See also CA 116; 123

Sherwin, Judith Johnson
See Johnson, Judith (Emlyn)

Sherwood, Frances 1940-   **CLC 81**
See also CA 146

Sherwood, Robert E(mmet) 1896-1955**T C L C
3; DAM DRAM**
See also CA 104; 153; DLB 7, 26

Shestov, Lev 1866-1938   **TCLC 56**

Shevchenko, Taras 1814-1861   **NCLC 54**

Shiel, M(atthew) P(hipps) 1865-1947**TCLC 8**
See Holmes, Gordon
See also CA 106; 160; DLB 153; MTCW 2

Shields, Carol 1935-   **CLC 91, 113; DAC**
See also CA 81-84; CANR 51, 74; MTCW 2

Shields, David 1956-   **CLC 97**
See also CA 124; CANR 48

Shiga, Naoya 1883-1971   **CLC 33; SSC 23**
See also CA 101; 33-36R; DLB 180

Shikibu, Murasaki c. 978-c. 1014   **CMLC 1**

Shilts, Randy 1951-1994   **CLC 85**
See also AAYA 19; CA 115; 127; 144; CANR
45; INT 127; MTCW 2

Shimazaki, Haruki 1872-1943
See Shimazaki Toson
See also CA 105; 134

Shimazaki Toson 1872-1943   **TCLC 5**
See also Shimazaki, Haruki
See also DLB 180

Sholokhov, Mikhail (Aleksandrovich) 1905-
1984   **CLC 7, 15**
See also CA 101; 112; MTCW 1, 2; SATA-Obit
36

Shone, Patric
See Hanley, James

Shreve, Susan Richards 1939-   **CLC 23**
See also CA 49-52; CAAS 5; CANR 5, 38, 69;
MAICYA; SATA 46, 95; SATA-Brief 41

Shue, Larry 1946-1985**CLC 52; DAM DRAM**
See also CA 145; 117

Shu-Jen, Chou 1881-1936
See Lu Hsun
See also CA 104

Shulman, Alix Kates 1932-   **CLC 2, 10**
See also CA 29-32R; CANR 43; SATA 7

Shuster, Joe 1914-   **CLC 21**

Shute, Nevil   **CLC 30**
See also Norway, Nevil Shute
See also MTCW 2

Shuttle, Penelope (Diane) 1947-   **CLC 7**
See also CA 93-96; CANR 39; DLB 14, 40

Sidney, Mary 1561-1621   **LC 19, 39**

Sidney, Sir Philip 1554-1586 **LC 19, 39; DA;
DAB; DAC; DAM MST, POET**
See also CDBLB Before 1660; DLB 167

Siegel, Jerome 1914-1996   **CLC 21**
See also CA 116; 169; 151

Siegel, Jerry
See Siegel, Jerome
Sienkiewicz, Henryk (Adam Alexander Pius)
1846-1916   **TCLC 3**
See also CA 104; 134
Sierra, Gregorio Martinez
See Martinez Sierra, Gregorio
Sierra, Maria (de la O'LeJarraga) Martinez
See Martinez Sierra, Maria (de la O'LeJarraga)
Sigal, Clancy 1926-   **CLC 7**
See also CA 1-4R
Sigourney, Lydia Howard (Huntley) 1791-1865
NCLC 21
See also DLB 1, 42, 73
Siguenza y Gongora, Carlos de 1645-1700**L C**
8; HLCS 1
Sigurjonsson, Johann 1880-1919   **TCLC 27**
See also CA 170
Sikelianos, Angelos 1884-1951   **TCLC 39**
Silkin, Jon 1930-   **CLC 2, 6, 43**
See also CA 5-8R; CAAS 5; DLB 27
Silko, Leslie (Marmon) 1948-**CLC 23, 74, 114;**
DA; DAC; DAM MST, MULT, POP;
WLCS
See also AAYA 14; CA 115; 122; CANR 45,
65; DLB 143, 175; MTCW 2; NNAL
Sillanpaa, Frans Eemil 1888-1964   **CLC 19**
See also CA 129; 93-96; MTCW 1
Sillitoe, Alan 1928-   **CLC 1, 3, 6, 10, 19, 57**
See also AITN 1; CA 9-12R; CAAS 2; CANR
8, 26, 55; CDBLB 1960 to Present; DLB 14,
139; MTCW 1, 2; SATA 61
Silone, Ignazio 1900-1978   **CLC 4**
See also CA 25-28; 81-84; CANR 34; CAP 2;
MTCW 1
Silver, Joan Micklin 1935-   **CLC 20**
See also CA 114; 121; INT 121
Silver, Nicholas
See Faust, Frederick (Schiller)
Silverberg, Robert 1935- **CLC 7; DAM POP**
See also AAYA 24; CA 1-4R; CAAS 3; CANR
1, 20, 36; CLR 58; DLB 8; INT CANR-20;
MAICYA; MTCW 1, 2; SATA 13, 91; SATA-
Essay 104
Silverstein, Alvin 1933-   **CLC 17**
See also CA 49-52; CANR 2; CLR 25; JRDA;
MAICYA; SATA 8, 69
Silverstein, Virginia B(arbara Opshelor) 1937-
CLC 17
See also CA 49-52; CANR 2; CLR 25; JRDA;
MAICYA; SATA 8, 69
Sim, Georges
See Simenon, Georges (Jacques Christian)
Simak, Clifford D(onald) 1904-1988**CLC 1, 55**
See also CA 1-4R; 125; CANR 1, 35; DLB 8;
MTCW 1; SATA-Obit 56
Simenon, Georges (Jacques Christian) 1903-
1989   **CLC 1, 2, 3, 8, 18, 47; DAM POP**
See also CA 85-88; 129; CANR 35; DLB 72;
DLBY 89; MTCW 1, 2
Simic, Charles 1938-   **CLC 6, 9, 22, 49, 68;**
DAM POET
See also CA 29-32R; CAAS 4; CANR 12, 33,
52, 61; DLB 105; MTCW 2
Simmel, Georg 1858-1918   **TCLC 64**
See also CA 157
Simmons, Charles (Paul) 1924-   **CLC 57**
See also CA 89-92; INT 89-92
Simmons, Dan 1948-   **CLC 44; DAM POP**
See also AAYA 16; CA 138; CANR 53
Simmons, James (Stewart Alexander) 1933-
CLC 43
See also CA 105; CAAS 21; DLB 40

Simms, William Gilmore 1806-1870 **NCLC 3**
See also DLB 3, 30, 59, 73
Simon, Carly 1945-   **CLC 26**
See also CA 105
Simon, Claude 1913-1984   **CLC 4, 9, 15, 39;**
DAM NOV
See also CA 89-92; CANR 33; DLB 83; MTCW
1
Simon, (Marvin) Neil 1927-**CLC 6, 11, 31, 39,**
70; DAM DRAM
See also AITN 1; CA 21-24R; CANR 26, 54;
DLB 7; MTCW 1, 2
Simon, Paul (Frederick) 1941(?)-   **CLC 17**
See also CA 116; 153
Simonon, Paul 1956(?)-   **CLC 30**
Simpson, Harriette
See Arnow, Harriette (Louisa) Simpson
Simpson, Louis (Aston Marantz) 1923-**CLC 4,**
7, 9, 32; DAM POET
See also CA 1-4R; CAAS 4; CANR 1, 61; DLB
5; MTCW 1, 2
Simpson, Mona (Elizabeth) 1957-   **CLC 44**
See also CA 122; 135; CANR 68
Simpson, N(orman) F(rederick) 1919-**CLC 29**
See also CA 13-16R; DLB 13
Sinclair, Andrew (Annandale) 1935- **CLC 2,**
14
See also CA 9-12R; CAAS 5; CANR 14, 38;
DLB 14; MTCW 1
Sinclair, Emil
See Hesse, Hermann
Sinclair, Iain 1943-   **CLC 76**
See also CA 132
Sinclair, Iain MacGregor
See Sinclair, Iain
Sinclair, Irene
See Griffith, D(avid Lewelyn) W(ark)
Sinclair, Mary Amelia St. Clair 1865(?)-1946
See Sinclair, May
See also CA 104
Sinclair, May 1863-1946   **TCLC 3, 11**
See also Sinclair, Mary Amelia St. Clair
See also CA 166; DLB 36, 135
Sinclair, Roy
See Griffith, D(avid Lewelyn) W(ark)
Sinclair, Upton (Beall) 1878-1968 **CLC 1, 11,**
15, 63; DA; DAB; DAC; DAM MST, NOV;
WLC
See also CA 5-8R; 25-28R; CANR 7; CDALB
1929-1941; DLB 9; INT CANR-7; MTCW
1, 2; SATA 9
Singer, Isaac
See Singer, Isaac Bashevis
Singer, Isaac Bashevis 1904-1991**CLC 1, 3, 6,**
9, 11, 15, 23, 38, 69, 111; DA; DAB; DAC;
DAM MST, NOV; SSC 3; WLC
See also AITN 1, 2; CA 1-4R; 134; CANR 1,
39; CDALB 1941-1968; CLR 1; DLB 6, 28,
52; DLBY 91; JRDA; MAICYA; MTCW 1,
2; SATA 3, 27; SATA-Obit 68
Singer, Israel Joshua 1893-1944   **TCLC 33**
See also CA 169
Singh, Khushwant 1915-   **CLC 11**
See also CA 9-12R; CAAS 9; CANR 6
Singleton, Ann
See Benedict, Ruth (Fulton)
Sinjohn, John
See Galsworthy, John
Sinyavsky, Andrei (Donatevich) 1925-1997
CLC 8
See also CA 85-88; 159
Sirin, V.
See Nabokov, Vladimir (Vladimirovich)

Sissman, L(ouis) E(dward) 1928-1976**CLC 9,**
18
See also CA 21-24R; 65-68; CANR 13; DLB 5
Sisson, C(harles) H(ubert) 1914-   **CLC 8**
See also CA 1-4R; CAAS 3; CANR 3, 48; DLB
27
Sitwell, Dame Edith 1887-1964 **CLC 2, 9, 67;**
DAM POET; PC 3
See also CA 9-12R; CANR 35; CDBLB 1945-
1960; DLB 20; MTCW 1, 2
Siwaarmill, H. P.
See Sharp, William
Sjoewall, Maj 1935-   **CLC 7**
See also CA 65-68; CANR 73
Sjowall, Maj
See Sjoewall, Maj
Skelton, John 1463-1529   **PC 25**
Skelton, Robin 1925-1997   **CLC 13**
See also AITN 2; CA 5-8R; 160; CAAS 5;
CANR 28, DLD 27, 53
Skolimowski, Jerzy 1938-   **CLC 20**
See also CA 128
Skram, Amalie (Bertha) 1847-1905 **TCLC 25**
See also CA 165
Skvorecky, Josef (Vaclav) 1924- **CLC 15, 39,**
69; DAC; DAM NOV
See also CA 61-64; CAAS 1; CANR 10, 34,
63; MTCW 1, 2
Slade, Bernard   **CLC 11, 46**
See also Newbound, Bernard Slade
See also CAAS 9; DLB 53
Slaughter, Carolyn 1946-   **CLC 56**
See also CA 85-88
Slaughter, Frank G(ill) 1908-   **CLC 29**
See also AITN 2; CA 5-8R; CANR 5; INT
CANR-5
Slavitt, David R(ytman) 1935-   **CLC 5, 14**
See also CA 21-24R; CAAS 3; CANR 41; DLB
5, 6
Slesinger, Tess 1905-1945   **TCLC 10**
See also CA 107; DLB 102
Slessor, Kenneth 1901-1971   **CLC 14**
See also CA 102; 89-92
Slowacki, Juliusz 1809-1849   **NCLC 15**
Smart, Christopher 1722-1771   **LC 3; DAM**
POET; PC 13
See also DLB 109
Smart, Elizabeth 1913-1986   **CLC 54**
See also CA 81-84; 118; DLB 88
Smiley, Jane (Graves) 1949-**CLC 53, 76; DAM**
POP
See also CA 104; CANR 30, 50, 74; INT CANR-
30
Smith, A(rthur) J(ames) M(arshall) 1902-1980
CLC 15; DAC
See also CA 1-4R; 102; CANR 4; DLB 88
Smith, Adam 1723-1790   **LC 36**
See also DLB 104
Smith, Alexander 1829-1867   **NCLC 59**
See also DLB 32, 55
Smith, Anna Deavere 1950-   **CLC 86**
See also CA 133
Smith, Betty (Wehner) 1896-1972   **CLC 19**
See also CA 5-8R; 33-36R; DLBY 82; SATA 6
Smith, Charlotte (Turner) 1749-1806 **N C L C**
23
See also DLB 39, 109
Smith, Clark Ashton 1893-1961   **CLC 43**
See also CA 143; MTCW 2
Smith, Dave   **CLC 22, 42**
See also Smith, David (Jeddie)
See also CAAS 7; DLB 5
Smith, David (Jeddie) 1942-

See Smith, Dave
  See also CA 49-52; CANR 1, 59; DAM POET
Smith, Florence Margaret 1902-1971
  See Smith, Stevie
  See also CA 17-18; 29-32R; CANR 35; CAP 2;
    DAM POET; MTCW 1, 2
Smith, Iain Crichton 1928-1998   **CLC 64**
  See also CA 21-24R; 171; DLB 40, 139
Smith, John 1580(?)-1631   **LC 9**
  See also DLB 24, 30
Smith, Johnston
  See Crane, Stephen (Townley)
Smith, Joseph, Jr. 1805-1844   **NCLC 53**
Smith, Lee 1944-   **CLC 25, 73**
  See also CA 114; 119; CANR 46; DLB 143;
    DLBY 83; INT 119
Smith, Martin
  See Smith, Martin Cruz
Smith, Martin Cruz 1942-   **CLC 25; DAM**
    MULT, POP
  See also BEST 89:4; CA 85-88; CANR 6, 23,
    43, 65; INT CANR-23; MTCW 2; NNAL
Smith, Mary-Ann Tirone 1944-   **CLC 39**
  See also CA 118; 136
Smith, Patti 1946-   **CLC 12**
  See also CA 93-96; CANR 63
Smith, Pauline (Urmson) 1882-1959**TCLC 25**
Smith, Rosamond
  See Oates, Joyce Carol
Smith, Sheila Kaye
  See Kaye-Smith, Sheila
Smith, Stevie   **CLC 3, 8, 25, 44; PC 12**
  See also Smith, Florence Margaret
  See also DLB 20; MTCW 2
Smith, Wilbur (Addison) 1933-   **CLC 33**
  See also CA 13-16R; CANR 7, 46, 66; MTCW
    1, 2
Smith, William Jay 1918-   **CLC 6**
  See also CA 5-8R; CANR 44; DLB 5; MAICYA;
    SAAS 22; SATA 2, 68
Smith, Woodrow Wilson
  See Kuttner, Henry
Smolenskin, Peretz 1842-1885   **NCLC 30**
Smollett, Tobias (George) 1721-1771**LC 2, 46**
  See also CDBLB 1660-1789; DLB 39, 104
Snodgrass, W(illiam) D(e Witt) 1926-**CLC 2,**
    6, 10, 18, 68; DAM POET
  See also CA 1-4R; CANR 6, 36, 65; DLB 5;
    MTCW 1, 2
Snow, C(harles) P(ercy) 1905-1980 **CLC 1, 4,**
    6, 9, 13, 19; DAM NOV
  See also CA 5-8R; 101; CANR 28; CDBLB
    1945-1960; DLB 15, 77; DLBD 17; MTCW
    1, 2
Snow, Frances Compton
  See Adams, Henry (Brooks)
Snyder, Gary (Sherman) 1930-**CLC 1, 2, 5, 9,**
    32, 120; DAM POET; PC 21
  See also CA 17-20R; CANR 30, 60; DLB 5,
    16, 165, 212; MTCW 2
Snyder, Zilpha Keatley 1927-   **CLC 17**
  See also AAYA 15; CA 9-12R; CANR 38; CLR
    31; JRDA; MAICYA; SAAS 2; SATA 1, 28,
    75
Soares, Bernardo
  See Pessoa, Fernando (Antonio Nogueira)
Sobh, A.
  See Shamlu, Ahmad
Sobol, Joshua   **CLC 60**
Socrates 469B.C.-399B.C.   **CMLC 27**
Soderberg, Hjalmar 1869-1941   **TCLC 39**
Sodergran, Edith (Irene)
  See Soedergran, Edith (Irene)

Soedergran, Edith (Irene) 1892-1923   **T C L C**
  31
Softly, Edgar
  See Lovecraft, H(oward) P(hillips)
Softly, Edward
  See Lovecraft, H(oward) P(hillips)
Sokolov, Raymond 1941-   **CLC 7**
  See also CA 85-88
Solo, Jay
  See Ellison, Harlan (Jay)
Sologub, Fyodor   **TCLC 9**
  See also Teternikov, Fyodor Kuzmich
Solomons, Ikey Esquir
  See Thackeray, William Makepeace
Solomos, Dionysios 1798-1857   **NCLC 15**
Solwoska, Mara
  See French, Marilyn
Solzhenitsyn, Aleksandr I(sayevich) 1918-
  CLC 1, 2, 4, 7, 9, 10, 18, 26, 34, 78; DA;
  DAB; DAC; DAM MST, NOV; SSC 32;
  WLC
  See also AITN 1; CA 69-72; CANR 40, 65;
    MTCW 1, 2
Somers, Jane
  See Lessing, Doris (May)
Somerville, Edith 1858-1949   **TCLC 51**
  See also DLB 135
Somerville & Ross
  See Martin, Violet Florence; Somerville, Edith
Sommer, Scott 1951-   **CLC 25**
  See also CA 106
Sondheim, Stephen (Joshua) 1930- **CLC 30,**
    39; DAM DRAM
  See also AAYA 11; CA 103; CANR 47, 68
Song, Cathy 1955-   **PC 21**
  See also CA 154; DLB 169
Sontag, Susan 1933-**CLC 1, 2, 10, 13, 31, 105;**
  DAM POP
  See also CA 17-20R; CANR 25, 51, 74; DLB
    2, 67; MTCW 1, 2
Sophocles 496(?)B.C.-406(?)B.C.   **CMLC 2;**
  DA; DAB; DAC; DAM DRAM, MST; DC
  1; WLCS
  See also DLB 176
Sordello 1189-1269   **CMLC 15**
Sorel, Georges 1847-1922   **TCLC 91**
  See also CA 118
Sorel, Julia
  See Drexler, Rosalyn
Sorrentino, Gilbert 1929-**CLC 3, 7, 14, 22, 40**
  See also CA 77-80; CANR 14, 33; DLB 5, 173;
    DLBY 80; INT CANR-14
Soto, Gary 1952- **CLC 32, 80; DAM MULT;**
  HLC
  See also AAYA 10; CA 119; 125; CANR 50,
    74; CLR 38; DLB 82; HW 1, 2; INT 125;
    JRDA; MTCW 2; SATA 80
Soupault, Philippe 1897-1990   **CLC 68**
  See also CA 116; 147; 131
Souster, (Holmes) Raymond 1921-**CLC 5, 14;**
  DAC; DAM POET
  See also CA 13-16R; CAAS 14; CANR 13, 29,
    53; DLB 88; SATA 63
Southern, Terry 1924(?)-1995   **CLC 7**
  See also CA 1-4R; 150; CANR 1, 55; DLB 2
Southey, Robert 1774-1843   **NCLC 8**
  See also DLB 93, 107, 142; SATA 54
Southworth, Emma Dorothy Eliza Nevitte
  1819-1899   **NCLC 26**
Souza, Ernest
  See Scott, Evelyn
Soyinka, Wole 1934-**CLC 3, 5, 14, 36, 44; BLC**
  3; DA; DAB; DAC; DAM DRAM, MST,

  MULT; DC 2; WLC
  See also BW 2, 3; CA 13-16R; CANR 27, 39;
    DLB 125; MTCW 1, 2
Spackman, W(illiam) M(ode) 1905-1990**C L C**
  46
  See also CA 81-84; 132
Spacks, Barry (Bernard) 1931-   **CLC 14**
  See also CA 154; CANR 33; DLB 105
Spanidou, Irini 1946-   **CLC 44**
Spark, Muriel (Sarah) 1918-**CLC 2, 3, 5, 8, 13,**
  18, 40, 94; DAB; DAC; DAM MST, NOV;
  SSC 10
  See also CA 5-8R; CANR 12, 36, 76; CDBLB
    1945-1960; DLB 15, 139; INT CANR-12;
    MTCW 1, 2
Spaulding, Douglas
  See Bradbury, Ray (Douglas)
Spaulding, Leonard
  See Bradbury, Ray (Douglas)
Spence, J. A. D.
  See Eliot, T(homas) S(tearns)
Spencer, Elizabeth 1921-   **CLC 22**
  See also CA 13-16R; CANR 32, 65; DLB 6;
    MTCW 1; SATA 14
Spencer, Leonard G.
  See Silverberg, Robert
Spencer, Scott 1945-   **CLC 30**
  See also CA 113; CANR 51; DLBY 86
Spender, Stephen (Harold) 1909-1995**CLC 1,**
  2, 5, 10, 41, 91; DAM POET
  See also CA 9-12R; 149; CANR 31, 54; CDBLB
    1945-1960; DLB 20; MTCW 1, 2
Spengler, Oswald (Arnold Gottfried) 1880-1936
  TCLC 25
  See also CA 118
Spenser, Edmund 1552(?)-1599**LC 5, 39; DA;**
  DAB; DAC; DAM MST, POET; PC 8;
  WLC
  See also CDBLB Before 1660; DLB 167
Spicer, Jack 1925-1965 **CLC 8, 18, 72; DAM**
  POET
  See also CA 85-88; DLB 5, 16, 193
Spiegelman, Art 1948-   **CLC 76**
  See also AAYA 10; CA 125; CANR 41, 55, 74;
    MTCW 2
Spielberg, Peter 1929-   **CLC 6**
  See also CA 5-8R; CANR 4, 48; DLBY 81
Spielberg, Steven 1947-   **CLC 20**
  See also AAYA 8, 24; CA 77-80; CANR 32;
    SATA 32
Spillane, Frank Morrison 1918-
  See Spillane, Mickey
  See also CA 25-28R; CANR 28, 63; MTCW 1,
    2; SATA 66
Spillane, Mickey   **CLC 3, 13**
  See also Spillane, Frank Morrison
  See also MTCW 2
Spinoza, Benedictus de 1632-1677   **LC 9**
Spinrad, Norman (Richard) 1940-   **CLC 46**
  See also CA 37-40R; CAAS 19; CANR 20; DLB
    8; INT CANR-20
Spitteler, Carl (Friedrich Georg) 1845-1924
  TCLC 12
  See also CA 109; DLB 129
Spivack, Kathleen (Romola Drucker) 1938-
  CLC 6
  See also CA 49-52
Spoto, Donald 1941-   **CLC 39**
  See also CA 65-68; CANR 11, 57
Springsteen, Bruce (F.) 1949-   **CLC 17**
  See also CA 111
Spurling, Hilary 1940-   **CLC 34**
  See also CA 104; CANR 25, 52

Spyker, John Howland
See Elman, Richard (Martin)
Squires, (James) Radcliffe 1917-1993 **CLC 51**
See also CA 1-4R; 140; CANR 6, 21
Srivastava, Dhanpat Rai 1880(?)-1936
See Premchand
See also CA 118
Stacy, Donald
See Pohl, Frederik
Stael, Germaine de 1766-1817
See Stael-Holstein, Anne Louise Germaine
Necker Baronn
See also DLB 119
Stael-Holstein, Anne Louise Germaine Necker
Baronn 1766-1817 **NCLC 3**
See also Stael, Germaine de
See also DLB 192
Stafford, Jean 1915-1979 **CLC 4, 7, 19, 68; SSC**
26
See also CA 1-4R; 85-88; CANR 3, 65; DLB 2,
173; MTCW 1, 2; SATA-Obit 22
Stafford, William (Edgar) 1914-1993 **CLC 4,**
7, 29; DAM POET
See also CA 5-8R; 142; CAAS 3; CANR 5, 22;
DLB 5, 206; INT CANR-22
Stagnelius, Eric Johan 1793-1823 **NCLC 61**
Staines, Trevor
See Brunner, John (Kilian Houston)
Stairs, Gordon
See Austin, Mary (Hunter)
Stalin, Joseph 1879-1953 **TCLC 92**
Stannard, Martin 1947- **CLC 44**
See also CA 142; DLB 155
Stanton, Elizabeth Cady 1815-1902 **TCLC 73**
See also CA 171; DLB 79
Stanton, Maura 1946- **CLC 9**
See also CA 89-92; CANR 15; DLB 120
Stanton, Schuyler
See Baum, L(yman) Frank
Stapledon, (William) Olaf 1886-1950 **T C L C**
22
See also CA 111; 162; DLB 15
Starbuck, George (Edwin) 1931-1996 **CLC 53;**
DAM POET
See also CA 21-24R; 153; CANR 23
Stark, Richard
See Westlake, Donald E(dwin)
Staunton, Schuyler
See Baum, L(yman) Frank
Stead, Christina (Ellen) 1902-1983 **CLC 2, 5,**
8, 32, 80
See also CA 13-16R; 109; CANR 33, 40;
MTCW 1, 2
Stead, William Thomas 1849-1912 **TCLC 48**
See also CA 167
Steele, Richard 1672-1729 **LC 18**
See also CDBLB 1660-1789; DLB 84, 101
Steele, Timothy (Reid) 1948- **CLC 45**
See also CA 93-96; CANR 16, 50; DLB 120
Steffens, (Joseph) Lincoln 1866-1936 **T C L C**
20
See also CA 117
Stegner, Wallace (Earle) 1909-1993 **CLC 9, 49,**
81; DAM NOV; SSC 27
See also AITN 1; BEST 90:3; CA 1-4R; 141;
CAAS 9; CANR 1, 21, 46; DLB 9, 206;
DLBY 93; MTCW 1, 2
Stein, Gertrude 1874-1946 **TCLC 1, 6, 28, 48;**
DA; DAB; DAC; DAM MST, NOV, POET;
PC 18; WLC
See also CA 104; 132; CDALB 1917-1929;
DLB 4, 54, 86; DLBD 15; MTCW 1, 2
Steinbeck, John (Ernst) 1902-1968 **CLC 1, 5, 9,**

13, 21, 34, 45, 75; DA; DAB; DAC; DAM
DRAM, MST, NOV; SSC 11; WLC
See also AAYA 12; CA 1-4R; 25-28R; CANR
1, 35; CDALB 1929-1941; DLB 7, 9, 212;
DLBD 2; MTCW 1, 2; SATA 9
Steinem, Gloria 1934- **CLC 63**
See also CA 53-56; CANR 28, 51; MTCW 1, 2
Steiner, George 1929- **CLC 24; DAM NOV**
See also CA 73-76; CANR 31, 67; DLB 67;
MTCW 1, 2; SATA 62
Steiner, K. Leslie
See Delany, Samuel R(ay, Jr.)
Steiner, Rudolf 1861-1925 **TCLC 13**
See also CA 107
Stendhal 1783-1842 **NCLC 23, 46; DA; DAB;**
DAC; DAM MST, NOV; SSC 27; WLC
See also DLB 119
Stephen, Adeline Virginia
See Woolf, (Adeline) Virginia
Stephen, Sir Leslie 1832-1904 **TCLC 23**
See also CA 123; DLB 57, 144, 190
Stephen, Sir Leslie
See Stephen, Sir Leslie
Stephen, Virginia
See Woolf, (Adeline) Virginia
Stephens, James 1882(?)-1950 **TCLC 4**
See also CA 104; DLB 19, 153, 162
Stephens, Reed
See Donaldson, Stephen R.
Steptoe, Lydia
See Barnes, Djuna
Sterchi, Beat 1949- **CLC 65**
Sterling, Brett
See Bradbury, Ray (Douglas); Hamilton,
Edmond
Sterling, Bruce 1954- **CLC 72**
See also CA 119; CANR 44
Sterling, George 1869-1926 **TCLC 20**
See also CA 117; 165; DLB 54
Stern, Gerald 1925- **CLC 40, 100**
See also CA 81-84; CANR 28; DLB 105
Stern, Richard (Gustave) 1928- **CLC 4, 39**
See also CA 1-4R; CANR 1, 25, 52; DLBY 87;
INT CANR-25
Sternberg, Josef von 1894-1969 **CLC 20**
See also CA 81-84
Sterne, Laurence 1713-1768 **LC 2, 48; DA;**
DAB; DAC; DAM MST, NOV; WLC
See also CDBLB 1660-1789; DLB 39
Sternheim, (William Adolf) Carl 1878-1942
TCLC 8
See also CA 105; DLB 56, 118
Stevens, Mark 1951- **CLC 34**
See also CA 122
Stevens, Wallace 1879-1955 **TCLC 3, 12, 45;**
DA; DAB; DAC; DAM MST, POET; PC
6; WLC
See also CA 104; 124; CDALB 1929-1941;
DLB 54; MTCW 1, 2
Stevenson, Anne (Katharine) 1933- **CLC 7, 33**
See also CA 17-20R; CAAS 9; CANR 9, 33;
DLB 40; MTCW 1
Stevenson, Robert Louis (Balfour) 1850-1894
NCLC 5, 14, 63; DA; DAB; DAC; DAM
MST, NOV; SSC 11; WLC
See also AAYA 24; CDBLB 1890-1914; CLR
10, 11; DLB 18, 57, 141, 156, 174; DLBD
13; JRDA; MAICYA; SATA 100; YABC 2
Stewart, J(ohn) I(nnes) M(ackintosh) 1906-
1994 **CLC 7, 14, 32**
See also CA 85-88; 147; CAAS 3; CANR 47;
MTCW 1, 2
Stewart, Mary (Florence Elinor) 1916- **CLC 7,**

35, 117; DAB
See also AAYA 29; CA 1-4R; CANR 1, 59;
SATA 12
Stewart, Mary Rainbow
See Stewart, Mary (Florence Elinor)
Stifle, June
See Campbell, Maria
Stifter, Adalbert 1805-1868 **NCLC 41; SSC 28**
See also DLB 133
Still, James 1906- **CLC 49**
See also CA 65-68; CAAS 17; CANR 10, 26;
DLB 9; SATA 29
Sting 1951-
See Sumner, Gordon Matthew
See also CA 167
Stirling, Arthur
See Sinclair, Upton (Beall)
Stitt, Milan 1941- **CLC 29**
See also CA 69-72
Stockton, Francis Richard 1834-1902
See Stockton, Frank R.
See also CA 108; 137; MAICYA; SATA 44
Stockton, Frank R. **TCLC 47**
See also Stockton, Francis Richard
See also DLB 42, 74; DLBD 13; SATA-Brief
32
Stoddard, Charles
See Kuttner, Henry
Stoker, Abraham 1847-1912
See Stoker, Bram
See also CA 105; 150; DA; DAC; DAM MST,
NOV; SATA 29
Stoker, Bram 1847-1912 **TCLC 8; DAB; WLC**
See also Stoker, Abraham
See also AAYA 23; CDBLB 1890-1914; DLB
36, 70, 178
Stolz, Mary (Slattery) 1920- **CLC 12**
See also AAYA 8; AITN 1; CA 5-8R; CANR
13, 41; JRDA; MAICYA; SAAS 3; SATA 10,
71
Stone, Irving 1903-1989 **CLC 7; DAM POP**
See also AITN 1; CA 1-4R; 129; CAAS 3;
CANR 1, 23; INT CANR-23; MTCW 1, 2;
SATA 3; SATA-Obit 64
Stone, Oliver (William) 1946- **CLC 73**
See also AAYA 15; CA 110; CANR 55
Stone, Robert (Anthony) 1937- **CLC 5, 23, 42**
See also CA 85-88; CANR 23, 66; DLB 152;
INT CANR-23; MTCW 1
Stone, Zachary
See Follett, Ken(neth Martin)
Stoppard, Tom 1937- **CLC 1, 3, 4, 5, 8, 15, 29,**
34, 63, 91; DA; DAB; DAC; DAM DRAM,
MST; DC 6; WLC
See also CA 81-84; CANR 39, 67; CDBLB
1960 to Present; DLB 13; DLBY 85; MTCW
1, 2
Storey, David (Malcolm) 1933- **CLC 2, 4, 5, 8;**
DAM DRAM
See also CA 81-84; CANR 36; DLB 13, 14, 207;
MTCW 1
Storm, Hyemeyohsts 1935- **CLC 3; DAM**
MULT
See also CA 81-84; CANR 45; NNAL
Storm, Theodor 1817-1888 **SSC 27**
Storm, (Hans) Theodor (Woldsen) 1817-1888
NCLC 1; SSC 27
See also DLB 129
Storni, Alfonsina 1892-1938 **TCLC 5; DAM**
MULT; HLC
See also CA 104; 131; HW 1
Stoughton, William 1631-1701 **LC 38**
See also DLB 24

Stout, Rex (Todhunter) 1886-1975   CLC 3
   See also AITN 2; CA 61-64; CANR 71
Stow, (Julian) Randolph 1935-   CLC 23, 48
   See also CA 13-16R; CANR 33; MTCW 1
Stowe, Harriet (Elizabeth) Beecher 1811-1896
   NCLC 3, 50; DA; DAB; DAC; DAM MST,
   NOV; WLC
      See also CDALB 1865-1917; DLB 1, 12, 42,
      74, 189; JRDA; MAICYA; YABC 1
Strachey, (Giles) Lytton 1880-1932 TCLC 12
   See also CA 110; DLB 149; DLBD 10; MTCW
   2
Strand, Mark 1934- CLC 6, 18, 41, 71; DAM
   POET
      See also CA 21-24R; CANR 40, 65; DLB 5;
      SATA 41
Straub, Peter (Francis) 1943-   CLC 28, 107;
   DAM POP
      See also BEST 89:1; CA 85-88; CANR 28, 65;
      DLBY 84; MTCW 1, 2
Strauss, Botho 1944-   CLC 22
<indexSee also CA 157; DLB 124
Streatfeild, (Mary) Noel 1895(?)-1986CLC 21
   See also CA 81-84; 120; CANR 31; CLR 17;
   DLB 160; MAICYA; SATA 20; SATA-Obit
   48
Stribling, T(homas) S(igismund) 1881-1965
   CLC 23
      See also CA 107; DLB 9
Strindberg, (Johan) August 1849-1912TCLC
   1, 8, 21, 47; DA; DAB; DAC; DAM DRAM,
   MST; WLC
      See also CA 104; 135; MTCW 2
Stringer, Arthur 1874-1950   TCLC 37
   See also CA 161; DLB 92
Stringer, David
   See Roberts, Keith (John Kingston)
Stroheim, Erich von 1885-1957   TCLC 71
Strugatskii, Arkadii (Natanovich) 1925-1991
   CLC 27
      See also CA 106; 135
Strugatskii, Boris (Natanovich) 1933-CLC 27
   See also CA 106
Strummer, Joe 1953(?)-   CLC 30
Strunk, William, Jr. 1869-1946   TCLC 92
   See also CA 118; 164
Stuart, Don A.
   See Campbell, John W(ood, Jr.)
Stuart, Ian
   See MacLean, Alistair (Stuart)
Stuart, Jesse (Hilton) 1906-1984CLC 1, 8, 11,
   14, 34; SSC 31
      See also CA 5-8R; 112; CANR 31; DLB 9, 48,
      102; DLBY 84; SATA 2; SATA-Obit 36
Sturgeon, Theodore (Hamilton) 1918-1985
   CLC 22, 39
      See also Queen, Ellery
      See also CA 81-84; 116; CANR 32; DLB 8;
      DLBY 85; MTCW 1, 2
Sturges, Preston 1898-1959   TCLC 48
   See also CA 114; 149; DLB 26
Styron, William 1925-CLC 1, 3, 5, 11, 15, 60;
   DAM NOV, POP; SSC 25
      See also BEST 90:4; CA 5-8R; CANR 6, 33,
      74; CDALB 1968-1988; DLB 2, 143; DLBY
      80; INT CANR-6; MTCW 1, 2
Su, Chien 1884-1918
   See Su Man-shu
   See also CA 123
Suarez Lynch, B.
   See Bioy Casares, Adolfo; Borges, Jorge Luis
Suckow, Ruth 1892-1960   SSC 18
   See also CA 113; DLB 9, 102

Sudermann, Hermann 1857-1928 TCLC 15
   See also CA 107; DLB 118
Sue, Eugene 1804-1857   NCLC 1
   See also DLB 119
Sueskind, Patrick 1949-   CLC 44
   See also Suskind, Patrick
Sukenick, Ronald 1932-   CLC 3, 4, 6, 48
   See also CA 25-28R; CAAS 8; CANR 32; DLB
   173; DLBY 81
Suknaski, Andrew 1942-   CLC 19
   See also CA 101; DLB 53
Sullivan, Vernon
   See Vian, Boris
Sully Prudhomme 1839-1907   TCLC 31
Su Man-shu   TCLC 24
   See also Su, Chien
Summerforest, Ivy B.
   See Kirkup, James
Summers, Andrew James 1942-   CLC 26
Summers, Andy
   See Summers, Andrew James
Summers, Hollis (Spurgeon, Jr.) 1916-CLC 10
   See also CA 5-8R; CANR 3; DLB 6
Summers, (Alphonsus Joseph-Mary Augustus)
   Montague 1880-1948   TCLC 16
      See also CA 118; 163
Sumner, Gordon Matthew   CLC 26
   See also Sting
Surtees, Robert Smith 1803-1864   NCLC 14
   See also DLB 21
Susann, Jacqueline 1921-1974   CLC 3
   See also AITN 1; CA 65-68; 53-56; MTCW 1,
   2
Su Shih 1036-1101   CMLC 15
Suskind, Patrick
   See Sueskind, Patrick
   See also CA 145
Sutcliff, Rosemary 1920-1992 CLC 26; DAB;
   DAC; DAM MST, POP
      See also AAYA 10; CA 5-8R; 139; CANR 37;
      CLR 1, 37; JRDA; MAICYA; SATA 6, 44,
      78; SATA-Obit 73
Sutro, Alfred 1863-1933   TCLC 6
   See also CA 105; DLB 10
Sutton, Henry
   See Slavitt, David R(ytman)
Svevo, Italo 1861-1928 TCLC 2, 35; SSC 25
   See also Schmitz, Aron Hector
Swados, Elizabeth (A.) 1951-   CLC 12
   See also CA 97-100; CANR 49; INT 97-100
Swados, Harvey 1920-1972   CLC 5
   See also CA 5-8R; 37-40R; CANR 6; DLB 2
Swan, Gladys 1934-   CLC 69
   See also CA 101; CANR 17, 39
Swarthout, Glendon (Fred) 1918-1992CLC 35
   See also CA 1-4R; 139; CANR 1, 47; SATA 26
Sweet, Sarah C.
   See Jewett, (Theodora) Sarah Orne
Swenson, May 1919-1989CLC 4, 14, 61, 106;
   DA; DAB; DAC; DAM MST, POET; PC
   14
      See also CA 5-8R; 130; CANR 36, 61; DLB 5;
      MTCW 1, 2; SATA 15
Swift, Augustus
   See Lovecraft, H(oward) P(hillips)
Swift, Graham (Colin) 1949-   CLC 41, 88
   See also CA 117; 122; CANR 46, 71; DLB 194;
   MTCW 2
Swift, Jonathan 1667-1745   LC 1, 42; DA;
   DAB; DAC; DAM MST, NOV, POET; PC
   9; WLC
      See also CDBLB 1660-1789; CLR 53; DLB 39,
      95, 101; SATA 19

Swinburne, Algernon Charles 1837-1909
   TCLC 8, 36; DA; DAB; DAC; DAM MST,
   POET; PC 24; WLC
      See also CA 105; 140; CDBLB 1832-1890;
      DLB 35, 57
Swinfen, Ann   CLC 34
Swinnerton, Frank Arthur 1884-1982CLC 31
   See also CA 108; DLB 34
Swithen, John
   See King, Stephen (Edwin)
Sylvia
   See Ashton-Warner, Sylvia (Constance)
Symmes, Robert Edward
   See Duncan, Robert (Edward)
Symonds, John Addington 1840-1893 NCLC
   34
      See also DLB 57, 144
Symons, Arthur 1865-1945   TCLC 11
   See also CA 107; DLB 19, 57, 149
Symons, Julian (Gustave) 1912-1994 CLC 2,
   14, 32
      See also CA 49-52; 147; CAAS 3; CANR 3,
      33, 59; DLB 87, 155; DLBY 92; MTCW 1
Synge, (Edmund) J(ohn) M(illington) 1871-
   1909   TCLC 6, 37; DAM DRAM; DC 2
      See also CA 104; 141; CDBLB 1890-1914;
      DLB 10, 19
Syruc, J.
   See Milosz, Czeslaw
Szirtes, George 1948-   CLC 46
   See also CA 109; CANR 27, 61
Szymborska, Wislawa 1923-   CLC 99
   See also CA 154; DLBY 96; MTCW 2
T. O., Nik
   See Annensky, Innokenty (Fyodorovich)
Tabori, George 1914-   CLC 19
   See also CA 49-52; CANR 4, 69
Tagore, Rabindranath 1861-1941TCLC 3, 53;
   DAM DRAM, POET; PC 8
      See also CA 104; 120; MTCW 1, 2
Taine, Hippolyte Adolphe 1828-1893 NCLC
   15
Talese, Gay 1932-   CLC 37
   See also AITN 1; CA 1-4R; CANR 9, 58; DLB
   185; INT CANR-9; MTCW 1, 2
Tallent, Elizabeth (Ann) 1954-   CLC 45
   See also CA 117; CANR 72; DLB 130
Tally, Ted 1952-   CLC 42
   See also CA 120; 124; INT 124
Talvik, Heiti 1904-1947   TCLC 87
Tamayo y Baus, Manuel 1829-1898 NCLC 1
Tammsaare, A(nton) H(ansen) 1878-1940
   TCLC 27
      See also CA 164
Tam'si, Tchicaya U
   See Tchicaya, Gerald Felix
Tan, Amy (Ruth) 1952- CLC 59, 120; DAM
   MULT, NOV, POP
      See also AAYA 9; BEST 89:3; CA 136; CANR
      54; CDALBS; DLB 173; MTCW 2; SATA
      75
Tandem, Felix
   See Spitteler, Carl (Friedrich Georg)
Tanizaki, Jun'ichiro 1886-1965CLC 8, 14, 28;
   SSC 21
      See also CA 93-96; 25-28R; DLB 180; MTCW
      2
Tanner, William
   See Amis, Kingsley (William)
Tao Lao
   See Storni, Alfonsina
Tarassoff, Lev
   See Troyat, Henri

Tarbell, Ida M(inerva) 1857-1944 **TCLC 40**
See also CA 122; DLB 47

Tarkington, (Newton) Booth 1869-1946**TCLC 9**
See also CA 110; 143; DLB 9, 102; MTCW 2;
SATA 17

Tarkovsky, Andrei (Arsenyevich) 1932-1986
CLC 75
See also CA 127

Tartt, Donna 1964(?)- **CLC 76**
See also CA 142

Tasso, Torquato 1544-1595 **LC 5**

Tate, (John Orley) Allen 1899-1979**CLC 2, 4, 6, 9, 11, 14, 24**
See also CA 5-8R; 85-88; CANR 32; DLB 4, 45, 63; DLBD 17; MTCW 1, 2

Tate, Ellalice
See Hibbert, Eleanor Alice Burford

Tate, James (Vincent) 1943- **CLC 2, 6, 25**
See also CA 21-24R; CANR 29, 57; DLB 5, 169

Tavel, Ronald 1940- **CLC 6**
See also CA 21-24R; CANR 33

Taylor, C(ecil) P(hilip) 1929-1981 **CLC 27**
See also CA 25-28R; 105; CANR 47

Taylor, Edward 1642(?)-1729 **LC 11; DA; DAB; DAC; DAM MST, POET**
See also DLB 24

Taylor, Eleanor Ross 1920- **CLC 5**
See also CA 81-84; CANR 70

Taylor, Elizabeth 1912-1975 **CLC 2, 4, 29**
See also CA 13-16R; CANR 9, 70; DLB 139;
MTCW 1; SATA 13

Taylor, Frederick Winslow 1856-1915 **TCLC 76**

Taylor, Henry (Splawn) 1942- **CLC 44**
See also CA 33-36R; CAAS 7; CANR 31; DLB 5

Taylor, Kamala (Purnaiya) 1924-
See Markandaya, Kamala
See also CA 77-80

Taylor, Mildred D. **CLC 21**
See also AAYA 10; BW 1; CA 85-88; CANR 25; CLR 9, 58; DLB 52; JRDA; MAICYA;
SAAS 5; SATA 15, 70

Taylor, Peter (Hillsman) 1917-1994**CLC 1, 4, 18, 37, 44, 50, 71; SSC 10**
See also CA 13-16R; 147; CANR 9, 50; DLBY 81, 94; INT CANR-9; MTCW 1, 2

Taylor, Robert Lewis 1912-1998 **CLC 14**
See also CA 1-4R; 170; CANR 3, 64; SATA 10

Tchekhov, Anton
See Chekhov, Anton (Pavlovich)

Tchicaya, Gerald Felix 1931-1988 **CLC 101**
See also CA 129; 125

Tchicaya U Tam'si
See Tchicaya, Gerald Felix

Teasdale, Sara 1884-1933 **TCLC 4**
See also CA 104; 163; DLB 45; SATA 32

Tegner, Esaias 1782-1846 **NCLC 2**

Teilhard de Chardin, (Marie Joseph) Pierre 1881-1955 **TCLC 9**
See also CA 105

Temple, Ann
See Mortimer, Penelope (Ruth)

Tennant, Emma (Christina) 1937-**CLC 13, 52**
See also CA 65-68; CAAS 9; CANR 10, 38, 59; DLB 14

Tenneshaw, S. M.
See Silverberg, Robert

Tennyson, Alfred 1809-1892 **NCLC 30, 65; DA; DAB; DAC; DAM MST, POET; PC 6; WLC**

See also CDBLB 1832-1890; DLB 32

Teran, Lisa St. Aubin de **CLC 36**
See also St. Aubin de Teran, Lisa

Terence c. 184B.C.-c. 159B.C.**CMLC 14; DC 7**
See also DLB 211

Teresa de Jesus, St. 1515-1582 **LC 18**

Terkel, Louis 1912-
See Terkel, Studs
See also CA 57-60; CANR 18, 45, 67; MTCW 1, 2

Terkel, Studs **CLC 38**
See also Terkel, Louis
See also AITN 1; MTCW 2

Terry, C. V.
See Slaughter, Frank G(ill)

Terry, Megan 1932- **CLC 19**
See also CA 77-80; CABS 3; CANR 43; DLB 7

Tertullian c. 155-c. 245 **CMLC 29**

Tertz, Abram
See Sinyavsky, Andrei (Donatevich)

Tesich, Steve 1943(?)-1996 **CLC 40, 69**
See also CA 105; 152; DLBY 83

Tesla, Nikola 1856-1943 **TCLC 88**

Teternikov, Fyodor Kuzmich 1863-1927
See Sologub, Fyodor
See also CA 104

Tevis, Walter 1928-1984 **CLC 42**
See also CA 113

Tey, Josephine **TCLC 14**
See also Mackintosh, Elizabeth
See also DLB 77

Thackeray, William Makepeace 1811-1863
NCLC 5, 14, 22, 43; DA; DAB; DAC; DAM MST, NOV; WLC
See also CDBLB 1832-1890; DLB 21, 55, 159, 163; SATA 23

Thakura, Ravindranatha
See Tagore, Rabindranath

Tharoor, Shashi 1956- **CLC 70**
See also CA 141

Thelwell, Michael Miles 1939- **CLC 22**
See also BW 2; CA 101

Theobald, Lewis, Jr.
See Lovecraft, H(oward) P(hillips)

Theodorescu, Ion N. 1880-1967
See Arghezi, Tudor
See also CA 116

Theriault, Yves 1915-1983 **CLC 79; DAC; DAM MST**
See also CA 102; DLB 88

Theroux, Alexander (Louis) 1939- **CLC 2, 25**
See also CA 85-88; CANR 20, 63

Theroux, Paul (Edward) 1941- **CLC 5, 8, 11, 15, 28, 46; DAM POP**
See also AAYA 28; BEST 89:4; CA 33-36R;
CANR 20, 45, 74; CDALBS; DLB 2; MTCW 1, 2; SATA 44

Thesen, Sharon 1946- **CLC 56**
See also CA 163

Thevenin, Denis
See Duhamel, Georges

Thibault, Jacques Anatole Francois 1844-1924
See France, Anatole
See also CA 106; 127; DAM NOV; MTCW 1, 2

Thiele, Colin (Milton) 1920- **CLC 17**
See also CA 29-32R; CANR 12, 28, 53; CLR 27; MAICYA; SAAS 2; SATA 14, 72

Thomas, Audrey (Callahan) 1935-**CLC 7, 13, 37, 107; SSC 20**
See also AITN 2; CA 21-24R; CAAS 19; CANR 36, 58; DLB 60; MTCW 1

Thomas, D(onald) M(ichael) 1935- **CLC 13, 22, 31**
See also CA 61-64; CAAS 11; CANR 17, 45, 75; CDBLB 1960 to Present; DLB 40, 207;
INT CANR-17; MTCW 1, 2

Thomas, Dylan (Marlais) 1914-1953**TCLC 1, 8, 45; DA; DAB; DAC; DAM DRAM, MST, POET; PC 2; SSC 3; WLC**
See also CA 104; 120; CANR 65; CDBLB 1945-1960; DLB 13, 20, 139; MTCW 1, 2;
SATA 60

Thomas, (Philip) Edward 1878-1917 **TCLC 10; DAM POET**
See also CA 106; 153; DLB 98

Thomas, Joyce Carol 1938- **CLC 35**
See also AAYA 12; BW 2, 3; CA 113; 116;
CANR 48; CLR 19; DLB 33; INT 116;
JRDA; MAICYA; MTCW 1, 2; SAAS 7;
SATA 40, 78

Thomas, Lewis 1913-1993 **CLC 35**
See also CA 85-88; 143; CANR 38, 60; MTCW 1, 2

Thomas, M. Carey 1857-1935 **TCLC 89**

Thomas, Paul
See Mann, (Paul) Thomas

Thomas, Piri 1928- **CLC 17; HLCS 1**
See also CA 73-76; HW 1

Thomas, R(onald) S(tuart) 1913- **CLC 6, 13, 48; DAB; DAM POET**
See also CA 89-92; CAAS 4; CANR 30;
CDBLB 1960 to Present; DLB 27; MTCW 1

Thomas, Ross (Elmore) 1926-1995 **CLC 39**
See also CA 33-36R; 150; CANR 22, 63

Thompson, Francis Clegg
See Mencken, H(enry) L(ouis)

Thompson, Francis Joseph 1859-1907**TCLC 4**
See also CA 104; CDBLB 1890-1914; DLB 19

Thompson, Hunter S(tockton) 1939- **CLC 9, 17, 40, 104; DAM POP**
See also BEST 89:1; CA 17-20R; CANR 23, 46, 74, 77; DLB 185; MTCW 1, 2

Thompson, James Myers
See Thompson, Jim (Myers)

Thompson, Jim (Myers) 1906-1977(?)**CLC 69**
See also CA 140

Thompson, Judith **CLC 39**

Thomson, James 1700-1748 **LC 16, 29, 40; DAM POET**
See also DLB 95

Thomson, James 1834-1882 **NCLC 18; DAM POET**
See also DLB 35

Thoreau, Henry David 1817-1862**NCLC 7, 21, 61; DA; DAB; DAC; DAM MST; WLC**
See also CDALB 1640-1865; DLB 1

Thornton, Hall
See Silverberg, Robert

Thucydides c. 455B.C.-399B.C. **CMLC 17**
See also DLB 176

Thurber, James (Grover) 1894-1961 **CLC 5, 11, 25; DA; DAB; DAC; DAM DRAM, MST, NOV; SSC 1**
See also CA 73-76; CANR 17, 39; CDALB 1929-1941; DLB 4, 11, 22, 102; MAICYA;
MTCW 1, 2; SATA 13

Thurman, Wallace (Henry) 1902-1934**TCLC 6; BLC 3; DAM MULT**
See also BW 1, 3; CA 104; 124; DLB 51

Ticheburn, Cheviot
See Ainsworth, William Harrison

Tieck, (Johann) Ludwig 1773-1853 **NCLC 5, 46; SSC 31**
See also DLB 90

Tiger, Derry

See Ellison, Harlan (Jay)

Tilghman, Christopher 1948(?)- **CLC 65**
See also CA 159

Tillinghast, Richard (Williford) 1940-**CLC 29**
See also CA 29-32R; CAAS 23; CANR 26, 51

Timrod, Henry 1828-1867 **NCLC 25**
See also DLB 3

Tindall, Gillian (Elizabeth) 1938- **CLC 7**
See also CA 21-24R; CANR 11, 65

Tiptree, James, Jr. **CLC 48, 50**
See also Sheldon, Alice Hastings Bradley
See also DLB 8

Titmarsh, Michael Angelo
See Thackeray, William Makepeace

Tocqueville, Alexis (Charles Henri Maurice Clerel, Comte) de 1805-1859**NCLC 7, 63**

Tolkien, J(ohn) R(onald) R(euel) 1892-1973
CLC 1, 2, 3, 8, 12, 38; DA; DAB; DAC; DAM MST, NOV, POP; WLC
See also AAYA 10; AITN 1; CA 17-18; 45-48; CANR 36; CAP 2; CDBLB 1914-1945; CLR 56; DLB 15, 160; JRDA; MAICYA; MTCW 1, 2; SATA 2, 32, 100; SATA-Obit 24

Toller, Ernst 1893-1939 **TCLC 10**
See also CA 107; DLB 124

Tolson, M. B.
See Tolson, Melvin B(eaunorus)

Tolson, Melvin B(eaunorus) 1898(?)-1966
CLC 36, 105; BLC 3; DAM MULT, POET
See also BW 1, 3; CA 124; 89-92; CANR 80; DLB 48, 76

Tolstoi, Aleksei Nikolaevich
See Tolstoy, Alexey Nikolaevich

Tolstoy, Alexey Nikolaevich 1882-1945**TCLC 18**
See also CA 107; 158

Tolstoy, Count Leo
See Tolstoy, Leo (Nikolaevich)

Tolstoy, Leo (Nikolaevich) 1828-1910**TCLC 4, 11, 17, 28, 44, 79; DA; DAB; DAC; DAM MST, NOV; SSC 9, 30; WLC**
See also CA 104; 123; SATA 26

Tomasi di Lampedusa, Giuseppe 1896-1957
See Lampedusa, Giuseppe (Tomasi) di
See also CA 111

Tomlin, Lily **CLC 17**
See also Tomlin, Mary Jean

Tomlin, Mary Jean 1939(?)-
See Tomlin, Lily
See also CA 117

Tomlinson, (Alfred) Charles 1927-**CLC 2, 4, 6, 13, 45; DAM POET; PC 17**
See also CA 5-8R; CANR 33; DLB 40

Tomlinson, H(enry) M(ajor) 1873-1958**TCLC 71**
See also CA 118; 161; DLB 36, 100, 195

Tonson, Jacob
See Bennett, (Enoch) Arnold

Toole, John Kennedy 1937-1969 **CLC 19, 64**
See also CA 104; DLBY 81; MTCW 2

Toomer, Jean 1894-1967**CLC 1, 4, 13, 22; BLC 3; DAM MULT; PC 7; SSC 1; WLCS**
See also BW 1; CA 85-88; CDALB 1917-1929; DLB 45, 51; MTCW 1, 2

Torley, Luke
<indexhanSee Blish, James (Benjamin)

Tornimparte, Alessandra
See Ginzburg, Natalia

Torre, Raoul della
See Mencken, H(enry) L(ouis)

Torrey, E(dwin) Fuller 1937- **CLC 34**
See also CA 119; CANR 71

Torsvan, Ben Traven

See Traven, B.

Torsvan, Benno Traven
See Traven, B.

Torsvan, Berick Traven
See Traven, B.

Torsvan, Berwick Traven
See Traven, B.

Torsvan, Bruno Traven
See Traven, B.

Torsvan, Traven
See Traven, B.

Tournier, Michel (Edouard) 1924-**CLC 6, 23, 36, 95**
See also CA 49-52; CANR 3, 36, 74; DLB 83; MTCW 1, 2; SATA 23

Tournimparte, Alessandra
See Ginzburg, Natalia

Towers, Ivar
See Kornbluth, C(yril) M.

Towne, Robert (Burton) 1936(?)- **CLC 87**
See also CA 108; DLB 44

Townsend, Sue **CLC 61**
See also Townsend, Susan Elaine
See also AAYA 28; SATA 55, 93; SATA-Brief 48

Townsend, Susan Elaine 1946-
See Townsend, Sue
See also CA 119; 127; CANR 65; DAB; DAC; DAM MST

Townshend, Peter (Dennis Blandford) 1945-
CLC 17, 42
See also CA 107

Tozzi, Federigo 1883-1920 **TCLC 31**
See also CA 160

Traill, Catharine Parr 1802-1899 **NCLC 31**
See also DLB 99

Trakl, Georg 1887-1914 **TCLC 5; PC 20**
See also CA 104; 165; MTCW 2

Transtroemer, Tomas (Goesta) 1931-**CLC 52, 65; DAM POET**
See also CA 117; 129; CAAS 17

Transtromer, Tomas Gosta
See Transtroemer, Tomas (Goesta)

Traven, B. (?)-1969 **CLC 8, 11**
See also CA 19-20; 25-28R; CAP 2; DLB 9, 56; MTCW 1

Treitel, Jonathan 1959- **CLC 70**

Tremain, Rose 1943- **CLC 42**
See also CA 97-100; CANR 44; DLB 14

Tremblay, Michel 1942- **CLC 29, 102; DAC; DAM MST**
See also CA 116; 128; DLB 60; MTCW 1, 2

Trevanian **CLC 29**
See also Whitaker, Rod(ney)

Trevor, Glen
See Hilton, James

Trevor, William 1928-**CLC 7, 9, 14, 25, 71, 116; SSC 21**
See also Cox, William Trevor
See also DLB 14, 139; MTCW 2

Trifonov, Yuri (Valentinovich) 1925-1981
CLC 45
See also CA 126; 103; MTCW 1

Trilling, Lionel 1905-1975 **CLC 9, 11, 24**
See also CA 9-12R; 61-64; CANR 10; DLB 28, 63; INT CANR-10; MTCW 1, 2

Trimball, W. H.
See Mencken, H(enry) L(ouis)

Tristan
See Gomez de la Serna, Ramon

Tristram
See Housman, A(lfred) E(dward)

Trogdon, William (Lewis) 1939-

See Heat-Moon, William Least
See also CA 115; 119; CANR 47; INT 119

Trollope, Anthony 1815-1882**NCLC 6, 33; DA; DAB; DAC; DAM MST, NOV; SSC 28; WLC**
See also CDBLB 1832-1890; DLB 21, 57, 159; SATA 22

Trollope, Frances 1779-1863 **NCLC 30**
See also DLB 21, 166

Trotsky, Leon 1879-1940 **TCLC 22**
See also CA 118; 167

Trotter (Cockburn), Catharine 1679-1749**LC 8**
See also DLB 84

Trout, Kilgore
See Farmer, Philip Jose

Trow, George W. S. 1943- **CLC 52**
See also CA 126

Troyat, Henri 1911- **CLC 23**
See also CA 45-48; CANR 2, 33, 67; MTCW 1

Trudeau, G(arretson) B(eekman) 1948-
See Trudeau, Garry B.
See also CA 81-84; CANR 31; SATA 35

Trudeau, Garry B. **CLC 12**
See also Trudeau, G(arretson) B(eekman)
See also AAYA 10; AITN 2

Truffaut, Francois 1932-1984 **CLC 20, 101**
See also CA 81-84; 113; CANR 34

Trumbo, Dalton 1905-1976 **CLC 19**
See also CA 21-24R; 69-72; CANR 10; DLB 26

Trumbull, John 1750-1831 **NCLC 30**
See also DLB 31

Trundlett, Helen B.
See Eliot, T(homas) S(tearns)

Tryon, Thomas 1926-1991 **CLC 3, 11; DAM POP**
See also AITN 1; CA 29-32R; 135; CANR 32, 77; MTCW 1

Tryon, Tom
See Tryon, Thomas

Ts'ao Hsueh-ch'in 1715(?)-1763 **LC 1**

Tsushima, Shuji 1909-1948
See Dazai Osamu

Tsvetaeva (Efron), Marina (Ivanovna) 1892-1941 **TCLC 7, 35; PC 14**
See also CA 104; 128; CANR 73; MTCW 1, 2

Tuck, Lily 1938- **CLC 70**
See also CA 139

Tu Fu 712-770 **PC 9**
See also DAM MULT

Tunis, John R(oberts) 1889-1975 **CLC 12**
See also CA 61-64; CANR 62; DLB 22, 171; JRDA; MAICYA; SATA 37; SATA-Brief 30

Tuohy, Frank **CLC 37**
See also Tuohy, John Francis
See also DLB 14, 139

Tuohy, John Francis 1925-
See Tuohy, Frank
See also CA 5-8R; CANR 3, 47

Turco, Lewis (Putnam) 1934- **CLC 11, 63**
See also CA 13-16R; CAAS 22; CANR 24, 51; DLBY 84

Turgenev, Ivan 1818-1883 **NCLC 21; DA; DAB; DAC; DAM MST, NOV; DC 7; SSC 7; WLC**

Turgot, Anne-Robert-Jacques 1727-1781 **LC 26**

Turner, Frederick 1943- **CLC 48**
See also CA 73-76; CAAS 10; CANR 12, 30, 56; DLB 40

Tutu, Desmond M(pilo) 1931-**CLC 80; BLC 3;**

DAM MULT
See also BW 1, 3; CA 125; CANR 67

Tutuola, Amos 1920-1997 **CLC 5, 14, 29; BLC 3; DAM MULT**
See also BW 2, 3; CA 9-12R; 159; CANR 27, 66; DLB 125; MTCW 1, 2

Twain, Mark **TCLC 6, 12, 19, 36, 48, 59; SSC 34; WLC**
See Clemens, Samuel Langhorne
See also AAYA 20; DLB 11, 12, 23, 64, 74

Tyler, Anne 1941- **CLC 7, 11, 18, 28, 44, 59, 103; DAM NOV, POP**
See also AAYA 18; BEST 89:1; CA 9-12R; CANR 11, 33, 53; CDALBS; DLB 6, 143; DLBY 82; MTCW 1, 2; SATA 7, 90

Tyler, Royall 1757-1826 **NCLC 3**
See also DLB 37

Tynan, Katharine 1861-1931 **TCLC 3**
See also CA 104; 167; DLB 153

Tyutchev, Fyodor 1803-1873 **NCLC 34**

Tzara, Tristan 1896-1963 **CLC 47; DAM POET**
See also CA 153; 89-92; MTCW 2

Uhry, Alfred 1936- **CLC 55; DAM DRAM, POP**
See also CA 127; 133; INT 133

Ulf, Haerved
See Strindberg, (Johan) August

Ulf, Harved
See Strindberg, (Johan) August

Ulibarri, Sabine R(eyes) 1919-**CLC 83; DAM MULT; HLCS 1**
See also CA 131; DLB 82; HW 1, 2

Unamuno (y Jugo), Miguel de 1864-1936 **TCLC 2, 9; DAM MULT, NOV; HLC; SSC 11**
See also CA 104; 131; DLB 108; HW 1, 2; MTCW 1, 2

Undercliffe, Errol
See Campbell, (John) Ramsey

Underwood, Miles
See Glassco, John

Undset, Sigrid 1882-1949 **TCLC 3; DA; DAB; DAC; DAM MST, NOV; WLC**
See also CA 104; 129; MTCW 1, 2

Ungaretti, Giuseppe 1888-1970 **CLC 7, 11, 15**
See also CA 19-20; 25-28R; CAP 2; DLB 114

Unger, Douglas 1952- **CLC 34**
See also CA 130

Unsworth, Barry (Forster) 1930- **CLC 76**
See also CA 25-28R; CANR 30, 54; DLB 194

Updike, John (Hoyer) 1932-**CLC 1, 2, 3, 5, 7, 9, 13, 15, 23, 34, 43, 70; DA; DAB; DAC; DAM MST, NOV, POET, POP; SSC 13, 27; WLC**
See also CA 1-4R; CABS 1; CANR 4, 33, 51; CDALB 1968-1988; DLB 2, 5, 143; DLBD 3; DLBY 80, 82, 97; MTCW 1, 2

Upshaw, Margaret Mitchell
See Mitchell, Margaret (Munnerlyn)

Upton, Mark
See Sanders, Lawrence

Upward, Allen 1863-1926 **TCLC 85**
See also CA 117; DLB 36

Urdang, Constance (Henriette) 1922-**CLC 47**
See also CA 21-24R; CANR 9, 24

Uriel, Henry
See Faust, Frederick (Schiller)

Uris, Leon (Marcus) 1924- **CLC 7, 32; DAM NOV, POP**
See also AITN 1, 2; BEST 89:2; CA 1-4R; CANR 1, 40, 65; MTCW 1, 2; SATA 49

Urmuz

See Codrescu, Andrei

Urquhart, Jane 1949- **CLC 90; DAC**
See also CA 113; CANR 32, 68

Ustinov, Peter (Alexander) 1921- **CLC 1**
See also AITN 1; CA 13-16R; CANR 25, 51; DLB 13; MTCW 2

U Tam'si, Gerald Felix Tchicaya
See Tchicaya, Gerald Felix

U Tam'si, Tchicaya
See Tchicaya, Gerald Felix

Vachss, Andrew (Henry) 1942- **CLC 106**
See also CA 118; CANR 44

Vachss, Andrew H.
See Vachss, Andrew (Henry)

Vaculik, Ludvik 1926- **CLC 7**
See also CA 53-56; CANR 72

Vaihinger, Hans 1852-1933 **TCLC 71**
See also CA 116; 166

Valdez, Luis (Miguel) 1940- **CLC 84; DAM MULT; DC 10; HLC**
See also CA 101; CANR 32; DLB 122; HW 1

Valenzuela, Luisa 1938- **CLC 31, 104; DAM MULT; HLCS 1; SSC 14**
See also CA 101; CANR 32, 65; DLB 113; HW 1, 2

Valera y Alcala-Galiano, Juan 1824-1905 **TCLC 10**
See also CA 106

Valery, (Ambroise) Paul (Toussaint Jules) 1871-1945 **TCLC 4, 15; DAM POET; PC 9**
See also CA 104; 122; MTCW 1, 2

Valle-Inclan, Ramon (Maria) del 1866-1936 **TCLC 5; DAM MULT; HLC**
See also CA 106; 153; CANR 80; DLB 134; HW 2

Vallejo, Antonio Buero
See Buero Vallejo, Antonio

Vallejo, Cesar (Abraham) 1892-1938 **TCLC 3, 56; DAM MULT; HLC**
See also CA 105; 153; HW 1

Valles, Jules 1832-1885 **NCLC 71**
See also DLB 123

Vallette, Marguerite Eymery
See Rachilde

Valle Y Pena, Ramon del
See Valle-Inclan, Ramon (Maria) del

Van Ash, Cay 1918- **CLC 34**

Vanbrugh, Sir John 1664-1726 **LC 21; DAM DRAM**
See also DLB 80

Van Campen, Karl
See Campbell, John W(ood, Jr.)

Vance, Gerald
See Silverberg, Robert

Vance, Jack **CLC 35**
See also Kuttner, Henry; Vance, John Holbrook
See also DLB 8

Vance, John Holbrook 1916-
See Queen, Ellery; Vance, Jack
See also CA 29-32R; CANR 17, 65; MTCW 1

Van Den Bogarde, Derek Jules Gaspard Ulric Niven 1921-
See Bogarde, Dirk
See also CA 77-80

Vandenburgh, Jane **CLC 59**
See also CA 168

Vanderhaeghe, Guy 1951- **CLC 41**
See also CA 113; CANR 72

van der Post, Laurens (Jan) 1906-1996**CLC 5**
See also CA 5-8R; 155; CANR 35; DLB 204

van de Wetering, Janwillem 1931- **CLC 47**
See also CA 49-52; CANR 4, 62

Van Dine, S. S. **TCLC 23**

See also Wright, Willard Huntington

Van Doren, Carl (Clinton) 1885-1950 **TCLC 18**
See also CA 111; 168

Van Doren, Mark 1894-1972 **CLC 6, 10**
See also CA 1-4R; 37-40R; CANR 3; DLB 45; MTCW 1, 2

Van Druten, John (William) 1901-1957**TCLC 2**
See also CA 104; 161; DLB 10

Van Duyn, Mona (Jane) 1921- **CLC 3, 7, 63, 116; DAM POET**
See also CA 9-12R; CANR 7, 38, 60; DLB 5

Van Dyne, Edith
See Baum, L(yman) Frank

van Itallie, Jean-Claude 1936- **CLC 3**
See also CA 45-48; CAAS 2; CANR 1, 48; DLB 7

van Ostaijen, Paul 1896-1928 **TCLC 33**
See also CA 163

Van Peebles, Melvin 1932- **CLC 2, 20; DAM MULT**
See also BW 2, 3; CA 85-88; CANR 27, 67

Vansittart, Peter 1920- **CLC 42**
See also CA 1-4R; CANR 3, 49

Van Vechten, Carl 1880-1964 **CLC 33**
See also CA 89-92; DLB 4, 9, 51

Van Vogt, A(lfred) E(lton) 1912- **CLC 1**
See also CA 21-24R; CANR 28; DLB 8; SATA 14

Varda, Agnes 1928- **CLC 16**
See also CA 116; 122

Vargas Llosa, (Jorge) Mario (Pedro) 1936- **CLC 3, 6, 9, 10, 15, 31, 42, 85; DA; DAB; DAC; DAM MST, MULT, NOV; HLC**
See also CA 73-76; CANR 18, 32, 42, 67; DLB 145; HW 1, 2; MTCW 1, 2

Vasiliu, Gheorghe 1881-1957
See Bacovia, George
See also CA 123

Vassa, Gustavus
See Equiano, Olaudah

Vassilikos, Vassilis 1933- **CLC 4, 8**
See also CA 81-84; CANR 75

Vaughan, Henry 1621-1695 **LC 27**
See also DLB 131

Vaughn, Stephanie **CLC 62**

Vazov, Ivan (Minchov) 1850-1921 **TCLC 25**
See also CA 121; 167; DLB 147

Veblen, Thorstein B(unde) 1857-1929 **TCLC 31**
See also CA 115; 165

Vega, Lope de 1562-1635 **LC 23; HLCS 1**

Venison, Alfred
See Pound, Ezra (Weston Loomis)

Verdi, Marie de
See Mencken, H(enry) L(ouis)

Verdu, Matilde
See Cela, Camilo Jose

Verga, Giovanni (Carmelo) 1840-1922 **TCLC 3; SSC 21**
See also CA 104; 123

Vergil 70B.C.-19B.C. **CMLC 9; DA; DAB; DAC; DAM MST, POET; PC 12; WLCS**
See also Virgil

Verhaeren, Emile (Adolphe Gustave) 1855-1916 **TCLC 12**
See also CA 109

Verlaine, Paul (Marie) 1844-1896**NCLC 2, 51; DAM POET; PC 2**

Verne, Jules (Gabriel) 1828-1905**TCLC 6, 52**
See also AAYA 16; CA 110; 131; DLB 123; JRDA; MAICYA; SATA 21

Very, Jones 1813-1880   NCLC 9
    See also DLB 1
Vesaas, Tarjei 1897-1970   CLC 48
    See also CA 29-32R
Vialis, Gaston
    See Simenon, Georges (Jacques Christian)
Vian, Boris 1920-1959   TCLC 9
    See also CA 106; 164; DLB 72; MTCW 2
Viaud, (Louis Marie) Julien 1850-1923
    See Loti, Pierre
    See also CA 107
Vicar, Henry
    See Felsen, Henry Gregor
Vicker, Angus
    See Felsen, Henry Gregor
Vidal, Gore 1925-CLC 2, 4, 6, 8, 10, 22, 33, 72;
        DAM NOV, POP
    See also AITN 1; BEST 90:2; CA 5-8R; CANR
        13, 45, 65; CDALBS; DLB 6, 152; INT
        CANR-13; MTCW 1, 2
Viereck, Peter (Robert Edwin) 1916- CLC 4
    See also CA 1-4R; CANR 1, 47; DLB 5
Vigny, Alfred (Victor) de 1797-1863NCLC 7;
        DAM POET; PC 26
    See also DLB 119, 192
Vilakazi, Benedict Wallet 1906-1947TCLC 37
    See also CA 168
Villa, Jose Garcia 1904-1997   PC 22
    See also CA 25-28R; CANR 12
Villaurrutia, Xavier 1903-1950   TCLC 80
    See also HW 1
Villiers de l'Isle Adam, Jean Marie Mathias
        Philippe Auguste, Comte de 1838-1889
        NCLC 3; SSC 14
    See also DLB 123
Villon, Francois 1431-1463(?)   PC 13
    See also DLB 208
Vinci, Leonardo da 1452-1519   LC 12
Vine, Barbara   CLC 50
    See also Rendell, Ruth (Barbara)
    See also BEST 90:4
Vinge, Joan (Carol) D(ennison) 1948-CLC 30;
        SSC 24
    See also CA 93-96; CANR 72; SATA 36
Violis, G.
    See Simenon, Georges (Jacques Christian)
Virgil 70B.C.-19B.C.
    See Vergil
    See also DLB 211
Visconti, Luchino 1906-1976   CLC 16
    See also CA 81-84; 65-68; CANR 39
Vittorini, Elio 1908-1966   CLC 6, 9, 14
    See also CA 133; 25-28R
Vivekananda, Swami 1863-1902   TCLC 88
Vizenor, Gerald Robert 1934-CLC 103; DAM
        MULT
    See also CA 13-16R; CAAS 22; CANR 5, 21,
        44, 67; DLB 175; MTCW 2; NNAL
Vizinczey, Stephen 1933-   CLC 40
    See also CA 128; INT 128
Vliet, R(ussell) G(ordon) 1929-1984 CLC 22
    See also CA 37-40R; 112; CANR 18
Vogau, Boris Andreyevich 1894-1937(?)
    See Pilnyak, Boris
    See also CA 123
Vogel, Paula A(nne) 1951-   CLC 76
    See also CA 108
Voigt, Cynthia 1942-   CLC 30
    See also AAYA 3, 30; CA 106; CANR 18, 37,
        40; CLR 13, 48; INT CANR-18; JRDA;
        MAICYA; SATA 48, 79; SATA-Brief 33
Voigt, Ellen Bryant 1943-   CLC 54
    See also CA 69-72; CANR 11, 29, 55; DLB 120

Voinovich, Vladimir (Nikolaevich) 1932-CLC
        10, 49
    See also CA 81-84; CAAS 12; CANR 33, 67;
        MTCW 1
Vollmann, William T. 1959- CLC 89; DAM
        NOV, POP
    See also CA 134; CANR 67; MTCW 2
Voloshinov, V. N.
    See Bakhtin, Mikhail Mikhailovich
Voltaire 1694-1778 LC 14; DA; DAB; DAC;
        DAM DRAM, MST; SSC 12; WLC
von Aschendrof, BaronIgnatz
    See Ford, Ford Madox
von Daeniken, Erich 1935-   CLC 30
    See also AITN 1; CA 37-40R; CANR 17, 44
von Daniken, Erich
    See von Daeniken, Erich
von Heidenstam, (Carl Gustaf) Verner
    See Heidenstam, (Carl Gustaf) Verner von
von Heyse, Paul (Johann Ludwig)
    See Heyse, Paul (Johann Ludwig von)
von Hofmannsthal, Hugo
    See Hofmannsthal, Hugo von
von Horvath, Odon
    See Horvath, Oedoen von
von Horvath, Oedoen
    See Horvath, Oedoen von
von Liliencron, (Friedrich Adolf Axel) Detlev
    See Liliencron, (Friedrich Adolf Axel) Detlev
        von
Vonnegut, Kurt, Jr. 1922-CLC 1, 2, 3, 4, 5, 8,
        12, 22, 40, 60, 111; DA; DAB; DAC; DAM
        MST, NOV, POP; SSC 8; WLC
    See also AAYA 6; AITN 1; BEST 90:4; CA 1-
        4R; CANR 1, 25, 49, 75; CDALB 1968-
        1988; DLB 2, 8, 152; DLBD 3; DLBY 80;
        MTCW 1, 2
Von Rachen, Kurt
    See Hubbard, L(afayette) Ron(ald)
von Rezzori (d'Arezzo), Gregor
    See Rezzori (d'Arezzo), Gregor von
von Sternberg, Josef
    See Sternberg, Josef von
Vorster, Gordon 1924-   CLC 34
    See also CA 133
Vosce, Trudie
    See Ozick, Cynthia
Voznesensky, Andrei (Andreievich) 1933-
        CLC 1, 15, 57; DAM POET
    See also CA 89-92; CANR 37; MTCW 1
Waddington, Miriam 1917-   CLC 28
    See also CA 21-24R; CANR 12, 30; DLB 68
Wagman, Fredrica 1937-   CLC 7
    See also CA 97-100; INT 97-100
Wagner, Linda W.
    See Wagner-Martin, Linda (C.)
Wagner, Linda Welshimer
    See Wagner-Martin, Linda (C.)
Wagner, Richard 1813-1883   NCLC 9
    See also DLB 129
Wagner-Martin, Linda (C.) 1936-   CLC 50
    See also CA 159
Wagoner, David (Russell) 1926- CLC 3, 5, 15
    See also CA 1-4R; CAAS 3; CANR 2, 71; DLB
        5; SATA 14
Wah, Fred(erick James) 1939-   CLC 44
    See also CA 107; 141; DLB 60
Wahloo, Per 1926-1975   CLC 7
    See also CA 61-64; CANR 73
Wahloo, Peter
    See Wahloo, Per
Wain, John (Barrington) 1925-1994 CLC 2,
        11, 15, 46

    See also CA 5-8R; 145; CAAS 4; CANR 23,
        54; CDBLB 1960 to Present; DLB 15, 27,
        139, 155; MTCW 1, 2
Wajda, Andrzej 1926-   CLC 16
    See also CA 102
Wakefield, Dan 1932-   CLC 7
    See also CA 21-24R; CAAS 7
Wakoski, Diane 1937- CLC 2, 4, 7, 9, 11, 40;
        DAM POET; PC 15
    See also CA 13-16R; CAAS 1; CANR 9, 60;
        DLB 5; INT CANR-9; MTCW 2
Wakoski-Sherbell, Diane
    See Wakoski, Diane
Walcott, Derek (Alton) 1930-CLC 2, 4, 9, 14,
        25, 42, 67, 76; BLC 3; DAB; DAC; DAM
        MST, MULT, POET; DC 7
    See also BW 2; CA 89-92; CANR 26, 47, 75,
        80; DLB 117; DLBY 81; MTCW 1, 2
Waldman, Anne (Lesley) 1945-   CLC 7
    See also CA 37-40R; CAAS 17; CANR 34, 69;
        DLB 16
Waldo, E. Hunter
    See Sturgeon, Theodore (Hamilton)
Waldo, Edward Hamilton
    See Sturgeon, Theodore (Hamilton)
Walker, Alice (Malsenior) 1944- CLC 5, 6, 9,
        19, 27, 46, 58, 103; BLC 3; DA; DAB;
        DAC; DAM MST, MULT, NOV, POET,
        POP; SSC 5; WLCS
    See also AAYA 3; BEST 89:4; BW 2, 3; CA
        37-40R; CANR 9, 27, 49, 66; CDALB 1968-
        1988; DLB 6, 33, 143; INT CANR-27;
        MTCW 1, 2; SATA 31
Walker, David Harry 1911-1992   CLC 14
    See also CA 1-4R; 137; CANR 1; SATA 8;
        SATA-Obit 71
Walker, Edward Joseph 1934-
    See Walker, Ted
    See also CA 21-24R; CANR 12, 28, 53
Walker, George F. 1947- CLC 44, 61; DAB;
        DAC; DAM MST
    See also CA 103; CANR 21, 43, 59; DLB 60
Walker, Joseph A. 1935-   CLC 19; DAM
        DRAM, MST
    See also BW 1, 3; CA 89-92; CANR 26; DLB
        38
Walker, Margaret (Abigail) 1915-1998CLC 1,
        6; BLC; DAM MULT; PC 20
    See also BW 2, 3; CA 73-76; 172; CANR 26,
        54, 76; DLB 76, 152; MTCW 1, 2
Walker, Ted   CLC 13
    See also Walker, Edward Joseph
    See also DLB 40
Wallace, David Foster 1962-   CLC 50, 114
    See also CA 132; CANR 59; MTCW 2
Wallace, Dexter
    See Masters, Edgar Lee
Wallace, (Richard Horatio) Edgar 1875-1932
        TCLC 57
    See also CA 115; DLB 70
Wallace, Irving 1916-1990 CLC 7, 13; DAM
        NOV, POP
    See also AITN 1; CA 1-4R; 132; CAAS 1;
        CANR 1, 27; INT CANR-27; MTCW 1, 2
Wallant, Edward Lewis 1926-1962CLC 5, 10
    See also CA 1-4R; CANR 22; DLB 2, 28, 143;
        MTCW 1, 2
Wallas, Graham 1858-1932   TCLC 91
Walley, Byron
    See Card, Orson Scott
Walpole, Horace 1717-1797   LC 49
    See also DLB 39, 104
Walpole, Hugh (Seymour) 1884-1941TCLC 5

See also CA 104; 165; DLB 34; MTCW 2
Walser, Martin 1927-   **CLC 27**
    See also CA 57-60; CANR 8, 46; DLB 75, 124
Walser, Robert 1878-1956 **TCLC 18; SSC 20**
    See also CA 118; 165; DLB 66
Walsh, Jill Paton   **CLC 35**
    See also Paton Walsh, Gillian
    See also AAYA 11; CLR 2; DLB 161; SAAS 3
Walter, Villiam Christian
    See Andersen, Hans Christian
Wambaugh, Joseph (Aloysius, Jr.) 1937-**C L C 3, 18; DAM NOV, POP**
    See also AITN 1; BEST 89:3; CA 33-36R;
      CANR 42, 65; DLB 6; DLBY 83; MTCW 1,
      2
Wang Wei 699(?)-761(?)   **PC 18**
Ward, Arthur Henry Sarsfield 1883-1959
    See Rohmer, Sax
    See also CA 108; 173
Ward, Douglas Turner 1930-   **CLC 19**
    See also BW 1; CA 81-84; CANR 27; DLB 7,
      38
Ward, Mary Augusta
    See Ward, Mrs. Humphry
Ward, Mrs. Humphry 1851-1920   **TCLC 55**
    See also DLB 18
Ward, Peter
    See Faust, Frederick (Schiller)
Warhol, Andy 1928(?)-1987   **CLC 20**
    See also AAYA 12; BEST 89:4; CA 89-92; 121;
      CANR 34
Warner, Francis (Robert le Plastrier) 1937-
    CLC 14
    See also CA 53-56; CANR 11
Warner, Marina 1946-   **CLC 59**
    See also CA 65-68; CANR 21, 55; DLB 194
Warner, Rex (Ernest) 1905-1986   **CLC 45**
    See also CA 89-92; 119; DLB 15
Warner, Susan (Bogert) 1819-1885 **NCLC 31**
    See also DLB 3, 42
Warner, Sylvia (Constance) Ashton
    See Ashton-Warner, Sylvia (Constance)
Warner, Sylvia Townsend 1893-1978 **CLC 7, 19; SSC 23**
    See also CA 61-64; 77-80; CANR 16, 60; DLB
      34, 139; MTCW 1, 2
Warren, Mercy Otis 1728-1814   **NCLC 13**
    See also DLB 31, 200
Warren, Robert Penn 1905-1989 **CLC 1, 4, 6, 8, 10, 13, 18, 39, 53, 59; DA; DAB; DAC; DAM MST, NOV, POET; SSC 4; WLC**
    See also AITN 1; CA 13-16R; 129; CANR 10,
      47; CDALB 1968-1988; DLB 2, 48, 152;
      DLBY 80, 89; INT CANR-10; MTCW 1, 2;
      SATA 46; SATA-Obit 63
Warshofsky, Isaac
    See Singer, Isaac Bashevis
Warton, Thomas 1728-1790   **LC 15; DAM POET**
    See also DLB 104, 109
Waruk, Kona
    See Harris, (Theodore) Wilson
Warung, Price 1855-1911   **TCLC 45**
Warwick, Jarvis
    See Garner, Hugh
Washington, Alex
    See Harris, Mark
Washington, Booker T(aliaferro) 1856-1915
    TCLC 10; BLC 3; DAM MULT
    See also BW 1; CA 114; 125; SATA 28
Washington, George 1732-1799   **LC 25**
    See also DLB 31
Wassermann, (Karl) Jakob 1873-1934 **T C L C**

6
    See also CA 104; 163; DLB 66
Wasserstein, Wendy 1950-   **CLC 32, 59, 90; DAM DRAM; DC 4**
    See also CA 121; 129; CABS 3; CANR 53, 75;
      INT 129; MTCW 2; SATA 94
Waterhouse, Keith (Spencer) 1929- **CLC 47**
    See also CA 5-8R; CANR 38, 67; DLB 13, 15;
      MTCW 1, 2
Waters, Frank (Joseph) 1902-1995   **CLC 88**
    See also CA 5-8R; 149; CAAS 13; CANR 3,
      18, 63; DLB 212; DLBY 86
Waters, Roger 1944-   **CLC 35**
Watkins, Frances Ellen
    See Harper, Frances Ellen Watkins
Watkins, Gerrold
    See Malzberg, Barry N(athaniel)
Watkins, Gloria 1955(?)-
    See hooks, bell
    See also BW 2; CA 143; MTCW 2
Watkins, Paul 1964-   **CLC 55**
    See also CA 132; CANR 62
Watkins, Vernon Phillips 1906-1967 **CLC 43**
    See also CA 9-10; 25-28R; CAP 1; DLB 20
Watson, Irving S.
    See Mencken, H(enry) L(ouis)
Watson, John H.
    See Farmer, Philip Jose
Watson, Richard F.
    See Silverberg, Robert
Waugh, Auberon (Alexander) 1939- **CLC 7**
    See also CA 45-48; CANR 6, 22; DLB 14, 194
Waugh, Evelyn (Arthur St. John) 1903-1966
    CLC 1, 3, 8, 13, 19, 27, 44, 107; DA; DAB; DAC; DAM MST, NOV, POP; WLC
    See also CA 85-88; 25-28R; CANR 22; CDBLB
      1914-1945; DLB 15, 162, 195; MTCW 1, 2
Waugh, Harriet 1944-   **CLC 6**
    See also CA 85-88; CANR 22
Ways, C. R.
    See Blount, Roy (Alton), Jr.
Waystaff, Simon
    See Swift, Jonathan
Webb, (Martha) Beatrice (Potter) 1858-1943
    TCLC 22
    See also Potter, (Helen) Beatrix
    See also CA 117; DLB 190
Webb, Charles (Richard) 1939-   **CLC 7**
    See also CA 25-28R
Webb, James H(enry), Jr. 1946-   **CLC 22**
    See also CA 81-84
Webb, Mary (Gladys Meredith) 1881-1927
    TCLC 24
    See also CA 123; DLB 34
Webb, Mrs. Sidney
    See Webb, (Martha) Beatrice (Potter)
Webb, Phyllis 1927-   **CLC 18**
    See also CA 104; CANR 23; DLB 53
Webb, Sidney (James) 1859-1947   **TCLC 22**
    See also CA 117; 163; DLB 190
Webber, Andrew Lloyd   **CLC 21**
    See also Lloyd Webber, Andrew
Weber, Lenora Mattingly 1895-1971 **CLC 12**
    See also CA 19-20; 29-32R; CAP 1; SATA 2;
      SATA-Obit 26
Weber, Max 1864-1920   **TCLC 69**
    See also CA 109
Webster, John 1579(?)-1634(?)   **LC 33; DA; DAB; DAC; DAM DRAM, MST; DC 2; WLC**
    See also CDBLB Before 1660; DLB 58
Webster, Noah 1758-1843   **NCLC 30**
    See also DLB 1, 37, 42, 43, 73

Wedekind, (Benjamin) Frank(lin) 1864-1918
    TCLC 7; DAM DRAM
    See also CA 104; 153; DLB 118
Weidman, Jerome 1913-1998   **CLC 7**
    See also AITN 2; CA 1-4R; 171; CANR 1; DLB
      28
Weil, Simone (Adolphine) 1909-1943**TCLC 23**
    See also CA 117; 159; MTCW 2
Weininger, Otto 1880-1903   **TCLC 84**
Weinstein, Nathan
    See West, Nathanael
Weinstein, Nathan von Wallenstein
    See West, Nathanael
Weir, Peter (Lindsay) 1944-   **CLC 20**
    See also CA 113; 123
Weiss, Peter (Ulrich) 1916-1982**CLC 3, 15, 51; DAM DRAM**
    See also CA 45-48; 106; CANR 3; DLB 69, 124
Weiss, Theodore (Russell) 1916-**CLC 3, 8, 14**
    See also CA 9-12R, CAAS 2; CANR 46; DLB
      5
Welch, (Maurice) Denton 1915-1948**TCLC 22**
    See also CA 121; 148
Welch, James 1940-   **CLC 6, 14, 52; DAM MULT, POP**
    See also CA 85-88; CANR 42, 66; DLB 175;
      NNAL
Weldon, Fay 1931-   **CLC 6, 9, 11, 19, 36, 59; DAM POP**
    See also CA 21-24R; CANR 16, 46, 63; CDBLB
      1960 to Present; DLB 14, 194; INT CANR-
      16; MTCW 1, 2
Wellek, Rene 1903-1995   **CLC 28**
    See also CA 5-8R; 150; CAAS 7; CANR 8; DLB
      63; INT CANR-8
Weller, Michael 1942-   **CLC 10, 53**
    See also CA 85-88
Weller, Paul 1958-   **CLC 26**
Wellershoff, Dieter 1925-   **CLC 46**
    See also CA 89-92; CANR 16, 37
Welles, (George) Orson 1915-1985**CLC 20, 80**
    See also CA 93-96; 117
Wellman, John McDowell 1945-
    See Wellman, Mac
    See also CA 166
Wellman, Mac 1945-   **CLC 65**
    See also Wellman, John McDowell; Wellman,
      John McDowell
Wellman, Manly Wade 1903-1986   **CLC 49**
    See also CA 1-4R; 118; CANR 6, 16, 44; SATA
      6; SATA-Obit 47
Wells, Carolyn 1869(?)-1942   **TCLC 35**
    See also CA 113; DLB 11
Wells, H(erbert) G(eorge) 1866-1946**TCLC 6, 12, 19; DA; DAB; DAC; DAM MST, NOV; SSC 6; WLC**
    See also AAYA 18; CA 110; 121; CDBLB 1914-
      1945; DLB 34, 70, 156, 178; MTCW 1, 2;
      SATA 20
Wells, Rosemary 1943-   **CLC 12**
    See also AAYA 13; CA 85-88; CANR 48; CLR
      16; MAICYA; SAAS 1; SATA 18, 69
Welty, Eudora 1909- **CLC 1, 2, 5, 14, 22, 33, 105; DA; DAB; DAC; DAM MST, NOV; SSC 1, 27; WLC**
    See also CA 9-12R; CABS 1; CANR 32, 65;
      CDALB 1941-1968; DLB 2, 102, 143;
      DLBD 12; DLBY 87; MTCW 1, 2
Wen I-to 1899-1946   **TCLC 28**
Wentworth, Robert
    See Hamilton, Edmond
Werfel, Franz (Viktor) 1890-1945   **TCLC 8**
    See also CA 104; 161; DLB 81, 124

Wergeland, Henrik Arnold 1808-1845 **N C L C 5**

Wersba, Barbara 1932- **CLC 30**
See also AAYA 2, 30; CA 29-32R; CANR 16, 38; CLR 3; DLB 52; JRDA; MAICYA; SAAS 2; SATA 1, 58; SATA-Essay 103

Wertmueller, Lina 1928- **CLC 16**
See also CA 97-100; CANR 39, 78

Wescott, Glenway 1901-1987 **CLC 13**
See also CA 13-16R; 121; CANR 23, 70; DLB 4, 9, 102

Wesker, Arnold 1932- **CLC 3, 5, 42; DAB; DAM DRAM**
See also CA 1-4R; CAAS 7; CANR 1, 33; CDBLB 1960 to Present; DLB 13; MTCW 1

Wesley, Richard (Errol) 1945- **CLC 7**
See also BW 1; CA 57-60; CANR 27; DLB 38

Wessel, Johan Herman 1742-1785 **LC 7**

West, Anthony (Panther) 1914-1987 **CLC 50**
See also CA 45-48; 124; CANR 3, 19; DLB 15

West, C. P.
See Wodehouse, P(elham) G(renville)

West, (Mary) Jessamyn 1902-1984 **CLC 7, 17**
See also CA 9-12R; 112; CANR 27; DLB 6; DLBY 84; MTCW 1, 2; SATA-Obit 37

West, Morris L(anglo) 1916- **CLC 6, 33**
See also CA 5-8R; CANR 24, 49, 64; MTCW 1, 2

West, Nathanael 1903-1940 **TCLC 1, 14, 44; SSC 16**
See also CA 104; 125; CDALB 1929-1941; DLB 4, 9, 28; MTCW 1, 2

West, Owen
See Koontz, Dean R(ay)

West, Paul 1930- **CLC 7, 14, 96**
See also CA 13-16R; CAAS 7; CANR 22, 53, 76; DLB 14; INT CANR-22; MTCW 2

West, Rebecca 1892-1983 **CLC 7, 9, 31, 50**
See also CA 5-8R; 109; CANR 19; DLB 36; DLBY 83; MTCW 1, 2

Westall, Robert (Atkinson) 1929-1993 **CLC 17**
See also AAYA 12; CA 69-72; 141; CANR 18, 68; CLR 13; JRDA; MAICYA; SAAS 2; SATA 23, 69; SATA-Obit 75

Westermarck, Edward 1862-1939 **TCLC 87**

Westlake, Donald E(dwin) 1933- **CLC 7, 33; DAM POP**
See also CA 17-20R; CAAS 13; CANR 16, 44, 65; INT CANR-16; MTCW 2

Westmacott, Mary
See Christie, Agatha (Mary Clarissa)

Weston, Allen
See Norton, Andre

Wetcheek, J. L.
See Feuchtwanger, Lion

Wetering, Janwillem van de
See van de Wetering, Janwillem

Wetherald, Agnes Ethelwyn 1857-1940 **T C L C 81**
See also DLB 99

Wetherell, Elizabeth
See Warner, Susan (Bogert)

Whale, James 1889-1957 **TCLC 63**

Whalen, Philip 1923- **CLC 6, 29**
See also CA 9-12R; CANR 5, 39; DLB 16

Wharton, Edith (Newbold Jones) 1862-1937 **TCLC 3, 9, 27, 53; DA; DAB; DAC; DAM MST, NOV; SSC 6; WLC**
See also AAYA 25; CA 104; 132; CDALB 1865-1917; DLB 4, 9, 12, 78, 189; DLBD 13; MTCW 1, 2

Wharton, James
See Mencken, H(enry) L(ouis)

Wharton, William (a pseudonym) **CLC 18, 37**
See also CA 93-96; DLBY 80; INT 93-96

Wheatley (Peters), Phillis 1754(?)-1784 **LC 3, 50; BLC 3; DA; DAC; DAM MST, MULT, POET; PC 3; WLC**
See also CDALB 1640-1865; DLB 31, 50

Wheelock, John Hall 1886-1978 **CLC 14**
See also CA 13-16R; 77-80; CANR 14; DLB 45

White, E(lwyn) B(rooks) 1899-1985 **CLC 10, 34, 39; DAM POP**
See also AITN 2; CA 13-16R; 116; CANR 16, 37; CDALBS; CLR 1, 21; DLB 11, 22; MAICYA; MTCW 1, 2; SATA 2, 29, 100; SATA-Obit 44

White, Edmund (Valentine III) 1940- **CLC 27, 110; DAM POP**
See also AAYA 7; CA 45-48; CANR 3, 19, 36, 62; MTCW 1, 2

White, Patrick (Victor Martindale) 1912-1990 **CLC 3, 4, 5, 7, 9, 18, 65, 69**
See also CA 81-84; 132; CANR 43; MTCW 1

White, Phyllis Dorothy James 1920-
See James, P. D.
See also CA 21-24R; CANR 17, 43, 65; DAM POP; MTCW 1, 2

White, T(erence) H(anbury) 1906-1964 **C L C 30**
See also AAYA 22; CA 73-76; CANR 37; DLB 160; JRDA; MAICYA; SATA 12

White, Terence de Vere 1912-1994 **CLC 49**
See also CA 49-52; 145; CANR 3

White, Walter
See White, Walter F(rancis)
See also BLC; DAM MULT

White, Walter F(rancis) 1893-1955 **TCLC 15**
See also White, Walter
See also BW 1; CA 115; 124; DLB 51

White, William Hale 1831-1913
See Rutherford, Mark
See also CA 121

Whitehead, E(dward) A(nthony) 1933- **CLC 5**
See also CA 65-68; CANR 58

Whitemore, Hugh (John) 1936- **CLC 37**
See also CA 132; CANR 77; INT 132

Whitman, Sarah Helen (Power) 1803-1878 **NCLC 19**
See also DLB 1

Whitman, Walt(er) 1819-1892 **NCLC 4, 31; DA; DAB; DAC; DAM MST, POET; PC 3; WLC**
See also CDALB 1640-1865; DLB 3, 64; SATA 20

Whitney, Phyllis A(yame) 1903- **CLC 42; DAM POP**
See also AITN 2; BEST 90:3; CA 1-4R; CANR 3, 25, 38, 60; CLR 58; JRDA; MAICYA; MTCW 2; SATA 1, 30

Whittemore, (Edward) Reed (Jr.) 1919- **CLC 4**
See also CA 9-12R; CAAS 8; CANR 4; DLB 5

Whittier, John Greenleaf 1807-1892 **NCLC 8, 59**
See also DLB 1

Whittlebot, Hernia
See Coward, Noel (Peirce)

Wicker, Thomas Grey 1926-
See Wicker, Tom
See also CA 65-68; CANR 21, 46

Wicker, Tom **CLC 7**
See also Wicker, Thomas Grey

Wideman, John Edgar 1941- **CLC 5, 34, 36, 67; BLC 3; DAM MULT**
See also BW 2, 3; CA 85-88; CANR 14, 42,

67; DLB 33, 143; MTCW 2

Wiebe, Rudy (Henry) 1934- **CLC 6, 11, 14; DAC; DAM MST**
See also CA 37-40R; CANR 42, 67; DLB 60

Wieland, Christoph Martin 1733-1813 **N C L C 17**
See also DLB 97

Wiene, Robert 1881-1938 **TCLC 56**

Wieners, John 1934- **CLC 7**
See also CA 13-16R; DLB 16

Wiesel, Elie(zer) 1928- **CLC 3, 5, 11, 37; DA; DAB; DAC; DAM MST, NOV; WLCS**
See also AAYA 7; AITN 1; CA 5-8R; CAAS 4; CANR 8, 40, 65; CDALBS; DLB 83; DLBY 87; INT CANR-8; MTCW 1, 2; SATA 56

Wiggins, Marianne 1947- **CLC 57**
See also BEST 89:3; CA 130; CANR 60

Wight, James Alfred 1916-1995
See Herriot, James
See also CA 77-80; SATA 55; SATA-Brief 44

Wilbur, Richard (Purdy) 1921- **CLC 3, 6, 9, 14, 53, 110; DA; DAB; DAC; DAM MST, POET**
See also CA 1-4R; CABS 2; CANR 2, 29, 76; CDALBS; DLB 5, 169; INT CANR-29; MTCW 1, 2; SATA 9

Wild, Peter 1940- **CLC 14**
See also CA 37-40R; DLB 5

Wilde, Oscar 1854(?)-1900 **TCLC 1, 8, 23, 41; DA; DAB; DAC; DAM DRAM, MST, NOV; SSC 11; WLC**
See also CA 104; 119; CDBLB 1890-1914; DLB 10, 19, 34, 57, 141, 156, 190; SATA 24

Wilder, Billy **CLC 20**
See also Wilder, Samuel
See also DLB 26

Wilder, Samuel 1906-
See Wilder, Billy
See also CA 89-92

Wilder, Thornton (Niven) 1897-1975 **CLC 1, 5, 6, 10, 15, 35, 82; DA; DAB; DAC; DAM DRAM, MST, NOV; DC 1; WLC**
See also AAYA 29; AITN 2; CA 13-16R; 61-64; CANR 40; CDALBS; DLB 4, 7, 9; DLBY 97; MTCW 1, 2

Wilding, Michael 1942- **CLC 73**
See also CA 104; CANR 24, 49

Wiley, Richard 1944- **CLC 44**
See also CA 121; 129; CANR 71

Wilhelm, Kate **CLC 7**
See also Wilhelm, Katie Gertrude
See also AAYA 20; CAAS 5; DLB 8; INT CANR-17

Wilhelm, Katie Gertrude 1928-
See Wilhelm, Kate
See also CA 37-40R; CANR 17, 36, 60; MTCW 1

Wilkins, Mary
See Freeman, Mary Eleanor Wilkins

Willard, Nancy 1936- **CLC 7, 37**
See also CA 89-92; CANR 10, 39, 68; CLR 5; DLB 5, 52; MAICYA; MTCW 1; SATA 37, 71; SATA-Brief 30

William of Ockham 1285-1347 **CMLC 32**

Williams, Ben Ames 1889-1953 **TCLC 89**
See also DLB 102

Williams, C(harles) K(enneth) 1936- **CLC 33, 56; DAM POET**
See also CA 37-40R; CAAS 26; CANR 57; DLB 5

Williams, Charles
See Collier, James L(incoln)

Williams, Charles (Walter Stansby) 1886-1945

TCLC 1, 11
See also CA 104; 163; DLB 100, 153
Williams, (George) Emlyn 1905-1987 CLC 15;
DAM DRAM
See also CA 104; 123; CANR 36; DLB 10, 77;
MTCW 1
Williams, Hank 1923-1953 TCLC 81
Williams, Hugo 1942- CLC 42
See also CA 17-20R; CANR 45; DLB 40
Williams, J. Walker
See Wodehouse, P(elham) G(renville)
Williams, John A(lfred) 1925-CLC 5, 13; BLC
3; DAM MULT
See also BW 2, 3; CA 53-56; CAAS 3; CANR
6, 26, 51; DLB 2, 33; INT CANR-6
Williams, Jonathan (Chamberlain) 1929-
CLC 13
See also CA 9-12R; CAAS 12; CANR 8; DLB
5
Williams, Joy 1944- CLC 31
See also CA 41-44R; CANR 22, 48
Williams, Norman 1952- CLC 39
See also CA 118
Williams, Sherley Anne 1944-CLC 89; BLC 3;
DAM MULT, POET
See also BW 2, 3; CA 73-76; CANR 25; DLB
41; INT CANR-25; SATA 78
Williams, Shirley
See Williams, Sherley Anne
Williams, Tennessee 1911-1983CLC 1, 2, 5, 7,
8, 11, 15, 19, 30, 39, 45, 71, 111; DA; DAB;
DAC; DAM DRAM, MST; DC 4; WLC
See also AITN 1, 2; CA 5-8R; 108; CABS 3;
CANR 31; CDALB 1941-1968; DLB 7;
DLBD 4; DLBY 83; MTCW 1, 2
Williams, Thomas (Alonzo) 1926-1990CLC 14
See also CA 1-4R; 132; CANR 2
Williams, William C.
See Williams, William Carlos
Williams, William Carlos 1883-1963CLC 1, 2,
5, 9, 13, 22, 42, 67; DA; DAB; DAC; DAM
MST, POET; PC 7; SSC 31
See also CA 89-92; CANR 34; CDALB 1917-
1929; DLB 4, 16, 54, 86; MTCW 1, 2
Williamson, David (Keith) 1942- CLC 56
See also CA 103; CANR 41
Williamson, Ellen Douglas 1905-1984
See Douglas, Ellen
See also CA 17-20R; 114; CANR 39
Williamson, Jack CLC 29
See also Williamson, John Stewart
See also CAAS 8; DLB 8
Williamson, John Stewart 1908-
See Williamson, Jack
See also CA 17-20R; CANR 23, 70
Willie, Frederick
See Lovecraft, H(oward) P(hillips)
Willingham, Calder (Baynard, Jr.) 1922-1995
CLC 5, 51
See also CA 5-8R; 147; CANR 3; DLB 2, 44;
MTCW 1
Willis, Charles
See Clarke, Arthur C(harles)
Willis, Fingal O'Flahertie
See Wilde, Oscar
Willy
See Colette, (Sidonie-Gabrielle)
Willy, Colette
See Colette, (Sidonie-Gabrielle)
Wilson, A(ndrew) N(orman) 1950- CLC 33
See also CA 112; 122; DLB 14, 155, 194;
MTCW 2
Wilson, Angus (Frank Johnstone) 1913-1991

CLC 2, 3, 5, 25, 34; SSC 21
See also CA 5-8R; 134; CANR 21; DLB 15,
139, 155; MTCW 1, 2
Wilson, August 1945- CLC 39, 50, 63, 118;
BLC 3; DA; DAB; DAC; DAM DRAM,
MST, MULT; DC 2; WLCS
See also AAYA 16; BW 2, 3; CA 115; 122;
CANR 42, 54, 76; MTCW 1, 2
Wilson, Brian 1942- CLC 12
Wilson, Colin 1931- CLC 3, 14
See also CA 1-4R; CAAS 5; CANR 1, 22, 33,
77; DLB 14, 194; MTCW 1
Wilson, Dirk
See Pohl, Frederik
Wilson, Edmund 1895-1972CLC 1, 2, 3, 8, 24
See also CA 1-4R; 37-40R; CANR 1, 46; DLB
63; MTCW 1, 2
Wilson, Ethel Davis (Bryant) 1888(?)-1980
CLC 13; DAC; DAM POET
See also CA 102; DLB 68; MTCW 1
Wilson, John 1785-1854 NCLC 5
Wilson, John (Anthony) Burgess 1917-1993
See Burgess, Anthony
See also CA 1-4R; 143; CANR 2, 46; DAC;
DAM NOV; MTCW 1, 2
Wilson, Lanford 1937- CLC 7, 14, 36; DAM
DRAM
See also CA 17-20R; CABS 3; CANR 45; DLB
7
Wilson, Robert M. 1944- CLC 7, 9
See also CA 49-52; CANR 2, 41; MTCW 1
Wilson, Robert McLiam 1964- CLC 59
See also CA 132
Wilson, Sloan 1920- CLC 32
See also CA 1-4R; CANR 1, 44
Wilson, Snoo 1948- CLC 33
See also CA 69-72
Wilson, William S(mith) 1932- CLC 49
See also CA 81-84
Wilson, (Thomas) Woodrow 1856-1924TCLC
79
See also CA 166; DLB 47
Winchilsea, Anne (Kingsmill) Finch Counte
1661-1720
See Finch, Anne
Windham, Basil
See Wodehouse, P(elham) G(renville)
Wingrove, David (John) 1954- CLC 68
See also CA 133
Wintergreen, Jane
See Duncan, Sara Jeannette
Winters, Janet Lewis CLC 41
See also Lewis, Janet
See also DLBY 87
Winters, (Arthur) Yvor 1900-1968 CLC 4, 8,
32
See also CA 11-12; 25-28R; CAP 1; DLB 48;
MTCW 1
Winterson, Jeanette 1959-CLC 64; DAM POP
See also CA 136; CANR 58; DLB 207; MTCW
2
Winthrop, John 1588-1649 LC 31
See also DLB 24, 30
Wirth, Louis 1897-1952 TCLC 92
Wiseman, Frederick 1930- CLC 20
See also CA 159
Wister, Owen 1860-1938 TCLC 21
See also CA 108; 162; DLB 9, 78, 186; SATA
62
Witkacy
See Witkiewicz, Stanislaw Ignacy
Witkiewicz, Stanislaw Ignacy 1885-1939
TCLC 8

See also CA 105; 162
Wittgenstein, Ludwig (Josef Johann) 1889-1951
TCLC 59
See also CA 113; 164; MTCW 2
Wittig, Monique 1935(?)- CLC 22
See also CA 116; 135; DLB 83
Wittlin, Jozef 1896-1976 CLC 25
See also CA 49-52; 65-68; CANR 3
Wodehouse, P(elham) G(renville) 1881-1975
CLC 1, 2, 5, 10, 22; DAB; DAC; DAM
NOV; SSC 2
See also AITN 2; CA 45-48; 57-60; CANR 3,
33; CDBLB 1914-1945; DLB 34, 162;
MTCW 1, 2; SATA 22
Woiwode, L.
See Woiwode, Larry (Alfred)
Woiwode, Larry (Alfred) 1941- CLC 6, 10
See also CA 73-76; CANR 16; DLB 6; INT
CANR-16
Wojciechowska, Maia (Teresa) 1927-CLC 26
See also AAYA 8; CA 9-12R; CANR 4, 41; CLR
1; JRDA; MAICYA; SAAS 1; SATA 1, 28,
83; SATA-Essay 104
Wolf, Christa 1929- CLC 14, 29, 58
See also CA 85-88; CANR 45; DLB 75; MTCW
1
Wolfe, Gene (Rodman) 1931- CLC 25; DAM
POP
See also CA 57-60; CAAS 9; CANR 6, 32, 60;
DLB 8; MTCW 2
Wolfe, George C. 1954- CLC 49; BLCS
See also CA 149
Wolfe, Thomas (Clayton) 1900-1938TCLC 4,
13, 29, 61; DA; DAB; DAC; DAM MST,
NOV; SSC 33; WLC
See also CA 104; 132; CDALB 1929-1941;
DLB 9, 102; DLBD 2, 16; DLBY 85, 97;
MTCW 1, 2
Wolfe, Thomas Kennerly, Jr. 1930-
See Wolfe, Tom
See also CA 13-16R; CANR 9, 33, 70; DAM
POP; DLB 185; INT CANR-9; MTCW 1, 2
Wolfe, Tom CLC 1, 2, 9, 15, 35, 51
See also Wolfe, Thomas Kennerly, Jr.
See also AAYA 8; AITN 2; BEST 89:1; DLB
152
Wolff, Geoffrey (Ansell) 1937- CLC 41
See also CA 29-32R; CANR 29, 43, 78
Wolff, Sonia
See Levitin, Sonia (Wolff)
Wolff, Tobias (Jonathan Ansell) 1945- C L C
39, 64
See also AAYA 16; BEST 90:2; CA 114; 117;
CAAS 22; CANR 54, 76; DLB 130; INT 117;
MTCW 2
Wolfram von Eschenbach c. 1170-c. 1220
CMLC 5
See also DLB 138
Wolitzer, Hilma 1930- CLC 17
See also CA 65-68; CANR 18, 40; INT CANR-
18; SATA 31
Wollstonecraft, Mary 1759-1797 LC 5, 50
See also CDBLB 1789-1832; DLB 39, 104, 158
Wonder, Stevie CLC 12
See also Morris, Steveland Judkins
Wong, Jade Snow 1922- CLC 17
See also CA 109
Woodberry, George Edward 1855-1930
TCLC 73
See also CA 165; DLB 71, 103
Woodcott, Keith
See Brunner, John (Kilian Houston)
Woodruff, Robert W.

See Mencken, H(enry) L(ouis)

Woolf, (Adeline) Virginia 1882-1941TCLC 1, 5, 20, 43, 56; DA; DAB; DAC; DAM MST, NOV; SSC 7; WLC
See also Woolf, Virginia Adeline
See also CA 104; 130; CANR 64; CDBLB 1914-1945; DLB 36, 100, 162; DLBD 10; MTCW 1

Woolf, Virginia Adeline
See Woolf, (Adeline) Virginia
See also MTCW 2

Woollcott, Alexander (Humphreys) 1887-1943 **TCLC 5**
See also CA 105; 161; DLB 29

Woolrich, Cornell 1903-1968　　　**CLC 77**
See also Hopley-Woolrich, Cornell George

Wordsworth, Dorothy 1771-1855　**NCLC 25**
See also DLB 107

Wordsworth, William 1770-1850　**NCLC 12, 38; DA; DAB; DAC; DAM MST, POET; PC 4; WLC**
See also CDBLB 1789-1832; DLB 93, 107

Wouk, Herman 1915-CLC 1, 9, 38; DAM NOV, POP
See also CA 5-8R; CANR 6, 33, 67; CDALBS; DLBY 82; INT CANR-6; MTCW 1, 2

Wright, Charles (Penzel, Jr.) 1935-CLC 6, 13, 28, 119
See also CA 29-32R; CAAS 7; CANR 23, 36, 62; DLB 165; DLBY 82; MTCW 1, 2

Wright, Charles Stevenson 1932-　**CLC 49; BLC 3; DAM MULT, POET**
See also BW 1; CA 9-12R; CANR 26; DLB 33

Wright, Frances 1795-1852　　　**NCLC 74**
See also DLB 73

Wright, Jack R.
See Harris, Mark

Wright, James (Arlington) 1927-1980CLC 3, 5, 10, 28; DAM POET
See also AITN 2; CA 49-52; 97-100; CANR 4, 34, 64; CDALBS; DLB 5, 169; MTCW 1, 2

Wright, Judith (Arandell) 1915- CLC 11, 53; PC 14
See also CA 13-16R; CANR 31, 76; MTCW 1, 2; SATA 14

Wright, L(aurali) R. 1939-　　　**CLC 44**
See also CA 138

Wright, Richard (Nathaniel) 1908-1960 C L C 1, 3, 4, 9, 14, 21, 48, 74; BLC 3; DA; DAB; DAC; DAM MST, MULT, NOV; SSC 2; WLC
See also AAYA 5; BW 1; CA 108; CANR 64; CDALB 1929-1941; DLB 76, 102; DLBD 2; MTCW 1, 2

Wright, Richard B(ruce) 1937-　　　**CLC 6**
See also CA 85-88; DLB 53

Wright, Rick 1945-　　　　　　**CLC 35**

Wright, Rowland
See Wells, Carolyn

Wright, Stephen 1946-　　　　　**CLC 33**

Wright, Willard Huntington 1888-1939
See Van Dine, S. S.
See also CA 115; DLBD 16

Wright, William 1930-　　　　　**CLC 44**
See also CA 53-56; CANR 7, 23

Wroth, LadyMary 1587-1653(?)　　**LC 30**
See also DLB 121

Wu Ch'eng-en 1500(?)-1582(?)　　**LC 7**

Wu Ching-tzu 1701-1754　　　　**LC 2**

Wurlitzer, Rudolph 1938(?)-　**CLC 2, 4, 15**
See also CA 85-88; DLB 173

Wycherley, William 1641-1715LC 8, 21; DAM DRAM

See also CDBLB 1660-1789; DLB 80

Wylie, Elinor (Morton Hoyt) 1885-1928 **TCLC 8; PC 23**
See also CA 105; 162; DLB 9, 45

Wylie, Philip (Gordon) 1902-1971　　**CLC 43**
See also CA 21-22; 33-36R; CAP 2; DLB 9

Wyndham, John　　　　　　　　**CLC 19**
See also Harris, John (Wyndham Parkes Lucas) Beynon

Wyss, Johann David Von 1743-1818NCLC 10
See also JRDA; MAICYA; SATA 29; SATA-Brief 27

Xenophon c. 430B.C.-c. 354B.C.　　**CMLC 17**
See also DLB 176

Yakumo Koizumi
See Hearn, (Patricio) Lafcadio (Tessima Carlos)

Yamamoto, Hisaye 1921-SSC 34; DAM MULT

Yanez, Jose Donoso
See Donoso (Yanez), Jose

Yanovsky, Basile S.
See Yanovsky, V(assily) S(emenovich)

Yanovsky, V(assily) S(emenovich) 1906-1989 **CLC 2, 18**
See also CA 97-100; 129

Yates, Richard 1926-1992　　　**CLC 7, 8, 23**
See also CA 5-8R; 139; CANR 10, 43; DLB 2; DLBY 81, 92; INT CANR-10

Yeats, W. B.
See Yeats, William Butler

Yeats, William Butler 1865-1939TCLC 1, 11, 18, 31, 93; DA; DAB; DAC; DAM DRAM, MST, POET; PC 20; WLC
See also CA 104; 127; CANR 45; CDBLB 1890-1914; DLB 10, 19, 98, 156; MTCW 1, 2

Yehoshua, A(braham) B. 1936-　**CLC 13, 31**
See also CA 33-36R; CANR 43

Yep, Laurence Michael 1948-　　**CLC 35**
See also AAYA 5; CA 49-52; CANR 1, 46; CLR 3, 17, 54; DLB 52; JRDA; MAICYA; SATA 7, 69

Yerby, Frank G(arvin) 1916-1991　**CLC 1, 7, 22; BLC 3; DAM MULT**
See also BW 1, 3; CA 9-12R; 136; CANR 16, 52; DLB 76; INT CANR-16; MTCW 1

Yesenin, Sergei Alexandrovich
See Esenin, Sergei (Alexandrovich)

Yevtushenko, Yevgeny (Alexandrovich) 1933- CLC 1, 3, 13, 26, 51; DAM POET
See also CA 81-84; CANR 33, 54; MTCW 1

Yezierska, Anzia 1885(?)-1970　　**CLC 46**
See also CA 126; 89-92; DLB 28; MTCW 1

Yglesias, Helen 1915-　　　　**CLC 7, 22**
See also CA 37-40R; CAAS 20; CANR 15, 65; INT CANR-15; MTCW 1

Yokomitsu Riichi 1898-1947　　**TCLC 47**
See also CA 170

Yonge, Charlotte (Mary) 1823-1901TCLC 48
See also CA 109; 163; DLB 18, 163; SATA 17

York, Jeremy
See Creasey, John

York, Simon
See Heinlein, Robert A(nson)

Yorke, Henry Vincent 1905-1974　　**CLC 13**
See also Green, Henry
See also CA 85-88; 49-52

Yosano Akiko 1878-1942　　**TCLC 59; PC 11**
See also CA 161

Yoshimoto, Banana　　　　　　**CLC 84**
See also Yoshimoto, Mahoko

Yoshimoto, Mahoko 1964-
See Yoshimoto, Banana
See also CA 144

Young, Al(bert James) 1939-CLC 19; BLC 3; DAM MULT
See also BW 2, 3; CA 29-32R; CANR 26, 65; DLB 33

Young, Andrew (John) 1885-1971　　**CLC 5**
See also CA 5-8R; CANR 7, 29

Young, Collier
See Bloch, Robert (Albert)

Young, Edward 1683-1765　　　**LC 3, 40**
See also DLB 95

Young, Marguerite (Vivian) 1909-1995 C L C 82
See also CA 13-16; 150; CAP 1

Young, Neil 1945-　　　　　　**CLC 17**
See also CA 110

Young Bear, Ray A. 1950-　**CLC 94; DAM MULT**
See also CA 146; DLB 175; NNAL

Yourcenar, Marguerite 1903-1987CLC 19, 38, 50, 87; DAM NOV
See also CA 69-72; CANR 23, 60; DLB 72; DLBY 88; MTCW 1, 2

Yurick, Sol 1925-　　　　　　**CLC 6**
See also CA 13-16R; CANR 25

Zabolotsky, Nikolai Alekseevich 1903-1958 **TCLC 52**
See also CA 116; 164

Zamiatin, Yevgenii
See Zamyatin, Evgeny Ivanovich

Zamora, Bernice (B. Ortiz) 1938-　**CLC 89; DAM MULT; HLC**
See also CA 151; CANR 80; DLB 82; HW 1, 2

Zamyatin, Evgeny Ivanovich 1884-1937 **TCLC 8, 37**
See also CA 105; 166

Zangwill, Israel 1864-1926　　　**TCLC 16**
See also CA 109; 167; DLB 10, 135, 197

Zappa, Francis Vincent, Jr. 1940-1993
See Zappa, Frank
See also CA 108; 143; CANR 57

Zappa, Frank　　　　　　　　**CLC 17**
See also Zappa, Francis Vincent, Jr.

Zaturenska, Marya 1902-1982　　**CLC 6, 11**
See also CA 13-16R; 105; CANR 22

Zeami 1363-1443　　　　　　　　**DC 7**

Zelazny, Roger (Joseph) 1937-1995 CLC 21
See also AAYA 7; CA 21-24R; 148; CANR 26, 60; DLB 8; MTCW 1, 2; SATA 57; SATA-Brief 39

Zhdanov, Andrei Alexandrovich 1896-1948 **TCLC 18**
See also CA 117; 167

Zhukovsky, Vasily (Andreevich) 1783-1852 **NCLC 35**
See also DLB 205

Ziegenhagen, Eric　　　　　　　**CLC 55**

Zimmer, Jill Schary
See Robinson, Jill

Zimmerman, Robert
See Dylan, Bob

Zindel, Paul 1936-CLC 6, 26; DA; DAB; DAC; DAM DRAM, MST, NOV; DC 5
See also AAYA 2; CA 73-76; CANR 31, 65; CDALBS; CLR 3, 45; DLB 7, 52; JRDA; MAICYA; MTCW 1, 2; SATA 16, 58, 102

Zinov'Ev, A. A.
See Zinoviev, Alexander (Aleksandrovich)

Zinoviev, Alexander (Aleksandrovich) 1922- **CLC 19**
See also CA 116; 133; CAAS 10

Zoilus
See Lovecraft, H(oward) P(hillips)

Zola, Emile (Edouard Charles Antoine) 1840-

1902TCLC 1, 6, 21, 41; DA; DAB; DAC;
     DAM MST, NOV; WLC
   See also CA 104; 138; DLB 123
Zoline, Pamela 1941-   **CLC 62**
   See also CA 161
Zorrilla y Moral, Jose 1817-1893   **NCLC 6**
Zoshchenko, Mikhail (Mikhailovich) 1895-1958
     TCLC 15; SSC 15
   See also CA 115; 160
Zuckmayer, Carl 1896-1977   **CLC 18**
   See also CA 69-72; DLB 56, 124
Zuk, Georges
   See Skelton, Robin
Zukofsky, Louis 1904-1978CLC 1, 2, 4, 7, 11,
     18; DAM POET; PC 11
   See also CA 9-12R; 77-80; CANR 39; DLB 5,
     165; MTCW 1
Zweig, Paul 1935-1984   **CLC 34, 42**
   See also CA 85-88; 113
Zweig, Stefan 1881-1942   **TCLC 17**
   See also CA 112; 170; DLB 81, 118
Zwingli, Huldreich 1484-1531   **LC 37**
   See also DLB 179

Literary Criticism Series
Cumulative Topic Index

This index lists all topic entries in Gale's *Classical and Medieval Literature Criticism, Contemporary Literary Criticism, Literature Criticism from 1400 to 1800, Nineteenth-Century Literature Criticism,* and *Twentieth-Century Literary Criticism.*

Aesopic Fable, the LC 51: 1-100
the British Aesopic fable, 1-55
the Aesopic tradition in non-English-speaking countries, 55-89
political uses of the Aesopic fable, 89-100

Age of Johnson LC 15: 1-87
Johnson's London, 3-15
aesthetics of neoclassicism, 15-36
"age of prose and reason," 36-45
clubmen and bluestockings, 45-56
printing technology, 56-62
periodicals: "a map of busy life," 62-74
transition, 74-86

AIDS in Literature CLC 81: 365-416

American Abolitionism NCLC 44: 1-73
overviews, 2-26
abolitionist ideals, 26-46
the literature of abolitionism, 46-72

American Black Humor Fiction TCLC 54: 1-85
characteristics of black humor, 2-13
origins and development, 13-38
black humor distinguished from related literary trends, 38-60
black humor and society, 60-75
black humor reconsidered, 75-83

American Civil War in Literature NCLC 32: 1-109
overviews, 2-20
regional perspectives, 20-54
fiction popular during the war, 54-79
the historical novel, 79-108

American Frontier in Literature NCLC 28: 1-103
definitions, 2-12
development, 12-17
nonfiction writing about the frontier, 17-30
frontier fiction, 30-45
frontier protagonists, 45-66
portrayals of Native Americans, 66-86
feminist readings, 86-98
twentieth-century reaction against frontier literature, 98-100

American Humor Writing NCLC 52: 1-59
overviews, 2-12
the Old Southwest, 12-42
broader impacts, 42-45
women humorists, 45-58

American Popular Song, Golden Age of TCLC 42: 1-49
background and major figures, 2-34
the lyrics of popular songs, 34-47

American Proletarian Literature TCLC 54: 86-175
overviews, 87-95
American proletarian literature and the American Communist Party, 95-111
ideology and literary merit, 111-17
novels, 117-36
Gastonia, 136-48
drama, 148-54
journalism, 154-59
proletarian literature in the United States, 159-74

American Romanticism NCLC 44: 74-138
overviews, 74-84
sociopolitical influences, 84-104
Romanticism and the American frontier, 104-15
thematic concerns, 115-37

American Western Literature TCLC 46: 1-100
definition and development of American Western literature, 2-7
characteristics of the Western novel, 8-23
Westerns as history and fiction, 23-34
critical reception of American Western literature, 34-41
the Western hero, 41-73
women in Western fiction, 73-91
later Western fiction, 91-99

Art and Literature TCLC 54: 176-248
overviews, 176-93
definitions, 193-219
influence of visual arts on literature, 219-31
spatial form in literature, 231-47

Arthurian Literature CMLC 10: 1-127
historical context and literary beginnings, 2-27
development of the legend through Malory, 27-64
development of the legend from Malory to the Victorian Age, 65-81
themes and motifs, 81-95
principal characters, 95-125

Arthurian Revival NCLC 36: 1-77
overviews, 2-12
Tennyson and his influence, 12-43
other leading figures, 43-73
the Arthurian legend in the visual arts, 73-76

Australian Literature TCLC 50: 1-94
origins and development, 2-21
characteristics of Australian literature, 21-33
historical and critical perspectives, 33-41
poctry, 41-58
fiction, 58-76

drama, 76-82
Aboriginal literature, 82-91

Beat Generation, Literature of the TCLC
42: 50-102
overviews, 51-59
the Beat generation as a social phenomenon, 59-62
development, 62-65
Beat literature, 66-96
influence, 97-100

Bildungsroman **in Nineteenth-Century
Literature** NCLC 20: 92-168
surveys, 93-113
in Germany, 113-40
in England, 140-56
female *Bildungsroman,* 156-67

Bloomsbury Group TCLC 34: 1-73
history and major figures, 2-13
definitions, 13-17
influences, 17-27
thought, 27-40
prose, 40-52
and literary criticism, 52-54
political ideals, 54-61
response to, 61-71

Bly, Robert, *Iron John: A Book about Men
and Men's Work* CLC 70: 414-62

The Book of J CLC 65: 289-311

Businessman in American Literature
TCLC 26: 1-48
portrayal of the businessman, 1-32
themes and techniques in business
fiction, 32-47

Celtic Twilight
See **Irish Literary Renaissance**

Children's Literature, Nineteenth-Century
NCLC 52: 60-135
overviews, 61-72
moral tales, 72-89
fairy tales and fantasy, 90-119
making men/making women, 119-34

Civic Critics, Russian NCLC 20: 402-46

principal figures and background, 402-09
and Russian Nihilism, 410-16
aesthetic and critical views, 416-45

**Colonial America: The Intellectual
Background** LC 25: 1-98
overviews, 2-17
philosophy and politics, 17-31
early religious influences in Colonial
America, 31-60
consequences of the Revolution, 60-78
religious influences in post-revolutionary America, 78-87
colonial literary genres, 87-97

**Columbus, Christopher, Books on the
Quincentennial of His Arrival in the New
World** CLC 70: 329-60

Connecticut Wits NCLC 48: 1-95
general overviews, 2-40
major works, 40-76
intellectual context, 76-95

Crime in Literature TCLC 54: 249-307
evolution of the criminal figure in
literature, 250-61
crime and society, 261-77
literary perspectives on crime and
punishment, 277-88
writings by criminals, 288-306

**Czechoslovakian Literature of the
Twentieth Century** TCLC 42: 103-96
through World War II, 104-35
de-Stalinization, the Prague Spring,
and contemporary literature, 13572
Slovak literature, 172-85
Czech science fiction, 185-93

Dadaism TCLC 46: 101-71
background and major figures, 102-16
definitions, 116-26
manifestos and commentary by
Dadaists, 126-40
theater and film, 140-58
nature and characteristics of Dadaist
writing, 158-70

Darwinism and Literature NCLC 32: 110-
206
background, 110-31
direct responses to Darwin, 131-71

collateral effects of Darwinism, 171-205

de Man, Paul, Wartime Journalism of
CLC 55: 382-424

Detective Fiction, Nineteenth-Century
NCLC 36: 78-148
origins of the genre, 79-100
history of nineteenth-century detective
fiction, 101-33
significance of nineteenth-century
detective fiction, 133-46

Detective Fiction, Twentieth-Century
TCLC 38: 1-96
genesis and history of the detective
story, 3-22
defining detective fiction, 22-32
evolution and varieties, 32-77
the appeal of detective fiction, 77-90

**The Double in Nineteenth-Century
Literature** NCLC 40: 1-95
genesis and development of the theme,
2-15
the double and Romanticism, 16-27
sociological views, 27-52
psychological interpretations, 52-87
philosophical considerations, 87-95

Dramatic Realism NCLC 44: 139-202
overviews, 140-50
origins and definitions, 150-66
impact and influence, 166-93
realist drama and tragedy, 193-201

**Electronic "Books": Hypertext and
Hyperfiction** CLC 86: 367-404
books vs. CD-ROMS, 367-76
hypertext and hyperfiction, 376-95
implications for publishing, libraries,
and the public, 395-403

Eliot, T. S., Centenary of Birth CLC 55:
345-75

Elizabethan Drama LC 22: 140-240
origins and influences, 142-67
characteristics and conventions, 167-83
theatrical production, 184-200
history, 200-12
comedy, 213-20
tragedy, 220-30

The Encyclopedists LC 26: 172-253
  overviews, 173-210
  intellectual background, 210-32
  views on esthetics, 232-41
  views on women, 241-52

English Caroline Literature LC 13: 221-307
  background, 222-41
  evolution and varieties, 241-62
  the Cavalier mode, 262-75
  court and society, 275-91
  politics and religion, 291-306

English Decadent Literature of the 1890s NCLC 28: 104-200
  fin de siècle: the Decadent period, 105-19
  definitions, 120-37
  major figures: "the tragic generation," 137-50
  French literature and English literary Decadence, 150-57
  themes, 157-61
  poetry, 161-82
  periodicals, 182-96

English Essay, Rise of the LC 18: 238-308
  definitions and origins, 236-54
  influence on the essay, 254-69
  historical background, 269-78
  the essay in the seventeenth century, 279-93
  the essay in the eighteenth century, 293-307

English Realist Novel, 1740-1771 LC 51: 102-198
  overviews, 103-23
  from romanticism to realism, 123-59
  women and the novel, 159-76
  the novel and other literary forms, 176-198

English Romantic Poetry NCLC 28: 201-327
  overviews and reputation, 202-37
  major subjects and themes, 237-67
  forms of Romantic poetry, 267-78
  politics, society, and Romantic poetry, 278-99
  philosophy, religion, and Romantic poetry, 299-324

Espionage Literature TCLC 50: 95-159
  overviews, 96-113
  espionage fiction/formula fiction, 113-26
  spies in fact and fiction, 126-38
  the female spy, 138-44
  social and psychological perspectives, 144-58

European Romanticism NCLC 36: 149-284
  definitions, 149-77
  origins of the movement, 177-82
  Romantic theory, 182-200
  themes and techniques, 200-23
  Romanticism in Germany, 223-39
  Romanticism in France, 240-61
  Romanticism in Italy, 261-64
  Romanticism in Spain, 264-68
  impact and legacy, 268-82

Existentialism and Literature TCLC 42: 197-268
  overviews and definitions, 198-209
  history and influences, 209-19
  Existentialism critiqued and defended, 220-35
  philosophical and religious perspectives, 235-41
  Existentialist fiction and drama, 241-67

Familiar Essay NCLC 48: 96-211
  definitions and origins, 97-130
  overview of the genre, 130-43
  elements of form and style, 143-59
  elements of content, 159-73
  the Cockneys: Hazlitt, Lamb, and Hunt, 173-91
  status of the genre, 191-210

Feminism in the 1990s: Commentary on Works by Naomi Wolf, Susan Faludi, and Camille Paglia CLC 76: 377-415

Feminist Criticism in 1990 CLC 65: 312-60

Fifteenth-Century English Literature LC 17: 248-334
  background, 249-72
  poetry, 272-315
  drama, 315-23
  prose, 323-33

Film and Literature TCLC 38: 97-226
  overviews, 97-119
  film and theater, 119-34
  film and the novel, 134-45
  the art of the screenplay, 145-66
  genre literature/genre film, 167-79
  the writer and the film industry, 179-90
  authors on film adaptations of their works, 190-200
  fiction into film: comparative essays, 200-23

French Drama in the Age of Louis XIV LC 28: 94-185
  overview, 95-127
  tragedy, 127-46
  comedy, 146-66
  tragicomedy, 166-84

French Enlightenment LC 14: 81-145
  the question of definition, 82-89
  Le siècle des lumières, 89-94
  women and the salons, 94-105
  censorship, 105-15
  the philosophy of reason, 115-31
  influence and legacy, 131-44

French Realism NCLC 52: 136-216
  origins and definitions, 137-70
  issues and influence, 170-98
  realism and representation, 198-215

French Revolution and English Literature NCLC 40: 96-195
  history and theory, 96-123
  romantic poetry, 123-50
  the novel, 150-81
  drama, 181-92
  children's literature, 192-95

Futurism, Italian TCLC 42: 269-354
  principles and formative influences, 271-79
  manifestos, 279-88
  literature, 288-303
  theater, 303-19
  art, 320-30
  music, 330-36
  architecture, 336-39
  and politics, 339-46
  reputation and significance, 346-51

Gaelic Revival
See **Irish Literary Renaissance**

Topic Index

Gates, Henry Louis, Jr., and African-American Literary Criticism CLC 65: 361-405

Gay and Lesbian Literature CLC 76: 416-39

German Exile Literature TCLC 30: 1-58
the writer and the Nazi state, 1-10
definition of, 10-14
life in exile, 14-32
surveys, 32-50
Austrian literature in exile, 50-52
German publishing in the United States, 52-57

German Expressionism TCLC 34: 74-160
history and major figures, 76-85
aesthetic theories, 85-109
drama, 109-26
poetry, 126-38
film, 138-42
painting, 142-47
music, 147-53
and politics, 153-58

***Glasnost* and Contemporary Soviet Literature** CLC 59: 355-97

Gothic Novel NCLC 28: 328-402
development and major works, 328-34
definitions, 334-50
themes and techniques, 350-78
in America, 378-85
in Scotland, 385-91
influence and legacy, 391-400

Graphic Narratives CLC 86: 405-32
history and overviews, 406-21
the "Classics Illustrated" series, 421-22
reviews of recent works, 422-32

Greek Historiography CMLC 17: 1-49

Harlem Renaissance TCLC 26: 49-125
principal issues and figures, 50-67
the literature and its audience, 67-74
theme and technique in poetry, fiction, and drama, 74-115
and American society, 115-21
achievement and influence, 121-22

Havel, Václav, Playwright and President CLC 65: 406-63

Historical Fiction, Nineteenth-Century NCLC 48: 212-307
definitions and characteristics, 213-36
Victorian historical fiction, 236-65
American historical fiction, 265-88
realism in historical fiction, 288-306

Holocaust Denial Literature TCLC 58: 1-110
overviews, 1-30
Robert Faurisson and Noam Chomsky, 30-52
Holocaust denial literature in America, 52-71
library access to Holocaust denial literature, 72-75
the authenticity of Anne Frank's diary, 76-90
David Irving and the "normalization" of Hitler, 90-109

Holocaust, Literature of the TCLC 42: 355-450
historical overview, 357-61
critical overview, 361-70
diaries and memoirs, 370-95
novels and short stories, 395-425
poetry, 425-41
drama, 441-48

Hungarian Literature of the Twentieth Century TCLC 26: 126-88
surveys of, 126-47
Nyugat and early twentieth-century literature, 147-56
mid-century literature, 156-68
and politics, 168-78
since the 1956 revolt, 178-87

Indian Literature in English TCLC 54: 308-406
overview, 309-13
origins and major figures, 313-25
the Indo-English novel, 325-55
Indo-English poetry, 355-67
Indo-English drama, 367-72
critical perspectives on Indo-English literature, 372-80
modern Indo-English literature, 380-89
Indo-English authors on their work, 389-404

Irish Literary Renaissance TCLC 46: 172-287
overview, 173-83
development and major figures, 184-202
influence of Irish folklore and mythology, 202-22
Irish poetry, 222-34
Irish drama and the Abbey Theatre, 234-56
Irish fiction, 256-86

Irish Nationalism and Literature NCLC 44: 203-73
the Celtic element in literature, 203-19
anti-Irish sentiment and the Celtic response, 219-34
literary ideals in Ireland, 234-45
literary expressions, 245-73

Italian Futurism
See **Futurism, Italian**

Italian Humanism LC 12: 205-77
origins and early development, 206-18
revival of classical letters, 218-23
humanism and other philosophies, 224-39
humanisms and humanists, 239-46
the plastic arts, 246-57
achievement and significance, 258-76

Lake Poets, The NCLC 52: 217-304
characteristics of the Lake Poets and their works, 218-27
literary influences and collaborations, 227-66
defining and developing Romantic ideals, 266-84
embracing Conservatism, 284-303

Larkin, Philip, Controversy CLC 81: 417-64

Latin American Literature, Twentieth-Century TCLC 58: 111-98
historical and critical perspectives, 112-36
the novel, 136-45
the short story, 145-49
drama, 149-60
poetry, 160-67
the writer and society, 167-86

Native Americans in Latin American literature, 186-97

The Levellers 51:200-312
overviews, 201-30
principal figures, 230-87
religion, political philosophy, and pamphleteering, 287-312

Madness in Twentieth-Century Literature TCLC 50: 160-225
overviews, 161-71
madness and the creative process, 171-86
suicide, 186-91
madness in American literature, 191-207
madness in German literature, 207-13
madness and feminist artists, 213-24

Metaphysical Poets LC 24: 356-439
early definitions, 358-67
surveys and overviews, 367-92
cultural and social influences, 392-406
stylistic and thematic variations, 407-38

Modern Essay, The TCLC 58: 199-273
overview, 200-07
the essay in the early twentieth century, 207-19
characteristics of the modern essay, 219-32
modern essayists, 232-45
the essay as a literary genre, 245-73

Muckraking Movement in American Journalism TCLC 34: 161-242
development, principles, and major figures, 162-70
publications, 170-79
social and political ideas, 179-86
targets, 186-208
fiction, 208-19
decline, 219-29
impact and accomplishments, 229-40

Multiculturalism in Literature and Education CLC 70: 361-413

Native American Literature CLC 76: 440-76

Natural School, Russian NCLC 24: 205-40
history and characteristics, 205-25

contemporary criticism, 225-40

Naturalism NCLC 36: 285-382
definitions and theories, 286-305
critical debates on Naturalism, 305-16
Naturalism in theater, 316-32
European Naturalism, 332-61
American Naturalism, 361-72
the legacy of Naturalism, 372-81

Negritude TCLC 50: 226-361
origins and evolution, 227-56
definitions, 256-91
Negritude in literature, 291-343
Negritude reconsidered, 343-58

New Criticism TCLC 34: 243-318
development and ideas, 244-70
debate and defense, 270-99
influence and legacy, 299-315

The New World in Renaissance Literature LC 31: 1-51
overview, 1-18
utopia vs. terror, 18-31
explorers and Native Americans, 31-51

New York Intellectuals and *Partisan Review* TCLC 30: 117-98
development and major figures, 118-28
influence of Judaism, 128-39
Partisan Review, 139-57
literary philosophy and practice, 157-75
political philosophy, 175-87
achievement and significance, 187-97

The New Yorker TCLC 58: 274-357
overviews, 274-95
major figures, 295-304
New Yorker style, 304-33
fiction, journalism, and humor at *The New Yorker,* 333-48
the new *New Yorker,* 348-56

Newgate Novel NCLC 24: 166-204
development of Newgate literature, 166-73
Newgate Calendar, 173-77
Newgate fiction, 177-95
Newgate drama, 195-204

Nigerian Literature of the Twentieth Century TCLC 30: 199-265

surveys of, 199-227
English language and African life, 227-45
politics and the Nigerian writer, 245-54
Nigerian writers and society, 255-62

Northern Humanism LC 16: 281-356
background, 282-305
precursor of the Reformation, 305-14
the Brethren of the Common Life, the Devotio Moderna, and education, 314-40
the impact of printing, 340-56

Nuclear Literature: Writings and Criticism in the Nuclear Age TCLC 46: 288-390
overviews, 290-301
fiction, 301-35
poetry, 335-38
nuclear war in Russo-Japanese literature, 338-55
nuclear war and women writers, 355-67
the nuclear referent and literary criticism, 367-88

Occultism in Modern Literature TCLC 50: 362-406
influence of occultism on literature, 363-72
occultism, literature, and society, 372-87
fiction, 387-96
drama, 396-405

Opium and the Nineteenth-Century Literary Imagination NCLC 20: 250-301
original sources, 250-62
historical background, 262-71
and literary society, 271-79
and literary creativity, 279-300

Periodicals, Nineteenth-Century British NCLC 24: 100-65
overviews, 100-30
in the Romantic Age, 130-41
in the Victorian era, 142-54
and the reviewer, 154-64

Plath, Sylvia, and the Nature of Biography CLC 86: 433-62
the nature of biography, 433-52
reviews of *The Silent Woman,* 452-61

Polish Romanticism NCLC 52: 305-71

overviews, 306-26
major figures, 326-40
Polish Romantic drama, 340-62
influences, 362-71

Pre-Raphaelite Movement NCLC 20: 302-401
overview, 302-04
genesis, 304-12
Germ and *Oxford and Cambridge Magazine,* 312-20
Robert Buchanan and the "Fleshly School of Poetry," 320-31
satires and parodies, 331-34
surveys, 334-51
aesthetics, 351-75
sister arts of poetry and painting, 375-94
influence, 394-99

Presocratic Philosophy CMLC 22: 1-56
overviews, 3-24
the Ionians and the Pythagoreans, 25-35
Heraclitus, the Eleatics, and the Atomists, 36-47
the Sophists, 47-55

Psychoanalysis and Literature TCLC 38: 227-338
overviews, 227-46
Freud on literature, 246-51
psychoanalytic views of the literary process, 251-61
psychoanalytic theories of response to literature, 261-88
psychoanalysis and literary criticism, 288-312
psychoanalysis as literature/literature as psychoanalysis, 313-34

Rap Music CLC 76: 477-50

Renaissance Natural Philosophy LC 27: 201-87
cosmology, 201-28
astrology, 228-54
magic, 254-86

Restoration Drama LC 21: 184-275
general overviews, 185-230
Jeremy Collier stage controversy, 230-39
other critical interpretations, 240-75

Revising the Literary Canon CLC 81: 465-509

Revolutionary Astronomers LC 51: 314-365
overviews, 316-25
principal figures, 325-52
revolutionary astronomical models, 352-65

Robin Hood, Legend of LC 19: 205-58
origins and development of the Robin Hood legend, 206-20
representations of Robin Hood, 220-44
Robin Hood as hero, 244-56

Rushdie, Salman, *Satanic Verses* Controversy CLC 55: 214-63; 59: 404-56

Russian Nihilism NCLC 28: 403-47
definitions and overviews, 404-17
women and Nihilism, 417-27
literature as reform: the Civic Critics, 427-33
Nihilism and the Russian novel: Turgenev and Dostoevsky, 433-47

Russian Thaw TCLC 26: 189-247
literary history of the period, 190-206
theoretical debate of socialist realism, 206-11
Novy Mir, 211-17
Literary Moscow, 217-24
Pasternak, *Zhivago,* and the Nobel Prize, 224-27
poetry of liberation, 228-31
Brodsky trial and the end of the Thaw, 231-36
achievement and influence, 236-46

Salinger, J. D., Controversy Surrounding *In Search of J. D. Salinger* CLC 55: 325-44

Science Fiction, Nineteenth-Century NCLC 24: 241-306
background, 242-50
definitions of the genre, 251-56
representative works and writers, 256-75
themes and conventions, 276-305

Scottish Chaucerians LC 20: 363-412

Scottish Poetry, Eighteenth-Century LC 29: 95-167

overviews, 96-114
the Scottish Augustans, 114-28
the Scots Vernacular Revival, 132-63
Scottish poetry after Burns, 163-66

Sherlock Holmes Centenary TCLC 26: 248-310
Doyle's life and the composition of the Holmes stories, 248-59
life and character of Holmes, 259-78
method, 278-79
Holmes and the Victorian world, 279-92
Sherlockian scholarship, 292-301
Doyle and the development of the detective story, 301-07
Holmes's continuing popularity, 307-09

Slave Narratives, American NCLC 20: 1-91
background, 2-9
overviews, 9-24
contemporary responses, 24-27
language, theme, and technique, 27-70
historical authenticity, 70-75
antecedents, 75-83
role in development of Black American literature, 83-88

Spanish Civil War Literature TCLC 26: 311-85
topics in, 312-33
British and American literature, 333-59
French literature, 359-62
Spanish literature, 362-73
German literature, 373-75
political idealism and war literature, 375-83

Spanish Golden Age Literature LC 23: 262-332
overviews, 263-81
verse drama, 281-304
prose fiction, 304-19
lyric poetry, 319-31

Spasmodic School of Poetry NCLC 24: 307-52
history and major figures, 307-21
the Spasmodics on poetry, 321-27
Firmilian and critical disfavor, 327-39
theme and technique, 339-47
influence, 347-51

Steinbeck, John, Fiftieth Anniversary of *The Grapes of Wrath* CLC 59: 311-54

Sturm und Drang NCLC 40: 196-276
    definitions, 197-238
    poetry and poetics, 238-58
    drama, 258-75

Supernatural Fiction in the Nineteenth Century NCLC 32: 207-87
    major figures and influences, 208-35
    the Victorian ghost story, 236-54
    the influence of science and occultism,
        254-66
    supernatural fiction and society, 266-86

Supernatural Fiction, Modern TCLC 30: 59-116
    evolution and varieties, 60-74
    "decline" of the ghost story, 74-86
    as a literary genre, 86-92
    technique, 92-101
    nature and appeal, 101-15

Surrealism TCLC 30: 334-406
    history and formative influences, 335-43
    manifestos, 343-54
    philosophic, aesthetic, and political
        principles, 354-75
    poetry, 375-81
    novel, 381-86
    drama, 386-92
    film, 392-98
    painting and sculpture, 398-403
    achievement, 403-05

Symbolism, Russian TCLC 30: 266-333
    doctrines and major figures, 267- 92
    theories, 293-98
    and French Symbolism, 298-310
    themes in poetry, 310-14
    theater, 314-20
    and the fine arts, 320-32

Symbolist Movement, French NCLC 20: 169-249
    background and characteristics, 170-86
    principles, 186-91
    attacked and defended, 191-97
    influences and predecessors, 197-211
    and Decadence, 211-16
    theater, 216-26
    prose, 226-33
    decline and influence, 233-47

Theater of the Absurd TCLC 38: 339-415
    "The Theater of the Absurd," 340-47

major plays and playwrights, 347-58
and the concept of the absurd, 358-86
theatrical techniques, 386-94
predecessors of, 394-402
influence of, 402-13

Tin Pan Alley
See **American Popular Song, Golden Age of**

Transcendentalism, American NCLC 24: 1-99
    overviews, 3-23
    contemporary documents, 23-41
    theological aspects of, 42-52
    and social issues, 52-74
    literature of, 74-96

Travel Writing in the Nineteenth Century NCLC 44: 274-392
    the European grand tour, 275-303
    the Orient, 303-47
    North America, 347-91

Travel Writing in the Twentieth Century TCLC 30: 407-56
    conventions and traditions, 407-27
    and fiction writing, 427-43
    comparative essays on travel writers,
        443-54

***Ulysses* and the Process of Textual Reconstruction** TCLC 26: 386-416
    evaluations of the new *Ulysses,* 386-94
    editorial principles and procedures, 394-
        401
    theoretical issues, 401-16

Utopian Literature, Nineteenth-Century NCLC 24: 353-473
    definitions, 354-74
    overviews, 374-88
    theory, 388-408
    communities, 409-26
    fiction, 426-53
    women and fiction, 454-71

Vampire in Literature TCLC 46: 391-454
    origins and evolution, 392-412
    social and psychological perspectives,
        413-44
    vampire fiction and science fiction, 445-
        53

Victorian Autobiography NCLC 40: 277-363
    development and major characteristics,
        278-88
    themes and techniques, 289-313
    the autobiographical tendency in
        Victorian prose and poetry,313-47
    Victorian women's autobiographies,
        347-62

Victorian Novel NCLC 32: 288-454
    development and major characteristics,
        290-310
    themes and techniques, 310-58
    social criticism in the Victorian novel,
        359-97
    urban and rural life in the Victorian
        novel, 397-406
    women in the Victorian novel, 406-25
    Mudie's Circulating Library, 425-34
    the late-Victorian novel, 434-51

Women's Diaries, Nineteenth-Century NCLC 48: 308-54
    overview, 308-13
    diary as history, 314-25
    sociology of diaries, 325-34
    diaries as psychological scholarship,
        334-43
    diary as autobiography, 343-48
    diary as literature, 348-53

Women Writers, Seventeenth-Century LC 30: 2-58
    overview, 2-15
    women and education, 15-19
    women and autobiography, 19-31
    women's diaries, 31-39
    early feminists, 39-58

World War I Literature TCLC 34: 392-486
    overview, 393-403
    English, 403-27
    German, 427-50
    American, 450-66
    French, 466-74
    and modern history, 474-82

Yellow Journalism NCLC 36: 383-456
    overviews, 384-96
    major figures, 396-413

Young Playwrights Festival

Topic Index

1988–CLC 55: 376-81
1989–CLC 59: 398-403
1990–CLC 65: 444-48

LC Cumulative Nationality Index

AFGHAN
Babur 18

AMERICAN
Bradstreet, Anne 4, 30
Edwards, Jonathan 7
Eliot, John 5
Franklin, Benjamin 25
Hathorne, John 38
Hopkinson, Francis 25
Knight, Sarah Kemble 7
Mather, Cotton 38
Mather, Increase 38
Munford, Robert 5
Penn, William 25
Sewall, Samuel 38
Stoughton, William 38
Taylor, Edward 11
Washington, George 25
Wheatley (Peters), Phillis 3, 50
Winthrop, John 31

BENINESE
Equiano, Olaudah 16

CANADIAN
Marie de l'Incarnation 10

CHINESE
Lo Kuan-chung 12
P'u Sung-ling 3
Ts'ao Hsueh-ch'in 1
Wu Ch'eng-en 7
Wu Ching-tzu 2

DANISH
Holberg, Ludvig 6
Wessel, Johan Herman 7

DUTCH
Erasmus, Desiderius 16
Lipsius, Justus 16
Spinoza, Benedictus de 9

ENGLISH
Addison, Joseph 18
Amory, Thomas 48
Andrewes, Lancelot 5
Arbuthnot, John 1
Aubin, Penelope 9
Bacon, Francis 18, 32
Barker, Jane 42
Beaumont, Francis 33
Behn, Aphra 1, 30, 42
Bradstreet, Anne 4, 30
Brooke, Frances 6, 48
Bunyan, John 4
Burke, Edmund 7, 36
Butler, Samuel 16
Carew, Thomas 13
Cary, Elizabeth, Lady Falkland 30
Cavendish, Margaret Lucas 30
Caxton, William , 17
Chapman, George 22
Charles I 13
Chatterton, Thomas 3
Chaucer, Geoffrey 17
Churchill, Charles 3
Cleland, John 2, 48
Collier, Jeremy 6
Collins, William 4, 40
Congreve, William 5, 21
Crashaw, Richard 24
Daniel, Samuel 24
Davys, Mary 1
Day, Thomas 1
Dee, John 20

Defoe, Daniel 1, 42
Dekker, Thomas 22
Delany, Mary (Granville Pendarves) 12
Deloney, Thomas 41
Dennis, John 11
Devenant, William 13
Donne, John 10, 24
Drayton, Michael 8
Dryden, John 3, 21
Elyot, Sir Thomas 11
Equiano, Olaudah 16
Fanshawe, Ann 11
Farquhar, George 21
Fielding, Henry 1
Fielding, Sarah 1
Fletcher, John 33
Foxe, John 14
Garrick, David 15
Gray, Thomas 4, 40
Greene, Robert 41
Hakluyt, Richard 31
Hawes, Stephen 17
Haywood, Eliza (Fowler) 1
Henry VIII 10
Herbert, George 24
Herrick, Robert 13
Hobbes, Thomas 36
Howell, James 13
Hunter, Robert 7
Johnson, Samuel 15
Jonson, Ben(jamin) 6, 33
Julian of Norwich 6
Kempe, Margery 6
Killigrew, Anne 4
Kyd, Thomas 22
Langland, William 19
Lanyer, Aemilia 10, 30
Lilly, William 27

Locke, John 7
Lodge. Thomas 41
Lovelace, Richard 24
Lyly, John 41
Lyttelton, George 10
Malory, (Sir) Thomas 11
Manley, Delarivier 1, 42
Marlowe, Christopher 22
Marston, John 33
Marvell, Andrew 4
Middleton, Thomas 33
Milton, John 9
Montagu, Mary (Pierrepont) Wortley 9
More, Henry 9
More, Sir Thomas 10, 32
Nashe, Thomas 41
Parnell, Thomas 3
Pepys, Samuel 11
Philips, Katherine 30
Pix, Mary (Griffith) 8
Pope, Alexander 3
Prior, Matthew 4
Raleigh, Sir Walter 31, 39
Reynolds, Joshua 15
Richardson, Samuel 1
Roper, William 10
Rowe, Nicholas 8
Sheridan, Frances 7
Sidney, Mary 19, 39
Sidney, Sir Philip 19, 39
Smart, Christopher 3
Smith, John 9
Spenser, Edmund 5, 39
Steele, Richard 18
Swift, Jonathan 1, 42
Trotter (Cockburn), Catharine 8
Vanbrugh, Sir John 21
Vaughan, Henry 27
Walpole, Horace 2
Warton, Thomas 15
Webster, John 33
Winchilsea, Anne (Kingsmill) Finch
    Counte 3
Winthrop, John 31
Wollstonecraft, Mary 5, 50
Wroth, Mary 30
Wycherley, William 8, 21
Young, Edward 3, 40

FRENCH
Boileau-Despreaux, Nicolas 3
Calvin, John 37
Christine dc Pizan 9
Condillac, Etienne Bonnot de 26
Corneille, Pierre 28
Crebillon, Claude Prosper Jolyot de
    (fils) 1
Descartes, Rene 20
Diderot, Denis 26
Duclos, Charles Pinot 1
Helvetius, Claude-Adrien 26
Holbach, Paul Henri Thiry Baron 14

La Bruyere, Jean de 17
La Fayette, Marie (Madeleine Pioche de la
    Vergne Comtes 2
La Fontaine, Jean de 50
Lesage, Alain-Rene 2
Malherbe, Francois de 5
Marat, Jean Paul 10
Marie de l'Incarnation 10
Marivaux, Pierre Carlet de Chamblain de 4
Marmontel, Jean-Francois 2
Moliere 10
Montaigne, Michel (Eyquem) de 8
Montesquieu, Charles-Louis de Secondat 7
Nostradamus 27
Perrault, Charles 2
Prevost, Abbe (Antoine Francois) 1
Rabelais, Francois 5
Racine, Jean 28
Ronsard, Pierre de 6
Rousseau, Jean-Baptiste 9
Scudery, Madeleine de 2
Sevigne, Marie (de Rabutin-Chantal)
    Marquise de 11
Turgot, Anne-Robert-Jacques 26
Voltaire 14

GERMAN
Agrippa von Nettesheim, Henry Cornelius 27
Andreae, Johann V(alentin) 32
Beer, Johann 5
Grimmelshausen, Johann Jakob Christoffel von
    6
Hutten, Ulrich von 16
Kempis, Thomas a 11
Lessing, Gotthold Ephraim 8
Luther, Martin 9, 37
Moritz, Karl Philipp 2
Schlegel, Johann Elias (von) 5

ICELANDIC
Petursson, Halligrimur 8

IRANIAN
Jami, Nur al-Din 'Abd al-Rahman 9

IRISH
Brooke, Henry 1
Burke, Edmund 7
Farquhar, George 21
Goldsmith, Oliver 2, 48
Sterne, Laurence 2, 48
Swift, Jonathan 1

ITALIAN
Aretino, Pietro 12
Ariosto, Ludovico 6
Boiardo, Matteo Maria 6
Bruno, Giordano 27
Campanella, Tommaso 32
Casanova de Seingalt, Giovanni Jacopo 13
Castelvetro, Lodovico 12
Castiglione, Baldassare 12

Cellini, Benvenuto 7
Ficino, Marsilio 12
Goldoni, Carlo 4
Machiavelli, Niccolo 8, 36
Michelangelo 12
Pico della Mirandola, Giovanni 15
Sannazaro, Jacopo 8
Tasso, Torquato 5
Vinci, Leonardo da 12

MEXICAN
Juana Ines de la Cruz 5
Siguenza y Gongora, Carlos de 8

NORWEGIAN
Holberg, Ludvig 6
Wessel, Johan Herman 7

POLISH
Kochanowski, Jan 10

RUSSIAN
Chulkov, Mikhail Dmitrievich 2
Frederick the Great 14
Ivan IV 17

SCOTTISH
Boswell, James 4, 50
Buchanan, George 4
Burns, Robert 3, 29, 40
Douglas, Gavin 20
Dunbar, William 20
Henryson, Robert 20
Hume, David 7
James I 20
Knox, John 37
Lyndsay, Sir David 20
Smith, Adam 36
Smollett, Tobias (George) 2
Thomson, James 16, 29, 40

SPANISH
Calderon de la Barca, Pedro 23
Castro, Guillen de 19
Cervantes (Saavedra), Miguel de 6, 23
Cortes, Hernan 31
Diaz del Castillo, Bernal 31
Gracian y Morales, Baltasar 15
John of the Cross, St. 18
Las Casas, Bartolome de 31
Quevedo, Francisco de 23
Rojas, Fernando de 23
Teresa de Jesus, St. 18
Vega, Lope de 23

SWISS
Paracelsus 14
Rousseau, Jean-Jacques 14 , 36
Zwingli, Huldrych 37

WELSH
Vaughan, Henry 27

LC Cumulative Title Index

"2nd Olympique Ode" (Cowley) **43**:142

"The 21th: and last booke of the Ocean to Scinthia" (Raleigh) **31**:265, 271-80, 282-4, 286-8

"The 23rd Psalme" (Herbert) **24**:274-75

"The 34. Chapter of the Prophet Isaiah" (Cowley) **43**:168, 170

XCVI Sermons (Andrewes) **5**:19, 22-5, 28, 33, 41

"A Chaulieu" (Rousseau) **9**:344

"A Chretophle de Choiseul" (Ronsard) **6**:433

"A Courtin" (Rousseau) **9**:343-44

"A de Lannoy" (Rousseau) **9**:345

"A Denyse sorciere" (Ronsard) **6**:430

"A Gui Peccate Prieur de Sougé" (Ronsard) **6**:437

"A Guillaume Des Autels" (Ronsard) **6**:433

"A Janne impitoyable" (Ronsard) **6**:419

"A Jean de Morel" (Ronsard) **6**:433

"A la fontaine Bellerie" (Ronsard) **6**:419, 430

"A la paix" (Rousseau) **9**:344

"A la reine sur sa bien-venüe en France" (Malherbe)
See "Ode à Marie de Médicis, sur sa Bienvenue en France"

"A la reyne mère sur les heureux succez de sa régence" (Malherbe)
See "Ode pour la Reine Mère du Roy pendant sa Régence"

"A l'ambassadeur de Venise" (Rousseau) **9**:344

"A l'empereur, après la conclusion de la quadruple alliance" (Rousseau) **9**:344

"A l'impératrice Amélie" (Rousseau) **9**:343

"A M. de Grimani" (Rousseau) **9**:340

A Mme Denis nièce de l'auteur, la vie de Paris et de Versailles (Voltaire) **14**:390

"A Monseigneur le Duc de Bellegarde, grand escuyer de France" (Malherbe) **5**:184

"A Philippe de Vendôme" (Rousseau) **9**:344

"A Philomèle" (Rousseau) **9**:345

"A Pierre L'Escot" (Ronsard) **6**:433

"A Robert de La Haye, Conseiller du Roi en son Parlement à Paris" (Ronsard) **6**:433

"A sa Muse" (Ronsard) **6**:430

"A son ame" (Ronsard) **6**:436

"A son livre" (Ronsard) **6**:425-27, 433-34

"A' the Airts" (Burns)
See "Of A' the Airts"

"A une jeune veuve" (Rousseau)
See "A une veuve"

"A une veuve" (Rousseau) **9**:340, 344

"A Zinzindorf" (Rousseau)
See "Ode au comte de Sinzendorff"

"Aaron" (Herbert) **24**:237

"Abbatis Eurditae" (Erasmus) **16**:128

"Abbot and the Learned Lady" (Erasmus) **16**:123, 142, 193

L'abbrégé de l'art poétique françois (Ronsard) **6**:406, 419, 427

L'A.B.C. (Voltaire) **14**:405

Abdelazer; or, The Moor's Revenge (Behn) **1**:28, 33, 39; **30**:67, 70-1, 77, 81; **42**:164

Abecedarium Naturae (Bacon) **18**:187

"Abel's blood" (Vaughan) **27**:300, 377-79

Der abenteuerliche Simplicissimus, Teutsch, das hist: Die Beschreibun dess Lebens eines seltzamen Vaganten, gennant Melchio Sternfels von Fuchsheim (Grimmelshausen) **6**:235-48, 252

Der abentheuerliche, wunderbare und unerhörte Ritter Hopffen-sack (Beer) **5**:54-5

Abhandlung von der Nachahmung (Schlegel) **5**:274, 282-83

Abhandlung von der Unähnlichkeit in der Nachahmung (Schlegel) **5**:274

Abode of Spring (Jami)
See *Baháristán*

"Abra; or, The Georgian Sultana" (Collins) **4**:210

Abraham and Isaac (Chester)
See *Abraham, Lot, and Melchysedeck* (Chester)

Abraham and Isaac (N-Town) **34**:181, 208

Abraham and Isaac (Towneley) **34**:251, 267, 288-9, 325

Abraham and Isaac (York)
See *Abraham's Sacrifice* (York)

Abraham, Lot, and Melchysedeck (Chester) **34**:92, 107-8, 111, 126-7, 131, 139

Abraham's Sacrifice (York) **34**:332, 364, 386-7

Abrege de la vie de Jesus Christ (Pascal) **35**:365

Abridgements of the History of Rome and England (Goldsmith) **2**:71

Abridgment of English History (Burke)
See *An Essay towards an Abridgement of the English History*

Absalom and Achitophel (Dryden) **3**:180, 185, 187, 189-92, 199, 201, 205, 213, 216-22, 225, 228, 231, 234, 240-43, 246; **21**:51, 53-7, 64-5, 86-7, 90-1, 94, 101-03, 111-13

Absalom's Hair (Calderon de la Barca)
See *Los cabellos de Absalón*

Absalom's Locks (Calderon de la Barca) **23**:64

"Absolute Retreat" (Winchilsea)
See "The Petition for an Absolute Retreat"

The Abuses of Conscience Considered (Sterne) **48**:258

Acajou et Zirphile (Duclos) **1**:185, 187

Accedence Commenc't Grammar (Milton) **43**:397

An Accidence; or, The Path-Way to Experience (Smith) **9**:381-82

The Accomplish'd Rake; or, Modern Fine Gentleman (Davys) **1**:99-100; **46**:20, 24-8, 32, 35-6

An Account of a Battel between the Ancient and Modern Books in St. James's Library (Swift)
See *A Tale of a Tub, Written for the Universal Improvement of Mankind, to Which is Added an Account of a Battel between the Ancient*

and Modern Books in St. James's Library

Account of a Journey from Paris to Limousin (La Fontaine)

    See *Relation d'un voyage de Paris en Limousin*

An Account of Corsica (Boswell)

    See *An Account of Corsica, The Journal of a Tour to that Island; and the Memoirs of Pascal Paoli*

An Account of Corsica, The Journal of a Tour to that Island; and the Memoirs of Pascal Paoli (Boswell) **4**:16, 25, 31, 33, 60, 71, 77-8; **50**:20, 23

"An Account of the English Poets" (Addison) **18**:6, 16, 38-9, 41, 61

"Account of the Ensuing Poem" (Dryden) **21**:90

The Account of the Fish Pool (Steele) **18**:354

An Account of the Growth of Popery and Arbitrary Power in England (Marvell) **4**:394

An Account of the Life of Mr. Richard Savage, Son of Earl Rivers (Johnson) **15**:188, 195, 199, 203, 206, 287

Account of the Life of Shakespear (Rowe) **8**:296, 303

Accustoria (Guicciardini) **49**:260

El acero de Madrid (Vega) **23**:393

Acertar Errando (Vega) **23**:355

Achilles (Gay) **49**:3, 92-93, 101, 123-124, 148-149, 152-162, 164-165

Achmet et Almanzine (Lesage) **28**:210

Acis and Galatea (Gay) **49**:100-101, 108

Act for Abolishing (Henry VIII) **10**:125, 131, 136-38, 141

"Act Sederunt of the Session" (Burns) **3**:99-100

Actes and Monumentes of these latter perilous dayes touching matters of the Church (Foxe) **14**:5, 7-10, 12-15, 17, 19-22, 24-29, 32, 36, 38-39, 41, 43, 46-50, 54

Les acteurs de bonnefoi (Marivaux) **4**:369, 377

The Actors of Good Faith (Marivaux)

    See *The Actors of Good Faith*

Ad Caesarem Maximilianum ut bellum in Venetos coeptum prosequatur exhortatorium (Hutten) **16**:238

"Ad Patrem" (Milton) **43**:391, 396

Ad Vitellionem, etc (Kepler) **45**:343

Adages (Erasmus)

    See *Adagia*

Adagia (Erasmus) **16**:106, 132, 136, 154, 171, 173, 191, 193, 195-98

Adagiorum chiliades (Erasmus) **16**:132

Adagiorum Opus (Erasmus) **16**:195

"Adam Armour's Prayer" (Burns) **29**:29

Adam; ou, La création de l'homme, sa chûte et sa réparation (Perrault) **2**:256

Adam (Towneley) **34**:289

Additional Articles to the Specimen of an Etimological Vocabulary (Behn) **2**:54

Address (Washington)

    See *Farewell Address*

"Address of Beelzebub" (Burns) **3**:78, 95-6; **29**:28, 41, 46

"Address to a Haggis" (Burns) **3**:52, 67, 71, 85; **29**:29

"Address to a Louse" (Burns)

    See "To a Louse, on Seeing One on a Lady's Bonnet at Church"

Address to All the Estates of the German Nation (Hutten) **16**:234

"Address to Edinburgh" (Burns) **3**:83; **29**:91, 92

"Address to Lord Provost Drummond" (Ramsay) **29**:336

Address to Protestants of all Persuasions (Penn) **25**:297-98, 332

"Address to "Ruin"" (Burns) **3**:48, 67; **29**:28, 79

"Address to Saxham" (Carew) **13**:17, 32, 59, 61

"Address to the Atheist" (Wheatley) **3**:424

Address to the British Colonists in North America (Burke) **36**:79

"Address to the De'il" (Burns) **3**:67, 71, 87, 95-6, 102-03; **29**:5, 7, 32-3, 35, 41, 44, 63, 93; **40**:71, 119

"An Address to the Deist" (Wheatley) **50**:162

The Address to the German Nobility (Luther)

    See *An den Christlichen Adel deutscher Nation: Von des Christlichen Standes Besserung*

"Address to the Noblest and Best of Ladies, the Countess Denbigh Against Irresolution and Delay in Matters of Religion" (Crashaw) **24**:15-6, 48, 53-4, 62

"Address to the Shade of Thomson" (Burns) **29**:32, 89

"An Address to the Soul Occasioned by a Rain" (Taylor) **11**:394

"Address to the Toothache" (Burns) **40**:63, 115

    See "To the Toothache"

"Address to the Unco Guid, or the Rigidly Righteous" (Burns) **3**:51; **29**:91

"Address to William Tytler" (Burns) **40**:110

Adélaide du Guesclin (Voltaire) **14**:397

Adjunta al Parnaso (Cervantes)

    See "Viage del Parnaso"

Admiralty Letters (Pepys) **11**:238

"Admiring Chrysanthemums in Sun Shengzuo's Studio, the Tenth Month" (P'u Sung-ling)

    See "Shiyue Sun Shengzuo zhaizhong shang ju"

Admonition or Warning (Knox) **37**:212-13

Admonitioun (Buchanan)

    See *Ane Admonitioun Direct to the Trew Lordis, Maintenaris of Justice and Obedience to the Kingis Grace*

****Adonis**** (La Fontaine) **50**:55, 87, 129, 131

Adonis y Venus (Vega) **23**:355

The Adoration of the Magi (N-Town)

    See *The Magi* (N-Town)

The Adoration of the Magi (Towneley)

    See *Oblacio Magorum* (Towneley)

Adoration of the Shepherds (Chester)

    See *The Shepherds* (Chester)

Adoration of the Shepherds (N-Town) **34**:170, 174, 184, 188, 192, 224

Adoration of the Shepherds (Towneley) **34**:288

"Adoro te" (Crashaw) **24**:55

The Advancement and Reformation of Modern Poetry (Dennis) **11**:16, 19, 22-4, 26, 30, 33, 36-8, 40, 43-4, 51-3

The Advantages and Disadvantages (Calderon de la Barca)

    See *Dicha y desdicha del nombre*

The Advantages that the Establishment of Christianity Has Conferred upon the Human Race (Turgot)

    See *Les Avantages que l'établissement du christianisme a procurÉs au genre humain*

The Adventure of the Black Lady (Behn) **1**:34, 38, 46; **42**:145, 152

The Adventures and Surprizing Deliverences of James Dubourdien and His Wife (Defoe) **42**:262

The Adventures in Madrid (Pix) **8**:262, 269, 271-72, 277

The Adventures of Alexander Vend church (Defoe) **42**:262

The Adventures of Covent Garden (Farquhar) **21**:135

The Adventures of David Simple (Fielding) **1**:270-

75, 278-79; **44**:48-52, 55, 65, 67, 69, 72-4, 77-8, 81-3, 93-4, 98, 100, 105, 110, 112, 121, 124

The Adventures of Ferdinand, Count Fathom (Smollett) **2**:319-22, 324, 326, 330-32, 335, 337, 340, 346, 351-52, 354, 356-57, 359; **46**:189, 192, 194, 202, 220-23, 232, 266, 274

The Adventures of Gargantua and Pantagruel (Rabelais)

    See *Gargantua and Pantagruel*

The Adventures of Gil Blas (Lesage)

    See *Histoire de Gil Blas de Santillane*

The Adventures of Guzman d'Alfarache (Lesage)

    See *Histoire de Guzman d'Alfarache*

The Adventures of Peregrine Pickle (Smollett) **2**:319-21, 324, 326, 328, 330, 332-34, 336-44, 352-57, 359, 361; **46**:189, 191, 193, 196, 202, 204, 206, 216-17, 219, 234, 250-60, 269

The Adventures of Rivella (Manley) **1**:308, 312, 315-17, 321, 323-24; **42**:261-62, 267, 269-70, 273-76, 283-84

Adventures of Robinson Crusoe, with His Vision of the Angelick World (Defoe) **42**:178, 192, 194, 196, 202, 211-12, 228-29, 232, 239

The Adventures of Roderick Random (Smollett) **2**:319-21, 324-30, 333-34, 336-38, 341-42, 344-47, 351, 353-57, 359-62, 366; **46**:187-90, 193, 198, 201-05, 207-10, 214-17, 219-20, 232-35, 239, 242-48, 257, 266, 269

The Adventures of Sir Launcelot Greaves (Smollett) **2**:319-20, 322, 324, 329-30, 333, 336-37, 352, 357, 359-60

Adventures of the Chevalier de Beauchêne (Lesage)

    See *Les aventures de Monsieur Robert Chevalier*

The Adventures of the Prince of Clermont, and Madame de Ravezan (Aubin) **9**:6

The Adventurous Simplicissimus's Perpetual Calendar (Grimmelshausen)

    See *Des abenteuerlichen Simplicissimi Ewigwahrender Calender*

"Adversity" (Gray)

    See "Ode to Adversity"

An Advertisement Touching An Holy War (Bacon) **32**:139, 141, 171

"Advertisements" (Garrick) **15**:122

Advertisements for the Unexperienced Planters of New England, or Any Where (Smith) **9**:379, 383-85, 388

"The Advice" (Raleigh) **39**:97

Advice (Smollett) **2**:352, 358-59; **46**:188, 194, 233

The Advice of William Penn to his Children (Penn) **25**:344

"Advice on Choosing a Mistress" (Franklin) **25**:141

Advice to a Lady (Lyttelton) **10**:200

"Advice to a Young Tradesman, Written by an Old One" (Franklin) **25**:181

Advice to Belinda (Lyttelton) **10**:203

"Advice to my Best Brother, Coll. Francis Lovelace" (Lovelace) **24**:321, 340, 348

"Ae Fond Kiss" (Burns) **3**:78, 83, 85; **29**:87-8, 93; **40**:97, 122

Aedes Walpolianae; or, A Description of the Pictures at Houghton Hall in Norfolk (Walpole) **2**:487

Aesop (Vanbrugh) **21**:284, 287, 294-95, 334

"Affectation" (Hopkinson) **25**:253

The Affected Ladies (Moliere)

    See *Les précieuses ridicules*

"Affected (Man)" (Butler) **16**:51

"Afflication II" (Herbert) **24**:274
"Afflication III" (Herbert) **24**:225, 250, 263, 274
"Afflication V" (Herbert) **24**:225, 250, 263, 274
"Affliction" (Herbert) **24**:233, 250, 274
"Affliction" (Vaughan) **27**:322, 332, 338, 396
"Affliction I" (Herbert) **24**:225-26, 233, 271, 274, 276
"Affliction IV" (Herbert) **24**:263, 274
"African Eclogues" (Chatterton) **3**:121, 123, 132
"After Autumne, Winter" (Herrick) **13**:341
"Afton Water" (Burns)
    See "Sweet Afton"
"Afuera, afuera, ansias mías" (Juana Ines de la Cruz) **5**:155
"Against Love" (Philips) **30**:287
Against the Fear of Death (Dryden)
    See *Translation of the Latter Part of the Third Book of Lucretius: Against the Fear of Death*
Against the Robbing and Murdering Hordes of Peasants (Luther) **37**:263, 303
Agamemnon. A tragedy (Thomson) **16**:385, 396; **29**:416-17, 421, 433
"The Ages of Man" (Bradstreet)
    See "The Four Ages of Man"
Agésilas (Corneille) **28**:31, 33, 35, 39, 41
Agesilaus (Corneille)
    See *Agésilas*
Agincourt
    See *The Battaile of Agincourt*
Agnes de Castro (Trotter) **8**:350, 352, 355, 357-59, 363-66, 368, 371-74
Agnes de Castro; or, The Force of Generous Blood (Behn) **1**:42, 44, 50-1
"The Agony" (Herbert) **24**:257-59, 266, 271, 273, 293
The Agony and the Betrayal (Chester)
    See *The Last Supper* (Chester)
Agony at Olivet (N-Town) **34**:209
Agony in the Garden and the Betrayal (York) **34**:333, 388
Agreeable Ugliness; or, The Triumph of the Graces (Scott) **44**:356-57, 364
"Agrippina" (Gray) **4**:332
Agudeza de Ingenio (Gracian y Morales)
    See *Agudeza y arte de ingenio*
Agudeza y arte de ingenio (Gracian y Morales) **15**:136, 139, 141, 143-45, 147, 150
Ah, ha, Tumulus thalamus (Howell) **13**:427
"Aire and Angels" (Donne) **10**:26, 36, 48, 55, 57-8, 82, 108-09; **24**:152, 155
Akakia (Voltaire) **14**:328
Alarum Against Usurers (Lodge) **41**:193, 199-201
Albovine (Davenant) **13**:175, 196, 216
El alcade de Zalamea (Calderon de la Barca) **23**:12, 39-42, 46, 52, 58, 64-5, 70
El Alcalde mayor (Vega) **23**:393
Alcestis (Buchanan) **4**:134-36
The Alchemist (Jonson) **6**:291, 294-95, 297, 300, 303, 305-07, 310-14, 319-20, 323-24, 328, 330-31, 334-36, 340, 343-44; **33**:106, 110, 112-13, 115, 132, 136, 146, 155-56, 160-61, 165-68, 170, 175-76, 179, 181
Alcida **41**:156, 174, 177
"The Alcoholic" (P'u Sung-ling)
    See "Jiu Kuang"
"Aldarhéttur" (Petursson) **8**:252
al-Durrah al-Fákhira (Jami) **9**:58, 73
Alexander and Campaspe (Lyly)
    See *Campaspe*
Alexander the Great (Racine)
    See *Alexandre le Grand*
"Alexander's Feast; or, The Power of Musique.

An Ode, in Honour of St. Cecilia's Day" (Dryden) **3**:186-87, 190, 213, 243; **21**:59, 61-4, 83, 88
Alexandre le Grand (Racine) **28**:293, 315, 339, 342, 358, 380, 382, 384
"Alexandreis" (Killigrew) **4**:350
Alfred. A Masque (Thomson) **16**:396; **29**:416, 433, 436; **40**:274
"Alfred, Father of the State" (Hopkinson) **25**:260
El alguacil endemoniado (Quevedo) **23**:187-89
All Fools (Chapman) **22**:6, 10, 13, 15-16, 60, 63, 65
All Fools but the Fool (Chapman)
    See *All Fools*
All for Love; or, The World Well Lost (Dryden) **3**:186, 194, 209-10, 214, 216, 222, 232-35, 237, 242; **21**:52-3, 91
"All Is Vanity" (Winchilsea) **3**:441
"All kings and all their favourites" (Donne)
    See "The Anniversarie"
All Men Are Brothers (Lo Kuan-chung)
    See *Shui Hu Chuan*
"All Saints" (Smart) **3**:378
"Allegoria del poema" (Tasso) **5**:402, 405
"An Allegory on Man" (Parnell) **3**:252, 254
"L'Allegro" (Milton) **9**:177, 192, 197-98, 201, 204, 212, 224-33
"L'allegro" (Smart) **3**:374
L'Allegro (Marvell) **43**:303
"Alliance" (Gray) **4**:333
"Alliance of Education and Government" (Gray)
    See "Essay on the Alliance of Education and Government"
All's Right at Last; or, The History of Frances West (Brooke) **6**:119-22; **48**:52-54, 57
"L'alma, che sparge e versa" (Michelangelo) **12**:370
"Alma; or, The Progress of the Mind" (Prior) **4**:455-56, 459-60, 464, 467-73
Almanach du Bonhomme Richard (Franklin)
    See *Poor Richard's Almanack*
Almanack (Franklin)
    See *Poor Richard's Almanack*
Las Almenas de Toro (Vega) **23**:350
Almindelig kirke-historie fra christendommens første begyndelse til Lutheri reformation... (Holberg) **6**:282
Almyna; or, The Arabian Vow (Manley) **1**:316
Alphonsus, Emperor of Germany (Chapman) **22**:7, 10, 12
"Alt eins og blómstrió eina" (Petursson) **8**:252, 254
"The Altar" (Herbert) **24**:228, 253-54, 267, 271, 274-75, 278-79
"Alte Reime von der praktischen Theologie" (Andreae) **32**:92
"Althea" (Lovelace)
    See "To Althea: From Prison"
Alzire; ou, Les Américains (Voltaire) **14**:328, 330, 332, 397
"L'amant heureux" (Rousseau) **9**:341
"El amante liberal" (Cervantes) **23**:99
Les amants magnifiques (Moliere) **10**:283, 313, 320; **28**:255, 257, 262
Amar después de la muerte (Calderon de la Barca) **23**:12-13
"Amarantha's Shining Hair" (Lovelace) **24**:302
"Amarilis" (Vega)
    See "Eclogue to Amaryllis"
Amasie (Racine) **28**:342
Amazonum cantilena (Erasmus) **16**:196
"The Amber Bead" (Herrick) **13**:397
The Ambitious Step-Mother (Rowe) **8**:282, 285-

86, 292, 295-96, 298, 302-05
Amelia (Fielding) **1**:209-10, 212, 215, 215-18, 224-26, 229, 233-35, 238, 241-42, 249-50, 252, 255, 258-61, 263; **46**:50-1, 74, 80, 88, 93-4, 99-100, 104-07, 136-37, 148, 172-73, 177-79
Amendments of Mr. Collier's False and Imperfect Citations from the "Old Batchelour," "Double-Dealer," "Love for Love," "Mourning Bride" (Congreve) **5**:104-05
"America" (Wheatley) **3**:435; **50**:162, 179
L'Ami du Peuple (Marat)
    See *Le publiciste parisien, journal politique, libre et impartial . . .*
El amigo hasta la muerte (Vega) **23**:393
Aminta (Tasso) **5**:388, 390-92, 401, 407
"Aminta of Tasso" (Winchilsea) **3**:445
Amistad Pagada (Vega) **23**:347
Among the Remedies (Las Casas) **31**:206
El amor constante (Castro) **19**:7-8, 13-15
"Amor constante más allá de la muerte" (Quevedo) **23**:177
Amor es más laberinto (Juana Ines de la Cruz) **5**:150, 151, 159
L'amor paterno (Goldoni) **4**:261
Amor secreto hasta celos (Vega) **23**:393
Amoretti (Spenser) **39**:373
Amoretti (Spenser) **5**:313, 332, 341-42, 355-56, 363-64
"An Amorist" (Butler) **16**:54
The Amorous Prince; or, The Curious Husband (Behn) **1**:33, 39, 52; **30**:80; **42**:150
L'amour de Dieu (Boileau-Despreaux) **3**:22
"L'amour dévoilé" (Rousseau) **9**:341
L'amour et la vérité (Marivaux) **4**:367
L'amour médecin (Moliere) **10**:282-83, 312-13, 327
l'Amour Médecin (Moliere) **28**:228, 236, 255-56, 259, 265
"Amourette" (Ronsard) **6**:427
Amours de Cassandre (Ronsard) **6**:406, 409, 417
Amours de Marie (Ronsard) **6**:409, 417
Les amours de Psyche et de Cupidon (La Fontaine) **50**:50, 52-53, 55-56, 58, 106-109, 112-113
Les amours de Ronsard (Ronsard) **6**:406, 411, 415-16, 425-27, 430-31
Les Amours déquisés (Lesage) **28**:204
The Amours of Philander and Sylvia (Behn) **42**:125
Amphitryon (Dryden) **3**:180, 210, 222, 230
Amphitryon (Moliere) **10**:268, 272, 283, 287, 312-13, 323; **28**:229, 235-37, 255, 258-59, 266
"Amymone" (Rousseau) **9**:343
"Amyntas goe, thou art undone" (Vaughan) **27**:363
"Amynthor's Grove" (Lovelace) **24**:328
An den Christlichen Adel deutscher Nation: Von des Christlichen Standes Besserung (Luther) **9**:102, 105, 108, 125-27, 134, 140, 143-44, 148; **37**:252, 254, 261, 300-02
"L'an se rajeunissoit" (Ronsard) **6**:427
"An Anabaptist" (Butler) **16**:27
"Anacreontic" (Parnell) **3**:256
"Anacreontike" (Herrick) **13**:341
Anacreontiques (Cowley) **43**:141
Analytical Geometry (Descartes) **35**:74
Anatomie of absurditie (Nashe) **41**:302
An Anatomie of the World (Donne)
    See *The First Anniversarie. An Anatomie of the World. Wherein By Occasion of the untimely death of Mistris Elizabeth Drury, the frailtie*

Title Index

and decay of this whole World is represented
"And do they so?" (Vaughan) **27**:325, 336

"And must I sing? what subject shall I chuse?" (Jonson) **6**:350

Andreas Hartknopf: Eine Allegorie (Moritz) **2**:233, 244-46

Andreas Hartknopfs Predigerjahre (Moritz) **2**:244

"Andrew Turner" (Burns) **3**:86

Andria (Lesage) **28**:201

Androboros: A Biographical Farce in Three Acts, Viz. The Senate, The Consistory, and The Apotheosis (Hunter) **7**:209-17

Andromache (Racine)
    See *Andromaque*

Andromaque (Racine) **28**:292-93, 297, 299, 302, 304-05, 308, 310, 312, 314 316-18, 327-28, 330-31, 337-39, 342, 346-47, 350, 352, 355, 363-64, 366, 369-70, 374, 376, 379-82, 384

Andromea and Perseus (Calderon de la Barca) **23**:9

Andromeda (Corneille)
    See *Andromède*

Andromède (Corneille) **28**:29, 31, 35, 41, 55

Ane Admonitioun Direct to the Trew Lordis, Maintenaris of Justice and Obedience to the Kingis Grace (Buchanan) **4**:118

Ane Opinion anent the University of St. Andrews (Buchanan)
    See *Opinion Anent the Reformation of the Universities of St Androis*

Anecdotes of Painting in England (Walpole) **2**:455-56, 487; **49**:358

"Anelida and Arcite" (Chaucer) **17**:71, 123

The Angel of Bethesda (Mather) **38**:203, 230, 234, 236-37

Angelographia (Mather) **38**:294-95

The Angels and the Shepherds (York) **34**:334

Anglicus (Lilly)
    See *Merlinus Anglicus*

"Anguish" (Vaughan) **27**:339

Anima magica abscondita (More) **9**:310

Animadversions upon the Remonstrants Defence (Milton) **9**:250

"Un Animal dans la lune" (La Fontaine) **50**:100, 104, 124-125

"Les Animaux malades de la peste" (La Fontaine) **50**:81, 85, 88, 99, 101, 103

Annaei Senecae Philosopli Opera, quae exstant, onmia (Lipsius) **16**:274

Annales de l'empire (Voltaire) **14**:338, 411

"Anne Hay" (Carew)
    See "Obsequies to the Lady Anne Hay"

Annibal (Marivaux) **4**:366

"The Anniversarie" (Donne) **10**:18, 36, 48, 52

The Anniversaries (Donne) **10**:17, 25-6, 39, 53, 63, 67, 74, 83-4, 89, 95, 97-9, 103; **24**:152-53, 182, 184-87

"Anniversary" (Marvell)
    See "The First Anniversary of the Government under O. C."

Anno 7603 (Wessel) **7**:390

The Annual Register (Burke) **7**:63

Annunciatio (Towneley) **34**:251, 278, 311, 326

The Annunciation and the Nativity (Chester) **34**:96, 102, 109, 121, 124-6, 128, 136, 153

Annunciation and Visit of Elizabeth to Mary (York) **34**:386

Annunciation (N-Town) **34**:203, 218, 240

Annunciation (Towneley)
    See *Annunciatio* (Towneley)

"The Annuntiation and the Passion" (Donne) **10**:40, 84

"Annus Mirabilis: The Year of Wonders, 1666" (Dryden) **3**:178, 190, 192-93, 201, 213, 215-16, 221-24, 226, 234-35, 239-40, 243; **21**:53, 85-6, 88, 91, 107, 111, 116

"Another" (Lovelace) **24**:322, 324, 335, 344

"Another Epistle to the Reader" (Cavendish) **30**:203

"Another Grace for a Child" (Herrick) **13**:357

"Answer" (Crashaw) **24**:22

"Answer" (Winchilsea)
    See "Ardelia's Answer to Ephelia"

"The Answer" (Wycherley) **8**:410

The Answer (Montagu) **9**:282

"An Answer to Another Perswading a Lady to Marriage" (Philips) **30**:279

"Answer to Mr. J.S.'s Epistle" (Fergusson) **29**:217

"The Answer to Sir Thomas Wortley's Sonnet" (Lovelace) **24**:

An Answer to Some Exceptions in Bishop Burnet's Third Part of the History of the Reformation (Collier) **6**:209

"Answer to the Guidwife of Wauchope House" (Burns) **3**:94

Answer to the Poisoned Book (More) **10**:398, 400, 437

"An Answer to the Rebus" (Wheatley) **3**:420

"Answer to the Secret Committee" (Prior) **4**:467

An Answer to the...Book Which a Nameless Heretic hath named: The Supper of the Lord (More) **10**:370

Answer to Valentin Compar (Zwingli) **37**:368, 374-75

"The Ant" (Lovelace) **24**:306-07, 315, 320-21, 328, 336, 338, 340

"An Anthem from the 114th Psalm" (Hopkinson) **25**:260

Anthon Reiser (Moritz)
    See *Anton Reiser*

Antibarbari (Erasmus) **16**:134, 142, 145-46

The Antichrist (Chester) **34**:96, 105, 122, 128, 131, 134-5, 137, 139-40, 160-1

An Antidote Against Atheism (More) **9**:300, 302, 306, 311

The Antient and Present State of Great Britain (Amory) **48**:16

Anti-Goeze (Lessing) **8**:98, 107

Anti-Machiavel (Frederick the Great) **14**:59, 62, 77-8

"Antimonopsychia: or, That All Souls are not One" (More) **9**:313-14, 331

Antinomians and Familists condemned by the synod of elders in New-England (Winthrop) **31**:359, 380

Anti-Pamela; or Feigned Innocence Detected in a Series of Syrena's Adventures (Haywood) **44**:145-6

"Antiphon" (Herbert) **24**:274

"Antiphon II" (Herbert) **24**:254, 274

"Antipsychopannychia" (More) **9**:313, 330-31

The Antiquarian's Family (Goldoni)
    See *La famiglia dell' antiquario*

"Antiquary" (Donne) **10**:95

Anton Reiser (Moritz) **2**:228-48

"Antonie" (Sidney)
    See "The Tragedie of Antonie"

Antonio and Mellida (Marston) **33**:186, 190-91, 193, 198-200, 202-03, 207-08, 234-35, 239, 241-44, 252-54

Antonio's Revenge (Marston) **33**:198, 200-03, 207-09, 213-14, 235-36, 238, 241, 243-44, 252, 254, 256

"Antonius" (Sidney)
    See "The Tragedie of Antonie"

Antony and Cleopatra (Brooke) **1**:62

Anything for a Quiet Life (Middleton) **33**:263, 272-73, 277-78, 280, 298, 303

Anything for a Quiet Life (Webster) **33**:339-40

Anzoig (Hutten) **16**:246

"A-pao" (P'u Sung-ling) **49**:278

Apearance of Mary to Thomas (York)
    See *The Appearance of Our Lady to Thomas* (York)

Aphorismi et Consilia, de Auxiliis Mentis, et Accensione (Bacon) **18**:187

Apologética historia sumaria (Las Casas) **31**:194-97, 211

Apologia (Agrippa von Nettesheim) **27**:22, 23

Apología (Las Casas) **31**:182-91, 192, 208-9, 210

Apologia (Erasmus) **16**:149

Apologia (Kepler)
    See *Defense of Tycho against Ursus*

Apologia (Pico della Mirandola) **15**:321-22, 327

Apologia pro Galileo (Campanella) **32**:204

"Apologie" (Crashaw)
    See "An Apology"

Apologie de l'Abbé Galiani (Diderot) **26**:156

"Apologie de Raimond Sebond" (Montaigne) **8**:191-92, 205, 209, 211, 218,221-22, 225, 228, 230-31, 234, 236-37, 240, 245, 247-48

L'apologie des femmes (Perrault) **2**:279

An Apologie for Poetrie (Sidney)
    See *The Defence of Poesie*

"An Apology" (Bradstreet) **4**:111; **30**:132-3

"The Apology" (Churchill) **3**:144, 150, 152-53, 155-57, 162-63

"An Apology" (Crashaw) **24**:53

An Apology (Luther) **37**:246, 249

Apology (Pascal)
    See *Pensees*

Apology for Heroic Poetry (Dryden)
    See *The Author's Apology for Heroic Poetry and Poetic License*

Apology for Smectymnuus (Milton) **9**:192, 210, 252; **43**:354, 356, 379

The Apology for the Clergy (Fielding) **46**:95

"An Apology for the Ladies" (Montagu) **9**:281

An Apology for the Life of Mrs. Shamela Andrews (Fielding) **1**:238-39, 242-43, 258, 260-61; **46**:54-8, 62, 64, 95-8, 104, 119, 122-23

"An Apology of Raymond Sebond" (Montaigne)
    See "Apologie de Raimond Sebond"

The apologye of syr Thomas More knyght (More) **10**:366, 370, 398; **32**:258, 262, 263, 269, 270, 274

Apophthegms New and Old (Bacon) **18**:136, 192

"Apostate Will" (Chatterton) **3**:127, 132

"Apostrophe to Fergusson" (Burns) **29**:91

Apotheosis of John Reuchlin (Erasmus) **16**:121

"The Apparition" (Donne) **10**:34, 36, 52, 73, 82; **24**:150-51, 155

"The Apparition of His Mistress Calling Him to Elizium" (Herrick) **13**:316, 365

An Appeal from the New, to the Old Whigs in Consequence of Some Late Discussions in Parliament, Relative to the Reflections on the French Revolution (Burke) **7**:27, 64; **36**:73-74, 76, 80-81, 99

An Appeal to Honour and Justice (Defoe) **42**:204

Appeal to the Old Whigs (Burke)
    See *An Appeal from the New, to the Old Whigs in Consequence of Some Late Discussions in Parliament, Relative to the Reflections on the French Revolution*

The Appearance of Our Lady to Thomas (York) **34**:343

The Appearance to Mary Magdalen (N-Town)

34:172, 199

The Appearance to the Three Maries (N-Town) **34**:172, 199, 223

Appearance to Two Disciples (Chester) **34**:116

Appel à toutes les nations de l'Europe (Voltaire) **14**:353

Appellation of John Knox (Knox)
See *Appellation to the Nobility and Estates of Scotland*

Appellation to the Nobility and Estates of Scotland (Knox) **37**:199, 203, 212, 218, 223, 225-27, 236-40

Appius and Virginia (Dennis) **11**:9, 12

Appius and Virginia (Webster) **33**:338-40

Applause (Boswell) **50**:31, 35

"Appleton House" (Marvell)
See "Upon Appleton House"

"Appologie for the ill success of his enterprise to Guiana" (Raleigh) **31**:272

"The Appology" (Winchilsea) **3**:446

The Apprentice's Vade Mecum (Richardson) **1**:416, 418; **44**:245

"L'apprentie coquette" (Marivaux) **4**:379

Det arabiske pulver (Holberg) **6**:277-78

"Aramantha" (Lovelace) **24**:334, 346-48, 352, 354

Araminta (Gay) **49**:33

"Arcades" (Milton) **9**:197, 202-03, 205

Arcadia **41**:139

Arcadia (Sannazaro) **8**:322, 326-28, 330-33, 336-37

Arcadia (Sidney)
See *The Countess of Pembroke's Arcadia*

The Arcadia (Vega)
See *Arcadia*

Arcadia (Vega) **23**:339, 374

Arcadia Reformed (Daniel)
See *The Queens Arcadia, A Pastoral Traj-Comedy*

Archidoxa (Paracelsus) **14**:198, 200

Archidoxis magica (Paracelsus)
See *Archidoxa*

"Ardelia's Answer to Ephelia" (Winchilsea) **3**:449, 451, 456

Arenal de Sevilla (Vega) **23**:359

Areopagitica (Milton) **9**:191, 195-6, 223-4, 249-57; **43**:357, 383, 405-7, 421

Argel fingido y renegado de amor (Vega) **23**:393

An Argument against Abolishing Christianity (Swift) **1**:460, 509, 519

"The Argument of His Book" (Herrick) **13**:336, 340, 346, 349, 351, 361, 363-64, 374-76, 391, 393, 398

Argumentum de summo bono (Ficino) **12**:168

Aristomène (Marmontel) **2**:213, 216

"Aristomenes" (Winchilsea) **3**:440

Arleouin Colombine (Lesage) **28**:205

Arlequin baron allemand, ou Le Triomphe de la Folie (Lesage) **28**:200

Arlequin colonel (Lesage) **28**:199

Arlequin colonel (Lesage)
See *La Tontine*

Arlequin empereur dans la lune (Lesage) **28**:200

Arlequin Endymion (Lesage) **28**:205

Arlequin Hulla (Lesage) **28**:205

Arlequin invisible (Lesage) **28**:204

Arlequin Mahomet (Lesage) **28**:205

Arlequin poli par l'amour (Marivaux) **4**:365-66, 368, 376

Arlequin, roi de Serendib (Lesage) **28**:205, 210

Arlequin, roi des Ogres (Lesage) **28**:205

Las Armas de la hermosura (Calderon de la Barca) **23**:11

The Arrogant Spaniard (Vega)
See *Not So Stupid After All*

"Ars memoriae" (Bruno) **27**:66-67

Arsace et Isménie (Montesquieu) **7**:320

Arstis Logicae Plenior Institutio (Milton) **43**:397

"Art above Nature, to Julia" (Herrick) **13**:351, 369, 393

Art de penser (Condillac) **26**:10, 28-9, 54

L'Art de Persuader (Pascal) **35**:340, 362

Art de raisonner (Condillac) **26**:7, 10, 28-9, 54

Art d'écrire (Condillac) **26**:10, 28-9, 54

Art of Comedy (Vega)
See *Arte nuevo de hacer comedias en este tiempo*

"Art of Conversation" (Montaigne)
See "De l'art de conferer"

"The Art of Memory" (Bruno)
See "Ars memoriae"

The Art of Poetry (Boileau-Despreaux)
See *L'art poétique*

"The Art of Procuring Pleasant Dreams" (Franklin) **25**:141

Art of Reasoning (Condillac)
See *Art de raisonner*

"The Art of Sinking in Poetry" (Pope)
See "Peri Bathous; or, The Art of Sinking in Poetry"

"The Art of the Paper War" (Hopkinson) **25**:271

Art of Thinking (Condillac)
See *Art de penser*

The Art of War (Machiavelli)
See *Libro della arte della guerra*

Art of Writing (Condillac)
See *Art d'écrire*

L'art poétique (Boileau-Despreaux) **3**:16, 22, 25-35, 39

Art Poétique (Ronsard)
See *L'abbrégé de l'art poétique françois*

Artamène; ou, Le Grand Cyrus (Marivaux) **4**:365-66, 368, 376

Arte de hacer Comedias (Vega)
See *Arte nuevo de hacer comedias en este tiempo*

El Arte de ingenio, tratado de la Agudeza (Gracian y Morales)
See *Agudeza y arte de ingenio*

Arte nuevo (Vega)
See *Arte nuevo de hacer comedias en este tiempo*

Arte nuevo de hacer comedias en este tiempo (Vega) **23**:338-40, 362-64, 383-94, 397-98, 401

De Arte Versificandi (Hutten) **16**:229

"Artem quaevis alit terra" (Erasmus) **16**:198

The Artful Widow (Goldoni)
See *La vedova scaltra*

"Articles of Belief and Acts of Religion" (Franklin) **25**:162, 175

"Articles proposed by the Earl of Warwick to the lords and council for their approbation, as preceptor to King Henry VI" **17**:436

Articles . . . to Stabliyshe Christen Quietnes (Henry VIII) **10**:129-30, 135

Articuli centum et sexaginta adversus huius tempestatis mathematicas atque philosophos (Bruno) **27**:123

"Artillerie" (Herbert) **24**:272-73

"Artillery" (Herbert)
See "Artillerie"

Arud risalesi (Babur) **18**:89-90

"As Love and I, Late Harbour'd in One Inne"
See "Sonnet LIX"

"As Spring the Winter Doth Succeed" (Bradstreet)

4:99

"As virtuous men pass mildly away" (Donne)
See "A Valediction: forbidding mourning"

"As Weary Pilgrim" (Bradstreet) **4**:98, 102, 108

"As you come from the holy land" (Raleigh) **39**:123

Ascencio Domini (Towneley) **34**:252, 262, 311

"Ascension" (Donne) **24**:167

The Ascension (Chester) **34**:115, 121, 125

"Ascension Day" (Vaughan) **27**:323, 340, 383

Ascension (N-Town) **34**:192

"The Ascension of Our Lord Jesus Christ" (Smart) **3**:378

The Ascension (Towneley)
See *Ascencio Domini* (Towneley)

"Ascension-Hymn" (Vaughan) **27**:323, 327

Ascent of Mount Carmel (John of the Cross)
See *Subida del Monte Carmelo*

"Asclepiads" (Sidney) **19**:326

The Ash Wednesday Supper (Bruno)
See *La cena de le ceneri*

Ash'i'atu 'l Lama'át (Jami) **9**:67

"L'asino d'oro" (Machiavelli) **8**:128, 135, 178-79

"Ask me no more where Jove bestows" (Carew) **13**:11, 20, 28-9, 58

"Aspiración" (Quevedo) **23**:178

"Aspiration" (Quevedo)
See "Aspiración"

"The Ass" (Vaughan) **27**:300, 315, 338, 340

The Ass of Silenius (Bruno) **27**:96

"Assaulted and Pursued Chastity" (Cavendish) **30**:186, 188-189

The Assayer (Galilei) **45**:219, 297-301, 303

Assertio septem sacramentorum adversus Martinum Lutherum haeresiarchon (Henry VIII) **10**:117-118, 120-22, 133-34, 138-39, 141-43, 146-47

An assertion of the Seven Sacraments, against Martin Luther (Henry VIII)
See *Assertio septem sacramentorum adversus Martinum Lutherum haeresiarchon*

The Assignation (Dryden) **3**:230

"The Ass's Skin" (Perrault)
See "Peau d'ane"

The Assumption of Mary (N-Town)
See *The Assumption of the Virgin* (N-Town)

Assumption of Our Lady (Chester)
See *Assumption of the Virgin* (Chester)

Assumption of the Virgin (Chester) **34**:123, 127-8, 130, 136

The Assumption of the Virgin (N-Town) **34**:169, 172-3, 187-90, 193, 199-200, 206-7, 216-17, 220, 240

The Assumption (Towneley) **34**:266

"Astrea Redux. A Poem on the Happy Restoration and Return of His Sacred Majesty Charles the Second" (Dryden) **3**:178, 223, 225-26; **21**:85

"Les Astres" (Ronsard) **6**:410, 422, 429

"Astrologer" (Butler) **16**:55

Astronomia magna, or the Whole Sagacious Philosophy of the Great and Small World (Paracelsus) **14**:199

Astronomia Nova: Physica Coelestis (Kepler) **45**:320-23, 325- 336-37, 339, 343-44, 346, 358, 360-62, 367-68

Astronomia pars optica (Kepler) **45**:337

Astronomiae instauratae mechanica (Brahe) **45**:80

Astronomiae instauratae progymnasmata (Brahe) **45**:4, 9, 46, 68

Astronomical Libra (Siguenza y Gongora)

See *Libra astronomica y philosophica*
"Astrophel: A Pastoral Elegy" (Spenser) **5**:312, 314, 354
Astrophel and Stella (Sidney) **19**:318-19, 329, 334, 345, 352, 354, 358, 360-61, 374-76, 391-97, 406, 409, 413-15, 421-22, 424; **39**:213, 214-23, 227-29, 233-37, 242, 247, 259-61, 267, 269, 279, 287-95
"At a Solemn Music" (Milton)
See "At a Solemn Music"
"At Roslin Inn" (Burns) **29**:59; **40**:100
Athaliah (Racine)
See *Athalie*
Athalie (Racine) **28**:295-97, 302, 305, 309, 311-13, 315-16, 344, 346, 349, 351-53, 355-58, 365, 371, 374, 378-79, 381
Athalie (Voltaire) **14**:354
Atheism Conquered (Campanella)
See *Atheismus triumphatus*
Atheismus triumphatus (Campanella) **32**:222-25, 227, 236
"The Atheist" (Donne) **10**:30
"The Atheist and the Acorn" (Winchilsea) **3**:451
Atom (Smollett)
See *The History and Adventures of an Atom*
Attila (Corneille) **28**:5, 16, 29, 33, 35, 37
"Attributes of the Supreme Being" (Smart) **3**:399
"Au beuf qui tout le jour" (Ronsard) **6**:433-34
"Au feu roi sur l'heureux succez du voyage de Sedan" (Malherbe) **5**:184
"Au prince de Vendôme" (Rousseau) **9**:340
"Au prince Eugêne de Savoie, après la paix de Passarowitz" (Rousseau) **9**:340, 344-45
"Au roi de la Grande-Bretagne" (Rousseau) **9**:344
"Au roi de Pologne" (Rousseau) **9**:344
Audiencias del rey Don Pedro (Vega) **23**:402
De augmentis scientiarum (Bacon) **18**:111, 117-18, 120, 126, 146, 152-53, 161-62, 168, 174, 178, 187, 193, 195, **32**:116, 139-40, 171
Aui maux raisonnables (Lesage) **28**:208
Aula (Hutten) **16**:239-41, 246
"The Auld Farmer's New Year Morning Saluta-tion" (Burns)
See "The Auld Farmer's New Year Morning Salutation"
"The Auld Farmer's New Year's Day Address to His Auld Mare Maggie" (Burns) **3**:57, 60, 64, 67, 87, 93; **29**:4-6, 29, 64; **40**:119
"Auld Lang Syne" (Burns) **3**:561, 62, 66, 78; **29**:93; **40**:96, 98
"Auld Lang Syne" (Ramsay) **29**:320
Auld Reikie (Fergusson) **29**:179, 181-84, 186-87
Aunswere to Frithes Letter agaynst the Blessed Sacramen of the Aulter (More) **10**:366, 398
Aureng-Zebe (Dryden) **3**:193, 222, 232-33; **21**:72, 75, 88, 120
La Aurora en Copacavana (Calderon de la Barca) **23**:19, 22
Aussichten zu einer Experimentalseelenlehre (Moritz) **2**:235-36
The Austrian in Love; or, The Love and Life Story of Sorona, Incomparable in Virtues and Beauty (Beer)
See *Der verliebte Österreicher*
Aut regem aut fatuum (Erasmus) **16**:198
"The Author" (Churchill) **3**:150-51, 155-56, 159-60, 163
"The Author to her Book" (Bradstreet) **4**:107, 112; **30**:130-1, 140-1
"Author to His Book" (Beer) **5**:59
"The Author upon Himself" (Swift) **1**:482, 523
The Author's Apology for Heroic Poetry and Po-etic License (Dryden) **3**:197, 236, 238;

21:66, 85
The Authors Dreame to the Ladie Marie the Countesse Dowager of Pembroke (Lanyer) **30**:251
"The Author's Earnest Cry and Prayer" (Burns) **40**:80
The Author's Farce and the Pleasures of the Town (Fielding) **1**:203, 219; **46**:55, 94-5, 102, 106, 113, 161
"The Author's Life" (Fergusson) **29**:194
"Authors Motto" (Crashaw) **24**:75
Autobiography (Cellini)
See *Vita di Benvenuto Cellini*
Autobiography (Fanshawe)
See *Memoirs of Lady Fanshawe*
The Autobiography and Correspondence of Mary Granville (Mrs. Delany) (Delany) **12**:135, 140, 143, 148-51, 154
The Autobiography of Benjamin Franklin (Franklin) **25**:113, 117-24, 129-30, 132, 134, 138, 144-49, 151-53, 155, 157, 161-63, 166, 168-73, 175-76, 179-83, 185-86, 188-89
The Autobiography of Venerable Marie of the Incarnation (Marie de l'Incarnation)
See *Relation autobiographique*
Autres balades (Christine de Pizan) **9**:41
"Autumn" (Pope) **3**:334
Autumn (Thomson) **16**:363-64, 372-74, 380-84, 395, 402-05, 411-13, 415, 419, 424-26, 432; **29**:378-79, 381, 384-85, 387, 393-94, 403, 415; **40**:272-73, 276, 281-82, 285-87, 290-91, 295, 300, 304-05, 307-09, 321, 323
"Aux princes chrétiens" (Rousseau) **9**:340, 344
"Aux Suisses" (Rousseau) **9**:344
Les Avantages que l'établissement du christianisme a procurÉs au genre humain (Turgot) **26**:348, 370
"Avant-entrée" (Ronsard) **6**:431
L'avare (Moliere) **10**:268, 271, 280, 283-85, 287, 290-91, 293, 297, 313, 341, 343, 345-46; **28**:245, 255-56, 258-59, 261, 266, 270, 275
Aventure indienne (Voltaire) **14**:346
Les aventures de Monsieur Robert Chevalier (Lesage) **2**:176, 182; **28**:200, 203-07, 210-11
Avision (Christine de Pizan)
See *Lavision-Christine*
Le avventure della villeggiatura (Goldoni) **4**:265-66
L'avvocato veneziano (Goldoni) **4**:262
"Away, away, my cares" (Juana Ines de la Cruz)
See "Afuera, afuera, ansias mías"
"Ay waukin O" (Burns) **29**:52
"B—, A Song" (Boswell) **4**:52, 61
B. D. S. Opera posthuma (Spinoza) **9**:397
Bababec (Voltaire) **14**:346
The Babbling Barber (Holberg)
See *Mester Gert Westphaler; eller, Den meget talende barbeer*
The Babur-nama (Babur) **18**:84-96
"Babylon" (Fergusson) **29**:237
The Babylonian Captivity of the Chruch (Luther)
See *De captivitate Babylonica ecclesiae praeludium*
Le bachelier de Salamanque (Lesage) **2**:177, 179, 182, 184, 202; **28**:200, 204
The Bachelor of Salamanca (Lesage)
See *Le bachelier de Salamanque*
Bachelor's Banquet (Dekker) **22**:96, 112
"The Bad Season Makes the Poet Sad" (Herrick) **13**:365, 383, 392-93, 396
Badman (Bunyan)

See *The Life and Death of Mr. Badman*
"The Bag" (Herbert) **24**:273
"The Bag Wig and the Tobacco-pipe" (Smart) **3**:366
The Bagatelles (Franklin) **25**:112, 115, 134, 140-44, 155
Baháristán (Jami) **9**:61, 63-4, 67-8, 70-1
"Bai Qiulian" (P'u Sung-ling) **49**:306
"Les bains de Thomery" (Rousseau) **9**:343
Bajazet (Racine) **28**:340-41, 346, 362, 366, 369-70, 373-74, 376, 383-84
Balaam and Balaak (Chester) **34**:118, 123, 129, 136
The Ball **22**:13
"Ballad of Down-Hall" (Prior) **4**:461, 464, 467
"A Ballad on Ale" (Gay) **49**:4, 7
Ballad on Ale (Gay) **49**:6
Ballad on the Want of Corn **41**:74, 79
"Ballad Second the Election" (Burns) **29**:89
"A Banker" (Butler) **16**:55
The Bankette of Sapience (Elyot) **11**:62, 73, 81, 83, 90
"The Banks of Doon" (Burns) **40**:63, 97
"The Banner, or Homage from Prussia" (Kochanowski)
See "Proporzec albo Hold Pruski"
"Bannocks o' Barley Meal" (Burns) **3**:84
Banns (N-Town) **34**:198
Los baños de Argel (Cervantes) **6**:180-81; **23**:100, 121
"The Banquet" (Herbert) **24**:274
Banquet (Chapman)
See *Ovid's Banquet of Sense, A Coronet for My Mistress Philosophy*
The Banquet of Sapience (Elyot)
See *The Bankette of Sapience*
"A Bao" (P'u Sung-ling) **49**:313
The Baptism (N-Town) **34**:188, 199
Baptistes: sive Calumnia, tragoedia, auctore Georgio Buchanano Scoto (Buchanan) **4**:120, 133-34, 136-37
"La barbe bleue" (Perrault) **2**:254, 258, 260, 267, 280, 284
"The Bard" (Gray) **4**:280, 282-85, 288-89, 292-93, 300-02, 309-10, 312-15, 317-18, 321, 333; **40**:199-200, 212, 216-20, 226, 231-32, 235, 238, 240-43
"A Bard's Epitaph" (Burns) **3**:67
"Barrenness" (Parnell) **3**:252
The Barrenness of Anna (N-Town) **34**:170, 199
The Barrons Wars in the Raigne of Edward the Second **8**:8, 10-11, 14-15, 19-20, 27, 33
Barselstuen (Holberg) **6**:277
Bartholomew Fair (Jonson) **6**:292, 304-06, 313-14, 320, 323-24, 330-31, 334-36, 340, 343; **33**:106, 113, 115, 137, 155, 157-61, 163, 166-67
Der Bart-Krieg (Grimmelshausen) **6**:247
Le baruffe chiozzotte (Goldoni) **4**:257, 264, 266, 275
"The Bashful Lover" (Thomson) **16**:427
The Basque Impostor (Cervantes) **6**:190-91
La batalla de honor (Vega) **23**:393, 402
The Battaile of Agincourt **8**:8, 14-18, 23, 25-7, 30, 33, 41-2, 44-5
"Battle of Hastings" (Chatterton) **3**:118, 120, 126, 128, 135
The Battle of Honor (Vega)
See *La batalla de honor*
"The Battle of Ramellies" (Dennis)
See "The Battle of Ramilla: or, The Power of Union"
"The Battle of Ramilla: or, The Power of Union"

(Dennis) **11**:13, 15, 26, 49

The Battle of the Cats (Vega)
　See *Gatomaquia*

"The Battle of the Frogs and Mice" (Parnell) **3**:251-54

"The Battle of the Kegs" (Hopkinson) **25**:245, 251-52, 255, 259, 261, 265, 272

The Beard War (Grimmelshausen)
　See *Der Bart-Krieg*

"Beau" (Marmontel) **2**:223

The Beau Defeated; or, The Lucky Younger Brother (Pix) **8**:262, 268-69, 272-73, 276

Beautie (Jonson)
　See *Masque of Beauty*

The Beauties of English Poetry (Goldsmith) **2**:80

"A Beautiful Young Nymph Going to Bed. Written for the Honour of the Fair Sex" (Swift) **1**:453, 483

"A beautifull Mistris" (Carew) **13**:34

The Beaux' Stratagem (Farquhar) **21**:127-29, 133-35, 138-39, 143-47, 149-54, 158-61, 167-72, 174-76, 178-79

"The Bee" (Vaughan) **27**:297, 306

"Before a Journey" (Andrewes) **5**:35

"Before the Birth of one of her Children" (Bradstreet) **4**:107; **30**:126, 143-4

"The Beggar to Mab, the Fairies' Queen" (Herrick) **13**:368

Beggar's Bush (Fletcher) **33**:60

The Beggar's Opera (Gay) **49**:5, 12-14, 16-23, 25, 28, 30, 70-71, 73 75-78, 88-89, 91-92, 98-104, 107-114, 118, 121-125, 147-148, 155, 160-161, 165, 171-179, 182-183, 186-187

"Begging" (Vaughan) **27**:339

Behemoth or a Dialogue on the Civil Wars (Hobbes) **36**:132-33, 139

Behemoth; or the Long Parliament (Hobbes)
　See *Behemoth or a Dialogue on the Civil Wars*

"Being once blind, his request to Bianncha" (Herrick) **13**:398

Beiträge zur Historie und Aufnahme des Theaters (Lessing) **8**:84, 111-12

Beiträge zur Philosophie des Lebens aus dem Tagebuch eines Freimaurers (Moritz) **2**:230, 241-42

"Bel Aubepin" (Ronsard) **6**:425-26

Belardo furioso (Vega) **23**:393

Bélisaire (Marmontel) **2**:208, 213-14, 217-20

Belisario (Goldoni) **4**:249

Belisarius (Marmontel)
　See *Bélisaire*

Bell in Campo (Cavendish) **30**:189, 217, 226, 229

Bell of Arragon (Collins) **40**:147

"Bella Bona Roba" (Lovelace) **24**:306, 326

La bella malmaridada (Vega) **23**:390

"La belle au bois dormant" (Perrault) **2**:253-54, 260-61, 266, 280-84

The Bellman of London, or Roque's Horn-Book (Dekker) **22**:97, 101, 121

Bellum Erasmi (Erasmus) **16**:159

Belshazzar's Feast (Calderon de la Barca) **23**:9-10, 64

"Beneath a Weeping Willow's Shade" (Hopkinson) **25**:250

"Béni soit le Dieu des armées" (Rousseau) **9**:338

Berenice (Racine)
　See *Bérénice*

Bérénice (Racine) **28**:293, 295, 300, 305-06, 308-09, 312, 315-16, 339-41, 344, 346, 349-50, 353, 358, 362, 364, 370, 376, 378, 381, 383-84

"Bermudas" (Marvell) **4**:400, 403-04, 410, 412, 441-42; **43**:300

"Bessy Bell and Mary Gray" (Ramsay) **29**:309, 320, 329

Bestia Civitatis (Beer) **5**:56

The Bethlehem Shepherds (Vega)
　See *Los Pastores de Belen*

The Betrayal of Christ (Chester)
　See *The Last Supper* (Chester)

The Betrothal of Mary (N-Town) **34**:170, 174, 181-2, 188, 192, 202

Betsy Thoughtless (Haywood)
　See *The History of Sir Francis Drake*

"A Better Answer" (Prior) **4**:466

Beware of Smooth Water (Calderon de la Barca)
　See *Guárdate del agua mensa*

"Beyond the Veil" (Vaughan) **27**:293

Biathanatos. A declaration of that paradoxe, or thesis, that self-homicide is not so naturally sinne, that it may never be otherwise. (Donne) **10**:11, 36, 77-9; **24**:176-79, 184, 186-87

La Bible enfin expliquée (Voltaire) **14**:370

Biblia Americana (Mather) **38**:161, 203

Bibliotheca (Elyot)
　See *The Dictionary*

Bibliotheca Eliotae (Elyot)
　See *The Dictionary*

"Bid me to live" (Herrick) **13**:332, 338

Les Bijoux indescrets (Diderot) **26**:104, 112, 129, 143, 161, 166

Le bilboquet (Marivaux) **4**:378

"The Bird" (Winchilsea) **3**:445, 451, 454

"The Bird" (Vaughan) **27**:290, 300, 315, 337, 339-40

"The Birds, the Beasts, and the Bat" (Hopkinson) **25**:247

"The Birks of Aberfeldy" (Burns) **40**:64

The Birth of Christ (N-Town) **34**:179, 184, 188

"Birth of Love" (Jonson) **6**:326

The Birth of Orson and Valentine (Vega)
　See *El nacimiento de Ursón y Valentín*

"The Birth of the Squire" (Gay) **49**:26

Bishops' Book (Henry VIII)
　See *The Institution of a Christen Man*

The Bitter (Rowe) **8**:292, 299, 310-12

"A Bitter Fate" (Chulkov)
　See "Gor'kaia uchast"

"Bitter-Sweet" (Herbert) **24**:272

La Bizarrias de Belisa (Vega) **23**:346

"Black Beginnings" (Wheatley) **50**:15

"The Black Lady" (Behn) **42**:119

"A Black Patch on Lucasta's Face" (Lovelace) **24**:329

"The Blacke Bookes Messenger, laying open the Life and Death of Ned Browne" **41** :**45, 150, 152, 155-56, 181-82**

Blacknesse (Jonson)
　See *Masque of Blacknesse*

Blast The First Blast to awake Women degenerate (Knox)
　See *First Blast of the Trumpet against the Monstrous Regiment of Women*

The Blazing World (Cavendish)
　See *The Description of a New Blazing World*

"The Bleeding Heart" (Crashaw) 24:13

Blenheim (Lyttelton) **10**:196, 198, 205, 215

Blenheim Castle (Lyttelton)
　See *Blenheim*

"Blessed be the paps Thou has sucked" (Crashaw) **24**:

The Blind Beggar of Alexandria (Chapman) **22**:10, 12, 60-1

The Bloody Brother, or Rollo Duke of Normandy (Fletcher) **33**:58

"The Blossome" (Donne) **10**:13, 36, 77-9; **24**:155, 183

"Bluebeard" (Perrault)
　See "La barbe bleue"

Blunt oder der Gast (Moritz) **2**:228, 242

Blurt, Master Constable (Dekker) **22**:132

Blurt, Master Constable (Middleton) **33**:261

The Boasting Soldier (Holberg) **6**:259

"Boatmen on Old Dragon River" (P'u Sung-ling) **3**:345

"The Bob of Dunblane" (Ramsay) **29**:320

La boba para los otros y discreta para sí (Vega) **23**:393

Le Bocage (Ronsard) **6**:410, 429, 431, 434

"Body and Soul" (More) **9**:298

The Body of Polycye (Christine de Pizan)
　See *Le livre du corps de policie*

Boece (Chaucer) **17**:214

La Boite de Pandore (Lesage) **28**:208, 211

The Boke named the Governour (Elyot)
　See *The Boke of the Governor, devised by Sir Thomas Elyot*

The Boke of the Cyte of Ladies (Christine de Pizan)
　See *Le livre de la cité des dames*

The Boke of the Governor, devised by Sir Thomas Elyot (Elyot) **11**:58-64, 68-9, 71-6, 78-91

"Boldness in Love" (Carew) **13**:15

Bon Ton; or, High Life Below Stairs (Garrick) **15**:91, 93, 101-03, 121

The Bondage of the Will (Luther)
　See *De servo arbitrio*

Bonduca (Fletcher) **33**:49, 57-8

"Bonie Dundee" (Burns) **29**:55

"The Bonie Moor-Hen" (Burns) **29**:21

"Bonie Wee Thing" (Burns) **40**:98

Bonifacius (Mather) **38**:167, 197-205, 226-33

"The Bonniest Lass" (Burns) **3**:98

"Bonny Doon" (Burns) **3**:62, 78

"Bonny Heck" (Fergusson) **29**:203

"Bonny Kate" (Ramsay) **29**:309

Bon-Sens (Holbach) **14**:152, 154, 156-58, 168

"The Book" (Vaughan) **27**:300, 337, 389

Book against the Barbarians (Erasmus)
　See *Antibarbari*

A Book for Boys and Girls; or, Country Rhimes for Children (Bunyan) **4**:170, 172, 182

Book for the Silk Weavers **41**:79

Book of Discipline (Knox) **37**:214-16

Book of Essays (Collier) (Collier)
　See *Essays upon Several Moral Subjects*

Book of Fame (Chaucer)
　See *House of Fame*

The Book of Fayttes of Armes and of Chyvalrye (Christine de Pizan)
　See *Le livre des faits d'armes et de chevalerie*

Book of foundations (Teresa de Jesus)
　See *Libro de las fundaciones de Santa Teresa de Jesús*

The Book of King Arthur and His Noble Knights of the Round Table (Malory)
　See *Morte Darthur*

The Book of Margery Kempe (Kempe) **6**:388-89, 391-93, 395-96, 398-400

The Book of Martyrs (Foxe)
　See *Actes and Monumentes of these latter perilous dayes touching matters of the Church*

Book of Saint Valentines Day of the Parlement of Briddes (Chaucer)
　See *Parlement of Foules*

Book of the Beatific Life (Paracelsus)
　See *Vita beata*

The Book of the Courtier (Castiglione)
See *Il libro del cortegiano*
Book of the Duchess (Chaucer) **17**:45, 58, 72-9,
91, 97, 105-06, 112-13, 178, 189
Book of the Duchesse (Chaucer)
See *Book of the Duchess*
The Book of the Duke of True Lovers (Christine
de Pizan)
See *Le livre du duc des vrais amans*
Book of the Five and Twenty Ladies (Chaucer)
See *Legend of Good Women*
The book of The Gentle Craft **41**:73, 75, 77-78,
81, 93, 97-98, 106, 111, 113-15, 117, 120,
127, 131
Book of the Governor (Elyot)
See *The Boke of the Governor, devised by Sir
Thomas Elyot*
Book of the Leon (Chaucer)
See *The Book of the Lion*
The Book of the Lion (Chaucer) **17**:45, 216
Book of the Reed (Jami)
See *Nay-namá*
Book of Troilus (Chaucer)
See *Troilus and Criseyde*
Books of Hospitals (Paracelsus) **14**:198
Books of the Greater Surgery (Paracelsus) **14**:199
"Bookworm" (Parnell) **3**:252
"The Bookworm" (P'u Sung-ling)
See "Shu chi"
The Bores (Moliere)
See *Les fâcheux*
"Borne I Was to meet with Age" (Herrick) **13**:341
"Boswell: A Song" (Boswell)
See "B—, A Song"
Boswell for the Defence (Boswell) **50**:31
Boswell in Extremes (Boswell) **50**:18, 31
Boswell in Holland (Boswell) **50**:31
Boswell on the Grand Tour (Boswell) **4**:64
Boswell's London Journal (Boswell) **4**:55, 57-8,
62-3, 71-2; **50**:11, 31
La bottega del caffè (Goldoni) **4**:264, 266
Le bourgeois gentilhomme (Moliere) **10**:270,
277-78, 280, 282-83, 286, 288, 290-93, 313;
28:229, 243-44, 246-49, 252-53, 255, 257,
259-62, 265-66, 275
The Bourgeois Gentleman (Moliere)
See *Le bourgeois gentilhomme*
Le bourru bienfaisant (Goldoni) **4**:252-53, 255,
268
"The Boy's Piety" (Erasmus) **16**:142
A Brand Pluck'd Out of the Burning (Mather)
38:178
The Brazen Serpent (Calderon de la Barca) **23**:9
"Breake of Day" (Donne) **10**:32; **24**:151, 154
Breaths of Familiarity (Jami)
See *Nafah al-uns*
Brevísima relación de la destrucción de las Indias
(Las Casas) **31**:174-75, 177-82, 190, 196,
202-7, 218
*A Brief and Plain Scheme how the English Colo-
nies in the North Parts of America...may be
made more useful to the Crown and one
another's Peace and Safety with a Univer-
sal Concurrence* (Penn) **25**:343, 346
A Brief Answer to a False and Foolish Libel (Penn)
25:289
*Brief Architecture of the Art of Lully with its
Completion* (Bruno)
See *De compendiosa architectura et
complemento artis Lullii*
*A Brief Character of the Low Countries under the
States* (Howell) **13**:424
A Brief Christian Introduction (Zwingli) **37**:368-

69, 371-72
"A Brief Description or Character...of the
Phanatiques" (Butler) **43**:78-9
*A Brief Explanation of a Late Pamphlet Entitled
"The Shortest Way with the Dissenters"*
(Defoe) **1**:161
A Brief History of Moscovia (Milton) **43**:397
*Brief Notes upon a Late Sermon, Titl'd, "The Fear
of God and the King"* (Milton) **9**:161;
43:338-40
Briefe, die neueste Litteratur betreffend (Lessing)
8:101
Der briefwechsel des Spinoza (Spinoza)
See *Correspondence*
Brieve Instruction (Calvin) **37**:134
"The Brigs of Ayr" (Burns) **3**:52, 67, 71; **29**:29,
65, 90; **40**:109
"Bristowe Tragedie; or, The Dethe of Syr Charles
Bawdin" (Chatterton) **3**:119, 126, 130, 135
"Britain" (Thomson) **16**:384
Britannia. A Poem (Thomson) **16**:375, 384, 393,
395, 423; **29**:368-69, 436
*Britannia Rediviva: A Poem on the Birth of the
Prince* (Dryden) **21**:65, 82, 87
Britannia Triumphans (Davenant) **13**:189
"Britannia Triumphans: or a Poem on the Battle
of Blenheim" (Dennis)
See "Britannia Triumphans: or, The Empire
Sav'd, and Europe Delivered"
"Britannia Triumphans: or, The Empire Sav'd, and
Europe Delivered" (Dennis) **11**:13, 15, 26,
48
Britannia's Honour (Dekker) **22**:95, 130
Britannicus (Racine) **28**:294-95, 309, 317, 327-
28, 330-31, 339, 343, 346, 348-50, 356, 365,
368-70, 372, 376, 379, 381
"The British Church" (Herbert) **24**:252, 254-55
"The British Church" (Vaughan) **27**:371
"British Debts Case" (Henry) **25**:198, 206, 232
The British Recluse (Haywood) **1**:283; **44**:142,
157
"The Brocaded Gown and the Linen Rag" (Smart)
3:366
"The broken heart" (Donne) **10**:82; **24**:150, 183
"Brose and Butter" (Burns) **3**:100
"The Brothers" (Young) **3**:467, 487-88; **40**:334
The Brothers at Cross-purposes (Holberg) **6**:259
"Bruar Water" (Burns) **3**:85
Bruder Blau-Mantel (Beer)
See *Der kurtzweilige Bruder Blau-Mantel*
"Brutus" (Cowley) **43**:173, 180, 187
Brutus (Voltaire) **14**:397
Das Buch Paragranum (Paracelsus) **14**:194, 196-
99
The Buffeting (Towneley)
See *Coliphizacio* (Towneley)
"The Bugs" (Fergusson) **29**:209, 231
Building of Noah's Ark (York) **34**:362, 369
The Bull Killer (Hutten) **16**:225-27, 234, 239-
41, 246
Bulla (Hutten)
See *The Bull Killer*
*Bulla Decimi Leonis, contra errores Martini
Lutheri* (Hutten) **16**:233
"Bumpkin or Country Squire" (Butler) **16**:50
"The Bunch of Grapes" (Herbert) **24**:247, 279
La buona famiglia (Goldoni) **4**:251, 260, 265
La buona madre (Goldoni) **4**:257
La buona moglie (Goldoni) **4**:265-66
Il burbero benefico (Goldoni)
See *Le bourru bienfaisant*
"The Bureau of Frauds" (P'u Sung-ling)
See "K'ao-pi ssu"

The Burial and the Guarding of the Sepulchre (N-
Town) **34**:172, 186-7
"A Burlesque Elegy on the Amputation of a
Student's Hair, before his Orders"
(Fergusson) **29**:198, 219
"Burlesque Lament for Creech" (Burns) **3**:86
El Buscón (Quevedo)
See *Historia de la Buscón*
"Busie old foole" (Donne)
See "The Sunne Rising"
"Busiris, King of Egypt" (Young) **3**:467, 485,
487-88
Bussy D'Ambois (Chapman)
See *The Tragedy of Bussy D'Ambois*
The Busy Idler (Schlegel)
See *Der geschäftige Müssiggänger*
The Busy-Body Papers (Franklin) **25**:134, 138-
40
"But now they have seen and hated" (Crashaw)
24:
"Buxom Joan of Deptford" (Congreve) **5**:85
"By Night When Others Soundly Slept"
(Bradstreet) **30**:148
"By the Delicious Warmness of Thy Mouth"
(Ramsay) **29**:330, 341, 345
*C. C. Taciti historiarum et annaliem libri qui
exstant* (Lipsius) **16**:257, 265, 269, 274
"Ca' the Yowes to the Knowes" (Burns) **3**:81;
29:35, 40; **40**:97
Cabala del cavallo Pegaseo (Bruno) **27**:96-97,
104
El cabalero de Olmedo (Vega) **23**:362, 365, 368,
372, 391, 393
El caballero bobo (Castro) **19**:8
Los cabellos de Absalón (Calderon de la Barca)
23:11, 20-1
Le cabinet du philosophe (Marivaux) **4**:359, 376,
378, 380
Las cadenas del demonio (Calderon de la Barca)
23:17-19, 22
"Cadenus and Vanessa" (Swift) **1**:481
Caesar and Pompey (Chapman)
See *The Tragedy of Caesar and Pompey*
Caesar Augustus (Towneley) **34**:250, 267, 325
"'Caesar-Brutus' Speech" (Henry) **25**:222-23,
225, 228
Caesar's Commentaries (Lipsius) **16**:276
Caesar's Fall (Dekker) **22**:106
Le café (Rousseau) **9**:337
Cain and Abel (Chester)
See *Creation and Fall* (Chester)
Cain and Abel (N-Town) **34**:172, 174, 181, 188,
200, 208
Cain (Towneley) **34**:389
The Calender (Spenser)
See *The Shepheardes Calender: Conteyning
Twelve <AElig>glogues Proportionable to
the Twelve Monethes*
"The Call" (Herbert) **24**:274
"The Call of Blood" (Cervantes)
See "La fuerza de la sangre"
"Caller Oysters" (Fergusson) **29**:170, 178, 189,
201, 205, 218, 238
"Caller Water" (Fergusson) **29**:177, 189, 192,
206, 216-17
"Calling Lucasta from Her Retirement" (Lovelace)
24:304, 346
"The Calm" (Donne) **10**:4, 97
"Camelion" (Prior)
See "The Chameleon"
Camino de perfección (Teresa de Jesus) **18**:389,
391, 392, 400
"A Camp Ballad" (Hopkinson) **25**:272

The Campaign (Addison)　**18**:6, 16, 19, 30-2
Campaspe (Lyly)　**41**:222,273
Il campiello (Goldoni)　**4**:251, 264, 267
Canaans Calamitie　**41**:75
Canaan's Calamitie (Dekker)　**22**:104
"Cancion entre el Alma y el Esposo" (John of the Cross)　**18**:202
"Canciones de la Esposa" (John of the Cross)　**18**:203, 223
"The Candidate" (Churchill)　**3**:143-44, 150, 152, 154-55, 158, 160, 162-63, 167-70
"The Candidate" (Gray)　**4**:312
The Candidates (Munford)
　　See *The Candidates; or, The Humors of a Virginia Election*
The Candidates; or, The Humors of a Virginia Election (Munford)　**5**:189-92, 195-97
Candide; or, Optimism (Voltaire)
　　See *Candide; ou, L'optimisme*
Candide; ou, L'optimisme (Voltaire)　**14**:322, 325, 328, 334, 338, 341-42, 344-46, 353-54, 358-59, 361, 364, 366-67, 373, 378-82, 386-92, 398, 402
"Candidus" (More)
　　See "To Candidus: How to Choose a Wife"
"The Canongate Playhouse in Ruins: A Burlesque Poem" (Fergusson)　**29**:201, 219, 222
"The Canonization" (Donne)　**10**:13, 32-3, 36, 49, 58-61, 103; **24**:153-54, 195-96
"Canon's Yeoman's Prologue" (Chaucer)　**17**:202
"Canon's Yeoman's Tale" (Chaucer)　**17**:66, 202, 205
Canterburie-Tales (Chaucer)
　　See *Canterbury Tales*
Canterbury Tales (Chaucer)　**17**:45, 47-50, 57-8, 60, 66-9, 75, 84, 87, 89-90, 98, 105, 112, 121-23, 136, 142, 146-47, 162, 167, 172-80, 183-84, 189, 195-96, 198, 200-02, 204-06, 209-10, 212-18, 220-21, 224-25, 230-33, 236-38, 240-44
La Cantica (Campanella)　**32**:243
"Canticle to Bacchus" (Herrick)　**13**:327
"Cántico Espiritual" (John of the Cross)　**18**:212-15, 219, 221-24, 232-34
Cántico Espiritual (John of the Cross)　**18**:206, 213, 229, 230, 234
"Cantos of Mutabilitie" (Spenser)　**39**:343
Cantus circaeus (Bruno)　**27**:67, 122
Canut (Schlegel)　**5**:273, 281, 283-86, 289
Canut, ein Trauerspiel (Schlegel)
　　See *Canut*
Capcio (Towneley)　**34**:53
Capitoli (Aretino)　**12**:31
Capricci (Aretino)　**12**:20
Le capricieux (Rousseau)　**9**:337-38
The Captain (Fletcher)　**33**:91
Captain Carleton (Defoe)
　　See *The Military Memoirs of Captain Carleton*
"Captain Grose" (Burns)
　　See "On the Late Captain Grose's Peregrinations Thro' Scotland"
Captain Singleton (Defoe)
　　See *The Life, Adventures, and Pyracies of the Famous Captain Singleton*
"The Captivated Bee" (Herrick)　**13**:367
The Captives (Gay)　**49**:89, 114, 121, 123, 173
The Captivity (Goldsmith)　**2**:104
The Capture (Towneley)　**34**:268
Caractères (La Bruyere)
　　See *The Characters; or, Manners of the Age*
"Caravellers and Peyncters" (Chatterton)　**3**:135
La Carbonera (Vega)　**23**:393, 402
The Card of Fancy　**41**:172-74, 176, 178

"Cardoness" (Burns)　**3**:86
"Care and Generosity" (Smart)　**3**:366
A Careful and Strict Enquiry into the Modern Prevailing Notions of That Freedom of Will, Which Is Supposed to Be Essential to Moral Agency, Vertue and Vice, Reward and Punishment, Praise and Blame (Edwards)　**7**:91-2, 95-6, 99, 101-03, 118, 121, 124, 126-27
"The Carle He Came O'er the Croft" (Ramsay)　**29**:330
"The Carle o'Kellyburn Braes" (Burns)　**40**:97
Carlos el perseguido (Vega)　**23**:390
Carmen Deo Nostro (Crashaw)　**24**:44, 68
"Carmen Seculare for the Year 1700" (Prior)　**4**:454-55, 459, 461, 465, 475
"Caro m' è 'l sonno, e più l' esser di sasso" (Michelangelo)　**12**:314
"Carol to St. Peter" (Juana Ines de la Cruz)　**5**:146
"Carrion Comfort" (Herbert)　**24**:229
"Carta del Rey don Fernando el Católico al Primer Virrey de Nápoles" (Quevedo)　**23**:169
Cartas de relación de la conquista de Méjico (CORTES)　**31**:52-88
"Carte de tendre" (Scudery)
　　See *Clélie: Histoire romaine*
"The Carthusian" (Erasmus)　**16**:119, 195
Casa con dos puertas, mala es de guardar (Calderon de la Barca)　**23**:52-7, 65-8
La casa de los celos (Cervantes)　**6**:180; **23**:101-02
La casa nova (Goldoni)　**4**:257, 264, 266
"El casamiento engañoso" (Cervantes)　**6**:171-73; **23**:95, 97, 99, 144
The Case is Altered (Jonson)　**6**:304; **33**:117, 132, 150, 152
"The Case of Conscience" (Burns)　**3**:97-8
Cases of Conscience Concerning Evil Spirits (Mather)　**38**:259, 265-8, 288-9, 295, 302-4, 311-15, 317-23
La cassaria (Ariosto)　**6**:59-61
"Cassinus and Peter, a Tragic Elegy" (Swift)　**1**:461, 483-84, 502-03, 509-10
Castel of Health (Elyot)
　　See *The Castel of Helth*
The Castel of Helth (Elyot)　**11**:58, 60, 62-3, 73, 83
Castelvines y Monteses (Vega)　**23**:351, 354
El castigo (Vega)
　　See *El castigo sin venganza*
El castigo del discreto (Vega)　**23**:390
El castigo sin venganza (Vega)　**23**:364-65, 369-70, 391-96, 398
Castillo interior, o las moradas (Teresa de Jesus)　**18**:389, 391-94, 396-99, 400, 402-05, 409
"The Castle Barber's Soliloquy" (Warton)　**15**:462
Castle Le Chareau d'Otranto Otranto (Walpole)
　　See *The Castle of Otranto*
The Castle of Health (Elyot)
　　See *The Castel of Helth*
The Castle of Indolence: an Allegorical Poem. Written in Immitation of Spenser (Thomson)　**16**:367-68, 370, 376-79, 382, 384, 387-88, 392, 395, 398, 406, 416, 418-19, 423-24, 426, 432; **29**:401, 405-07, 409-10, 414, 436-39, 441-43, 445-46, 448; **40**:267-71, 273-74, 307-08, 311-12, 315-16
The Castle of Otranto (Walpole)　**2**:447-52, 456, 458-60, 462, 464, 466-80, 486-89, 495-99, 501, 503-07; **49**:326-404
Castruccio (Machiavelli)
　　See *La vita di Castruccio Castracani da Lucca*
A Catalogue of the Royal and Noble Authors of England (Walpole)　**2**:456, 486-87

Catechism (Andrewes)　**5**:39
Catechistical Doctrine (Andrewes)
　　See *A Patterne of Catechisticall Doctrine*
Catharos (Lodge)　**41**:198-99, 204
Catiline (Jonson)　**33**:119, 131-2, 156
Catiline His Conspiracy (Jonson)　**6**:291, 294, 296, 300-01, 305-06, 308, 314, 318-20, 323-24, 330-33, 336
Catiline's Conspiracy (Jonson)
　　See *Catiline His Conspiracy*
"The Causes of the American Discontents" (Franklin)　**25**:125
The Causes of the Decay and Defects of Dramatick Poetry, and of the Degeneracy of the Public Taste (Dennis)　**11**:17
Causes of the Magnificency and Opulency of Cities (Raleigh)　**31**:224
The Causes of the Progress and Decline of the Sciences and the Arts (Turgot)
　　See *Considérations philosophiques sur les sciences et les savants*
The Cavalier and the Lady (Goldoni)
　　See *Il cavaliere e la dama*
Cave of Fancy (Wollstonecraft)
　　See *The Cave of Fancy, a Tale*
The Cave of Fancy, a Tale (Wollstonecraft)　**5**:426, 442
The Cave of Salamanca (Cervantes)
　　See *La cuerva de Salamanca*
CCXI Sociable Letters (Cavendish)　**30**:191-2
Ce qu'on ne fait pas et ce qu'on pourrait faire (Voltaire)　**14**:380
Ceci n'est pas un conte (Diderot)　**26**:136
The Celebrated Letter from Samuel Johnson, LL.D. to Philip Dormer Stanhope, Earl of Chesterfield (Johnson)　**15**:203, 301
A Celebration of Charis in Ten Lyric Pieces (Jonson)　**6**:305, 326, 336
La Celestina (Rojas)　**23**:202-61, 63
Célinte: Nouvelle première (Scudery)　**2**:307
"El celoso extremeño" (Cervantes)　**6**:171-72, 177; **23**:95, 97, 99
La cena de le ceneri (Bruno)　**27**:74-75, 78, 97, 100, 105-11, 113-17
"Cendrillon" (Perrault)　**2**:253-54, 260-65, 267, 280-82, 284-85
Censure to Philantus　**41**:178
Les cent balades (Christine de Pizan)　**9**:40
Cent balades d'amant et de dame (Christine de Pizan)　**9**:48
Cent histoires (Christine de Pizan)　**9**:29
Centaur (Young)
　　See *The Centaur Not Fabulous, in Six Letters to a Friend on the Life in Vogue*
The Centaur Not Fabulous, in Six Letters to a Friend on the Life in Vogue (Young)　**3**:488, 492; **40**:334
Centura prima ad Belgas (Lipsius)　**16**:269
The Centuries (Nostradamus)
　　See *Les Prophéties de M. Michel Nostradamus*
"Céphale" (Rousseau)　**9**:343
Cephise et l'Amour (Montesquieu)　**7**:320
El cerco de Numancia (Cervantes)　**6**:143, 177-78, 180, 189; **23**:100-02
"Ceremonies for Christmasse" (Herrick)　**13**:331, 336
"Cerrar podrá mis ojos" (Quevedo)　**23**:198, 200
Certain Epistles after the manner of Horace (Daniel)　**24**:
Certain Satires (Marston)　**33**:221-23, 234
Certain Small Poems (Daniel)　**24**:145
Certain Sonnets (Sidney)　**19**:391, 395-96, 424; **39**:216, 267, 280

El cetro de José (Juana Ines de la Cruz) **5**:158
Chabot (Chapman)
    See *The Tragedy of Chabot, Admiral of France*
Chain of Gold (Jami)
    See *Silsilatu'dh-Dhahab*
The Chains of Slavery, a Work Wherein the Clandestine and Villainous Attempts of Princes to Ruin Liberty Are Pointed out, and the Dreadful Scenes of Despotism Disclosed . . . (Marat) **10**:226, 231, 236
"Chai-p'ing kung-tzu" (P'u Sung-ling) **49**:281
A Challenge at Tilt (Jonson) **33**:170
"The Chameleon" (Prior) **4**:456, 461
The Chandler (Bruno)
    See *Il Candelaio*
"Ch'ang-ê" (P'u Sung-ling) **49**:297, 300
The Changeling (Middleton) **33**:261, 266-70, 272, 275, 280-82, 291-93, 298, 327
"Chang-shih fu" (P'u Sung-ling) **49**:283
"Chanon's Yeoman's Tale" (Chaucer)
    See "Canon's Yeoman's Tale"
"The Character of a Good Parson" (Dryden) **21**:56
"Character of a Lawyer" (Butler)
    See "A Lawyer"
"The Character of a Presbyter" (Butler) **43**:78
"The Character of Holland" (Marvell) **4**:395, 398, 429
"The Character of Polybius" (Dryden) **3**:237
"Character of St. Evremond" (Dryden) **3**:236
"A Character of the Anti-Covenanter" (Burns) **29**:43
Character of the Long Parliament and Assembly of Divines (Milton) **43**:383, 397
"The Character, to Etesia" (Vaughan) **27**:361, 363-64
Characteristica Universalis (Leibniz) **35**:132
"Characters" (Butler) **16**:18, 26-8, 30, 50-5; **43**:70-1, 74, 110
Characters and Miscellaneous Observations (Butler) **43**:69
Characters and Passages from Note-Books (Butler) **16**:18; **43**:91, 93-4, 99
Characters Historical and Panegyrical of the Greatest Men (Perrault)
    See *Les hommes illustres qui ont paru en France pendant ce siècle*
The Characters; or, Manners of the Age (La Bruyere) **17**:409-15, 417, 419-21, 423-27, 429
The Charcoal-Boal Girl (Vega)
    See *La Carbonera*
"Charitas Nimia" (Crashaw) **24**:19, 38, 41, 53, 65-6, 76
"Charity and Humility" (More) **9**:296
Charity and Its Fruits (Edwards) **7**:119
"Charms and Knots" (Herbert) **24**:274
Charms of Study (Marmontel) **2**:213
"The Charnel-house" (Vaughan) **27**:314, 319-21
"Charon" (Erasmus) **16**:114, 116, 132, 142, 155
Charter (Penn)
    See *Charter of Liberties*
Charter of Liberties (Penn) **25**:311, 314, 320-22
Charter of Privileges (Penn) **25**:317-18, 341
"Le chartier embourbe" (La Fontaine) **50**:128
Chaste Joseph (Grimmelshausen)
    See *Der keusche Joseph*
A Chaste Maid in Cheapside (Middleton) **33**:263, 272-73, 277-78, 280, 298, 303, 322-23
"Le chat" (Ronsard) **6**:424, 436
"Le Chat, la Belette et le petit Lapin" (La Fontaine) **50**:98, 100-101
"La Chauve-Souris et les deux Belettes" (La Fontaine) **50**:79

"Che yü" (P'u Sung-ling) **3**:350
"A Cheat" (Butler) **16**:50
The Cheats of Scapin (Moliere)
    See *Les fourberies de Scapin*
"The Check" (Vaughan) **27**:320-21, 325
"Le chemin de la fortune" (Marivaux) **4**:380
"Le Chene et le Roseau" (La Fontaine) **50**:51
"Ch'eng hsien" (P'u Sung-ling) **3**:350, 352
"Cheng the Fairy" (P'u Sung-ling) **3**:344
"Ch'eng the Immortal" (P'u Sung-ling)
    See "Ch'eng hsien"
"Cherche, Cassandre, un poëte nouveau" (Ronsard) **6**:433-34
"Cherry Ripe" (Herrick) **13**:332
"The Chess Ghost" (P'u Sung-ling)
    See "Qi gui"
"Chi shêng" (P'u Sung-ling) **49**:294-295
"Chia êrh" (P'u Sung-ling) **49**:299
"Chia Feng chih" (P'u Sung-ling) **49**:281, 287
"Chiang Ch'eng" (P'u Sung-ling) **3**:346
"Chiao Mi" (P'u Sung-ling) **49**:294
"Chiao-na" (P'u Sung-ling) **49**:295-96, 300
"Ch'iao-niang" (P'u Sung-ling) **49**:298, 300
"Chiao-no" (P'u Sung-ling) **3**:354
"Chiao-nu" (P'u Sung-ling) **49**:278
"Childe-hood" (Vaughan) **27**:300, 306, 337-38, 340-41, 389
"Child-Song" (Sidney) **19**:330
Chiliades (Erasmus) **16**:171
Chilias Logarithmmorum (Kepler) **45**:320
"Ch'in Kuei" (P'u Sung-ling) **49**:283
Chin p'ing mei **19**:16-55
"Ch'in shêng" (P'u Sung-ling) **49**:295-296, 298
"Chinese Letters" (Goldsmith) **48**:189, 191
"Ch'ing-mei" (P'u Sung-ling) **49**:297, 300-01
The Chioggian Brawls (Goldoni)
    See *Le baruffe chiozzotte*
Chiose (Castelvetro) **12**:67-8
Chirurgia minor quam Bertheoneam intitulaut (Paracelsus) **14**:198-99
"Chiu yu" (P'u Sung-ling) **49**:296
"Chiu-shan wang" (P'u Sung-ling) **49**:298-299
"Chloris Appearing in the Looking-Glass" (Parnell) **3**:255
Choosing a Councilman in Daganzo (Cervantes) **6**:190
"The Chorus of Slaves" (Talvik)
    See "The Chorus of Slaves"
"Ch'ou hu" (P'u Sung-ling) **49**:294, 297
"Chou hu" (P'u Sung-ling) **49**:299
"Chou San" (P'u Sung-ling) **49**:295-296
Christ among the Doctors (Chester) **34**:125-6
Christ and the Doctors (N-Town) **34**:180, 183-4, 188-9, 192, 200, 204, 216, 240
Christ before Annas and Caiaphas (York)
    See *Peter Denies Jesus: Jesus Examined by Caiaphas* (York)
Christ before Herod (York)
    See *Trial Before Herod* (York)
Christ Before Pilate (York)
    See *Dream of Pilate's Wife: Jesus Before Pilate* (York)
Christ Led Up to Calvary (York) **34**:334
Christ on the Road to Emmaus (Chester) **34**:121
Christ, the Adultress, Chelidonius (Chester) **34**:110
Christ with the Doctors in the Temple (York) **34**:386
Die Christenberg (Andreae)
    See *Dichtungen*
Christenburg, ein schön geistlich Gedicht (Andreae) **32**:92
Christian Astrology Modestly Treated in Three

Books (Lilly) **27**:143-46
Christian Commonwealth (Eliot)
    See *The Christian Commonwealth; or, The Civil Policy of the Rising Kingdom of Jesus Christ.*
The Christian Commonwealth; or, The Civil Policy of the Rising Kingdom of Jesus Christ. . . (Eliot) **5**:129-30, 139-40
Christian Doctrine (Milton)
    See *De doctrina christiana*
Christian Epistle upon Penitence (Perrault) **2**:256
"Christian Experience" (Winthrop) **31**:342-44
The Christian Hero (Steele) **18**:314, 328-29, 332, 338, 340, 345-46, 348, 350, 353-59, 364-65, 376, 378, 380
Christian Introduction (Zwingli)
    See *A Brief Christian Introduction*
Christian Liberty (Luther)
    See *Dissertatio de libertate christiana per autorem recognita*
"The Christian Militant" (Herrick) **13**:333, 371-72
"Christian Morals" (Pascal) **35**:362
Christian Philosopher, A Collection of the Best Discoveries in Nature with Religious Improvements (Mather) **38**:165, 197, 202, 212-13, 218, 230, 234-37
The Christian Quaker (Penn) **25**:291, 295-97, 335
"The Christian Triumph" (Young)
    See "The Complaint; or, Night Thoughts: Night the Fourth"
"Christian Triumph" (Young)
    See "The Complaint; or, Night Thoughts: Night the Fourth"
Christianae Fidei Expositio (Zwingli)
    See *Explanation of the Christian Faith*
Christiani Matrimonii Institutio (Erasmus) **16**:154-55, 193
Christianisme dévoilé (Holbach) **14**:152-53, 157-59, 166-67
Christianity Unveiled (Holbach)
    See *Christianisme dévoilé*
Christianopolis (Andreae) **32**:68-9, 71, 77-9, 85-6, 89, 90-1, 93-5
"The Christians Reply" (Davenant) **13**:204-07
"Christmas" (Herbert) **24**:274
"A Christmas Caroll" (Herrick) **13**:310, 404-05
The Christmas Party (Holberg)
    See *Julestuen*
A Christmas Tale (Garrick) **15**:124
Christographia (Taylor) **11**:369-70, 373-74, 382, 386-88, 390, 398
Christ's Descent into Hell (Chester) **34**:131-5
"Christ's Kirk on the Green" (Ramsay) **29**:305, 314, 316, 321, 324, 327, 330, 336, 353-5, 362-3
"Christs Nativity" (Vaughan) **27**:325, 330, 372, 392-93
"Christ's Reply" (Taylor) **11**:361
Christ's tears over Jerusalem (Nashe) **41**:342, 374
Christus Triumphans (Foxe) **14**:43, 46-47
The Chronology of the Ancient Kingdoms Amended (Newton) **35**:321-23, 326-27
"The Chrysanthemum Spirit" (P'u Sung-ling) **3**:348
"The Church" (Herbert) **24**:273-76, 278, 280
"The Church Floore" (Herbert) **24**:278
Church History (Holberg)
    See *Almindelig kirke-historie fra christendommens første begyndelse til Lutheri reformation...*

"The Church Militant" (Herbert)　**24**:268-69, 275-76

"Church Monuments" (Herbert)　**24**:246, 248-49

"Church Music" (Herbert)　**24**:274

"The Church Porch" (Herbert)　**24**:236, 251, 267-70

"Church-lock and Key" (Herbert)　**24**:228

"Churchwarden" (Butler)　**16**:53

"Churchyard" (Gray)
　　See "Elegy Written in a Country Churchyard"

"Ch'u-sheng" (P'u Sung-ling)　**49**:291

Chymische Hochzeit Christiani Rosenkreutz anno 1459 (Andreae)　**32**:67, 87-93, 100

Ciceronianus (Erasmus)　**16**:175, 177, 182

Ciceronis Amor: Tullies Love　**41**:165-69, 174, 176, 177

The Cid (Castro)
　　See *Las mocedades del Cid*

Le Cid (Corneille)　**28**:3-6, 9-12, 14, 16, 18-23, 25, 30, 32-34, 38, 42, 55-58

The Cid (Corneille)
　　See *Le Cid*

Lo cierto por lo dudoso (Vega)　**23**:402

"La Cigale et la Fourmi" (La Fontaine)　**50**:74, 78, 92-93, 124-125

"Cinderella" (Perrault)
　　See "Cendrillon"

Cinna, ou La Clémence d'Auguste (Corneille)　**28**:4, 9, 12, 14-15, 21-3, 25, 34-5, 38, 53-8

Le cinquième et dernier livre des faicts et dictz heroiques du noble Pantagruel (Rabelais)　**5**:215-16, 219, 230, 233, 239, 251

"Circé" (Rousseau)　**9**:341-43, 345

Circe (Vega)　**23**:374

The Citizen of the World; or, Letters from a Chinese Philosopher (Goldsmith)　**2**:65, 70-1, 74-6, 83-5, 95, 97, 102-05, 107, 116, 127-28; **48**:189, 223, 226

La Citta del sole (Campanella)　**32**:193-222, 231, 235, 242-43

The City Heiress; or, Sir Timothy Treat-all (Behn)　**1**:29, 33, 37, 40, 48; **30**:81; **42**:125, 151

The City Jilt; or, The Alderman Turned Beau: A Secret History (Haywood)　**44**:145-6

"City Mouse and Country Mouse" (Marvell)
　　See *The Hind and the Panther, Transvers'd to the Story of the Country and the City-Mouse*

"A City Night-Piece" (Goldsmith)　**2**:103

The City of the Sun (Campanella)
　　See *La Citta del sole*

"A City-Wit" (Butler)　**16**:55

De Cive (Hobbes)　**36**:111, 113-14, 116, 118, 128, 133, 140, 143, 149-50, 160, 166, 169

The Civil War (Cowley)　**43**:175-82

Civil Wars (Daniel)　**24**:82-3, 87, 95, 98, 100-12, 122, 127, 130, 139, 141-43

The Civile Wares between the Howses of Lancaster and Yorke, corrected and continued (Daniel)　**24**:84-5, 89

De Civilitate (Erasmus)　**16**:154

Civility for Boys (Erasmus)　**16**:124

Civis christianus (Andreae)　**32**:93

Civitas Solis (Campanella)
　　See *La Citta del sole*

The Clandestine Marriage (Garrick)　**15**:98, 101-02, 105, 108-09, 111, 114, 116, 121, 124

Clarissa Harlowe (Richardson)
　　See *Clarissa; or, The History of a Young Lady*

Clarissa; or, The History of a Young Lady (Richardson)　**1**:367-69, 371-72, 374, 377-78, 380-82, 385-86, 388-95, 399-413, 415-16, 418; **44**:182, 185, 189-92, 194, 197-8, 200, 211-3, 215, 218, 221-3, 225, 228-30,

232-35, 237, 239, 242, 244-5, 248-50, 258, 260-2, 265-6, 268-70, 292

"Clasping of Hands" (Herbert)　**24**:273

"Clavis" (Newton)　**35**:294

A Clear State of the case of Elizabeth Canning (Fielding)　**46**:154-55

Clélie: Histoire romaine (Scudery)　**2**:293, 300, 302-04, 306-09, 311-14

De Clementia (Calvin)　**37**:135

Clementia; or, The History of an Italian Lady, Who Made Her Escape from a Monastery, for the Love of a Scots Nobleman (Haywood)　**1**:283

Cleomenes (Dryden)　**3**:222

Cleopatra (Daniel)
　　See *The Tragedy of Cleopatra*

Cléopâtre (Marmontel)　**2**:213, 216-17

"Clerk's Prologue" (Chaucer)　**17**:218

"Clerk's Tale" (Chaucer)　**17**:65, 142, 195-97, 205, 226, 228, 236-37, 241

"The Clever Offcome" (Ramsay)　**29**:340

The Clever Woman (Goldoni)
　　See *La donna di garbo*

"Clifton" (Chatterton)　**3**:131

Clitandre (Corneille)　**28**:42-4, 55

La Clizia (Machiavelli)　**8**:126, 170, 176

Clodius and Scipiana (Barker)　**42**:59

"Cloe Jealous" (Prior)　**4**:463

"Cloe Weeping" (Prior)　**4**:459

"Clorinda and Damon" (Marvell)　**4**:397, 438

"Clothes do but cheat and cousen us" (Herrick)　**13**:369

"Clothes for Continuance" (Herrick)　**13**:313

"Clout the Caldron" (Ramsay)　**29**:320, 330

"Coaches" (Montaigne)
　　See "Des coches"

"Le Coche et la Mouche" (La Fontaine)　**50**:98, 100

"The Cock and the Fox" (Chaucer)
　　See "Nun's Priest's Tale"

"Cock-crowing" (Vaughan)　**27**:300, 325, 337

Codex A (Vinci)　**12**:420

Codex Atlanticus (Vinci)　**12**:385, 387, 395, 411, 413-14, 417, 419, 433

Codex B (Vinci)　**12**:419-20, 422

Codex C (Vinci)　**12**:421

Codex E (Vinci)　**12**:421

Codex G (Vinci)　**12**:421

Codex H (Vinci)　**12**:420

Codex Huygens (Vinci)　**12**:394

Codex I (Vinci)　**12**:420

Codex Trivulziano (Vinci)　**12**:386, 420, 422

Codex Urbinas (Vinci)　**12**:393, 435

Codice Atlantico (Vinci)
　　See *Codex Atlanticus*

Codicetto Trivulziano (Vinci)
　　See *Codex Trivulziano*

Codici (Vinci)　**12**:419

"Codicil to Rob. Fergusson's Last Will" (Fergusson)　**29**:173, 213

Coelum Britannicum (Carew)　**13**:6-8, 10-11, 13, 20, 24, 26, 38-9, 41-2, 46-7

The Coffee-House Politician (Fielding)
　　See *Rape upon Rape; or, The Justice Caught in His Own Trap*

"Cogitata et Visa" (Bacon)　**18**:153

Cogitationes de Natura Rarum (Bacon)　**18**:187

Cogitationes de Scientia Humana (Bacon)　**18**:187

"Colin Clout" (Spenser)
　　See *Colin Clouts Come Home Againe*

Colin Clouts Come Home Againe (Spenser)　**5**:313-14, 335, 343, 345-47, 355, 359-62; **39**:352

Coliphizacio (Towneley)　**34**:250, 257-60, 299,

311, 321

"The Collar" (Herbert)　**24**:228, 238, 240, 265, 272, 274, 279, 292

Collectanea (Erasmus)　**16**:171, 195

Collectaneorum mathematicorum decades XI (Andreae)　**32**:90, 100

Collected Letters (Wollstonecraft)　**50**:278

"Collected out of his own Works, and other Primitive Authors by Henry Vaughan, Silurist" (Vaughan)　**27**:313

Collected Works (Lyttelton)　**10**:210

Collected Works (Wu Ch'eng-en)
　　See *She-yan hsien-sheng ts'un-kao*

Collection of Poems (Dennis)　**11**:4

A Collection of Psalm Tunes, with a few Anthems and Hymns (Hopkinson)　**25**:260

A Collection of Several Philosophical Writings (More)　**9**:309

The Collection of the Historie of England from the Conquest to the Reign of Edward III (Daniel)　**24**:85, 90-6, 98, 102, 104, 122, 139, 141

A Collection of the Moral and Instructive Sentiments, Maxims, Cautions, and Reflexions, Contained in the Histories of Pamela, Clarissa, and Sir Charles Grandison (Richardson)　**1**:416; **44**:245-6, 259-63

"College Exercise" (Prior)　**4**:455

Colloquia, Familiar Colloquies, Colloquies, Colloquiorum Opus (Erasmus)
　　See *Familiorum Colloquiorum*

"Colloquium Senile" (Erasmus)　**16**:129

"Colloquy of Funerals" (Erasmus)
　　See "Funus"

"Collos. 3.3" (Herbert)　**24**:252, 255, 257, 274

The Colonel (Davenant)　**13**:175

Colonel Jack (Defoe)
　　See *The History of the Most Remarkable Life and Extraordinary Adventures of the Truly Honourable Colonel Jacque, Vulgarly Called Colonel Jack*

La colonie (Marivaux)　**4**:367, 378

"El coloquio de los perros" (Cervantes)　**6**:171-73; **23**:99, 104, 111, 149

Colours of Good and Evil (Bacon)　**18**:149, 196,

Come and Welcome, to Jesus Christ (Bunyan)　**4**:174-75, 177

"Come, Fair Rosina" (Hopkinson)　**25**:250

"Come Live with Me and Be My Love" (Marlowe)
　　See *The Passionate Shepherd to His Love*

"Come, see the place where the Lord lay" (Crashaw)　**24**:5

"Come, thou monarch" (Garrick)　**15**:130

Comedia de Calisto y Melibea (Rojas)
　　See *La Celestina*

Comedias (Cervantes)
　　See *Ocho comedias y ocho entremeses nunca representados*

Comedias y entremeses (Cervantes)
　　See *Ocho comedias y ocho entremeses nunca representados*

Comedy about Life at Court (Aretino)
　　See *Cortigiana errante*

The Comedy Named the Several Wits (Cavendish)　**30**:227

The Comely Cook (Chulkov)
　　See *Prigozhaya povarikha*

Comentarius Solutus (Bacon)　**18**:133, 153

"Com'esser, donna, può quel c'alcun vede" (Michelangelo)　**12**:363, 365

Comfort of Lovers (Hawes)　**17**:345-49, 351-54, 362-63

The Comic Illusion (Corneille)

See *L'illusion comique*
The Comical Gallant (Dennis) **11**:12, 20
The Comical Hash (Cavendish) **30**:189
The Coming of Antichrist (Chester)
   See *The Antichrist* (Chester)
"Comme on voit sur la branche" (Ronsard) **6**:425,
   435
Commedia di Callimaco: E di Lucretia
   (Machiavelli) **8**:126, 131-32, 147, 162-63,
   168-72, 175-80
"Commencement" (Pascal) **35**:369-70
Los commendadores de Cordoba (Vega) **23**:391,
   401
Commentaire sur Corneille (Voltaire) **14**:339
Commentaire sur Desportes (Malherbe) **5**:169,
   173, 180
Commentaire sur Hemsterhuis (Diderot) **26**:143
Commentarii (Foxe)
   See *Actes and Monumentes of these latter per-
   ilous dayes touching matters of the Church*
Commentariolus (Copernicus) **45**:91-2, 94-5,
   103, 122, 124, 129, 166
Commentarium in convivium Platonis de amore
   (Ficino) **12**:184, 197, 201
Commentary (Pico della Mirandola)
   See *Commento*
Commentary on Desportes (Malherbe)
   See *Commentaire sur Desportes*
Commentary on John (Calvin) **37**:180
Commentary on Prudentius' Hymn to the Nativity
   (Erasmus) **16**:124
"Commentary on Psalm 118" (Luther) **9**:136
Commentary on Romans (Calvin) **37**:89
Commentary on the Four Gospels (Taylor)
   11:373
Commentary on the "Lama'át" (Jami) **9**:67
Commentary on the Psalms (Luther)
   See *Die sieben Busspsal mit deutscher au-
   siegung nach dem schrifftlichen synne tzu
   Christi und gottes gnaden, neben seynes
   selben, ware erkentniss grundlich gerichtet...*
Commentary on the Symposium (Ficino) **12**:176,
   180, 201-03
Commentary on the True and False Religion
   (Zwingli) **37**:352, 357-58, 268, 390, 394
Commento (Pico della Mirandola) **15**:325, 338-
   39, 346, 356-58
Comments on Livy (Machiavelli)
   See *Discorsi di Nicolo Machiavelli... sopra la
   prima deca di Tito Livio, a Zanobi
   Buondelmonte, et a Cosimo Rucellai*
*Le Commerce et le gouvernement considérés
   relativement l'un à l'autre* (Condillac)
   See *Du commerce et du gouvernement
   considérés relativement l'un à l'autre*
"Common Amusements" (Hopkinson) **25**:271
Commonplace Book (Milton) **43**:332-3
Commonplace Book (Newton) **35**:274
"Communicacion de amor invisible por los ojos"
   (Quevedo) **23**:184
"Communities" (Donne) **24**:154
"Les Compagnons d'Ulysse" (La Fontaine)
   50:84-85, 88, 124-125, 131-132, 135
"Companion to the Guide to Oxford" (Warton)
   15:449
The Companion to the Theatre (Haywood)
   44:170-1
Comparative Histories of Heroes (Holberg) **6**:282
Comparative Histories of Heroines (Holberg)
   6:282
"The Comparison" (Carew) **13**:27, 58-9
*A Comparison of Early Christians with Those of
   Today* (Pascal) **35**:392

Comparison of the Arts (Vinci) **12**:416
"Compartlement" (Herrick) **13**:321
*De compendiosa architectura et complemento
   artis Lullii* (Bruno) **27**:67-68
Compendium of Voyages (Smollett) **46**:190
"The Complaint" (Fergusson) **29**:197
"Complaint" (Young)
   See "The Complaint; or, Night Thoughts"
"Complaint of Cherwell" (Warton) **15**:431
Complaint of Great Want and Scarcity of Corn
   See *Ballad on the Want of Corn*
Complaint of Peace Ejected from All Countries
   (Erasmus)
   See *Querela Pacis*
The Complaint of Rosamond (Daniel) **24**:84, 86,-
   7, 89, 97-8, 107, 118, 121-2, 130, 132-4
"The Complaint; or, Night Thoughts" (Young)
   3:462, 464, 466-78, 480-84, 486-89, 491-
   500; **40**:330, 334-35, 337, 339-40, 344-48,
   351-57, 358-70, 370-77, 377-85, 385-88
"The Complaint; or, Night Thoughts: Night the
   Eighth" (Young) **3**:464, 466, 498-99
"The Complaint; or, Night Thoughts: Night the
   Fifth" (Young) **3**:464, 466, 480, 491;
   40:341, 344-45, 379
"The Complaint; or, Night Thoughts: Night the
   First" (Young) **3**:491, 498; **40**:339-40, 344-
   45
"The Complaint; or, Night Thoughts: Night the
   Fourth" (Young) **3**:464, 465, 478, 491, 498-
   99; **40**:341, 344-45
"The Complaint; or, Night Thoughts: Night the
   Ninth" (Young) **3**:464, 466, 498-99;
   40:328-32, 337-38, 343-44, 347, 359, 361-
   62, 369
"The Complaint; or, Night Thoughts: Night the
   Second" (Young) **3**:464, 480, 491; **40**:340-
   41, 344-45
"The Complaint; or, Night Thoughts: Night the
   Seventh" (Young) **3**:464, 466, 498; **40**:342,
   347
"The Complaint; or, Night Thoughts: Night the
   Sixth" (Young) **3**:466, 498; **40**:341-42, 347
"The Complaint; or, Night Thoughts: Night the
   Third" (Young) **3**:465, 472, 491; **40**:344-
   45
*Complaint They Have Made that He Is Too Rig-
   orous* (Calvin) **37**:90
*Complaints: Containing Sundrie Small Poemes of
   the Worlds Vanitie* (Spenser) **5**:311-12
The Compleat English Gentleman (Defoe) **42**:202
A Compleat History of England (Smollett) **2**:342,
   344; **46**:190, 248, 262-63
*The Complete Letters of Lady Mary Wortley
   Montagu, Vol. III: 1752-62* (Montagu)
   9:269
The Complete Vindication (Johnson) **15**:206
"Compleynt of Mars" (Chaucer) **17**:99
Comprobatory Treatise (Las Casas) **31**:203
La Comtesse de Tende (La Fayette) **2**:138-39,
   144, 149-50, 152, 157-59, 165-67, 169
La comtesse d'Escarbagnas (Moliere) **10**:272,
   283, 293, 313; **28**:245-46, 255, 274-75
El Comulgatorio (Gracian y Morales) **15**:144,
   148
Comus: A Maske (Milton) **9**:178, 183, 189, 191-
   2, 195, 197-9, 202-5, 208, 214-5, 229-30,
   234-5, 238, 250-1; **43**:396
Con supan se lo coman (Vega) **23**:393
"Conan" (Gray) **40**:232
Conception of Mary (N-Town)
   See *Conception of the Virgin* (N-Town)
Conception of the Virgin (N-Town) **34**:174, 178,

   181, 188, 192, 200-1, 215, 239-40, 242
*Conceptions of Divine Love, Conceptions of the
   Love of God* (Teresa de Jesus)
   See *Conceptos del amor de dios sobre algunas
   palabras de los Cantares de Salomón*
*Conceptos del amor de dios sobre algunas
   palabras de los Cantares de Salomón* (Teresa
   de Jesus) **18**:389, 392, 409
Concerning Christian Liberty (Luther)
   See *Dissertatio de libertate christiana per
   autorem recognita*
"Concerning Humour in Comedy" (Congreve)
   See "Letter Concerning Humour in Comedy"
Concerning the Cause, Principle, and One (Bruno)
   See *De la causa, principio et uno*
Concerning the Christian Religion (Ficino)
   See *De religione christiana*
*Concerning the End for Which God Created the
   World* (Edwards) **7**:93, 95, 101-03, 117-
   18, 121
Concerning the Nature of Love (Dryden) **21**:77-
   8
*Concerning the Revolutions of the Heavenly
   Spheres* (Copernicus)
   See *Nicolai Copernici Torunensi De
   Revolutionibus orbium coelestium, Libri VI*
Concerning the Unity of the Church in Love
   (Erasmus) **16**:114
Conciones et meditationes (Kempis) **11**:410
"Concluding Hymn" (Burns) **29**:35
"Conclusio" (Newton) **35**:296, 298
"Conclusion" (Pascal) **35**:371
"The Conclusion, After the Manner of Horace"
   (Ramsay) **29**:339
Conclusion of the Memoirs of Miss Sidney Bidulph
   (Sheridan) **7**:371, 378, 383-84
"Conclusions" (Winthrop) **31**:321
Conclusions (Pico della Mirandola) **15**:321, 324-
   25, 329, 334
Concord of Plato and Aristotle (Pico della
   Mirandola) **15**:342
El Conde Alarcos (Castro) **19**:4, 14
Conduct of Human Understanding (Locke)
   35:225, 228-29, 241
The Conduct of the Minority (Burke) **7**:47
The Confederacy (Vanbrugh) **21**:287-89, 292,
   295, 301-02, 319-20
"The Conference" (Churchill) **3**:150-52, 155-56,
   160, 163
Confessio (Andreae) **32**:67, 71, 87
"The Confession of Faith of a Savoyard Vicar"
   (Rousseau)
   See "Profession du vicaire Savoyard"
Confessionario (Las Casas) **31**:209
Les Confessions (Rousseau) **14**:218, 220-23, 226,
   247-51, 254, 256-60, 263-64, 267-68, 295,
   297, 301, 303-10, 312-14; **36**:268
Les confessions du Comte de *** (Duclos) **1**:187-
   88, 190-93, 198
"Confined Love" (Donne) **24**:154
The Confutation of Tyndale's Answer (More)
   10:362-63, 366, 370, 396-98, 408-09, 441;
   32:270, 348
*Congratulation to the Venerable Presbyter
   Gabriel of Saconay* (Calvin) **37**:95
Conjectures (Young)
   See *Conjectures on Original Composition in a
   Letter to the Author of Sir Charles Grandison*
*Conjectures on Original Composition in a Letter
   to the Author of Sir Charles Grandison*
   (Young) **3**:474, 479, 481-82, 484, 489, 492-
   96, 499; **40**:334, 338, 350, 353, 356, 359,
   363, 371, 373-74

"Conjuration to Electra" (Herrick) **13**:336

"Le connaisseur" (Marmontel) **2**:214, 221

"The Connoisseur" (Marmontel)
See "Le connaisseur"

"Connubii Flores, or the Well-Wishes at Weddings" (Herrick) **13**:380

The Conquest of Granada by the Spaniards (Dryden) **3**:179, 208, 221, 232

The Conquest of Spain (Pix) **8**:261-63, 269, 271-72, 277

Conquistata (Tasso)
See *Di Gerusalemme conquistata*

"Conscience. An Elegy" (Fergusson) **29**:199

The Conscious Lovers (Steele) **18**:320, 330, 345-46, 348, 352-54, 358, 368-75, 377-80, 382-83

De conscribendis Epistolis (Erasmus) **16**:146

"A Consideration upon Cicero" (Montaigne) **8**:232

Considerations on the Causes of the Grandeur and the Decadence of the Romans (Montesquieu)
See *Considérations sur les causes de la grandeur des Romains, et de leurdécadence*

Considérations philosophiques sur les sciences et les savants (Turgot) **26**:370

Considerations sur le goût (Duclos) **1**:188

Considérations sur le Gouvernement de Pologne (Rousseau) **36**:249

Considérations sur les causes de la grandeur des Romains, et de leur décadence (Montesquieu) **7**:309-12, 319, 321-25, 332, 342, 347, 356-57, 360, 362

Considerations sur les moeurs de ce siècle (Duclos) **1**:184-85, 187-88, 191, 199

Considerations Touching the Likeliest Means to Remove Hirelings Out of the Church (Milton) **40**:336, 397

Considerations Upon the Reputation of T. Hobbes (Hobbes) **36**:139-40

Considerations upon Two Bills (Swift) **1**:489

Consideraziono sui "Discorsi" del Machiavelli (Guicciardini) **49**:198, 201, 225, 229, 260, 264

"Consolation" (Malherbe)
See "Consolation à Du Perier"

"The Consolation" (Young)
See "The Complaint; or, Night Thoughts: Night the Ninth"

"Consolation à Du Perier" (Malherbe) **5**:168, 170

"Consolation au Président de Verdun" (Malherbe) **5**:171

"Consolation for the Old Bachelor" (Hopkinson) **25**:270

Consolatoria (Guicciardini) **49**:217, 225

The Consolidator (Defoe) **1**:162

Conspiracio (Towneley) **34**:251, 267-8, 288, 311, 326-7

The Conspiracy and Tragedy of Charles, Duke of Byron (Chapman) **22**:7-8, 15, 18-19, 20-1, 30, 33, 39, 40-3, 46-7, 55

Conspiracy (Chester) **34**:114

The Conspiracy of the Jews and Judas (N-Town) **34**:176, 188

The Conspiracy to Take Jesus (York) **34**:333-4, 342, 388

The Conspiracy (Towneley)
See *Conspiracio* (Towneley)

The Constant Couple; or, A Trip to he Jubilee (Farquhar) **21**:126, 128-29, 135-36, 139-40, 142, 144, 146, 148, 150, 152-55, 161, 163-64, 170, 176

The Constant Prince (Calderon de la Barca)
See *El Principe constante*

"Constantia" (Brooke) **1**:62

De Constantia in Publicis Malis (Lipsius)
See *De constantia libri duo*

De constantia libri duo (Lipsius) **16**:252, 257-58, 262, 265-73, 276

Constantine Donation (Hutten)
See *De falso credita et ementita Donatione Constatini Magni*

"The Constellation" (Vaughan) **27**:307, 325, 340-41, 373, 376, 379, 383

The Constellation of the Great Bear (Jami)
See *Haft Aurang*

La Constitution ou Projet de déclaration des Droits de l'homme et du citoyen, suivi d'un Plan de constitution juste, sage et libre (Marat) **10**:221, 226

Constitutions (Teresa de Jesus) **18**:392

Contagion sacrée (Holbach) **14**:152-53, 157-59, 168-69

"Conte" (Marmontel) **2**:220

Contemplacio (N-Town) **34**:172-3, 220

A Contemplation on Night (Gay) **49**:33

"Contemplations" (Bradstreet) **4**:85-6, 90-3, 95-6, 100-04, 108, 112; **30**:113-16, 120-125, 142, 151-3,

De contemptu mundi (Erasmus) **16**:133, 144, 146

The Contending Brothers (Brooke) **1**:63

"Content" (Ramsay) **29**:308-9, 353

"Contented Wi' Little" (Burns) **40**:97

Contes et nouvelles en vers (La Fontaine) **50**:66-71, 79, 115-116, 122, 128-129, 131-132

Contes moraux (Marmontel) **2**:208-15, 220-22, 224

Contes persans (Lesage) **28**:210

"Contes tires d'Athenee" (La Fontaine) **50**:69

Continuation of the Compleat History of England (Smollett) **46**:248-9

"Continuation of the Yellow Millet" (P'u Sung-ling)
See "Hsü huang-liang"

The Continued Cry of the Oppressed (Penn) **25**:332

Contra valor no hay desdicha (Vega) **23**:393

"The Contract" (Cavendish) **30**:188

Le Contrat Social (Rousseau)
See *Du Contrat social*

"Contre ceux qui ont le gout difficile" (La Fontaine) **50**:64

"Contre les bûcherons de la forêt de Gastine" (Ronsard) **6**:417

"Contre les détracteurs de l'antiquité" (Rousseau) **9**:346

Contributions to the History and Improvement of the Theater (Lessing)
See *Beiträge zur Historie und Aufnahme des Theaters*

The Convent of Pleasure (Cavendish) **30**:227-30

"The Conversation" (Prior) **4**:459

Conversation of a Father with His Children (Diderot)
See *Entretien d'un père avec ses enfants*

Conversations (Jonson) **6**:324

Conversations sur divers sujets (Scudery) **2**:293-94, 303, 307

"Conversion of St. Paul" (Smart) **3**:403

Conversion of St. Paul (Lyttelton)
See *Observations on the Conversion and Apostleship of St. Paul, in a Letter to Gilbert West*

Conversion of Swearers (Hawes) **17**:345-49, 352, 354, 361-62

"The Convert's Love" (Parnell) **3**:255

Convivium (Ficino)

See *Commentarium in convivium Platonis de amore*

Convivium Religiosum (Erasmus) **16**:116, 121, 172

"Cook's Prologue" (Chaucer) **17**:206

"Cook's Tale" (Chaucer) **17**:201

Cool Thoughts (Franklin) **25**:127

A Cooling Carde for all Fond Lovers (Lyly) **41**:239, 253

"The Cooper o'Cuddy" (Burns) **29**:24

"The Copernican System" (Chatterton) **3**:127

Copia (Erasmus)
See *De Copia*

De Copia (Erasmus) **16**:112, 136, 140, 146, 154, 196, 198, 202

The Coquet Mother and Coquet Daughter (Gay) **49**:5-6

"Le Corbeau et le Renard" (La Fontaine) **50**:62, 73, 79, 85, 92, 132

Cordial for Cavaliers (Howell) **13**:420

"Corinna's Going a-Maying" (Herrick) **13**:316, 323, 330, 332, 337, 343, 348-51, 357, 361, 364, 366-67, 377, 383-86, 397, 402

Coriolanus (Dennis)
See *The Invader of His Country: or, The Fatal Resentment*

Coriolanus. A Tragedy (Thomson) **16**:396; **29**:419-21, 434-35

"Corn Rigs" (Burns) **3**:87; **40**:72-3, 93

Cornelia (Kyd) **22**:244-5, 252, 275

La Corona (Donne) **10**:40, 84; **24**:165-67, 173, 198

Corona Tragica (Vega) **23**:340

"The Coronet" (Marvell) **4**:396, 403, 426, 437-38, 443; **43**:300, 306

"A Coronet for his Mistresse Philosophy" (Chapman) **22**:

De Corpore Politico (Hobbes) **36**:111, 123, 128, 139, 149, 151, 160, 169-70

Correction of the Understanding (Spinoza)
See *De intellectus emendatione*

Correspondance (Marie de l'Incarnation)
See *Lettres de la Vénérable Mère Marie de l'Incarnation*

Correspondance (Sevigne)
See *Correspondance de Mme de Sévigné*

Correspondance (Voltaire) **14**:337

Correspondance de Mme de Sévigné (Sevigne) **11**:336-38

Correspondence (Diderot) **26**:73, 119, 121

Correspondence (Ivan IV) **17**:401

Correspondence (Spinoza) **9**:438

Correspondence (Young) **40**:371

The Correspondence of Isaac Newton (Newton) **35**:319

The Correspondence of Samuel Richardson (Richardson) **44**:231, 233, 245

The Correspondence of Swift (Swift) **1**:449

"Corruption" (Vaughan) **27**:305, 325, 327, 338, 356, 391-93

Il cortegiano (Castiglione)
See *Il libro del cortegiano*

El cortesan o l'uomo di mondo (Goldoni) **4**:249

Cortigiana (Aretino)
See *Cortigiana errante*

Cortigiana errante (Aretino) **12**:6, 9, 19-20, 23, 26-7, 29-30, 35-6

Corylo (Beer) **5**:56

Cose fiorentine (Guicciardini) **49**:198, 214, 225-26, 260

Cosi-Sancta (Voltaire) **14**:345, 359, 398

"The Cottar's Saturday Night" (Burns) **3**:48, 50, 52, 54-6, 65, 67, 72, 77, 79, 81, 83-5, 93,

Title Index

102-04; **29**:8-9, 29-30, 32, 61, 63, 71-4, 91, 93; **40**:69, 72, 74-6, 80, 92, 94-5, 100, 105, 113

The Council of the Jews I (N-Town) **34**:185, 188, 208, 210-11

Counsel and Advice (Penn) **25**:330

Counsels and Reflections of Fr. Guicciardini (Guicciardini) **49**:196

Count Alarcos (Castro)
    See *El Conde Alarcos*

Count d'Irlos (Castro) **19**:4

Count Fathom Ferdinand, Count Falthom (Smollett)
    See *The Adventures of Ferdinand, Count Fathom*

The Counterfeit Bridegroom; or, The Defeated Widow (Behn) **1**:33; **30**:71, 80

The Counterfeit Christian Detected and the Real Quaker Justified (Penn) **25**:287, 291

The Countess of Dellwyn (Fielding) **1**:273, 278; **44**:66-8, 72, 75-6, 81, 94, 98

"Countess of Denbigh" (Crashaw)
    See "Address to the Noblest and Best of Ladies, the Countess Denbigh Against Irresolution and Delay in Matters of Religion"

The Countess of Pembroke's Arcadia (Sidney) **19**:318-27, 329-30, 334-36, 338-45, 347-49, 351-58, 360-62, 364-74, 376-80, 389-91, 396-97, 399-415, 420-30, 432-33; **39**:199-203, 209-14, 226, 227-29, 238, 241, 259, 270, 274, 280-84

The Countesse of Mountgomeries Urania (Wroth) **30**:334-38, 340, 342-44, 346-59, 363-65, 367, 369, 371, 383, 393

The Country Girl (Garrick) **15**:122-23

The Country House (Vanbrugh) **21**:293, 319

"The Country Lass" (Burns) **3**:85; **29**:49

"Country Life" (Philips) **30**:326

"A Country Life: To His Brother, Master Thomas Herrick" (Herrick) **13**:377-82

"The Country Life, to the Honoured Master Endimion Porter, Groome of the Bed-Chamber to His Majesty" (Herrick) **13**:327, 364, 368, 377, 395

The Country Parson (Herbert) **24**:225-26, 255, 266-67

The Country-Wife (Wycherley) **8**:379-81, 383, 385-92, 394, 396-97, 400-02, 406, 409-16, 419-23, 425-26, 428-29; **21**:347, 355-57, 359-70, 372-76, 379-80, 383, 387-88, 390-91, 393-98

"La Coupe enchantee" (La Fontaine) **50**:116-119

"La Cour du lion" (La Fontaine) **50**:92-98, 100-101, 103-104

Courage (Grimmelshausen)
    See *Die Erzbetrugerin und Landstortzerin Courasche*

"Courante Monsieur" (Lovelace) **24**:327

Cours d'étude (Condillac) **26**:7, 10, 29, 31, 47, 54

"The Court Life. To a Friend, Disswading Him from Attending for Places" (Wycherley) **8**:416

Court of Carimania (Haywood)
    See *The Secret History of the Present Intrigues of the Court of Caramania*

"The Court of Death: a Pindarique Poem, dedicated to the memory of her Most Sacred Majesty, Queen Mary" (Dennis) **11**:14, 49-50

"The Court of Equity" (Burns)
    See "Libel Summons"

"Court of Honor" (Addison) **18**:27

The Court of the King of Bantam (Behn) **1**:34, 38, 45-6, 48; **30**:88

Court Poems (Montagu) **9**:276

The Courtesan (Aretino)
    See *Cortigiana errante*

The Courtier (Castiglione)
    See *Il libro del cortegiano*

The Courtier's Library (Donne) **10**:82

"La Courtisane Amoureuse" (La Fontaine) **50**:69-70

"Courtship" (Erasmus) **16**:193

The Cousins (Davys) **1**:97; **46**:20, 24, 26, 35

The Covent-Garden Tragedy (Fielding) **1**:239

"A Covetous Man" (Butler) **16**:50

The Coxcomb (Fletcher) **33**:56, 60, 63, 71, 97

"The Coy Mistress" (Marvell)
    See "To His Coy Mistress"

The Crafty Whore (Aretino) **12**:21, 25

"The Craven Street Gazette" (Franklin) **25**:141

Creation and Fall (Chester) **34**:105-6, 121, 127, 131, 141

Creation and Fall of Lucifer (York) **34**:342

The Creation and Fall of Man (N-Town) **34**:172, 180, 184-5, 188, 199, 208

Creation and Fall of the Angels (York) **34**:388

Creation of Heaven and Earth (York)
    See *Creation to the Fifth Day* (York)

The Creation of Heaven and the Angels and the fall of Lucifer (N-Town) **34**:172, 178

Creation of the World (Chester)
    See *Creation and Fall* (Chester)

Creation to the Fifth Day (York) **34**:366, 374

The Creation (Towneley) **34**:251, 266, 296, 299, 325

"The Cricket" (P'u Sung-ling) **49**:306
    See "Ts'u-chih"

Criminal Legislation (Marat)
    See *Plan de législation criminelle, ouvrage dans lequel on traite des délits et des peines, de la force des preuves et des présomptions . . .*

"Cripples" (Montaigne) **8**:221

The Crisis (Steele) **18**:352, 354

Crispin, rival de son maitre (Lesage) **2**:182, 201; **28**:199-202, 209, 211-12, 215

The Critic (Gracian y Morales)
    See *El Criticón*

"The Critic and the Writer of Fables" (Winchilsea) **3**:443, 457

Critical Examination of the Apologists of the Christian Religion (Holbach) **14**:167

The Critical History of Jesus Christ; or, Reasoned Analysis of the Gospels (Holbach)
    See *Ecce Homo! or, A Critical Inquiry into the History of Jesus of Nazareth; Being a Rational Analysis of the Gospels*

Critical Observations (Dennis)
    See *Remarks on a Book, entituled Prince Arthur, an Heroick Poem*

El Criticón (Gracian y Morales) **15**:136-52, 154-55, 157-72, 174-75

La critique de L'école des femmes (Moliere) **10**:278, 281, 283, 287, 297, 311, 321; **28**:255-56, 258, 274

Critique de l'Opera (Perrault) **2**:259

Critique de Turcaret (Lesage) **28**:204

The Critique upon Milton (Addison) **18**:7

Le crocheteur borgne (Voltaire) **14**:359

"Cromwell"
    See "Thomas Cromwell, Earle of Essex"

"The Crosse" (Donne) **10**:16, 40, 84; **24**:165, 167, 198-99

"The Crosse" (Herbert) **24**:268. 272-74

"Crowne of Sonnets" (Wroth) **30**:342, 390, 399

De cruce (Lipsius)
    See *De cruce libi tres*

De cruce libi tres (Lipsius) **16**:269

Crucifixio Cristi (York) **34**:334, 342, 355, 371, 380-1, 384-8

Crucifixion (Chester) **34**:100, 111, 115, 121, 128-9

The Crucifixion (N-Town) **34**:186, 188

The Crucifixion (Towneley) **34**:265, 278, 321

The Crucifixion (York)
    See *Crucifixio Cristi* (York)

"Crucifying" (Donne) **24**:167

The Cruel Brother (Davenant) **13**:175, 216

"The Cruel Mistress" (Carew) **13**:11

"The Cruell Maid" (Herrick) **13**:364

The Cruelty of the Spaniards in Peru (Davenant) **13**:190

"The Crusade" (Warton) **15**:432-33, 442, 445, 454

The Cry: A New Dramatic Fable (Fielding) **1**:270, 273; **44**:62-5, 67-8, 70-1, 77, 96, 100, 105, 110

"The Cryer" **8**:27

The Cub at Newmarket. A Letter to the People of Scotland (Boswell) **4**:50, 52-3

El Cubo de la Almundena (Calderon de la Barca) **23**:14

Cuento de cuentos (Quevedo) **23**:154

El cuerdo loco (Vega) **23**:393

La cuerva de Salamanca (Cervantes) **6**:189-92; **23**:139, 142

"Culex" (Spenser) **5**:312

"A Cully" (Butler) **16**:50

La cuna y la sepultura (Quevedo) **23**:190

"Cupid and Ganymede" (Prior) **4**:461

"Cupid Fargone" (Lovelace) **24**:340

"Cupid, I Hate Thee, Which I'de Have Thee Know"
    See "Sonnet 48"

"Cupid's Conflict" (More) **9**:298, 302

Cupid's Revenge (Fletcher) **33**:40-52, 54-6, 67-9, 71-2, 76, 91

The Cure and the Sickness (Calderon de la Barca) **23**:9

"Le Cure et le Mort" (La Fontaine) **50**:98-102

A Cure for a Cuckold (Webster) **33**:337, 340-41, 358

"Curiosa Americana" (Mather) **38**:230

De Curiositatis pernicic (Andreae) **32**:100

"El curioso" (Cervantes) **23**:95

El curioso impertinente (Cervantes) **23**:99, 130, 141, 144-45

"A Curious Man" (Butler) **16**:52

"The Curse" (Donne) **10**:52, 82

"The Curse" (Herrick) **13**:341

"A Custom of the Island of Cea" (Montaigne) **8**:238

"Cyclops" (Erasmus) **16**:154

Cymon (Garrick) **15**:124

"Cymon and Iphigenia" (Dryden) **3**:184, 205, 213, 243

"A Cynic Satire" (Marston) **33**:203

"Cynthia" (Jonson) **6**:322

Cynthia (Raleigh)
    See *The Ocean to Cynthia*

Cynthia's Revels (Jonson) **6**:300, 302, 306, 308, 311, 335-36, 342; **33**:103, 105, 139, 141, 143, 145-56, 159, 161, 173, 177

The Czar of Muscovy (Pix) **8**:260-61, 263, 269, 271-72, 276

"Czego chcesz od nas, panie?" (Kochanowski)
    See "Piesn"

"The Daft Days" (Fergusson) **29**:170-71, 175, 178, 181, 189, 194, 198, 205, 214, 234-37
"Les daimons" (Ronsard) **6**:407, 411, 422, 424
"Daintie Davie" (Burns) **3**:56
D'Alembert's Dream (Diderot)
  See *Le Rêve de d'Alembert*
La dama boba (Vega) **23**:372, 393
La dama duende (Calderon de la Barca) **23**:38, 41-2, 44, 46, 57, 59, 64, 66
"A Damask Rose Sticking upon a Lady's Breast" (Carew) **13**:18, 30
D'Ambois (Chapman)
  See *The Tragedy of Bussy D'Ambois*
"Damon the Mower" (Marvell) **43**:300
"Damon the Mower" (Wheatley) **3**:410-11, 441-42
"Damon to his Friends" (Fergusson) **29**:201
"The Dampe" (Donne) **10**:36-7, 82; **24**:154
The Dancing-Master (Wycherley)
  See *The Gentleman Dancing-Master*
The Danger of Priestcraft to Religion and Government (Dennis) **11**:26
"The dangers of speaking and of not speaking and the function of language in silence" (Quevedo)
  See "Peligros de habler y de caller y lenguaje en el silencio"
"Dangers wait on Kings" (Herrick) **13**:394
Dannemarks og Norges beskrivelse (Holberg) **6**:266, 281
Dannemarks riges historie (Holberg) **6**:266, 278, 281-82
Den danske comoedies ligbegænglese (Holberg) **6**:278
"Daphnaida" (Spenser) **5**:312-13; **39**:347
"Daphnis and Chloe" (Marvell) **4**:408-10
"Dark Night of the Soul" (John of the Cross)
  See "Noche Oscura del alma"
The Dark Night of the Soul (John of the Cross)
  See *Noche Escura del Alma*
"Date Obolum Belesario" (Hopkinson) **25**:251, 255
"Um daudans óvíssan tíma" (Petursson) **8**:253
Daughter of the Air (Calderon de la Barca)
  See *La hija del aire*
"The Daughter of the Yen Family" (P'u Sung-ling)
  See "Yen Shih"
"David" (Parnell) **3**:255
David, ou l'Histoire de l'homme selon le cœur de Dieu (Holbach) **14**:153
David Simple, Volume the Last (Fielding)
  See *The Adventures of David Simple*
Davideis: A Sacred Poem on the Troubles of David (Cowley) **43**:141, 144, 146, 148-50, 153, 159, 180, 189, 193
"Dawn of Day and Sunset" (More) **9**:298
"The Dawning" (Herbert) **24**:274
"The Dawning" (Vaughan) **27**:291, 312, 314, 330, 336, 341, 365-66
"The Day of Judgement" (Swift) ·**1**:522, 524
"Day of Judgment" (Vaughan) **27**:338, 340-41, 375, 390
The Day of Pentecost (N-Town) **34**:199
Day of Preparation (Bacon)
  See *Parasceve*
The Day of Trouble is Near (Mather) **38**:309
Daybreak in Copacabana (Calderon de la Barca) **23**:9
De IV Novissimis (More) **10**:398-99
De captivitate Babylonica ecclesiae praeludium (Luther) **9**:87, 105, 107-08, 125, 141, 151; **37**:247, 252, 254, 261
De Christiana religione (Ficino)

  See *De religione christiana*
De disciplina claustralium (Kempis) **11**:411
De doctrina christiana (Milton) **9**:247-8, 250; **43**:341-2, 366, 397-401, 408-9
De felici liberalitate (Paracelsus) **14**:199
De generatione hominis (Paracelsus) **14**:198
De imitatione Christi (Kempis) **11**:406-13, 415-22, 424-26
De intellectus emendatione (Spinoza) **9**:402, 423-24, 433, 435, 442-44
De iure regni apud Scotos: dialogus, authore Georgio Buchanano Scoto (Buchanan) **4**:118, 120, 125, 127, 130, 134, 136-37
"De la coustume" (Montaigne) **8**:236-37
"De la cruauté" (Montaigne) **8**:240
De la Littérature Allemande (Frederick the Great) **14**:65, 77
"De la phisionomie" (Montaigne) **8**:221-22, 242
De la politique (Montesquieu) **7**:360-63
"De la praesumption" (Montaigne) **8**:211, 233, 242
"De la vanité" (Montaigne) **8**:197, 211, 232, 240-41
"De l'affection des peres aux enfants" (Montaigne) **8**:240
"De l'art de conferer" (Montaigne) **8**:197, 240
"De l'election de son sepulchre" (Ronsard) **6**:417, 430
De l'esprit des loix (Montesquieu) **7**:304-06, 308-13, 315-17, 319-20, 322-29, 331, 333-37, 339, 341-45, 347-50, 356-57, 359-60, 362-64
"De l'excellence de l'esprit de l'homme" (Ronsard) **6**:424
"De l'experience" (Montaigne) **8**:211, 221, 236, 239, 241-42
De l'homme (Marat)
  See *A Philosophical Essay on Man, Being an Attempt to Investigate the Principles and Laws of the Reciprocal Influence of the Soul on the Body*
"De l'institution des enfans" (Montaigne) **8**:241
De magnificentia (Ficino) **12**:168
De Maria Scotorum regina, totaque ejus contra regem conjuratione (Buchanan) **4**:120, 121, 125-26
"De Monachis S. Antonii" (Buchanan) **4**:122
De morbus amentium (Paracelsus) **14**:198
De musica (Ficino) **12**:197
De Non Plectendis Morte Adulteris (Foxe) **14**:26
De prosodia libellus (Buchanan) **4**:129
De Rebus Memorabilibus Angliae (Elyot) **11**:62, 73
De religione christiana (Ficino) **12**:172-73, 177, 182, 185, 188-89, 195, 201
De religione perpetua (Paracelsus) **14**:199
De renovatione et restauratione (Paracelsus) **14**:198
De ressurectione et corporum glorificatione (Paracelsus) **14**:199
De' segni de' tempi (Bruno) **27**:112
De sphaera (Buchanan)
  See *Sphaera in quinque libros distributa*
De summo bono et aeterno bono (Paracelsus) **14**:199
De testamentis (Casanova de Seingalt) **13**:126
De usynlige (Holberg) **6**:273, 278
De vita (Ficino) **12**:171-72, 180
De vita longa (Paracelsus) **14**:198
The Dead Term (Dekker) **22**:97
"The Dean of the Faculty" (Burns) **3**:96
The Dean's Provocation for Writing the "Lady's Dressing Room" (Montagu) **9**:282

"Dear Bargain" (Crashaw) **24**:19, 41
"Dear Patron of My Virgin Muse" (Burns) **29**:41
"Dear Roger if your Jenny geck" (Ramsay) **29**:343
"Death" (Herbert) **24**:214, 227, 238, 241, 243, 269, 274
"Death" (Vaughan) **27**:338, 390
Death and Assumption (N-Town) **34**:206
"Death and Daphne" (Swift) **1**:459
"Death and Doctor Hornbook" (Burns) **3**:50, 82, 87, 90; **29**:4-6, 45, 61-2, 91; **40**:63, 71, 78-9, 118
"The Death and Dying Words of Poor Mailie" (Burns) **3**:57, 60, 67, 71, 87, 90; **29**:29, 63; **40**:65
A Death and Execution of Courteen Most Wicked Traitors **41**:73
"Death of a Favorite Cat" (Gray)
  See "Ode on the Death of a Favourite Cat, Drowned in a Tub of Gold Fishes"
"The Death of Astragon" (Davenant) **13**:204, 206
The Death of Blanche the Duchess (Chaucer)
  See *Book of the Duchess*
Death of Christ (York)
  See *Mortificacio Christi* (York)
Death of Herod (Chester) **34**:96, 122, 124
The Death of Herod (N-Town) **34**:175-6, 178, 192, 199, 215, 227
"Death of Hoel" (Gray) **40**:231-32
"The Death of Oscur" (Macpherson) **29**:252-54
The Death of Pompey (Corneille)
  See *La mort de pompée*
"Death of Sir Roger de Coverley" (Addison) **18**:28
"Death of the Lord Protector" (Marvell)
  See "Poem upon the Death of O. C."
"Death's Duel" (Crashaw) **24**:50
Deaths Duell; or, A Consolation to the Soule, against the dying Life, and living Death of the Body (Donne) **10**:64, 85, 102-05; **24**:192, 201
Le debat de deux amans (Christine de Pizan) **9**:28, 42, 48
The Debate of Poissy (Christine de Pizan)
  See *Le livre du dit de Poissy*
"Debates in Magna Lilliputia" (Johnson)
  See "Debates in the Senate of Magna Lilliputia"
"Debates in the Senate of Magna Lilliputia" (Johnson) **15**:194, 206
The Debauchee; or, The Credulous Cuckold (Behn) **1**:33; **30**:71, 80
The debellation of Salem and Bizance (More) **10**:366, 370, 398, 408
"Deborah" (Parnell) **3**:255
Decannali (Machiavelli)
  See *Decennale primo*
"Decay" (Herbert) **24**:258
"The Decay of Friendship" (Fergusson) **29**:198
"The Deceitful Marriage" (Cervantes)
  See "El casamiento engañoso"
The Deceiver Deceived (Pix) **8**:259-62, 268-69, 271-73, 275
Decennale primo (Machiavelli) **8**:128
Déclamation sur l'incertitude, vanité et abus des sciences (Agrippa von Nettesheim)
  See *De incertitudine et vanitate scientiarium declamatio inuectiua et excellentia verbi Dei*
"Declamations on Natural Philosophy" (Mather) **38**:230
A Declaration made by the Archbishop of Cullen upon the Deede of his Marriage **41**:73
Declaration of Gentlemen Merchants and Inhabitants of Boston and Country Adjacent

(Mather) **38**:165

Declaration of the Articles Condemned by Leo X (Luther) **9**:84

"The Dedication" (Churchill)
See "Fragment of a Dedication to Dr. W. Warburton, Bishop of Gloucester"

"The Dedication" (Herbert) **24**:244, 258

"The Dedication" (Vaughan) **27**:351

"Dedication of Examen Poeticum" (Dryden) **3**:214

"The Dedication of the Aeneis" (Dryden) **3**:242; **21**:109-10, 116

"Dedication to G—— H——, Esq." (Burns) **3**:48, 86; **29**:22-3, 29

"The Dedication to the Sermons" (Churchill) **3**:157

The Deeds of Bernardo del Carpio's Youth (Vega) **23**:348

"Deep Riddle of Mysterious State" (Lovelace) **24**:347

"The Defence" (Chatterton) **3**:133

Defence (Elyot)
See *The Defence of Good Women*

Defence of an Essay of Dramatic Poesy (Dryden) **3**:238; **21**:117

"Defence of Conny-catching" **41**:151-52, 181-83

The Defence of Good Women (Elyot) **11**:58, 61, 68-9, 71, 83-6, 91-2, 95-6

"Defence of Poesie" (Burns) **29**:30

The Defence of Poesie (Sidney) **19**:324, 326, 330, 333, 336-37, 340-41, 345, 352, 355-56, 363-64, 368-69, 380-81, 393-94, 401-02, 404, 407-13, 415-18, 420-24, 432-33; **39**:199, 204-09, 212, 226-29, 234-35, 238-46, 242, 244, 247-58, 270, 278-79, 280, 283, 295-99

Defence of the Duke of Buckingham's Book (Penn) **25**:333

Defence of the Earl of Leicester (Sidney) **39**:266, 279

"Defence of the Epilogue (to The Conquest of Granada)" (Dryden) **3**:238; **21**:116-17

A Defence of the "Essay of Human Understanding" (Trotter) **8**:353, 355, 358, 361-63, 365, 370, 374

A Defence of the People of England (Milton)
See *Pro populo anglicano defensio, contra Claudii Anonymi*

A Defence of the Reasons for Restoring Some Prayers and Directions of King Edward the Sixth's First Liturgy (Collier) **6**:209

A Defence of the Short View of the Profaneness and Immorality of the English Stage (Collier) **6**:229

Defense (Elyot)
See *The Defence of Good Women*

Défense de "L'esprit des loix" (Montesquieu) **7**:324

La Defense du mondain (Voltaire) **14**:406

Defense of Good Women (Elyot)
See *The Defence of Good Women*

Defense of Himself (Milton) **43**:378-9

A Defense of Rime (Daniel) **24**:85, 89, 92, 97, 103-05

Defense of the Seven Sacraments against Martin Luther (Henry VIII)
See *Assertio septem sacramentorum adversus Martinum Lutherum haeresiarchon*

Defense of the Sound and Orthodox Doctrine of the Bondage and Deliverance of the Human Will against the False Accusations of Albert Pighins (Calvin) **37**:91

Defense of Tycho against Ursus (Kepler) **45**:346-47, 351

Defensio Seconda (Milton)
See *Second Defence of the English People*

Defensiones (Paracelsus) **14**:200

Defensoria (Guicciardini) **49**:260

Defensorium bonarum mulierum (Elyot)
See *The Defence of Good Women*

"The Definition of Love" (Marvell) **4**:403, 411, 425, 434, 441-43; **43**:304-6

Defoe's Review (Defoe) **42**:228

Dehortatio gentilis theologiae (Agrippa von Nettesheim) **27**:22-23

"The Deil's Awa' wi' th' Exciseman" (Burns) **3**:96; **40**:97

Dekker his Dream (Dekker) **22**:96, 112, 119, 121-2

Del governo (Guicciardini) **49**:259

Del modo (Guicciardini) **49**:259

The Delectable History of Forbonius and Prisceria (Lodge) **41**:188, 194-95, 200, 212, 214

"Delia" (Ramsay) **29**:329

Delia (Daniel) **24**:85, 88, 97, 109, 116-18, 122, 132, 134

"Delight in Disorder" (Herrick) **13**:330, 333, 351, 358, 359, 369, 379-80, 382

Delights of the Muses (Crashaw) **24**:7, 9, 42, 60

"The Delights of virtue" (Fergusson) **29**:206

"Deliverance From a Fit of Fainting" (Bradstreet) **30**:148-9

Deliverance of Souls (Towneley) **34**:326

Della fortuna (Ficino) **12**:169

The Deluge (Chester)
See *Noah's Flood* (Chester)

"Democritus and Heraclitus" (Prior) **4**:464-65

Democritus plantonissans: or, An Essay upon the Infinity of Worlds Out of Platonic Principles (More) **9**:307, 320, 330

"Demonology" (Ronsard)
See "Les daimons"

Dendrologia: Dodona's Grove; or, The Vocall Forest (Howell) **13**:415, 419, 424, 426, 433

"Denial" (Herbert) **24**:216, 228, 251, 272-74

Denys le tyran (Marmontel) **2**:213, 215

Le dépit amoureux (Moliere) **10**:275-77, 280, 283, 286, 291, 310, 318; **28**:255-56, 258, 261-63, 267

"Deposition from love" (Carew) **13**:11, 15, 61

Les derniers vers de Pierre de Ronsard, gentilhomne vandomois (Ronsard) **6**:436

Des abenteuerlichen Simplicissimi Ewig-wahrender Calender (Grimmelshausen) **6**:248

Des abentheuerlichen Jan Rebhu Ritter Spiridon aus Perusina (Beer) **5**:54-5

Des berühmten Spaniers Francisci Sambelle wolausgepolirte Weiber-Hächel (Beer) **5**:53, 56

"Des cannibales" (Montaigne) **8**:222, 233, 236, 238

"Des coches" (Montaigne) **8**:197, 204, 236

"Des senteurs" (Montaigne) **8**:234

The Descent of Anima Christi into Hell (N-Town) **34**:172, 185, 188

"The Descent of Odin, an Ode" (Gray) **4**:310, 312, 318; **40**:199, 201, 231, 243

"Descripcion del ardor canicular, que respeta al llanto enamorado yno le enjuga" (Quevedo) **23**:196

Descriptio (Andreae)
See *Confessio*

Descriptio Globi Intellectualis (Bacon) **18**:186-87, 195

Description du Corps Humain (Descartes) **35**:88, 91

"Description of a Church" (Hopkinson) **25**:259

"Description of a City Shower" (Swift) **1**:439, 458

The Description of a New Blazing World (Cavendish) **30**:199, 203-4, 210, 217, 226, 228, 230-36

"Description of a Tapestry at Longleat" (Winchilsea) **3**:457

"The Description of a Woman" (Herrick) **13**:398

"Description of an Author's Bedroom" (Goldsmith) **2**:74

"A Description of Cannynge's Feast" (Chatterton) **3**:135

"A Description of Constancy" (Cavendish) **30**:186

"The Description of Cooke-ham" (Lanyer) **30**:243, 249, 256

Description of Denmark and Norway (Holberg)
See *Dannemarks og Norges beskrivelse*

A Description of Millenium Hall, and the Country Adjacent, by a Gentleman on His Travels (Scott) **44**:325, 329, 331, 334, 338-41, 343-44, 346, 348-49, 352-53, 361-62, 367-70, 372, 374, 376-77, 380-86, 401, 407, 410

A Description of New England (Smith) **9**:375, 382-84

A Description of the Intellectual Globe (Bacon)
See *Descriptio Globi Intellectualis*

"Description of the Morning" (Swift) **1**:439, 458, 480-81

Descriptions of Strawberry (Valentine) **49**:358

The Deserted Village (Goldsmith) **2**:68, 71, 74-5, 79-80, 82, 90, 94-6, 98, 104-05, 107, 114; **48**:182, 193, 215

The Desolation of America (Day) **1**:105

"The Despairing Shepherd" (Prior) **4**:461

The Despairing Shepherd (Gay) **49**:7

"Despondency, an Ode" (Burns) **3**:48, 67, 86; **29**:28, 32-3, 79

El desposorio encubierto (Vega) **23**:390

El Desprecio Agradecido (Vega) **23**:352

"Destinie" (Cowley) **43**:187

Determinations (Taylor)
See *Gods Determinations touching his Elect: and The Elects Combat in their Conversion, and Coming up to God in Christ: together with the Comfortable Effects Thereof*

Deudsch Catechismus (Luther) **9**:134, 147, 151

"The Deuk's Dang o'er My Daddy" (Burns) **6**:81; **29**:24; **40**:89

Les Deux amis de Bourbonne (Diderot) **26**:118, 136-37, 150

Les deux consolés (Voltaire) **14**:398

"Les Deux Coqs" (La Fontaine) **50**:98-102

"Les Deux Pigeons" (La Fontaine) **50**:61, 78, 87, 99, 128-132, 134

Devastation of the Indies: A Brief Account (Las Casas)
See *Brevísima relación de la destrucción de las Indias*

The Devil Conjured (Lodge) **41**:199, 204

The Devil is an Ass (Jonson) **6**:297, **30**:311, 314, 320, 327-30, 335; **33**:106, 113, 132-3, 159, 165

The Devil upon Two Sticks (Lesage)
See *Le diable boiteux*

The Devil's Chains (Calderon de la Barca)
See *Las cadenas del demonio*

THe Devil's Champions Defeated (Penn) **25**:287

The Devil's Law-Case (Webster) **33**:338-40, 344

Le Devin du village (Rousseau) **14**:287

"Les Devineresses" (La Fontaine) **50**:98-101

La devoción de la cruz (Calderon de la Barca) **23**:15, 18, 20, 40, 64

Dévoilé (Holbach)
 See *Christianisme dévoilé*

"Devotion makes the Deity" (Herrick) **13**:319

The Devotion of the Cross (Calderon de la Barca)
 See *La devoción de la cruz*

Devotions on Sundrie Occasions (Donne)
 See *Devotions upon Emergent Occasions, and Severall steps in my sicknes*

Devotions upon Emergent Occasions, and Severall steps in my sicknes (Donne) **10**:31, 40, 64, 84, 89, 103-04; **24**:173, 175

Devout Exercises of the Heart in Meditation and Soliloquy (Rowe) **44**:291, 317

Devout Treatise upon the Pater Noster (Erasmus) **16**:124

Di Gerusalemme conquistata (Tasso) **5**:375-76, 383, 394, 403

Le diable boiteux (Lesage) **2**:175-77, 181-85, 189, 201-04; **28**:190, 199-200, 202, 204-11

Dialectic of Enlightenment (Bacon) **32**:188

A dialoge of comfort against tribulacion (More) **10**:367, 370, 389, 393-96, 398-99, 404, 407, 409, 413, 431, 435-41; **32**:259, 260, 268-70

Dialoghi (Aretino)
 See *Ragionamento della Nanna e della Antonia*

Dialoghi italiani (Chapman) **27**:97, 100, 103-04

Dialoghi metafisici e morali (Bruno) **27**:116

Dialogi (Hutten) **16**:233

Dialogo dei due massimi sistemi del mondo—Tolemaico e Copernicano (Galilei) **45**:200-01, 203-04, 207-08, 202-13, 218-20, 225-26, 229, 239, 248-49, 252, 259, 261:, 269-70, 312

Dialogo del reggimento di Firenze (Guicciardini) **49**:199-203, 228-29, 251, 259-65

Dialogo nel quale la Nanna insegna a la Pippa (Aretino) **12**:36

Dialogo politico contra Luterani, Calvinisti ed altri eretici (Campanella) **32**:211

"A Dialogue" (Herbert) **24**:271, 273-74, 281, 283

"Dialogue" (Lovelace) **24**:327

Dialogue (Galilei)
 See *Dialogo dei due massimi sistemi del mondo—Tolemaico e Copernicano*

A Dialogue (Hume) **7**:184

Dialogue Between a Pilosopher and a Student of the Common Law of England (Hobbes) **36**:142

"Dialogue between Brandy and Whisky" (Fergusson) **29**:170

"The Dialogue between Daphne and Apollo" (Prior) **4**:466

"Dialogue between Franklin and the Gout" (Franklin) **25**:104, 112, 141, 144

"Dialogue between Mr. John Lock and Seigneur de Montaigne" (Prior) **4**:470

"A Dialogue between Old England and New" (Bradstreet) **4**:85, 90, 95, 109

"Dialogue between Philocles and Horatio Concerning Virtue and Pleasure" (Franklin) **25**:111

"A Dialogue between the Resolved Soul, and Created Pleasure" (Marvell) **4**:410, 425-27, 442

"A Dialogue between the Soul and Body" (Marvell) **4**:412, 420-23, 426, 429, 439; **43**:305

"Dialogue between the Writer and a Maypole Dresser" (Taylor) **11**:366

"Dialogue betweene pail Truth and Blind Ignorance" **41**:80

"A Dialogue betweene two shepheards, Thenot

and Piers, in praise of Astraea" (Sidney) **19**:292-93, 296; **39**:143, 151, 168, 176

"A Dialogue betwixt Lucasia and Rosania Imitating that of Gentle Thyrsis" (Philips) **30**:288

Dialogue Concerning the Two Chief World Systems (Galilei)
 See *Dialogo dei due massimi sistemi del mondo—Tolemaico e Copernicano*

A Dialogue Concernynge heresyes and matters of religion (More) **10**:366, 388, 408-09, 438, 441-42

Dialogue de l'Amour et de l'Amitié (Perrault) **2**:280

Dialogue de Sylla et Eucrate (Montesquieu) **7**:321, 324

Dialogue des héros de roman (Boileau-Despreaux) **3**:24, 29, 33

"A Dialogue of Absence 'twixt Lucasia and Orinda" (Philips) **30**:280, 288

"A Dialogue of Absence 'Twixt Lucasia and Orinda set by Mr Henry Lawes" (Philips) **30**:280

"The Dialogue of the Dogs" (Cervantes)
 See "El coloquio de los perros"

The Dialogue of the Two Systems (Galilei)
 See *Dialogo dei due massimi sistemi del mondo—Tolemaico e Copernicano*

Dialogue on Florentine Government and Dialogue on the Government of Florence (Guicciardini)
 See *Dialogo del reggimento di Firenze*

Dialogue on the Great World Systems (Galilei)
 See *Dialogo dei due massimi sistemi del mondo—Tolemaico e Copernicano*

Dialogue; ou, Satire X (Boileau-Despreaux) **3**:37-9

Dialogue Upon the Common Law (Hobbes) **36**:114, 131-32

"Dialogue with the Nine Sisters" (Ronsard) **6**:412

Dialogues (Aretino)
 See *Ragionamento della Nanna e della Antonia*

Dialogues (Bruno)
 See *Dialoghi italiani*

Dialogues (Eliot)
 See *Indian Dialogues, for Their Instruction in that Great Service of Christ, in Calling Home Their Countrymen to the Knowledge of God and of Themselves, and of Jesus Christ*

Dialogues (Lyttelton)
 See *Dialogues of the Dead*

Dialogues (More) **10**:370

Dialogues (Reynolds)
 See *Johnson & Garrick*

Dialogues avec moi-même (Rousseau)
 See *Rousseau juge de Jean Jacques*

Dialogues concerning Natural Religion (Hume) **7**:144, 154-58, 196-98

Dialogues of Freemasons (Lessing)
 See *Lessing's Masonic Dialogues*

"Dialogues of the Dead" (Prior) **4**:467-68, 472-73

"Dialogues of the Dead" (Prior)
 See "Dialogue between Mr. John Lock and Seigneur de Montaigne"

"Dialogues of the Dead" (Prior)
 See "The Dialogue between Daphne and Apollo"

Dialogues of the Dead (Lyttelton) **10**:196, 198-201, 204, 207-10, 212, 214-15

"Dialogues of the Dogs" (Burns)
 See "The Twa Dogs"

Dialogues upon Medals (Addison) **18**:6, 8, 30, 39

Dialogus de homine (Agrippa von Nettesheim) **27**:21

Dialogus novitiorum (Kempis) **11**:411

"Diane" (Rousseau) **9**:343

Diaries (Johnson) **15**:288

Diary (Sewall) **38**:352-57, 362, 364, 366-76

Diary in North Wales (Johnson)
 See *A Diary of a Journey into North Wales, in the year 1774*

A Diary of a Journey into North Wales, in the year 1774 (Johnson) **15**:209

The Diary of Cotton Mather (Mather)
 See *Paterna*

The Diary of Samuel Pepys (Pepys) **11**:208-89

Diatriba de Signo Filii Hominis et de Secundo Messiae Adventu (Mather) **38**:306

"The Dice Box" (Walpole) **2**:500

Dicha y desdicha del nombre (Calderon de la Barca) **23**:67

Dichtungen (Andreae) **32**:67

Dicing (Towneley) **34**:321-2, 325

The Dictionary (Elyot) **11**:58, 61-3, 68, 73, 84-5, 87, 90-1

Dictionary (Johnson)
 See *Dictionary of the English Language*

Dictionary of the English Language (Johnson) **15**:182, 195-99, 203, 207-08, 221, 225, 239, 241, 250-51, 270, 276, 278-80, 282-83, 298-302, 306, 310-11, 313

Dictionnaire des synonymes (Condillac) **26**:29

Dictionnaire philosophique (Voltaire) **14**:339, 343, 351-53, 358, 367, 369-70, 391-96, 402

Diderich Menschenskræk (Holberg) **6**:277

Diderich the Terrible (Holberg)
 See *Diderich Menschenskræk*

Dido (Schlegel) **5**:280

Dido, Queen of Carthage (Marlowe)
 See *The Tragedy of Dido, Queen of Carthage*

Dido y Eneas (Castro) **19**:7-8

"'Dies Irae,' The Hymn of the church, in Meditation of the Day of Judgement" (Crashaw) **24**:4, 19-20, 36, 70-1, 73-4, 77-8

Dietwald und Amerlinde (Grimmelshausen) **6**:247-48

"The Difference Betwixt Kings and Subjects" (Herrick) **13**:394

The Different Widows; or, Intrigue all-a-Mode (Pix) **8**:260, 269, 271-72, 276

De Dignitate et Augmentis Scientiarum (Bacon)
 See *De augmentis scientiarum*

"Dimmi di gratia, Amor, se gli ochi mei" (Michelangelo) **12**:360

Dione: A Pastoral Tragedy (Gay) **49**:19, 33, 37, 121, 148, 164

Dioptrice (Kepler) **45**:320, 343

Dioptrics (Descartes) **35**:74, 99-105

"Direct" (Marmontel) **2**:220

"Directions for a Birthday Song" (Swift) **42**:336

Directions for a Candidate of the Ministry (Mather)
 See *Menudictio ad Minsterium*

"The Dirge" (Sidney) **19**:329

Dirge (Gay) **49**:43

"Dirge for Cymbeline" (Collins)
 See "A Song from Cymbeline"

"Dirge in <AElig>lla" (Chatterton)
 See "<AElig>lla: A Tragycal Enterlude"

"Dirge of Jephthah's Daughter" (Herrick) **13**:317, 342

"The Disappointment" (Behn) **1**:52, 54; **30**:69-70

"The Discharge" (Herbert) **24**:274

"Discipline" (Herbert)

See "Throw Away Thy Rod"
"Discontents in Devon" (Herrick) **13**:387
Discorsi (Tasso) **5**:383, 387, 392-94, 408
Discorsi del poema eroico (Tasso) **5**:383, 393
Discorsi dell'arte poetica (Tasso) **5**:383, 392, 394
Discorsi di Nicolo Machiavelli... sopra la prima deca di Tito Livio, a Zanobi Buondelmonte, et a Cosimo Rucellai (Machiavelli) **8**:124-28, 130, 133, 135-37, 139, 142, 145, 148-49, 151, 155-56, 158, 160-62, 167, 169-71, 175, 179; **36**:192, 196, 201, 205-06, 209, 211, 216, 218, 220-23, 225, 232-37
Discorsi e dimonstrazioni matematiche intorno a due nuove scienze (Galilei) **45**:206, 219, 248-49, 271, 302
Discorsi Tasso (Tasso)
See *Discorsi dell'arte poetica*
Discorsi Tusso (Tasso)
See *Discorsi del poema eroico*
Discorso di Logrogno (Guicciardini) **49**:197, 199, 202, 224, 229, 259-60, 263-64
Discorso intorno alle cose che stanno su l'acqua (Galilei) **45**:257, 260-61, 278
Discours (Corneille) **28**:5, 23, 38, 41, 52, 56
Discours (Ronsard)
See *Discours des misères de ce temps*
"Discours a Madame de La Sabliere sur l'ame des betes" (La Fontaine) **50**:134
"Discours a Monsieur de la Rochefoucauld"des (La Fontaine) **50**:64
"Discours au Roy" (Boileau-Despreaux) **3**:39
Discours de metaphysique (Leibniz) **35**:130, 132-33, 137, 142, 165, 167-72, 179
Discours des misères de ce temps (Ronsard) **6**:409-11, 414, 417-18
Discours en Sorbonne (Turgot) **26**:381
Discours en vers sur l'homme (Voltaire) **14**:364, 379
Discours préliminaire (Diderot) **26**:108
Discours sur la poésie dramatique (Diderot) **26**:89, 104, 108, 117, 141, 150
Discours sur l'Histoire Universelle (Turgot) **26**:381, 392
Discours sur l'Inégalité (Rousseau)
See *Discours sur l'origine et les fondements de l'inégalité parmi les hommes*
Discours sur l'origine et les fondements de l'inégalité parmi les hommes (Rousseau) **14**:214, 223, 227-28, 239-41, 253, 270, 276, 288-91, 293-95, 297, 306, 309, 313; **36**:245-46, 257, 267-68, 275-76, 288, 299
Discourse (Bacon) **32**:175
A Discourse By Way of Vision, Concerning the Government of Oliver romwell (Cowley) **43**:160, 180, 187
Discourse Concering the Danger of Apostasy (Mather) **38**:284
A Discourse concerning a Guide in Controversies, in Two Letters (Trotter) **8**:355, 362, 370
A Discourse Concerning the Faith and Fervency in Prayer and the Glorious Kingdom of the Lord Jesus Christ (Mather) **38**:307
Discourse concerning the Government of Oliver Cromwell (Cowley)
See *A Discourse By Way of Vision, Concerning the Government of Oliver romwell*
A Discourse Concerning the Mechanical Operation of the Spirit (Swift) **1**:509, 513-14, 517
A Discourse Concerning the Original and Progress of Satire (Dryden) **3**:210, 214, 231, 237; **21**:111, 118
"Discourse II" (Reynolds)

See "The Second Discourse"
"Discourse of Laws" (Hobbes) **36**:174, 182-84
"A Discourse of Life and Death" (Sidney) **39**:143-45, 150, 173, 176, 177
Discourse of Logrogno (Guicciardini)
See *Discorso di Logrogno*
"Discourse of Rome" (Hobbes) **36**:180-81
A Discourse of the Contests and Dissentions between the Nobles and the Commons in Athens and Rome (Swift) **42**:338
A Discourse of the Original and Fundamental Cause of Natural, Customary, Arbitrary, Voluntary and Necessary War (Raleigh) **31**:236, 239
"A Discourse on Arbitrary Gouerment" (Winthrop) **31**:383
Discourse on Bodies in Water (Galilei)
See *Discorso intorno alle cose che stanno su l'acqua*
Discourse on Dramatic Poetry (Diderot)
See *Discours sur la poésie dramatique*
Discourse on Floating Bodies (Galilei)
See *Discorsi e dimonstrazioni matematiche intorno a due nuove scienze*
Discourse on Inequality (Rousseau)
See *Discours sur l'origine et les fondements de l'inégalité parmi les hommes*
Discourse on Metaphysics (Leibniz)
See *Discours de metaphysique*
Discourse on Method (Descartes) **35**:74, 79, 81-9, 91-5, 99-100, 110, 114-15, 117, 123
"Discourse on Ode" (Young) **40**:348
Discourse on Pastoral Poetry (Pope) **3**:322-23
Discourse on Political Economy (Rousseau)
See *Economie Politique*
Discourse on the Arts and Sciences (Rousseau) **14**:255, 276, 286, 288, 297, 305, 309, 313; **36**:264, 268, 297, 301
Discourse on the Changes Which Have Occurred on Our Globe (Voltaire) **14**:390
Discourse on the Origins of Inequality (Rousseau)
See *Discours sur l'origine et les fondements de l'inégalité parmi les hommes*
Discourse on the seven days of the creation (Pico della Mirandola)
See *Heptaplus*
Discourse on Two New Sciences (Galilei)
See *Discorsi e dimonstrazioni matematiche intorno a due nuove scienze*
A Discourse on Western Planting (Hakluyt) **31**:143, 151, 155
"Discourse Three" (Reynolds)
See "The Third Discourse"
A Discourse Touching the Spanish Monarchy (Campanella)
See *Monarchia di Spagna*
Discourse Upon Comedy (Farquhar) **21**:128, 133, 139, 141-43, 146, 161, 182
A Discourse Upon Gondibert, An Heroic Poem written by Sir William D'Avenant. With an Answer to It by Mr. Hobbes (Davenant) **13**:183, 195, 207
"Discourse Upon the Beginning of Tacitus" (Hobbes) **36**:174, 179, 182
"Discourse XI" (Reynolds)
See "The Eleventh Discourse"
"Discourse XII" (Reynolds)
See "The Twelfth Discourse"
Discourses (Hobbes) **36**:173-74, 176, 178-79
The Discourses (Reynolds)
See *Discourses on Art*
Discourses on Art (Reynolds) **15**:364, 366, 371-72, 376-77, 379-80, 382, 384-91, 394, 399-

402, 404-05, 407-08, 411-18, 420-21, 422
Discourses on Livy (Machiavelli)
See *Discorsi di Nicolo Machiavelli... sopra la prima deca di Tito Livio, a Zanobi Buondelmonte, et a Cosimo Rucellai*
Discourses on Universal History (Turgot)
See *Discours sur l'Histoire Universelle*
The Discoverie of the Large, rich and Bewitful Empire of Guiana (Raleigh) **31**:233-6, 246, 254, 291-3, 295-301, 304-6; **39**:78, 91, 121, 123-24
Discoveries (Jonson)
See *Timber; or, Discoveries*
"Discovery"
See "A Notable Discouery of Coosnage"
The Discovery (Sheridan) **7**:370, 372-74, 376-77
El Discreto (Gracian y Morales) **15**:135-36, 143-45, 165
"Disdaine Returned" (Carew) **13**:11, 62
The Dismissal of the Grecian Envoys (Kochanowski)
See *Odprawa posłów grekich*
"Disorder and Frailty" (Vaughan) **27**:318, 326
Disputatio contra iudicium astrologorum (Ficino) **12**:171-72, 199-200
Disputatio in prologum instauratarum scientiarum ad scholas christianas (Campanella) **32**:239
Disputatio pro declaratione virtutia indulgentiarum (Luther) **9**:91, 109, 119, 123-24, 129, 146-47; **37**:260, 269, 296, 300, 323, 325, 329-31, 333, 335
"A Disputation Between a Hee Conny-catcher and a Shee Conny-catcher" **41**:150, 152, 155-56, 180-82
Disputation (N-Town) **34**:172
Disputationes (Pico della Mirandola) **15**:354
La dispute (Marivaux) **4**:369
"Disquisition" (Davenant)
See "The Philosophers Disquisition to the Dying Christian"
Dissertatio Cum Sidereo Nuncio (Kepler) **45**:320, 343
Dissertatio de libertate christiana per autorem recognita (Luther) **9**:105-06, 108, 123, 125, 134-35, 142; **37**:252-54, 261, 299
Dissertation (Boileau-Despreaux)
See *Dissertation sur la Joconde*
Dissertation Concerning the Future Conversion of the Jewish Nation (Mather) **38**:307
Dissertation on Liberty and Necessity, Pleasure and Pain (Franklin) **25**:116, 132, 174-77
Dissertation sur la Joconde (Boileau-Despreaux) **3**:29, 33
Dissertation sur la liberté (Condillac) **26**:47
Dissertation sur l'existence de Dieu (Condillac) **26**:47
Dissertation sur l'harmonie du style (Condillac) **26**:29
"The Dissolution" (Donne) **10**:58
"A Disswasive to His Mistress on Her Resolving to Turn Nun" (Wycherley) **8**:400
Distichs of Cato (Erasmus) **16**:123
"Distraction" (Vaughan) **27**:331, 339
The Distress'd Wife (Gay) **49**:114, 123-124, 148-149, 153-155
The Distresses (Davenant) **13**:176, 181, 196, 200
Distributio Operis (Bacon) **18**:146
Le dit de la pastoure (Christine de Pizan) **9**:48
Le dit de la rose (Christine de Pizan) **9**:25, 49
"Dithyrambes" (Ronsard) **6**:429
Le dittie de Jehanne d'Arc (Christine de Pizan)
See *Le dittie sur Jeanne d'Arc*
Le dittie sur Jeanne d'Arc (Christine de Pizan)

9:39

Divers Voyages Touching the Discovery of America and the Islands Adjacent unto the Same (Hakluyt) **31**:143, 155, 157, 162

"Diversion" (Montaigne) **8**:221

"Divination by a Daffodil" (Herrick) **13**:367

"A Divine and Supernatural Light, Immediately Imparted to the Soul By the Spirit of God, Shown to Be Both a Scriptural, and Rational Doctrine" (Edwards) **7**:101, 123, 131

Divine Dialogues (More) **9**:293, 297, 300, 307-08

Divine Emblems; or, Temporal Things Spiritualized (Bunyan) **4**:182

Divine Epigrams (Crashaw) **24**:5

The Divine in Mode (Marvell) See *Mr. Smirk; or, The Divine in Mode*

"A Divine Mistris" (Carew) **13**:33-4, 62

The Divine Narcissus (Juana Ines de la Cruz) See *El divino Narciso*

Divine Poems (Donne) **10**:40, 45, 96, 98-99, 106; **24**:169, 173, 198-203

Divine Providence (Zwingli) **37**:352

El divino Narciso (Juana Ines de la Cruz) **5**:143-45, 151-52, 158-59

The Divorce-Court Judge (Cervantes) See *El juez de los divorcios*

Diwan (Babur) **18**:90

"Do Millosci" (Kochanowski) **10**:160

"Do paniej" (Kochanowski) **10**:160

"Do snu" (Kochanowski) **10**:161

Doctor Faustus (Marlowe) See *The Tragicall History of the Life and Death of Doctor Faustus*

The Doctor in spite of Himself (Moliere) See *Le médecin malgré lui*

The Doctor of His Honor (Calderon de la Barca) See *El médico de su honra*

The Doctors (Towneley) See *Pagina Doctorum* (Towneley)

Doctrinae christianae Summa (Andreae) **32**:90

The Doctrinal of Princes (Elyot) **11**:61, 82, 84-5, 89

Doctrinale seu manuale juvenum (Kempis) **11**:411

The Doctrine and Discipline of Divorce (Milton) **9**:192, 250, 253; **43**:396

The Doctrine of Divine Providence (Mather) **38**:295-6

Dodona's Grove (Howell) See *Dendrologia: Dodona's Grove; or, The Vocall Forest*

"Does Haughty Gaul" (Burns) **3**:81

"The Dog & the Scunk" (Hopkinson) **25**:257

The Dog in the Manger (Vega) See *El perro del hortelano*

The Dogood Papers (Franklin) **25**:134-38, 161

The Dogs' Colloquy (Cervantes) See "El coloquio de los perros"

"The Dolefull Lay of Clorinda" (Sidney) **19**:292, 296, 309-10; **39**:150, 165, 166, 167

Dom Garcie de Navarre; ou, Le prince jaloux (Moliere) **10**:277, 280, 283, 291, 297-300, 310, 319-20, 325; **28**:230-32, 255, 260

Dom Juan (Moliere) See *Don Juan; ou Le festin de Pierre*

Dom Sanche d'Aragon (Corneille) **28**:4-5, 29-30, 33, 36, 41

Don César Ursin (Lesage) **28**:199

Don Felix de Mendoce (Lesage) **28**:199

Don Garcia of Navarre (Moliere) See *Dom Garcie de Navarre; ou, Le prince jaloux*

Don Garcie de Navarre (Moliere) See *Dom Garcie de Navarre; ou, Le prince jaloux*

Don Giovanni tenorio (Goldoni) **4**:262

Don Juan; or, The Banquet of Stone (Moliere) See *Don Juan; ou Le festin de Pierre*

Don Juan; ou Le festin de Pierre (Moliere) **10**:266, 282-84, 289-91, 298-99, 312, 318-21, 327, 329, 333-34, 345, 347-48; **28**:227-30, 232-40, 242-43, 246, 249, 251, 253-57, 269, 271, 275

Don Quixote (Calderon de la Barca) **23**:63

Don Quixote (Castro) **19**:2

Don Quixote (Cervantes) See *El ingenioso hidalgo Don Quixote de la Mancha*

Don Quixote in England (Fielding) **1**:250; **46**:60, 97-8, 101

Don Ranudo de Colibrados (Holberg) **6**:277

Don Sebastian, King of Portugal (Dryden) **3**:186, 209-10, 214, 222, 232-33, 235, 241; **21**:56, 71

La donna di garbo (Goldoni) **4**:250, 265, 267

La donna di governo (Goldoni) **4**:260

Le donne de casa soa (Goldoni) **4**:265-66

Le donne gelose (Goldoni) **4**:257

Donne's Sermons (Donne) **10**:47, 106

"Dooms-day" (Herbert) **24**:269

Doomsday (N-Town) See *Judgement Day* (N-Town)

Dorastus and Fawnia **41**:139

"Doris" (Congreve) **5**:85, 106-07

La Dorotea (Vega) **23**:359, 379

Dorothea (Vega) See *La Dorotea*

Los Dos Amantes de cielo (Calderon de la Barca) **23**:18-22

"Las dos doncelas" (Cervantes) **6**:171, 177; **23**:95-6, 99

The Double Dealer (Congreve) **5**:64, 66, 68, 71, 74, 76, 78-9, 84, 86-7, 90, 92-3, 96, 98-9, 101, 103, 109-13; **21**:3, 5-9, 26-8, 32, 38-41, 45

The Double Distress (Pix) **8**:260-63, 269, 271-72, 276

La double inconstance (Marivaux) **4**:366-67, 371-72, 376-77, 379-83

The Double Inconstancy (Marivaux) See *The Double Inconstancy*

The Double PP. A Papist in Arms. Bearing Ten several Shields. Encountered by the Protestant. At ten several Weapons. A Jesuit Marching before them. Cominus and Eminus. (Dekker) **22**:96, 104

Double Supply of Words and Matter (Erasmus) **16**:123

Doules sur la religion (Holbach) **14**:153

"The Dove" (Prior) **4**:467

Dowel, Dobet, and Dobest (Langland) See *Piers Plowman*

"Down Hall" (Prior) See "Ballad of Down-Hall"

Le doyen de Killérine (Prevost) **1**:329-30, 334-37, 343-44, 346-47

"Dr. Scarborough" (Cowley) **43**:187

Drafts and Fragments (Collins) **40**:150, 153

The Dramatic Historiographer (Haywood) See *The Companion to the Theatre*

Dramatic Works (Garrick) **15**:94

"Dramatizes the brevity of life in progress and the apparent nothingness of past life" (Quevedo) See "Representase la Brevedad de lo que se vive y cuan nada parece lo que se vivio"

The Drapier's Letters (Swift) **1**:441, 458, 497, 514, 516

"Draw-Gloves" (Herrick) **13**:331

"A Dream" (Burns) **3**:87, 96; **29**:13-14, 16, 18, 46, 91

"Dream" (Juana Ines de la Cruz) See "Primero sueño"

"The Dream" (Kochanowski) See "Tren XIX"

Dream (Dekker) See *Dekker his Dream*

Dream of Pilate's Wife: Jesus Before Pilate (York) **34**:333-4, 388

Dream of the Red Chamber (Ts'ao Hsueh-ch'in) See *Hung-lou meng*

"A Dream of Wolves" (P'u Sung-ling) **3**:344

"The Dreame" (Donne) **24**:183

"Dressing" (Vaughan) **27**:354, 364, 372

"A Drink Eclogue" (Fergusson) **29**:189, 192, 212, 218, 228, 231, 237

"Drink to Me Only with Thine Eyes" (Jonson) See "Song to Celia"

"The Drummer" (Ramsay) **29**:336

The Drummer (Addison) **18**:20

Du commerce et du gouvernement considérés relativement l'un à l'autre (Condillac) **26**:10, 47, 50

Du Contrat social (Rousseau) **14**:215, 223, 227-29, 241, 247-49, 252, 254, 256, 261, 263, 270, 273, 273, 275-78, 284, 288, 292, 297, 300-03, 309, 313-14; **36**:245-52, 268-69, 275, 279, 281, 285-86, 289, 291, 294, 296, 298-301

"Du Fu" (P'u Sung-ling) **49**:312

"Du repentir" (Montaigne) **8**:211, 226, 231, 242

The Duchess of Malfi (Webster) **33**:334, 336-38, 340-60, 364-67, 370, 382-85, 388-403

Due Preparations for the Plague (Defoe) **1**:168

Due trattati uno intorna alle otto principale arti dell oreficeria. L'altro in materia dell'arte della scultura... (Cellini) **7**:74-5, 79

"The Duellist" (Churchill) **3**:144-48, 152, 154-55, 158, 160, 163

The Duke of Guise (Dryden) **3**:210; **21**:53, 55-8, 65, 107

"Duke of Marlborough" (Wycherley) **8**:380

Dulce Bellum inexpertis (Erasmus) **16**:132, 173, 198

"Dulnesse" (Herbert) **24**:272, 274

The Dumb Virgin; or, The Force of Imagination (Behn) **1**:42-3; **30**:88; **42**:146

"Duncan Gray" (Burns) **3**:61, 66, 71; **29**:22-3, 55; **40**:63, 87-8, 97

"A Dunce" (Butler) **16**:30

"The Dunciad" (Pope) **3**:269, 272, 276-77, 279, 281, 287-91, 295-96, 298-301, 304-07, 313-14, 317-22, 324, 327-31, 333, 336-38

"Dunciad Variorum" (Pope) **3**:319-20, 328

The Dupe (Sheridan) **7**:370, 373, 377

The Dutch Courtesan (Marston) **33**:193-94, 197-98, 204-05, 210, 216-17, 235, 243, 246

The Dutch Lover (Behn) **1**:29, 33, 39, 52; **30**:67, 70, 74-5, 80,84; **42**:149

"Duty to Tyrants" (Herrick) **13**:394

"Dweller in Yon Dungeon Dark" (Burns) **3**:60

"The Dwelling-Place" (Vaughan) **27**:340, 343-44, 347

A dyaloge of syr Thomas More knyghte (More) **10**:362, 397-98

The Dying Negro (Day) **1**:105-07

"The Eagle" (More) **9**:298

"The Eagle and Robin Red-Breist" (Ramsay) **29**:332

"The Eagle, the Sow, and the Cat" (Winchilsea) 3:457

The Earl of Essex (Brooke) 1:62

The Earl of Westmoreland (Brooke) 1:62

Eassays in Prose and Verse (Cowley) 43:150

"Easter" (Herbert) 24:274-75, 280

"Easter" (Vaughan) 27:331

"Easter Day" (Crashaw) 24:

"Easter Wings" (Herbert) 24:228, 271, 274

Eastern Evangelical Planeta (Siguenza y Gongora)
See *Oriental planeta evangelica epopeya sacro-panegyrica al apostol grande de las Indias S. Francisco Xavier*

Eastward Ho! (Jonson) 33:146

Eastward Hoe (Chapman) 22:6, 10, 13, 64

"The Ebb and Flow" (Taylor) 11:352, 356, 386

"Eben as a Little Flower" (Petursson)
See "Alt eins og blómstrió eina"

Ecce Homo! or, A Critical Inquiry Into the History of Jesus of Nazareth; Being a Rational Analysis of the Gospels (Holbach) 14:148, 168

Ecclesiastes (Erasmus) 16:115, 154

Ecclesiastical History (Collier)
See *An Ecclesiastical History of Great Britain*

Ecclesiastical History (Foxe)
See *Actes and Monumentes of these latter perilous dayes touching matters of theChurch*

An Ecclesiastical History of Great Britain (Collier) 6:208, 210

Eclogae piscatoriae (Sannazaro) 8:326-27, 332, 334, 336

"Eclogue I" 8:34-5

"Eclogue II" 8:35

"Eclogue IV" 8:35

"Eclogue V" 8:35

"Eclogue VII" 8:35

"Eclogue VIII" 8:35

"Eclogue IX" 8:35

"Eclogue to Amaryllis" (Vega) 23:381

Eclogue to Claudio (Vega) 23:337-38

"An Eclogue to the Memory of Dr. William Wilkie, Late Professor of Natural Philosophy in the University of St. Andrews" (Fergusson) 29:189, 193, 222, 225, 227

"Eclogues" (Chatterton)
See "African Eclogues"

"Eclogues" (Warton)
See "Five Pastoral Eclogues: The Scenes of Which are Supposed to Lie Among the Shepherds, Oppressed by the War in Germany"

Eclogues
See *Eglogs*

Eclogues (Ronsard) 6:411

L'école des femmes (Moliere) 10:261-65, 272, 279, 281, 283, 285-88, 297, 300, 302-06, 310, 319, 335, 341; 28:228, 236, 239, 243-44, 246, 255, 261, 266-69, 275

L'école des maris (Moliere) 10:275, 277, 280-81, 283, 286-87, 291, 295, 299-300, 302-04, 310, 312, 341; 28:244, 255-56, 258, 260, 267

L'écoles des mères (Marivaux) 4:354, 365, 368

"Ecologue 1613 Dec. 26" (Donne) 24:159-61

Ecologues (Dryden) 21:119

"An Economical Project" (Franklin) 25:141

Economie Politique (Rousseau) 36:256, 264-66, 268, 275, 289, 299

Ecossaise (Voltaire) 14:338

Écrits spirituels et historiques (Marie de l'Incarnation) 10:251

Ecrits sur la grace (Pascal) 35:365, 367

"The Ecstasy" (Donne)

See "The Exstasie"

L'ecumoire; ou, Tanzai et Néadarné, histoire Japonaise (Crebillon) 1:75, 79, 81, 89-90; 28:70, 72, 81-3, 86, 92

"An Eddy" (Carew) 13:34

"An Edict by the King of Prussia" (Franklin) 25:112

"Edina, Scotia's Darling Seat!" (Burns) 40:69, 72

"Edinburgh's Salutation to the Most Honourable, My Lord Marquess of Carnarvon" (Ramsay) 29:330, 355

Edmond and Eleonora (Thomson)
See *Edward and Eleonora. A Tragedy*

"Education and Government" (Gray)
See "Essay on the Alliance of Education and Government"

The Education of a Christian Prince (Erasmus)
See *Institutio principis christiani*

The Education of the Human Race (Lessing) 8:61-2, 84, 100, 105, 107, 112

The Education of Women (Defoe) 1:148

The Education or bringinge up of Children (Elyot) 11:61

Edward and Eleonora. A Tragedy (Thomson) 16:396; 29:418-20, 422, 433; 40:274

Edward II (Cary)
See *The History of the Life, Reign, and Death of Edward II*

Edward II (Marlowe)
See *The Troublesome Raigne and Lamentable Death of Edward the Second, King of England*

Edwin and Angelina (Goldsmith) 2:74, 104

Les effets surprenants de la sympathie; ou, Les aventures de *** (Marivaux) 4:361

Les egarements du coeur et de l'esprit; ou, Memoires de Monsieur de Meilcour (Crebillon) 1:75, 79, 84, 86, 88-95; 28:70-6, 78, 80-1, 86-7, 89-93

Eglogs 8:17, 34-5

Egyptus (Marmontel) 2:213, 217

Eight Plays (Cervantes)
See *Ocho comedias y ocho entremeses nunca representados*

Eight Plays and Eight Interludes: New and Never Performed (Cervantes)
See *Ocho comedias y ocho entremeses nunca representados*

"The Eighth Discourse" (Reynolds) 15:382, 396, 403, 405

Eikon Basilike: The Portraicture of His Sacred Majestie in His Solitudes and Sufferings (Charles I) 13:130-54

Eikonoklastes (Milton) 9:161; 43:358, 363-8, 370-1, 374-5, 383, 396, 407

"Ein' feste Burg ist unser Gott" (Luther) 9:142, 151

"Elder Rock" (P'u Sung-ling) 49:309-10

La elección de los alcaldes de Daganzo (Cervantes) 23:138-40

"The Election" (Fergusson) 29:189, 203

Electricity (Marat) 10:222

"An Elegiac Epistle to a Friend" (Gay) 49:4, 7

An Elegiac Epistle to a Friend, written by Mr. Gay, When He Labored under a Dejection of Spirits*** (Gay) 49:4, 6-7

"An Elegiac Poem on the Death of George Whitefield" (Wheatley) 3:412, 415, 422, 436; 50:141, 162

"Elegiarum Liber" (Buchanan) 4:122

"Elegie I: Jealosie" (Donne) 10:66-8; 24:151, 154

"Elegie II: The Anagram" (Donne) 10:82; 24:151

"Elegie III: Change" (Donne) 10:82

"Elegie IV: The Perfume" (Donne) 10:36, 67-8, 89; 24:151, 208

"Elegie V: His Picture" (Donne) 10:67-8; 24:151, 183

"Elegie VII: `Nature's lay ideot'" (Donne) 10:55

"Elegie VIII: The Comparison" (Donne) 10:10, 82

"Elegie IX: The Autumnall" (Donne) 10:82

"Elegie 10, `Image and Dream'" (Donne) 24:152, 183

"Elegie XI: The Bracelet" (Donne) 10:4; 24:151

"Elegie XII: His parting from her" (Donne) 10:36, 67-8, 82; 24:154, 183

"Elegie XIV: A Tale of a Citizen and His Wife" (Donne) 10:39

"Elegie XV: The Expostulation" (Donne) 10:67-8

"Elegie XVI: On his mistris" (Donne) 10:36, 52, 56, 67-8, 82; 24:151, 207

"Elegie XVII: Variety" (Donne) 10:81-2

"Elegie XVII: Loves Progress" (Donne) 10:68; 24:151, 183

"Elegie XIX: Going to Bed" (Donne) 10:43, 51-2, 54, 68, 82-4, 88, 103

"Elegie XX: Loves Warr" (Donne) 10:43, 68; 24:151, 154

"Elegie à Cassandre" (Ronsard) 6:432-34

"L'Elégie à Guillaume des Autels sur le Tumulte d'Amboise" (Ronsard) 6:411

"Elegie A Ian Brinon" (Ronsard) 6:433

"Elegie A J. De La Peruse" (Ronsard) 6:433

"Elegie á Janet, peintre du Roi" (Ronsard) 6:433

"Elegie A Loïs Des Masures Tournisien" (Ronsard) 6:433, 436

"Elégie à Marie Stuart" (Ronsard) 6:426-27, 433

"Elegie A M. A. De Muret" (Ronsard) 6:433

"Elegie A Tresillustre et Reverendissime Cardinal de Chastillon" (Ronsard) 6:433

"Elegie au Seigneur L'Huillier" (Ronsard) 6:433

"Elegie du Verre à Jan Brinon" (Ronsard) 6:433

"An Elegie on the death of Mr. R. Hall, slain at Pontefract, 1648" (Vaughan) 27:369

"An Elegie on the death of Mr. R. W." (Vaughan) 27:369

"An Elegie. On the Death of Mrs. Cassandra Cotton" (Lovelace) 24:342

"An Elegie on the La: Pen: sent to my Mistresse out of France" (Carew) 13:50-1

"An Elegie On the Lady Jane Pawlet" (Jonson) 6:346-47

"Elegie Sur Le Trepas d'Antoine Chateignier" (Ronsard) 6:432-34

"Elégie (to Mary, Queen of Scots)" (Ronsard) 6:432

"Elegie Traduite du Grec d'Ergasto" (Ronsard) 6:433-34

"*An Elegie upon that Honourable and renowned Knight Sir Philip Sidney*, who was untimely slaine at the Seige of *Zutphon*, Anno1586" (Bradstreet) 4:94; 30:134

"An Elegie upon the Death of the Deane of Pauls, Dr. John Donne" (Carew) 13:19, 26, 28, 52

"Elegie upon the untimely death of the incomparable Prince Henry" (Donne) 10:4

Elegies (Donne) 10:26, 36, 46-7, 50, 54-5, 88-9, 92-3, 96, 98, 106; 24:150-51, 153, 184

Elégies (Ronsard) 6:407, 410-11

Elegies upon Sundry Occasions 8:7, 17

"Elegy" (Marvell)
See "Poem upon the Death of O. C."

"Elegy" (Rowe) 44:291

"Elegy" (Warton) **15**:461

"Elegy on Captain Matthew Henderson" (Burns) **40**:114

"Elegy on John Cowper, the Kirk-Treasurer's Man" (Ramsay) **29**:305, 320, 358, 360, 362-3

"Elegy on John Hogg the College Porter" (Fergusson) **29**:172, 211, 216, 224, 227

"An Elegy on Leaving—" (Wheatley) **50**:242-43

"Elegy on Lucky Wood" (Ramsay) **29**:305, 320, 327, 358-60

"Elegy on Maggy Johnston" (Ramsay) **29**:301, 305, 357, 360, 362

"An Elegy on Mr. Samuel Clerk Running Stationer" (Ramsay) **29**:360

"Elegy on Poor Mailie" (Burns)
    See "The Death and Dying Words of Poor Mailie"

"Elegy on Sir Henry" (Cowley) **43**:156, 167

"Elegy on Sir Henry Wotton" (Cowley) **43**:147

"Elegy on the Death of a Mad Dog" (Goldsmith) **2**:74, 109

"An Elegy on the Death of an Amiable Young Lady" (Boswell) **4**:51

"Elegy on the Death of an Auld Bawd" (Ramsay) **29**:327

"Elegy on the Death of Mr. David Gregory, Late Professor of Mathematics in the University of St. Andrew" (Fergusson) **29**:194, 205, 213, 216, 223

"Elegy on the Death of Scots Music" (Fergusson) **29**:170, 178, 189, 193, 195, 198, 205, 212, 215, 232, 237

"Elegy on the Marquis of Blanford" (Congreve) **5**:75

"Elegy on the Year 1788" (Burns) **40**:117

"Elegy to an Old Beauty" (Parnell) **3**:252-54

"Elegy to the Memory of an Unfortunate Lady" (Pope) **3**:267-68, 270, 290-91, 302-03, 305, 315-16

"An Elegy upon the Death of My Lord Francis Villiers" (Marvell) **4**:409; **43**:252

Elegy VI (Milton) **43**:379

"Elegy Written in a Country Churchyard" (Gray) **4**:283, 285, 287-92, 294, 300-05, 308-13, 315-17, 319, 321-23, 326-29, 332, 336-38, 340; **40**:198-200, 205-9, 212, 217-19, 221, 223, 226-27, 229-32, 235-46, 248-58

"The Elements" (Bradstreet)
    See "The Four Elements"

Eléments de la philosophie de Newton (Voltaire) **14**:366-67

Les éléments de littérature (Marmontel) **2**:213, 220-21, 223

Eléments de physiologie (Diderot) **26**:113-16, 132, 136, 139, 143

The Elements of Law Natural and Politic (Hobbes) **36**:127-28, 166, 171-72

Elements of Natural Philosophy (Locke) **35**:225

Elements of Philosophy (Hobbes) **36**:143

Elements of Physiology (Diderot)
    See *Eléments de physiologie*

"Elephant in the Moon" (Butler) **16**:4, 16; **43**:108, 130

De elevatione mentis ad acquirendum summum bonum (Kempis) **11**:411

"The Eleventh Discourse" (Reynolds) **15**:383, 397, 403, 416, 421

Les Elevthéromahes (Diderot) **26**:191

"Elinda's Glove" (Lovelace) **24**:303, 316, 342

"Elinoure and Juga" (Chatterton) **3**:118, 135

"The Elixir" (Herbert) **24**:214-15, 256

Den ellefte juni (Holberg) **6**:259, 273, 277

Éloge de Gournay (Turgot) **26**:374

Eloge de Richardson (Diderot) **26**:73, 105

"Eloisa to Abelard" (Pope) **3**:267-68, 271, 273, 276, 290, 296, 307, 315-16

"Eloquence" (Hume) **7**:167

"The Elysian Fields" (Franklin) **25**:141-43

Emblems (Bunyan)
    See *Divine Emblems; or, Temporal Things Spiritualized*

Los Embustes de Fabia (Vega) **23**:390

Émile, ou de l'éducation (Rousseau) **14**:220, 235, 237, 240-41, 247-48, 251-53, 260, 269, 273, 276-77, 279-84, 287-88, 291-92, 294-97, 301-02, 306, 308-10, 313-14; **36**:247-48, 250, 295

Emilia Galotti (Lessing) **8**:58-9, 61-3, 66, 68-70, 72, 85, 88, 94-5, 99, 102, 105, 107, 112, 114, 116

Emily Montague (Brooke)
    See *The History of Emily Montague*

Los empeños de una casa (Juana Ines de la Cruz) **5**:144, 150-52, 157, 159

The Emperor of the Moon (Behn) **1**:29, 37, 40; **30**:80

Emperor of the Turks (Pix)
    See *Ibrahim, the Thirteenth Emperour of the Turks*

The Empiric (Holberg) **6**:259

"Employment II" (Herbert) **24**:274, 276

"En una Noche escura" (John of the Cross) **18**:201, 224

Los encantos de la culpa (Calderon de la Barca) **23**:9

Enchiridion ethicum (More) **9**:300, 322

Enchiridion metaphysicum (More) **9**:305, 307, 325-26

Enchiridion militis christiani (Erasmus) **16**:106, 110, 135, 137-38, 149-51, 154, 162, 170-71, 179-80, 186-88, 193, 198, 203-04

Encomion musices (Luther) **9**:97

Encomium moriae (Erasmus)
    See *Moriae encomium*

Encyclopédie (Diderot) **26**:69-71, 75, 78, 81-3, 92-3, 103, 106, 112-14, 120-21, 129-32, 134-35, 138-41, 146, 149-56, 165-68, 170

End of Life (Jami)
    See *Khátimat al-hayát*

Endimion (Lyly) **41**:222, 252, 273

Endimion and Phoebe. Ideas Latmus **8**:19-21, 29, 32, 34, 36-7, 41

Los enemigos en casa (Vega) **23**:393

Los enemigos hermanos (Castro) **19**:7-8

Enesta vida todo es verdad y todo es mentira (Calderon de la Barca) **23**:12

England's Great Inerest in the Choice of this Parliament (Penn) **25**:277

Englands Heroicall Epistles **8**:7-8, 10-12, 14-16, 19, 27-8, 30-1, 33, 43, 50-1, 53-4

England's Present Interest Considered (Penn) **25**:296, 301, 332

England's Prophetical Merline (Lilly) **27**:140-41

England's Teares for the Present Wars (Howell) **13**:424

English Dictionary (Johnson)
    See *Dictionary of the English Language*

"English Epigram" (Crashaw) **24**:

English Faust-Book (Anonymous author of *Historie*)
    See *Historie of the damnable life, and deserved death of Doctor Iohn Faustus*

"English Metamorphosis" (Chatterton) **3**:119-20

"An English Padlock" (Prior) **4**:461, 464, 467

"The English Spanish Girl" (Cervantes)
    See "La Española inglesa"

English Voyages (Hakluyt)
    See *The Principal Navigations, Voyages, Traffiques and Discoveries of theEnglish Nation*

The Englishman (Steele) **18**:350, 352-53

The Englishman, 9 (Steele) **18**:349

"Ennui without Cause" (Scudery) **2**:294

"Enquiry" (Herrick)
    See "Inquiry"

An Enquiry Concerning Faith (Erasmus)
    See *Inquisitio de Fide*

Enquiry concerning Human Understanding (Hume) **7**:170, 176, 179, 183, 185, 192-93, 199

Enquiry Concerning Merit and Virtue (Diderot)
    See *Essai sur le mérite et la vertu*

Enquiry concerning the Principles of Morals (Hume) **7**:157-58, 160-61, 163, 176, 188

Enquiry into Human Nature (Hume) **7**:163

Enquiry into the Age of Oil Painting (Lessing) **8**:105

An Enquiry into the Occasional Conformity of Dissenters (Defoe) **1**:161

An Enquiry into the Present State of Polite Learning in Europe (Goldsmith) **2**:64-5, 73-4, 81, 86, 102, 104, 109-11; **48**:209-10

Les Enragés (Lesage) **28**:206, 209

"Enraptured I Gaze" (Hopkinson) **25**:250

Enseignemens moraux (Christine de Pizan) **9**:45, 48

"Enseña cómo todas las cosas avisan de la muerte" (Quevedo) **23**:198

De ente et uno (Pico della Mirandola) **15**:325, 329, 334, 338, 342, 349, 356

The Entertaining Novels of Mrs. Jane Barker (Barker) **42**:58

Entertainment (Davenant)
    See *First Day's Entertainment at Rutland House*

Entertainment (Marston) **33**:195

"Die entführte Dose" (Schlegel) **5**:277, 282

Enthusiasmus triumphatus: or, A Discourse of the Nature, Causes, Kinds, and Cure of Enthusiasme (More) **9**:310-11, 317-20

Entre Los Remedios (Las Casas) **31**:212

"Entréme" (John of the Cross) **18**:232-33

Entremeses (Cervantes)
    See *Ocho comedias y ocho entremeses nunca representados*

La entretenida (Cervantes) **6**:180-81; **23**:101-02

Entretien d'un père avec ses enfants (Diderot) **26**:119, 144, 149

Entretien entre d'Alembert et Diderot (Diderot) **26**:73, 108, 114

Entretiens des cheminées de Madrid (Lesage) **28**:200

Entretiens sur le Fils naturel (Diderot) **26**:102, 104-05, 108, 117, 119, 141

Entry into Jerusalem (N-Town) **34**:174, 192

The Entry into Jerusalem (York) **34**:374-7

"L'Envoy" (Vaughan) **27**:379, 389

"The Ephemera" (Franklin) **25**:112, 141, 143-44

Epicene (Jonson)
    See *Epicœne; or, the Silent Woman*

Epicœne; or, the Silent Woman (Jonson) **6**:291, 294-95, 297, 299, 301, 306, 310-11, 313-14, 318-20, 323-24, 329, 334-36, 341, 343-45; **33**:108, 110, 113-15, 132, 153, 158-59, 161, 165, 167, 170, 173

Title Index

"The Epicurean" (Hume) 7:153

Epigrammata (More) 10:364, 372, 374, 426, 428, 430-31

Epigrammatical Expostulations (Gay) 49:7

The Epigrammatical Petition (Gay) 49:7

Epigrammatum Sacrorum Liber (Crashaw) 24:7, 9, 23, 41-2, 52-3, 75-6

Epigrammes (More)
See *Epigrammata*

Epigrams (Jonson) 6:304, 315, 337, 347-48, 351; 33:173-74, 179

Epigrams (Kochanowski) 10:153, 167

Epilog (Wessel) 7:390

"An Epilogue for a Scoolplay" (Ramsay) 29:337

"An Epilogue Spoken to the King at the Opening of the Play-House at Oxford on Saturday Last. Being March the Nineteenth 1681" (Dryden) 21:82

"Epilogue to Earl Rivers's *Dictes*" (Caxton)
See "Epilogue to *The Dictes or Sayengs*"

"Epilogue to *Eneydos*" (Caxton) 17:11

"Epilogue to *The Book of Fame*" (Caxton) 17:11

"Epilogue to *The Consolation of Philosophy*" (Caxton) 17:11

"Epilogue to *The Dictes or Sayengs*" (Caxton) 17:6, 11

"Epilogue to *The Order of Chivalry*" (Caxton) 17:11

Epilogue to the Satires (Pope) 3:273, 318, 332-36

"Epilogue...in the Character of an Edinburgh Buck" (Fergusson) 29:214, 218, 220

"Epiphanie" (Crashaw)
See "In the Glorious Epiphany of our Lord; a hymn sung as by the Three Kings"

"Epiphany Hymn" (Crashaw)
See "In the Glorious Epiphany of our Lord; a hymn sung as by the Three Kings"

"The Epistle" (Chatterton)
See "Epistle to Catcott"

"Epistle" (Churchill)
See "An Epistle to William Hogarth"

"Epistle" (Warton) 15:450

"Epistle III" (Pope) 3:303

"Epistle IV" (Pope) 3:303

Epistle Addressed to Sir Thomas Hanmer (Collins) 40:131, 141

"The Epistle Dedicatory" (Cavendish) 30:29

"An Epistle from Lycidas to Menalcas" (Boswell) 4:51

"Epistle from Mrs. Y[onge] to Her Husband" (Montagu) 9:282

The Epistle of Othea to Hector; or, The Boke of Knyghthode (Christine de Pizan)
See *L'epitre d'Othéa*

"The Epistle of Rosamond to King Henry the Second" 8:31, 33, 52

"Epistle to a Lady" (Burns) 29:34

The Epistle to a Lady on her Fondness for Old China (Gay) 49:5, 8, 49

"An Epistle to a Lady, Who Desired the Author to Make Verses on Her, in the Heroick Style" (Swift) 1:524

"Epistle to a Young Friend" (Burns) 3:48, 86; 29:20, 29, 77, 79; 40:85, 94

"Epistle to Augustus" (Pope) 3:332

"Epistle to Blacklock" (Burns) 3:86

"Epistle to Boileau" (Prior) 4:455

Epistle to Burlington (Gay) 49:35, 159

"Epistle to Catcott" (Chatterton) 3:118, 126, 132-33

"Epistle to Colonel de Peyster" (Burns) 3:85; 40:78

"Epistle to Davie, a Brother Poet" (Burns) 40:115

"Epistle to Dr. Arbuthnot" (Pope) 3:273, 284, 286, 288, 296, 332, 334

"Epistle to Fleetwood Sheppard" (Prior) 4:465

Epistle to Germanus Brixius (More)
See *Epistola ad German. Brixium*

"Epistle to Henry Reynolds"
See "To My Most Dearely-Loved Friend Henery Reynolds Esquire, of Poets and Poesie"

"Epistle to James Smith" (Wessel)
See "Smith"

"Epistle to James Tennant of Glenconner" (Burns) 40:109

"Epistle to John Rankine, Enclosing Some Poems" (Burns) 3:67, 85, 87; 29:21, 41; 40:86, 103

"Epistle to J.R******" (Burns)
See "Epistle to John Rankine, Enclosing Some Poems"

"Epistle to J.S." (Fergusson) 29:173, 217

"Epistle to Ladie Margaret, Countess of Cumberland" (Daniel) 24:85, 114, 122

"Epistle to Lord Bathurst" (Pope) 3:273, 318

"Epistle to Lord Burlington" (Pope) 3:273, 317, 332

"An Epistle to Mistris Toppe" (Cavendish) 30:201

"Epistle to Monsieur Duhan" (Frederick the Great) 14:62

"An Epistle to Mr. Dryden" (Wycherley) 21:353

"Epistle to Mr. Jervas, With Dryden's Translation of Fresnoy's Art of Painting"(Pope) 3:315

Epistle to Paul Methuen (Gay) 49:22

"Epistle to Pulteney" (Gay) 49:126-27

"Epistle to Somerville" (Ramsay) 29:318

"Epistle to the King" (Wycherley) 8:399

"Epistle to the Ladie Lucie, Countess of Bedford" (Daniel) 24:128-30

"Epistle to the Reader" (Cavendish) 30:200

"Epistle to the Reader" (Locke) 35:236

Epistle to the Reader (More) 9:298

"Epistle to the Right Honourable Paul Metheun, Esq." (Gay) 49:27

Epistle to the Student In Astrology (Lilly) 27:143

"Epistle to the Vertuous Reader" (Lanyer)
See "To the Vertuous Reader"

"An Epistle to William Hogarth" (Churchill) 3:140, 144, 146, 148, 150, 152, 154, 157-58, 160, 163-64

"Epistle to William Simpson of Ochiltree, May 1785" (Burns) 3:48, 91, 92; 29:36, 81, 89; 40:94

"An Epistle Wrote From Mavisbank March 1748 to a Friend in Edr" (Ramsay) 29:339, 350

Epistler befattende adskillige historiske, politiske, metaphysiske, moralske, philosophiske, item skjemtsomme materier... (Holberg) 6:266, 273, 278

"The Epistles" (Burns) 3:53, 72, 77, 84, 87, 93; 29:9, 20, 32-3, 36, 38, 78-80, 91; 40:85-6

Epistles
See *Englands Heroicall Epistles*

Epistles (Daniel) 24:130-31

Epistles (Ficino) 12:165

Epistles (Holberg)
See *Epistler befattende adskillige historiske, politiske, metaphysiske, moralske, philosophiske, item skjemtsomme materier...*

Epistles and Defense of Ryme (Daniel) 24:130

Epistles for the Ladies (Haywood) 1:286

Epistles to Mr. Pope (Young) 3:486, 490

"Epistles to Several Persons" (Pope) 3:273

Epistolæ Obscurorum Vivorum (Hutten)
See *Literæ obscurorum Vivorum*

Epistola ad German. Brixium (More) 10:364, 431

Epistola contra J. Pomeranum (More)
See *Epistola in qua...respondet literis Pomerani*

Epistola de felicitate (Ficino) 12:168

Epistola de tolerantia ad clarissimum virum T.A.R.P.T.O.L.A. scripta à P.A.P.O.I.L.A. (Locke) 7:261

Epistola in qua...respondet literis Pomerani (More) 10:365, 369

Epistolae Ho-Elianae: Familiar Letters Domestic and Forren (Howell) 13:415-27, 430-34, 436, 441-46

Epistolario Completo (Quevedo) 23:190

Épistre II: À M. de l'Abbé des Roches (Boileau-Despreaux) 3:39

Épistre V: À M. de Guilleragues (Boileau-Despreaux) 3:22

Épistre VI: À M. de Lamoignon, avocat general (Boileau-Despreaux) 3:22

Épistre VII: À M. Racine (Boileau-Despreaux) 3:19, 21

Épistre IX: À M. le Marquis de Seignelay (Boileau-Despreaux) 3:39

L'epistre au dieu d'amours (Christine de Pizan) 9:25, 27-8, 38

Épistres (Boileau-Despreaux) 3:38-9, 42

"Epistulae Obscurorum Virorum" (Buchanan) 4:123

"Epitaph" (Crashaw)
See "Epitaph upon the Death of Mr. Ashton, a conformable citizen"

"An Epitaph" (Prior)
See "Epitaph on Sauntering Jack and Idle Joan"

"Epitaph" (Raleigh) 39:123

Epitaph (Marvell) 43:283, 285

"Epitaph on a Scolding Wife by her Husband" (Franklin) 25:157

"Epitaph on Habbie Simson" (Fergusson) 29:203

"Epitaph on Lady Mary Villiers" (Carew) 13:8

"Epitaph on Miss Elizabeth Stanley" (Thomson) 16:428

"Epitaph on Mr. John Lloyd" (Philips) 30:278

"Epitaph on Robert Canynge" (Chatterton) 3:119

"Epitaph on Salathiel Pavy" (Jonson)
See "Epitaph on Salomon Pavy"

"Epitaph on Salomon Pavy" (Jonson) 6:326, 347

"Epitaph on Sauntering Jack and Idle Joan" (Prior) 4:456, 461-62, 470

"Epitaph on the Lady S. Wife to Sir W.S." (Carew) 13:52, 58

"Epitaph on the Marchioness of Winchester" (Milton) 9:205

"An Epitaph upon a Child" (Herrick) 13:341

"Epitaph upon Husband and Wife, who died and were buried together" (Crashaw) 24:9

"An Epitaph upon Lady Elizabeth" (Vaughan) 27

"Epitaph upon the Death of Mr. Ashton, a conformable citizen" (Crashaw) 24:4, 16, 20

"Epitaphe de Loyse de Mailly" (Ronsard) 6:436

Epitaphium Damonis (Milton) 43:360

Epithalamia (Donne) 24:155, 161

"Epithalamie on Sir Clipseby Crew and His Lady" (Herrick)
See "A Nuptiall Song, or Epithalamie on Sir Clipseby Crew and His Lady"

"Epithalamion" (Herrick)
See "A Nuptiall Song, or Epithalamie on Sir Clipseby Crew and His Lady"

"Epithalamion" (Spenser) 5:307, 311, 313-15, 329, 332, 347-49, 355-56, 364; 39:321

"Epithalamion at the Marriage of the Earl of Somerset" (Donne) 24:183

"Epithalamion made at Lincolnes Inne" (Donne) **10**:97
"An Epithalamion, or mariage song on the Lady Elizabeth, and Count Palatinebeing married on St. Valentines day" (Donne) **10**:9, 40, 55
"Epithalamium" (Buchanan) **4**:122
"Epithalamium" (Crashaw) **24**:46, 61
"Epithalamium" (Donne) **24**:161
Epitome of Copernican Astronomy (Book 4) (Kepler) **45**:322, 331, 357, 360-62
Épître XII (On Love for God) (Boileau-Despreaux) **3**:38
Epitre à Uranie (Voltaire) **14**:369
"Epître aux muses" (Rousseau) **9**:346
L'epitre d'Othéa (Christine de Pizan) **9**:30-1, 37, 48
"An Epode" (Jonson) **33**:174
L'epreuve (Marivaux) **4**:358, 364, 369, 371-72
"Equité des Vieux Gaulois" (Ronsard) **6**:410
Erasmus Montanus (Holberg) **6**:269, 272, 274-77, 283-85
"Êrh-lang Sou-shan-t'u Ko" (Wu Ch'eng-en) **7**:397
Eriphyle (Voltaire) **14**:397
Der erste Beernhäuter (Grimmelshausen) **6**:247
Eruditissimi viri Guilielmi Rossei opus elegans (More) **10**:365, 369, 409; **32**:331, 332
Die Erzbetrugerin und Landstortzerin Courasche (Grimmelshausen) **6**:238, 249, 251-52
"La Española inglesa" (Cervantes) **6**:171; **23**:95, 99
"Espiración" (Quevedo) **23**:178
L'Esprit (Helvetius)
   See *De l'esprit*
L'esprit des moeurs (Voltaire) **14**:328
Esprit du clergé (Holbach) **14**:153
Esprit du judaïsme (Holbach) **14**:154
"L'esprit fort" (Perrault) **2**:253
Essai sur la poésie épique (Voltaire)
   See *Essay upon the Epic Poetry of the European Nations from Homer down to Milton*
Essai sur la Vie de Sénèque (Diderot) **26**:74, 119
Essai sur le goût (Marmontel) **2**:214, 222
Essai sur le mérite et la vertu (Diderot) **26**:117, 119
Essai sur les causes qui peuvent affecter les esprits et les caractères (Montesquieu) **7**:348, 358
Essai sur les moeurs (Voltaire) **14**:334, 353, 358, 364, 380, 383-88, 395, 402
Essai sur les préjugés (Holbach) **14**:152, 154, 168
Essai sur les révolutions de la musique en France (Marmontel) **2**:222
Essai sur les romans (Marmontel) **2**:213, 215, 220
Essai sur l'histoire générale et sur les moeurs et l'esprit des nations (Voltaire) **14**:411
Essai sur l'origine des connaissances humaines (Condillac) **26**:5-6, 8-11, 13-14, 23, 25, 27, 29-31, 40-1, 44, 47-8, 50-6, 59
Essai sur l'origine des connoissances humaines (Condillac)
   See *Essai sur l'origine des connaissances humaines*
Essai sur l'origine des langues (Rousseau) **14**:292, 294-95
Les essais de Messire Michel Seigneur de Montaigne (Montaigne) **8**:189, 191-94, 196-97, 199, 201-06, 210, 212-14, 216-20, 223, 225, 229-31, 233-42, 244, 247
Essais de Theodicee (Leibniz) **35**:130, 142, 148, 164, 166-67, 171-72, 175
Essais sur la peinture (Diderot) **26**:69, 120, 124-25, 127, 163
Essais sur le règnes de Claude et de Néron (Diderot) **26**:119
"Essay" (Prior)
   See "Essay upon Opinion"
An Essay concerning Human Understanding (Locke) **7**:236, 238-39, 244, 246-48, 251, 253, 255-56, 258, 266, 269, 271-72, 281, 284-91, 296; **35**:197-267
An Essay concerning the True Original, Extent, and End of Civil Government (Locke) **7**:273
An Essay for the Recording of Illustrious Providences Illustrious Providences (Mather)
   See *Remarkable Providences*
An Essay for the Understanding of St. Paul's Epistles by Consulting St. Paul Himself (Locke) **7**:282-83
Essay of Dramatic Poesy (Dryden)
   See *Of Dramatick Poesie: An Essay*
"Essay of Heroic Plays" (Dryden)
   See "Of Heroic Plays"
"An Essay of Heroic Plays" (Dryden) **3**:236
Essay on Comedy (Farquhar)
   See *Discourse Upon Comedy*
Essay on Conversation (Fielding) **1**:234; **46**:74
"An Essay on Criticism" (Pope) **3**:263-64, 267-70, 273, 275-76, 291, 295, 307, 313, 322, 324-28, 337
Essay on Dramatic Discourse Concerning Satire (Dryden) **21**:111-12, 115
"Essay on Homer" (Parnell) **3**:253
"Essay on Learning" (Prior)
   See "Essay upon Learning"
Essay on Lyric Poetry (Young) **40**:333
An Essay on Man (Pope) **3**:269, 272-73, 276, 279, 287-89, 291, 297, 300, 304, 306-07, 313, 315-16, 318-19, 326, 334, 337
An Essay on publick Spirit (Dennis)
   See *An Essay upon Public Spirit; being a Satire in Prose upon the Manners and Luxury of the Times, the chief Sources of our present Parties and Divisions*
"Essay on the Alliance of Education and Government" (Gray) **40**:198, 228-29
"Essay on the Different Styles of Poetry" (Parnell) **3**:255
An Essay on the External Use of Water (Smollett) **46**:189
An Essay on the Genius of Shakespear (Dennis) **11**:16, 19, 21, 30, 32, 38-9
"Essay on the Georgics" (Addison) **18**:20
An Essay on the Human Soul (Marat) **10**:231
"Essay on the Imagination" (Addison) **18**:58, 62
Essay on the Knowledge of the Character of Men (Fielding) **46**:63, 88, 91, 153, 155
Essay on the Knowledge of the Characters of Men (Moritz) **1**:234
An Essay on the Navy (Dennis) **11**:19
An Essay on the Operas, after the Italian manner, which are about to be established on the English Stage: with some Reflections on the Damage which they may bring to the Public (Dennis) **11**:15, 19, 26
Essay on the Origin of Human Knowledge (Condillac)
   See *Essai sur l'origine des connaissances humaines*
Essay on the Origin of Knowledge (Condillac)
   See *Essai sur l'origine des connaissances humaines*
Essay on the Prejudices and the Influence of Opinions on Customs and the Happiness of Mankind (Holbach)
   See *Essai sur les préjugés*
"Essay on the Real Secret of the Freemasons" (Cleland) **2**:53
Essay on the Sublime and Beautiful (Burke)
   See *A Philosophical Enquiry into the Origin of Our Ideas of the Sublime and Beautiful*
An Essay on the Theatre; or A Comparison Between Laughing and Sentimental Comedy (Goldsmith) **2**:126
An Essay towards an Abridgement of the English History (Burke) **7**:49
An Essay Towards the Present and Future Peace of Europe By the Establishment of an European Dyet, Parliament, or Estates (Penn) **25**:302-03, 342, 346
"An Essay upon Acting" (Garrick) **15**:122
Essay upon Human Understanding (Condillac)
   See *Essai sur l'origine des connaissances humaines*
"Essay upon Learning" (Prior) **4**:465, 467, 474
"Essay upon Opinion" (Prior) **4**:467-71
An Essay upon Projects (Defoe) **1**:160
An Essay upon Public Spirit; being a Satire in Prose upon the Manners and Luxury of the Times, the chief Sources of our present Parties and Divisions (Dennis) **11**:8-9, 15, 17, 19, 26
Essay upon the Civil Wars of France (Voltaire) **14**:382
Essay upon the Epic Poetry of the European Nations from Homer down to Milton (Voltaire) **14**:349-50, 352
Essayes in Divinity (Donne) **10**:40, 76-7, 83
Essays (Bacon) **18**:104, 108, 110, 114-15, 116, 118, 123-24, 128, 132-34, 136-37, 141-42, 146, 149, 178-79, 183, 187, 192; **32**:118, 136, 183
Essays (Hume) **7**:145, 167
Essays (Montagu)
   See *The Nonsense of Common-Sense*
Essays (Montaigne)
   See *Les essais de Messire Michel Seigneur de Montaigne*
Essays and Poems and Simplicity, a Comedy (Montagu) **9**:271, 276, 279
Essays and Treatises on Several Subjects (Hume) **7**:153
Essays, Moral and Political (Hume) **7**:152, 189
Essays Moral, Political, and Literary (Hume) **7**:163
Essays on Painting (Diderot)
   See *Essais sur la peinture*
Essays on the Law of Nature (Locke) **35**:209, 229
Essays to do Good (Mather)
   See *Bonifacius*
Essays upon Several Moral Subjects (Collier) **6**:200, 227
Essays upon Wit (Addison) **18**:7, 18, 60
Esther (Andreae) **32**:101
Esther (Racine) **28**:295-97, 313, 315, 344, 346, 349, 351-53, 355-56, 358, 371-72, 381-82, 384
Est-il bon? Est-il méchant? (Diderot) **26**:103, 110, 117, 119, 137, 143
La Estrelle (Vega) **23**:343, 350, 402-03
"Etenim res Creatae exerto Capite observantes expectant revelationem filiorum Dei" (Vaughan) **27**:306
"Eternity" (Herrick) **13**:334, 358

Eternity (Smart)
  See *On the Eternity of the Supreme Being*
"Etesia absent" (Vaughan) **27**:362
"The Ethereal Rock" (P'u Sung-ling)
  See "Shi Qingxu"
Ethic (Spinoza)
  See *Ethic ordine geometrico demonstrata*
Ethic ordine geometrico demonstrata (Spinoza)
  9:397-99, 402-04, 408, 415-17, 419-26, 428,
  431-36, 438-39, 441-42, 444-47
"Ethick Epistles" (Pope)
  See "Epistles to Several Persons"
Ethics (Leibniz) **35**:132
Ethocratie (Holbach) **14**:152, 155-56, 160, 174
"Eton" (Gray)
  See "Ode on a Distant Prospect of Eton Col-
  lege"
"Eton College Ode" (Gray)
  See "Ode on a Distant Prospect of Eton Col-
  lege"
L'étourdi (Moliere) **10**:260, 275-77, 280, 283,
  286-87, 293, 309-10; **28**:255-58, 260-61,
  265-67
Les Etrennes (Lesage)
  See *Turcaret*
Eugenia and Adelaide (Sheridan) **7**:371, 378
Euphues and His England (Lyly) **41**:222, 240-
  42, 247, 249, 253, 255-56, 262, 264, 271,
  275, 278-81, 291
Euphues and his Ephoebus (Lyly) **41**:239
Euphues' Golden Legacy bequeathed to Philastus'
  Son (Lodge)
  See *Rosalynde*
"Euphues his censure to Philantus" **41**:141, 148
Euphues' Shadow, the Battaile of the Sences
  (Lodge) **41**:194-95, 199, 203-04
Euphues. The Anatomy of Wit (Lyly) **41**:218-24,
  226-34, 235-43 243-46, 247, 249, 252-56,
  259-65, 265-74, 274-83, 289-09
Eurydice Hiss'd (Fielding) **1**:220; **46**:166
Euvres de Descartes (Descartes) **35**:109
Evaai (Haywood) **44**:130
"Even now that Care which on thy Crown attends"
  (Sidney) **19**:293-94, 296, 299, 309-10;
  39:162
"Even Song" (Herbert) **24**:246, 271, 274
"Evening" (Parnell)
  See "A Hymn for Evening"
"Evening" (Wheatley)
  See "An Hymn to the Evening"
"An Evening Prayer" (Swift) **1**:488
"An Evening Walk in the Abbey-Church of
  Holyroodhouse" (Boswell) **4**:50, 60
An Evening's Love; or, The Mock-Astrologer
  (Dryden) **3**:177, 179, 230, 236, 238
"Evensong" (Herrick) **13**:386
The Evergreen (Ramsay) **29**:301-02, 305, 308,
  310, 316, 321-2, 324-7, 330-32
Every Man in his Humour (Jonson) **6**:297, 300-
  01, 305-06, 310-12, 320-21, 323, 336, 342;
  33:103-5, 132-3, 142, 144-45, 147, 149, 151,
  158, 160-61, 167, 173
Every Man out of His Humour (Jonson) **6**:297,
  301, 3C3, 306, 335, 339, 344; **33**:126, 132,
  139-48, 150-51, 154-56, 158, 160-61, 164,
  166, 173-74
"Eve's Apologie in defence of Women" (Lanyer)
  30:253, 262, 264-65
"An Evill Spirit Your Beautie Haunts Me Still"
  8:27
Ex Libro de Numphis, Sylvanus, Pygmæs,
  Salamandris et Gigantibus (Paracelsus)
  14:189

Examen des prophéties (Holbach) **14**:153-54
Examen important de Milord Bolingbroke
  (Voltaire) **14**:370
Examen Poeticum (Dryden) **21**:119
Examens (Corneille) **28**:5, 38
Examination (Franklin) **25**:125
An Examination Concerning Faith (Erasmus)
  See *Inquisitio de Fide*
An Examination of Dr. Woodward's Account of
  the Deluge, & c. (Arbuthnot) **1**:15
Example of Vertu (Hawes)
  See *Example of Virtue*
Example of Virtue (Hawes) **17**:344-54, 362-63,
  365
"The Excellency of Christ" (Edwards) **7**:120, 122-
  23
"An Excellente Balade of Charitie as wroten bie
  the gode Prieste Thomas Rowley, 1464"
  (Chatterton) **3**:123-24, 127, 135
Exclamations (Teresa de Jesus) **18**:392
The Excursion (Brooke) **6**:107-08, 110-11, 115,
  117, 119, 121-22; **48**:53-54, 61, 112-120
"Execration upon Vulcan" (Jonson) **33**:175
Exemplary Novels (Cervantes)
  See *Novelas exemplares*
Exemplary Stories (Cervantes)
  See *Novelas exemplares*
Exemplary Tales (Cervantes)
  See *Novelas exemplares*
Exercitia spiritualia (Kempis) **11**:411
"The Exhibition" (Chatterton) **3**:126, 132
"Exhorta a Lisi efectos semejantes de la vibora"
  (Quevedo) **23**:196
Exhortation for all Christians Warming Them
  Against Insurrection and Rebillion (Luther)
  37:263, 303
Exhortation to Emperor Charles V (Hutten)
  16:234
Exhortation to Penitence (Machiavelli) **36**:223
Exhortation to the German Princes to Undertake
  War against the Turks (Hutten) **16**:235
Exhortatorium (Hutten)
  See *Ad Caesarem Maximilianum ut bellum in*
  Venetos coeptum prosequatur exhortatorium
Exilius; or, the Banish'd Roman (Barker) **42**:61-
  3, 65-6, 68-9, 77-9
"Existence" (Turgot) **26**:350, 355-56, 357, 381
Exodus (Towneley) **34**:250
"Exorcising Against Jealousy" (P'u Sung-ling)
  3:346
"Exorcism, or The Spectater" (Erasmus) **16**:194-
  95
"Expansibilitie" (Turgot) **26**:356
The Expedition of Humphry Clinker (Smollett)
  2:319-20, 322-26, 329-30, 332, 336-37, 341-
  44, 347-51, 353, 357, 359, 362-66; **46**:190-
  93, 195, 197-200, 204, 224-33, 235, 237,
  252, 260-69, 277-88
"An Expedition to Fife and the Island of May"
  (Fergusson) **29**:231
"The Experience" (Taylor) **11**:359, 363, 384, 389,
  396
"Experience" (Winthrop) **31**:342, 352
Experiences nouvelles touchant le vide (Pascal)
  35:389
Experimental Philosophy (Campanella)
  See *Philosophia sensibus demonstrata*
Experiments and Observations on Electricity,
  Made at Philadelphia (Franklin) **25**:111
"The Expiration" (Donne) **10**:36; **24**:150
Explanation of the Christian Faith (Zwingli)
  37:352, 356, 391
An Explanation of the San-kuo-chih, Done in the

Popular Style (Lo Kuan-chung)
  See *San-kuo-chih yeni-i*
Explanation on the New System (Leibniz) **35**:166
Explanations of the 95 Theses (Luther)
  See *Resolutiones disputationum de*
  indulgentiarum
Explicatio triginita sigillorum (Bruno) **27**:94, 100
The Exploits of Garcilaso de la Vega and the Moor
  Tarfe (Vega)
  See *Los hechos de Garcilaso de la Vega y Moro*
  Tarfe
Expositio passionis Christi (More)
  See *Expositio passionis Domini*
Expositio passionis Domini (More) **10**:365, 413-
  14
Exposition des origines des connaissances
  humaines (Condillac)
  See *Essai sur l'origine des connaissances*
  humaines
An Exposition of the Faith (Zwingli)
  See *Explanation of the Christian Faith*
Expostulatio (Hutten) **16**:232, 234-35
Expostulation (Agrippa von Nettesheim) **27**:13
"An Expostulation with Inigo Jones" (Jonson)
  6:350
Expulsion from the Garden (York) **34**:359
The Expulsion of the Triumphant Beast (Bruno)
  See *Lo spaccio de la bestia trionfante*
"The Exstasie" (Donne) **10**:13, 18, 26, 33, 35-6,
  46, 51-2, 55, 81-2, 85, 87, 103; **24**:154, 162,
  194-97
"The Exstasy: A Pindarique Ode to Her Majesty
  the Queen" (Aubin) **9**:4
"Extemporaneous Effusion on Being Appointed
  to the Excise" (Burns) **6**:89; **29**:47
"Extempore-to Mr. Gavin Hamilton" (Burns)
  40:87-8
Extraccio Animarum (Towneley) **34**:251, 291,
  308
Extrait des sentiments de Jean Meslier (Voltaire)
  14:370
"Eyes and Tears" (Marvell) **4**:397, 403, 439
Eyn Sermon von Ablass und Gnade (Luther) **9**:91,
  146
"Fable 14" (Gay) **49**:186
"Fable No. 50" (Gay)
  See "The Hare and Many Friends"
"Fable of the Cock and the Fox" (Chaucer)
  See "Nun's Priest's Tale"
Fable XVIII (Gay) **49**:79
Fables (Gay) **49**:10-11, 13, 16, 18, 21, 26, 28,
  49, 71, 78, 172, 178, 183, 186-188
Fables Ancient and Modern; Translated into
  Verse, from Homer, Ovid, Boccace, &
  Chaucer (Dryden) **3**:184, 187, 190, 204-
  05, 216, 221, 237-38, 242-43; **21**:118-19
Fables choisies (La Fontaine) **50**:60, 66-67, 71,
  77, 79, 82, 85-96, 100, 104-106, 122-126,
  128-129, 132
Fables II (Gay) **49**:147
Les fâcheux (Moliere) **10**:275, 277, 281, 283,
  291, 299, 302, 310; **28**:255, 257, 267
The Faerie Queene, Disposed into Twelve Bookes
  Fashioning XII Morall Vertues (Spenser)
  5:295, 297, 299-302, 304-05, 307-25, 328,
  331, 333-37, 341-42, 349, 355-56, 360, 364-
  66; **39**:303-14, 317, 320-29, 329-42, 342-47,
  351-53, 354-62, 373-87, 388-95
The Fair Captive (Haywood) **44**:150
"Fair copy of my Celia's face" (Carew) **13**:20
"Fair Daffodils" (Herrick)
  See "To Daffadills"
The Fair Favorite (Davenant) **13**:175, 181-82,

196
"The Fair Hypocrite" (Manley) **1**:306, 308
The Fair Jilt; or, The History of Prince Tarquin and Miranda (Behn) **1**:30-1, 42-3, 46, 49-53, 55; **30**:87, 89; **42**:109, 117, 136, 145-46
The Fair Penitent (Rowe) **8**:285, 287, 291-300, 302-05, 307, 312-14, 316-17
A Fair Quarrel (Middleton) **33**:264, 270, 276, 280, 282, 321, 323-26
"Fair Recluse" (Smart) **3**:399
"The Fair Singer" (Marvell) **4**:403, 409, 436
The Fair Vow-Breaker (Behn)
  See *The History of the Nun; or, The Fair Vow-Breaker*
"The Faire Begger" (Lovelace) **24**:306-07
"The Fairie Temple: or, Oberons Chappell. Dedicated to Mr. John Merrifield, Counsellor at Law" (Herrick) **13**:351, 372-73
"The Fairies" (Perrault)
  See "Les Fées"
The Fairies (Garrick) **15**:95-6, 128
"The Fairy Feast" (Parnell) **3**:255
"A Fairy Tale in the Ancient English Style" (Parnell) **3**:251, 254, 256-57
"Faith" (Herbert) **24**:259, 268
"Faith" (Vaughan) **27**:383
Faith Encouraged (Mather) **38**:229
A Faithful Account of the Discipline Professed and Practised in the Churches of New England (Mather)
  See *Ratio Disciplinae*
Faithful Admonition to the Professors of God's Truth in England (Knox) **37**:200-01
A Faithful Narrative of the Surprizing Work of God in the Conversion of Many Hundred Souls in Northampton, and the Neighboring Towns and Villages (Edwards) **7**:101, 118
Faithful Shepard (Calderon de la Barca) **23**:63
The Faithful Shepherdess (Fletcher) **33**:45, 53, 63-71, 75-6, 78, 81-83, 91
The Faithful Wife (Marivaux)
  See *The Faithful Wife*
"The Falcon" (Lovelace) **24**:302, 315, 330, 336-40, 346, 348
Fall of Lucifer (Chester) **34**:105-6, 123, 126, 128-9, 131-5
Fall of Man (Chester)
  See *Creation and Fall* (Chester)
Fall of Man (York)
  See *Man's Disobedience and Fall* (York)
Fall of the Angels (Chester) **34**:138
The False Alarm (Johnson) **15**:202, 208
False Confidences (Marivaux)
  See *False Confidences*
The False Count; or, A New Way to Play an Old Game (Behn) **1**:34, 37; **30**:81
The False Friend (Vanbrugh) **21**:295, 319
The False Friend; or, The Fate of Disobedience (Pix) **8**:259, 261-63, 268-70, 272, 276, 278
The False Friend' or, The Treacherous Portuguese (Davys)
  See *The Cousins*
"False Knight" (Erasmus) **16**:114
The False Maid (Marivaux)
  See *The False Maid*
De falso credita et ementita Donatione Constatini Magni (Hutten) **16**:212, 224, 231, 234, 245
Fama Fraternitatis (Andreae) **32**:22, 67, 71, 85, 87
"The Fame Machine" (Goldsmith)
  See "A Reverie"
La famiglia dell' antiquario (Goldoni) **4**:250, 260, 266

Familiar Letters (Howell)
  See *Epistolae Ho-Elianae: Familiar Letters Domestic and Forren*
Familiar Letters between the Principal Characters in "David Simple" (Fielding) **1**:270-73; **44**:68, 72-3, 100
Familiar Letters betwixt a Gentleman and a Lady (Davys) **1**:101-02; **46**:19-20, 23-8, 33-7
Familiar Letters on Important Occasions (Richardson) **1**:398, 416-17; **44**:229-31, 234-5, 244-5, 248
"Familier" (Marmontel) **2**:221
Familiorum Colloquiorum (Erasmus) **16**:113-14, 116-17, 121-24, 128, 132, 139-40, 142-43, 146, 152, 154-57, 162, 174, 176, 192-95
The Family Instructor (Defoe) **1**:122, 170, 176; **42**:177, 184, 201-02, 205
Family Memoirs (Guicciardini) **49**:215-15
The Family of Love (Middleton) **33**:262, 275, 277, 310
Family Religion Excited (Mather) **38**:167
"A Famous Prediction of Merlin" (Swift) **1**:516-17
The Famous Tragedy of the Rich Jew of Malta (Marlowe) **22**:328,331,335-36, 339, 347-48, 361-64, 366, 370-72, 378; **47**:252, 254, 275, 284, 341, 365
The Fan (Gay) **49**:33, 60, 65, 69, 141, 152
The Fan (Goldoni)
  See *Il ventaglio*
"A Fanatic" (Butler)
  See "A (Puritan) Fanatic"
"Fanatic" (Butler) **16**:52-3
"A Fancy" (Carew) **13**:63
Fanny Hill (Cleland)
  See *Memoirs of a Woman of Pleasure*
"Fanscombe Barn" (Winchilsea) **3**:443, 452, 457
"Fantastic" (Butler) **16**:51
Fantomina; or, Love in a Maze (Haywood) **44**:145, 152-3
"The Farewell" (Churchill) **3**:151-52, 155-56, 163
Farewell Address (Washington) **25**:363, 365, 367-68, 378-86, 388, 393, 397-98
"A Farewell to America" (Wheatley) **3**:416
"Farewell to Eliza" (Burns)
  See "From Thee Eliza"
"Farewell to Follie" **41**:148, 177
"Farewell to Lochaber" (Ramsay) **29**:309
"Farewell to love" (Donne) **10**:82
"Farewell to Nancy" (Burns) **3**:65
"Farewell to Poetry" (Herrick) **13**:328, 342, 365, 392
"A Farewell to Poetry, with a Long Digression on Anatomy" (Barker) **42**:96
"An Farewell to Poetry, with a Long digression on Anatomy" (Barker) **42**:96, 98-9
"Farewell to the Court" (Raleigh) **31**:269-71
"A Farewel-Sermon Preached at the First Precinct in Northampton after the Peoples' Publick Rejection of Their Minister" (Edwards) **7**:118
"The Farmer's Ingle" (Fergusson) **29**:170, 173, 176, 179, 180-81, 189, 192, 194-95, 207, 209, 218, 235, 237, 239
The Farmer's Letters to the Protestants of Ireland (Brooke) **1**:62
The Farmer's Return from London (Garrick) **15**:100
"Farmer's Salutation to his Old Mare" (Burns) **40**:65
The Farrier (Aretino)
  See *Marescalco*

The Farther Adventures of Robinson Crusoe (Defoe) **42**:177, 192-98, 205, 207, 228-29, 233
A Farther Vindication of the Short View (Collier) **6**:229-30
"Farwell Frost, or Welcome the Spring" (Herrick) **13**:354, 396
"Fashion. A Poem" (Fergusson) **29**:198, 230
Fatal Friendship (Trotter) **8**:352, 355, 357, 360, 363, 368-69, 371-74
The Fatal Secret; or, Constancy in Distress (Haywood) **1**:285; **44**:145, 149, 152-3
"The Fatal Sisters. An Ode (From the Norse Tongue) in the Orcades of Thormodus Torfaeus . . . and also in Bartholinus" (Gray) **4**:312, 317-18; **40**:199-200, 231, 243
Father Abraham's Speech at an Auction (Franklin)
  See *The Way to Wealth*
Fatihat al-shabáb (Jami) **9**:65, 68
"Le Faucon" (La Fontaine) **50**:69
La fausse suivante (Marivaux) **4**:363, 377
Les fausses confidences (Marivaux) **4**:354, 358, 360, 365, 368, 371-72
Faust (Lessing) **8**:71, 111-12
Faust-Buch (Anonymous author of *Historia*)
  See *Historia von D. Johann Fausten*
Favola: Belfagor arcidiavolo che prese moglie (Machiavelli) **8**:126, 128, 137, 178
"The Favour" (Vaughan) **27**:325, 340
The Fawne (Marston)
  See *Parasitaster; or, The Fawn*
Fayerie Court
  See *Nimphidia, the Court of Fayrie*
"The Feast" (Vaughan) **27**:338, 341, 379
the Feast Over Dust (Bruno)
  See *La cena de le ceneri*
"A Feaver" (Donne) **10**:13, 26-7, 36, 52, 82; **24**:154
Febris II (Hutten) **16**:230, 232, 241-42, 246
Febris Prima (Hutten) **16**:230, 232-33, 246
"February" (Chatterton) **3**:131
"Les Fées" (Perrault) **2**:254, 260, 280
The Feigned Courtesans; or, A Night's Intrigue (Behn) **1**:33-4, 37, 39; **30**:71, 78, 80, 82; **42**:150
Félicie (Marivaux) **4**:369
La félicité des temps; ou, Eloge de la France (Voltaire) **14**:380
"Felix's Behaviour towards Paul" (Sterne) **2**:430
The Female Academy (Cavendish) **30**:227-8
"Female Glory" (Lovelace) **24**:302
The Female Officer (Brooke) **1**:63
"The Female Phaeton" (Prior) **4**:460
The Female Reader (Wollstonecraft) **5**:460
The Female Spectator (Haywood) **1**:286, 288-89, 300-02; **44**:129-32, 136-7, 144, 150-1, 167, 169, 172
The Female Tatler (Manley) **1**:310
"La femme comme il y en a peu" (Marmontel) **2**:212
La femme fidèle (Marivaux) **4**:369
"La Femme noyee" (La Fontaine) **50**:85
Les femmes savantes (Moliere) **10**:268, 272-73, 275, 277, 282-83, 287-88, 291, 293-99, 305, 313, 320-21, 338; **28**:248-50, 252, 256-61, 267, 269-70, 274-75
Le femmine puntigliose (Goldoni) **4**:258-59, 265
"Fên-chou hu" (P'u Sung-ling) **49**:298
"Fêng hsien" (P'u Sung-ling) **49**:300
"Fêng San-niang" (P'u Sung-ling) **49**:300
Las Ferias de Madrid (Vega) **23**:390-93
"Le Fermier, le Chien, et le Renard" (La Fontaine) **50**:81

Fernan Gonzalez (Vega) **23**:348

"Feronde, ou le purgatoire" (La Fontaine) **50**:116, 120

le Festin de Pierre (Moliere)
See *le Festin de Pierre*

"A Fever" (Donne)
See "A Feaver"

Fever the First (Hutten)
See *Febris Prima*

Fever the Second (Hutten)
See *Febris II*

A Few Sighs from Hell; or, The Groans of a Damned Soul (Bunyan) **4**:172, 175

"La Fiancee du roi de Garbe" (La Fontaine) **50**:68

"FIDA: or the Country-beauty" (Vaughan) **27**:360

Fidei Christianae Expositio (Zwingli)
See *Explanation of the Christian Faith*

De fideli dispensatore (Kempis) **11**:411

Fiendly Exposition (Zwingli)
See *Explanation of the Christian Faith*

Fifteen Discourses (Reynolds)
See *Discourses on Art*

"The Fifteenth Discourse" (Reynolds) **15**:365, 398, 404-05

"The Fifth Discourse" (Reynolds) **15**:380, 394, 403

"A Fifth-Monarchy Man" (Butler) **16**:27, 54

La figlia obbediente (Goldoni) **4**:260-61

"Le filets de Vulcain" (Rousseau) **9**:343

"La Fille" (La Fontaine) **50**:98-101, 103-104

Le Fils naturel (Diderot) **26**:69, 104, 110, 117, 148-49, 150

"Filum Labyrinthi sive Formula Inquisitionis" (Bacon) **18**:148, 187

Fimmtíu passíusálmar (Petursson) **8**:251-54

Fingal (Macpherson) **29**:242-3, 245-50, 252, 254-59, 263, 265, 270, 272, 279-80, 290, 292, 296-99

"Finjamos que soy feliz" (Juana Ines de la Cruz) **5**:155

The First American Composer. Six Songs by Francis Hopkinson (Hopkinson) **25**:250

The First and Second Anniversaries (Donne)
See *The Anniversaries*

The First and Second Isaac (Calderon de la Barca) **23**:9

The First Anniversarie. An Anatomie of the World. Wherein By Occasion of the untimely death of Mistris Elizabeth Drury, the frailtie and decay of this whole World is represented (Donne) **10**:4, 44, 64, 74-7, 83, 89-90, 98; **24**:165, 182-87

"The First Anniversary of the Government Under His Highness the Lord Protector" (Marvell)
See "The First Anniversary of the Government under O. C."

"The First Anniversary of the Government under O. C." (Marvell) **4**:398, 417, 429-31; **43**:252-4, 256-8, 260-1, 263, 268, 277-8, 280-1, 283-7, 289, 290, 295, 318, 325

First Blast of the Trumpet against the Monstrous Regiment of Women (Knox) **37**:192-98, 199, 202-03, 212, 218-22, 225, 227, 232, 235, 237-39

"The First Book Concerning the Language of the Prophets" (Newton) **35**:326

First Book of Discipline (Knox) **37**:199, 204

"First Book of the American Chronicle" (Hopkinson) **25**:249

First Day's Entertainment at Rutland House (Davenant) **13**:194-95

First Decennale (Machiavelli) **36**:232

First Defense and *Defension Prima* (Milton)
See *Pro populo anglicano defensio, contra Claudii Anonymi*

"The First Discourse" (Reynolds) **15**:377, 402, 405, 412

First Discourse (Rousseau)
See *Discourse on the Arts and Sciences*

"First Eclogue" (Collins) **4**:229

"First Epistle of the First Book of Horace" (Pope)
See *Satires and Epistles of Horace, Imitated*

"The First of April" (Warton) **15**:443

First Shepherds' Play (Towneley)
See *Prima Pastorum* (Towneley)

The First Sluggard (Grimmelshausen)
See *Der erste Beernhäuter*

"A Fish Diet" (Erasmus)
See "Ichthyophagia"

"Fish-Eating" (Erasmus)
See "Ichthyophagia"

Fishers (Towneley) **34**:252

"Fit of Fainting" (Bradstreet)
See "Deliverance From a Fit of Fainting"

"Five Pastoral Eclogues: The Scenes of Which are Supposed to Lie Among the Shepherds, Oppressed by the War in Germany" (Warton) **15**:430, 459-60

Five Questions concerning the Mind (Ficino) **12**:175

Flagellacio (Towneley) **34**:250, 311, 313, 316, 321, 326

"The Flaming Heart: Upon the Book and Picture of the Seraphical Saint Teresa (as she is usually expressed with a Seraphim Beside her)." (Crashaw) **24**:8, 18, 20, 23, 33, 44, 48, 50, 63, 66

Flashes of Light (Jami)
See *Lawá'ih*

Le flatteur (Rousseau) **9**:337-38

"The Flea" (Donne) **10**:12, 50, 81-2, 96; **24**:150, 154

"Fleckno" (Marvell) **4**:409

"The Flesh and the Spirit" (Bradstreet) **4**:90, 96; **30**:114, 124

"The Flies" (Franklin) **25**:141

Flight into Egypt (York)
See *The Israelites in Egypt, the ten Plagues, and Passage of the Red Sea* (York)

The Flight of Birds (Vinci) **12**:405

The Flight to Egypt (Towneley)
See *Fugacio Joseph & Marie in Egiptum* (Towneley)

The Flights (Gay) **49**:43

Florentine Affairs and Le Cose Fioretine (Guicciardini)
See *Cose fiorentine*

Florentine History and History of Florence (Guicciardini)
See *Storie Fiorentine*

Flores Solitudinis (Vaughan) **27**:304, 311-313, 337

Florizel and Perdita (Garrick) **15**:129

"Flow Gently Sweet Afton" (Burns)
See "Sweet Afton"

"The Flower" (Herbert) **24**:215, 237, 243, 268, 274, 276

"The Flower" (Vaughan) **27**

"The Flower and the Leaf" (Chaucer) **17**:49, 54, 60

"The Flower and the Leaf" (Dryden) **3**:190

"The Flower Maiden Hsiang-yu" (P'u Sung-ling) **3**:354

"A Fly about a Glass of Burnt Claret" (Lovelace) **24**:329, 333, 354

"A Fly Caught in a Cobweb" (Lovelace) **24**:320, 330-31, 337-40, 347, 353

"A Fly that flew into my Mistress her Eye" (Carew) **13**:18

The Flying Doctor (Moliere)
See *Le médecin volant*

Flying Mercury (Siguenza y Gongora)
See *Mercurio volante con la noticia de la recuperacion de las provincias del Nuevo México conseguida por D. Diego de Vargas, Zapato, y Luxan Ponze de Leon*

"fMy Generous Heart Disdains" (Hopkinson) **25**:250-51

La Foire des fées (Lesage) **28**:204

Folly (Erasmus)
See *Moriae encomium*

"A Fool" (Butler) **16**:51

The Fool of Quality; or, The History of Henry, Earl of Moreland (Brooke) **1**:59-68, 70-2

"Foolish Men" (Juana Ines de la Cruz)
See "Hombres necios que acusáis"

The Fop Corrected (Marivaux)
See *The Fop Corrected*

"For A' That and A' That" (Burns)
See "Is There for Honest Poverty"

"For Deliverance from a Fever" (Bradstreet) **4**:100

"For Godsake hold your tongue, and let me love" (Donne)
See "The Canonization"

"For His Own Epitaph" (Prior) **4**:461, 471, 474

"For My Own Monument" (Prior)
See "For His Own Epitaph"

"For Solitude and Retirement against the Publick Active Life" (Wycherley) **8**:399

"For the Publick Active Life, against Solitude" (Wycherley) **8**:399

"For the Restoration of My Dear Husband from a Burning Ague" (Bradstreet) **4**:100; **30**:149

"For the sake o' Somebody" (Burns) **29**:51

"For the sake of Somebody" (Ramsay) **29**:330

"The Force of Blood" (Cervantes)
See "La fuerza de la sangre"

"The Force of Religion; or, Vanquished Love" (Young) **3**:466, 485, 487

The Forced Marriage (Moliere)
See *Le mariage forcé*

The Forced Marriage; or, The Jealous Bridegroom (Behn) **1**:29, 33, 39; **30**:73-4, 80, 83; **42**:149, 151

"The Forervnners" (Herbert) **24**:232-33, 236-37, 259, 274-75

The Forest (Jonson) **6**:312, 315, 325, 337, 347-50; **33**:129, 171

Forest of Forests, Silva Silvarum (Bacon)
See *Sylva Sylvarum: Or a Natural History*

The Forest of Scholars (Wu Ching-tzu)
See *Ju-lin wai-shih*

"Les forges de Lemnos" (Rousseau) **9**:343

"The Fork" (Wessel) **7**:390

"Forma Bonum Fragile" (Prior) **4**:461

"The Fornicator" (Burns) **3**:97; **29**:21, 28; **40**:86

"A Forsaken Lady to Her False Servant" (Lovelace) **24**:315, 332

Fortuna (Hutten) **16**:232-33, 241-42

The Fortunate Isles and Their Union (Jonson) **33**:176-77, 179, 181

The Fortunate Mistress (Defoe) **1**:129, 134, 139-40, 142, 145, 147, 149-50, 173, 177-80

The Fortunate Son (Vega)
See *El hijo venturoso*

Fortunatus (Dekker)
See *Old Fortunatus*

"Fortune hathe taken away my love" (Raleigh) **31**:265

The Fortune of Diana (Vega) **23**:374-75

The Fortunes and Misfortunes of the Famous Moll Flanders (Defoe) **1**:125, 127, 134-35, 137, 139-40, 142, 145, 147, 151-59, 169, 176-78

"The Four Ages of Man" (Bradstreet) **4**:89, 94-5, 103

Four Birds of Noah's Ark (Dekker) **22**:97-8, 104, 112, 118

"The Four Elements" (Bradstreet) **4**:86, 89, 94, 109, 111

The Four Foster Children of Desire (Sidney) **39**:265-77, 277

The Four Last Things (More) **10**:370, 415, 430, 435-36

"The Four Monarchies" (Bradstreet) **4**:86, 89-90, 95-6, 102-04, 111; **30**:117, 119, 132-3, 137

Four Plays in One; or, Moral Representations in One (Fletcher) **33**:40-52

"The Four Seasons of the Year" (Bradstreet) **4**:86, 88-9, 94-5, 103-11; **30**:125

"Four Soliloquies" (Vega) **23**:381

Les fourberies de Scapin (Moliere) **10**:268, 272, 275, 283, 285, 293, 297, 299, 313, 335; **28**:236, 255-56, 258-59, 266-67, 269

"The Fourteenth Discourse" (Reynolds) **15**:398, 404

"The Fourth Discourse" (Reynolds) **15**:365, 379, 380, 383, 393, 402

Fourth Letter on a Regicide Peace (Burke) **7**:64; **36**:95

"The Fourth Monarchy" (Bradstreet) **30**:133

Fowre Hymnes (Spenser) **5**:313, 323-24, 335, 338, 350, 353-54, 356; **39**:326, 346

"The Fox and the Crow" (La Fontaine)
See "Le Corbeau et le Renard"

The Fox; or, Volpone (Jonson)
See *Volpone; or, the Foxe*

"Fragment" (Chatterton) **3**:123

"Fragment" (Winchilsea) **3**:451

"Fragment of a Dedication to Dr. W. Warburton, Bishop of Gloucester" (Churchill) **3**:143, 152, 154, 158-67, 169-71

Fragment of an Original Letter on the Slavery of the Negroes (Day) **1**:105

Fragmente eines Ungenannten (Lessing) **8**:105

Fragments échappés (Diderot) **26**:158

Fragments of Ancient Poetry, Collected in the Highlands of Scotland, and Translated from the Gaelic or Erse Language (Macpherson) **29**:242, 250, 252-57, 262, 265, 278-79, 285, 290, 294-98

"Frailty" (Herbert) **24**:272

The Frame of Government of Pennsylvania (Penn) **25**:315-17, 320-23, 345

Francesco's Fortuner **41**:178

La Franciade (Ronsard)
See *Les quatre premiers livres de la Franciade*

Franciscanus (Buchanan)
See *Georgii Buchanani Scoti, franciscanus: varia eiusdem authoris poemata*

Franklin Papers (Franklin)
See *The Papers of Benjamin Franklin*

"Franklin's Prologue" (Chaucer) **17**:140

"Franklin's Tale" (Chaucer) **17**:71-2, 133-35, 137, 140-46, 148-49, 153, 201-02, 208, 237

Fraski (Kochanowski) **10**:160-61, 176

"Fratres Fraterrimi" (Buchanan) **4**:120, 122, 134

"Fratres Fraterrimi XXII" (Buchanan)
See "Fratres Fraterrimi"

Frederick, Duke of Lunenburg-Saxon (Haywood)

44:150, 170

Free Commentaries (Bacon)
See *Comentarius Solutus*

The Freedom of a Christian Man (Luther)
See *Dissertatio de libertate christiana per autorem recognita*

The Freedom of the Will (Edwards)
See *A Careful and Strict Enquiry into the Modern Prevailing Notions of That Freedom of Will, Which Is Supposed to Be Essential to Moral Agency, Vertue and Vice, Reward and Punishment, Praise and Blame*

Free-Grace Maintained (Mather) **38**:226

The Freeholder (Addison) **18**:8

The Free-Thinker (Lessing)
See *Der Freygeist*

A French Grammar, and a Dialogue consisting of all Gallicisms with Additions of the most useful and significant Proverbs (Howell) **13**:427

French Revolution (Wollstonecraft)
See *An Historical and Moral View of the Origin and Progress of the French Revolution, and the Effect It Has Produced in Europe*

Der Freygeist (Lessing) **8**:66, 112

Friar Bacon and Friar Bungay **41**:159-63, 165, 168

"Friar's Tale" (Chaucer) **17**:198, 205

"The Fribbleriad" (Garrick) **15**:115

Friday (Gay) **49**:39, 42, 45, 47-48

"Friday; or, The Dirge" (Gay) **49**:67-68, 79, 85, 138

"A Friend" (Philips) **30**:289, 304-5

The Friend of the People (Marat)
See *Le publiciste parisien, journal politique, libre et impartial . . .*

"A Friend Unknown" (Herbert) **24**:292

"Friendly Reproof to Ben Jonson" (Carew) **13**:9

"Friendship" (Ramsay) **29**:308-9

Friendship in Death: In Twenty Letters from the Dead to the Living (Rowe) **44**:277-78, 290, 292-93, 296, 300, 302, 309-10, 312-13

"Friendship in Embleme or the Seal To My Dearest Lucasia" (Philips) **30**:278, 280, 289, 292, 304-5, 308-9

"Friendship Put to the Test" (Marmontel) **2**:214

"Friendship's Mystery. To My Dearest Lucasia" (Philips) **30**:280, 288

"The Frog Song" (P'u Sung-ling)
See "Wa-ch'u"

"A Frolick" (Herrick) **13**:365

"From Another Sore Fit" (Bradstreet) **30**:148-9

From Bad to Worse (Calderon de la Barca)
See *Poeresta que estaba*

"From Esopus to Maria" (Burns) **29**:92

"From Thee Eliza" (Burns) **3**:86; **40**:73

"Frozen Words" (Addison) **18**:27

"The Frozen Zone" (Herrick) **13**:368

The Fruitless Enquiry (Haywood) **1**:284

Fruits of Solitude (Penn)
See *Some Fruits of Solitude in Reflections and Maxims Relating to the Conduct of Human Life*

"Fu hu" (P'u Sung-ling) **49**:299

Fuenteovejuna (Vega) **23**:358, 362, 364-68, 372-73, 391, 393, 398-99, 401

"La fuerza de la sangre" (Cervantes) **6**:171, 176-77; **23**:96, 99, 144

Fuerza lastimosa (Vega) **23**:402

Fugacio Joseph & Marie in Egiptum (Towneley) **34**:251, 325

The Fugitive (Davys)
See *The Merry Wanderer*

The Fundamental Constitutions of Carolina (Locke) **7**:295

"The Funeral" (Erasmus)
See "Funus"

The Funeral (Steele) **18**:314, 329-30, 332-33, 336-40, 348-49, 352-54, 359, 362-65, 370-72, 374, 383

"A Funeral Poem on the Death of C.E. and Infant of Twelve Months" (Wheatley) **50**:195

A Funeral Poem upon the Death of the...Earl of Devonshire (Daniel) **24**:89, 145

"The Funerall" (Donne) **10**:26, 36; **24**:152, 155

"The Funerall Rites of the Rose" (Herrick) **13**:348-51, 353, 373, 384

"Funus" (Erasmus) **16**:116, 119, 141, 155

Furioso (Ariosto)
See *Orlando furioso*

A Further Defence: Being an Answer to a Reply to the Vindication of the Reasons and Defence for Restoring, &c. (Collier) **6**:209

"The Future Punishment of the Wicked Unavoidable and Intolerable" (Edwards) **7**:98, 107

"La Gageure des trois commeres" (La Fontaine) **50**:116-119, 121

El galán fantasma (Calderon de la Barca) **23**:70

El Galante (Gracian y Morales) **15**:135

La Galatea (Cervantes) **6**:130, 143-44, 151, 160, 164, 174, 177, 189; **23**:94, 96, 98-99, 111, 114, 145

La galerie du palais, ou l'amie rivale (Corneille) **28**:30, 44-5, 55

Das Galgen-Männlin (Grimmelshausen) **6**:247

"The gallant Weaver" (Burns) **29**:49

El gallardo español (Cervantes) **6**:180; **23**:100, 149

Gallathea (Lyly) **41**:222, 271, 273

"The Gallery" (Marvell) **4**:403, 408-09, 435

"Gallo crocitanti" (Kochanowski) **10**:175

"The Gambling Charm" (P'u Sung-ling)
See "Du Fu"

A Game at Chess (Middleton) **33**:264-65, 268, 270, 276-77, 282, 308-14

"The Game of Chess" (Kochanowski)
See "Szachy"

The Game of Hide and Seek (Calderon de la Barca) **23**:

The Game of Love and Chance (Marivaux)
See *The Game of Love and Chance*

The Game of Love and Fortune (Calderon de la Barca) **23**:64

"The Garden" (Marvell) **4**:400, 404-07, 410, 412, 426-27, 430, 435, 437, 439, 441-42, 445-48; **43**:278, 288, 299, 302-5

"Garden of Adonis" (Herrick) **13**:361

Garden of Roses (Kempis)
See *Hortulus rosarii de valle lachrymarum continens egreias & devotas sentecias*

Gargantua and Pantagruel (Rabelais) **5**:203, 214-15, 220, 221, 230, 234-35, 244, 248, 250

"The Garland" (Hopkinson) **25**:250-51, 260

"The Garland" (Prior) **4**:460-61

"The Garland" (Vaughan) **27**:321

The Garland of Good Will **41**:80

"Gather Ye Rosebuds while Ye May" (Herrick)
See "To the Virgins, to Make Much of Time"

Gatomaquia (Vega) **23**:339-40

"Gaveston"
See "Pierce Gaveston, Earle of Cornwall"

"Gay Bacchus" (Parnell) **3**:251-52

"Ge Jin" (P'u Sung-ling) **49**:306, 310

Gedanken zur Aufnahme des dänischen Theaters (Schlegel) **5**:272-74, 279

Der Geheimnisvolle (Schlegel) **5**:275, 278-79

Geistliche Kurtzweil (Andreae) **32**:92

"General Prologue" (Chaucer) **17**:60, 67, 69, 84, 98, 133, 141, 147, 162-63, 166, 168, 173-74, 176-78, 189, 194, 197, 200-01, 204-07, 209-10, 213-15, 218, 224-26, 230, 232, 234, 236, 238, 242-43

"A General Prologue to all my Playes" (Cavendish) **30**:225

The Generall Historie of Virginia, New-England, and the Summer Isles **9**:352-56, 358-61, 364-66, 373-79, 381-87

"The Generous Lover" (Cervantes)
See "El amante liberal"

Genesis (Aretino) **12**:13, 20, 36

Genesis (Towneley) **34**:250

"Genethliacon et Epicedion" (Crashaw) **24**:27

Geneva Manuscript (Rousseau) **36**:285, 293

Le Génie (Marmontel) **2**:222, 259

"La Genisse, la Chevre et la Brebis en societe avec le Lion" (La Fontaine) **50**:81

De Gentilismo non retinendo (Campanella) **32**:236-42

"Gentillesse" (Chaucer) **17**:60, 145, 236, 240

The Gentle Craft
See *The book of The Gentle Craft*

The Gentle Craft I
See *The book of The Gentle Craft*

The Gentle Craft I
See *The book of The Gentle Craft*

The Gentle Craft II **41**:74-75, 77, 87, 112, 114, 120

The Gentle Shepherd, A Pastoral Comedy (Ramsay) **29**:301-03, 305, 308-18, 320-23, 325, 328, 330-36, 340, 342, 345-47, 349, 351-53, 355-56

The Gentleman Dancing-Master (Wycherley) **8**:384-86, 388-92, 395, 401, 404-05, 408-09, 411; **21**:342-44, 346, 351-52, 355-56, 359, 361, 372, 387, 392

"Gentleman in the Navy" (Wheatley)
See "To a Gentleman in the Navy"

The Gentleman Usher (Chapman) **22**:6, 10, 15, 63, 65-6

The Genuine Remains (Butler) **16**:4, 11, 50; **43**:62, 106

Géographie Politique (Turgot)
See *Plan d'un ouvrage sur la géographie politique*

The Geometrical School (Vinci) **12**:405

"Geordie and Davie" (Fergusson) **29**:205

George Dandin; or, The Baffled Husband (Moliere)
See *George Dandin; ou, Le mari confondu*

George Dandin; ou, Le mari confondu (Moliere) **10**:275, 280, 283-85, 297, 312-13, 320, 335, 343-45; **28**:229, 236, 255, 257, 260, 269, 274-75

Georgics (Dryden) **21**:119

Georgii Buchanani Scoti, franciscanus: varia eiusdem authoris poemata (Buchanan) **4**:118-20, 123, 134-35, 138

German Michael (Grimmelshausen)
See *Der Teutsche Michel*

German Requiem for the Burnt Bulls and Papal Laws (Hutten) **16**:232

Gerusalemme (Tasso)
See *La Gierusalemme liberata*

Der geschäftige Müssiggänger (Schlegel) **5**:273, 277, 282

Geschicht und Histori von Land-Graff Ludwig dem Springer (Beer) **5**:52

Die Geschwister in Taurien (Schlegel) (Schlegel) **5**:280

Gesprächbüchlein (Hutten) **16**:234

Gesta Grayorum (Bacon) **18**:196, **32**:133

"The Ghaists: A Kirk-yard Eclogue" (Fergusson) **29**:170, 189, 209, 217, 227, 230, 237

Ghiribizzi (Machiavelli) **36**:236-37

"The Ghost" (Churchill) **3**:143-45, 148, 151, 153-55, 158-60, 162-64

"Ghost of John Dennis" (Gray) **4**:333

The Ghost of Lucrece (Middleton) **33**:286-87

The Ghostly Lover (Calderon de la Barca) **23**:64

Gibraltar, a Comedy (Dennis) **11**:8

Gideon's Fleece (Calderon de la Barca) **23**:9

La Gierusalemme liberata (Tasso) **5**:372-80, 382-88, 392-95, 398-99, 401, 406-08

"The Gift of Poetry" (Parnell) **3**:255

Gift of the Free (Jami)
See *Tuhfatu'l-Ahrár*

"The Gifts of Jacquet to Isabeau" (Ronsard) **6**:420

The Gifts of the Magi (Towneley)
See *Oblacio Magorum* (Towneley)

"Gilderoy" (Fergusson) **29**:205

"The Girl of Pohsing" (P'u Sung-ling) **3**:347

"Girl Who Did Not Want to Marry" (Erasmus) **16**:123, 141, 193

"The Girl with No Interest in Marriage" (Erasmus)
See "Girl Who Did Not Want to Marry"

"La gitanilla" (Cervantes) **6**:171-72; **23**:96, 99, 144-45, 149

Giudizi (Aretino) **12**:22, 26

"Giudizzio sovra la Gerusalemme" (Tasso) **5**:384

Giunte (Castelvetro) **12**:67-8

"Giunto è già 'l corso della vita mia" (Michelangelo) **12**:368, 375

"Give Me Thy Heart" (Hopkinson) **25**:250

Giving Alms to Charity and Employing the Poor (Defoe) **1**:124

The Giving of the Law Balaam (Chester)
See *Balaam and Balaak* (Chester)

"The Glance" (Herbert) **24**:259, 272, 278

"The Glass Scholar" (Cervantes)
See "El licenciado vidriera"

A glasse for Europe (Lyly) **41**:252, 255

A Glasse of the Truthe: An Argument by Way of Dialogue between a Lawyer and a Divine; That the Marriage of Henry VIII. with Catherine of Aragon Was Unlawful; And That the Cause Ought to Be Heard and Ordered within the Realm (Henry VIII) **10**:119, 127, 129, 142-45

De gli eroici furori (Bruno) **27**:62, 70-72, 74-82, 95, 100-04

Gl'innamorati (Goldoni) **4**:267-68

Glorias de Querétaro en la neuva congregacion eclecsiastica de María Santissimade Guadalupe (Siguenza y Gongora) **8**:339-40

Glories of Querétaro (Siguenza y Gongora)
See *Glorias de Querétaro en la neuva congregacion eclecsiastica de María Santissima de Guadalupe*

"The Glorious Success of Her Majesty's Arms" (Prior)
See "The Ode on the Glorious Success of Her Majesty's Arms"

"The Glory and Grace in the Church Set Out" (Taylor) **11**:394

Gnothi Seauton (Arbuthnot) **1**:19

God Glorified in the Work of Redemption, by the Greatness of Man's Dependence upon Him in the Whole of It (Edwards) **7**:95

God Not the Author of Evil (Collier) **6**:210

"Goddwyn" (Chatterton) **3**:119, 129

"Godly Girzie" (Burns) **3**:97

Gods Determinations touching his Elect: and The Elects Combat in their Conversion, and Coming up to God in Christ: together with the Comfortable Effects Thereof (Taylor) **11**:343-45, 350-51, 354, 356, 358-59, 362-63, 368, 373-74, 376, 381-82, 385, 393-94, 401, 403

Godwin & Mary (Wollstonecraft) **5**:444

"Goe, and catche a falling starre" (Donne)
See "Song. 'Goe, and catche a falling starre'"

The Golden Age Restored (Jonson) **33**:169, 176

"The Golden Ass" (Machiavelli)
See "L'asino d'oro"

"Golden Chord of Ecstasy" (Crashaw) **24**:18

The Golden Fleece (Corneille)
See *La toison d'or*

The Golden Fleece (Vega) **23**:385

"Goldie" (Burns)
See "On Commissary Goldie's Brains"

"Goliath of Gath. 1 Sam. Chap. XVII." (Wheatley) **3**:413, 418, 430, 436; **50**:245

Gondibert: An Heroick Poem (Davenant) **13**:158-60, 164, 167-75, 182-83, 185, 195-96, 199, 202-10, 215

Good Advice to the Church of England (Penn) **25**:297

"Good and Ill in Every Nation" (Wessel) **7**:391

"The Good Conscience, the Only Certain, Lasting Good" (Wycherley) **8**:399

"Good Counsel" (Petursson)
See "Heilrædauísur"

"Good Counsel to a Young Maid" (Carew) **13**:23, 57

"Good Eating" (Fergusson) **29**:206, 218, 220

"Good Friday" (Donne)
See "Goodfriday 1613: Riding Westward"

"Good Friday" (Herbert) **24**:272, 293

"The Good Husband" (Marmontel) **2**:214

The Good Mother (Goldoni)
See *La buona madre*

The Good Natured Man (Goldsmith) **2**:67-8, 70-1, 73, 76, 81, 84, 86-8, 99, 105-06, 112, 114, 119-21, 126-28

Good Sense (Holbach)
See *Bon-Sens*

"Goodfriday, 1613" (Chapman) **22**:

"Goodfriday 1613: Riding Westward" (Donne) **10**:40, 61, 84, 96, 105, 107; **24**:165, 169, 173, 198-02

"The good-morrow" (Donne) **10**:12, 26, 32, 36, 49, 52, 54, 57-8; **24**:153-54, 183, 206

"The Goodness of his God" (Herrick) **13**:358

"Gor'kaia uchast'" (Chulkov) **2**:14, 18

Gospel of Nicodemus (York) **34**:334

"Gotham" (Churchill) **3**:141, 145, 149, 152-53, 155-56, 158, 160, 162-63, 172

Gothrika (Schlegel) **5**:273

"Götterlehre; oder, Mythologische Dichtungen der Alten" (Moritz) **2**:231, 246

The Governess; or, Little Female Academy (Fielding) **1**:273, 275-78; **44**:59-61, 65, 67-8, 72, 77, 86, 88, 90-1, 95, 100, 104, 110-7

The Governor (Elyot)
See *The Boke of the Governor, devised by Sir Thomas Elyot*

"Governor Yu" (P'u Sung-ling) **3**:345

The Governour (Elyot)
See *The Boke of the Governor, devised by Sir Thomas Elyot*

"Grace" (Herbert) **24**:274

Grace Abounding to the Chief of Sinners (Bunyan) **4**:149, 152, 159, 164, 166, 169, 172, 174, 180, 196-202

Grammaire (Condillac) **26**:10, 29, 31, 35, 50, 54
El Gran Príncipe de Fez (Calderon de la Barca)
  23:18-22
La gran sultana (Cervantes) **6**:180; **23**:100
El gran teatro del mundo (Calderon de la Barca)
  23:9, 57, 60-1, 64
Le Grand Cyrus (Marivaux)
  See *Artamène; ou, Le Grand Cyrus*
The Grand Duke of Gandia (Calderon de la Barca)
  23:64
"The Grand Question Debated" (Swift) **1**:459
The Grand Tour (Boswell)
  See *Boswell on the Grand Tour*
Grandison (Richardson)
  See *The History of Sir Charles Grandison*
"The Grasshopper" (Lovelace)
  See "The Grasshopper, To My Noble Friend,
  Charles Cotton"
"The Grasshopper, To My Noble Friend, Charles
  Cotton" (Lovelace) **24**:301, 303-04, 306,
  311-12, 315-16, 321-23, 325-26, 333, 335-
  36, 342, 344-45, 348, 350, 353
"Gratiana Dancing and Singing" (Lovelace)
  24:302, 306, 316, 342
"Grato e felice, a' tuo feroci mali" (Michelangelo)
  12:369
"The Grave of King Arthur" (Warton) **15**:432-
  33, 442, 445, 454-55
De gravitatione et equipondio fluidorum (New-
  ton) **35**:296-96
The Great Case of Liberty of Conscience Debated
  (Penn) **25**:296, 301, 307, 332
*The Great Christian Doctrine of Original Sin
  Defended* (Edwards) **7**:94-6, 98
*The Great Historical, Geographical, Genealogi-
  cal and Poetical Dictionary* (Collier) **6**:208,
  210
Great Instauration (Bacon)
  See *Summi Angliae Instauratio magna*
The Great Theater of the World (Calderon de la
  Barca)
  See *El gran teatro del mundo*
*Great Works of Nature for the Particular Use of
  Mankind* (Bacon)
  See *Magnalia naturae praecipue quoad usus
  humanos*
Greater Surgery (Paracelsus)
  See *Books of the Greater Surgery*
The Greatest Monster of the World (Calderon de
  la Barca)
  See *El mayor monstruo del mundo*
Greaves (Smollett)
  See *The Life and Adventures of Sir Lancelot
  Greaves*
"Green Grow the Rashes O" (Burns) **3**:71, 87;
  29:20; **40**:85, 97
Greene's Vision **41**:166, 177
"La grenouille et le rat" (La Fontaine) **50**:88,
  129, 131
"La Grenouille qui se veut faire aussi grosse que
  le boeuf" (La Fontaine) **50**:84, 88
"Grief" (Herbert) **24**:274
"Grim Grizzle" (Burns) **3**:99
"Griselidis" (Perrault) **2**:253-56, 279
"Groatsworth of Wit bought with a Million of
  Repentance" **41**:148, 157-58, 179
The Grounds of Criticism in Poetry (Dennis) **11**:8,
  16, 18, 22-6, 30, 33, 36-7, 40-1, 44, 51-3
The Grounds of Criticism in Tragedy (Dryden)
  3:236-37; **21**:52, 114-15
Grounds of Natural Philosophy (Cavendish)
  30:224
The Grub Street Opera (Fielding) **1**:249; **46**:94,

166
La guarda cuidadosa (Cervantes) **23**:137, 139
Guárdate del agua mensa (Calderon de la Barca)
  23:64
The Guardian (Addison) **18**:7, 20-1, 24
The Guardian (Garrick) **15**:93, 98, 101, 105, 121,
  124
The Guardian (Steele) **18**:318, 333, 344, 347,
  350, 353-54, 369, 372
The Guardian, 15 (Steele) **18**:349
The Guardian, 21 (Steele) **18**:358
The Guardian, 26 (Steele) **18**:346
The Guardian, 45 (Steele) **18**:349
The Guardian, 172 (Steele) **18**:347
"Gude Ale Keeps the Heart Aboon" (Burns) **3**:86
"Gude Braid Claith" (Fergusson) **29**:170, 179,
  189-91, 202, 205
"Gude E'en to You, Kimmer" (Burns) **3**:67
La guerro (Goldoni) **4**:262
Guiana (Ralcigh)
  See *The Discoverie of the Large, rich and
  Bewitful Empire of Guiana*
"Guid Mornin' to your Majesty" (Burns) **3**:71
The Guide Mistaken, and temporizing Rebuked
  (Penn) **25**:283, 287-88, 334
"Guiltless Lady Imprisoned, after Penanced"
  (Lovelace) **24**:307, 334-35
The Guise (Webster) **33**:340
Gulliver's Travels (Swift)
  See *Travels into Several Remote Nations of the
  World, in Four Parts; By Lemuel Gulliver*
Gull's Horn-Book (Dekker) **22**:96, 106
Gustavus, King of Swithland (Dekker) **22**:88
Gustavus Vasa, the Deliverer of His Country
  (Brooke) **1**:62, 67
"Das Gute Leben cines recht schaffenen Dieners
  Gottes" (Andreae) **32**:92
Der gute Rat (Schlegel) **5**:278-79
Guy, Eàrl of Warwick (Dekker) **22**:88
Guzman the Valiant (Vega) **23**:347
Gwydonius **41**:156, 176
The Gypsies Metamorphosed (Jonson) **6**:317, 337
"The Gypsy Maid" (Cervantes)
  See "La gitanilla"
"H. Scriptures" (Vaughan) **27**:341, 354, 392
"H:W: in Hiber: `belligeranti'" (Donne) **10**:39
"Habbakuk" (Parnell) **3**:255
"Had I the Wyte" (Burns) **29**:20; **40**:85
Haft Aurang (Jami) **9**:59, 62, 65-8, 71
"The Hag Is Astride" (Herrick) **13**:331, 336
Hakluyt's Voyages (Hakluyt)
  See *The Principal Navigations, Voyages,
  Traffiques and Discoveries of theEnglish
  Nation*
"Hallelujah" (Winchilsea) **3**:451
"Hallow Fair" (Fergusson) **29**:172, 179, 181, 189-
  93, 107, 204-05, 210, 224, 227, 237-39
"Hallowe'en" (Burns) **3**:48, 52, 54, 56, 65, 67,
  72-3, 84, 86; **29**:4, 6-9, 13-16, 18, 28, 64,
  72-4; **40**:82, 96, 103-4
Hamburg Dramaturgy (Lessing)
  See *Die Hamburgische Dramaturgie*
Die Hamburgische Dramaturgie (Lessing) **8**:61-
  3, 65, 67-9, 71, 73-4, 76-8, 80-7, 94, 98-104,
  107, 110-11, 114-16
"Hame Content: A Satire" (Fergusson) **29**:189,
  210, 217-18
"The Hamlet" (Warton)
  See "Hamlet, an Ode written in Whichwood
  Forest"
Hamlet (Kyd)
  See *The Tragedie of Soliman and Perseda*
"Hamlet, an Ode written in Whichwood Forest"

(Warton) **15**:432, 434, 443
"Han Fang" (P'u Sung-ling) **3**:344; **49**:280
Handbook of the Militant Christian (Erasmus)
  See *Enchiridion militis christiani*
"The Handsome and the Deformed Leg" (Franklin)
  25:141, 147
"Handsome Nell" (Burns) **40**:93
The Hanging of Judas (Towneley)
  See *Suspencio Jude* (Towneley)
"Hannah" (Parnell) **3**:255
Hannibal (Marivaux)
  See *Hannibal*
"Hans Carvel" (Prior) **4**:455, 461, 467
Hans Frandsen (Holberg)
  See *Jean de France; eller, Hans Frandsen*
"Happiness" (Philips) **30**:279, 287
"The Happy Fugitives" (Manley) **1**:306-08
"The Happy Lover's Reflections" (Ramsay)
  29:329
"An Haranguer" (Butler) **16**:53
"The Hare and Many Friends" (Gay) **49**:172
Harlequin Refined by Love (Marivaux)
  See *Harlequin Refined by Love*
Harlequin's Invasion (Garrick) **15**:100, 104, 114,
  124
*The Harmonie of the Church. Containing the
  Spirituall Songes and Holy Hymnes, of
  Godley Men, Patriarkes and Prophetes: All,
  Sweetly Sounding, to the Praise and Glory
  of the Highest* **8**:19, 29
Harmonies of the World (Kepler)
  See *Hormonice Mundi*
"Harmony" (Kochanowski)
  See "Zgoda"
"Harriet's Birth Day" (Smart) **3**:366
"The Harrow" (Franklin) **25**:141
The Harrowing of Hell, and the Resurrection (N-
  Town) **34**:172-3, 178, 187-8
Harrowing of Hell (Chester) **34**:109, 120, 124-
  5, 130, 138
Harrowing of Hell (N-Town) **34**:180
Harrowing of Hell (York) **34**:334, 353, 374, 387
The Harrowing (Towneley)
  See *Extraccio Animarum* (Towneley)
Le hasard du coin du feu (Crebillon) **1**:76-7, 79;
  28:69-72, 79, 87, 91-3
"Hassan; or, The Camel-Driver" (Collins) **4**:210
*The Haunch of Venison, a Poetical Epistle to Lord
  Clare* (Goldsmith) **48**:74, 104
The Hawk-Eyed Sentinel (Cervantes) **6**:190
Hazañas del Cid (Castro)
  See *Las mocedades del Cid II*
"he Apostacy of One, and But One Lady"
  (Lovelace) **24**:307
"He Expresses Joy at Finding...Her Whom He Had
  Loved as a Mere Boy" (More) **10**:427
"He that loves a rosy cheek" (Carew)
  See "Disdaine Returned"
"He that loves a rosy lip" (Carew) **13**:20
"Heads of an Answer to Rymer" (Dryden) **3**:236-
  37; **21**:114-15
"Health" (Ramsay) **29**:309, 353
"The Heart" **8**:9, 30
"Heart of Oak" (Garrick) **15**:114, 124
Heat (Marat) **10**:222
"Heaven" (Herbert) **24**:269, 273
The Heavenly Footman (Bunyan) **4**:172, 177
Heavens Alarm to the World (Mather) **38**:283,
  294
Heaven's Favourite (Marvell) **43**:297
Hebrides Journal (Boswell)
  See *Journal of a Tour to the Hebrides with
  Samuel Johnson, LL. D.*

"Hê-chien shêng" (P'u Sung-ling)   49:295
Los hechos de Garcilaso de la Vega y Moro Tarfe
    (Vega)   23:362, 400
Heedless Hopalong (Grimmelshausen)
    See *Der seltsame Springinsfeld*
"Heilrædauisur" (Petursson)   8:253
Heinrich der Löws (Schlegel)   5:273
Hekuba (Schlegel)   5:280
"Helter Skelter; or, The Hue and Cry after the
    Attorneys Going to Ride the Circuit" (Swift)
    1:459
"Hêng-niang" (P'u Sung-ling)   49:295
"The Henpecked Husband" (Burns)   29:24; 40:89
La Henriade (Marmontel)   2:222-23
La henriade (Voltaire)   14:328, 338, 342, 349,
    358, 379, 382, 391, 414
Henrich and Pernille (Holberg)
    See *Henrik og Pernille*
Henrik og Pernille (Holberg)   6:277, 283
Henry (Lyttelton)
    See *The History of the Life of King Henry the
    Second and of the Age in Which He Lived*
Henry II. (Lyttelton)
    See *The History of the Life of King Henry the
    Second and of the Age in Which He Lived*
"Henry and Emma" (Prior)   4:455, 458, 460, 467,
    474-79
Heptaplus (Pico della Mirandola)   15:319, 324,
    329-30, 334, 338, 340-41, 345, 350-57, 359-
    60
"Her Man Described by Her Own Dictamen"
    (Jonson)   6:305
"Her Muffe" (Lovelace)   24:347
"Her Right Name" (Prior)   4:460-61, 466
Les Héraclides (Marmontel)   2:213, 216
*Heráclito cristiano y Segunda harpa a imitación
    de la de David* (Quevedo)   23:176-77
"Heraclitus" (Prior)
    See "Democritus and Heraclitus"
Héraclius (Corneille)   28:4-5, 21, 28-9, 34-5, 41,
    57
Heraclius (Corneille)
    See *Héraclius*
Herbarius (Paracelsus)   14:198
Hercule Chrestien (Ronsard)   6:437
Herculis christiani luctae (Andreae)   32:92
"Here she lies, a pretty bud" (Herrick)
    See "Upon a Child That Died"
"Here's a Health to them that's awa'" (Burns)
    40:102
"Here's his health in water" (Burns)   29:54
L'héritier du village (Marivaux)   4:367
Hermann (Schlegel)   5:273, 280-81
The Hermetic and Alchmical Writings (Paracelsus)
    14:185
"An Hermetic Philosopher" (Butler)   16:28, 52
Hermetical Physick (Vaughan)   27:324
"The Hermit" (Parnell)   3:252-54, 256-58
The Hermit (Goldsmith)   2:68
Hermosura de Angelica (Vega)   23:340
The Hero (Gracian y Morales)
    See *El Héroe*
Hero and Leander (Chapman)   22:8, 14, 19, 22-
    4, 26, 28, 69, 71, 73
Hero and Leander (Marlowe)   22:334, 337, 340,
    370; 47:257, 275
Herod and the Three Kings (N-Town)   34:208
Herod the Great (Towneley)
    See *Magnus Herodes* (Towneley)
El Héroe (Gracian y Morales)   15:135-36, 143-
    45, 165
The Heroic Frenzies (Bruno)
    See *De gli eroici furori*

*Heroic Piety of Don Fernando Cortés, Marqués
    del Valle* (Siguenza y Gongora)   8:343
"Heroical Epistle" (Butler)
    See "Heroical Epistle of Hudibras to his Lady"
"Heroical Epistle of Hudibras to his Lady" (But-
    ler)   16:24, 39, 49; 43:68
"The Heroine" (P'u Sung-ling)
    See "Hsieh-nü"
"Heroique Stanzas to the Glorious Memory of
    Cromwell" (Dryden)   3:223-26; 21:85
"Le Heron" (La Fontaine)   50:99, 101, 103
"Le Heron et la fille" (La Fontaine)   50:124-125
Héros (Gracian y Morales)   15:142
Les héros de Roman (Boileau-Despreaux)
    See *Dialogue des héros de roman*
Herrmann (Schlegel)
    See *Hermann*
"Hesiod; or, The Rise of Woman" (Parnell)   3:251,
    254, 257
*Hesperides: or, The Works Both Humane & Di-
    vine of Robert Herrick, Esq.* (Herrick)
    13:310, 312-13, 315-19, 321-22, 326, 328,
    331-33, 335, 340-41, 346, 349-54, 356-58,
    360-63, 365, 367, 370, 372-75, 378, 389-92,
    394-99, 401-04, 408-11
Les Heureux Orphelins (Crebillon)   28:72, 77-8,
    80-1, 93
L'heureux stratagème (Marivaux)   4:359, 368,
    370
Hexerei; eller, Blind allarm (Holberg)   6:273, 277
"Hey Ca; thro'" (Burns)   3:86
"Hey for a lass wi'a tocher" (Burns)   40:87
"Hey, the Dusty Miller" (Burns)   3:81
"Hezekiah" (Parnell)   3:255
The Hid Treasure (Calderon de la Barca)   23:9
"The Hidden Treasure" (Vaughan)   27:338, 340
Hieroglyphic Tales (Walpole)   2:481, 488, 499-
    501, 507; 49:357
Hieronimo (Kyd)
    See *Soliman and Perseda*
"A Highland Lad" (Burns)   40:98
"The Highland Laddie" (Ramsay)   29:304
"Highland Mary" (Burns)   3:56, 67, 72; 29:42;
    40:64
The Highlander (Macpherson)   29:252, 255, 262-
    5
La hija del aire (Calderon de la Barca)   23:58,
    61, 64-5
El hijo de Reduán (Vega)   23:400
El hijo venturoso (Vega)   23:400
"The Hill and Grove at Bill-Borrow" (Marvell)
    See "Upon the Hill and Grove at Billborow"
The Hilliad (Smart)   3:367, 372, 394, 399
The Hind and the Panther (Dryden)   3:184, 190-
    91, 199, 203-04, 208, 220-21, 234-35, 340-
    42; 21:67-72, 79-80, 87
*The Hind and the Panther, Transvers'd to the Story
    of the Country and the City-Mouse* (Marvell)
    4:454, 458, 464
"L'hinne de Bacus" (Ronsard)   6:420, 429
"Hints" (Wollstonecraft)   50:284
"Hints to Those Who Would Be Rich" (Franklin)
    25:181
"L'Hirondelle et les petits oiseaux" (La Fontaine)
    50:79
Hirsau Stained Glass Windows (Lessing)   8:105
Der Hirt (Zwingli)
    See *The Shepherd*
"His Age, Dedicated to His Peculiar Friend, M.
    John Wickes, under the Name Posthumus"
    (Herrick)   13:365, 378, 381-82, 394
"His Answer to a Question" (Herrick)   13:337
"His Cloe Hunting" (Prior)   4:459

"His Creed" (Herrick)   13:342, 366
"His Defence against the Idle Critick"   8:27
"His Farewell to Sack" (Herrick)   13:326, 333,
    392-93, 397
"His farwell unto Poetrie" (Herrick)
    See "Farewell to Poetry"
"His Grange, or Private Wealth" (Herrick)   13:335
"His Lachrimae, or Mirth, Turn'd to Mourning"
    (Herrick)   13:387
"His Letanie, to the Holy Spirit" (Herrick)
    See "Litany to the Holy Spirit"
"His Litany to the Holy Spirit" (Herrick)
    See "Litany to the Holy Spirit"
His Majesties Declaration Defended (Dryden)
    21:57, 65
"His Meditation upon Death" (Herrick)   13:342,
    391
*His Noble Numbers: or, His Pious Pieces, Wherein
    (amongst Other Things) He Sings the Birth
    of His Christ: and Sighes for His Saviours
    Suffering on the Crosse* (Herrick)   13:310,
    312-13, 315, 317, 319, 322, 324, 328, 333-
    35, 338, 340-41, 353-54, 357-58, 361-63,
    366-67, 371, 373, 390-91, 397, 401, 404-05,
    411
"His Poetry His Pillar" (Herrick)   13:327, 341
"His Prayer for Absolution" (Herrick)   13:328
"His Prayer to Ben Jonson" (Herrick)
    See "Prayer to Ben Jonson"
"His request to Julia" (Herrick)   13:355
"His Returne to London" (Herrick)   13:352, 387-
    88
"His Sailing from Julia" (Herrick)   13:327, 402
"His Saviour's words, going to the Cross"
    (Herrick)   13:358
"His Tears to Thamasis" (Herrick)   13:403
"His Winding-Sheet" (Herrick)   13:352, 354, 357
Histoire de Brandebourg (Frederick the Great)
    14:58, 69
L'histoire de Charles XII (Voltaire)   14:328, 382,
    386-87, 408
L'histoire de Fenni (Voltaire)   14:359, 361
Histoire de Gil Blas de Santillane (Lesage)   2:174-
    88, 190-202, 204; 28:188-191, 194-98, 200-
    08, 210-11, 219, 221, 223-24
Histoire de Guzman d'Alfarache (Lesage)   2:177,
    182, 202-03; 28:200, 203
L'histoire de Jenni (Voltaire)   14:346
Histoire de la guerre de 1741 (Voltaire)   14:383
*Histoire de l'empire de Russie sous Pierre le
    Grand* (Voltaire)   14:383, 408
Histoire de Louis XI (Duclos)   1:186, 189
Histoire de ma Vie jusqu'à l'an 1797 (Casanova
    de Seingalt)
    See *Mémoires de J. Casanova de Seingalt écrits
    par lui-même*
Histoire de Madame de Luz (Duclos)   1:187-97
Histoire de Madame Henriette d'Angleterre (La
    Fayette)   2:156
Histoire de mon temps (Frederick the Great)
    14:64, 69, 71, 75
*Histoire d'Edouard et d'Elisabeth qui passèrent
    quatre vingt un ans chez les Megamicres*
    (Casanova de Seingalt)
    See *Icosameron*
L'Histoire des deux Indes (Diderot)   26:159
Histoire des voyages de Scarmentado (Voltaire)
    14:359, 378, 386
Histoire d'Estevanille Gonzalez (Lesage)   2:182,
    202, 204; 28:197, 200
*Histoire du Chevalier de Grieux et de Manon
    Lescaut* (Prevost)   1:328-33, 335-38, 340,
    343-44, 346-62

Histoire d'une Grecque moderne (Prevost) **1**:330, 334-35, 343-45

Histoire générale des hommes et des empires (Condillac) **26**:10

Histoire véritable (Montesquieu) **7**:348

Histoires ou Contes du temps passé, avec des moralités: Contes de Ma Mère l'Oye (Perrault) **2**:252-74, 279-86

Historia (Anonymous author of *Historia*)
    See *Historia von D. Johann Fausten*

Historia (Buchanan)
    See *Rerum Scoticarum Historia, auctore Georgio Buchanano Scoto*

Historia de la Buscón (Quevedo) **23**:154, 156-57, 160, 162-63, 166, 168, 180

Historia de las Indias (Las Casas) **31**:176, 197, 201-7, 217

Historia Densi et Rari (Bacon) **18**:132

Historia e dimonstrazioni intorno alle macchie solari (Galilei) **45**:258, 264, 279, 295, 299

Historia Prima (Bacon) **18**:149

Historia Ricardi Tertii (More)
    See *The Life of Kinge Richarde the Thirde*

Historia Ventorum (Bacon) **18**:132, 149

Historia verdadera de la conquista de la Nueva España (Diaz del Castillo) **31**:89-129

Historia Vitae et Mortis (Bacon) **18**:131-32, 149-50, 187

Historia von D. Johann Fausten (Anonymous author of *Historia*) **47**:119-75

Historic Doubts on the Life and Reign of King Richard the Third (Walpole) **2**:456, 488; **49**:345, 358, 402

Historical Account of two Notable Corruptions of the Scriptures, in a Letter to a Friend (Newton) **35**:274-76, 278-79, 324, 327

An Historical and Moral View of the Origin and Progress of the French Revolution, and the Effect It Has Produced in Europe (Wollstonecraft) **5**:416, 426, 429, 431, 436, 443, 461; **50**:325, 361

Historical Description of Russian Commerce (Wollstonecraft) **5**:436

Historical Dictionary (Collier)
    See *The Great Historical, Geographical, Genealogical and Poetical Dictionary*

The Historical Register for the year 1736 (Fielding) **46**:56, 90, 95, 112, 159

"An Historical Review of the Constitution and Government of Pennsylvania" (Franklin) **25**:111

Historie (Anonymous author of *Historie*)
    See *Historie of the damnable life, and deserved death of Doctor Iohn Faustus*

Historie di Nicolo Machiavegli (Machiavelli) **8**:125, 128, 133, 136, 151, 174-75; **36**:232

Historie of the damnable life, and deserved death of Doctor Iohn Faustus (Anonymous author of *Historie*) **47**:177-201

The Histories and Novels of the Late Ingenious Mrs. Behn (Behn) **1**:48

Historiomastrix (Jonson) **33**:149

The History and Adventures of an Atom (Smollett) **2**:319-20, 329, 331-32, 341; **46**:190, 193-94, 212, 248-50

The History and Secret of Painting in Wax (Diderot) **26**:159

History of a Foundling (Fielding)
    See *The History of Tom Jones, a Foundling*

"The History of a New Roof" (Hopkinson)
    See "The New Roof"

"History of Astronomy" (Smith) **36**:332

History of Brandenburg (Frederick the Great)

See *Histoire de Brandebourg*

History of Britain (Milton) **43**:376-8, 380-3, 397, 406-8

The History of Charles Mandeville (Brooke) **6**:111; **48**:119

The History of Cornelia (Scott) **44**:344, 402

History of Edward V. and Richard III. (More) **10**:374

The History of Emily Montague (Brooke) **6**:108-15, 117-22; **48**:52-55, 57-58, 60-63, 65-66, 68-78, 83-84, 88, 92, 94, 98, 101-104, 108, 110

History of England (Hume) **7**:140, 153, 159, 166-68, 191-93, 199-200

History of England (Smollett)
    See *A Compleat History of England*

The History of English Poetry (Warton) **15**:429-30, 435-38, 449, 451-54, 457-59

The History of Florence (Machiavelli)
    See *Historie di Nicolo Machiavegli*

A History of Forbonius and Prisceria
    See *The Delectable History of Forbonius and Prisceria*

The History of Genghizcan the Great, First Emperor of the Antient Moguls and Tartars (Aubin) **9**:3, 7

History of Great Britain and Ireland (Macpherson) **29**:275

The History of Great Britain, under the House of Stuart (Hume) **7**:138, 151

The History of Gustavus Ericson, King of Sweden. With an Introductory History of Sweden from the Middle of the Twelfth Century (Scott) **44**:340, 406

The History of Henry II (Lyttelton)
    See *The History of the Life of King Henry the Second and of the Age in Which He Lived*

History of Henry the Second (Lyttelton)
    See *The History of the Life of King Henry the Second and of the Age in Which He Lived*

History of Italy (Guicciardini)
    See *Storia d'Italia*

The History of Jemmy and Jenny Jessamy (Haywood) **1**:283, 287, 294; **44**:129-30, 156

The History of John Bull (Arbuthnot) **1**:12-17, 20-2

The History of Jonathan Wild the Great (Fielding)
    See *The Life of Mr. Jonathan Wild the Great*

History of Joseph (Rowe) **44**:277, 291

The History of Joseph Andrews (Fielding) **1**:204-05, 207, 209-11, 217-19, 221-24, 228, 230-33, 238, 241-43, 246, 249, 251-55, 258-63, 265; **46**:50, 54-63, 65-7, 70, 74, 78, 80-1, 84, 88, 90, 94-7, 99-104, 106-07, 118-125, 135, 142-48, 159-63, 165-66, 169, 172-77

The History of Lady Julia Mandeville (Brooke) **6**:107-110, 115, 118-22; **48**:53, 58-59, 60-62, 67, 70, 73, 76, 87-88, 92, 112-113, 115, 119

History of Life and Death (Bacon)
    See *Historia Vitae et Mortis*

The History of Little Jack (Day) **1**:106, 108, 111

History of Louis le Grand (Boileau-Despreaux) **3**:17

The History of Mecklenburgh from the First Settlement of the Vandals in that Country to the Present Time (Scott) **44**:340

The History of Miss Betsy Thoughtless (Haywood) **1**:282-84, 286-87, 291, 293; **44**:129-30, 137, 156-79, 164-6, 172

"The History of Miss Stanton" (Goldsmith)
    See "To the Authors of the British Magazine"

History of My Life (Casanova de Seingalt)
    See *Mémoires de J. Casanova de Seingalt écrits par lui-même*

The History of New England from 1630 to 1649 (Winthrop)
    See *A Journal of the Transactions and Occurrences in the Settlement of Massachusetts and the Other New-England Colonies*

The History of Nourjahad (Sheridan) **7**:373-74, 378-79, 384-85

The History of Ophelia (Fielding) **1**:271-73, 278; **44**:68-9, 81

The History of Pompey the Little; or, The Life and Adventures of a Lap-Dog (Coventry) **46**:3-9

The History of Rasselas, Prince of Abissinia (Johnson) **15**:191-93, 196-99, 201-02, 204, 207-08, 213-14, 216-17, 225-29, 233, 237-38, 240, 244-45, 247, 251-61, 267, 269-70, 273, 286, 298, 305-07

History of Redemption (Edwards)
    See *History of the Work of Redemption*

The History of Richard III (More)
    See *The Life of Kinge Richarde the Thirde*

The History of Rivella (Manley)
    See *The Adventures of Rivella*

The History of Sandford and Merton (Day) **1**:105-14

The History of Sir Charles Grandison (Richardson) **1**:369-71, 374-76, 379-80, 383, 388-90, 399-401, 407-10, 413-15, 418; **44**:181-2, 185, 189, 192-4, 197-200, 211-3, 215, 218, 223, 225, 230, 235, 239

The History of Sir Francis Drake (Davenant) **13**:190

The History of Sir George Ellison (Scott) **44**:339, 343-44, 346, 361, 363-64, 370, 388-89, 392, 395, 401, 403, 407, 410, 412

History of Tastes in Gardens (Valentine) **49**:358

"The History of the Beautiful Captive" (Goldsmith) **48**:217

History of the Canons Regular of Mount St. Agnes (Kempis) **11**:411

History of the Civil Wars (Daniel)
    See *The Civile Wares between the Howses of Lancaster and Yorke, corrected and continued*

The History of the Countess of Ellwyn (Fielding)
    See *The Countess of Dellwyn*

History of the Earth and Animated Nature (Goldsmith) **2**:68, 72, 76, 80; **48**:221

History of the Indies (Las Casas)
    See *Historia de las Indias*

History of the Kingdom of Denmark (Holberg)
    See *Dannemarks riges historie*

History of the League (Dryden) **21**:58, 68, 72

The History of the Life and Adventures of Mr. Duncan Campbell, a Gentleman (Defoe) **1**:136

The History of the Life of King Henry the Second and of the Age in Which He Lived (Lyttelton) **10**:196-97, 199-201, 209

The History of the Life, Reign, and Death of Edward II (Cary) **30**:158, 162-64, 166-68

The History of the Most Remarkable Life and Extraordinary Adventures of the Truly Honourable Colonel Jacque, Vulgarly Called Colonel Jack (Defoe) **1**:125, 128, 134, 139-40, 142, 147, 176

The History of the Nun; or, The Fair Vow-Breaker (Behn) **1**:42-4, 46, 50-1; **30**:86, 88; **42**:146

A History of the Plague (Defoe)
    See *A Journal of the Plague Year*

Title Index

History of the Reformation in Scotland (Knox)
  See *The History of the Reformation of Religion in Scotland*
The History of the Reformation of Religion in Scotland (Knox) **37**:213, 234, 240
The History of the Reign of King Henry the Seventh (Bacon) **18**:132, 134, 136, 177, 187; **32**:187; **32**:187
History of the Russian Empire under Peter the Great (Voltaire)
  See *Histoire de l'empire de Russie sous Pierre le Grand*
History of the Six Worthy Yeomen of the West **41**:78
The History of the Union of Great Britain (Defoe) **1**:124, 162
The History of the Union with Scotland (Defoe)
  See *The History of the Union of Great Britain*
History of the Work of Redemption (Edwards) **7**:117, 119-20
The History of the World (Raleigh) **39**:77-78, 80-87, 88-93, 98-106, 109-21, 123, 124-27
The History of Tom Jones, a Foundling (Fielding) **1**:205-07, 209-13, 215, 217-19, 221-25, 228, 230-38, 240-48, 254-63; **46**:50-1, 63, 66, 73-4, 77-81, 83-4, 86, 88-9, 91-2, 94-5, 97-102, 104-07, 125, 131-37, 149-53, 155-57, 172-79
History of Winds (Bacon)
  See *Historia Ventorum*
Histriomastix; or, The Player Whipt (Marston) **33**:193, 196
"The Hock-Cart, or Harvest Home" (Herrick) **13**:351, 368-69, 383, 395
"Hohsien" (P'u Sung-ling) **49**:288
"The Holdfast" (Herbert) **24**:267, 271
"Holy Baptisme I" (Herbert) **24**:273, 272
The Holy Bible: Containing the Old Testament and the New (Eliot)
  See *Mamusse wunneetupanatamwe Up-Biblum God Naneeswe Nukkone TestamentKah Wonk Wusku Testament*
The Holy City; or, The New Jerusalem (Bunyan) **4**:169-70
"Holy Communion" (Herbert) **24**:274
"Holy Communion" (Herbert) **24**:274
"The Holy Communion" (Vaughan) **27**:341, 394
"The Holy Fair" (Burns) **3**:59, 65, 68, 71-2, 76-8, 84, 86, 95-7, 104-06; **29**:13, 16-18, 24, 32-5, 40-2, 44-5, 61, 64, 76, 91, 93; **40**:63, 70-2, 89, 94, 97, 105, 109, 117
"Holy Scriptures" (Vaughan)
  See "H. Scriptures"
"Holy Scriptures I" (Herbert) **24**:274, 276
"Holy Sonnet 3, `O might those sighs and teares returne againe'" (Donne) **24**:169
"Holy Sonnet 4" (Donne) **24**:170
"Holy Sonnet 5, `I am a little world cunningly made'" (Donne) **24**:170, 186
"Holy Sonnet 6, `This is my playes last scene'" (Donne) **24**:170
"Holy Sonnet VII: At the round earths imagin'd corners blow" (Donne) **10**:96; **24**:170, 202
"Holy Sonnet 8, `If faithful soules be alike glorified'" (Donne) **24**:170
"Holy Sonnet 9, `If povsonous mineralls'" (Donne) **24**:170
"Holy Sonnet 10, `Death be not proud'" (Donne) **24**:164, 171
"Holy Sonnet 11, `Spit in my face yee Jewes'" (Donne) **24**:
"Holy Sonnet 12, `Why are wee by all creatures waited on?'" (Donne) **24**:171

"Holy Sonnet XIII: What if this present were the world's last night?" (Donne) **10**:73; **24**:171
"Holy Sonnet XIV: Batter my heart, three-person'd God" (Donne) **10**:96; **24**:171
"Holy Sonnet 15, `Wilt thou love God as he thee!'" (Donne) **24**:172
"Holy Sonnet XVII: Since she whom i lov'd hath paid her last debt" (Donne) **10**:54; **24**:172
"Holy Sonnet XVII: `Show me deare Christ, thy spouse'" (Donne) **10**:84; **24**:172
"Holy Sonnet 19, `Oh to vex me contraryes meete in one'" (Donne) **24**:173
Holy Sonnets (Donne) **10**:26, 40, 45, 52, 55, 63-4, 84, 93, 96, 99; 165, 169, 173, 198-99, 202
"The Holy Tulzie" (Burns) **6**:83-8; **29**:41-5, 63
The Holy War (Bunyan) **4**:156-57, 159, 161, 169-70, 172, 180-82, 203-04, 206
An Holy War and Considerations Touching a War with Spain (Bacon) **32**:133
"Holy Willie's Prayer" (Burns) **3**:67-9, 71-2, 78, 82, 85, 87, 90, 93, 95, 97-8; **29**:13-15, 24, 32, 39-45, 47, 61, 63, 65, 71-2, 74-6; **40**:63, 70, 72, 79-80, 89, 95
"Holyhead" (Swift) **1**:482
"Hombres necios que acusáis" (Juana Ines de la Cruz) **5**:150, 156
"Home" (Herbert) **24**:216
Homer (Chapman) **22**:5, 14
Homer (Pope)
  See *The Odyssey of Homer*
L'Homère travesti; ou, L'Iliade en vers burlesques (Marivaux) **4**:385
De Homine (Hobbes) **36**:160
De hominis dignitate (Pico della Mirandola)
  See *Oratio de dignitate hominis*
L'homme aux quarante écus (Voltaire) **14**:338, 346, 359, 363
"L'homme et la Couleuvre" (La Fontaine) **50**:80, 84, 119
"L'homme qui court apres la Fortune et l'Homme qui l'attend en son lit" (La Fontaine) **50**:100-102
Les hommes illustres qui ont paru en France pendant ce siècle (Perrault) **2**:276, 279, 283
Honest Excuses (Lodge) **41**:200
The Honest Whore (Dekker) **22**:88-9, 93, 99-100, 103, 106, 108-9, 119, 123, 125-7, 131-2
The Honest Whore (Middleton) **33**:267, 272
Den honnette ambition (Holberg) **6**:267, 275, 277
The Honorable Girl (Goldoni)
  See *La putta onorata*
"Honored Friend" (Dryden) **21**:88
"Honoria" (Dryden)
  See *Theodore and Honoria*
Honour Restored (Calderon de la Barca) **23**:24
"Hop o' My Thumb" (Perrault)
  See "Le petit poucet"
"Hope" (Crashaw) **24**:4, 42, 45, 53
"Hope" (Herbert) **24**:254, 264, 266
Hopffen-Sack (Beer)
  See *Der abentheuerliche, wunderbare und unerhörte Ritter Hopffen-sack*
"The Hop-Garden" (Smart) **3**:362, 363, 371-72, 375, 394, 399
La hora de todos (Quevedo) **23**:154
Horace (Corneille) **28**:4, 12, 16, 21, 23-4, 34-5, 43, 55, 57-8
Horace (Philips) **30**:277, 283, 291, 311, 319-20
Horace (Smart)
  See *The Works of Horace, Translated into Verse*
Horace, Epod. iv. Imitated by Sir James Baker Kt. (Gay) **49**:7
"Horace to Virgil, on His Taking a Voyage to Ath-

ens" (Ramsay) **29**:330, 338
"An Horatian Ode upon Cromwell's Return from Ireland" (Marvell) **4**:397-98, 404, 413-17, 425, 430-31, 436, 438, 440, 442; **43**:252-6, 258, 262, 264-80, 283-4, 287, 290, 293, 295-9; **43**:300, 301, 307-14, 317-8
The Horatii (Aretino)
  See *Orazia*
Horatius (Corneille)
  See *Horace*
Hormonice Mundi (Kepler) **45**:325-26, 343, 346, 348, 367-68
"Horoscope" (Crashaw)
  See "Love's Horoscope"
Les horribles et espouvantables faictz et prouesses du tres renommé Pantagruel Roy des Dipsodes, filz du grand géant Gargantua (Rabelais) **5**:208-09, 216-17, 223, 225-26, 233, 235-38, 241, 248, 252-54, 257-59, 264-68
The Horse Doctor (Aretino)
  See *Marescalco*
"Horse-Courser" (Butler) **16**:53
"Horses" (More) **9**:298
Hortelano era Belardo (Vega) **23**:359
Hortulus rosarii de valle lachrymarum continens egreias & devotas sentecias (Kempis) **11**:410
"Hortus" (Marvell) **4**:448
Hospitale pauperum (Kempis) **11**:411
Hous of Fame (Chaucer)
  See *House of Fame*
House of Fame (Chaucer) **17**:45, 58, 78, 87, 97, 108, 178, 206, 217-19
A House with Two Doors Is Difficult to Guard (Calderon de la Barca)
  See *Casa con dos puertas, mala es de guardar*
"Housewifery" (Taylor)
  See "Huswifery"
The Housholders Philosophie (Kyd) **22**:251, 253
"How Lang and Dreary Is the Night" (Burns) **6**:82; **29**:52
"How Lilies Came White" (Herrick) **13**:346, 367
"How Marigolds Came Yellow" (Herrick) **13**:365
How Sleep the Brave (Collins) **40**:132
"How the Wallflower Came First" (Herrick) **13**:365
"Hoy nos viene a redimir" (Teresa de Jesus) **18**:389
"Hsi Fang-ping" (P'u Sung-ling) **3**:347
"Hsiang Kao" (P'u Sung-ling) **3**:347
"Hsiang-nu" (P'u Sung-ling) **49**:278
"Hsiang-yu" (P'u Sung-ling) **49**:278, 280
"Hsiang-yü" (P'u Sung-ling) **3**:354
"Hsia-nü" (P'u Sung-ling) **3**:354; **49**:294
"Hsiao Ts'ui" (P'u Sung-ling) **49**:298, 300
"Hsieh-nü" (P'u Sung-ling) **3**:351
"Hsien-jen tao" (P'u Sung-ling) **3**:354; **49**:278, 281
"Hsin Shih-ssu niang" (P'u Sung-ling) **49**:278, 296-97, 299-300
Hsing-shih yin-yuan chuan (P'u Sung-ling) **3**:346, 356
Hsi-yu chi (Wu Ch'eng-en) **7**:395-408, 410-12, 414-15, 417
"Hsü huang-liang" (P'u Sung-ling) **3**:350; **49**:281, 292
"Hu ch'eng yin" (P'u Sung-ling) **49**:294
"Hu hsieh" (P'u Sung-ling) **49**:295
"Hu lien" (P'u Sung-ling) **49**:295
"Hu Ssu-chieh" (P'u Sung-ling) **49**:294-95
"Hu Ssu-hsiang-kung" (P'u Sung-ling) **49**:295
"Huan Niang" (P'u Sung-ling) **49**:310

"Huang Chiang-chün" (P'u Sung-ling) **49**:283
"Huang Jiulang" (P'u Sung-ling) **49**:313
"Huang Ying" (P'u Sung-ling) **49**:310, 314-15
Hudibras (Butler) **16**:2, 4-12, 14-27, 30-9, 41-8, 50-1; **43**:62-4, 67-71, 74-6, 78-80, 81-7, 90-7, 99-100, 103, 107, 110-7, 120-8, 132-3
Hudibras (Smart) **3**:374
Hudibras, the first part (Butler)
　See *Hudibras*
"Huffing Courtier" (Butler) **16**:51, 53
"The Human Nature" (Taylor) **11**:370
Human Nature (Hobbes) **36**:128, 138-39
Human Rhymes (Vega)
　See *Rimas Humas*
L'Humanità di Christo (Aretino) **12**:6, 13-4, 20, 35
Humanity of Christ (Aretino)
　See *L'Humanità di Christo*
Humble Exhortation to Charles V (Calvin)
　See *Humble Exhortation to the Invincible Emperor Charles V and the Most Illustrious Princes*
Humble Exhortation to the Invincible Emperor Charles V and the Most Illustrious Princes (Calvin) **37**:92
"Humilitie" (Herbert) **24**:252, 254-55, 266, 274
An Humorous Day's Mirth (Chapman) **22**:10, 12, 34, 60-61
The Humourous Lieutenant, or Demetrius and Enanthe (Fletcher) **33**:57, 60, 86-8
Humourous Pieces (Warton) **15**:434-35
"The Humours" (Bradstreet)
　See "Of the Four Humours in Man's Constitution"
"Humours" (Marston) **33**:235
Humphry Clinker (Smollett)
　See *The Expedition of Humphry Clinker*
Hung-lou meng (Ts'ao Hsueh-ch'in) **1**:533-61
"Hung-yü" (P'u Sung-ling) **49**:300
The Hunting of the hare (Cavendish) **30**:209
"The Hunting Song" (Burns) **40**:103
"The Hurricane" (Winchilsea)
　See "A Pindarick Poem upon the Hurricane"
The Husband in Answer to the Wife (Haywood) **44**:150
"Husbanding Your Will" (Montaigne) **8**:221
"The Husband's Resentment" (Manley) **1**:306, 308
"Hu-shih" (P'u Sung-ling) **49**:295
"Huswifery" (Taylor) **11**:352, 355-56, 360, 386, 393, 402
Hyacinth (Andreae) **32**:101
"Hyme" (Donne)
　See "Hymne to God my God, in my sicknesse"
"L'hymen" (Rousseau) **9**:343
Hymenaei (Jonson) **6**:315, 349; **33**:129, 174, 177-8
Hymen's Triumph (Daniel) **24**:83, 89, 97-8, 122, 134-35, 139-41
"Hymme to God My God, in My Sicknesse" (Donne)
　See "Hymne to God my God, in my sicknesse"
"A Hymn for Christmas Day" (Chatterton) **3**:127
"A Hymn for Evening" (Parnell) **3**:255
"A Hymn for Morning" (Parnell) **3**:255
"Hymn for the Circumcision" (Crashaw)
　See "Hymn for the Circumcision day of our Lord"
"Hymn for the Circumcision day of our Lord" (Crashaw) **24**:29, 47
"Hymn for the Day of St. Philip and St. James" (Smart) **3**:370, 378, 390-91
"Hymn of St. Thomas" (Crashaw) **24**:77-8

"The Hymn of the Church" (Crashaw)
　See "'Dies Irae,' The Hymn of the church, in Meditation of the Day of Judgement"
"Hymn of the Nativity" (Crashaw)
　See "Hymn of the Nativity, Sung by the Shepherds"
"Hymn of the Nativity, Sung by the Shepherds" (Crashaw) **24**:6, 8, 13, 19, 25, 30, 35-6, 39-40, 44, 49, 54, 59
"Hymn on Solitude" (Thomson) **16**:406; **29**:444
"Hymn on the Nativity of Our Lord and Saviour Jesus Christ" (Smart) **3**:376, 378, 390, 392
"Hymn on the Power of God" (Thomson) **16**:418
"A Hymn on the Seasons" (Thomson) **16**:375-76, 384-85, 405-06, 419, 430-31; **29**:392, 398, 404
"Hymn to Adversity" (Gray)
　See "Ode to Adversity"
"Hymn to Beauty" (Spenser)
　See "An Hymne in Honour of Beautie"
"A Hymn to Contentment" (Parnell) **3**:252-58
"An Hymn to Diana" (Jonson) **6**:325
"An Hymn to God the Father" (Jonson) **6**:326
"An Hymn to Humanity" (Wheatley) **3**:412, 415-16, 420; **50**:179, 195, 259
"Hymn to Ignorance" (Gray) **4**:301, 333; **40**:235, 238-40, 243
"Hymn to Musique" (Herrick) **13**:324
"Hymn to Saint Teresa" (Crashaw)
　See "Hymn to the Name and Honor of the Admirable Saint Teresa, Foundress of the Reformation of the Discalced Carmelites, both men and Women"
"Hymn to St. Philip and St. James" (Smart)
　See "Hymn for the Day of St. Philip and St. James"
"An Hymn to the Evening" (Wheatley) **3**:413, 418, 420, 430, 435-37; **50**:204, 206-07, 241
"An Hymn to the Morning" (Wheatley) **3**:413, 418, 435; **50**:192-93, 204-07, 209, 227, 240-41
"Hymn to the Name above every Name—the Name of Jesus" (Crashaw) **24**:18, 27-8, 32, 38, 53, 59-60, 64, 66-70
"Hymn to the Name and Honor of the Admirable Saint Teresa, Foundress of the Reformation of the Discalced Carmelites, both men and Women" (Crashaw) **24**:8, 13, 16-8, 20, 25, 28, 31, 36, 44, 63, 74
"Hymn to the Name and Honor of the Admirable St. Teresa" (Crashaw)
　See "Hymn to the Name and Honor of the Admirable Saint Teresa, Foundress of the Reformation of the Discalced Carmelites, both men and Women"
A Hymn to the Pillory (Defoe) **1**:161
"Hymn to the Supreme Being, on Recovery from a Dangerous Fit of Illness" (Smart) **3**:366, 371, 375-76, 378, 381-82, 395
"L'Hymne de Henri II" (Ronsard) **6**:439
"Hymne de la Mort" (Ronsard) **6**:422-23, 429, 435-37
"Hymne de la Philosophie" (Ronsard) **6**:422-23, 429
"Hymne de l'autonne" (Ronsard) **6**:429
"L'Hymne de l'Esté" (Ronsard) **6**:438
"Hymne de l'éternité" (Ronsard) **6**:422-23, 429, 437, 439
"Hymne de Mercure" (Ronsard) **6**:429
"Hymne des astres" (Ronsard)
　See "Les Astres"
"Hymne des estoilles" (Ronsard) **6**:424
"Hymne du ciel" (Ronsard) **6**:422, 424, 429

"An Hymne in Honour of Beautie" (Spenser) **5**:309, 311, 323-24, 352-53
"An Hymne in Honour of Love" (Spenser) **5**:323, 350-52
"Hymne of Beauty" (Spenser)
　See "An Hymne in Honour of Beautie"
"An Hymne of Heavenly Beautie" (Spenser) **5**:309, 311, 351-53
"An Hymne of Heavenly Love" (Spenser) **5**:324, 350-53
"Hymne of Love" (Spenser)
　See "An Hymne in Honour of Love"
"A Hymne to Bacchus" (Herrick) **13**:351, 410
"A Hymne to Christ, at the authors last going into Germany" (Donne) **10**:16, 40, 84
"Hymne to God my God, in my sicknesse" (Donne) **10**:16, 40, 65, 85, 97, 106; **24**:165, 169, 173-74, 199-201
"A Hymne to God the Father" (Donne) **10**:16, 40, 65, 85; **24**:167, 168
"A Hymne to His Ladies Birth-Place" **8**:42-3
"A Hymne to Hymen" (Chapman) **22**:77
"A Hymne to Our Savior on the Crosse" (Chapman) **22**:
"An hymne to the Saints, and to Marquesse Hamylton" (Donne) **10**:84
Hymnes (Ronsard) **6**:407, 409-11, 424, 431-32, 434
Hymnes (Spenser)
　See *Fowre Hymnes*
Hymnes retranchées (Ronsard) **6**:410, 422
Hymns (Ronsard)
　See *Hymnes*
Hymns and Spiritual Songs for the Fasts and Festivals of the Church of England (Smart) **3**:375-78, 390, 400, 402-04
Hymns for Children (Smart)
　See *Hymns for the Amusement of Children*
Hymns for the Amusement of Children (Smart) **3**:375, 393, 395, 397
Hymns for the Fasts and Festivals (Smart)
　See *Hymns and Spiritual Songs for the Fasts and Festivals of the Church of England*
Hymns of the Passion (Petursson)
　See *Fimmtíu passiusálmar*
"Hymnus Epiphanie" (Crashaw)
　See "In the Glorious Epiphany of our Lord; a hymn sung as by the Three Kings"
"Hymnus in Cynthiam" (Chapman) **22**:
"Hymnus in Noctem" (Chapman) **22**:
"Hymnus in Noctem" (Chapman)
　See "Hymnus in Noctem"
The Hypochondriac (Moliere)
　See *Le malade imaginaire*
The Hypochondriack (Boswell) **4**:34, 36-8, 57-9, 64, 71-2, 74; **50**:31
L'hypocondre; ou, La femme qui ne parle point (Rousseau) **9**:335-36
"An Hypocrite" (Butler) **16**:27
The Hypocrite (Aretino)
　See *Lo ipocrito*
"Hypocrites Deficient in the Duty of Prayer" (Edwards) **7**:113
"An Hypocritical Nonconformist" (Butler) **16**:28, 55
"Hypothesis explaining the Properties of Light" (Newton) **35**:296, 298, 303
Hypothesis physica nova (Leibniz) **35**:154
"I dare not ask" (Herrick) **13**:322
"I had eight birds hacht in one nest" (Bradstreet) **4**:106
"I Hae a Wife" (Burns) **3**:81
"I have in me a great care" (Juana Ines de la Cruz)

5:152

"I Heare Some Say, this Man Is Not in Love"
See "Sonnet 24"

"I' ho gia fatto un gozzo in questo stento"
(Michelangelo) **12**:365

"I look to the North" (Burns) **29**:57

"I love my Jean" (Burns) **29**:85, 87; **40**:64, 102

"I love unloved" (Henry VIII) **10**:145

"I' mi son caro assai più ch'i' non soglio"
(Michelangelo) **12**:367

"I Murder Hate by Field or Flood" (Burns) **29**:23

I pettegolezzi delle donne (Goldoni) **4**:256

I rusteghi (Goldoni) **4**:257, 261, 265, 268, 274-
75

I sette salmi de la penitenzia di David (Aretino)
12:13, 20-1, 25, 35

I suppositi (Pope) **3**:334

"I tell thee, Charmion, could I Time retrieve"
(Congreve) **5**.85

"I walkt the other day" (Vaughan) **27**:325, 360

"I wonder by my troth" (Donne)
See "The good-morrow"

Iacke of Newbery
See *The Pleasant Historie of John Winchcomb,
in his younger years called Iacke ofNewberie*

Ibrahim; ou, L'illustre Bassa (Scudery) **2**:306-
09, 311

Ibrahim; ou, L'illustre Bassa (Scudery)
See *Isabelle Grimaldi*

Ibrahim, the Thirteenth Emperour of the Turks
(Pix) **8**:258, 260-61, 263, 265, 267, 269-
74, 276-78

Ichabod: or, The Glory Departing (Mather)
38:306, 309

"Ichthyophagia" (Erasmus) **16**:129, 141, 194-
95, 198

Icon Basilike (Charles I)
See *Eikon Basilike: The Portraicture of His
Sacred Majestie in His Solitudes and Suf-
ferings*

Iconoclastes (Milton)
See *Eikonoklastes*

Icosameron (Casanova de Seingalt) **13**:98, 112

Idalia; or, The Unfortunate Mistress (Haywood)
1:283; **44**:139, 142, 145, 148, 152-4

Idea **8**:14, 19

"Idea 61"
See "Sonnet 61"

"Idea of a Perfect Commonwealth" (Hume)
7:189-90

*Idea the Shepheards Garland, Fashioned in Nine
Eglogs. Rowlands Sacrifice to the Nine
Muses* **8**:20-1, 29, 31-2, 34-9, 50, 54

Ideal einer vollkommenen Zeitung (Moritz) **2**:240

Ideas Mirrour. Amours in Quatorzains **8**:19, 32,
37, 52, 54

Idées républicaines (Voltaire) **14**:401, 405-06

"Identity and Diversity" (Locke) **35**:233

"Idle Verse" (Vaughan) **27**:392

"Idleness of Business" (Wycherley) **8**:380

The Idler (Johnson) **15**:196, 199, 207, 225, 261-
62, 267, 269, 284, 287, 289

"The Idler, 50" (Johnson) **15**:287

"The Idler, 64" (Johnson) **15**:266

"The Idler, 73" (Johnson) **15**:262

"The Idler, 89" (Johnson) **15**:290

If it be not Good, the Devil is in it (Dekker) **22**:88,
94, 102, 104, 107-8, 127, 132

"If perchance, my Fabio" (Juana Ines de la Cruz)
See "Si acaso, Fabio mío"

"If Synthia be a Queene, a princes, and supreame"
(Raleigh) **31**:272

If This Be Not a Good Play, the Devil Is in It

(Dekker)
See *If it be not Good, the Devil is in it*

"If yet I have not all thy love" (Donne)
See "Lovers infinitenesse"

*Ignatius, His Conclave; or His Inthronisation in
a Late Election in Hell: wherein many things
are mingled by way of satyr* (Donne) **10**:39,
62-3; **24**:186

"Ignorance" (Wycherley) **8**:380

The Ignorance and Calumny of H. Hallywell
(Penn) **25**:287

"An Ignorant Man" (Butler) **16**:54

Il Candelaio (Bruno) **27**:68-69, 104, 117

Il Candelajo (Bruno)
See *Il Candelaio*

Il cavaliere e la dama (Goldoni) **4**:250, 265

Il festino (Goldoni) **4**:262

Il filosofo (Aretino) **12**:19, 26-7, 30, 36

Il gondoliere veneziano (Goldoni) **4**:267

Il libro del cortegiano (Castiglione) **12**:76-127

Il libro dello amore (Ficino) **12**:176

Il mondo creato (Tasso)
See *Le sette giornate del mondo creato*

Il negromante (Ariosto) **6**:60-1

"Il Penseroso" (Milton) **9**:177, 192, 198, 204,
212, 224-30, 232

Il principe di Niccholo Machivello (Machiavelli)
8:123, 125-28, 130-37, 139-40, 142, 145-49,
151-55, 157-62, 167-68, 170, 172-73, 175-
79; **36**:192-200, 200-20, 222-30, 235-37

Il ritorno dalla villeggiatura (Goldoni) **4**:265

Il servitore di due padroni (Goldoni) **4**:272-73

Il teatro comico (Goldoni) **4**:266, 268

Il ventaglio (Goldoni) **4**:255, 264, 266-67

Il vero amico (Goldoni) **4**:259

L'ile de la raison; ou, Les petits hommes
(Marivaux) **4**:367, 377, 388

"Île de Ré" (Malherbe)
See "Pour le roy allant chastier la rebellion des
Rochelois et chasser les Anglois qui en leur
faveur estoient descendus en l'isle de Ré"

L'ile des esclaves (Marivaux) **4**:361, 465-68, 377,
388

Iliad (Chapman) **22**:3-4, 10, 29

"Ill Government" (Herrick) **13**:395

"I'll Never Leave Thee" (Ramsay) **29**:320

"I'll tell thee now (dear love) what thou shalt doe"
(Donne)
See "A Valediction: of the booke"

L'illusion comique (Corneille) **28**:30, 32, 46-8,
55-7

*The Illustrious French Lovers: Being the True
Histories of the Amours of Several French
Persons of Quality* (Aubin) **9**:3-4

"The Illustrious Kitchen Maid" (Cervantes)
See "La ilustre fregona"

"The Illustrious Serving Wench" (Cervantes)
See "La ilustre fregona"

"La ilustre fregona" (Cervantes) **6**:170-71, 176;
23:104, 146, 149

"I'm o'er young to Marry Yet" (Burns) **29**:22,
48; **40**:87

Image
See *The Image of Governance compiled of the
actes and sentences notable of the moste
noble Emperour Alexander Severus, late
translated out of Greke into Englyshe by syr
Thomas Elyot, Knight, in the fauour of
nobylitie*

The Image of Death in Ancient Art (Lessing)
8:104

*The Image of Governance compiled of the actes
and sentences notable of the moste noble*

*Emperour Alexander Severus, late translated
out of Greke into Englyshe by syr Thomas
Elyot, Knight, in the fauour of nobylitie*
(Elyot) **11**:60-1, 68, 71, 73-4, 76, 91

Images and Shadows of Divine Things (Edwards)
7:128

The Imaginary Invalid (Moliere)
See *Le malade imaginaire*

"Imagination" (Marmontel) **2**:221

"Imagination" (Wheatley)
See "On Imagination"

De imaginum signorum et idearum compostione
(Bruno) **27**:91-95, 124

The Imitation of Christ (Kempis)
See *De imitatione Christi*

Imitation of Jesus Christ (Corneille) **28**:5

"An Imitation of Some French Verses" (Parnell)
3:257

"Imitations of Horace" (Swift) **1**:439, 523

Imitations of Horace (Pope)
See *Satires and Epistles of Horace, Imitated*

"Imitative Arts" (Smith) **36**:319

"Imitée d'Horace" (Rousseau) **9**:344

De immenso (Bruno)
See *De innumerabilibus immenso et
infigurabili; sue de universo et mundis*

"Immoderately Mourning My Brother's Untimely
Death" (Lovelace) **24**:332

The Immortality of the Soul (More) **9**:305-06,
314, 323-24, 329

The Impartial Critick (Dennis) **11**:5, 20, 30, 39

The Imperial Crown of Otón (Vega)
See *La imperial de Otón*

La imperial de Otón (Vega) **23**:398

Impertinent Curiosity (Castro) **19**:4

"The importunate Fortune" (Vaughan) **27**:325,
361, 366

The Imposter (Brooke) **1**:62

The Imposter (Moliere)
See *Le tartuffe*

L'imposteur (Moliere)
See *Le tartuffe*

L'impostore (Goldoni) **4**:262

Imposture sacerdotale (Holbach) **14**:153

The Impromptu at Versailles (Moliere)
See *L'impromptu de Versailles*

L'impromptu de Versailles (Moliere) **10**:278, 281,
283, 287, 311, 318, 321; **28**:230-32, 236,
255, 274-75

"Impromptu on Lord Holland's House" (Gray)
See "On Lord Holland's Seat near Margate,
Kent"

"In Amicum Foeneatorem" (Vaughan) **27**:325,
360

"In Answer of an Elegiacal Letter, upon the Death
of the King of Sweden, from Aurelian
Townsend, inviting me to write on that subject" (Carew) **13**:22, 42

"In Answer to a Mistress, Who Desir'd Her Lover
to Marry Her" (Wycherley) **8**:415

In arrtem brevem Raymundi Lullii commentaria
(Agrippa von Nettesheim) **27**:25

"In celebration of the yearely Preserver of the
Games" (Davenant) **13**:205

In Defense of the Indians (Las Casas)
See *Apologia*

In geomanticam disciplinem lectura (Agrippa von
Nettesheim) **27**:23

"In Honour of Du Bartas" (Bradstreet) **30**:137

"In Honour of that High and Mighty Princess,
Queen Elizabeth, of Happy Memory"
(Bradstreet) **4**:88, 110, 114; **30**:153

"In Matters of General Concern to the People"

(Franklin) **25**:126

"In Memory of My Dear Grandchild Elizabeth Bradstreet" (Bradstreet) **30**:126

"In memory of the Virtuous and Learned Lady Madre de Teresa that sought an early Martyrdom" (Crashaw) **24**:47, 53

"In My Solitary Hours" (Bradstreet) **30**:150

"In Praise of Ignorance" (Wycherley) **21**:356

In Praise of Knowledge (Bacon) **32**:186, 188

"In Pursuit of Benefices" (Erasmus) **16**:194

"In Quintum Novembris" (Milton) **9**:204

"In reference to her children" (Bradstreet) **4**:94; **30**:146

"In Thankful Remembrance for My Dear Husband's Safe Arrival" (Bradstreet) **30**:147-8, 151

"In the Due Honor of the Author Master Robert Norton, and His Work" **9**:382

In the Garden (Marvell) **43**:261

"In the Glorious Assumption of Our Lady, The Hymn" (Crashaw) **24**:25, 37, 53, 74-5

"In the Glorious Epiphany of our Lord; a hymn sung as by the Three Kings" (Crashaw) **24**:19, 30, 33, 38-40, 53, 56-9, 65

"In the praise of the Spring" (Crashaw) **24**:43

In This Life Everything is True and Everything is False (Calderon de la Barca) **23**:64

"In vita humana" (Bacon) **18**:192

"In what torne ship" (Donne)
See "A Hymne to Christ, at the authors last going into Germany"

"In Yonder Grave a Druid Lies" (Collins)
See "An Ode Occasion'd by the Death of Mr. Thomson"

"In Zodiacum Marcelli Palingenii" (Vaughan) **27**:325

Inamorato Curio (Marston) **33**:223

The Incantation of Circe (Bruno)
See *Cantus circaeus*

"The Incarnation and Passion" (Vaughan) **27**:325, 337

Les Incas (Marmontel) **2**:212-14

The Incas (Marmontel)
See *Les Incas*

De incertitudine et vanitate scientiarium declamatio inuectiua et excellentia verbiDei (Agrippa von Nettesheim) **27**:4-5, 9-11, 13-14, 16, 19-24, 26, 28-31, 34-53, 56

Incognita; or, Love and Duty Reconcil'd (Congreve) **5**:83, 95, 108-09; **21**:11-14, 35-9, 44-5

The Inconstant; or, The Way to Win Him (Farquhar) **21**:128-29, 133-36, 139-42, 148, 150, 154, 161, 169

"Independence" (Churchill) **3**:141, 150-51, 155-56, 163-64

Indian Dialogues, for Their Instruction in that Great Service of Christ, in Calling Home Their Countrymen to the Knowledge of God and of Themselves, and of Jesus Christ (Eliot) **5**:135-36, 138

The Indian Emperour; or, The Conquest of Mexico by the Spaniards, Being the Sequel of the Indian Queen (Dryden) **3**:177-78, 232, 235; **21**:56, 66, 88, 102, 105-07

The Indian Grammar Begun; or, An Essay to Bring the Indian Language into Rules, for the Help of Such as Desire to Learn the Same, for the Furtherance of the Gospel Among Them (Eliot) **5**:134

The Indian Primer; or, The Way of Training up of Our Indian Youth in the Good Knowledge of God, in the Knowledge of the Scriptures and

in an Ability to Read (Eliot) **5**:132

The Indian Queen (Dryden) **3**:231; **21**:104-05, 107

Indian Spring (Siguenza y Gongora) **8**:340

Indiculus librorum (Andreae) **32**:90

"The Indifferent" (Donne) **10**:12, 52, 82; **24**:151, 153-54, 207

L'indigent philosophe (Marivaux) **4**:376, 378-80, 386-87

The Indiscreet Jewels (Diderot)
See *Les Bijoux indescrets*

The Indiscreet Vows (Marivaux)
See *The Indiscreet Vows*

"The Infidel Reclaimed" (Young)
See "The Complaint; or, Night Thoughts: Night the Sixth"

"Information to Those Who Would Remove to America" (Franklin) **25**:140, 144

Los infortunios de Alonso Ramírez (Siguenza y Gongora)
See *Infortunios que Alonso Ramírez natural de la ciudad de S. Juan de Puerto Rico*

Infortunios que Alonso Ramírez natural de la ciudad de S. Juan de Puerto Rico (Siguenza y Gongora) **8**:341, 344-47

El ingenioso hidalgo Don Quixote de la Mancha (Cervantes) **6**:130-37, 139-53, 157-58, 160-64, 166-72, 174, 177, 180, 183-92; **23**:85-6, 88, 90, 92-98, 100, 102-11, 120-23, 125-33, 137-39, 141, 143, 145, 148-49

L'Ingénu (Voltaire) **14**:334, 346, 354, 359, 361, 398, 400

"Ingrateful Beauty Threatened" (Carew) **13**:23, 28, 33, 63

"L'Ingratitude et l'injustice des hommes envers la Fortune" (La Fontaine) **50**:100-102

The Inhumane Cardinal; or, Innocence Betrayed (Pix) **8**:260, 267, 277

The Injured Husband; or, The Mistaken Resentment (Haywood) **1**:292

Innamorato (Boiardo)
See *Orlando innamorato*

Innocency with her Open Face (Penn) **25**:286-88

The Innocent Mistress (Pix) **8**:258, 260-62, 268-69, 271-73, 275

De innumerabilibus immenso et infigurabili; sue de universo et mundis (Bruno) **27**:117, 123

"Inquiry" (Herrick) **13**:311

Inquisitio de Fide (Erasmus) **16**:142, 155, 193

The Insatiate Countess (Marston) **33**:204, 212, 243

"Inscription in a Hermitage" (Warton) **15**:444, 454

Inscription to Mr. Tommy Potter (Gay) **49**:7

Inspicientes (Hutten)
See *The Spectators*

"Installation Ode" (Gray) **4**:312

Institute of a Christian Prince (Erasmus)
See *Institutio principis christiani*

Institutes (Calvin) **37**:86-87, 89, 104, 108, 111, 117, 127-28, 134-136, 151-61

The Institutes of Health (Cleland) **2**:50, 54

Institutio (Calvin)
See *Institutes*

Institutio Christiani Matrimoni (Erasmus)
See *Christiani Matrimonii Institutio*

Institutio magica pro Curiosis (Andreae) **32**:100

Institutio principis (Erasmus) **16**:198

Institutio principis christiani (Erasmus) **16**:112, 120-21, 132, 154-55, 186

The Institution of a Christen Man (Henry VIII) **10**:130-31, 133, 135-39, 141

"Institution pour l'adolescence du Roi, Charles IX" (Ronsard) **6**:409, 411

Instructions for Forreine Travel (Howell) **13**:420, 424, 427-28, 430, 433, 437

Instructions for the Organization of a Community Chest (Luther) **9**:134

Instructions to his Son and to Posterity (Raleigh) **31**:237-9, 260

The Insufficiency of Reason as a Substitute for Revelation (Edwards) **7**:129

Interesting Narrative (Equiano)
See *The Interesting Narrative of the Life of Olaudah Equiano, or Gustavus Vassa, the African*

The Interesting Narrative of Olaudah Equiano (Equiano)
See *The Interesting Narrative of the Life of Olaudah Equiano, or Gustavus Vassa, the African*

Interesting Narrative of the Life (Equiano)
See *The Interesting Narrative of the Life of Olaudah Equiano, or Gustavus Vassa, the African*

The Interesting Narrative of the Life of Olaudah Equiano, or Gustavus Vassa, the African (Equiano) **16**:60-71, 75-8, 82, 85, 91, 94, 97-9

The Interior Castle; or, The Mansions (Teresa de Jesus)
See *Castillo interior, o las moradas*

Interludes (Cervantes)
See *Ocho comedias y ocho entremeses nunca representados*

Interpretation and Substantiation of the Conclusions (Zwingli) **37**:369-70

"De Interpretationae Naturae Proemium" (Bacon) **18**:187-88

De Interpretationae Naturae Sententiae XII (Bacon) **18**:187

The Intriguing Chambermaid (Fielding) **46**:163

Introduction to a Secret Encyclopaedia (Leibniz) **35**:167

An Introduction to Astrology (Lilly) **27**:133, 143

"Introduction to the Pardoner's Tale" (Chaucer) **17**:122

Inundación Castálida (Juana Ines de la Cruz) **5**:159

The Invader of His Country; or, The Fatal Resentment (Dennis) **11**:10, 18

The Invalidity of John Faldo's Vindication (Penn) **25**:290

Invective against Aleander (Hutten) **16**:234

Invective against the Luther-chewing Priests (Hutten) **16**:234

"The Inventory" (Burns) **3**:87; **29**:29; **40**:96

"Invisible Communication of Love through Our Eyes" (Quevedo)
See "Communicacion de amor invisible por los ojos"

The Invisible Spy (Haywood) **1**:292; **44**:137

"The Invitation" (Herbert) **24**:293

"Invitation to Brecknock" (Vaughan) **27**

An Invitation to Women to look after their Inheritance in the Heavenly Mansion (Sewall)
See *Talitha Cumi*

"An Invocation to Sleep" (Winchilsea) **3**:453

"Io crederrei, se tu fussi di sasso" (Michelangelo) **12**:362

Iphigenia (Dennis) **11**:12, 34-6

Iphigenia (Racine)
See *Iphigénie*

Iphigénie (Racine) **28**:315, 343, 346, 358, 369-74, 376, 378-81, 383-84

Lo ipocrito (Aretino) **12**:9, 19, 26, 29-30, 36
Irene: A Tragedy (Johnson) **15**:187, 195, 207, 224
Irenicum, or Ecclesiastical Polity tending to Peace (Newton) **35**:280-81
Irish Widow (Garrick) **15**:93, 101-02, 104
"Is There for Honest Poverty" (Burns) **3**:65, 72, 78
Isaac (Towneley) **34**:250-1
"Isaacs Marriage" (Vaughan) **27**:305
Isabelle Grimaldi (Scudery) **2**:308
"Isaiah LXII: 1-8" (Wheatley) **3**:434; **50**:245
"Ishui hsiu-ts'ai" (P'u Sung-ling) **49**:281
"The Island of Fairies" (P'u Sung-ling)
   See "Hsien-jen tao"
The Isle of Dogs (Nashe) **41**:302, 381-82
The Isle of Reason (Marivaux)
   See *The Isle of Reason*
The Isle of Slaves (Marivaux)
   See *The Isle of Slaves*
The Israelites in Egypt, the ten Plagues, and Passage of the Red Sea (York) **34**:332, 342-3
Istoriceskoe opisanie Rossijskoj kommercii (Chulkov) **2**:12-3
Istoriceskoe opisanie Rossijskoj kommercii (Wollstonecraft)
   See *Historical Description of Russian Commerce*
"It is Not Growing Like a Tree" (Jonson) **6**:322
"It Was a' for Our Rightfu' King" (Burns) **40**:98
Jack of Newbery
   See *The Pleasant Historie of John Winchcomb, in his younger years called Iacke of Newberie*
Jack the Fatalist (Diderot)
   See *Jacques le fataliste*
Jack Wilton (Nashe)
   See *The Unfortunate Traveller or the life of Jack Wilton*
Jacke Drum's Entertainment (Marston) **33**:193, 197, 235
Jacob and Esau (Towneley) **34**:250
Jacob and Tyboe (Holberg)
   See *Jacob von Tyboe*
Jacob (Towneley) **34**:250-1, 325
Jacob von Tyboe (Holberg) **6**:277, 283-84
"Jacobs Pillow, and Pillar" (Vaughan) **27**:378-79
Jacques le fataliste (Diderot) **26**:69-70, 90, 103, 118-19, 131-32, 135-37, 143-44, 148-49, 155, 161
La jalousie de Barbouillé (Moliere) **10**:281-83, 309, 312, 314, 344-45; **28**:25, 260
James the Fourth **41**:159-63
"Jamie come try me" (Burns) **29**:53, 83-4
Jane (Rowe)
   See *The Tragedy of Lady Jane Gray*
Jane Shore (Rowe)
   See *The Tragedy of Jane Shore*
"January and May" (Chaucer)
   See "Miller's Tale"
"Le Jardinier et son seigneur" (La Fontaine) **50**:84
"Ie ne suis point, ma guerrière Cassandre" (Ronsard) **6**:416
"Je vous envoye un bouquet" (Ronsard) **6**:417
The Jealous Bridegroom (Behn) **42**:149
"The Jealous Extremaduran" (Cervantes)
   See "El celoso extremeño"
"The Jealous Hidalgo" (Cervantes)
   See "El celoso extremeño"
The Jealous Old Husband (Cervantes) **6**:190-92
The Jealous Women (Goldoni)
   See *Le donne gelose*
The Jealousy of Le Barbouillé (Moliere)

   See *La jalousie de Barbouillé*
Jealousy, the Greatest Monster of the World (Calderon de la Barca)
   See *El mayor monstruo del mundo*
Jean de France; eller, Hans Frandsen (Holberg) **6**:258, 277
Jeannot et Colin (Voltaire) **14**:342, 344
"A Jeat Ring Sent" (Donne) **24**:183
Jemmy and Jenny Jessamy (Haywood)
   See *The History of Jemmy and Jenny Jessamy*
"Jenny said to Jocky, 'Gin ye winna tell'" (Ramsay) **29**:330, 341
Jephtha (Buchanan)
   See *Jephthes, sive votum: tragoedia; auctore Georgio Buchanano Scoto*
Jephthah (Dekker) **22**:105
Jephthes, sive votum: tragoedia; auctore Georgio Buchanano Scoto (Buchanan) **4**:120, 128-30, 133, 136-37
Jeppe of the Hill; or, The Peasant Metamorphosed (Holberg)
   See *Jeppe paa bjerget; eller, Den forvandlede bonde*
Jeppe paa bjerget; eller, Den forvandlede bonde (Holberg) **6**:258, 271-72, 276, 278, 282, 285-86
Jeronimo (Marston) **33**:208
Jerusalem Carriage (Chester) **34**:128
Jerusalem Delivered (Brooke) **1**:62
The Jerusalem Sinner Saved (Bunyan) **4**:172
Jesse Tree Play (N-Town) **34**:191
Jests to make you merry (Dekker) **22**:96
"Jesu" (Herbert) **24**:255-56, 266, 272
"Jesus Christ Gloriously Exalted" (Edwards) **7**:123
Jesus' Entry into Jerusalem (N-Town) **34**:211
Le jeu de l'amour et du hasard (Marivaux) **4**:354, 359-60, 365, 367-70, 372-73, 377-79
Le Jeune vieillard (Lesage) **28**:208
The Jew of Malta (Marlowe)
   See *The Famous Tragedy of the Rich Jew of Malta*
The Jew of Venice (Dekker) **22**:88
Jewish History (Holberg)
   See *Jødiske historie fra verdens begyndelse, fortsatt til disse tider, deelt udi svende parter...*
"The Jews" (Vaughan) **27**:375, 379
The Jews (Lessing)
   See *Die Juden*
"Jinny the Just" (Marvell) **4**:471
"Jiu Kuang" (P'u Sung-ling) **49**:313
"Job" (Young)
   See "A Paraphrase on Part of the Book of Job"
"Joconde" (La Fontaine) **50**:66, 115-116, 129, 131
Jocondo and Astolfo (Dekker)
   See *The Tale of Jocondo and Astolpho*
Jødiske historie fra verdens begyndelse, fortsatt til disse tider, deelt udi svende parter... (Holberg) **6**:282
Johann Beer: Sein Leben von ihm selbst erzählt (Beer) **5**:52
Johannes Baptista (Towneley) **34**:251, 261
"John Anderson, My Jo" (Burns) **3**:52, 62, 78, 85; **29**:40; **40**:98
"John Barleycorn" (Burns) **3**:67; **29**:64
"John Smith of His Friend Master John Taylor and His Armado" **9**:382
John the Baptist (Towneley)
   See *Johannes Baptista* (Towneley)
Johnson & Garrick (Reynolds) **15**:388, 399
"The Jolly Beggars" (Burns) **3**:49, 61, 64, 66-9,

72-3, 75-9, 82, 84, 93, 105-06; **29**:9-10, 13, 15-6, 18, 20, 25, 32, 35, 64; **40**:63, 69, 72, 76-7, 90, 98, 121
"Jonah" (Parnell) **3**:255
Jonathan Wild (Fielding)
   See *The Life of Mr. Jonathan Wild the Great*
"Jones and Walker" (Henry)
   See "British Debts Case"
"Jordan" (Herbert) **24**:283, 285
"Jordan I" (Herbert) **24**:216, 227, 232-33, 253, 273, 275, 279, 285, 287
"Jordan II" (Herbert) **24**:216, 227, 232-33, 273, 279, 285
El Jose de las mujeres (Calderon de la Barca) **23**:15, 18-20
Joseph and the Midwives (N-Town) **34**:199
Joseph Andrews (Fielding)
   See *The History of Joseph Andrews*
Joseph Musai (Grimmelshausen) **6**:248
"Joseph's Coat" (Herbert) **24**:274, 279
Joseph's Return (N-Town) **34**:183, 188, 192
Joseph's Scepter (Juana Ines de la Cruz) **5**:152
Joseph's Trouble About Mary (York) **34**:338
"Le jour que la beauté" (Ronsard) **6**:433
Journal (Knight)
   See *The Journal of Madam Knight*
Journal (Marat)
   See *Le publiciste parisien, journal politique, libre et impartial . . .*
Journal du voyage de Michel de Montaigne en Italie par la Suisse et l'Allemagne en 1580 et 1581 (Montaigne) **8**:234-37, 246
Journal in France (Gray) **40**:201
Journal in the Lakes (Gray) **40**:202
"The Journal of a Modern Lady" (Swift) **1**:482
Journal of a Tour to Corsica (Boswell) **50**:
Journal of a Tour to the Hebrides with Samuel Johnson, LL. D. (Boswell) **4**:24-6, 31, 47, 54, 60, 75-8
The Journal of a Voyage to Lisbon (Fielding) **1**:203; **46**:73, 88, 93, 118, 137
Journal of his Tour in the Netherlands (Reynolds)
   See *Journey to Flanders and Holland in the year 1781*
The Journal of John Winthrop 1630-1649 (Winthrop)
   See *A Journal of the Transactions and Occurrences in the Settlement of Massachusetts and the Other New-England Colonies*
The Journal of Madam Knight (Knight) **7**:218-30
The Journal of Major George Washington, Sent by the Hon. Robert Dinwiddie, Esq; . . . Commander in Chief of Virginia to the Commandant of the French Forces on Ohio (Washington) **25**:387
A Journal of the Plague Year (Defoe) **1**:124, 133, 135, 140, 142, 168-70; **42**:203, 219, 222
"Journal of the Retired Citizen" (Addison) **18**:28
A Journal of the Transactions and Occurrences in the Settlement of Massachusetts and the Other New-England Colonies (Winthrop) **31**:327, 342-44, 350-63, 379-89, 389-98
"Journal Sixth" (Chatterton) **3**:123
The Journal to Eliza (Sterne) **2**:393, 396, 402, 413, 422-24, 426-28, 439
The Journal to Stella (Swift) **1**:453, 463, 516-17
Une Journée des Pargues (Lesage) **28**:200
"The Journey" (Churchill) **3**:143, 150-51, 155-56, 163
Journey from this World to the Next (Fielding) **1**:211, 219, 221, 234; **46**:99
Journey of Niels Klim to the World Underground

(Holberg)
   See *Nicolai Klimii iter subterraneum...*
A Journey through Every Stage of Life, Described in a Variety of Interesting Scenes, Drawn from Real Characters (Scott) **44**:344, 362, 404
A Journey to Bath (Sheridan) **7**:369-70, 377-78
Journey to Flanders and Holland in the year 1781 (Reynolds) **15**:386, 388, 390
A Journey to London (Vanbrugh) **21**:286, 291, 293-96, 298-99, 314, 316, 319-22, 328
Journey to the Hebrides (Johnson)
   See *A Journey to the Western Islands of Scotland*
Journey to the Spring (Holberg)
   See *Kildereisen*
The Journey to the West (Wu Ch'eng-en)
   See *Hsi-yu chi*
A Journey to the Western Islands of Scotland (Johnson) **15**:198-99, 208, 246, 248, 250, 297
"The Joy of Church Fellowship rightly attended" (Taylor) **11**:368
"Joy of My Life" (Vaughan) **27**:328, 340, 383
A Joyful Meditation (Hawes) **17**:346-47, 349, 352, 362
A Joyful Meditation of the Coronation of Henry the Eyght (Hawes)
   See *A Joyful Meditation*
"Jubilate Agno" (Smart) **3**:373-74, 376, 378-80, 382, 384-86, 390, 394-400, 403
The Jubilee (Garrick) **15**:100, 122, 126
Jucundi Jucundissimi wunderliche Lebens-Beschreibung (Beer) **5**:49-51, 56
Jucundus Jucundissimus (Beer)
   See *Jucundi Jucundissimi wunderliche Lebens-Beschreibung*
Judas Macabeo (Calderon de la Barca) **23**:21
Die Juden (Lessing) **8**:79, 95, 112-13
"Judge Lu" (P'u Sung-ling)
   See "Lu p'an"
Judgement Day (Chester)
   See *Last Judgement* (Chester)
Judgement Day (N-Town) **34**:180, 187-88, 192, 236-7, 240
The Judgement Day (York) **34**:371, 374, 379
The Judgement of Martin Luther on Monastic Vows (Luther) **37**:262, 301
"Judgment" (Herbert) **24**:269
The Judgment of Paris (Congreve) **5**:72
Judicium (Towneley) **34**:250-1, 262, 264, 291, 302-3, 305, 307, 311, 313, 315, 321-2
El juez de los divorcios (Cervantes) **6**:190-92; **23**:137, 140
"Le juge arbitre, l'hospitalier el le solitaire" (La Fontaine) **50**:134
"Le jugement de Pluton" (Rousseau) **9**:345
"Jui-yun" (P'u Sung-ling) **3**:348
Julestuen (Holberg) **6**:259, 277
Julia Mandeville (Brooke)
   See *The History of Lady Julia Mandeville*
"Julia's Petticoat" (Herrick) **13**:351, 370
Julie, ou La Nouvelle Héloïse (Rousseau)
   See *La Nouvelle Héloïse*
Juliet Grenville; or, The History of the Human Heart (Brooke) **1**:62, 67, 70, 72
Ju-lin wai-shih (Wu Ching-tzu) **2**:511-38
Julius Excluded from Heaven (Erasmus)
   See *Julius secundus exlusus*
Julius exclusus (Erasmus)
   See *Julius secundus exlusus*
Julius secundus exlusus (Erasmus) **16**:132, 169, 172, 175-76, 182, 191-92

"July 8, 1656" (Bradstreet) **30**:147
"La Jument du compere Pierre" (La Fontaine) **50**:116, 120-121
"Jumpin John" (Burns) **29**:22
Der junge Gelehrte (Lessing) **8**:63, 94, 98, 113
Jungfer-Hobel (Beer)
   See *Der neu ausgefertigte Jungfer-Hobel*
"Jupiter et Europe" (Rousseau) **9**:341
Jure Divino (Defoe) **1**:162
The Just and Prudent Father (Marivaux)
   See *The Just and Prudent Father*
The Just Italian (Davenant) **13**:175
A Just Rebuke (Penn) **25**:290-91
"A Just Verdict" (P'u Sung-ling)
   See "Che yü"
Justi Lipsii Diva Sichemiensis sive Aspricollis: nova ejus beneficia & admiranda (Lipsius) **16**:253
Justi Lipsii Diva Virgo Hallensis: beneficia ejus & miracula fide atque ordine descripta (Lipsius) **16**:253
"Justice II" (Herbert) **24**:257-59, 266
The Justice of God in the Damnation of Sinners (Edwards) **7**:98, 117
Justice without Revenge (Vega)
   See *El castigo sin venganza*
Justification of Andromeda Liberata (Chapman) **22**:51, 73-4
"Juvenilia" (Thomson) **16**:418; **40**:312
Juvenilia; or, Certaine paradoxes, and problems (Donne) **10**:76, 95-6; **24**:151, 205
"Kalendae Maiae" (Buchanan) **4**:120, 122-23
"K'ao ch'eng-huang" (P'u Sung-ling) **49**:287
"K'ao-pi ssu" (P'u Sung-ling) **3**:354; **49**:280
Katharine and Petruchio (Garrick) **15**:94
Keep the Widow Waking (Dekker) **22**:107
"Kellyburn Braes" (Burns) **29**:24; **40**:89
Der keusche Joseph (Grimmelshausen) **6**:247-48
"Kew Gardens" (Chatterton) **3**:125-26, 132, 134-35
A Key Opening a Way (Penn) **25**:334
Khátimat al-hayát (Jami) **9**:65, 68
Khirad-náma-yi Iskandarí (Jami) **9**:68, 70-1
Kierlighed uden strømper (Wessel) **7**:388-92
Kildereisen (Holberg) **6**:259, 277
The Kind Keeper; or, Mr. Limberham (Dryden) **3**:222, 229-30; **21**:55
"The Kind Reception" (Ramsay) **29**:329, 352
Kinderlogik (Moritz)
   See *Versuch einer kleinen praktischen Kinderlogik*
"The King and His Three Daughters" (Walpole) **2**:500, 507
A King and No. King (Fletcher) **33**:40-52, 54, 60-61, 63, 75-6, 78-81, 97
"King Arthur; or, The British Worthy" (Dryden) **3**:222; **21**:88
King Charles's Works (Charles I) **13**:134
The King is the Best Judge (Vega)
   See *El mejor alcalde, el rey*
The King is the Best Magistrate (Vega)
   See *El mejor alcalde, el rey*
King Peter in Madrid and the Liege Lord of Illescas (Vega)
   See *El rey don Pedro en Madrid y el infazón de Illescas*
King Vamba (Vega) **23**:348
The King without a Kingdom (Vega)
   See *El rey sin reino*
"The King's Birthday in Edinburgh" (Fergusson) **29**:170, 175, 178, 189-90, 199, 205, 214, 218-19

King's Book (Henry VIII)
   See *A Necessary Doctrine and Erudition for any Christen Man, Sette Furthe by the Kynges Majestie of Englande*
Kings Daughter of France **41**:73
"The Kirk of Scotland's Garland" (Burns) **6**:89; **29**:47, 59; **40**:100
"The Kirk's Alarm" (Burns) **3**:71, 78, 96
Kjælighed uden Strömper (Wessel)
   See *Kierlighed uden strømper*
Der kleine Catechismus (Luther) **9**:151
Kleine Schriften (Lessing) **8**:82
Kleine Schriften, die deutsche Sprache betreffend (Moritz) **2**:241
Kleonnis (Lessing) **8**:109
"Knave" (Butler) **16**:52, 55
The Knight from Olmedo (Vega)
   See *El cabalero de Olmedo*
The Knight of the Burning Pestle (Fletcher) **33**:45, 60-61, 63-4, 71, 91, 98
The Knight-Commanders of Cordova (Vega)
   See *Los commendadores de Cordoba*
"Knight's" (Chaucer)
   See "Knight's Tale"
A Knight's Conjuring, done in earnest, discovered in jest (Dekker) **22**:95
"Knight's Tale" (Chaucer) **17**:49, 53, 55, 69-70, 72, 117, 123-28, 130-31, 133-36, 149, 183-84, 195, 202, 205, 214, 218, 226-27, 230, 232-35, 237, 243
"Knight's Tale" (Dryden) **3**:184-85, 187, 196, 204, 243
Know Yourself (Arbuthnot) **1**:19
The Knowledge that Maketh a Wise Man (Elyot)
   See *Of the Knowledge Which Maketh a Wise Man*
Kometographia, or a Discourse Concerning Comets (Mather) **38**:283-4, 294
Korte Verhandeling van God, de Mensch und deszelhs Welstand (Spinoza) **9**:423
"Ko-yi" (P'u Sung-ling) **49**:279
Kritische Briefe (Lessing) **8**:112
"Kuei-li" (P'u Sung-ling) **49**:282
"Kung-sun Chiu-niang" (P'u Sung-ling) **49**:282
"Kung-sun Hsia" (P'u Sung-ling) **3**:352
"Kuo shêng" (P'u Sung-ling) **49**:295-296
Der kurtzweilige Bruder Blau-Mantel (Beer) **5**:56
Die kurtzweiligen Sommer-Täge (Beer) **5**:46, 48, 50-2, 57-60
"A la Bourbon" (Lovelace) **24**:327
De la causa, principio et uno (Bruno) **27**:83, 86, 90, 96-97, 104
"A la Chabot" (Lovelace) **24**:327
"La: Pen" (Carew)
   See "An Elegie on the La: Pen: sent to my Mistresse out of France"
De la poésie dramatique (Diderot)
   See *Discours sur la poésie dramatique*
El laberinto de amor (Cervantes) **6**:180-81; **23**:101-02, 143, 147
El laberinto de Creta (Vega) **23**:393
The Labyrinth (Zwingli) **37**:378
Le labyrinthe de Versailles (Perrault) **2**:266, 280
Labyrinthus medicorum (Paracelsus) **14**:200
Ladies' Library (Steele) **18**:347, 349-50, 380
The Ladies Subscription (Cleland) **2**:51, 53
"The Ladle" (Prior) **4**:455, 461, 467, 473
"The Lady A. L., My Asylum in a Great Extremity" (Lovelace) **24**:304
"The Lady Cornelia" (Cervantes)
   See "La Señora Cornelia"
The Lady in Child-bed (Holberg) **6**:259
"The Lady Knight-Errant" (P'u Sung-ling)

See "Hsia-nü"
The Lady of May (Sidney) **19**:328-29, 374, 391, 393, 396-98, 400, 409-10, 421; **39**:228, 238, 241, 266, 277-78
"The Lady of Quality" (Smollett)
    See "The Memoirs of a Lady"
"A Lady with a Falcon in Her Fist" (Lovelace) **24**:336, 346
"The Lady's Answer To The Knight" (Butler) **16**:30, 39, 49
"The Lady's Dressing Room" (Swift) **1**:453, 461, 483-84, 502, 510
The Lady's Pacquet of Letters Broke Open (Manley)
    See *The New Atalantis*
The Lady's Tale (Davys) **1**:97, 100, 102-03; **46**:18, 20-6, 29, 32, 34-47
Lágrimas de un penitente (Quevedo) **23**:176-77
Lailá u Majnún (Jaml) **9**:66, 70-1
"La Laitiere et le pot au lait" (La Fontaine) **50**:99-102
"The Lament" (Burns) **3**:48, 52, 86; **29**:28, 32, 91
"Lament I" (Kochanowski) **10**:166-68
"Lament II" (Kochanowski) **10**:165-67
"Lament III" (Kochanowski) **10**:153, 166
"Lament IV" (Kochanowski) **10**:153, 166-68, 170
"Lament V" (Kochanowski)
    See "Threnody V"
"Lament VI" (Kochanowski) **10**:153, 157, 166, 170
"Lament VII" (Kochanowski)
    See "Tren VII"
"Lament VIII" (Kochanowski)
    See "Tren VIII"
"Lament IX" (Kochanowski)
    See "Tren IX"
"Lament X" (Kochanowski) **10**:157-58, 166, 170
"Lament XI" (Kochanowski)
    See "Threnody XI"
"Lament XII" (Kochanowski) **10**:153, 157-58, 166-67
"Lament XIII" (Kochanowski) **10**:153, 166-67
"Lament XIV" (Kochanowski) **10**:153, 159, 165, 169
"Lament XV" (Kochanowski) **10**:153, 165-66, 170
"Lament XVI" (Kochanowski)
    See "Tren XVI"
"Lament XVII" (Kochanowski)
    See "Tren XVII"
"Lament XVII" (Kochanowski)
    See "Threnody XVII"
"Lament XIX" (Kochanowski)
    See "Tren XIX"
Lament and Exhortation aginst the excessive un-Christian Power of the Bishop of Rome and the unministerial Ministers (Hutten) **16**:225, 234
"Lament for Creech" (Burns)
    See "Burlesque Lament for Creech"
"Lament for James, Earl of Glencairn" (Burns) **3**:84
"Lamentation for the Queen" (More) **10**:430
The Lamentation of Beckles **41**:73
"The Lamentations of Jeremy, for the most part according to Tremelius" (Donne) **10**:84
Laments (Kochanowski)
    See *Treny*
Lamon's Tale (Sidney) **19**:422
De lampade combinatoria Lulliana (Bruno) **27**:119
"The Lampe" (Vaughan) **27**:325, 328

Langue des calculs (Condillac) **26**:10, 12, 18, 29, 37, 42, 47, 49-50, 53-4
Lantern and Candle-light, or the Bellman's Second Night-walk (Dekker) **22**:97, 122, 130, 135
Laocoon; or, The Limits of Poetry and Painting (Lessing)
    See *Laokoon; oder, Über die Grenzen der Mahlerey und Poesie*
Laokoon; oder, Über die Grenzen der Mahlerey und Poesie (Lessing) **8**:59-62, 64, 67, 69-71, 73, 76, 80, 82-4, 86-7, 89, 92-3, 98, 100-02, 104-06, 110-11, 114
"Lapides flere" (Erasmus) **16**:198
"Lapraik II" (Burns)
    See "Second Epistle to John Lapraik"
Large Account of the Taste in Poetry (Dennis) **11**:22, 28, 30
The Large Catechism (Luther)
    See *Deudsch Catechismus*
"Lark" (Herrick) **13**:317
"The Lark now leaves his watry Nest" (Davenant) **13**:195
"Les Larmes de Saint Pierre" (Malherbe) **5**:165-66, 175, 178, 181
"Larmes du Sieur Malherbe" (Malherbe) **5**:178-79
"The Lass of Balloch myle" (Burns) **3**:71
"The Lass of Cessnock Banks" (Burns) **40**:93
"The Lass of Patie's Mill" (Ramsay) **29**:309, 320, 329
"A Lass wi' a Tocher" (Burns) **29**:22
Lasselia; or, The Self-Abandoned (Haywood) **44**:145, 147
"The Last Day" (Young)
    See "Poem on the Last Day"
The Last Goth (Vega) **23**:348
"The Last Instructions to a Painter" (Marvell) **4**:398, 443-45
Last Judgement (Chester) **34**:105, 109, 111, 113, 115, 121, 128, 161
The Last Judgement (Towneley)
    See *Judicium* (Towneley)
Last Judgement (York)
    See *The Judgement Day* (York)
"Last May a braw Wooer" (Burns) **3**:67, 71, 82, 85; **29**:22; **40**:87, 97
"The Last Speech and Dying Words of Ebenezor Elliston" (Swift) **42**:342-43
"The Last Speech of a Wretched Miser" (Ramsay) **29**:306, 361-3
The Last Speech of John Good (Brooke) **1**:62
The Last Supper (Chester) **34**:121, 127-8
The Last Supper (N-Town) **34**:176, 179, 188
The Last Supper (York) **34**:334, 369, 387
"The Last Time I Came O'er the Moor" (Ramsay) **29**:309, 315
"Late Wars" (Butler) **16**:27
The Latest from the Realm of Wit (Lessing) **8**:112
Latin-English Dictionary (Elyot)
    See *The Dictionary*
"A Latitudinarian" (Butler) **16**:52
The Latter Sign (Mather) **38**:294
"Lauda Sion Salvatorem, The Hymn for the Blessed Sacrament" (Crashaw) **24**:19-20, 70, 77
Launen und Phantasien (Moritz) **2**:243
Laurel de Apolo (Vega) **23**:337, 339
"Lauretta" (Marmontel) **2**:214
Laus philosophiae (Ficino) **12**:170, 174
Laus Stultitiae (Erasmus) **16**:126-27
Lavision-Christine (Christine de Pizan) **9**:24, 33, 36-8, 48

The Law against Lovers (Davenant) **13**:185-86, 192-93, 195, 200
Lawá'ih (Jami) **9**:61-2, 67-8
"The Lawne" (Herrick) **13**:393
"A Lawyer" (Butler) **16**:50, 55; **43**:68
"Lay" (Sidney)
    See "The Dolefull Lay of Clorinda"
Laylá and Majnún (Jami)
    See *Lailá u Majnún*
"The Layman's Lamentations upon the Civil Death of the Late Laborers in the Lord's Vineyard, by way of Dialogue between a Proud Prelate and a Poor Professour Silenced on Bartholomew Day, 1662" (Taylor) **11**:365-66
Lazarus (Chester) **34**:127
Lazarus (Towneley) **34**:252, 311, 320
"Laziness" (Wycherley) **8**:380
"The Lea-Rig" (Burns) **3**:85, **40**:96
The Learned Ladies (Moliere)
    See *Les femmes savantes*
"A Lecture upon the Shadow" (Donne) **10**:18, 52; **24**:207
Lectures on Genesis (Luther) **9**:136
Lectures on Jurisprudence (Smith) **36**:369
Lectures on Justice, Police, Revenue and Arms (Smith) **36**:366
"The Lee Ring" (Fergusson) **29**:196
"The Legacie" (Donne) **10**:26; **24**:150, 155
The Legacy (Marivaux)
    See *The Legacy*
Legend (Chaucer)
    See *Legend of Good Women*
Legend of Good Women (Chaucer) **17**:45-6, 71, 87, 97, 106, 108, 123, 201, 213-18, 229
Legende of Good Women (Chaucer)
    See *Legend of Good Women*
The Legends **8**:10, 14, 33
"The Legion Club" (Swift) **1**:513, 524
Legion's Memorial (Defoe) **1**:161
Le legs (Marivaux) **4**:354, 358, 363, 365, 368-69
"Leith Races" (Fergusson) **29**:170, 181, 189-93, 210-11, 221, 224, 227, 230, 237-39
"Lei-ts'ao" (P'u Sung-ling) **49**:291
La Lena (Ariosto) **6**:61
"Lêng shêng" (P'u Sung-ling) **49**:295-296, 298
Lenten Stuff (Nashe)
    See *Nashe's Lenten Stuffe*
"Lenvoy de Chaucer a Bukton" (Chaucer) **17**:236
The Leprosy of Constantine (Calderon de la Barca) **23**:9
De l'esprit (Helvetius) **26**:256, 259-63, 265, 267-69, 272-81, 284-86, 291, 293-94, 298-309, 312-14, 316-17, 324-26
De l'Esprit geometrique (Pascal) **35**:387
Lessing's Masonic Dialogues (Lessing) **8**:61
"Lessius" (Crashaw) **24**:4
"Let us pretend I am happy" (Juana Ines de la Cruz)
    See "Finjamos que soy feliz"
"Letanie" (Herrick)
    See "Litany"
Lethe, or Esop in the Shades (Garrick) **15**:98, 101-02, 111-14
Letter (More)
    See *Aunswere to Frithes Letter agaynst the Blessed Sacramen of the Aulter*
Letter against Werner (Copernicus) **45**:125
"Letter and Discourse to Henry Sevill Touching Helps for the Intellecual Powers" (Bacon) **18**:187; **32**:163
Letter Book (Sewall) **38**:369
"Letter Concerning Humour in Comedy"

(Congreve) **5**:92, 97, 104-05

A Letter concerning Toleration, Humbly Submitted (Locke) **7**:290; **35**:202

"A Letter From China" (Franklin) **25**:141

A Letter from Edmund Burke, Esq., One of the Representatives in Parliament for the City of Bristol, to John Farr and John Harris, Esqrs., Sheriffs of That City, on the Affairs ofAmerica (Burke) **7**:39

"Letter from Franklin to the Abbé Morellet" (Franklin) **25**:141

Letter from H. . . . G. . . .g Esq. (Haywood) **44**:130

Letter from Italy (Addison) **18**:19

A Letter from Mr. Burke, to a Member of the National Assembly: In Answer to Some Objections to His Book on French Affairs (Burke) **7**:8, 24, 47, 57; **36**:99

"A Letter from Octavia to Marcus Antonius" (Daniel) **24**:89

A Letter from the Right Honourable Edmund Burke to a Noble Lord, on the Attacks Made upon Him and His Pension, in the House of Lords (Burke) **7**:14, 23, 41-2, 47, 59, 61-2; **36**:65, 90, 99

Letter from Thrasybulus to Leucippus (Holbach) **14**:167

Letter Impugning Frith (More) **10**:436

Letter of Advice to the Earl of Rutland on His Travels (Bacon) **18**:133

The Letter of Cupid (Christine de Pizan)
   See *L'epistre au dieu d'amours*

"Letter on Ancient and Modern Tragedy" (Schlegel)
   See "Schreiben an den Herrn N. N. über die Komödie in Versen"

Letter on French Music (Rousseau) **14**:286

Letter on the Blind (Diderot)
   See *Lettre sur les aveugles*

Letter on the Deaf and Dumb (Diderot)
   See *Lettre sur les sourds et muets*

Letter on the Present Character of the French Nation (Wollstonecraft) **5**:426

"A Letter to a Brother of the Pen in Tribulation" (Behn) **30**:68

Letter to a Friend, Concerning the Ruptures of the Commonwealth (Milton) **43**:337, 397

Letter to a Lady (Gay) **49**:17

A Letter to a Member of the National Assembly (Burke)
   See *A Letter from Mr. Burke, to a Member of the National Assembly: In Answer to Some Objections to His Book on French Affairs*

Letter to Castelli (Galilei) **45**:258-59

"Letter to Chesterfield" (Johnson)
   See *The Celebrated Letter from Samuel Johnson, LL.D. to Philip Dormer Stanhope, Earl of Chesterfield*

Letter to Christina (Galilei)
   See *Lettera a Madama Cristina de Lorena*

A Letter to Dr. Holdsworth (Trotter) **8**:362

"Letter to G.N. from Wrest" (Carew) **13**:17, 32, 59-61

"A Letter to Her Husband, Absent upon Public Employment" (Bradstreet) **30**:126, 131

Letter to Lord Arlington (Penn) **25**:301

"Letter to Lord Chesterfield" (Johnson)
   See *The Celebrated Letter from Samuel Johnson, LL.D. to Philip Dormer Stanhope, Earl of Chesterfield*

Letter to M. d'Alembert on the Theatre (Rousseau)
   See *Lettre à d'Alembert sur les spectacles*

Letter to Madame Christina of Lorraine, Grand Duchess of Tuscany (Galilei)

See *Lettera a Madama Cristina de Lorena*

"Letter to Mme. La Freté (Bilked for Breakfast)" (Franklin) **25**:141

A Letter to Mr. Harding (Swift) **1**:515

"Letter to Mr. Pope" (Parnell) **3**:250-51

A Letter to Queen Elizabeth (Sidney)
   See *A Letter Written by Sir Philip Sidney...*

"Letter to Raleigh" (Spenser) **5**:364-65

A Letter to Shopkeepers (Swift) **1**:515

Letter to the Commanlty of Scotland (Knox) **37**:199, 203, 218, 225, 237, 239

"Letter to the Countess Denbigh" (Crashaw)
   See "Address to the Noblest and Best of Ladies, the Countess Denbigh Against Irresolution and Delay in Matters of Religion"

Letter to the Queen Regent (Knox) **37**:223, 237

Letter to the Reader (Erasmus)
   See *De Utilitate Colloquiorum*

Letter to the Regent (Knox) **37**:218

Letter to the Regent (Knox)
   See *Letter to the Queen Regent*

"A Letter to the Rev. Dr. White on the Conduct of a Church Organ" (Hopkinson) **25**:260

Letter to the Reverend Mr. Douglas, Occasioned by his Vindication of Milton (Johnson) **15**:306

"Letter to the Royal Academy" (Franklin) **25**:141

Letter to the Sheriffs of Bristol (Burke) **36**:88

A Letter to the Whole People of Ireland (Swift) **1**:515

Letter to William Elliot (Burke) **7**:23, 61-2

"Letter VIII" (Cavendish) **30**:202

"Letter Written by a Foreigner on His Travels" (Hopkinson) **25**:246

A Letter Written by Sir Philip Sidney... (Sidney) **39**:279, 287-87

Lettera a Madama Cristina de Lorena (Galilei) **45**:225-26, 229, 233-34, 259, 265, 268, 281-82, 298-300

Lettere (Tasso) **5**:394

Letters (Aretino) **12**:4-6, 18, 31, 34, 36-8

Letters (Dennis)
   See *Original Letters, Familiar, Moral and Critical*

Letters (Erasmus) **16**:167

Letters (Ficino) **12**:174

Letters (Frederick the Great) **14**:58

Letters (Gray)
   See *The Letters of Thomas Gray*

Letters (Howell)
   See *Epistolae Ho-Elianae: Familiar Letters Domestic and Forren*

Letters (Lyttelton)
   See *Letters from a Persian in England to His Friend at Ispahan*

Letters (Richardson)
   See *Familiar Letters on Important Occasions*

Letters (Sevigne)
   See *Lettres de Mme de Sévigné, de sa famille et de ses amis*

Letters (Sevigne)
   See *Lettres choisies de Mme la marquise de Sévignéà Mme de Grignan sa fille qui contiennent beaucoup de particularitiés de l'histoire de Louis XIV*

The Letters and the Life of Francis Bacon, Including all His Occasional Works (Bacon) **18**:188, 190

The Letters and Works of Lady Mary Wortley Montagu (Montagu)
   See *The Works of the Right Honourable Lady Mary Wortley Montague*

Letters between the Honourable Andrew Erskine

and James Boswell, Esq. (Boswell) **4**:15, 57

Letters concerning Contemporary Literature (Lessing)
   See *Literaturbrief*

Letters concerning the English Nation (Voltaire) **14**:350, 364, 380, 383, 390, 393, 403-04

Letters concerning Toleration (Locke) **7**:252, 285, 290

Letters during the Embassy (Montagu)
   See *Letters of the Right Honourable Lady Mary Wortley Montague*

Letters from a Persian in England to His Friend at Ispahan (Lyttelton) **10**:196, 198, 200, 202-07, 209-10, 212-13

Letters from Mexico (CORTES)
   See *Cartas de relación de la conquista de Méjico*

Letters from Mrs. Delany (Widow of Doctor Patrick Delany) to Mrs. Frances Hamilton (Delany) **12**:133-34

Letters from Orinda to Poliarchus (Philips) **30**:274, 284-5, 313, 318-19

Letters from the Dead to the Living (Rowe)
   See *Friendship in Death: In Twenty Letters from the Dead to the Living*

"Letters from the Devil" (Munford) **5**:192

Letters from the Mountains (Rousseau)
   See *Lettres de la montagne*

Letters from Yorick to Eliza (Sterne) **2**:424; **48**:275, 349

Letters Moral and Entertaining in Prose and Verse (Rowe) **44**:277, 291, 293-94, 300-02, 309

Letters of Advice to Queen Elizabeth (Bacon) **18**:133

Letters of King Henry VIII: A Selection, with Other Documents (Henry VIII) **10**:124

Letters of Obscure Men (Hutten)
   See *Literæ obscurorum Vivorum*

Letters of Sir Joshua Reynolds (Reynolds) **15**:400

Letters of the Right Honourable Lady Mary Wortley Montague (Montagu) **9**:273, 276, 283-84, 286

The Letters of Thomas Gray (Gray) **4**:295-96, 310-11

Letters of Two Lovers (Rousseau)
   See *La Nouvelle Héloïse*

Letters on a Regicide Peace (Burke) **36**:99-100

Letters on Sunspots (Galilei)
   See *Historia e dimonstrazioni intorno alle macchie solari*

Letters on the Genius and Writings of Shakespeare (Dennis)
   See *An Essay on the Genius of Shakespear*

Letters on the History of England (Goldsmith) **2**:71

The Letters, Speeches and Proclamations of King Charles I (Charles I) **13**:144

Letters to a Young Clergyman (Swift) **1**:471

Letters to Arnauld (Leibniz)
   See *Lettres a Arnauld*

Letters to Clarinda, by Robert Burns (Burns) **3**:50

Letters to Eugénie; or, Preservative Against Prejudice (Holbach)
   See *Lettres à Eugénie*

Letters to Horace Walpole (Walpole) **2**:452, 456, 464-66, 484, 491-94; **49**:400

Letters to Imlay (Wollstonecraft) **5**:424, 426, 443-44, 458

Letters to Mrs. Bunbury (Goldsmith) **2**:74

Letters to Poliarchus (Philips) **30**.284-5

Letters to Severall Personages (Donne) **10**:53, 83

Title Index

Letters Written by Mrs. Manley (Manley) **1**:307-09, 313; **42**:261

Letters Written during a Short Residence in Sweden, Norway, and Denmark (Wollstonecraft) **5**:418, 426, 443, 448, 450-52, 461; **50**:325-327, 361

Lettre à d'Alembert sur les spectacles (Rousseau) **14**:247, 290-93, 297, 301

Lettre à M. de Beaumont (Rousseau) **14**:247

Lettre de l'imposteur (Moliere) **10**:316

Lettre d'un Turc (Voltaire) **14**:380

Lettre sur les aveugles (Diderot) **26**:93, 112, 114, 116-17, 146-48, 161, 166

Lettre sur les sourds et muets (Diderot) **26**:94, 106, 114, 120, 122-23, 151, 166

Lettres (Sevigne)
See *Lettres de Mme de Sévigné, de sa famille et de ses amis*

Lettres a Arnauld (Leibniz) **35**:130, 137, 142

Lettres à Eugénie (Holbach) **14**:153, 168

Lettres Athéniennes, extraites du porte-feuille d'Alcibiade (Crebillon) **28**:93

Lettres choisies de Mme la marquise de Sévignéà Mme de Grignan sa fille qui contiennent beaucoup de particularités de l'histoire de Louis XIV (Sevigne) **11**:301, 315

"Les lettres contenant une aventure" (Marivaux) **4**:378-79

Lettres d'Amabed (Voltaire) **14**:345-46

Les lettres d'Annabel (Voltaire) **14**:359

Lettres de la Duchesse de*** au Duc de*** (Crebillon) **1**:86; **28**:81, 93

Lettres de la Marquise de M*** au Comte de R*** (Crebillon) **1**:86, 88; **28**:70, 72, 79, 93

Lettres de la montagne (Rousseau) **14**:247, 288; **36**:247, 249, 279, 293

Lettres de la Vénérable Mère Marie de l'Incarnation (Marie de l'Incarnation) **10**:245, 247, 249, 251

Lettres de Mme de Sévigné, de sa famille et de ses amis (Sevigne) **11**:301, 315, 336-38

Lettres galantes d'Aristénète (Lesage) **28**:199

Lettres persanes (Montesquieu) **7**:309-11, 313, 317, 319-25, 327, 339-40, 342-45, 347-49, 356-58, 360, 362-63

Lettres philosophiques (Holbach) **14**:153

Lettres philosophiques (Voltaire)
See *Letters concerning the English Nation*

Lettres provinciales (Pascal) **35**:337, 342, 356, 358-59, 361, 364, 367, 375-77, 379-81, 384-86, 390-91

"Les lettres sur les habitants de Paris" (Marivaux) **4**:378

The Leviathan or the Matter, Form and Power of a Commonwealth Ecclesiastical and Civil (Hobbes) **36**:111, 114, 116, 118-19, 122-26, 128-30, 132-33, 136-37, 139-40, 142, 148, 150-52, 156-66, 166-74, 176-81

Lexicon Tetraglotton: An English-French-Italian-Spanish Dictionary (Howell) **13**:427

De l'homme (Helvetius) **26**:257, 268-69, 272-78, 280, 282-84, 286-89, 293-95, 300-06, 308, 310, 312-17, 320, 323-26

Liao-chai chih-i (P'u Sung-ling) **3**:342-49, 353-55; **49**:270-273, 275-287, 290, 294-297

Liaozhai zhiui (P'u Sung-ling)
See *Liao-chai chih-i*

Liaozhai's Records of the Strange (P'u Sung-ling)
See *Liao-chai chih-i*

The Liar (Corneille)
See *Le menteur*

"Libel Summons" (Burns) **3**:99; **29**:4, 28

Libell über die Pest (Paracelsus) **14**:199

Libels no Proofs (Penn) **25**:287

"The Liberal Lover" (Cervantes)
See "El amante liberal"

De Libero Arbitro (Erasmus) **16**:155, 193

Liberty (Thomson) **16**:363, 369, 374, 382, 384, 386, 388, 395, 406-07, 421, 423; **29**:369, 430-31, 448-51, 453; **40**:274, 312-13, 315

"Liberty and Peace" (Wheatley) **3**:409-11, 416, 432, 435; **50**:179-80, 203, 234, 241

Liberty Asserted (Dennis) **11**:12

"'Liberty or Death' Speech" (Henry) **25**:206-12, 217, 229, 231-33, 237, 239-40, 242

Libra astronomica y philosophica (Siguenza y Gongora) **8**:339-42

Libro de las fundaciones de Santa Teresa de Jesús (Teresa de Jesus) **18**:389, 391, 393

Libro de su vida (Teresa de Jesus) **18**:389, 391, 392, 397-98, 400-03, 405-06, 409-18

Libro dell'arte della guerra (Machiavelli) **8**:128, 133, 171-73, 178; **36**:197

"El licenciado vidriera" (Cervantes) **6**:171-73, 176-77; **23**:99

"The Lie" (Raleigh) **39**:74, 94-95, 123, 125

"Lien-hsiang" (P'u Sung-ling) **49**:300

"Lien-hua kung-chu" (P'u Sung-ling) **3**:350

"Life" (Herbert) **24**:274

Life (Casanova de Seingalt)
See *Mémoires de J. Casanova de Seingalt écrits par lui-même*

Life (Equiano)
See *The Interesting Narrative of the Life of Olaudah Equiano, or Gustavus Vassa, the African*

Life (Mather) **38**:323-26

The Life, Adventures, and Pyracies of the Famous Captain Singleton (Defoe) **1**:126, 133, 139-40, 142, 147, 174-75

"The Life and Acts of, or An Elegy on Patie Birnie" (Ramsay) **29**:306, 359-60, 363

The Life and Adventures of Sir Lancelot Greaves (Smollett) **46**:192-93, 196, 234, 269-77

The Life and Adventures of the Lady Lucy, the Daughter of an Irish Lord (Aubin) **9**:3-4, 8-9, 14-15

The Life and Adventures of the Young Count Albertus, the Son of Count Lewis Augustus, by the Lady Lucy (Aubin) **9**:3-4, 8

The Life and Amorous Adventures of Lucinda, an English Lady (Aubin) **9**:4, 17

Life and Correspondence (Delany)
See *The Autobiography and Correspondence of Mary Granville (Mrs. Delany)*

The Life and Death of Mr. Badman (Bunyan) **4**:156, 159, 161, 163-64, 166-67, 169, 172, 178-79, 190, 202-03

"Life and Death of Ned Browne"
See "The Blacke Bookes Messenger, laying open the Life and Death of Ned Browne"

The Life and Death of Sir Thomas Moore (Roper)
See *The Mirrour of Vertue in Worldly Greatnes; or, The Life of syr Thomas More Knight*

The Life and Death of that Reverand Man of God, Dr. Richard Mather (Mather) **38**:277-82

The Life and Opinions of Tristram Shandy, Gentleman (Sterne) **2**:372-83, 385-96, 398-426, 428-41; **48**:246-53, 157-8, 261, 264-8, 270-1, 274-6, 278-81, 283-6, 288-93, 298, 303-4, 309-10, 312-13, 316, 321-29, 331-39, 341-2, 344-52, 355-63, 368-70, 372-75

The Life and Strange Surprising Adventures of Robinson Crusoe, of York, Mariner (Defoe) **1**:118-19, 122-26, 130-31, 134, 137-40, 142-47, 152, 155, 159, 163-74, 176-78; **42**:174-

256

Life Is a Dream (Calderon de la Barca)
See *La vida es sueño*

Life of Charles I (Lilly)
See *Life of Charles the First*

Life of Charles the First (Lilly) **27**:135

The Life of Charlotta du Pont, an English Lady (Aubin) **9**:4-6, 9, 17-18

Life of Christ (Aretino)
See *L'Humanità di Christo*

"Life of Cowley" (Johnson) **15**:215, 231-32, 241

The Life of David Hume, Esq., Written by Himself (Hume) **7**:146

Life of Destouches (Lessing) **8**:101

"Life of Dryden" (Johnson) **15**:270, 312

Life of Johan Picus, Earl of Mirandula (More) **10**:366, 429, 431-32, 435

The Life of John Buncle, Enq. (Amory) **48**:7-11, 13 16, 22 28, 30, 35 38, 40-47

Life of John Eliot (Mather) **38**:165

Life of Johnson (Boswell)
See *The Life of Samuel Johnson, LL. D.*

Life of King Charles (Lilly) **27**:135

The Life of Kinge Richarde the Thirde (More) **10**:364, 369-70, 372, 378, 395, 409, 415-16, 419-20, 429-31, 433-34, 450

The Life of Madam de Beaumount, a French Lady Who Lived in a Cave in Wales above Fourteen Years Undiscovered... (Aubin) **9**:3, 7, 9-13, 17-18

The Life of Madam de Villesache (Haywood) **44**:145, 147

Life of Marianne (Marivaux)
See *La vie de Marianne; ou, Les aventures de Mme la Comtesse de****

Life of Molière (Voltaire) **14**:339

Life of More (Roper)
See *The Mirrour of Vertue in Worldly Greatnes; or, The Life of syr Thomas More Knight*

The Life of Mr. Jonathan Wild the Great (Fielding) **1**:211, 214, 216-18, 221-22, 226-30, 233, 242-44, 255, 260-63; **46**:50, 55-6, 59, 65, 70, 78, 88-9, 92, 94, 99-100, 104-05, 113-19, 122, 124, 136-37, 173, 175-79

The Life of Mrs. Christian Davies (Defoe) **1**:146

The Life of Olaudah Equiano (Equiano)
See *The Interesting Narrative of the Life of Olaudah Equiano, or Gustavus Vassa, the African*

The Life of Pico della Mirandula (More)
See *Life of Johan Picus, Earl of Mirandula*

Life of Picus (More)
See *Life of Johan Picus, Earl of Mirandula*

Life of Plautus (Lessing) **8**:101

"The Life of Plutarch" (Parnell) **3**:237

"Life of Pope" (Johnson) **15**:270-71

Life of Richard III (More)
See *The Life of Kinge Richarde the Thirde*

Life of Robert, Second Duke of Normandy (Lodge) **41**:188, 199, 203-04

Life of Saint Catherine (Aretino)
See *Vita di santa Caterina da Siena*

Life of Saint Thomas Aquinas (Aretino) **12**:13, 36

The Life of Samuel Johnson, LL. D. (Boswell) **4**:18-19, 21-6, 30, 36-7, 39-41, 46-8, 50, 53-4, 56-60, 65-71, 75, 77-9; **50**:4-12, 17-22, 24-36, 38-40

"Life of Savage" (Johnson)
See *An Account of the Life of Mr. Richard Savage, Son of Earl Rivers*

Life of Shakespeare (Rowe)
See *Account of the Life of Shakespear*

Life of Sophocles (Lessing) **8**:101, 109-10
The Life of the Countess de Gondez (Aubin) **9**:6
The Life of the Mother Teresa of Jesus (Teresa de Jesus)
  See *Libro de su vida*
"The Life of the Soul" (More)
  See "Psychozoia: or, A Christiano-Platonicall Display of Life"
Life of the Thrice noble high and puissant Prince William Cavendish Duke of Newcastle (Cavendish) **30**:185, 192, 194-99
Life of the Virgin Mary (Aretino) **12**:13, 36
The Life of Theodore Agrippa D'Aubigné, Containing a Succinct Account of the Most Remarkable Occurences during the Civil Wars of France in the Reigns of Charles IX, Henry III, Henry IV, and in the Minority of Lewis XIII*** (Scott) **44**:409
The Life of Thomas More (Roper)
  See *The Mirrour of Vertue in Worldly Greatnes; or, The Life of syr Thomas More Knight*
"Life of Waller" (Johnson) **15**:225, 230
"Life of Watts" (Johnson) **15**:225
The Life of William Cavendish (1) (Cavendish)
  See *Life of the Thrice noble high and puissant Prince William Cavendish Duke of Newcastle*
The Life of William Lilly, Student in Astrology, wrote by himself in the 66th year of his age (Lilly) **27**:132
Life's Progress through the Passions; or, The Adventures of Natura (Haywood) **1**:291
Like Father Like Son; or, The Mistaken Brothers (Behn) **1**:31, 38; **30**:62, 68-70, 87-8
The Likeliest Means (Milton)
  See *Considerations Touching the Likeliest Means to Remove Hirelings Out of the Church*
Lilliput (Garrick) **15**:101-03, 123-24
"The Lilly in a Christal" (Herrick) **13**:350-51, 369, 380-82, 392-94
"Lines by Ladgate" (Chatterton) **3**:119
"Lines on Fergusson the Poet" (Burns) **29**:91
"Lines to Amoret" (Vaughan) **27**:333
"Lines to Sour-Faced Gila" (Juana Ines de la Cruz) **5**:146
"Lines Written in Mezeray" (Prior)
  See "Written in the Beginning of Mezeray's History of France"
De l'infinito universo et mondi (Bruno) **27**:84, 90, 97, 111
The Lining for the Patch-Work Screen: Design'd for the Farther Entertainment of the Ladies (Barker) **42**:64-5, 74, 77, 80, 83
De l'Interprétation de la Nature (Diderot)
  See *Pensées sur l'interprétation de la nature*
"Le Lion Malade et le Renard" (La Fontaine) **50**:79
"Lisetta's Reply" (Prior) **4**:461, 466
"The Litanie" (Donne) **10**:40, 56, 84, 92; **24**:165, 167
"Litany" (Herrick) **13**:317, 320, 334, 336-38
"Litany in Time of Plague" (Nashe) **41**:346, 357
Litany to the Germans (Hutten) **16**:234
"Litany to the Holy Spirit" (Herrick) **13**:314, 319, 328, 342, 357
Literæ obscurorum Vivorum (Hutten) **16**:212, 214-15, 218-25, 228, 230-33, 235-37, 245
Literaturbrief (Lessing) **8**:70, 98, 100, 103-04, 106, 109-12, 115
The Litigants (Racine)
  See *Les plaideurs*
"A Litigious Man" (Butler) **16**:50

Little Female Academy (Fielding)
  See *The Governess; or, Little Female Academy*
The Little French Lawyer (Fletcher) **33**:60
The Little Garden of Roses (Kempis)
  See *Hortulus rosarii de valle lachrymarum continens egreias & devotas sentecias*
"Little Red Riding Hood" (Perrault)
  See "Le petit chaperon rouge"
The Little Surgery (Paracelsus)
  See *Chirurgia minor quam Bertheoneam intitulaut*
"Little T. C." (Marvell)
  See "The Picture of Little T. C. in a Prospect of Flowers"
"La liturgie de Cythère" (Rousseau) **9**:345
"Liu Liang-ts'ai" (P'u Sung-ling) **49**:296
The Lives of Cleopatra and Octavia (Fielding) **1**:273; **44**:66, 68, 72, 74, 82, 100-1, 103-7
Lives of Do-wel, Do-bet, and Do-best (Langland)
  See *Piers Plowman*
The Lives of the Poets (Johnson)
  See *Prefaces, Biographical and Critical, to the Works of the English Poets*
"Living Flame of Love" (John of the Cross)
  See "Llama de amor viva"
The Living Flame of Love (John of the Cross)
  See *Llama de Amor Viva*
Le livre de la cité des dames (Christine de Pizan) **9**:23, 25, 28, 33-4, 38-9, 44-5
Le livre de la mutacion de fortune (Christine de Pizan) **9**:24, 28, 34-5, 38-9, 48
Le livre de la paix (Christine de Pizan) **9**:25, 48
Livre de la prod'hommie de l'homme (Christine de Pizan) **9**:48
Le livre des fais et bonnes meurs du sage roy Charles V (Christine de Pizan) **9**:23-4, 26, 48
Le livre des faits d'armes et de chevalerie (Christine de Pizan) **9**:23, 25, 28-9, 35,45, 47
Le livre du chemin de long estude (Christine de Pizan) **9**:24, 27, 46, 48
Le livre du corps de policie (Christine de Pizan) **9**:25, 46-8
Le livre du dit de Poissy (Christine de Pizan) **9**:28, 41, 43
Le livre du duc des vrais amans (Christine de Pizan) **9**:27, 42, 48
"Livret de Folastries" (Ronsard) **6**:417, 431
"Ella: A Tragycal Enterlude" (Chatterton) **3**:118-20, 123-24, 127, 129-30, 135
"Llama de amor viva" (John of the Cross) **18**:213, 216-17, 222, 224
Llama de Amor Viva (John of the Cross) **18**:202, 205, 221, 229-30
Loa a los años del rey (Juana Ines de la Cruz) **5**:159
Loa en las huertas donde fue a divertirse la Excelentísima Señora Condesa de Paredes, Marquesa de la Laguna (Juana Ines de la Cruz) **5**:159
La locandiera (Goldoni) **4**:262, 264, 267, 273-74
"Lo-ch'a hai-shih" (P'u Sung-ling) **49**:282
"Lochaber No More" (Ramsay) **29**:315, 319-20, 352
Logic (Condillac)
  See *Logique*
The Logick Primer (Eliot)
  See *The Logick Primer, Some Logical Notions to Initiate the Indians in Knowledge of the Rule of Reason; and to Know How to Make Use Thereof*
The Logick Primer, Some Logical Notions to Ini-

tiate the Indians in Knowledge of the Rule of Reason; and to Know How to Make Use Thereof (Eliot) **5**:132, 134-35
Logique (Condillac) **26**:10, 12, 20, 28-9, 46-7, 50, 59
Londinopolis; An Historical Discourse or Perlustration of the City of London (Howell) **13**:424
"London: A Poem, In Imitation of the Third Satire of Juvenal" (Johnson) **15**:187-90, 194, 206, 288, 291-95, 302-05
London Journal (Boswell)
  See *Boswell's London Journal*
London journal (Boswell) **50**:13-19
London's Tempe (Dekker) **22**:95, 130
The Long Road of Learning (Christine de Pizan)
  See *Le livre du chemin de long estude*
"A Long Story" (Gray) **4**:301, 312, 315-17, 333-34; **40**:239
"Longing" (Herbert) **24**:272, 274
"Longing for Heaven" (Bradstreet) **4**:85, 112
A Looking Glass for Ladies and England (Lodge) **41**:199
"A Looking-Glasse" (Carew) **13**:28
"A Loose Sarabande" (Lovelace) **24**:303, 306, 315, 320, 347, 350, 354
"Lord Daer" (Burns)
  See "Meeting with Lord Daer"
"The Loss of his Mistresses" (Herrick) **13**:337
Lost Fight of the Revenge (Raleigh) **39**:78, 121, 124-25
The Lost Lover; or, A Jealous Husband (Manley) **1**:315; **42**:261
The Lottery (Fielding) **46**:101
The Loud Secret (Calderon de la Barca) **23**:60, 64
"Le Loup et l'Agneau" (La Fontaine) **50**:80, 94
"Le Loup et le chien" (Warde) **50**:84-85, 96, 133
"Love" (Herbert) **24**:234, 268, 272, 274
"Love I" (Herbert) **24**:234, 268, 272, 274
"Love II" (Herbert) **24**:235, 238, 272, 282
"Love III" (Herbert) **24**:230, 234, 252, 259, 262-64, 266, 269, 273, 275, 280, 282
Love and a Bottle (Farquhar) **21**:128, 135-36, 139-40, 145-46, 148, 150-52, 154, 161-63, 170, 176
Love and Business (Farquhar) **21**:130, 133, 142
Love and Honor (Davenant) **13**:175-77, 181, 192, 196, 215
"Love and Liberty" (Burns) **29**:25, 64-6, 69; **40**:85, 90
"Love Arm'd" (Behn) **1**:31, 38; **30**:62, 68-70, 87
Love at a Loss; or, Most Votes Carry It (Trotter) **8**:355, 357, 361, 368-69, 372-74
"Love Banish'd Heav'n, in Earth Was Held in Scorne"
  See "Sonnet 23"
"Love Conquered" (Lovelace) **24**:350
"Love Disarm'd" (Prior) **4**:459
Love Elegies (Donne)
  See *Elegies*
Love for Love (Congreve) **5**:66, 68, 70-1, 74, 76, 78-9, 81, 83, 84, 86-90, 92, 94, 96-101, 105-06, 109, 111; **21**:4, 9-10, 15, 17, 22-3, 25-7, 29-32, 40-1, 43
Love in a Bottle (Farquhar)
  See *Love and a Bottle*
"Love, in a Humor, Play'd the Prodigall"
  See "Sonnet 7"
Love in a Wood; or, St. James's Park (Wycherley) **8**:384, 388, 390-92, 395, 397, 402, 407, 410, 432-34; **21**:351-52, 354, 356, 359-60, 370-73, 376-78, 380-81, 391, 396-97

Love in Excess; or, The Fatal Enquiry (Haywood) 1:284-85, 290, 292, 295-300; 44:128, 130-1, 138-42, 168-9

"Love in Fantastic Triumph Sat" (Behn)
See "Love Arm'd"

Love in Several Masques (Fielding) 1:250; 46:94, 101, 160

Love Intrigues; or, the History of the Amours of Bosvil and Galesia (Barker) 42:59, 61, 63-4, 70, 72, 77-8, 80-4, 88

Love Is the Best Doctor (Moliere)
See *l'Amour Médecin*

"Love Joy" (Herbert) 24:255, 262, 266

Love Letters between a Nobleman and His Sister (Behn) 1:34, 43, 48; 30:87-8, 99-102, 105-6, 110; 42:152, 153

Love Letters on All Occasions (Haywood) 44:150

Love Letters to a Gentleman (Behn) 1:38

Love Lyrics. Six Songs by Francis Hopkinson (Hopkinson) 25:250

"Love Made in the First Age" (Lovelace) 24:316, 347

"The Love of Fame" (Young)
See "The Universal Passion; or, The Love of Fame"

Love, the Greater Labyrinth (Juana Ines de la Cruz)
See *Amor es más laberinto*

Love the Greatest Enchanter (Calderon de la Barca)
See *El mayor encanto, amor*

Love Triumphant (Dryden) 3:230

"Love Unknown" (Herbert) 24:252, 256, 263-64, 266, 272-73, 278

"Love-Begotten Daughter" (Burns)
See "A Poet's Welcome to His Love-Begotten Daughter"

Love-Letters from King Henry VIII. to Anne Boleyn (Henry VIII) 10:119

The Lover (Steele) 18:354

"Lover and the Maiden" (Erasmus) 16:140

"A Lover's Anger" (Prior) 4:460

"Lovers infinitenesse" (Donne) 10:36, 82; 24:154, 183

Lovers' Reunion (Marivaux)
See *Lovers' Reunion*

Lovers' Spite (Moliere)
See *Le dépit amoureux*

The Lovers Watch (Behn)
See *La Montre; or, The Lover's Watch*

Love's Adventures (4) (Cavendish) 30:189, 205, 227, 229

"Loves Alchymie" (Donne) 10:82; 24:150, 152, 155

"Love's Cure" (Ramsay) 29:329

Love's Cure; or, The Martial Maid (Fletcher) 33:41

"Loves Deitie" (Donne) 10:26, 81; 24:152, 155

"Love's Diet" (Donne) 24:152

"Love's Exchange" (Donne) 24:151

"Loves Growth" (Donne) 10:18, 57; 24:150, 153, 181-82

"Love's Horoscope" (Crashaw) 24:10, 14, 45

Love's Metamorphosis (Lyly) 41:273

"Loves Usury" (Donne) 10:52; 24:151, 153

Love's Victorie (Wroth) 30:345, 362-68, 375-82

"Love-Sick" (Vaughan) 27:338-39

The Loyal Subject (Fletcher) 33:60-61

"Lu p'an" (P'u Sung-ling) 3:350

"Lucasta at the Bath" (Lovelace) 24:306, 347

Lucasta: Epodes, Odes, Sonnets, Songs, etc. (Lovelace) 24:303, 313-14, 336-37, 340-42, 350-51, 353

"Lucasta Laughing" (Lovelace) 24:347

"Lucasta Paying Her Obsequies" (Lovelace) 24:302

Lucasta: Posthume Poems of Richard Lovelace, Esq. (Lovelace) 24:303, 305, 328, 336-37, 340, 346-49, 352-54

"Lucasta, Taking the Waters at Tunbridge" (Lovelace) 24:305, 316, 347

"Lucasta Weeping" (Lovelace) 24:303

"Lucasta's Fan, with a Looking-Glass in It" (Lovelace) 24:353

"Lucasta's Muff" (Lovelace) 24:303

"Lucia" (Young) 3:472

"Lucius" (Prior) 4:455

The Lucky Chance; or, An Alderman's Bargain (Behn) 1:27-9, 34, 37, 40-1, 47-8; 30:66, 80-1, 85-7, 95; 42:151-52

The Lucky Mistake (Behn) 1:32, 46, 51-2; 42:109

"Lucky Spence's Last Advice" (Ramsay) 29:305, 320, 327, 361-2

"Luke 2, "'Quaerit Jesum suum Maria.'" (Crashaw) 24:74-5, 77-8

Luminalia (Davenant) 13:189

Luminis Naturalis (Bacon) 18:187

"Lung-fei hsiang kung" (P'u Sung-ling) 3:350

Lung-hu feng-yün hui (Lo Kuan-chung) 12:282

"Le lutrin" (Boileau-Despreaux) 3:16-17, 19, 21-2, 24, 29, 37-43

"The Luxury of Vain Imagination" (Johnson)
See *The Rambler, 89*

"Lycidas" (Milton) 9:177, 197, 199, 203-11, 213, 229-30, 238-41, 243; 43:360, 396

Lycidus; or, The Lover in Fashion (Behn) 1:41

The Lyfe of Sir Thomas Moore, Knighte (Roper)
See *The Mirrour of Vertue in Worldly Greatnes; or, The Life of syr Thomas More Knight*

The Lying Lover (Steele) 18:314-15, 330, 333, 338-40, 346, 348, 353-54, 359, 364-66, 371

The Lying Valet (Garrick) 15:98, 100-01, 113, 121, 124

The Lying-in Room (Holberg)
See *Barselstuen*

Det lykkelige skibbrud (Holberg) 6:263, 278

Lykken bedre end Forstanden (Wessel) 7:390

"La Lyre" (Ronsard) 6:427-28

"A Lyrick to Mirth" (Herrick) 13:365

M. Fabre, 'envoyé extraordinaire de Louis XIV en Perse' (Lesage) 28:200

"Ma Chieh-fu" (P'u Sung-ling) 49:296-297

Macbeth (Davenant) 13:185-87, 212 214-16

Macbeth (Johnson)
See *Miscellaneous Observations on the Tragedy of Macbeth*

MacFlecknoe; or, A Satire upon the Trew-Blew-Protestant Poet, T. S. (Dryden) 3:189, 192, 199, 205, 212, 222, 231, 242; 21:51-2, 66, 83, 90-2, 94, 111, 113

"Macpherson's Farewell" (Burns) 3:60

Mactacio Abel (Towneley) 34:252, 254, 258-9, 267, 278, 282, 288, 298-99, 302, 310-12, 321, 324-5

"The Mad Maid's Song" (Herrick) 13:319-20, 324, 326, 332, 336-37

A Mad World My Masters (Middleton) 33:263, 276-77, 290-91, 298

Madagascar; With Other Poems (Davenant) 13:204-05

Madame de la Carlière (Diderot)
See *Mme. de La Carlière*

The Madmen of Valencia (Vega) 23:385, 388-90

Madon (Fletcher) 33:91

La madre amorosa (Goldoni) 4:260

Magazin zur Erfahrungsseelenkunde (Moritz)

2:236

"Maggie Johnstone" (Ramsay) 29:320

Magi (Chester) 34:121-22, 124-5, 153

The Magi (N-Town) 34:172-3, 184, 188, 192, 199, 201, 205-6

Magi (York) 34:386

De magia (Bruno) 27:94

The Magic Bird's Nest (Grimmelshausen)
See *Das wunderbarliche Vogelnest (I and II)*

El mágico prodigioso (Calderon de la Barca) 23:8, 12, 15, 18, 20, 22, 43, 64

Magnalia Christi Americana: or, The Ecclesiatical History of New England (Mather) 38:158, 161, 164-65, 170, 173-4, 178, 181-97, 205-36

Magnalia naturae praecipue quoad usus humanos (Bacon) 18:152

The Magnetic Lady (Jonson) 6:306, 311, 314, 327, 339; 33:117, 140, 159, 162

The Magnificent Entertainment (Dekker) 22:130

The Magnificent Lovers (Moliere)
See *Les amants magnifiques*

Magnus Herodes (Towneley) 34:253, 258-60, 267, 288, 301, 311, 321

"Magy Dickson" (Ramsay) 29:360, 363

Mahomet (Defoe) 1:162

Mahomet (Voltaire) 14:328, 397

Mahomet and Irene (Johnson)
See *Irene: A Tragedy*

"Maidenhead" (Cowley) 43:147

The Maid's Tragedy (Fletcher) 33:40-52, 58-60, 71-5, 80-81, 84-7

The Maidservant (Corneille)
See *La Suivante*

"Mailie's Dying Words and Elegy" (Burns)
See "The Death and Dying Words of Poor Mailie"

"Le maître chat; ou, Le chat botté" (Perrault) 2:254, 257-58, 260, 266-71, 280-81, 284

"La Mal Marie" (La Fontaine) 50:100-101, 103

Le malade imaginaire (Moliere) 10:270, 272, 274-75, 282-83, 285-86, 290-91, 299, 304, 306, 313, 318, 327-29, 336, 339; 28:228-29, 243, 246-47, 249, 252-53, 256, 258-59, 261, 265-67

The Malcontent (Marston) 33:187, 189, 191, 193-94, 198-200, 202-05, 208-09, 211, 213, 215, 227, 233-37, 239, 242-43, 247

The Male Coquette (Garrick) 15:98, 101-03

Malpiglio (Tasso) 5:407

Mamillia: A Mirror or Looking-Glass for the Ladies of England 41:141, 148, 156-57, 171-72, 176, 178

Mamusse wunneetupanatamwe Up-Biblum God Naneeswe Nukkone Testament KahWonk Wusku Testament (Eliot) 5:124, 126-28, 130-32, 134

"Man" (Herbert) 24:274

"Man" (Vaughan) 27:306, 340, 342, 391

Man (Marat)
See *A Philosophical Essay on Man, Being an Attempt to Investigate the Principles and Laws of the Reciprocal Influence of the Soul on the Body*

"Man in Darkness" (Vaughan) 27:311-12, 314

"Man in Glory" (Vaughan) 27:312

The Man in the Moone 8:14, 17, 27, 32, 34, 36-7

"Man Naturally God's Enemies" (Edwards) 7:98

The Man of Discretion (Gracian y Morales)
See *El Discreto*

"Man of Lawe's Tale" (Chaucer)
See "Man of Law's Tale"

"Man of Law's Prologue" (Chaucer) 17:214

"Man of Law's Tale" (Chaucer) **17**:60, 63, 83, 119, 176, 196, 205, 232, 237

The Man of Real Sensibility (Scott)
See *The History of Sir George Ellison*

"Man Was Made to Mourn" (Burns) **3**:48, 52, 67, 74, 87; **29**:28, 32-3, 64, 79

The Man with Forty Ecus (Voltaire)
See *L'homme aux quarante écus*

"Manciple's Tale" (Chaucer) ·**17**:173

Mandragola (Machiavelli)
See *Commedia di Callimaco: E di Lucretia*

The Mandrake (Grimmelshausen)
See *Das Galgen-Männlin*

Manductio ad Stoicam philosophiam (Lipsius)
See *Manductionis ad philosophiam stoicam libri tres*

Manductionis ad philosophiam stoicam libri tres (Lipsius) **16**:257-58

Manifest (Siguenza y Gongora)
See *Manifesto philosophico contra los cometas despojados del imperio que tenian sobre los timidos*

Manifesto philosophico contra los cometas despojados del imperio que tenian sobre los timidos (Siguenza y Gongora) **8**:341-42

"Manliness" (Donne) **10**:95

"The Man-Mountain's Answer to the Lilliputian Verses" (Gay) **49**:4, 7

The Man-Mountain's Answer to the Lilliputian Verses (Gay) **49**:6, 9

"Manne, Womanne, Syr Rogerre" (Collins) **4**:214, 229, 231, 237, 239-43

"The Manner of Writing History" (Racine) **28**:294

The Manners (Collins) **40**:132, 159, 163, 174

"A Man's a Man for a' That" (Burns) **1**:518; **29**:93; **40**:73, 98

Man's Disobedience and Fall (York) **34**:343, 359

"Mans Fall and Recovery" (Vaughan) **27**:325, 327

"Man's Injustice toward Providence" (Winchilsea) **3**:451

The Man's the Master (Davenant) **13**:186-87, 189

Manual of Metaphysics (More) **9**:297

Manual of the Christian Knight (Erasmus)
See *Enchiridion militis christiani*

The Manual Oracle and Art of Prudence (Gracian y Morales)
See *Oráculo manual y arte de prudencia*

Map of the Bay and the Rivers, with an Annexed Relation of the Countries and Nations That Inhabit Them
See *A Map of Virginia. With a Description of the Countrey, the Commodities, People, Government, and Religion*

A Map of Virginia. With a Description of the Countrey, the Commodities, People, Government, and Religion **9**:352, 355, 357, 359, 374, 380-81, 383

"Marc Antonie" (Sidney)
See "The Tragedie of Antonie"

Marco Bruto (Quevedo)
See *La vida de Marco Bruto*

Marcus heroicum (Hutten) **16**:238, 241

Marescalco (Aretino) **12**:19, 26-7, 29-30, 35-7

Marfisa (Aretino) **12**:35

A Margarite of America (Lodge) **41**:188, 199, 203-04, 211-15

"Le mari sylphide" (Marmontel) **2**:212; **30**:

Maria (Wollstonecraft)
See *The Wrongs of Woman; or, Maria*

"Maria Wentworth" (Carew) **13**:48

Le mariage forcé (Moliere) **10**:283, 287, 311; **28**:229, 255

Les Mariages de Canada (Lesage) **28**:210-11

Mariam (Cary)
See *The Tragedie of Mariam, Faire Queene of Jewry*

Mariamne (Voltaire) **14**:397

Marian: A Comic Opera, in Two Acts (Brooke) **6**:107-09; **48**:119

El marido más firme (Vega) **23**:393

Marina regina di Scozia (Campanella) **32**:211

Marmor Norfolciense (Johnson) **15**:206

Marriage as Retribution (P'u Sung-ling)
See *Hsing-shih yin-yuan chuan*

Marriage at Cana (York) **34**:369

A Marriage Booklet for Simple Pastors (Luther) **9**:151

The Marriage Contract (Brooke) **1**:63

"Marriage that was no Marriage" (Erasmus) **16**:141, 193

Marriage-à-la-Mode (Dryden) **3**:208, 210, 214, 222, 230-33

"The Marrow Ballad" (Ramsay) **29**:362-3

Martin Mar-All (Dryden)
See *Sir Martin Mar-All; or, The Feign'd Innocence*

El mártir de Sacramento (Juana Ines de la Cruz) **5**:158

"Martyrdome" (Vaughan) **27**:370

Mary: A Fiction (Wollstonecraft) **5**:426-28, 442-43, 453, 460-61; **50**:271-274, 279-280, 293, 295, 298, 320, 322-324

"Mary Blaize" (Goldsmith) **2**:74

"Mary in Heaven" (Burns)
See "To Mary in Heaven"

Mary in the Temple (N-Town) **34**:174, 181-2, 184, 188-9, 192, 201-2

"Mary Morison" (Burns)
See "Ye Are Na Mary Morison"

"Mary Scot" (Ramsay) **29**:329

Mascarade (Holberg) **6**:259, 269, 277

Masculine Birth of Time (Bacon)
See *Temporis partus masculus*

Mask of Comus (Milton)
See *Comus: A Maske*

Mask of Semele (Congreve) **5**:72; **21**:44

Maskarade (Holberg)
See *Mascarade*

"Le masque de Laverne" (Rousseau) **9**:345

Masque of Beauty (Jonson) **6**:338; **33**:128

Masque of Blacknesse (Jonson) **6**:321, 337-38

The Masque of Queens (Jonson) **6**:315, 337, 339; **33**:172

The Masquerade (Fielding) **46**:94, 105

The Masqueraders (Haywood) **44**:152

Masques (Jonson) **6**:323

The Massacre at Paris: with the Death of the Duke of Guise (Marlowe) **22**:336, 339, 348, 361, 364, 368; **47**:252, 256, 275, 343, 358

Massacre of the Innocents (Towneley) **34**:288

Massacre of the Innocents (York) **34**:332

Le massere (Goldoni) **4**:264-66

The Master Critic (Gracian y Morales)
See *El Criticón*

"Master Glass" (Cervantes)
See "El licenciado vidriera"

"Master Herrick's Farewell unto Poetry" (Herrick)
See "Farewell to Poetry"

"The Match" (Marvell) **4**:403, 408

"The Match" (Vaughan) **27**:351

Match Me in London (Dekker) **22**·88, 95, 107-9, 111, 126-7, 132

The Mathemathical Principles of Natural Philoso-

phy (Newton) **35**:279-80, 285, 287, 289-90, 292-93, 296-300, 303-06, 308, 313, 317-19, 323-24, 330-32

Mathematical Bellerophon against the Astrological Chimera of Don Martin de la Torre, etc. (Siguenza y Gongora) **8**:341

"A Mathematician" (Butler) **16**:50

"Matilda the Faire" **8**:30, 33

The Matrimonial Trouble (2) (Cavendish) **30**:227

De matrimonio (Agrippa von Nettesheim) **27**:25, 42

La Matrone d'Ephèse (Lesage) **28**:208

"Mattens" (Herbert) **24**:272, 274

"A Mauchline Wedding" (Burns) **6**:91; **29**:3-4, 13, 16, 63

Maundy II (N-Town) **34**:211

Maundy III (N-Town) **34**:208, 211

Maximes (Gracian y Morales) **15**:142

The Maxims of Fr. Guicciardini (Guicciardini) **49**:196, 259-60, 264

May Day (Chapman) **22**:6, 12, 15, 64

May Day (Garrick) **15**:121

El mayor encanto, amor (Calderon de la Barca) **23**:9, 64

El mayor monstruo del mundo (Calderon de la Barca) **23**:13, 64-5

The Mayor of Queenborough; or, Hengist of Kent (Middleton) **33**:264

The Mayor of Zalamea (Calderon de la Barca)
See *El alcade de Zalamea*

La mayor virtud de un rey (Vega) **23**:392-93

"The Maypole Is Up" (Herrick) **13**:331, 364

"Me Thinks I See Some Crooked Mimicke Jeere"
See "Sonnet 31"

"Mechanical Operation of the Spirit" (Swift) **42**:354

The Medall. A Satire Against Sedition (Dryden) **3**:187, 199, 222, 234-35, 240; **21**:51, 57, 59, 65, 68, 86, 90

Medea (Buchanan)
See *Medea Euripidis poetae tragici Georgio Buchanano Scoto interprete*

Medea (Corneille)
See *Médée*

Medea Euripidis poetae tragici Georgio Buchanano Scoto interprete (Buchanan) **4**:134-35

Le médecin malgré lui (Moliere) **10**:278, 283, 291, 312, 327; **28**:236, 255-56, 266, 269

Le médecin volant (Moliere) **10**:281, 283, 309, 314, 327; **28**:258

Médée (Corneille) **28**:20, 23, 31, 38, 43, 47

Medicine for a Cursed Wife (Dekker) **22**:110

"A Medicine-Taker" (Butler) **16**:50

El médico de su honra (Calderon de la Barca) **23**:13-14, 39, 41, 54-5, 64, 70, 72, 74, 79

Medico olandese (Goldoni) **4**:259

Meditata (Copernicus)
See *Monetae cudendae ratio*

"Meditation 7" (Taylor) **11**:360

"Meditation 19" (Taylor) **11**:360

"Meditation 30" (Taylor) **11**:360

"Meditation 77" (Taylor) **11**:359

"A Meditation at the setting of the Sun, or the souls Elevation to the true light" (Vaughan) **27**:323

"Meditation before the receiving of the holy Communion" (Vaughan) **27**:304

"Meditation Eight" (Taylor) **11**:351-52

"A Meditation for His Mistresse" (Herrick) **13**:364

"A Meditation on a Quart Mug" (Franklin) **25**:111

"Meditation One" (Taylor) **11**:349

"Meditation Six" (Taylor) **11**:356

"Meditation upon a Broomstick" (Swift) **42**:342-46

Meditationes sobre el Cantar (Teresa de Jesus) **18**:400-05

Meditationis Sacrae (Bacon) **18**:149; **32**:187

Meditations (Taylor) **11**:344, 347-48, 355, 359, 365, 367-68, 373, 376-77, 382-84, 396

"Meditations Divine and Moral" (Bradstreet) **4**:96-7, 99-100, 114; **30**:114

Meditations of the Glory of the Heavenly World (Mather) **38**:309

Meditations on Death (Mather) **38**:309

Meditations on First Philosophy (Descartes) **35**:74-6, 79, 82, 84, 90, 92, 104, 109, 113-14, 117-18

Meditations on Knowledge Truth and Ideas (Leibniz) **35**:176

"Meditations upon an Egg" (Bunyan) **4**:182

The Meeting of the Company; or, Baye's Art of Acting (Garrick) **15**:100, 102, 122

"Meeting with Lord Daer" (Burns) **3**:71, 86; **29**:29

"Mei-nü" (P'u Sung-ling) **49**:280

El mejor alcalde, el rey (Vega) **23**:372-73, 401-02

"Mejor vida es morir que vivir muetro" (Quevedo) **23**:191

Melampe (Holberg) **6**:259, 277

Melampus (Holberg)
    See *Melampe*

Mélange amusant de saillies d'espirit et de traits historiques des plus frappants (Lesage) **28**:200

Mélanges (Voltaire) **14**:337, 367

"Melibee" (Chaucer)
    See "Tale of Melibee"

"Melibeus" (Chaucer) **17**:169

Mélicerte (Moliere) **10**:275, 283

Mélite; or, The False Letters (Corneille)
    See *Mélite, oules fausses lettres*

Mélite, oules fausses lettres (Corneille) **28**:20, 42-4, 48, 55

Memnon; ou, La sagesse humaine (Voltaire) **14**:346, 398

"Memoir" (Boswell) **4**:61

Mémoire d'un honnête homme (Prevost) **1**:343-44

Mémoire sur les jugements de Dieu (Duclos) **1**:186

Memoires (Voltaire) **14**:364

Mémoires de J. Casanova de Seingalt écrits par lui-même (Casanova de Seingalt) **13**:76, 78, 80-7, 89-93, 95-6, 98, 103-11, 113-18, 121, 123, 126

Mémoires de ma vie (Perrault) **2**:277, 283

Les Mémoires de M. de Montcal (Prevost) **1**:335, 337

Mémoires de M. Goldoni, pour servir à l'histoire de sa vie, et à celle de son théâtre(Goldoni) **4**:255, 262-64, 268, 275

Mémoires d'un honnête homme (Prevost)
    See *Mémoire d'un honnête homme*

Mémoires d'un père pour servir à l'instruction de ses enfans (Marmontel) **2**:208-12, 221, 223

Mémoires et aventures d'un homme de qualité, qui s'est retiré du monde (Prevost) **1**:327, 329, 333-37, 343-44, 347, 351-52, 356

Memoires of the Last Ten Years of the Reign of George the Second (Walpole) **2**:453-54, 456, 481-82, 485-88, 498

Memoires of the Navy (Pepys)

    See *Memoires relating to the State of the Royal Navy*

Memoires of the Royal Navy, 1679-88 (Pepys)
    See *Memoires relating to the State of the Royal Navy*

Mémoires pour Catherine II (Diderot) **26**:158

Mémoires pour servir à l'histoire de la Maison de Brandebourg (Frederick the Great) **14**:58, 69

Mémoires pour servir de suite aux "Considérations sur les moeurs de ce siècle" (Duclos) **1**:187, 191-92, 198

Memoires relating to the State of the Royal Navy (Pepys) **11**:208, 230, 238, 240

Mémoires secrets sur le règne de Louis XIV, la règence, et le règne de Louis XV (Duclos) **1**:186, 189

Memoirs (Babur)
    See *The Babur-nama*

Memoirs (Fanshawe)
    See *Memoirs of Lady Fanshawe*

Memoirs (Holberg)
    See *Memoirs of Lewis Holberg*

Memoirs and Correspondence of George, Lord Lyttelton, 1734 to 1773 (Lyttelton) **10**:198

Memoirs: Containing the Lives of Several Ladies of Great Britain (Amory) **48**:7, 11, 13, 15-16, 23, 25, 27-29, 31-32, 34-37, 43

Memoirs from Europe Towards the Close of the Eighth Century (Manley)
    See *The New Atalantis*

Memoirs of a Cavalier (Defoe) **1**:124, 133, 139-40, 146, 175-76; **42**:219, 222

Memoirs of a Certain Island Adjacent to the Kingdom of Utopia (Haywood) **1**:283, 286, 290; **44**:129, 131

Memoirs of a Coxcomb (Cleland) **2**:33, 42, 50-1, 53-7

"The Memoirs of a Lady" (Smollett) **46**:219, 257

Memoirs of a Man of Honour (Haywood) **44**:172

The Memoirs of a Protestant (Goldsmith) **2**:101-02

Memoirs of a Woman of Pleasure (Cleland) **2**:32-51, 53-60; **48**:125, 127-30, 132-37, 139-43, 145-47, 150-51, 153, 156-69, 172, 174, 178

Memoirs of Ann Lady Fanshawe (Fanshawe)
    See *Memoirs of Lady Fanshawe*

Memoirs of Lady Fanshawe (Fanshawe) **11**:100-110

"Memoirs of Learned Ladies" (Amory) **48**:2

Memoirs of Lewis Holberg (Holberg) **6**:280

Memoirs of Marmontel (Marmontel)
    See *Mémoires d'un père pour servir à l'instruction de ses enfans*

The Memoirs of Martinus Scriblerus (Arbuthnot)
    See *The Memoirs of the Extraordinary Life, Works, and Discoveries of Martinus Scriblerus*

Memoirs of Miss Sidney Bidulph, Extracted from Her Own Journal (Sheridan) **7**:369, 371-76, 378-79, 381-85

"Memoirs of M. de Voltaire" (Goldsmith) **2**:101-02

Memoirs of Pascal Paoli (Boswell)
    See *An Account of Corsica, The Journal of a Tour to that Island; and the Memoirs of Pascal Paoli*

"Memoirs of Scriblerus" (Swift) **42**:351-52

The Memoirs of the Extraordinary Life, Works, and Discoveries of Martinus Scriblerus (Arbuthnot) **1**:12-13, 15, 17-20, 23-4

Memoirs of the Reign of George the Third (Walpole) **2**:456, 481-82, 485-88, 498

"Memoirs of the Shilling" (Addison) **18**:27

The Memorable Maske of the two Honorable Houses or Inns of Court; the Middle Temple of Lyncolns Inne (Chapman) **22**:13

Memorable Providences Relating to Witchcraft and Possesions (Mather) **38**:221, 236, 243-4

"Memoria immortal de don Pedro Girón, duque do Osuna, muerto enlas prosión" (Quevedo) **23**:155

Memorial (Pascal) **35**:358, 365, 389

"The Men of War" (Vaughan) **27**:377, 379

Menaphon **41**:145, 156, 159-60, 163, 165, 168, 171-73, 176-77

"Meng-lang" (P'u Sung-ling) **49**:279

Menippus Inanitatum Nostratuum Speculum (Andreae) **32**:67, 93

Le menteur (Corneille) **28**:4, 6, 42

Menudictio ad Minsterium (Mather) **38**:165, 181, 235

La méprise (Marivaux) **4**:368

"Merchant" (Young) **3**:467

The Merchant of Women (Calderon de la Barca) **23**:64

"The Merchant to Secure His Treasure" (Prior) **4**:466

"Merchant's Prologue" (Chaucer) **17**:167-68

"Merchant's Tale" (Chaucer) **17**:137, 142, 147-54, 167-68, 170-71, 189, 191, 197-98, 201-02, 209, 217, 236-37, 239, 243

Mercurio volante con la noticia de la recuperacion de las provincias del Nuevo México conseguida por D. Diego de Vargas, Zapato, y Luxan Ponze de Leon (Siguenza y Gongora) **8**:344

"Mercury and Cupid" (Prior) **4**:461

Mercury Vindicated from the Alchemists at Court (Jonson) **6**:328; **33**:177

Mercy and Justice (Castro) **19**:2

La mère confidente (Marivaux) **4**:368-69

"A meri iest how a sergeant would learne to playe the frere" (More) **10**:430

Merlinus Anglicus (Lilly) **27**:133-34, 140-42

Mérope (Voltaire) **14**:328, 332, 338, 358, 397, 415-16, 418-19

"The Merry Beggars" (Burns) **29**:9

"Merry Hae I Been Teething a Heckle" (Burns) **3**:67

The Merry Masqueraders; or, The Humorous Cuckold (Aubin) **9**:6

The Merry Muses of Caledonia (Burns) **6**:67; **29**:58, 82

"The Merry Tales of Lynn" (Boswell) **4**:61

The Merry Wanderer (Davys) **1**:99; **46**:20, 24-6, 28, 33-6

"The Message" (Donne) **24**:150

"The Messiah" (Pope) **3**:270, 292

Mester Gert Westphaler; eller, Den meget talende barbeer (Holberg) **6**:258-59, 273, 277

The Metamorphosed Gipsies (Jonson)
    See *The Gypsies Metamorphosed*

Metamorphosis (Holberg) **6**:266

The Metamorphosis of Pygmalion's Image (Marston) **33**:195, 201, 203, 207, 213, 222, 234

Metaphysics (Campanella) **32**:234

Le métempsychosiste (Montesquieu) **7**:348

Meteorology (Descartes) **35**:79, 85-8, 91-3, 100, 102, 110

The Method of Preaching (Erasmus)
    See *Ecclesiastes*

Method of Study (Erasmus) **16**:123

Metrical History of Christianity (Taylor) **11**:373-

74, 393

"The Metropolis of Great Britain" (Dryden) **3**:239

"Le Meunier, son fils, et l'ane" (La Fontaine) **50**:84

"Mi Li: A Chinese Fairy Tale" (Walpole) **2**:500

Michaelmas Term (Middleton) **33**:262, 271, 274, 277-78, 295, 310, 313

Micro-cynicon. Sixe Snarling Satyres (Middleton) **33**:287-88, 297

Micromégas (Voltaire) **14**:341, 346, 359-60, 366

"Midas" (Rousseau) **9**:345

Midas (Lyly) **41**:222, 272

Middle of the Necklace (Jami)
　　See *Wásitat al-Iqd*

"Midnight" (Vaughan) **27**:330, 383

Midsummer Night (Vega)
　　See *La noche de San Juan*

Migajas sentenciosas (Quevedo) **23**:177

"A Mighty Fortress Is Our God" (Luther)
　　See "Ein' feste Burg ist unser Gott"

"Mignonne, allons voir si la rose" (Ronsard)
　　See "Ode à Cassandre: `Mignonne, allon voir'"

Militaire philosophe (Holbach) **14**:153, 167

The Military Memoirs of Captain Carleton (Defoe) **1**:133, 140, 146

The Military Orders (Calderon de la Barca) **23**:8

The Military Philosopher; or, Difficulties of Religion (Holbach)
　　See *Militaire philosophe*

De militia romana libri quinque (Lipsius) **16**:265, 267, 269, 277-78

"Miller's" (Chaucer)
　　See "Miller's Tale"

"Miller's Prologue" (Chaucer) **17**:183, 204

"Miller's Tale" (Chaucer) **17**:55, 168, 170, 183-88, 191, 193-94, 197-98, 201-02, 209, 217, 220, 233-35

Milton (Warton) **15**:438

Mind (Edwards)
　　See *Notes on the Mind*

"Minerva" (Rousseau) **9**:345

"Minister Dragon's Flight" (P'u Sung-ling)
　　See "Lung-fei hsiang kung"

Minna von Barnhelm (Lessing) **8**:58, 60-3, 66, 68-70, 72, 74-5, 83, 85, 87-8, 92, 94-5, 98, 105-07, 112, 114, 116

"Minute Philosopher of Bishop Berkley" (Addison) **18**:20

The Mirrour of Vertue in Worldly Greatnes; or, The Life of syr Thomas More Knight (Roper) **10**:459-87

Le misanthrope (Moliere) **10**:268-69, 271-73, 275-78, 280, 282-88, 290-93, 295-99, 308, 312-13, 318-21, 335, 338; **28**:227-28, 231, 234-36, 239, 242-43, 246, 248-50, 254-57, 259, 265-66, 268-71, 274

"The Misanthrope Corrected" (Marmontel)
　　See "Le misanthrope corrigé"

"Le misanthrope corrigé" (Marmontel) **2**:214, 218

"Miscell. IV" (Buchanan) **4**:134

The Miscellaneous Essays (Hopkinson)
　　See *The Miscellaneous Essays and Occasional Writings of Francis Hopkinson*

The Miscellaneous Essays and Occasional Writings of Francis Hopkinson (Hopkinson) **25**:253-54, 262, 269-70

Miscellaneous Observations (Butler) **16**:26

Miscellaneous Observations on Important Theological Subjects (Edwards) **7**:114

Miscellaneous Observations on the Tragedy of Macbeth (Johnson) **15**:206, 241, 307, 312-13

Miscellaneous Poems (Marvell) **43**:278

Miscellaneous Poetry (Dennis)
　　See *Miscellanies in Verse and Prose by Mr. Dennis*

The Miscellaneous Works in Prose and Verse of Mrs. Elizabeth Rowe (Rowe) **44**:278, 291

Miscellanies (Congreve) **5**:69, 75

Miscellanies (Cowley) **43**:140-1, 167, 170

Miscellanies (Fielding) **1**:211, 219, 221; **46**:63, 99-100, 104, 114

Miscellanies (Wycherley)
　　See *Miscellany Poems*

Miscellanies in Verse and Prose by Mr. Dennis (Dennis) **11**:4-5, 15, 47

Miscellany (Dennis)
　　See *Miscellanies in Verse and Prose by Mr. Dennis*

Miscellany Poems (Dryden) **21**:119

Miscellany Poems (Wycherley) **8**:380, 415-16

Miscellany Poems on Several Occasions, Written by a Lady, 1713 (Winchilsea) **3**:456

"The Miser" (Butler) **16**:50

The Miser (Moliere)
　　See *L'avare*

"Miserie" (Herbert) **24**:229-30, 274

The Miseries of Enforced Marriage (Behn) **1**:49

"The Miseries of Queene Margarite" **8**:8, 17, 33

"Miserly Riches" (Erasmus) **16**:142

"Misery" (Vaughan) **27**:339

The Misery of a Prison, and a Prisoner (Dekker) **22**:96

"The Misery of Unbelievers" (Edwards) **7**:98

Mishap through Honor (Vega) **23**:374, 378

Mismatches in Valencia (Castro) **19**:2

"Miss Chia-no" (P'u Sung-ling)
　　See "Ying-ning"

"Miss Huan-niang" (P'u Sung-ling) **3**:352

Miss in Her Teens; or, The Medley of Lovers (Garrick) **15**:93, 98, 101-02, 104, 113, 115, 124

Miss Lucy in Town, A Sequel to the Virgin Unmasked (Fielding) **1**:251

Miss Sara Sampson (Lessing) **8**:58, 66, 70, 72, 80, 85, 94-5, 98, 105, 107-09, 112, 116

Miss Sarah Sampson (Lessing)
　　See *Miss Sara Sampson*

The Mistake (Vanbrugh) **21**:293, 295, 319

The Mistresse; or, Seuerall Copies of Love Verses (Cowley) **43**:141, 147, 156-7, 166-7, 170-1, 189

The Misunderstanding (Marivaux)
　　See *The Misunderstanding*

Mithridate (Racine) **28**:312, 316, 341, 343, 346, 365, 372, 374, 376, 378-80

Mithridates (Racine)
　　See *Mithridate*

Mme. de La Carlière (Diderot) **26**:118, 149

"A Mme de Montespan" (La Fontaine) **50**:98

"Mnemon" (More) **9**:298

Las mocedades del Cid (Castro) **19**:3, 8, 11-14

Las mocedades del Cid I (Castro) **19**:5, 8

Las mocedades del Cid II (Castro) **19**:4-5, 8, 12-15

"A Mock Charon" (Lovelace) **24**:

"A Mock Song" (Lovelace) **24**:315, 320, 322, 348

The Mock-Astrologer (Dryden)
　　See *An Evening's Love; or, The Mock-Astrologer*

The Mocker (Chulkov)
　　See *Peremešnik*

"A Modell of Christian Charity" (Winthrop) **31**:320-24, 354, 363-78, 380, 383, 387, 393

"A Modern Critic" (Butler) **16**:50

The Modern Fine Gentleman (Garrick)
　　See *The Male Coquette*

The Modern Husband (Fielding) **1**:203-04, 250; **46**:59, 90, 105

The Modern Poet (Davys) **46**:19

"A Modern Politician" (Butler) **16**:30

A Modest Inquiry into the Nature and Necessity of Paper Currency (Franklin) **25**:111

A Modest Proposal for Preventing the Children of the Poor People from Being a Burthen (Swift) **1**:442, 447-48, 459-60, 481-82, 484-85, 490, 497, 513, 517, 519-22

Modus cudendi monetam (Copernicus)
　　See *Monetae cudendae ratio*

Modus Orandi Deum (Erasmus) **16**:154

La moglie saggia (Goldoni) **4**:261-62

The Mohocks: A Tragi-Comical Farce (Gay) **49**:33, 60, 114-115, 117, 121, 179

"A Mole in Celia's Bosom" (Carew) **13**:18

Moll Flanders (Defoe)
　　See *The Fortunes and Misfortunes of the Famous Moll Flanders*

Molly Mog (Gay) **49**:4-5, 12

De monade, numero et figura (Bruno) **27**:117, 123

Monadologie (Leibniz) **35**:137, 148, 170, 177, 179

Monadology (Leibniz)
　　See *Monadologie*

Monarchia del Messia (Campanella) **32**:201, 210

Monarchia di Spagna (Campanella) **32**:210, 225, 231

Le mondain (Voltaire) **14**:364, 379, 406

"Monday" (Gay) **49**:69

Monday (Gay) **49**:39-40, 46-47

Le monde comme il va (Voltaire) **14**:364, 398

Le Monde de M. Descartes, ou e traite de a lumiere (Descartes) **35**:79, 84-5, 91, 99, 103, 109, 111, 114

Le Monde renversé (Lesage) **28**:205, 211

Monetae cudendae ratio (Copernicus) **45**:88-90

Money, Its Interest and Coinage (Locke) **35**:217

The Monitor (Hutten) **16**:216, 234, 246

Monitor II (Hutten) **16**:241, 246

Monitor for Communicants (Mather) **38**:167

"The Monk and the Miller's Wife" (Ramsay) **29**:321

"Monk's Prologue" (Chaucer)
　　See "Prologue to the Monk's Tale"

"Monk's Tale" (Chaucer) **17**:61, 119, 136, 196, 201, 218, 220-21

Monody (Lyttelton)
　　See *To the Memory of a Lady Lately Deceased: A Monody*

"Monody, Written near Stratford upon Avon" (Warton) **15**:442

Monsieur de Pourceaugnac (Moliere) **10**:272, 277-78, 282-84, 286, 290-91, 296, 313, 327; **28**:255-56

Monsieur D'Olive (Chapman) **22**:6, 10, 15, 63, 66

Monsieur Thomas; or, Father's Own Son (Fletcher) **33**:41

La Montre; or, The Lover's Watch (Behn) **1**:41

"The Monument: a Poem, Sacred to the Immortal Memory of the Best and Greatest of Kings, William the Third, King of Great Britain, &c." (Dennis) **11**:15, 48-50

A Monumental Column (Webster) **33**:342, 344-45

Monuments of the Martyrs (Foxe)
　　See *Actes and Monumentes of these latter*

Title Index

perilous dayes touching matters of the Church

The Moone-Calfe **8**:9, 17

"Moral Essays" (Pope) **3**:273, 319

Moral Fables (Holberg)
  See *Moralske fabler*

The Moral Law Expounded (Andrewes) **5**:28

Moral Proverbs (Christine de Pizan)
  See *Prouverbes moraux*

Moral Reflections (Holberg)
  See *Moralske tanker*

Moral Sentiments (Smith)
  See *Theory of Moral Sentiments*

Moral Tales (Marmontel)
  See *Contes moraux*

Moral Teachings (Christine de Pizan)
  See *Enseignemens moraux*

Morale universelle (Holbach) **14**:152, 155-56, 160, 168, 175

"The Morals of Chess" (Franklin) **25**:112, 141, 147

Moralske fabler (Holberg) **6**:278

Moralske tanker (Holberg) **6**:266, 273, 278

More Dissemblers Besides Women (Middleton) **33**:263, 311, 321, 323-27

More Fruits (Penn) **25**:334

Moria (Erasmus)
  See *Moriae encomium*

Moriae encomium (Erasmus) **16**:107-17, 127, 130-33, 135-39, 142, 149, 152-55, 157-62, 165-73, 175-76, 181-83, 185-92, 194-95, 202-07

"Morning" (Fergusson) **29**:171, 196, 219

"Morning" (Parnell)
  See "A Hymn for Morning"

"Morning" (Smart) **3**:366

"Morning" (Wheatley)
  See "An Hymn to the Morning"

"The Morning Interview" (Ramsay) **29**:327

"Morning. The Author confined to College" (Warton) **15**:440, 463

"The Morning-watch" (Vaughan) **27**:322-23, 330, 333, 339, 392-94

"La morosophie" (Rousseau) **9**:345

La mort de pompée (Corneille) **28**:4, 6, 16, 21, 28-9, 32, 34, 38, 55

"La Mort et le bucheron" (La Fontaine) **50**:92

"La Mort et le mourant" (La Fontaine) **50**:84

Morte Darthur (Malory) **11**:113-202

Mortificacio Christi (York) **34**:334-5, 388

"Mortification" (Herbert) **24**:238

Mortimer His Fall (Jonson) **6**:311

Mortimeriados. The Lamentable Civell Warres of Edward the Second and the Barrons **8**:19-20, 30, 33

"Moses" (Parnell) **3**:255

Moses and Balaam and Balaack (Chester)
  See *Balaam and Balaak* (Chester)

Moses and Pharaoh (York) **34**:365-6, 372, 374, 386-7

Moses (N-Town) **34**:178, 181, 192, 208

The Mother as Confidant (Marivaux)
  See *The Mother as Confidant*

Mother Bombie (Lyly) **41**:272

"Mother Hubberd's Tale" (Spenser)
  See "Prosopopoia; or, Mother Hubberds Tale"

"The Motto" (Cowley) **43**:189

A Motto for an Opera (Gay) **49**:7

De motu (Galilei) **45**:253-54
  See *The Assayer*

De motu (Newton) **35**:317

"La Mouche et la Fourmi" (La Fontaine) **50**:77

"The Mount of Olives" (Vaughan) **27**:325, 355

The Mount of Olives; or, Solitary Devotions (Vaughan) **27**:293, 303-04, 308, 311-12, 314, 323-24, 328, 335, 371, 382

"A Mountebank" (Butler) **16**:50

"Mourning" (Marvell) **4**:397, 408-10, 425, 439

The Mourning Bride (Congreve) **5**:68-9, 72, 74-6, 79, 85, 88, 101-02, 110-11; **21**:10

"Mourning Garment" **41**:148, 156, 177-78

"Mourning Muses" (Congreve) **5**:75

"Mouse Performance" (P'u Sung-ling)
  See "Shu'hsi"

Movements of Water (Vinci)
  See *On the Motion and Power of Water*

"The Mower against gardens" (Marvell) **4**:403, 410, 441-42

"The Mower to the Glo-Worms" (Marvell) **4**:411, 425, 441-42

"The Mower's Song" (Marvell) **4**:411, 442; **43**:300

"Mr. Ashton" (Crashaw)
  See "Epitaph upon the Death of Mr. Ashton, a conformable citizen"

Mr. Burke's Speech, on the 1st December 1783, upon the Question for the Speaker's Leaving the Chair, in Order for the House to Resolve Itself into a Committee on Mr. Fox's East Indian Bill (Burke) **7**:34

Mr. Collier's Dissuasive from the Playhouse (Collier) **6**:229

Mr. Howell's Poems upon divers Emergent Occasions (Howell) **13**:427, 431

Mr. Limberham (Dryden)
  See *The Kind Keeper; or, Mr. Limberham*

Mr. Smirk; or, The Divine in Mode (Marvell) **4**:394, 399

Mr. Steele's Apology for Himself and His Writings (Steele) **18**:336, 338, 340

Mubayyan (Babur) **18**:89-91

Mubin (Babur) **18**:87

"Muiopotmos; or, the Fate of the Butterflie" (Spenser) **5**:305, 312, 329-31, 345, 347-49

De Mundi (Brahe)
  See *Tychonis Brahe Dani, De Mundi aetherei recentioribus phaenomenis Liber secundus, qui est de illustri stella caudata ab elapso fere triente Nouembris anno MDLXXVII usque in finem Januarii sequentis conspecta.*

"The Murder of the Dog" (Wessel) **7**:391

"Les murs de Troie" (Perrault) **2**:274

Musa II (Quevedo) **23**:155

Musa IV (Quevedo) **23**:155

Musa V (Quevedo) **23**:155

Musa VI (Quevedo) **23**:155

Musa IX (Quevedo) **23**:155

"The Muse" (Cowley) **43**:153, 164, 167, 171, 187

"The Muse" (Kochanowski)
  See "Muza"

"Muse's Duel" (Crashaw) **24**:9

The Muses Elizium, Lately Discovered, by a New Way over Parnassus. The Passages Therein, Being the Subject of Ten Sundry Nymphalls **8**:21, 28, 31, 34, 37, 40-1, 50

"Musicks Duell" (Crashaw)
  See "Music's Duel"

"Musicks Empire" (Marvell) **4**:442-43

"Music's Duel" (Crashaw) **24**:4-5, 9, 20, 26, 28, 43, 46

Musophilus; or, Defense of All Learning (Daniel) **24**:89, 93, 99-100, 123, 127-28, 132

"Mutabilitie Cantos" (Spenser)
  See "Cantos of Mutabilitie"

"The Mutiny" (Vaughan) **27**:339

"The Mutual Complaint of Plainstanes and Causey in their Mother-tongue" (Fergusson) **29**:170, 179, 181, 189-190, 192, 196, 206, 220

"Muza" (Kochanowski) **10**:160

"My ain kind Dearie" (Burns) **3**:71

"My boddy in the walls captived" (Raleigh) **31**:271, 286

"My Days Have Been So Wondrous Free" (Hopkinson) **25**:250, 260

"My Dear and Loving Husband" (Bradstreet)
  See "To My Dear and Loving Husband His Goeing into England"

My Dear Belladine (Gay) **49**:7

"My Harry was a Gallant Gay" (Burns) **29**:51-2

"My Heart Was Slaine, and None But You and I"
  See "Sonnet 2"

"My Last Will" (Fergusson) **29**:173

"My Lord" (Cavendish) **30**:225

My Lord General Hastings (Marvell)
  See *My Lord General Hastings*

"My Love Has Gone to Sea" (Hopkinson) **25**:250-51

"My Luve Is Like a Red, Red Rose" (Burns) **3**:76, 78, 83; **29**:26-8, 35; **40**:93, 98

"My Nanie O" (Burns) **3**:71

"My Noble Lovely Little Peggy" (Prior) **4**:464

"My Patie is a Lover Gay" (Ramsay) **29**:309, 330, 341

"My Peggy is a Young Thing" (Ramsay) **29**:320, 322, 331, 333, 342

"My Picture Left in Scotland" (Jonson) **6**:347

"My Soul" (Bradstreet) **30**:148

"My thankful heart with glorying tongue" (Bradstreet) **4**:107

"My Touchers the Jewel" (Burns) **29**:22, 49

"My Wife's a Wanton, Wee thing" (Burns) **40**:89

"Myrrour of Modestie" **41**:141, 172

The Mysteries of the Sacred Mass Divine Orpheus (Calderon de la Barca) **23**:64

The Mysterious Mother (Walpole) **2**:451, 459-60, 473-75, 486, 488, 501, 505-06; **49**:331, 337-41, 344-45, 347, 369, 371-72, 377

Mysterium Cosmographicum (Kepler) **45**:320, 324, 326, 335, 341, 343-47, 351-52, 354, 359, 361-62, 365-68
  See *Hormonice Mundi*

"Mystery of Godliness" (More) **9**:300

"Mystery of Iniquity" (More) **9**:300

The Mystery of Israel's Salvation (Mather)
  See *The Mystery of Salvation*

The Mystery of Jesus (Pascal) **35**:358

The Mystery of Salvation (Mather) **38**:305-7, 310

"Mystification" (Diderot) **26**:161

Mythologiae Christianae sive virtutum and vitiorum vitae humanae imaginum libri tres (Andreae) **32**:93

"Na lipe" (Kochanowski) **10**:161

"Na nabozna" (Kochanowski) **10**:160

El nacimiento de Montesinos (Castro) **19**:13-15

El nacimiento de Ursón y Valentín (Vega) **23**:399

Nafah al-uns (Jami) **9**:67, 71

Naked truth needs no Shift (Penn) **25**:287

"The Name of Jesus" (Crashaw)
  See "Hymn to the Name above every Name—the Name of Jesus"

"Die Namen" (Lessing) **8**:69

Nanine (Voltaire) **14**:338

"Nany" (Ramsay) **29**:320

"Narcissa" (Young)
  See "The Complaint; or, Night Thoughts: Night the Third"

"Narcissa" (Young)

See "The Complaint; or, Night Thoughts: Night the Third"

Narcisse (Rousseau) **14**:309

Narrative (Equiano)
See *The Interesting Narrative of the Life of Olaudah Equiano, or Gustavus Vassa, the African*

Der Narrenspital (Beer) **5**:53-4

"Narva and Mored" (Chatterton) **3**:123

Nashe's Lenten Stuffe (Nashe) **41**:309, 375-87

Nathan der Weise (Lessing) **8**:59, 61-3, 66-9, 71, 77-9, 83-7, 89, 94-100, 106-07, 112, 114-16

Nathan the Wise (Lessing)
See *Nathan der Weise*

"Nativitie" (Donne) **24**:167

The Nativity (N-Town) **34**:192, 204-5

"Nativity Ode" (Milton)
See "On the Morning of Christ's Nativity"

"The Nativity of Our Lord and Savior Jesus Christ" (Smart)
See "Hymn on the Nativity of Our Lord and Saviour Jesus Christ"

"De natura acidorum" (Newton) **35**:299

Natural and Experimental History (Bacon)
See *Sylva Sylvarum: Or a Natural History*

The Natural Son (Diderot)
See *Le Fils naturel*

"Nature" (Herbert) **24**:278

The Nature of Christianity (Luther) **37**:269

The Nature of True Virtue (Edwards) **7**:93, 95, 102, 108-09, 118-20, 124, 131

"Nature that washt her hands in milke" (Raleigh) **39**:96, 123

"Nature's Law" (Burns) **29**:23, 29

Natures Pictures drawn by Francie's Pencil (1) (Cavendish) **30**:184, 186, 188, 201, 213, 219, 226

"Naufragium" (Erasmus) **16**:128, 141, 174, 194

Naval Minutes (Pepys) **11**:239-41

Nay-namá (Jami) **9**:66

A Necessary Doctrine and Erudition for any Christen Man, Sette Furthe by the Kynges Majestie of Englande (Henry VIII) **10**:131, 133, 135-37, 139, 141

The Necessity for Reforming the Church (Calvin) **37**:92

"Necessity of Fate" (Barker) **42**:96

Necessity of Reformation (Mather) **38**:257

Neck or Nothing (Garrick) **15**:98, 101-02

"Negli anni molti e nelle molte pruove" (Michelangelo) **12**:363, 371

"Nemaean Ode" (Cowley) **43**:142

Nemo (Hutten) **16**:224, 230, 232-33, 245

Neptunes Triumph (Jonson) **6**:337-38

Neptuno Alegórico (Juana Ines de la Cruz) **5**:144

"N'ésperons plus, mon âme, aux promesses du monde" (Malherbe) **5**:181

Der neu ausgefertigte Jungfer-Hobel (Beer) **5**:53, 56

Ein neu Lied (Hutten) **16**:242, 247

Die neue Cecilia (Moritz) **2**:244-45

"Neuer too late" **41**:148, 156-58, 177-78

Neues ABC Buch, welches zugleich eine Anleitung zum Denken für Kinderenthält (Moritz) **2**:246

"Ein neues Lied wir heben an" (Luther) **9**:143

La neuvaine de Cythère (Marmontel) **2**:213

Le Neveu de Rameau (Diderot) **26**:69-70, 89, 92, 94-96, 103, 106, 117-19, 125, 130, 136, 144, 162, 165, 168-69

"A New Arabian Night's Entertainment" (Walpole) **2**:500

New Arcadia (Sidney) **39**:228-29, 243, 269, 270, 271, 273, 274

New Art (Vega)
See *Arte nuevo de hacer comedias en este tiempo*

The New Art of Playwriting in this Age (Vega)
See *Arte nuevo de hacer comedias en este tiempo*

The New Art of Writing Comedies (Vega)
See *Arte nuevo de hacer comedias en este tiempo*

The New Art of Writing Plays (Vega)
See *Arte nuevo de hacer comedias en este tiempo*

The New Astronomy (Kepler)
See *Astronomia Nova: Physica Coelestis*

The New Atalantis (Manley) **1**:306-24; **42**:261, 263-67, 269-79, 281-86

The New Athenians no noble Bereans (Penn) **25**:289

New Atlantis (Bacon)
See *Nova Atlantis*

New Eloise (Rousseau)
See *La Nouvelle Héloïse*

New Englands Trials **9**:352, 355, 358, 383

A New English Grammar Prescribing as certain Rules as the Language will have for Forrenners to learn English. There is also another Grammar of the Spanish or Castillian Toung. (Howell) **13**:427

New Essays (Leibniz) **35**:130, 132, 169-70, 173, 179

The New House (Goldoni)
See *La casa nova*

The New Inn (Jonson) **6**:302, 304, 306, 311, 314, 339; **33**:117, 145, 154, 159

" New Jerusalem" (Mather) **38**:306, 308-11

New Organon (Bacon)
See *Summi Angliae Instauratio magna*

New Physical Hypothesis (Leibniz)
See *Hypothesis physica nova*

"A New Psalm for the Chapel of Kilmarnock" (Burns) **3**:95; **29**:47

"The New Roof" (Hopkinson) **25**:252-53, 259, 268, 271, 273

"A New Song" (Hopkinson) **25**:262

A New Song (Hutten)
See *Ein neu Lied*

New Song of New Similies (Gay) **49**:4

New System (Leibniz) **35**:166, 179

A New Voyage Round the World (Defoe) **1**:133, 174, 176

The New Witnesses proved Old Hereticks (Penn) **25**:287, 291-92

"New Year's Day" (Crashaw)
See "Our Lord in his Circumcision to his Father"

"New Year's Gift" (Herrick)
See "A New-Yeares Gift Sent to Sir Simeon Steward"

New Year's Wishes (Hutten) **16**:225

Das newe Testament deutzsche (Luther) **9**:152

"Newgate's Garland" (Gay) **49**:171, 178

Newgate's Garland (Gay) **49**:4-5, 19

"Newmarket, a Satire" (Warton) **15**:440, 449, 462

News from Hell, Brought by the Devil's Carrier and containing The Devil's Answer to Pierce Penniless (Dekker) **22**:95

News from Plymouth (Davenant) **13**:175, 187

News From the New World (Jonson) **33**:169

"A New-Yeares Gift Sent to Sir Simeon Steward" (Herrick) **13**:310, 351-52, 365

"A New-yeares gift. To the King" (Carew) **13**:44

"Nicaise" (La Fontaine) **50**:69

Nicolai Copernici Torunensi De Revolutionibus orbium coelestium. Libri VI (Copernicus) **45**:91-3, 95, 96-101, 103, 105, 108, 110-2, 114-6, 120-1, 123-6, 128-9, 145, 147, 165, 173, 175, 178, 185

Nicolai Klimii iter subterraneum... (Holberg) **6**:260-61, 266, 270, 273, 278-79

Nicomède (Corneille) **28**:4-5, 15-16, 21, 30, 32, 35, 38, 41, 49

Nicomedes (Corneille)
See *Nicomède*

"Nieh Hsiao-ch'ien" (P'u Sung-ling) **3**:352

"Nien yang" (P'u Sung-ling) **49**:296

Nifo (Tasso) **5**:407

"Night" (Churchill) **3**:148, 150, 153, 155-56, 159, 162-63

"Night" (Lovelace) **24**:321

"Night" (Smart) **3**:366

"The Night" (Vaughan) **27**:291, 305, 314, 328, 346, 380-81, 383-91, 393

"Night I" (Young)
See "The Complaint: or, Night Thoughts: Night the First"

"Night II" (Young)
See "The Complaint; or, Night Thoughts: Night the Second"

"Night VI" (Young)
See "The Complaint; or, Night Thoughts: Night the Sixth"

"Night VIII" (Young)
See "The Complaint; or, Night Thoughts: Night the Eighth"

"A Night Piece" (Smart) **3**:399

"Night the Fifth" (Young)
See "The Complaint; or, Night Thoughts: Night the Fifth"

"Night the Ninth" (Young)
See "The Complaint; or, Night Thoughts: Night the Ninth"

"The Nightingale" (Winchilsea)
See "To the Nightingale"

"Night-Piece" (Parnell)
See "Night-Piece on Death"

"Night-Piece on Death" (Parnell) **3**:251-52, 254-59

"The Night-Piece to Julia" (Herrick) **13**:332, 336-37, 360, 403

Nimphidia, the Court of Fayrie **8**:9, 11, 13-21, 23, 25-6, 28, 33-4, 36-7, 41, 46, 48-50

Nine Books of Archidoxus (Paracelsus)
See *Archidoxa*

La niñe de plata (Vega) **23**:402

Ninety-Five Theses (Luther)
See *Disputatio pro declaratione virtutia indulgentiarum*

"The Ninth Discourse" (Reynolds) **15**:396, 403, 411-12, 416

"Niobe in Distress for Her Children Slain by Apollo" (Wheatley) **3**:412, 430; **50**:241

"Nitidia's Answer" (Hopkinson) **25**:270

No Abolition of Slavery (Boswell) **4**:52

No Cross, No Crown (Penn) **25**:285, 294, 298, 301, 316, 330, 333-34

No hay cosa como callar (Calderon de la Barca) **23**:70

"No Luck in Love" (Herrick) **13**:327

No Monster like Jealousy (Calderon de la Barca)
See *El mayor monstruo del mundo*

"No Spouse but a sister" (Herrick) **13**:367

No Wit No Help Like a Woman's (Middleton) **33**:264, 275

Noah and the Flood (York) **34**:342, 362-3, 374

Noah (N-Town) **34**:174, 181, 200, 208, 215

Noah (Towneley) **34**:252-3, 278, 293-4, 296, 321

Noah's Flood (Chester) **34**:92, 106-07, 111, 129-31, 156, 160

Noahs Floud **8**:31

De nobilitate et praeccelentia foeminei sexus (Agrippa von Nettesheim) **27**:5-6, 25, 48, 54-55

The Noble and Joyous Book Entytled Le Morte Darthur (Malory)
     See *Morte Darthur*

The Noble Gentleman (Fletcher) **33**:60

Noble Numbers, or Pious Pieces (Herrick)
     See *His Noble Numbers: or, His Pious Pieces, Wherein (amongst Other Things) He Sings the Birth of His Christ: and Sighes for His Saviours Suffering on the Crosse*

The Noble Slaves; or, The Lives and Adventures of Two Lords and Two Ladies Who Were Shipwreck'd upon a desolate Island (Aubin) **9**:3-6, 8, 16-17

The Noble Spanish Soldier (Dekker) **22**:106, 110-1, 125-6, 132

The Nobody (Hutten)
     See *Nemo*

La noche de San Juan (Vega) **23**:372

Noche Escura del Alma (John of the Cross) **18**:202, 214-15, 220, 229-30, 234-35

"Noche Oscura del alma" (John of the Cross) **18**:213-14, 216, 222-24, 230, 232-35

"A Nocturnal Reverie" (Winchilsea) **3**:441-42, 444-47, 451-52, 455, 457-58

"A Nocturnal upon S. Lucies day, Being the shortest day" (Donne) **10**:26, 36, 48, 50, 78-80, 82, 89; **24**:155

Noe and His Wife (York) **34**:333

"Non è sempre di colpa aspra e mortale" (Michelangelo) **12**:366

"Non ha l'ottimo artista alcun concetto" (Michelangelo) **12**:314, 366, 371, 373

"Non posso non mancar d'ingegno e d'arte" (Michelangelo) **12**:371

"Non pur d'argento o d'oro" (Michelangelo) **12**:368-69

"Non so se s'è la desiata luce" (Michelangelo) **12**:356

"Nonne Preestes Tale" (Chaucer)
     See "Nun's Priest's Tale"

The Nonsense of Common-Sense (Montagu) **9**:281

"Noon" (Smart) **3**:366

The Northern Heiress; or, The Humours of York (Davys) **1**:97-8; **46**:19, 24-5, 28-9

Northward Ho (Dekker) **22**:106, 110-1, 125-6, 132

Northward Ho! (Webster) **33**:345

"Not Every Day Fit for Verse" (Herrick) **13**:382

Not So Stupid After All (Vega) **23**:385-86

"A Notable Discouery of Coosnage" **41**:149, 152, 155-56, 165, 181-83

Note-Books (Butler)
     See *Characters and Passages from Note-Books*

Notebooks (Vinci) **12**:392-93, 397-401, 404-06, 410, 428-29

Notebooks (Voltaire) **14**:380, 391, 395

Notes on the Mind (Edwards) **7**:99, 120, 124

Notes on Universal History (Turgot)
     See *Sur l'histoire universelle*

The Notion of a Spirit (More)
     See *Enchiridion metaphysicum*

Nourjahad (Sheridan)
     See *The History of Nourjahad*

"Nous ne sommes pas nez de la dure semence" (Ronsard) **6**:433-34

Nouvelle continuation des amours (Ronsard) **6**:425-26, 431, 433

La Nouvelle Héloïse (Rousseau) **14**:216, 218, 220, 235, 237, 239, 247-49, 251-52, 264, 273, 278, 291, 297, 301, 309, 311, 313; **36**:254

Nouvelles Aventures de l'admirable Don Quichotte de la Manche (Lesage) **28**:199, 203

Nova Atlantis (Bacon) **18**:118, 121, 126, 129, 132, 136, 141, 143, 153, 157-58, 163, 173, 176-77, 179-80, 185, 187, 189-92, 196-97; **32**:106-10, 114, 119-27, 129-42, 144-5, 148-53, 156, 158-62, 165-89

Nova Stereometria (Kepler) **45**:320
     See *Harmonice Mundi*

Novelas exemplares (Cervantes) **6**:144, 148, 171-72, 174, 176-77, 183; **23**:94, 97-99, 137

Novellas to Marcia Leonarda (Vega) **23**:378

Los novios de Hornachuelos (Vega) **23**:348

Novum instrumentum (Erasmus) **16**:159, 163, 171

Novum Organum (Bacon)
     See *Summi Angliae Instauratio magna*

Novum Scientiarum Organum (Bacon) **18**:104-05, 108, 115, 118-20, 130-32, 135-36, 140, 142-44, 146-47, 149-50, 152-53, 155, 157, 160-61, 163, 165, 168, 172, 174, 187-88, 193

"Now Rosy May" (Burns) **29**:36

"Now wat ye wha I met yestreen" (Ramsay) **29**:309

"Now we have present made" (Raleigh) **31**:279-80

La Nueva Ira de Dios y Gran Tamorlan de Persia (Vega) **23**:351-52

El Nuevo mondo descubierto por Cristobal Colon (Vega) **23**:348

La nuit et le moment; ou, Les matines de Cythere (Crebillon) **1**:76-7, 79, 90; **28**:65, 70-2, 79, 88, 90-3

La Numancia (Cervantes)
     See *El cerco de Numancia*

Numitor (Marmontel) **2**:213, 217

The Nun (Diderot)
     See *La Religieuse*

The Nun; or, The Perjur'd Beauty (Behn) **30**:88; **42**:109, 146

"Nung-jên" (P'u Sung-ling) **49**:294

"Nun's Priest's Tale" (Chaucer) **17**:55, 58, 71, 82, 136-37, 140, 185, 195-98, 205, 220-22, 242

"Nuovo piacere e di maggiore stima" (Michelangelo) **12**:363

"A Nuptiall Song, or Epithalamie on Sir Clipseby Crew and His Lady" (Herrick) **13**:350, 352, 364

The Nuptials of Peleus and Thetis (Howell) **13**:414

"Nut-brown Maid" (Prior)
     See "Henry and Emma"

"Nygelle" (Chatterton) **3**:129

"A Nymph" (More) **9**:298

"A Nymph and a Swain to Apollo once pray'd" (Congreve) **5**:85

"The Nymph and the Faun" (Marvell)
     See "The Nymph Complaining for the Death of Her Faun"

"The Nymph Complaining for the Death of Her Faun" (Marvell) **4**:395, 397, 401-02, 404, 412, 419, 423, 425, 435, 438, 443; **43**:278, 300

Nympha Caledoniæ (Buchanan) **4**:117

Nymphes de la Seine (Racine) **28**:293

"A Nymph's Passion" (Jonson) **6**:351

"Nymph's Reply to the Shepherd" (Raleigh) **39**:96, 121

"O An Ye Were Dead Guidman" (Burns) **29**:24; **40**:89

"O Ay My Wife She Dang Me" (Burns) **29**:24; **40**:88

"O, Bony Jean" (Ramsay) **29**:320

"O doktorze Hiszpanie" (Kochanowski) **10**:160

"O For Ane and Twenty, Tam" (Burns) **3**:67; **29**:22, 49

"O Gloriosa Domina" (Crashaw) **24**:

"O Happy Golden Age" (Daniel) **24**:134

"O hermosura que excedéis" (Teresa de Jesus) **18**:390

"O Kapelanie" (Kochanowski) **10**:160

"O Lay Thy Loof in Mine, Lass" (Burns) **3**:67

"O, Let Me In This Ae Night" (Burns) **29**:82-3

"O Lord the Maker of All Things" (Henry VIII) **10**:146

"O Madness! terror of mankind" (Prior) **4**:60

"O Mither Dear, I 'Gin to Fear" (Ramsay) **29**:330

"O once I lov'd" (Burns) **40**:103

"O Ruddier than the Cherry!" (Gay) **49**:157

"O Saw ye Bonnie Lesly" (Burns) **40**:64

"O smierci Jana Tarnowskiego" (Kochanowski) **10**:173

"O Thou, omnipotent, eternal Lord!" (Boswell) **4**:61

"O Wert Thou in the Cauld, Cauld Blast" (Burns) **3**:67, 82; **40**:98

"O Whistle an' I'll Come to Ye My Lad" (Burns) **29**:22

"Obedience" (Herbert) **24**:272

"Obedience in Subjects" (Herrick) **13**:394

Oberon, the Fairy Prince (Jonson) **6**:327

"Oberon's Chappell" (Herrick)
     See "The Fairie Temple: or, Oberons Chappell. Dedicated to Mr. John Merrifield, Counsellor at Law"

"Oberon's Feast" (Herrick) **13**:368

"Oberon's Palace" (Herrick) **13**:367

Oblacio Magorum (Towneley) **34**:251, 265, 267, 308, 326

Obras (Juana Ines de la Cruz) **5**:144

Los Obras de gracián (Gracian y Morales) **15**:142

Obris Espirituales (John of the Cross) **18**:202

Obscure Men (Hutten)
     See *Literæ obscurorum Vivorum*

Obsecratio (Erasmus) **16**:106

"Les Obseques de la Lionne" (La Fontaine) **50**:79

"The Obsequies" (Vaughan) **27**:338

"Obsequies to the Lady Anne Hay" (Carew) **13**:31, 48-9, 54, 61

"Obsequies to the Lord Harrington, brother to the Lady Lucy, Countesse of Bedford" (Donne) **10**:97

Observations, Good or Bad, Stupid or Clever, Serious or Jocular, on Squire Foote's Dramatic Entertainment entitled "The Minor," by a Genius (Boswell) **4**:51

Observations on a Late Publication Intituled "The Present State of the Nation" (Burke) **7**:54, 57; **36**:94

Observations on Blackmore's Prince Arthur (Dennis)
     See *Remarks on a Book, entituled Prince Arthur, an Heroick Poem*

"Observations on English Metre" (Gray) **40**:201

Observations on Experimental Philosophy (Cavendish) **30**:202-3, 207, 210, 220, 223-4

Observations on Macbeth (Johnson)
See *Miscellaneous Observations on the Tragedy of Macbeth*
"Observations on Reading History" (Franklin) **25**:165
Observations on Spenser (Warton)
See *Observations on the Faerie Queene of Spenser*
Observations on St. Paul's Conversion (Lyttelton)
See *Observations on the Conversion and Apostleship of St. Paul, in a Letter to Gilbert West*
Observations on the Conversion and Apostleship of St. Paul, in a Letter to Gilbert West (Lyttelton) **10**:196-97, 200-03, 207, 214
Observations on the "Discourses" of Machiavelli and Observations on Machiavelli's Discourses (Guicciardini)
See *Consideraziono sui "Discorsi" del Machiavelli*
Observations on the Faerie Queene of Spenser (Warton) **15**:427, 429, 436-38, 446-48, 451-53, 457
Observations on the Life of Cicero (Lyttelton) **10**:200
Observations on "The Minor" (Boswell)
See *Observations, Good or Bad, Stupid or Clever, Serious or Jocular, on Squire Foote's Dramatic Entertainment entitled "The Minor," by a Genius*
Observations sur la Nakaz (Diderot) **26**:158
Observations sur les instructions de Catherine II à ses députés (Diderot) **26**:120
Observations upon Anthrophia theomagica (More) **9**:310
Observations upon the Prophecies of Daniel and the Apocalypse of St. John (Newton) **35**:275-76, 321, 323, 326-27
L'obstacle Favorable (Lesage) **28**:209
"An Obstinate Man" (Butler) **16**:27
Occidental Paradise (Siguenza y Gongora)
See *Parayso occidental, plantado y cultivado por la liberal benefica mano de los muy Catholicos*
Occult Philosophy (Agrippa von Nettesheim)
See *De occulta Philosophia libri tres*
Occulta philosophia (Paracelsus) **14**:200
De occulta Philosophia libri tres (Agrippa von Nettesheim) **27**:3, 6, 10, 12-13, 15, 20-21, 23-26, 28, 32, 34, 42, 44-45, 47-54
"Ocean: An Ode" (Young) **3**:467, 488; **40**:333, 371
The Ocean to Cynthia (Raleigh) **31**:266, 272-80, 292; **39**:76, 94-95, 102, 122, 125, 128-36
Ocho comedias y ocho entremeses nunca representados (Cervantes) **6**:177, 189; **23**:135, 142
"October, a Poem" (Boswell) **4**:50
"Ode" (Crashaw)
See "Ode on a Prayer-Booke"
"Ode" (Killigrew) **4**:350
"Ode" (Marvell)
See "An Horatian Ode upon Cromwell's Return from Ireland"
"Ode" (Marvell)
See "An Horatian Ode upon Cromwell's Return from Ireland"
"An Ode" (Prior) **4**:465
"Ode XIX" (Warton) **15**:454
"Ode à Bonneval" (Rousseau) **9**:340, 344
"Ode à Cassandre: 'Mignonne, allon voir'" (Ronsard) **6**:408-09, 412-13, 417-18, 425
"Ode à Caumartin" (Rousseau) **9**:339, 344

"Ode à Duché" (Rousseau) **9**:339, 344
"Ode à Henri II" (Ronsard) **6**:439
"Ode à la fare" (Rousseau) **9**:339, 344
"Ode à la fortune" (Rousseau) **9**:339-40, 344
"Ode à la postérité" (Rousseau) **9**:345
"Ode à Malherbe" (Rousseau) **9**:340, 345
"Ode à Marie de Médicis, sur sa Bienvenue en France" (Malherbe) **5**:171, 183
"Ode à Michel de l'Hospital" (Ronsard) **6**:427-30
"Ode à Monseigneur le Dauphin" (Ronsard) **6**:438-39
"Ode au comte de Luc" (Rousseau) **9**:340-41, 343
"Ode au comte de Sinzendorff" (Rousseau) **9**:340, 344
"Ode au marquis d'Ussé" (Rousseau) **9**:339, 344
"Ode by Dr. Samuel Johnson to Mrs. Thrale upon their supposed approaching Nuptials" (Boswell) **4**:50
"Ode de la Paix" (Ronsard) **6**:431
"Ode for General Washington Birthday" (Burns) **40**:88
"Ode for Music" (Gray) **4**:316-17, 332-33; **40**:257
"Ode for Music" (Warton) **15**:441, 447, 454, 461
"Ode for St. Cecilia's Day" (Pope) **3**:270, 290, 292, 295
"Ode for St. Cecilia's Day" (Smart) **3**:366, 374
"Ode from Ossian's Poems" (Hopkinson) **25**:250-51
"An Ode Occasion'd by the Death of Mr. Thomson" (Collins) **4**:218, 220, 227, 229, 231
"Ode: Of Wit" (Cowley) **43**:140, 152-3, 156, 161, 164, 166-7, 170, 173
"Ode on a Distant Prospect of Eton College" (Gray) **4**:284, 287, 289, 310-12, 315, 322, 324, 332, 334; **40**:198-99, 205, 220, 223, 229-31, 235-38, 242
"Ode on a Drop of Dew" (Marvell) **4**:396-97, 403, 426-27, 438, 441, 443; **43**:306
"Ode on a Prayer-Booke" (Crashaw) **24**:
"Ode on Colonel Ross" (Collins)
See "Ode to a Lady on the Death of Colonel Ross in the Action of Fontenoy"
"Ode on Shakespeare" (Garrick) **15**:114
"Ode on Solitude" (Pope) **3**:268
"Ode on Spring" (Gray) **4**:283-84, 300, 302, 311, 315, 319, 322-24, 332-33; **40**:198, 200-1, 206, 218, 220-24, 229, 235-38, 240, 242-43, 251
"Ode on St. Cecilia" (Addison) **18**:16
"Ode On the Approach of Summer" (Warton) **15**:434-35, 441, 454
The Ode on the Battle of Fontenoy (Marmontel) **2**:213
"Ode on the Death of a Favourite Cat, Drowned in a Tub of Gold Fishes" (Gray) **4**:284, 301, 303, 309-10, 328-29, 332-33; **40**:209, 239, 251
"Ode on the Death of a Lamb" (Boswell) **4**:52, 61
The Ode on the Death of Mr. Crashaw (Cowley) **43**:159, 171
"An Ode on the Death of Mr. Henry Purcell" (Dryden) **21**:89
"Ode on the Death of Mr. Pelham" (Garrick) **15**:114
"Ode on the Death of Mr. Thomson" (Collins) **40**:134, 137, 144-45, 153, 169
"The Ode on the Glorious Success of Her Majesty's Arms" (Prior) **4**:466
"Ode on the Music of the Grecian Theatre"

(Collins) **4**:214, 220; **40**:141
"Ode on the New Year"
See "To the New Yeere"
"Ode on the Pleasure Arising from Vicissitude" (Gray) **4**:301, 315, 332; **40**:242
"Ode on the Poetical Character" (Collins) **4**:211, 214, 216, 220, 229, 234, 236, 242, 245; **40**:132, 135, 142, 145, 147, 153, 155-57, 159, 162-64, 166-68, 170, 172, 189, 191
"An Ode on the Popular Superstitions of the Highlands of Scotland, etc." (Collins) **4**:214, 217, 219, 223, 226, 231, 234, 236, 244; **40**:131, 134, 135-37, 148, 159, 165-66
"Ode on the Progress of Poesy" (Gray)
See "The Progress of Poesy"
"Ode on the Spring" (Gray)
See "Ode on Spring"
"Ode on Vale Royal Abbey" (Warton)
See "Ode Written at Vale-Royal Abbey in Cheshire"
"Ode on Vicissitude" (Gray)
See "Ode on the Pleasure Arising from Vicissitude"
"Ode on Whistling" (Boswell) **4**:52
"Ode pour la Reine Mère du Roy pendant sa Régence" (Malherbe) **5**:171, 185
"An Ode, Presented to the King, on His Majesty's Arrival in Holland, After the Queen's Death, 1695" (Prior) **4**:465
"Ode sent to Mr. Upton, on his Edition of the Faerie Queene" (Warton) **15**:442
"Ode sur la mort du prince de Conti" (Rousseau) **9**:339, 343
"Ode sur la naissance du duc de Bretagne" (Rousseau) **9**:339-40, 343
"Ode sur les miseres des hommes" (Ronsard) **6**:437
"Ode to a Grizzle Wig" (Warton) **15**:441, 462
"Ode to a Lady on the Death of Colonel Ross" (Collins) **40**:132, 154, 189
"Ode to a Lady on the Death of Colonel Ross in the Action of Fontenoy" (Collins) **4**:226, 229-30
"Ode to Adversity" (Gray) **4**:282, 311-12, 332; **40**:198, 218-19, 226, 229-30, 235, 237-40
"Ode to Ambition" (Boswell) **4**:52
"Ode to Evening" (Collins) **4**:211-13, 216-19, 221-22, 225-29, 231-36, 239-40, 242, 244; **40**:132-35, 137, 139, 144, 146-54, 159, 165-66, 171-72, 188-92
"Ode to Fear" (Collins) **4**:211, 216, 229, 231, 236, 238, 244; **40**:131, 132-33, 141, 145-48, 159-60, 162, 165-65, 170-72, 184
"Ode to His Valentine"
See "To His Valentine"
"Ode to Hope" (Fergusson) **29**:175, 205
"Ode to Ill-Nature" (Smart) **3**:361, 366
Ode to Independence (Smollett) **2**:332, 359
"Ode to Jesus" (Herrick) **13**:317
"Ode to John Rouse" (Milton) **9**:241
"Ode to Liberty" (Collins) **4**:213, 216, 229, 232, 234; **40**:132, 140-41, 146, 148, 153, 170, 173, 190
"Ode to Mæcenas" (Wheatley) **3**:408, 412, 415-17, 419-20, 423, 426, 430, 432, 436
"Ode to Mercy" (Collins) **4**:216, 229; **40**:132, 146, 164
"Ode to Music" (Hopkinson) **25**:259
"Ode to Neptune" (Wheatley) **3**:430; **50**:143; **50**:143
"Ode to Peace" (Collins) **4**:229, 234
"Ode to Pity" (Collins) **4**:214, 216; **40**:169
"Ode to Pity" (Fergusson) **29**:180, 205

"Ode to Simplicity" (Collins) **4**:214, 216, 229; **40**:134, 140-41, 169-70, 173, 189-90

"An Ode to Sir Clipsebie Crew" (Herrick) **13**:365

"Ode to Sleep" (Wessel) **7**:389

"Ode to Solitude, at an Inn" (Warton) **15**:444

"Ode to Spring" (Burns) **3**:99

"Ode to St. Cecilia" (Smart)
    See "Ode for St. Cecilia's Day"

"Ode to the Bee" (Fergusson) **29**:177, 190, 238

"Ode to the Butterfly" (Fergusson) **29**:190

"Ode to the Cicada" (Lovelace) **24**:303

"Ode to the Elves" (Boswell) **4**:52, 61

"Ode to the Gowdspink" (Fergusson) **29**:177, 190, 196

"Ode to the King Pater Patriae" (Young) **40**:333

"Ode to the Queen" (Prior) **4**:462

"Ode to the Spleen" (Winchilsea) **3**·441, 446-47, 449, 451, 453, 457

"Ode to the Spring" (Gray)
    See "Ode on Spring"

"Ode to the Sun" (Copernicus) **45**:121

Ode to Tragedy (Boswell) **4**:51

"An Ode upon Dedicating a Building, and Erecting a Statue to Shakespeare, at Stratford-upon-Avon" (Garrick) **15**:91, 97

"Ode. Upon his Majesties Restoration and Return" (Cowley) **43**:173

"Ode Written at Vale-Royal Abbey in Cheshire" (Warton) **15**:442, 447, 454

"Ode Written in the Beginning of the Year 1746" (Collins) **4**:216-17, 219, 222, 225-26, 230-32, 235, 243-44; **40**:137, 148, 165-66

"An Ode Written in the Peake" **8**:42-3

Odes **8**:14, 17-18, 21, 30

Odes (Dryden) **21**:76

Odes (Gray) **4**:279; **40**:199

Odes (Ronsard) **6**:409, 411, 414, 429-31

Odes (Young) **3**:476

Odes on Several Descriptive and Allegoric Subjects (Collins) **4**:210, 212, 215-17, 221, 223, 225, 229, 234, 242-43

Odes on Several Descriptive and Allegorical Subjects (Collins) **40**:131-35, 163, 167-70, 174

Odes with Other Lyrick Poesies **8**:27

"The Odour" (Herbert) **24**:272

Odprawa posłów grekich (Kochanowski) **10**:152-53, 161, 164, 167, 176-77

Odyssey (Chapman) **22**:3-4, 29

The Odyssey of Homer (Pope) **3**:291

The Oeconomy of a Winter's Day (Cleland) **2**:50, 54

Oedipe (Corneille) **28**:21, 28, 35, 38, 41, 56, 58

Oedipe (Voltaire) **14**:352, 397, 401

Oedipus (Corneille)
    See *Oedipe*

Oedipus (Dryden) **21**:90

"O'er Bogie" (Ramsay) **29**:329

"O'er the Hills Far Away" (Hopkinson) **25**:250-51

"O'er the Moor to Maggy" (Ramsay) **29**:329

Oeuvres choisies (Prevost) **1**:343

Oeuvres complétes (Condillac) **26**:52-3

Oeuvres complètes (Montesquieu) **7**:357

Oeuvres completes (Pascal) **35**:368

Oeuvres de Turgot (Turgot) **26**:381, 390

Oeuvres politiques (Diderot) **26**:135

"Of a Country Life" (Thomson) **16**:418, 432

"Of A' the Airts" (Burns) **3**:71, 85; **40**:98

"Of Age" (Montaigne) **8**:239

Of an Organum or Ars Magna of Thinking (Leibniz) **35**:167

"Of Books" (Montaigne) **8**:232

"Of Cannibals" (Montaigne)
    See "Des cannibales"

Of Civil Power (Milton)
    See *A Treatise of Civil Power in Ecclesiastic Causes*

Of Comfort against Tribulation (More)
    See *A dialoge of comfort against tribulacion*

"Of Commerce" (Hume) **7**:190-91

Of Constancy (Lipsius)
    See *De constantia libri duo*

Of Counsel (Bacon) **32**:136

"Of Death" (Bacon) **18**:148

Of Density and Rarity (Bacon) **18**:143

Of Dramatick Poesie: An Essay (Dryden) **3**:182, 188, 190, 197, 202, 211, 214, 222, 229, 236-37, 240; **21**:52, 111

"Of earthly Hope" (Bacon) **18**:149

Of Education (Milton) **9**:252, 257-59, 261-62; **43**:381, 411

Of Empire (Bacon) **32**:136, 186

"Of Endless Punishment" (Edwards) **7**:98

"Of Experience" (Montaigne)
    See "De l'experience"

Of Faction (Bacon) **32**:136

Of Friendship (Bacon) **32**:118

"Of Giving the Lie" (Montaigne) **8**:230

"Of Glory" (Montaigne) **8**:245

Of Goodness and Goodness of Nature (Bacon) **32**:118

Of Great Place (Bacon) **32**:118

Of Heaviness and Lightness (Bacon) **18**:143

"Of Heroic Plays" (Dryden) **3**:236-38; **21**:114

Of Innovations (Bacon) **32**:164

"Of Interest" (Hume) **7**:190

"Of Liberty and Necessity" (Hume) **7**:151

Of Life and Death (Bacon) **18**:143

Of Love (Bacon) **32**:118

"Of Luxury" (Hume) **7**:190

Of Marriage (Bacon) **32**:118

"Of Masques and Triumphs" (Bacon) **18**:195

"Of Miracles" (Hume) **7**:151, 155, 157, 175

"Of Moderation of Cares" (Bacon) **18**:149

"Of Money" (Hume) **7**:190

Of Negotiating (Bacon) **32**:118

Of Nobility (Bacon) **32**:136

Of Occult Philosophy (Agrippa von Nettesheim)
    See *De occulta Philosophia libri tres*

Of Plantations (Bacon) **32**:172

"Of Popularity" (Holberg) **6**:227

Of Prelatical Episcopacy (Milton) **9**:249

"Of Presumption" (Montaigne)
    See "De la praesumption"

"Of Public Credit" (Hume) **7**:190-91

Of Reformation Touching Church-Discipline in England (Milton) **9**:252; **43**:383

"Of Repentance" (Montaigne)
    See "Du repentir"

Of Revenge (Bacon) **32**:118

Of Riches (Bacon) **32**:118

Of Seditions and Troubles (Bacon) **32**:136, 173-74

"Of Some Verses of Virgil" (Montaigne)
    See "Sur des vers de Virgile"

Of Sulpher, Mercury, and Salt (Bacon) **18**:143

"Of Taxes" (Hume) **7**:190

"Of Temperance and Patience" (Vaughan) **27**:312

"Of the Academic or Sceptical Philosophy" (Hume) **7**:164

"Of the Balance of Power" (Hume) **7**:190

"Of the Balance of Trade" (Hume) **7**:190-91

"Of the Benefit we may get from our Enemies" (Vaughan) **27**:311

"Of the Diseases of the Mind and Body" (Vaughan) **27**:311

"Of the faithful friendship that lasted between two faithful friends" **41**:80

"Of the First Principles of Government" (Hume) **7**:188

"Of the Four Humours in Man's Constitution" (Bradstreet) **4**:89, 94, 102, 106, 111

"Of the Idea of Necessary Connexion" (Hume) **7**:164

"Of the Independency of Parliament" (Hume) **7**:152, 199

"Of the Jealousy of Trade" (Hume) **7**:190-91

Of the Knowledge Which Maketh a Wise Man (Elyot) **11**:58, 60-1, 71-2, 74-5, 81, 84, 89, 90, 92

"Of the Liberty of the Press" (Hume) **7**:152, 189

"Of the Modern Philosophy" (Hume) **7**:198

"Of the Origin of Government" (Hume) **7**:189

"Of the Origin of Romantic Fiction in Europe" (Warton) **15**:457

"Of the Original Contract" (Hume) **7**:189

"Of the Populousness of Antient Nations" (Hume) **7**:190

Of the Proficience and Advancement of Learning Divine and Human (Bacon)
    See *On the Advancement of Learning*

Of the Progres of the Soule (Donne)
    See *The Second Anniversarie. Of the Progres of the Soule. Wherein, By Occasion Of the Religious death of Mistris Elizabeth Drury, the incommodities of the Soule in this life, and her exaltation in the next, are Contemplated*

"Of the Standard of Taste" (Hume) **7**:163, 201-02

Of the Supreme Mysteries of Nature (Paracelsus) **14**:182

Of the Sympathy and Antipathy of Things (Bacon) **18**:143

Of The True Greatness of Britain (Bacon) **32**:136

Of the True Greatness of Kingdoms and Estates (Bacon) **32**:136, 162, 173

Of the true Theologia Mystica (Leibniz) **35**:155

Of the Use and Abuse of the Tongue (Erasmus) **16**:127

"Of the Vanity of All Worldly Creatures" (Bradstreet)
    See "The Vanity of All Worldly Things"

Of the Vicissitudes of Things (Bacon) **32**:171

Of the Wisdom of the Ancients (Bacon)
    See *De sapienta veterum*

"Of the Worshipping of False Imaginations" (Andrewes) **5**:22, 34, 42

"Of the Worshipping of Imaginations" (Andrewes)
    See "Of the Worshipping of False Imaginations"

"Of Three Kinds of Association with Others" (Montaigne) **8**:221, 243

Of True Greatness. An Epistle to the Right Henourable George Dodington, Esq. (Fielding) **46**:71, 178

Of True Religion, Heresy, Schism, Toleration, and what best means may be used against the growth of Popery (Milton) **43**:396

Of Truth (Bacon) **32**:115, 118, 126

Of Universal Synthesis and Analysis (Leibniz) **35**:167

Of Usury (Bacon) **32**:162

"Of Vanity" (Montaigne)
    See "De la vanité"

Of Winds (Bacon) **18**:143

Of Wisdom for a Man's Self (Bacon) **32**:118

"Of Wit" (Cowley)
    See "Ode: Of Wit"

"Of Youth and Age" (Bacon) **18**:194

"An Offering" (Herbert) **24**:276, 278

The Offering of the Magi (Towneley)
    See *Oblacio Magorum* (Towneley)

Offering of the Shepherds (York) **34**:366

The Offerings of the Three Kings (Chester)
    34:124-5

"Office of a Chaplain" (Collier) **6**:200

"Office of the Holy Cross" (Crashaw) **24**:

"An Officer" (Butler) **16**:52

Offrande (Marat)
    See *Offrande à la patrie; ou, Discours au Tiers
    État de France*

*Offrande à la patrie; ou, Discours au Tiers État
    de France* (Marat) **10**:225, 228-29, 232-
    33, 236

"Oh! Come to Mason Borough's Grove"
    (Hopkinson) **25**:260

"Oh do not die" (Donne)
    See "A Feaver"

"Oh Doe Not Wanton with Those Eyes" (Jonson)
    6:346

"Oh My Black Soule" (Donne) **24**:201, 203

"Les Oies de Frere Philippe" (La Fontaine) **50**:70

The Old Bachelor (Congreve)
    See *The Old Batchelour*

The Old Batchelour (Congreve) **5**:66, 68, 71, 74,
    76, 78, 81, 84, 86-8, 91-3, 95-6, 99, 101, 108-
    09, 112, 117; **21**:9, 12, 26-7, 29, 32, 34-9,
    44

The Old Farm and the New Farm (Hopkinson)
    See *A Pretty Story*

Old Fortunatus (Dekker) **22**:88, 91, 99-105, 108,
    111, 119, 127, 131-3

The Old Joiner (Chapman) **22**:64

The Old Law; or, A New Way to Please You
    (Middleton) **33**:264, 277

The Old Maid by Mary Singleton, Spinster
    (Brooke) **6**:108, 114-15; **48**:60-61, 66, 74,
    86, 87, 102, 118

*An Old Man Taught Wisdom; Or, The Virgin Un-
    masked* (Fielding) **1**:251

*Olinda's Adventures; or, The Amours of a Young
    Lady* (Trotter) **8**:364-65, 368

"Ollas Ostentare" (Erasmus) **16**:166, 173, 175

Olor Iscanus (Vaughan) **27**:294, 303, 308, 311,
    313, 315, 319, 329, 333, 335, 337, 364-65,
    369

"Olsztyn Bread Tariff" (Copernicus)
    See *Ratio panaria Allensteinensis*

Olympie (Voltaire) **14**:331

"Olympique Ode" (Cowley) **43**:142

Ominous Years (Boswell) **50**:31

Omniscience (Smart)
    See *On the Omniscience of the Supreme Being*

"On a Bank of Flowers" (Burns) **29**:22; **40**:87

"On a Bed of Guernsey Lilies" (Smart) **3**:375

"On a Cherry Stone Sent to Weare in his Mistress'
    Eare, a Death's Head on the one Side and
    Her Owne Face on the Other Side" (Herrick)
    13:341

"On a Damaske Rose" (Carew)
    See "A Damask Rose Sticking upon a Lady's
    Breast"

"On a Distant Prospect of Eton College" (Gray)
    See "Ode on a Distant Prospect of Eton Col-
    lege"

"On a Drop of Dew" (Marvell)
    See "Ode on a Drop of Dew"

"On a Picture Painted by her self, representing two
    Nimphs of Diana's, one in a posture to Hunt,
    the other Batheing" (Killigrew) **4**:349

"On a Prayer-book Sent to Mrs. M. E." (Crashaw)

"On a Prayer-book Sent to Mrs. M. R." (Crashaw)
    24:

"On a Scotch Bard Gone to the West Indies"
    (Burns) **3**:86, 92

"On a Solemn Music" (Milton) **9**:198

"On Affliction" (Winchilsea) **3**:451

"On Atheism" (Wheatley) **50**:194

On Being and the One (Pico della Mirandola)
    See *De ente et uno*

"On Being Brought from Africa to America"
    (Wheatley) **3**:412-13, 415, 417, 420, 425,
    427, 429, 431-32; **50**:146, 161, 214, 233,
    240, 245, 258

"On Blake's Victory over the Spaniards" (Marvell)
    See "On the Victory Obtained by Blake over
    the Spaniards"

On Cause, the Principle, and the One (Bruno)
    See *De la causa, principio et uno*

"On Censure" (Boswell) **4**:36

"On Commissary Goldie's Brains" (Burns) **3**:86,
    92

On Conciliation with the Colonies (Burke)
    See *Speech on Moving His Resolutions for Con-
    ciliation with the Colonies*

On Constancy (Lipsius)
    See *De constantia libri duo*

"On Conversation" (Franklin) **25**:134, 140

On Converting the Heathen (Campanella)
    See *Quod reminiscentur*

"On Cripples" (Montaigne)
    See "Cripples"

"On Cutting Down an Old Thorn" (Swift) **1**:459

"On Death" (Boswell) **4**:36

"On Deism" (Wheatley) **50**:194

"On Desire. A Pindarick" (Behn) **1**:52; **30**:68,
    76

"On Diaries" (Boswell) **50**:31

On Divine and Human Righteousness (Zwingli)
    37:378

"On Dreams: An Imitation of Petronius" (Swift)
    1:522

"On Early Marriages" (Franklin) **25**:141

"On Fear" (Boswell) **4**:36

On Free Will (Erasmus)
    See *De Libero Arbitro*

"On Gelliflowers begotten" (Herrick) **13**:367

On Gentilism (Campanella)
    See *De Gentilismo non retinendo*

"On Glenriddell's Fox Breaking His Chain"
    (Burns) **3**:77

"On Great Place" (Bacon) **18**:114-15

"On Hapinesse" (Chatterton) **3**:126

"On Himselfe" (Herrick) **13**:340-41, 370

"On His Mistris" (Donne)
    See "Elegie XVI: On his mistris"

*On How the Medici Family Should Secure Power
    for Themselves* (Guicciardini) **49**:259

"On Imagination" (Wheatley) **3**:412-13, 429-30,
    435; **50**:173, 192-93, 204-06, 212, 227, 234,
    238, 240, 243

On Imitation (Schlegel)
    See *Abhandlung von der Nachahmung*

On Infinite Universe and its Worlds (Bruno)
    See *De l'infinito universo et mondi*

On Infintiy, the Universe, and the Worlds (Bruno)
    See *De l'infinito universo et mondi*

"On James Cumming" (Fergusson) **29**:222

"On Julia's Clothes" (Herrick)
    See "Upon Julia's Clothes"

"On Justice and Generosity" (Goldsmith) **2**:87,
    128

"On King Arthur's Round Table, at Winchester"

    (Warton) **15**:442

"On Life, Death, and Immortality" (Young)
    See "The Complaint; or, Night Thoughts: Night
    the First"

"On Little Hector Philips" (Philips) **30**:314

"On Lord Holland's Seat near Margate, Kent"
    (Gray) **4**:301, 303, 316

"On Love" (Boswell) **4**:36

"On Major General Lee" (Wheatley)
    See "Thoughts on His Excellency Major Gen-
    eral Lee"

On Man (Helvetius)
    See *De l'homme*

"On Michael Angelo's Famous Piece of the Cru-
    cifixion" (Young) **3**:488

On Mind (Helvetius)
    See *De l'esprit*

On Minting Money (Copernicus)
    See *Monetae cudendae ratio*

On Monastic Vows (Luther)
    See *The Judgement of Martin Luther on Mo-
    nastic Vows*

"On Mr. G. Herbert's Book sent to a Gentleman"
    (Crashaw) **24**:

"On My First Daughter" (Jonson) **6**:347

"On My Son's Return out of England" (Bradstreet)
    4:100; **30**:147

"On Night" (Fergusson) **29**:194

"On Observing a lock of Miss B-D-N's Hair sepa-
    rated from her Head-dress, and hanging to-
    wards the Author" (Boswell) **4**:61

On Occult Philosophy (Agrippa von Nettesheim)
    See *De occulta Philosophia libri tres*

On our Religion to God, to Christ, and the Church
    (Newton) **35**:281

On Our Ridiculous Imitation of the French (But-
    ler) **43**:62

"On Parents & Children" (Boswell) **4**:36

"On Poetry" (Wollstonecraft) **50**:284

"On Poetry: A Rhapsody" (Swift) **1**:435

*On Poetry and Our Relish for the Beauties of Na-
    ture* (Wollstonecraft) **5**:426, 450

On Political Geography (Turgot)
    See *Plan d'un ouvrage sur la géographie
    politique*

"On Quotations" (Boswell) **4**:35, 37

"On Recollection" (Wheatley) **3**:413, 415, 419,
    432; **50**:173, 179, 189, 205, 211, 214, 227,
    234, 259-60

"On Reserve" (Boswell) **4**:34

On Royal Power (Las Casas) **31**:203

"On Sanazar's Being Honoured with Six Hundred
    Duckets by the Clarissimi of Venice, for
    Composing an Elegiak Hexastick of the City.
    A Satyre" (Lovelace) **24**:348, 354

On Scandals (Calvin)
    See *On the Scandals by Which Many Today Are
    Deterred and Some Even Alienated from the
    Pure Doctrine of the Gospel*

"On Seeing a Butterfly in the Street" (Fergusson)
    29:209, 230

"On Seeing a Wounded Hare Limp by Me Which
    a Fellow Had Just Shot at" (Burns) **3**:59

"On Sight of a Gentlewoman's Face in the Wa-
    ter" (Carew) **13**:18

"On Similarity among Authors" (Boswell) **4**:35

"On Sir Thomas Bodley's Library" (Vaughan)
    27:311

"On Sleeping in Church" (Swift) **1**:465

"On Some Commemorations of Thomson" (Burns)
    29:89

"On Suicide" (Boswell) **4**:35-6

"On the Accession of King George to the British

Throne" (Dennis)
See "A Poem upon the Death of Her Late Sacred Majesty Queen Anne, and the Most Happy and Most Auspicious Accession of His Sacred Majesty King George"
On the Advancement of Learning (Bacon) **18**:104, 108, 113, 131, 133-34, 136-37, 140, 142, 144, 146, 148, 153, 161, 163, 168, 170, 173-75, 177-79, 183, 186-87, 193, 195-96 **32**:107, 114-16, 133, 138-40, 144-45, 161, 163
"On the Alliance of Education and Government" (Gray)
See "Essay on the Alliance of Education and Government"
"On the Anniversary of Her Husband's Death" (Rowe) **44**:310
"On the Apothecary's Filling my Bills amongst the Doctors" (Barker) **42**:96
"On the Approach of Summer" (Warton)
See "Ode On the Approach of Summer"
On the Art of Persuasion (Pascal)
See *L'Art de Persuader*
"On the Assumption" (Crashaw)
See "In the Glorious Assumption of Our Lady, The Hymn"
On the Birth of Perceptible Things in Reason (Paracelsus) **14**:198
"On the Birth of the Prince of Wales" (Warton) **15**:461
"On the Birth-Day of Queen Katherine" (Killigrew) **4**:350
"On the bleeding wounds..." (Crashaw) **24**:53-4
"On the Choice of a Mistress" (Franklin)
See "Advice on Choosing a Mistress"
On the Christian Religion (Ficino)
See *De religione christiana*
"On the Cold Month of April 1771" (Fergusson) **29**:197, 219
On the Composition of Images, Signs and Ideas (Bruno)
See *De imaginum signorum et idearum compostione*
"On the Coronation of the Most August Monarch K. James II, and Queen Mary" (Prior) **4**:475
On the Councils of the Church (Luther) **37**:300
On the Creative Imitation of the Beautiful (Moritz)
See *Über die bildende Nachahmung des Schönen*
"On the Death of a Squirrel" (Franklin) **25**:141
"On the Death of a Very Young Gentleman" (Dryden) **21**:87
"On the Death of an Infant" (Wheatley) **3**:410
"On the Death of Dr. Toshack of Perth, a Great Homourist" (Fergusson) **29**:201
"On the Death of General Wooster" (Wheatley) **50**:242
"On the Death of George the Second" (Warton) **15**:461
"On the Death of His Mother" (Thomson) **16**:428-29
"On the Death of Lord President Dundas" (Burns) **29**:89
"On the Death of Mr. Richard West" (Gray)
See "Sonnet on the Death of Mr. Richard West"
"On the Death of Mr. Snider Killed by Richardson" (Wheatley) **3**:435
"On the Death of Mr. William Aikman, the Painter" (Thomson) **16**:428; **29**:428
"On the Death of My Dear Friend and Play-Fellow, Mrs. E. D. Having Dream'd the night before I heard thereof, that I had lost a Pearl" (Barker) **42**:100

"On the Death of the Rev. Mr. George Whitefield" (Wheatley) **50**:162, 191, 209, 212
See "An Elegiac Poem on the Death of George Whitefield"
"On the Death of the Reverend Dr. Sewall" (Wheatley) **3**:416, 436
On the Diseases That Deprive Man of Reason (Paracelsus)
See *De morbus amentium*
"On the distresses of the poor, exemplified in the life of a private centinel" (Goldsmith) **2**:103; **48**:
"On the Duke of Buckingham" (Carew) **13**:50
On the Eternity of God (Smart)
See *On the Eternity of the Supreme Being*
On the Eternity of the Supreme Being (Smart) **3**:366, 379, 394, 402
"On the Famous Voyage" (Jonson) **6**:347
"On the First of January 1657" (Philips) **30**:277
On the Formation and Distribution of Riches (Turgot)
See *Réflexions sur la formation et la distribution des richesses*
"On the Frontispiece of Isaacson's Chronology" (Crashaw) **24**:
On the Goodness of the Supreme Being (Smart) **3**:380, 395-97
On the Government of Florence after the Medici Restoration in 1512 (Guicciardini) **49**:259
"On the Hill and Grove at Billborow" (Marvell)
See "Upon the Hill and Grove at Billborow"
On the Immensity of the Supreme Being (Smart) **3**:379, 394, 399, 402
On the Interpretation of Nature (Diderot)
See *Pensées sur l'interprétation de la nature*
"On the Introduction of Learning into England" (Warton) **15**:458
"On the Juice of a Lemon" (Cowley) **43**:156
"On the Last Epiphany, or Christ Coming to Judgment" (Chatterton) **3**:127
"On the Late Captain Grose's Peregrinations Thro' Scotland" (Burns) **3**:71, 85-6
"On the Late Massacre in Piemont" (Milton) **9**:191
"On the Marriage of the King" (Warton) **15**:455; **15**:461
"On the Marriage of T.K. and C.C. the morning stormie" (Carew) **13**:57
On the Medium of Moral Government—Particularly Conversation (Edwards) **7**:129-30
On the Method of Minting Money (Copernicus)
See *Monetae cudendae ratio*
"On the Morning of Christ's Nativity" (Milton) **9**:198, 204-05, 228, 230; **43**:362, 396
On the Motion and Power of Water (Vinci) **12**:385, 405
"On the Music-bells" (Fergusson) **29**:217
On the Natural History of Religion (Hume) **7**:154-55, 157-58, 186, 196-99
On the Nobleness and Superiority of the Female Sex (Agrippa von Nettesheim)
See *De nobilitate et praeccelentia foeminei sexus*
On the Omniscience of the Supreme Being (Smart) **3**:366, 380, 394
On the Origin of Man (Paracelsus)
See *De generatione hominis*
On the Papacy in Rome, Against the Most Celebrated Romanist in Leipzig (Luther) **9**:125, 140, 148
On the Power of the Supreme Being (Smart) **3**:380, 394
On the Pretended Donation of Constantine

(Hutten)
See *De falso credita et ementita Donatione Constaini Magni*
"On the Profession of a Player" (Boswell) **4**:71
On the Progress of the Human Mind (Turgot)
See *Tableau philosophique des progrés successifs de lesprit humain*
"On the Province of God in the Government of the World" (Franklin) **25**:176
"On the Resemblance of Children to their Fathers" (Montaigne)
See "De l'affection des peres aux enfants"
On the Revolutions of Heavenly Bodies (Copernicus)
See *Nicolai Copernici Torunensi De Revolutionlbus orbium coelestium, Libri VI*
On the Roman Trinity (Hutten)
See *Vadiscus, sive Trias Romana*
On the Scandals by Which Many Today Are Deterred and Some Even Alienated from the Pure Doctrine of the Gospel (Calvin) **37**:93-94
"On the Shadow of Ideas" (Bruno)
See "De umbris idearum"
On the Spirit (Helvetius)
See *De l'esprit*
"On the Spring" (Gray)
See "Ode on Spring"
"On the Still surviving marks of our Savior's wounds" (Crashaw) **24**:
On the Sublime (Dennis) **11**:33
"On the Testimony of Conscience" (Swift) **1**:488
"On the Theatre: A Comparison between Laughing and Sentimental Comedy" (Goldsmith) **2**:107
"On the Third of September 1651" (Philips) **30**:278
"On the Townes Honest Man" (Jonson) **6**:342
On the Trinity (Swift) **1**:495
On the Ultimate Origination of Things (Leibniz) **35**:168
"On the Uncertain Hour of Death" (Petursson)
See "Um daudans óvíssan tíma"
On the Uncertainty and Vanity of the Arts and Sciences (Agrippa von Nettesheim)
See *De incertitudine et vanitate scientiarum declamatio inuectiua et excellentia verbi Dei*
On the Usefulness of the Stage (Dennis)
See *The Usefulness of the Stage to the Happiness of Mankind, to Government and to Religion*
On the Vanity of the Sciences (Agrippa von Nettesheim)
See *De incertitudine et vanitate scientiarum declamatio inuectiua et excellentia verbi Dei*
"On the Victory Obtained by Blake over the Spaniards" (Marvell) **4**:431
"On the water" (Crashaw) **24**:
"On the Works of Providence" (Wheatley)
See "Thoughts on the Works of Providence"
"On the wounds of Our Crucified Lord" (Crashaw) **24**:
"On Time" (Boswell) **4**:71
"On Time, Death, and Friendship" (Young)
See "The Complaint; or, Night Thoughts: Night the Second"
"On Tragedy" (Hume) **7**:163, 167
On Translating: An Open Letter (Luther) **9**:150
On True and False Religion (Zwingli) **37**:365
"On Truth" (Boswell) **4**:37
"On Two Green Apricots sent to Cowley by Sir Crashaw" (Crashaw) **24**:
On Universal History (Turgot)

See *Discours sur l'Histoire Universelle*
On Usury (Luther) **9**:134
"On Virtue" (Wheatley) **3**:412-13, 418, 432
"On Youth and Age" (Boswell) **4**:37
One Project for the Good of England; that is, our civil union is our civil safety (Penn) **25**:278, 298
"One that died of the Wind Colic" (Carew) **13**:18
1 The Honest Whore (Dekker)
   See *The Honest Whore*
The Onlookers (Hutten)
   See *The Spectators*
The Only Method of Attracting All Peoples to the True Faith (Las Casas) **31**:184, 187-88
"Onn Oure Ladies Chyrche" (Chatterton) **3**:130
"Open the Door to Me, O" (Burns) **3**:76
Opening of Youth (Jami)
   See *Fatihat al-shabáb*
"Opéra" (Marmontel) **2**:223
"L'opéra de Naples" (Rousseau) **9**:345
The Opera of Operas (Haywood) **44**:
Opera Omnia (Lipsius) **16**:271
Opera omnia (More) **9**:312
Opera Philosophica (Hobbes) **36**:151
Opera posthuma (Spinoza)
   See *B. D. S. Opera posthuma*
Opere (Machiavelli) **8**:135
Opere and Opere inedite (Guicciardini)
   See *Opere inedite de Francesco Guicciardini*
Opere inedite de Francesco Guicciardini (Guicciardini) **49**:196, 214, 266
Opere Varie Critiche (Castelvetro) **12**:45-6, 71
Ophelia (Fielding)
   See *The History of Ophelia*
Opinion Anent the Reformation of the Universities of St Androis (Buchanan) **4**:129
Opinion par alphabet (Voltaire) **14**:392
The Opportunities of the Fireside (Crebillon)
   See *Le hasard du coin du feu*
Optice (Newton)
   See *Opticks, or a Treatise of the Reflections Refractions Inflections and Colours of Light*
Opticks, or a Treatise of the Reflections Refractions Inflections and Colours of Light (Newton) **35**:285, 287, 292, 299, 303-04, 306-08, 323, 326, 328
Optics (Descartes) **35**:85-7, 91-3, 110
Optics (Marat) **10**:222
Opus Paramirum (Paracelsus) **14**:187, 198, 198-99
Opuscula (Andrewes)
   See *Opuscula quaedam posthuma*
Opuscula Latina (Holberg) **6**:266
Opuscula quaedam posthuma (Andrewes) **5**:22
Oráculo manual y arte de prudencia (Gracian y Morales) **15**:135-36, 139, 141, 143-48
"L'Oraison de Saint Julien" (La Fontaine) **50**:68
L'oraison Notre Dame (Christine de Pizan)
   See *L'oryson Notre Dame*
Oratio accusatoria (Guicciardini) **49**:264-65
Oratio consolatoria (Bruno) **27**:123
Oratio de dignitate hominis (Pico della Mirandola) **15**:321, 324-27, 333-35, 338, 341, 345-46, 348, 350, 354-57, 360
Oratio valedictoria (Bruno) **27**:120
Oration on the Dignity of Man (Pico della Mirandola)
   See *Oratio de dignitate hominis*
Orations of Divers Sorts Accomodated to Divers Places (Cavendish) **30**:190-1, 204, 207, 209, 235-36
Oratorio pro quodam doctorando (Agrippa von Nettesheim) **27**:40

Orazia (Aretino) **12**:6, 19, 26-7, 36
Order of the Gospel (Mather) **38**:260
"The Ordination" (Burns) **3**:71, 93, 95-6; **29**:13-14, 16, 18, 28, 41, 45, 59, 64; **40**:63, 100, 109
"Ordre" (Pascal) **35**:362, 372
Les oreilles du comte de Chesterfield (Voltaire) **14**:346, 359, 360
"Les Oreilles du Lievre" (La Fontaine) **50**:79
Orest und Pylades (Schlegel) **5**:280
Oreste (Voltaire) **14**:328
Oriental Eclogues (Collins)
   See *Persian Eclogues*
Oriental planeta evangelica epopeya sacropanegyrica al apostol grande de las Indias S. Francisco Xavier (Siguenza y Gongora) **8**:340
The Original and Progress of Satire (Dryden)
   See *A Discourse Concerning the Original and Progress of Satire*
Original Composition (Young)
   See *Conjectures on Original Composition in a Letter to the Author of Sir Charles Grandison*
"An Original Letter from a Gentleman of Scotland to the Earl of *** in London" (Boswell) **4**:53
Original Letters, Familiar, Moral and Critical (Dennis) **11**:17
Original Letters written during the reigns of Henry VI., Edward IV., and Richard III.
   See *Paston Letters*
The Original Power of the Collective Body of the People of England, Examined and Asserted (Defoe) **1**:121
Original Sin (Edwards)
   See *The Great Christian Doctrine of Original Sin Defended*
Original Stories from Real Life; with Conversations, Calculated to Regulate the Affections, and Form the Mind to Truth and Goodness (Wollstonecraft) **5**:426, 460
De originali peccato (Agrippa von Nettesheim) **27**:21
Origines (Newton)
   See *A Short Scheme of the True Religion*
Orlando furioso (Ariosto) **6**:21-3, 25-7, 29-41, 43-6, 48-59, 62-3, 65-6, 68-76, 79, 81-3
Orlando innamorato (Boiardo) **6**:86-91, 93-9, 101-04
Ornaments for the Daughters of Zion (Mather) **38**:167
Oroonoko; or, The Royal Slave (Behn) **1**:29-32, 34-6, 38, 41-2, 44-6, 49-51, 53-6; **30**:62-64, 66, 79, 86-9, 91; **42**:107-71
Orpharion **41**:177-78
Orthodox Confession (Calvin) **37**:91
L'oryson Notre Dame (Christine de Pizan) **9**:25, 46
Otho (Corneille)
   See *Othon*
Othon (Corneille) **28**:5, 31, 34-5, 41
"Our Lord in his Circumcision to his Father" (Crashaw) **24**:35, 39, 54
Outlaws of the Marshes (Lo Kuan-chung)
   See *Shui Hu Chuan*
Ovid's Banquet of Sense, A Coronet for My Mistress Philosophy (Chapman) **22**:51, 62, 69, 70-1, 76-7, 79
Ovid's Epistles (Dryden) **21**:72
"The Owl Describing Her Young Ones" (Winchilsea) **3**:456
The Owle **8**:14, 27, 30-1
Ox (Zwingli) **37**:378

Oxford Newsman's Verses (Warton) **15**:441, 462
The Oxford Sausage; or, Select Poetical Pieces: Written by the Most Celebrated Wits of the University of Oxford (Warton) **15**:441-42, 449-50
Paean (Erasmus) **16**:106
Page of Plymouth (Dekker) **22**:105
Pagina Doctorum (Towneley) **34**:251, 326
The Painter of His Own Dishonor (Calderon de la Barca)
   See *El pintor de su deshonra*
"The Painter Who Pleased No Body and Every Body" (Gay) **49**:30
"Painture" (Lovelace) **24**:328
The Palace Corridor; or, The Rival Friend (Corneille)
   See *La galerie du palais, ou l'amie rivale*
The Palace Disordered (Vega) **23**:385
"Palamon and Arcite" (Chaucer)
   See "Knight's Tale"
"Palamon and Arcite" (Dryden)
   See "Knight's Tale"
Palinodiæ (Buchanan) **4**:119, 138
"Palinodie" (Rousseau) **9**:340, 345
"Palm-Sunday" (Vaughan) **27**:300, 338
Pamela (Goldoni) **4**:273
Pamela; or, Virtue Rewarded (Richardson) **1**:365-66, 368, 371-72, 374, 377, 382-91, 395-99, 401-04, 406-10, 414-15, 418; **44**:192, 194, 197-200, 203-6, 209, 211-2, 215, 218-20, 223, 225, 229-30, 232, 237-40, 242, 244-6, 248-50, 252-3, 258, 272
Pamphilia to Amphilanthus (Wroth) **30**:340-41, 346-47, 353, 359-62, 369-71, 382-400
Pamphlet on the Plague (Paracelsus)
   See *Libell über die Pest*
Pandosto **41**:141-44, 148, 156-57, 159, 161, 165-66, 168, 171-72, 174-79
"A Panegerick to Sir Lewis Pemberton" (Herrick) **13**:341, 365, 376
"Panegyric" (Crashaw) **24**:60, 64
"Panegyric on Oxford Ale" (Warton) **15**:440, 450, 462-63
"Panegyrical Epistle to Mr. Thomas Snow" (Gay) **49**:28
"A Panegyrick on the Dean in the Person of a Lady in the North" (Swift) **1**:504
Panegyricus (Erasmus) **16**:106, 110
A Panegyrike Congratulatorie to the King's Majesty (Daniel) **24**:89, 125, 127
Panthea (Gay) **49**:33
Den pantsatte bondedreng (Holberg) **6**:278
"Pao Chu" (P'u Sung-ling) **3**:348
The Papers of Benjamin Franklin (Franklin) **25**:144
"Papers on the Imagination" (Addison) **18**:61
"Para quién escribo" (Aleixandre)
   See *Vidua Christiana*
"Parable Against Persecution" (Franklin) **25**:141
"Parables of Our Lord and Saviour Jesus Christ" (Smart) **3**:395
Parabolae (Erasmus) **16**:136
Paraclesis (Erasmus)
   See *Paraclesis ad Lectorem Pium*
Paraclesis ad Lectorem Pium (Erasmus) **16**:138, 149, 154
"Paradise" (Herbert) **24**:229, 277
Paradise Lost (Milton) **9**:165-73, 175-83, 185-93, 196-9, 201, 204, 206, 208, 211-22, 228-30, 233-7, 240-50, 252, 257-8, 260-62; **43**:333, 361-3, 365-71, 381, 391, 393, 396-7, 399, 401, 403-6, 408-9, 421
Paradise Regained (Milton) **9**:183, 189, 192, 200,

214, 217, 230, 233, 235-7, 246-9; **43**:332-4, 361-2, 379, 390, 393-4, 396, 401, 409

"A Paradox" (Lovelace)   **24**:305, 342, 346, 349

Paradoxe sur le comédien (Diderot)   **26**:103, 109, 117, 120, 131, 144, 161, 168

Paradoxes and Problems (Donne)
   See *Juvenilia; or, Certaine paradoxes, and problems*

Paradoxical Questions... (Newton)
   See *The Mathemathical Principles of Natural Philosophy*

Paragranum (Paracelsus)
   See *Das Buch Paragranum*

A Parallel of Poetry and Painting (Dryden)   **3**:236-38; **21**:90

"Parallel with other great cities" (Howell)   **13**:424

Parallèle des anciens et des modernes en ce qui regarde les arts et les sciences (Perrault)   **2**.259, 274-80, 283

Paramirum (Paracelsus)
   See *Opus Paramirum*

"A Paranaeticall, or Advisive Verse, to his friend, Master John Wicks" (Herrick)   **13**:378

Paraphrase and Notes on the Epistles of St. Paul (Locke)   **35**:203

Paraphrase of Hebrews (Erasmus)   **16**:157

Paraphrase of the Psalms (Buchanan)
   See *Psalmorum Dauidis paraphrasis poetica, nunc primum edita, authore Georgio Buchanano, Scoto, poetarum nostri saeculi facilè principe*

"A Paraphrase on Part of the Book of Job" (Young)   **3**:467, 492, 497; **40**:352, 371

"Paraphrase on 'Te Deum'" (Dennis)
   See "Part of the 'Te Deum' Paraphras'd, in Pindarick Verse"

Parasceve (Bacon)   **18**:148, 152, 187

Parasitaster; or, The Fawn (Marston)   **33**:187, 195, 197, 199, 204, 211, 215, 234, 237, 239

Parayso occidental, plantado y cultivado por la liberal benefica mano de los muy Catholicos (Siguenza y Gongora)   **8**:343

"Pardoner's Prologue" (Chaucer)   **17**:118, 122-23

"Pardoner's Tale" (Chaucer)   **17**:98, 118, 121-23, 178, 195-200

Parlement (Chaucer)
   See *Parlement of Foules*

Parlement of Foules (Chaucer)   **17**:45, 72, 77-8, 82, 91-7, 105, 108, 114-17, 149, 173, 189, 223, 227

The Parlement of hefne (N-Town)   **34**:178-85, 188-9, 192, 202-3, 209, 240, 243

Parley of Beasts (Howell)   **13**:424

Parley of Trees (Howell)   **13**:424

Parliament (Burke)   **36**:73, 77

Parliament of Fowls (Chaucer)
   See *Parlement of Foules*

Parliament of Heaven (N-Town)
   See *The Parlement of hefne* (N-Town)

"The Parliament of Roses, to Julia" (Herrick)   **13**:389, 402

Parliamenti Angliae Declaratio, & c. (Marvell)   **4**:395

"The Parlyamente of Sprytes" (Chatterton)   **3**:129

Parmentator (Mather)   **38**:158

Parnassus (Quevedo)   **23**:155

"A Parodie" (Herbert)   **24**:225, 273-74

Parrot (Haywood)   **44**:129-30

"Parsons' Cause" (Henry)   **25**:213, 217, 235

"Parson's Prologue" (Chaucer)   **17**:215-16

"Parson's Tale" (Chaucer)   **17**:47, 119-21, 172-73, 176, 178-80, 189, 200, 209, 213, 220,

241-44

"Part of the 'Te Deum' Paraphras'd, in Pindarick Verse" (Dennis)   **11**:14, 51

"Partes Instauratio Secundae Delineatio et Argumentum" (Bacon)   **18**:187

Parthenopoeia (Howell)   **13**:441

Parthian Truimph (Siguenza y Gongora)
   See *Triumpho parthenico que en glorias de María Santissima immaculadamente concebida*

"A Particular Providence and a Future State" (Hume)   **7**:155

"The Parties of Great Britain" (Hume)   **7**:152

"Parting with Lucasia A Song" (Philips)   **30**:287

De partu virginis (Sannazaro)   **8**:320, 322-23, 326-28, 330, 332, 336-37

Parva magna, magna nulla (Marston)   **33**:222

The Parvenu Countryman (Marivaux)
   See *Le paysan parvenu*

Pasquil the Playne (Elyot)   **11**:61, 71-2, 84, 89, 92

Pasquin (Fielding)   **1**:249; **46**:55-6, 81, 95, 161, 166

Pasquinades (Aretino)
   See *Giudizi*

Passio Discrepta (Herbert)   **24**:294

"The Passion" (Milton)   **9**:204, 206

"The Passion" (Vaughan)   27

The Passion (Chester)
   See *Crucifixion* (Chester)

Passion I (N-Town)   **34**:172-3, 175-6, 186, 197-200, 208, 210-11, 220, 225-32, 239-45

Passion II (N-Town)   **34**:172-3, 175-6, 197-200, 208, 210-11, 220, 225-31, 129-41, 243

"Passion of Byblis" (Dennis)   **11**:4-5, 15

"The Passion of Christ" (Lanyer)   **30**:249

The Passion of Jesus (Aretino)
   See *La Passione di Gesù*

Passion Play (York)
   See *Crucifixio Cristi* (York)

"The Passionate Man's Pilgrimage..." (Raleigh)   **39**:97, 121, 123

"The Passionate Shepherd to his Love" (Herrick)   **13**:318

The Passionate Shepherd to His Love (Marlowe)   **22**:337; **47**:383

La Passione di Gesù (Aretino)   **12**:20, 35

"The Passions: An Ode for Music" (Collins)   **4**:211-12, 214, 216, 220-22, 232, 234; **40**:132, 135, 139-41, 144, 146, 152, 159, 162, 170, 172-73

The Pastime of Pleasure (Hawes)   **17**:336-43, 347-59, 361-67

"Pastime with Good Company" (Henry VIII)   **10**:145

Paston Correspondence
   See *Paston Letters*

Paston Letters   **17**:431-74

"Pastoral Dialogue" (Killigrew)   **4**:350

"Pastoral II. Noon" (Fergusson)   **29**:171, 196-97, 219, 236

"Pastoral III. Night" (Fergusson)   **29**:171, 196-97, 214, 238

"Pastoral in the Manner of Spenser" (Warton)   **15**:441

"Pastoral: To Amarantha" (Lovelace)   **24**:303, 306, 316

La pastorale comique (Moliere)   **10**:283

"A Pastorall Dialogue" (Carew)   **13**:59, 62

"A Pastorall upon the birth of Prince Charles" (Herrick)   **13**:395

"Pastorals" (Pope)   **3**:266-67, 270, 274, 290, 294, 322, 334-35

Pastorals   **8**:10, 31

Pastorals (Lyttelton)   **10**:202

"Eine Pastoraltheologie in Versen" (Andreae)   **32**:92

Los Pastores de Belen (Vega)   **23**:356, 359

"A Pastrolall Dialogue..." (Sidney)
   See "A Dialogue betweene two shepheards, Thenot and Piers, in praise of Astraea"

A Patch-Work Screen for the Ladies; or Love and Virtue Recommended: In a collection of Instructive Novels (Barker)   **42**:58-9, 63-6, 69-70, 73, 75, 77-85, 87-93, 96, 98-9

Paterna (Mather)   **38**:173, 202-03, 217

"Patie and Pegie" (Ramsay)   **29**:330

"Patie and Roger" (Ramsay)   **29**:322, 328, 330, 332

"Patient Griselda" (Perrault)
   See "Griselidis"

Patient Grissil (Dekker)   **22**:93, 108, 111, 119, 127, 132, 138

"The Patriarch" (Burns)   **3**:98

The Patriot (Johnson)   **15**:208

The Patriots (Munford)   **5**:189-97

A Patterne of Catechisticall Doctrine (Andrewes)   **5**:23, 28

"Paulo Purganti" (Prior)   **4**:455, 461-62, 467

Pax Vobiscum (Aretino)   **12**:16

Le paysan parvenu (Marivaux)   **4**:353-57, 360-62, 368, 373-75, 379, 387

"Un paysan son seigneur offensa" (La Fontaine)   **50**:67

"Peace" (Herbert)   **24**:265, 274

"Peace" (Vaughan)   **27**:293, 339, 380

"The Peace Which Christ Gives His True Followers" (Hume)   **7**:119

"The Peach in Brandy" (Walpole)   **2**:500, 507

"The Pearl" (Herbert)   **24**:234, 238-41, 243, 250, 272

The Peasant in His Nook (Vega)
   See *El villano en su rincón*

"Peau d'ane" (Perrault)   **2**:253-57, 261, 279, 286

"A Pedant" (Butler)   **16**:52

Peder Paars (Holberg)   **6**:258, 265-66, 269-71, 273, 278, 282

Pedro de Urdemalas (Cervantes)   **6**:180-81; **23**:100, 102

A Peep behind the Curtain (Garrick)   **15**:98, 101-02, 122

"Peggy and Jenny" (Ramsay)   **29**:322

"Peggy, Now the King's Come" (Ramsay)   **29**:

La Peinture (Perrault)   **2**:259

Pelegrino (Vega)
   See *El peregrino en su patria*

"Peligros de habler y de caller y lenguaje en el silencio" (Quevedo)   **23**:183

La Pénélope moderne (Lesage)   **28**:207, 210

Penelope's Web   **41**:165, 178

Penetential Psalms (Aretino)
   See *I sette salmi de la penitenzia di David*

Pennsylvania Charter (Penn)
   See *Charter of Liberties*

Pensees (Pascal)   **35**:337-43, 346, 348-51, 355-72, 388-89, 391-93

Pensées chrétiennes (Perrault)   **2**:283

Pensées et fragments inédits de Montesquieu (Montesquieu)   **7**:329, 332, 339, 342, 346, 348-49, 357, 361

Pensées philosophiques (Diderot)   **26**:71, 94, 112, 120, 146-47, 166-67

"Pensées sur la clarté du discours" (Marivaux)   **4**:371

Pensées sur le gouvernement (Voltaire)   **14**:401

Pensées sur l'interprétation de la nature (Diderot)

26:71, 73, 85-6, 114, 119, 140, 145-46, 148, 157, 167-68

Pentecost (Chester) **34**:121

Le Père de famille (Diderot) **26**:69, 104-06, 110, 117

Pere Pickle (Smollett)
See *The Adventures of Peregrine Pickle*

Le père prudent et equitable; ou, Crispin l'heureux forbe (Marivaux) **4**:358

Peregrini in Patria errores (Andreae) **32**:93

Peregrini (Towneley) **34**:251-2, 311, 321, 326

El peregrino en su patria (Vega) **23**:338, 388, 400

Peremešnik (Chulkov) **2**:14-15, 17-24, 26-7

Perfect Description of the People and Country of Scotland (Howell) **13**:420, 424

El perfecto caballero (Castro) **19**:13-14

"Peri Bathous; or, The Art of Sinking in Poetry" (Pope) **3**:317, 321, 323-24, 328-29

Peribáñez (Vega)
See *Peribáñez y el comendador de Ocaña*

Peribáñez and the Commander of Ocaña (Vega)
See *Peribáñez y el comendador de Ocaña*

Peribáñez y el comendador de Ocaña (Vega) **23**:360, 362, 365-68, 370, 372-73, 391, 393, 401

Perimedes, the Blacksmith **41**:156, 176

"The Perjured Beauty" (Manley) **1**:306-08

Pernille's Brief Ladyship (Holberg)
See *Pernilles korte frøikenstand*

Pernilles korte frøikenstand (Holberg) **6**:263, 277

The Perplex'd Duchess (Haywood) **44**:139, 145

El perro del hortelano (Vega) **23**:344, 364-65, 367-68, 370, 372

El Perseo (Vega) **23**:393

Persian Eclogues (Collins) **4**:209-11, 215, 217, 229, 233; **40**:132, 134, 139-41, 144, 146, 152, 159, 162, 170, 172-73

The Persian Letters (Lyttelton)
See *Letters from a Persian in England to His Friend at Ispahan*

Persian Letters (Montesquieu)
See *Lettres persanes*

Persiles y Sigismunda (Cervantes)
See *Los trabajos de Persiles y Sigismunda*

Personal Narrative (Edwards) **7**:98, 101, 116

"The Personal Union" (Taylor) **11**:370

"Persuasions to Love" (Carew)
See "To A.L. Perswasions to Love"

"Perswasions to Enjoy" (Carew) **13**:59

A Perswasive to Moderation (Penn) **25**:333

Pertharite, roi des Lombards (Corneille) **28**:5, 28, 35, 38, 58

Pertharites, King of the Lombards (Corneille)
See *Pertharite, roi des Lombards*

"Pervigilium Veneris" (Parnell) **3**:251, 253-54

Peter Denies Jesus: Jesus Examined by Caiaphas (York) **34**:333, 388

"The Peter-Penny" (Herrick) **13**:331

"Le petit chaperon rouge" (Perrault) **2**:254-55, 257-58, 260, 262, 266-67, 271-74, 280, 282, 285

"Le Petit Chien qui secoue de l'argent et des pierreries" (La Fontaine) **50**:66, 116, 120, 122

Le petit maître corrigé (Marivaux) **4**:368, 378

"Le petit poucet" (Perrault) **2**:254-56, 258, 260-61, 266, 280-81, 284

"The Petition for an Absolute Retreat" (Winchilsea) **3**:451-52, 454-56, 458

"The Petition of the Left Hand" (Franklin) **25**:104, 141

"Phaedra" (Prior) **4**:455

Phaenomena Quaedam Apocalyptica (Sewall) **38**:347, 354

Phaenomena Universi (Bacon) **18**:187

Phaethon (Dekker) **22**:111

"The Phaeton and the One-Horse Chair" (Warton) **15**:441, 462

Phaeton in the Suds (Fielding) **1**:220

Phalarismus (Hutten) **16**:239-41, 245

The Phantom Lady (Calderon de la Barca)
See *La dama duende*

Pharaoh (Towneley) **34**:249, 251-2, 267, 273, 320, 325

Pharsamon; ou, Les nouvelles folies romanesques (Marivaux) **4**:378, 385-86

Phèdre (Racine) **28**:293-95, 301-02, 303-06, 308-09, 313, 315-17, 331-37, 343-44, 346-47, 350-52, 355-56, 358, 363, 370-71, 374, 378-80, 382, 384

"Philander" (Young) **3**:472

Philaster; or, Love Lies a-Bleeding (Fletcher) **33**:40-52, 54, 59-61, 63, 69-71, 75, 77, 80, 83-86, 90-91, 97

Philebus Commentary (Ficino) **12**:194

Philidore and Placentia (Haywood) **1**:283; **44**:139-40, 142

Philip Chabot, Admiral of France (Chapman)
See *The Tragedy of Chabot, Admiral of France*

"Phillis's Age" (Prior) **4**:461

"Phillis's Reply to the Answer..." (Wheatley) **3**:437; **50**:148, 241

"Philomela" (Sidney) **19**:329

Philomela **41**:140, 156, 177-78

Philomela (Vega) **23**:374

Le philosophe anglais; ou, Histoire de Monsieur Cléveland, Fils naturel de Cromwell (Prevost) **1**:328-29, 333-35, 337-39, 341, 343, 347, 352, 357-59

"A Philosopher" (Butler) **16**:50

The Philosopher (Aretino)
See *Il filosofo*

"The Philosopher and the Lover; to a Mistress dying" (Davenant) **13**:195, 205

"The Philosopher's Devotion" (More) **9**:296

"The Philosophers Disquisition to the Dying Christian" (Davenant) **13**:204-06

Philosophia Christi (Erasmus) **16**:142

Philosophia Ethica rejicienda (Campanella) **32**:236

De philosophia occulta (Agrippa von Nettesheim)
See *De occulta Philosophia libri tres*

Philosophia Pythagorica (Campanella) **32**:211

Philosophia realis (Campanella) **32**:226, 239-40

Philosophia sagax (Paracelsus) **14**:200, 203

Philosophia sensibus demonstrata (Campanella) **32**:236

Philosophical and Physical Opinions (Cavendish) **30**:186, 200, 204, 207, 209, 220-1, 229

A Philosophical Enquiry into the Origin of Our Ideas of the Sublime and Beautiful (Burke) **7**:4, 6, 39

A Philosophical Essay on Man, Being an Attempt to Investigate the Principles and Laws of the Reciprocal Influence of the Soul on the Body (Marat) **10**:220, 222-23, 231, 239

Philosophical Essays (Hume) **7**:138, 154

Philosophical Essays concerning Human Understanding (Hume) **7**:164

Philosophical Fancies (Cavendish) **30**:200, 220

Philosophical Letters (Cavendish) **30**:202, 219-20, 222-3

Philosophical Poems (More) **9**:295, 298, 303, 306, 308, 320

The Philosophical recognition of the True, Universal Religion against Antichristianism and Machiavellism (Campanella)
See *Atheismus triumphatus*

Philosophical Review of the Successive Advances of the Human Mind (Turgot) **26**:370

Philosophical Rudiments (Hobbes) **36**:140, 143

Philosophical Thoughts (Diderot)
See *Pensées philosophiques*

The Philosophical Writings of Descartes (Descartes) **35**:109-10

La philosophie de l'histoire (Voltaire) **14**:357, 383, 387

"Philosophy and Religion Are Sisters" (Ficino) **12**:174

Philotas (Daniel)
See *The Tragedy of Philotas*

Philotas (Lessing) **8**:66, 109

The Phoenix (Middleton) **33**:262, 276-77, 288-89, 291, 310-11

"The Physician's Stratagem" (Manley) **1**:306-08

"Physician's Tale" (Chaucer) **17**:117, 196-97, 200

"Physiognomy" (Montaigne)
See "De la phisionomie"

Physiologia (Lipsius) **16**:258

"The Picture of Little T. C. in a Prospect of Flowers" (Marvell) **4**:427, 434-35, 438, 442

Pieces (Howell) **13**:437

"Pierce Gaveston, Earle of Cornwall" **8**:29-30, 33

Pierce Penilesse his supplication to the Divell (Nashe) **41**:302, 308, 370-71, 375

Piers Plowman (Langland) **19**:56-204

"Piesn" (Kochanowski) **10**:154, 156, 160-61, 170, 175-76

"Piesn Swietojanska o Sobótce" (Kochanowski) **10**:151-54, 161

Piesni (Kochanowski) **10**:161, 167, 176

"Piety, a Vision" (Parnell)
See "Piety; or, The Vision"

"Piety; or, The Vision" (Parnell) **3**:255, 257-58

"The Pig, the Goat, and the Sheep" (Dennis) **11**:47

"The Pigmies and the Cranes" (Addison) **18**:29

Pilate's Wife's Dream and the Trial before Pilate (N-Town) **34**:179, 186, 188

The Pilfered Snuffbox (Schlegel)
See "Die entführte Dose"

"A Pilgrim" (Bradstreet)
See "As Weary Pilgrim"

The Pilgrim in his Homeland (Vega)
See *El peregrino en su patria*

Pilgrim in His Own Land (Vega)
See *El peregrino en su patria*

"The Pilgrimage" (Herbert) **24**:262, 264-66

"A Pilgrimage for Religion's Sake" (Erasmus)
See "Religious Pilgrimage"

The Pilgrim's Progress from This World to That Which Is to Come (Bunyan) **4**:143-73, 178-99, 202

The Pilgrims (Towneley)
See *Peregrini* (Towneley)

"The Pillar of Fame" (Herrick) **13**:358, 391

"A Pimp" (Butler) **16**:54

Pindaric Odes (Cowley)
See *Pindarique Odes*

Pindaric Odes (Ronsard) **6**:411

"A Pindarick Ode on the King...Occasion'd by the Victory at Aghrim" (Dennis) **11**:48

"Pindarick Poem on Habbakuk" (Rowe) **44**:279

"A Pindarick Poem upon the Hurricane" (Winchilsea) **3**:451, 454

"Pindarick to the Athenian Society" (Rowe) **44**:280

Pindarique Odes (Cowley) **43**:142, 153, 159, 166, 168, 170, 173, 187.

"A Pindarique on His Majesties Birth-Day" (Prior) **4**:475

El pintor de su deshonra (Calderon de la Barca) **23**:9, 13, 41, 43, 45, 64

"Pious Selinda" (Congreve) **5**:85

"Pious Thoughts and Ejaculations" (Vaughan) **27**:337

"The Pious Woman" (Kochanowski)
  See "Na nabozna"

"Piscatoria II" (Sannazaro) **8**:334-35

"Piscatoria III" (Sannazaro) **8**:332, 335

Piscatoriae (Sannazaro)
  See *Eclogae piscatoriae*

Piscatura (Hutten)
  See *De piscatura Venetorum heroicum*

De piscatura Venetorum heroicum (Hutten) **16**:238, 241

Place royale; or, The Extravagant Lover (Corneille)
  See *La place royale, ou l'amoureux extravagant*

La place royale, ou l'amoureux extravagant (Corneille) **28**:32, 46-8, 55-6

Placets au roi (Moliere) **10**:281

Les plaideurs (Racine) **28**:297-98, 302, 312, 321, 343, 369, 381, 383

The Plain-Dealer (Wycherley) **8**:380, 382, 384-97, 402-03, 406, 409, 415, 420, 423-26, 429-30, 432; **21**:346-49, 354, 359-60, 363, 374-76, 379-81, 385, 388-89, 391-94, 396

Plain-Dealing with a traducing Anabaptist (Penn) **25**:287, 291

"Plaine-Path'd Experience, th'Unlearneds Guide"
  See "Sonnet 46"

"Plainte pour une Absence" (Malherbe) **5**:171

Plaisirs de l'ile enchantée (Moliere) **10**:311; **28**:229

Plan de législation criminelle, ouvrage dans lequel on traite des délits et des peines, de la force des preuves et des présomptions . . . (Marat) **10**:221

Plan d'un ouvrage sur la géographie politique (Turgot) **26**:364, 371-72, 381, 392, 394

Plan d'une université pour le gouvernement de Russie (Diderot) **26**:120

Plan for a Campaign (Zwingli) **37**:393

Plan for the Union of the Colonies (Penn) **25**:318, 322

Plan for Two Discourses on Universal History (Turgot) **26**:344

Plan of a Constitution (Marat)
  See *La Constitution ou Projet de déclaration des Droits de l'homme et du citoyen, suivi d'un Plan de constitution juste, sage et libre*

The Plan of a Dictionary of the English Language; Addressed to the Right Honourable Philip Dormer, Earl of Chesterfield (Johnson) **15**:197, 206, 250-51

Plan of a Mémoire on Taxes (Turgot) **26**:374

Plan of a Work on Commerce, the Circulation and Interest of Money, the Wealth of States (Turgot) **26**:374

Plan of Union (Penn)
  See *Plan for the Union of the Colonies*

Planetomachia **41**:165, 172, 176, 178

Plantarum (Cowley) **43**:153-4

The Platonic Lovers (Davenant) **13**:175-76, 181, 187, 196-200, 215

Platonic Theology (Ficino)
  See *Theologia platonica de immortalitate animorum*

"Platonick Philosopher" (Vaughan) **27**:311

"The Platonist" (Hume) **7**:153

"A Player" (Butler) **16**:26

A Playhouse to Let (Davenant) **13**:190

Plays (Cavendish) **30**:225

Plays (Gay) **49**:184

The Plays, Histories, and Novels of the Late Ingenious Mrs. Behn (Behn) **1**:29

Plays Never Before Printed (Cavendish) **30**:225

The Plays of John Marston (Marston) **33**:202

The Plays of William Shakespeare, in Eight Volumes, with the Corrections and Illustrations of Various Commentators; To which are added Notes by Sam Johnson (Johnson) **15**:197, 225, 307, 313

Pleasant Comedie of the Gentle Craft (Dekker)
  See *The Shoemaker's Holiday, or the Gentle Craft*

The Pleasant Historie of John Winchcomb, in his younger years called Iacke of Newberie **41**:73-75, 77-78, 82, 87-89, 92-95, 97-98, 100-01, 104-11, 115, 117-18, 120, 125, 127-32

Pleasure Reconcild to Vertue (Jonson) **6**:337; **33**:178-79

"The Pleasures of Melancholy" (Warton) **15**:431, 433, 435, 439, 445, 448, 454, 456, 460

The Pleasures of the Imagination (Addison) **18**:7, 18, 20, 37, 61

The Plebian (Steele) **18**:352-54

A Plot and No Plot (Dennis) **11**:5, 12, 14

"The Plots" (Davenant) **13**:205

"Plutarch's Lives" (Dryden) **21**:52, 58

Plutus's Council-Chamber (Grimmelshausen)
  See *Rathstübel Plutonis*

El poder en el discreto (Vega) **23**:402

"A Poem as the Corpus Delicti" (P'u Sung-ling)
  See "Shih-yen"

Poem on the Disaster of Lisbon (Voltaire)
  See *Poème sur le désastre de Lisbonne*

"Poem on the Last Day" (Young) **3**:466-69, 483, 485, 487, 497; **40**:352, 359, 371

A Poem Sacred to the Memory of Sir Isaac Newton (Thomson) **16**:384-85, 399, 401, 406, 419, 421, 423, 425, 428; **29**:404, 415, 424, 429; **40**:309

"A Poem to the Memory of Mr. Congreve" (Thomson)
  See "To the Memory of Mr. Congreve"

"A Poem upon the Death of Her Late Sacred Majesty Queen Anne, and the Most Happy and Most Auspicious Accession of His Sacred Majesty King George" (Dennis) **11**:15, 26, 50

"A Poem Upon the Death of His Late Highness the Lord Protector" (Marvell)
  See "Poem upon the Death of O. C."

"Poem upon the Death of O. C." (Marvell) **4**:398, 417, 431; **43**:252, 255, 278, 280-1, 297

"Poème lyrique" (Marmontel) **2**:223

Poème sur la loi naturelle (Voltaire) **14**:378, 380

Poème sur le désastre de Lisbonne (Voltaire) **14**:364, 378, 381, 388, 390

Poèmes (Ronsard) **6**:407, 410, 427

Poems **8**:18, 26, 42

Poems (Bradstreet) **4**:87

Poems (Chapman) **22**:51-2, 54, 74-7

Poems (Cowley) **43**:187

Poems (Winchilsea) **3**:448

Poems (Killigrew) **4**:347

Poems (Milton) **9**:262

Poems (More)
  See *Philosophical Poems*

Poems (Philips) **30**:286, 298, 303, 313, 316, 320-3, 327

Poems (Ramsay) **29**:324, 337, 348-50, 359

Poems (Ronsard)
  See *Poèmes*

Poems (Taylor) **11**:381

Poems & a Defense of Rime (Daniel) **24**:96

Poems and Fables (Gay) **49**:5

Poems and Fancies (Cavendish) **30**:199-201, 206, 220, 226

"Poems and Letters" (Wheatley) **50**:146

Poems and Letters by Mr. Dennis (Dennis) **11**:4

Poems Ascribed to Robert Burns, the Ayrshire Bard (Burns) **3**:49

Poems by Christopher Smart (Smart) **3**:392

Poems by Thomas Carew, Esquire (Carew) **13**:9, 27-8, 30, 52

Poems, Chiefly in the Scottish Dialect (Burns) **3**:47-8; **29**:28, 90, 92-3

Poems for Young Ladies, in Three Parts (Goldsmith) **2**:81

Poems in Burlesque (Dennis) **11**:47

Poems Lyrick and Pastorall **8**:17

The Poems of Ossian (Macpherson) **29**:242, 252, 254, 273, 286

The Poems of Phillis Wheatley (Wheatley) **3**:421

The Poems of the Late Christopher Smart, M. A., Fellow of Pembroke College, Cambridge, Consisting of His Prize Poems, Odes, Sonnets, and Fables, Latin and English Translations (Smart) **3**:371

Poems on Several Occasions (Parnell) **3**:258

Poems on Several Occasions (Prior) **4**:466

Poems on Several Occasions (Smart) **3**:375

Poems on Several Occasions, Never Before Printed (Davenant) **13**:206

Poems on Several Occasions, written by Philomela (Rowe) **44**:278-79, 281, 309-10, 313

Poems on Various Subjects, Religious and Moral, by Phillis Wheatley, Negro Servant to Mr. John Wheatley of Boston, in New England, 1773 (Wheatley) **3**:407, 409-11, 417, 421, 431; **50**:157, 159, 161-63, 201-02, 211, 217-21, 223, 231-32, 235, 237-39, 242, 245, 249, 255, 257-59, 261.

Poems upon Several Occasions (Gay) **49**:5

Poems upon Several Occasions, with a Voyage to the Island of Love (Behn) **1**:29; **42**:125

Poems, with the Tenth Satyre of Iuvenal Englished (Vaughan) **27**:294, 315-17, 329, 369

Poeresta que estaba (Calderon de la Barca) **23**:67

The Poetaster (Jonson) **6**:302, 304, 306, 335-36; **33**:103-6, 132, 139, 141, 149-55, 157, 159-60, 163, 173-74

"Poetesses hasty Resolution" (Cavendish) **30**:200

Poetica (Campanella) **32**:234

Poetica d'Aristotele vulgarizzata et sposta (Castelvetro) **12**:46, 50, 62, 69, 71

"Poetical Banquet" (Erasmus) **16**:140

"Poetical Question" (Rowe) **44**:280

Poetical Recreations: Consisting of Original Poems, Songs, Odes, etc. With Several New Translations (Barker) **42**:58, 62, 74-5, 81, 96, 98-102

Poetical Works (Butler) **43**:117

The Poetical Works of David Garrick, Esq. (Garrick) **15**:97, 114

The Poetical Works of Edward Taylor (Taylor) **11**:343, 355

Poetical Works of Samuel Daniel (Daniel) **24**:

Poeticall Blossoms (Cowley) **43**:189

Poetics (Dennis)   **11**:33

Poétique française (Marmontel)   **2**:223

"A Poet's Welcome to His Love-Begotten Daughter" (Burns)   **3**:85, 87; **29**:21, 28; **40**:86

"The Poet's Wish" (Ramsay)   **29**:330

Le point d'honneur (Lesage)   **28**:199, 201

The Poison and The Antidote (Calderon de la Barca)   **23**:9

Poisoned and Cured (Calderon de la Barca)   **23**:64

Pokazi (Beer)   **5**:56

Politica (Lipsius)
    See *Politicorum sive civilis doctrinae libri sex, qui ad principatum maxime spectant*

Política de Dios, Gobierno de Cristo (Quevedo)   **23**:154, 169-73, 180

Political Discourses (Hume)   **7**:190

The Political History of the Devil (Defoe)   **1**:136

Political Tracts (Johnson)   **15**:208

Political Treatise (Spinoza)   **9**.423

The Politician (Gracian y Morales)
    See *El Político Don Fernando el Católico*

Político (Gracian y Morales)
    See *El Político Don Fernando el Católico*

El Político Don Fernando el Católico (Gracian y Morales)   **15**:143-45, 165

Politicorum libri sex (Lipsius)
    See *Politicorum sive civilis doctrinae libri sex, qui ad principatum maxime spectant*

Politicorum sive civilis doctrinae libri sex, qui ad principatum maxime spectant (Lipsius)   **16**:251, 254, 262, 265-66, 268-69, 277-79

Politics (Lipsius)
    See *Politicorum sive civilis doctrinae libri sex, qui ad principatum maxime spectant*

Politique naturelle (Holbach)   **14**:152, 154-56, 160, 162, 168

Der politische Feuermäuer-kehrer (Beer)   **5**:56

Den politiske kandestøber (Holberg)   **6**:258, 273, 276, 282-83

Polly (Gay)   **49**:8, 19, 30, 71, 76-77, 87-88, 93, 96, 101, 123-124, 147-148, 153-155, 159-160, 162, 173

"Polwarth on the Green" (Ramsay)   **29**:315, 329

Polyeucte (Corneille)   **28**:4, 9-12, 14, 16-17, 19, 21-3, 27, 30, 33, 38, 41, 56, 58

Polyeuctes (Corneille)
    See *Polyeucte*

Poly-Olbion   **8**:5-8, 10-15, 17-21, 24-6, 29, 40-3, 45-7

Pompey: A Tragedy (Philips)   **30**:275-6, 283-6, 289, 291, 293-4, 303, 306, 309-11, 313, 315-19, 322,

Pompey the Great; his faire Cornelias Tragedie; effected by her Father andHusbands downecast death and fortune (Kyd)
    See *Tragedy*

"Poor Mailie's Elegy" (Burns)
    See "The Death and Dying Words of Poor Mailie"

Poor Richard's Almanack (Franklin)   **25**:109, 111, 114-15, 117-18, 122, 133, 140, 145, 149, 156-62, 166

Pope ein Metaphysiker (Lessing)   **8**:98

"Popish Pamphlet cast in London streets not long after the city was burned" (Taylor)   **11**:366

"A Popish Priest" (Butler)   **16**:50, 53

Popular Elaboration of the Chronicle of the Three Kingdoms (Lo Kuan-chung)
    See *San-kuo-chih yeni-i*

"The Popular Superstitions of the Highlands of Scotland" (Collins)
    See "An Ode on the Popular Superstitions of the Highlands of Scotland, etc."

Porfiar hasta morir (Vega)   **23**:391

Portatif (Voltaire)
    See *Dictionnaire philosophique*

Portefeuille de J.-B. Rousseau (Rousseau)   **9**:335

Portraits (Reynolds)   **15**:407, 419

The Posthumous Poems of Dr. Thomas Parnell Containing Poems Moral and Divine (Parnell)   **3**:257

Posthumous Works (Butler)   **16**:30; **43**:74

Posthumous Works (Locke)   **35**:203

Posthumous Works of the Author of a Vindication of the Rights of Woman (Wollstonecraft)
    See *Letters to Imlay*

The Posthumous Works of William Wycherley, Esq., in Prose and Verse (Wycherley)   **8**:416

"Posting" (Montaigne)   **8**:203

El postrer duelo de España (Calderon de la Barca)   **23**:70

" Le pot de terre et le pot de fer" (La Fontaine)   **50**:128

"Pour le roy allant chastier la rebellion des Rochelois et chasser les Anglois qui en leur faveur estoient descendus en l'isle de Ré" (Malherbe)   **5**:166, 168, 171, 185

"Pour le Sonnet de Cassandre" (Malherbe)   **5**:171

"Pour Mme la D... de N... sur le gain d'un procès" (Rousseau)   **9**:344

"Pour une personne convalescente" (Rousseau)   **9**:342-43

"The power in the people" (Herrick)   **13**:395

The Power of Being Discreet (Vega)
    See *El poder en el discreto*

The Power of Love (Manley)   **1**:306, 308, 312

Die Pracht zu Landheim (Schlegel)   **5**:277-79

Practica (Paracelsus)   **14**:199

Praedones (Hutten)
    See *The Robbers*

De Praeparatione ad Mortem (Erasmus)   **16**:154-55

Praescriptio (Lipsius)   **16**:271-73

"Praise II" (Herbert)   **24**:274-75

"The Praise and Happinesse of the Countrie-Life; Written Originally in Spanish by Don Antonio de Guevara" (Vaughan)   **27**:311

The Praise of Folly (Erasmus)
    See *Moriae encomium*

Praise of Matrimony (Erasmus)   **16**:146

"Praised be Dianas faire and harmleslight" (Raleigh)   **31**:268-70, 273, 280

"Praxis" (Newton)   **35**:295, 297, 300

"The Prayer" (Herbert)   **24**:263, 271

Prayer (Andrewes)
    See *Scala coeli: Nineteene Sermons concerning Prayer*

"Prayer II" (Herbert)   **24**:268

"Prayer before Sermon" (Andrewes)   **5**:42-3

"Prayer for the King on his going to Limoges" (Malherbe)   **5**:167

"A Prayer in the Prospect of Death" (Burns)   **29**:79

"Prayer to Ben Jonson" (Herrick)   **13**:323

"A Prayer to the Wind" (Carew)   **13**:28

Prayers and Meditations (Johnson)   **15**:209, 225, 240, 243, 246

Preces (Andrewes)
    See *Preces privatae, graece, et latine*

Preces privatae, graece, et latine (Andrewes)   **5**:21-4, 26-7, 33-6, 38, 42

Les précieuses ridicules (Moliere)   **10**:275, 277, 280-81, 283, 286, 290-93, 299-300, 310, 316-20; **28**:243-44, 255-56, 260, 265-66, 269, 274

The Precious Pearl (Jami)
    See *al-Durrah al-Fákhira*

"Predestination" (Prior)   **4**:473

"The Preexistency of the Soul" (More)   **9**:313, 330-31

"Preface" (Luther)   **9**:118

"Preface" (Ramsay)   **29**:337

"The Preface" (Taylor)   **11**:393, 401-03

Preface (Schlegel)
    See *Vorrede des Uebersetzers zu Der Ruhmredige*

"Preface to *Eneydos*" (Caxton)   **17**:13

Preface to Gondibert (Davenant)   **13**:202-03, 207, 209-10, 212

Preface to Ovid's Epistles (Dryden)   **3**:217; **21**:113

"Preface to *Polychronicon*" (Caxton)   **17**:22, 25-6

"Preface to Shakespeare" (Johnson)   **15**:214-15, 220, 236, 270, 307-08, 310-13

"Preface (to the Dictionary)" (Johnson)   **15**:250-51

"Preface to the Fables" (Dryden)   **3**:217; **21**:112

Prefaces, Biographical and Critical, to the Works of the English Poets (Johnson)   **15**:199-200, 203-04, 209-10, 220-21, 229, 231, 237, 241, 243, 251, 270, 285, 287, 298

Prejudice Corrected (Marivaux)
    See *Prejudice Corrected*

Le Préjugé vaincu (Marivaux)   **4**:364, 369

Prelude on the Babylonian Captivity of the Church (Luther)
    See *De captivitate Babylonica ecclesiae praeludium*

"A Preparation to Prayer" (Winchilsea)   **3**:451

Preparatory Meditations before my Approach to the Lords Supper. Chiefly upon the Doctrin preached upon the Day of administration. (Taylor)   **11**:343-44, 346, 351, 354-55, 358-59, 363, 367-68, 372-73, 377-78, 380-82, 384-86, 392, 394-95, 397-400

The Prerogative of Parliaments in England (Raleigh)   **31**:237, 252

The Presence (Cavendish)   **30**:226, 229

"The Present" (Herrick)   **13**:317

Present Discontents (Burke)
    See *Thoughts on the Cause of the Present Discontents*

A Present for a Serving Maid (Haywood)   **1**:293

The Present Means and Brief Delineation of a Free Commonwealth (Milton)   **9**:185; **43**:338, 397

The Present State of Affairs (Burke)   **7**:47

The Present State of All Nations (Smollett)   **46**:190, 204

The Present State of Wit (Gay)   **49**:23-24

"The Presentation of Christ in the Temple" (Smart)   **3**:376, 378. 401-02

Presentation of Mary (N-Town)
    See *Presentation of the Virgin* (N-Town)

Presentation of the Virgin (N-Town)   **34**:223

A Preservative agaynste Deth (Elyot)   **11**:62, 71, 83

Prêtres démasqués (Holbach)   **14**:153

A Pretty Story (Hopkinson)   **25**:246-47, 253-54, 265, 268-70

A Pretty Story Written in the Year of our Lord 1774, by Peter Grievous, Esq; A. B. C. D. E. (Hopkinson)
    See *A Pretty Story*

"The Priest" (Kochanowski)
    See "O Kapelanie"

Priestcraft Dangerous to Religion and Government (Dennis)
    See *The Danger of Priestcraft to Religion and*

Government

Priestcraft distinguished from Christianity (Dennis) **11**:15, 26

Prigozhaya povarikha (Chulkov) **2**:13-18, 23-5

Prima Pastorum (Towneley) **34**:251, 253-4, 256-60, 265, 267, 274-6, 278, 284-87, 311, 318, 321-4

Primal History (Bacon)
See *Historia Prima*

"Primero sueño" (Juana Ines de la Cruz) **5**:146-54, 156

Primitive Christianity Revived (Penn) **25**:331

"The Primrose" (Carew) **13**:30

"The Primrose" (Donne) **10**:13, 33, 36-7; **24**:152

"Primrose" (Herrick) **13**:311

The Prince (Machiavelli)
See *Il principe di Niccholo Machivello*

The Prince in Disguise (Marivaux)
See *The Prince in Disguise*

The Prince or Maxims of State (Raleigh) **31**:237, 239

Le prince travesti (Marivaux) **4**:366-67

"The Princess Lily" (Pope) **3**:335

"Princess Lotus Bloom" (P'u Sung-ling)
See "Lien-hua kung-chu"

The Princess of Clèves (La Fayette)
See *La Princesse de Clèves*

The Princess of Elis (Moliere)
See *La princesse d'Élide*

La princesse de Babylon (Voltaire) **14**:346, 359

La Princesse de Chine (Lesage) **28**:210

La Princesse de Clèves (La Fayette) **2**:136-40, 142-51, 153-71

La Princesse de Montpensier (La Fayette) **2**:138-39, 144, 151-52, 155-58, 161, 165-66

La princesse d'Élide (Moliere) **10**:282-83, 291, 311, 320, 325, 327; **28**:229, 236, 256, 260

The Principal Navigations, Voyages, Traffiques and Discoveries of theEnglish Nation (Hakluyt) **31**:132, 136-9, 141, 143, 147, 149, 152, 158-62, 168

El Príncipe constante (Calderon de la Barca) **23**:14, 18-19, 32, 36, 61, 64-5

Principes de la Nature et de la Grace fondes en Raison (Leibniz) **35**:130, 148, 179

Principia (Newton)
See *The Mathemathical Principles of Natural Philosophy*

Principia Philosophiae (Descartes) **35**:72, 74, 79, 84-5, 87, 91-6, 99-100, 102, 109, 112-14, 116, 118

De principiis (Gray)
See *De principiis cogitandi*

De Principiis atque Originibus (Bacon) **18**:187

De principiis cogitandi (Gray) **4**:329; **40**:198, 218, 228

De Principio Individui (Leibniz) **35**:132

The Principles of Descartes (Spinoza)
See *Renati Des cartes principiorum philosophiae pars I. et II. more geometrico demonstratae per Benedictum de Spinoza*

Principles of Nature and of Grace (Leibniz)
See *Principes de la Nature et de la Grace fondes en Raison*

The Principles of Philosophy (Descartes)
See *Principia Philosophiae*

Principles of Political Right (Rousseau) **36**:289

"Principles Which Lead and Direct Philosophical Enquiries Illustrated by the History of Astronomy" (Smith) **36**:331

Printz Adimantus und der königlichen Princessin Ormizella Liebes-Geschict (Beer) **5**:52, 54-5

"Prioress's Tale" (Chaucer) **17**:60, 68, 119, 177-78

Private Correspondence (Pepys) **11**:241

"Pro Lena apologia" (Buchanan)
See "Pro Lena apologia, Eleg. III"

"Pro Lena apologia, Eleg. III" (Buchanan) **4**:134-35

Pro populo anglicano defensio, contra Claudii Anonymi (Milton) **9**:159, 163, 201, 252; **43**:332, 339, 360-1, 364, 366, 370-2, 374, 377-81, 391, 401, 411, 413, 415, 420

Processus Crucis (Towneley) **34**:311

Processus Noe cum Filius (Towneley) **34**:258-60, 281, 311

Processus Prophetarum (Chester) **34**:96

Processus Prophetarum (Towneley) **34**:270-5, 282, 312

Processus Talentorum (Towneley) **34**:250, 252, 308, 311, 313

Proclamation (N-Town) **34**:238-43

"The Prodigal Son" (Marvell) **4**:431

Prodromi sive Anticipatationes Philosophiae Secundae (Bacon) **18**:187

Profane Feast (Erasmus) **16**:143, 145

"Profession du vicaire Savoyard" (Rousseau) **14**:247, 260, 301, 310; **36**:249

"Profession of Faith" (Rousseau)
See "Profession du vicaire Savoyard"

"The Proffer" (Vaughan) **27**:376-77, 379

Profitable Meditations Fitted to Man's Different Condition (Bunyan) **4**:167-68

Progne y Filomena (Castro) **19**:7-8

Prognostications (Paracelsus) **14**:187

Prognosticon vetus in Aggripinarum archivis inventum (Agrippa von Nettesheim) **27**:42-43

"The Progress of Beauty, 1720" (Swift) **1**:458, 461, 483-84

"The Progress of Discontent" (Warton) **15**:434, 440, 463

The Progress of Love, in Four Eclogues (Lyttelton) **10**:196-97, 200, 203-05

"The Progress of Marriage" (Swift) **1**:453

"The Progress of Poesy" (Gray) **4**:280-81, 283-84, 291-92, 300-02, 309, 312-13, 317, 321, 332-33; **40**:199-200, 205, 218, 231-32, 235, 237, 239-41, 243

"The Progress of Poetry" (Gray)
See "The Progress of Poesy"

"The Progress of Virtue" (Swift) **1**:458

The Progresse of the Soule (Donne) **10**:4, 14, 19-23, 52-3, 62

"Progymnasmata" (More) **10**:430

Progymnasmata (Brahe)
See *Astronomiae instauratae progymnasmata*

"Prohemye to *Polychronicon*" (Caxton)
See "Preface to *Polychronicon*"

"The Prohibition" (Donne) **10**:36

A Project for the Advancement of Religion (Swift) **1**:492

Project on the Corsican Constitution (Rousseau) **36**:301

Prólogo (Gracian y Morales) **15**:171

"The Prologue" (Bradstreet) **4**:95, 105-06, 110, 114; **30**:117-20, 137, 139

"Prologue" (Chaucer)
See "General Prologue"

"Prologue" (Taylor) **11**:384, 394, 401-03

"Prologue before the Queen" (Prior) **4**:455

"Prologue in Praise of Music" (Hopkinson) **25**:259

The Prologue of Demon (N-Town) **34**:176, 179, 183, 185-6, 188-9

The Prologue of Johannes Baptista (N-Town) **34**:189

"Prologue of the Nun's Priest's Tale" (Chaucer) **17**:137

"Prologue on the Old Winchester Playhouse" (Warton) **15**:462

"Prologue, Spoke by One of the Young Gentlemen" (Ramsay) **29**:337

"Prologue Spoken by Mr Woods" (Burns) **40**:110

"Prologue to Aurenzebe" (Ramsay) **29**:336

"Prologue to *Blanchardin and Eglantine*" (Caxton) **17**:29

"Prologue to *Charles the Great*" (Caxton) **17**:16, 23

"Prologue to *Eneydos*" (Caxton) **17**:7, 10, 16-17, 19

"Prologue to *Le Morte d'Arthur*" (Caxton) **17**:30-1, 33

"Prologue to the *Golden Legend*" (Caxton) **17**:14

"Prologue to the Monk's Tale" (Chaucer) **17**:122, 137

"Prologue to *The Recuyell*" (Caxton) **17**:7

"Prologue to the University of Oxford" (Dryden) **21**:83, 88

"Prologue to the Wife of Bath's Tale" (Chaucer) **17**:55, 81, 122, 181, 189, 202, 206, 210-11, 213, 229-31, 236-38, 240-41

Promenade du sceptique (Diderot) **26**:112

Promus of Formularies and Elegancies (Bacon) **18**:133

Prophecies (Vinci) **12**:418

"The Prophecy" (Chatterton) **3**:123

"A Prophecy" (Hopkinson) **25**:248, 258

"The Prophecy of Famine" (Churchill) **3**:140, 142-46, 148, 152-56, 160, 163

A Prophesy of the White Kings Dreadful Deadman Explaned (Lilly) **27**:135, 142, 146

Prophetical Merline (Lilly)
See *England's Prophetical Merline*

Les Prophéties de M. Michel Nostradamus (Nostradamus) **27**:151-52, 161-63, 173, 178, 188, 190-92, 195-98

The Prophets (N-Town) **34**:170, 178-9, 181, 183-5, 188-9, 191-2, 200

Prophets of Antichrist (Chester) **34**:126, 134

Prophets of Doomsday (Chester) **34**:121

The Prophets (Towneley) **34**:282, 326

"Proporzec albo Hold Pruski" (Kochanowski) **10**:175

Proposal for Establishing a High Court of Honour (Hopkinson) **25**:252

A Proposal for Putting a Speedy End to the War (Dennis) **11**:19

A Proposal for the Universal Use of Irish Manufacture (Swift) **1**:513-14

"Proposalls of Certaine Expedients for the Preventing of a Civil r Now Feard" (Milton) **43**:337

Proposals for Printing the Dramatick Works of William Shakespeare (Johnson) **15**:311, 313

"The Proposed New Version of the Bible" (Franklin) **25**:141

A Proposition for the Advancement of Experimental Philosophy (Cowley) **43**:152

Prose Observations (Butler) **16**:50; **43**:133-4

"A Proselite" (Butler) **16**:50

Prosopopeia, Containing the Tears of the Holy, Blessed, and Sanctified Mary, Mother of God (Lodge) **41**:204-05

"Prosopopoia; or, Mother Hubberds Tale" (Spenser) **5**:312, 329, 345, 356; **39**:338

The Prospect: being the Fifth Part of Liberty (Thomson) **16**:374

"Prospectus" (Johnson)
See *The Plan of a Dictionary of the English Language; Addressed to the Right Honourable Philip Dormer, Earl of Chesterfield*
The Prostation of the Faith (Calderon de la Barca) **23**:8
"The Protégé" (Chulkov)
See "Stavlennik"
"Protestation to Julia" (Herrick) **13**:327
Prothalamion; or, A Spousall Verse (Spenser) **5**:311, 313, 329, 332, 347, 349, 356; **39**:305
"Protogenes and Apelles" (Prior) **4**:455
Proud Melchio (Grimmelshausen)
See *Der stoltze Melcher*
Prouverbes moraux (Christine de Pizan) **9**:45
"Providence" (Herbert) **24**:274-75
"Providence" (Vaughan) **27**:338
Providencia de Dios, padeciada de los que la niegan y gozada de los que las confiesan: doctrina estudiada en los gusanos y persecuciones de Job (Quevedo) **23**:154
Provincial Letters (Pascal)
See *Lettres provinciales*
La provinciale (Marivaux) **4**:369
The Provok'd Husband (Vanbrugh)
See *A Journey to London*
The Provok'd Wife (Vanbrugh) **21**:278, 281-84, 287, 289-90, 292-94, 296, 298-99, 301, 314-15, 318-20, 322-28, 333-36
The Provoked Wife (Vanbrugh)
See *The Provok'd Wife*
Proximus and Lympida (Grimmelshausen)
See *Proximus und Lympida*
Proximus und Lympida (Grimmelshausen) **6**:247-48
The Prudent Man (Goldoni) **4**:250
The Prudent Revenge (Vega) **23**:374, 378
La prueba de los amigos (Vega) **23**:393, 398
Psallterz Dawidów (Kochanowski) **10**:151, 155, 158, 161-62, 167, 170, 173-74
"Psalm 23" (Crashaw) **24**:4, 20, 53, 55, 76-7
"A Psalme or Hymne to the Graces" (Herrick) **13**:391
Psalmes (Sidney) **19**:309-10, 312, 315; **39**:143, 150-53, 155-62, 163, 165, 180-89, 191
Psalmorum Dauidis paraphrasis poetica, nunc primum edita, authore Georgio Buchanano, Scoto, poetarum nostri saeculi facilè principe (Buchanan) **4**:119, 124, 130
"Psalms" (Smart)
See *A Translation of the Psalms of David, Attempted in the Spirit of Christianity, and Adapted to the Divine Service*
Psalms (Kochanowski) **10**:172
Psalms of David (Smart)
See *A Translation of the Psalms of David, Attempted in the Spirit of Christianity, and Adapted to the Divine Service*
Psalter of David (Kochanowski)
See *Psallterz Dawidów*
Psalterium Americanum (Mather) **38**:229
Pseudo-Martyr: Wherein Out of Certaine Propositions and Gradations, This Conclusion is evicted. That Those Which Are of the Romane Religion in this Kingdome, may and ought to take the Oath of Allegiance (Donne) **10**:11, 39, 89; **24**:176-77, 179, 181, 186, 205, 209
Psiché (Moliere) **10**:275, 283
"Psychathanasia platonica: or, A Platonicall Poem of the Immortality of Souls" (More) **9**:295, 311-15, 327-31

"Psyche's Song" (More) **9**:320
Psychodia platonica: or, A Platonicall Song of the Soul (More) **9**:294, 296, 302, 312, 320, 330-31
Psychopannychia (Calvin) **37**:131, 133-36
"Psychozoia: or, A Christiano-Platonicall Display of Life" (More) **9**:302-04, 309, 312-13, 315, 320-21, 327-28, 330
Publiciste de la Révolution française (Marat)
See *Le publiciste parisien, journal politique, libre et impartial . . .*
Le Publiciste parisien (Marat)
See *Le publiciste parisien, journal politique, libre et impartial . . .*
Le publiciste parisien, journal politique, libre et impartial . . . (Marat) **10**:220-21, 227-29, 232, 234, 236
Publick Spirit (Dennis)
See *An Essay upon Public Spirit; being a Satire in Prose upon the Manners and Luxury of the Times, the chief Sources of our present Parties and Divisions*
The Publick Wooing (Cavendish) **30**:189
La pucelle (Voltaire) **14**:328, 338, 354, 396-97, 399-400, 413
"De pueris" (Erasmus) **16**:198-202
Pulcheria (Corneille)
See *Pulchérie*
Pulchérie (Corneille) **28**:5, 16, 33-5, 41
"The Pulley" (Herbert) **24**:233, 273
The Punctilious Ladies (Goldoni)
See *Le femmine puntigliose*
Punishment without Revenge (Vega)
See *El castigo sin venganza*
Purgation (N-Town) **34**:198, 200
El purgatono de San Patricio (Calderon de la Barca) **23**:17-22
Purgatorio de l'inferno (Bruno) **27**:68
Purgatory of Hell (Bruno)
See *Purgatorio de l'inferno*
The Purgatory of St. Patrick (Calderon de la Barca) **23**:8
Purificacio Marie (Towneley) **34**:326
Purification (Chester)
See *Christ among the Doctors* (Chester)
Purification of Mary (N-Town) **34**:170, 172-3, 188, 192, 216
Purification of Mary: Simeon and Anna Prophesy (York) **34**:343
The Purification (Towneley)
See *Purificacio Marie* (Towneley)
The Puritan and the Papist (Cowley) **43**:181
"A (Puritan) Fanatic" (Butler) **16**:27
La putta onorata (Goldoni) **4**:250, 256, 265-67, 269-70, 272-73
Pygmalion's Image (Marston)
See *The Metamorphosis of Pygmalion's Image*
Le Pyrrhonisme de l'histoire (Voltaire) **14**:383
"Qi gui" (P'u Sung-ling) **49**:313
"Qua si fa elmi di calici e spade" (Michelangelo) **12**:369
"Quaerit Jesum" (Crashaw)
See "Luke 2, 'Quaerit Jesum suum Maria.'"
Quaestiones Physiologicae, ethicae et politicae (1613) (Campanella) **32**:202-04, 226, 236
"Quaestiones quaedam philosophicae" (Newton) **35**:295, 298
The Quaker a Christian (Penn) **25**:291
Quakerism a New Nick-Name for Old Christianity (Penn) **25**:290
"Quam Pulchra Es" (Henry VIII) **10**:146
"Quand je suis vingt ou trente mois sans retourner en Vendômois" (Ronsard) **6**:417

"Quand j'estois libre" (Ronsard) **6**:432-33
"Quand vous serez bien vieille" (Ronsard) **6**:409, 417
"A Quarreler" (Butler) **16**:27
Le quart livre des faicts et dictz heroiques du noble Pantagruel (Rabelais) **5**:215-16, 224-25, 233-35, 238-40, 249-50, 252, 255-56, 258-59
Les quatre premiers livres de la Franciade (Ronsard) **6**:406-07, 409-10, 414, 416-17, 420-22, 424, 431-32
"Que philosopher, c'est apprendre à mourir" (Montaigne) **8**:236, 238
"Queen and Huntress" (Jonson) **6**:305
Queen Catharine; or, The Ruines of Love (Pix) **8**:257, 260-63, 268-69, 271-72, 275
Queenes (Jonson)
See *The Masque of Queens*
The Queens Arcadia, A Pastoral Traj-Comedy (Daniel) **24**:98, 122, 134-37, 140
"The Queer" (Vaughan) **27**:323
Querela (Agrippa von Nettesheim) **27**:48
Querela Pacis (Erasmus) **16**:132, 154-55, 173, 182, 198
Querelae (Hutten) **16**:229
"Queries" (Newton) **35**:285
Querimonia Pacis (Erasmus)
See *Querela Pacis*
The Quest of Cynthia **8**:9, 17, 34
"The Question" (Prior)
See "The Question, to Lisetta"
"The Question, to Lisetta" (Prior) **4**:460-61, 466
Questions (Turgot) **26**:373
Questions sur l'Encyclopédie (Voltaire) **14**:367, 370, 380, 392
La Queue de la vérité (Lesage) **28**:206
"Quickness" (Vaughan) **27**:338, 344, 394
"Quip"
See "Qvippe for an Vpstart Courtier"
"The Quip" (Herbert) **24**:239, 284, 287
Quis aberret a janua (Erasmus) **16**:196
Quod reminiscentur (Campanella) **32**:234
Quotidiana (Mather) **38**:202
Quæstiones Epistolicæ (Lipsius) **16**:263
"Qvippe for an Vpstart Courtier" **41**:151, 179
"A Rabble" (Butler) **16**:54
Ragionamenti (Aretino)
See *Ragionamento della Nanna e della Antonia*
Ragionamento de le Corti (Aretino) **12**:20
Ragionamento della Nanna e della Antonia (Aretino) **12**:4-6, 12, 14, 20-1, 23-6, 31-2, 35-7
The Raising of Lazarus (N-Town) **34**:192
La raison par alphabet (Voltaire) **14**:392
The Rambler (Johnson) **15**:189-91, 195-96, 198-201, 207, 218, 251, 259-61, 266-67, 273-74, 285, 287, 289, 306-07, 309
The Rambler, 4 (Johnson) **15**:237
The Rambler, 20 (Johnson) **15**:262
The Rambler, 32 (Johnson) **15**:243
The Rambler, 68 (Johnson) **15**:309
The Rambler, 73 (Johnson) **15**:267
The Rambler, 76 (Johnson) **15**:268
The Rambler, 78 (Johnson) **15**:266
The Rambler, 86 (Johnson) **15**:239
The Rambler, 89 (Johnson) **15**:213, 240
The Rambler, 92 (Johnson) **15**:239
The Rambler, 125 (Johnson) **15**:309
The Rambler, 154 (Johnson) **15**:237
The Rambler, 159 (Johnson) **15**:268
The Rambler, 167 (Johnson) **15**:309
The Rambler, 168 (Johnson) **15**:239
The Rambler, 177 (Johnson) **15**:241

Title Index

The Rambler, 183 (Johnson) **15**:267
The Rambler, 188 (Johnson) **15**:266
The Rambler, 190 (Johnson) **15**:244
The Rambler, 203 (Johnson) **15**:291
Rameau's Nephew (Diderot)
    See *Le Neveu de Rameau*
"A Ranter" (Butler) **16**:52
"The Rantin' Dog the Daddy o't" (Burns) **3**:86;
    29:22, 55; **40**:87
The Rape of the Lock (Pope) **3**:267-71, 273, 275-
    76, 279-82, 287, 289-91, 295-96, 298-99,
    304, 307, 310-14, 317, 335
*Rape upon Rape; Or, The Justice Caught in His
    Own Trap* (Fielding) **1**:250; **46**:102, 105
*Rape upon Rape; or, The Justice Caught in His
    Own Trap* (Fielding) **46**:
"A Rapture" (Carew) **13**:11-12, 19-20, 24, 26,
    28, 30-1, 34-7, 39, 56-60
The Rash Resolve (Haywood) **1**:292; **44**:160
Rasselas (Johnson)
    See *The History of Rasselas, Prince of Abissinia*
"Le Rat de ville et le rat des champs" (La Fontaine)
    50:94
"Le Rat et l'huitre" (La Fontaine) **50**:88
"Le Rat qui s'est retire du monde" (La Fontaine)
    50:84, 98, 100-101, 103
Rathstübel Plutonis (Grimmelshausen) **6**:247
Ratio Disciplinae (Mather) **38**:165
Ratio Fidei (Zwingli) **37**:352,354
Ratio panaria Allensteinensis (Copernicus) **45**:91
*Ratio seu Methodus compendio perveniendi ad
    veram theologiam* (Erasmus) **16**:149, 151
Ratio Status (Grimmelshausen) **6**:247-48
Ratio Verea Theologiae (Erasmus) **16**:154
*Rational Account of the Main Doctrines of the
    Christian Religion Attempted* (Edwards)
    7:128
De ratione studii (Erasmus) **16**:136, 146-47, 154,
    187
"Rattlin' Roarin' Willie" (Burns) **3**:67, 86
The Raven's Almanack (Dekker) **22**:97, 118
Rays of the Flashes (Jami)
    See *Ash'i'atu 'l Lama'át*
"Reactio" (Marston) **33**:221-23
The Reader (Steele) **18**:354
*The Readie and Easie Way to Establish a Free
    Commonwealth* (Milton) **9**:162-63, 184;
    43:333-5, 337-8, 340-42, 358, 384-5, 396,
    404
*Reason against Railing, and Truth against Fic-
    tion* (Penn) **25**:287, 291
The Reason of Church Government (Milton)
    9:192, 203, 250, 252; **43**:349, 391, 407, 414
*The Reasonableness of Christianity, as Delivered
    in the Scriptures* (Locke) **7**:259, 281-82,
    290; **35**:202, 204, 217, 265
*Reasons for Restoring Some Prayers and Direc-
    tions as They Stand in the Communion Ser-
    vice of the First English Reformed Liturgy*
    (Collier) **6**:209
"Rebel Families" (P'u Sung-ling)
    See "Tao-hu"
"A Rebus by I. B." (Wheatley) **3**:4ll, 433
A Receipt for Stewing Veal (Gay) **49**:7
*Recent Phenomena in the Celestial World, Book
    II, about the brilliant Comet (stella caudata)
    which was seen from the end of the
    (first)third of November in the year 1577 to
    the end of Jan. in the following year* (Brahe)
    See *Tychonis Brahe Dani, De Mundi aetherei
    recentioribus phaenomenis Liber secundus,
    qui est de illustri stella caudata ab elapso
    fere triente Nouembris anno MDLXXVII*

*usque in finem Januarii sequentis conspecta.
    Recmil des pièces mises au théâtre franeais*
    (Lesage) **28**:205
"Recollection" (Wheatley)
    See "On Recollection"
Records of the Strange (P'u Sung-ling)
    See *Liao-chai chih-i*
The Recruiting Officer (Farquhar) **21**:126, 128-
    29, 132-33, 135, 138-39, 143-44, 149-54,
    157-58, 161, 166-69, 171-72, 176, 178-81
"Red and white roses" (Carew) **13**:11
"A Red, Red Rose" (Burns)
    See "My Luve Is Like a Red, Red Rose"
Redargutio philosophiarum (Bacon) **18**:153-54,
    187; **32**:114, 126, 187
"Redemption" (Brooke) **1**:62
"Redemption" (Herbert) **24**:252, 256, 262-63,
    273-74, 292-93
"Reeve's Tale" (Chaucer) **17**.171, 193, 201-02
Reflections (Turgot)
    See *Réflexions sur la formation et la distribu-
    tion des richesses*
*Reflections Critical and Satyrical, upon a Late
    Rhapsody call'd An Essay upon Criticism*
    (Dennis) **11**:22
Reflections on the French Revolution (Burke)
    See *Reflections on the Revolution in France and
    on the Proceedings in Certain Societies in
    London Relative to That Event*
*Reflections on the Revolution in France and on
    the Proceedings in Certain Societies in Lon-
    don Relative to That Event* (Burke) **7**:7-9,
    14, 20, 23, 26-7, 32, 34, 37, 41, 50-1, 55,
    60-2; **36**:73-74, 81, 91, 95-100
Reflections upon an Essay on Criticism (Dennis)
    See *Reflections Critical and Satyrical, upon a
    Late Rhapsody call'd An Essay upon Criti-
    cism*
*Reflections upon the Present State of England, and
    the Independence of America* (Day) **1**:106,
    108
"The Reflexion" (Taylor) **11**:352, 360, 363, 384
Réflexions critiques sur Longin (Boileau-
    Despreaux) **3**:29, 39
*Reflexions on the Public Situation of the King-
    dom* (Young) **40**:334
*Réflexions sur la formation et la distribution des
    richesses* (Turgot) **26**:345,373-76
*Réflexions sur le caractère de quelques princes et
    sur quelques événements de leur vie*
    (Montesquieu) **7**:360-62
"Réflexions sur les coquettes" (Marivaux) **4**:380
Réflexions sur les langues (Turgot) **26**:362
Réflexions sur Longin (Boileau-Despreaux)
    See *Réflexions critiques sur Longin*
Reformation Writings (Luther)
    See *Die Reformationsschriften*
Die Reformationsschriften (Luther) **9**:140
*The Reform'd Coquet; or, The Memoirs of
    Amoranda* (Davys) **1**:98-102; **46**:19-21, 23-
    5, 27, 30-5, 37-8, 41-3
Réfutation d'Helvétius (Diderot) **26**:118, 143,
    149, 155, 170
Refutation of Helvetius (Diderot)
    See *Réfutation d'Helvétius*
The Refutation of Machiavelli's Prince (Frederick
    the Great)
    See *Anti-Machiavel*
Refutation of Philosophies (Bacon)
    See *Redargutio philosophiarum*
"Regeneration" (Herbert) **24**:264-65
"Regeneration" (Vaughan) **27**:328, 340, 352-56,
    364, 386, 389-90

The Regicide (Perrault) **2**:357-58
Regicide (Smollett) **46**:187, 233, 239, 257
Register (Burke)
    See *The Annual Register*
Régrets sur ma Vieille Robe de Chambre (Diderot)
    26:73, 119
Regulae ad Directionem Ingenii (Descartes)
    35:72, 74-5, 79-85, 91 94-6, 100, 110, 114,
    118, 123
Rehabilitations of Horace (Lessing)
    See *Rettungen des Horaz*
The Rehearsal at Goatham (Gay) **49**:123-124
The Rehearsall Transpros'd (Marvell) **4**:394,
    399-400, 429, 455; **43**:291, 298, 300-1
Rei Christianae et Litterariae Subsidia (Andreae)
    32:102
Reign of Henry the Second (Lyttelton)
    See *The History of the Life of King Henry the
    Second and of the Age in Which He Lived*
Reisen eines Deutschen in England im Jahr 1782
    (Moritz) **2**:227, 229, 233-34, 244-46
*Reisen eines Deutschen in Italien in den Jahren
    1786 bis 1788* (Moritz) **2**:233, 246
Rejectiuncula (Lipsius) **16**:254
"Rejoice in the Lamb" (Smart)
    See "Jubilate Agno"
"The Relapse" (Vaughan) **27**:339
"The Relapse" (Young)
    See "The Complaint; or, Night Thoughts: Night
    the Fifth"
The Relapse; or, Vertue in Danger (Vanbrugh)
    See *The Relapse; or, Virtue in Danger*
The Relapse; or, Virtue in Danger (Vanbrugh)
    21:278-84, 286, 288-90, 293-94, 296-306,
    308-11, 313-14, 316, 318-24, 326-29, 331-
    36
The Relapser (Vanbrugh)
    See *The Relapse; or, Virtue in Danger*
Relation (Cavendish) **30**:212
Relation autobiographique (Marie de
    l'Incarnation) **10**:251-54
Relation du banissement des Jésuites de la Chine
    (Voltaire) **14**:370
Relation d'un voyage de Paris en Limousin (La
    Fontaine) **50**:128
Relations (Marie de l'Incarnation)
    See *Relation autobiographique*
Relazioni (Machiavelli) **8**:128
La Religieuse (Diderot) **26**:95, 129, 136, 147,
    149, 155, 161-62, 169
Religio Laici; or, A Layman's Faith (Dryden)
    3:184, 188, 191, 196, 204, 208, 216, 221,
    235, 240-43; **21**:51, 56, 58, 67-9, 71-2, 88,
    115, 120
"Religion" (Vaughan) **27**:328, 353, 371, 379,
    390
Religious Affections (Edwards)
    See *A Treatise concerning Religious Affections*
"Religious Banquet" (Erasmus)
    See "Religious Treat"
Religious Courtship (Defoe) **1**:122
"Religious Pilgrimage" (Erasmus) **16**:118, 141,
    194-95
Religious Symposium (Erasmus)
    See *Convivium Religiosum*
"Religious Treat" (Erasmus) **16**:117-18, 142
"The Relique" (Donne) **10**:13, 18, 36, 55, 62,
    103; **24**:155, 195-97
*Reliques of Robert Burns, Consisting Chiefly of
    Original Letters, Poems, and Critical Ob-
    servations on Scottish Songs* (Burns) **3**:49
Remains (Butler)
    See *The Genuine Remains*

Remains (Butler)
See *The Genuine Remains*
Remains (Raleigh) **31**:224
Remarkable Providences (Mather) **38**:253, 259, 265, 267-8, 276-7, 285-6, 291, 294-9, 301-2
Remarks (Dennis)
See *Remarks on a Book, entituled Prince Arthur, an Heroick Poem*
"Remarks Concerning the Savages of North America" (Franklin) **25**:140-41, 147
Remarks on a Book, entituled Prince Arthur, an Heroick Poem (Dennis) **11**:5, 8-9, 15, 17, 19, 22, 30, 36-7, 39, 41, 46
Remarks on Clarissa (Fielding) **44**:100
Remarks on Italy (Addison) **18**:39
"Remarks on Ovid" (Addison) **18**:18
Remarks on Prince Arthur (Dennis)
See *Remarks on a Book, entituled Prince Arthur, an Heroick Poem*
Remarks on the Policy of the Allies (Burke) **7**:23
Remarks on the Rape of the Lock (Dennis) **11**:21
Remarks upon Cato, a Tragedy (Dennis) **11**:22, 30
Remarks upon Mr. Pope's Translation of Homer (Dennis) **11**:22
Remarks upon Some Writers in the Controversy concerning the Foundation of Moral Duty and Moral Obligation (Trotter) **8**:363
Remarks upon the Principles and Reasonings of Dr. Rutherforth's "Essay on the Nature and Obligations of Virtue" (Trotter) **8**:362-63, 370
El remedio en la desdicha (Vega) **23**:339, 358
Remedy of Affliction for the Loss of Our Friends (Fielding) **1**:234
"The Remedy worse than the Disease" (Prior) **4**:459
Remembrances (Guicciardini) **49**:214
A Remonstrance and a Warning against the Presumptuous, Unchristian Power of the Bishop of Rome and the Unspiritual Spiritual Estate (Hutten)
See *Lament and Exhortation aginst the excessive un-Christian Power of the Bishop of Rome and the unministerial Ministers*
Remonstrance au Peuple de France (Ronsard) **6**:411, 418
"Le Renard et le Bouc" (La Fontaine) **50**:62
Renati Des cartes principiorum philosophiae pars I. et II. more geometrico demonstratae per Benedictum de Spinoza (Spinoza) **9**:396, 402, 423, 433, 442, 444
Le Renommée aux Muses (Racine) **28**:293
"The Repentant Girl" (Erasmus)
See "Virgin Repentant"
"Repentence" (Vaughan) **27**:326, 383
"Repentence of Robert Greene, Maister of Artes" **41**:148, 171, 179
"Reply" (Wheatley) **50**:162
See "Phillis's Reply to the Answer..."
The Reply of the Most Illustrious Cardinall of Perron, to the Answeare of the Most Excellent King of Great Britaine (Cary) **30**:166-67
"Reply to a Tailor" (Burns) **3**:92; **29**:21
Reply to Burke (Wollstonecraft)
See *A Vindication of the Rights of Men, in a Letter to the Right Honourable Edmund Burke; Occasioned by His Reflections on the Revolution in France*
Reply to Gosson (Lodge) **41**:189, 191-92
Reply to Sadoleto (Calvin) **37**:89
Reply to the Objections of M Bayles (Leibniz)

35:155
"Reponse à quelque ministre de Génève" (Ronsard) **6**:417
Report from Spain (Guicciardini) **49**:223
Report of the Jesuit Berthier's Illness, Confession, Death and Revelation (Voltaire) **14**:340
A Report of the Truth of the fight about the Iles of Acores (Raleigh) **31**:235
A Report of the Truth of the Fight about the Isles of Azores... (Raleigh) **39**:79, 123
"Reports of the Debates of the Senate of Lilliput" (Johnson)
See "Debates in the Senate of Magna Lilliputia"
"Representase la Brevedad de lo que se vive y cuan nada parece lo que se vivio" (Quevedo) **23**:182
"The Reprisal" (Herbert) **24**:231, 271
The Reprisal (Smollett) **2**:358; **46**:190, 257
Reproof (Smollett) **2**:352, 358-59; **46**:188, 194, 233
"Republican" (Butler) **16**:51
"A Request to the Graces" (Herrick) **13**:393
Rerum in Ecclesia History (Foxe)
See *Actes and Monumentes of these latter perilous dayes touching matters of the Church*
De Rerum Natura (Dryden) **21**:78-9
Rerum Scoticarum Historia, auctore Georgio Buchanano Scoto (Buchanan) **4**:118-23, 125-27, 129-30, 136-37
"The Resignation" (Chatterton) **3**:125-27, 135
"Resignation" (Young) **3**:467, 477, 490, 492; **40**:335
"Resolution" (More) **9**:296
Resolutiones disputationum de indulgentiarum (Luther) **9**:91, 109, 146-47
"Resolved never to Versifie more" (Barker) **42**:96, 98-9
"Respiration" (Quevedo)
See "Espiración"
Responde stulto secundum stultitiam eius (More) **10**:365
Responsio ad Lutherum (More)
See *Eruditissimi viri Guilielmi Rossei opus elegans*
"Respuesta a Sor Filotea de la Cruz" (Juana Ines de la Cruz) **5**:147, 150, 152, 156
Resurreccio Domini (Towneley) **34**:251-2, 261, 267, 289, 326
"The Resurrection" (Cowley) **43**:143, 164, 169, 187
"Resurrection" (Donne) **10**:17; **24**:167
"Resurrection and Immortality" (Vaughan) **27**:305, 325, 338, 390
Resurrection (Chester) **34**:128-9, 154
Resurrection: Fright of the Jews (York) **34**:334, 350, 352-3, 355-6, 373-4
The Resurrection (N-Town) **34**:173, 204
The Resurrection of Christ (York)
See *Resurrection: Fright of the Jews* (York)
The Resurrection (Towneley)
See *Resurreccio Domini* (Towneley)
De Resurrectione (Chester)
See *Resurrection* (Chester)
El retablo de las maravillas (Cervantes) **23**:139-40, 142
Retaliation (Goldsmith) **2**:70-1, 74, 104
"A Retir'd Friendship To Ardelia" (Philips) **30**:278
"Retirement" (Fergusson) **29**:180, 214
"Retirement" (Vaughan) **27**:312
"Retraction" (Chaucer) **17**:209, 213, 216, 242
"Retractions" (Chaucer)
See "Retraction"

"The Retreate" (Vaughan) **27**:291, 293, 295, 298, 301, 305-10, 312, 326, 330, 337-38, 341, 345-46, 357, 364-65, 391-92
Rettungen des Horaz (Lessing) **8**:105, 112
"The Return" (Taylor) **11**:363, 368, 384, 389, 396
The Return of Several Ministers (Mather) **38**:221-22
La réunion des amours (Marivaux) **4**:367
Le Rêve de d'Alembert (Diderot) **26**:92, 94, 96, 109, 114, 116-17, 119, 130-31, 143-49, 151, 157, 161, 168
Revelations (Julian of Norwich)
See "Revelations of Divine Love"
"Revelations of Divine Love" (Julian of Norwich) **6**:357-59, 362, 366, 369, 373-74, 376, 379-82
"The Revenge" (Chatterton)
See "The Revenge, a Burletta"
"The Revenge" (Young) **3**:467, 485, 487-88
Revenge (Raleigh)
See *Lost Fight of the Revenge*
"The Revenge, a Burletta" (Chatterton) **3**:123, 132
Revenge for Honor (Chapman) **22**:7, 12
The Revenge of Bussy D'Ambois (Chapman) **22**:6, 11, 13, 15, 18-19, 20-2, 30-1, 34, 42, 43, 46-7, 54-5
The Revenge; or, A Match in Newgate (Behn) **30**:80
Revenger's Tragedie (Marston) **33**:200
The Revenger's Tragedy (Middleton) **33**:266, 301
"A Reverie" (Goldsmith) **48**:217
"A Reverie at the Boar's-Head Tavern" (Goldsmith) **2**:84
Rêveries du promeneur solitaire (Rousseau) **14**:222, 257, 249, 254-55, 266-68, 303-04, 306, 312, 314
"The Reverse: or, The Tables Turn'd" (Dennis) **11**:51-2
"The Review" (Defoe) **1**:137, 155, 161-62
"The Revival" (Vaughan) **27**:364-65
La Révolution de l'Amérique anglaise (Diderot) **26**:158-59
"The Revolution in Low Life" (Goldsmith) **2**:105
The Revolution of Sweden (Trotter) **8**:354-55, 358, 361, 363, 369-70, 372, 374
De Revolutionibus (Copernicus)
See *Nicolai Copernici Torunensi De Revolutionibus orbium coelestium, Libri VI*
De Revolutionibus orbium coelestium (Copernicus)
See *Nicolai Copernici Torunensi De Revolutionibus orbium coelestium, Libri VI*
Revolutions (Copernicus)
See *Nicolai Copernici Torunensi De Revolutionibus orbium coelestium, Libri VI*
Revolutions of the Heavenly Spheres (Copernicus)
See *Nicolai Copernici Torunensi De Revolutionibus orbium coelestium, Libri VI*
El rey don Pedro en Madrid y el infazón de Illescas (Vega) **23**:402
El rey sin reino (Vega) **23**:398
"A Rhapsodie. Occasionally written upon a meeting with some of his friends at the Globe Taverne" (Vaughan) **27**:302
Rhymes of the Lawyer Burguillos (Vega) **23**:381
"The Rich Beggars" (Erasmus) **16**:118, 143
"Richard Cromwell" (Marvell) **4**:398
Richarde the thirde (More)
See *The Life of Kinge Richarde the Thirde*
"Richy and Sandy" (Ramsay) **29**:328
"Ricky with the Tuft" (Perrault)

See "Riquet à la houppe"
Ricordanze (Guicciardini) **49**:196, 229, 250
Ricordi (Guicciardini) **49**:195-98, 201-03, 205, 207-09, 211-12, 218-19, 224-29, 240-46, 250-52, 255, 259
"The Ridiculous Wishes" (Perrault)
  See "Les souhaits ridicules"
"Riding Westward" (Chapman) **22**:
"Le Rieiur et les poissons" (La Fontaine) **50**:105
"The Right Hon. My Lady Anne Lovelace" (Lovelace) **24**:314
"Righteousness" (Vaughan) **27**:378
Rights of Woman (Wollstonecraft)
  See *A Vindication of the Rights of Woman, with Strictures on Political and Moral Subjects*
"Rigs o'Barley" (Burns) **3**:67, 71
Rimas Humas (Vega) **23**:340, 380
Rimas Sacras (Vega) **23**:359, 381
Rime (Michelangelo) **12**:354, 356-60, 362-63, 365-68, 371, 374-76
Le Rime del Petrarca brevemente sposte per Ludovico Castelvetro (Castelvetro) **12**:68
Rinaldo (Tasso) **5**:375, 383-84, 392
Rinaldo and Armida (Dennis) **11**:12, 34
"Rinconete y Cortadillo" (Cervantes) **6**:171-72; **23**:99
"Riquet à la houppe" (Perrault) **2**:254, 257, 260, 280
Risale-i aruz (Babur) **18**:91
"The Rise and Fall of the Stocks" (Ramsay) **29**:308, 361
Rise and Progress of the People Called Friends (Penn)
  See *Rise and Progress of the People Called Quakers*
Rise and Progress of the People Called Quakers (Penn) **25**:301, 331, 341-42
"Rise of Peyncteynge in Englande" (Chatterton) **3**:119
"The Rise of the Freeman's Journal/an abusive libellous Paper printed in the Year 1781" (Hopkinson) **25**:257
"The Rise of Woman" (Parnell)
  See "Hesiod; or, The Rise of Woman"
"The Rising of the Session" (Fergusson) **29**:172, 179, 189, 191, 205
Ritter Spiridon aus Perusina (Beer)
  See *Des abentheuerlichen Jan Rebhu Ritter Spiridon aus Perusina*
The Rival Ladies (Dryden) **3**:230-31
The Rivals (Davenant) **13**:185-87, 200
"The Rivers of Scotland: An Ode" (Fergusson) **29**:205, 217
The Roaring Girl (Dekker) **22**:106, 110, 126, 132
The Roaring Girl (Middleton) **33**:263, 368, 270-73, 277-78, 300, 316, 318, 320
"Rob Fergusson's Last Will" (Fergusson) **29**:212, 222
The Robbers (Hutten) **16**:216, 225, 227, 234, 241, 246
"Robert and Raufe" (Chatterton) **3**:129
"Robert Burns' Answer" (Burns) **29**:86; **40**:86
"Robert, Duke of Normandie" **8**:30, 33
"Robert of Normandy"
  See "Robert, Duke of Normandie"
Robert of Normandy (Lodge)
  See *Life of Robert, Second Duke of Normandy*
"Robert, Richy and Sandy" (Ramsay) **29**:326
Robert the Devil (Lodge)
  See *Life of Robert, Second Duke of Normandy*
"Robin Shure in Hairst" (Burns) **3**:86; **29**:22
"The Rock of Rubies and the Quarry of Pearls"

(Herrick) **13**:312, 338
A Rod for Runaways (Dekker) **22**:97
Roderick Random (Smollett)
  See *The Adventures of Roderick Random*
Rodogune, Princess of Parthia (Corneille)
  See *Rodogune, Princesse des Parthes*
Rodogune, Princesse des Parthes (Corneille) **28**:4, 16, 21-2, 29, 34-5, 38, 41, 56
"Roger and Jenny" (Ramsay) **29**:322
Roger de Sicile (Lesage) **28**:204, 208
The Rogueries of Scapin (Moliere)
  See *Les fourberies de Scapin*
"Le Roi Candaule" (La Fontaine) **50**:70
Roland amoureux (Lesage) **28**:200
Roman Triads (Hutten)
  See *Vadiscus, sive Trias Romana*
The Romance of a Morning (Cleland) **2**:52
The Romance of a Night; or, A Covent-Garden-Adventure (Cleland) **2**:52
The Romance of an Evening (Cleland) **2**:52
"Romance of the Knight" (Chatterton) **3**:118, 124
The Romance of Three Kingdoms (Lo Kuan-chung)
  See *San-kuo-chih yeni-i*
The Romance of Yúsuf (Joseph) and Zulaykhá (Potiphar's Wife) (Jami)
  See *Yúsuf u Zulaikhá*
Romans (Voltaire) **14**:337
Romaunt (Chaucer)
  See *Romaunt of the Rose*
Romaunt of the Rose (Chaucer) **17**:47, 58, 116, 195
"Romaunte of the Cnyghte" (Chatterton)
  See "Romance of the Knight"
Romulus and Hersilia (Behn) **30**:81
Roper's More (Roper)
  See *The Mirrour of Vertue in Worldly Greatnes; or, The Life of syr Thomas More Knight*
Rosalynde (Lodge) **41**:188, 194-95, 198-203, 205-212, 214
"Rosamond"
  See "The Epistle of Rosamond to King Henry the Second"
Rosamond (Addison) **18**:7, 17, 19, 32
"Rosania shadowed whilst Mrs Mary Aubrey" (Philips) **30**:288
Rosary of the Pious (Jami)
  See *Tuhfat al-ahrár*
"The Rosciad" (Churchill) **3**:139, 143-45, 148-49, 151, 153, 157-59, 161-63, 171-73
"The Rose" (Herbert) **24**:260, 262, 287
"A Rosebud by my Early Walk" (Burns) **40**:98
"The Rosemarie Branch" (Herrick) **13**:352
Rosina; or, Love in a Cottage: A Comic Opera, in Two Acts (Brooke) **6**:107, 109; **48**:116-117, 119
The Roundheads; or the Good Old Cause (Behn) **1**:29, 33, 37, 40; **30**:81
Rousseau juge de Jean Jacques (Rousseau) **14**:225, 247, 254, 256, 267, 303-04, 312
Les Routes du Monde (Lesage) **28**:211
The Rover; or, The Banished Cavalier (Behn) **1**:28, 33-4, 37, 39-40; **30**:71, 73, 75, 77, 80-2, 84, 86-7; **42**:150
Rowley Poems (Chatterton) **3**:126-27
Roxana (Defoe)
  See *The Fortunate Mistress*
The Royal Convert (Rowe) **8**:292, 299-302, 305, 308
The Royal Hearings of King Pedro (Vega)
  See *Audiencias del rey Don Pedro*
"The Royal Man" (P'u Sung-ling)
  See "Wang-che"

The Royal Mischief (Manley) **1**:315-16; **42**:261
"Rubelet" (Herrick) **13**:321
Rudiments (Hobbes)
  See *Philosophical Rudiments*
Rudolphine Tables (Kepler)
  See *Hormonice Mundi*
El rufián dichoso (Cervantes) **6**:180; **23**:101-02
El rufian viudo (Cervantes) **23**:137
"A Ruful Lamentacion" (More) **10**:428-29
"Ruin" (Burns)
  See "Address to "Ruin""
"The Ruines of Time" (Spenser) **5**:312, 314
"Rule, Brittania" (Thomson) **16**:374, 385, 396; **29**:434, 452; **40**:273, 315
"Rules and Lessons" (Vaughan) **27**:290, 300, 312, 314, 325, 331, 353, 371, 383
"Rules by which A Great Empire My Be Reduced to A Small One" (Franklin) **25**:112, 125
"Rules for diminishing a Great Empire" (Franklin)
  See "Rules by which A Great Empire My Be Reduced to A Small One"
Rules for the Direction of the Mind (Descartes)
  See *Regulae ad Directionem Ingenii*
Rules of a Christian Life (Elyot)
  See *The Rules of a Christian lyfe made by Picus erle of Mirandula*
The Rules of a Christian lyfe made by Picus erle of Mirandula (Elyot) **11**:62, 84
Rural Sports (Gay) **49**:31, 33, 35, 38, 49, 60, 62-65, 67, 69, 78-79, 95, 138, 141
"Ruth's Resolution" (Edwards) **7**:119
"Ryse of Peyncteynge in Englande" (Chatterton)
  See "Rise of Peyncteynge in Englande"
Sab'a (Jami) **9**:65-7, 72
The Sacramental Meditations (Taylor)
  See *Preparatory Meditations before my Approach to the Lords Supper. Chiefly upon the Doctrin preached upon the Day of administration.*
De sacramento matrimonii (Agrippa von Nettesheim)
  See *De matrimonio*
Sacred Contagion; or, The Natural History of Superstition (Holbach)
  See *Contagion sacrée*
Sacred Rhymes (Vega)
  See *Rimas Sacras*
The Sacred Year of Madrid (Calderon de la Barca) **23**:9
"The Sacrifice" (Herbert) **24**:222, 257, 271, 273, 290-93
"The Sacrifice" (Vaughan) **27**:353
"The Sacrifice, by way of Discourse betwixt himselfe and Julia" (Herrick) **13**:403
The Sacrifice of Isaac (Chester)
  See *Abraham, Lot, and Melchysedeck* (Chester)
"The Sacrifice to Apollo" **8**:41
Sacrificium of Cayme et Abell (York) **34**:333, 335, 361-2, 365
The Sad Shepherd (Jonson) **6**:304-06, 309, 311, 321-22, 325; **33**:132, 137, 150
"The sadnesse of things for Sapho's sicknesse" (Herrick) **13**:365
"Sae Flaxen Were Her Ringlets" (Burns) **29**:36
Saint Cyprian (Elyot)
  See *A Swete and devoute Sermon of Holy saynt Ciprian of Mortalitie of Man*
Saint Paulin (Perrault) **2**:260
Salámán and Absál (Jami)
  See *Salámán u Absál*
Salámán u Absál (Jami) **9**:59, 62, 65, 68, 71-2
Salmacida Spolia (Davenant) **13**:182, 189
Salmacis and Hermaphroditus (Fletcher) **33**:89-

90, 94-5

Salon de 1761 (Diderot)   **26**:103

Salon de 1765 (Diderot)   **26**:89, 107-08, 124

Salon de 1767 (Diderot)   **26**:96, 99, 103, 107-08, 122-24, 126, 134, 144

Salons (Diderot)   **26**:69, 72-3, 95, 104, 106-09, 119-21, 123-24, 127-29, 144, 155, 168

The Salutation and Conception (N-Town) **34**:173, 179, 183, 192, 203, 223

"The Salutation and Sorrow of the Virgine Marie" (Lanyer)   **30**:262, 264

Salutation (Chester)   **34**:109

Salutation (Towneley)   **34**:325

The Salvation of the Soul (Mather)   **38**:226

"Salve Deus Rex Judaeorum" (Lanyer)   **30**:259, 260, 262-67

Salve Deus Rex Judaeorum (Lanyer)   **30**:238, 242-45, 248-49, 252, 258-61, 264

Samson Agonistes (Milton)   **9**:183, 189, 192-3, 198, 200, 204, 217, 229-30, 236-8, 243, 249; **43**:361-2, 384, 392, 394, 411-2, 416, 420-1

Samuel Henzi (Lessing)   **8**:105, 114

San Hermenegildo (Juana Ines de la Cruz)   **5**:158

San Kuo (Lo Kuan-chung)
   See *San-kuo-chih yeni-i*

"San-ch'ao Yüan-lao" (P'u Sung-ling)   **49**:283

"Sancta Maria" (Crashaw)
   See "Santca Maria Dolorum"

"Sandie and Willie, an Eclogue" (Fergusson) **29**:205

The Sandy Foundation Shaken (Penn)   **25**:284, 286-88, 294, 296, 324, 334

Sanford and Merton (Day)
   See *The History of Sandford and Merton*

San-kuo-chih yeni-i (Lo Kuan-chung)   **12**:279-80, 282, 284-97

"San-sheng" (P'u Sung-ling)   **49**:293

San-Sui p'ing-yao chuan (Lo Kuan-chung) **12**:282

Santa Bárbara, or the Mountain Miracle and Heaven's Martyr (Castro)   **19**:2

"Santca Maria Dolorum" (Crashaw)   **24**:28, 30, 53, 75, 78

"The Sap" (Vaughan)   **27**:325, 354, 391

De sapienta veterum (Bacon)   **18**:117, 132, 174, 185, 195; **32**:107, 137, 172

De Sapierta Vetuum (Bacon)
   See *Valerius Terminus of the Interpretation of Nature*

Sappho and Phao (Lyly)   **41**:273

"Satira Nova" (Marston)   **33**:222-23

Satire (Ariosto)   **6**:31-3, 59, 71-2

Satire II: À M. de Molière (Boileau-Despreaux) **3**:39

Satire III (Boileau-Despreaux)   **3**:37

Satire IV (On Human Folly) (Boileau-Despreaux) **3**:39

Satire VI (Boileau-Despreaux)   **3**:23, 37-8

Satire VIII: A M. Morel, Docteur en Sorbonne (Boileau-Despreaux)   **3**:25

Satire IX (Boileau-Despreaux)   **3**:35

Satire XII: Sur l'équivoque (Boileau-Despreaux) **3**:22, 25

Satire of Truth (Boileau-Despreaux)   **3**:21

Satires (Ariosto)
   See *Satire*

Satires (Boileau-Despreaux)   **3**:38-9, 42-3

Satires (Marston)   **33**:202, 207, 213

Satires (Young)   **3**:474, 478, 492-93

Satires and Epistles of Horace, Imitated (Pope) **3**:273, 289, 296, 314, 319

Satires and Epistles of Horace, Imitated and Satires of Dr. Donne Versified (Pope)   **3**:289,

292, 302-03

Satires of Dr. Donne Versified (Pope)   **3**:289, 292, 302-03

Satiromastix; of the Untrussing of the Humorous Poet (Dekker)   **22**:88, 92, 106, 108, 119, 130-1

"Saturday" (Gay)   **49**:38, 66

Saturday (Gay)   **49**:41, 43, 45, 47

"A Saturday's Expedition. In Mock Heroics" (Fergusson)   **29**:198

"Satyr albo Dziki Maz" (Kochanowski)   **10**:175

"The Satyr, or The Wild Man" (Kochanowski)
   See "Satyr albo Dziki Maz"

"Satyr upon the Licentious Age of Charles 2D" (Butler)   **16**:52; **43**:106-8

"Satyr upon the weakness and Misery of Man" (Butler)   **43**:108-9

"Satyre I" (Donne)   **10**:100-02

"Satyre II" (Donne)   **10**:38, 100-02

"Satyre III" (Donne)   **10**:12, 38, 48-9, 84, 93, 100-02; **24**:204-05, 208-09

"Satyre IV" (Donne)   **10**:100-02; **24**:204, 206

"Satyre V" (Donne)   **10**:99-102

Satyres (Donne)   **10**:7, 24-5, 38, 42, 47, 98-102

The Satyrical Pilgrim (Grimmelshausen)
   See *Der satyrische Pilgram*

Der satyrische Pilgram (Grimmelshausen)   **6**:244-48, 251

"The Satyr's Comic Project for Recovering a Young Bankrupt Stock-jobber" (Ramsay) **29**:308

Saul smitten to the Ground (Penn)   **25**:287

Sausage (Warton)
   See *The Oxford Sausage; or, Select Poetical Pieces: Written by the Most Celebrated Wits of the University of Oxford*

Sayings of Light and Love (John of the Cross) **18**:229

Scala coeli: Nineteene Sermons concerning Prayer (Andrewes)   **5**:23

Scala Intellectualis (Bacon)   **18**:187

Scarabaeus (Erasmus)   **16**:176

Scelta d'alcune Poesie filosofiche (Campanella) **32**:243-51

"Sceptic" (Butler)   **16**:53

"The Sceptic" (Hume)   **7**:153, 188

The Schism in England (Calderon de la Barca) **23**:64

De Schismate extinguendo, et de vera Ecclesiastica Libertate adverenda (Hutten) **16**:213, 233

The Scholars (Lovelace)   **24**:351

"The School for Fathers" (Marmontel)   **2**:214

The School for Husbands (Moliere)
   See *L'école des maris*

The School for Mothers (Marivaux)
   See *The School for Mothers*

The School for Wives (Moliere)
   See *L'école des femmes*

The School for Wives Criticized (Moliere)
   See *La critique de L'école des femmes*

"The School or Perl of Putney" (Herrick)   **13**:353

"Schoolmaster" (Butler)   **16**:50

"Schreiben an den Herrn N. N. über die Komödie in Versen" (Schlegel)   **5**:272, 282

Science (Hopkinson)   **25**:263

La Science du Bonhomme Richard (Franklin)
   See *The Way to Wealth*

Scilla's Metamorphosis (Lodge)   **41**:199

Scipina (Barker)   **42**:59

The Scornful Lady (Fletcher)   **33**:86-8, 91

"Scotch Drink" (Burns)   **3**:52, 67, 84-5, 87; **29**:29; **40**:80, 94

"Scotish Ballad" (Burns)   **29**:50

Scots Confession (Knox)   **37**:210

"Scots Wha Hae wi' Wallace Bled" (Burns)   **3**:52, 60-1, 67, 72, 78, 83; **29**:41; **40**:62, 98

The Scourge of Villany (Marston)   **33**:203, 207, 218-19, 221-26, 235, 250, 252

The Scourging (Towneley)
   See *Flagellacio* (Towneley)

Scriptorum philosophicum (More)   **9**:311

"Scrutinie" (Lovelace)   **24**:306, 315-16, 318-19, 349

Gli sdegni amorosi (Goldoni)
   See *Il gondoliere veneziano*

"Se ben concetto ha la divina parte" (Michelangelo)   **12**:372

A Sea Grammar (Smith)
   See *An Accidence; or, The Path-Way to Experience*

"The Sea Marke"   **9**:382-83

The Sea Voyage (Fletcher)   **33**.60

"The Search" (Herbert)   **24**:272

"The Search" (Vaughan)   **27**:305, 330, 339, 380

"Search All the World About" (Davenant)   **13**:204

A Seasonable Argument to Persuade All the Grand Juries in England to Petition for a New Parliament; or, A List of the Principal Labourers in the Great Design of Popery and Arbitrary Power, &c. (Marvell)   **4**:394

A Seasonable Caveat against Popery (Penn) **25**:287

A Seasonable Question, & c. (Marvell)   **4**:394

"Seasons" (Bradstreet)
   See "The Four Seasons of the Year"

The Seasons. A Poem (Thomson)   **16**:359, 361-63, 365-76, 378-79, 381-86, 388-89, 391-95, 397-98, 401-09, 411-15, 418-19, 421-26, 429-34; **29**:370-71, 373-75, 377, 380, 384-85, 388-391, 394-400, 402-04, 410-11, 413, 422, 429, 432, 444, 447; **40**:263-67, 269, 271, 273-76, 278, 280, 282, 284-85, 289-308, 311-15, 321-22

Seat of Government (Raleigh)   **31**:224

"A Sea-Voyage from Tenby to Bristol" (Philips) **30**:287

Second Accusation before Pilate: Remorse of Judas: Purchase of Field of Blood (York) **34**:333, 388

The Second Anniversarie. Of the Progres of the Soule. Wherein, By Occasion Of the Religious death of Mistris Elizabeth Drury, the incommodities of the Soule in this life, and her exaltation in the next, are Contemplated (Donne)   **10**:39, 44, 74-5, 77, 89, 95, 98; **24**:165, 185-88

Second Blast of the Trumpet (Knox)   **37**:203, 237, 240

Second Defence of the English People (Milton) **9**:235, 250; **43**:339-40, 369, 372, 375, 377-81, 384, 391, 406

Second Defense against Westphal (Calvin)
   See *Second Defense of the Godly and Orthodox Faith Concerning the Sacraments against the False Accusations of Joachim Westphal*

Second Defense of the Godly and Orthodox Faith Concerning the Sacraments against the False Accusations of Joachim Westphal (Calvin)   **37**:93-4

A Second Defense of the Prophaneness and Immorality of the English Stage (Collier) **6**:222, 229

Second Diary (Pepys)   **11**:246

"The Second Discourse" (Reynolds)   **15**:377, 389,

Title Index

391, 397, 402, 418-19

Second Discourse (Rousseau)
  See *Discours sur l'origine et les fondements de l'inégalité parmi les hommes*

Second Discourse (Turgot) **26**:350, 381, 384

"Second Epistle to John Lapraik" (Burns) **3**:87, 92-3; **29**:10

"A Second Epistle, To . . .Mr. E.S." (Barker) **42**:97

"Second Nun's Tale" (Chaucer) **17**:189, 214, 220, 237

"Second part of Conny-catching" **41**:149, 155-56, 181-82

The Second Part; or, A Continuance of Poly-Olbion from the Eighteenth Song.
  See *Poly-Olbion*

"The Second Rapture" (Carew) **13**:26, 34, 57

The Second Shepherds' Play (Towneley)
  See *Secunda Pastorum* (Towneley)

The Second Surprise of Love (Marivaux)
  See *The Second Surprise of Love*

Second Treatise of Government (Locke) **7**:277-78, 291, 296; **35**:221, 226, 241

Second Trial before Pilate Continued (York)
  See *Second Trial Continued: Judgement on Jesus* (York)

Second Trial Continued: Judgement on Jesus (York) **34**:333-4, 385, 387

La seconde surprise de l'amour (Marivaux) **4**:367, 368, 381

"Secresie Protected" (Carew) **13**:26

The Secret History of Queen Zarah and the Zarazians (Manley) **1**:307, 309, 311,313, 316, 319-23; **42**:261, 263-65, 270-71, 273, 277, 281

The Secret History of the Present Intrigues of the Court of Caramania (Haywood) **1**:290; **44**:129-31

Secret Love; or, The Maiden Queen (Dryden) **3**:177, 193, 197, 210, 230

The Secret Memoirs and Manners of Several Persons of Quality (Manley)
  See *The New Atalantis*

The Secret of Pegasus (Bruno)
  See *Cabala del cavallo Pegaseo*

The Secret Spoken Aloud (Calderon de la Barca)
  See *El secreto a voces*

Secret Vengeance for a Secret Insult (Calderon de la Barca)
  See *A secreto agravio secreta venganza*

"The Secretary" (Prior) **4**:460-62, 466

El secreto a voces (Calderon de la Barca) **23**:67

A secreto agravio secreta venganza (Calderon de la Barca) **23**:13-14, 39, 41, 43, 45, 70

Secular Authority, To What Extent It Should Be Obeyed (Luther) **9**:134, 151

"The Secular Masque" (Dryden) **3**:199; **21**:64

"Secular Ode on the Jubilee at Pembroke College, Cambridge, in 1743" (Smart) **3**:394

Secunda Pastorum (Towneley) **34**:251, 253-6, 258-9, 261, 265, 267, 274-5, 277, 280-82, 286-7, 289, 297-99, 304, 311-12, 316-19, 321-4

"See Down Maria's Blushing Cheek" (Hopkinson) **25**:250

"See the Chariot at Hand" (Jonson) **6**:305

"S'egli è, donna, che puoi" (Michelangelo) **12**:366

Sei giornate (Aretino)
  See *Ragionamento della Nanna e della Antonia*

Sejanus (Jonson) **33**:106, 119, 131-2, 150, 153, 155, 159-60

Sejanus His Fall (Jonson) **6**:291, 294, 296, 300-

01, 305-06, 308, 314, 318, 323, 327, 329-32, 334, 336, 341

The Select Works of Mr. John Dennis (Dennis) **11**:15-6, 20, 50

"A Self Accuser" (Donne) **10**:95

Selfishness of a False Philosophy (Marmontel) **2**:213

The Self-Rival (Davys) **1**:97-8; **46**:24, 29, 35

"Selim; or, The Shepherd's Moral" (Collins) **4**:210

The Selling of Joseph (Sewall) **38**:347, 355, 367-8

Der seltsame Springinsfeld (Grimmelshausen) **6**:238, 247, 249-51

Semele (Congreve)
  See *Mask of Semele*

La Semilla y la cizaña (Calderon de la Barca) **23**:14

Sémlramis (Voltaire) **14**:397

La S<etilda>n y la Criada (Calderon de la Barca) **23**:11

Sending of the Holy Ghost (Chester) **34**:114

Seneca (Lipsius)
  See *Annaei Senecae Philosopli Opera, quae exstant, onmia*

"La Señora Cornelia" (Cervantes) **6**:171, 177; **23**:99

"Sensibility" (Burns) **3**:83-4

"Sentencia" (Quevedo) **23**:192

"Sentencia 24" (Quevedo) **23**:199

A Sentimental Journey through France and Italy (Sterne) **2**:377, 384-86, 389, 391, 393-96, 398, 400, 402, 411, 413-14, 426-28, 439; **48**:286, 312-19, 335-6, 338-40, 342, 346-48, 350-1, 353-4, 359, 377-8, 381

Sentiments (Richardson)
  See *A Collection of the Moral and Instructive Sentiments, Maxims, Cautions, and Reflexions, Contained in the Histories of Pamela, Clarissa, and Sir Charles Grandison*

"Separatio elementorum" (Newton) **35**:294

"Separation of Lovers" (Carew) **13**:62

September Bibel (Luther)
  See *Das newe Testament deutzsche*

Septet (Jami)
  See *Sab'a*

Septiform Narration of the Six Days of Creation (Pico della Mirandola)
  See *Heptaplus*

"Sepulchre" (Herbert) **24**:248

Sequel to The Liar (Corneille)
  See *La suite du menteur*

El Serafin Humano (Vega) **23**:347

A Serious Apology for the Principles and Practices of the People called Qyuakers against the Malicious Aspersions, Erroneous Doctrines and Horrid Blasphemies of Thomas Jenner and Timothy Taylor (Penn) **25**:287, 290, 310

Serious Reflections during the Life and Surprising (Defoe) **42**:

Les serments indiscrets (Marivaux) **4**:358-59, 363, 368, 378-79

"Sermon" (Erasmus) **16**:142

"Sermon 4 Of Repentance" (Andrewes) **5**:34

"Sermon 6 Of the Resurrection" (Andrewes) **5**:33

"Sermon 7" (Andrewes) **5**:33

"Sermon 9 Of the Nativitie" (Andrewes) **5**:33

"Sermon 11 Of the Nativitie" (Andrewes) **5**:34

"Sermon 14 Of the Resurrection" (Andrewes) **5**:34

"Sermon 15 Of the Nativitie" (Andrewes) **5**:34

"Sermon 17 Of the Resurrection" (Andrewes) **5**:34

Sermon de J. Rossette (Voltaire) **14**:357

Sermon des cinquante (Voltaire) **14**:369, 370

The Sermon on Good Works (Luther)
  See *Von den guten Wercken*

Sermon on Indulgences and Grace (Luther)
  See *Eyn Sermon von Ablass und Gnade*

"A Sermon on Painting" (Walpole) **2**:487

Sermons (Churchill) **3**:141, 167, 169

Sermons (Donne) **24**:197

Sermons (Johnson) **15**:209, 289-90

"Sermons, 3" (Donne) **24**:176

"Sermons 4" (Donne) **24**:176

"Sermons, 5" (Donne) **24**:176-77

"Sermons 9" (Donne) **24**:176

The Sermons of Mr. Yorick (Sterne) **2**:374, 429-30, 433, 34; **48**:257-60, 274-76, 292, 341, 350

Sermons to Novices (Kempis) **11**:410

Sertorius (Corneille) **28**:9, 21, 29-30, 33, 35, 38, 54, 56

La serva amorosa (Goldoni) **4**:261, 265

La serva reconoscente (Goldoni) **4**:261

The Servant of Two Masters (Goldoni)
  See *Il servitore di due padroni*

"La Servante Justifiee" (La Fontaine) **50**:67

Servir con mala estrella (Vega) **23**:402

De servo arbitrio (Luther) **9**:138; **37**:272, 297

Le sette giornate del mondo creato (Tasso) **5**:375, 398

Sette Salmi (Aretino)
  See *I sette salmi de la penitenzia di David*

"Seven Characteristical Satires" (Young) **40**:359

The Seven Deadly Sins of London (Dekker) **22**:95, 101, 117-118, 121, 130

The Seven Penetential Psalms of David (Aretino)
  See *I sette salmi de la penitenzia di David*

Seven Philosophical Problems (Hobbes) **36**:139

Seven Songs for the Harpsichord (Hopkinson) **25**:250, 259-60

Seventeen Sermons on the Nativity (Andrewes) **5**:27

"The Seventh Discourse" (Reynolds) **15**:381, 395, 403

Several Discourses upon Practical Subjects (Collier) **6**:210

Several Reasons Proving that Inculating or Transplanting the Small Pox is a Lawful Practice... (Mather) **38**:294

Sganarelle; or, The Cuckold in His Own Imagination (Moliere)
  See *Sganarelle, ou le cocu imaginaire*

Sganarelle, ou le cocu imaginaire (Moliere) **10**:277, 280, 283, 286, 302, 306, 310; **28**:243, 255, 259, 262-63

The Shadow of Night (Chapman) **22**:10, 14, 51, 76

"The Shadows of Ideas" (Bruno)
  See "De umbris idearum"

Shakespeare (Johnson)
  See *The Plays of William Shakespeare, in Eight Volumes, with the Corrections and Illustrations of Various Commentators; To which are added Notes by Sam Johnson*

Shamela (Fielding)
  See *An Apology for the Life of Mrs. Shamela Andrews*

"Shao nü" (P'u Sung-ling) **49**:297

"She Chiang-chün" (P'u Sung-ling) **49**:283

"She Play'd the Loon or She Was Married" (Burns) **29**:24

She Stoops to Conquer (Goldsmith) **2**:67, 69,

72-4, 76, 79-81, 86-7, 89, 98-9, 105-07, 112, 119-21, 126-28

The Sheaves of Ruth (Calderon de la Barca) **23**:9

The Sheep Well (Vega)
See *Fuenteovejuna*

"Shephardling" (Herrick) **13**:321

The Shepheardes Calender: Conteyning Twelve <AElig>glogues Proportionable to the Twelve Monethes (Spenser) **5**:294, 297, 304, 311-12, 323, 326, 329, 354, 359-62; **39**:305, 307, 316-17, 328, 338, 350-52, 354, 374

The Shepheards Sirena **8**:9, 17-19, 21, 33-4, 36-7

The Shepherd (Zwingli) **37**:379-80

"The Shepherdess of the Alps" (Marmontel) **2**:214

The Shepherds (Chester) **34**:102, 109-10, 123, 126-9, 138

Shepherd's Garland
See *Idea the Shepheards Garland, Fashioned in Nine Eglogs. Rowlands Sacrifice to the Nine Muses*

The Shepherd's Week (Gay) **49**:31-33, 35, 37-43, 45-49, 60, 65-69, 78-79, 138, 141, 147, 157, 171, 185

Shepherds (York) **34**:333, 386

She-yan hsien-sheng ts'un-kao (Wu Ch'eng-en) **7**:396-99

"Shi Qingxu" (P'u Sung-ling) **49**:307, 309-12

"Shih Ch'ing-hsü" (P'u Sung-ling) **3**:350; **49**:278

"Shih-yen" (P'u Sung-ling) **3**:350

"Shipman's" (Chaucer)
See "Shipman's Tale"

"Shipman's Tale" (Chaucer) **17**:170, 194, 201-02, 212, 214, 225, 239

"The Shipwreck" (Erasmus)
See "Naufragium"

"Shiyue Sun Shengzuo zhaizhong shang ju" (P'u Sung-ling) **49**:314

The Shoemaker's Holiday, or the Gentle Craft (Dekker) **22**:91, 99-100, 103-106, 108-109, 112, 116-123, 125-9, 133-8

"The Shoe-tying" (Herrick) **13**:367

"A Shopkeeper" (Butler) **16**:55

A Short Account of the Destruction of the Indies (Las Casas)
See *Brevísima relación de la destrucción de las Indias*

A Short Historical Essay Touching General Councils, Creeds, and Impositions in Religion (Marvell) **4**:394

A Short Scheme of the True Religion (Newton) **35**:281

A Short Story of the rise, reign, and ruin of the Antinomians, Familists & Libertines (Winthrop)
See *Antinomians and Familists condemned by the synod of elders in New-England*

Short Treatise (Spinoza)
See *Korte Verhandeling van God, de Mensch und deszelhs Welstand*

Short Treatise on the Lord's Supper (Calvin) **37**:91, 97

Short Treatise Showing what a Faithful Man Should Do Knowing the Truth of theGospel When He Is among the Papists (Calvin) **37**:90

A Short View (Collier)
See *A Short View of the Immorality and Profaneness of the English Stage, Together with the Sense of Antiquity upon This Argument*

A Short View of the Immorality and Profaneness of the English Stage, Together with the Sense

of Antiquity upon This Argument (Collier) **6**:204-08, 210-12, 215, 217-18, 220-31

A Short Vindication of The Relapse and The Provok'd Wife from Immorality and Prophaneness (Vanbrugh) **21**:289, 292, 297, 321, 324, 326-27, 334

A shorte and briefe narration of the two nauigations and discoueries to the Northweast partes called Newe Fraunce (Hakluyt) **31**:155

The Shortest Way with the Dissenters; or, Proposals for the Establishment of the Church (Defoe) **1**:118, 121, 144, 161, 163, 166

"Shower" (Swift)
See "Description of a City Shower"

The Showing forth of Christ: Sermons of John Donne (Donne) **10**:92

"The Showre" (Vaughan) **27**:300, 318

"The Shrew-Wife" (More) **9**:298

"Shu chi" (P'u Sung-ling) **49**:314-15

"Shuang teng" (P'u Sung-ling) **49**:298

"Shu-chih" (P'u Sung-ling) **49**:278

"Shu'hsi" (P'u Sung-ling) **3**:352

Shui Hu Chuan (Lo Kuan-chung) **12**:279-84, 286, 291-94, 296-97

"Si acaso, Fabio mío" (Juana Ines de la Cruz) **5**:155

"Si come nella penna e nell'inchiosto" (Michelangelo) **12**:360

"Sì come per levar, Donna, si pone" (Michelangelo) **12**:338, 373

La Sibila del Oriente (Calderon de la Barca) **23**:20

"Sic a Wife as Willie Had" (Burns) **3**:86

The Sicilian; or, Love the Painter (Moliere)
See *Le sicilien; ou, L'amour peintre*

Le sicilien; ou, L'amour peintre (Moliere) **10**:283-84, 291, 312, 328; **28**:255-56, 261, 274

The Sick Monkey (Garrick) **15**:122

The Sidereal Messenger (Galilei)
See *Sidereus Nuncius*

Sidereus Nuncius (Galilei) **45**:217-18, 224-26, 228, 239, 243-45, 247-49, 255-56, 264, 274, 278-79, 295, 299, 304

Sidereus Nuntius (Galilei)
See *Sidereus Nuncius*

Sidney Bidulph (Sheridan)
See *Memoirs of Miss Sidney Bidulph, Extracted from Her Own Journal*

Die sieben Busspsal mit deutscher au-siegung nach dem schrifftlichen synne tzu Christi und gottes gnaden, neben seynes selben, ware erkentniss grundlich gerichtet... (Luther) **9**:79, 119-21, 123

Le siècle de Louis le Grand (Perrault) **2**:259, 274, 276

Le siècle de Louis XIV (Voltaire) **14**:338-39, 352, 364, 372, 383, 388, 409-11

Le siècle de Louis XV (Voltaire) **14**:338-39, 383

The Siege of Rhodes (Davenant) **13**:175-83, 185, 189-90, 192, 194, 215

The Siege of Sinope: A Tragedy (Brooke) **6**:109; **48**:116-117

"A Sigh" (Winchilsea) **3**:447

"Sighs and Groans" (Herbert)
See "Sighs and Grones"

"Sighs and Grones" (Herbert) **24**:274, 276

"Sigismunda and Guiscardo" (Dryden) **3**:184, 204, 216

"The Sign" (Winchilsea) **3**:447

"Silence, and stealth of dayes" (Vaughan) **27**:303, 337, 357

Silenei Alcibia dis (Erasmus) **16**:198

The Silent Woman (Dryden) **3**:236

The Silent Woman (Jonson)
See *Epicœne; or, the Silent Woman*

Silex Scintillans; or, Sacred Poems and Priuate Eiaculations (Vaughan) **27**:293-95, 299, 301-04, 307, 309, 311-18, 320-21, 329-32, 334-35, 337-39, 342, 350-51, 357, 364-66, 370-71, 373-79, 382, 389-90, 393, 395

The Silly Lady (Vega)
See *La dama boba*

Silsilatu'dh-Dhahab (Jami) **9**:65, 68, 71

Silvae (Buchanan) **4**:133, 135

"The Silver Tassie" (Burns) **3**:77-8, 85

"The Simile" (Fergusson) **29**:201

"A Simile" (Prior) **4**:460, 475

The Simplician World-Observer (Beer)
See *Der symplicianische Welt-Kucker; oder, Abentheuerliche Jan Rebhu, Parts I-IV*

Simplician Writings (Grimmelshausen)
See *Der abenteuerliche Simplicissimus, Teutsch, das hist: Die Beschreibun dess Lebens eines seltzamen Vaganten, gennant Melchio Sternfels von Fuchsheim*

Simplicissimi wunderliche Gauckel-Tasche (Grimmelshausen) **6**:247

Simplicissimus's Bag of Tricks (Grimmelshausen)
See *Simplicissimi wunderliche Gauckel-Tasche*

"Simplicity and Refinement in Writing" (Hume) **7**:163, 167

"Simulation and Dissimulation" (Bacon) **18**:124, 128

"Sin I" (Herbert) **24**:257

"Since I am comming" (Donne)
See "Hymne to God my God, in my sicknesse"

Sincere Admonition (Luther)
See *Exhortation for all Christians Warming Them Against Insurrection and Rebillion*

The Sincere Ones (Marivaux)
See *The Sincere Ones*

Les sincères (Marivaux) **4**:369-70, 372

"The Sinner" (Herbert) **24**:291

"Sinners in the Hands of an Angry God" (Edwards) **7**:92, 98, 102-08, 110, 117-18

"Sion" (Herbert) **24**:275, 278, 280

Sir Charles Grandison (Richardson)
See *The History of Sir Charles Grandison*

Sir Giles Goosecap (Chapman) **22**:62, 65

Sir Giles Goosecap (Marston) **33**:193

Sir Harry Wildair: Being the Sequel of The Trip to the Jubilee (Farquhar) **21**:132, 135-36, 139-40, 146, 150, 153-54, 161, 163, 170, 176

Sir Lancelot Greaves (Smollett)
See *The Life and Adventures of Sir Lancelot Greaves*

Sir Martin Mar-All; or, The Feign'd Innocence (Dryden) **3**:179, 210, 230

Sir Miracle Comes a Cropper (Vega) **23**:385-86

Sir Patient Fancy (Behn) **1**:33, 37, 39, 41; **30**:67, 71, 72, 75, 78-80, 84-5; **42**:149-50

"Sir Roger at Church" (Addison) **18**:56

Sir Roger de Coverley Papers (Addison) **18**:43, 70

"Sir Tho. Southwell" (Herrick) **13**:368

Sir Thomas Wiat (Dekker) **22**:109

"Sir Thopas" (Chaucer) **17**:61, 177, 201-02, 205

"Sir Walter Raleigh's Pilgrimage" (Raleigh) **39**:775

Sir Walter Raleigh's Sceptick; or, Speculations (Raleigh) **31**:223-6, 230, 238

"The Sitting of the Session" (Fergusson) **29**:189, 205, 218

Six Articles (Henry VIII)

See *Act for Abolishing*
Six Bookes of Politickes or Civil Doctrine (Lipsius)
See *Politicorum sive civilis doctrinae libri sex, qui ad principatum maxime spectant*
"The Sixth Discourse" (Reynolds) **15**:380, 394, 397, 403
Sixty-Seven Articles (Zwingli) **37**:352
Sixty-Seven Conclusions (Zwingli)
See *Sixty-Seven Articles*
"Skazka o rozdenii taftjanoj muški" (Chulkov) **2**:22-3, 26-9
The Skeptic (Raleigh)
See *Sir Walter Raleigh's Sceptick; or, Speculations*
The Skills of the Guild-Masters
See "A Notable Discouery of Coosnage"
The Skimmer; or The History of Tanzai and Néadarné (Crebillon)
See *L'ecumoire; ou, Tanzai et Néadarné, histoire Japonaise*
The Skirmisher Defeated (Penn) **25**:290
"The Skylark" (Ronsard) **6**:408
Slaughter of the Innocents (Chester) **34**:96, 98, 100, 110
The Slaughter of the Innocents (N-Town) **34**:172, 178, 184, 192, 215, 240, 244
The Slaying of Abel (Towneley)
See *Mactacio Abel* (Towneley)
"Sleeping Beauty" (Perrault)
See "La belle au bois dormant"
Small Catechism (Luther)
See *Der kleine Catechismus*
"A Small Poet" (Butler) **16**:23, 54-5
Le smanie della villeggiatura (Goldoni) **4**:268
"Smith" (Wessel) **7**:391-92
"Snail" (Lovelace) **24**:302-04, 315, 322-29, 331, 342, 344
"So, so breake off this last lamenting kisse" (Donne)
See "The Expiration"
Sober and Seasonable Memorandum (Howell) **13**:440
Sober Inspections (Howell)
See *Some Sober Inspections Made into the Carriage and Consults of the Late Long Parliament*
Sociable Letters (Cavendish) **30**:205
The Social Contract (Rousseau)
See *Du Contrat social*
"Soeur Jeanne" (La Fontaine) **50**:67
The Sofa (Crebillon)
See *Le Sopha*
"The Soger Laddie" (Ramsay) **29**:320
"The Soldier" (Erasmus) **16**:119, 195
"The Soldier and the Carthusian" (Erasmus)
See "The Soldier"
"The Soldier and the Carthusian" (Erasmus)
See "The Carthusian"
"The Soldier going to the Field" (Davenant) **13**:195
The Soldier's Fortune (Behn) **1**:33
Soliloquium animae (Kempis) **11**:410
Soliloquy of a Beauty in the Country (Lyttelton) **10**:197, 203
Soliman and Perseda (Kyd) **22**:247, 252-256, 259, 275
"Solitary Devotions" (Vaughan) **27**:314
De solitudine et silentio (Kempis) **11**:411
"Solomon" (Parnell) **3**:255
"Solomon" (Prior)
See "Solomon on the Vanity of the World"
"Solomon on the Vanity of the World" (Prior) **4**:455-56, 458-62, 464, 466-68, 470-73

"Solving a Difficult Case" (P'u Sung-ling) **3**:345
Solyman and Perseda (Kyd)
See *Tragedy*
Some Considerations on Doctor Kennet's Second and Third Letters (Collier) **6**:209
Some Fruits of Solitude in Reflections and Maxims Relating to the Conduct of Human Life (Penn) **25**:299, 302-03, 309, 334, 343-46
Some Papers proper to be read before the R-l Society, concerning the terrestrial Chrysipus, Golden-foot, or Guinea; an insect, or vegetable, resembling the Polypus (Fielding) **46**:67
Some Proposals for a Second Settlement (Penn) **25**:346
"Some Reflections" (Winchilsea) **3**:451
Some Sober Inspections Made into the Carriage and Consults of the Late Long Parliament (Howell) **13**:419-20
Some Thoughts concerning Education (Locke) **7**:271, 280-81; **35**:200, 202, 217, 225, 241-42
"Some Thoughts on the Diseases of the Mind; with a Scheme for purging the Moral Faculties" (Hopkinson) **25**:271
"Some Verses Upon the Burning of Our House, July 10th, 1666" (Bradstreet) **4**:90, 98, 112, 114
Somnium (Buchanan) **4**:119, 123, 134, 138
Somnium (Kepler) **45**:352
See *Hormonice Mundi*
"The Son of God" (More) **9**:298
Sonets amoureux (Ronsard) **6**:426
Sonetti Lussuriosi (Aretino) **12**:14, 18, 21-2, 25
"Song" (Behn)
See "Love Arm'd"
"Song" (Herrick)
See "To the Rose. Song"
"A Song" (Prior) **4**:465
"Song 1" **8**:46
"Song III" (Kochanowski) **10**:161
"Song 5" **8**:46
"Song IX" (Kochanowski) **10**:161
"Song 18" **8**:46
"Song 26" **8**:48
"Song 30" **8**:48
"Song. Endymion Porter and Olivia" (Davenant) **13**:195
"A Song from Cymbeline" (Collins) **4**:214, 217, 224, 230; **40**:181-82, 184
"Song. "'Goe, and catche a falling starre'" (Donne) **10**:50, 52; **24**:153
"Song: My Days Have Been so Wondrous Free" (Parnell) **3**:255
"Song of Death" (Burns) **3**:81; **40**:102
"A Song of Scipina" (Barker) **42**:76
"The Song of the Spirit" (John of the Cross) **18**:209-11
"A Song on a Painting Depicting the God Êrh-lang Hunting in the Surrounding Country with His Followers" (Wu Ch'eng-en)
See "Êrh-lang Sou-shan-t'u Ko"
"Song. 'Sweetest love, I do not goe'" (Donne) **10**:12, 26, 31-2, 36, 52, 58, 82, 96; **24**:154
"A Song to Amoret" (Vaughan) **27**:363
"Song to Celia" (Jonson) **6**:304-05, 317, 322-23, 346, 349
A Song to David (Smart) **3**:365, 369-82, 285-89, 391, 393, 395-401, 403
"A Song to the Maskers" (Herrick) **13**:351, 399, 401
"Song, To Two Lovers Condemn'd to Die" (Davenant) **13**:205

"A Song upon Sylvia" (Herrick) **13**:367
Songe de Vaux (La Fontaine) **50**:50-51, 55
Songs (Kochanowski)
See *Piesni*
Songs and Sonets (Donne) **10**:32-3, 35-6, 47, 50, 52, 54-5, 57, 63, 66, 81-2, 84, 88, 92-3, 96, 98, 106; **24**:151-53, 181-84, 194-97
"The Songs of Selma" (Macpherson) **29**:245-46
"Songs of the Bride" (John of the Cross)
See "Canciones de la Esposa"
"Songs of the Soul" (John of the Cross) **18**:216
"Sonnet 2" **8**:39
"Sonnet 7" **8**:39
"Sonnet VIII" **8**:23
"Sonnet 22" **8**:39
"Sonnet 23" **8**:39
"Sonnet 24" **8**:38
"Sonnet 31" **8**:38
"Sonnet 36" **8**:39
"Sonnet XLII" (Ronsard) **6**:413
"Sonnet XLIII" (Ronsard) **6**:413
"Sonnet 46" **8**:39
"Sonnet 48" **8**:39
"Sonnet LVII" (Ronsard) **6**:430
"Sonnet LIX" **8**:23
"Sonnet 61" **8**:39
"Sonnet 62" **8**:39
"Sonnet LXVI" (Spenser) **5**:363
"Sonnet LXXVI" (Ronsard) **6**:430
"Sonnet CLXXIV" (Ronsard) **6**:431
"Sonnet CXXVII" (Ronsard) **6**:430
"Sonnet on Bathing" (Warton) **15**:441
"Sonnet on Hope" (Juana Ines de la Cruz) **5**:144
"Sonnet on the Death of Mr. Richard West" (Gray) **4**:286, 294, 296, 314-15, 322-23; **40**:220, 222, 229
"Sonnet, on the Death of Robert Riddel, Esq. *of Glen Riddel, April 1794*" (Burns) **40**:102
"Sonnet to Sleep" (Daniel) **24**:
"Sonnet Written after seeing Wilton-House" (Warton) **15**:444
"Sonnet Written at Winslade in Hampshire" (Warton) **15**:441
"Sonnet Written in a Blank Leaf of Dugdale's 'Monasticon'" (Warton) **15**:435, 443, 455
Sonnets (Aretino)
See *Sonetti Lussuriosi*
Sonnets (Warton) **15**:435
Sonnets for Hélène (Ronsard)
See *Sonnets pour Hélène*
Sonnets pour Hélène (Ronsard) **6**:413, 417
Sonnets to Delia (Daniel) **24**:
Sonnets to Idea
See *Idea*
Le Sopha (Crebillon) **1**:75-7, 79, 81, 88-9; **28**:70-2, 75, 80, 92
Sophonisba (Corneille)
See *Sophonisbe*
Sophonisba (Thomson) **16**:393, 395; **40**:274
Sophonisba; or, The Wonder of Women (Marston) **33**:191-93, 199, 205-06, 211-12, 215, 239, 243
Sophonisbe (Corneille) **28**:21, 30, 33, 35
"Sophronyme" (Rousseau) **9**:345
The Sorceries of Sin (Calderon de la Barca)
See *Los encantos de la culpa*
"Sore Fit" (Bradstreet)
See "From Another Sore Fit"
"Sot" (Butler) **16**:50-1
"Les Souhaits" (La Fontaine) **50**:100-101, 103
"Les souhaits ridicules" (Perrault) **2**:253-56, 261, 266, 279-80
"The Soul" (Philips) **30**:279

"The soul is the salt" (Herrick) **13**:341

"The Sow of Feeling" (Fergusson) **29**:180, 207, 215, 219-20, 239

Lo spaccio de la bestia trionfante (Bruno) **27**:75, 85-87, 89-93, 98, 100, 104, 106, 110-11, 118, 120, 122

"The Spanish Doctor" (Kochanowski)
See "O doktorze Hiszpanie"

The Spanish Friar (Behn) **1**:47

The Spanish Friar (Dryden) **3**:186, 193, 210, 214, 229-30, 233; **21**:55-7

The Spanish Gypsy (Middleton) **33**:264, 268, 276, 282

The Spanish Lovers (Davenant) **13**:176

The Spanish Tragedie of Don Horatio and Bellmipeia (Kyd) **22**:254

The Spanish Tragedy (Marston) **33**:256

Spanish Tragedy; or, Hieronimo is mad again (Kyd) **22**:246

The Spanish Wives (Pix) **8**:259-61, 263, 265, 267-69, 271-72, 274-77

Spartam nactus es (Erasmus) **16**:198

"A speach according to Horace" (Jonson) **6**:350

Specimen of an Etimological Vocabulary (Cleland) **2**:53

A Specimen of Discoveries (Leibniz) **35**:168

"Specimens of a Modern Law Suit" (Hopkinson) **25**:249

Le spectateur Français (Marivaux) **4**:358-60, 371-72, 378-80

The Spectator (Addison) **18**:4, 7, 13-15, 20-1, 24, 26-8, 32-7, 39, 42-4, 46-9, 50-1, 53-4, 58, 60, 63-8, 69-71, 72-6, 78

The Spectator (Steele) **18**:313, 318, 320-22, 330-31, 333-37, 340-44, 348, 351-55, 359, 368-70, 372, 376-77, 384-85

The Spectator, 5 (Addison) **18**:51

The Spectator, 10 (Addison) **18**:50, 65

The Spectator, 26 (Addison) **18**:54

The Spectator, 26 (Steele) **18**:324

The Spectator, 35 (Addison) **18**:77

The Spectator, 38 (Addison) **18**:74

The Spectator, 39 (Addison) **18**:8, 39

The Spectator, 40 (Addison) **18**:39, 77

The Spectator, 42 (Addison) **18**:39

The Spectator, 42 (Steele) **18**:326

The Spectator, 44 (Addison) **18**:39

The Spectator, 45 (Addison) **18**:39

The Spectator, 47 (Steele) **18**:372

The Spectator, 62 (Addison) **18**:56

The Spectator, 65 (Steele) **18**:372, 383

The Spectator, 66 (Steele) **18**:347

The Spectator, 69 (Addison) **18**:35

The Spectator, 70 (Addison) **18**:56

The Spectator, 74 (Addison) **18**:56

The Spectator, 79 (Steele) **18**:318

The Spectator, 84 (Steele) **18**:318

The Spectator, 85 (Addison) **18**:77

The Spectator, 94 (Addison) **18**:57

The Spectator, 120 (Addison) **18**:57

The Spectator, 125 (Addison) **18**:33, 35

The Spectator, 126 (Addison) **18**:55

The Spectator, 144 (Steele) **18**:346

The Spectator, 158 (Addison) **18**:35

The Spectator, 160 (Addison) **18**:57

The Spectator, 219 (Addison) **18**:71

The Spectator, 237 (Addison) **18**:57

The Spectator, 249 (Steele) **18**:372

The Spectator, 259 (Steele) **18**:318

The Spectator, 267 (Addison) **18**:40, 78

The Spectator, 290 (Steele) **18**:318

The Spectator, 315 (Addison) **18**:78

The Spectator, 342 (Steele) **18**:350

The Spectator, 356 (Steele) **18**:358

The Spectator, 381 (Addison) **18**:54

The Spectator, 399 (Addison) **18**:34

The Spectator, 409 (Addison) **18**:60, 76

The Spectator, 411 (Addison) **18**:40

The Spectator, 414 (Addison) **18**:37

The Spectator, 428 (Steele) **18**:379

The Spectator, 434 (Addison) **18**:35

The Spectator, 445 (Addison) **18**:50

The Spectator, 446 (Addison) **18**:34

The Spectator, 449 (Steele) **18**:382

The Spectator, 466 (Steele) **18**:318

The Spectator, 489 (Addison) **18**:57

The Spectator, 502 (Steele) **18**:372

The Spectator, 525 (Addison) **18**:34

The Spectator, 58-63 (Addison) **18**:39, 65

The Spectators (Hutten) **16**:225-27, 230, 233, 239, 241, 247

"The Speech of a Fife Laird, Newly Come from the Grave" (Fergusson) **29**:237

"The Speech of Polly Baker" (Franklin) **25**:141

Speech on Economical Reform (Burke) **36**:65, 79

Speech on Moving His Resolutions for Conciliation with the Colonies (Burke) **7**:39, 63; **36**:88

Speech on the East India Bill (Burke)
See *Mr. Burke's Speech, on the 1st December 1783, upon the Question for the Speaker's Leaving the Chair, in Order for the House to Resolve Itself into a Committee on Mr. Fox's East Indian Bill*

Speech on the Nabob of Arcot's Debts (Burke) **7**:62

"A speeche between Ladies, being shepherds on Salilsbury Plaine" **41**:80

Speech...on Presenting, on the 11 of February 1780—a Plan for the Better Security of the Independence of Parliament and the Economical Reformation of the Civil and Other Establishments (Burke) **7**:15-16, 26, 46

The Spell (Gay) **49**:43

Sphaera in quinque libros distributa (Buchanan) **4**:123-25, 129, 134-37

"Spirit of Mogunce" **41**:73

The Spirit of Truth vindicated against...a late Malicious Libel (Penn) **25**:287, 289, 291

"Spiritual Canticle" (John of the Cross) **18**:216

"Spiritual Canticle" (John of the Cross)
See "Cántico Espiritual"

The Spiritual Canticle (John of the Cross)
See *Cántico Espiritual*

Spiritual Letters (Marie de l'Incarnation)
See *Lettres de la Vénérable Mère Marie de l'Incarnation*

Spiritual Relations (Teresa de Jesus) **18**:393, 410

"The Spleen" (Winchilsea)
See "Ode to the Spleen"

Sposizione ai primi XXIX canti dell'Inferno dantesco (Castelvetro) **12**:67-8

"The Spring" (Carew) **13**:20, 32-3

"Spring" (Gray)
See "Ode on Spring"

"Spring" (More) **9**:298

"Spring" (Pope) **3**:334

Spring. A Poem (Thomson) **16**:363-64, 373, 381-83, 393, 401, 405-06, 410,414-15, 423-24, 426, 430-32; **29**:368, 370-71, 373-74, 376, 378-79, 382, 386, 388-89, 393-95, 402-03, 415, 426; **40**:272-73, 275-76, 293-301, 304, 306-09, 321, 323

"Squieres Tale" (Chaucer)
See "Squire's Tale"

"Squire's Tale" (Chaucer) **17**:71, 81, 201, 205

"Ssu-hsün" (P'u Sung-ling) **49**:296

"Ssu-wen lang" (P'u Sung-ling) **49**:280-281, 286

"St. John's Eve" (Kochanowski)
See "Piesn Swietojanska o Sobótce"

"St. Lucies Day" (Donne)
See "A Nocturnal upon S. Lucies day, Being the shortest day"

The St. Marco Place (Goldoni)
See *Il campiello*

"St. Mary Magdalene or The Weeper" (Crashaw)
See "The Weeper"

"St. Teresa" (Crashaw)
See "Hymn to the Name and Honor of the Admirable Saint Teresa, Foundress of the Reformation of the Discalced Carmelites, both men and Women"

The Stablemaster (Aretino)
See *Marescalco*

The Stage Coach (Farquhar) **21**:151, 169

A Stage-Coach Journey to Exeter (Manley)
See *Letters Written by Mrs. Manley*

"Stamp Act Resolves" (Henry)
See "Virginia Resolves"

"Stamp Act Speech" (Henry)
See "Caesar-Brutus' Speech"

Stange Histories of Kings, Princes, Dukes **41**:80

"Stanzas by Mr. Prior" (Prior) **4**:465

"Stanzas to Alcandre on the Return of Oranthe to Fontainebleau" (Malherbe) **5**:168

The Staple of News (Jonson) **6**:300, 306, 308, 310-12, 314, 328, 336; **33**:159, 165

"The Starre" (Herbert) **24**:274

"The Starre" (Vaughan) **27**:325, 338, 341, 364

The Starry Messenger (Galilei)
See *Sidereus Nuncius*

The State of Innocence, and Fall of Man (Dryden) **3**:206, 221, 233; **21**:66

La Statue merveilleuse (Lesage) **28**:208

De Statv Romano (Hutten) **16**:231

"Stavlennik" (Chulkov) **2**:22

"Stay my Charmer can you leave me?" (Burns) **29**:53

"Steer Her Up" (Burns) **3**:86

"Stella's Birthday, March 13, 1727" (Swift) **1**:481, 523

Steps (Crashaw)
See *Steps to the Temple, several poems with other delights of the Muses*

Steps to the Temple, several poems with other delights of the Muses (Crashaw) **24**:

"Still to Be Neat" (Jonson) **6**:305

"The Stoic" (Hume) **7**:153

Stoic Philosophy (Lipsius)
See *Manductionis ad philosophiam stoicam libri tres*

Der stoltze Melcher (Grimmelshausen) **6**:247

"Stone from Heaven" (P'u Sung-ling)
See "Shih Ch'ing-hsü"

Storia d'Italia (Guicciardini) **49**:201, 205, 209-10, 212-13, 216-21, 224-229, 231-32, 234-35, 237-38, 240, 243, 249, 250-51, 253, 255-56

Storie Fiorentine (Guicciardini) **49**:197-99, 201, 210-12, 214-17, 219-20, 224-27, 229, 251, 253, 255, 262

"The Storm" (Donne) **10**:97

"The Storm" (Vaughan) **27**:339

The Storm (Defoe) **1**:162; **42**:202-03

"The Story of Cephisa" (Gay) **49**:4

The Story of Cephisa (Gay) **49**:6

Story of Unnion and Valentine (Steele) **18**:335

The Strait Gate; or, Great Difficulty of Going to

Heaven (Bunyan) **4**:175

The Strange Adventures of the Count de Vinevil and His Family. Being an Account of What Happen'd to Them Whilst They Resided at Constantinople (Aubin) **9**:3-5, 7, 10, 13-14, 16-17

A Strange Horse Race (Dekker) **22**:97, 102

Strange Newes Of the Intercepting Certaine Letters (Nashe) **41**:374, 380

Strange Stories from a Chinese Studio (P'u Sung-ling) **49**:270-271
   See *Liao-chai chih-i*

Strange stories from the Refuge of My Study (P'u Sung-ling)
   See *Liao-chai chih-i*

"A Strange Tale of Pigeons" (P'u Sung-ling) **3**:348; **49**:306, 313-314

The Strange Tales of Liao-chai (P'u Sung-ling)
   See *Liao chai chih i*

"Strephon and Chloe" (Swift) **1**:453, 484, 502-03, 510

Stricturae Politicae (Lipsius) **16**:254

"The Stuarts: A Pindarique Ode" (Aubin) **9**:4

Gli studenti (Ariosto) **6**:61

Stultatia (Erasmus) **16**:169

Die stumme Schönheit (Schlegel) **5**:275, 278

Den stundesløse (Holberg) **6**:264, 267, 273, 276-77

The Stunning Beauty (Vega)
   See *La niñe de plata*

Subhat al-abrár (Jami) **9**:66, 68, 71

Subida del Monte Carmelo (John of the Cross) **18**:202-03, 214, 229-30, 233-36

"Submission" (Herbert) **24**:226

The Successful Strategem (Marivaux)
   See *The Successful Strategem*

"Such a Parcel of Rogues in a Nation" (Burns) **29**:90

Sueño del infierno (Quevedo) **23**:187, 189

Sueno doel juicio final (Quevedo) **23**:186-89

Sueños (Quevedo) **23**:186, 190

"The Suicide" (Warton)
   See "To Suicide"

Sui-T'ang chih-chuan (Lo Kuan-chung) **12**:282

Sui-T'ang liang-ch'ao chih-chuan (Lo Kuan-chung) **12**:282

Suite de l'entretien (Diderot) **26**:116

La suite du menteur (Corneille) **28**:31

La Suivante (Corneille) **28**:45-6

Summa doctrinae christianae trigemina (Andreae) **32**:91

Summary Apologetical History (Las Casas)
   See *Apológetica historia sumaria*

Summer. A Poem (Thomson) **16**:363-64, 369, 373, 375, 381-83, 400-03, 405-06, 409-10, 412, 415, 423-24, 426, 430-32; **29**:367-69, 373-74, 378, 380-84, 386, 392, 395, 402-04, 412, 426, 431; **40**:272, 275-76, 280, 282-85, 288-89, 293-95, 300-01, 305-06, 308-09, 321-22

Summers Last Will and testament (Nashe) **41**:346, 379

Summi Angliae Instauratio magna (Bacon) **32**:106, 108, 111-14, 116, 128, 136-39, 164-166, 181, 183, 187-88

Summi Angliae Instauratio magna (Bacon)
   See *Novum Scientiarum Organum*

"Summoner's Tale" (Chaucer) **17**:169-70, 194, 197, 202, 231, 243

"The Sun Rising" (Donne)
   See "The Sunne Rising"

"The Sunbeams" (More) **9**:298, 314

"Sunday" (Gay) **49**:

"Sunday" (Gay) **49**:

"The Sunne Rising" (Donne) **10**:12, 18, 32, 34, 49, 55; **24**:153-5, 163-64

The Sun's Darlinf (Dekker) **22**:107, 111

Superiority of the Female Sex (Agrippa von Nettesheim)
   See *De nobilitate et praeccelentia foeminei sexus*

"Superliminare" (Herbert) **24**:237, 253, 267

Supper at Emmaus (York)
   See *Travellers to Emmaus* (York)

Supplément au Voyage de Bougainville (Diderot) **26**:91, 118, 144, 149-50, 153, 159, 161, 169

Supplement to Bougainville's Voyage (Diderot)
   See *Supplément au Voyage de Bougainville*

The Supplication of Souls (More) **10**:362, 370, 397-99, 408-09; **32**:269

"Sur des vers de Virgile" (Montaigne) **8**:204, 221, 231, 235, 242

"Sur la bataille de Peterwardein" (Rousseau) **9**:340, 344

Sur la Russie (Diderot) **26**:157

"Sur l'attentat commis en la personne de sa majesté le 19 de Décembre 1605" (Malherbe) **5**:183

"Sur l'aveuglement des hommes du siècle" (Rousseau) **9**:342, 345

"Sur le devoir et le sort des grands hommes" (Rousseau) **9**:344

"Sur les divinités poétiques" (Rousseau) **9**:345

Sur l'histoire universelle (Turgot) **26**:370-73, 378, 381, 390

"Sur un arbrisseau" (Rousseau) **9**:341

"Sur un baiser" (Rousseau) **9**:341

"Sur un commencement d'année" (Rousseau) **9**:344

Suréna (Corneille) **28**:5, 16, 29, 35, 41, 48, 52-5

Surenas (Corneille)
   See *Suréna*

The Surgeon of His Honor (Calderon de la Barca)
   See *El médico de su honra*

La surprise de l'amour (Marivaux) **4**:354, 366-68, 370, 376-78, 381

The Surprise of Love (Marivaux)
   See *The Surprise of Love*

Surprise or Constancy Rewarded (Haywood) **44**:130

The Surprises of Love, Exemplified in the Romance of a Day (Cleland) **2**:52-4

Suspencio Jude (Towneley) **34**:308, 320

"Suspetto d'Herode" (Crashaw) **24**:20, 32

"Suspicion of Herod" (Crashaw)
   See "Suspetto d'Herode"

"Sweet Afton" (Burns) **3**:76, 86; **29**:36, 84-5

"Sweet lover of the soul" (Juana Ines de la Cruz) **5**:152

"Sweetest love, I do not goe" (Donne)
   See "Song. 'Sweetest love, I do not goe'"

"Sweetly breathing vernal air" (Carew) **13**:20

A Swete and devoute Sermon of Holy saynt Ciprian of Mortalitie of Man (Elyot) **11**:62, 84

Sylla et Eucrate (Montesquieu)
   See *Dialogue de Sylla et Eucrate*

"The Sylph Husband" (Marmontel) **2**:214

Le Sylphe; ou, songe de madame de R*** Ecrit par Elle-meme a madame de S*** (Crebillon) **28**:70, 79

Sylva Sylvarum: Or a Natural History (Bacon) **18**:115, 132, 137, 143, 149-50, 187; **32**:106, 117, 185

Sylvae (Dryden) **21**:72, 74-5, 77, 79-80, 119-20

Der symplicianische Welt-Kucker; oder, Abentheuerliche Jan Rebhu, Parts I-IV (Beer) **5**:52-3, 55-6, 59-60

System of Nature (Holbach)
   See *Système de la nature*

Système de la nature (Holbach) **14**:152, 154-56, 158-59, 166, 168-71, 175

Système social (Holbach) **14**:152, 154-56, 175

"Szachy" (Kochanowski) **10**:175

Table of Colours or Appearance of Good and Evil (Bacon)
   See *Colours of Good and Evil*

Table Talk (Luther)
   See *Tischreden; oder, Colloquia ...*

"Le Tableau" (La Fontaine) **50**:70

Tableau des vices de la Constitution anglaise (Marat) **10**:226

Le Tableau du mariage (Lesage) **28**:205, 207

Tableau Économique (Turgot) **26**:373

Tableau philosophique des progrés successifs de l'esprit humain (Turgot) **26**:345, 358

"Tabula smaragdina" (Newton) **35**:295

Tabulae Rudolphinae (Kepler) **45**:339, 343
   See *Hormonice Mundi*

Tacaño (Quevedo) **23**:180

Tacitus (Lipsius)
   See *C. C. Taciti historiarum et annaliem libri qui exstant*

"The Tailor Fell Thro' the Bed" (Burns) **29**:20, 22, 48; **40**:85, 87

"Take heed of loving mee" (Donne)
   See "The Prohibition"

The Taking of Jesus (N-Town) **34**:207

Talanta (Aretino) **12**:19, 26, 30, 36

"A Tale" (Fergusson) **29**:205

"A Tale" (Franklin) **25**:141

Tale of a Tub (Jonson) **6**:300, 306, 311, 314; **33**:159, 166

A Tale of a Tub, Written for the Universal Improvement of Mankind, to Which is Added an Account of a Battel between the Ancient and Modern Books in St. James's Library (Swift) **1**:425, 431, 435, 437, 439-40, 449, 453-59, 470-71, 473, 484-85, 490-91, 495, 497, 504, 509, 513-17, 524

The Tale of Jocondo and Astolpho (Dekker) **22**:88

"Tale of Melibee" (Chaucer) **17**:137, 177, 202, 205, 227, 237, 241, 243-44

The Tale of the Foolish Curiosity (Cervantes)
   See *El curioso impertinente*

"A Tale of the Miser and the Poet" (Winchilsea) **3**:457

"The Tale of Three Bonnets" (Ramsay) **29**:308, 355-57, 362

The Talents (Towneley)
   See *Processus Talentorum* (Towneley)

"Tales" (Prior) **4**:460, 464

Tales (Chaucer)
   See *Canterbury Tales*

Tales (La Fontaine)
   See *Contes et nouvelles en vers*

Tales and Fables (Ramsay) **29**:301, 316, 321, 329, 323, 331-33, 340-2, 352

Tales of Canterbury (Chaucer)
   See *Canterbury Tales*

Talitha Cumi (Sewall) **38**:347

"Tam Glen" (Burns) **3**:66, 74, 78; **29**:7, 47, 49; **40**:97, 104

"Tam o' Shanter" (Burns) **3**:49, 52, 55-6, 61, 64, 66-7, 69, 71-2, 75-6, 78-9, 82-3, 85, 87, 89-91, 96, 106; **29**:5, 24, 32, 35, 40, 47, 58, 60-3, 65-70, 73-6, 92-3; **40**:63, 69, 71, 77-8, 89, 94, 96, 114, 118-19

"Tam Samson's Elegy" (Burns) **29**:6, 29; **40**:96, 114

Tamburlaine the Great: Divided into two Tragicall

Discourses (Marlowe) **22**:329-30, 335-38, 341-42, 344-47, 349, 351-52, 356, 358, 360-63, 367, 369-70, 372, 386-87, 400; **47**:214, 221, 240, 243, 249, 250, 252, 275, 279-84, 301, 340-41, 358-59

Tamerlane (Rowe) **8**:282, 285, 289, 292, 298, 302-04, 308

The Taminge of the Tamer (Fletcher)
    See *The Woman's Prize; or, The Tamer Tamed*

Tamorlan (Vega)
    See *La Nueva Ira de Dios y Gran Tamorlan de Persia*

"Tancred and Sigismunda" (Dryden) **3**:190

Tancred and Sigismunda. A Tragedy (Thomson) **16**:369, 396; **29**:416, 419, 421, 423, 434

Tancréde (Voltaire) **14**:358

Tangier Journal (Pepys) **11**:238

Tanzai (Crebillon)
    See *L'ecumoire; ou, Tanzai et Néadarné, histoire Japonaise*

"Tao-hu" (P'u Sung-ling) **3**:351; **49**:294

Tarquin (Vega) **23**:355

"Tartana: Or, The Plaid" (Ramsay) **29**:327

Tartuffe (Moliere)
    See *Le tartuffe*

Le tartuffe (Moliere) **10**:265, 267-69, 272-73, 275, 277-91, 293-94, 296-99, 304, 307-08, 311-13, 319-21, 325, 329-30, 332-35, 338-40; **28**:227-29, 232-37, 243-44, 246, 248-50, 253, 258-60, 262-67, 269-70, 275-80, 284-85

"Taste" (Smart) **3**:393

The Tatler (Addison) **18**:7, 13-14, 16, 21, 24, 26-7, 31, 35, 37, 39, 42, 46-7, 49, 54, 65, 69

The Tatler (Steele) **18**:312-13, 315-18, 320-29, 331-37, 340-44, 346-49, 351-55, 359-61, 367-69, 372, 376-78, 380-85

The Tatler, 1 (Steele) **18**:334, 383

The Tatler, 3 (Steele) **18**:376

The Tatler, 4 (Steele) **18**:341

The Tatler, 5 (Steele) **18**:317

The Tatler, 8 (Steele) **18**:381

The Tatler, 11 (Steele) **18**:326

The Tatler, 33 (Steele) **18**:349

The Tatler, 45 (Steele) **18**:381

The Tatler, 49 (Steele) **18**:326

The Tatler, 53 (Steele) **18**:326

The Tatler, 63 (Steele) **18**:349

The Tatler, 68 (Steele) **18**:371, 381

The Tatler, 79 (Steele) **18**:345

The Tatler, 82 (Steele) **18**:381

The Tatler, 113 (Steele) **18**:384

The Tatler, 118 (Steele) **18**:384

The Tatler, 141 (Steele) **18**:347

The Tatler, 144 (Steele) **18**:377

The Tatler, 149 (Steele) **18**:381

The Tatler, 163 (Addison) **18**:79

The Tatler, 165 (Addison) **18**:76

The Tatler, 172 (Steele) **18**:345, 382

The Tatler, 178 (Steele) **18**:318

The Tatler, 181 (Steele) **18**:384

The Tatler, 188 (Steele) **18**:318

The Tatler, 198 (Steele) **18**:382

The Tatler, 199 (Steele) **18**:318

The Tatler, 201 (Steele) **18**:346

The Tatler, 219 (Steele) **18**:372

The Tatler, 244 (Steele) **18**:318

The Tatler, 248 (Steele) **18**:347

The Tatler, 271 (Steele) **18**:335, 378

Le taureau blanc (Voltaire) **14**:346, 359

Taxation No Tyranny (Johnson) **15**:198, 203, 208, 276

"Te Deum" (Dennis)

See "Part of the 'Te Deum' Paraphras'd, in Pindarick Verse"

"The Tea-pot and the Scrubbing-brush" (Smart) **3**:366

"The Teare" (Crashaw) **24**:15, 35

The Teares of Peace (Chapman) **22**:29, 32, 34, 51, 74-6

"The Teares of the Daughters of Jerusalem" (Lanyer) **30**:262

"The Teares of the Muses" (Spenser) **5**:312; **39**:321, 342-43

"Tears" (Vaughan) **27**:364, 379

The Tears of Caledonia (Smollett) **46**:188

"The Tears of Scotland" (Smollett) **2**:332-33, 358

"The Tears of St. Peter" (Malherbe)
    See "Les Larmes de Saint Pierre"

The Tea-Table Miscellany (Ramsay) **29**:301, 316, 321, 329, 331-33, 341-2, 352

Teatro (Aretino) **12**:19

"Tedious Man" (Butler) **16**:55

Le télémaque travesti (Marivaux) **4**:385-87

Temora (Macpherson) **29**:242, 246-47, 250, 252, 254-55, 257-59, 265, 270, 272, 276, 279-80, 290, 292-93, 296, 298

"The Temper" (Herbert) **24**:238, 240-41, 258

"The Temper I" (Herbert) **24**:238, 241, 245-46

"The Temper 2" (Herbert) **24**:274

"The Tempest" (Vaughan) **27**:355, 391

The Tempest (Dryden) **21**:88, 107

The Tempest; or, The Enchanted Island (Davenant) **13**:185-87, 216-19

"Temple" (Donne) **24**:167

"The Temple" (Herrick)
    See "The Fairie Temple: or, Oberons Chappell. Dedicated to Mr. John Merrifield, Counsellor at Law"

The Temple Beau (Dryden) **3**:219, 250

The Temple Beau (Fielding) **46**:70, 101-02, 105

Le temple de Gnide (Montesquieu) **7**:320, 324, 342, 348

Le Temple de me\<macute\>moire (Lesage) **28**:204

"Temple des Messeigneurs" (Ronsard) **6**:439

"The Temple of Fame" (Pope) **3**:270, 316

The Temple of Gnidus (Montesquieu)
    See *Le temple de Gnide*

The Temple of Love (Davenant) **13**:175, 181, 189, 196-97

The Temple of Minerva (Hopkinson) **25**:251, 260, 267

The Temple: Sacred Poems and Private Ejaculations (Herbert) **24**:213, 218-21, 231, 234, 252, 254-56, 260, 262-63, 266-68, 274, 276, 278, 283, 286, 290, 293

Temporis partus masculus (Bacon) **18**:121, 144, 154, 187 **32**:137

Temptation (Chester) **34**:125-7, 132

The Temptation (N-Town) **34**:172, 178, 183, 185-6, 188-9, 199

Temptation of Jesus (York) **34**:374

"Le tems" (Rousseau) **9**:345

Ten Articles (Henry VIII)
    See *Articles . . . to Stabliyshe Christen Quietnes*

The Tender Husband (Steele) **18**:314-15, 329-30, 339-40, 343, 353-54, 359, 365, 367

Tentamen Anagogicum (Leibniz) **35**:174

"The Tenth Discourse" (Reynolds) **15**:382, 388, 396, 403

The Tenth Muse Lately sprung up in America (Bradstreet) **4**:84-7, 89-90, 94, 102, 107, 109-11, 114; **30**:117-19, 130-2, 139-41, 146, 152, 154

The Tenure of Kings and Magistrates (Milton) **9**:161

Tercera Orden de San Francisco (Vega) **23**:337

"A Ternary of Littles" (Herrick) **13**:356

Terrors of the Night (Nashe) **41**:356, 370-71, 374

The Test (Marivaux)
    See *The Test*

The Test of Filial Duty, in a Series of Letters between Miss Emilia Leonard and Miss Charlotte Arlington (Scott) **44**:362-64, 409-09

The Test of Friendship (Vega)
    See *La prueba de los amigos*

"Testament explique par Esope" (La Fontaine) **50**:124

Testament of Love (Chaucer)
    See *Legend of Good Women*

"La Tete et la queue du Serpent" (La Fontaine) **50**:99-101, 104

Tethys Festival; or, The Queens Wake (Daniel) **24**:123-24, 126

Tetrachordon (Milton) **9**:163, 208

Der Teutsche Michel (Grimmelshausen) **6**:247

Thalia Rediviva (Vaughan) **27**:306, 309, 324, 337, 364, 366

"The Thanksgiving" (Herbert) **24**:229, 271

"The Thanksgiving" (Herrick) **13**:317, 319, 362

"The Thanksgiving to God" (Herrick) **13**:324

"Thanksgiving to God for his House" (Herrick) **13**:333, 358, 362

"That Politics May Be Reduced to a Science" (Hume) **7**:188, 204

"That to Philosophize Is to Learn to Die" (Montaigne)
    See "Que philosopher, c'est apprendre à mourir"

Theatralische Bibliothek (Lessing) **8**:100

Theatralische Werke (Schlegel) **5**:273

The Theatre (Steele) **18**:346, 354, 372-73

The Theatre, 19 (Steele) **18**:372

Le Théâtre de la foire (Lesage) **28**:200, 204-05, 208

Théâtre espagnol (Lesage) **28**:199

Théâtre forain (Lesage) **28**:208

The Theatrical Candidates (Garrick) **15**:100

La Thébaïde, ou Les frères ennemis (Racine) **28**:293, 312, 339, 34, 380, 383-84

The Thebans, or The Enemy Brothers (Racine)
    See *La Thébaïde, ou Les frères ennemis*

Theca gladii spiritus (Andreae) **32**:91-2

"Theend of the 22 Boock, entreatings of Sorrow" (Raleigh) **31**:265, 279, 283

Theodora, Virgin and Martyr (Corneille)
    See *Théodore, vierge et martyre*

Theodore and Honoria (Dryden) **3**:184, 190, 204-05, 216

Théodore, vierge et martyre (Corneille) **28**:29, 31, 34, 38, 41, 43, 58

Theologia (Campanella) **32**:234

Theologia (Ficino)
    See *Theologia platonica de immortalitate animorum*

Theologia Platonica (Ficino)
    See *Theologia platonica de immortalitate animorum*

Theologia platonica de immortalitate animorum (Ficino) **12**:166-68, 170-72, 174, 177, 182, 185-87, 189, 191, 193, 195, 197-98, 200

Theological Works (More) **9**:309

Theological-Political Treatise (Spinoza)
    See *Tractatus theologico-politicus continens dissertationes all quot, quibus ostenditur libertatem philosophandi non tantum salva pietate, & reipublicae*

Théologie portative (Holbach) **14**:152-53

Theophilus (Andreae) **32**:

Theory of Moral Sentiments (Smith) **36**:314-20, 329-30, 332-36, 353, 369, 371, 376, 378-80, 382, 385, 388-91

"There Was a Lad Was Born in Kyle" (Burns) **3**:87, 92; **40**:97

"There's a Youth in This City" (Burns) **29**:22; **40**:87

"There's Nothing Grieves Me, But that Age Should Haste"
See "Sonnet VIII"

"Thermometer of Zeal" (Addison) **18**:27

"Thétis" (Rousseau) **9**:343

"They are all gone into the world of light!" (Vaughan) **27**:327

Thierry and Theodoret (Fletcher) **33**:40-52

"A Thing Done" (Jonson) **33**:126

"Third and last Part of Conny catching" **41**:149, 151-52, 144-56,181

"The Third Discourse" (Reynolds) **15**:368, 378-80, 383, 391, 395-96, 402, 412, 422

A Third Letter on Toleration (Locke) **35**:217

"The Thirteenth Discourse" (Reynolds) **15**:398, 404

Thirty Propositions (Las Casas) **31**:209

This and That (Chulkov) **2**:19

This Is My Body: These Words Still Stand (Luther) **9**:136

"This is No my ain Hoose" (Ramsay) **29**:330

"This Is Not a Story" (Diderot) **26**:149, 161

"Thomas Cromwell, Earle of Essex" **8**:30, 33

Thomas Indie (Towneley) **34**:326

Thomas of India (Towneley)
See *Thomas Indie* (Towneley)

Thomas of Reading **41**:74-77, 81, 86, 88-90, 100, 102, 106, 113-15, 117-18, 120, 127

"Those eies which set my fancie on a fire" (Raleigh) **31**:269-70, 273

"Thou Lingering Star" (Burns) **3**:56

"Thou Purblind Boy, since Thou Hast Beene So Slacke"
See "Sonnet 36"

"Thou that knowst for whom I mourn" (Vaughan) **27**:337

"An Thou wert my ain Thing" (Ramsay) **29**:330

"Thought and Vision" (Bacon)
See "Cogitata et Visa"

A Thought on Eternity (Gay) **49**:6

Thoughts (Pascal)
See *Pensees*

Thoughts (Wollstonecraft)
See *Thoughts on the Education of Daughters: With Reflections on Female Conduct, in the More Important Duties of Life*

Thoughts and Conclusions (Bacon) **32**:137

Thoughts and Details on Scarcity Originally Presented to the Right Hon. William Pitt in the Month of November, 1795 (Burke) **7**:57, 59-60; **36**:91

Thoughts on French Affairs (Burke) **36**:99

"Thoughts on His Excellency Major General Lee" (Wheatley) **3**:411, 413, 437

Thoughts on Knowledge Truth and Ideas (Leibniz) **35**:132, 135

Thoughts on Religion (Swift) **1**:486, 491

Thoughts on the Cause of the Present Discontents (Burke) **7**:14, 26, 46, 49, 57, 60-3; **36**:88

Thoughts on the Education of Daughters: With Reflections on Female Conduct, in the More Important Duties of Life (Wollstonecraft) **5**:425, 427, 441-42, 460; **50**:293, 324-325,361

Thoughts on the Interpretation of Nature (Diderot)

See *Pensées sur l'interprétation de la nature*

Thoughts on the late Transactions respecting the Falkland Islands (Johnson) **15**:208

"Thoughts on the Works of Providence" (Wheatley) **3**:408, 414, 419, 424, 435-36; **50**:174, 205

Thoughts on Various Subjects (Swift) **1**:480

"Thoughts Upon Various Subjects" (Butler) **16**:49

"A Thousand Martyrs I Have Made" (Behn) **30**:62, 87

Thraseas (Lipsius) **16**:254

Three Bertheonei Books (Paracelsus)
See *Chirurgia minor quam Bertheoneam intitulaut*

"The Three Bonnets" (Ramsay) **29**:321, 353

Three Essays, Moral and Political (Hume) **7**:189

Three Hours after Marriage (Arbuthnot) **1**:17-19

Three Hours after Marriage (Gay) **49**:3, 16, 119, 121-123, 148, 154

Three Justices in One (Calderon de la Barca) **23**:41

The Three Kingdoms (Lo Kuan-chung)
See *San-kuo-chih yeni-i*

Three Letters on the Genius and Writings of Shakespeare (Dennis)
See *An Essay on the Genius of Shakespear*

Threnodia Augustalis (Chethimattam) **3**:186, 216; **21**:65, 67, 82, 86-7

Threnodia Augustalis (Goldsmith) **2**:104

The Threnodies (Kochanowski)
See *Treny*

"Threnody V" (Kochanowski) **10**:153, 163, 166-67, 169

"Threnody VIII" (Kochanowski)
See "Tren VIII"

"Threnody XI" (Kochanowski) **10**:157-58, 163

"Threnody XVII" (Kochanowski)
See "Tren XVII"

"Threnody XVII" (Kochanowski) **10**:153, 158-59, 163, 165, 173

"The Throne" (Vaughan) **27**:338, 379

"Through the Wood, Laddie" (Ramsay) **29**:304, 320

"Throw Away Thy Rod" (Herbert) **24**:277

"Thumbs" (Montaigne) **8**:203

Thursday (Gay) **49**:39, 41,46

"Thursday; or, The Spell" (Gay) **49**:66, 68, 80

"Thy Human Frame, My Glorious Lord, I Spy" (Taylor) **11**:402

"La tia fingida" (Cervantes) **6**:171

"Tibbie, I hae Seen the day" (Burns) **40**:93

Le tiers livre des faictz et dictz heroiques du noble Pantagruel (Rabelais) **5**:216-19, 233-34, 239-41, 243-44, 249, 255-56, 258-59, 267

"The Timber" (Vaughan) **27**:337, 340

Timber; or, Discoveries (Jonson) **6**:291, 312-13, 316, 322, 324, 328, 343, 347, 349-50; **33**:116, 131, 141, 173, 175, 177, 179, 181

"The Times" (Churchill) **3**:141, 143, 155, 162-63

Timon (Boiardo)
See *Timone*

Timone (Boiardo) **6**:88

"Tinker's Song" (Herrick) **13**:331

Tischreden; oder, Colloquia ... (Luther) **9**:110, 127-28; **37**:298

Tite et Bérénice (Corneille) **28**:31, 33, 35, 37, 40-1, 44, 52

Titus and Berenice (Corneille)
See *Tite et Bérénice*

Titus et Gesippus (Foxe) **14**:42-44, 46-47

Titus Vespasian (Cleland) **2**:51

"To a Child of Quality Five Years Old, the Author Forty, Written in 1704" (Prior) **4**:460, 463, 465-66, 475

"To a Child of Quality of Five Years Old, the Author Suppos'd Forty" (Prior)
See "To a Child of Quality Five Years Old, the Author Forty, Written in 1704"

"To a Clergyman on the Death of His Lady" (Wheatley) **3**:433

"To a Clergyman on the Death of Their Relations" (Wheatley) **50**:195

"To a Crowing Cock" (Kochanowski)
See "Gallo crocitanti"

"To a Crowing Gaul" (Kochanowski)
See "Gallo crocitanti"

"To a Fine Young Woman, Who, Being Asked by Her Lover, Why She Kept So Filthy a Thing as a Snake in Her Bosom; Answer'd, 'Twas to Keep a Filthier Thing out of it, His Hand'" (Wycherley) **8**:415

"To a Gentleman in the Navy" (Wheatley) **3**:420; **50**:162, 241

"To a Gentleman on His Voyage to Great Britain for the Recovery of His Health" (Wheatley) **50**:188-90

"To a Girl" (Kochanowski) **10**:160

"To a Haggis" (Burns)
See "Address to a Haggis"

"To a Kiss" (Burns) **3**:86

"To a Lady" (Kochanowski)
See "Do paniej"

"To a Lady" (Prior) **4**:466

"To a Lady and Her Children, On the Death of Her Son and Their Brother" (Wheatley) **50**:195

To a Lady on her Passion for Old China (Gay) **49**:25

"To a Lady on her Passion for Old China" (Guicciardini) **49**:25

"To a Lady on Her Remarkable Preservation in an Hurricane in North Carolina" (Wheatley) **3**:430-31; **50**:189, 225

"To a Lady on the Death of Three Relations" (Wheatley) **3**:422, 428; **50**:195

"To a Lady, Who Wore Drawers in an Ill Hour" (Wycherley) **8**:399

"To a Lady with Child that Ask'd an Old Shirt" (Lovelace) **24**:306, 348, 354

"To a Louse, on Seeing One on a Lady's Bonnet at Church" (Burns) **3**:63, 67, 71, 87, 94-5; **29**:10-11, 30, 32

"To a Mountain Daisy, on Turning One Down with the Plough in April, 1786" (Burns) **3**:48, 67, 87, 94-5; **29**:30, 79, 93; **40**:95, 116

"To a Mouse, on Turning Her Up in Her Nest with the Plough, November, 1785" (Burns) **3**:48, 60, 67, 71, 77, 79, 87, 73-5; **29**:4, 10, 30, 32-3, 64, 91; **40**:95, 119

"To a Supposed Mistress" (Crashaw)
See "Wishes to His Suppos'd Mistress"

"To a Vain Young Courtier" (Wycherley) **21**:342

"To A Young Friend" (Burns)
See "Epistle to a Young Friend"

"To a Young Gentleman, Who Was Blam'd for Marrying Young" (Dennis) **11**:47

"To a Young Lady Fond of Fortune Telling" (Prior) **4**:461

"To a Young Lady, with Some Lampreys" (Gay) **49**:25

"To A.D., unreasonable distrustfull of her owne beauty" (Carew) **13**:37

"To Adversity" (Gray)

See "Ode to Adversity"

"To A.L. Perswasions to Love" (Carew) **13**:11, 18, 21, 27, 29-30, 34, 54-7

"To all Noble and Worthy Ladies" (Cavendish) **30**:200, 203

"To all vertuous Ladies in generall" (Lanyer) **10**:183, 188-89; **30**:250

"To Althea: From Prison" (Lovelace) **24**:303-04, 306-07, 309, 313, 316, 319-21, 333-36, 350

"To Amarantha" (Lovelace)
See "To Amarantha, That She Would Dishevell Her Hair"

"To Amarantha, That She Would Dishevell Her Hair" (Lovelace) **24**:326

"To Amaranthe" (Lovelace)
See "Pastoral: To Amarantha"

"To Amoret gone from him" (Vaughan) **27**:289, 302, 316, 324, 330-31, 362-63

"To Amoret Walking in a Starry Evening" (Vaughan) **27**:289, 323-24, 363, 368, 396

"To Amoret Weeping" (Vaughan) **27**:289, 363

"To Amoret,of the difference twixt him, and other Lovers, and what true Love is" (Vaughan) **27**:289, 302, 317-18, 320, 329, 363, 396

"To an University Wit, or Poet; Who Had Written Some Ill Verses, with an Ill Play or Two; Which, Not Succeeding, He Resolv'd to Turn Parson" (Wycherley) **8**:399

"To Antenor on a paper of mine" (Philips) **30**:301

"To Antenor on a Paper of mine which J J threatens to publish to prejudice him" (Philips) **30**:289, 306

"To Anthea" (Herrick) **13**:336, 341, 351-52, 365

"To Anthea Lying in Bed" (Herrick) **13**:351

"To Anthea, Who May Command Him Any Thing" (Herrick) **13**:355

"To Ben Jonson Upon occasion of his Ode of defiance annext to his play of the new Inne" (Carew) **13**:32, 65

"To Blossoms" (Herrick) **13**:336

"To Candidus: How to Choose a Wife" (More) **10**:428-29

"To Celimena" (Philips) **30**:295

"To Charis" (Jonson)
See "To Charis"

"To Cherry-Blossomes" (Herrick) **13**:350

"To Colonel De Peyster" (Burns)
See "Epistle to Colonel de Peyster"

"To Cooke-ham" (Lanyer) **30**:246-48

"To Cupid" (Herrick) **13**:341

"To Daffadills" (Herrick) **13**:336-37, 349-50, 353-54, 364, 402

"To Deanbourn, a rude River in Devon" (Herrick) **13**:387-88

"To Dianeme" (Herrick) **13**:389

"To Dr. R.S. my indifferent Lover, who complain'd of my Indifferency" (Barker) **42**:76

"To Dr. Samuel Johnson: Food for a new Edition of his Dictionary" (Fergusson) **29**:194, 211

"To Dr. Sherlock, on His Practical Discourse Concerning Death" (Prior) **4**:466

"To drink is a Christian diversion" (Congreve) **5**:85

"To Electra" (Herrick) **13**:337, 353

"To Esesia looking from her Casement at the Full Moon" (Vaughan) **27**:360

"To Etesia (for Timander,) the first Sight" (Vaughan) **27**:360

"To Etesia going beyond Sea" (Vaughan) **27**:362

"To Etesia parted from him, and looking back" (Vaughan) **27**:361

"To fair Fidelle's grassy tomb" (Collins) **4**:218

"To Find God" (Herrick) **13**:319, 374

"To Flavia Who Fear'd She Was Too Kind" (Dennis) **11**:48

"To Flowers" (Herrick) **13**:364

"To God" (Herrick) **13**:317

"To Henry Higden" (Behn) **30**:68

"To Henry Jarmin" (Davenant) **13**:206

"To Her Most Honoured Father Thomas Dudley" (Bradstreet) **30**:137, 139

"To Him Who Hates Me" (Bruno) **27**:96

"To His Book" (Herrick) **13**:393

"To his Books" (Vaughan) **27**:311

"To his Conscience" (Herrick) **13**:319

"To His Coy Love" **8**:27

"To His Coy Mistress" (Marvell) **4**:397, 400-01, 403-4, 411, 425, 427, 430, 432-34, 439, 441-42, 445-57; **43**:261

"To His Dear Brother, Colonel F. L." (Lovelace) **24**:304

"To his Dying Brother, Master William Herrick" (Herrick) **13**:353

"To His Excellency General George Washington" (Wheatley) **3**:416; 234-35, 241

"To His Friend, Being in Love" (Vaughan) **27**:316

"To His Honor the Lieutenant Governor on the Death of His Lady" (Wheatley) **3**:415

"To his Kinswoman, Mistresse Penelope Wheeler" (Herrick) **13**:391

"To his Mistress confined" (Carew) **13**:10

"To His Mistresses" (Herrick) **13**:393

"To his Mistris Going to Bed" (Donne) **24**:151

"To his Muse" (Herrick) **13**:393

"To his retired friend, an invitation to Brecknock" (Vaughan) **27**:303

"To His Rivall" **8**:27

"To His Sacred Majesty, A Panegyrick on His Coronation" (Dryden) **3**:223; **21**:81-2, 85

"To his Son" (Raleigh) **39**:122

"To His Valentine" **8**:17

"To his Valentine" (Herrick) **13**:338

"To his worthy Kinsman, Master Stephen Soame" (Herrick) **13**:391

"To Honor Dryden" (Dryden) **3**:239

"To I. Morgan . . . upon his sudden Journey and succeeding Marriage" (Vaughan) **27**:358

"To Imagination" (Wheatley)
See "On Imagination"

"To J. S****" (Burns) **40**:85

"To John Donn" (Jonson) **33**:173

"To John Hoddesdon, on His Divine Epigrams" (Dryden) **3**:223

"To John I Ow'd Great Obligation" (Prior) **4**:459

"To Julia" (Herrick) **13**:340, 353, 391, 403-04

"To Julia, in Her Dawne, or Day-breake" (Herrick) **13**:403

"To Julia, the Flaminica Dialis, or Queen-Priest" (Herrick) **13**:353

"To Lady Crew, upon the Death of Her Child" (Herrick)
See "To the Lady Crew, upon the Death of Her Child"

"To Laurels" (Herrick) **13**:341

"To Live Merrily, and to Trust to Good Verses" (Herrick) **13**:350, 365-67, 382

"To Love" (Kochanowski)
See "Do Millosci"

"To Love" (Wycherley) **8**:399

"To Lucasta: From Prison" (Lovelace) **24**:301, 304-05, 316, 320, 334-35, 337, 343, 344-45, 353

"To Lucasta Going Beyond the Sea" (Lovelace)

24:303-04, 341-42, 346, 350, 352

"To Lucasta on Going to the Wars" (Lovelace) **24**:301-04, 306, 310, 316, 318, 320-21, 333, 341-42, 346, 350, 352

"To Lucasta. The Rose" (Lovelace) **24**:306, 315, 326

"To Maevis Junior" (Ramsay) **29**:339

"To Major Logan" (Burns) **29**:20

"To Mary in Heaven" (Burns) **3**:61, 72, 74; **40**:63, 97

"To Marygolds" (Herrick) **13**:353

To Matthew Prior, Esq; Upon the Roman Satirists (Dennis) **11**:40

"To Mæcenas" (Wheatley) **50**:161-62, 191-92, 196, 203, 212, 226-27, 232, 238, 241, 252, 255-57, 259
See "Ode to Mæcenas"

"To Meadows" (Herrick) **13**:337

"To Mr. and Mrs. ******* on the Death of TheirInfant Son" (Wheatley) **3**:436

"To Mr. E. H. Physician and Poet" (Dennis) **11**:47

"To Mr. Gray" (Warton) **15**:442

"To Mr. Gray, on the Publication of His Odes" (Garrick) **15**:114, 125

"To Mr. Henry Lawes" (Philips) **30**:278

"To Mr. Hill, on his Verses to the Dutchess of York when she was at Cambridge" (Barker) **42**:97

"To Mr. Hobbes" (Cowley) **43**:153, 167, 170

"To Mr. Hobs" (Cowley)
See "To Mr. Hobbes"

"To Mr. Pope" (Parnell)
See "Letter to Mr. Pope"

"To Mr R. W. 'If as mine is'" (Donne) **10**:9, 39

"To Mr S. B. 'O Thou which'" (Donne) **10**:97

"To Mr T. W. 'All haile sweet Poet'" (Donne) **10**:97

"To Mr. Tilman after he had taken orders" (Donne) **24**:173

"To Mr. Waller in His Old Age" (Wycherley) **8**:380

To Mr. West at Wickham (Lyttelton) **10**:199

"To Mrs. Leonard, on the Death of Her Husband" (Wheatley) **50**:195

"To Mrs M. H. 'Mad paper, stay'" (Donne) **10**:83

"To Music" (Herrick) **13**:317

"To Musique, to becalme his Fever" (Herrick) **13**:336

"To My Auld Breeks" (Fergusson) **29**:173, 190-91, 212

"To My Booke" (Jonson) **6**:351

"To My Booke-seller" (Jonson) **6**:352

"To my Cousin, C.R., Marrying my Lady A" (Carew) **13**:15

"To My Dear and Loving Husband His Goeing into England" (Bradstreet) **4**:94; **30**:126,

"To My Dear Children" (Bradstreet) **4**:104; **30**:124, 145, 148, 151

"To My Dear Cousin Mrs. M.T. after the Death of her Husband and Son" (Barker) **42**:97

"To My Dear Sister Mrs CP on Her Marriage" (Philips) **30**:278, 287

"To my dearest Antenor on his Parting" (Philips) **30**:289

"To my Excellent Lucasia on our Friendship" (Philips)
See "Friendship in Embleme or the Seal To My Dearest Lucasia"

"To my friend G.N. from Wrest" (Carew)
See "Letter to G.N. from Wrest"

"To my Friend Mr. Ogilby Upon the Fables of Aesop Paraphras'd in Verse" (Davenant) **13**:204, 206

"To my Friend S. L. on his Receiving the Name of Little Tom King" (Barker) **42**:97

"To My Friends against Poetry" (Barker) **42**:97-8

"To My Honored Friend, Dr. Charleton" (Dryden) **3**:223

"To My Honored Friend, Sir Robert Howard" (Dryden) **3**:223

"To My Honour'd Kinsman, John Driden, of Chesterton, in the County ofHuntingdon, Esq." (Dryden) **3**:246

"To my Honoured friend, Master Thomas May, upon his Comedie, The Heire" (Carew) **13**:45

"To my Inconstant Mistress" (Carew) **13**:13, 33

"To My Ingenious and worthy Friend, W.L., Esq., Author of that Celebrated Treatise in Folio Called the 'Land Tax Bill'" (Gay) **49**:27

"To my Ingenuous Friend, R. W." (Vaughan) **27**:359

"To my Lady Elizabeth Boyle Singing now affairs &c" (Philips) **30**:303, 318

"To My Lord Chancellor" (Dryden) **3**:223; **21**:85, 87

"To My Lord Colrane" (Killigrew) **4**:350

To my Lord Hervey (Lyttelton) **10**:215

"To my Lucasia in defence of declared Friendship" (Philips) **30**:291, 301

"To My Mistresse in Absence" (Carew) **13**:62

"To My Most Dearely-Loved Friend Henery Reynolds Esquire, of Poets and Poesie" **8**:9, 25

"To my much honoured Friend, Henry Lord Carey of Lepington, upon his translation of Malvezzi" (Carew) **13**:54, 65

"To My Muse" (Cowley) **43**:140

"To My Muse" (Jonson) **33**:179

"To My Noble Friend Master William Browne, of the Evill Time" **8**:9

"To My Reader" (Jonson) **6**:352

"To my Unkind Strephon" (Barker) **42**:76

"To my worthy Friend, M. D'Avenant, Upon his Excellent Play, The Just Italian" (Carew) **13**:66

"To my Worthy Friend Master George Sandys, on his Translation of the Psalms" (Carew) **13**:25, 31

"To My Worthy Friend Mr. Peter Lilly" (Lovelace) **24**:327, 337, 340, 345

"To Nath. Lee, in Bethlem" (Wycherley) **21**:344

"To Ovid's Heroines in his Epistles" (Barker) **42**:76, 96

"To Penshurst" (Jonson) **6**:342, 347; **33**:169, 171-72, 174

"To Perilla" (Herrick) **13**:350, 352

"To Philaster on His Melancholy for Regina" (Philips) **30**:279

"To Phyllis, to Love and Live with Him" (Herrick) **13**:323, 332, 360

"To Pontius washing the blood-stained hands" (Crashaw) **24**:45

"To Primroses fill'd with Morning-Dew" (Herrick) **13**:350

"To Regina Collier on Her Cruelty to Philaster" (Philips) **30**:279

"To Rosania & Lucasia" (Philips) **30**:309

"To S. M., A Young African Painter, on Seeing His Works" (Wheatley) **3**:412, 420, 423, 436; **50**:196, 242

"To Saxham" (Carew)
    See "Address to Saxham"

To Serve with Bad Luck (Vega)
    See *Servir con mala estrella*

"To Shakespeare" (Jonson) **33**:173

"To Sir Clipesby Crew" (Herrick) **13**:368, 392-93

"To Sir Edward Dering (the Noble Silvander) on His Dream and Navy" (Philips) **30**:279

"To Sir Edward Herbert, at Julyers. 'Man is a lumpe'" (Donne) **10**:103

"To Sir Godfrey Knelles" (Dryden) **21**:89

"To Sir Henry Wotton. 'Here's no more newes'" (Donne) **10**:39

"To Sir Henry Wotton. 'Sir, more then kisses'" (Donne) **10**:39

"To Sir Robert Wroth" (Jonson) **33**:172

"To Sir William Davenant" (Cowley) **43**:168

"To Sleep" (Kochanowski)
    See "Do snu"

"To Sleep" (Warton) **15**:444

"To Suicide" (Warton) **15**:444, 447

"To Sylvia" (Herrick) **13**:313

"To the Abbé de la Roche at Auteuil" (Franklin) **25**:141

"To the Angell spirit of the most excellent Sir Phillip Sidney" (Sidney) **19**:296, 299, 303, 309-10; **39**:162, 163, 166, 167, 189-95

"To the Author of The Touchstone of Truth" (Jonson) **6**:325

"To the Authors of the British Magazine" (Goldsmith) **48**:216-19

"To the best, and most accomplish'd Couple" (Vaughan) **27**:330, 359

To the Children of the Light (Penn) **25**:331

To the Christian Nobility... (Luther)
    See *An den Christlichen Adel deutscher Nation: Von des Christlichen Standes Besserung*

"To the Countess Denbigh" (Crashaw)
    See "Address to the Noblest and Best of Ladies, the Countess Denbigh Against Irresolution and Delay in Matters of Religion"

"To the Countess of Anglesie upon the immoderately-by-her lamented death of her Husband" (Carew) **13**:49-50

"To the Countess of Burlington" (Garrick) **15**:97

"To the Countess of Roscommon" (Philips) **30**:315

"To the Countesse of Bedford. 'Madame, reason is'" (Donne) **10**:9

"To the Countesse of Bedford. 'Madame, You have refin'd'" (Donne) **10**:83

"To the Countesse of Bedford. 'This twilight of'" (Donne) **10**:9

"To the Countesse of Huntingdon. 'That unripe side'" (Donne) **10**:36

"To the De'il" (Burns)
    See "Address to the De'il"

"To the doubtfull Reader" (Lanyer) **30**:249

"To the Duchess of Ormond" (Dryden) **3**:243; **21**:87

"To the E. of D." (Donne) **24**:169

"To the Earle of Portland, Lord Treasurer; on the marriage of his Sonne" (Davenant) **13**:205

"To the Eccho" (Winchilsea) **3**:454

"To the Empire of America Beneath the Western Hemisphere. Farewell to America" (Wheatley) **50**:242

"To the Excellent Mrs Anne Owen upon receiving the Name of Lucasia and Adoption into our Society December 28 1651" (Philips) **30**:308

"To the Holy Bible" (Vaughan) **27**:337, 389

"To the Honour of Pimps and Pimping; dedicated to the Court; and written at a Time when such were most considerable there" (Wycherley) **21**:348

"To the Honourable Charles Montague, Esq." (Prior) **4**:461, 465

"To the Importunate Address of Poetry" (Barker) **42**:96

"To the King" (Herrick) **13**:395

"To the King" (Young) **3**:488

"To the King at his entrance into Saxham" (Carew) **13**:61

"To the King on New-yeares day 1630" (Davenant) **13**:205

"TO THE KING, to cure the Evill" (Herrick) **13**:395-96

"TO THE KING, upon His Comming with His Army into the West" (Herrick) **13**:389

"To the King's Most Excellent Majesty" (Wheatley) **50**:191, 240

"To the Lady Castlemaine, upon Her Incouraging His First Play" (Dryden) **3**:223

"To the Lady Crew, upon the Death of Her Child" (Herrick) **13**:353, 366

"To the Linden Tree" (Kochanowski)
    See "Na lipe"

"To the little Spinners" (Herrick) **13**:374

"To the Lord Cary of Lepington" (Davenant) **13**:206

"To the Maids to walk abroad" (Herrick) **13**:360

"To the Majestie of King James" **8**:30

To the Memory of a Lady Lately Deceased: A Monody (Lyttelton) **10**:198-99, 201, 203, 207, 209-10, 215

"To the Memory of Master Newbery" (Smart) **3**:374

"To the Memory of Mr. Congreve" (Thomson) **16**:428-29

"To the Memory of Mr. Oldham" (Dryden) **3**:201

"To the Memory of My Beloved, the Author, Mr. William Shakespeare, and What He Hath Left Us" (Jonson) **6**:348, 350

To the Memory of Sir Isaac Newton (Thomson)
    See *A Poem Sacred to the Memory of Sir Isaac Newton*

"To the Memory of the Right Honourable the Lord Talbot" (Thomson) **16**:428

"To the morning" (Crashaw)
    See "To the morning in satisfaction for sleep"

"To the morning in satisfaction for sleep" (Crashaw) **24**:9, 53

"To the Name Above Every Name" (Crashaw)
    See "Hymn to the Name above every Name—the Name of Jesus"

"To the Name of Jesus" (Crashaw)
    See "Hymn to the Name above every Name—the Name of Jesus"

"To the New Yeere" **8**:17, 27

"To the Nightengale" (Thomson) **16**:427

"To the Nightingale" (Winchilsea) **3**:441-42, 444, 447, 451, 454

To the Nobility of the Gerrman Nation... (Luther)
    See *An den Christlichen Adel deutscher Nation: Von des Christlichen Standes Besserung*

"To the Noble Palemon on His Incomparable Discourse of Friendship" (Philips) **30**:281

"To the Painter" (Carew) **13**:63

"To the Ph—an Ode" (Ramsay) **29**:330, 337

"To the Pious Memory of C. W. Esquire" (Vaughan) **27**:376

"To the Pious Memory of the Accomplisht Young Lady Mrs. Anne Killigrew" (Dryden) **3**:186, 216, 223

"To the Principal and Professors of the University of St. andrews, on their superb treat to Dr. Samuel Johnson" (Fergusson) **29**:189, 191, 194, 211, 216, 231

"To the Queen" (Carew) **13**:59
"To the Queen of inconstancie" (Philips) **30**:309
"To the Queenes most Excellent Majestie" (Lanyer) **10**:183
"To the Queen's Majesty" (Crashaw) **24**:38-9
"To the Queen's most excellent Majestie" (Lanyer) **30**:245
"To the Reader of Master William Davenant's Play" (Carew) **13**:67
"To the Reader of My Works" (Cavendish) **30**:200-03, 225
"To the Reader of These Sonnets" **8**:37
"To the Rev John M'Math" (Burns) **29**:32
"To the Reverend Dr. Thomas Amory on Reading His Sermons on Daily Devotion, in Which theat Duty is Recommended and Assisted" (Wheatley) **50**:225-26
"To the Reverend Shade of his Religious Father" (Herrick) **13**:350
"To the Right Honorable William, Earl of Dartmouth, His Majesty's Principal Secretary of State for North America" (Wheatley) **3**:415, 423, 427, 429, 434; **50**:150, 180, 202, 212, 225, 232-33, 244
"To the River Isca" (Vaughan) **27**:359
"To the River Lodon" (Warton) **15**:435, 443
"To the Rose" (Herrick) **13**:334
"To the Rose. Song" (Herrick) **13**:398
"To the Royal Academy" (Franklin)
  See "Letter to the Royal Academy"
"To the Royal Society" (Cowley) **43**:150, 152, 167, 170-1
"To the Same (i.e., to Celia)" (Jonson) **6**:349
"To the same Party Counsel concerning her choice" (Crashaw) ·**24**:62
"To the Students at Cambridge" (Wheatley) **50**:194
"To the Toothache" (Burns) **3**:67, 85
"To the Translator of Lucan" (Raleigh) **39**:122
"To the Tron-Kirk Bell" (Fergusson) **29**:169, 179, 189, 193, 205, 217, 225
"To the truly Noble Mrs Anne Owne on my first Approaches" (Philips) **30**:300
"To the two Universities" (Cavendish) **30**:200
"To the University of Cambridge, in New England" (Wheatley) **3**:413, 415-16, 423, 427, 429; **50**:149, 162, 179, 214, 232-33
"To the Vertuous Reader" (Lanyer) **10**:181-82, 184, 190; **30**:243-44, 249, 252, 260
"To the Virginian Voyage" **8**:18, 25-7, 30, 42-5
"To the Virgins, to Make Much of Time" (Herrick) **13**:319, 337, 354, 357, 361, 367
"To the Weaver's gin ye go" (Burns) **29**:22, 54-5; **40**:87
"To the Woodlark" (Burns) **3**:81
"To Violets" (Herrick) **13**:337
"To William Simpson of Ochiltree, May 1785" (Burns)
  See "Epistle to William Simpson of Ochiltree, May 1785"
"Toad and Spyder" (Lovelace) **24**:308, 315, 330, 334, 336, 348
La toison d'or (Corneille) **28**:32, 34, 36, 38
Tom Jones (Fielding)
  See The History of Tom Jones, a Foundling
"Tom May's Death" (Marvell) **4**:439; **43**:252, 274
Tombeau de Marguerite de Valois (Ronsard) **6**:434
"Le Tombeau du feu Roy Tres-Chrestien Charles IX" (Ronsard) **6**:437
Tombo-Chiqui; or, The American Savage (Cleland) **2**:51, 53

Tommorow is a New Day (Calderon de la Barca) **23**:64
La Tontine (Lesage) **28**:199-200, 206, 209
"The Toothache cured by a Kiss" (Carew) **13**:18
The Topsy-Turvy World (Grimmelshausen)
  See Die Verkehrte Welt
Los torneos de Aragón (Vega) **23**:393
"Torticolis" (Rousseau) **9**:345
"La Tortue et les deux canards" (La Fontaine) **50**:85, 128, 131
Totum in Toto (Marston) **33**:223
Tour of Corsica (Boswell)
  See An Account of Corsica, The Journal of a Tour to that Island; and the Memoirs of Pascal Paoli
A Tour through the Whole Island of Great Britain (Defoe) **1**:173-74; **42**:203
"The Tournament" (Chatterton) **3**:124, 135
"The Town and Country Contrasted. In an Epistle to a Friend" (Fergusson) **29**:205
Town Eclogues (Montagu)
  See Court Poems
The Town Fop; or, Sir Timothy Tawdrey (Behn) **1**:33, 39, 46-7; **30**:71-4, 81
"The Town Mouse and the Country Mouse" (Cowley) **43**:160
Los trabajos de Persiles y Sigismunda (Cervantes) **6**:142-43, 151, 169-70, 174-76, 178, 180; **23**:94-99, 111, 115, 120-21, 132-34, 143-44
"Tract on the Popery Laws" (Burke) **7**:46; **36**:80, 85
"A Tract Relatives to the Laws Against Popery in Ireland" (Burke)
  See "Tract on the Popery Laws"
Tractatus theologico-politicus continens dissertationes all quot, quibus ostenditur libertatem philosophandi non tantum salva pietate, & reipublicae (Spinoza) **9**:393, 397-98, 402, 408-09, 418-19, 423-24, 431, 436, 438-40
La tragedia por los celos (Castro) **19**:7-8
"The Tragedie of Antonie" (Sidney) **39**:143-45, 150, 172, 173, 176
The Tragedie of Mariam, Faire Queene of Jewry (Cary) **30**:158-159, 162-64, 166-71
The Tragedie of Soliman and Perseda (Kyd) **22**:248, 254-55, 257, 259, 271
Tragedy (Kyd) **22**:246, 254
The Tragedy of Bussy D'Ambois (Chapman) **22**:3, 5, 7-8, 11, 15, 18-19, 20-2, 30-1, 34, 36-9, 40, 42, 44, 52, 54, 56, 57, 78-9, 80-1
·The Tragedy of Caesar and Pompey (Chapman) **22**:7, 12-13, 15, 30, 34, 46-7, 54
Tragedy of Cato (Addison) **18**:7, 10-11, 14-15, 17-19, 31-2, 46-7, 76-7
The Tragedy of Chabot, Admiral of France (Chapman) **22**:7, 13, 15, 45-6
The Tragedy of Cleopatra (Daniel) **24**:85, 89, 98, 107, 112-15, 118, 122, 130-31, 134
The Tragedy of Dido, Queen of Carthage (Marlowe) **22**:339, 347, 361-63; **47**:275, 283
The Tragedy of Jane Shore (Rowe) **8**:285, 287, 292-97, 299-302, 304-08, 314, 316
The Tragedy of Lady Jane Gray (Rowe) **8**:293, 297, 300, 302, 305, 307-08
The Tragedy of Philotas (Daniel) **24**:85, 89, 90, 98, 122, 128, 134, 141-42, 145
The Tragedy of Sophonisba (Thomson) **16**:387
The Tragedy of the Horatii (Aretino)
  See Orazia
The Tragedy of Tragedies; or, The Life and Death of Tom Thumb The Great (Fielding) **1**:203,

239; **46**:75, 94, 161, 166, 177
A Tragic Play in the Christian World **23**:65
The Tragicall History of the Life and Death of Doctor Faustus (Marlowe) **22**:328-29, 333-36, 338-39, 347, 349-51, 361-67, 371-73, 378-86, 389-91, 394-96, 398-400; ·**47**:201-408
Tragicomedia de Calisto y Melibea (Rojas)
  See La Celestina
The Tragicomedy of Calisto and Melibea (Rojas)
  See La Celestina
Trail and Flagellation of Christ (Chester) **34**:121, 135
Traité de métaphysique (Voltaire) **14**:339, 366-67, 379
Traité des animaux (Condillac) **26**:45, 47, 50, 53
Traité des devoirs (Montesquieu) **7**:339, 356, 360
Traité des sensations (Condillac) **26**:6, 8, 10, 12-15, 23, 27·9, 44, 47, 50-3, 55-6, 59-60
Traité des systèmes (Condillac) **26**:6, 8, 11-12, 17, 38, 44, 47
Traite du vide (Pascal) **35**:392
Traité sur la tolérance (Voltaire) **14**:370, 379, 402
Le Traitre puni (Lesage) **28**:199, 206, 208, 210
Trampagos, the Pimp Who Lost His Moll (Cervantes) **6**:190-92
"The Transfiguration" (Herrick) **13**:353, 403
The Transfiguration (York) **34**:387
"Transition" (Pascal) **35**:369
Translation of the Latter Part of the Third Book of Lucretius: Against the Fear of Death (Dryden) **21**:72-4, 76-7
A Translation of the Psalms of David, Attempted in the Spirit of Christianity, and Adapted to the Divine Service (Smart) **3**:371, 376-78, 382, 395, 398
Translations from Ariosto (Gay) **49**:7, 127
"Transmigrations of Pug the Monkey" (Addison) **18**:28
Transportata (Bacon) **32**:133
El trato de Argel (Cervantes) **6**:177-78, 180-81; **23**:100
Los tratos de Argel (Cervantes)
  See El trato de Argel
Trattato della Pittura (Vinci) **12**:384, 391, 393-96, 406, 412, 417-18, 420-21, 423-25, 427
Travel Journal (Montaigne)
  See Journal du voyage de Michel de Montaigne en Italie par la Suisse et l'Allemagne en 1580 et 1581
The Traveller (Berry)
  See The Unfortunate Traveller or the life of Jack Wilton
The Traveller: A Prospect of Society (Goldsmith) **2**:66, 68, 71-5, 80-2, 94-5, 97, 102, 104-05, 112-15, 128-31; **48**:193, 221
"The Traveller Benighted and Lost" (Hopkinson) **25**:250-51
Travellers to Emmaus (York) **34**:371
"The Travelling Spirit" (Cavendish) **30**:188
Travels (Addison) **18**:30
Travels, Chiefly on Foot, through Several Parts of England in 1782 (Moritz)
  See Reisen eines Deutschen in England im Jahr 1782
Travels into Several Remote Nations of the World, in Four Parts. By Lemuel Gulliver (Swift) **1**:426-29, 432-37, 439-42, 444-52, 456, 460-79, 483-91, 497-502, 504-10, 513-17, 519, 527-29; **42**:290-378
Travels through France and Italy (Smollett)

2:322, 329, 331, 344, 363, 365-67; **46**:190, 193-95, 206, 249
The Treasure (Lessing) **8**:112
The Treasure of the City of Ladies, or, The Book of the Three Virtues (Christine de Pizan)
　See *La trésor de la cité des dames; or, Le livre des trois vertus*
Treatise (Taylor)
　See *Treatise Concerning the Lord's Supper*
Treatise Concerning Enthusiasm (More) **9**:318
A Treatise concerning Religious Affections (Edwards) **7**:94, 96, 101-02, 118-21
Treatise Concerning the Lord's Supper (Taylor) **11**:373, 385-86
A Treatise Historical containing the Bitter Passion of our Saviour Christ (More) **10**:370
Treatise of Civil Government (Locke) **7**:269, 273
A Treatise of Civil Power in Ecclesiastic Causes (Milton) **43**:336, 384-5
A Treatise of Human Nature: Being an Attempt to Introduce the Experimental Method of Reasoning into Moral Subjects (Hume) **7**:136-41, 154-55, 157-58, 160-61, 163, 165-66, 168, 171, 174, 176, 178, 183, 188, 197-99, 202
A Treatise of the Art of Political Lying (Arbuthnot) **1**:15
"Treatise on Charity" (Crashaw) **24**:16
Treatise on Man (Descartes) **35**:99, 104
Treatise on Minting Money (Copernicus)
　See *Monetae cudendae ratio*
Treatise on Painting (Vinci)
　See *Trattato della Pittura*
A Treatise on Polite Conversation (Swift) **1**:437
"Treatise on Predestination" (Knox) **37**:205-10
Treatise on Religion and the State (Spinoza) **9**:421
Treatise on Shadows (Vinci) **12**:405
Treatise on Systems (Condillac)
　See *Traité des systèmes*
Treatise on the Animals (Condillac)
　See *Traité des animaux*
A Treatise on the Astrolabe (Chaucer) **17**:214-15
Treatise on the Fable (Lessing) **8**:104
Treatise on the New Testament (Luther) **9**:140
A Treatise on the Nobilitie and excellencye of woman kynde (Agrippa von Nettesheim)
　See *De nobilitate et praeccelentia foeminei sexus*
Treatise on the Sensations (Condillac)
　See *Traité des sensations*
A Treatise to Receaue the Blessed Sacrament (More) **10**:367
Treatise upon the Christian Religion (Addison) **18**:8
A Treatise upon the Passion (More) **10**:367, 399-400, 405, 436, 440
"The Tree" (Winchilsea) **3**:442, 444, 451, 454
"The Tree of Knowledge" (Cowley) **43**:159,167
The Tree of the Choicest Fruit (Calderon de la Barca) **23**:9
"Tren VII" (Kochanowski) **10**:153, 157, 166-67, 170
"Tren VIII" (Kochanowski) **10**:153, 157, 159, 163, 166-67, 170
"Tren IX" (Kochanowski) **10**:158, 170, 174
"Tren XVI" (Kochanowski) **10**:153, 158, 165, 170, 174
"Tren XVII" (Kochanowski) **10**:153, 157-59, 165, 173-74
"Tren XIX" (Kochanowski) **10**:153, 157-58, 165, 170, 173

Treny (Kochanowski) **10**:151-53, 156-59, 162, 164-65, 167-76
La trésor de la cité des dames; or, Le livre des trois vertus (Christine de Pizan) **9**:25, 33-5, 38-9, 45, 47
Trial Before Herod (York) **34**:333, 374, 386, 388
The Trial of Joseph and Mary (N-Town) **34**:174, 183, 188, 192, 200, 208-9, 243
"The Trials of a Noble House" (Juana Ines de la Cruz)
　See *Los empeños de una casa*
Trias Romana (Hutten)
　See *Vadiscus, sive Trias Romana*
De tribus tabernaculis (Kempis) **11**:411
A Trick to Catch the Old One (Middleton) **33**:263, 268, 272-74, 277, 298-99, 313
The Tricks of Scapin (Moliere)
　See *Les fourberies de Scapin*
Trifles (Kochanowski)
　See *Fraski*
La trilogia della villeggiatura (Goldoni) **4**:275
"Trinitie Sunday" (Herbert) **24**:229
"Triomphe de l'amour" (Rousseau) **9**:343
Le triomphe de l'amour (Marivaux) **4**:367, 377
"Le Triomphe de l'Hiver" (Ronsard) **6**:438
Le triomphe de Plutus (Marivaux) **4**:367
Trip to the Jubilee (Farquhar)
　See *The Constant Couple; or, A Trip to he Jubilee*
Triparadisus (Mather) **38**:236-7
"The Triple Fool" (Donne) **10**:12, 82; **24**:150, 155
De triplici ratione cognoscendi Deum (Agrippa von Nettesheim) **27**:21
De triplicia minimo et mensura ad trium speculativarum scientiarum et multarum activarum atrium pricipie (Bruno) **27**:117, 123
De Tristitia Christi (More) **10**:436
Tristram Shandy (Sterne)
　See *The Life and Opinions of Tristram Shandy, Gentleman*
Der Triumph der guten Frauen (Schlegel) **5**:275, 278-79
"Triumph of Charis" (Jonson)
　See *A Celebration of Charis in Ten Lyric Pieces*
Triumph of Death (Fletcher) **33**:41
"The Triumph of Isis" (Warton) **15**:431, 433, 440, 449, 460-61
The Triumph of Love (Marivaux)
　See *The Triumph of Love*
The Triumph of Plutus (Marivaux)
　See *The Triumph of Plutus*
Triumph of the Four Foster Childern of Desire (Sidney) **19**:421
Triumph of Time (Fletcher) **33**:51
"The Triumphe of death" (Sidney) **39**:143, 146, 151, 153, 177
Triumpho parthenico que en glorias de María Santissima immaculadamente concebida (Siguenza y Gongora) **8**:340
The Triumphs of Integrity (Middleton) **33**:325
"The Triumphs of Owen. A Fragment" (Gray) **4**:312-13, 318; **40**:199, 226, 231
"The Triumphs of Philamore and Amoret" (Lovelace) **24**:
Triumphus Capnionis (Hutten) **16**:220, 231, 238-41
Trivia; or, The Art of Walking the Streets of London (Gay) **49**:7, 32, 68, 78, 80-81, 83, 86, 100, 127-135, 137-145, 147, 152, 171, 187
Troilus (Chaucer)
　See *Troilus and Criseyde*

Troilus and Cressida (Dekker) **22**:105
Troilus and Cressida; or, Truth Found Too Late (Dryden) **3**:197, 233; **21**:52-4, 56, 114
Troilus and Criseyde (Chaucer) **17**:45, 47, 58, 78, 84, 92, 99-100, 104-05, 117, 124, 131-32, 138, 154, 156, 159, 178, 194, 204-05, 213-14, 216-19
Troilus and Cryseide (Chaucer)
　See *Troilus and Criseyde*
Les Trois commères (Lesage) **28**:204, 209
Les trois livres du recueil des nouvelles poesies (Ronsard) **6**:432
Die Trojanerinnen (Schlegel) **5**:273, 280-81
Troja-Nova Triumphans (Dekker) **22**:130
Trophy of Spanish Justice (Siguenza y Gongora) **8**:343
The Troublesome Raigne and Lamentable Death of Edward the Second, King of England (Marlowe) **22**:329-31, 335, 339, 361-67; **47**:275, 281-84, 341, 357-60
"A True Estimate" (Young) **3**:491; **40**:342, 344, 346
The True Friend (Goldoni)
　See *Il vero amico*
The True God Pan (Calderon de la Barca) **23**:9
"The True History for the Ladies" (Goldsmith) **48**:218
"A true Hymne" (Herbert) **24**:235, 273, 287
"A True Love Story" (Walpole) **2**:500
The True Patriot (Fielding) **1**:234
A True Relation of My Birth Breeding and Life (Cavendish) **30**:184-86, 212-13, 215, 219, 235
A True Relation of Such Occurrences and Accidents of Noate As Hath Hapned in Virginia **9**:352-55, 357-60, 365-66, 369-71, 380-81, 383, 385-87
A True Relation of the Apparition of One Mrs. Veal (Defoe) **1**:144, 163
The True Travels, Adventures, and Observations of Captaine John Smith **9**:352-53, 361-62, 365, 367, 372, 375, 381-84, 388
The True-Born Englishman (Defoe) **1**:118, 160
A Trumpet sounded in the ears of the Inhabitants of both the High & Low Dutch Nation (Penn) **25**:331
Truth Exalted (Penn) **25**:283, 287-88, 292
Truth rescued from Imposture, or A Brief Reply to a meer Rhapsody of Lies, Folly and Slander (Penn) **25**:287, 289
The Tryal of the Cause of the Roman Catholics (Brooke) **1**:62
Ts'an-T'ang wu-tai-shih yen-i (Lo Kuan-chung) **12**:282
"Ts'u-chih" (P'u Sung-ling) **3**:347, 350; **49**:279
"Tsui Meng" (P'u Sung-ling) **3**:345
"Tu ha' 'l uiso" (Michelangelo) **12**:362
"Tuesday; or, The Ditty (Gay) **49**:66-67
Tuesday; or, The Ditty (Gay) **49**:39, 41, 43-44, 46-47
Tuhfat al-ahrár (Jami) **9**:68
Tuhfatu'l-Ahrár (Jami) **9**:66, 68, 70-1
Tumble-Down Dick (Fielding) **1**:239
"Tung shêng" (P'u Sung-ling) **49**:294
Turbo (Andreae) **32**:93, 99-100
Turcaret (Lesage) **2**:175, 180, 182-85, 188, 201-02; **28**:199-202, 204-05, 207, 210, 212-15
Tusculan Disputations (Erasmus) **16**:172
"Tutelage" (Donne) **24**:151
"The Twa Dogs" (Burns) **3**:48, 52, 57, 64, 71, 73, 77, 84-5, 96, 103-05; **29**:29, 41, 45-6, 65, 91; **40**:65, 94, 98, 119
"The Twa Herds" (Burns) **3**:78, 87, 93, 95-6;

29:42; **40**:80

"Tweedside" (Fergusson) **29**:205

"The Twelfth Discourse" (Reynolds) **15**:383, 389, 397, 403, 405, 419

"Twelfth-Night, or King and Queen" (Herrick) **13**:331

"Twenty-Four Songs Set to Music by Several Eminent Masters" (Prior) **4**:466-67

"The Twenty-Third Psalm" (Hopkinson) **25**:260

Twice or thrice had I loved thee (Donne)
    See "Aire and Angels"

"Twicknam Garden" (Donne) **10**:10, 36, 50; **24**:152, 155, 195-97

The Twin Rivals (Farquhar) **21**:128-29, 132, 135-36, 139-42, 144, 146-47, 149-54, 156-57, 161-66, 169-71, 176

"Two Extra Commandments" (Franklin) **25**:141

The Two Friends from Bourbonne (Diderot)
    See *Les Deux amis de Bourbonne*

Two Kinds of Righteousness (Luther) **37**:298-99

Two Letters from Sir Isaac Newton to M. Le Clerc, the former containing a Dissertation upon the Reading of the Greek Testament, 1 John v. 7, the latter upon 1 Timothy iii (Newton) **35**:275

Two Letters...on the Proposals for Peace, with the Regicide Directory of France (Burke) **7**:14, 23, 26, 39, 46, 53, 61

"The Two Maidens" (Cervantes)
    See "Las dos doncelas"

Two Noble Kinsmen (Fletcher) **33**:56

"Two Pastoralls" (Sidney) **19**:393; **39**:228, 269

2 The Honest Whore (Dekker)
    See *The Honest Whore*

Two Treatises of Government (Locke) **7**:263, 273, 295-96; **35**:202, 209, 217, 226-28, 240

"Two went up into the Temple to pray" (Crashaw) **24**:5

Tychonis Brahe Dani, De Mundi aetherei recentioribus phaenomenis Liber secundus, qui est de illustri stella caudata ab elapso fere triente Nouembris anno MDLXXVII usque in finem Januarii sequentis conspecta. (Brahe) **45**:4, 41-2, 45-6, 55-6, 65, 68-70

Tyrannick Love; or, The Royal Martyr (Dryden) **3**:210, 232-33, 235, 237; **21**:88, 102, 105-07

"The Tyrant Wife" (Burns) **29**:24

Über den märkischen Dialekt (Moritz) **2**:241

Über die bildende Nachahmung des Schönen (Moritz) **2**:234, 243, 245

Uden hoved og hale (Holberg) **6**:277

"Ugadciki" (Chulkov) **2**:22

"La uita del me amor'" (Michelangelo) **12**:360

Ulysses (Rowe) **8**:285, 287, 292, 295, 299, 302, 305

Ulysses von Ithacia; eller, En tysk comoedie (Holberg) **6**:259, 263, 277

"De umbris idearum" (Bruno) **27**:65-67, 86, 91, 108-10

Una delle ultime sere di carnovale (Goldoni) **4**:264, 266

"Underneath This Sable Hearse" (Jonson) **6**:304-05

"The undertaking" (Donne) **10**:18, 26, 51, 54-5; **24**:153, 155

"An Undeserving Favourite" (Butler) **16**:54

The Unfortunate Bride; or, The Blind Lady a Beaut (Behn) **30**:88; **42**:146

The Unfortunate Happy Lady (Behn) **1**:34, 38, 42, 46, 49, 51-2, 55; **30**:88; **42**:119

"The Unfortunate Lover" (Marvell) **4**:408-10, 442-43

The Unfortunate Lovers (Davenant) **13**:176, 181-82, 196

The Unfortunate Princess (Haywood) **1**:290-91

The Unfortunate Traveller or the life of Jack Wilton (Nashe) **41**:302, 304, 306, 308, 311-70, 374, 377-80

The Unhappy Mistake; or, The Impious Vow Punished (Behn) **1**:51

The Unhappy Penitent (Trotter) **8**:355, 357, 361, 363, 369, 371-74

De Unico Vocationis Modo (Las Casas) **31**:211

The Union: or Select Scots and English Poems (Warton) **15**:441

De unitate ecclesia conservanda (Hutten) **16**:213, 231, 233

Universal Beauty (Brooke) **1**:62, 64-5, 68-9

The Universal Gallant; or, The Different Husbands (Fielding) **1**:250; **46**:101

Universal History (Smollett) **46**:190-91

"The Universal Passion; or, The Love of Fame" (Young) **3**:467, 476-77, 486; **40**:332, 351, 359

"The Universal Prayer" (Pope) **3**:284

"University of Oxon." (Dryden)
    See "Prologue to the University of Oxford"

"Unkindnesse" (Herbert) **24**:273

"Unprofitablenes" (Vaughan) **27**:392

Unterhaltungen mit seinen Schülern (Moritz) **2**:240

The Untrussing of the Humorous Poet (Dekker)
    See *Satiromastix; of the Untrussing of the Humorous Poet*

"Up in the Air" (Ramsay) **29**:320, 330

"Up Tails All" (Herrick) **13**:331

"Upon a Beautiful Young Nymph Going to Bed" (Swift)
    See "A Beautiful Young Nymph Going to Bed. Written for the Honour of the Fair Sex"

"Upon a Child. An Epitaph" (Herrick) **13**:340

"Upon a Child That Died" (Herrick) **13**:340, 367, 409

"Upon a fit of Sickness, Anno 1632" (Bradstreet) **4**:90; **30**:146

"Upon a Lady that Died in Childbirth" (Herrick) **13**:409

"Upon a Lady's Fall over a Stile, Gotten by Running from Her Lover; by Which She Show'd Her Fair Back-Side, Which Was Her Best Side, and Made Him More Her Pursuer than He Was Before" (Wycherley) **8**:415

"Upon a Ribband" (Carew) **13**:33-4

"Upon a Spider Catching a Fly" (Taylor) **11**:356, 369, 385, 394

"Upon a Wasp Child with Cold" (Taylor) **11**:369, 386

"Upon a Wife that dyed mad with Jealousie" (Herrick) **13**:340

"Upon an Old Worn-Out Picture of Justice, Hung... in a Court of Judicature" (Wycherley) **8**:416

"Upon Appleton House" (Marvell) **4**:397, 401-04, 409-10, 412, 425, 429, 435-36, 438-41, 448

"Upon Electra" (Herrick) **13**:369

"Upon Friendship, preferre'd to Love" (Wycherley) **21**:396

"Upon Gut" (Herrick) **13**:356

"Upon Happiness" (Thomson) **16**:418

"Upon her Numerous Progeny" (Crashaw) **24**:27

"Upon Himself" (Herrick) **13**:387

"Upon His Departure Hence" (Herrick) **13**:333

"Upon his Verses" (Herrick) **13**:392

"Upon Julia's Clothes" (Herrick) **13**:338-39, 351, 368-70, 402

"Upon Julia's Fall" (Herrick) **13**:367

"Upon Julia's Recovery" (Herrick) **13**:349-50, 365, 388-89, 402

"Upon Julia's Voice" (Herrick) **13**:397

"Upon Julia's Washing Her Self in the River" (Herrick) **13**:393

"Upon Mr. Staninough's Death" (Crashaw) **24**:53

"Upon My Daughter Hannah Wiggin Her Recovery from a Dangerous Fever" (Bradstreet) **4**:100

"Upon My Dear and Loving Husband His Goeing into England" (Bradstreet) **30**:150
    See "To My Dear and Loving Husband His Goeing into England"

"Upon My Son Samuel His Going to England, November 6, 1959" (Bradstreet) **30**:150

"Upon occasion of his Ode of defiance annext to his Play of the new Inne" (Carew)
    See "To Ben Jonson Upon occasion of his Ode of defiance annext to his play of the new Inne"

"Upon our Victory at Sea, and Burning the French Fleet at La Hogu" (Dennis) **11**:48

"Upon Roses" (Herrick) **13**:389

"Upon some verses of Vergil" (Donne) **10**:81

"Upon Sudds" (Herrick) **13**:398

"Upon the Annunciation and Passion" (Donne) **24**:165-67, 198-99

"Upon the Death of Her Husband. By Mrs. Elizabeth Singer." (Rowe) **44**:310

"Upon the death of his Sparrow" (Herrick) **13**:340

"Upon the Death of Mr. Herrys" (Crashaw) **24**:35

"Upon the Death of O.C." (Marvell)
    See "Poem upon the Death of O. C."

"Upon the Death of that Holy and Reverend Man of God, Mr. Samuel Hooker" (Taylor) **11**:368

"Upon the Death of the Lord Hastings" (Donne) **3**:223, 239

Upon the Death of the Lord Hastings (Marvell) **43**:252, 274

"Upon the Death of the Lord Protector" (Marvell)
    See "Poem upon the Death of O. C."

"Upon the Discretion of Folly" (Wycherley) **21**:356

"Upon the Double Murther of King Charles I" (Philips) **30**:278, 282, 287

Upon the Excellency of Christianity (Swift) **1**:487

"Upon the Graving of her Name Upon a Tree in Barnelmes Walk" (Philips) **30**:787

"Upon the Hill and Grove at Billborow" (Marvell) **4**:397, 403, 429, 440

"Upon the Idleness of Business: A Satyr. To One, Who Said, a Man Show'd His Sense, Spirit, Industry, and Parts, by His Love of Bus'ness" (Wycherley) **8**:416

"Upon the Impertinence of Knowledge, the Unreasonableness of Reason, and the Brutality of Humanity; Proving the Animal Life the Most Reasonable Life, since the Most Natural, and Most Innocent" (Wycherley) **8**:399, 415; **21**:356

"Upon the Infant Martyrs" (Crashaw) **24**:54

"Upon the Nipples of Julia's Breast" (Herrick) **13**:368, 393

"Upon the Sepulchre" (Crashaw) **24**:54

"Upon the troublesome times" (Herrick) **13**:396

Upon the Types of the Old Testament (Taylor) **11**:399-400

"Upon Wedlock and Death of Children" (Taylor) **11**:367-68

Urania Titani (Brahe) **45**:74

Ur-Hamlet (Kyd) **22**:248-251, 267, 269-271, 276,

279

Urim and Thummim (Penn) **25**:289

Ursus Murmurat (Beer) **5**:52

"The Use and Objects of the Faculties of the Mind" (Bacon) **18**:105

The Usefullness of the Colloquies (Erasmus)
  See *De Utilitate Colloquiorum*

The Usefulness of the Stage to the Happiness of Mankind, to Government and to Religion (Dennis) **11**:20, 30, 37

De Utilitate Colloquiorum (Erasmus) **16**:122, 156, 194

Utopia (Haywood)
  See *Memoirs of a Certain Island Adjacent to the Kingdom of Utopia*

Utopia (More) **10**:357-58, 360, 365, 368-69, 373-75, 377-83, 385-97, 400-01, 404-06, 409-15, 420-26, 430-31, 434-36, 441, 443, 449-54; **32**:254-358

Utrum Hebraei possint construere novas synagogas (Casanova de Seingalt) **13**:126

Vade Mecum (Richardson)
  See *The Apprentice's Vade Mecum*

Vadiscus, sive Trias Romana (Hutten) **16**:213, 218, 230-31, 233, 235, 246

"A Valediction: forbidding mourning" (Donne) **10**:6, 10-11, 13, 18, 31, 36, 51, 54, 58, 67, 69, 94, 105; **24**:150, 152, 154

"A Valediction: of my name, in the window" (Donne) **10**:31, 82

"A Valediction: of the booke" (Donne) **10**:31, 36

"A Valediction: of weeping" (Donne) **10**:9, 26, 31, 36, 50, 58, 71

The Valencian Widow (Vega) **23**:376, 378

Valentinian (Fletcher) **33**:56, 58, 60

Valerius Terminus of the Interpretation of Nature (Bacon) **18**:131, 161, 186-87; **32**:160-1, 187

La Valise trouvée (Lesage) **28**:200

El Valle de la Zarzuela (Calderon de la Barca) **23**:14

The Valley of Lilies (Kempis) **11**:410

De vanitate Scientiarium (Agrippa von Nettesheim)
  See *De incertitudine et vanitate scientiarium declamatio inuectiua et excellentia verbi Dei*

Vanitie and Uncertaintie (Agrippa von Nettesheim)
  See *De incertitudine et vanitate scientiarium declamatio inuectiua et excellentia verbi Dei*

The Vanity and Nothingness of Human Knowledge (Agrippa von Nettesheim)
  See *De incertitudine et vanitate scientiarium declamatio inuectiua et excellentia verbi Dei*

"The Vanity of All Worldly Things" (Bradstreet) **4**:90, 99, 109

"The Vanity of Human Wishes, being the Tenth Satire of Juvenal imitated" (Johnson) **15**:186-89, 194-96, 199, 201, 204, 206, 217, 219, 228, 233-36, 242, 244, 268-75, 277-81, 291-93

Vanity of Sciences and Arts and the Excellence of the Word of God (Agrippa von Nettesheim)
  See *De incertitudine et vanitate scientiarium declamatio inuectiua et excellentia verbi Dei*

"Vanity of Spirit" (Vaughan) **27**:323, 354-55, 390-91, 394

"The Vanity of the World" (Rowe) **44**:280

Variae Lectiones (Lipsius) **16**:262

El Varon Atento (Gracian y Morales) **15**:135

"Les Vautours et les Pigeons" (La Fontaine) **50**:98-100

Veber die Babylonische Gefangenschaft der

Kirche (Luther)
  See *De captivitate Babylonica ecclesiae praeludium*

La vedova scaltra (Goldoni) **4**:250, 266-67

La vedova spiritosa (Goldoni) **4**:261

"The Vegetation of Metals" (Newton) **35**:297

"Veggio co be uostr'ochi" (Michelangelo)
  See "Veggio co bei vostr'occhi un dolce lume"

"Veggio co bei vostr'occhi un dolce lume" (Michelangelo) **12**:360, 367

"Veggio nel tuo bel uiso" (Michelangelo) **12**:360

La venganza venturoza (Vega) **23**:393

De vera compunctione animae (Kempis) **11**:411

Vergleichung Shakespears und Andreas Gryphs (Schlegel) **5**:273

"La vérité" (Rousseau) **9**:345

Der verkehrte Staats-Mann; oder, Nasen-weise Secretarius (Beer) **5**:57

Die Verkehrte Welt (Grimmelshausen) **6**:247

Verkehrter Staatsmann (Beer)
  See *Der verkehrte Staats-Mann; oder, Nasen-weise Secretarius*

Der verliebte Österreicher (Beer) **5**:48, 57-9

"Verses in Friars' Case Hermitage" (Burns) **29**:92

"Verses Intended to Be Written Below a Noble Earl's Picture" (Burns) **3**:86

"Verses Made for Women Who Cry Apples" (Swift) **1**:459

"Verses on Reynold's Window" (Warton)
  See "Verses on Sir Joshua's Painted Window at New College"

"Verses on Sir Joshua's Painted Window at New College" (Warton) **15**:432-33, 444, 448, 456

"Verses on the Death of Dr. Swift" (Swift) **1**:439, 475, 482, 523-24

"Verses to a Lady" (Chatterton) **3**:123

"Verses to Collector Mitchell" (Burns) **3**:85

"Verses to Sir Joshua Reynolds" (Warton)
  See "Verses on Sir Joshua's Painted Window at New College"

"Verses Upon the Burning of Our House" (Bradstreet) **30**:114
  See "Some Verses Upon the Burning of Our House, July 10th, 1666"

"Verses Written at the Age of Fourteen, and Sent to Mr. Beville Higgons, on His Sickness and Recovery from the Small-Pox" (Trotter) **8**:358, 368

"Versicles on Sign-posts" (Burns) **40**:105

Versuch einer deutschen Prosodie (Moritz) **2**:231, 242-43, 245

Versuch einer kleinen praktischen Kinderlogik (Moritz) **2**:240-41, 246

"Vertue" (Herbert) **24**:274

"La veuve et le magicien" (Marivaux) **4**:380

La veuve, ou Le traître trahi (Corneille) **28**:43-5, 48

"Vexilla Regis" (Crashaw) **24**:20, 38

Den vægelsindede (Holberg) **6**:258, 263, 267, 273, 277

"Viage del Parnaso" (Cervantes) **6**:148, 174; **23**:135

The Vicar of Wakefield (Goldsmith) **2**:66-7, 69-72, 74-6, 79-86, 89-94, 98-102, 104-09, 111-12, 114, 116-19, 121-28; **48**:181-242

Vice and Luxury Public Mischiefs (Dennis) **11**:19, 26

Vice and Luxury Public Mishaps (Dennis)
  See *Vice and Luxury Public Mischiefs*

"Vicissitude" (Gray)
  See "Ode on the Pleasure Arising from Vicissitude"

La victoria de la honra (Vega) **23**:393

La vida de Marco Bruto (Quevedo) **23**:154

La vida es sueño (Calderon de la Barca) **23**:9, 12, 23, 31, 36-8, 42, 44, 46-7, 52, 56, 58, 60, 65

Vidua Christiana (Erasmus) **16**:193

La vie de Marianne; ou, Les aventures de Mme la Comtesse de*** (Marivaux) **4**:353-56, 359-60, 362, 368, 372-75, 378-81, 383-84, 387

La Vie d'Esope (La Fontaine) **50**:63

La vie inestimable du grand Gargantua, père de Pantagruel (Rabelais) **5**:216-17, 223, 226, 233, 235, 239-41, 249, 251, 254, 256-58, 260

"Le Vieillard et l 'Ane" (La Fontaine) **50**:78

El viejo celoso (Cervantes) **23**:139-40, 142

A View of the Edinburgh Theatre during the Summer Season, 1759 (Boswell) **4**:50

View of the Present State of Ireland (Spenser) **39**:320, 333, 362-73

"Vigil of Venus" (Parnell) **3**:258

The Village Heir (Marivaux)
  See *The Village Heir*

El villano en su rincón (Vega) **23**:372-73

De vinculis in genere (Bruno) **27**:100

"Vindication" (Dryden) **3**:210

A Vindication of Mr. Locke's Christian Principles from the Injurious Imputations of Dr. Holdsworth (Trotter) **8**:362

A Vindication of Natural Society (Burke)
  See *A Vindication of Natural Society; or, A View of the Miseries and Evils Arising to Mankind from Every Species of Artificial Society*

A Vindication of Natural Society; or, A View of the Miseries and Evils Arising to Mankind from Every Species of Artificial Society (Burke) **7**:57, 61

A Vindication of the Reasonableness of Christianity (Locke) **7**:281; **35**:217

A Vindication of the Reasons and Defence, &c. Part I being a Reply to the First Part of No Sufficient Reason. Part II being a Reply to the Second Part of No Sufficient Reason (Collier) **6**:209

Vindication of the Relapse and the Provok'd Wife from Immorality and Prophaneness (Vanbrugh)
  See *A Short Vindication of The Relapse and The Provok'd Wife from Immorality and Prophaneness*

A Vindication of the Rights of Men, in a Letter to the Right Honourable Edmund Burke; Occasioned by His Reflections on the Revolution in France (Wollstonecraft) **5**:415, 417, 426, 428, 432, 435-41, 444, 451-53, 460-61; **50**:307-308, 320, 325, 329-334, 336, 344, 361

A Vindication of the Rights of Woman, with Strictures on Political and Moral Subjects (Wollstonecraft) **5**:415-16, 418, 420-29, 431-34, 437, 439-41, 443-44, 446, 448-53, 456-61; **50**:271-273, 279-284, 292-295, 298-299, 304-317, 320-322, 325, 328-331, 334-336, 341-348, 351-358, 361-364, 366-368

The Vindication of Wives (Perrault)
  See *L'apologie des femmes*

Vindications (Lessing) **8**:79

"Vine" (Herrick) **13**:320

The Vineyard of the Lord (Calderon de la Barca) **23**:9

"The Vintage to the Dungeon" (Lovelace) **24**:308-09, 319, 334-35, 342

"A Vintner" (Butler) **16**:55

Violenta; or, The Rewards of Virtue (Pix) **8**:277-78

Virelays (Christine de Pizan) **9**:43

La Virgen del Sagrario (Calderon de la Barca) **23**:22

"Virgils Gnat" (Spenser) **5**:312

"The Virgin Averse to Marriage" (Erasmus)
See "Girl Who Did Not Want to Marry"

"A Virgin Life" (Barker) **42**:96, 100-01

The Virgin Martyr (Dekker) **22**:99-100, 107, 126-7, 131-3

"Virgin Repentant" (Erasmus) **16**:141, 193

Virginia: A Tragedy, with Odes, Pastorals, and Translations (Brooke) **6**:108-09

"Virginia Resolves" (Henry) **25**:213, 223-24

"Virginian Ode"
See "To the Virginian Voyage"

"The Virgin's Choice" (Chatterton) **3**:132

"Virgin-shrine" (Vaughan) **27**:347

Virgo Aspricollis (Lipsius) **16**:254

Virgo Sichemiensis (Lipsius) **16**:254

"Virtue" (Herbert)
See "Vertue"

"Virtue" (Wheatley)
See "On Virtue"

"Virtue's Apology" (Bowman)
See "The Complaint; or, Night Thoughts: Night the Seventh"

"A Virtuoso" (Butler) **16**:50-2

Virtuous Villager (Haywood) **44**:129

"The Visible and Invisible: Soul and Sense" (More) **9**:298

Visio de Petro Plowman, Vita de Dowel, Vita de Dobet, Vita de Dobest (Langland)
See *Piers Plowman*

"The Vision" (Burns) **3**:47, 50, 71, 86; **29**:5, 30, 64, 66, 91; **40**:95, 102, 109-110

"A Vision" (Herrick) **13**:351, 367, 393

"Vision" (Ramsay) **29**:305, 308, 312, 316, 321, 332

Vision
See *Greene's Vision*

La vision de Babouc (Voltaire) **14**:359, 360

"Vision of Beauty" (Jonson) **6**:326

"Vision of Mirza" (Addison) **18**:28

Vision of Noah (Aretino) **12**:13

The Vision of the Twelve Goddesses (Daniel) **24**:123-26, 137

Vision of William concerning Piers the Plowman (Langland)
See *Piers Plowman*

"A Vision upon this Conceit of The Fairy Queen" (Raleigh) **39**:76

Visions of Petrarch and Du Bellay (Spenser) **39**:305

"Visions of the Worlds Vanitie" (Spenser) **5**:312

The Visit of the Magi (N-Town)
See *The Magi* (N-Town)

The Visit to Elizabeth (N-Town) **34**:170, 183, 188, 192, 200

"Visit to the Exchange" (Addison) **18**:28

"Visits to the Abbey" (Addison) **18**:28

Vita ab ipso conscripta (Andreae) **32**:67-8, 71, 94, 100-101

Vita beata (Paracelsus) **14**:199

Vita di Benvenuto Cellini (Cellini) **7**:68-74, 76-85

La vita di Castruccio Castracani da Lucca (Machiavelli) **8**:133, 161, 174-75

Vita di Cristo (Aretino)
See *L'Humanità di Christo*

Vita di santa Caterina da Siena (Aretino) **12**:6, 8, 13, 36

El vizcaino fingido (Cervantes) **23**:137, 139-40

The Vocal Forest (Howell)
See *Dendrologia: Dodona's Grove; or, The Vocall Forest*

La voiture embourbée (Marivaux) **4**:385-87

La voix du sage et du peuple (Voltaire) **14**:403

"La volière" (Rousseau) **9**:345

Volpone; or, the Foxe (Jonson) **6**:291, 294-95, 297, 299-300, 303, 306, 308, 310-13, 319-20, 322-24, 328, 330-36, 339-41, 343, 349-50; **33**:106-7, 113-15, 133, 135-6, 146, 157, 159-60, 165, 167-68

Volumen Paramirum (Paracelsus) **14**:199

Vom Besten und Edelsten Beruff. Des wahren Diensts Gottes (Andreae) **32**:92

Von den guten Wercken (Luther) **9**:125, 134-35, 139, 147, 150

Von den hinfallenden Siechtagen (Paracelsus) **14**:199

Von den hinfallenden Siechtagen der Mutter (Paracelsus) **14**:199

Von der Freiheit eines Christenmenschen (Luther)
See *Dissertatio de libertate christiana per autorem recognita*

Vorlesungen über den Stil (Moritz) **2**:244

Vorrede des Uebersetzers zu Der Ruhmredige (Schlegel) **5**:283

"Vorrei voler, Signor, quel ch'io non voglio" (Michelangelo) **12**:367

Le voyage à Paphos (Montesquieu) **7**:320, 324, 348

"Le Voyage de Tours, ou les amoureus Thoinet et Perrot" (Ronsard) **6**:426-27

A Voyage to Lisbon (Fielding)
See *The Journal of a Voyage to Lisbon*

"Voyage to Parnassus" (Cervantes)
See "Viage del Parnaso"

Voyage to the Island of Love (Behn)
See *Poems upon Several Occasions, with a Voyage to the Island of Love*

"Le voyageur dans le nouveau monde" (Marivaux) **4**:376, 380

"Wa-ch'u" (P'u Sung-ling) **3**:352

"Wae is my heart" (Burns) **29**:51, 53

The Wanderer (Vega) **23**:374

The Wandering Beauty (Behn) **1**:42, 46, 51, 53

"Wang Ch'eng" (P'u Sung-ling) **3**:350-51; **49**:296

"Wang Tzu-an" (P'u Sung-ling) **3**:345; **49**:281

"Wang-che" (P'u Sung-ling) **3**:351

"War" (Butler) **16**:50

The Warners (Hutten) **16**:228

"A Warning to Professors" (Edwards) **7**:98

Wásitat al-Iqd (Jami) **9**:65, 68

"The Wasp" (Hopkinson) **25**:248

"The Wassaile" (Herrick) **13**:366

"The water blushed into wine" (Crashaw) **24**:4

The Water Margin (Lo Kuan-chung)
See *Shui Hu Chuan*

"The Watercourse" (Herbert) **24**:267

"The Water-fall" (Vaughan) **27**:307, 337-38

"A Waukrife Minnie" (Burns) **3**:86

The Wavering Nymph; or, Mad Amyntas (Behn) **30**:80

The Way of Perfection (Teresa de Jesus)
See *Camino de perfección*

The Way of the Cross (Towneley)
See *Processus Crucis* (Towneley)

The Way of the World (Congreve) **5**:70-1, 73, 75-6, 78-88, 90-5, 97-100, 103-05, 107, 109-11, 113, 117; **21**:4-5, 8-10, 13, 15-18, 20, 23, 26-8, 32-4, 43-4

The Way to Things by Words and to Words by Things (Cleland) **2**:53

The Way to Wealth (Franklin) **25**:114, 147, 149, 157-58

"Ways of the Present World" (Petursson)
See "Aldarhéttur"

The Wayward Head and Heart (Crebillon)
See *Les egarements du coeur et de l'esprit; ou, Memoires de Monsieur de Meilcour*

"We Raise a New Song" (Luther)
See "Ein neues Lied wir heben an"

Wealth of Nations (Smith) **36**:318, 320-30, 333-36, 342, 344, 347-48, 355-56, 360-78, 382-91

"Wealth, or the Woody" (Ramsay) **29**:307

"The Weary Pund o' Tow" (Burns) **29**:24

The Wedding Day (Fielding) **1**:208, 220, 250; **46**:102

"Wednesday; or, The Dumps" (Gay) **49**:66, 68-69

Wednesday; or, The Dumps (Gay) **49**:39, 41, 43-45, 47

"The Weeper" (Crashaw) **24**:4-5, 8, 12, 15, 21-4, 30, 32, 35, 37, 40, 41-4, 46, 49-50, 54-6, 59, 70, 74, 77

Weiberhächel (Beer)
See *Des berühmten Spaniers Francisci Sambelle wolausgepolirte Weiber-Hächel*

"The Welcome: A Poem to His Grace the Duke of Marlborough" (Aubin) **9**:4

A Welcome from Greece (Gay) **49**:7

"The Welcome to Sack" (Herrick) **13**:365, 397

"We'll hide the Couper" (Burns) **40**:89

The Welsh Embassador (Dekker) **22**:132

Wesen des Christentums (Luther)
See *The Nature of Christianity*

Westward Ho (Dekker) **22**:88, 104, 106, 110-111, 125-6, 132

Westward Ho! (Webster) **33**:345

"Wha Is That at My Bower-Door" (Burns) **3**:100; **29**:23, 50; **40**:88

"Wha'll Mow Me Now" (Burns) **3**:100

"What Can a Young Lassie" (Burns) **29**:24; **40**:89

"What Do You Want from Us, Lord?" (Kochanowski)
See "Piesn"

"What Do You Wish, O Lord, In Return For Your Bounteous Gifts?" (Kochanowski)
See "Piesn"

The What D'Ye Call It: A Tragi-Comi-Pastoral Farce (Gay) **49**:32-33, 36, 100, 117-119, 121-124, 147-148, 155, 161, 173, 179, 182-183, 185

"What Kind of Mistresse He Would Have" (Herrick) **13**:351, 359, 393

"What wilt Thou from us, Lord?" (Kochanowski)
See "Piesn"

What you Will (Marston) **33**:187, 190, 193-94, 197, 199, 215, 207, 234, 239

The Wheat and the Tares (Calderon de la Barca) **23**:9

"When First I Ended, Then I First Began"
See "Sonnet 62"

"When He Would Have His Verses Read" (Herrick) **13**:349, 351, 393, 402

"When Laurell spirts 'ith fire" (Herrick) **13**:360

"When Lovely Woman Stoops to Folly" (Goldsmith) **2**:104

"When Phoebe formed a wanton smile" (Collins) **4**:225

"When Spring Came on with Fresh Delight" (Parnell)
See "When Spring Comes On"

"When Spring Comes On" (Parnell) **3**:251-52

"Whether Day or Night Is the More Excellent" (Milton) 9:225

Whether Soldiers too can be Saved (Luther) 37:303

"Whether the British Government Inclines More to Absolute Monarchy, or to a Republic" (Hume) 7:189

"While Grace doth stir me" (Juana Ines de la Cruz) 5:152

"The Whistle" (Burns) 40:81

"The Whistle" (Franklin) 25:112, 115, 141, 144

"Whistle and I'll Come tae Ye, My Lad" (Burns)
See "Whistle and I'll Come tae Ye, My Lad"

"Whistle and I'll Come tae Ye, My Lad" (Burns) 3:66, 74, 78; 29:22; 40:87, 97

"Whistle o'er the Lave o't" (Burns) 29:24; 40:88, 97

"White Autumn Silk" (P'u Sung-ling)
See "Bai Qiulian"

The White Devil (Webster) 33:334-36, 340-42, 344-46, 351, 353, 360-67, 370-72, 374-86, 389-90, 395, 397, 401

"The White Island: or place of the Blest" (Herrick) 13:319-20, 330, 334, 336, 338, 374, 401

White King (Lilly)
See *A Prophesy of the White Kings Dreadful Dead-man Explaned*

"White Sunday" (Vaughan) 27:376

"Who did it" (Jonson) 33:126

"Who ever comes to shroud me do not harme" (Donne)
See "The Funerall"

"The Whore" (Chatterton)
See "The Whore of Babylon"

"The Whore of Babylon" (Chatterton) 3:126, 133-34

The Whore of Babylon (Dekker) 22:88, 94, 108, 110, 119, 127, 132

"Why Doth the Pox so much Affect to Undermine the Nose?" (Donne) 10:96

"Why Hath the Common Opinion Afforded Women Souls?" (Donne) 10:96

"Why I Write Not of Love" (Jonson) 6:347-48

Why we ought to unite with Constance, Lindau, Strasbourg, etc. (Zwingli) 37:386

The Wicked Man's Portion (Mather) 38:309

"Wicked Men Useful in Their Destruction Only" (Edwards) 7:93, 122

The Widow (Middleton) 33:277

"The Widow Can Bake, and the Widow Can Brew" (Ramsay) 29:330

The Widow; or, The Betrayer Betrayed (Corneille)
See *La veuve, ou Le traître trahi*

The Widow Ranter; or, The History of Bacon in Virginia (Behn) 1:35; 30:81, 83, 94; 42:121-22, 138, 150

The Widows Tears (Chapman) 22:6, 12, 15, 34, 60, 63, 67

"The Widow's Tears; or Dirge of Dorcas" (Herrick) 13:317

Wie die Alten den Tod gebildeten (Lessing) 8:82

The Wife (Haywood) 44:150

"Wife of Bath" (Pope) 3:269

The Wife of Bath (Gay) 49:37, 115-117, 119, 123, 171

"Wife of Bath's Prologue" (Chaucer)
See "Prologue to the Wife of Bath's Tale"

"Wife of Bath's Tale" (Chaucer) 17:142, 145, 181, 189, 191, 202, 213, 229-33, 236-37, 240-41

"A Wife of Ten Thousand" (Marmontel) 2:214

A Wife to be Lett (Haywood) 44:150

"The Wife's Resentment" (Manley) 1:306-08

"Wife's Tale" (Chaucer)
See "Wife of Bath's Tale"

"The Wild Boar and the Ram" (Gay) 49:30

The Wild Gallant (Dryden) 3:193, 230-31

The Wild Goose Chase (Fletcher) 33:56, 60, 79, 86-8

"The Will" (Donne) 10:13, 18, 50

Willenhag-Romane (Beer) 5:47-8

"Willie Brew'd a Peck o' Maut" (Burns) 3:61, 78; 29:59; 40:97, 100

"Willie Wastle" (Burns) 29:7

"The Willing Mistress" (Behn) 1:52, 54; 30:68

"Wilt thou forgive" (Donne)
See "A Hymne to God the Father"

A Winding-Sheet for Controversie Ended (Penn) 25:287, 291

"The Windows" (Herbert) 24:259-60, 266

"Windsor-Forest" (Pope) 3:268, 270, 273-74, 290, 292, 306-07, 315-16, 334, 336-38

Wine (Gay) 49:3, 7, 31, 33, 35, 60-62, 69, 141

"Winning of Calers" 41 58

"Winter" (Pope) 3:334

"Winter, a Dirge" (Burns) 3:48; 29:79

Winter. A Poem (Thomson) 16:363-64, 366, 369, 372-73, 381, 383, 385, 387, 393, 397-98, 402-03, 405, 409, 413, 415, 419-24, 426, 429, 431, 433; 29:374, 376, 378, 383, 385, 387, 391-93, 399, 403, 407, 413-14, 431; 40:273, 275, 280-81, 289, 288, 290-91, 293-95, 297-98, 300, 304-09, 321-22

Winter Meditations (Mather) 38:161-2, 230

"A Winter Night" (Burns) 3:86; 29:92

Wisdom Justified of her Children (Penn) 25:291, 296

Wisdom of Alexander (Jami)
See *Khirad-náma-yi Iskandarí*

The Wisdom of Solomon Paraphrased (Middleton) 33:285-87

The Wisdom of the Ancients (Bacon)
See *De sapienta veterum*

"The Wish" (Rowe) 44:280

"Wishes" (Crashaw)
See "Wishes to His Suppos'd Mistress"

"Wishes to His Suppos'd Mistress" (Crashaw) 24:4, 9-10, 13, 17, 20, 27, 29, 43, 45-6

"Wishes to his (supposed) Mistress" (Crashaw)
See "Wishes to His Suppos'd Mistress"

The Witch (Middleton) 33:265, 281-82, 310, 321-22

The Witch of Edmonton (Dekker) 22:100, 107-111, 132-3

"A Witch Trial at Mount Holly" (Franklin) 25:111, 141

"With Fooles and Children Good Discretion Beares"
See "Sonnet 22"

"With Pleasures Have I Past My Days" (Hopkinson) 25:250, 260

Without Head or Tail (Holberg)
See *Uden hoved og hale*

The Wits (Davenant) 13:175, 187

The Wits Cabal (Cavendish) 30:227

Wits Recreations (Crashaw) 24:43

Wives (Pix)
See *The Spanish Wives*

Wolfenbüttel Fragments (Lessing) 8:64, 79

The Woman Hater (Fletcher) 33:44, 60, 63-4, 66, 69, 71, 74, 91, 94-5, 97-8

The Woman of Honor (Cleland) 2:53-4

The Woman Taken in Adultery (Chester)
See *Temptation* (Chester)

The Woman Taken in Adultery (N-Town) 34:172, 175-6, 235-6

Woman Taken in Adultery, Raising of Lazarus (York) 34:387

The Woman Turned Bully (Behn) 30:80

"The Woman with a Sausage on Her Nose" (Perrault) 2:255

"Woman's Constancy" (Donne) 10:12, 50, 52; 24:151, 153-54, 181

The Woman's Prize; or, The Tamer Tamed (Fletcher) 33:63, 74-5

"Women" (Butler) 16:47

Women Beware Women (Middleton) 33:268, 270, 276-77, 280-81, 284, 303-07

Women's Tittle-Tattle (Goldoni)
See *I pettegolezzi delle donne*

The Wonder of a Kingdom (Dekker) 22:95, 108-109, 111

The Wonder Show (Cervantes) 6:190-91

Wonderful Works of God Commemorated (Mather) 38:230, 235

The Wonderful Year (Dekker) 22:95, 101

Wonders of Babylon (Castro) 19:4

Wonders of the Invisible World (Mather) 38:149, 162, 170, 173, 177-8, 222, 236-7

The Wonder-Working Magician (Calderon de la Barca)
See *El mágico prodigioso*

Work for Armourers, of the Peace is Broken,—God help the Poor, the rich can shift 22:97, 118-119

Work of Redemption (Edwards)
See *God Glorified in the Work of Redemption, by the Greatness of Man's Dependence upon Him in the Whole of It*

Works (Jonson) 6:323, 347; 33:166

Works (Philips) 30:291

"The Works and Wonders of Almighty Power" (Thomson) 16:418

The Works of Allan Ramsay (Ramsay) 29:331

The Works of George Lord Lyttelton (Lyttelton) 10:196

The Works of Henry Fielding, Esq.; With the Life of the Author (Fielding) 1:208, 219

The Works of Henry Vaughan (Vaughan) 27

The Works of Horace, Translated into Verse (Smart) 3:397-98

The Works of Michael Drayton 8:48

The Works of Mrs. Davys (Davys) 1:97-8; 46:19-20, 24, 29-30

The Works of Mrs. Eliza Haywood (Haywood) 44:139

The Works of Mrs. Elizabeth Rowe and Mr. Thomas Rowe (Rowe) 44:280, 303-08

The Works of Ossian (Macpherson)
See *The Poems of Ossian*

The Works of Samuel Daniel (Daniel) 24:134

The Works of Sir Thomas Malory (Malory)
See *Morte Darthur*

The Works of Sir Thomas More Knyght (More) 10:370

The Works of the Right Honourable Lady Mary Wortley Montague (Montagu) 9:270, 272

The Works of Virgil...Translated into English Verse (Dryden) 3:201

"The World" (Herbert) 24:255, 262

"The World" (Philips) 30:279

"The World" (Vaughan) 27:295, 305, 322-25, 340, 368, 373, 376, 383, 386, 390-91, 394

"The world Contemned, in a Parenetical Epistle written by the Reverend Father Eucherius, Bishop of Lyons, to his kinsman Valerianus" (Vaughan) 27:313, 325

The World Runs on Wheels (Chapman)
See *All Fools*

The Worlds Great Fair (Calderon de la Barca) 23:9-10

The World's Olio (Cavendish) 30:209

The Worst Doesn't Always Happen (Calderon de la Barca) 23:66, 68

The Worthy Tract of Paulus Jovius, contayning a discourse of Rare Inventions both Militarie & Amorous called Imprese (Daniel) 24:124

"Would you know what's soft?" (Carew) 13:11

"Wounded Hare" (Burns)
　See "On Seeing a Wounded Hare Limp by Me Which a Fellow Had Just Shot at"

"The Wounded Heart" (Herrick) 13:337

"Wrath upon the Wicked to the Uttermost" (Edwards) 7:98

"A Wreath" (Herbert) 24:286

The Writings of Benjamin Franklin (Franklin) 25:120

"Written at the Hermitage of Braid, near Edinburgh" (Fergusson) 29:197

"Written at Vale-Royal Abbey" (Warton)
　See "Ode Written at Vale-Royal Abbey in Cheshire"

"Written in the Beginning of Mezeray's History of France" (Prior) 4:466, 472

The Wrongs of Woman; or, Maria (Wollstonecraft) 5:416, 424, 426-27, 429-31, 443-44, 453-56, 461; 50:271-277, 280, 282, 284, 292, 295, 298-299, 320, 324, 361-362, 364-368

"Wu hsiao-lien" (P'u Sung-ling) 49:297, 299, 300

Das wunderbarliche Vogelnest (I and II) (Grimmelshausen) 6:238, 247

"Ya-t'ou" (P'u Sung-ling) 49:278-279, 297, 300

"Ye Are Na Mary Morison" (Burns) 3:71, 78, 87; 40:63, 93

"Ye Genii who in secret state" (Collins) 40:150

"Ye have been fresh and green" (Herrick) 13:319

"Ye yin zaifu" (P'u Sung-ling) 49:314

"Yeh-ch'a kuo" (P'u Sung-ling) 49:282

"Yeh-kou" (P'u Sung-ling) 49:282

"Yeh-sheng" (P'u Sung-ling) 49:290

"Yellow Pride" (P'u Sung-ling)
　See "Huang Ying"

"The Yellowhair'd Laddie" (Ramsay) 29:309

"Yen Shih" (P'u Sung-ling) 3:354; 49:278

"Yestreen I Had a Pint o' Wine" (Burns) 29:23, 35, 87; 40:88

"Yi yüan kuan" (P'u Sung-ling) 49:294-295

"Ying-ning" (P'u Sung-ling) 3:348, 352, 354; 49:278-279

You Can't Play with Love (Calderon de la Barca) 23:64

"Young Damon of the vale is dead" (Collins) 4:225

"The Young Gentleman in Love" (Prior) 4:455, 461

"Young Jockey was the blythest lad" (Burns) 29:54

The Young King; or, The Mistake (Behn) 1:33, 39; 30:70-1, 79, 81-3; 42:121, 148

The Young Lady (Haywood) 44:172

"The Young Laird and Edinburgh Katy" (Ramsay) 29:329

"Young Love" (Marvell) 4:435

The Young Savant (Lessing)
　See *Der junge Gelehrte*

The Younger Brother; or, The Amorous Jilt (Behn) 1:56; 30:81

Your Five Gallants (Middleton) 33:262, 277

"Youthful Piety" (Erasmus) 16:195

Youths Glory and Deaths Banquet (Cavendish) 30:189-90, 226-7, 229

"Yu Chu-ngo" (P'u Sung-ling) 3:345

"Yu Ch'u-wo" (P'u Sung-ling) 49:281

"Yü-ch'ien" (P'u Sung-ling) 49:281

"Yu-ch'u-e" (P'u Sung-ling) 49:287

Yúsuf u Zulaikhá (Jami) 9:60, 62, 66-7, 70-1

Zadig (Voltaire) 14:328, 338, 345, 358-60, 378, 389, 397

Zahurdas de Plutón, in fine (Quevedo) 23:154

Zaïde (La Fayette) 2:138-39, 151-52, 157-58, 160, 168-69

Zaïre (Voltaire) 14:323-25, 328, 338, 342, 358, 397

Zayde (La Fayette)
　See *Zaïde*

"Zealot" (Butler) 16:53

Zelmane; or, The Corinthian Queen (Pix) 8:276

Zendorii à Zendoriis teutsche Winternächte; oder, Die ausführliche und denckwürdige Beschreibung seiner Lebens-Geschict (Beer) 5:47-8, 50, 54, 57-8, 60

Zenobia (Calderon de la Barca) 23:65

Zermine et Almanzor (Lesage) 28:208

"Zgoda" (Kochanowski) 10:175

"Zu zha" (P'u Sung-ling) 49:310

Zulime (Voltaire) 14:397

Title Index

ISBN 0-7876-3266-X

9 780787 632663

90000